United Nations Resolutions on Palestine
and
the Arab-Israeli Conflict

Volume III: 1982–1986

UNITED NATIONS RESOLUTIONS ON PALESTINE
AND
THE ARAB-ISRAELI CONFLICT
Volume III: 1982–1986

Editor

Michael Simpson

Institute for Palestine Studies

Washington, D.C.

The Institute for Palestine Studies, founded in Beirut in 1963, is
an independent, non-profit Arab research and publication center,
which is not affiliated with any political organization or government.
The opinions expressed in its publications do not necessarily
reflect those of the Institute.

Library of Congress Cataloging-in-Publication Data

United Nations resolutions on Palestine and the Arab-Israeli conflict.

   Includes index.
   Contents: v.1. 1947-1974 / edited by George J.
Tomeh — v.2. 1975-1981 / edited by Regina Sharif —
v.3. 1982-1986 / edited by Michael Simpson.
   1. United Nations—Palestine.   2. Jewish-Arab
relations—1949-   —Sources.   I. Tomeh, George J.
(George Joseph)   II. Sharif, Regina, 1942-   .
III. Simpson, Michael, 1948-   .   IV. United Nations.
V. Institute for Palestine Studies (Washington, D.C.)
JX1977.2.P34U575   1988   341.23'5694   88-2791
v.1 ISBN 0-88728-161-3   ISBN 0-88728-171-0 (pbk.)
v.2 ISBN 0-88728-162-1   ISBN 0-88728-172-9 (pbk.)
v.3 ISBN 0-88728-163-X   ISBN 0-88728-173-7 (pbk.)

Cover designed by Afaf Zurayk, Washington, D.C.

Typeset by Graftec Corp., Washington, D.C.

Printed in the United States of America by Progressive Litho, Inc., Alexandria, Virginia.

On the occasion of the
twenty-fifth anniversary of the establishment
of the
Institute for Palestine Studies,

these volumes are dedicated

to

CONSTANTINE K. ZURAYK

Distinguished Professor Emeritus of History,
American University of Beirut

Co-founder,
Chairman (1963 - 1984), and
Honorary Chairman (1984 -)
of the
Institute for Palestine Studies

CONTENTS

LIST OF RESOLUTIONS

General Assembly

Security Council

Economic and Social Council and its subsidiary organs

A. Economic and Social Council

B. Commission on Human Rights

D. Governing Council of the United Nations Develoment Program

United Nations Educational, Scientific and Cultural Organization

A. General Conference

B. Executive Board

World Health Organization (World Health Assembly)

International Atomic Energy Agency

I. RESOLUTIONS OF THE GENERAL ASSEMBLY

Resolution No. ES-9/1 of 5 February 1982

DECLARING ISRAEL'S DECISION TO IMPOSE ITS LAWS, JURIS-
DICTION AND ADMINISTRATION ON THE GOLAN HEIGHTS
TO BE NULL AND VOID

The General Assembly,

Having considered the item entitled "The situation in the occupied Arab territories" at its ninth emergency special session in accordance with Security Council resolution 500 (1982) of 28 January 1982,

Noting with regret and concern that the Security Council at its 2329th meeting, on 20 January 1982, failed to take appropriate measures against Israel, as requested by the Council in resolution 497 (1981) of 17 December 1981, as the result of the negative vote of a permanent member of the Council,

Recalling Security Council resolution 497 (1981),

Recalling its resolution 35/122 E of 11 December 1980,

Reaffirming its resolution 36/226 B of 17 December 1981,

Having considered the reports of the Secretary-General of 21 December 1981[1] and 31 December 1981,[2]

Recalling its resolution 3314 (XXIX) of 14 December 1974, in which it defined an act of aggression as, *inter alia,* "the invasion or attack by the armed forces of a State of the territory of another State, or any military occupation, however temporary, resulting from such invasion or attack, or any annexation by the use of force of the territory of another State or part thereof", and provided that "no consideration of whatever nature, whether political, economic, military or otherwise, may serve as a justification for aggression",

Stressing once again that the acquisition of territory by force is inadmissible under the Charter of the United Nations, the principles of international law and relevant United Nations resolutions,

Reaffirming once more the applicability of the Geneva Convention relative to the Protection of Civilian Persons in Time of War, of 12 August 1949,[3] to the occupied Syrian territory,

Noting that Israel's record and actions establish conclusively that it is not a peace-loving Member State and that it has not carried out its obligations under the Charter,

Noting further that Israel has refused, in violation of Article 25 of the Charter, to accept and carry out the numerous relevant decisions of the Security Council, the latest being resolution 497 (1981),

1. *Strongly condemns* Israel for its failure to comply with Security Council resolution 497 (1981) and General Assembly resolution 36/226 B;

2. *Declares* that Israel's decision of 14 December 1981 to impose its laws, jurisdiction and administration on the occupied Syrian Golan Heights constitutes an act of aggression under the provisions of Article 39 of the Charter

of the United Nations and General Assembly resolution 3314 (XXIX);

3. *Declares once more* that Israel's decision to impose its laws, jurisdiction and administration on the occupied Syrian Golan Heights is null and void and has no legal validity and/or effect whatsoever;

4. *Determines* that all actions taken by Israel to give effect to its decision relating to the occupied Syrian Golan Heights are illegal and invalid and shall not be recognized;

5. *Reaffirms its determination* that all the provisions of the Hague Conventions of 1907[4] and the Geneva Convention relative to the Protection of Civilian Persons in Time of War, of 12 August 1949, continue to apply to the Syrian territory occupied by Israel since 1967, and calls upon all parties thereto to respect and ensure respect of their obligations under these instruments in all circumstances;

6. *Determines* that the continued occupation of the Syrian Golan Heights since 1967 and its effective annexation by Israel on 14 December 1981, following Israel's decision to impose its laws, jurisdiction and administration on that territory, constitute a continuing threat to international peace and security;

7. *Strongly deplores* the negative vote by a permanent member of the Security Council which prevented the Council from adopting against Israel, under Chapter VII of the Charter, the "appropriate measures" referred to in resolution 497 (1981) unanimously adopted by the Council;

8. *Further deplores* any political, economic, military and technological support to Israel, which encourages Israel to commit acts of aggression and to consolidate and perpetuate its occupation and annexation of occupied Arab territories;

9. *Firmly emphasizes* its demands that Israel, the occupying Power, rescind forthwith its decision of 14 December 1981 to impose its laws, jurisdiction and administration on the Syrian Golan Heights, which has resulted in the effective annexation of that territory;

10. *Reaffirms* the overriding necessity of the total and unconditional withdrawal by Israel from all the Palestinian and other Arab territories occupied since 1967, including Jerusalem, which is a primary requirement for the establishment of a comprehensive and just peace in the Middle East;

11. *Declares* that Israel's record and actions confirm that it is not a peace-loving Member State and that it has carried out neither its obligations under the Charter nor its commitment under General Assembly resolution 273 (III) of 11 May 1949;

12. *Calls upon* all Member States to apply the following measures:

(*a*) To refrain from supplying Israel with any weapons and related equipment and to suspend any military assistance which Israel receives from them;

---

[1] A/36/846 and Corr.1-S/14805 and Corr. 1.

[2] S/14821.

[3] United Nations, *Treaty Series,* vol. 75, no. 973, p. 287.

[4] Carnegie Endowment for International Peace, *The Hague Conventions and Declarations 1899-1907* (New York, Oxford University Press, 1918).

(b) To refrain from acquiring any weapons or military equipment from Israel;

(c) To suspend economic, financial and technological assistance to and co-operation with Israel;

(d) To sever diplomatic, trade and cultural relations with Israel;

13. *Also calls upon* all Member States to cease forthwith, individually and collectively, all dealings with Israel in order totally to isolate it in all fields;

14. *Urges* non-Member States to act in accordance with the provisions of the present resolution;

15. *Calls upon* all specialized agencies of the United Nations system and international institutions to conform their relations with Israel to the terms of the present resolution;

16. *Requests* the Secretary-General to follow up the implementation of the present resolution and to report thereon at intervals of two months to Member States as well as to the Security Council and to submit a comprehensive report to the General Assembly at its thirty-seventh session under the item entitled "The situation in the Middle East".

Adopted at the 12th plenary meeting:
In favour: 86
Afghanistan, Albania, Algeria, Angola, Bahrain, Bangladesh, Benin, Bhutan, Botswana, Bulgaria, Burma, Burundi, Byelorussia, Cape Verde, China, Congo, Cuba, Cyprus, Czechoslovakia, Democratic Yemen, Djibouti, Ethiopia, Gambia, German Democratic Republic, Ghana, Greece, Grenada, Guinea, Guinea-Bissau, Guyana, Hungary, India, Indonesia, Iran, Iraq, Ivory Coast, Jordan, Kenya, Kuwait, Lao People's Democratic Republic, Lebanon, Lesotho, Libya, Madagascar, Malaysia, Maldives, Mali, Malta, Mauritania, Mongolia, Morocco, Mozambique, Nepal, Nicaragua, Niger, Nigeria, Oman, Pakistan, Peru, Poland, Qatar, Rwanda, Sao Tome and Principe, Saudi Arabia, Senegal, Seychelles, Sierra Leone, Somalia, Sri Lanka, Sudan, Suriname, Syria, Togo, Tunisia, Uganda, Ukraine, USSR, United Arab Emirates, United Republic of Cameroon, United Republic of Tanzania, Upper Volta, Viet Nam, Yemen, Yugoslavia, Zambia, Zimbabwe.
Against: 21
Australia, Belgium, Canada, Denmark, Fiji, Finland, France, Federal Republic of Germany, Iceland, Ireland, Israel, Italy, Japan, Luxembourg, Netherlands, New Zealand, Norway, Portugal, Sweden, United Kingdom, United States.
Abstentions: 34
Argentina, Austria, Bahamas, Barbados, Bolivia, Brazil, Chile, Colombia, Costa Rica, Dominican Republic, Ecuador, Egypt, El Salvador, Gabon, Guatemala, Haiti, Honduras, Liberia, Malawi, Panama, Papua New Guinea, Paraguay, Saint Lucia, Saint Vincent, Samoa, Singapore, Spain, Swaziland, Thailand, Trinidad and Tobago, Turkey, Uruguay, Venezuela, Zaire.
Absent: 13
Antigua and Barbuda, Belize, Central African Republic, Chad, Comoros, Democratic Kampuchea,* Dominica,

Equatorial Guinea, Jamaica, Mauritius, Mexico, Solomon Islands, Vanuatu.

The Philippines and Romania did not participate in the vote.

---

* Later announced that it was not participating in the vote.

Decision No. 36/462 of 16 March 1982

ON THE FINANCING OF THE UNITED NATIONS RELIEF AND WORKS AGENCY FOR PALESTINE REFUGEES IN THE NEAR EAST

At its 106th plenary meeting, on 16 March 1982, the General Assembly, having considered the recommendations of the Working Group on the Financing of the United Nations Relief and Works Agency for Palestine Refugees in the Near East:[5]

(a) Took note of the report of the Working Group;[6]

(b) Urged the Commissioner-General of the United Nations Relief and Works Agency for Palestine Refugees in the Near East to continue his efforts to make the most efficient use of the resources of the Agency and requested the Joint Inspection Unit to carry out a comprehensive review of the Agency's organization, budget and operations with a view to assisting the Commissioner-General to make the most effective and economical use of the limited funds available to the Agency;

(c) Called upon:
(i) Governments that had not yet contributed to the United Nations Relief and Works Agency For Palestine Refugees in the Near East to start contributing;
(ii) Governments that had hitherto only made relatively small contributions to contribute more generously;
(iii) Governments in a special position to do so to increase their contributions;
(iv) Governments that in the past had made generous contributions to continue to make generous contributions and strive whenever possible to increase their contributions;

(d) Called upon Governments and organizations making contributions in kind either to give cash instead or to allow the United Nations Relief and Works Agency for Palestine Refugees in the Near East to sell their contributions for cash;

(e) Decided to suspend temporarily the consideration of agenda item 60 (United Nations Relief and Works Agency for Palestine Refugees in the Near East).

Adopted at the 106th Plenary Meeting without a vote.

---

[5] A/36/866 and Corr.1, para. 26.
[6] A/36/866 and Corr.1.

4

Resolution No. 36/138 C of 19 March 1982

ON THE FINANCING OF THE UNITED NATIONS INTERIM FORCE IN LEBANON

The General Assembly,

Having considered the report of the Secretary-General on the financing of the United Nations Interim Force in Lebanon[7] and the related report of the Advisory Committee on Administrative and Budgetary Questions,[8]

Bearing in mind Security Council resolutions 425 (1978) and 426 (1978) of 19 March 1978, 427 (1978) of 3 May 1978, 434 (1978) of 18 September 1978, 444 (1979) of 19 January 1979, 450 (1979) of 14 June 1979, 459 (1979) of 19 December 1979, 474 (1980) of 17 June 1980, 483 (1980) of 17 December 1980, 488 (1981) of 19 June 1981, 498 (1981) of 18 December 1981 and 501 (1982) of 25 February 1982,[9]

Recalling its resolutions S-8/2 of 21 April 1978, 33/14 of 3 November 1978, 34/9 B of 17 December 1979, 35/44 of 1 December 1980, 35/115 A of 10 December 1980 and 36/138 A of 16 December 1981,

Reaffirming its previous decisions regarding the fact that, in order to meet the expenditures caused by such operations, a different procedure from the one applied to meet expenditures of the regular budget of the United Nations is required,

Taking into account the fact that the economically more developed countries are in a position to make relatively large contributions and that the economically less developed countries have a relatively limited capacity to contribute towards peace-keeping operations involving heavy expenditures,

Bearing in mind the special responsibilities of the States permanent members of the Security Council in the financing of peace-keeping operations decided upon in accordance with the Charter of the United Nations,

1. *Authorizes* the Secretary-General to enter into commitments for the United Nations Interim Force in Lebanon in an amount not to exceed $9,825,000 gross ($9,822,000 net) for the period from 25 February to 18 June 1982 inclusive, in addition to the amounts authorized for the Force under General Assembly resolution 36/138 A, to finance the increase in the strength of the Force approved by the Security Council under its resolution 501 (1982), the said amount to be apportioned among Member States in accordance with the scheme set out in Assembly resolution 33/14 and the provisions of section V, paragraph 1, of resolution 34/9 B, section VI, paragraph 1, of resolution 36/138 A, in the proportions determined by the scale of assessments for the years 1980, 1981 and 1982;

2. *Further authorizes* the Secretary-General to enter into commitments for the United Nations Interim Force in Lebanon, for the same purpose, at a rate not to exceed $1,913,000 gross ($1,910,333 net) per month for the period from 19 June to 18 December 1982 inclusive, in addition to the amounts authorized for the Force under General Assembly resolution 36/138 A, should the Security Council decide to continue the Force beyond the period of six months authorized under its resolution 498 (1981), the said amount to be apportioned among Member States in accordance with the scheme set out in Assembly resolution 33/14 and the provisions of section V, paragraph 1, of resolution 34/9 B, section VI, paragraph 1, of resolution 35/115 A and section VI, paragraph 1, of resolution 36/138 A, in the proportions determined by the scale of assessments for the years 1980, 1981 and 1982.

Adopted at the 108th plenary meeting:

In favour: 90

Argentina, Australia, Austria, Bahamas, Bahrain, Bangladesh, Barbados, Belgium, Bhutan, Bolivia, Brazil, Burma, Canada, Chile, China, Colombia, Costa Rica, Denmark, Djibouti, Ecuador, Egypt, Ethiopia, Fiji, Finland, France, Gabon, Federal Republic of Germany, Ghana, Greece, Iceland, India, Indonesia, Ireland, Israel, Italy, Ivory Coast, Jamaica, Japan, Jordan, Kenya, Kuwait, Lebanon, Luxembourg, Madagascar, Malawi, Malaysia, Maldives, Mali, Malta, Mauritania, Mexico, Morocco, Nepal, Netherlands, New Zealand, Niger, Norway, Oman, Pakistan, Panama, Paraguay, Peru, Philippines, Portugal, Qatar, Romania, Rwanda, Saint Lucia, Samoa, Saudi Arabia, Senegal, Sierra Leone, Singapore, Spain, Sweden, Thailand, Togo, Trinidad and Tobago, Tunisia, Turkey, United Arab Emirates, United Kingdom, United Republic of Cameroon, United Republic of Tanzania, United States, Uruguay, Venezuela, Yugoslavia, Zaire, Zambia.

Against: 12

Albania, Byelorussia, Czechoslovakia, German Democratic Republic, Hungary, Lao People's Democratic Republic, Mongolia, Poland, Syria, Ukraine, USSR, Viet Nam.

Abstentions: 3

Chad, Democratic Yemen, Guinea.

Absent: 51

Afghanistan, Algeria, Angola, Antigua and Barbuda, Belize, Benin, Botswana, Bulgaria, Burundi, Cape Verde, Central African Republic, Comoros, Congo, Cuba, Cyprus, Democratic Kampuchea, Dominica, Dominican Republic, El Salvador, Equatorial Guinea, Gambia, Grenada, Guatemala, Guinea-Bissau, Guyana, Haiti, Honduras, Iran, Iraq, Lesotho, Liberia, Libya, Mauritius,* Mozambique, Nicaragua, Nigeria, Papua New Guinea, Saint Vincent, Sao Tome and Principe, Seychelles, Solomon Islands, Somalia, Sri Lanka, Sudan, Suriname, Swaziland, Uganda, Upper Volta, Vanuatu, Yemen, Zimbabwe.

---

[7]A/36/865 and Corr.1.

[8]A/36/868.

[9]The resolutions cited in this paragraph and the next provide for the establishment, renewed mandate and financing of the United Nations Interim Force in Lebanon (UNIFIL) (in 1978) for the withdrawal of Israeli forces from Lebanese territory. [ed. note]

---

* Later advised the Secretariat it had intended to vote in favour.

Resolution No. ES-7/4 of 28 April 1982

ON THE QUESTION OF PALESTINE: CONDEMNING ISRAEL FOR ITS POLICIES IN THE OCCUPIED TERRITORIES, URGING STATES NOT TO PROVIDE ISRAEL WITH ASSISTANCE, AND URGING THE SECURITY COUNCIL TO RECOGNIZE THE INALIENABLE RIGHTS OF THE PALESTINIAN PEOPLE

The General Assembly,

Having considered the question of Palestine at its resumed seventh emergency special session,[10]

Noting with regret and concern that the Security Council, at its 2348th meeting, on 2 April 1982, and at its 2357th meeting, on 20 April 1982, failed to take a decision as a result of the negative votes of the United States of America,

Having heard the statement by the Head of the Political Department of the Palestine Liberation Organization, the representative of the Palestinian people,[11]

Convinced that the worsening situation in the Middle East and the failure to find a solution to this question pose a grave threat to international peace and security,

Deploring the repressive measures taken by the Israeli authorities in the illegally occupied Palestinian Arab territories, including Jerusalem,

Recalling the relevant United Nations resolutions pertaining to the status and unique character of the Holy City of Jerusalem, in particular Security Council resolutions 465 (1980) of 1 March 1980, 476 (1980) of 30 June 1980 and 478 (1980) of 20 August 1980,

Affirming once more that the Geneva Convention relative to the Protection of Civilian Persons in Time of War, of 12 August 1949,[12] is applicable to all territories occupied by Israel since 1967, including Jerusalem,

Noting with regret that, owing to the negative vote of one of its permanent members, the Security Council has, so far, failed to take a decision on the recommendations of the Committee on the Exercise of the Inalienable Rights of the Palestinian People endorsed by the General Assembly in its resolution 31/20 of 24 November 1976, 32/40 A of 2 December 1977, 33/28 A of 7 December 1978, 34/65 A of 29 November 1979, 35/169 A of 15 December 1980 and 36/120 D of 10 December 1981,

1. *Reaffirms* its resolution ES-7/2 of 29 July 1980 and 3236 (XXIX) and 3237 (XXIX) of 22 November 1974 and all other relevant United Nations resolutions pertinent to the question of Palestine;

2. *Reaffirms* the fundamental principle of the inadmissibility of the acquisition of territory by force;

3. *Reaffirms* that all the provisions of the Hague Conventions of 1907[13] and the Geneva Convention relative to the Protection of Civilian Persons in Time of War, of 12 August 1949, apply to all territories occupied by Israel since 1967, including Jerusalem, and calls upon all parties to these instruments to respect and ensure respect of their obligations in all circumstances;

4. *Demands* that Israel should comply with the provisions of Security Council resolutions 465 (1980);

5. *Further demands* that Israel should comply with all United Nations resolutions relevant to the status and unique character of the Holy City of Jerusalem, in particular with Security Council resolutions 476 (1980) and 478 (1980);

6. *Expresses its rejection* of all policies and plans aiming at the resettlement of the Palestinians outside their homeland;

7. *Condemns* Israel, the occupying Power, for its:

(*a*) Failure to fulfill its obligations under the provisions of the Geneva Convention relative to Protection of Civilian Persons in Time of War;

(*b*) Disbanding of the elected municipal council of El-Bireh;

(*c*) Dismissal of the elected mayors of Ramallah and Nablus;

(*d*) Violation of the sanctity of the Holy Places, particularly of Al-Haram Al-Shareef, in Jerusalem;

(*e*) Shooting and killing and wounding of worshippers in the precincts of Al-Haram Al-Shareef by members of the Israeli army on 11 April 1982;

(*f*) Repressive measures, including shooting at the unarmed civilian population in the occupied Palestinian territory and in the occupied Syrian Golan Heights, resulting in death and injury;

(*g*) Attacks against and interference with the functions of various civic and religious institutions in the occupied Palestine territory, including Jerusalem, in particular educational institutions;

8. *Condemns* all policies which frustrate the exercise of the inalienable rights of the Palestinian people, in particular providing Israel with military, economic and political assistance and the misuse of the veto by a permanent member of the Security Council, thus enabling Israel to continue its aggression, occupation and unwillingness to carry out its obligations under the Charter and the relevant resolutions of the United Nations;

9. *Urges* all Governments which have not yet done so:

(*a*) To recognize the inalienable rights of the Palestinian people;

(*b*) To renounce the policy of providing Israel with military, economic and political assistance, thus discouraging Israel from continuing its aggression, occupation and disregard of its obligations under the Charter and the relevant resolutions of the United Nations;

(*c*) To act accordingly in all the organs of the United Nations;

10. *Condemns* the policies which encourage the flow of human resources to Israel, enabling it to implement and to proceed with its colonization and settlement policies in the occupied Arab territories;

11. *Declares once again* that Israel's record and actions confirm that it is not a peace-loving Member State and

---

[10]The seventh emergency special session of the General Assembly held its first meeting to consider the Palestine question on 22 July 1980. [ed. note]

[11]A/ES-7/PV.12, p. 16.

[12]United Nations, *Treaty Series*, vol. 75, no. 973, p. 287.

[13]Carnegie Endowment for International Peace, *The Hague Conventions and Declarations of 1899 and 1907* (New York, Oxford University Press, 1915).

that it has carried out neither its obligations under the Charter nor its commitment under General Assembly resolution 273 (III) of 11 May 1949;

12. *Calls again upon* Israel, the occupying Power, to observe and apply scrupulously the provisions of the Geneva Convention relative to the Protection of Civilian Persons in Time of War and the principles of international law governing military occupation in all the occupied Palestinian and other Arab territories, including Jerusalem;

13. *Demands* that Israel, the occupying Power, should permit entry into the occupied territories of the Special Committee to Investigate Israeli Practices Affecting the Human Rights of the Population of the Occupied Territories and of the Commission established by Security Council resolution 446 (1979), in order to facilitate the fulfilment of the mandates entrusted to them by the General Assembly and by the Council, respectively;

14. *Urges* the Security Council to recognize the inalienable rights of the Palestinian people as defined in General Assembly resolution ES-7/2 and to endorse the recommendations of the Committee on the Exercise of the Inalienable Rights of the Palestinian People, as endorsed by the Assembly in its resolution 31/20 and in subsequent resolutions;

15. *Calls upon* the Secretary-General, in concurrence with the Security Council and in consultation as appropriate with the Committee on the Exercise of the Inalienable Rights of the Palestinian People, to initiate contacts with all parties to the Arab-Israeli conflict in the Middle East, including the Palestine Liberation Organization, the representative of the Palestinian people, with a view to finding concrete ways and means to achieve a comprehensive, just and lasting solution, conducive to peace, in conformity with the principles of the Charter and relevant resolutions and based on the implementation of the recommendations of the Committee as endorsed by the General Assembly at its thirty-first session;

16. *Requests* the Secretary-General to follow up the implementation of the present resolution and to report thereon at appropriate intervals to Member States as well as to the Security Council and to submit a comprehensive report to the General Assembly at its thirty-seventh session under the item entitled "Question of Palestine";

17. *Decides* to adjourn the seventh emergency special session temporarily and to authorize the President of the latest regular session of the General Assembly to resume its meetings upon request from Member States.

Adopted at the 20th plenary meeting:
In favour: 86
Afghanistan, Albania, Algeria, Angola, Bahrain, Bangladesh, Benin, Bhutan, Botswana, Bulgaria, Burundi, Byelorussia, Cape Verde, Chad, China, Congo, Cuba, Cyprus, Czechoslovakia, Democratic Yemen, Djibouti, Ethiopia, Gambia, German Democratic Republic, Ghana, Greece, Grenada, Guinea, Guinea-Bissau, Guyana, Hungary, India, Indonesia, Iran, Iraq, Jordan, Kenya, Kuwait, Lao People's Democratic Republic, Lebanon, Libya,

Madagascar, Malaysia, Maldives, Mali, Malta, Mauritania, Mongolia, Morocco, Mozambique, Nepal, Nicaragua, Niger, Nigeria, Oman, Pakistan, Poland, Qatar, Romania, Rwanda, Sao Tome and Principe, Saudi Arabia, Senegal, Seychelles, Sierra Leone, Somalia, Sri Lanka, Sudan, Suriname, Syria, Togo, Trinidad and Tobago, Tunisia, Turkey, Uganda, Ukraine, USSR, United Arab Emirates, United Republic of Cameroon, United Republic of Tanzania, Upper Volta, Viet Nam, Yemen, Yugoslavia, Zambia, Zimbabwe.

Against: 20
Australia, Austria, Belgium, Canada, Denmark, Finland, France, Federal Republic of Germany, Iceland, Ireland, Israel, Italy, Luxembourg, Netherlands, New Zealand, Norway, Portugal, Sweden, United Kingdom, United States.

Abstentions: 36
Argentina, Bahamas, Barbados, Bolivia, Brazil, Burma, Chile, Colombia, Costa Rica, Dominican Republic, Ecuador, Egypt, El Salvador, Fiji, Guatemala, Haiti, Honduras, Ivory Coast, Jamaica, Japan, Liberia, Malawi, Mexico, Panama, Papua New Guinea, Paraguay, Peru, Philippines, Samoa, Singapore, Spain, Swaziland, Thailand, Uruguay, Venezuela, Zaire.

Absent: 14
Antigua and Barbuda, Belize, Central African Republic, Comoros, Democratic Kampuchea, Dominica, Equatorial Guinea, Gabon, Lesotho, Mauritius, Saint Lucia, Saint Vincent, Solomon Islands, Vanuatu.

Resolution No. ES-7/5 of 26 June 1982

ON THE QUESTION OF PALESTINE: DEMANDING A CEASE-FIRE IN LEBANON, AND THE WITHDRAWAL OF ISRAELI FORCES FROM LEBANESE TERRITORY

The General Assembly,

Having considered the question of Palestine at its resumed seventh emergency special session,

Having heard the statement of the Palestine Liberation Organization, the representative of the Palestinian people,[14]

Alarmed by the worsening situation in the Middle East resulting from Israel's acts of aggression against the sovereignty of Lebanon and the Palestinian people in Lebanon,

Recalling Security Council resolutions 508 (1982) of 5 June 1982, 509 (1982) of 6 June 1982 and 512 (1982) of 19 June 1982,[15]

Taking note of the reports of the Secretary-General relevant to this situation, particularly his report of 7 June 1982,[16]

Taking note of the two positive replies to the Secretary-

---

[14]See A/ES-7/PV.22.
[15]On Israel's invasion of Lebanon. [ed. note]
[16]S/15178.

7

General by the Government of Lebanon[17] and the Palestine Liberation Organization,[18]

Noting with regret that the Security Council has, so far, failed to take effective and practical measures, in accordance with the Charter of the United Nations, to ensure implementation of its resolutions 508 (1982) and 509 (1982),

Referring to the humanitarian principles of the Geneva Convention relative to the Protection of Civilian Persons in Time of War, of 12 August 1949,[19] and to the obligations arising from the regulations annexed to the Hague Conventions of 1907,[20]

Deeply concerned at the sufferings of the Palestinian and Lebanese civilian populations,

Reaffirming once again its conviction that the question of Palestine is the core of the Arab-Israeli conflict and that no comprehensive, just and lasting peace in the region will be achieved without the full exercise by the Palestinian people of its inalienable national rights,

Reaffirming further that a just and comprehensive settlement of the situation in the Middle East cannot be achieved without the participation on an equal footing of all the parties to the conflict, including the Palestine Liberation Organization as the representative of the Palestinian people,

1. *Reaffirms* the fundamental principle of the inadmissibility of the acquisition of territory by force;

2. *Demands* that all Member States and other parties observe strict respect for Lebanon's sovereignty, territorial integrity, unity and political independence within its internationally recognized boundaries;

3. *Decides* to support fully the provisions of Security Council resolutions 508 (1982) and 509 (1982) in which the Council, *inter alia*, demanded that:

(*a*) Israel withdraw all its military forces forthwith and unconditionally to the internationally recognized boundaries of Lebanon;

(*b*) All parties to the conflict cease immediately and simultaneously all military activities within Lebanon and across the Lebanese-Israeli border;

4. *Condemns* Israel for its non-compliance with resolutions 508 (1982) and 509 (1982);

5. *Demands* that Israel comply with all the above provisions no later than 0600 hours, (Beirut time) on Sunday, 27 June 1982;

6. *Calls upon* the Security Council to authorize the Secretary-General to undertake necessary endeavours and practical steps to implement the provisions of resolution 508 (1982), 509 (1982) and 512 (1982);

7. *Urges* the Security Council, in the event of continued failure by Israel to comply with the demands contained in resolutions 508 (1982) and 509 (1982), to meet in order to consider practical ways and means in accordance with the Charter of the United Nations;

8. *Calls upon* all States and international agencies and organizations to continue to provide the most extensive humanitarian aid possible to the victims of the Israeli invasion of Lebanon;

9. *Requests* the Secretary-General to delegate a high-level commission to investigate and assess the extent of loss of human life and material damage and to report, as soon as possible, on the result of this investigation, to the General Assembly and the Security Council;

10. *Decides* to adjourn the seventh emergency special session temporarily and to authorize the President of the latest regular session of the General Assembly to resume its meetings upon request from Member States.

Adopted at the 24th plenary meeting:
In favour: 127
Afghanistan, Albania, Algeria, Angola, Argentina, Australia, Austria, Bahamas, Bahrain, Bangladesh, Barbados, Belgium, Benin, Bhutan, Bolivia, Botswana, Brazil, Bulgaria, Burma, Burundi, Byelorussia, Canada, Cape Verde, Chile, China, Colombia, Congo, Costa Rica, Cuba, Cyprus, Czechoslovakia, Democratic Kampuchea, Democratic Yemen, Denmark, Djibouti, Ecuador, Egypt, Fiji, Finland, France, Gabon, Gambia, German Democratic Republic, Federal Republic of Germany, Ghana, Greece, Guinea-Bissau, Guyana, Hungary, Iceland, India, Indonesia, Iran, Iraq, Ireland, Italy, Jamaica, Japan, Jordan, Kenya, Kuwait, Lao People's Democratic Republic, Lebanon, Lesotho, Liberia, Libya, Luxembourg, Madagascar, Malaysia, Maldives, Mali, Malta, Mauritania, Mauritius, Mexico, Mongolia, Morocco, Mozambique, Nepal, Netherlands, New Zealand, Nicaragua, Niger, Norway, Oman, Pakistan, Panama, Paraguay, Peru, Philippines, Poland, Portugal, Qatar, Romania, Sao Tome and Principe, Saudi Arabia, Senegal, Seychelles, Sierra Leone, Singapore, Somalia, Spain, Sri Lanka, Sudan, Suriname, Sweden, Syria, Thailand, Togo, Trinidad and Tobago, Tunisia, Turkey, Uganda, Ukraine, USSR, United Arab Emirates, United Kingdom, United Republic of Cameroon, United Republic of Tanzania, Upper Volta, Uruguay, Venezuela, Viet Nam, Yemen, Yugoslavia, Zaire, Zambia.
Against: 2
Israel, United States.
Abstentions: 0
Absent: 27
Antigua and Barbuda, Belize, Central African Republic, Chad, Comoros, Dominica, Dominican Republic, El Salvador,* Equatorial Guinea, Ethiopia,* Grenada, Guatemala, Guinea, Haiti, Honduras, Ivory Coast, Malawi, Nigeria, Papua New Guinea, Rwanda,* Saint Lucia, Saint Vincent, Samoa,* Solomon Islands, Swaziland, Vanuatu, Zimbabwe.

---

[17]S/15178, para.3.
[18]S/15178, para.4.
[19]United Nations, *Treaty Series*, vol. 75, no. 973, p. 287.
[20]Carnegie Endowment for International Peace, *The Hague Conventions and Declarations of 1899 and 1907* (New York, Oxford University Press, 1915).

---

*Later advised the Secretariat it had intended to vote in favour.

Resolution No. ES-7/6 of 19 August 1982

ON THE QUESTION OF PALESTINE: CALLING FOR THE FREE EXERCISE OF THE RIGHTS OF THE PALESTINIAN PEOPLE TO SELF-DETERMINATION AND INDEPENDENCE, DEMANDING THAT ISRAEL CARRY OUT PREVIOUS RESOLUTIONS OF THE GENERAL ASSEMBLY RELATING TO THE OCCUPIED TERRITORIES, AND URGING THE SECRETARY-GENERAL TO TAKE MEASURES TO GUARANTEE THE SAFETY OF THE PALESTINIAN AND LEBANESE CIVILIAN POPULATION

The General Assembly,

Having considered the question of Palestine at its resumed seventh emergency special session,

Having heard the statement of the Palestine Liberation Organization, the representative of the Palestinian people,[21]

Guided by the purposes and principles of the United Nations, in particular the respect for the principle of equal rights and self-determination of peoples,

Aware of the functions of the Security Council during its meetings relevant to the situation in the Middle East, in particular since 4 June 1982,

Expressing its deep regret that the Security Council has, so far, failed to take effective and practical measures in accordance with the Charter of the United Nations to ensure implementation of its resolutions 508 (1982) of 5 June 1982 and 509 (1982) of 6 June 1982,

Alarmed that the situation in the Middle East has further worsened as a result of Israel's acts of aggression against the sovereignty of Lebanon and the Palestinian people in Lebanon,

Guided further by the purposes and principles of the United Nations in particular to take effective collective measures for the prevention and removal of threats to the peace and for the suppression of acts of aggression,

Mindful of the humanitarian principles and provisions of the Geneva Conventions of 1949[22] and Additional Protocol I thereto[23] and the obligations arising from the regulations annexed to the Hague Conventions of 1907,[24]

Reaffirming its conviction that the question of Palestine is the core of the Arab-Israeli conflict and that no comprehensive, just and lasting peace in the region will be achieved without the full exercise by the Palestinian people of its inalienable rights in Palestine,

Reaffirming once again that a just and comprehensive settlement of the situation in the Middle East cannot be achieved without the participation on an equal footing of all the parties to the conflict, including the Palestine Liberation Organization as the representative of the Palestinian people,

Expressing its indignation at the continuation and intensification of military activities by Israel within Lebanon, particularly in and around Beirut,

Recalling all its resolutions relevant to the question of Palestine,

Recalling Security Council resolutions 508 (1982) of 5 June 1982, 509 (1982) of 6 June 1982, 511 (1982) of 18 June 1982, 512 (1982) of 19 June 1982, 513 (1982) of 4 July 1982, 515 (1982) of 29 July 1982, 516 (1982) of 1 August 1982, 517 (1982) of 4 August 1982 and 518 (1982) of 12 August 1982,[25]

1. *Reiterates* its affirmation of the fundamental principle of the inadmissibility of the acquisition of territory by force;

2. *Calls* for the free exercise in Palestine of the inalienable rights of the Palestinian people to self-determination without external interference and to national independence;

3. *Reaffirms* its rejection of all policies and plans aiming at the resettlement of the Palestinians outside their homeland;

4. *Demands* that Israel respect and carry out the provisions of the previous resolutions of the General Assembly relating to the occupied Palestinian and other Arab territories, including Jerusalem, as well as the provisions of Security Council resolution 465 (1980) of 1 March 1980, in which the Council, *inter alia*:

(a) Determined that all measures taken by Israel to change the physical character, demographic composition, institutional structure or status of the Palestinian and other Arab territories occupied since 1967, including Jerusalem, or any part thereof, had no legal validity and that Israel's policy and practices of settling parts of its population and new immigrants in those territories constituted a flagrant violation of the Geneva Convention relative to the Protection of Civilian Persons in Time of War, of 12 August 1949,[26] and also constituted a serious obstruction to achieving a comprehensive, just and lasting peace in the Middle East;

(b) Strongly deplored the continuation and persistence of Israel in pursuing those policies and practices and called upon the Government and people of Israel to rescind those measures, to dismantle the existing settlements and in particular to cease, on an urgent basis, the establishment, construction and planning of settlements in the Arab territories occupied since 1967, including Jerusalem;

5. *Demands also* that Israel carry out the provisions of Security Council resolutions 509 (1982), 511 (1982), 512 (1982), 513 (1982), 515 (1982), 516 (1982), 517 (1982) and 518 (1982);

6. *Urges* the Secretary-General, with the concurrence of the Security Council and the Government of Lebanon and pending the withdrawal of Israel from Lebanon, to undertake effective measures to guarantee the safety and

---

[21]A/ES-7/PV.25, p. 7.

[22]United Nations, *Treaty Series,* vol. 75, nos. 970-973.

[23]A/32/144, annex I.

[24]Carnegie Endowment for International Peace, *The Hague Conventions and Declarations of 1899 and 1907* (New York, Oxford University Press, 1915).

[25]On Israel's invasion of Lebanon. [ed. note]

[26]United Nations, *Treaty Series,* vol. 75, no. 973, p. 287.

security of the Palestinian and Lebanese civilian population in South Lebanon;

7. *Condemns* Israel for its non-compliance with resolutions of the Security Council, in defiance of Article 25 of the Charter of the United Nations;

8. *Urges once again* the Security Council, in the event of continued failure by Israel to comply with the demands contained in its resolutions 465 (1980), 508 (1982), 509 (1982), 515 (1982) and 518 (1982), to meet in order to consider practical ways and means in accordance with the relevant provisions of the Charter;

9. *Requests once again* the Secretary General to delegate a high-level commission to investigate and make an up-to-date assessment of the extent of loss of human life and material damage and to report, as soon as possible, on the result of this investigation to the General Assembly and the Security Council;

10. *Requests* the Secretary-General and organizations of the United Nations system, in co-operation with the International Committee of the Red Cross and other non-governmental organizations, to investigate the strict application by Israel of the provisions of the Geneva Conventions of 1949 and other instruments in the case of those detained;

11. *Calls once again upon* the Secretary-General to initiate contacts with all the parties to the Arab-Israeli conflict in the Middle East, including the Palestine Liberation Organization, the representative of the Palestinian people, with a view to convening an international conference, under the auspices of the United Nations, to find concrete ways and means of achieving a comprehensive, just and lasting solution, conducive to peace in conformity with the principles of the Charter and relevant resolutions;

12. *Decides* to adjourn the seventh emergency special session temporarily and to authorize the President of the latest regular session of the General Assembly to resume its meetings upon request from Member States.

Adopted at the 31st plenary meeting:

In favour: 120

Afghanistan, Albania, Algeria, Angola, Argentina, Austria, Bahamas, Bahrain, Bangladesh, Barbados, Benin, Bhutan, Bolivia, Botswana, Brazil, Bulgaria, Burma, Burundi, Byelorussia, Cape Verde, Chad, Chile, China, Colombia, Congo, Cuba, Cyprus, Czechoslovakia, Democratic Kampuchea, Democratic Yemen, Djibouti, Ecuador, Egypt, El Salvador, Ethiopia, Fiji, Finland, Gabon, Gambia, German Democratic Republic, Ghana, Greece, Grenada, Guinea, Guinea-Bissau, Guyana, Honduras, Hungary, India, Indonesia, Iran, Iraq, Ivory Coast, Japan, Jordan, Kenya, Kuwait, Lao People's Democratic Republic, Lebanon, Lesotho, Liberia, Libya, Madagascar, Malaysia, Maldives, Mali, Malta, Mauritania, Mauritius, Mexico, Mongolia, Morocco, Mozambique, Nepal, Nicaragua, Niger, Nigeria, Oman, Pakistan, Panama, Paraguay, Peru, Philippines, Poland, Qatar, Romania, Rwanda, Samoa, Sao Tome and Principe, Saudi Arabia, Senegal, Seychelles, Sierra Leone, Singapore, Somalia, Spain, Sri Lanka, Sudan, Swaziland, Syria, Thailand, Togo, Trinidad and Tobago, Tunisia, Turkey, Uganda, Ukraine, USSR, United Arab Emirates, United Republic of Cameroon, United Republic of Tanzania, Upper Volta, Uruguay, Venezuela, Viet Nam, Yemen, Yugoslavia, Zambia, Zaire, Zimbabwe.

Against: 2

Israel, United States.

Abstentions: 20

Australia, Belgium, Canada, Denmark, Dominican Republic, France, Federal Republic of Germany, Haiti, Iceland, Ireland, Italy, Jamaica, Luxembourg, Malawi, Netherlands, New Zealand, Norway, Portugal, Sweden, United Kingdom.

Absent: 14

Antigua and Barbuda, Belize, Central African Republic, Comoros, Costa Rica, Dominica, Equatorial Guinea, Guatemala, Papua New Guinea, Saint Lucia, Saint Vincent, Solomon Islands, Suriname, Vanuatu.

Resolution No. ES-7/7 of 19 August 1982

DECIDING TO CONVENE AN INTERNATIONAL CONFERENCE ON THE QUESTION OF PALESTINE

The General Assembly,

Recalling its resolution 36/120 C of 10 December 1981, by which it decided to convene an International Conference on the Question of Palestine, not later than 1984, for a comprehensive effort to seek effective ways and means of enabling the Palestinian people to attain and exercise its rights,

Deeply alarmed at the explosive situation in the Middle East resulting from the Israeli aggression against the sovereign State of Lebanon and the Palestinian people, which poses a threat to international peace and security,

Deeply aware of the responsibility of the United Nations under its Charter for the maintenance of international peace,

Gravely concerned that no just solution to the problem of Palestine has been achieved and that this problem therefore continues to aggravate the Middle East conflict, of which it is the core, and to endanger international peace and security,

Taking note of the final communiqué of the Extraordinary Ministerial Meeting of the Co-ordinating Bureau of the Non-Aligned Countries on the Question of Palestine, held at Nicosia from 15 to 17 July 1982,[27]

Recognizing the need to intensify all efforts by the international community to enable the Palestinian people to attain and exercise its inalienable rights as defined and reaffirmed in United Nations resolutions,

Stressing the importance of the work of the Preparatory Committee for the International Conference on the Question of Palestine and the need for securing the broadest possible involvement of Member States in the prepara-

---

[27] A/37/366, annex.

tory processes leading up to the Conference, and in the Conference itself,

1. *Decides* to convene the International Conference on the Question of Palestine at the headquarters of the United Nations Educational, Scientific and Cultural Organization, in Paris, from 16 to 27 August 1983;

2. *Requests* the Secretary-General to ensure that adequate resources from the regular budget of the United Nations are provided urgently in order to enable the successful holding of the Conference and to carry out the necessary preparations and follow-up activities for the Conference;

3. *Calls upon* all States to co-operate with the Preparatory Committee in the implementation of the present resolution and invites them to establish national focal points for effective co-ordination of preparations at the national level.

Adopted at the 31st plenary meeting:
In favour: 123
Afghanistan, Albania, Algeria, Angola, Argentina, Austria, Bahamas, Bahrain, Bangladesh, Barbados, Benin, Bhutan, Bolivia, Botswana, Brazil, Bulgaria, Burma, Burundi, Byelorussia, Cape Verde, Chad, Chile, China, Colombia, Congo, Costa Rica, Cuba, Cyprus, Czechoslovakia, Democratic Kampuchea, Democratic Yemen, Djibouti, Dominican Republic, Ecuador, Egypt, El Salvador, Ethiopia, Fiji, Gabon, Gambia, German Democratic Republic, Ghana, Greece, Grenada, Guinea, Guinea-Bissau, Guyana, Haiti, Honduras, Hungary, India, Indonesia, Iran, Iraq, Ivory Coast, Jamaica, Jordan, Kenya, Kuwait, Lao People's Democratic Republic, Lebanon, Lesotho, Liberia, Libya, Madagascar, Malawi, Malaysia, Maldives, Mali, Malta, Mauritania, Mauritius, Mexico, Mongolia, Morocco, Mozambique, Nepal, Nicaragua, Niger, Nigeria, Oman, Pakistan, Panama, Paraguay, Peru, Philippines, Poland, Qatar, Romania, Rwanda, Samoa, Sao Tome and Principe, Saudi Arabia, Senegal, Seychelles, Sierra Leone, Singapore, Somalia, Spain, Sri Lanka, Sudan, Swaziland, Syria, Thailand, Togo, Trinidad and Tobago, Tunisia, Turkey, Uganda, Ukraine, USSR, United Arab Emirates, United Republic of Cameroon, United Republic of Tanzania, Upper Volta, Uruguay, Venezuela, Viet Nam, Yemen, Yugoslavia, Zaire, Zambia, Zimbabwe.
Against: 2
Israel, United States.
Abstentions: 18
Australia, Belgium, Canada, Denmark, Finland, France, Federal Republic of Germany, Iceland, Ireland, Italy, Japan, Luxembourg, Netherlands, New Zealand, Norway, Portugal, Sweden, United Kingdom.
Absent: 13
Antigua and Barbuda, Belize, Central African Republic, Comoros, Dominica, Equatorial Guinea, Guatemala, Papua New Guinea, Saint Lucia, Saint Vincent, Solomon Islands, Suriname, Vanuatu.

Resolution No. ES-7/8 of 19 August 1982

DECIDING TO COMMEMORATE INNOCENT CHILDREN WHO ARE VICTIMS OF AGGRESSION

The General Assembly,
Having considered the question of Palestine at its resumed seventh emergency special session,
Appalled by the great number of innocent Palestinian and Lebanese children victims of Israel's acts of aggression,
Decides to commemorate 4 June of each year as the International Day of Innocent Children Victims of Aggression.

Adopted at the 31st plenary meeting:
In favour: 102
Afghanistan, Albania, Algeria, Angola, Argentina, Bahamas, Bahrain, Bangladesh, Barbados, Benin, Bhutan, Botswana, Brazil, Bulgaria, Burundi, Byelorussia, Cape Verde, Chad, China, Congo, Cuba, Cyprus, Czechoslovakia, Democratic Kampuchea, Democratic Yemen, Djibouti, Ecuador, Egypt, Ethiopia, Gabon, Gambia, German Democratic Republic, Ghana, Greece, Grenada, Guinea, Guinea-Bissau, Guyana, Hungary, India, Indonesia, Iran, Iraq, Jamaica, Jordan, Kenya, Kuwait, Lao People's Democratic Republic, Lebanon, Lesotho, Libya, Madagascar, Malaysia, Maldives, Mali, Malta, Mauritania, Mauritius, Mexico, Mongolia, Morocco, Mozambique, Nepal, Nicaragua, Niger, Nigeria, Oman, Pakistan, Panama, Peru, Philippines, Poland, Qatar, Romania, Rwanda, Sao Tome and Principe, Saudi Arabia, Senegal, Seychelles, Sierra Leone, Singapore, Somalia, Spain, Sri Lanka, Sudan, Syria, Thailand, Trinidad and Tobago, Tunisia, Turkey, Uganda, Ukraine, USSR, United Arab Emirates, United Republic of Cameroon, United Republic of Tanzania, Venezuela, Viet Nam, Yemen, Yugoslavia, Zambia, Zimbabwe.
Against: 2
Israel, United States.
Abstentions: 34
Australia, Austria, Belgium, Bolivia, Burma, Canada, Colombia, Denmark, Dominican Republic, El Salvador, Fiji, Finland, France, Federal Republic of Germany, Haiti, Honduras, Iceland, Ireland, Italy, Japan, Liberia, Luxembourg, Malawi, Netherlands, New Zealand, Norway, Paraguay, Portugal, Samoa, Swaziland, Sweden, United Kingdom, Uruguay, Zaire.
Absent: 18
Antigua and Barbuda, Belize, Central African Republic, Chile, Comoros, Costa Rica, Dominica, Equatorial Guinea, Guatemala, Ivory Coast, Papua New Guinea, Saint Lucia, Saint Vincent, Solomon Islands, Suriname, Togo, Upper Volta, Vanuatu.

Resolution No. ES-7/9 of 24 September 1982

ON THE QUESTION OF PALESTINE: URGING AN INVESTIGATION OF THE MASSACRE OF INNOCENT CIVILIANS IN BEIRUT, DEMANDING A CEASE-FIRE IN LEBANON AND A WITHDRAWAL OF ISRAELI FORCES FROM LEBANESE TERRITORY,

AND RESOLVING THAT THE PALESTINIAN REFUGEES SHOULD BE ENABLED TO RETURN TO THEIR HOMES

The General Assembly,

Having considered the question of Palestine at its resumed seventh emergency special session,

Having heard the statement of the Palestine Liberation Organization, the representative of the Palestinian people,[28]

Recalling and reaffirming, in particular, its resolution 194 (III) of 11 December 1948,

Appalled at the massacre of Palestinian civilians in Beirut,

Recalling Security Council resolutions 508 (1982) of 5 June 1982, 509 (1982) of 6 June 1982, 513 (1982) of 4 July 1982, 520 (1982) of 17 September 1982 and 521 (1982) of 19 September 1982,[29]

Taking note of the reports of the Secretary-General relevant to the situation, particularly his report of 18 September 1982,[30]

Noting with regret that the Security Council has so far not taken effective and practical measures, in accordance with the Charter of the United Nations, to ensure implementation of its resolutions 508 (1982) and 509 (1982),

Referring to the humanitarian principles of the Geneva Convention relative to the Protection of Civilian Persons in Time of War, of 12 August 1949,[31] and to the obligations arising from the regulations annexed to the Hague Conventions of 1907,[32]

Deeply concerned at the sufferings of the Palestinian and Lebanese civilian populations,

Noting the homelessness of the Palestinian people,

Reaffirming the imperative need to permit the Palestinian people to exercise their legitimate rights,

1. *Condemns* the criminal massacre of Palestinian and other civilians in Beirut on 17 September 1982;

2. *Urges* the Security Council to investigate, through the means available to it, the circumstances and extent of the massacre of Palestinian and other civilians in Beirut on 17 September 1982, and to make public the report on its findings as soon as possible;

3. *Decides* to support fully the provisions of Security Council resolutions 508 (1982) and 509 (1982), in which the Council, *inter alia,* demanded that:

(*a*) Israel withdraw all its military forces forthwith and unconditionally to the internationally recognized boundaries of Lebanon;

(*b*) All parties to the conflict cease immediately and simultaneously all military activities within Lebanon and across the Lebanese-Israeli border;

4. *Demands* that all Member States and other parties observe strict respect for the sovereignty, territorial integrity, unity and political independence of Lebanon within its internationally recognized boundaries;

5. *Reaffirms* the fundamental principle of the inadmissibility of the acquisition of territory by force;

6. *Resolves* that, in conformity with its resolution 194 (III) and subsequent relevant resolutions, the Palestinian refugees should be enabled to return to their homes and property from which they have been uprooted and displaced, and demands that Israel comply unconditionally and immediately with the present resolution;

7. *Urges* the Security Council, in the event of continued failure by Israel to comply with the demands contained in resolutions 508 (1982) and 509 (1982) and the present resolution, to meet in order to consider practical ways and means in accordance with the Charter of the United Nations;

8. *Calls upon* all States and international agencies and organizations to continue to provide the most extensive humanitarian aid possible to the victims of the Israeli invasion of Lebanon;

9. *Requests* the Secretary-General to prepare a photographic exhibit of the massacre of 17 September 1982 and to display it in the United Nations visitors' hall;

10. *Decides* to adjourn the seventh emergency special session temporarily and to authorize the President of the latest regular session of the General Assembly to resume its meetings upon request from Member States.

Adopted at the 32nd plenary meeting:

In favour: 147

Afghanistan, Albania, Algeria, Angola, Argentina, Australia, Austria, Bahamas, Bahrain, Bangladesh, Barbados, Belgium, Benin, Bhutan, Bolivia, Botswana, Brazil, Bulgaria, Burma, Burundi, Byelorussia, Canada, Cape Verde, Chad, Chile, China, Colombia, Comoros, Congo, Costa Rica, Cuba, Cyprus, Czechoslovakia, Democratic Kampuchea, Democratic Yemen, Denmark, Djibouti, Dominican Republic, Ecuador, Egypt, El Salvador, Ethiopia, Fiji, Finland, France, Gabon, Gambia, German Democratic Republic, Federal Republic of Germany, Ghana, Greece, Grenada, Guatemala, Guinea, Guinea-Bissau, Guyana, Haiti, Honduras, Hungary, Iceland, India, Indonesia, Iran, Iraq, Ireland, Italy, Ivory Coast, Jamaica, Japan, Jordan, Kenya, Kuwait, Lao People's Democratic Republic, Lebanon, Lesotho, Liberia, Libya, Luxembourg, Madagascar, Malaysia, Maldives, Mali, Malta, Mauritania, Mauritius, Mexico, Mongolia, Morocco, Mozambique, Nepal, Netherlands, New Zealand, Nicaragua, Niger, Nigeria, Norway, Oman, Pakistan, Panama, Papua New Guinea, Paraguay, Peru, Philippines, Poland, Portugal, Qatar, Romania, Rwanda, Saint Lucia, Samoa, Sao Tome and Principe, Saudi Arabia, Senegal, Seychelles, Sierra Leone, Singapore, Solomon Islands, Somalia, Spain, Sri Lanka, Sudan, Suriname, Swaziland, Sweden, Syria, Thailand, Togo, Trinidad and Tobago, Tunisia, Turkey, Uganda, Ukraine, USSR, United Arab Emirates, United Kingdom, United Republic of Cameroon, United Republic of Tanzania, Upper Volta, Uruguay, Vanuatu, Venezu-

---

[28]See A/ES-7/PV.32.

[29]On Israel's invasion of Lebanon. [ed.note]

[30]S/15400.

[31]United Nations, *Treaty Series,* vol. 75, no. 973, p. 287.

[32]Carnegie Endowment for International Peace, *The Hague Conventions and Declarations of 1899 and 1907* (New York, Oxford University Press, 1915).

ela, Viet Nam, Yemen, Yugoslavia, Zaire, Zambia, Zimbabwe.
Against: 2
Israel, United States.
Abstentions: 0
Absent: 6
Antigua and Barbuda, Belize, Dominica, Equatorial Guinea, Malawi, Saint Vincent.

Resolution No. 37/18 of 16 November 1982

CONDEMNING ISRAEL'S THREAT TO REPEAT ITS ATTACK AGAINST IRAQI NUCLEAR INSTALLATIONS AND DEMANDING THAT IT BE WITHDRAWN

The General Assembly,

Having considered the item entitled "Armed Israeli aggression against the Iraqi nuclear installations and its grave consequences for the established international system concerning the peaceful uses of nuclear energy, the non-proliferation of nuclear weapons and international peace and security",

Recalling the relevant resolutions of the Security Council and the General Assembly,

Taking note of the report of the Secretary-General,[33]

Taking note also of the relevant resolution of the International Atomic Energy Agency and the Commission on Human Rights,

Viewing with deep concern Israel's refusal to comply with those resolutions, particularly Security Council resolution 487 (1981) of 19 June 1981,

Gravely alarmed by the dangerous escalation of Israel's acts of aggression in the region,

Gravely concerned that Israel continues to maintain its threats to repeat such attacks against nuclear installations,

Reiterating its alarm over the information and evidence regarding the acquisition and development of nuclear weapons by Israel,

Recalling the Declaration and the Programme of Action on the Establishment of a New International Economic Order,[34] the Charter of Economic Rights and Duties of States[35] and the Declaration on the Use of Scientific and Technological Progress in the Interests of Peace and for the Benefit of Mankind,[36]

Affirming the need to ensure against the repetition of such an attack on nuclear facilities by Israel or any other State,

1. *Condemns* Israel's refusal to implement resolution 487 (1981), unanimously adopted by the Security Council;

2. *Strongly condemns* Israel's threats to repeat such attacks, which would gravely endanger international peace and security;

3. *Condemns* Israel's threats to repeat such attacks, which would gravely endanger international peace and security;

4. *Demands* that Israel withdraw forthwith its officially declared threat to repeat its armed attack against nuclear facilities;

5. *Considers* the Israeli act of aggression to be a violation and a denial of the inalienable sovereign right of States to scientific and technological progress for achieving social and economic development and raising the standards of peoples and the dignity of the human person, as well as a violation and a denial of inalienable human rights and the sovereign right of States to scientific and technological development;

6. *Requests* the Security Council to consider the necessary measures to deter Israel from repeating such an attack on nuclear facilities;

7. *Calls* for the continuation of the consideration, at the international level, of legal measures to prohibit armed attacks against nuclear facilities, and threats thereof as a contribution to promoting and ensuring the safe development of nuclear energy for peaceful purposes;

8. *Requests* the Secretary-General to prepare, with the assistance of a group of experts,[37] a comprehensive study on the consequences of the Israeli armed attack against the Iraqi nuclear installations devoted to peaceful purposes, and to submit that study to the General Assembly at its thirty-eighth session;

9. *Further requests* the Secretary-General to report to the General Assembly at its thirty-eighth session on the implementation of the present resolution;

10. *Decides* to include in the provisional agenda of its thirty-eighth session the item entitled "Armed Israeli aggression against the Iraqi nuclear installations and its grave consequences for the established international system concerning the peaceful uses of nuclear energy, the non-proliferation of nuclear weapons and international peace and security".

Adopted at the 70th plenary meeting:
In favour: 119
Albania, Algeria, Angola, Argentina, Austria, Bahrain, Bangladesh, Barbados, Belgium, Benin, Bhutan, Brazil, Bulgaria, Burundi, Byelorussia, Cape Verde, Central African Republic, Chad, China, Comoros, Congo, Cuba, Cyprus, Czechoslovakia, Democratic Kampuchea, Democratic Yemen, Denmark, Djibouti, Ecuador, Egypt, El Salvador, Equatorial Guinea, Ethiopia, Finland, France, Gabon, Gambia, German Democratic Republic, Federal Republic of Germany, Ghana, Greece, Grenada, Guinea, Guyana, Honduras, Hungary, Iceland, India, Indonesia, Iraq, Ireland, Italy, Japan, Jordan, Kenya, Kuwait, Lao People's Democratic Republic, Liberia, Libya, Luxembourg, Madagascar, Malaysia, Maldives, Mali, Malta, Mauritania, Mauritius, Mexico, Mongolia, Morocco, Mozam-

---

[33]A/37/365 and Add.1-S/15320 and Add.1. For the printed text, see *Official Records of the Security Council, Thirty-seventh year, Supplement for July, August and September 1982,* documents S/15320 and Add.1.
[34]Resolutions 3201 (S-VI) and 3202 (S-VI)
[35]Resolution 3281 (XXIX).
[36]Resolution 3384 (XXX).

[37]Subsequently named Group of Experts on the Consequences of the Israeli Armed Attack against the Iraqi Nuclear Installations.

bique, Nepal, Netherlands, New Zeland, Nicaragua, Niger, Nigeria, Norway, Oman, Pakistan, Panama, Papua New Guinea, Peru, Philippines, Poland, Portugal, Qatar, Romania, Sao Tome and Principe, Saudi Arabia, Senegal, Seychelles, Singapore, Somalia, Spain, Sri Lanka, Sudan, Suriname, Swaziland, Sweden, Syria, Thailand, Togo, Trinidad and Tobago, Tunisia, Turkey, Uganda, Ukraine, USSR, United Kingdom, United Republic of Cameroon, United Republic of Tanzania, Upper Volta, Uruguay, Venezuela, Viet Nam, Yemen, Yugoslavia, Zambia.

Against: 2

Israel, United States.

Abstentions: 13

Australia, Bahamas, Canada, Chile, Colombia, Dominican Republic, Fiji, Guatemala, Haiti, Ivory Coast, Jamaica, Malawi, Paraguay.

Absent: 22

Afghanistan, Antigua and Barbuda, Belize, Bolivia, Botswana, Burma, Costa Rica, Dominica, Guinea-Bissau, Iran, Lebanon, Lesotho, Rwanda, Saint Lucia, Saint Vincent, Samoa, Sierra Leone, Solomon Islands, United Arab Emirates,* Vanuatu, Zaire, Zimbabwe.

---

* Later advised the Secretariat it had intended to vote in favour.

Resolution No. 37/19 of 19 November 1982

CONSIDERING THAT ISRAEL'S THREAT TO REPEAT ITS ATTACK AGAINST IRAQI NUCLEAR INSTALLATIONS IS A SERIOUS THREAT TO THE ROLE AND ACTIVITIES OF THE INTERNATIONAL ATOMIC ENERGY AGENCY

The General Assembly,

Having received the report of the International Atomic Energy Agency to the General Assembly for the year 1981,[38]

Taking note of the statement by the Director General of the International Atomic Energy Agency of 18 November 1982,[39] which provides additional information on developments in the Agency's activities during 1982,

Recognizing the importance of the work and the relevance for the International Atomic Energy Agency to promote further the application of nuclear energy for peaceful purposes, as envisaged in its statute, and to improve further its technical assistance and promotional programmes for the benefit of developing countries,

Conscious of the importance of the work of the International Atomic Energy Agency in the implementation of the relevant provisions of the Treaty on the Non-Proliferation of Nuclear Weapons[40] and other international

treaties, conventions and agreements designed to achieve similar objectives, as well as in ensuring, so far as it is able, that the assistance provided by the Agency or at its request or under its supervision or control is not used in such a way as to further any military purpose, as stated in article II of its statute,

Taking note of the decision of the General Conference of the International Atomic Energy Agency of 20 September 1982 to grant membership of the Agency to Namibia, represented by the United Nations Council for Namibia, in conformity with the request contained in General Assembly resolution 36/121 D of 10 December 1981,

Conscious of the useful outcome of the Conference on Nuclear Power Experience, held at Vienna from 13 to 17 September 1982 by the International Atomic Energy Agency,

Aware that on 29 July 1982 twenty-five years had elapsed since the International Atomic Energy Agency came into being,

1. *Takes note* of the report of the International Atomic Energy Agency;

2. *Urges* all States to strive for effective and harmonious international co-operation in carrying out the work of the International Atomic Energy Agency and to implement strictly the mandate of its statute, in promoting the use of nuclear energy and the application of nuclear science and technology for peaceful purposes; in strengthening technical assistance and co-operation for developing countries; and in ensuring the effectiveness of the Agency's safeguards system;

3. *Considers* that Israel's threat to repeat its armed attack against nuclear facilities as well as any other armed attack against such facilities constitute, *inter alia*, a serious threat to the role and activities of the International Atomic Energy Agency in the development and further promotion of nuclear energy for peaceful purposes;

4. *Affirms* its confidence in the role of the International Atomic Energy Agency in the application of nuclear energy for peaceful purposes;

5. *Requests* the Secretary-General to transmit to the Director General of the International Atomic Energy Agency the records of the thirty-seventh session of the General Assembly relating to the Agency's activities;

Adopted at the 73rd plenary meeting:

In favour: 105

Afghanistan, Albania, Algeria, Angola, Argentina, Bahrain, Bangladesh, Barbados, Benin, Bhutan, Brazil, Bulgaria, Burundi, Byelorussia, Cape Verde, Central African Republic, Chad, Chile, Colombia, Congo, Cuba, Cyprus, Czechoslovakia, Democratic Yemen, Dominican Republic, Ecuador, Egypt, Equatorial Guinea, Ethiopia, Fiji, Gabon, Gambia, German Democratic Republic, Ghana, Guatemala, Guinea, Guinea-Bissau, Guyana, Honduras, Hungary, India, Indonesia, Iraq, Ivory Coast, Jamaica, Jordan, Kenya, Kuwait, Lao People's Democratic Republic, Lebanon, Libya, Madagascar, Malaysia, Maldives, Mali, Malta, Mauritania, Mauritius, Mexico, Mongolia, Morocco, Mozambique, Nepal, Nicaragua, Niger, Nigeria, Oman,

---

[38] International Atomic Energy Agency, *The Annual Report for 1981* (Austria, July 1982); transmitted to the members of the General Assembly by a note of the Secretary-General (A/37/382 and Corr.1).

[39] *Official Records of the General Assembly, Thirty-seventh Session, Plenary Meetings,* 71st meeting, paras. 2-44.

[40] Resolution 2373 (XXII), annex.

Pakistan, Panama, Papua New Guinea, Peru, Philippines, Poland, Qatar, Romania, Saint Lucia, Samoa, Sao Tome and Principe, Saudi Arabia, Senegal, Sierra Leone, Singapore, Solomon Islands, Somalia, Sri Lanka, Sudan, Suriname, Syria, Thailand, Togo, Trinidad and Tobago, Tunisia, Uganda, Ukraine, USSR, United Arab Emirates, United Republic of Cameroon, United Republic of Tanzania, Uruguay, Vanuatu, Venezuela, Viet Nam, Yemen, Yugoslavia, Zambia.

Against: 2

Israel, United States.

Abstention: 25

Australia, Austria, Belgium, Canada, Denmark, Finland, France, Federal Republic of Germany, Greece, Iceland, Ireland, Italy, Japan, Liberia, Luxembourg, Malawi, Netherlands, New Zealand, Norway, Paraguay, Portugal, Spain, Sweden, Turkey, United Kingdom.

Absent: 24

Antigua and Barbuda, Bahamas, Belize, Bolivia, Botswana, Burma, China, Comoros, Costa Rica, Democratic Kampuchea, Djibouti, Dominica, El Salvador, Grenada, Haiti, Iran, Lesotho, Rwanda, Saint Vincent, Seychelles, Swaziland, Upper Volta, Zaire, Zimbabwe.

Resolution No. 37/38 A, B of 30 November 1982

ON THE FINANCING OF THE UNITED NATIONS DISENGAGEMENT OBSERVER FORCE

A

The General Assembly,

Having considered the report of the Secretary-General on the financing of the United Nations Disengagement Observer Force,[41] as well as the related report of the Advisory Committee on Administrative and Budgetary Questions,[42]

Bearing in mind Security Council resolutions 350 (1974) of 31 May 1974, 363 (1974) of 29 November 1974, 369 (1975) of 28 May 1975, 381 (1975) of 30 November 1975, 390 (1976) of 28 May 1976, 398 (1976) of 30 November 1976, 408 (1977) of 26 May 1977, 420 (1977) of 30 November 1977, 429 (1978) of 31 May 1978, 441 (1978) of 30 November 1978, 449 (1979) of 30 May 1979, 456 (1979) of 30 November 1979, 470 (1980) of 30 May 1980, 481 (1980) of 26 November 1980, 485 (1981) of 22 May 1981, 493 (1981) of 23 November 1981, 506 (1982) of 26 May 1982 and 524 (1982) of 29 November 1982,[43]

---

[41]A/37/534 and Corr.1.

[42]A/37/597.

[43]The United Nations Disengagement Observer Force (UNDOF) between Israeli and Syrian forces in the Golan Heights was established by virtue of Security Council Resolution No. 350 (1974) for an initial period of six months, subject to renewal by further resolution of the Security Council. The resolutions in this and the next paragraph provide for the financing and the renewal of the mandate of UNDOF. [ed. note]

Recalling its resolutions 3101 (XXVIII) of 11 December 1973, 3211 B (XXIX) of 29 November 1974, 3374 C (XXX) of 2 December 1975, 31/5 D of 22 December 1976, 32/4 C of 2 December 1977, 33/13 D of 8 December 1978, 34/7 C of 3 December 1979, 35/44 of 1 December 1980, 35/45 A of 1 December 1980 and 36/66 A of 30 November 1981,

Reaffirming its previous decisions regarding the fact that, in order to meet the expenditures caused by such operations, a different procedure is required from that applied to meet expenditures of the regular budget of the United Nations,

Taking into account the fact that the economically more developed countries are in a position to make relatively larger contributions and that the economically less developed countries have a relatively limited capacity to contribute towards peace-keeping operations involving heavy expenditures,

Bearing in mind the special responsibilities of the States permanent members of the Security Council in the financing of such operations, as indicated in General Assembly resolution 1874 (S-IV) of 27 June 1963 and other resolutions of the Assembly,

I

Decides to appropriate to the Special Account referred to in section II, paragraph 1, of General Assembly resolution 3211 B (XXIX) the amount of $15,973,998 gross ($15,784,998 net) authorized and apportioned by section III of Assembly resolution 36/66 A for the operation of the United Nations Disengagement Observer Force for the period from 1 June to 30 November 1982, inclusive;

II

1. *Decides* to appropriate to the Special Account an amount of $17,186,500 for the operation of the United Nations Disengagement Observer Force for the period from 1 December 1982 to 31 May 1983, inclusive;

2. *Decides further,* as an *ad hoc* arrangement, without prejudice to the positions of principle that may be taken by Member States in any consideration by the General Assembly of arrangement for the financing of peace-keeping operations, to apportion the amount of $17,186,500 among Member States in accordance with the scheme set out in Assembly resolution 3101 (XXVIII) and the provisions of section II, paragraph 2 (*b*) and 2 (*c*), and section V, paragraph 1, of resolution 3374 C (XXX), section V, paragaph 1, of resolution 31/5 D, section V, paragraph 1, of resolution 32/4 C, section V, paragraph 1, of resolution 33/13 D, section V, paragraph 1, of resolution 34/7 C, section V, paragraph 1, of resolution 35/45 A and section V, paragraph 1, of resolution 36/66 A; the scale of assessments for the years 1980, 1981, and 1982 shall be applied against a portion thereof, that is $2,864,417, being the amount pertaining on a *pro rata* basis to the month of December 1982, and the scale of assessments for the years 1983, 1984 and 1985 shall be applied against the balance for the period thereafter;

3. *Decides* that there shall be set off against the appor-

tionment among Member States, as provided in paragraph 2 above, their respective share in the estimated income of $10,000 other than staff assessment income approved for the period from 1 December 1982 to 31 May 1983, inclusive;

4. *Decides* that, in accordance with the provisions of its resolution 973 (X) of 15 December 1955 there shall be set off against the apportionment among Member States, as provided for in paragraph 2 above, their respective share in the Tax Equalization Fund of the estimated staff assessment income of $192,500 approved for the period from 1 December 1982 to 31 May 1983, inclusive;

III

Authorizes the Secretary-General to enter into commitments for the United Nations Disengagement Observer Force at a rate not to exceed $2,864,416 gross ($2,830,666 net) per month for the period from 1 June to 30 November 1983 inclusive, should the Security Council decide to continue the Force beyond the period of six months authorized under its resolution 524 (1982), the said amount to be apportioned among Member States in accordance with the scheme set out in the present resolution;

IV

1. *Stresses* the need for voluntary contributions to the United Nations Disengagement Observer Force both in cash and in the form of services and supplies acceptable to the Secretary-General;

2. *Requests* the Secretary-General to take all necessary action to ensure that the United Nations Disengagement Observer Force is conducted with a maximum of efficiency and economy;

V

1. *Decides* that Antigua and Barbuda, Belize and Vanuatu shall be included in the group of Member States mentioned in paragraph 2(*d*) of General Assembly resolution 3101 (XXVIII) and the that their contributions to the United Nations Disengagement Observer Force shall be calculated in accordance with the provisions of the resolution adopted by the Assembly at the current session regarding the scale of assessments;

2. *Decides further* that, in accordance with regulation 5.2(*c*) of the Financial Regulations of the United Nations, the contributions to the United Nations Disengagement Observer Force until 30 November 1982 of the Member States referred to in paragraph 1 of the present section shall be treated as miscellaneous income to be set off against the appropriations apportioned in section II above.

Adopted at the 85th plenary meeting:
In favour: 95
Argentina, Australia, Austria, Bahamas, Bahrain, Bangladesh, Barbados, Belgium, Bhutan, Brazil, Burma, Burundi, Canada, Central African Republic, Chile, China, Colombia, Comoros, Congo, Costa Rica, Cyprus, Denmark, Ecuador, Egypt, Fiji, Finland, France, Gabon, Gambia, Federal Republic of Germay, Ghana, Greece, Guy-

ana, Honduras, Iceland, India, Indonesia, Ireland, Israel, Italy, Ivory Coast, Japan, Jordan, Kenya, Kuwait, Lesotho, Luxembourg, Malawi, Malaysia, Mali, Malta, Mauritania, Mauritius, Mexico, Morocco, Nepal, Netherlands, New Zealand, Niger, Nigeria, Norway, Oman, Pakistan, Paraguay, Peru, Philippines, Poland, Portugal, Qatar, Romania, Rwanda, Samoa, Senegal, Singapore, Solomon Islands, Somalia, Spain, Sri Lanka, Sudan, Sweden, Thailand, Togo, Trinidad and Tobago, Tunisia, Turkey, United Arab Emirates, United Kingdom, United Republic of Cameroon, United Republic of Tanzania, United States, Uruguay, Venezuela, Yugoslavia, Zaire, Zambia.
Against: 3
Albania, Iraq, Syria.
Abstentions: 17
Algeria, Bulgaria, Byelorussia, Cuba, Czechoslovakia, Democratic Yemen, Dominican Republic, Ethiopia, German Democratic Republic, Grenada, Hungary, Lao People's Democratic Republic,* Mongolia, Ukraine, USSR, Viet Nam, Yemen.
Absent: 41
Afghanistan, Angola, Antigua and Barbuda, Belize, Benin, Bolivia, Botswana, Cape Verde, Chade, Democratic Kampuchea, Djibouti, Dominica, El Salvador, Equatorial Guinea, Guatemala, Guinea, Guinea-Bissau, Haiti, Iran, Jamaica,** Lebanon,** Liberia, Libya, Madagascar, Maldives, Mozambique, Nicaragua, Panama, Papua New Guinea, Saint Lucia, Saint Vincent, Sao Tome and Principe, Saudi Arabia, Seychelles, Sierra Leone,** Suriname, Swaziland, Uganda, Upper Volta, Vanuatu, Zimbabwe.

---

*Later advised the Secretariat it had intended not to participate in the vote.
**Later advised the Secretariat it had intended to vote in favour.

B

The General Assembly,

Having regard to the financial position of the Special Account for the United Nations Emergency Force and the United Nations Disengagement Observer Force, as set forth in the report of the Secretary-General,[44] and referring to paragraph 5 of the report of the Advisory Committee on Administrative and Budgetary Questions,[45]

Mindful of the fact that it is essential to provide the United Nations Disengagement Observer Force with the necessary financial resources to enable it to fulfill its responsibilities under the relevant resolutions of the Security Council,

Concerned that the Secretary-General is continuing to face growing difficulties in meeting the obligations of the Forces on a current basis, particularly those due to the Governments of troop-contributing States,

---

[44] A/37/534 and Corr.1.
[45] A/37/597.

Recalling its resolutions 33/13 E of 14 December 1978, 34/7 D of 17 December 1979, 35/45 B of 1 December 1980 and 36/66 B of 30 November 1981,

Recognizing that, in consequence of the withholding of contributions by certain Member States, the surplus balances in the Special Account for the United Nations Emergency Force and the United Nations Disengagement Observer Force have, in effect, been drawn upon to the full extent to supplement the income received from contributions for meeting expenses of the Forces,

Concerned that the application of the provisions of regulations 5.2 (*b*), 5.2 (*d*), 4.3 and 4.4 of the Financial Regulations of the United Nations would aggravate the already difficult financial situation of the Forces,

Decides that the provisions of regulations 5.2 (*b*), 5.2 (*d*), 4.3 and 4.4 of the Financial Regulations of the United Nations shall be suspended in respect of the amount of $7,403,489, which otherwise would have to be surrendered pursuant to those provisions, this amount to be entered in the account referred to in the operative part of General Assembly resolution 33/13 E and held in suspense until a further decision is taken by the Assembly.

Adopted at the 85th plenary meeting:
In favour: 95
Argentina, Australia, Austria, Bahamas, Bahrain, Bangladesh, Barbados, Belgium, Bhutan, Brazil, Burma, Burundi, Canada, Central African Republic, Chile, China, Colombia, Comoros, Congo, Costa Rica, Cyprus, Denmark, Ecuador, Egypt, Fiji, Finland, France, Gabon, Gambia, Federal Republic of Germany, Ghana, Greece, Guyana, Honduras, Iceland, India, Indonesia, Ireland, Israel, Italy, Ivory Coast, Japan, Jordan, Kenya, Kuwait, Lesotho, Luxembourg, Malawi, Malaysia, Mali, Malta, Mauritania, Mauritius, Mexico, Morocco, Nepal, Netherlands, New Zealand, Niger, Nigeria, Norway, Oman, Pakistan, Paraguay, Peru, Philippines, Portugal, Qatar, Rwanda, Samoa, Senegal, Sierra Leone, Singapore, Solomon Islands, Somalia, Spain, Sri Lanka, Sudan, Swaziland, Sweden, Thailand, Togo, Trinidad and Tobago, Tunisia, Turkey, United Arab Emirates, United Kingdom, United Republic of Cameroon, United Republic of Tanzania, United States, Uruguay, Venezuela, Yugoslavia, Zaire, Zambia.
Against: 11
Albania, Bulgaria, Byelorussia, Czechoslovakia, German Democratic Republic, Hungary, Iraq, Mongolia, Syria, Ukraine, USSR.
Abstentions: 11
Algeria, Cuba, Democratic Yemen, Dominican Republic, Ethiopia, Grenada, Lao People's Democratic Republic,* Poland, Romania, Viet Nam, Yemen.
Absent: 39
Afghanistan, Angola, Antigua and Barbuda, Belize, Benin, Bolivia, Botswana, Cape Verde, Chad, Democratic Kampuchea, Djibouti, Dominica, El Salvador, Equatorial Guinea, Guatemala, Guinea, Guinea-Bissau, Haiti, Iran, Jamaica,** Lebanon,** Liberia, Libya, Madagascar, Maldives, Mozambique, Nicaragua, Panama, Papua New Guinea, Saint Lucia, Saint Vincent, Sao Tome and Princi-

pe, Saudi Arabia, Seychelles, Suriname, Uganda, Upper Volta, Vanuatu, Zimbabwe.

---

* Later advised the Secretariat it had intended not to participate in the vote.
** Later advised the Secretariat it had intended to vote in favour.

Resolution No. 37/39 of 3 December 1982

CONDEMNING ISRAEL AND CERTAIN WESTERN STATES FOR COLLABORATION WITH SOUTH AFRICA IN THE ECONOMIC, MILITARY AND NUCLEAR FIELDS [EXCERPTS FROM A RESOLUTION ON ASSISTANCE TO SOUTH AFRICA]

The General Assembly,

....

Alarmed at the continued collaboration of certain Western States and Israel with the racist regime of South Africa in the nuclear field,

....

3. *Vigorously condemns* the collaboration of certain Western States, Israel and other States, as well as the transnational corporations and other organizations which maintain or continue to increase their collaboration with the racist regime of South Africa, especially in the political, economic, military and nuclear fields, thus encouraging that regime to persist in its inhuman and criminal policy of brutal oppression of the peoples of southern Africa and denial of their human rights;

....

Adopted at the 90th plenary meeting:
In favour: 121
Albania, Algeria, Angola, Antigua and Barbuda, Argentina, Bahamas, Bahrain, Bangladesh, Barbados, Belize, Benin, Bhutan, Bolivia, Botswana, Brazil, Bulgaria, Burma, Burundi, Byelorussia, Cape Verde, Central African Republic, Chad, Chile, China, Colombia, Comoros, Costa Rica, Cuba, Cyprus, Czechoslovakia, Democratic Kampuchea, Democratic Yemen, Djibouti, Dominican Republic, Ecuador, Egypt, El Salvador, Equatorial Guinea, Ethiopia, Fiji, Gabon, German Democratic Republic, Ghana, Grenada, Guinea, Buinea-Bissau, Guyana, Haiti, Hungary, India, Indonesia, Iran, Iraq, Jamaica, Jordan, Kenya, Kuwait, Lao People's Democratic Republic, Lebanon, Lesotho, Liberia, Libya, Madagascar, Malaysia, Maldives, Mali, Malta, Mauritania, Mauritius, Mexico, Mongolia, Morocco, Mozambique, Nepal, Nicaragua, Niger, Nigeria, Oman, Pakistan, Panama, Papua New Guinea, Peru, Philippines, Poland, Qatar, Romania, Rwanda, Saint Lucia, Samoa, Sao Tome and Principe, Saudi Arabia, Senegal, Sierra Leone, Singapore, Solomon Islands, Somalia, Sri Lanka, Sudan, Suriname, Swaziland, Syria, Thailand, Togo, Trinidad and Tobago, Tunisia, Turkey, Uganda, Ukraine, USSR, United Arab Emirates, United

Republic of Tanzania, Upper Volta, Uruguay, Vanuatu, Venezuela, Viet Nam, Yemen, Yugoslavia, Zaire, Zambia, Zimbabwe.
Against: 10
Belgium, Canada, France, Federal Republic of Germany, Israel, Italy, Luxembourg, Netherlands, United Kingdom, United States.
Abstentions: 14
Australia, Austria, Denmark, Finland, Greece, Iceland, Ireland, Ivory Coast, Japan, New Zealand, Norway, Portugal, Spain, Sweden.
Absent: 11
Afghanistan,* Congo, Dominica, Gambia,* Guatemala, Honduras, Malawi,** Paraguay, Saint Vincent, Seychelles, United Republic of Cameroon.

---

* Later advised the Secretariat it had intended to vote in favour.
** Later advised the Secretariat it had intended to abstain.

Resolution No. 37/40 of 3 December 1982

CONDEMNING RACISM IN SOUTH AFRICA AND THE OCCUPIED ARAB TERRITORIES [EXCERPTS FROM A RESOLUTION ON THE IMPLEMENTATION OF THE PROGRAMME FOR THE DECADE FOR ACTION TO COMBAT RACISM AND RACIAL DISCRIMINATION]

The General Assembly,

....

Alarmed at the persistent collaboration of certain Western States and Israel with the racist régime of South Africa in the nuclear field,

....

2. *Strongly condemns* the policies of *apartheid*, racism and racial discrimination pursued in southern Africa, all occupied Arab territories and elsewhere, including the denial of the right of peoples to self-determination and independence;

3. *Reaffirms* its strong support for the national liberation struggle against racism, racial discrimination, *apartheid*, colonialism and foreign domination and for self-determination by all available means, including armed struggle;

....

10. *Vigorously condemns* the collaboration of certain Western States, Israel and other States and of transnational corporations and other organizations which are maintaining or continuing to increase their collaboration with the racist régime of South Africa, particularly in the political, economic, military and nuclear fields, thereby encouraging that régime to persist in its inhuman and criminal policy of brutal oppression of the peoples of southern Africa and in its denial of human rights;

....

Adopted at the 90th plenary meeting:
In favour: 122
Albania, Algeria, Angola, Antigua and Barbuda, Argentina, Bahamas, Bahrain, Bangladesh, Barbados, Belize, Benin, Bhutan, Bolivia, Botswana, Brazil, Bulgaria, Burma, Burundi, Byelorussia, Cape Verde, Central African Republic, Chad, Chile, China, Colombia, Comoros, Costa Rica, Cuba, Cyprus, Czechoslovakia, Democratic Kampuchea, Democratic Yemen, Djibouti, Dominican Republic, Ecuador, Egypt, El Salvador, Equatorial Guinea, Ethiopia, Fiji, Gabon, German Democratic Republic, Ghana, Grenada, Guinea, Guinea-Bissau, Guyana, Haiti, Hungary, India, Indonesia, Iran, Iraq, Ivory Coast, Jamaica, Jordan, Kenya, Kuwait, Lao People's Democratic Republic, Lebanon, Lesotho, Liberia, Libya, Madagascar, Malaysia, Maldives, Mali, Malta, Mauritania, Mauritius, Mexico, Mongolia, Morocco, Mozambique, Nepal, Nicaragua, Niger, Nigeria, Oman, Pakistan, Panama, Papua New Guinea, Peru, Philippines, Poland, Qatar, Romania, Rwanda, Saint Lucia, Samoa, Sao Tome and Principe, Saudi Arabia, Senegal, Sierra Leone, Singapore, Solomon Islands, Somalia, Sri Lanka, Sudan, Suriname, Swaziland, Syria, Thailand, Togo, Trinidad and Tobago, Tunisia, Turkey, Uganda, Ukraine, USSR, United Arab Emirates, United Republic of Tanzania, Upper Volta, Uruguay, Vanuatu, Venezuela, Viet Nam, Yemen, Yugoslavia, Zaire, Zambia, Zimbabwe.
Against: 19
Australia, Austria, Belgium, Canada, Denmark, Finland, France, Federal Republic of Germany, Iceland, Ireland, Israel, Italy, Luxembourg, Netherlands, New Zealand, Norway, Sweden, United Kingdom, United States.
Abstentions: 5
Greece, Japan, Paraguay, Portugal, Spain.
Absent: 10
Afghanistan,* Congo, Dominica, Gambia,* Guatemala, Honduras, Malawi,** Saint Vincent, Seychelles, United Republic of Cameroon.

---

*Later advised the Secretariat it had intended to vote in favour.
**Later advised the Secretariat it had intended to abstain.

Resolution No. 37/43 of 3 December 1982

REAFFIRMING THE RIGHT OF THE PALESTINIAN PEOPLE TO SELF-DETERMINATION, CONDEMNING ISRAELI ATTACKS ON CIVILIANS IN LEBANON AND CALLING FOR SUPPORT FOR THE PALESTINE LIBERATION ORGANIZATION [EXCERPTS FROM A RESOLUTION ON THE RIGHT OF PEOPLES UNDER COLONIAL AND FOREIGN DOMINATION TO SELF-DETERMINATION AND INDEPENDENCE]

The General Assembly,

....

Considering that the denial of the inalienable rights of

the Palestinian people to self-determination, sovereignty, independence and return to Palestine and the repeated acts of aggression by Israel against the peoples of the region constitute a serious threat to international peace and security,

Deeply shocked and alarmed at the deplorable consequences of the Israeli invasion of Beirut on 3 August 1982, and recalling all the resolutions of the Security Council, in particular resolutions 520 (1982) of 17 September 1982 and 521 (1982) of 19 September 1982,

Reaffirming its faith in the importance of the implementation of the Declaration on the Granting of Independence to Colonial Countries and Peoples, contained in General Assembly resolution 1514 (XV) of 14 December 1960,

Reaffirming the importance of the universal realization of the right of peoples to self-determination, national sovereignty and territorial integrity and of the speedy granting of independence to colonial countries and peoples as imperatives for the full enjoyment of all human rights,

....

3. *Reaffirms* the inalienable right of the Namibian people, the Palestinian people and all peoples under foreign and colonial domination to self-determination, national independence, territorial integrity, national unity and sovereignty without outside interference;

....

18. *Strongly condemns* those Governments that do not recognize the right to self-determination and independence of all peoples still under colonial and foreign domination and alien subjugation, notably the peoples of Africa and the Palestinian people;

19. *Strongly condemns* the increasingly widespread massacres of innocent and defenceless people, including women and children, by the racist minority Pretoria régime in its desperate attempt to thwart the legitimate demands of the people;

20. *Strongly condemns* the massacre of Palestinians and other civilians at Beirut on 17 September 1982;

21. *Strongly condemns* the expansionist activities of Israel in the Middle East and the continual bombing of Palestinian civilians, which constitute a serious obstacle to the realization of the self-determination and independence of the Palestinian people;

22. *Strongly condemns* the Israeli aggression against Lebanon in June 1982, which endangers stability, peace and security in the region, and reiterates its support for the efforts undertaken to implement the resolutions of the Security Council, in particular those demanding the immediate and unconditional withdrawal of Israeli forces from Lebanese territory to internationally recognized boundaries and respect for the sovereignty and territorial integrity of Lebanon;

23. *Urges* all States, competent organizations of the United Nations system, specialized agencies and other international organizations to extend their support to the Palestinian people through its sole and legitimate representative, the Palestine Liberation Organization, in its struggle to regain its right to self-determination and independence in accordance with the Charter of the United Nations;

24. *Demands* the immediate and unconditional release of all persons detained or imprisoned as a result of their struggle for self-determination and independence, full respect for their fundamental individual rights and the observance of article 5 of the Universal Declaration of Human Rights,[46] under which no one shall be subjected to torture or to cruel, inhuman or degrading treatment;

....

Adopted at the 90th plenary meeting:
In favour: 120
Albania, Algeria, Angola, Antigua and Barbuda, Argentina, Bahamas, Bahrain, Bangladesh, Barbados, Belize, Benin, Bhutan, Bolivia, Botswana, Brazil, Bulgaria, Burundi, Byelorussia, Cape Verde, Central African Republic, Chad, Chile, China, Colombia, Comoros, Congo, Cuba, Cyprus, Czechoslovakia, Democratic Kampuchea, Democratic Yemen, Djibouti, Dominican Republic, Ecuador, Egypt, El Salvador, Equatorial Guinea, Ethiopia, Fiji, Gabon, German Democratic Republic, Ghana, Grenada, Guinea, Guinea-Bissau, Guyana, Haiti, Hungary, India, Indonesia, Iran, Iraq, Ivory Coast, Jamaica, Jordan, Kenya, Kuwait, Lao People's Democratic Republic, Lesotho, Liberia, Libya, Madagascar, Malaysia, Maldives, Mali, Malta, Mauritania, Mauritius, Mexico, Mongolia, Morocco, Mozambique, Nepal, Nicaragua, Niger, Nigeria, Oman, Pakistan, Panama, Papua New Guinea, Peru, Philippines, Poland, Qatar, Romania, Rwanda, Saint Lucia, Samoa, Sao Tome and Principe, Saudi Arabia, Senegal, Sierra Leone, Singapore, Solomon Islands, Somalia, Sri Lanka, Sudan, Suriname, Swaziland, Syria, Thailand, Togo, Trinidad and Tobago, Tunisia, Turkey, Uganda, Ukraine, USSR, United Arab Emirates, United Republic of Tanzania, Upper Volta, Uruguay, Vanuatu, Venezuela, Viet Nam, Yemen, Yugoslavia, Zaire, Zambia, Zimbabwe.
Against: 17
Australia, Belgium, Canada, Denmark, Finland, France, Federal Republic of Germany, Iceland, Israel, Italy, Luxembourg, Netherlands, New Zealand, Norway, Sweden, United Kingdom, United States.
Abstentions: 6
Austria, Greece, Ireland, Japan, Portugal, Spain.
Absent: 13
Afghanistan,* Burma, Costa Rica, Dominica, Gambia,* Guatemala, Honduras, Lebanon, Malawi,** Paraguay, Saint Vincent, Seychelles, United Republic of Cameroon.

---

* Later advised the Secretariat it had intended to vote in favour.
** Later advised the Secretariat it had intended to abstain.
[46] Resolution 217 A (III).

Resolution No. 37/46 of 3 December 1982

EXPRESSING CONCERN AT ISRAEL'S DEFIANCE OF THE INTERNATIONAL CONVENTION ON THE ELIMINATION OF ALL FORMS OF RACIAL DISCRIMINATION [EXCERPTS FROM A RESOLUTION ON RACIAL DISCRIMINATION]

The General Assembly,

Recalling its resolutions 36/12 of 28 October 1981 on the report of the Committee on the Elimination of Racial Discrimination and 37/45 of 3 December 1982 on the status of the International Convention on the Elimination of All Forms of Racial Discrimination,[47] as well as its other relevant resolutions on the implementation of the Programme for the Decade for Action to Combat Racism and Racial Discrimination,[48]

Having considered the report of the Committee on the Elimination of Racial Discrimination on its twenty-fifth and twenty-sixth sessions,[49] submitted under article 9, paragraph 2, of the International Convention on the Elimination of All Forms of Racial Discrimination,

Emphasizing the importance for the success of the struggle against all practices of racial discrimination, including vestiges and manifestations of racist ideologies wherever they exist, that all Member States be guided in their internal and foreign policy by the basic provisions of the Convention,

Mindful of the obligation of all States parties to comply fully with the provisions of the Convention,

Welcoming the continued cooperation of the Committee on the Elimination of Racial Discrimination with the competent specialized agencies, especially the United Nations Educational, Scientific and Cultural Organization and the International Labour Organisation, and with other United Nations bodies,

Noting the decisions adopted and recommendations made by the Committee at its twenty-fifth and twenty-sixth sessions,

....

7. *Expresses grave concern* at the Israeli policy of defiance of the basic principles and objectives of the Convention, as reflected in the report of the Committee, and calls for the respect and preservation of the national and cultural identity of the Palestinian people;

....

Adopted at the 90th plenary meeting:
In favour: 131
Albania Algeria, Angola, Antigua and Barbuda, Argentina, Bahamas, Bahrain, Bangladesh, Barbados, Benin, Bhutan, Bolivia, Botswana, Brazil, Bulgaria, Burma, Burundi, Byelorussia, Cape Verde, Central African Republic, Chad, Chile, China, Colombia, Comoros, Congo, Costa Rica, Cuba, Cyprus, Czechoslovakia, Democratic Kampuchea, Democratic Yemen, Djibouti, Dominican Republic, Ecuador, Egypt, El Salvador, Equatorial Guinea, Ethiopia, Fiji, France, Gabon, German Democratic Republic, Ghana, Greece, Grenada, Guinea, Guinea-Bissau, Guyana, Haiti, Hungary, Iceland, India, Indonesia, Iran, Iraq, Italy, Ivory Coast, Jamaica, Japan, Jordan, Kenya, Kuwait, Lao People's Democratic Republic, Lebanon, Lesotho, Liberia, Libya, Madagascar, Malaysia, Maldives, Mali, Malta, Mauritania, Mauritius, Mexico, Mongolia, Morocco, Mozambique, Nepal, Netherlands, Nicaragua, Niger, Nigeria, Oman, Pakistan, Panama, Papua New Guinea, Peru, Philippines, Poland, Portugal, Qatar, Romania, Rwanda, Saint Lucia, Samoa, Sao Tome and Principe, Saudi Arabia, Senegal, Sierra Leone, Singapore, Solomon Islands, Somalia, Spain, Sri Lanka, Sudan, Suriname, Swaziland, Syria, Thailand, Togo, Trinidad and Tobago, Tunisia, Turkey, Uganda, Ukraine, USSR, United Arab Emirates, United Republic of Cameroon, United Republic of Tanzania, Upper Volta, Uruguay, Vanuatu, Venezuela, Viet Nam, Yemen, Yugoslavia, Zaire, Zambia, Zimbabwe.
Against: 2
Israel, United States.
Abstentions: 15
Australia, Austria, Belgium, Belize,* Canada, Denmark, Finland, Federal Republic of Germany, Ireland, Luxembourg, Malawi, New Zealand, Norway, Sweden, United Kingdom.
Absent: 8
Afghanistan,* Dominica, Gambia,* Guatemala, Honduras, Paraguay, Saint Vincent, Seychelles.

---

* Later advised the Secretariat it had intended to vote in favour.

Resolution No. 37/69 A, C, D, F of 9 December 1982

CONDEMNING COLLABORATION BETWEEN ISRAEL AND CERTAIN WESTERN STATES AND SOUTH AFRICA, ESPECIALLY IN THE MILITARY AND NUCLEAR FIELDS [EXCERPTS FROM A RESOLUTION ON SOUTH AFRICAN POLICIES OF *APARTHEID*]

A

SITUATION IN SOUTH AFRICA

The General Assembly,

....

Condemning all military, nuclear and other collaboration by certain Western States and Israel with South Africa,

Gravely concerned at the pronouncements, policies and actions of the Government of the United States of America which have provided comfort and encouragement to the racist régime of South Africa,

Concerned that some Western States and Israel continue military and nuclear co-operation with South Africa, in gross violation of the provisions of Security Council resolution 418 (1977), of 4 November 1977, and have failed to

---

[47] Resolution 2106 A (XX), annex.
[48] Resolution 3057 (XXVIII), annex.
[49] *Official Records of the General Assembly, Thirty-seventh Session, Supplement No. 18* (A/37/18).

prevent corporations, institutions and individuals within their jurisdiction from carrying out such co-operation,

....

4. *Condemns* the policies of certain Western States, especially the United States of America, and of Israel, and of their transnational corporations and financial institutions that have increased political, economic and military collaboration with the racist régime of South Africa despite repeated appeals by the General Assembly;

....

Adopted at the 97th plenary meeting:
In favour: 118
Afghanistan, Albania, Algeria, Angola, Antigua and Barbuda, Argentina, Bahamas, Bahrain, Bangladesh, Barbados, Benin, Bhutan, Bolivia, Botswana, Brazil, Bulgaria, Burma, Burundi, Byelorussia, Cape Verde, Central African Republic, Chad, China, Colombia, Comoros, Congo, Costa Rica, Cuba, Cyprus, Czechoslovakia, Democratic Kampuchea, Democratic Yemen, Djibouti, Dominican Republic, Ecuador, Egypt, Equatorial Guinea, Ethiopia, Fiji, Gabon, Gambia, German Democratic Republic, Ghana, Grenada, Guinea, Guinea-Bissau, Guyana, Haiti, Hungary, India, Indonesia, Iran, Iraq, Jamaica, Jordan, Kenya, Kuwait, Lao People's Democratic Republic, Lesotho, Liberia, Libya, Madagascar, Malaysia, Maldives, Mali, Malta, Mauritania, Mauritius, Mexico, Mongolia, Morocco, Mozambique, Nepal, Nicaragua, Niger, Nigeria, Oman, Pakistan, Panama, Papua New Guinea, Peru, Philippines, Poland, Qatar, Romania, Rwanda, Sao Tome and Principe, Saudi Arabia, Senegal, Sierra Leone, Solomon Islands, Somalia, Sri Lanka, Sudan, Suriname, Swaziland, Syria, Thailand, Togo, Trinidad and Tobago, Tunisia, Turkey, Uganda, Ukraine, USSR, United Arab Emirates, United Republic of Cameroon, United Republic of Tanzania, Upper Volta, Uruguay, Vanuatu, Venezuela, Viet Nam, Yemen, Yugoslavia, Zaire, Zambia, Zimbabwe.
Against: 14
Belgium, Canada, Denmark, France, Federal Republic of Germany, Iceland, Italy, Luxembourg, Netherlands, New Zealand, Norway, Portugal, United Kingdom, United States.
Abstentions: 11
Australia, Austria, Finland, Greece, Ireland, Ivory Coast, Japan,* Malawi, Singapore, Spain, Sweden.
Absent: 12
Belize, Chile, Dominica, El Salvador, Guatemala, Honduras, Lebanon, Paraguay, Saint Lucia, Saint Vincent, Samoa,** Seychelles.**

Israel announced that it was not participating in the vote.

---

*Later advised the Secretariat it had intended to vote against.
**Later advised the Secretariat it had intended to vote in favour.

C

COMPREHENSIVE AND MANDATORY SANCTIONS AGAINST SOUTH AFRICA

The General Assembly,

....

Deploring the attitude of those Western permanent members of the Security Council that have so far prevented the Council from adopting comprehensive sanctions against South Africa under Chapter VII of the Charter,
Deploring also the attitude of those States, in particular the United States of America and Israel, that have continued and increased their political, economic and other collaboration with South Africa,

....

2. *Requests* all States, especially Western States concerned and Israel, to cease all collaboration with the racist régime of South Africa and to implement the relevant resolutions of the United Nations;

....

Adopted at the 97th plenary meeting:
In favour: 114
Afghanistan, Albania, Algeria, Angola, Antigua and Barbuda, Argentina, Bahamas, Bahrain, Bangladesh, Barbados, Benin, Bhutan, Bolivia, Brazil, Bulgaria, Burma, Burundi, Byelorussia, Cape Verde, Central African Republic, Chad, China, Colombia, Comoros, Congo, Costa Rica, Cuba, Cyprus, Czechoslovakia, Democratic Kampuchea, Democratic Yemen, Djibouti, Dominican Republic, Ecuador, Egypt, Equatorial Guinea, Ethiopia, Fiji, Gabon, Gambia, German Democratic Republic, Ghana, Grenada, Guinea, Guinea-Bissau, Guyana, Haiti, Hungary, India, Indonesia, Iran, Iraq, Jamaica, Jordan, Kenya, Kuwait, Lao People's Democratic Republic, Liberia, Libya, Madagascar, Malaysia, Mali, Malta, Mauritania, Mauritius, Mexico, Mongolia, Morocco, Mozambique, Nepal, Nicaragua, Niger, Nigeria, Oman, Pakistan, Panama, Papua New Guinea, Peru, Philippines, Poland, Qatar, Romania, Rwanda, Sao Tome and Principe, Saudi Arabia, Senegal, Sierra Leone, Solomon Islands, Somalia, Sri Lanka, Sudan, Suriname, Syria, Thailand, Togo, Trinidad and Tobago, Tunisia, Turkey, Uganda, Ukraine, USSR, United Arab Emirates, United Republic of Cameroon, United Republic of Tanzania, Upper Volta, Uruguay, Vanuatu, Venezuela, Viet Nam, Yemen, Yugoslavia, Zaire, Zambia, Zimbabwe.
Against: 10
Belgium, Canada, France, Federal Republic of Germany, Japan, Luxembourg, Netherlands, Portugal, United Kingdom, United States.
Abstentions: 19
Australia, Austria, Botswana, Denmark, Finland, Greece, Iceland, Ireland, Italy, Ivory Coast, Lesotho, Malawi, Maldives, New Zealand, Norway, Singapore, Spain, Swaziland, Sweden.
Absent: 12
Belize, Chile, Dominica, El Salvador, Guatemala, Honduras, Lebanon, Paraguay, Saint Lucia, Saint Vincent, Samoa,* Seychelles.*

Israel announced that it was not participating in the vote.

_____

*Later advised the Secretariat it had intended to vote in favour.

D

MILITARY AND NUCLEAR COLLABORATION WITH SOUTH AFRICA

The General Assembly,

....

Expressing deep concern over the stepped-up arms build-up and war preparations by the racist régime of South Africa and strongly condemning the growing violation of the arms embargo as well as the continued nuclear collaboration by the United States of America and some other Western States and Israel with the *apartheid* régime,

....

2. *Deplores* the actions of several Western States and Israel which have provided the racist régime of South Africa with an enormous arsenal of military equipment and technology, as well as assistance in its nuclear plans, and which have allowed corporations under their jurisdiction to invest in the armaments industry in South Arica;

....

Adopted at the 97th plenary meeting:
In favour: 120
Afghanistan, Albania, Algeria, Angola, Antigua and Barbados, Argentina, Bahamas, Bahrain, Bangladesh, Barbados, Benin, Bhutan, Bolivia, Botswana, Brazil, Bulgaria, Burma, Burundi, Byelorussia, Cape Verde, Central African Republic, Chad, Chile, China, Colombia, Comoros, Congo, Costa Rica, Cuba, Cyprus, Czechoslovakia, Democratic Kampuchea, Democratic Yemen, Djibouti, Dominican Republic, Ecuador, Egypt, Equatorial Guinea, Ethiopia, Fiji, Gabon, Gambia, German Democratic Republic, Ghana, Grenada, Guinea, Guinea-Bissau, Guyana, Haiti, Hungary, India, Indonesia, Iran, Iraq, Jamaica, Jordan, Kenya, Kuwait, Lao People's Democratic Republic, Lesotho, Liberia, Libya, Madagascar, Malaysia, Maldives, Mali, Malta, Mauritania, Mauritius, Mexico, Mongolia, Morocco, Mozambique, Nepal, Nicaragua, Niger, Nigeria, Oman, Pakistan, Panama, Papua New Guinea, Peru, Philippines, Poland, Qatar, Romania, Rwanda, Sao Tome and Principe, Saudi Arabia, Senegal, Sierra Leone, Singapore, Solomon Islands, Somalia, Sri Lanka, Sudan, Suriname, Swaziland, Syria, Thailand, Togo, Trinidad and Tobago, Tunisia, Turkey, Uganda, Ukraine, USSR, United Arab Emirates, United Republic of Cameroon, United Republic of Tanzania, Upper Volta, Uruguay, Vanuatu, Venezuela, Viet Nam, Yemen, Yugoslavia, Zaire, Zambia, Zimbabwe.
Against: 8
Belgium, Canada, France, Luxembourg, New Zealand, Portugal, United Kingdom, United States.
Abstentions: 16
Australia, Austria, Denmark, Finland, Federal Republic of Germany, Greece, Iceland, Ireland, Italy, Ivory Coast, Japan, Malawi, Netherlands, Norway, Spain, Sweden.

Absent: 11
Belize, Dominica, El Salvador, Guatemala, Honduras, Lebanon, Paraguay, Saint Lucia, Saint Vincent, Samoa,* Seychelles.*

Israel announced that it was not participating in the vote.

_____

*Later advised the Secretariat it had intended to vote in favour.

F

RELATIONS BETWEEN ISRAEL AND SOUTH AFRICA

The General Assembly,
Reaffirming its resolutions on relations between Israel and South Africa,
Having considered the special report of the Special Committee against *Apartheid* on recent developments concerning relations between Israel and South Africa,[50]
Alarmed at the increasing collaboration by Israel with the racist régime of South Africa, especially in the military and nuclear fields, in defiance of resolutions of the General Assembly and the Security Council,
Considering that such collaboration is a serious hindrance to international action for the eradication of *apartheid,* an encouragement to the racist régime of South Africa to persist in its criminal policy of *apartheid* and a hostile act against the oppressed people of South Africa and the entire African continent, and constitutes a threat to international peace and security,
1. *Again strongly condemns* the continuing and increasing collaboration of Israel with the racist régime of South Africa, especially in the military and nuclear fields;
2. *Demands* that Israel desist from and terminate all forms of collaboration with South Africa forthwith, particularly in the military and nuclear fields, and abide scrupulously by the relevant resolutions of the General Assembly and the Security Council;
3. *Calls upon* all Governments and organizations to exert their influence to persuade Israel to desist from such collaboration and abide by the resolutions of the General Assembly;
4. *Requests* the Special Committee against *Apartheid* to publicize, as widely as possible, information on the relations between Israel and South Africa;
5. *Further requests* the Special Committee to keep the matter under constant review and to report to the General Assembly and the Security Council as appropriate.

Adopted at the 97th plenary meeting:
In favour: 113
Afghanistan, Albania, Algeria, Angola, Antigua and Barbuda, Argentina, Bahamas, Bahrain, Bangladesh, Barbados, Benin, Bhutan, Bolivia, Botswana, Brazil, Bulgaria, Burundi, Byelorussia, Cape Verde, Central African Republic, Chad, China, Colombia, Comoros, Congo, Cuba,

_____

[50]*Official Records of the General Assembly, Thirty-seventh Session, Supplement No. 22A (A/37/22/Add. 1 and 2),* document A/37/22/Add. 1.

Cyprus, Czechoslovakia, Democratic Kampuchea, Democratic Yemen, Djibouti, Dominican Republic, Ecuador, Egypt, Ethiopia, Gabon, Gambia, German Democratic Republic, Ghana, Greece, Grenada, Guinea, Guinea-Bissau, Guyana, Haiti, Hungary, India, Indonesia, Iran, Iraq, Jamaica, Jordan, Kenya, Kuwait, Lao People's Democratic Republic, Lesotho, Liberia, Libya, Madagascar, Malaysia, Maldives, Mali, Malta, Mauritania, Mauritius, Mexico, Mongolia, Morocco, Mozambique, Nepal, Nicaragua, Niger, Nigeria, Oman, Pakistan, Panama, Papua New Guinea, Peru, Philippines, Poland, Qatar, Romania, Rwanda, Sao Tome and Principe, Saudi Arabia, Senegal, Sierra Leone, Somalia, Spain, Sri Lanka, Sudan, Suriname, Syria, Thailand, Togo, Trinidad and Tobago, Tunisia, Turkey, Uganda, Ukraine, USSR, United Arab Emirates, United Republic of Cameroon, United Republic of Tanzania, Upper Volta, Vanuatu, Venezuela, Viet Nam, Yemen, Yugoslavia, Zaire, Zambia, Zimbabwe.

Against: 18

Australia, Austria, Belgium, Canada, Denmark, Finland, France, Federal Republic of Germany, Iceland, Ireland, Italy, Luxembourg, Netherlands, New Zealand, Norway, Sweden, United Kingdom, United States.

Abstentions: 10

Burma, Chile, Fiji, Ivory Coast, Japan, Malawi, Portugal, Singapore, Solomon Islands, Uruguay.

Absent: 13

Belize, Dominica, El Salvador, Equatorial Guinea, Guatemala, Honduras, Lebanon, Paraguay, Saint Lucia, Saint Vincent, Samoa, Seychelles,* Swaziland.

Costa Rica and Israel announced that they were not participating in the vote.

---

* Later advised the Secretariat it had intended to vote in favour.

Resolution No. 37/75 of 9 December 1982

URGING THE CREATION OF A NUCLEAR-WEAPON-FREE ZONE IN THE MIDDLE EAST, AND CALLING ON ALL COUNTRIES OF THE REGION TO PLACE THEIR NUCLEAR ACTIVITIES UNDER INTERNATIONAL ATOMIC ENERGY AGENCY SAFEGUARDS

The General Assembly,

Recalling its resolutions 3263 (XXIX) of 9 December 1974, 3474 (XXX) of 11 December 1975, 31/71 of 10 December 1976, 32/82 of 12 December 1977, 33/64 of 14 December 1978, 34/77 of 11 December 1979, 35/147 of 12 December 1980 and 36/87 of 9 December 1981 on the establishment of a nuclear-weapon-free zone in the region of the Middle East,

Recalling also the recommendations for the establishment of such a zone in the Middle East consistent with paragraphs 60 to 63, in particular paragraph 63 (*d*), of the Final Document of the Tenth Special Session of the General Assembly,[51]

Emphasizing the basic provisions of the above-mentioned

resolutions, which call upon all parties directly concerned to consider taking the practical and urgent steps required for the implementation of the proposal to establish a nuclear-weapon-free zone in the region of the Middle East and, pending and during the establishment of such a zone, to declare solemnly that they will refrain, on a reciprocal basis, from producing, acquiring or in any other way possessing nuclear weapons and nuclear explosive devices and from permitting the stationing of nuclear weapons on their territory by any third party, to agree to place all their nuclear facilities under International Atomic Energy Agency safeguards and to declare their support for the establishment of the zone and deposit such declarations with the Security Council for consideration, as appropriate,

Reaffirming the inalienable right of all States to acquire and develop nuclear energy for peaceful purposes,

Emphasizing further the need for appropriate measures on the question of the prohibition of military attacks on nuclear facilities,

Bearing in mind the consensus reached by the General Assembly at its thirty-fifth session that the establishment of a nuclear-weapon-free zone in the region of the Middle East would greatly enhance international peace and security,

Desirous to build on that consensus so that substantial progress can be made towards establishing a nuclear-weapon-free zone in the region of the Middle East,

1. *Urges* all parties directly concerned to consider seriously taking the practical and urgent steps required for the implementation of the proposal to establish a nuclear-weapon-free zone in the region of the Middle East in accordance with the relevant resolutions of the General Assembly and, as a means of promoting this objective, invites the countries concerned to adhere to the Treaty on the Non-Proliferation of Nuclear Weapons;[52]

2. *Calls upon* all countries of the region that have not done so, pending the establishment of the zone, to agree to place all their nuclear activities under International Atomic Energy Agency safeguards;

3. *Invites* those countries, pending the establishment of a nuclear-weapon-free zone in the region of the Middle East, to declare their support for establishing such a zone, consistent with the relevant paragraph of the Final Document of the Tenth Special Session of the General Assembly, and to deposit those declarations with the Security Council;

4. *Invites further* those countries, pending the establishment of the zone, not to develop, produce, test, or otherwise acquire nuclear weapons or permit the stationing on their territories, or territories under their control, of nuclear weapons or nuclear explosive devices;

5. *Invites* the nuclear-weapon States and all other States to render their assistance in the establishment of the zone and at the same time to refrain from any action that runs

---

[51]Resolution S-10/2.

[52]A/37/148.

counter to both the letter and spirit of the present resolution;

6. *Requests* the Secretary-General to report to the General Assembly at its thirty-eighth session on the implementation of the present resolution;

7. *Decides* to include in the provisional agenda of its thirty-eighth session the item entitled "Establishment of a nuclear-weapon-free zone in the region of the Middle East".

Adopted at the 98th plenary meeting without a vote.

Resolution No. 37/82 of 9 December 1982

DEMANDING THAT ISRAEL RENOUNCE THE POSSESSION OF NUCLEAR WEAPONS AND PLACE ITS NUCLEAR ACTIVITIES UNDER INTERNATIONAL SAFEGUARDS

The General Assembly,

Recalling its resolutions 35/157 of 12 December 1980 and 36/98 of 9 December 1981 on Israeli nuclear armament,

Recalling also its relevant resolutions on the establishment of a nuclear-weapon-free zone in the region of the Middle East,

Recalling further its resolution 33/71 A of 14 December 1978 on military and nuclear collaboration with Israel,

Recalling its repeated condemnation of the nuclear collaboration between Israel and South Africa,

Recalling Security Council resolution 487 (1981) of 19 June 1981 and taking note of the first special report of the Special Committee against *Apartheid* on recent developments concerning relations between Israel and South Africa,[53]

Noting with grave concern Israel's persistent refusal to adhere to the Treaty on the Non-Proliferation of Nuclear Weapons,[54] despite repeated calls by the General Assembly, the Security Council and the International Atomic Energy Agency, and to place its nuclear facilities under Agency safeguards,

Conscious of the grave consequences which endanger international peace and security as a result of Israel's nuclear-weapon capability and its collaboration with South Africa to develop nuclear weapons and their delivery systems,

Taking note of the report of the Secretary-General on Israeli nuclear armament,[55]

1. *Reaffirms* its demand that Israel renounce, without delay, any possession of nuclear weapons and place all its nuclear activities under international safeguards;

2. *Calls again upon* all States and other parties and institutions to terminate forthwith all nuclear collaboration with Israel;

3. *Requests again* the Security Council to investigate Isra-

el's nuclear activities and the collaboration of other States, parties and institutions in these activities;

4. *Calls upon* all States to submit to the Secretary-General all information in their possession concerning the Israeli nuclear programme or any public or private assistance thereto;

5. *Requests* the Security Council to consider taking effective action so as to prevent Israel from endangering international peace and security by pursuing its policy of aggression, expansion and annexation of territories;

6. *Condemns* Israel's officially declared intention to repeat its armed attack against nuclear facilities;

7. *Requests* the Secretary-General to keep Israeli nuclear activities under constant review and to report thereon as appropriate;

8. *Also requests* the Secretary-General, in co-operation with the Organization of African Unity and the League of Arab States, to follow closely the nuclear and military collaboration between Israel and South Africa and the dangers it constitutes to peace and security and to efforts aimed at the establishment of nuclear-weapon-free zones in Africa and the Middle East;

9. *Decides* to include in the provisional agenda of its thirty-eighth session the item entitled "Israeli nuclear armament".

Adopted at the 98th plenary meeting:

In favour: 106

Afghanistan, Albania, Algeria, Angola, Argentina, Bahamas, Bahrain, Bangladesh, Barbados, Belize, Benin, Bhutan, Bolivia, Botswana, Brazil, Bulgaria, Burundi, Byelorussia, Cape Verde, Central African Republic, Chad, China, Comoros, Congo, Cuba, Cyprus, Czechoslovakia, Democratic Kampuchea, Democratic Yemen, Djibouti, Ecuador, Egypt, El Salvador, Ethiopia, Gambia, German Democratic Republic, Ghana, Greece, Grenada, Guinea, Guinea-Bissau, Guyana, Hungary, India, Indonesia, Iran, Iraq, Jordan, Kenya, Kuwait, Lao People's Democratic Republic, Lebanon, Liberia, Libya, Madagascar, Malaysia, Maldives, Mali, Malta, Mauritania, Mauritius, Mexico, Mongolia, Morocco, Mozambique, Nicaragua, Niger, Nigeria, Oman, Pakistan, Panama, Peru, Philippines, Poland, Qatar, Romania, Rwanda, Sao Tome and Principe, Saudi Arabia, Senegal, Sierra Leone, Solomon Islands, Somalia, Spain, Sri Lanka, Sudan, Suriname, Syria, Thailand, Togo, Trinidad and Tobago, Tunisia, Turkey, Uganda, Ukraine, USSR, United Arab Emirates, United Republic of Cameroon, United Republic of Tanzania, Upper Volta, Vanuatu, Venezuela, Viet Nam, Yemen, Yugoslavia, Zambia.

Against: 2

Israel, United States.

Abstentions: 34

Australia, Austria, Belgium, Burma, Canada, Chile, Colombia, Denmark, Dominican Republic, Fiji, Finland, France, Federal Republic of Germany, Guatemala, Haiti, Iceland, Ireland, Italy, Ivory Coast, Jamaica, Japan, Luxembourg, Malawi, Nepal, Netherlands, New Zealand, Norway, Papua New Guinea, Paraguay, Portugal, Saint Lucia,

---

[53] *Official Records of the General Assembly, Thirty-seventh Session, Supplement No. 22A* (A/37/22/Add. 1 and 2), document A/37/22/Add. 1.
[54] Resolution 2373 (XXII), annex.
[55] A/37/434.

Sweden, United Kingdom, Uruguay.
Absent: 14
Antigua and Barbuda, Costa Rica, Dominica, Equatorial Guinea, Gabon, Honduras, Lesotho, Saint Vincent, Samoa,* Seychelles, Singapore, Swaziland, Zaire, Zimbabwe.

---

* Later advised the Secretariat it had intended to vote in favour.

Resolution No. 37/86 A, B, C, D, E of 10 December 1982

ON THE QUESTION OF PALESTINE: CALLING FOR THE COMPLETE WITHDRAWAL OF ISRAEL FROM THE ARAB TERRITORIES OCCUPIED SINCE 1967, FOR THE EXERCISE OF SELF-DETERMINATION BY THE PALESTINIAN PEOPLE, INCLUDING THE RIGHT TO ESTABLISH AN INDEPENDENT STATE, AND FOR THE UNITED NATIONS TO SUPERVISE THE OCCUPIED TERRITORIES FOR A SHORT TRANSITIONAL PERIOD

A

The General Assembly,

Recalling its resolutions 3376 (XXX) of 10 November 1975, 31/20 of 24 November 1976, 32/40 of 2 December 1977, 33/28 of 7 December 1978, 34/65 of 29 November and 12 December 1979, ES-7/2 of 29 July 1980, 35/169 of 15 December 1980, 36/120 of 10 December 1981, ES-7/4 of 28 April 1982, ES-7/5 of 26 June 1982 and ES-7/9 of 24 September 1982,[56]

Having considered the report of the Committee on the Exercise of the Inalienable Rights of the Palestinian People,[57]

1. *Expresses its appreciation* to the Committee on the Exercise of the Inalienable Rights of the Palestinian People for its efforts in performing the tasks assigned to it by the General Assembly;

2. *Endorses* the recommendations of the Committee contained in paragraphs 114 to 119 of its report and draws the attention of the Security Council to the fact that action on the Committee's recommendations, as endorsed by the General Assembly in its resolution 31/20, is long overdue;

3. *Requests* the Committee to keep the situation relating to the question of Palestine under review and to report and make suggestions to the General Assembly or the Security Council, as appropriate;

4. *Authorizes* the Committee to continue to exert all efforts to promote the implementation of its recommendations, to send delegations or representatives to international conferences where such representation would be considered by it to be appropriate, and to report thereon to the General Assembly at its thirty-eighth session and thereafter;

5. *Requests* the United Nations Conciliation Commission for Palestine, established under General Assembly resolution 194 (III) of 11 December 1948, as well as other United Nations bodies associated with the question of Palestine, to co-operate fully with the Committee and to make available to it, at its request, the relevant information and documentation which they have at their disposal;

6. *Decides* to circulate the report of the Committee to all the competent bodies of the United Nations and urges them to take the necessary action, as appropriate, in accordance with the Committee's programme of implementation;

7. *Requests* the Secretary-General to continue to provide the Committee with all the necessary facilities for the performance of its tasks.

Adopted at the 99th plenary meeting:
In favour: 119
Afghanistan, Albania, Algeria, Angola, Antigua and Barbuda, Argentina, Bahamas, Bahrain, Bangladesh, Barbados, Belize, Benin, Bhutan, Brazil, Bulgaria, Burundi, Byelorussia, Cape Verde, Central African Republic, Chad, Chile, China, Colombia, Comoros, Congo, Cuba, Cyprus, Czechoslovakia, Democratic Kampuchea, Democratic Yemen, Djibouti, Dominican Republic, Ecuador, Egypt, El Salvador, Equatorial Guinea, Ethiopia, Gabon, Gambia, Democratic Republic of Germany, Ghana, Greece, Guinea, Guinea-Bissau, Guyana, Haiti, Honduras, Hungary, India, Indonesia, Iran, Iraq, Ivory Coast, Jamaica, Jordan, Kenya, Kuwait, Lao People's Democratic Republic, Lebanon, Liberia, Libya, Madagascar, Malawi, Malaysia, Maldives, Mali, Malta, Mauritania, Mauritius, Mexico, Mongolia, Morocco, Mozambique, Nepal, Nicaragua, Niger, Nigeria, Oman, Pakistan, Panama, Papua New Guinea, Peru, Philippines, Poland, Portugal, Qatar, Romania, Rwanda, Sao Tome and Principe, Saudi Arabia, Senegal, Sierra Leone, Singapore, Somalia, Spain, Sri Lanka, Sudan, Suriname, Syria, Thailand, Togo, Tunisia, Turkey, Uganda, Ukraine, USSR, United Arab Emirates, United Republic of Cameroon, United Republic of Tanzania, Upper Volta, Uruguay, Vanuatu, Venezuela, Viet Nam, Yemen, Yugoslavia, Zaire, Zambia, Zimbabwe.
Against: 2
Israel, United States.
Abstentions: 21
Australia, Austria, Belgium, Burma, Canada, Costa Rica, Denmark, Fiji, Finland, France, Federal Republic of Germany, Iceland, Ireland, Italy, Japan, Luxembourg, Netherlands, New Zealand, Norway, Sweden, United Kingdom.
Absent: 14
Bolivia,* Botswana, Dominica, Grenada, Guatemala, Lesotho, Paraguay, Saint Lucia, Saint Vincent, Samoa,* Seychelles,* Solomon Islands, Swaziland, Trinidad and Tobago.*

---

* Later advised the Secretariat it had intended to vote in favour.

B

The General Assembly,
Having considered the report of the Committee on the Exercise of the Inalienable Rights of the Palestinian

---

[56]The resolutions cited are previous resolutions on the question of Palestine. [ed. note]
[57]*Official Records of the General Assembly, Thirty-seventh Session, Supplement No. 35* (A/37/35 and Corr. 1).

People,[58]

Noting, in particular, the information contained in paragraphs 103 to 111 of that report,

Recalling its resolutions 32/40 B of 2 December 1977, 33/28 C of 7 December 1978, 34/65 D of 12 December 1979, 35/169 D of 15 December 1980 and 36/120 B of 10 December 1981,

1. *Takes note with appreciation* of the action taken by the Secretary-General in compliance with General Assembly resolution 36/120 B;

2. *Requests* the Secretary-General to ensure that the Division for Palestinian Rights of the Secretariat continues to discharge the tasks detailed in paragraph 1 of General Assembly resolution 32/40 B, paragraph 2 (*b*) of resolution 34/65 D and paragraph 3 of resolution 36/120 B, in consultation with the Committee on the Exercise of the Inalienable Rights of the Palestinian People and under its guidance;

3. *Also requests* the Secretary-General to provide the Division for Palestinian Rights with the necessary resources to carry out its tasks as urged in paragraph 109 of the Committee's report;

4. *Further requests* the Secretary-General to ensure the continued co-operation of the Department of Public Information and other units of the Secretariat in enabling the Division for Palestinian Rights to perform its tasks and in covering adequately the various aspects of the question of Palestine;

5. *Invites* all Governments and organizations to lend their co-operation to the Committee and the Division for Palestinian Rights in the performance of their tasks;

6. *Takes note with appreciation* of the action taken by Member States to observe annually on 29 November the International Day of Solidarity with the Palestinian People and the issuance by them of special postage stamps for the occasion.

Adopted at the 99th plenary meeting:

In favour: 121

Afghanistan, Albania, Algeria, Angola, Antigua and Barbuda, Argentina, Bahamas, Bahrain, Bangladesh, Barbados, Belize, Benin, Bhutan, Brazil, Bulgaria, Burma, Burundi, Byelorussia, Cape Verde, Central African Republic, Chad, Chile, China, Colombia, Comoros, Congo, Cuba, Cyprus, Czechoslovakia, Democratic Kampuchea, Democratic Yemen, Djibouti, Dominican Republic, Ecuador, Egypt, El Salvador, Equatorial Guinea, Ethiopia, Fiji, Gabon, Gambia, German Democratic Republic, Ghana, Greece, Guinea, Guinea-Bissau, Guyana, Haiti, Honduras, Hungary, India, Indonesia, Iran, Iraq, Ivory Coast, Jamaica, Jordan, Kenya, Kuwait, Lao People's Democratic Republic, Lebanon, Liberia, Libya, Madagascar, Malawi, Malaysia, Maldives, Mali, Malta, Mauritania, Mauritius, Mexico, Mongolia, Morocco, Mozambique, Nepal, Nicaragua, Niger, Nigeria, Oman, Pakistan, Panama, Papua New Guinea, Peru, Philippines, Poland, Portugal, Qatar, Romania, Rwanda, Sao Tome and Principe, Saudi Arabia, Senegal, Sierra Leone, Singapore, Somalia, Spain, Sri Lanka, Sudan, Suriname, Syria, Thailand, Togo, Tunisia, Turkey, Uganda, Ukraine, USSR, United Arab Emirates, United Republic of Cameroon, United Republic of Tanzania, Upper Volta, Uruguay, Vanuatu, Venezuela, Viet Nam, Yemen, Yugoslavia, Zaire, Zambia, Zimbabwe.

Against: 3

Canada, Israel, United States.

Abstentions: 18

Australia, Austria, Belgium, Costa Rica, Denmark, Finland, France, Federal Republic of Germany, Iceland, Ireland, Italy, Japan, Luxembourg, Netherlands, New Zealand, Norway, Sweden, United Kingdom.

Absent: 14

Bolivia,* Botswana, Dominica, Grenada, Guatemala, Lesotho, Paraguay, Saint Lucia, Saint Vincent, Samoa,* Seychelles,* Solomon Islands, Swaziland, Trinidad and Tobago.*

---

* Later advised the Secretariat it had intended to vote in favour.

C

The General Assembly,

Recalling its resolutions 3236 (XXIX) and 3237 (XXIX) of 22 November 1974 and all other United Nations resolutions, including resolution ES-7/2 of 29 July 1980, pertinent to the question of Palestine,

Recalling also its resolutions 36/120 C of 10 December 1981, in which it decided to convene an International Conference on the Question of Palestine for a comprehensive effort to seek effective ways and means to enable the Palestinian people to attain and to exercise their rights, and ES-7/7 of 19 August 1982, in which it decided to convene the Conference at the headquarters of the United Nations Educational, Scientific, and Cultural Organization, in Paris, from 16 to 27 August 1983,

Convinced that a comprehensive, just and lasting peace in the Middle East can be established, in acordance with the Charter and the relevant resolutions of the United Nations, through a just solution to the problem of Palestine on the basis of the attainment of the legitimate rights of the Palestinian people,

Convinced that the Conference will provide a unique opportunity to heighten awareness of the underlying causes of the question of Palestine and to contribute actively and constructively to a solution of the question on the basis of relevant United Nations resolutions,

Stressing the need to assure the participation of all Member States in the Conference and their support for its preparation,

Taking note with appreciation of the report of the Preparatory Committee for the International Conference on the Question of Palestine,[59]

---

[58]*Official Records of the General Assembly, Thirty-seventh Session, Supplement No. 35* (A/37/35 and Corr.1).

[59]*Ibid., Supplement No. 49* (A/37/49 and Corr.1).

1. *Reiterates* the responsibility of the United Nations to strive for a lasting peace in the Middle East through a just solution of the problem of Palestine;

2. *Endorses* the recommendations of the Preparatory Committee for the International Conference on the Question of Palestine, contained in paragraph 32 of its report,[60] concerning the preparatory activities for the Conference, the objectives, the documentation, the draft provisional agenda and the draft provisional rules of procedure of the Conference, the participation in the Conference and the organization of work of the Preparatory Committee;

3. *Calls upon* all organizations of the United Nations system to continue to extend their fullest support to the Conference and to its preparation;

4. *Urges* all Member States to promote heightened awareness of the importance of the Conference and to intensify preparations at the national, subregional and regional levels in order to ensure its success;

5. *Calls upon* all Member States to contribute to the achievement of Palestinian rights and to support modalities for their implementation, and to participate in the Conference and the regional preparatory meetings preceding it;

6. *Decides* to consider the results of the Conference at its thirty-eighth session.

Adopted at the 99th plenary meeting:
In favour: 123
Afghanistan, Albania, Algeria, Angola, Antigua and Barbuda, Argentina, Austria, Bahamas, Bahrain, Bangladesh, Barbados, Belize, Benin, Bhutan, Brazil, Bulgaria, Burma, Burundi, Byelorussia, Cape Verde, Central African Republic, Chad, Chile, China, Colombia, Comoros, Congo, Cuba, Cyprus, Czechoslovakia, Democratic Kampuchea, Democratic Yemen, Djibouti, Dominican Republic, Ecuador, Egypt, El Salvador, Equatorial Guinea, Ethiopia, Fiji, Gabon, Gambia, German Democratic Republic, Ghana, Greece, Guinea, Guinea-Bissau, Guyana, Haiti, Honduras, Hungary, India, Indonesia, Iran, Iraq, Ivory Coast, Jamaica, Jordan, Kenya, Kuwait, Lao People's Democratic Republic, Lebanon, Liberia, Libya, Madagascar, Malawi, Malaysia, Maldives, Mali, Malta, Mauritania, Mauritius, Mexico, Mongolia, Morocco, Mozambique, Nepal, Nicaragua, Niger, Nigeria, Oman, Pakistan, Panama, Papua New Guinea, Peru, Philippines, Poland, Portugal, Qatar, Romania, Rwanda, Sao Tome and Principe, Saudi Arabia, Senegal, Sierra Leone, Singapore, Somalia, Spain, Sri Lanka, Sudan, Suriname, Sweden, Syria, Thailand, Togo, Tunisia, Turkey, Uganda, Ukraine, USSR, United Arab Emirates, United Republic of Cameroon, United Republic of Tanzania, Upper Volta, Uruguay, Vanuatu, Venezuela, Viet Nam, Yemen, Yugoslavia, Zaire, Zambia, Zimbabwe.
Against: 2
Israel, United States.
Abstentions: 17

Australia, Belgium, Canada, Costa Rica, Denmark, Finland, France, Federal Republic of Germany, Iceland, Ireland, Italy, Japan, Luxembourg, Netherlands, New Zealand, Norway, United Kingdom.
Absent: 14
Bolivia,* Botswana, Dominica, Grenada, Guatemala, Lesotho, Paraguay, Saint Lucia, Saint Vincent, Samoa,* Seychelles,* Solomon Islands, Swaziland, Trinidad and Tobago.*

---

* Later advised the Secretariat it had intended to vote in favour.

D

The General Assembly,

Recalling its resolutions relevant to the question of Palestine, in particular resolutions 181 (II) of 29 November 1947, 194 (III) of 11 December 1948, 3210 (XXIX) of 14 October 1974, 3236 (XXIX) of 22 November 1974 and ES-7/2 of 29 July 1980,

Recalling the resolutions of the Security Council relevant to Palestine,

Having heard the statement of the representative of the Palestine Liberation Organization,[61]

1. *Takes note* of the declaration of the Palestine Liberation Organization of 19 April 1981 of its intention to pursue its role in the solution of the question of Palestine on the basis of the attainment by the Palestinian people of its inalienable rights in Palestine, in accordance with the relevant resolutions of the United Nations;

2. *Reaffirms* the principle of the inadmissibility of the acquisition of territory by force;

3. *Reaffirms once again* that a comprehensive, just and lasting peace in the Middle East cannot be established without the unconditional withdrawal of Israel from the Palestinian and other Arab territories occupied since 1967, including Jerusalem, and without the exercise and attainment by the Palestinian people of its inalienable rights in Palestine, in accordance with the principles of the Charter and the relevant resolutions of the United Nations;

4. *Requests* the Security Council to discharge its responsibilities under the Charter and recognize the inalienable rights of the Palestinian Arab people, including the right to self-determination and the right to establish its independent Arab State in Palestine;

5. *Reiterates* its request that the Security Council take the necessary measures, in execution of the relevant United Nations resolutions, to implement the plan which, *inter alia*, recommends that an independent Arab State shall come into existence in Palestine;

6. *Requests* the Secretary-General to report on the progress made in implementing the present resolution as soon as possible.

Adopted at the 99th plenary meeting:
In favour: 113

---

[60] *Ibid.*

[61] *Ibid., Thirty-seventh Session, Plenary Meetings,* 84th meeting, paras. 110-153.

Afghanistan, Albania, Algeria, Angola, Antigua and Barbuda, Argentina, Austria, Bahrain, Bangladesh, Belize, Benin, Bhutan, Brazil, Bulgaria, Burma, Burundi, Byelorussia, Cape Verde, Central African Republic, Chad, Chile, China, Colombia, Comoros, Congo, Cuba, Cyprus, Czechoslovakia, Democratic Kampuchea, Democratic Yemen, Djibouti, Ecuador, Egypt, El Salvador, Equatorial Guinea, Ethiopia, Fiji, Gabon, Gambia, German Democratic Republic, Ghana, Guinea, Guyana, Honduras, Hungary, India, Indonesia, Iran, Iraq, Jamaica, Jordan, Kenya, Kuwait, Lao People's Democratic Republic, Lebanon, Liberia, Libya, Madagascar, Malawi, Malaysia, Maldives, Mali, Malta, Mauritania, Mauritius, Mexico, Mongolia, Morocco, Mozambique, Nepal, Nicaragua, Niger, Nigeria, Oman, Pakistan, Panama, Papua New Guinea, Peru, Philippines, Poland, Qatar, Romania, Rwanda, Sao Tome and Principe, Saudi Arabia, Senegal, Sierra Leone, Singapore, Somalia, Spain, Sri Lanka, Sudan, Suriname, Syria, Thailand, Togo, Tunisia, Turkey, Uganda, Ukraine, USSR, United Arab Emirates, United Republic of Cameroon, United Republic of Tanzania, Upper Volta, Uruguay, Vanuatu, Viet Nam, Yemen, Yugoslavia, Zaire, Zambia, Zimbabwe.

Against: 4

Canada, Costa Rica, Israel, United States.

Abstentions: 23

Australia, Bahamas, Barbados, Belgium, Denmark, Dominican Republic, Finland, France, Federal Republic of Germany, Greece, Guinea-Bissau, Haiti, Iceland, Ireland, Italy, Japan, Luxembourg, Netherlands, New Zealand, Norway, Portugal, Sweden, United Kingdom.

Absent: 16

Bolivia,* Botswana, Dominica, Grenada, Guatemala, Ivory Coast, Lesotho, Paraguay, Saint Lucia, Saint Vincent, Samoa,* Seychelles,* Solomon Islands, Swaziland, Trinidad and Tobago,* Venezuela.

---

* Later advised the Secretariat it had intended to vote in favour.

E

The General Assembly,

Having considered the report of the Committee on the Exercise of the Inalienable Rights of the Palestinian People,[62]

Expressing its extreme concern that no just solution to the problem of Palestine has been achieved and that this problem therefore continues to aggravate the Middle East conflict, of which it is the core, and to endanger international peace and security,

Recalling its previous relevant resolutions, particularly resolutions 181 (II) of 29 November 1947, 194 (III) of 11 December 1948, 3236 (XXIX) of 22 November 1974, ES-7/2 of 29 July 1980, 36/120 D of 10 December 1981

---

[62]*Official Records of the General Assembly, Thirty-seventh Session,* Supplement No. 35 (A/37/35 and Corr. 1).

and ES-7/9 of 24 September 1982,

Recalling, in particular, the principles relevant to the question of Palestine that have been accepted by the international community, including the right of all States in the region to existence within internationally recognized boundaries, and justice and security for all the peoples, which requires recognition and attainment of the legitimate rights of the Palestinian people,

Recognizing the necessity of participation by all parties concerned in any efforts aimed at the attainment of a just and lasting solution,

1. *Reaffirms* the inalienable legitimate rights of the Palestinian people, including the right to self-determination and the right to establish, once it so wishes, its independent State in Palestine;

2. *Declares* all Israeli policies and practices of, or aimed at, annexation of the occupied Palestinian and other Arab territories, including Jerusalem, to be in violation of international law and of the relevant United Nations resolutions;

3. *Demands,* in conformity with the fundamental principle of the inadmissibility of the acquisition of territory by force, that Israel should withdraw completely and unconditionally from all the Palestinian and other Arab territories occupied since June 1967, including Jerusalem, with all property and services intact;

4. *Urges* the Security Council to facilitate the process of Israeli withdrawal;

5. *Recommends* that, following the withdrawal of Israel from the occupied Palestinian territories, those territories should be subjected to a short transitional period under the supervision of the United Nations, during which period the Palestinian people would exercise its right to self-determination;

6. *Urgently calls* for the achievement of a comprehensive, just and lasting peace, based on the resolutions of the United Nations and under its auspices, in which all parties concerned, including the Palestine Liberation Organization, the representative of the Palestinian people, participate on an equal footing;

7. *Recommends* that the Security Council should take early action to promote a just and comprehensive solution to the question of Palestine;

8. *Requests* the Secretary-General to report to the General Assembly at its thirty-eighth session on the progress made in implementing the present resolution.

Adopted at the 112th plenary meeting:
In favour: 123

Afghanistan, Algeria, Angola, Argentina, Austria, Bahamas, Bahrain, Bangladesh, Barbados, Benin, Bhutan, Bolivia, Botswana, Brazil, Bulgaria, Burundi, Byelorussia, Cape Verde, Central African Republic, Chad, Chile, China, Colombia, Comoros, Congo, Cuba, Cyprus, Czechoslovakia, Democratic Kampuchea, Democratic Yemen, Djibouti, Dominican Republic, Ecuador, Egypt, El Salvador, Equatorial Guinea, Ethiopia, Fiji, Finland, Gabon, German Democratic Republic, Ghana, Greece, Grenada, Guinea, Guinea-Bissau, Guyana, Hungary, India, Indonesia, Iran,

Iraq, Ivory Coast, Jamaica, Jordan, Kenya, Kuwait, Lao People's Democratic Republic, Lebanon, Lesotho, Liberia, Madagascar, Mozambique, Nepal, New Zealand, Nicaragua, Niger, Nigeria, Oman, Pakistan, Panama, Papua New Guinea, Paraguay, Peru, Philippines, Poland, Qatar, Romania, Rwanda, Saint Lucia, Samoa, Sao Tome and Principe, Saudi Arabia, Senegal, Seychelles, Sierra Leone, Singapore, Somalia, Spain, Sri Lanka, Sudan, Suriname, Sweden, Syria, Thailand, Togo, Trinidad and Tobago, Tunisia, Turkey, Uganda, Ukraine, USSR, United Arab Emirates, United Republic of Cameroon, United Republic of Tanzania, Upper Volta, Uruguay, Venezuela, Viet Nam, Yemen, Yugoslavia, Zaire, Zambia, Zimbabwe.

Against: 2

Israel, United States.

Abstentions: 19

Australia, Belgium, Burma, Canada, Denmark, France, Federal Republic of Germany, Guatemala, Haiti, Iceland, Ireland, Italy, Japan, Luxembourg, Malawi, Netherlands, Norway, Portugal, United Kingdom.

Absent: 11

Antigua and Barbuda, Belize, Costa Rica, Dominica, Gambia, Honduras, Libya, Saint Vincent,* Solomon Islands, Swaziland, Vanuatu.

Albania announced that it was not participating in the vote.

---

* Later advised the Secretariat it had intended to vote in favour.

Resolution No. 37/88 A, B, C, D, E, F, G of 10 December 1982

ON ISRAELI PRACTICES AFFECTING HUMAN RIGHTS IN THE OCCUPIED TERRITORIES: CONDEMNING ISRAEL'S POLICIES OF ANNEXATION AND SETTLEMENT IN THE OCCUPIED ARAB TERRITORIES, AS WELL AS THE MEASURES OF THE OCCUPATION AUTHORITIES AGAINST CIVIL, POLITICAL AND EDUCATIONAL FREEDOM AND THEIR FAILURE TO APPREHEND AND PROSECUTE PERSONS GUILTY OF ASSASSINATION ATTEMPTS AGAINST ARAB MAYORS

A

The General Assembly,

Recalling its resolutions 3092 A (XXVIII) of 7 December 1973, 3240 B (XXIX) of 29 November 1974, 3525 B (XXX) of 15 December 1975, 31/106 B of 16 December 1976, 32/91 A of 13 December 1977, 33/113 A of 18 December 1978, 34/90 B of 12 December 1979, 35/122 A of 11 December 1980 and 36/147 A of 16 December 1981,[63]

Recalling also Security Council resolution 465 (1980) of 1 March 1980 in which, *inter alia*, the Council affirmed that the Geneva Convention relative to the Protection of Civilian Persons in Time of War, of 12 August 1949,[64] is

---

[63]The resolutions cited are previous resolutions on Israeli practices in the occupied territories. [ed. note]
[64]United Nations, *Treaty Series*, vol. 75, no. 973, p. 287.

applicable to the Arab territories occupied by Israel since 1967, including Jerusalem,

Considering that the promotion of respect for the obligations arising from the Charter of the United Nations and other instruments and rules of international law is among the basic purposes and principles of the United Nations,

Bearing in mind the provisions of the Geneva Convention,

Noting that Israel and those Arab States whose territories have been occupied by Israel since June 1967 are parties to that Convention,

Taking into account that States parties to that Convention undertake, in accordance with article 1 thereof, not only to respect but also to ensure respect for the Convention in all circumstances,

1. *Reaffirms* that the Geneva Convention relative to the Protection of Civilian Persons in Time of War, of 12 August 1949, is applicable to Palestinian and other Arab territories occupied by Israel since 1967, including Jerusalem;

2. *Condemns once again* the failure of Israel as the occupying Power to acknowledge the applicability of that Convention to the territories it has occupied since 1967, including Jerusalem;

3. *Strongly demands* that Israel acknowledge and comply with the provisions of that Convention in Palestinian and other Arab territories it has occupied since 1967, including Jerusalem;

4. *Urgently calls upon* all States parties to that Convention to exert all efforts in order to ensure respect for and compliance with its provisions in Palestinian and other Arab territories occupied by Israel since 1967, including Jerusalem.

Adopted at the 100th plenary meeting:
In favour: 134

Afghanistan, Albania, Algeria, Argentina, Australia, Austria, Bahrain, Bangladesh, Barbados, Belgium, Benin, Bhutan, Bolivia, Botswana, Brazil, Bulgaria, Burma, Burundi, Byelorussia, Canada, Central African Republic, Chad, Chile, China, Colombia, Comoros, Congo, Costa Rica, Cuba, Cyprus, Czechoslovakia, Democratic Kampuchea, Democratic Yemen, Denmark, Djibouti, Dominican Republic, Ecuador, Egypt, El Salvador, Ethiopia, Fiji, Finland, France, Gabon, Gambia, German Democratic Republic, Federal Republic of Germany, Ghana, Greece, Guyana, Haiti, Honduras, Hungary, Iceland, India, Indonesia, Iran, Iraq, Ireland, Italy, Jamaica, Japan, Jordan, Kenya, Kuwait, Lao People's Democratic Republic, Lebanon, Liberia, Libya, Luxembourg, Madagascar, Malawi, Malaysia, Maldives, Mali, Malta, Mauritania, Mauritius, Mexico, Mongolia, Morocco, Mozambique, Nepal, Netherlands, New Zealand, Nicaragua, Niger, Nigeria, Norway, Oman, Pakistan, Panama, Papua New Guinea, Peru, Philippines, Poland, Portugal, Qatar, Romania, Rwanda, Sao Tome and Principe, Saudi Arabia, Senegal, Sierra Leone, Singapore, Solomon Islands, Somalia, Spain, Sri Lanka, Sudan, Suriname, Sweden, Syria, Thailand, Togo, Trinidad and Tobago, Tunisia, Turkey, Uganda, Ukraine, USSR, United Arab Emirates, United Kingdom, United

Republic of Cameroon, United Republic of Tanzania, Upper Volta, Uruguay, Vanuatu, Venezuela, Viet Nam, Yemen, Yugoslavia, Zaire, Zambia.

Against: 1

Israel.

Abstention: 1

United States.

Absent: 20

Angola, Antigua and Barbuda, Bahamas, Belize, Cape Verde, Dominica, Equatorial Guinea, Grenada, Guatemala, Guinea, Guinea-Bissau, Ivory Coast, Lesotho, Paraguay, Saint Lucia, Saint Vincent, Samoa, Seychelles, Swaziland, Zimbabwe.

B

The General Assembly,

Recalling its resolutions 32/5 of 28 October 1977, 33/113 B of 18 December 1978, 34/90 C of 12 December 1979, 35/122 B of 11 December 1980 and 36/147 B of 16 December 1981,

Recalling also Security Council resolution 465 (1980) of 1 March 1980,

Expressing grave anxiety and concern at the present serious situation in the occupied Palestinian and other Arab territories, including Jerusalem, as a result of the continued Israeli occupation and the measures and actions taken by the Government of Israel, the occupying Power, designed to change the legal status, geographical nature and demographic composition of those territories,

Considering that the Geneva Convention relative to the Protection of Civilian Persons in Time of War, of 12 August 1949,[65] is applicable to all Arab territories occupied since 5 June 1967, including Jerusalem,

1. *Determines* that all such measures and actions taken by Israel in the Palestinian and other Arab territories occupied since 1967, including Jerusalem, are in violation of the relevant provisions of the Geneva Convention relative to the Protection of Civilian Persons in Time of War, of 12 August 1949, and constitute a serious obstruction of efforts to achieve a just and lasting peace in the Middle East and therefore have no legal validity;

2. *Strongly deplores* the persistence of Israel in carrying out such measures, in particular the establishment of settlements in the Palestinian and other occupied Arab territories, including Jerusalem;

3. *Demands* that Israel comply strictly with its international obligations in accordance with the principles of international law and the provisions of the Geneva Convention;

4. *Demands once more* that the Government of Israel, the occupying Power, desist forthwith from taking any action which would result in changing the legal status, geographical nature or demographic composition of the Palestinian and other Arab territories occupied since 1967, including Jerusalem;

5. *Urgently calls upon* all States parties to the Geneva Convention to respect and to exert all efforts in order to ensure respect and compliance with its provisions in all Arab territories occupied by Israel since 1967, including Jerusalem.

Adopted at the 100th plenary meeting:

In favour: 134

Afghanistan, Albania, Algeria, Argentina, Australia, Austria, Bahrain, Bangladesh, Barbados, Belgium, Benin, Bhutan, Bolivia, Botswana, Brazil, Bulgaria, Burma, Burundi, Byelorussia, Canada, Central African Republic, Chad, Chile, China, Colombia, Comoros, Congo, Costa Rica, Cuba, Cyprus, Czechoslovakia, Democratic Kampuchea, Democratic Yemen, Denmark, Djibouti, Dominican Republic, Ecuador, Egypt, El Salvador, Ethiopia, Fiji, Finland, France, Gabon, Gambia, German Democratic Republic, Federal Republic of Germany, Ghana, Greece, Guyana, Haiti, Honduras, Hungary, Iceland, India, Indonesia, Iran, Iraq, Ireland, Italy, Jamaica, Japan, Jordan, Kenya, Kuwait, Lao People's Democratic Republic, Lebanon, Liberia, Libya, Luxembourg, Madagascar, Malawi, Malaysia, Maldives, Mali, Malta, Mauritania, Mauritius, Mexico, Mongolia, Morocco, Mozambique, Nepal, Netherlands, New Zealand, Nicaragua, Niger, Nigeria, Norway, Oman, Pakistan, Panama, Papua New Guinea, Peru, Philippines, Poland, Portugal, Qatar, Romania, Rwanda, Sao Tome and Principe, Saudi Arabia, Senegal, Sierra Leone, Singapore, Solomon Islands, Somalia, Spain, Sri Lanka, Sudan, Suriname, Sweden, Syria, Thailand, Togo, Trinidad and Tobago, Tunisia, Turkey, Uganda, Ukraine, USSR, United Arab Emirates, United Kingdom, United Republic of Cameroon, United Republic of Tanzania, Upper Volta, Uruguay, Vanuatu, Venezuela, Viet Nam, Yemen, Yugoslavia, Zaire, Zambia.

Against: 1

Israel.

Abstention: 1

United States.

Absent: 20

Angola, Antigua and Barbuda, Bahamas, Belize, Cape Verde, Dominica, Equatorial Guinea, Grenada, Guatemala, Guinea, Guinea-Bissau, Ivory Coast, Lesotho, Paraguay, Saint Lucia, Saint Vincent, Samoa, Seychelles, Swaziland, Zimbabwe.

C

The General Assembly,

Guided by the purposes and principles of the Charter of the United Nations and by the principles and provisions of the Universal Declaration of Human Rights,[66]

Bearing in mind the provisions of the Geneva Convention relative to the Protection of Civilian Persons in Time of War, of 12 August 1949,[67] as well as of other relevant conventions and regulations,

---

[65]United Nations, *Treaty Series*, vol. 75, no. 973, p. 287.

[66]Resolution 217 A (III).

[67]United Nations, *Treaty Series*, vol. 75, no. 973, p. 287.

Recalling all its resolutions on the subject, in particular resolutions 32/91 B and C of 13 December 1977, 33/113 C of 18 December 1978, 34/90 A of 12 December 1979, 35/122 C of 11 December 1980 and 36/147 C of 16 December 1981, and also those adopted by the Security Council, the Commission on Human Rights and other United Nations organs concerned and by the specialized agencies,

Having considered the report of the Special Committee to Investigate Israeli Practices Affecting the Human Rights of the Population of the Occupied Territories,[68] which contains, *inter alia,* public statements made by the leaders of the Government of Israel,

1. *Commends* the Special Committee to Investigate Israeli Practices Affecting the Human Rights of the Population of the Occupied Territories for its efforts in performing the tasks assigned to it by the General Assembly and for its thoroughness and impartiality;

2. *Deplores* the continued refusal by Israel to allow the Special Committee access to the occupied territories;

3. *Demands* that Israel allow the Special Committee access to the occupied territories;

4. *Reaffirms* the fact that occupation itself constitutes a grave violation of the human rights of the civilian population of the occupied Arab territories;

5. *Condemns* the continued and persistent violation by Israel of the Geneva Convention relative to the Protection of Civilian Persons in Time of War, of 12 August 1949, and other applicable international instruments, and condemns in particular those violations which that Convention designates as "grave breaches" thereof;

6. *Declares once more* that Israel's grave breaches of that Convention are war crimes and an affront to humanity;

7. *Strongly condemns* the following Israeli policies and practices:

(*a*) Annexation of parts of the occupied territories, including Jerusalem;

(*b*) Imposition of Israeli laws, jurisdiction and administration on the Syrian Golan Heights, which has resulted in the effective annexation of the Syrian Golan Heights;

(*c*) Establishment of new Israeli settlements and expansion of the existing settlements on private and public Arab lands, and transfer of an alien population thereto;

(*d*) Evacuation, deportation, expulsion, displacement and transfer of Arab inhabitants of the occupied territories and denial of their right to return;

(*e*) Confiscation and expropriation of private and public Arab property in the occupied territories and all other transactions for the acquisition of land involving the Israeli authorities, institutions or nationals on the one hand and the inhabitants or institutions of the occupied territories on the other;

(*f*) Excavations and transformations of the landscape and the historical, cultural and religious sites, especially at Jerusalem;

(*g*) Destruction and demolition of Arab houses;

(*h*) Collective punishment, mass arrests, administrative detention and ill-treatment of the Arab population;

(*i*) Ill-treatment and torture of persons under detention;

(*j*) Pillaging of archaeological and cultural property;

(*k*) Interference with religious freedoms and practices as well as family rights and customs;

(*l*) Interference with the system of education and with the social and economic development of the population in the occupied Palestinian and other Arab territories;

(*m*) Interference with the freedom of movement of individuals within the occupied Palestinian and other Arab territories;

(*n*) Illegal exploitation of the natural wealth, resources and population of the occupied territories;

8. *Reaffirms* that all measures taken by Israel to change the physical character, demographic composition, institutional structure or status of the occupied territories, or any part thereof, including Jerusalem, are null and void, and that Israel's policy of settling parts of its population and new immigrants in the occupied territories constitutes a flagrant violation of the Geneva Convention and of the relevant resolutions of the United Nations;

9. *Demands* that Israel desist forthwith from the policies and practices referred to in paragraphs 7 and 8 above;

10. *Urges* the international organizations and the specialized agencies, in particular the International Labour Organisation, to examine the conditions of Arab workers in the occupied Palestinian and other Arab territories, including Jerusalem;

11. *Reiterates its call* upon all States, in particular those States parties to the Geneva Convention, in accordance with article 1 of that Convention, and upon international organizations and the specialized agencies not to recognize any changes carried out by Israel in the occupied territories and to avoid actions, including those in the field of aid, which might be used by Israel in its pursuit of the policies of annexation and colonization or any of the other policies and practices referred to in the present resolution;

12. *Requests* the Special Committee, pending the early termination of Israeli occupation, to continue to investigate Israeli policies and practices in the Arab territories occupied by Israel since 1967, to consult, as appropriate, with the International Committee of the Red Cross in order to ensure the safeguarding of the welfare and human rights of the population of the occupied territories and to report to the Secretary-General as soon as possible and whenever the need arises thereafter;

13. *Requests* the Special Committee to continue to investigate the treatment of civilians in detention in the Arab territories occupied by Israel since 1967;

14. *Condemns* Israel's refusal to permit persons from the occupied territories to appear as witnesses before the Special Committee;

15. *Requests* the Secretary-General:

(*a*) To provide all necessary facilities to the Special Committee, including those required for its visits to the occu-

---

[68]See A/37/485.

pied territories, with a view to investigating the Israeli policies and practices referred to in the present resolution;

(b) To continue to make available additional staff as may be necessary to assist the Special Committee in the performance of its tasks;

(c) To ensure the widest circulation of the reports of the Special Committee, and of information regarding its activities and findings, by all means available through the Department of Public Information of the Secretariat and, where necessary, to reprint those reports of the Special Committee which are no longer available;

(d) To report to the General Assembly at its thirty-eighth session on the tasks entrusted to him in the present paragraph;

16. *Requests* the Security Council to ensure Israel's respect for and compliance with all the provisions of the Geneva Convention relative to the Protection of Civilian Persons in Time of War, of 12 August 1949, in Palestinian and other Arab territories occupied since 1967, including Jerusalem, and to initiate measures to halt Israeli policies and practices in those territories;

17. *Decides* to include in the provisional agenda of its thirty-eighth session the item entitled "Report of the Spécial Committee to Investigate Israeli Practices Affecting the Human Rights of the Population of the Occupied Territories".

Adopted at the 100th plenary meeting:
In favour: 112
Afghanistan, Albania, Algeria, Argentina, Bahrain, Bangladesh, Benin, Bhutan, Bolivia, Botswana, Brazil, Bulgaria, Burma, Burundi, Byelorussia, Central African Republic, Chad, China, Colombia, Comoros, Congo, Cuba, Cyprus, Czechoslovakia, Democratic Kampuchea, Democratic Yemen, Djibouti, Ecuador, Egypt, El Salvador, Ethiopia, Fiji, Gabon, Gambia, German Democratic Republic, Ghana, Greece, Guyana, Haiti, Honduras, Hungary, India, Indonesia, Iran, Iraq, Jamaica, Jordan, Kenya, Kuwait, Lao People's Democratic Republic, Lebanon, Liberia, Libya, Madagascar, Malawi, Malaysia, Maldives, Mali, Malta, Mauritania, Mauritius, Mexico, Mongolia, Morocco, Mozambique, Nepal, Nicaragua, Niger, Nigeria, Oman, Pakistan, Panama, Papua New Guinea, Peru, Philippines, Poland, Portugal, Qatar, Romania, Rwanda, Sao Tome and Principe, Saudi Arabia, Senegal, Sierra Leone, Singapore, Solomon Islands, Somalia, Spain, Sri Lanka, Sudan, Suriname, Syria, Thailand, Togo, Trinidad and Tobago, Tunisia, Turkey, Uganda, Ukraine, USSR, United Arab Emirates, United Republic of Cameroon, United Republic of Tanzania, Upper Volta, Uruguay, Vanuatu, Venezuela, Viet Nam, Yemen, Yugoslavia, Zaire, Zambia.
Against: 2
Israel, United States.
Abstentions: 21
Australia, Austria, Barbados, Belgium, Canada, Costa Rica, Denmark, Dominican Republic, Finland, France, Federal Republic of Germany, Iceland, Ireland, Italy, Japan, Luxembourg, Netherlands, New Zealand, Norway, Sweden, United Kingdom.

Absent: 21
Angola, Antigua and Barbuda, Bahamas, Belize, Cape Verde, Chile, Dominica, Equatorial Guinea, Grenada, Guatemala, Guinea, Guinea-Bissau, Ivory Coast, Lesotho, Paraguay, Saint Lucia, Saint Vincent, Samoa, Seychelles, Swaziland, Zimbabwe.

D

The General Assembly,

Recalling Security Council resolutions 468 (1980) of 8 May 1980, 469 (1980) of 20 May 1980 and 484 (1980) of 19 December 1980 and General Assembly resolution 36/147 D of 16 December 1981,[69]

Deeply concerned at the expulsion by the Israeli military occupation authorities of the Mayors of Hebron and Halhul and of the Sharia Judge of Hebron,

Recalling the Geneva Convention relative to the Protection of Civilian Persons in Time of War, of 12 August 1949,[70] in particular article 1 and the first paragraph of article 49, which read as follows:

"Article 1

"The High Contracting Parties undertake to respect and to ensure respect for the present Convention in all circumstances."

"Article 49

"Individual or mass forcible transfers as well as deportations of protected persons from occupied territory to the territory of the occupying Power or to that of any other country, occupied or not, are prohibited, regardless of their motive . . .",

Reaffirming the applicability of the Geneva Convention to the Palestinian and other Arab territories occupied by Israel since 1967, including Jerusalem,

1. *Demands once more* that the Government of Israel, the occupying Power, rescind the illegal measures taken by the Israeli military occupation authorities in expelling and imprisoning the Mayors of Hebron and Halhul and in expelling the Sharia Judge of Hebron and that it facilitate the immediate return of the expelled Palestinian leaders so that they can resume the functions for which they were elected and appointed;

2. *Requests* the Secretary-General to report to the General Assembly as soon as possible on the implementation of the present resolution.

Adopted at the 100th plenary meeting:
In favour: 132
Afghanistan, Albania, Algeria, Argentina, Australia, Austria, Bahrain, Bangladesh, Barbados, Belgium, Benin, Bhutan, Bolivia, Botswana, Brazil, Bulgaria, Burma, Burundi, Byelorussia, Canada, Central African Repub-

---

[69]These resolutions refer to Israeli measures against Palestinian leaders. [ed. note]
[70]United Nations, *Treaty Series*, vol. 75, no. 973, p. 287.

lic, Chad, Chile, China, Comoros, Congo, Costa Rica, Cuba, Cyprus, Czechoslovakia, Democratic Kampuchea, Democratic Yemen, Denmark, Djibouti, Dominican Republic, Ecuador, Egypt, El Salvador, Ethiopia, Fiji, Finland, France, Gabon, Gambia, German Democratic Republic, Federal Republic of Germany, Ghana, Greece, Guyana, Haiti, Honduras, Hungary, Iceland, India, Indonesia, Iran, Iraq, Ireland, Italy, Jamaica, Japan, Jordan, Kenya, Kuwait, Lao People's Democratic Republic, Lebanon, Liberia, Libya, Luxembourg, Madagascar, Malawi, Malaysia, Maldives, Mali, Malta, Mauritania, Mauritius, Mexico, Mongolia, Morocco, Mozambique, Nepal, Netherlands, New Zealand, Nicaragua, Niger, Nigeria, Norway, Oman, Pakistan, Panama, Papua New Guinea, Peru, Philippines, Poland, Portugal, Qatar, Romania, Rwanda, Sao Tome and Principe, Saudi Arabia, Senegal, Sierra Leone, Singapore, Solomon Islands, Somalia, Spain, Sri Lanka, Sudan, Suriname, Sweden, Syria, Thailand, Togo, Trinidad and Tobago, Tunisia, Turkey, Uganda, Ukraine, USSR, United Arab Emirates, United Kingdom, United Republic of Cameroon, United Republic of Tanzania, Upper Volta, Uruguay, Vanuatu, Venezuela, Yemen, Yugoslavia, Zaire, Zambia.

Against: 1

Israel.

Abstention: 1

United States.

Absent: 22

Angola, Antigua and Barbuda, Bahamas, Belize, Cape Verde, Colombia,* Dominica, Equatorial Guinea, Grenada, Guatemala, Guinea, Guinea-Bissau, Ivory Coast, Lesotho, Paraguay, Saint Lucia, Saint Vincent, Samoa, Seychelles, Swaziland, Viet Nam, Zimbabwe.

---

* Later advised the Secretariat it had intended to vote in favour.

E

The General Assembly,

Deeply concerned that the Arab territories occupied since 1967 have been under continued Israeli military occupation,

Recalling Security Council resolution 497 (1981) of 17 December 1981 and General Assembly resolutions 36/226 B of 17 December 1981 and ES-9/1 of 5 February 1982,

Recalling its previous resolutions, in particular resolutions 3414 (XXX) of 5 December 1975, 31/61 of 9 December 1976, 32/20 of 25 November 1977, 33/28 and 33/29 of 7 December 1978, 34/70 of 6 December 1979 and 35/122 E of 11 December 1980, in which it, *inter alia,* called upon Israel to put an end to its occupation of the Arab territories and to withdraw from all those territories,

Reaffirming once more the illegality of Israel's decision of 14 December 1981 to impose its laws, jurisdiction and administration on the occupied Syrian Golan Heights, which has resulted in the effective annexation of that territory,

Reaffirming that the acquisition of territory by force is inadmissible under the Charter of the United Nations

and that all territories thus occupied by Israel must be returned,

Recalling the Geneva Convention relative to the Protection of Civilian Persons in Time of War, of 12 August 1949,[71]

1. *Strongly condemns* Israel, the occupying Power, for its refusal to comply with the relevant resolutions of the General Assembly and the Security Council, particularly Council resolution 497 (1981), in which the Council, *inter alia,* decided that the Israeli decision to impose its laws, jurisdiction and administration in the occupied Syrian Golan Heights was null and void and without international legal effect and demanded that Israel, the occupying Power, should rescind forthwith its decision;

2. *Condemns* the persistence of Israel in changing the physical character, demographic composition, institutional structure and legal status of the occupied Syrian Arab Golan Heights;

3. *Determines* that all legislative and administrative measures and actions taken or to be taken by Israel, the occupying Power, that purport to alter the character and legal status of the Syrian Arab Golan Heights are null and void and constitute a flagrant violation of international law and of the Geneva Convention relative to the Protection of Civilian Persons in Time of War, of 12 August 1949, and have no legal effect;

4. *Strongly condemns* Israel for its attempts and measures to impose forcibly Israeli citizenship and Israeli identity cards on the Syrian citizens in the occupied Syrian Arab Golan Heights and calls upon it to desist from its repressive measures against the population of the Syrian Arab Golan Heights;

5. *Calls upon* Member States not to recognize any of the legislative or administrative measures and actions referred to above;

6. *Requests* the Secretary-General to report to the General Assembly at its thirty-eighth session on the implementation of the present resolution.

Adopted at the 100th plenary meeting:

In favour: 133

Afghanistan, Albania, Algeria, Argentina, Australia, Austria, Bahrain, Bangladesh, Barbados, Belgium, Benin, Bhutan, Bolivia, Botswana, Brazil, Bulgaria, Burma, Burundi, Byelorussia, Canada, Central African Republic, Chad, Chile, China, Colombia, Comoros, Congo, Costa Rica, Cuba, Cyprus, Czechoslovakia, Democratic Kampuchea, Democratic Yemen, Denmark, Djibouti, Dominican Republic, Ecuador, Egypt, El Salvador, Ethiopia, Fiji, Finland, France, Gabon, Gambia, German Democratic Republic, Federal Republic of Germany, Ghana, Greece, Guyana, Haiti, Honduras, Hungary, Iceland, India, Indonesia, Iran, Iraq, Ireland, Italy, Jamaica, Japan, Jordan, Kenya, Kuwait, Lao People's Democratic Republic, Lebanon, Liberia, Libya, Luxembourg, Madagascar, Malaysia, Maldives, Mali, Malta, Mauritania, Mauritius, Mexico, Mongolia, Morocco, Mozambique, Nepal, Netherlands,

---

[71]United Nations, *Treaty Series,* vol. 75, no. 973, p. 287.

New Zealand, Nicaragua, Niger, Nigeria, Norway, Oman, Pakistan, Panama, Papua New Guinea, Peru, Philippines, Poland, Portugal, Qatar, Romania, Rwanda, Sao Tome and Principe, Saudi Arabia, Senegal, Sierra Leone, Singapore, Solomon Islands, Somalia, Spain, Sri Lanka, Sudan, Suriname, Sweden, Syria, Thailand, Togo, Trinidad and Tobago, Tunisia, Turkey, Uganda, Ukraine, USSR, United Arab Emirates, United Kingdom, United Republic of Cameroon, United Republic of Tanzania, Upper Volta, Uruguay, Vanuatu, Venezuela, Viet Nam, Yemen, Yugoslavia, Zaire, Zambia.

Against: 1
Israel.

Abstentions: 2
Malawi, United States.

Absent: 20
Angola, Antigua and Barbuda, Bahamas, Belize, Cape Verde, Dominica, Equatorial Guinea, Grenada, Guatemala, Guinea, Guinea-Bissau, Ivory Coast, Lesotho, Paraguay, Saint Lucia, Saint Vincent, Samoa, Seychelles, Swaziland, Zimbabwe.

F

The General Assembly,

Bearing in mind the Geneva Convention relative to the Protection of Civilian Persons in Time of War, of 12 August 1949,[72]

Deeply shocked by the most recent atrocities committed by Israel, the occupying Power, against educational institutions in the occupied Palestinian territories,

1. *Reaffirms* the applicability of the Geneva Convention relative to the Protection of Civilian Persons in Time of War, of 12 August 1949, to the Palestinian and other Arab territories occupied by Israel since 1967, including Jerusalem;

2. *Condemns* Israeli policies and practices against Palestinian students and faculties in schools, universities and other educational institutions in the occupied Palestinian territories, especially the policy of opening fire on defenseless students, causing many casualties;

3. *Condemns* the systematic Israeli campaign of repression against and closing of universities in the occupied Palestinian territories, restricting and impeding academic activities of Palestinian universities by subjecting the selection of courses, textbooks and eduational programmes, the admission of students and the appointment of faculty members to the control and supervision of the military occupation authorities, in clear contravention of the Geneva Convention;

4. *Demands* that Israel, the occupying Power, comply with the provisions of that Convention, rescind all actions and measures against all educational institutions, ensure the freedom of these institutions and refrain forthwith from hindering the effective operation of the universities and other educational institutions;

5. *Requests* the Secretary-General to report on the implementation of the present resolution before the end of 1983.

Adopted at the 100th plenary meeting:

In favour: 110
Afghanistan, Albania, Algeria, Argentina, Austria, Bahrain, Bangladesh, Benin, Bhutan, Bolivia, Botswana, Brazil, Bulgaria, Burundi, Byelorussia, Central African Republic, Chad, China, Colombia, Comoros, Congo, Cuba, Cyprus, Czechoslovakia, Democratic Kampuchea, Democratic Yemen, Djibouti, Dominican Republic, Ecuador, Egypt, El Salvador, Ethiopia, Fiji, Gabon, Gambia, German Democratic Republic, Ghana, Greece, Guyana, Haiti, Honduras, Hungary, India, Indonesia, Iran, Iraq, Jamaica, Jordan, Kenya, Kuwait, Lao People's Democratic Republic, Lebanon, Liberia, Libya, Madagascar, Malaysia, Maldives, Mali, Malta, Mauritania, Mauritius, Mexico, Mongolia, Morocco, Mozambique, Nepal, Nicaragua, Niger, Nigeria, Oman, Pakistan, Panama, Papua New Guinea, Peru, Philippines, Poland, Portugal, Qatar, Romania, Rwanda, Sao Tome and Principe, Saudi Arabia, Senegal, Sierra Leone, Singapore, Solomon Islands, Somalia, Spain, Sri Lanka, Sudan, Suriname, Syria, Thailand, Togo, Trinidad and Tobago, Tunisia, Turkey, Uganda, Ukraine, USSR, United Arab Emirates, United Republic of Cameroon, United Republic of Tanzania, Upper Volta, Vanuatu, Venezuela, Viet Nam, Yemen, Yugoslavia, Zambia.

Against: 2
Israel, United States.

Abstentions: 24
Australia, Barbados, Belgium, Burma, Canada, Chile, Costa Rica, Denmark, Finland, France, Federal Republic of Germany, Iceland, Ireland, Italy, Japan, Luxembourg, Malawi, Netherlands, New Zealand, Norway, Sweden, United Kingdom, Uruguay, Zaire.

Absent: 20
Angola, Antigua and Barbuda, Bahamas, Belize, Cape Verde, Dominica, Equatorial Guinea, Grenada, Guatemala, Guinea, Guinea-Bissau, Ivory Coast, Lesotho, Paraguay, Saint Lucia, Saint Vincent, Samoa, Seychelles, Swaziland, Zimbabwe.

G

The General Assembly,

Recalling Security Council resolution 471 (1980) of 5 June 1980, in which the Council condemned the assassination attempts against the Mayors of Nablus, Ramallah and Al Bireh and called for the immediate apprehension and prosecution of the perpetrators of those crimes,

Recalling also General Assembly resolution 36/147 G of 16 December 1981,

Recalling once again the Geneva Convention relative to the Protection of Civilian Persons in Time of War, of 12 August 1949,[73] in particular article 27, which states, *inter*

---

[72]United Nations, *Treaty Series,* vol. 75, no. 973, p. 287.

[73]United Nations, *Treaty Series,* vol. 75, no. 973, p. 287.

alia:

"Protected persons are entitled, in all circumstances, to respect for their persons . . . . They shall at all times be humanely treated, and shall be protected especially against all acts of violence or threats thereof . . .",

Reaffirming the applicability of that Convention to the Arab territories occupied by Israel since 1967, including Jerusalem,

1. *Expresses deep concern* that Israel, the occupying Power, has failed for two years to apprehend and prosecute the perpetrators of the assassination attempts;

2. *Demands once more* that Israel, the occupying Power, inform the Secretary-General of the results of the investigations relevant to the assassination attempts;

3. *Requests* the Secretary-General to report to the General Assembly at its thirty-eighth session on the implementation of the present resolution.

Adopted at the 100th plenary meeting:

In favour: 134

Afghanistan, Albania, Algeria, Argentina, Australia, Austria, Bahrain, Bangladesh, Barbados, Belgium, Benin, Bhutan, Bolivia, Botswana, Brazil, Bulgaria, Burma, Burundi, Byelorussia, Canada, Central African Republic, Chad, Chile, China, Colombia, Comoros, Congo, Costa Rica, Cuba, Cyprus, Czechoslovakia, Democratic Kampuchea, Democratic Yemen, Denmark, Djibouti, Dominican Republic, Ecuador, Egypt, El Salvador, Ethiopia, Fiji, Finland, France, Gabon, Gambia, German Democratic Republic, Federal Republic of Germany, Ghana, Greece, Guyana, Haiti, Honduras, Hungary, Iceland, India, Indonesia, Iran, Iraq, Ireland, Italy, Jamaica, Japan, Jordan, Kenya, Kuwait, Lao People's Democratic Republic, Lebanon, Liberia, Libya, Luxembourg, Madagascar, Malawi, Malaysia, Maldives, Mali, Malta, Mauritania, Mauritius, Mexico, Mongolia, Morocco, Mozambique, Nepal, Netherlands, New Zealand, Nicaragua, Niger, Nigeria, Norway, Oman, Pakistan, Panama, Papua New Guinea, Peru, Philippines, Poland, Portugal, Qatar, Romania, Rwanda, Sao Tome and Principe, Saudi Arabia, Senegal, Sierra Leone, Singapore, Solomon Islands, Somalia, Spain, Sri Lanka, Sudan, Suriname, Sweden, Syria, Thailand, Togo, Trinidad and Tobago, Tunisia, Turkey, Uganda, Ukraine, USSR, United Arab Emirates, United Kingdom, United Republic of Cameroon, United Republic of Tanzania, Upper Volta, Uruguay, Vanuatu, Venezuela, Viet Nam, Yemen, Yugoslavia, Zaire, Zambia.

Against: 1

Israel.

Abstention: 1

United States.

Absent: 20

Angola, Antigua and Barbuda, Bahamas, Belize, Cape Verde, Dominica, Equatorial Guinea, Grenada, Guatemala, Guinea, Guinea-Bissau, Ivory Coast, Lesotho, Paraguay, Saint Lucia, Saint Vincent, Samoa, Seychelles, Swaziland, Zimbabwe.

Resolution No. 37/104 of 16 December 1982

CALLING ON ALL STATES TO ACCORD THE NECESSARY FACILITIES, PRIVILEGES AND IMMUNITIES TO DELEGATIONS OF NATIONAL LIBERATION MOVEMENTS RECOGNIZED BY THE ORGANIZATION OF AFRICAN UNITY AND/OR THE LEAGUE OF ARAB STATES AND ACCORDED OBSERVER STATUS BY INTERNATIONAL ORGANIZATIONS

The General Assembly,

Recalling its resolution 35/167 of 15 December 1980,

Taking note of the report of the Secretary-General,[74]

Bearing in mind the resolution of the United Nations Conference on the Representation of States in Their Relations with International Organizations relating to the observer status of national liberation movements recognized by the Organization of African Unity and/or by the League of Arab States,[75]

Noting that the Vienna Convention on the Representation of States in Their Relations with International Organizations of a Universal Character, of 14 March 1975,[76] regulates only the representation of States in their relations with international organizations,

Taking into account the current practice of inviting the above-mentioned national liberation movements to participate as observers in the sessions of the General Assembly, specialized agencies and other organizations of the United Nations system and in the work of the conferences held under the auspices of such international organizations,

Convinced that the participation of the national liberation movements referred to above in the work of international organizations helps to strengthen international peace and co-operation,

Desirous of ensuring the effective participation of the above-mentioned national liberation movements as observers in the work of international organizations and of regulating, to that end, their status and the facilities, privileges and immunities necessary for the performance of their functions,

1. *Invites* all States that have not done so, in particular those that are hosts to international organizations or to conferences convened by, or held under the auspices of, international organizations of a universal character, to consider as soon as possible the question of ratifying, or acceding to, the Vienna Convention on the Representation of States in Their Relations with International Organizations of a Universal Character;

2. *Calls once more upon* the States concerned to accord to the delegations of the national liberation movements recognized by the Organization of African Unity and/or by the League of Arab States, and accorded observer status by international organizations, the facilities, privileges and immunities necessary for the performance of their func-

---

[74]A/37/326 and Add. 1.

[75]See *Official Records of the United Nations Conference on the Representation of States in Their Relations with International Organizations, Vienna, 4 February-14 March 1975*, vol. II (United Nations publication, Sales No. E.75.V.12), document A/CONF.67/15, annex.

[76]*Ibid.*, vol. II, p. 207.

tions in accordance with the provisions of the Vienna Convention on the Representation of States in Their Relations with International Organizations of a Universal Character;

3. *Requests* the Secretary-General to report to the General Assembly at its thirty-ninth session on the implementation of the present resolution.

Adopted at the 107th plenary meeting:
In favour: 110
Afghanistan, Albania, Algeria, Angola, Argentina, Bahamas, Bahrain, Bangladesh, Barbados, Belize, Benin, Bhutan, Bolivia, Brazil, Bulgaria, Burundi, Byelorussia, Central African Republic, Chad, Chile, China, Colombia, Comoros, Congo, Cuba, Cyprus, Czechoslovakia, Democratic Kampuchea, Democratic Yemen, Djibouti, Ecuador, Egypt, Ethiopia, Gabon, Gambia, German Democratic Republic, Ghana, Greece, Grenada, Guinea, Guyana, Hungary, India, Indonesia, Iran, Iraq, Ivory Coast, Jamaica, Jordan, Kenya, Kuwait, Lao People's Democratic Republic, Lebanon, Lesotho, Libya, Madagascar, Malawi, Malaysia, Maldives, Mali, Malta, Mauritania, Mauritius, Mexico, Mongolia, Morocco, Mozambique, Nepal, Nicaragua, Niger, Nigeria, Oman, Pakistan, Panama, Papua New Guinea, Peru, Philippines, Poland, Qatar, Romania, Rwanda, Sao Tomе and Principe, Saudi Arabia, Senegal, Sierra Leone, Singapore, Somalia, Sri Lanka, Sudan, Syria, Thailand, Togo, Trinidad and Tobago, Tunisia, Turkey, Uganda, Ukraine, USSR, United Arab Emirates, United Republic of Cameroon, United Republic of Tanzania, Upper Volta, Vanuatu, Venezuela, Viet Nam, Yemen, Yugoslavia, Zaire, Zambia, Zimbabwe.
Against: 10
Belgium, Canada, France, Germany, Israel, Italy, Luxembourg, Netherlands, United Kingdom, United States.
Abstentions: 17
Australia, Austria, Burma, Denmark, Fiji, Finland, Guatemala, Iceland, Ireland, Japan, New Zealand, Norway, Paraguay, Portugal, Spain, Sweden, Uruguay.
Absent: 19
Antigua and Barbuda, Botswana, Cape Verde, Costa Rica, Dominica, Dominican Republic, El Salvador, Equatorial Guinea, Guinea-Bissau, Haiti, Honduras, Liberia, Saint Lucia, Saint Vincent, Samoa, Seychelles, Solomon Islands, Suriname, Swaziland.

Resolution No. 37/120 A, B, C, D, E, F, G, H, I, J, K of 16 December 1982

ON THE UNITED NATIONS RELIEF AND WORKS AGENCY FOR PALESTINE REFUGEES IN THE NEAR EAST: ENDORSING ASSISTANCE TO PALESTINIAN REFUGEES, CALLING UPON ISRAEL TO REMOVE OBSTACLES TO THE ESTABLISHMENT OF A UNIVERSITY OF JERUSALEM FOR PALESTINIAN REFUGEES AND TO PERMIT THE RETURN OF DISPLACED PALESTINIANS, AND REQUESTING THE SECRETARY-GENERAL TO TAKE ALL APPROPRIATE STEPS FOR THE PROTECTION AND ADMINISTRATION OF ARAB PROPERTY, ASSETS AND PROPERTY RIGHTS IN ISRAEL, AND TO ISSUE IDENTIFICATION CARDS TO ALL PALESTINIAN REFUGEES AND THEIR DESCENDENTS

A

WORKING GROUP ON THE FINANCING OF THE UNITED NATIONS RELIEF AND WORKS AGENCY FOR PALESTINE REFUGEES IN THE NEAR EAST

The General Assembly,
Recalling its resolutions 2656 (XXV) of 7 December 1970, 2728 (XXV) of 15 December 1970, 2791 (XXVI) of 6 December 1971, 2964 (XXVII) of 13 December 1972, 3090 (XXVIII) of 7 December 1973, 3330 (XXIX) of 17 December 1974, 3419 D (XXX) of 8 December 1975, 31/15 C of 23 November 1976, 32/90 D of 13 December 1977, 33/112 D of 18 December 1978, 34/52 D of 23 November 1979, 35/13 D of 3 November 1980 and 36/146 E of 16 December 1981,[77]

Recalling also its decision 36/462 of 16 March 1982, whereby the General Assembly took note of the special report of the Working Group on the Financing of the United Nations Relief and Works Agency for Palestine Refugees in the Near East[78] and adopted the recommendations contained therein,

Having considered the report of the Working Group on the Financing of the United Nations Relief and Works Agency for Palestine Refugees in the Near East,[79]

Taking into account the report of the Commissioner-General of the United Nations Relief and Works Agency for Palestine Refugees in the Near East, covering the period from 1 July 1981 to 30 June 1982,[80] and his special report issued on 28 September 1982,[81]

Gravely concerned at the critical financial situation of the United Nations Relief and Works Agency for Palestine Refugees in the Near East, which has already reduced the essential minimum services being provided to the Palestine refugees and which threatens even greater reductions in the future,

Emphasizing the urgent need for extraordinary efforts in order to maintain, at least at their present minimum level, the activities of the United Nations Relief and Works Agency for Palestine Refugees in the Near East,

1. *Commends* the Working Group on the Financing of the United Nations Relief and Works Agency for Palestine Refugees in the Near East for its efforts to assist in ensuring the Agency's financial security;

2. *Takes note with approval* of the report of the Working Group;

3. *Requests* the Working Group to continue its efforts, in co-operation with the Secretary-General and the Commissioner-General of the United Nations Relief and Works Agency for Palestine Refugees in the Near East, for the financing of the Agency for a further period of one year;

4. *Requests* the Secretary-General to provide the neces-

---

[77]These resolutions focus on the financing of the United Nations Relief and Works Agency for Palestine Refugees in the Near East. [ed. note]
[78]A/36/866 and Corr.1.
[79]A/37/591.
[80]*Official Records of the General Assembly, Thirty-seventh Session, Supplement No. 13* (A/37/13).
[81]A/37/479.

sary services and assistance to the Working Group for the conduct of its work.

Adopted at the 108th plenary meeting without a vote.

B

ASSISTANCE TO PERSONS DISPLACED AS A RESULT OF THE JUNE 1967 AND SUBSEQUENT HOSTILITIES

The General Assembly,

Recalling its resolution 36/146 D of 16 December 1981 and all previous resolutions on the question,

Taking note of the report of the Commissioner-General of the United Nations Relief and Works Agency for Palestine Refugees in the Near East covering the period from 1 July 1981 to 30 June 1982,[82] and his special report covering the period from 6 June to 31 August 1982,[83]

Concerned about the continued human suffering resulting from the hostilities in the Middle East,

1. *Reaffirms* its resolution 36/146 D and all previous resolutions on the question;

2. *Endorses,* bearing in mind the objectives of those resolutions, the efforts of the Commissioner-General of the United Nations Relief and Works Agency for Palestine Refugees in the Near East to continue to provide humanitarian assistance as far as practicable, on an emergency basis and as a temporary measure, to other persons in the area who are at present displaced and in serious need of continued assistance as a result of the June 1967 and subsequent hostilities;

3. *Strongly appeals* to all Governments and to organizations and individuals to contribute generously for the above purposes to the United Nations Relief and Works Agency for Palestine Refugees in the Near East and to the other intergovernmental and non-governmental organizations concerned.

Adopted at the 108th plenary meeting without a vote.

C

UNIVERSITY OF JERUSALEM FOR PALESTINE REFUGEES

The General Assembly,

Recalling its resolution 36/146 G of 16 December 1981,

Having examined with appreciation the report of the Secretary-General[84] concerning the establishment of a university at Jerusalem in pursuance of paragraphs 5 and 6 of resolution 36/146 G,

Having also examined with appreciation the report of the Commissioner-General of the United Nations Relief and Works Agency for Palestine Refugees in the Near East covering the period from 1 July 1981 to 30 June 1982,[85]

1. *Commends* the constructive efforts made by the Secretary-General, the Commissioner-General of the United Nations Relief and Works Agency for Palestine Refugees in the Near East, the Council of the United Nations University and the United Nations Educational, Scientific and Cultural Organization, which worked diligently towards the implementation of General Assembly resolution 36/146 G;

2. *Further commends* the close co-operation of the competent educational authorities concerned;

3. *Emphasizes* the need for strengthening the educational system in the Arab territories occupied since 5 June 1967, including Jerusalem, and specifically the need for the establishment of the proposed university;

4. *Endorses* the various steps recommended in the report of the Secretary-General, including the creation of a voluntary fund to be administered by the Department of Technical Co-operation for Development of the Secretariat, in order to provide graduate and post-doctoral fellowships for a highly trained core faculty of the proposed university;

5. *Requests* the Secretary-General to continue to take all necessary measures, including the conduct of a functional feasibility study, for establishing the University of Jerusalem in accordance with the recommendations contained in the report of the Secretary-General;

6. *Calls upon* Israel as the occupying Power to cooperate in the implementation of the present resolution and to remove the hindrances which it has put in the way of establishing the University of Jerusalem;

7. *Requests* the Secretary-General to report to the General Assembly at its thirty-eighth session on the progress made in the implementation of the present resolution.

Adopted at the 108th plenary meeting:
In favour: 141

Afghanistan, Albania, Algeria, Angola, Argentina, Australia, Austria, Bahamas, Bahrain, Bangladesh, Barbados, Belgium, Belize, Benin, Bhutan, Bolivia, Botswana, Brazil, Bulgaria, Burma, Burundi, Byelorussia, Canada, Central African Republic, Chad, Chile, China, Colombia, Comoros, Congo, Costa Rica, Cuba, Cyprus, Czechoslovakia, Democratic Kampuchea, Democratic Yemen, Denmark, Djibouti, Dominican Republic, Ecuador, Egypt, El Salvador, Ethiopia, Fiji, Finland, France, Gabon, Gambia, German Democratic Republic, Germany, Ghana, Greece, Grenada, Guatemala, Guinea, Guinea-Bissau, Guyana, Honduras, Hungary, Iceland, India, Indonesia, Iran, Iraq, Ireland, Italy, Ivory Coast, Jamaica, Japan, Jordan, Kenya, Kuwait, Lao People's Democratic Republic, Lebanon, Liberia, Libya, Luxembourg, Madagascar, Malawi, Malaysia, Maldives, Mali, Malta, Mauritania, Mauritius, Mexico, Mongolia, Morocco, Mozambique, Nepal, Netherlands, New Zealand, Nicaragua, Nigeria, Norway, Oman, Pakistan, Panama, Paraguay, Peru, Philippines, Poland, Portugal, Qatar, Romania, Rwanda, Samoa, Sao Tome and Principe, Saudi Arabia, Senegal, Seychelles, Sierra Leone, Singapore, Somalia, Spain, Sri Lanka, Sudan, Suriname, Sweden, Syria, Thailand, Togo, Trinidad and Tobago, Tunisia, Turkey, Uganda, Ukraine, USSR, United

---

[82]*Official Records of the General Assembly, Thirty-seventh Session, Supplement No. 13* (A/37/13).

[83]A/37/479.

[84]A/37/599.

[85]*Official Records of the General Assembly, Thirty-seventh Session, Supplement No. 13* (A/37/13).

Arab Emirates, United Kingdom, United Republic of Cameroon, United Republic of Tanzania, Upper Volta, Uruguay, Vanuatu, Venezuela, Viet Nam, Yemen, Yugoslavia, Zaire, Zambia.

Against: 2

Israel, United States.

Abstentions: 0

Absent: 13

Antigua and Barbuda, Cape Verde, Dominica, Equatorial Guinea, Haiti, Lesotho, Niger, Papua New Guinea, Saint Lucia, Saint Vincent, Solomon Islands, Swaziland, Zimbabwe.

D

OFFERS BY MEMBER STATES OF GRANTS AND SCHOLARSHIPS FOR HIGHER EDUCATION, INCLUDING VOCATIONAL TRAINING, FOR PALESTINE REFUGEES

The General Assembly,

Recalling its resolution 212 (III) of 19 November 1948 on assistance to Palestine refugees,

Recalling also its resolutions 35/13 B of 3 November 1980 and 36/146 H of 16 December 1981,

Cognizant of the fact that the Palestine refugees have, for the last three decades, lost their lands and means of livelihood,

Having examined with appreciation the report of the Secretary-General[86] on offers of grants and scholarships for higher education for Palestine refugees and on the scope of the implementation of resolution 36/146 H,

Having also examined the report of the Commissioner-General of the United Nations Relief and Works Agency for Palestine Refugees in the Near East, covering the period from 1 July 1981 to 30 June 1982,[87] dealing with this subject,

Noting that fewer than one per thousand of the Palestine refugee students have the chance to continue higher education, including vocational training,

Noting also that over the past several years the number of scholarships offered by the United Nations Relief and Works Agency for Palestine Refugees in the Near East has dwindled to half of what it was because of the Agency's recurring budgetary difficulties,

1. *Urges* all States to respond to the appeal contained in General Assembly resolution 32/90 F of 13 December 1977 in a manner commensurate with the needs of Palestine refugees for higher education and vocational training;

2. *Strongly appeals* to all States, specialized agencies and non-governmental organizations to augment the special allocations for grants and scholarships to Palestine refugees in addition to their contributions to the regular budget of the United Nations Relief and Works Agency for Palestine Refugees in the Near East;

3. *Expresses its appreciation* to all Governments, specialized agencies and non-governmental organizations that responded favourably to General Assembly resolution 36/146 H;

4. *Invites* the relevant United Nations agencies to continue, within their respective spheres of competence, to expand assistance for higher education to Palestine refugee students;

5. *Appeals* to all States, specialized agencies and the United Nations University to contribute generously to the Palestinian universities in the territories occupied by Israel since 1967;

6. *Also appeals* to all States, specialized agencies and other international bodies to contribute towards the establishment of vocational training centres for Palestine refugees;

7. *Requests* the United Nations Relief and Works Agency for Palestine Refugees in the Near East to act as recipient and trustee for such special allocations and scholarships and to award them to qualified Palestine refugee candidates;

8. *Requests* the Secretary-General to report to the General Assembly at its thirty-eighth session on the implementation of the present resolution.

Adopted at the 108th plenary meeting:

In favour: 143

Afghanistan, Algeria, Angola, Argentina, Australia, Austria, Bahamas, Bahrain, Bangladesh, Barbados, Belgium, Belize, Benin, Bhutan, Bolivia, Botswana, Brazil, Bulgaria, Burma, Burundi, Byelorussia, Canada, Central African Republic, Chad, Chile, China, Colombia, Comoros, Congo, Costa Rica, Cuba, Cyprus, Czechoslovakia, Democratic Kampuchea, Democratic Yemen, Denmark, Djibouti, Dominican Republic, Ecuador, Egypt, El Salvador, Ethiopia, Fiji, Finland, France, Gabon, Gambia, German Democratic Republic, Germany, Ghana, Greece, Grenada, Guatemala, Guinea, Guinea-Bissau, Guyana, Honduras, Hungary, Iceland, India, Indonesia, Iran, Iraq, Ireland, Italy, Ivory Coast, Jamaica, Japan, Jordan, Kenya, Kuwait, Lao People's Democratic Republic, Lebanon, Liberia, Libya, Luxembourg, Madagascar, Malawi, Malaysia, Maldives, Mali, Malta, Mauritania, Mauritius, Mexico, Mongolia, Morocco, Mozambique, Nepal, Netherlands, New Zealand, Nicaragua, Nigeria, Norway, Oman, Pakistan, Panama, Papua New Guinea, Paraguay, Peru, Philippines, Poland, Portugal, Qatar, Romania, Rwanda, Samoa, Sao Tome and Principe, Saudi Arabia, Senegal, Seychelles, Sierra Leone, Singapore, Somalia, Spain, Sri Lanka, Sudan, Suriname, Sweden, Syria, Thailand, Togo, Trinidad and Tobago, Tunisia, Turkey, Uganda, Ukraine, USSR, United Arab Emirates, United Kingdom, United Republic of Cameroon, United Republic of Tanzania, United States, Upper Volta, Uruguay, Vanuatu, Venezuela, Viet Nam, Yemen, Yugoslavia, Zaire, Zambia, Zimbabwe.

Against: 0

Abstention: 1

Israel.

Absent: 12

Albania, Antigua and Barbuda, Cape Verde, Dominica, Equatorial Guinea, Haiti, Lesotho, Niger, Saint Lucia, Saint Vincent, Solomon Islands, Swaziland.

---

[86]A/37/427.

[87]*Official Records of the General Assembly, Thirty-seventh Session, Supplement No. 13* (A/37/13).

E

PALESTINE REFUGEES IN THE GAZA STRIP

The General Assembly,

Recalling Security Council resolution 237 (1967) of 14 June 1967,

Recalling also General Assembly resolutions 2792 C (XXVI) of 6 December 1971, 2963 C (XXVII) of 13 December 1972, 3089 C (XXVIII) of 7 December 1973, 3331 D (XXIX) of 17 December 1974, 3419 C (XXX) of 8 December 1975, 31/15 E of 23 November 1976, 32/90 C of 13 December 1977, 33/112 E of 18 December 1978, 34/52 F of 23 November 1979, 35/13 F of 3 November 1980 and 36/146 A of 16 December 1981,[88]

Having considered the report of the Commissioner-General of the United Nations Relief and Works Agency for Palestine Refugees in the Near East, covering the period from 1 July 1981 to 30 June 1982,[89] and the report of the Secretary-General of 17 September 1982,[90]

Recalling the provisions of paragraph 11 of its resolution 194 (III) of 11 December 1948 and considering that measures to resettle Palestine refugees in the Gaza Strip away from the homes and property from which they were displaced constitute a violation of their inalienable right of return,

Alarmed by the reports received from the Commissioner-General that the Israeli occupying authorities persist in their policy of demolishing, on punitive grounds, shelters occupied by refugee families,

1. *Reiterates its demand* that Israel desist from the removal and resettlement of Palestine refugees in the Gaza Strip and from the destruction of their shelters;

2. *Requests* the Secretary-General, after consulting with the Commissioner-General of the United Nations Relief and Works Agency for Palestine Refugees in the Near East, to report to the General Assembly, before the opening of its thirty-eighth session, on Israel's compliance with paragraph 1 above.

Adopted at the 108th plenary meeting:

In favour: 143

Afghanistan, Albania, Algeria, Angola, Argentina, Australia, Austria, Bahamas, Bahrain, Bangladesh, Barbados, Belgium, Belize, Benin, Bhutan, Bolivia, Botswana, Brazil, Bulgaria, Burma, Burundi, Byelorussia, Canada, Cape Verde, Central African Republic, Chad, Chile, China, Colombia, Comoros, Congo, Costa Rica, Cuba, Cyprus, Czechoslovakia, Democratic Kampuchea, Democratic Yemen, Denmark, Djibouti, Dominican Republic, Ecuador, Egypt, El Salvador, Ethiopia, Fiji, Finland, France, Gabon, Gambia, German Democratic Republic, Germany, Ghana, Greece, Grenada, Guinea, Guinea-Bissau, Guyana, Honduras, Hungary, Iceland, India, Indonesia, Iran, Iraq, Ireland, Italy, Ivory Coast, Jamaica, Japan, Jordan, Kenya, Kuwait, Lao People's Democratic Republic, Lebanon, Liberia, Libya, Luxembourg, Madagascar, Malawi, Malaysia, Maldives, Mali, Malta, Mauritania, Mauritius, Mexico, Mongolia, Morocco, Mozambique, Nepal, Netherlands, New Zealand, Nicaragua, Nigeria, Norway, Oman, Pakistan, Panama, Papua New Guinea, Paraguay, Peru, Philippines, Poland, Portugal, Qatar, Romania, Rwanda, Samoa, Sao Tome and Principe, Saudi Arabia, Senegal, Seychelles, Sierra Leone, Singapore, Somalia, Spain, Sri Lanka, Sudan, Suriname, Sweden, Syria, Thailand, Togo, Trinidad and Tobago, Tunisia, Turkey, Uganda, Ukraine, USSR, United Arab Emirates, United Kingdom, United Republic of Cameroon, United Republic of Tanzania, Upper Volta, Uruguay, Vanuatu, Venezuela, Viet Nam, Yemen, Yugoslavia, Zaire, Zambia, Zimbabwe.

Against: 2

Israel, United States.

Abstentions: 0

Absent: 11

Antigua and Barbuda, Dominica, Equatorial Guinea, Guatemala, Haiti, Lesotho, Niger, Saint Lucia, Saint Vincent, Solomon Islands, Swaziland.

F

RESUMPTION OF THE RATION DISTRIBUTION TO PALESTINE REFUGEES

The General Assembly,

Recalling its resolution 36/146 F of 16 December 1981 and all previous resolutions on the question, including resolution 302 (IV) of 8 December 1949,

Having considered the report of the Commissioner-General of the United Nations Relief and Works Agency for Palestine Refugees in the Near East, covering the period from 1 July 1981 to 30 June 1982,[91] and his special report covering the period from 6 June to 31 August 1982,[92]

Deeply concerned at the interruption by the United Nations Relief and Works Agency for Palestine Refugees in the Near East, owing to financial difficulties, of the general ration distribution to Palestine refugees in all fields in the occupied Palestinian territories, Jordan and the Syrian Arab Republic,

1. *Calls upon* all Governments, as a matter of urgency, to make the most generous efforts possible to meet the needs of the United Nations Relief and Works Agency for Palestine Refugees in the Near East, particularly in the light of the interruption by the Agency of the general ration distribution to Palestine refugees in all fields, and therefore urges noncontributing Governments to contribute regularly and contributing Governments to consider increasing their regular contributions;

2. *Requests* the Commissioner-General of the United Na-

---

[88]On Israeli actions harmful to Palestinian refugees in the Gaza Strip. [ed. note]

[89]*Official Records of the General Assembly, Thirty-seventh Session, Supplement No. 13* (A/37/13).

[90]A/37/425 and Corr.1.

[91]*Official Records of the General Assembly, Thirty-seventh Session, Supplement No. 13* (A/37/13).

[92]A/37/479.

tions Relief and Works Agency for Palestine Refugees in the Near East to resume on a continuing basis and as soon as possible the interrupted general ration distribution to Palestine refugees in all fields.

Adopted at the 108th plenary meeting:
In favour: 121
Afghanistan, Algeria, Angola, Argentina, Bahamas, Bahrain, Bangladesh, Barbados, Belize, Benin, Bhutan, Bolivia, Botswana, Brazil, Bulgaria, Burma, Burundi, Byelorussia, Cape Verde, Central African Republic, Chad, Chile, China, Colombia, Comoros, Congo, Costa Rica, Cuba, Cyprus, Czechoslovakia, Democratic Kampuchea, Democratic Yemen, Djibouti, Dominican Republic, Ecuador, Egypt, El Salvador, Ethiopia, Fiji, Gabon, Gambia, German Democratic Republic, Ghana, Greece, Grenada, Guinea, Guinea-Bissau, Guyana, Honduras, Hungary, India, Indonesia, Iran, Iraq, Ivory Coast, Jamaica, Jordan, Kenya, Kuwait, Lao People's Democratic Republic, Lebanon, Liberia, Libya, Madagascar, Malawi, Malaysia, Maldives, Mali, Malta, Mauritania, Mauritius, Mexico, Mongolia, Morocco, Mozambique, Nepal, Nicaragua, Nigeria, Oman, Pakistan, Panama, Papua New Guinea, Paraguay, Peru, Philippines, Poland, Qatar, Romania, Rwanda, Samoa, Sao Tome and Principe, Saudi Arabia, Senegal, Seychelles, Sierra Leone, Somalia, Sri Lanka, Sudan, Suriname, Syria, Thailand, Togo, Trinidad and Tobago, Tunisia, Turkey, Uganda, Ukraine, USSR, United Arab Emirates, United Republic of Cameroon, United Republic of Tanzania, Upper Volta, Uruguay, Vanuatu, Venezuela, Viet Nam, Yemen, Yugoslavia, Zaire, Zambia, Zimbabwe.
Against: 13
Belgium, Denmark, France, Germany, Iceland, Ireland, Israel, Italy, Japan, Luxembourg, Netherlands, United Kingdom, United States.
Abstentions: 10
Australia, Austria, Canada, Finland, Guatemala, New Zealand, Norway, Portugal, Spain, Sweden.
Absent: 12
Albania, Antigua and Barbuda, Dominica, Equatorial Guinea, Haiti, Lesotho, Niger, Saint Lucia, Saint Vincent, Singapore, Solomon Islands, Swaziland.

G

POPULATION AND REFUGEES DISPLACED SINCE 1967

The General Assembly,
Recalling Security Council resolution 237 (1967) of 14 June 1967,
Recalling also General Assembly resolutions 2252 (ES-V) of 4 July 1967, 2452 A (XXIII) of 19 December 1968, 2535 B (XXIV) of 10 December 1969, 2672 D (XXV) of 8 December 1970, 2792 E (XXVI) of 6 December 1971, 2963 C and D (XXVII) of 13 December 1972, 3089 C (XXVIII) of 7 December 1973, 3331 D (XXIX) of 17 December 1974, 3419 C (XXX) of 8 December 1975, 31/15 D of 23 November 1976, 32/90 E of 13 December 1977, 33/112 F of 18 December 1978, 34/52 E of 23 November 1979, ES-7/2 of 29 July 1980, 35/13 E of 3 November 1980 and 36/146B of 16 December 1981,[93]

Having considered the report of the Commissioner-General of the United Nations Relief and Works Agency for Palestine Refugees in the Near East, covering the period from 1 July 1981 to 30 June 1982,[94] and the report of the Secretary-General of 20 September 1982,[95]

1. *Reaffirms* the inalienable right of all displaced inhabitants to return to their homes or former places of residence in the territories occupied by Israel since 1967 and declares once more that any attempt to restrict, or to attach conditions to, the free exercise of the right of return by any displaced person is inconsistent with that inalienable right and inadmissible;

2. *Considers* any and all agreements embodying any restriction on or condition for the return of the displaced inhabitants as null and void;

3. *Strongly deplores* the continued refusal of the Israeli authorities to take steps for the return of the displaced inhabitants;

4. *Calls once more upon* Israel:

(a) To take immediate steps for the return of all displaced inhabitants;

(b) To desist from all measures that obstruct the return of the displaced inhabitants, including measures affecting the physical and demographic structure of the occupied territories;

5. *Requests* the Secretary-General, after consulting with the Commissioner-General of the United Nations Relief and Works Agency for Palestine Refugees in the Near East, to report to the General Assembly before the opening of its thirty-eighth session on Israel's compliance with paragraph 4 above.

Adopted at the 108th plenary meeting:
In favour: 126
Afghanistan, Albania, Algeria, Angola, Argentina, Bahamas, Bahrain, Bangladesh, Barbados, Belize, Benin, Bhutan, Bolivia, Botswana, Brazil, Bulgaria, Burma, Burundi, Byelorussia, Cape Verde, Central African Republic, Chad, Chile, China, Colombia, Comoros, Congo, Costa Rica, Cuba, Cyprus, Czechoslovakia, Democratic Kampuchea, Democratic Yemen, Djibouti, Dominican Republic, Ecuador, Egypt, El Salvador, Ethiopia, Fiji, Gabon, Gambia, German Democratic Republic, Ghana, Greece, Grenada, Guinea, Guinea-Bissau, Guyana, Honduras, Hungary, India, Indonesia, Iran, Iraq, Ivory Coast, Jamaica, Japan, Jordan, Kenya, Kuwait, Lao People's Democratic Republic, Lebanon, Lesotho, Liberia, Libya, Madagascar, Malaysia, Maldives, Mali, Malta, Mauritania, Mauritius, Mexico, Mongolia, Morocco, Mozambique, Nepal, Nicaragua, Nigeria, Oman, Pakistan, Panama, Papua New Guinea, Paraguay, Peru, Philippines, Poland, Portugal, Qatar, Romania, Rwanda, Samoa, Sao Tome

---

[93]Concerning persons displaced since 1967. [ed. note]
[94]*Official Records of the General Assembly, Thirty-seventh Session, Supplement No. 13* (A/37/13).
[95]A/37/426.

and Principe, Saudi Arabia, Senegal, Seychelles, Sierra Leone, Singapore, Somalia, Spain, Sri Lanka, Sudan, Suriname, Syria, Thailand, Togo, Trinidad and Tobago, Tunisia, Turkey, Uganda, Ukraine, USSR, United Arab Emirates, United Republic of Cameroon, United Republic of Tanzania, Upper Volta, Uruguay, Vanuatu, Venezuela, Viet Nam, Yemen, Yugoslavia, Zaire, Zambia, Zimbabwe.

Against: 2

Israel, United States.

Abstentions: 19

Australia, Austria, Belgium, Canada, Denmark, Finland, France, Germany, Guatemala, Iceland, Ireland, Italy, Luxembourg, Malawi, Netherlands, New Zealand, Norway, Sweden, United Kingdom.

Absent: 9

Antigua and Barbuda, Dominica, Equatorial Guinea, Haiti, Niger, Saint Lucia, Saint Vincent, Solomon Islands, Swaziland.

H

REVENUES DERIVED FROM PALESTINE REFUGEE PROPERTIES

The General Assembly,

Recalling its resolutions 35/13 A to F of 3 November 1980, 36/146 C of 16 December 1981 and all its previous resolutions on the question, including resolution 194 (III) of 11 December 1948,

Taking note of the report of the Secretary-General of 28 September 1982,[96]

Taking note also of the report of the United Nations Conciliation Commission for Palestine, covering the period from 1 October 1981 to 30 September 1982,[97]

Recalling that the Universal Declaration of Human Rights[98] and the prnciples of international law uphold the principle that no one shall be arbitrarily deprived of one's private property,

Considering that the Palestinian Arab refugees are entitled to their property and to the income derived from their property, in conformity with the principles of justice and equity,

Recalling, in particular, its resolution 394 (V) of 14 December 1950, in which it directed the United Nations Conciliation Commission for Palestine, in consultation with the parties concerned, to prescribe measures for the protection of the rights, property and interests of the Palestinian Arab refugees,

Taking note of the completion of the programme of identification and evaluation of Arab property, as announced by the United Nations Conciliation Commission for Palestine in its twenty-second progress report,[99] of 11 May 1964, and of the fact that the Land Office had a schedule of Arab owners and file of documents defining the location, area and other particulars of Arab property,

1. *Requests* the Secretary-General to take all appropriate steps, in consultation with the United Nations Conciliation Commission for Palestine, for the protection and administration of Arab property, assets and property rights in Israel, and to establish a fund for the receipt of income derived therefrom, on behalf of their rightful owners;

2. *Calls once again upon* the Governments concerned, especially Israel, to render all facilities and assistance to the Secretary-General in the implementation of the present resolution;

3. *Requests* the Secretary-General to report to the General Assembly at its thirty-eighth session on the implementation of the present resolution.

Adopted at the 108th plenary meeting:
In favour: 121

Afghanistan, Albania, Algeria, Angola, Argentina, Bahrain, Bangladesh, Barbados, Belize, Benin, Bhutan, Bolivia, Botswana, Brazil, Bulgaria, Burma, Burundi, Byelorussia, Cape Verde, Central African Republic, Chad, Chile, China, Colombia, Comoros, Congo, Costa Rica, Cuba, Cyprus, Czechoslovakia, Democratic Kampuchea, Democratic Yemen, Djibouti, Dominican Republic, Ecuador, Egypt, El Salvador, Ethiopia, Gabon, Gambia, German Democratic Republic, Ghana, Greece, Grenada, Guinea, Guinea-Bissau, Guyana, Honduras, Hungary, India, Indonesia, Iran, Iraq, Ivory Coast, Jamaica, Jordan, Kenya, Kuwait, Lao People's Democratic Republic, Lebanon, Lesotho, Liberia, Libya, Madagascar, Malawi, Malaysia, Maldives, Mali, Malta, Mauritania, Mauritius, Mexico, Mongolia, Morocco, Mozambique, Nepal, Nicaragua, Nigeria, Oman, Pakistan, Panama, Paraguay, Peru, Philippines, Poland, Portugal, Qatar, Romania, Rwanda, Sao Tome and Principe, Saudi Arabia, Senegal, Seychelles, Sierra Leone, Singapore, Somalia, Spain, Sri Lanka, Sudan, Suriname, Syria, Thailand, Togo, Trinidad and Tobago, Tunisia, Turkey, Uganda, Ukraine, United Arab Emirates, USSR, United Republic of Cameroon, United Republic of Tanzania, Upper Volta, Uruguay, Vanuatu, Venezuela, Viet Nam, Yemen, Yugoslavia, Zambia, Zimbabwe.

Against: 2

Israel, United States.

Abstentions: 24

Australia, Austria, Bahamas, Belgium, Canada, Denmark, Fiji, Finland, France, Germany, Guatemala, Iceland, Ireland, Italy, Japan, Luxembourg, Netherlands, New Zealand, Norway, Papua New Guinea, Samoa,* Sweden, United Kingdom, Zaire.

Absent: 9

Antigua and Barbuda, Dominica, Equatorial Guinea, Haiti, Niger, Saint Lucia, Saint Vincent, Solomon Islands, Swaziland.

---

[96]A/37/488 and Corr.1.

[97]A/37/497, annex.

[98]Resolution 217 A (III).

[99]*Official Records of the General Assembly, Nineteenth Session, Annex No. 11,* document A/5700.

---

* Later advised the Secretariat it had intended to vote in favour.

I

SPECIAL IDENTIFICATION CARDS TO ALL PALESTINE REFUGEES

The General Assembly,

Recalling its resolution 36/146 F of 16 December 1981 and all previous resolutions on the question,

Recalling, in particular, its resolutions 194 (III) of 11 December 1948 and 302 (IV) of 8 December 1949,

Recognizing the concern of the United Nations with the problem of the Palestine refugees,

1. *Reiterates its regret* that paragraph 11 of General Assembly resolution 194 (III) has not thus far been implemented;

2. *Requests* the Secretary-General, in co-operation with the Commissioner-General of the United Nations Relief and Works Agency for Palestine Refugees in the Near East, to issue identification cards to all Palestine refugees and their descendants, irrespective of whether they are recipients or not of rations and services from the Agency, as well as to all displaced persons and to those who have been prevented from returning to their homes as a result of the 1967 hostilities, and their descendants;

3. *Requests* the Secretary-General to report to the General Assembly at its thirty-eighth session on the implementation of the present resolution.

Adopted at the 108th plenary meeting:

In favour: 106

Afghanistan, Albania, Algeria, Angola, Argentina, Bahrain, Bangladesh, Benin, Bhutan, Bolivia, Botswana, Brazil, Bulgaria, Burundi, Byelorussia, Cape Verde, Central African Republic, Chad, China, Colombia, Comoros, Congo, Cuba, Cyprus, Czechoslovakia, Democratic Kampuchea, Democratic Yemen, Djibouti, Dominican Republic, Ecuador, Egypt, El Salvador, Ethiopia, Gabon, Gambia, German Democratic Republic, Ghana, Greece, Grenada, Guinea, Guinea-Bissau, Guyana, Honduras, Hungary, India, Indonesia, Iran, Iraq, Ivory Coast, Jordan, Kenya, Kuwait, Lao People's Democratic Republic, Lesotho, Liberia, Libya, Madagascar, Malaysia, Maldives, Mali, Malta, Mauritania, Mauritius, Mexico, Mongolia, Morocco, Mozambique, Nepal, Nicaragua, Nigeria, Oman, Pakistan, Panama, Peru, Poland, Qatar, Romania, Rwanda, Sao Tome and Principe, Saudi Arabia, Senegal, Seychelles, Sierra Leone, Somalia, Sri Lanka, Sudan, Suriname, Syria, Thailand, Togo, Trinidad and Tobago, Tunisia, Turkey, Uganda, Ukraine, USSR, United Arab Emirates, United Republic of Cameroon, United Republic of Tanzania, Upper Volta, Vanuatu, Venezuela, Viet Nam, Yemen, Yugoslavia, Zambia.

Against: 16

Australia, Belgium, Canada, Denmark, France, Germany, Iceland, Israel, Italy, Japan, Lebanon, Luxembourg, Netherlands, Norway, United Kingdom, United States.

Abstentions: 20

Austria, Bahamas, Barbados, Chile, Costa Rica, Fiji, Finland, Guatemala, Ireland, Jamaica, Malawi, New Zealand, Papua New Guinea, Paraguay, Philippines, Portugal,
Spain, Sweden, Uruguay, Zaire.

Absent: 14

Antigua and Barbuda, Belize, Burma, Dominica, Equatorial Guinea, Haiti, Niger, Saint Lucia, Saint Vincent, Somoa, Singapore, Solomon Islands, Swaziland, Zimbabwe.

J

PROTECTION OF PALESTINE REFUGEES

The General Assembly,

Recalling Security Council resolutions 508 (1982) of 5 June 1982, 509 (1982) of 6 June 1982, 511 (1982) of 18 June 1982, 512 (1982) of 19 June 1982, 513 (1982) of 4 July 1982, 515 (1982) of 29 July 1982, 517 (1982) of 4 August 1982, 518 (1982) of 12 August 1982, 519 (1982) of 17 August 1982, 520 (1982) of 17 September 1982 and 523 (1982) of 18 October 1982,[100]

Recalling General Assembly resolutions ES-7/5 of 26 June 1982, ES-7/6 of 24 August 1982, ES-7/8 of 19 August 1982 and ES-7/9 of 24 September 1982,

Having considered the report of the Commissioner-General of the United Nations Relief and Works Agency for Palestine Refugees in the Near East, covering the period from 1 July 1981 to 30 June 1982,[101] and his special report covering the period from 6 June to 31 August 1982,[102]

Referring to the humanitarian principles of the Geneva Convention relative to the Protection of Civilian Persons in Time of War, of 12 August 1949,[103] and to the obligations arising from the regulations annexed to the Hague Convention of 1907,

Deeply distressed at the sufferings of the Palestinians resulting from the Israeli invasion of Lebanon,

1. *Urges* the Secretary-General, in consultation with the United Nations Relief and Works Agency for Palestine Refugees in the Near East, and pending the withdrawal of Israeli forces from the Palestinian and other Arab territories occupied by Israel since 1967, including Jerusalem, to undertake effective measures to guarantee the safety and security and the legal and human rights of the Palestine refugees in the occupied territories;

2. *Calls upon* Israel, the occupying Power, to release forthwith all detained Palestine refugees, including the employees of the United Nations Relief and Works Agency for Palestine Refugees in the Near East;

3. *Also calls upon* Israel to desist forthwith from preventing those Palestinians registered by the United Nations Relief and Works Agency for Palestine Refugees in the Near East as refugees in Lebanon from returning to their camps in Lebanon;

4. *Further calls upon* Israel to allow the resumption of health, medical, educational and social services rendered

---

[100]The resolutions in this and the next paragraph focus on Israel's 1982 invasion of Lebanon. [ed. note]

[101]*Official Records of the General Assembly, Thirty-seventh Session, Supplement No. 13* (A/37/13).

[102]A/37/479.

[103]United Nations, *Treaty Series*, vol. 75, no. 973, p. 287.

by the United Nations Relief and Works Agency for Palestine Refugees in the Near East to the Palestinians in the refugee camps in southern Lebanon;

5. *Requests* the Commissioner-General of the United Nations Relief and Works Agency for Palestine Refugees in the Near East to co-ordinate his activities in rendering those services with the Government of Lebanon, the host country;

6. *Urges* the Commissioner-General to provide housing, in consultation with the Government of Lebanon, to the Palestine refugees whose houses were demolished or razed by the Israeli forces, in order to protect them from the severity of the weather;

7. *Requests* the Commissioner-General, in consultation with the Government of Lebanon, to prepare a report on the totality of the damage caused to the Palestine refugees and their property and to the Agency's facilities, as well as those of other international bodies, as a result of the Israeli aggression;

8. *Requests* the Secretary-General, in consultation with the Commissioner-General, to report to the General Assembly before the opening of its thirty-eighth session on the implementation of the present resolution.

Adopted at the 108th plenary meeting:
In favour: 127
Afghanistan, Albania, Algeria, Angola, Argentina, Austria, Bahamas, Bahrain, Bangladesh, Barbados, Belize, Benin, Bhutan, Bolivia, Botswana, Brazil, Bulgaria, Burma, Burundi, Byelorussia, Cape Verde, Central African Republic, Chad, Chile, China, Colombia, Comoros, Congo, Cuba, Cyprus, Czechoslovakia, Democratic Kampuchea, Democratic Yemen, Djibouti, Dominican Republic, Ecuador, Egypt, El Salvador, Ethiopia, Fiji, Finland, France, Gabon, Gambia, German Democratic Republic, Ghana, Greece, Grenada, Guinea, Guinea-Bissau, Guyana, Honduras, Hungary, India, Indonesia, Iran, Iraq, Ivory Coast, Jamaica, Japan, Jordan, Kenya, Kuwait, Lao People's Democratic Republic, Lebanon, Lesotho, Liberia, Libya, Madagascar, Malawi, Malaysia, Maldives, Mali, Malta, Mauritania, Mauritius, Mexico, Mongolia, Morocco, Mozambique, Nepal, New Zealand, Nicaragua, Nigeria, Oman, Pakistan, Panama, Papua New Guinea, Peru, Philippines, Poland, Qatar, Romania, Rwanda, Samoa, Sao Tome and Principe, Saudi Arabia, Senegal, Seychelles, Sierra Leone, Somalia, Spain, Sri Lanka, Sudan, Suriname, Sweden, Syria, Thailand, Togo, Trinidad and Tobago, Tunisia, Turkey, Uganda, Ukraine, USSR, United Arab Emirates, United Republic of Cameroon, United Republic of Tanzania, Upper Volta, Uruguay, Vanuatu, Venezuela, Viet Nam, Yemen, Yugoslavia, Zaire, Zambia.
Against: 2
Israel, United States.
Abstentions: 16
Australia, Belgium, Canada, Costa Rica, Denmark, Germany, Guatemala, Iceland, Ireland, Italy, Luxembourg, Netherlands, Norway, Paraguay, Portugal, United Kingdom.
Absent: 11

Antigua and Barbuda, Dominica, Equatorial Guinea, Haiti, Niger, Saint Lucia, Saint Vincent, Singapore, Solomon Islands, Swaziland, Zimbabwe.

K

The General Assembly,

Recalling its resolution 36/146 F of 16 December 1981 and all previous resolutions on the question, including resolution 194 (III) of 11 December 1948,

Taking note of the report of the Commissioner-General of the United Nations Relief and Works Agency for Palestine Refugees in the Near East, covering the period from 1 July 1981 to 30 June 1982,[104]

1. *Notes with regret* that repatriation or compensation of the refugees as provided for in paragraph 11 of General Assembly resolution 194 (III) has not been effected, that no substantial progress has been made in the programme endorsed by the Assembly in paragraph 2 of its resolution 513 (VI) of 26 January 1952 for the reintegration of refugees either by repatriation or resettlement and that, therefore, the situation of the refugees continues to be a matter of serious concern;

2. *Expresses its thanks* to the Commissioner-General and to all the staff of the United Nations Relief and Works Agency for Palestine Refugees in the Near East, recognizing that the Agency is doing all it can within the limits of available resources, and also expresses its thanks to the specialized agencies and private organizations for their valuable work in assisting the refugees;

3. *Reiterates its request* that the headquarters of the United Nations Relief and Works Agency for Palestine Refugees in the Near East should be relocated to its former site within its area of operations as soon as practicable;

4. *Notes with regret* that the United Nations Conciliation Commission for Palestine has been unable to find a means of achieving progress in the implementation of paragraph 11 of General Assembly resolution 194 (III) and requests the Commission to exert continued efforts towards the implementation of that paragraph and to report to the Assembly as appropriate, but not later than 1 October 1983;

5. *Directs attention* to the continuing seriousness of the financial position of the United Nations Relief and Works Agency for Palestine Refugees in the Near East, as outlined in the report of the Commissioner-General;

6. *Notes with concern* that, despite the commendable and successful efforts of the Commissioner-General to collect additional contributions, this increased level of income to the United Nations Relief and Works Agency for Palestine Refugees in the Near East is still insufficient to cover essential budget requirements in the present year and that, at currently foreseen levels of giving, deficits will recur each year;

7. *Calls upon* all Governments as a matter of urgency to

---

[104]*Official Records of the General Assembly, Thirty-seventh Session, Supplement No. 13* (A/37/13).

make the most generous efforts possible to meet the anticipated needs of the United Nations Relief and Works Agency for Palestine Refugees in the Near East, particularly in the light of the budgetary deficit projected in the report of the Commissioner-General, and therefore urges non-contributing Governments to contribute regularly and contributing Governments to consider increasing their regular contributions.

Adopted at the 108th plenary meeting:
In favour: 144

Afghanistan, Algeria, Angola, Argentina, Australia, Austria, Bahamas, Bahrain, Bangladesh, Barbados, Belgium, Belize, Benin, Bhutan, Bolivia, Botswana, Brazil, Bulgaria, Burma, Burundi, Byelorussia, Canada, Cape Verde, Central African Republic, Chad, Chile, China, Colombia, Comoros, Congo, Costa Rica, Cuba, Cyprus, Czechoslovakia, Democratic Kampuchea, Democratic Yemen, Denmark, Djibouti, Dominican Republic, Ecuador, Egypt, El Salvador, Ethiopia, Fiji, Finland, France, Gabon, Gambia, German Democratic Republic, Germany, Ghana, Greece, Grenada, Guatemala, Guinea, Guinea-Bissau, Guyana, Honduras, Hungary, Iceland, India, Indonesia, Iran, Iraq, Ireland, Italy, Ivory Coast, Jamaica, Japan, Jordan, Kenya, Kuwait, Lao People's Democratic Republic, Lebanon, Lesotho, Liberia, Libya, Luxembourg, Madagascar, Malawi, Malaysia, Maldives, Mali, Malta, Mauritania, Mauritius, Mexico, Mongolia, Morocco, Mozambique, Nepal, Netherlands, New Zealand, Nicaragua, Nigeria, Norway, Oman, Pakistan, Panama, Papua New Guinea, Paraguay, Peru, Philippines, Poland, Portugal, Qatar, Romania, Rwanda, Samoa, Sao Tome and Principe, Saudi Arabia, Senegal, Seychelles, Sierra Leone, Singapore, Somalia, Spain, Sri Lanka, Sudan, Suriname, Sweden, Syria, Thailand, Togo, Trinidad and Tobago, Tunisia, Turkey, Uganda, Ukraine, USSR, United Arab Emirates, United Kingdom, United Republic of Cameroon, United Republic of Tanzania, United States, Upper Volta, Uruguay, Vanuatu, Venezuela, Viet Nam, Yemen, Yugoslavia, Zaire, Zambia.

Against: 0

Abstention: 1

Israel.

Absent: 11

Albania, Antigua and Barbuda, Dominica, Equatorial Guinea, Haiti, Niger, Saint Lucia, Saint Vincent, Solomon Islands, Swaziland, Zimbabwe.

Resolution No. 37/122 of 16 December 1982

DEMANDING THAT ISRAEL CEASE ALL ACTIONS AND/OR PLANS TO BUILD A CANAL LINKING THE MEDITERRANEAN SEA TO THE DEAD SEA

The General Assembly,

Recalling its resolution 36/150 of 16 December 1981,

Recalling the rules and principles of international law relative to the fundamental rights and duties of States,

Bearing in mind the principles of international law relative to belligerent occupation of land, including the Ge-

neva Convention relative to the Protection of Civilian Persons in Time of War, of 12 August 1949,[105] and reaffirming their applicability to all Arab territories occupied since 1967, including Jerusalem,

Taking note of the report of the Secretary-General,[106]

Recognizing that the proposed canal, to be constructed partly through the Gaza Strip, a Palestinian territory occupied in 1967, would violate the principles of international law and affect the interests of the Palestinian people,

Confident that the canal linking the Mediterranean Sea with the Dead Sea, if constructed by Israel, will cause direct, serious and irreparable damage to Jordan's rights and legitimate vital interests in the economic, agricultural, demographic and ecological fields,

Noting with regret the non-compliance by Israel with General Assembly resolution 36/150,[107]

1. *Deplores* Israel's non-compliance with General Assembly resolution 36/150;

2. *Emphasizes* that the canal linking the Mediterranean Sea with the Dead Sea, if constructed, is a violation of the rules and principles of international law, especially those relating to the fundamental rights and duties of States and to belligerent occupation of land;

3. *Demands* that Israel not construct this canal and cease forthwith all actions and/or plans taken towards the implementation of this project;

4. *Calls upon* all States, specialized agencies, governmental and non-governmental organizations not to assist, directly or indirectly, in preparations for and execution of this project and strongly urges national, international and multinational corporations to do likewise;

5. *Requests* the Secretary-General to monitor and assess, on a continuing basis and through a competent expert organ, all aspects—juridical, political, economic, ecological and demographic—of the adverse effects on Jordan and on the Arab territories occupied since 1967, including Jerusalem, arising from the implementation of the Israeli decision to construct this canal and to forward the findings of that organ on a regular basis to the General Assembly;

6. *Requests* the Secretary-General to report to the General Assembly at its thirty-eighth session on the implementation of the present resolution;

7. *Decides* to include in the provisional agenda of its thirty-eighth session the item entitled "Israel's decision to build a canal linking the Mediterranean Sea to the Dead Sea."

Adopted at the 108th plenary meeting:
In favour: 139

Afghanistan, Albania, Algeria, Angola, Argentina, Australia, Austria, Bahamas, Bahrain, Bangladesh, Barbados,

---

[105]United Nations, *Treaty Series*, vol. 75, no. 973, p. 287.

[106]A/37/328-S/15277 and Corr.1. For the printed text, see *Official Records of the Security Council, Thirty-seventh Year, Supplement for April, May and June 1982*, document S/15277.

[107]On Israel's proposed canal between the Mediterranean and the Dead Seas. [ed. note]

44

Belgium, Belize, Benin, Bhutan, Bolivia, Botswana, Brazil, Bulgaria, Burma, Burundi, Byelorussia, Canada, Cape Verde, Central African Republic, Chad, Chile, China, Colombia, Comoros, Congo, Costa Rica, Cuba, Cyprus, Czechoslovakia, Democratic Kampuchea, Democratic Yemen, Denmark, Djibouti, Dominican Republic, Ecuador, Egypt, El Salvador, Ethiopia, Fiji, Finland, France, Gambia, German Democratic Republic, Germany, Ghana, Greece, Grenada, Guinea, Guinea-Bissau, Guyana, Hungary, Iceland, India, Indonesia, Iran, Iraq, Ireland, Italy, Ivory Coast, Jamaica, Japan, Jordan, Kenya, Kuwait, Lao People's Democratic Republic, Lebanon, Liberia, Libya, Luxembourg, Madagascar, Malaysia, Maldives, Mali, Malta, Mauritania, Mauritius, Mexico, Mongolia, Morocco, Mozambique, Nepal, Netherlands, New Zealand, Nicaragua, Nigeria, Norway, Oman, Pakistan, Panama, Papua New Guinea, Paraguay, Peru, Philippines, Poland, Portugal, Qatar, Romania, Rwanda, Samoa, Sao Tome and Principe, Saudi Arabia, Senegal, Seychelles, Sierra Leone, Singapore, Somalia, Spain, Sri Lanka, Sudan, Suriname, Sweden, Syria, Thailand, Togo, Trinidad and Tobago, Tunisia, Turkey, Uganda, Ukraine, USSR, United Arab Emirates, United Kingdom, United Republic of Cameroon, United Republic of Tanzania, Upper Volta, Uruguay, Vanuatu, Venezuela, Viet Nam, Yemen, Yugoslavia, Zaire, Zambia.

Against: 2

Israel, United States.

Abstention: 1

Malawi.

Absent: 14

Antigua and Barbuda, Dominica, Equatorial Guinea, Gabon, Guatemala, Haiti, Honduras, Lesotho, Niger, Saint Lucia, Saint Vincent, Solomon Islands, Swaziland, Zimbabwe.

Resolution No. 37/123 A, B, C, D, E, F of 16 December 1982

ON THE SITUATION IN THE MIDDLE EAST: CONDEMNING ISRAEL'S POLICIES IN THE OCCUPIED ARAB TERRITORIES AND CALLING FOR ITS COMPLETE WITHDRAWAL FROM THEM, CONDEMNING THE MASSACRES OF SABRA AND SHATILA IN LEBANON AND CALLING FOR THE RESTORATION OF THE AUTHORITY OF THE LEBANESE STATE IN LEBANESE TERRITORY, CONDEMNING ISRAELI PRACTICES IN LEBANON, CALLING FOR RECOGNITION OF THE RIGHT OF THE PALESTINIAN PEOPLE, UNDER THE LEADERSHIP OF THE PLO, TO SELF-DETERMINATION AND AN INDEPENDENT STATE, AND CALLING UPON ALL STATES TO PUT AN END TO THE FLOW OF AID TO ISRAEL

A

The General Assembly,

Having discussed the item entitled "The situation in the Middle East",

Taking note of the reports of the Secretary-General,[108]

Recalling Security Council resolution 497 (1981) of 17 December 1981,

Reaffirming its resolutions 36/226 B of 17 December 1981 and ES-9/1 of 5 February 1982,

Recalling its resolution 3314(XXIX) of 14 December 1974, in which it defined an act of aggression, *inter alia*, as "the invasion or attack by the armed forces of a State of the territory of another State, or any military occupation, however temporary, resulting from such invasion or attack, or any annexation by the use of force of the territory of another State or part thereof" and provided that "no consideration of whatever nature, whether political, economic, military or otherwise, may serve as a justification for aggression",

Reaffirming the fundamental principle of the inadmissibility of the acquisition of territory by force,

Reaffirming once more the applicability of the Geneva Convention relative to the Protection of Civilian Persons in Time of War, of 12 August 1949,[109] to the occupied Palestinian and other Arab territories, including Jerusalem,

Noting that Israel's record and actions establish conclusively that it is not a peace-loving Member State and that it has not carried out its obligations under the Charter of the United Nations,

Noting further that Israel has refused, in violation of Article 25 of the Charter, to accept and carry out the numerous relevant decisions of the Security Council, the latest of which was resolution 497 (1981), thus failing to carry out its obligations under the Charter,

1. *Strongly condemns* Israel for its failure to comply with Security Council resolution 497 (1981) and General Assembly resolutions 36/226B and ES-9/1;

2. *Declares once more* that Israel's decision of 14 December 1981 to impose its laws, jurisdiction and administration on the occupied Syrian Golan Heights constitutes an act of aggression under the provisions of Article 39 of the Charter of the United Nations and General Assembly resolution 3314 (XXIX);

3. *Declares once more* that Israel's decision to impose its laws, jurisdiction and administration on the occupied Syrian Golan Heights is null and void and has no legal validity and/or effect whatsoever;

4. *Declares* all Israeli policies and practices of, or aimed at, annexation of the occupied Palestinian and other Arab territories, including Jerusalem, to be in violation of international law and of the relevant United Nations resolutions;

5. *Determines once more* that all actions taken by Israel to give effect to its decision relating to the occupied Syrian Golan Heights are illegal and invalid and shall not be

---

[108]A/37/169 and Add.1-3-S/14953 and Add.1-3. For the printed text, see *Official Records of the Security Council, Thirty-seventh Year, Supplement for April, May and June 1982*, documents 5/14953 and Add.1; and *ibid., Supplement for October, November and December 1982*, documents S/14953/Add.2 and 3.

[109]United Nations, *Treaty Series*, vol. 75, no. 973, p. 287.

recognized;

6. *Reaffirms its determination* that all the provisions of the Hague Convention of 1907[110] and the Geneva Convention relative to the Protection of Civilian Persons in Time of War, of 12 August 1949, continue to apply to the Syrian territory occupied by Israel since 1967, and calls upon the parties thereto to respect and ensure respect of their obligations under these instruments in all circumstances;

7. *Determines once more* that the continued occupation of the Syrian Golan Heights since 1967 and their effective annexation by Israel on 14 December 1981, following Israel's decision to impose its laws, jurisdiction and administration on that territory, constitute a continuing threat to international peace and security;

8. *Strongly deplores* the negative vote by a permanent member of the Security Council which prevented the Council from adopting against Israel, under Chapter VII of the Charter, the "appropriate measures" referred to in resolution 497 (1981) unanimously adopted by the Council;

9. *Further deplores* any political, economic, financial, military and technological support to Israel that encourages Israel to commit acts of aggression and to consolidate and perpetuate its occupation and annexation of occupied Arab territories;

10. *Firmly emphasizes once more* its demands that Israel, the occupying Power, rescind forthwith its decision of 14 December 1981 to impose its laws, jurisdiction and administration on the Syrian Golan Heights, which has resulted in the effective annexation of that territory;

11. *Reaffirms once more* the overriding necessity of the total and unconditional withdrawal by Israel from all the Palestinian and other Arab territories occupied since 1967, including Jerusalem, which is an essential prerequisite for the establishment of a comprehensive and just peace in the Middle East;

12. *Determines once more* that Israel's record and actions confirm that it is not a peace-loving Member State, that it has persistently violated the principles contained in the Charter and that it has carried out neither its obligations under the Charter nor its commitment under General Assembly resolution 273 (III) of 11 May 1949;

13. *Calls once more upon* all Member States to apply the following measures:

(*a*) To refrain from supplying Israel with any weapons and related equipment and to suspend any military assistance that Israel receives from them;

(*b*) To refrain from acquiring any weapons or military equipment from Israel;

(*c*) To suspend economic, financial and technological assistance to and co-operation with Israel;

(*d*)To sever diplomatic, trade and cultural relations with Israel;

14. *Reiterates its call* to all Member States to cease forthwith, individually and collectively, all dealings with Israel in order totally to isolate it in all fields;

15. *Urges* non-member States to act in accordance with the provisions of the present resolution;

16. *Calls upon* the specialized agencies and other international organizations to conform their relations with Israel to the terms of the present resolution.

Adopted at the 108th plenary meeting:

In favour: 87

Afghanistan, Albania, Algeria, Angola, Bahrain, Bangladesh, Benin, Bhutan, Botswana, Bulgaria, Burundi, Byelorussia, Cape Verde, Chad, China, Comoros, Congo, Cuba, Cyprus, Czechoslovakia, Democratic Kampuchea, Democratic Yemen, Djibouti, Ethiopia, Gambia, German Democratic Republic, Ghana, Greece, Grenada, Guinea, Guinea-Bissau, Guyana, Hungary, India, Indonesia, Iran, Iraq, Jordan, Kenya, Kuwait, Lao People's Democratic Republic, Lebanon, Lesotho, Liberia, Libya, Madagascar, Malaysia, Maldives, Mali, Malta, Mauritania, Mauritius, Mexico, Mongolia, Morocco, Mozambique, Nepal, Nicaragua, Nigeria, Oman, Pakistan, Poland, Qatar, Rwanda, Sao Tome and Principe, Saudi Arabia, Senegal, Seychelles, Sierra Leone, Somalia, Sri Lanka, Sudan, Suriname, Syria, Togo, Tunisia, Turkey, Uganda, Ukraine, USSR, United Arab Emirates, United Republic of Cameroon, United Republic of Tanzania, Viet Nam, Yemen, Yugoslavia, Zambia.

Against: 22

Australia, Belgium, Canada, Costa Rica, Denmark, Finland, France, Germany, Guatemala, Iceland, Ireland, Israel, Italy, Japan, Luxembourg, Netherlands, New Zealand, Norway, Portugal, Sweden, United Kingdom, United States.

Abstentions: 31

Argentina, Austria, Bahamas, Barbados, Brazil, Burma, Central African Republic, Chile, Colombia, Dominican Republic, Ecuador, El Salvador, Fiji, Gabon, Ivory Coast, Jamaica, Malawi, Panama, Papua New Guinea, Paraguay, Peru, Philippines, Samoa, Singapore, Spain, Thailand, Trinidad and Tobago, Upper Volta, Uruguay, Venezuela, Zaire.

Absent: 16

Antigua and Barbuda, Belize, Bolivia, Dominica, Egypt, Equatorial Guinea, Haiti, Honduras, Niger, Romania, Saint Lucia, Saint Vincent, Solomon Islands, Swaziland, Vanuatu, Zimbabwe.

B

The General Assembly,

Recalling the relevant provisions of the Universal Declaration of Human Rights,[111]

Recalling also the Constitution of the United Nations Educational, Scientific and Cultural Organization[112] and

---

[110]Carnegie Endowment for International Peace, *The Hague Conventions and Declarations of 1899 and 1907* (New York, Oxford University Press, 1915), p. 100.

[111]Resolution 217 A (III).

[112]See *Manual of the General Conference,* 1981 edition (Paris, UNESCO, 1981).

all other relevant international instruments concerning the right to cultural identity in all its forms,

Having learned that the Israeli army, during its occupation of Beirut, seized and took away the archives and documents of every kind concerning Palestinian history and culture, including cultural articles belonging to Palestinian institutions—in particular the Palestine Research Centre—archives, documents, manuscripts and materials such as film documents, literary works by major authors, paintings, *objets d'art* and works of folklore, research works and so forth, serving as a foundation for the history, culture, national awareness, unity and solidarity of the Palestinian people,

1. *Condemns* those acts of plundering the Palestinian cultural heritage;

2. *Calls upon* the Government of Israel to make full restitution, through the United Nations Educational, Scientific and Cultural Organization, of all the cultural property belonging to Palestinian institutions, including the archives and documents removed from the Palestine Research Centre and arbitrarily seized by the Israeli forces.

Adopted at the 108th plenary meeting:

In favour: 138

Afghanistan, Albania, Algeria, Angola, Argentina, Australia, Austria, Bahamas, Bahrain, Bangladesh, Barbados, Belgium, Belize, Benin, Bhutan, Bolivia, Botswana, Brazil, Bulgaria, Burma, Burundi, Byelorussia, Canada, Cape Verde, Central African Republic, Chad, Chile, China, Colombia, Comoros, Congo, Costa Rica, Cuba, Cyprus, Czechoslovakia, Democratic Kampuchea, Democratic Yemen, Denmark, Djibouti, Ecuador, Egypt, Ethiopia, Fiji, Finland, France, Gabon, Gambia, German Democratic Republic, Germany, Ghana, Greece, Grenada, Guinea, Guinea-Bissau, Guyana, Honduras, Hungary, Iceland, India, Indonesia, Iran, Iraq, Ireland, Italy, Ivory Coast, Jamaica, Japan, Jordan, Kenya, Kuwait, Lao People's Democratic Republic, Lebanon, Lesotho, Liberia, Libya, Luxembourg, Madagascar, Malaysia, Maldives, Mali, Malta, Mauritania, Mauritius, Mexico, Mongolia, Morocco, Mozambique, Nepal, Netherlands, New Zealand, Nicaragua, Nigeria, Norway, Oman, Pakistan, Panama, Paraguay, Peru, Philippines, Poland, Portugal, Qatar, Romania, Rwanda, Samoa, Sao Tome and Principe, Saudi Arabia, Senegal, Seychelles, Sierra Leone, Singapore, Somalia, Spain, Sri Lanka, Sudan, Suriname, Sweden, Syria, Thailand, Togo, Trinidad and Tobago, Tunisia, Turkey, Uganda, Ukraine, USSR, United Arab Emirates, United Kingdom, United Republic of Cameroon, United Republic of Tanzania, Upper Volta, Uruguay, Venezuela, Viet Nam, Yemen, Yugoslavia, Zaire, Zambia.

Against: 1

Israel.

Abstentions: 4

Dominican Republic, Malawi, Papua New Guinea, United States.

Absent: 13

Antigua and Barbuda, Dominica, El Salvador, Equatorial Guinea, Guatemala, Haiti, Niger, Saint Lucia, Saint Vincent, Solomon Islands, Swaziland, Vanuatu,* Zimbabwe.

---

* Later advised the Secretariat it had intended to vote in favour.

C

The General Assembly,

Recalling its resolution 36/120 E of 10 December 1981, in which it determined that all legislative and administrative measures and actions taken by Israel, the occupying Power, which had altered or purported to alter the character and status of the Holy City of Jerusalem, in particular the so-called "Basic Law" on Jerusalem and the proclamation of Jerusalem as the capital of Israel, were null and void and must be rescinded forthwith,

Recalling Security Council resolution 478 (1980) of 20 August 1980, in which the Council, *inter alia*, decided not to recognize the "Basic Law" and called upon those States that had established diplomatic missions at Jerusalem to withdraw such missions from the Holy City,

1. *Deplores* the transfer by some States of their diplomatic missions to Jerusalem in violation of Security Council resolution 478 (1980);

2. *Calls upon* those States to abide by the provisions of the relevant United Nations resolutions, in conformity with the Charter of the United Nations.

Adopted at the 108th plenary meeting:

In favour: 137

Afghanistan, Albania, Algeria, Angola, Argentina, Australia, Austria, Bahamas, Bahrain, Bangladesh, Barbados, Belgium, Benin, Bhutan, Bolivia, Botswana, Brazil, Bulgaria, Burma, Burundi, Byelorussia, Canada, Cape Verde, Central African Republic, Chad, Chile, China, Colombia, Comoros, Congo, Cuba, Cyprus, Czechoslovakia, Democratic Kampuchea, Democratic Yemen, Denmark, Djibouti, Ecuador, Egypt, El Salvador, Ethiopia, Finland, France, Gabon, Gambia, German Democratic Republic, Germany, Ghana, Greece, Grenada, Guinea, Guinea-Bissau, Guyana, Honduras, Hungary, Iceland, India, Indonesia, Iran, Iraq, Ireland, Italy, Ivory Coast, Jamaica, Japan, Jordan, Kenya, Kuwait, Lao People's Democratic Republic, Lebanon, Lesotho, Liberia, Libya, Luxembourg, Madagascar, Malaysia, Maldives, Mali, Malta, Mauritania, Mauritius, Mexico, Mongolia, Morocco, Mozambique, Nepal, Netherlands, New Zealand, Nicaragua, Nigeria, Norway, Oman, Pakistan, Panama, Paraguay, Peru, Philippines, Poland, Portugal, Qatar, Romania, Rwanda, Samoa, Sao Tome and Principe, Saudi Arabia, Senegal, Seychelles, Sierra Leone, Singapore, Somalia, Spain, Sri Lanka, Sudan, Suriname, Sweden, Syria, Thailand, Togo, Trinidad and Tobago, Tunisia, Turkey, Uganda, Ukraine, United Arab Emirates, USSR, United Kingdom, United Republic of Cameroon, United Republic of Tanzania, Upper Volta, Uruguay, Vanuatu, Venezuela, Viet Nam, Yemen, Yugoslavia, Zaire, Zambia.

Against: 1

Israel.

Abstentions: 4

Dominican Republic, Guatemala, Malawi, United States.
Absent: 14
Antigua and Barbuda, Belize, Costa Rica, Dominica, Equatorial Guinea, Fiji, Haiti, Niger, Papua New Guinea, Saint Lucia, Saint Vincent, Solomon Islands, Swaziland, Zimbabwe.

D

The General Assembly,

Recalling its resolution 95 (I) of 11 December 1946,

Recalling also its resolution 96 (I) of 11 December 1946, in which it, *inter alia,* affirmed that genocide is a crime under international law which the civilized world condemns, and for the commission of which principals and accomplices—whether private individuals, public officials or statesmen, and whether the crime is committed on religious, racial, political or any other grounds—are punishable,

Referring to the provisions of the Convention on the Prevention and Punishment of the Crime of Genocide, adopted by the General Assembly on 9 December 1948,[113]

Recalling the relevant provisions of the Geneva Convention relative to the Protection of Civilian Persons in Time of War, of 12 August 1949,[114]

Appalled at the large-scale massacre of Palestinian civilians in the Sabra and Shatila refugee camps situated at Beirut,

Recognizing the universal outrage and condemnation of that massacre,

Recalling its resolution ES-7/9 of 24 September 1982,

1. *Condemns* in the strongest terms the large-scale massacre of Palestinian civilians in the Sabra and Shatila refugee camps;

2. *Resolves* that the massacre was an act of genocide.

Adopted at the 108th plenary meeting:

In favour: 123
Afghanistan, Albania, Algeria, Angola, Argentina, Austria, Bahamas, Bahrain, Bangladesh, Belize, Benin, Bhutan, Bolivia, Botswana, Brazil, Bulgaria, Burma, Burundi, Byelorussia, Cape Verde, Central African Republic, Chad, Chile, China, Colombia, Comoros, Congo, Costa Rica, Cuba, Cyprus, Czechoslovakia, Democratic Kampuchea, Democratic Yemen, Djibouti, Ecuador, Egypt, El Salvador, Ethiopia, Fiji, Finland, Gabon, Gambia, German Democratic Republic, Ghana, Greece, Grenada, Guatemala, Guinea, Guinea-Bissau, Guyana, Honduras, Hungary, India, Indonesia, Iran, Iraq, Jamaica, Japan, Jordan, Kenya, Kuwait, Lao People's Democratic Republic, Lesotho, Liberia, Libya, Madagascar, Malawi, Malaysia, Maldives, Mali, Malta, Mauritania, Mauritius, Mexico, Mongolia, Morocco, Mozambique, Nepal, Nicaragua, Nigeria, Oman, Pakistan, Panama, Paraguay, Peru, Philippines, Poland, Qatar, Romania, Rwanda, Samoa, Sao Tome and Principe, Saudi Arabia, Senegal, Seychelles, Sierra Leone, Singapore, Somalia, Spain, Sri Lanka, Sudan, Suriname, Syria, Thailand, Togo, Trinidad and Tobago, Tunisia, Turkey, Uganda, Ukraine, USSR, United Arab Emirates, United Republic of Cameroon, United Republic of Tanzania, Upper Volta, Uruguay, Vanuatu, Venezuela, Viet Nam, Yemen, Yugoslavia, Zaire, Zambia.

Against: 0

Abstentions: 22
Australia, Barbados, Belgium, Canada, Denmark, Dominican Republic, France, Germany, Iceland, Ireland, Israel, Italy, Ivory Coast, Luxembourg, Netherlands, New Zealand, Norway, Papua New Guinea, Portugal, Sweden, United Kingdom, United States.

Absent: 11
Antigua and Barbuda, Dominica, Equatorial Guinea, Haiti, Lebanon, Niger, Saint Lucia, Saint Vincent, Solomon Islands, Swaziland, Zimbabwe.

E

The General Assembly,

Having heard the address by the President of the Lebanese Republic on 18 October 1982,[115]

Taking note of the decision of the Government of Lebanon calling for the withdrawal from Lebanon of all non-Lebanese troops and forces which are not authorized by the Government to deploy therein,

Bearing in mind Security Council resolutions 508 (1982) of 5 June 1982 and 509 (1982) of 6 June 1982,

1. *Calls* for strict respect of the territorial integrity, sovereignty, unity and political independence of Lebanon and supports the efforts of the Government of Lebanon, with regional and international endorsement, to restore the exclusive authority of the Lebanese State throughout its territory up to the internationally recognized boundaries;

2. *Requests* the Secretary-General to report to the General Assembly on the implementation of the present resolution.

Adopted at the 108th plenary meeting:

In favour: 145
Afghanistan, Algeria, Angola, Argentina, Australia, Austria, Bahamas, Bahrain, Bangladesh, Barbados, Belgium, Belize, Benin, Bhutan, Bolivia, Botswana, Brazil, Bulgaria, Burma, Burundi, Byelorussia, Canada, Cape Verde, Central African Republic, Chad, Chile, China, Colombia, Comoros, Congo, Costa Rica, Cuba, Cyprus, Czechoslovakia, Democratic Kampuchea, Democratic Yemen, Denmark, Djibouti, Dominican Republic, Ecuador, Egypt, El Salvador, Ethiopia, Fiji, Finland, France, Gabon, Gambia, German Democratic Republic, Germany, Ghana, Greece, Grenada, Guatemala, Guinea, Guinea-Bissau, Guyana, Honduras, Hungary, Iceland, India, Indonesia, Iran, Iraq, Ireland, Israel, Italy, Ivory Coast, Jamaica, Japan, Jordan, Kenya, Kuwait, Lao People's Democratic Republic, Leba-

---

[113]Resolution 260 A (III).

[114]United Nations, *Treaty Series,* vol. 75, no. 973, p. 287.

[115]*Official Records of the General Assembly, Thirty-seventh Session, Plenary Meetings,* 35th meeting, paras. 2-18.

non, Lesotho, Liberia, Libya, Luxembourg, Madagascar, Malawi, Malaysia, Maldives, Mali, Malta, Mauritania, Mauritius, Mexico, Mongolia, Morocco, Mozambique, Nepal, Netherlands, New Zealand, Nicaragua, Nigeria, Norway, Oman, Pakistan, Panama, Papua New Guinea, Paraguay, Peru, Philippines, Poland, Portugal, Qatar, Romania, Rwanda, Samoa, Sao Tome and Principe, Saudi Arabia, Senegal, Seychelles, Sierra Leone, Singapore, Somalia, Spain, Sri Lanka, Sudan, Suriname, Sweden, Syria, Thailand, Togo, Trinidad and Tobago, Tunisia, Turkey, Uganda, Ukraine, USSR, United Arab Emirates, United Kingdom, United Republic of Cameroon, United Republic of Tanzania, United States, Upper Volta, Uruguay, Vanuatu, Venezuela, Viet Nam, Yemen, Yugoslavia, Zaire, Zambia.

Against: 0

Abstentions: 0

Absent: 10

Antigua and Barbuda, Dominica, Equatorial Guinea, Haiti, Niger, Saint Lucia, Saint Vincent, Solomon Islands, Swaziland, Zimbabwe.

Albania announced that it was not participating in the vote.

F

The General Assembly,

Having discussed the item entitled "The situation in the Middle East",

Reaffirming its resolutions 36/226 A and B of 17 December 1981 and ES-9/1 of 5 February 1982,

Recalling Security Council resolutions 425 (1978) of 19 March 1978, 497 (1981) of 17 December 1981, 508 (1982) of 5 June 1982, 509 (1982) of 6 June 1982, 511 (1982) of 18 June 1982, 512 (1982) of 19 June 1982, 513 (1982) of 4 July 1982, 515 (1982) of 29 July 1982, 516 (1982) of 1 August 1982, 517 (1982) of 4 August 1982, 518 (1982) of 12 August 1982, 519 (1982) of 17 August 1982, 520 (1982) of 17 September 1982 and 521 (1982) of 19 September 1982,[116]

Taking note of the report of the Secretary-General of 12 October 1982,[117]

Welcoming the world-wide support extended to the just cause of the Palestinian people and the other Arab countries in their struggle against Israeli aggression and occupation in order to achieve a comprehensive, just and lasting peace in the Middle East and the full exercise by the Palestinian people of its inalienable national rights, as affirmed by previous resolutions of the General Assembly relating to the question of Palestine and the situation in the Middle East,

Gravely concerned that the Arab and Palestinian territories occupied since 1967, including Jerusalem, still re-main under Israeli occupation, that the relevant resolutions of the United Nations have not been implemented and that the Palestinian people is still denied the restoration of its land and the exercise of its inalienable national rights in conformity with international law, as reaffirmed by resolutions of the United Nations,

Reaffirming the applicability of the Geneva Convention relative to the Protection of Civilian Persons in Time of War, of 12 August 1949,[118] to all the occupied Palestinian and other Arab territories, including Jerusalem,

Reiterating all relevant United Nations resolutions which emphasize that the acquisition of territory by force is inadmissible under the Charter of the United Nations and the principles of international law and that Israel must withdraw unconditionally from all the Palestinian and other Arab territories occupied by Israel since 1967, including Jerusalem,

Reaffirming further the imperative necessity of establishing a comprehensive, just and lasting peace in the region, based on full respect for the Charter and the principles of international law,

Gravely concerned also at recent Israeli actions involving the escalation and expansion of the conflict in the region, which further violate the principles of international law and endanger international peace and security,

Welcoming the Arab peace plan adopted unanimously at the Twelfth Arab Summit Conference, held at Fez, Morocco, on 25 November 1981 and 9 September 1982,[119]

Bearing in mind the address made, on 26 October 1982, by His Majesty King Hassan II of Morocco,[120] in his capacity as President of the Twelfth Arab Summit Conference,

1. *Condemns* Israel's continued occupation of the Palestinian and other Arab territories, including Jerusalem, in violation of the Charter of the United Nations, the principles of international law and the relevant resolutions of the United Nations, and demands the immediate, unconditional and total withdrawal of Israel from all these occupied territories;

2. *Reaffirms its conviction* that the question of Palestine is the core of the conflict in the Middle East and that no comprehensive, just and lasting peace in the region will be achieved without the full exercise by the Palestinian people of its inalienable national rights and the immediate, unconditional and total withdrawal of Israel from all the Palestinian and other occupied Arab territories;

3. *Reaffirms further* that a just and comprehensive settlement of the situation in the Middle East cannot be achieved without the participation on an equal footing of all the parties to the conflict, including the Palestine Liberation Organization, the representative of the Palestinian people;

4. *Declares once more* that peace in the Middle East is indivisible and must be based on a comprehensive, just

---

[116]All but one of these resolutions focused on the situation arising from Israel's invasions of Lebanon in 1978 and 1982. [ed. note]

[117]A/37/525-S/15451. For the printed text, see *Official Records of the Security Council, Thirty-seventh Year, Supplement for October, November and December 1982*, document S/15451.

[118]United Nations, *Treaty Series,* vol. 75, no. 973, p. 287.

[119]See A/37/696-S/15510, annex.

[120]*Official Records of the General Assembly, Thirty-seventh Session, Plenary Meetings,* 44th meeting, paras. 83-92.

and lasting solution of the Middle East problem, under the auspices of the United Nations, which ensures the complete and unconditional withdrawal of Israel from the Palestinian and other Arab territories occupied since 1967, including Jerusalem, and which enables the Palestinian people, under the leadership of the Palestine Liberation Organization, to exercise its inalienable rights, including the right to return and the right to self-determination, national independence and the establishment of its independent sovereign State in Palestine, in accordance with the resolutions of the United Nations relevant to the question of Palestine, in particular General Assembly resolutions ES-7/2 of 29 July 1980, 36/120 A to F of 10 December 1981, 37/86 A to D of 10 December 1982 and 37/86 E of 20 December 1982;

5. *Rejects* all agreements and arrangements in so far as they violate the recognized rights of the Palestinian people and contradict the principles of just and comprehensive solutions to the Middle East problem to ensure the establishment of a just peace in the area;

6. *Deplores* Israel's failure to comply with Security Council resolutions 476 (1980) of 30 June 1980 and 478 (1980) of 20 August 1980 and General Assembly resolutions 35/207 of 16 December 1980 and 36/226 A and B of 17 December 1981, determines that Israel's decision to annex Jerusalem and to declare it as its "capital" as well as the measures to alter its physical character, demographic composition, institutional structure and status are null and void and demands that they be rescinded immediately, and calls upon all Member States, the specialized agencies and all other international organizations to abide by the present resolution and all other relevant resolutions, including Assembly resolutions 37/86 A to E;

7. *Condemns* Israel's aggression and practices against the Palestinian people in the occupied Palestinian territories and outside these territories, particularly Palestinians in Lebanon, including the expropriation and annexation of territory, the establishment of settlements, assassination attempts and other terrorist, aggressive and repressive measures, which are in violation of the Charter and the principles of international law and the relevant international conventions;

8. *Strongly condemns* the imposition by Israel of its laws, jurisdiction and administration on the occupied Syrian Golan Heights, its annexationist policies and practices, the establishment of settlements, the confiscation of lands, the diversion of water resources and the imposition of Israeli citizenship on Syrian nationals, and declares that all these measures are null and void and constitute a violation of the rules and principles of international law relevant to belligerent occupation, in particular the Geneva Convention relative to the Protection of Civilian Persons in Time of War, of 12 August 1949;

9. *Considers* that the agreements on strategic cooperation between the United States of America and Israel signed on 30 November 1981 would encourage Israel to pursue its aggressive and expansionist policies and practices in the Palestinian and other Arab territories occupied since 1967, including Jerusalem, would have adverse effects on efforts for the establishment of a comprehensive, just and lasting peace in the Middle East and would threaten the security of the region;

10. *Calls upon* all States to put an end to the flow to Israel of any military, economic and financial aid, as well as of human resources, aimed at encouraging it to pursue its aggressive policies against the Arab countries and the Palestinian people;

11. *Requests* the Secretary-General to report to the Security Council periodically on the development of the situation and to submit to the General Assembly at its thirty-eighth session a comprehensive report covering the developments in the Middle East in all their aspects.

Adopted at the 112th plenary meeting:
In favour: 113
Afghanistan, Algeria, Angola, Argentina, Bahrain, Bangladesh, Benin, Bhutan, Bolivia, Botswana, Brazil, Bulgaria, Burundi, Byelorussia, Cape Verde, Central African Republic, Chad, Chile, China, Colombia, Comoros, Congo, Cuba, Cyprus, Czechoslovakia, Democratic Kampuchea, Democratic Yemen, Djibouti, Ecuador, Egypt, El Salvador, Equatorial Guinea, Ethiopia, Gabon, Gambia, German Democratic Republic, Ghana, Greece, Grenada, Guinea, Guinea-Bissau, Guyana, Hungary, India, Indonesia, Iran, Iraq, Jamaica, Jordan, Kenya, Kuwait, Lao People's Democratic Republic, Lebanon, Lesotho, Liberia, Libya, Madagascar, Malaysia, Maldives, Mali, Malta, Mauritania, Mauritius, Mexico, Mongolia, Morocco, Mozambique, Nepal, Nicaragua, Niger, Nigeria, Oman, Pakistan, Panama, Papua New Guinea, Paraguay, Peru, Philippines, Poland, Qatar, Romania, Rwanda, Samoa, Sao Tome and Principe, Saudi Arabia, Senegal, Seychelles, Sierra Leone, Singapore, Somalia, Spain, Sri Lanka, Sudan, Suriname, Syria, Thailand, Togo, Trinidad and Tobago, Tunisia, Turkey, Uganda, Ukraine, USSR, United Arab Emirates, United Kingdom, United Republic of Cameroon, United Republic of Tanzania, Upper Volta, Venezuela, Viet Nam, Yemen, Yugoslavia, Zambia, Zimbabwe.
Against: 17
Australia, Belgium, Canada, Denmark, France, Federal Republic of Germany, Iceland, Ireland, Israel, Italy, Luxembourg, Netherlands, New Zealand, Norway, Portugal, United Kingdom, United States.
Abstentions: 15
Antigua and Barbuda, Austria, Bahamas, Barbados, Burma, Dominican Republic, Fiji, Finland, Haiti, Ivory Coast, Japan, Malawi, Sweden, Uruguay, Zaire.
Absent: 10
Belize, Costa Rica, Dominica, Guatemala, Honduras, Saint Lucia, Saint Vincent, Solomon Islands, Swaziland, Vanuatu.

Albania announced that it was not participating in the vote.

Resolution No. 37/127 A, B of 17 December 1982

ON THE FINANCING OF THE UNITED NATIONS INTERIM FORCE IN LEBANON

A

The General Assembly,

Having considered the report of the Secretary-General on the financing of the United Nations Interim Force in Lebanon[121] and the related report of the Advisory Committee on Administrative and Budgetary Questions,[122]

Bearing in mind Security Council resolutions 425 (1978) and 426 (1978) of 19 March 1978, 427 (1978) of 3 May 1978, 434 (1978) of 18 September 1978, 444 (1979) of 19 January 1979, 450 (1979) of 14 June 1979, 459 (1979) of 19 December 1979, 474 (1980) of 17 June 1980, 483 (1980) of 17 December 1980, 488 (1981) of 19 June 1981, 498 (1981) of 18 December 1981, 501 (1982) of 25 February 1982, 511 (1982) of 18 June 1982, 519 (1982) of 17 August 1982 and 523 (1982) of 18 October 1982,[123]

Recalling its resolutions S-8/2 of 21 April 1978, 33/14 of 3 November 1978, 34/9 B of 17 December 1979, 35/44 of 1 December 1980, 35/115 A of 10 December 1980, 36/138 A of 16 December 1981 and 36/138 C of 19 March 1982,

Reaffirming its previous decisions regarding the fact that, in order to meet the expenditures caused by such operations, a different procedure from the one applied to meet expenditures of the regular budget of the United Nations is required,

Taking into account the fact that the economically more developed countries are in a position to make relatively larger contributions and that the economically less developed countries have a relatively limited capacity to contribute towards peace-keeping operations involving heavy expenditures,

Bearing in mind the special responsibilities of the States permanent members of the Security Council in the financing of peace-keeping operations decided upon in accordance with the Charter of the United Nations,

I

Decides to appropriate to the Special Account referred to in section I, paragraph 1, of General Assembly resolution S-8/2 an amount of $89,724,996 gross ($88,887,000 net), being the amount authorized and apportioned under the provisions of section III of Assembly resolution 36/138 A and paragraph 1 of resolution 36/138 C for the operation of the United Nations Interim Force in Lebanon from 19 December 1981 to 18 June 1982, inclusive;

II

Decides to appropriate to the Special Account referred to in section I, paragraph 1, of General Assembly resolution S-8/2 an amount of $30,459,332 gross ($30,175,666 net), being the amount authorized and apportioned under the provisions of section III of Assembly resolution 36/138 A and paragraph 1 of resolution 36/138 C for the operation of the United Nations Interim Force in Lebanon from 19 June to 18 August 1982, inclusive;

III

Decides to appropriate to the Special Account referred to in section I, paragraph 1, of General Assembly resolution S-8/2 an amount of $30,459,332 gross ($30,175,666 net), being the amount authorized and apportioned under the provisions of section III of Assembly resolution 36/138 A and paragraph 1 of resolution 36/138 C for the operation of the United Nations Interim Force in Lebanon from 19 August to 18 October 1982, inclusive;

IV

Decides to appropriate to the Special Account referred to in section I, paragraph 1, of General Assembly resolution S-8/2 an amount of $30,459,332 gross ($30,175,666 net), being the amount authorized and apportioned under the provisions of section III of Assembly resolution 36/138 A and paragraph 1 of resolution 36/138 C for the operation of the United Nations Interim Force in Lebanon from 19 October to 18 December 1982, inclusive;

V

Authorizes the Secretary-General to enter into commitments for the operation of the United Nations Interim Force in Lebanon from 19 December 1982 to 18 January 1983 inclusive, in an amount not to exceed $15,229,666 gross ($15,087,833 net), the said amount to be apportioned among Member States in accordance with the scheme set out in General Assembly resolution 33/14 and the provisions of section V, paragraph 1, of resolution 34/9 B, section VI, paragraph 1, of resolution 35/115 A; and section VI, paragraph 1, of resolution 36/138 A; the scale of assessments for the years 1980, 1981 and 1982 shall be applied against a portion thereof, that is, $6,386,634 gross ($6,327,156 net), being the amount pertaining on a *pro rata* basis to the period from 19 to 31 December 1982 inclusive, and the scale of assessments for the years 1983, 1984 and 1985 shall be applied against the balance for the period thereafter;

VI

Authorizes the Secretary-General to enter into commitments for the operation of the United Nations Interim Force in Lebanon at a rate not to exceed $15,229,666 gross ($15,087,833 net) per month for the period from 19 January 1983 to 18 December 1983 inclusive, should the Security Council decide to continue the Force beyond the period of three months authorized under its resolution 523 (1982), subject to obtaining the prior concurrence of the Advisory Committee on Administrative and Budgetary Questions for the actual level of commitments to be entered into for each mandate period that may be approved subsequent to 19 January 1983, the said amount to be apportioned among Member States in accordance with the scheme set out in General Assembly resolution 33/14 and the provisions of section V, paragraph 1, of resolution 34/9 B, section VI, paragraph 1, of resolution 35/115 A and section VI, paragraph 1, of resolution

---

[121]A/37/535.

[122]A/37/649.

[123]The resolutions cited in this and the next paragraph refer to the renewal of the mandate and the financing of the United Nations Interim Force in Lebanon. [ed. note]

36/138 A, in the proportions determined by the scale of assessments for the years 1983, 1984 and 1985;

VII

1. *Renews its invitation* to Member States to make voluntary contributions to the United Nations Interim Force in Lebanon both in cash and in the form of services and supplies acceptable to the Secretary-General;

2. *Invites* Member States to make voluntary contributions in cash to the Suspense Account established in accordance with its resolution 34/9 D of 17 December 1979;

VIII

Requests the Secretary-General to take all necessary action to ensure that the United Nations Interim Force in Lebanon shall be administered with a maximum of efficiency and economy;

IX

1. *Decides* that Antigua and Barbuda, Belize and Vanuatu shall be included in the group of Member States mentioned in section I, paragraph 2 (*d*), of General Assembly resolution S-8/2 and that their contributions to the United Nations Interim Force in Lebanon shall be calculated in accordance with the provisions of paragraphs 1 and 6 of Assembly resolution 37/125 A of 17 December 1982;

2. *Decides further* that, in accordance with regulation 5.2(*c*) of the Financial Regulations of the United Nations, the contributions to the United Nations Interim Force in Lebanon until 18 December 1982 of the Member States referred to in paragraph 1 of the present section shall be treated as miscellaneous income to be set off against the apportionments authorized in section V above.

Adopted at the 109th plenary meeting:
In favour: 119
Angola, Argentina, Australia, Austria, Bahamas, Bahrain, Bangladesh, Barbados, Belgium, Bhutan, Bolivia, Botswana, Burma, Burundi, Canada, Cape Verde, Central African Republic, Chad, Chile, China, Colombia, Comoros, Congo, Costa Rica, Cuba, Cyprus, Denmark, Djibouti, Dominica, Dominican Republic, Ecuador, Egypt, El Salvador, Fiji, Finland, France, Gabon, Gambia, Federal Republic of Germany, Ghana, Greece, Guatemala, Guinea, Guinea-Bissau, Guyana, Honduras, Iceland, India, Indonesia, Ireland, Israel, Italy, Ivory Coast, Jamaica, Japan, Jordan, Kenya, Kuwait, Lebanon, Lesotho, Liberia, Luxembourg, Madagascar, Malawi, Malaysia, Mali, Malta, Mauritania, Mauritius, Mexico, Morocco, Nepal, Netherlands, New Zealand, Nicaragua, Niger, Norway, Oman, Pakistan, Panama, Papua New Guinea, Paraguay, Peru, Philippines, Portugal, Qatar, Romania, Rwanda, Samoa, Saudi Arabia, Senegal, Sierra Leone, Singapore, Solomon Islands, Somalia, Spain, Sri Lanka, Sudan, Suriname, Swaziland, Sweden, Thailand, Togo, Trinidad and Tobago, Tunisia, Turkey, Uganda, United Arab Emirates, United Kingdom, United Republic of Cameroon, United Republic of Tanzania, United States, Upper Volta, Uruguay, Venezuela, Yugoslavia, Zaire, Zambia, Zimbabwe.
Against: 14

Afghanistan, Albania, Bulgaria, Byelorussia, Czechoslovakia, German Democratic Republic, Hungary, Iraq, Mongolia, Poland, Syria, Ukraine, USSR, Viet Nam.
Abstentions: 5
Cuba, Grenada, Maldives, Sao Tome and Principe, Yemen.
Absent: 18
Algeria, Antigua and Barbuda, Belize, Benin, Democratic Kampuchea, Democratic Yemen, Equatorial Guinea, Ethiopia, Haiti, Iran, Lao People's Democratic Republic, Libya, Mozambique, Nigeria, Saint Lucia, Saint Vincent, Seychelles, Vanuatu.

B

The General Assembly,

Having regard to the financial position of the Special Account for the United Nations Interim Force in Lebanon as set forth in the report of the Secretary-General,[124] and referring to paragraph 7 of the report of the Advisory Committee on Administrative and Budgetary Questions,[125]

Mindful of the fact that it is essential to provide the United Nations Interim Force in Lebanon with the necessary financial resources to enable it to fulfil its responsibilities under the relevant resolutions of the Security Council,

Concerned that the Secretary-General is continuing to face growing difficulties in meeting the obligations of the United Nations Interim Force in Lebanon on a current basis, particularly those due to the Governments of troop-contributing States,

Recalling its resolutions 34/9 E of 17 December 1979, 35/115 B of 10 December 1980 and 36/138 B of 16 December 1981,[126]

Recognizing that, in consequence of the withholding of contributions by certain Member States, the surplus balances in the Special Account for the United Nations Interim Force in Lebanon have, in effect, been drawn upon to the full extent to supplement the income received from contributions for meeting expenses of the Force,

Concerned that the application of the provisions of regulations 5.2 (*b*), 5.2 (*d*), 4.3 and 4.4 of the Financial Regulations of the United Nations would aggravate the already difficult situation of the United Nations Interim Force in Lebanon,

Decides that the provisions of regulations 5.2 (*b*), 5.2 (*d*), 4.3 and 4.4 of the Financial Regulations of the United Nations shall be suspended in respect of the amount of $5,939,256, which otherwise would have to be surrendered pursuant to those provisions, this amount to be entered in the account referred to in the operative part of General Assembly resolution 34/9 E and held in suspense until a further decision is taken by the Assembly.

Adopted at the 109th plenary meeting:

---

[124]A/37/535.
[125]A/37/649.
[126]These resolutions refer to the financing of the United Nations Interim Force in Lebanon. [ed. note]

In favour: 118

Angola, Argentina, Australia, Austria, Bahamas, Bahrain, Bangladesh, Barbados, Belgium, Bhutan, Bolivia, Botswana, Brazil, Burma, Burundi, Canada, Cape Verde, Central African Republic, Chad, Chile, China, Colombia, Comoros, Congo, Costa Rica, Cuba, Cyprus, Denmark, Djibouti, Dominica, Dominican Republic, Ecuador, Egypt, El Salvador, Fiji, Finland, France, Gabon, Gambia, Federal Republic of Germany, Ghana, Greece, Guatemala, Guinea, Guinea-Bissau, Guyana, Honduras, Iceland, India, Indonesia, Ireland, Israel, Italy, Ivory Coast, Jamaica, Japan, Jordan, Kenya, Kuwait, Lebanon, Lesotho, Liberia, Luxembourg, Madagascar, Malawi, Malaysia, Mali, Malta, Mauritania, Mauritius, Mexico, Morocco, Nepal, Netherlands, New Zealand, Nicaragua, Niger, Norway, Oman, Pakistan, Panama, Papua New Guinea, Paraguay, Peru, Philippines, Portugal, Qatar, Rwanda, Samoa, Saudi Arabia, Senegal, Sierra Leone, Singapore, Solomon Islands, Somalia, Spain, Sri Lanka, Sudan, Suriname, Swaziland, Sweden, Thailand, Togo, Trinidad and Tobago, Tunisia, Turkey, Uganda, United Arab Emirates, United Kingdom, United Republic of Cameroon, United Republic of Tanzania, United States, Upper Volta, Uruguay, Venezuela, Yugoslavia, Zaire, Zambia, Zimbabwe.

Against: 14

Afghanistan, Albania, Bulgaria, Byelorussia, Czechoslovakia, German Democratic Republic, Hungary, Iraq, Mongolia, Poland, Syria, Ukraine, USSR, Viet Nam.

Abstentions: 6

Cuba, Grenada, Maldives, Romania, Sao Tome and Principe, Yemen.

Absent: 18

Algeria, Antigua and Barbuda, Belize, Benin, Democratic Kampuchea, Democratic Yemen, Equatorial Guinea, Ethiopia, Haiti, Iran, Lao People's Democratic Republic, Libya, Mozambique, Nigeria, Saint Lucia, Saint Vincent, Seychelles, Vanuatu.

Resolution No. 37/134 of 17 December 1982

CALLING FOR THE PROVISION OF HUMANITARIAN ASSISTANCE TO THE PALESTINIAN PEOPLE, AND REQUESTING THAT UNITED NATIONS ASSISTANCE SHOULD BE RENDERED IN COOPERATION WITH THE PALESTINE LIBERATION ORGANIZATION

The General Assembly,

Recalling its resolution ES-7/5 of 26 June 1982,

Recalling also Security Council resolution 512 (1982) of 19 June 1982,

Recalling further Economic and Social Council resolution 1982/48 of 27 July 1982,

Expressing its deep alarm at the Israeli invasion of Lebanon, which claimed the lives of a very large number of civilian Palestinians,

Horrified by the Sabra and Shatila massacre,

Noting with deep concern the dire need of the Palestinian victims of the Israeli invasion for urgent humanitarian assistance,

Noting the need to provide economic and social assistance to the Palestinian people,

1. *Condemns* Israel for its invasion of Lebanon, which inflicted severe damage on civilian Palestinians, including heavy loss of human life, intolerable suffering and massive material destruction;

2. *Endorses* Economic and Social Council resolution 1982/48;

3. *Calls upon* Governments and relevant United Nations bodies to provide humanitarian assistance to the Palestinian victims of the Israeli invasion of Lebanon;

4. *Requests* the relevant programmes, agencies, organs and organizations of the United Nations system to intensify their efforts, in co-operation with the Palestine Liberation Organization, to provide economic and social assistance to the Palestinian people;

5. *Also requests* that United Nations assistance to the Palestinians in the Arab host countries should be rendered in co-operation with the Palestine Liberation Organization and with the consent of the Arab host Government concerned;

6. *Requests* the Secretary-General to report to the General Assembly at its thirty-eighth session, through the Economic and Social Council, on the progress made in the implementation of the present resolution.

Adopted at the 109th plenary meeting:

In favour: 143

Afghanistan, Albania, Algeria, Angola, Argentina, Australia, Austria, Bahamas, Bahrain, Bangladesh, Barbados, Belgium, Benin, Bhutan, Bolivia, Botswana, Brazil, Bulgaria, Burma, Burundi, Byelorussia, Canada, Cape Verde, Central African Republic, Chad, Chile, China, Colombia, Comoros, Congo, Costa Rica, Cuba, Cyprus, Czechoslovakia, Democratic Kampuchea, Democratic Yemen, Denmark, Djibouti, Dominican Republic, Ecuador, Egypt, El Salvador, Ethiopia, Fiji, Finland, France, Gabon, Gambia, German Democratic Republic, Federal Republic of Germany, Ghana, Greece, Grenada, Guinea, Guinea-Bissau, Guyana, Honduras, Hungary, Iceland, India, Indonesia, Iran, Iraq, Ireland, Italy, Ivory Coast, Jamaica, Japan, Jordan, Kenya, Kuwait, Lao People's Democratic Republic, Lebanon, Lesotho, Liberia, Libya, Luxembourg, Madagascar, Malawi, Malaysia, Maldives, Mali, Malta, Mauritania, Mauritius, Mexico, Mongolia, Morocco, Mozambique, Nepal, Netherlands, New Zealand, Nicaragua, Niger, Nigeria, Norway, Oman, Pakistan, Panama, Papua New Guinea, Paraguay, Peru, Philippines, Poland, Portugal, Qatar, Romania, Rwanda, Samoa, Sao Tome and Principe, Saudi Arabia, Senegal, Sierra Leone, Singapore, Solomon Islands, Somalia, Spain, Sri Lanka, Suriname, Swaziland, Sweden, Thailand, Togo, Trinidad and Tobago, Tunisia, Turkey, Uganda, Ukraine, USSR, United Arab Emirates, United Kingdom, United Republic of Cameroon, United Republic of Tanzania, Upper Volta, Uruguay, Vanuatu, Venezuela, Viet Nam, Yemen, Yugoslavia, Zaire, Zambia, Zimbabwe.

Against: 2

Israel, United States.

Abstentions: 0
Absent: 11
Antigua and Barbuda, Belize, Bolivia,* Equatorial Guinea, Guatemala, Haiti, Saint Lucia, Saint Vincent, Seychelles, Sudan,* Syria.*

---

* Later advised the Secretariat it had intended to vote in favour.

Resolution No. 37/135 of 17 December 1982

REAFFIRMING THE ILLEGALITY OF MEASURES TAKEN BY IS-RAEL TO EXPLOIT THE HUMAN AND NATURAL RESOURCES OF THE OCCUPIED ARAB AND PALESTINIAN TERRITORIES, AND CALLING UPON IT TO DESIST FROM SUCH MEASURES

The General Assembly,

Recalling its resolutions 3175 (XXVIII) of 17 December 1973, 3336 (XXIX) of 17 December 1974, 3516 (XXX) of 15 December 1975, 31/186 of 21 December 1976, 32/161 of 19 December 1977, 34/136 of 14 December 1979, 35/110 of 5 December 1980 and 36/173 of 17 December 1981 on permanent sovereignty over national resources in the occupied Palestinian and other Arab territories,

Recalling also its previous resolutions on permanent sovereignty over natural resources, particularly their provisions supporting resolutely the efforts of the developing countries and the peoples of territories under colonial and racial domination and foreign occupation in their struggle to regain effective control over their natural and all other resources, wealth and economic activities,

Bearing in mind the relevant principles of international law and the provisions of the international conventions and regulations, in particular Convention IV of the Hague of 1907,[127] and the fourth Geneva Convention of 12 August 1949,[128] concerning the obligations and responsibilities of the occupying Power,

Bearing in mind also the pertinent provisions of its resolutions 3201 (S-VI) and 3202 (S-VI) of 1 May 1974, containing the Declaration and the Programme of Action on the Establishment of a New International Economic Order, and 3281 (XXIX) of 12 December 1974, containing the Charter of Economic Rights and Duties of States,

Regretting that the report of the Secretary-General on permanent sovereignty over national resources in the occupied Palestinian and other Arab territories, requested in General Assembly resolution 36/173, was not submitted,

1. *Condemns* Israel for its exploitation of the national resources of the occupied Palestinian and other Arab territories;

2. *Emphasizes* the right of the Palestinian and other Arab peoples whose territories are under Israeli occupation to full and effective permanent sovereignty and control over their natural and all other resources, wealth and economic activities;

3. *Reaffirms* that all measures undertaken by Israel to exploit the human, natural and all other resources, wealth and economic activities in the occupied Palestinian and other Arab territories are illegal and calls upon Israel to desist immediately from such measures;

4. *Further reaffirms* the right of the Palestinian and other Arab peoples subjected to Israeli aggression and occupation to the restitution of and full compensation for the exploitation, depletion and loss of and damages to their natural, human and all other resources, wealth and economic activities, and calls upon Israel to meet their just claims;

5. *Calls upon* all States to support the Palestinian and other Arab peoples in the exercise of their above-mentioned rights;

6. *Calls upon* all States, international organizations, specialized agencies, business corporations and all other institutions not to recognize, or co-operate with or assist in any manner in, any measures undertaken by Israel to exploit the national resources of the occupied Palestinian and other Arab territories or to effect any changes in the demographic composition, the character and form of use of their natural resources or the institutional structure of those territories;

7. *Requests* the Secretary-General to prepare and submit to the General Assembly at its thirty-eighth session, through the Economic and Social Council, the two reports requested in Assembly resolution 36/173.

Adopted at the 109th plenary meeting:
In favour: 124
Afghanistan, Albania, Algeria, Angola, Argentina, Bahamas, Bahrain, Bangladesh, Barbados, Benin, Bhutan, Bolivia, Botswana, Brazil, Bulgaria, Burundi, Byelorussia, Cape Verde, Central African Republic, Chad, Chile, China, Colombia, Comoros, Congo, Costa Rica, Cuba, Cyprus, Czechoslovakia, Democratic Kampuchea, Democratic Yemen, Djibouti, Dominica, Dominican Republic, Ecuador, Egypt, El Salvador, Ethiopia, Gabon, Gambia, German Democratic Republic, Ghana, Greece, Grenada, Guinea, Guinea-Bissau, Guyana, Honduras, Hungary, India, Indonesia, Iran, Iraq, Jamaica, Japan, Jordan, Kenya, Kuwait, Lao People's Democratic Republic, Lebanon, Lesotho, Liberia, Libya, Madagascar, Malawi, Malaysia, Maldives, Mali, Malta, Mauritania, Mauritius, Mexico, Mongolia, Morocco, Mozambique, Nepal, Nicaragua, Niger, Nigeria, Oman, Pakistan, Panama, Papua New Guinea, Paraguay, Peru, Philippines, Poland, Portugal, Qatar, Romania, Rwanda, Samoa, Sao Tome and Principe, Saudi Arabia, Senegal, Sierra Leone, Singapore, Soloman Islands, Somalia, Spain, Sri Lanka, Suriname, Swaziland, Thailand, Togo, Trinidad and Tobago, Tunisia, Turkey, Uganda, Ukraine, USSR, United Arab Emirates, United Republic of Cameroon, United Republic of Tanzania, Upper Volta, Uruguay, Vanuatu, Venezuela, Viet Nam, Yemen, Yugoslavia, Zaire, Zambia, Zimbabwe.
Against: 2
Israel, United States.

---

[127]Carnegie Endowment for International Peace, *The Hague Conventions and Declarations of 1899 and 1907* (New York, Oxford University Press, 1915), p. 100.
[128]United Nations, *Treaty Series*, vol. 75, no. 973, p. 287.

Abstentions: 20

Australia, Austria, Belgium, Burma, Canada, Denmark, Fiji, Finland, France, Federal Republic of Germany, Iceland, Ireland, Italy, Ivory Coast, Luxembourg, Netherlands, New Zealand, Norway, Sweden, United Kingdom.

Absent: 10

Antigua and Barbuda, Belize, Equatorial Guinea, Guatemala, Haiti, Saint Lucia, Saint Vincent, Seychelles, Sudan,* Syria.*

---

* Later advised the Secretariat it had intended to vote in favour.

Resolution No. 37/163 of 17 December 1982

CALLING FOR ASSISTANCE FOR THE RECONSTRUCTION AND DEVELOPMENT OF LEBANON

The General Assembly,

Recalling its resolutions 33/146 of 20 December 1978, 34/135 of 14 December 1979, 35/85 of 5 December 1980 and 36/205 of 17 December 1981 on assistance for the reconstruction and development of Lebanon,

Recalling also Economic and Social Council resolution 1980/15 of 29 April 1980,

Deeply concerned about the heavy and tragic loss of life and the mass destruction of property as well as the extensive damage to the economic and social structures of Lebanon,

Taking into consideration the will and the determination of the Government of Lebanon to undertake a large-scale reconstruction and rehabilitation programme in the immediate future,

Affirming the urgent need for substantial international action to assist the Government of Lebanon in its efforts for reconstruction and development,

Taking note of the report of the Secretary-General[129] and of the statement made by the United Nations Co-ordinator of Assistance for the Reconstruction and Development of Lebanon,[130]

1. *Expresses its appreciation* to the Secretary-General for his report;

2. *Welcomes* the appeal of the Secretary-General for international assistance to Lebanon and urges all Governments to contribute substantially to this end;

3. *Commends* the United Nations Co-ordinator of Assistance for the Reconstruction and Development of Lebanon and his staff for their valuable and relentless efforts in the discharge of their duties under the most adverse circumstances;

4. *Expresses its appreciation* for the humanitarian and emergency relief assistance provided by the United Nations Children's Fund, the Food and Agricultural Organization of the United Nations, the World Food Programme, the Office of the United Nations Disaster Relief Co-

ordinator, the United Nations High Commissioner for Refugees, the World Health Organization, the International Committee of the Red Cross, the League of Red Cross and Red Crescent Societies and other benevolent agencies, and for their prompt and effective response;

5. *Requests* the Secretary-General to continue his intensive efforts to mobilize all possible assistance within the United Nations system to help the Government of Lebanon in its reconstruction and development efforts;

6. *Calls upon* the organs, organizations and bodies of the United Nations system to expand and intensify programmes of assistance in response to the needs of Lebanon;

7. *Requests* the Secretary-General to report to the Economic and Social Council at its first regular session of 1983 and to the General Assembly at its thirty-eighth session on the progress achieved in the implementation of the present resolution.

Adopted at the 109th plenary meeting without a vote.

Resolution No. 37/222 of 20 December 1982

AFFIRMING THAT ISRAELI OCCUPATION IS CONTRADICTORY TO THE SOCIAL AND ECONOMIC DEVELOPMENT OF THE PALESTINIAN PEOPLE IN THE OCCUPIED TERRITORIES AND THAT THE EXERCISE OF THEIR RIGHT TO SELF-DETERMINATION IS A PREREQUISITE TO THEIR SOCIAL AND ECONOMIC DEVELOPMENT

The General Assembly,

Recalling the Vancouver Declaration on Human Settlements, 1976,[131] and the relevant recommendations for national action[132] adopted by Habitat: United Nations Conference on Human Settlements,

Recalling also resolution 3, entitled "Living conditions of the Palestinians in occupied territories", contained in the recommendations for international co-operation adopted by Habitat: United Nations Conference on Human Settlements,[133]

Recalling further its resolution 36/73 of 4 December 1981,

1. *Takes note* of the report of the Secretary-General on the living conditions of the Palestinian people in the occupied Palestinian territories;[134]

2. *Takes note* of the statement made by the observer of the Palestine Liberation Organization;[135]

3. *Expresses its alarm* at the deterioration in the living conditions of the Palestinian people in the Palestinian territories occupied since 1967 as a result of the Israeli occupation;

4. *Affirms* that the Israeli occupation is contradictory to the basic requirements for the social and economic devel-

---

[129]A/37/508 and Add. 1.

[130]*Official Records of the General Assembly, Thirty-seventh Session, Second Committee,* 7th meeting, paras. 36-49.

[131]*Report of Habitat: United Nations Conference on Human Settlements, Vancouver, 31 May-11 June 1976* (United Nations publication, Sales No. E.76.IV.7 and corrigendum), chap. I.

[132]*Ibid.,* chap. II.

[133]*Ibid.,* chap. III.

[134]A/37/238.

[135]*Official Records of the General Assembly, Thirty-seventh Session, Second Committee,* 31st meeting, para. 86.

opment of the Palestinian people in the occupied West Bank and Gaza Strip;

5. *Affirms also* that the exercise by the Palestinian people of their right to self-determination is a prerequisite for their social and economic development in the Palestinian territories occupied since 1967;

6. *Calls upon* the Israeli occupation authorities to give United Nations bodies and experts access to the Palestinian territories occupied since 1967;

7. *Recognizes* the need for a comprehensive report on the social and economic conditions of the Palestinian people in the Palestinian territories occupied since 1967;

8. *Requests* the Secretary-General to prepare and submit to the General Assembly at its thirty-eighth session, through the Economic and Social Council, a comprehensive report on the living conditions of the Palestinian people in the occupied Palestinian territories.

Adopted at the 113th plenary meeting:
In favour: 145
Afghanistan, Albania, Algeria, Angola, Antigua and Barbuda, Argentina, Austria, Bahamas, Bahrain, Bangladesh, Barbados, Belgium, Benin, Bhutan, Bolivia, Botswana, Brazil, Bulgaria, Burundi, Byelorussia, Cape Verde, Central African Republic, Chad, Chile, China, Colombia, Comoros, Congo, Costa Rica, Cuba, Cyprus, Czechoslovakia, Democratic Kampuchea, Democratic Yemen, Denmark, Djibouti, Dominican Republic, Ecuador, Egypt, El Salvador, Ethiopia, Fiji, Finland, France, Gabon, Gambia, German Democratic Republic, Federal Republic of Germany, Ghana, Greece, Grenada, Guinea, Guinea-Bissau, Guyana, Honduras, Hungary, Iceland, India, Indonesia, Iran, Iraq, Ireland, Italy, Ivory Coast, Jamaica, Japan, Jordan, Kenya, Kuwait, Lao People's Democratic Republic, Lebanon, Lesotho, Liberia, Libya, Luxembourg, Madagascar, Malawi, Malaysia, Maldives, Mali, Malta, Mauritania, Mauritius, Mexico, Mongolia, Morocco, Mozambique, Nepal, Netherlands, New Zealand, Nicaragua, Nigeria, Norway, Oman, Pakistan, Panama, Papua New Guinea, Paraguay, Peru, Philippines, Poland, Portugal, Qatar, Romania, Rwanda, Saint Lucia, Saint Vincent, Samoa, Sao Tome and Principe, Saudi Arabia, Senegal, Sierra Leone, Singapore, Somalia, Spain, Sri Lanka, Sudan, Suriname, Swaziland, Sweden, Syria, Thailand, Togo, Trinidad and Tobago, Tunisia, Turkey, Uganda, Ukraine, USSR, United Arab Emirates, United Kingdom, United Republic of Cameroon, United Republic of Tanzania, Upper Volta, Uruguay, Vanuatu, Venezuela, Viet Nam, Yemen, Yugoslavia, Zaire, Zambia, Zimbabwe.
Against: 2
Israel, United States.
Abstentions: 3
Australia, Burma, Canada.
Absent: 6
Belize, Dominica, Equatorial Guinea, Guatemala, Seychelles, Solomon Islands.

Resolution No. 38/9 of 10 November 1983

REITERATING ITS DEMAND THAT ISRAEL WITHDRAW ITS THREAT TO ATTACK AND DESTROY NUCLEAR FACILITIES IN IRAQ AND OTHER COUNTRIES

The General Assembly,
Having considered the item entitled "Armed Israeli aggression against the Iraqi nuclear installations and its grave consequences for the established international system concerning the peaceful uses of nuclear energy, the non-proliferation of nuclear weapons and international peace and security",
Recalling the relevant resolutions of the Security Council and the General Assembly,
Taking note of the relevant resolutions of the International Atomic Energy Agency,
Taking note also with appreciation of the report of the Secretary-General,[136]
Viewing with deep concern Israel's continued refusal to comply with those resolutions,
Reiterating its alarm over the information and evidence regarding the acquisition and development of nuclear weapons by Israel,
Recalling Article 2, paragraph 4, of the Charter of the United Nations, which enjoins all Member States to refrain in their international relations from the threat or use of force against the territorial integrity or political independence of any State, or in any other manner inconsistent with the purposes of the United Nations,
Noting that serious radiological effects would result from an armed attack with conventional weapons on a nuclear installation, which could also lead to the initiation of radiological warfare,

1. *Reiterates its condemnation* of Israel's continued refusal to implement Security Council resolution 487 (1981), unanimously adopted by the Council on 19 June 1981;

2. *Notes* that the statements made so far by Israel have not removed apprehensions that its threat to repeat its armed attack against nuclear facilities, as well as any similar action against such facilities, will continue to endanger the role and activities of the International Atomic Energy Agency and other international instruments in the development of nuclear energy for peaceful purposes and in safeguarding against further proliferation of nuclear weapons;

3. *Considers* that any threat to attack and destroy nuclear facilities in Iraq and in other countries constitutes a violation of the Charter of the United Nations;

4. *Reiterates its demand* that Israel withdraw forthwith its threat to attack and destroy nuclear facilities in Iraq and in other countries;

5. *Once again requests* the Security Council to consider the necessary measures to deter Israel from repeating such an attack on nuclear facilities;

---

[136] A/38/342.

6. *Reaffirms its call* for the continuation of the consideration, at the international level, of legal measures to prohibit armed attacks against nuclear facilities, and threats thereof, as a contribution to promoting and ensuring the safe development of nuclear energy for peaceful purposes;

7. *Expresses its deep appreciation* to the Secretary-General and the Group of Experts on the Consequences of the Israeli Armed Attack against the Iraqi Nuclear Installations for their comprehensive study;[137]

8. *Requests* the Secretary-General to report to the General Assembly at its thirty-ninth session on the implementation of the present resolution;

9. *Decides* to include in the provisional agenda of its thirty-ninth session the item entitled "Armed Israeli aggression against the Iraqi nuclear installations and its grave consequences for the established international system concerning the peaceful uses of nuclear energy, the non-proliferation of nuclear weapons and international peace and security".

Adopted at the 52nd plenary meeting:
In favour: 123
Afghanistan, Albania, Algeria, Angola, Argentina, Austria, Bahrain, Bangladesh, Belgium, Benin, Bhutan, Bolivia, Brazil, Bulgaria, Burundi, Byelorussia, Canada, Cape Verde, Central African Republic, Chad, China, Comoros, Congo, Cuba, Cyprus, Czechoslovakia, Democratic Kampuchea, Democratic Yemen, Denmark, Djibouti, Ecuador, Egypt, El Salvador, Ethiopia, Finland, France, Gabon, Gambia, German Democratic Republic, Federal Republic of Germany, Ghana, Greece, Grenada, Guinea, Guinea-Bissau, Guyana, Hungary, Iceland, India, Indonesia, Iraq, Ireland, Italy, Japan, Jordan, Kenya, Kuwait, Lao People's Democratic Republic, Lebanon, Lesotho, Libya, Luxembourg, Madagascar, Malaysia, Maldives, Mali, Malta, Mauritania, Mauritius, Mexico, Mongolia, Morocco, Mozambique, Nepal, Netherlands, Nicaragua, Niger, Norway, Oman, Pakistan, Panama, Papua New Guinea, Peru, Philippines, Poland, Portugal, Qatar, Romania, Rwanda, Samoa, Sao Tome and Principe, Saudi Arabia, Senegal, Sierra Leone, Singapore, Solomon Islands, Somalia, Spain, Sri Lanka, Sudan, Sweden, Syria, Thailand, Togo, Trinidad and Tobago, Tunisia, Turkey, Uganda, Ukraine, USSR, United Arab Emirates, United Kingdom, United Republic of Cameroon, United Republic of Tanzania, Upper Volta, Uruguay, Zaire, Venezuela, Viet Nam, Yemen, Yugoslavia, Zambia, Zimbabwe.
Against: 2
Israel, United States.
Abstentions: 12
Australia, Bahamas, Barbados, Chile, Colombia, Fiji, Guatemala, Haiti, Ivory Coast, Jamaica, Malawi, Paraguay.
Absent: 20
Antigua and Barbuda, Belize, Botswana, Burma, Costa Rica, Dominica, Dominican Republic, Equatorial Guinea, Honduras, Iran,* Liberia, Nigeria, Saint Lucia, Saint Vincent, Seychelles,* St. Christopher and Nevis, Suriname, Swaziland, Vanuatu, Zaire.

---

*Later advised the Secretariat it had intended to vote in favour.

Resolution No. 38/17 of 22 November 1983

CONDEMNING ISRAEL'S EXPANSIONIST POLICIES AS AN OBSTACLE TO THE ACHIEVEMENT OF SELF-DETERMINATION AND INDEPENDENCE BY THE PALESTINIAN PEOPLE, AND CONDEMNING THE MASSACRE OF PALESTINIANS AND OTHER CIVILIANS IN BEIRUT, AS WELL AS ISRAEL'S POLICIES IN LEBANON [EXCERPTS FROM A RESOLUTION ON THE RIGHT TO SELF-DETERMINATION OF COLONIAL COUNTRIES AND PEOPLES]

The General Assembly,

....

Welcoming the holding of the International Conference in Support of the Struggle of the Namibian People for Independence in Paris from 25 to 29 April 1983,[138]
Welcoming also the holding of the International Conference on the Alliance between South Africa and Israel at Vienna from 11 to 13 July 1983,[139]

....

Recalling further its relevant resolutions on the question of Palestine, in particular resolutions 3236 (XXIX) and 3237 (XXIX) of 22 November 1974, 36/120 of 10 December 1981, ES-7/6 of 19 August 1982 and 37/86 of 10 December 1982,
Recalling the Geneva Declaration on Palestine and the Programme of Action for the Achievement of Palestinian Rights, adopted by the International Conference on the Question of Palestine,[140]
Considering that the denial of the inalienable rights of the Palestinian people to self-determination, sovereignty, independence and return to Palestine and the repeated acts of aggression by Israel against the people of the region constitute a serious threat to international peace and security,
Deeply shocked and alarmed at the deplorable consequences of the Israeli invasion of Lebanon and recalling all the relevant resolutions of the Security Council, in particular resolutions 508 (1982) of 5 June 1982, 509 (1982) of 6 June 1982, 520 (1982) of 17 September 1982 and 521 (1982) of 19 September 1982,

1. *Calls upon* all States to implement fully and faithfully all the resolutions of the United Nations regarding the exercise of the right to self-determination and independence by peoples under colonial and foreign domination;

2. *Reaffirms* the legitimacy of the struggle of peoples for

---

[137] A/38/337, annex.

[138] See A/CONF.120/13.
[139] See A/AC.115/L.595.
[140] *Report of the International Conference on the Question of Palestine, Geneva, 29 August-7 September 1983* (United Nations publication, Sales No. E.83.I.21), chap. I.

their independence, territorial integrity, national unity and liberation from colonial domination, *apartheid* and foreign occupation by all available means, including armed struggle;

3. *Reaffirms* the inalienable right of the Namibian people, the Palestinian people and all peoples under foreign and colonial domination to self-determination, national unity and sovereignty without foreign interference;

4. *Strongly condemns* those Governments that do not recognize the right to self-determination and independence of all peoples still under colonial domination and alien subjugation, notably the peoples of Africa and the Palestinian people;

5. *Endorses* the Paris Declaration on Namibia, adopted by the International Conference in Support of the Struggle of the Namibian People for Independence,[141] and the Geneva Declaration on Palestine, adopted by the International Conference on the Question of Palestine, as well as the Programmes of Action adopted by these Conferences, and calls for their immediate implementation;

....

15. *Strongly condemns* the continued violations of the human rights of the peoples still under colonial domination and alien subjugation, the continuation of the illegal occupation of Namibia, and South Africa's attempts to dismember its Territory, the perpetuation of the racist minority régime in southern Africa and the denial to the Palestinian people of their inalienable national rights;

....

18. *Takes note* of the Declaration of the International Conference on the Alliance between South Africa and Israel;[142]

19. *Strongly condemns* the policy of those Western States, Israel and other States whose political, economic, military, nuclear, strategic, cultural and sports relations with the racist minority régime in South Africa encourage that régime to persist in its suppression of the aspirations of peoples to self-determination and independence;

....

29. *Strongly condemns* the constant and deliberate violations of the fundamental rights of the Palestinian people, as well as the expansionist activities of Israel in the Middle East, which constitute an obstacle to the achievement of self-determination and independence by the Palestinian people and a threat to peace and stability in the region;

30. *Further strongly condemns* the massacre of Palestinians and other civilians at Beirut and the Israeli aggression against Lebanon, which endangers stability, peace and security in the region;

31. *Demands* the immediate and unconditional release of all persons detained or imprisoned as a result of their struggle for self-determination and independence, full respect for their fundamental individual rights and com-

pliance with article 5 of the Universal Declaration of Human Rights,[143] under which no one shall be subjected to torture or to cruel, inhuman or degrading treatment;

32. *Urges* all States, specialized agencies, competent organizations of the United Nations system and other international organizations to extend their support to the Palestinian people through its sole and legitimate representative, the Palestine Liberation Organization, in its struggle to regain its right to self-determination and independence in accordance with the Charter;

....

Adopted at the 66th plenary meeting:
In favour: 104
Afghanistan, Albania, Algeria, Angola, Argentina, Bahamas, Bahrain, Bangladesh, Bhutan, Bolivia, Botswana, Brazil, Bulgaria, Burma, Burundi, Byelorussia, Cape Verde, Chile, China, Congo, Cuba, Cyprus, Czechoslovakia, Democratic Kampuchea, Democratic Yemen, Djibouti, Dominican Republic, Ecuador, Egypt, El Salvador, Ethiopia, Fiji, Gabon, German Democratic Republic, Guinea, Guinea-Bissau, Guyana, Hungary, India, Indonesia, Iran, Iraq, Jamaica, Jordan, Kenya, Kuwait, Lao People's Democratic Republic, Lebanon, Lesotho, Libya, Madagascar, Malaysia, Maldives, Mali, Malta, Mauritania, Mauritius, Mexico, Mongolia, Morocco, Mozambique, Nepal, Nicaragua, Nigeria, Oman, Pakistan, Panama, Papua New Guinea, Paraguay,* Peru, Philippines, Poland, Qatar, Romania, Rwanda, Saint Lucia, Sao Tome and Principe, Saudi Arabia, Senegal, Singapore, Somalia, Sri Lanka, Sudan, Suriname, Swaziland, Syria, Thailand, Togo, Trinidad and Tobago, Tunisia, Turkey, Uganda, Ukraine, USSR, United Arab Emirates, United Republic of Cameroon, United Republic of Tanzania, Upper Volta, Uruguay, Venezuela, Viet Nam, Yemen, Yugoslavia, Zambia.
Against:17
Australia, Belgium, Canada, Denmark, Finland, France, Federal Republic of Germany, Iceland, Israel, Italy, Luxembourg, Netherlands, New Zealand, Norway, Sweden, United Kingdom, United States.
Abstentions: 6
Austria, Greece, Ireland, Japan, Portugal, Spain.
Absent: 30
Antigua and Barbuda, Barbados, Belize, Benin,** Central African Republic, Chad, Colombia,** Comoros, Costa Rica, Dominica, Equatorial Guinea, Gambia, Ghana, Grenada, Guatemala, Haiti, Honduras, Ivory Coast, Liberia, Malawi,*** Niger,** Saint Vincent, Samoa, Seychelles, Sierra Leone, Solomon Islands, St. Christopher and Nevis, Vanuatu, Zaire, Zimbabwe.

----

  * Later advised the Secretariat it had intended not to participate.
 ** Later advised the Secretariat it had intended to vote in favour.
*** Later advised the Secretariat it had intended to abstain.

----

[141]See A/CONF.120/13.
[142]A/38/311-S/15883, annex.

[143]Resolution 217 A (III).

Resolution No. 38/35 A, B of 1 December 1983

ON THE FINANCING OF THE UNITED NATIONS DISENGAGEMENT OBSERVER FORCE

A

The General Assembly,

Having considered the report of the Secretary-General on the financing of the United Nations Disengagement Observer Force,[144] as well as the related report of the Advisory Committee on Administrative and Budgetary Questions,[145]

Bearing in mind Security Council resolutions 350 (1974) of 31 May 1974, 363 (1974) of 29 November 1974, 369 (1975) of 28 May 1975, 381 (1975) of 30 November 1975, 390 (1976) of 28 May 1976, 398 (1976) of 30 November 1976, 408 (1977) of 26 May 1977, 420 (1977) of 30 November 1977, 429 (1978) of 31 May 1978, 441 (1978) of 30 November 1978, 449 (1979) of 30 May 1979, 456 (1979) of 30 November 1979, 470 (1980) of 30 May 1980, 481 (1980) of 26 November 1980, 485 (1981) of 22 May 1981, 493 (1981) of 23 November 1981, 506 (1982) of 26 May 1982, 524 (1982) of 29 November 1982, 531 (1983) of 26 May 1983 and 543 (1983) of 29 November 1983,[146]

Recalling its resolutions 3101 (XXVIII) of 11 December 1973, 3211 B (XXIX) of 29 November 1974, 3374 C (XXX) of 2 December 1975, 31/5 D of 22 December 1976, 32/4 C of 2 December 1977, 33/13 D of 8 December 1978, 34/7 C of 3 December 1979, 35/44 of 1 December 1980, 35/45 A of 1 December 1980, 36/66 A of 30 November 1981 and 37/38 A of 30 November 1982,

Reaffirming its previous decisions regarding the fact that, in order to meet the expenditures caused by such operations, a different procedure is required from that applied to meet expenditures of the regular budget of the United Nations,

Taking into account the fact that the economically more developed countries are in a position to make relatively larger contributions and that the economically less developed countries have a relatively limited capacity to contribute towards peace-keeping operations involving heavy expenditures,

Bearing in mind the special responsibilities of the States permanent members of the Security Council in the financing of such operations, as indicated in General Assembly resolution 1874 (S-IV) of 27 June 1963 and other resolutions of the Assembly,

I

Decides to appropriate to the Special Account referred to in section II, paragraph 1, of General Assembly resolution 3211 B (XXIX) the amount of $17,186,496 gross ($16,983,996 net) authorized and apportioned by section III of Assembly resolution 37/38 A for the operation of the United Nations Disengagement Observer Force for the period from 1 June to 30 November 1983, inclusive;

II

1. *Decides* to appropriate to the Special Account an amount of $17,489,500 for the operation of the United Nations Disengagement Observer Force for the period from 1 December 1983 to 31 May 1984, inclusive;

2. *Decides further,* as an *ad hoc* arrangement, without prejudice to the positions of principle that may be taken by Member States in any consideration by the General Assembly of arrangements for the financing of peace-keeping operations, to apportion the amount of $17,489,500 among Member States in accordance with the scheme set out in Assembly resolution 3101 (XXVIII) and the provisions of section II, paragraphs 2 (*b*) and 2(*c*), and section V, paragraph 1, of resolution 3374 C (XXX), section V, paragraph 1, of resolution 31/5 D, section V, paragraph 1, of resolution 32/4 C, section V, paragraph 1, of resolution 33/13 D, section V, paragraph 1, of resolution 34/7 C, section V, paragraph 1, of resolution 35/45 A, section V, paragraph 1, of resolution 36/66 A and section V, paragraph 1, of resolution 37/38 A, in the proportions determined by the scale of assessments for the years 1983, 1984 and 1985;

3. *Decides* that there shall be set off against the apportionment among Member States, as provided in paragraph 2 above, their respective share in the estimated income of $10,000 other than staff assessment income approved for the period from 1 December 1983 to 31 May 1984, inclusive;

4. *Decides* that, in accordance with the provisions of its resolution 973 (X) of 15 December 1955, there shall be set off against the apportionment among Member States, as provided for in paragraph 2 above, their respective share in the Tax Equalization Fund of the estimated staff assessment income of $199,500 approved for the period from 1 December 1983 to 31 May 1984, inclusive;

III

Authorizes the Secretary-General to enter into commitments for the United Nations Disengagement Observer Force at a rate not to exceed $2,914,916 gross ($2,880,000 net) per month for the period from 1 June to 30 November 1984 inclusive, should the Security Council decide to continue the Force beyond the period of six months authorized under its resolution 543 (1983), the said amount to be apportioned among Member States in accordance with the scheme set out in the present resolution;

IV

1. *Stresses* the need for voluntary contributions to the United Nations Disengagement Observer Force, both in cash and in the form of services and supplies acceptable to the Secretary-General;

2. *Requests* the Secretary-General to take all necessary action to ensure that the United Nations Disengagement

---

[144] A/38/472 and Corr.1.

[145] A/38/588.

[146] The resolutions cited in this paragraph and the next provide for the renewed mandate and financing of the United Nations Disengagement Observer Force. [ed. note]

Observer Force is conducted with a maximum of efficiency and economy.

Adopted at the 79th plenary meeting:
In favour: 109
Antigua and Barbuda, Argentina, Australia, Austria, Bangladesh, Barbados, Belgium, Belize, Bhutan, Botswana, Brazil, Burma, Canada, Cape Verde, Central African Republic, Chad, Chile, China, Colombia, Comoros, Costa Rica, Cyprus, Democratic Kampuchea, Democratic Yemen, Denmark, Ecuador, Egypt, El Salvador, Equatorial Guinea, Fiji, Finland, France, Gabon, Federal Republic of Germany, Ghana, Greece, Guatemala, Guinea-Bissau, Guyana, Honduras, Iceland, India, Indonesia, Ireland, Israel, Italy, Jamaica, Jordan, Kenya, Kuwait, Lebanon, Liberia, Luxembourg, Madagascar, Malawi, Malaysia, Mali, Malta, Mauritania, Mauritius, Mexico, Morocco, Nepal, Netherlands, New Zealand, Niger, Nigeria, Norway, Oman, Pakistan, Panama, Papua New Guinea, Peru, Philippines, Poland, Portugal, Qatar, Romania, Rwanda, Saint Lucia, Samoa, Saudi Arabia, Senegal, Singapore, Solomon Islands, Somalia, Spain, Sri Lanka, Sudan, Suriname, Sweden, Thailand, Togo, Trinidad and Tobago, Tunisia, Turkey, Uganda, United Arab Emirates, United Kingdom, United Republic of Cameroon, United Republic of Tanzania, United States, Upper Volta, Uruguay, Vanuatu, Venezuela, Yugoslavia, Zaire, Zambia, Zimbabwe.
Against: 3
Albania, Democratic Yemen, Syria.
Abstentions: 14
Algeria, Bulgaria, Byelorussia, Congo, Cuba, Czechoslovakia, German Democratic Republic, Hungary, Iraq, Ivory Coast, Mongolia, Ukraine, USSR, Yemen.
Absent: 30
Afghanistan, Angola, Bahamas,* Bahrain,* Benin, Bolivia, Burundi, Djibouti, Dominica, Dominican Republic, Ethiopia, Gambia, Grenada, Guinea, Haiti, Iran, Japan, Lao People's Democratic Republic, Lesotho, Maldives, Mozambique, Nicaragua, Paraguay, Saint Vincent, Sao Tome and Principe, Seychelles, Sierra Leone, St. Christopher and Nevis, Swaziland, Viet Nam.

Libya announced that it was not participating in the vote.

---

* Later advised the Secretariat it had intended to vote in favour.

B

The General Assembly,
Having regard to the financial position of the Special Account for the United Nations Emergency Force and the United Nations Disengagement Observer Force, as set forth in the report of the Secretary-General,[147] and referring to paragraph 5 of the report of the Advisory Committee on Administrative and Budgetary Questions,[148]

Mindful of the fact that it is essential to provide the United Nations Disengagement Observer Force with the necessary financial resources to enable it to fulfil its responsibilities under the relevant resolutions of the Security Council,

Concerned that the Secretary-General is continuing to face growing difficulties in meeting the obligations of the Forces on a current basis, particularly those due to the Governments of troop-contributing States,

Recalling its resolutions 33/13 E of 14 December 1978, 34/7 D of 17 December 1979, 35/45 B of 1 December 1980, 36/66 B of 30 November 1981 and 37/38 B of 30 November 1982,

Recognizing that, in consequence of the withholding of contributions by certain Member States, the surplus balances in the Special Account for the United Nations Emergency Force and the United Nations Disengagement Observer Force have, in effect, been drawn upon to the full extent to supplement the income received from contributions for meeting expenses of the Forces,

Concerned that the application of the provisions of regulations 5.2(*b*), 5.2(*d*), 4.3 and 4.4 of the Financial Regulations of the United Nations would aggravate the already difficult financial situation of the Forces,

Decides that the provisions of regulations 5.2(*b*), 5.2(*d*), 4.3 and 4.4 of the Financial Regulations of the United Nations shall be suspended in respect of the amount of $5,191,637, which otherwise would have to be surrendered pursuant to those provisions, this amount to be entered into the account referred to in the operative part of General Assembly resolution 33/13 E and held in suspense until a further decision is taken by the Assembly.

Adopted at the 79th plenary meeting:
In favour: 108
Antigua and Barbuda, Argentina, Australia, Austria, Bahrain, Bangladesh, Barbados, Belgium, Belize, Bhutan, Brazil, Burma, Canada, Cape Verde, Central African Republic, Chad, Chile, China, Colombia, Comoros, Costa Rica, Cyprus, Democratic Kampuchea, Denmark, Ecuador, Egypt, El Salvador, Equatorial Guinea, Fiji, Finland, France, Gabon, Federal Republic of Germany, Ghana, Greece, Guatemala, Guyana, Honduras, Iceland, India, Indonesia, Ireland, Israel, Italy, Ivory Coast, Jamaica, Jordan, Kenya, Kuwait, Lebanon, Liberia, Luxembourg, Madagascar, Malawi, Malaysia, Mali, Malta, Mauritania, Mauritius, Mexico, Morocco, Nepal, Netherlands, New Zealand, Nicaragua, Niger, Nigeria, Norway, Oman, Pakistan, Panama, Papua New Guinea, Peru, Philippines, Portugal, Qatar, Rwanda, Saint Lucia, Samoa, Saudi Arabia, Senegal, Singapore, Solomon Islands, Somalia, Spain, Sri Lanka, Sudan, Suriname, Sweden, Thailand, Togo, Trinidad and Tobago, Tunisia, Turkey, Uganda, United Arab Emirates, United Kingdom, United Republic of Cameroon, United Republic of Tanzania, United States, Upper Volta, Uruguay, Vanuatu, Venezuela, Yugoslavia, Zaire, Zambia, Zimbabwe.
Against: 12
Albania, Bulgaria, Byelorussia, Cuba, Czechoslovakia, Democratic Yemen, German Democratic Republic, Hungary, Mongolia, Syria, Ukraine, USSR.

---

[147] A/38/472 and Corr.1.
[148] A/38/588.

Abstentions: 6
Algeria, Congo, Iraq, Poland, Romania, Yemen.
Absent: 30
Afghanistan, Angola, Bahamas,* Benin, Bolivia, Botswana, Burundi, Djibouti, Dominica, Dominican Republic, Ethiopia, Gambia, Grenada, Guinea, Guinea-Bissau, Haiti, Iran, Japan, Lao People's Democratic Republic, Lesotho, Maldives, Mozambique, Paraguay, Saint Vincent, Sao Tome and Principe, Seychelles, Sierra Leone, St. Christopher and Nevis, Swaziland, Viet Nam.

Libya announced that it was not participating in the vote.

_____

* Later advised the Secretariat it had intended to vote in favour.

Resolution No. 38/36 A, D of 1 December 1983

CONDEMNING MILITARY AND NUCLEAR COLLABORATION ON THE PART OF ISRAEL AND CERTAIN WESTERN STATES AND SOUTH AFRICA [EXCERPTS FROM A RESOLUTION ON NAMIBIA]

A

SITUATION IN NAMIBIA RESULTING FROM THE ILLEGAL OCCUPATION OF THE TERRITORY BY SOUTH AFRICA

The General Assembly,

....

Deeply deploring the continued collaboration with South Africa of certain Western States, in particular the United States of America, as well as that of Israel, in disregard of the relevant resolutions of the General Assembly and the Security Council,

....

25. *Condemns* the increased assistance rendered by the major Western countries and Israel to South Africa in the political, economic, financial and particularly the military fields, expresses its conviction that this assistance constitutes a hostile action against the people of Namibia and the front-line States since it is bound to strengthen the military capability of the racist régime, and demands that such assistance be immediately terminated;

....

32. *Condemns* the continuing military and nuclear collaboration on the part of certain Western States and Israel with the racist régime of South Africa, which is encouraging the Pretoria régime in its defiance of the international community and obstructing efforts to eliminate *apartheid* and bring South Africa's illegal occupation of Namibia to an end, and urges those States to cease and desist forthwith from such collaboration with South Africa, which is in violation of the arms embargo imposed against South Africa under Security Council resolution 418 (1977) of 4 November 1977;

33. *Expresses its grave concern* at the acquisition of nuclear weapons capability by the racist régime of South Africa, with its record of violence and aggression, and declares that such acquisition constitutes a further attempt on its part to terrorize and intimidate independent States in the region into submission, while also posing a danger to all mankind;

34. *Strongly condemns* the collusion by the Governments of certain Western and other States, particularly those of the United States of America and Israel, with the racist régime of South Africa in the nuclear field and calls upon France and all other States to refrain from supplying the racist minority régime of South Africa, directly or indirectly, with installations that might enable it to produce uranium, plutonium or other nuclear materials, reactors or military equipment;

....

Adopted at the 79th plenary meeting:
In favour: 117
Afghanistan, Albania, Algeria, Angola, Antigua and Barbuda, Argentina, Bahamas, Bahrain, Bangladesh, Barbados, Belize, Benin, Bhutan, Bolivia, Botswana, Brazil, Bulgaria, Burma, Burundi, Byelorussia, Cape Verde, China, Comoros, Congo, Costa Rica, Cuba, Cyprus, Czechoslovakia, Democratic Kampuchea, Democratic Yemen, Djibouti, Dominican Republic, Ecuador, Egypt, El Salvador, Equatorial Guinea, Ethiopia, Fiji, Gabon, German Democratic Republic, Ghana, Greece, Guinea, Guinea-Bissau, Guyana, Haiti, Honduras, Hungary, India, Indonesia, Iran, Iraq, Jamaica, Jordan, Kenya, Kuwait, Lao People's Democratic Republic, Lebanon, Libya, Madagascar, Malaysia, Maldives, Mali, Malta, Mauritania, Mauritius, Mexico, Mongolia, Morocco, Mozambique, Nepal, Nicaragua, Niger, Nigeria, Oman, Pakistan, Panama, Papua New Guinea, Peru, Philippines, Poland, Qatar, Romania, Rwanda, Saint Vincent, Sao Tome and Principe, Saudi Arabia, Senegal, Seychelles, Sierra Leone, Singapore, Sri Lanka, Sudan, Suriname, Swaziland, Syria, Thailand, Togo, Trinidad and Tobago, Tunisia, Turkey, Uganda, Ukraine, USSR, United Arab Emirates, United Republic of Cameroon, United Republic of Tanzania, Upper Volta, Uruguay, Vanuatu, Venezuela, Viet Nam, Yemen, Yugoslavia, Zaire, Zambia, Zimbabwe.
Against: 0
Abstentions: 28
Australia, Austria, Belgium, Canada, Central African Republic, Chad, Denmark, Finland, France, Federal Republic of Germany, Iceland, Ireland, Italy, Ivory Coast, Japan, Luxembourg, Malawi, Netherlands, New Zealand, Norway, Portugal, Saint Lucia, Samoa, Solomon Islands, Spain, Sweden, United Kingdom, United States.
Absent: 12
Chile, Colombia, Dominica, Gambia,* Grenada, Guatemala, Israel, Lesotho,** Liberia, Paraguay, Somalia,* St. Christopher and Nevis.

_____

* Later advised the Secretariat it had intended to vote in favour.
** Later advised the Secretariat it had intended to abstain.

_____

D

DISSEMINATION OF INFORMATION AND MOBILIZATION OF INTERNATIONAL PUBLIC OPINION IN SUPPORT OF NAMIBIA

The General Assembly,

....

4. *Decides* to intensify its international campaign in support of the cause of Namibia and to expose and denounce the collusion of the United States of America, certain other Western States and Israel with the South African racists and, to this end, requests the United Nations Council for Namibia to include in its programme of dissemination of information for 1984 the following activities:

(*a*) Preparation and dissemination of publications on the political, economic, military and social consequences of the illegal occupation of Namibia by South Africa, as well as on legal matters, on the question of the territorial integrity of Namibia and on contacts between Member States and South Africa;

(*b*) Production and dissemination of radio programmes in English, French, German and Spanish designed to draw the attention of world public opinion to the current situation in Namibia;

(*c*) Production of material for publicity through radio and television broadcasts;

(*d*) Placement of advertisements in newspapers and magazines;

(*e*) Production of films, film-strips and slide sets on Namibia;

(*f*) Production and dissemination of posters;

(*g*) Full utilization of the resources related to press releases, press conferences and press briefings in order to maintain a constant flow of information to the public on all aspects of the question of Namibia;

(*h*) Production and dissemination of a comprehensive economic map of Namibia;

(*i*) Preparation and wide dissemination of a booklet containing resolutions of the General Assembly and the Security Council relating to Namibia, together with relevant portions of Assembly resolutions on the activities of foreign economic interests in Namibia and on military activities in Namibia;

(*j*) Publicity for and distribution of an indexed reference book on transnational corporations involved in Namibia;

(*k*) Preparation and dissemination of a booklet based on a study on the implementation of Decree No. 1 for the Protection of the Natural Resources of Namibia,[149] enacted by the Council on 27 September 1974;

(*l*) Acquisition of books, pamphlets and other materials relating to Namibia for further dissemination;

....

Adopted at the 79th plenary meeting:

In favour: 122

Afghanistan, Albania, Algeria, Angola, Antigua and Barbuda, Argentina, Bahamas, Bahrain, Bangladesh, Barbados, Belize, Benin, Bhutan, Bolivia, Botswana, Brazil, Bulgaria, Burma, Burundi, Byelorussia, Cape Verde, Chile, China, Colombia, Comoros, Congo, Costa Rica, Cuba, Cyprus, Czechoslovakia, Democratic Kampuchea, Democratic Yemen, Djibouti, Dominican Republic, Ecuador, Egypt, El Salvador, Equatorial Guinea, Ethiopia, Fiji, Gabon, German Democratic Republic, Ghana, Greece, Guinea, Guinea-Bissau, Guyana, Haiti, Honduras, Hungary, India, Indonesia, Iran, Iraq, Ivory Coast, Jamaica, Jordan, Kenya, Kuwait, Lao People's Democratic Republic, Lebanon, Libya, Madagascar, Malawi, Malaysia, Maldives, Mali, Malta, Mauritania, Mauritius, Mexico, Mongolia, Morocco, Mozambique, Nepal, Nicaragua, Niger, Nigeria, Oman, Pakistan, Panama, Papua New Guinea, Peru, Philippines, Poland, Qatar, Romania, Rwanda, Saint Lucia, Saint Vincent, Sao Tome and Principe, Saudi Arabia, Senegal, Seychelles, Sierra Leone, Singapore, Sri Lanka, Sudan, Suriname, Swaziland, Syria, Thailand, Togo, Trinidad and Tobago, Tunisia, Turkey, Uganda, Ukraine, USSR, United Arab Emirates, United Republic of Cameroon, United Republic of Tanzania, Upper Volta, Uruguay, Vanuatu, Venezuela, Viet Nam, Yemen, Yugoslavia, Zaire, Zambia, Zimbabwe.

Against: 0

Abstentions: 22

Australia, Austria, Belgium, Canada, Chad, Denmark, Finland, France, Federal Republic of Germany, Iceland, Ireland, Italy, Japan, Luxembourg, Netherlands, New Zealand, Norway, Portugal, Spain, Sweden, United Kingdom, United States.

Absent: 13

Central African Republic, Dominica, Gambia,* Grenada, Guatemala, Israel, Lesotho,* Liberia, Paraguay, Samoa, Solomon Islands, Somalia,* St. Christopher and Nevis.

----

* Later advised the Secretariat it had intended to vote in favour.

Resolution No. 38/38 A, B of 5 December 1983

ON THE FINANCING OF THE UNITED NATIONS INTERIM FORCE IN LEBANON

A

The General Assembly,

Having considered the report of the Secretary-General on the financing of the United Nations Interim Force in Lebanon[150] and the related report of the Advisory Committee on Administrative and Budgetary Questions,[151]

Bearing in mind Security Council resolutions 425 (1978) and 426 (1978) of 19 March 1978, 427 (1978) of 3 May 1978, 434 (1978) of 18 September 1978, 444 (1979) of 19 January 1979, 450 (1979) of 14 June 1979, 459 (1979) of 19 December 1979, 474 (1980) of 17 June 1980, 483

----

[149]*Official Records of the General Assembly, Thirty-fifth Session, Supplement No. 24* (A/35/24), vol.1, annex II.

[150]A/38/473 and Corr.1.
[151]A/38/589.

(1980) of 17 December 1980, 488 (1981) of 19 June 1981, 498 (1981) of 18 December 1981, 501 (1982) of 25 February 1982, 511 (1982) of 18 June 1982, 519 (1982) of 17 August 1982, 523 (1982) of 18 October 1982, 529 (1983) of 18 January 1983, 536 (1983) of 18 July 1983 and 538 (1983) of 18 October 1983,[152]

Recalling its resolutions S-8/2 of 21 April 1978, 33/14 of 3 November 1978, 34/9 B of 17 December 1979, 35/44 of 1 December 1980, 35/115 A of 10 December 1980, 36/138 A of 16 December 1981, 36/138 C of 19 March 1982 and 37/127 A of 17 December 1982,

Reaffirming its previous decisions regarding the fact that, in order to meet the expenditures caused by such operations, a different procedure from the one applied to meet expenditures of the regular budget of the United Nations is required,

Taking into account the fact that the economically more developed countries are in a position to make relatively larger contributions and that the economically less developed countries have a relatively limited capacity to contribute towards peace-keeping operations involving heavy expenditures,

Bearing in mind the special responsibilities of the States permanent members of the Security Council in the financing of peace-keeping operations decided upon in accordance with the Charter of the United Nations,

I

Decides to appropriate to the Special Account referred to in section 1, paragraph 1, of General Assembly resolution S-8/2 an amount of $15,229,666 gross ($15,087,833 net), being the amount authorized and apportioned under the provisions of section V of Assembly resolution 37/127 A for the operation of the United Nations Interim Force in Lebanon from 19 December 1982 to 18 January 1983, inclusive;

II

Decides to appropriate to the Special Account an amount of $80,331,000 gross ($79,466,000 net), being the amount authorized with the prior concurrence of the Advisory Committee on Administrative and Budgetary Questions and apportioned under the provisions of section VI of General Assembly resolution 37/127 A for the operation of the United Nations Interim Force in Lebanon from 19 January to 18 July 1983, inclusive;

III

Decides to appropriate to the Special Account an amount of $40,379,000 gross ($39,925,000 net), being the amount authorized with the prior concurrence of the Advisory Committee on Administrative and Budgetary Questions and apportioned under the provisions of section VI of General Assembly resolution 37/127 A for the operation

of the United Nations Interim Force in Lebanon from 19 July to 18 October 1983, inclusive;

IV

Decides to appropriate to the Special Account an amount of $23,482,000 gross ($23,162,000 net), being the amount authorized with the prior concurrence of the Advisory Committee on Administrative and Budgetary Questions and apportioned under the provisions of section VI of General Assembly resolution 37/127 A for the operation of the United Nations Interim Force in Lebanon from 19 October to 18 December 1983, inclusive;

V

1. *Decides* to appropriate to the Special Account an amount of $46,964,000 for the operation of the United Nations Interim Force in Lebanon for the period from 19 December 1983 to 18 April 1984, inclusive;

2. *Decides further,* as an *ad hoc* arrangement, without prejudice to the positions of principle that may be taken by Member States in any consideration by the General Assembly of arrangements for the financing of peace-keeping operations, to apportion the amount of $46,964,000 among Member States in accordance with the scheme set out in Assembly resolution 33/14 and the provisions of section V, paragraph 1, of resolution 34/9 B, section VI, paragraph 1, of resolution 35/115 A, section VI, paragraph 1, of resolution 36/138 A and section IX, paragraph 1, of resolution 37/127 A, in the proportions determined by the scale of assessments for the years 1983, 1984 and 1985;

3. *Decides* that there shall be set off against the apportionment among Member States, as provided in paragraph 2 above, their respective share in the estimated income of $13,333 other than staff assessment income approved for the period from 19 December 1983 to 18 April 1984, inclusive;

4. *Decides* that, in accordance with the provisions of its resolution 973 (X) of 15 December 1955, there shall be set off against the apportionment among Member States, as provided for in paragraph 2 above, their respective share in the Tax Equalization Fund of the estimated staff assessment income of $626,667 approved for the period from 19 December 1983 to 18 April 1984, inclusive;

VI

Authorizes the Secretary-General to enter into commitments for the operation of the United Nations Interim Force in Lebanon at a rate not to exceed $11,741,000 gross ($11,581,000 net) per month for the period from 19 April to 18 December 1984, inclusive, should the Security Council decide to continue the Force beyond the period of six months authorized under its resolution 538 (1983), subject to obtaining the prior concurrence of the Advisory Committee on Administrative and Budgetary Questions for the actual level of commitments to be entered into for each mandate period that may be approved subsequent to 19 April 1984, the said amount to be apportioned among Member States in accordance with the scheme set

---

[152]The resolutions cited in this and the next paragraph refer to the renewal of the mandate and the financing of the United Nations Interim Force in Lebanon. [ed. note]

out in the present resolution;

VII

1. *Renews its invitation* to Member States to make voluntary contributions to the United Nations Interim Force in Lebanon both in cash and in the form of services and supplies acceptable to the Secretary-General;

2. *Invites* Members States to make voluntary contributions in cash to the Suspense Account established in accordance with its resolution 34/9 D of 17 December 1979;

VIII

Requests the Secretary-General to take all necessary action to ensure that the United Nations Interim Force in Lebanon shall be administered with a maximum of efficiency and economy.

B

The General Assembly,

Having regard to the financial position of the Special Account for the United Nations Interim Force in Lebanon, as set forth in the report of the Secretary-General,[153] and referring to paragraph 7 of the report of the Advisory Committee on Administrative and Budgetary Questions,[154]

Mindful of the fact that it is essential to provide the United Nations Interim Force in Lebanon with the necessary financial resources to enable it to fulfil its responsibilities under the relevant resolutions of the Security Council,

Concerned that the Secretary-General is continuing to face growing difficulties in meeting the obligations of the United Nations Interim Force in Lebanon on a current basis, particularly those due to the Governments of troop-contributing States,

Recalling its resolutions 34/9 E of 17 December 1979, 35/115 B of 10 December 1980, 36/138 B of 16 December 1981 and 37/127 B of 17 December 1982,

Recognizing that, in consequence of the withholding of contributions by certain Member States, the surplus balances in the Special Account for the United Nations Interim Force in Lebanon have, in effect, been drawn upon to the full extent to supplement the income received from contributions for meeting expenses of the Force,

Concerned that the application of the provisions of regulations 5.2(*b*), 5.2(*d*), 4.3 and 4.4 of the Financial Regulations of the United Nations would aggravate the already difficult financial situation of the United Nations Interim Force in Lebanon,

Decides that the provisions of regulations 5.2(*b*), 5.2(*d*), 4.3 and 4.4 of the Financial Regulations of the United Nations shall be suspended in respect of the amount of $5,599,876, which otherwise would have to be surrendered pursuant to those provisions, this amount to be entered in the account referred to in the operative part of General Assembly resolution 34/9 E and held in suspense

until a further decision is taken by the Assembly.

Both resolutions were adopted together at the 83rd plenary meeting:

In favour: 80
Australia, Austria, Bahrain, Belgium, Bhutan, Bolivia, Brazil, Canada, Chad, Chile, China, Costa Rica, Cyprus, Denmark, Ecuador, Egypt, El Salvador, Ethiopia, Fiji, Finland, France, Gabon, Federal Republic of Germany, Ghana, Greece, Guatemala, Honduras, Iceland, India, Indonesia, Ireland, Israel, Italy, Ivory Coast, Japan, Jordan, Kuwait, Lebanon, Lesotho, Malaysia, Mali, Malta, Mauritania, Mexico, Nepal, Netherlands, New Zealand, Nicaragua, Nigeria, Norway, Oman, Pakistan, Panama, Philippines, Portugal, Romania, Saint Lucia, Samoa, Saudi Arabia, Singapore, Somalia, Spain, Sudan, Suriname, Swaziland, Sweden, Thailand, Trinidad and Tobago, Tunisia, Turkey, Uganda, United Arab Emirates, United Kingdom, United Republic of Cameroon, United Republic of Tanzania, United States, Uruguay, Venezuela, Yugoslavia, Zambia.

Against: 11
Albania, Bulgaria, Byelorussia, Cuba, German Democratic Republic, Hungary, Mongolia, Poland, Syria, Ukraine, USSR.

Abstentions: 7
Afghanistan, Burundi, Cape Verde, Congo, Iraq, Maldives, Yemen.

Absent: 58
Algeria, Angola, Antigua and Barbuda, Argentina, Bahamas, Bangladesh, Barbados, Belize, Benin, Botswana, Burma,* Central African Republic, Colombia, Comoros, Czechoslovakia, Democratic Kampuchea, Democratic Yemen, Djibouti, Dominica, Dominican Republic, Equatorial Guinea, Gambia, Grenada, Guinea, Guinea-Bissau, Guyana, Haiti, Iran, Jamaica, Kenya, Lao People's Democratic Republic, Liberia, Luxembourg, Madagascar, Malawi,* Mauritius, Morocco,* Mozambique, Niger, Papua New Guinea, Paraguay, Peru, Qatar,* Rwanda, St. Christopher and Nevis, Saint Vincent, Sao Tome and Principe, Senegal, Seychelles, Sierra Leone, Solomon Islands,* Sri Lanka, Togo,* Upper Volta, Vanuatu, Viet Nam,** Zaire,* Zimbabwe.

Libya announced that it was not participating in the vote.

---

* Later advised the Secretariat it had intended to vote in favour.
** Later advised the Secretariat it had intended to vote against.

Resolution No. 38/39 A, F, G of 5 December 1983

CONDEMNING COLLABORATION BETWEEN ISRAEL AND SOUTH AFRICA, ESPECIALLY IN THE MILITARY AND NUCLEAR FIELDS [EXCERPTS FROM A RESOLUTION ON THE *APARTHEID* POLICIES OF THE SOUTH AFRICAN GOVERNMENT]

A

SITUATION IN SOUTH AFRICA

---

[153]A/38/473 and Corr.1.
[154]A/38/589.

The General Assembly,

....

Having considered the report of the Special Committee against *Apartheid,*[155] as well as its special report on recent developments concerning relations between Israel and South Africa,[156]

....

Recognizing that the policies and actions of certain Western Powers and Israel are the main obstacles that have frustrated international efforts for the elimination of *apartheid,*

Condemning, in particular, the increased collaboration by the Government of the United States of America with the racist régime of South Africa, in pursuance of its policy of so-called "constructive engagement", which has encouraged the racist régime to entrench *apartheid,* intensify repression and escalate aggression against and destabilization of independent African States,

Condemning the increasing collaboration by Israel with the racist minority régime of South Africa, particularly in the military and nuclear fields,

....

1. *Endorses* the annual report of the Special Committee against *Apartheid* and its special report on recent developments concerning relations between Israel and South Africa;

....

12. *Condemns* the policies of certain Western States, especially the United States of America, and Israel, and of their transnational corporations and financial institutions that have increased political, economic and military collaboration with the racist minority régime of South Africa despite repeated appeals by the General Assembly;

....

22. *Requests* the Special Committee:

(*a*) To prepare a report reviewing the implementation of the resolutions of the General Assembly and the Security Council on the problem of *apartheid* and the acts of aggression by the racist régime of South Africa, and the policies and actions of States which have failed to co-operate in international action;

(*b*) To review developments concerning collaboration by the United States of America, Israel and other States with the racist régime of South Africa, and to report from time to time, as appropriate;

(*c*) To pay special attention to mobilizing public opinion and encouraging public action against collaboration with South Africa.

Adopted at the 83rd plenary meeting:

In favour: 124

Afghanistan, Albania, Algeria, Angola, Antigua and Barbuda, Argentina, Bahamas, Bahrain, Bangladesh, Barba-

dos, Belize, Benin, Bhutan, Bolivia, Botswana, Brazil, Bulgaria, Burma, Burundi, Byelorussia, Cape Verde, Central African Republic, Chad, China, Colombia, Comoros, Congo, Costa Rica, Cuba, Cyprus, Czechoslovakia, Democratic Kampuchea, Democratic Yemen, Djibouti, Dominican Republic, Ecuador, Egypt, El Salvador, Equatorial Guinea, Ethiopia, Fiji, Gabon, Gambia, German Democratic Republic, Ghana, Guinea, Guinea-Bissau, Guyana, Haiti, Honduras, Hungary, India, Indonesia, Iran, Iraq, Jamaica, Jordan, Kenya, Kuwait, Lao People's Democratic Republic, Lebanon, Lesotho, Libya, Madagascar, Malaysia, Maldives, Mali, Malta, Mauritania, Mauritius, Mexico, Mongolia, Morocco, Mozambique, Nepal, Nicaragua, Niger, Nigeria, Norway, Oman, Pakistan, Panama, Papua New Guinea, Peru, Philippines, Poland, Qatar, Romania, Rwanda, Saint Lucia, Saint Vincent, Samoa, Sao Tome and Principe, Saudi Arabia, Senegal, Seychelles, Sierra Leone, Singapore, Solomon Islands, Somalia, Sri Lanka, Sudan, Suriname, Syria, Thailand, Togo, Trinidad and Tobago, Tunisia, Turkey, Uganda, Ukraine, USSR, United Arab Emirates, United Republic of Cameroon, United Republic of Tanzania, Upper Volta, Uruguay, Vanuatu, Venezuela, Viet Nam, Yemen, Yugoslavia, Zaire, Zambia, Zimbabwe.

Against: 16

Australia, Belgium, Canada, France, Federal Republic of Germany, Iceland, Italy, Japan, Luxembourg, Netherlands, New Zealand, Norway, Paraguay, Portugal, United Kingdom, United States.

Abstentions: 10

Austria, Denmark, Finland, Greece, Guatemala, Ireland, Ivory Coast, Malawi, Spain, Sweden.

Absent: 6

Chile, Dominica, Grenada, Liberia, St. Christopher and Nevis, Swaziland.

Israel announced that it was not participating in the vote.

F

RELATIONS BETWEEN ISRAEL AND SOUTH AFRICA

The General Assembly,

Reaffirming its resolutions on relations between Israel and South Africa,

Having considered the special report of the Special Committee against *Apartheid* on recent developments concerning relations between Israel and South Africa, [157]

Taking note of the Declaration of the International Conference on the Alliance between South Africa and Israel,[158] and the Declaration of the Second World Conference to Combat Racism and Racial Discrimination,[159]

Alarmed at the increasing collaboration by Israel with

---

[155] *Official Records of the General Assembly, Thirty-eighth Session, Supplement No. 22* (A/38/22).

[156] *Ibid., Supplement No. 22A* (A/38/22/Add.1).

[157] *Ibid., Supplement No. 22A* (A/38/22/Add.1).

[158] A/38/311-S/15883, annex.

[159] See *Report of the Second World Conference to Combat Racism and Racial Discrimination, Geneva, 1-12 August 1983* (United Nations publication, Sales No. E.83.XIV.4 and corrigendum), chap. II.

the racist régime of South Africa, especially in the military and nuclear fields, in defiance of resolutions of the General Assembly and the Security Council,

Considering that such collaboration is a serious hindrance to international action for the eradication of *apartheid,* an encouragement to the racist régime of South Africa to persist in its criminal policy of *apartheid* and a hostile act against the oppressed people of South Africa and the entire African continent, and constitutes a threat to international peace and security,

1. *Again strongly condemns* the continuing and increasing collaboration by Israel with the racist régime of South Africa, especially in the military and nuclear fields;

2. *Demands* that Israel desist from and terminate forthwith all forms of collaboration with South Africa, particularly in the military and nuclear fields, and abide scrupulously by the relevant resolutions of the General Assembly and the Security Council;

3. *Calls upon* all Governments and organizations to exert their influence to persuade Israel to desist from such collaboration and abide by the resolutions of the General Assembly;

4. *Requests* the Special Committee against *Apartheid* to publicize, as widely as possible, information on the relations between Israel and South Africa and especially the Declaration of the International Conference on the Alliance between South Africa and Israel;

5. *Requests* the Secretary-General to render, through the Department of Public Information and the Centre against *Apartheid* of the Secretariat, all possible assistance to the Special Committee in disseminating information relating to the collaboration between Israel and South Africa;

6. *Further requests* the Special Committee to keep the matter under constant review and to report to the General Assembly and the Security Council as appropriate.

Adopted at the 83rd plenary meeting:
In favour: 106
Afghanistan, Albania, Algeria, Angola, Antigua and Barbuda, Argentina, Bahrain, Bangladesh, Benin, Bhutan, Bolivia, Botswana, Brazil, Bulgaria, Burma, Burundi, Byelorussia, Cape Verde, Central African Republic, Chad, China, Comoros, Congo, Cuba, Cyprus, Czechoslovakia, Democratic Kampuchea, Democratic Yemen, Djibouti, Ecuador, Egypt, Equatorial Guinea, Ethiopia, Gabon, Gambia, German Democratic Republic, Ghana, Greece, Grenada, Guinea, Guinea-Bissau, Guyana, Hungary, India, Indonesia, Iran, Iraq, Jordan, Kenya, Kuwait, Lao People's Democratic Republic, Lebanon, Lesotho, Libya, Madagascar, Malaysia, Maldives, Mali, Malta, Mauritania, Mauritius, Mexico, Mongolia, Morocco, Mozambique, Nepal, Nicaragua, Niger, Nigeria, Oman, Pakistan, Papua New Guinea, Peru, Philippines, Poland, Qatar, Romania, Rwanda, Sao Tome and Principe, Saudi Arabia, Senegal, Seychelles, Sierra Leone, Singapore, Somalia, Sri Lanka, Sudan, Syria, Thailand, Togo, Tunisia, Turkey, Uganda, Ukraine, USSR, United Arab Emirates, United Republic of Cameroon, United Republic of Tanzania, Upper Volta, Uruguay,* Vanuatu, Venezuela, Viet Nam, Yemen, Yugo-

slavia, Zambia, Zimbabwe.
Against: 18
Australia, Austria, Belgium, Canada, Denmark, Finland, France, Federal Republic of Germany, Iceland, Ireland, Italy, Luxembourg, Netherlands, New Zealand, Norway, Sweden, United Kingdom, United States.
Abstentions: 17
Bahamas, Colombia, Costa Rica, Dominican Republic, Fiji, Guatemala, Haiti, Ivory Coast, Jamaica, Japan, Malawi, Panama, Paraguay, Portugal, Samoa, Solomon Islands, Spain.
Absent: 15
Barbados, Belize, Chile, Dominica, El Salvador, Grenada, Honduras, Liberia, Saint Lucia, Saint Vincent, St. Christopher and Nevis, Suriname, Swaziland, Trinidad and Tobago, Zaire.

Israel announced that it was not participating in the vote.

---

* Later advised the Secretariat it had intended to abstain.

G

MILITARY AND NUCLEAR COLLABORATION WITH SOUTH AFRICA

The General Assembly,
Reaffirming its resolutions on military and nuclear collaboration with South Africa, in particular its resolution 37/69 D of 9 December 1982,
Recalling its resolutions concerning the denuclearization of the continent of Africa,

....

Gravely concerned that, despite the arms embargo imposed by the Security Council, the racist régime of South Africa has continued to obtain from certain Western States and Israel military equipment and ammunition, as well as technology and know-how to develop its armaments industry and nuclear-weapon capability,

Noting with grave concern that military and nuclear collaboration by certain Western States and Israel with South Africa has enabled the racist régime to develop its arms production and become an arms-exporting country,

Recognizing that the stepped-up arms buildup and nuclear-weapon capability, as well as escalating acts of aggression by the racist régime of South Africa, constitute a grave threat to international peace and security,

Expressing alarm at the growing violation of the arms embargo, as well as the continued nuclear collaboration by the United States of America and some other Western States and Israel with the *apartheid* régime,

Condemning the actions of those transnational corporations that continue, through their collaboration with the racist régime of South Africa, to enhance its military and nuclear capabilities, as well as the failure of the Governments of the home countries of those corporations to take effective action to prevent such collaboration in accordance with the relevant resolutions of the United Nations,

Considering the urgent need for mandatory decisions by the Security Council, under Chapter VII of the Charter, to prohibit any military and nuclear collaboration with the racist régime of South Africa,

1. *Urges* the Security Council to take mandatory decisions, under Chapter VII of the Charter of the United Nations, to ensure the total cessation of all military and nuclear co-operation with the racist régime of South Africa by Governments, corporations, institutions and individuals;

2. *Strongly condemns* the actions of certain Western States and Israel which have provided the racist régime of South Africa with an enormous arsenal of military equipment and technology, as well as assistance in its nuclear plans, and which have allowed corporations under their jurisdiction to invest in the armaments industry in South Africa;

....

Adopted at the 83rd plenary meeting:

In favour: 122

Afghanistan, Albania, Algeria, Angola, Antigua and Barbuda, Argentina, Bahamas, Bahrain, Bangladesh, Barbados, Belize, Benin, Bhutan, Bolivia, Botswana, Brazil, Bulgaria, Burma, Burundi, Byelorussia, Cape Verde, Central African Republic, Chad, Chile, China, Colombia, Comoros, Congo, Cuba, Cyprus, Czechoslovakia, Democratic Kampuchea, Democratic Yemen, Djibouti, Dominican Republic, Ecuador, Egypt, Equatorial Guinea, Ethiopia, Fiji, Gabon, Gambia, German Democratic Republic, Ghana, Guinea, Guinea-Bissau, Guyana, Haiti, Hungary, India, Indonesia, Iran, Iraq, Jamaica, Jordan, Kenya, Kuwait, Lao People's Democratic Republic, Lebanon, Lesotho, Libya, Madagascar, Malaysia, Maldives, Mali, Malta, Mauritania, Mauritius, Mexico, Mongolia, Morocco, Mozambique, Nepal, Nicaragua, Niger, Nigeria, Oman, Pakistan, Panama, Papua New Guinea, Peru, Philippines, Poland, Qatar, Romania, Rwanda, Saint Lucia, Saint Vincent, Samoa, Sao Tome and Principe, Saudi Arabia, Senegal, Seychelles, Sierra Leone, Singapore, Soloman Islands, Somalia, Sri Lanka, Sudan, Syria, Suriname, Swaziland, Thailand, Togo, Trinidad and Tobago, Tunisia, Turkey, Uganda, Ukraine, USSR, United Arab Emirates, United Republic of Cameroon, United Republic of Tanzania, Upper Volta, Uruguay, Vanuatu, Venezuela, Viet Nam, Yemen, Yugoslavia, Zambia, Zimbabwe.

Against: 9

Australia, Canada, France, Federal Republic of Germany, Italy, Paraguay, Portugal, United Kingdom, United States.

Abstentions: 17

Austria, Belgium, Denmark, Finland, Greece, Guatemala, Iceland, Ireland, Ivory Coast, Japan, Luxembourg, Malawi, Netherlands, New Zealand, Norway, Spain, Sweden.

Absent: 8

Costa Rica, Dominica, El Salvador, Grenada, Honduras, Liberia, St. Christopher and Nevis, Zaire.

Israel announced that it was not participating in the vote.

Resolution No. 38/58 A, B, C, D, E of 13 December 1983

ON THE QUESTION OF PALESTINE: ENDORSING THE RIGHT OF THE PALESTINIAN PEOPLE TO SELF-DETERMINATION, INCLUDING THE RIGHT TO ESTABLISH AN INDEPENDENT STATE, THE RIGHT OF THE PALESTINE LIBERATION ORGANIZATION TO PARTICIPATE IN PEACE NEGOTIATIONS ON AN EQUAL FOOTING, THE NEED FOR A COMPLETE WITHDRAWAL OF ISRAELI FORCES FROM THE OCCUPIED TERRITORIES, AND THE RIGHT OF ALL STATES IN THE REGION TO EXISTENCE WITHIN SECURE AND INTERNATIONALLY RECOGNIZED BOUNDARIES

A

The General Assembly,

Recalling its resolutions 3376 (XXX) of 10 November 1975, 31/20 of 24 November 1976, 32/40 of 2 December 1977, 33/28 of 7 December 1978, 34/65 A and B of 29 November 1979 and 34/65 C and D of 12 December 1979, ES-7/2 of 29 July 1980, 35/169 of 15 December 1980, 36/120 of 10 December 1981, ES-7/4 of 28 April 1982, ES-7/5 of 26 June 1982, ES-7/9 of 24 September 1982 and 37/86 A of 10 December 1982,[160]

Having considered the report of the Committee on the Exercise of the Inalienable Rights of the Palestinian People,[161]

1. *Expresses its appreciation* to the Committee on the Exercise of the Inalienable Rights of the Palestinian People for its efforts in performing the tasks assigned to it by the General Assembly;

2. *Endorses* the recommendations of the Committee contained in paragraphs 94 to 98 of its report and draws the attention of the Security Council to the fact that action on the Committee's recommendations, as repeatedly endorsed by the General Assembly, at its thirty-first session and subsequently, is long overdue;

3. *Requests* the Committee to keep under review the situation relating to the question of Palestine as well as the implementation of the Programme of Action for the Achievement of Palestinian Rights[162] adopted by the International Conference on the Question of Palestine and to report and make suggestions to the General Assembly or the Security Council, as appropriate;

4. *Requests* the United Nations Conciliation Commission for Palestine, established under General Assembly resolution 194 (III) of 11 December 1948, as well as other United Nations bodies associated with the question of Palestine, to co-operate fully with the Committee and to make available to it, at its request, the relevant information and documentation which they have at their disposal;

5. *Authorizes* the Committee to continue to exert all ef-

---

[160]The resolutions cited are previous resolutions on the question of Palestine. [ed. note]

[161]*Official Records of the General Assembly, Thirty-eighth Session, Supplement No. 35* (A/38/35).

[162]*Report of the International Conference on the Question of Palestine, Geneva, 29 August-7 September 1983* (United Nations publication, Sales No. E.83.I.21), chap. I, sect. B.

forts to promote the implementation of its recommendations, to send delegations or representatives to international conferences where such representation would be considered by it to be appropriate, and to report thereon to the General Assembly at its thirty-ninth session and thereafter;

6. *Decides* to circulate the report of the Committee to all the competent bodies of the United Nations and urges them to take the necessary action, as appropriate, in accordance with the Committee's programme of implementation;

7. *Requests* the Secretary-General to continue to provide the Committee with all the necessary facilities for the performance of its tasks.

Adopted at the 95th plenary meeting:

In favour: 126

Afghanistan, Albania, Algeria, Angola, Argentina, Bahamas, Bahrain, Bangladesh, Belize, Benin, Bhutan, Bolivia, Botswana, Brazil, Bulgaria, Burma, Burundi, Byelorussia, Cape Verde, Central African Republic, Chad, Chile, China, Colombia, Comoros, Congo, Cuba, Cyprus, Czechoslovakia, Democratic Kampuchea, Democratic Yemen, Djibouti, Dominican Republic, Ecuador, Egypt, El Salvador, Equatorial Guinea, Ethiopia, Fiji, Gabon, Gambia, German Democratic Republic, Ghana, Greece, Guinea, Guinea-Bissau, Guyana, Haiti, Honduras, Hungary, India, Indonesia, Iran, Iraq, Ivory Coast, Jamaica, Jordan, Kenya, Kuwait, Lao People's Democratic Republic, Lebanon, Lesotho, Liberia, Libya, Madagascar, Malawi, Malaysia, Maldives, Mali, Malta, Mauritania, Mauritius, Mexico, Mongolia, Morocco, Mozambique, Nepal, Nicaragua, Niger, Nigeria, Oman, Pakistan, Panama, Papua New Guinea, Paraguay, Peru, Philippines, Poland, Portugal, Qatar, Romania, Rwanda, Sao Tome and Principe, Saudi Arabia, Senegal, Seychelles, Sierra Leone, Singapore, Solomon Islands, Somalia, Spain, Sri Lanka, Sudan, Suriname, Syria, Thailand, Togo, Trinidad and Tobago, Tunisia, Turkey, Uganda, Ukraine, USSR, United Arab Emirates, United Republic of Cameroon, United Republic of Tanzania, Upper Volta, Uruguay, Vanuatu, Venezuela, Viet Nam, Yemen, Yugoslavia, Zaire, Zambia, Zimbabwe.

Against: 2

Israel, United States.

Abstentions: 19

Australia, Austria, Belgium, Canada, Costa Rica, Denmark, Finland, France, Federal Republic of Germany, Iceland, Ireland, Italy, Japan, Luxembourg, Netherlands, New Zealand, Norway, Sweden, United Kingdom.

Absent: 10

Antigua and Barbuda, Barbados, Dominica, Grenada, Guatemala, Saint Lucia, Saint Vincent, Samoa, St. Christopher and Nevis, Swaziland.

B

The General Assembly,

Having considered the report of the Committee on the Exercise of the Inalienable Rights of the Palestinian People,[163]

Noting, in particular, the information contained in paragraphs 86 to 91 of that report,

Recalling its resolutions 32/40 B of 2 December 1977, 33/28 C of 7 December 1978, 34/65 D of 12 December 1979, 35/169 D of 15 December 1980, 36/120 B of 10 December 1981 and 37/86 B of 10 December 1982,[164]

1. *Notes with appreciation* the action taken by the Secretary-General in compliance with General Assembly resolution 37/86 B;

2. *Requests* the Secretary-General to ensure that the Division for Palestinian Rights of the Secretariat continues to discharge the tasks detailed in paragraph 1 of General Assembly resolution 32/40 B, paragraph 2 (*b*) of resolution 34/65 D and paragraph 3 of resolution 36/120 B, in consultation with the Committee on the Exercise of the Inalienable Rights of the Palestinian People and under its guidance;

3. *Also requests* the Secretary-General to provide the Division for Palestinian Rights with the necessary resources to accomplish its task and to expand its work programme, *inter alia*, through:

(*a*) Closer contacts with the media and wider dissemination of the Division's information material, particularly where information on the question of Palestine is inadequate;

(*b*) Increased contacts with non-governmental organizations and the convening of symposia and meetings for non-governmental organizations in different regions in order to heighten awareness of the facts relating to the question of Palestine;

4. *Further requests* the Secretary-General to ensure the continued co-operation of the Department of Public Information and other units of the Secretariat in enabling the Division for Palestinian Rights to perform its tasks and in covering adequately the various aspects of the question of Palestine;

5. *Invites* all Governments and organizations to lend their co-operation to the Committee on the Exercise of the Inalienable Rights of the Palestinian People and the Division for Palestinian Rights in the performance of their tasks;

6. *Notes with appreciation* the action taken by Member States to observe annually on 29 November the International Day of Solidarity with the Palestinian People and the issuance by them of special postage stamps for the occasion.

Adopted at the 95th plenary meeting:

In favour: 127

Afghanistan, Albania, Algeria, Angola, Argentina, Bahamas, Bahrain, Bangladesh, Belize, Benin, Bhutan, Bolivia, Botswana, Brazil, Bulgaria, Burma, Burundi, Byelorussia, Cape Verde, Central African Republic, Chad, Chile, China,

---

[163]*Official Records of the General Assembly, Thirty-eighth Session, Supplement No. 35* (A/38/35).

[164]The resolutions cited are previous resolutions on Palestinian rights. [ed. note]

Colombia, Comoros, Congo, Costa Rica, Cuba, Cyprus, Czechoslovakia, Democratic Kampuchea, Democratic Yemen, Djibouti, Dominican Republic, Ecuador, Egypt, El Salvador, Equatorial Guinea, Ethiopia, Fiji, Gabon, Gambia, German Democratic Republic, Ghana, Greece, Guinea, Guinea-Bissau, Guyana, Haiti, Honduras, Hungary, India, Indonesia, Iran, Iraq, Ivory Coast, Jamaica, Jordan, Kenya, Kuwait, Lao People's Democratic Republic, Lebanon, Lesotho, Liberia, Libya, Madagascar, Malawi, Malaysia, Maldives, Mali, Malta, Mauritania, Mauritius, Mexico, Mongolia, Morocco, Mozambique, Nepal, Nicaragua, Niger, Nigeria, Oman, Pakistan, Panama, Papua New Guinea, Paraguay, Peru, Philippines, Poland, Portugal, Qatar, Romania, Rwanda, Sao Tome and Principe, Saudi Arabia, Senegal, Seychelles, Sierra Leone, Singapore, Solomon Islands, Somalia, Spain, Sri Lanka, Sudan, Suriname, Syria, Thailand, Togo, Trinidad and Tobago, Tunisia, Turkey, Uganda, Ukraine, USSR, United Arab Emirates, United Republic of Cameroon, United Republic of Tanzania, Upper Volta, Uruguay, Vanuatu, Venezuela, Viet Nam, Yemen, Yugoslavia, Zaire, Zambia, Zimbabwe.

Against: 3

Canada, Israel, United States.

Abstentions: 17

Australia, Austria, Belgium, Denmark, Finland, France, Federal Republic of Germany, Iceland, Ireland, Italy, Japan, Luxembourg, Netherlands, New Zealand, Norway, Sweden, United Kingdom.

Absent: 10

Antigua and Barbuda, Barbados, Dominica, Grenada, Guatemala, Saint Lucia, Saint Vincent, Samoa, St. Christopher and Nevis, Swaziland.

C

The General Assembly,

Recalling its resolution 36/120 C of 10 December 1981, in which it decided to convene, under the auspices of the United Nations, an International Conference on the Question of Palestine on the basis of its resolution ES-7/2 of 29 July 1980,

Recalling also its resolution 37/86 C of 10 December 1982 in which it, *inter alia,* reiterated the responsibility of the United Nations to strive for a lasting peace in the Middle East through a just solution of the problem of Palestine,

Having considered the report of the International Conference on the Question of Palestine,[165] held at Geneva from 29 August to 7 September 1983,

Convinced that the Conference, in adopting by acclamation the Geneva Declaration on Palestine[166] and the Programme of Action for the Achievement of Palestinian Rights,[167] made an important and positive contribution

to the attainment of a comprehensive, just and durable peace in the Middle East through a just solution of the problem of Palestine, the core of the Arab-Israeli conflict,

Conscious of the importance of the time factor in achieving a just solution of the problem of Palestine,

1. *Takes note with satisfaction* of the report of the International Conference on the Question of Palestine;

2. *Endorses* the Geneva Declaration on Palestine, adopted by acclamation on 7 September 1983;

3. *Welcomes and endorses* the call for convening an International Peace Conference on the Middle East in conformity with the following guidelines:

(a) The attainment by the Palestinian people of its legitimate inalienable rights, including the right to return, the right to self-determination and the right to establish its own independent State in Palestine;

(b) The right of the Palestine Liberation Organization, the representative of the Palestinian people, to participate on an equal footing with other parties in all efforts, deliberations and conference on the Middle East;

(c) The need to put an end to Israel's occupation of the Arab territories, in accordance with the principle of the inadmissibility of the acquisition of territory by force, and, consequently, the need to secure Israeli withdrawal from the territories occupied since 1967, including Jerusalem;

(d) The need to oppose and reject such Israeli policies and practices in the occupied territories, including Jerusalem, and any *de facto* situation created by Israel as are contrary to international law and relevant United Nations resolutions, particularly the establishment of settlements, as these policies and practices constitute major obstacles to the achievement of peace in the Middle East;

(e) The need to reaffirm as null and void all legislative and administrative measures and actions taken by Israel, the occupying Power, which have altered or purported to alter the character and status of the Holy City of Jerusalem, including the expropriation of land and property situated thereon, and in particular the so-called "Basic Law" on Jerusalem and the proclamation of Jerusalem as the capital of Israel;

(f) The right of all States in the region to existence within secure and internationally recognized boundaries, with justice and security for all the people, the *sine qua non* of which is the recognition and attainment of the legitimate, inalienable rights of the Palestinian people as stated in subparagraph (a) above;

4. *Invites* all parties to the Arab-Israeli conflict, including the Palestine Liberation Organization, as well as the United States of America, the Union of Soviet Socialist Republics and other concerned States, to participate in the International Peace Conference on the Middle East on an equal footing and with equal rights;

5. *Request* the Secretary-General, in consultation with the Security Council, urgently to undertake preparatory measures to convene the Conference;

6. *Invites* the Security Council to facilitate the organization of the Conference;

7. *Also requests* the Secretary-General to report on his

---

[165]United Nations publication, Sales No. E.83.I.21.

[166]*Ibid.,* chap. I, sect. A.

[167]*Report of the International Conference on the Question of Palestine, Geneva, 29 August-7 September 1983* (United Nations publication, Sales No. E.83.I.21), chap. I, sect. B.

efforts no later than 15 March 1984;

8. *Decides* to consider at its thirty-ninth session the report of the Secretary-General on the Conference.

Adopted at the 95th plenary meeting:
In favour: 124
Afghanistan, Albania, Algeria, Angola, Argentina, Austria, Bahamas, Bahrain, Bangladesh, Belize, Benin, Bhutan, Bolivia, Botswana, Brazil, Bulgaria, Burma, Burundi, Byelorussia, Cape Verde, Central African Republic, Chad, China, Colombia, Comoros, Congo, Cuba, Cyprus, Czechoslovakia, Democratic Kampuchea, Democratic Yemen, Djibouti, Dominican Republic, Ecuador, Egypt, El Salvador, Equatorial Guinea, Ethiopia, Fiji, Finland, Gabon, Gambia, German Democratic Republic, Ghana, Greece, Guinea, Guinea-Bissau, Guyana, Haiti, Hungary, India, Indonesia, Iran, Iraq, Ivory Coast, Jamaica, Jordan, Kenya, Kuwait, Lao People's Democratic Republic, Lebanon, Lesotho, Libya, Madagascar, Malawi, Malaysia, Maldives, Mali, Malta, Mauritania, Mauritius, Mexico, Mongolia, Morocco, Mozambique, Nepal, Nicaragua, Niger, Nigeria, Oman, Pakistan, Panama, Papua New Guinea, Paraguay, Peru, Philippines, Poland, Portugal, Qatar, Romania, Rwanda, Sao Tome and Principe, Saudi Arabia, Senegal, Seychelles, Sierra Leone, Singapore, Somalia, Spain, Sri Lanka, Sudan, Suriname, Sweden, Syria, Thailand, Togo, Trinidad and Tobago, Tunisia, Turkey, Uganda, Ukraine, USSR, United Arab Emirates, United Republic of Cameroon, United Republic of Tanzania, Upper Volta, Uruguay, Vanuatu, Venezuela, Viet Nam, Yemen, Yugoslavia, Zambia, Zimbabwe.
Against: 4
Australia, Canada, Israel, United States.
Abstentions: 15
Belgium, Costa Rica, Denmark, France, Federal Republic of Germany, Iceland, Ireland, Italy, Japan, Luxembourg, Netherlands, New Zealand, Norway, Solomon Islands, United Kingdom.
Absent: 13
Antigua and Barbuda, Barbados, Chile, Dominica, Grenada, Guatemala, Liberia, Saint Lucia, Saint Vincent, Samoa, St. Christopher and Nevis, Swaziland, Zaire.

Honduras announced that it was not participating in the vote.

D

The General Assembly,
Having considered the report of the International Conference on the Question of Palestine,[168] held at Geneva from 29 August to 7 September 1983,
Taking note of the Programme of Action for the Achievement of Palestinian Rights,[169]
Bearing in mind its resolution 38/145 of 19 December 1983 on assistance to the Palestinian people,

---

[168]United Nations publication, Sales No. E.83.I.21.
[169]*Report of the International Conference on the Question of Palestine, Geneva, 29 August-7 September 1983* (United Nations publication, Sales No. E.83.I.21), chap. I, sect. B.

Urges the meeting of specialized agencies and other organizations of the United Nations system to be convened in 1984, referred to in General Assembly resolution 38/145, to take into account the recommendations of the five regional preparatory meetings of the International Conference on the Question of Palestine[170] and the United Nations resolutions concerning economic and social assistance to the Palestinian people in developing a co-ordinated programme of economic and social assistance to the Palestinian people, and to ensure the implementation of that programme.

Adopted at the 95th plenary meeting:
In favour: 144
Afghanistan, Albania, Algeria, Angola, Argentina, Australia, Austria, Bahamas, Bahrain, Bangladesh, Belgium, Belize, Benin, Bhutan, Bolivia, Botswana, Brazil, Bulgaria, Burma, Burundi, Byelorussia, Canada, Cape Verde, Central African Republic, Chad, Chile, China, Colombia, Comoros, Congo, Costa Rica, Cuba, Cyprus, Czechoslovakia, Democratic Kampuchea, Democratic Yemen, Denmark, Djibouti, Dominican Republic, Ecuador, Egypt, El Salvador, Equatorial Guinea, Ethiopia, Fiji, Finland, France, Gabon, Gambia, German Democratic Republic, Federal Republic of Germany, Ghana, Greece, Guinea, Guinea-Bissau, Guyana, Haiti, Honduras, Hungary, Iceland, India, Indonesia, Iran, Iraq, Ireland, Italy, Ivory Coast, Jamaica, Japan, Kenya, Kuwait, Lao People's Democratic Republic, Lebanon, Lesotho, Liberia, Libya, Luxembourg, Madagascar, Malawi, Malaysia, Maldives, Mali, Malta, Mauritania, Mauritius, Mexico, Mongolia, Morocco, Mozambique, Nepal, Netherlands, New Zealand, Nicaragua, Niger, Nigeria, Norway, Oman, Pakistan, Papua New Guinea, Panama, Paraguay, Peru, Philippines, Poland, Portugal, Qatar, Romania, Rwanda, Sao Tome and Principe, Saudi Arabia, Senegal, Seychelles, Sierra Leone, Singapore, Solomon Islands, Somalia, Spain, Sri Lanka, Sudan, Suriname, Syria, Thailand, Togo, Trinidad and Tobago, Tunisia, Turkey, Uganda, Ukraine, USSR, United Arab Emirates, United Kingdom, United Republic of Cameroon, United Republic of Tanzania, Upper Volta, Uruguay, Vanuatu, Venezuela, Viet Nam, Yemen, Yugoslavia, Zaire, Zambia, Zimbabwe.
Against: 2
Israel, United States.
Abstentions: 0
Absent: 11
Antigua and Barbuda, Barbados, Dominica, Grenada, Guatemala, Jordan, Saint Lucia, Saint Vincent, Samoa, St. Christopher and Nevis, Swaziland.

E

The General Assembly,
Having considered the report of the International Conference on the Question of Palestine,[171] held at Geneva from 29 August to 7 September 1983,

---

[170]*Ibid.,* chap. II, paras. 10 and 11.
[171]United Nations publication, Sales No. E.83.I.21.

Convinced that the world-wide dissemination of accurate and comprehensive information and the role of non-governmental organizations and institutions remain of vital importance in heightening awareness of and support for the inalienable rights of the Palestinian people to self-determination and to the establishment of an independent sovereign Palestinian State,

Requests that the Department of Public Information of the Secretariat, in full co-operation and co-ordination with the Committee on the Exercise of the Inalienable Rights of the Palestinian People, should:

(*a*) Disseminate all information on the activities of the United Nations system relating to Palestine;

(*b*) Expand publications and audio-visual coverage of the facts and developments pertaining to the question of Palestine;

(*c*) Publish newsletters and articles in its relevant publications on Israeli violations of the human rights of the Arab inhabitants of the occupied territories, and organize fact-finding missions to the area for journalists;

(*d*) Organize regional encounters for journalists;

(*e*) Disseminate appropriate information on the results of the International Conference on the Question of Palestine.

Adopted at the 95th plenary meeting:
In favour: 125

Afghanistan, Albania, Algeria, Angola, Argentina, Austria, Bahamas, Bahrain, Bangladesh, Belize, Benin, Bhutan, Bolivia, Botswana, Brazil, Bulgaria, Burma, Burundi, Byelorussia, Cape Verde, Central African Republic, Chad, China, Colombia, Comoros, Congo, Cuba, Cyprus, Czechoslovakia, Democratic Kampuchea, Democratic Yemen, Djibouti, Dominican Republic, Ecuador, Egypt, El Salvador, Equatorial Guinea, Ethiopia, Fiji, Finland, Gabon, Gambia, German Democratic Republic, Ghana, Greece, Guinea, Guinea-Bissau, Guyana, Haiti, Honduras, Hungary, India, Indonesia, Iran, Iraq, Jamaica, Jordan, Kenya, Kuwait, Lao People's Democratic Republic, Lebanon, Lesotho, Liberia, Libya, Madagascar, Malawi, Malaysia, Maldives, Mali, Malta, Mauritania, Mauritius, Mexico, Mongolia, Morocco, Mozambique, Nepal, Nicaragua, Niger, Nigeria, Oman, Pakistan, Panama, Papua New Guinea, Paraguay, Peru, Philippines, Poland, Portugal, Qatar, Romania, Rwanda, Sao Tome and Principe, Saudi Arabia, Senegal, Seychelles, Sierra Leone, Singapore, Solomon Islands, Somalia, Spain, Sri Lanka, Sudan, Suriname, Sweden, Syria, Thailand, Togo, Trinidad and Tobago, Tunisia, Turkey, Uganda, Ukraine, USSR, United Arab Emirates, United Republic of Cameroon, United Republic of Tanzania, Upper Volta, Uruguay, Vanuatu, Venezuela, Viet Nam, Yemen, Yugoslavia, Zambia, Zimbabwe.

Against: 3
Canada, Israel, United States.

Abstentions: 15
Australia, Belgium, Denmark, France, Federal Republic of Germany, Iceland, Ireland, Italy, Ivory Coast, Japan, Luxembourg, Netherlands, New Zealand, Norway, United Kingdom.

Absent: 14
Antigua and Barbuda, Barbados, Chile, Costa Rica, Dominica, Grenada, Guatemala, Liberia, Saint Lucia, Saint Vincent, Samoa, St. Christopher and Nevis, Swaziland, Zaire.

Resolution No. 38/64 of 15 December 1983

CALLING UPON COUNTRIES OF THE MIDDLE EAST TO PLACE THEIR NUCLEAR ACTIVITIES UNDER INTERNATIONAL ATOMIC ENERGY AGENCY SAFEGUARDS

The General Assembly,

Recalling its resolutions 3263 (XXIX) of 9 December 1974, 3474 (XXX) of 11 December 1975, 31/71 of 10 December 1976, 32/82 of 12 December 1977, 33/64 of 14 December 1978, 34/77 of 11 December 1979, 35/147 of 12 December 1980, 36/87 of 9 December 1981 and 37/75 of 9 December 1982 on the establishment of a nuclear-weapon-free zone in the region of the Middle East,

Recalling also the recommendations for the establishment of such a zone in the Middle East consistent with paragraphs 60 to 63, in particular paragraph 63 (*d*), of the Final Document of the Tenth Special Session of the General Assembly,[172]

Emphasizing the basic provisions of the above-mentioned resolutions, which call upon all parties directly concerned to consider taking the practical and urgent steps required for the implementation of the proposal to establish a nuclear-weapon-free zone in the region of the Middle East and, pending and during the establishment of such a zone, to declare solemnly that they will refrain, on a reciprocal basis, from producing, acquiring or in any other way possessing nuclear weapons and nuclear explosive devices and from permitting the stationing of nuclear weapons on their territory by any third party, to agree to place all their nuclear facilities under International Atomic Energy Agency safeguards and to declare their support for the establishment of the zone and deposit such declarations with the Security Council for consideration, as appropriate,

Reaffirming the inalienable right of all States to acquire and develop nuclear energy for peaceful purposes,

Emphasizing further the need for appropriate measures on the question of the prohibition of military attacks on nuclear facilities,

Bearing in mind the consensus reached by the General Assembly at its thirty-fifth session that the establishment of a nuclear-weapon-free zone in the region of the Middle East would greatly enhance international peace and security,

Desirous to build on that consensus so that substantial progress can be made towards establishing a nuclear-weapon-free zone in the region of the Middle East,

Taking note of the report of the Secretary-General,[173]

---

[172]Resolution 5-10/2.
[173]A/38/197.

1. *Urges* all parties directly concerned to consider seriously taking the practical and urgent steps required for the implementation of the proposal to establish a nuclear-weapon-free zone in the region of the Middle East in accordance with the relevant resolutions of the General Assembly and, as a means of promoting this objective, invites the States concerned to adhere to the Treaty on the Non-Proliferation of Nuclear Weapons;[174]

2. *Calls upon* all States of the region that have not done so, pending the establishment of the zone, to agree to place all their nuclear activities under International Atomic Energy Agency safeguards;

3. *Invites* those States, pending the establishment of a nuclear-weapon-free zone in the region of the Middle East, to declare their support for establishing such a zone, consistent with the relevant paragraph of the Final Document of the Tenth Special Session of the General Assembly, and to deposit those declarations with the Security Council;

4. *Further invites* those States, pending the establishment of the zone, not to develop, produce, test or otherwise acquire nuclear weapons or permit the stationing on their territories, or territories under their control, of nuclear weapons or nuclear explosive devices;

5. *Invites* the nuclear-weapon States and all other States to render their assistance in the establishment of the zone and at the same time to refrain from any action that runs counter to both the letter and spirit of the present resolution;

6. *Requests* the Secretary-General to submit a report to the General Assembly at its thirty-ninth session on the implementation of the present resolution;

7. *Decides* to include in the provisional agenda of its thirty-ninth session the item entitled "Establishment of a nuclear-weapon-free zone in the region of the Middle East".

Adopted at the 97th plenary meeting without a vote.

Resolution No. 38/69 of 15 December 1983

CONDEMNING ISRAEL'S REFUSAL TO RENOUNCE ANY POSSESSION OF NUCLEAR WEAPONS AND TO PLACE ITS NUCLEAR ACTIVITIES UNDER INTERNATIONAL SAFEGUARDS

The General Assembly,

Recalling its previous resolutions on Israeli nuclear armament,

Recalling its relevant resolutions on the establishment of a nuclear-weapon-free zone in the region of the Middle East,

Recalling also its resolution 35/157 of 12 December 1980 on military and nuclear collaboration with Israel,

Recalling its repeated condemnation of nuclear collaboration between Israel and South Africa,

Recalling Security Council resolution 487 (1981) of 19 June 1981 and taking note of the special report of the Special Committee against *Apartheid* on recent developments concerning relations between Israel and South Africa,[175]

Noting with concern Israel's refusal to comply with Security Council resolution 487 (1981),

Further noting with grave concern Israel's persistent refusal to adhere to the Treaty on the Non-Proliferation of Nuclear Weapons,[176] despite repeated calls by the General Assembly, the Security Council and the International Atomic Energy Agency, and to place its nuclear facilities under Agency safeguards,

Conscious of the grave consequences which endanger international peace and security as a result of Israel's development and acquisition of nuclear weapons and Israel's collaboration with South Africa to develop nuclear weapons and their delivery systems,

Taking note of the report of the Secretary-General,[177]

1. *Condemns* Israel's refusal to renounce any possession of nuclear weapons and to place all its nuclear activities under international safeguards;

2. *Requests* the Security Council to take urgent and effective measures to implement its resolution 487 (1981) and to ensure that Israel complies with the resolution and places its nuclear facilities under International Atomic Energy Agency safeguards;

3. *Requests* the International Atomic Energy Agency to suspend any scientific co-operation with Israel which could contribute to Israel's nuclear capabilities;

4. *Reiterates* its condemnation of the Israeli threat, in violation of the Charter of the United Nations, to repeat its armed attack on peaceful nuclear facilities in Iraq and in other countries;

5. *Requests* the Secretary-General to continue to follow closely Israel's nuclear activities and the nuclear and military collaboration between Israel and South Africa and to report to the General Assembly at its thirty-ninth session thereon, as appropriate;

6. *Decides* to include in the provisional agenda of its thirty-ninth session the item entitled "Israeli nuclear armament".

Adopted at the 97th plenary meeting:
In favour: 99
Afghanistan, Albania, Algeria, Angola, Bahrain, Bangladesh, Barbados, Benin, Bhutan, Bolivia, Botswana, Brazil, Bulgaria, Burundi, Byelorussia, Cape Verde, Central African Republic, Chad, China, Congo, Cuba, Cyprus, Czechoslovakia, Democratic Kampuchea, Democratic Yemen, Djibouti, Ecuador, Egypt, Ethiopia, Gabon, Gambia, German Democratic Republic, Ghana, Greece, Grenada, Guinea, Guyana, Hungary, India, Indonesia, Iran, Iraq, Jordan, Kenya, Kuwait, Lao People's Democratic Republic, Lebanon, Libya, Madagascar, Malaysia, Maldives, Mali, Malta, Mauritania, Mexico, Mongolia, Morocco, Mozam-

---

[174]Resolution 2373 (XXII), annex.

[175] *Official Records of the General Assembly, Thirty-eighth Session, Supplement No. 22A* (A/38/22/Add.1).
[176]Resolution 2373 (XXII), annex.
[177]A/38/199.

bique, Nicaragua, Niger, Nigeria, Oman, Pakistan, Papua New Guinea, Peru, Poland, Qatar, Romania, Rwanda, Sao Tome and Principe, Saudi Arabia, Senegal, Seychelles, Sierra Leone, Somalia, Spain, Sri Lanka, Sudan, Suriname, Syria, Thailand, Togo, Trinidad and Tobago, Tunisia, Turkey, Uganda, Ukraine, USSR, United Arab Emirates, United Republic of Cameroon, United Republic of Tanzania, Upper Volta, Vanuatu, Venezuela, Viet Nam, Yemen, Yugoslavia, Zambia, Zimbabwe.

Against: 2

Israel, United States.

Abstentions: 39

Argentina, Australia, Austria, Bahamas, Belgium, Burma, Canada, Chile, Colombia, Denmark, Dominican Republic, Fiji, Finland, France, Federal Republic of Germany, Guatemala, Haiti, Honduras, Iceland, Ireland, Italy, Ivory Coast, Japan, Liberia, Luxembourg, Malawi, Nepal, Netherlands, New Zealand, Norway, Panama, Paraguay, Philippines, Portugal, Swaziland, Sweden, United Kingdom, Uruguay, Zaire.

Absent: 16

Antigua and Barbuda, Belize, Comoros, Dominica, El Salvador, Equatorial Guinea, Guinea-Bissau, Jamaica, Lesotho, Mauritius, Saint Lucia, Saint Vincent, Samoa, Singapore, Solomon Islands, St. Christopher and Nevis.

Costa Rica announced that it was not participating in the vote.

Resolution No. 38/79 A, B, C, D, E, F, G, H of 15 December 1983

ON ISRAELI PRACTICES AFFECTING HUMAN RIGHTS IN THE OCCUPIED TERRITORIES: CONDEMNING ISRAEL FOR FAILING TO HONOR A PRISONER RELEASE AGREEMENT NEGOTIATED THROUGH THE RED CROSS FOR ITS POLICIES OF ANNEXATION AND SETTLEMENT IN THE OCCUPIED TERRITORIES, AS WELL AS MEASURES AGAINST CIVIL, POLITICAL AND EDUCATIONAL FREEDOM THERE, AND FOR ITS EXPULSION OF PALESTINIAN LEADERS AND ITS FAILURE TO APPREHEND AND PROSECUTE PERSONS GUILTY OF ASSASSINATION ATTEMPTS AGAINST ARAB MAYORS

A

The General Assembly,

Having heard the statement of the representative of the Palestine Liberation Organization relative to the fate of Ziad Abu Eain,[178]

Taking note of the report of the International Committee of the Red Cross of 13 December 1983,[179]

1. *Condemns* Israel for the fact that one prisoner, Ziad Abu Eain, who had been registered before embarkation by delegates of the International Committee of the Red Cross at Tel Aviv Airport, was taken at the last minute by the Israeli authorities;

2. *Demands* the immediate release of Ziad Abu Eain, as well as the other prisoners who were duly registered to be freed from Insar Camp and other military command posts in southern Lebanon but have not in fact been released, and the securing of their transfer to Algiers in conformity with the agreement reached through the good offices of the International Committee of the Red Cross;

3. *Requests* the Secretary-General to report on the implementation of the present resolution.

Adopted at the 98th plenary meeting:

In favour: 110

Afghanistan, Albania, Algeria, Angola, Argentina, Austria, Bahrain, Bangladesh, Belgium, Benin, Bhutan, Botswana, Bulgaria, Burundi, Byelorussia, Cape Verde, Central African Republic, Chad, China, Congo, Cuba, Cyprus, Czechoslovakia, Democratic Kampuchea, Democratic Yemen, Denmark, Djibouti, Egypt, Equatorial Guinea, Ethiopia, Fiji, France, Gabon, Gambia, German Democratic Republic, Federal Republic of Germany, Ghana, Greece, Grenada, Guinea, Guinea-Bissau, Guyana, Hungary, India, Indonesia, Iran, Iraq, Ireland, Italy, Japan, Jordan, Kenya, Kuwait, Lao People's Democratic Republic, Lebanon, Libya, Luxembourg, Madagascar, Malaysia, Maldives, Mali, Malta, Mauritania, Mauritius, Mexico, Mongolia, Morocco, Mozambique, Netherlands, New Zealand, Nicaragua, Niger, Nigeria, Oman, Pakistan, Papua New Guinea, Poland, Portugal, Qatar, Romania, Rwanda, Sao Tome and Principe, Saudi Arabia, Senegal, Seychelles, Sierra Leone, Solomon Islands, Somalia, Spain, Sudan, Suriname, Syria, Togo, Tunisia, Turkey, Uganda, Ukraine, USSR, United Arab Emirates, United Kingdom, United Republic of Cameroon, United Republic of Tanzania, Upper Volta, Vanuatu, Venezuela, Viet Nam, Yemen, Yugoslavia, Zambia, Zimbabwe.

Against: 2

Israel, United States.

Abstentions: 29

Australia, Bahamas, Barbados, Belize, Bolivia,* Brazil, Canada, Colombia, Costa Rica, Dominican Republic, Ecuador, El Salvador, Finland, Iceland, Jamaica, Lesotho, Liberia, Malawi, Nepal, Norway, Panama, Paraguay, Peru, Sri Lanka, Swaziland, Sweden, Trinidad and Tobago, Uruguay, Zaire.

Absent: 16

Antigua and Barbuda, Burma, Chile, Comoros, Dominica, Guatemala, Haiti, Honduras, Ivory Coast, Philippines, Saint Lucia, Saint Vincent, Samoa, Singapore, St. Christopher and Nevis, Thailand.

---

* Later advised the Secretariat it had intended to vote in favour.

B

The General Assembly,

Recalling its resolutions 3092 A (XXVIII) of 7 December 1973, 3240 B (XXIX) of 29 November 1974, 3525 B (XXX) of 15 December 1975, 31/106 B of 16 December 1976, 32/91 A of 13 December 1977, 33/113 A of 18 December 1978, 34/90 B of 12 December 1979, 35/122 A of 11 December 1980, 36/147 A of 16 December 1981

---

[178]*Official Records of the General Assembly, Thirty-eighth Session, Special Political Committee,* 40th meeting, para. 1.
[179]See A/38/735.

and 37/88 A of 10 December 1982,[180]

Recalling also Security Council resolution 465 (1980) of 1 March 1980 in which, *inter alia*, the Council affirmed that the Geneva Convention relative to the Protection of Civilian Persons in Time of War, of 12 August 1949,[181] is applicable to the Arab territories occupied by Israel since 1967, including Jerusalem,

Considering that the promotion of respect for the obligations arising from the Charter of the United Nations and other instruments and rules of international law is among the basic purposes and principles of the United Nations,

Bearing in mind the provisions of the Geneva Convention,

Noting that Israel and those Arab States whose territories have been occupied by Israel since June 1967 are parties to that Convention,

Taking into account that States parties to that Convention undertaken in accordance with article 1 thereof, not only to respect but also to ensure respect for the Convention in all circumstances,

1. *Reaffirms* that the Geneva Convention relative to the Protection of Civilian Persons in Time of War, of 12 August 1949, is applicable to Palestinian and other Arab territories occupied by Israel since 1967, including Jerusalem;

2. *Condemns once again* the failure of Israel as the occupying Power to acknowledge the applicability of that Convention to the territories it has occupied since 1967, including Jerusalem;

3. *Strongly demands* that Israel acknowledge and comply with the provisions of that Convention in Palestinian and other Arab territories it has occupied since 1967, including Jerusalem;

4. *Urgently calls upon* all States parties to that Convention to exert every effort in order to ensure respect for and compliance with its provisions in Palestinian and other Arab territories occupied by Israel since 1967, including Jerusalem.

Adopted at the 98th plenary meeting:

In favour: 146

Afghanistan, Albania, Algeria, Angola, Argentina, Australia, Austria, Bahamas, Bahrain, Bangladesh, Barbados, Belgium, Belize, Benin, Bhutan, Bolivia, Botswana, Brazil, Bulgaria, Burma, Burundi, Byelorussia, Canada, Cape Verde, Central African Republic, Chad, Chile, China, Colombia, Congo, Costa Rica, Cuba, Cyprus, Czechoslovakia, Democratic Kampuchea, Democratic Yemen, Denmark, Djibouti, Dominica, Dominican Republic, Ecuador, Egypt, El Salvador, Equatorial Guinea, Ethiopia, Fiji, Finland, France, Gabon, Gambia, German Democratic Republic, Federal Republic of Germany, Ghana, Greece, Grenada, Guinea, Guinea-Bissau, Guyana, Hungary, Iceland, India, Indonesia, Iran, Iraq, Ireland, Italy, Ivory Coast, Jamaica, Japan, Jordan, Kuwait, Lao People's Democratic Republic, Lebanon, Lesotho, Liberia, Libya, Luxembourg, Madagascar, Malawi, Malaysia, Maldives, Mali, Malta, Mauritania, Mauritius, Mexico, Mongolia, Morocco, Mozambique, Nepal, Netherlands, New Zealand, Nicaragua, Niger, Nigeria, Norway, Oman, Pakistan, Panama, Papua New Guinea, Paraguay, Peru, Philippines, Poland, Portugal, Qatar, Romania, Rwanda, Saint Lucia, Sao Tome and Principe, Saudi Arabia, Senegal, Seychelles, Sierra Leone, Singapore, Somalia, Spain, Sri Lanka, Sudan, Suriname, Swaziland, Sweden, Syria, Thailand, Togo, Trinidad and Tobago, Tunisia, Turkey, Uganda, Ukraine, USSR, United Arab Emirates, United Kingdom, United Republic of Cameroon, United Republic of Tanzania, Upper Volta, Uruguay, Vanuatu, Venezuela, Viet Nam, Yemen, Yugoslavia, Zaire, Zambia, Zimbabwe.

Against: 1

Israel.

Abstention: 1

United States.

Absent: 9

Antigua and Barbuda, Comoros, Guatemala, Haiti, Honduras, Kenya, Saint Vincent, Samoa, St. Christopher and Nevis.

C

The General Assembly,

Recalling its resolutions 32/5 of 28 October 1977, 33/113 B of 18 December 1978, 34/90 C of 12 December 1979, 35/122 B of 11 December 1980, 36/147 B of 16 December 1981 and 37/88 B of 10 December 1982,[182]

Recalling also Security Council resolution 465 (1980) of 1 March 1980,

Expressing grave anxiety and concern at the present serious situation in the occupied Palestinian and other Arab territories, including Jerusalem, as a result of the continued Israeli occupation and the measures and actions taken by the Government of Israel, the occupying Power, designed to change the legal status, geographical nature and demographic composition of those territories,

Considering that the Geneva Convention relative to the Protection of Civilian Persons in Time of War, of 12 August 1949,[183] is applicable to all Arab territories occupied since June 1967, including Jerusalem,

1. *Determines* that all such measures and actions taken by Israel in the Palestinian and other Arab territories occupied since 1967, including Jerusalem, are in violation of the relevant provisions of the Geneva Convention relative to the Protection of Civilian Persons in Time of War, of 12 August 1949, and constitute a serious obstruction of efforts to achieve a just and lasting peace in the Middle East and therefore have no legal validity;

2. *Strongly deplores* the persistence of Israel in carrying out such measures, in particular the establishment of settlements in the Palestinian and other occupied Arab territories, including Jerusalem;

3. *Demands* that Israel comply strictly with its interna-

---

[180]The resolutions cited are previous resolutions on Israeli practices in the occupied territories. [ed. note]

[181]United Nations, *Treaty Series*, vol. 75, no. 973, p. 287.

[182]The resolutions cited are previous resolutions on Israeli practices in the occupied territories. [ed. note]

[183]United Nations *Treaty Series*, vol. 75, no. 973, p. 287.

tional obligations in accordance with the principles of international law and the provisions of the Geneva Convention;

4. *Demands once more* that the Government of Israel, the occupying Power, desist forthwith from taking any action which would result in changing the legal status, geographical nature or demographic composition of the Palestinian and other Arab territories occupied since 1967, including Jerusalem;

5. *Urgently calls upon* all States parties to the Geneva Convention to respect and to exert every effort in order to ensure respect for and compliance with its provisions in all Arab territories occupied by Israel since 1967, including Jerusalem.

Adopted at the 98th plenary meeting:

In favour: 147

Afghanistan, Albania, Algeria, Angola, Argentina, Australia, Austria, Bahamas, Bahrain, Bangladesh, Barbados, Belgium, Belize, Benin, Bhutan, Bolivia, Botswana, Brazil, Bulgaria, Burma, Burundi, Byelorussia, Canada, Cape Verde, Central African Republic, Chad, Chile, China, Colombia, Congo, Costa Rica, Cuba, Cyprus, Czechoslovakia, Democratic Kampuchea, Democratic Yemen, Denmark, Djibouti, Dominica, Dominican Republic, Ecuador, Egypt, El Salvador, Equatorial Guinea, Ethiopia, Fiji, Finland, France, Gabon, Gambia, German Democratic Republic, Federal Republic of Germany, Ghana, Greece, Grenada, Guinea, Guinea-Bissau, Guyana, Hungary, Iceland, India, Indonesia, Iran, Iraq, Ireland, Italy, Ivory Coast, Jamaica, Japan, Jordan, Kenya, Kuwait, Lao People's Democratic Republic, Lebanon, Lesotho, Liberia, Libya, Luxembourg, Madagascar, Malawi, Malaysia, Maldives, Mali, Malta, Mauritania, Mauritius, Mexico, Mongolia, Morocco, Mozambique, Nepal, Netherlands, New Zealand, Nicaragua, Niger, Nigeria, Norway, Oman, Pakistan, Panama, Papua New Guinea, Paraguay, Peru, Philippines, Poland, Portugal, Qatar, Romania, Rwanda, Saint Lucia, Sao Tome and Principe, Saudi Arabia, Senegal, Seychelles, Sierra Leone, Singapore, Solomon Islands, Somalia, Spain, Sri Lanka, Sudan, Suriname, Swaziland, Sweden, Syria, Thailand, Togo, Trinidad and Tobago, Tunisia, Turkey, Uganda, Ukraine, USSR, United Arab Emirates, United Kingdom, United Republic of Cameroon, United Republic of Tanzania, Upper Volta, Uruguay, Vanuatu, Venezuela, Viet Nam, Yemen, Yugoslavia, Zaire, Zambia, Zimbabwe.

Against: 1

Israel.

Abstentions: 1

United States.

Absent: 8

Antigua and Barbuda, Comoros, Guatemala, Haiti, Honduras, Saint Vincent, Samoa, St. Christopher and Nevis.

D

The General Assembly,

Guided by the purposes and principles of the Charter of the United Nations and by the principles and provisions of the Universal Declaration of Human Rights,[184]

Bearing in mind the provisions of the Geneva Convention relative to the Protection of Civilian Persons in Time of War, of 12 August 1949,[185] as well as of other relevant conventions and regulations,

Recalling all its resolutions on the subject, in particular resolutions 32/91 B and C of 13 December 1977, 33/113 C of 18 December 1978, 34/90 A of 12 December 1979, 35/122 C of 11 December 1980, 36/147 C of 16 December 1981 and 37/88 C of 10 December 1982, and also those adopted by the Security Council, the Commission on Human Rights, in particular its resolution 1983/1 of 15 February 1983,[186] and other United Nations organs concerned and by the specialized agencies,

Having considered the report of the Special Committee to Investigate Israeli Practices Affecting the Human Rights of the Population of the Occupied Territories,[187] which contains, *inter alia*, public statements made by officials of the Government of Israel,

1. *Commends* the Special Committee to Investigate Israeli Practices Affecting the Human Rights of the Population of the Occupied Territories for its efforts in performing the tasks assigned to it by the General Assembly and for its thoroughness and impartiality;

2. *Deplores* the continued refusal by Israel to allow the Special Committee access to the occupied territories;

3. *Demands* that Israel allow the Special Committee access to the occupied territories;

4. *Reaffirms* the fact that occupation itself constitutes a grave violation of the human rights of the civilian population of the occupied Arab territories;

5. *Condemns* the continued and persistent violation by Israel of the Geneva Convention relative to the Protection of Civilian Persons in Time of War, of 12 August 1949, and other applicable international instruments, and condemns in particular those violations which that Convention designates as "grave breaches" thereof;

6. *Declares once more* that Israel's grave breaches of that Convention are war crimes and an affront to humanity;

7. *Stongly condemns* the following Israeli policies and practices:

(*a*) Annexation of parts of the occupied territories, including Jerusalem;

(*b*) Imposition of Israeli laws, jurisdiction and administration on the Syrian Golan Heights, which has resulted in the effective annexation of the Syrian Golan Heights;

(*c*) Establishment of new Israeli settlements and expansion of the existing settlements on private and public Arab lands, and transfer of an alien population thereto;

(*d*) Evacuation, deportation, expulsion, displacement and transfer of Arab inhabitants of the occupied territories and denial of their right to return;

---

[184]Resolution 217 A (III).

[185]United Nations, *Treaty Series*, vol. 75, no. 973, p. 287.

[186]See *Official Records of the Economic and Social Council, 1983, Supplement No. 3* (3/1983/13 and Corr.1), chap. XXVII.

[187]See A/38/409.

(*e*) Confiscation and expropriation of private and public Arab property in the occupied territories and all other transactions for the acquisition of land involving the Israeli authorities, institutions or nationals on the one hand and the inhabitants or institutions of the occupied territories on the other;

(*f*) Excavation and transformation of the landscape and the historical, cultural and religious sites, especially at Jerusalem;

(*g*) Pillaging of archaeological and cultural property;

(*h*) Destruction and demolition of Arab houses;

(*i*) Collective punishment, mass arrests, administrative detention and ill-treatment of the Arab population;

(*j*) Ill-treatment and torture of persons under detention;

(*k*) Interference with religious freedoms and practices as well as family rights and customs;

(*l*) Interference with the system of education and with the social and economic development of the population in the occuped Palestinian and other Arab territories;

(*m*) Interference with the freedom of movement of individuals within the occupied Palestinian and other Arab territories;

(*n*) Illegal exploitation of the natural wealth, resources and population of the occupied territories;

8. *Strongly condemns* the arming of Israeli settlers in the occupied territories to commit acts of violence against Arab civilians and the perpetration of acts of violence by these armed settlers against individuals, causing injury and death and wide-scale damage to Arab property;

9. *Reaffirms* that all measures taken by Israel to change the physical character, demographic composition, institutional structure or status of the occupied territories, or any part thereof, including Jerusalem, are null and void, and that Israel's policy of settling parts of its population and new immigrants in the occupied territories constitutes a flagrant violation of the Geneva Convention and of the relevant resolutions of the United Nations;

10. *Demands* that Israel desist forthwith from the policies and practices referred to in paragraphs 7, 8 and 9 above;

11. *Calls upon* Israel, the occupying Power, to take immediate steps for the return of all displaced Arab and Palestinian inhabitants to their homes or former places of residence in the territories occupied by Israel since 1967;

12. *Urges* the international organizations and the specialized agencies, in particular the International Labour Organization, to examine the conditions of Arab workers in the occupied Palestinian and other Arab territories, including Jerusalem;

13. *Reiterates its call* upon all States, in particular those States parties to the Geneva Convention, in accordance with article 1 of that Convention, and upon international organizations and the specialized agencies not to recognize any changes carried out by Israel in the occupied territories and to avoid actions, including those in the field of aid, which might be used by Israel in its pursuit of the policies of annexation and colonization or any of the other policies and practices referred to in the present resolution;

14. *Requests* the Special Committee, pending the early termination of Israeli occupation, to continue to investigate Israeli policies and practices in the Arab territories occupied by Israel since 1967, to consult, as appropriate, with the International Committee of the Red Cross in order to ensure the safeguarding of the welfare and human rights of the population of the occupied territories and to report to the Secretary-General as soon as possible and whenever the need arises thereafter;

15. *Requests* the Special Committee to continue to investigate the treatment of civilians in detention in the Arab territories occupied by Israel since 1967;

16. *Condemns* Israel's refusal to permit persons from the occupied territories to appear as witnesses before the Special Committee and to participate in conferences and meetings held outside the occupied territories;

17. *Requests* the Secretary-General:

(*a*) To provide all necessary facilities to the Special Committee, including those required for its visits to the occupied territories, with a view to investigating the Israeli policies and practices referred to in the present resolution;

(*b*) To continue to make available additional staff as may be necessary to assist the Special Committee in the performance of its tasks;

(*c*) To ensure the widest circulation of the reports of the Special Committee, and of information regarding its activities and findings, by al means available through the Department of Public Information of the Secretariat and, where necessary, to reprint those reports of the Special Committee which are no longer available;

(*d*) To report to the General Assembly at its thirty-ninth session on the tasks entrusted to him in the present paragraph;

18. *Requests* the Security Council to ensure Israel's respect for and compliance with all the provisions of the Geneva Convention relative to the Protection of Civilian Persons in Time of War, of 12 August 1949, in Palestinian and other Arab territories occupied since 1967, including Jerusalem, and to initiate measures to halt Israeli policies and practices in those territories;

19. *Decides* to include in the provisional agenda of its thirty-ninth session the item entitled "Report of the Special Committee to Investigate Israeli Practices Affecting the Human Rights of the Population of the Occupied Territories".

Adopted at the 98th plenary meeting:
In favour: 115
Afghanistan, Albania, Algeria, Angola, Argentina, Bahrain, Bangladesh, Belize, Benin, Bhutan, Bolivia, Botswana, Brazil, Bulgaria, Burma, Burundi, Byelorussia, Cape Verde, Central African Republic, Chad, China, Colombia, Congo, Cuba, Cyprus, Czechoslovakia, Democratic Kampuchea, Democratic Yemen, Djibouti, Ecuador, Egypt, Equatorial Guinea, Ethiopia, Fiji, Gabon, Gambia, German Democratic Republic, Ghana, Greece, Grenada, Guinea, Guinea-Bissau, Guyana, Hungary, India, Indonesia, Iran, Iraq, Jamaica, Jordan, Kenya, Kuwait, Lao People's Democratic Republic, Lebanon, Lesotho, Libe-

ria, Libya, Madagascar, Malawi, Malaysia, Maldives, Mali, Malta, Mauritania, Mauritius, Mexico, Mongolia, Morocco, Mozambique, Nepal, Nicaragua, Niger, Nigeria, Oman, Pakistan, Panama, Papua New Guinea, Peru, Philippines, Poland, Portugal, Qatar, Romania, Rwanda, Sao Tome and Principe, Saudi Arabia, Senegal, Seychelles, Sierra Leone, Singapore, Somalia, Spain, Sri Lanka, Sudan, Suriname, Syria, Thailand, Togo, Trinidad and Tobago, Tunisia, Turkey, Uganda, Ukraine, USSR, United Arab Emirates, United Republic of Cameroon, United Republic of Tanzania, Upper Volta, Uruguay, Vanuatu, Venezuela, Viet Nam, Yemen, Yugoslavia, Zambia, Zimbabwe.

Against: 2
Israel, United States.
Abstentions: 27
Australia, Austria, Bahamas, Barbados, Belgium, Canada, Costa Rica, Denmark, Dominican Republic, Finland, France, Federal Republic of Germany, Iceland, Ireland, Italy, Ivory Coast, Japan, Luxembourg, Malawi, Netherlands, New Zealand, Norway, Paraguay, Swaziland, Sweden, United Kingdom, Zaire.
Absent: 13
Antigua and Barbuda, Chile, Comoros, Dominica, El Salvador, Guatemala, Haiti, Honduras, Saint Lucia, Saint Vincent, Samoa, Solomon Islands, St. Christopher and Nevis.

E

The General Assembly,
Recalling Security Council resolutions 468 (1980) of 8 May 1980, 469 (1980) of 20 May 1980 and 484 (1980) of 19 December 1980 and General Assembly resolutions 36/147 D of 16 December 1981 and 37/88 D of 10 December 1982,[188]
Deeply concerned at the expulsion by the Israeli military occupation authorities of the Mayors of Hebron and Halhul and of the Sharia Judge of Hebron,
Recalling the Geneva Convention relative to the Protection of Civilian Persons in Time of War, of 12 August 1949,[189] in particular article 1 and the first paragraph of article 49, which read as follows:

"Article 1

"The High Contracting Parties undertake to respect and to ensure respect for the present Convention in all circumstances."

"Article 49

"Individual or mass forcible transfers, as well as deportations of protected persons from occupied territory to the territory of the occupying Power or to that of any other country, occupied or not, are prohibited, regardless of their motive . . .",

Reaffirming the applicability of the Geneva Convention to the Palestinian and other Arab territories occupied by Israel since 1967, including Jerusalem,
1. *Demands once more* that the Government of Israel, the occupying Power, rescind the illegal measures taken by the Israeli military occupation authorities in expelling and imprisoning the Mayors of Hebron and Halhul and in expelling the Sharia Judge of Hebron and that it facilitate the immediate return of the expelled Palestinian leaders so that they can resume the functions for which they were elected and appointed;
2. *Requests* the Secretary-General to report to the General Assembly as soon as possible on the implementation of the present resolution.

Adopted at the 98th plenary meeting:
In favour: 146
Afghanistan, Albania, Algeria, Angola, Argentina, Australia, Austria, Bahamas, Bahrain, Bangladesh, Barbados, Belgium, Belize, Benin, Bhutan, Bolivia, Botswana, Brazil, Bulgaria, Burma, Burundi, Byelorussia, Canada, Cape Verde, Central African Republic, Chad, Chile, China, Colombia, Congo, Costa Rica, Cuba, Cyprus, Czechoslovakia, Democratic Kampuchea, Democratic Yemen, Denmark, Djibouti, Dominican Republic, Ecuador, Egypt, El Salvador, Equatorial Guinea, Ethiopia, Fiji, Finland, France, Gabon, Gambia, German Democratic Republic, Federal Republic of Germany, Ghana, Greece, Grenada, Guinea, Guinea-Bissau, Guyana, Hungary, Iceland, India, Indonesia, Iran, Iraq, Ireland, Italy, Ivory Coast, Jamaica, Japan, Jordan, Kenya, Kuwait, Lao People's Democratic Republic, Lebanon, Lesotho, Liberia, Libya, Luxembourg, Madagascar, Malawi, Malaysia, Maldives, Mali, Malta, Mauritania, Mauritius, Mexico, Mongolia, Morocco, Mozambique, Nepal, Netherlands, New Zealand, Nicaragua, Nigeria, Norway, Oman, Pakistan, Panama, Papua New Guinea, Paraguay, Peru, Philippines, Poland, Portugal, Qatar, Romania, Rwanda, Saint Lucia, Sao Tome and Principe, Saudi Arabia, Senegal, Seychelles, Sierra Leone, Singapore, Somalia, Spain, Sri Lanka, Sudan, Suriname, Swaziland, Sweden, Syria, Thailand, Togo, Trinidad and Tobago, Tunisia, Turkey, Uganda, Ukraine, USSR, United Arab Emirates, United Kingdom, United Republic of Cameroon, United Republic of Tanzania, Upper Volta, Uruguay, Vanuatu, Venezuela, Viet Nam, Yemen, Yugoslavia, Zaire, Zambia, Zimbabwe.
Against: 1
Israel.
Abstention: 1
United States.
Absent: 9
Antigua and Barbuda, Comoros, Dominica, Guatemala, Haiti, Honduras, Saint Vincent, Samoa, St. Christopher and Nevis.

F

The General Assembly,
Deeply concerned that the Arab territories occupied since 1967 have been under continued Israeli military occupation,

---

[188]These resolutions refer to Israeli measures against Palestinian leaders. [ed. note]
[189]United Nations, *Treaty Series,* vol. 75, no. 973, p. 287.

Recalling Security Council resolution 497 (1981) of 17 December 1981, and General Assembly resolutions 36/226B of 17 December 1981, ES-9/1 of 5 February 1982 and 37/88 E of 10 December 1982,

Recalling its previous resolutions, in particular resolutions 3414 (XXX) of 5 December 1975, 31/61 of 9 December 1976, 32/20 of 25 November 1977, 33/28 and 33/29 of 7 December 1978, 34/70 of 6 December 1979 and 35/122 E of 11 December 1980, in which it, *inter alia*, called upon Israel to put an end to its occupation of the Arab territories and to withdraw from all those territories,

Reaffirming once more the illegality of Israel's decision of 14 December 1981 to impose its laws, jurisdiction and administration on the occupied Syrian Golan Heights, which has resulted in the effective annexation of that territory,

Reaffirming that the acquisition of territory by force is inadmissible under the Charter of the United Nations and that all territories thus occupied by Israel must be returned,

Recalling the Geneva Convention relative to the Protection of Civilian Persons in Time of War, of 12 August 1949,[190]

1. *Strongly condemns* Israel, the occupying Power, for its refusal to comply with the relevant resolutions of the General Assembly and the Security Council, particularly Council resolution 497 (1981), in which the Council, *inter alia*, decided that the Israeli decision to impose its laws, jurisdiction and administration on the occupied Syrian Golan Heights was null and void and without international legal effect and demanded that Israel, the occupying Power, should rescind forthwith its decision;

2. *Condemns* the persistence of Israel in changing the physical character, demographic composition, institutional structure and legal status of the occupied Syrian Arab Golan Heights;

3. *Determines* that all legislative and administrative measures and actions taken or to be taken by Israel, the occupying Power, that purport to alter the character and legal status of the Syrian Arab Golan Heights are null and void and constitute a flagrant violation of international law and of the Geneva Convention relative to the Protection of Civilian Persons in Time of War, of 12 August 1949, and have no legal effect;

4. *Strongly condemns* Israel for its attempts and measures to impose forcibly Israeli citizenship and Israeli identity cards on the Syrian citizens in the occupied Syrian Arab Golan Heights and calls upon it to desist from its repressive measures against the population of the Syrian Arab Golan Heights;

5. *Calls once again upon* Member States not to recognize any of the legislative or administrative measures and actions referred to above;

6. *Requests* the Secretary-General to submit to the General Assembly at its thirty-ninth session a report on the implementation of the present resolution.

Adopted at the 98th plenary meeting:
In favour: 144
Afghanistan, Albania, Algeria, Angola, Argentina, Australia, Austria, Bahamas, Bahrain, Bangladesh, Barbados, Belgium, Belize, Benin, Bhutan, Bolivia, Botswana, Brazil, Bulgaria, Burma, Burundi, Byelorussia, Canada, Cape Verde, Central African Republic, Chad, Chile, China, Colombia, Congo, Costa Rica, Cuba, Cyprus, Czechoslovakia, Democratic Kampuchea, Democratic Yemen, Denmark, Djibouti, Dominican Republic, Ecuador, Egypt, El Salvador, Equatorial Guinea, Ethiopia, Fiji, Finland, France, Gabon, Gambia, German Democratic Republic, Federal Republic of Germany, Ghana, Greece, Grenada, Guinea, Guinea-Bissau, Guyana, Hungary, Iceland, India, Indonesia, Iran, Iraq, Ireland, Italy, Ivory Coast, Jamaica, Japan, Jordan, Kenya, Kuwait, Lao People's Democratic Republic, Lebanon, Lesotho, Liberia, Libya, Luxembourg, Madagascar, Malawi, Malaysia, Maldives, Mali, Malta, Mauritania, Mauritius, Mexico, Mongolia, Morocco, Mozambique, Nepal, Netherlands, New Zealand, Nicaragua, Nigeria, Norway, Oman, Pakistan, Panama, Papua New Guinea, Paraguay, Peru, Philippines, Poland, Portugal, Qatar, Romania, Rwanda, Sao Tome and Principe, Saudi Arabia, Senegal, Seychelles, Sierra Leone, Singapore, Solomon Islands, Somalia, Spain, Sri Lanka, Sudan, Suriname, Swaziland, Sweden, Syria, Thailand, Togo, Trinidad and Tobago, Tunisia, Turkey, Uganda, Ukraine, USSR, United Arab Emirates, United Kingdom, United Republic of Cameroon, United Republic of Tanzania, Upper Volta, Uruguay, Vanuatu, Venezuela, Viet Nam, Yemen, Yugoslavia, Zambia, Zimbabwe.
Against: 1
Israel.
Abstention: 1
United States.
Absent: 11
Antigua and Barbuda, Comoros, Dominica, Guatemala, Haiti, Honduras, Saint Lucia, Saint Vincent, Samoa, St. Christopher and Nevis, Zaire.

G

The General Assembly,

Bearing in mind the Geneva Convention relative to the Protection of Civilian Persons in Time of War, of 12 August 1949,[191]

Deeply shocked by the most recent atrocities committed by Israel, the occupying Power, against educational institutions in the occupied Palestinian territories,

1. *Reaffirms* the applicability of the Geneva Convention relative to the Protection of Civilian Persons in Time of War, of 12 August 1949, to the Palestinian and other Arab territories occupied by Israel since 1967, including Jerusalem;

---

[190]United Nations, *Treaty Series,* vol. 75, no. 973, p. 287.

[191]United Nations, *Treaty Series,* vol. 75, no. 973, p. 287.

2. *Condemns* Israeli policies and practices against Palestinian students and faculties in schools, universities and other educational institutions in the occupied Palestinian territories, especially the policy of opening fire on defenceless students, causing many casualties;

3. *Condemns* the systematic Israeli campaign of repression against and closing of universities in the occupied Palestinian territories, restricting and impeding the academic activities of Palestinian universities by subjecting the selection of courses, textbooks and educational programmes, the admission of students and the appointment of faculty members to the control and supervision of the military occupation authorities, in clear contravention of the Geneva Convention;

4. *Demands* that Israel, the occupying Power, comply with the provisions of that Convention, rescind all actions and measures against all educational institutions, ensure the freedom of those institutions and refrain forthwith from hindering the effective operation of the universities and other educational institutions;

5. *Requests* the Secretary-General to submit a report on the implementation of the present resolution before the end of 1984.

Adopted at the 98th plenary meeting:
In favour: 116
Afghanistan, Albania, Algeria, Angola, Argentina, Austria, Bahamas, Bahrain, Bangladesh, Belize, Benin, Bhutan, Bolivia, Botswana, Brazil, Bulgaria, Burundi, Byelorussia, Cape Verde, Central African Republic, Chad, China, Congo, Cuba, Cyprus, Czechoslovakia, Democratic Kampuchea, Democratic Yemen, Djibouti, Dominican Republic, Ecuador, Egypt, Equatorial Guinea, Ethiopia, Fiji, Gabon, Gambia, German Democratic Republic, Ghana, Greece, Grenada, Guinea, Guinea-Bissau, Guyana, Hungary, India, Indonesia, Iran, Iraq, Ivory Coast, Jamaica, Jordan, Kenya, Kuwait, Lao People's Democratic Republic, Lebanon, Lesotho, Libya, Madagascar, Malawi, Malaysia, Maldives, Mali, Malta, Mauritania, Mauritius, Mexico, Mongolia, Morocco, Mozambique, Nepal, Nicaragua, Niger, Nigeria, Oman, Pakistan, Panama, Papua New Guinea, Peru, Philippines, Poland, Portugal, Qatar, Romania, Rwanda, Sao Tome and Principe, Saudi Arabia, Senegal, Seychelles, Sierra Leone, Singapore, Somalia, Spain, Sri Lanka, Sudan, Suriname, Syria, Thailand, Togo, Trinidad and Tobago, Tunisia, Turkey, Uganda, Ukraine, USSR, United Arab Emirates, United Republic of Cameroon, United Republic of Tanzania, Upper Volta, Vanuatu, Venezuela, Viet Nam, Yemen, Yugoslavia, Zambia, Zimbabwe.
Against: 2
Israel, United States.
Abstentions: 28
Australia, Barbados, Belgium, Burma, Canada, Chile, Colombia, Costa Rica, Denmark, Finland, France, Federal Republic of Germany, Iceland, Ireland, Italy, Japan, Liberia, Luxembourg, Netherlands, New Zealand, Norway, Paraguay, Solomon Islands, Swaziland, Sweden, United

Kingdom, Uruguay, Zaire.
Absent: 11
Antigua and Barbuda, Comoros, Dominica, El Salvador, Guatemala, Haiti, Honduras, Saint Lucia, Saint Vincent, Samoa, St. Christopher and Nevis.

H

The General Assembly,

Recalling Security Council resolution 471 (1980) of 5 June 1980, in which the Council condemned the assassination attempts against the Mayors of Nablus, Ramallah and Al Bireh and called for the immediate apprehension and prosecution of the perpetrators of those crimes,

Recalling also General Assembly resolutions 36/147 G of 16 December 1981 and 37/88 G of 10 December 1982,

Recalling once again the Geneva Convention relative to the Protection of Civilian Persons in Time of War, of 12 August 1949,[192] in particular article 27, which states, *inter alia:*

"Protected persons are entitled, in all circumstances, to respect for their persons . . . They shall at all times be humanely treated, and shall be protected especially against all acts of violence or threats thereof . . . ",

Reaffirming the applicability of that Convention to the Arab territories occupied by Israel since 1967, including Jerusalem,

1. *Expresses deep concern* that Israel, the occupying Power, has failed for three years to apprehend and prosecute the perpetrators of the assassination attempts;

2. *Demands once more* that Israel, the occupying Power, inform the Secretary-General of the results of the investigations relative to the assassination attempts;

3. *Requests* the Secretary-General to submit to the General Assembly at its thirty-ninth session a report on the implementation of the present resolution.

Adopted at the 98th plenary meeting:
In favour: 145
Afghanistan, Albania, Algeria, Angola, Argentina, Australia, Austria, Bahamas, Bahrain, Bangladesh, Barbados, Belgium, Belize, Benin, Bhutan, Bolivia, Botswana, Brazil, Bulgaria, Burma, Burundi, Byelorussia, Canada, Cape Verde, Central African Republic, Chad, Chile, China, Colombia, Congo, Costa Rica, Cuba, Cyprus, Czechoslovakia, Democratic Kampuchea, Democratic Yemen, Denmark, Djibouti, Dominican Republic, Ecuador, Egypt, El Salvador, Equatorial Guinea, Ethiopia, Fiji, Finland, France, Gabon, Gambia, German Democratic Republic, Federal Republic of Germany, Ghana, Greece, Grenada, Guinea, Guinea-Bissau, Guyana, Hungary, Iceland, India, Indonesia, Iran, Iraq, Ireland, Italy, Ivory Coast, Jamaica, Japan, Jordan, Kenya, Kuwait, Lao People's Democratic Republic, Lebanon, Lesotho, Liberia, Libya, Luxembourg, Madagascar, Malawi, Malaysia, Maldives, Mali, Malta, Mauritania, Mauritius, Mexico, Mongolia, Morocco, Mozambique, Nepal, Netherlands, New Zealand, Nicara-

---

[192]United Nations, *Treaty Series*, vol. 75, no. 973, p. 287.

gua, Niger, Nigeria, Norway, Oman, Pakistan, Panama, Papua New Guinea, Paraguay, Peru, Philippines, Poland, Portugal, Qatar, Romania, Rwanda, Saint Lucia, Sao Tome and Principe, Saudi Arabia, Senegal, Seychelles, Sierra Leone, Singapore, Solomon Islands, Somalia, Spain, Sri Lanka, Sudan, Suriname, Swaziland, Sweden, Syria, Thailand, Togo, Trinidad and Tobago, Tunisia, Turkey, Uganda, Ukraine, USSR, United Arab Emirates, United Kingdom, United Republic of Cameroon, United Republic of Tanzania, Upper Volta, Uruguay, Vanuatu, Venezuela, Viet Nam, Yemen, Yugoslavia, Zambia, Zimbabwe.

Against: 1

Israel.

Abstention: 1

United States.

Absent: 10

Antigua and Barbuda, Comoros, Dominica, Guatemala, Haiti, Honduras, Saint Vincent, Samoa, St. Christopher and Nevis, Zaire.

Resolution No. 38/83 A, B, C, D, E, F, G, H, I, J, K of 15 December 1983

ON THE UNITED NATIONS RELIEF AND WORKS AGENCY FOR PALESTINE REFUGEES IN THE NEAR EAST: CALLING FOR CONTRIBUTIONS BY GOVERNMENTS TO THE AGENCY AND ENDORSING ASSISTANCE TO PALESTINIAN REFUGEES, CALLING ON ISRAEL TO PERMIT THE RETURN OF DISPLACED PALESTINIANS AND TO REMOVE OBSTACLES TO THE ESTABLISHMENT OF A UNIVERSITY OF JERUSALEM FOR PALESTINIAN REFUGEES, AND REQUESTING THE SECRETARY-GENERAL TO TAKE APPROPRIATE STEPS FOR THE PROTECTION AND ADMINISTRATION OF ARAB REFUGEE PROPERTY, ASSETS AND PROPERTY RIGHTS

A

ASSISTANCE TO PALESTINE REFUGEES

The General Assembly,

Recalling its resolution 37/120 K of 16 December 1982 and all previous resolutions on the question, including resolution 194 (III) of 11 December 1948,

Taking note of the report of the Commissioner-General of the United Nations Relief and Works Agency for Palestine Refugees in the Near East covering the period from 1 July 1982 to 30 June 1983,[193]

1. *Notes with deep regret* that repatriation or compensation of the refugees as provided for in paragraph 11 of General Assembly resolution 194 (III) has not been effected, that no substantial progress has been made in the programme endorsed by the Assembly in paragraph 2 of its resolution 513 (VI) of 26 January 1952 for the reintegration of refugees either by repatriation or resettlement and that, therefore, the situation of the refugees continues to be a matter of serious concern;

2. *Expresses its thanks* to the Commissioner-General and

to all the staff of the United Nations Relief and Works Agency for Palestine Refugees in the Near East, recognizing that the Agency is doing all it can within the limits of available resources, and also expresses its thanks to the specialized agencies and private organizations for their valuable work in assisting the refugees;

3. *Reiterates its request* that the headquarters of the United Nations Relief and Works Agency for Palestine Refugees in the Near East should be relocated to its former site within its area of operations as soon as practicable;

4. *Notes with regret* that the United Nations Conciliation Commission for Palestine has been unable to find a means of achieving progress in the implementation of paragraph 11 of General Assembly resolution 194 (III)[194] and requests the Commission to exert continued efforts towards the implementation of that paragraph and to report to the Assembly as appropriate, but not later than 1 October 1984;

5. *Directs attention* to the continuing seriousness of the financial position of the United Nations Relief and Works Agency for Palestine Refugees in the Near East, as outlined in the report of the Commissioner-General;

6. *Notes with profound concern* that, despite the commendable and successful efforts of the Commissioner-General to collect additional contributions, this increased level of income to the United Nations Relief and Works Agency for Palestine Refugees in the Near East is still insufficient to cover essential budget requirements in the present year and that, at currently foreseen levels of giving, deficits will recur each year;

7. *Calls upon* all Governments as a matter of urgency to make the most generous efforts possible to meet the anticipated needs of the United Nations Relief and Works Agency for Palestine Refugees in the Near East, particularly in the light of the budgetary deficit projected in the report of the Commissioner-General, and therefore urges non-contributing Governments to contribute regularly and contributing Governments to consider increasing their regular contributions;

8. *Decides* to extend until 30 June 1987, without prejudice to the provisions of paragraph 11 of General Assembly resolution 194 (III), the mandate of the United Nations Relief and Works Agency for Palestine Refugees in the Near East.

Adopted at the 98th plenary meeting:
In favour: 147

Afghanistan, Algeria, Angola, Australia, Austria, Bahamas, Bahrain, Bangladesh, Barbados, Belgium, Belize, Benin, Bhutan, Bolivia, Botswana, Brazil, Bulgaria, Burma, Burundi, Byelorussia, Canada, Cape Verde, Central African Republic, Chad, Chile, China, Colombia, Congo, Costa Rica, Cuba, Cyprus, Czechoslovakia, Democratic Kampuchea, Democratic Yemen, Denmark, Djibouti, Dominica, Dominican Republic, Ecuador, Egypt, El Salvador, Equatorial Guinea, Ethiopia, Fiji, Finland, France,

---

[193]*Official Records of the General Assembly, Thirty-eighth Session, Supplement No. 13* (A/38/13 and Corr.1).

[194]See A/38/397, annex.

Gabon, Gambia, German Democratic Republic, Federal Republic of Germany, Ghana, Greece, Grenada, Guinea, Guinea Bissau, Guyana, Honduras, Hungary, Iceland, India, Indonesia, Iran, Iraq, Ireland, Italy, Ivory Coast, Jamaica, Japan, Jordan, Kenya, Kuwait, Lao People's Democratic Republic, Lebanon, Lesotho, Liberia, Libya, Luxembourg, Madagascar, Malawi, Malaysia, Maldives, Mali, Malta, Mauritania, Mauritius, Mexico, Mongolia, Morocco, Mozambique, Nepal, Netherlands, New Zealand, Nicaragua, Niger, Nigeria, Norway, Oman, Pakistan, Panama, Papua New Guinea, Paraguay, Peru, Philippines, Poland, Portugal, Qatar, Romania, Rwanda, Saint Lucia, Sao Tome and Principe, Saudi Arabia, Senegal, Seychelles, Sierra Leone, Singapore, Somalia, Spain, Sri Lanka, Sudan, Suriname, Swaziland, Sweden, Syria, Thailand, Togo, Trinidad and Tobago, Tunisia, Turkey, Uganda, Ukraine, USSR, United Arab Emirates, United Kingdom, United Republic of Cameroon, United Republic of Tanzania, United States, Upper Volta, Uruguay, Vanuatu, Venezuela, Viet Nam, Yemen, Yugoslavia, Zaire, Zambia, Zimbabwe.

Against: 0

Abstention: 1

Israel.

Absent: 9

Albania, Antigua and Barbuda, Comoros, Guatemala, Haiti, Saint Vincent, Samoa, Solomon Islands, St. Christopher and Nevis.

B

WORKING GROUP ON THE FINANCING OF THE UNITED NATIONS RELIEF AND WORKS AGENCY FOR PALESTINE REFUGEES IN THE NEAR EAST

The General Assembly,

Recalling its resolutions 2656 (XXV) of 7 December 1970, 2728 (XXV) of 15 December 1970, 2791 (XXVI) of 6 December 1971, 2964 (XXVII) of 13 December 1972, 3090 (XXVIII) of 7 December 1973, 3330 (XXIX) of 17 December 1974, 3419 D (XXX) of 8 December 1975, 31/15 C of 23 November 1976, 32/90 D of 13 December 1977, 33/112 D of 18 December 1978, 34/52 D of 23 November 1979, 35/13 D of 3 November 1980, 36/146 E of 16 December 1981 and 37/120 A of 16 December 1982,[195]

Recalling also its decision 36/462 of 15 March 1982, whereby it took note of the special report of the Working Group on the Financing of the United Nations Relief and Works Agency for Palestine Refugees in the Near East[196] and adopted the recommendations contained therein,

Having considered the report of the Working Group on the Financing of the United Nations Relief and Works Agency for Palestine Refugees in the Near East,[197]

Taking into account the report of the Commissioner-General of the United Nations Relief and Works Agency for Palestine Refugees in the Near East, covering the period from 1 July 1982 to 30 June 1983,[198]

Gravely concerned at the critical financial situation of the United Nations Relief and Works Agency for Palestine Refugees in the Near East, which has already reduced the essential minimum services being provided to the Palestine refugees and which threatens even greater reductions in the future,

Emphasizing the urgent need for extraordinary efforts in order to maintain, at least at their present minimum level, the activities of the United Nations Relief and Works Agency for Palestine Refugees in the Near East,

1. *Commends* the Working Group on the Financing of the United Nations Relief and Works Agency for Palestine Refugees in the Near East for its efforts to assist in ensuring the Agency's financial security;

2. *Takes note with approval* of the report of the Working Group;

3. *Requests* the Working Group to continue its efforts, in co-operation with the Secretary-General and the Commissioner-General of the United Nations Relief and Works Agency for Palestine Refugees in the Near East, for the financing of the Agency for a further period of one year;

4. *Requests* the Secretary-General to provide the necessary services and assistance to the Working Group for the conduct of its work.

Adopted at the 98th plenary meeting without a vote.

C

ASSISTANCE TO PERSONS DISPLACED AS A RESULT OF THE JUNE 1967 AND SUBSEQUENT HOSTILITIES

The General Assembly,

Recalling its resolution 37/120B of 16 December 1982 and all previous resolutions on the question,

Taking note of the report of the Commissioner-General of the United Nations Relief and Works Agency for Palestine Refugees in the Near East, covering the period from 1 July 1982 to 30 June 1983,[199]

Concerned about the continued human suffering resulting from the hostilities in the Middle East,

1. *Reaffirms* its resolution 37/120 B and all previous resolutions on the question;

2. *Endorses,* bearing in mind the objectives of those resolutions, the efforts of the Commissioner-General of the United Nations Relief and Works Agency for Palestine Refugees in the Near East to continue to provide humanitarian assistance as far as practicable, on an emergency basis and as a temporary measure, to other persons in the area who are at present displaced and in serious need of

---

[195]These resolutions focus on the financing of the United Nations Relief and Works Agency for Palestine Refugees in the Near East. [ed. note]

[196]A/36/866; see also A/37/591.

[197]A/38/558.

[198]*Official Records of the General Assembly, Thirty-eighth Session, Supplement No. 13* (A/38/13 and Corr.1).

[199]*Official Records of the General Assembly, Thirty-eighth Session, Supplement No. 13* (A/38/13 and Corr.1).

continued assistance as a result of the June 1967 and subsequent hostilities;

3. *Strongly appeals* to all Governments and to organizations and individuals to contribute generously for the above purposes to the United Nations Relief and Works Agency for Palestine Refugees in the Near East and to the other intergovernmental and non-governmental organizations concerned.

Adopted at the 98th plenary meeting without a vote.

D

OFFERS BY MEMBER STATES OF GRANTS AND SCHOLARSHIPS FOR HIGHER EDUCATION, INCLUDING VOCATIONAL TRAINING, FOR PALESTINE REFUGEES

The General Assembly,

Recalling its resolution 212 (III) of 19 November 1948 on assistance to Palestine refugees,

Recalling also its resolutions 35/13 B of 3 November 1980, 36/146 H of 16 December 1981 and 37/120 D of 16 December 1982,

Cognizant of the fact that the Palestine refugees have, for the last three decades, lost their lands and means of livelihood,

Having examined with appreciation the report of the Secretary-General[200] on offers of grants and scholarships for higher education for Palestine refugees and on the scope of the implementation of resolution 37/120 D,

Having also examined the report of the Commissioner-General of the United Nations Relief and Works Agency for Palestine Refugees in the Near East covering the period from 1 July 1982 to 30 June 1983,[201] dealing with this subject,

1. *Urges* all States to respond to the appeal contained in General Assembly resolution 32/90 F of 13 December 1977 in a manner commensurate with the needs of Palestine refugees for higher education and vocational training;

2. *Strongly appeals* to all States, specialized agencies and non-governmental organizations to augment the special allocations for grants and scholarships to Palestine refugees in addition to their contributions to the regular budget of the United Nations Relief and Works Agency for Palestine Refugees in the Near East;

3. *Expresses its appreciation* to all Governments, specialized agencies and non-governmental organizations that responded favourably to General Assembly resolution 36/146 H;

4. *Invites* the relevant organizations of the United Nations system to continue, within their respective spheres of competence, to expand assistance for higher education to Palestine refugee students;

5. *Appeals* to all States, specialized agencies and the United Nations University to contribute generously to the Palestinian universities in the territories occupied by Israel since 1967, including, in due course, the proposed University of Jerusalem "Al-Quds" for Palestine refugees;

6. *Also appeals* to all States, specialized agencies and other international bodies to contribute towards the establishment of vocational training centres for Palestine refugees;

7. *Requests* the United Nations Relief and Works Agency for Palestine Refugees in the Near East to act as the recipient and trustee for such special allocations and scholarships and to award them to qualified Palestine refugee candidates;

8. *Requests* the Secretary-General to report to the General Assembly at its thirty-ninth session on the implementation of the present resolution.

Adopted at the 98th plenary meeting:
In favour: 147

Afghanistan, Algeria, Angola, Argentina, Australia, Austria, Bahamas, Bahrain, Bangladesh, Barbados, Belgium, Belize, Benin, Bhutan, Bolivia, Botswana, Brazil, Bulgaria, Burma, Burundi, Byelorussia, Canada, Cape Verde, Central African Republic, Chad, Chile, China, Colombia, Congo, Costa Rica, Cuba, Cyprus, Czechoslovakia, Democratic Kampuchea, Democratic Yemen, Denmark, Djibouti, Dominica, Dominican Republic, Ecuador, Egypt, El Salvador, Equatorial Guinea, Ethiopia, Fiji, Finland, France, Gabon, Gambia, German Democratic Republic, Federal Republic of Germany, Ghana, Greece, Grenada, Guinea, Guinea-Bissau, Guyana, Honduras, Hungary, Iceland, India, Indonesia, Iran, Iraq, Ireland, Italy, Ivory Coast, Jamaica, Japan, Jordan, Kenya, Kuwait, Lao People's Democratic Republic, Lebanon, Lesotho, Liberia, Libya, Luxembourg, Madagascar, Malawi, Malaysia, Maldives, Mali, Malta, Mauritania, Mauritius, Mexico, Mongolia, Morocco, Mozambique, Nepal, Netherlands, New Zealand, Nicaragua, Niger, Nigeria, Norway, Oman, Pakistan, Panama, Papua New Ginea, Paraguay, Peru, Philippines, Poland, Portugal, Qatar, Romania, Rwanda, Saint Lucia, Sao Tome and Principe, Saudi Arabia, Senegal, Seychelles, Sierra Leone, Singapore, Somalia, Spain, Sri Lanka, Sudan, Suriname, Swaziland, Sweden, Syria, Thailand, Togo, Trinidad and Tobago, Tunisia, Turkey, Uganda, Ukraine, USSR, United Arab Emirates, United Kingdom, United Republic of Cameroon, United Republic of Tanzania, United States, Upper Volta, Uruguay, Vanuatu, Venezuela, Viet Nam, Yemen, Yugoslavia, Zaire, Zambia, Zimbabwe.

Against: 0
Abstention: 1
Israel.
Absent: 9

Albania, Antigua and Barbuda, Comoros, Guatemala, Haiti, Saint Vincent, Samoa, Solomon Islands, St. Christopher and Nevis.

E

PALESTINE REFUGEES IN THE GAZA STRIP

The General Assembly,
Recalling Security Council resolution 237 (1967) of 14

---

[200]A/38/149.
[201]*Officiai Records of the General Assembly, Thirty-eighth Session, Supplement No. 13* (A/38/13 and Corr.1).

June 1967,

Recalling also General Assembly resolutions 2792 C (XXVI) of 6 December 1971, 2963 C (XXVII) of 13 December 1972, 3089 C (XXVIII) of 7 December 1973, 3331 D (XXIX) of 17 December 1974, 3419 C (XXX) of 8 December 1975, 31/15 E of 23 November 1976, 32/90 C of 13 December 1977, 33/112 E of 18 December 1978, 34/52 F of 23 November 1979, 35/13 F of 3 November 1980, 36/146 A of 16 December 1981 and 37/120 E of 16 December 1982,[202]

Having considered the report of the Commissioner-General of the United Nations Relief and Works Agency for Palestine Refugees in the Near East, covering the period from 1 July 1982 to 30 June 1983,[203] and the report of the Secretary-General of 3 October 1983,[204]

Recalling the provisions of paragraph 11 of its resolution 194 (III) of 11 December 1948 and considering that measures to resettle Palestine refugees in the Gaza Strip away from the homes and property from which they were displaced constitute a violation of their inalienable right of return,

Alarmed by the reports received from the Commissioner-General that the Israeli occupying authorities, in contravention of Israel's obligations under international law, persist in their policy of demolishing, on punitive grounds shelters occupied by refugee families,

1. *Reiterates. its demand* that Israel desist from the removal and resettlement of Palestine refugees in the Gaza Strip and from the destruction of their shelters;

2. *Requests* the Secretary-General, after consulting with the Commissioner-General of the United Nations Relief and Works Agency for Palestine Refugees in the Near East, to report to the General Assembly, before the opening of its thirty-ninth session, on Israel's compliance with paragraph 1 above.

Adopted at the 98th plenary meeting:
In favour: 146
Afghanistan, Albania, Algeria, Angola, Argentina, Australia, Austria, Bahamas, Bahrain, Bangladesh, Barbados, Belgium, Belize, Benin, Bhutan, Bolivia, Botswana, Brazil, Bulgaria, Burma, Burundi, Byelorussia, Canada, Cape Verde, Central African Republic, Chad, Chile, China, Colombia, Congo, Costa Rica, Cuba, Cyprus, Czechoslovakia, Democratic Kampuchea, Democratic Yemen, Denmark, Djibouti, Dominican Republic, Ecuador, Egypt, El Salvador, Equatorial Guinea, Ethiopia, Fiji, Finland, France, Gabon, Gambia, German Democratic Republic, Federal Republic of Germany, Ghana, Greece, Grenada, Guinea, Guinea-Bissau, Guyana, Honduras, Hungary, Iceland, India, Indonesia, Iran, Iraq, Ireland, Italy, Ivory Coast, Jamaica, Japan, Jordan, Kenya, Kuwait, Lao People's Democratic Republic, Lebanon, Lesotho, Liberia, Libya, Luxembourg, Madagascar, Malawi, Malaysia, Maldives, Mali, Malta, Mauritania, Mauritius, Mexico, Mongolia, Morocco, Mozambique, Nepal, Netherlands, New Zealand, Nicaragua, Niger, Nigeria, Norway, Oman, Pakistan, Panama, Papua New Guinea, Paraguay, Peru, Philippines, Poland, Portugal, Qatar, Romania, Rwanda, Saint Lucia, Sao Tome and Principe, Saudi Arabia, Senegal, Seychelles, Sierra Leone, Singapore, Somalia, Spain, Sri Lanka, Sudan, Suriname, Swaziland, Sweden, Syria, Thailand, Togo, Trinidad and Tobago, Tunisia, Turkey, Uganda, Ukraine, USSR, United Arab Emirates, United Kingdom, United Republic of Cameroon, United Republic of Tanzania, Upper Volta, Uruguay, Vanuatu, Venezuela, Viet Nam, Yemen, Yugoslavia, Zaire, Zambia, Zimbabwe.

Against: 2
Israel, United States.

Abstentions: 0

Absent: 9
Antigua and Barbuda, Comoros, Dominica, Guatemala, Haiti, Saint Vincent, Samoa, Solomon Islands, St. Christopher and Nevis.

F

RESUMPTION OF THE RATION DISTRIBUTION TO PALESTINE REFUGEES

The General Assembly,

Recalling its resolutions 36/146 F of 16 December 1981, 37/120 F of 16 December 1982 and all previous resolutions on the question, including resolution 302 (IV) of 8 December 1949,

Having considered the report of the Commissioner-General of the United Nations Relief and Works Agency for Palestine Refugees in the Near East, covering the period from 1 July 1982 to 30 June 1983,[205]

Taking note of the report of the Joint Inspection Unit of 1 August 1983,[206]

Deeply concerned at the interruption by the United Nations Relief and Works Agency for Palestine Refugees in the Near East, owing to financial difficulties, of the general ration distribution to Palestine refugees in all fields in the occupied Palestinian territories, Jordan and the Syrian Arab Republic,

1. *Regrets* that resolution 37/120 F of 16 December 1982 has not been implemented;

2. *Calls upon* all Governments, as a matter of urgency, to make the most generous efforts possible and to offer the necessary resources to meet the needs of the United Nations Relief and Works Agency for Palestine Refugees in the Near East, particularly in the light of the interruption by the Agency of the general ration distribution to Palestine refugees in all fields, and therefore urges noncontributing Governments to contribute regularly and con-

---

[202]On Israeli actions harmful to Palestinian refugees in the Gaza Strip. [ed. note]
[203]*Official Records of the General Assembly, Thirty-eighth Session, Supplement No. 13* (A/38/13 and Corr.1).
[204]A/38/418.

[205]*Official Records of the General Assembly, Thirty-eighth Session, Supplement No. 13* (A/38/13 and Corr.1).
[206]A/38/143.

tributing Governments to consider increasing their regular contributions;

3. *Requests* the Commissioner-General of the United Nations Relief and Works Agency for Palestine Refugees in the Near East to resume on a continuing basis the interrupted general ration distribution to Palestine refugees in all fields.

Adopted at the 98th plenary meeting:

In favour: 123

Afghanistan, Algeria, Angola, Argentina, Bahamas, Bahrain, Bangladesh, Barbados, Belize, Benin, Bhutan, Bolivia, Botswana, Brazil, Bulgaria, Burma, Burundi, Byelorussia, Cape Verde, Central African Republic, Chad, Chile, China, Colombia, Congo, Costa Rica, Cuba, Cyprus, Czechoslovakia, Democratic Kampuchea, Democratic Yemen, Djibouti, Dominican Republic, Ecuador, Egypt, El Salvador, Equatorial Guinea, Ethiopia, Fiji, Gabon, Gambia, German Democratic Republic, Ghana, Greece, Grenada, Guinea, Guinea-Bissau, Guyana, Honduras, Hungary, India, Indonesia, Iran, Iraq, Ivory Coast, Jamaica, Jordan, Kenya, Kuwait, Lao People's Democratic Republic, Lebanon, Lesotho, Liberia, Libya, Madagascar, Malawi, Malaysia, Maldives, Mali, Malta, Mauritania, Mauritius, Mexico, Mongolia, Morocco, Mozambique, Nepal, Nicaragua, Niger, Nigeria, Oman, Pakistan, Panama, Papua New Guinea, Paraguay, Peru, Philippines, Poland, Qatar, Romania, Rwanda, Sao Tome and Principe, Saudi Arabia, Senegal, Seychelles, Sierra Leone, Singapore, Somalia, Sri Lanka, Sudan, Suriname, Swaziland, Syria, Thailand, Togo, Trinidad and Tobago, Tunisia, Turkey, Uganda, Ukraine, USSR, United Arab Emirates, United Republic of Cameroon, United Republic of Tanzania, Upper Volta, Uruguay, Vanuatu, Venezuela, Viet Nam, Yemen, Yugoslavia, Zambia, Zimbabwe.

Against: 19

Australia, Belgium, Canada, Denmark, Finland, France, Federal Republic of Germany, Iceland, Ireland, Israel, Italy, Japan, Luxembourg, Netherlands, New Zealand, Norway, Sweden, United Kingdom, United States.

Abstentions: 3

Austria, Portugal, Spain.

Absent: 12

Albania, Antigua and Barbuda, Comoros, Dominica, Guatemala, Haiti, Saint Lucia, Saint Vincent, Samoa, Solomon Islands, St. Christopher and Nevis, Zaire.

G

POPULATION AND REFUGEES DISPLACED SINCE 1967

The General Assembly,

Recalling Security Council resolution 237 (1967) of 14 June 1967,

Recalling also General Assembly resolutions 2252 (ES-V) of 4 July 1967, 2452 A (XXII) of 19 December 1968, 2535 B (XXIV) of 10 December 1969, 2672 D (XXV) of 8 December 1970, 2792 E (XXVI) of 6 December 1971, 2963 C and D (XXVII) of 13 December 1972, 3089 C (XXVIII) of 7 December 1973, 3331 D (XXIX) of 17 December 1974, 3419 C (XXX) of 8 December 1975,

31/15 D of 23 November 1976, 32/90 E of 13 December 1977, 33/112 F of 18 December 1978, 34/52 E of 23 November 1979, ES-7/2 of 29 July 1980, 35/13 E of 3 November 1980, 36/146 B of 16 December 1981 and 37/120 G of 16 December 1982,[207]

Having considered the report of the Commissioner-General of the United Nations Relief and Works Agency for Palestine Refugees in the Near East, covering the period from 1 July 1982 to 30 June 1983,[208] and the report of the Secretary-General of 3 October 1983,[209]

1. *Reaffirms* the inalienable right of all displaced inhabitants to return to their homes or former places of residence in the territories occupied by Israel since 1967 and declares once more that any attempt to restrict, or to attach conditions to, the free exercise of the right of return by any displaced person is inconsistent with that inalienable right and inadmissible;

2. *Considers* any and all agreements embodying any restriction on or condition for the return of the displaced inhabitants as null and void;

3. *Strongly deplores* the continued refusal of the Israeli authorities to take steps for the return of the displaced inhabitants;

4. *Calls once more upon* Israel:

(*a*) To take immediate steps for the return of all displaced inhabitants;

(*b*) To desist from all measures that obstruct the return of the displaced inhabitants, including measures affecting the physical and demographic structure of the occupied territories;

5. *Requests* the Secretary-General, after consulting with the Commissioner-General of the United Nations Relief and Works Agency for Palestine Refugees in the Near East, to report to the General Assembly, before the opening of its thirty-ninth session, on Israel's compliance with paragraph 4 above.

Adopted at the 98th plenary meeting:

In favour: 128

Afghanistan, Albania, Algeria, Angola, Argentina, Bahamas, Bahrain, Bangladesh, Barbados, Belize, Benin, Bhutan, Bolivia, Botswana, Brazil, Bulgaria, Burma, Burundi, Byelorussia, Cape Verde, Central African Republic, Chad, Chile, China, Colombia, Congo, Costa Rica, Cuba, Cyprus, Czechoslovakia, Democratic Kampuchea, Democratic Yemen, Djibouti, Dominican Republic, Ecuador, Egypt, El Salvador, Equatorial Guinea, Ethiopia, Fiji, Gabon, Gambia, German Democratic Republic, Ghana, Greece, Grenada, Guinea, Guinea-Bissau, Guyana, Honduras, Hungary, India, Indonesia, Iran, Iraq, Ivory Coast, Jamaica, Japan, Jordan, Kenya, Kuwait, Lao People's Democratic Republic, Lebanon, Lesotho, Liberia, Libya, Madagascar, Malawi, Malaysia, Maldives, Mali, Malta, Mauritania, Mauritius, Mexico, Mongolia, Morocco, Mozam-

---

[207] Concerning persons displaced since 1967. [ed. note]
[208] *Official Records of the General Assembly, Thirty-eighth Session, Supplement No. 13* (A/38/13 and Corr.1).
[209] A/38/419.

bique, Nepal, Nicaragua, Niger, Nigeria, Oman, Pakistan, Panama, Papua New Guinea, Paraguay, Peru, Philippines, Poland, Portugal, Qatar, Romania, Rwanda, Sao Tome and Principe, Saudi Arabia, Senegal, Seychelles, Sierra Leone, Singapore, Somalia, Spain, Sri Lanka, Sudan, Suriname, Swaziland, Syria, Thailand, Togo, Trinidad and Tobago, Tunisia, Turkey, Uganda, Ukraine, USSR, United Arab Emirates, United Republic of Cameroon, United Republic of Tanzania, Upper Volta, Uruguay, Vanuatu, Venezuela, Viet Nam, Yemen, Yugoslavia, Zaire, Zambia, Zimbabwe.

Against: 2

Israel, United States.

Abstentions: 17

Australia, Austria, Belgium, Canada, Denmark, Finland, France, Federal Republic of Germany, Iceland, Ireland, Italy, Luxembourg, Netherlands, New Zealand, Norway, Sweden, United Kingdom.

Absent: 10

Antigua and Barbuda, Comoros, Dominica, Guatemala, Haiti, Saint Lucia, Saint Vincent, Samoa, Solomon Islands, St. Christopher and Nevis.

H

REVENUES DERIVED FROM PALESTINE REFUGEE PROPERTIES

The General Assembly,

Recalling its resolutions 35/13 A to F of 3 November 1980, 36/146 C of 16 December 1981, 37/120 H of 16 December 1982 and all its previous resolutions on the question, including resolution 194 (III) of 11 December 1948,

Taking note of the reports of the Secretary-General of 2 September and 8 November 1983,[210]

Taking note also of the report of the United Nations Conciliation Commission for Palestine, covering the period from 1 October 1982 to 30 September 1983,[211]

Recalling that the Universal Declaration of Human Rights[212] and the principles of international law uphold the principle that no one shall be arbitrarily deprived of his or her private property,

Considering that the Palestine Arab refugees are entitled to their property and to the income derived from their property, in conformity with the principles of justice and equity,

Recalling, in particular, its resolution 394 (V) of 14 December 1950, in which it directed the United Nations Conciliation Commission for Palestine, in consultation with the parties concerned, to prescribe measures for the protection of the rights, property and interests of the Palestinian Arab refugees,

Taking note of the completion of the programme of identification and evaluation of Arab property, as an-

nounced by the United Nations Conciliation Commission for Palestine in its twenty-second progress report,[213] of 11 May 1964, and of the fact that the Land Office had a schedule of Arab owners and file of documents defining the location, area and other particulars of Arab property,

1. *Requests* the Secretary-General to take all appropriate steps, in consultation with the United Nations Conciliation Commission for Palestine, for the protection and administration of Arab property, assets and property rights in Israel, and to establish a fund for the receipt of income derived therefrom, on behalf of the rightful owners;

2. *Calls once again upon* the Governments concerned, especially Israel, to render all facilities and assistance to the Secretary-General in the implementation of the present resolution;

3. *Requests* the Secretary-General to report to the General Assembly at its thirty-ninth session on the implementation of the present resolution.

Adopted at the 98th plenary meeting:
In favour: 125

Afghanistan, Albania, Algeria, Angola, Argentina, Bahamas, Bahrain, Bangladesh, Barbados, Belize, Benin, Bhutan, Bolivia, Botswana, Brazil, Bulgaria, Burma, Burundi, Byelorussia, Cape Verde, Central African Republic, Chad, Chile, China, Colombia, Congo, Costa Rica, Cuba, Cyprus, Czechoslovakia, Democratic Kampuchea, Democratic Yemen, Djibouti, Dominican Republic, Ecuador, Egypt, El Salvador, Equatorial Guinea, Ethiopia, Fiji, Gabon, Gambia, German Democratic Republic, Ghana, Greece, Grenada, Guinea, Guinea-Bissau, Guyana, Honduras, Hungary, India, Indonesia, Iran, Iraq, Ivory Coast, Jamaica, Jordan, Kenya, Kuwait, Lao People's Democratic Republic, Lebanon, Lesotho, Libya, Madagascar, Malawi, Malaysia, Maldives, Mali, Malta, Mauritania, Mauritius, Mexico, Mongolia, Morocco, Mozambique, Nepal, Nicaragua, Niger, Nigeria, Oman, Pakistan, Panama, Papua New Guinea, Paraguay, Peru, Philippines, Poland, Portugal, Qatar, Romania, Rwanda, Sao Tome and Principe, Saudi Arabia, Senegal, Seychelles, Sierra Leone, Singapore, Somalia, Spain, Sri Lanka, Sudan, Suriname, Swaziland, Syria, Thailand, Togo, Trinidad and Tobago, Tunisia, Turkey, Uganda, Ukraine, USSR, United Arab Emirates, United Republic of Cameroon, United Republic of Tanzania, Upper Volta, Uruguay, Vanuatu, Venezuela, Viet Nam, Yemen, Yugoslavia, Zambia, Zimbabwe.

Against: 2

Israel, United States.

Abstentions: 20

Australia, Austria, Belgium, Canada, Denmark, Finland, France, Federal Republic of Germany, Iceland, Ireland, Italy, Japan, Liberia, Luxembourg, Netherlands, New Zealand, Norway, Sweden, United Kingdom, Zaire.

Absent: 10

Antigua and Barbuda, Comoros, Dominica, Guatemala,

---

[210]A/38/361 and Add.1.
[211]A/38/397, annex.
[212]Resolution 217 A (III).

---

[213]*Official Records of the General Assembly, Nineteenth Session, Annex No. 11,* document A/5700.

Haiti, Saint Lucia, Saint Vincent, Samoa, Solomon Islands, St. Christopher and Nevis.

I

PROTECTION OF PALESTINE REFUGEES

The General Assembly,

Recalling Security Council resolutions 508 (1982) of 5 June 1982, 509 (1982) of 6 June 1982, 511 (1982) of 18 June 1982, 512 (1982) of 19 June 1982, 513 (1982) of 4 July 1982, 515 (1982) of 29 July 1982, 517 (1982) of 4 August 1982, 518 (1982) of 12 August 1982, 519 (1982) of 17 August 1982, 520 (1982) of 17 September 1982 and 523 (1982) of 18 October 1982,[214]

Recalling General Assembly resolutions ES-7/5 of 26 June 1982, ES-7/6 of 19 August 1982, ES-7/8 of 19 August 1982, ES-7/9 of 24 September 1982 and 37/120 J of 16 December 1982,

Having considered the report of the Secretary-General of 19 October 1983,[215]

Having also considered the report of the Commissioner-General of the United Nations Relief and Works Agency for Palestine Refugees in the Near East, covering the period from 1 July 1982 to 30 June 1983,[216]

Referring to the humanitarian principles of the Geneva Convention relative to the Protection of Civilian Persons in Time of War, of 12 August 1949,[217] and to the obligations arising from the Regulations annexed to the Hague Convention IV of 1907,[218]

Deeply distressed at the sufferings of the Palestinians resulting from the Israeli invasion of Lebanon,

Reaffirming its support for Lebanese sovereignty, unity and territorial integrity,

1. *Urges* the Secretary-General, in consultation with the United Nations Relief and Works Agency for Palestine Refugees in the Near East, to undertake effective measures to guarantee the safety and security and the legal and human rights of the Palestine refugees in all the territories under Israeli occuption;

2. *Calls once again upon* Israel, the occupying Power, to release forthwith all detained Palestine refugees, including the employees of the United Nations Relief and Works Agency for Palestine Refugees in the Near East;

3. *Also calls upon* Israel to desist forthwith from preventing those Palestinians registered by the United Nations Relief and Works Agency for Palestine Refugees in the Near East as refugees in Lebanon from returning to their camps in Lebanon;

4. *Further calls upon* Israel to allow the resumption of health, medical, educational and social sevices rendered by the United Nations Relief and Works Agency for Palestine Refugees in the Near East to the Palestinians in the refugee camps in southern Lebanon;

5. *Requests* the Commissioner-General of the United Nations Relief and Works Agency for Palestine Refugees in the Near East to co-ordinate his activities in rendering those services with the Government of Lebanon, the host country;

6. *Urges* the Commissioner-General to provide housing, in consultation with the Government of Lebanon, to the Palestine refugees whose houses were demolished or razed by the Israeli forces;

7. *Calls upon* Israel to compensate the United Nations Relief and Works Agency for Palestine Refugees in the Near East for the damage to its property and facilities resulting from the Israeli invasion of Lebanon, without prejudice to Israel's responsibility for all damage resulting from that invasion;

8. *Requests* the Secretary-General, in consultation with the Commissioner-General, to report to the General Assembly, before the opening of its thirty-ninth session, on the implementation of the present resolution.

Adopted at the 98th plenary meeting:

In favour: 129

Afghanistan, Albania, Algeria, Angola, Argentina, Austria, Bahamas, Bahrain, Bangladesh, Barbados, Belize, Benin, Bhutan, Bolivia, Botswana, Brazil, Bulgaria, Burma, Burundi, Byelorussia, Cape Verde, Central African Republic, Chad, Chile, China, Colombia, Congo, Cuba, Cyprus, Czechoslovakia, Democratic Kampuchea, Democratic Yemen, Djibouti, Dominican Republic, Ecuador, Egypt, El Salvador, Equatorial Guinea, Ethiopia, Fiji, Finland, France, Gabon, Gambia, German Democratic Republic, Ghana, Greece, Grenada, Guinea, Guinea-Bissau, Guyana, Honduras, Hungary, India, Indonesia, Iran, Iraq, Ivory Coast, Japan, Jordan, Kenya, Kuwait, Lao People's Democratic Republic, Lesotho, Liberia, Libya, Madagascar, Malawi, Malaysia, Maldives, Mali, Malta, Mauritania, Mauritius, Mexico, Mongolia, Morocco, Mozambique, Nepal, New Zealand, Nicaragua, Niger, Nigeria, Oman, Pakistan, Panama, Papua New Guinea, Paraguay, Peru, Philippines, Poland, Qatar, Romania, Rwanda, Sao Tome and Principe, Saudi Arabia, Senegal, Seychelles, Sierra Leone, Singapore, Somalia, Spain, Sri Lanka, Sudan, Suriname, Swaziland, Sweden, Syria, Thailand, Togo, Trinidad and Tobago, Tunisia, Turkey, Uganda, Ukraine, USSR, United Arab Emirates, United Republic of Cameroon, United Republic of Tanzania, Upper Volta, Uruguay, Vanuatu, Venezuela, Viet Nam, Yemen, Yugoslavia, Zaire, Zambia, Zimbabwe.

Against: 2

Israel, United States.

Abstentions: 15

Australia, Belgium, Canada, Costa Rica, Denmark, Federal Republic of Germany, Iceland, Ireland, Italy, Jamaica,* Luxembourg, Netherlands, Norway, Portugal, United Kingdom.

Absent: 11

---

[214]On Israel's invasion of Lebanon. [ed. note]

[215]A/38/420 and Corr.1.

[216]*Official Records of the General Assembly, Thirty-eighth Session, Supplement No. 13* (A/38/13 and Corr.1).

[217]United Nations, *Treaty Series,* vol. 75, no. 973, p. 287.

[218]Carnegie Endowment for International Peace, *The Hague Conventions and Declarations of 1899 and 1907* (New York, Oxford University Press, 1915), p. 100.

Antigua and Barbuda, Comoros, Dominica, Guatemala, Haiti, Lebanon, Saint Lucia, Saint Vincent, Samoa, Solomon Islands, St. Christopher and Nevis.

---

* Later advised the Secretariat it had intended to vote in favour.

J

PALESTINE REFUGEES IN THE WEST BANK

The General Assembly,

Recalling Security Council resolution 237 (1967) of 14 June 1967,

Having considered the report of the Commissioner-General of the United Nations Relief and Works Agency for Palestine Refugees in the Near East, covering the period from 1 July 1982 to 30 June 1983,[219]

Alarmed by the reports that Israel plans to remove and resettle the Palestine refugees of the West Bank and to destroy their camps,

Recalling the provisions of paragraph 11 of its resolution 194 (III) of 11 December 1948 and considering that measures to resettle Palestine refugees in the West Bank away from the homes and property from which they were displaced constitute a violation of their inalienable right of return,

1. *Calls upon* Israel to abandon its plans and to refrain from the removal, and from any action that may lead to the removal and resettlement, of Palestine refugees in the West Bank and from the destruction of their camps;

2. *Requests* the Secretary-General, in co-operation with the Commissioner-General of the United Nations Relief and Works Agency for Palestine Refugees in the Near East, to keep the matter under close supervision and to report to the General Assembly, before the opening of its thirty-ninth session, on any developments regarding this matter.

Adopted at the 98th plenary meeting:

In favour: 145

Afghanistan, Albania, Algeria, Angola, Argentina, Australia, Austria, Bahamas, Bahrain, Bangladesh, Barbados, Belgium, Belize, Benin, Bhutan, Bolivia, Botswana, Brazil, Bulgaria, Burma, Burundi, Byelorussia, Canada, Cape Verde, Central African Republic, Chad, Chile, China, Colombia, Congo, Costa Rica, Cuba, Cyprus, Czechoslovakia, Democratic Kampuchea, Democratic Yemen, Denmark, Djibouti, Dominican Republic, Ecuador, Egypt, El Salvador, Equatorial Guinea, Ethiopia, Fiji, Finland, France, Gabon, Gambia, German Democratic Republic, Federal Republic of Germany, Ghana, Greece, Grenada, Guinea, Guinea-Bissau, Guyana, Honduras, Hungary, Iceland, India, Indonesia, Iran, Iraq, Ireland, Italy, Ivory Coast, Jamaica, Japan, Jordan, Kenya, Kuwait, Lao People's Democratic Republic, Lebanon, Lesotho, Liberia, Libya, Luxembourg, Madagascar, Malawi, Malaysia, Maldives, Mali, Malta, Mauritania, Mauritius, Mexico, Mongolia, Morocco, Mozambique, Nepal, Netherlands, New Zealand, Nicaragua, Niger, Nigeria, Norway, Pakistan, Panama, Papua New Guinea, Paraguay, Peru, Philippines, Poland, Portugal, Qatar, Romania, Rwanda, Saint Lucia, Sao Tome and Principe, Saudi Arabia, Senegal, Seychelles, Sierra Leone, Singapore, Somalia, Spain, Sri Lanka, Sudan, Suriname, Swaziland, Sweden, Syria, Thailand, Togo, Trinidad and Tobago, Tunisia, Turkey, Uganda, Ukraine, USSR, United Arab Emirates, United Kingdom, United Republic of Cameroon, United Republic of Tanzania, Upper Volta, Uruguay, Vanuatu, Venezuela, Viet Nam, Yemen, Yugoslavia, Zaire, Zambia, Zimbabwe.

Against: 2

Israel, United States.

Abstentions: 0

Absent: 10

Antigua and Barbuda, Comoros, Dominica, Guatemala, Haiti, Oman, Saint Vincent, Samoa, Solomon Islands, St. Christopher and Nevis.

K

UNIVERSITY OF JERUSALEM "AL-QUDS" FOR PALESTINE REFUGEES

The General Assembly,

Recalling its resolutions 36/146 G of 16 December 1981 and 37/120 C of 16 December 1982,

Having examined the report of the Secretary-General on the question of the establishment of a university at Jerusalem,[220] prepared in pursuance of paragraphs 5 and 7 of resolution 37/120 C,

Having also examined the report of the Commissioner-General of the United Nations Relief and Works Agency for Palestine Refugees in the Near East, covering the period from 1 July 1982 to 30 June 1983,[221]

1. *Commends* the constructive efforts made by the Secretary-General, the Commissioner-General of the United Nations Relief and Works Agency for Palestine Refugees in the Near East, the Council of the United Nations University and the United Nations Educational, Scientific and Cultural Organization, which worked diligently towards the implementation of General Assembly resolution 37/120 C and other relevant resolutions;

2. *Further commends* the close co-operation of the competent educational authorities concerned;

3. *Emphasizes* the need for strengthening the educational system in the Arab territories occupied since 5 June 1967, including Jerusalem, and specifically the need for the establishment of the proposed university;

4. *Takes note* of the various steps recommended in the report of the Secretary-General;

5. *Requests* the Secretary-General to continue to take all

---

[219]*Official Records of the General Assembly, Thirty-eighth Session, Supplement No. 13* (A/38/13 and Corr.1).

[220]A/38/386.

[221]*Official Records of the General Assembly, Thirty-eighth Session, Supplement No. 13* (A/38/13 and Corr.1).

necessary measures for establishing the University of Jerusalem "Al-Quds" in accordance with General Assembly resolution 35/13 B of 3 November 1980, giving due consideration to the recommendations consistent with the provisions of that resolution;

6. *Calls upon* Israel, the occupying Power, to co-operate in the implementation of the present resolution and to remove the hindrances which it has put in the way of establishing the University of Jerusalem;

7. *Requests* the Secretary-General to report to the General Assembly at its thirty-ninth session on the progress made in the implementation of the present resolution.

Adopted at the 98th plenary meeting:
In favour: 146
Afghanistan, Albania, Algeria, Angola, Argentina, Australia, Austria, Bahamas, Bahrain, Bangladesh, Barbados, Belgium, Belize, Benin, Bhutan, Bolivia, Botswana, Brazil, Bulgaria, Burma, Burundi, Byelorussia, Canada, Cape Verde, Central African Republic, Chad, Chile, China, Colombia, Congo, Costa Rica, Cuba, Cyprus, Czechoslovakia, Democratic Kampuchea, Democratic Yemen, Denmark, Djibouti, Dominican Republic, Ecuador, Egypt, El Salvador, Equatorial Guinea, Ethiopia, Fiji, Finland, France, Gabon, Gambia, German Democratic Republic, Federal Republic of Germany, Ghana, Greece, Grenada, Guinea, Guinea-Bissau, Guyana, Honduras, Hungary, Iceland, India, Indonesia, Iran, Iraq, Ireland, Italy, Ivory Coast, Jamaica, Japan, Jordan, Kenya, Kuwait, Lao People's Democratic Republic, Lebanon, Lesotho, Liberia, Libya, Luxembourg, Madagascar, Malawi, Malaysia, Maldives, Mali, Malta, Mauritania, Mauritius, Mexico, Mongolia, Morocco, Mozambique, Nepal, Netherlands, New Zealand, Nicaragua, Niger, Nigeria, Norway, Oman, Pakistan, Panama, Papua New Giunea, Paraguay, Peru, Philippines, Poland, Portugal, Qatar, Romania, Rwanda, Saint Lucia, Sao Tome and Principe, Saudi Arabia, Senegal, Seychelles, Sierra Leone, Singapore, Somalia, Spain, Sri Lanka, Sudan, Suriname, Swaziland, Sweden, Syria, Thailand, Togo, Trinidad and Tobago, Tunisia, Turkey, Uganda, Ukraine, USSR, United Arab Emirates, United Kingdom, United Republic of Cameroon, United Republic of Tanzania, Upper Volta, Uruguay, Vanuatu, Venezuela, Viet Nam, Yemen, Yugoslavia, Zaire, Zambia, Zimbabwe.
Against: 2
Israel, United States.
Abstentions: 0
Absent: 9
Antigua and Barbuda, Comoros, Dominica, Guatemala, Haiti, Saint Vincent, Samoa, Solomon Islands, St. Christopher and Nevis.

Resolution No. 38/85 of 15 December 1983

DEMANDING THAT ISRAEL CEASE ALL ACTIONS AND/OR PLANS TO BUILD A CANAL LINKING THE MEDITERRANEAN SEA TO THE DEAD SEA

The General Assembly,

Recalling its resolutions 36/150 of 16 December 1981 and 27/122 of 16 December 1982,[222]

Recalling the rules and principles of international law relative to the fundamental rights and duties of States,

Bearing in mind the principles of international law relative to belligerent occupation of land, including the Geneva Convention relative to the Protection of Civilian Persons in Time of War, of 12 August 1949,[223] and reaffirming their applicability to all Arab territories occupied since 1967, including Jerusalem,

Taking note of the report of the Secretary-General,[224]

Recognizing that the proposed canal, to be constructed partly through the Gaza Strip, a Palestinian territory occupied in 1967, would violate the principles of international law and affect the interests of the Palestinian people,

Confident that the canal linking the Mediterranean Sea with the Dead Sea, if constructed by Israel, will cause direct, serious and irreparable damage to Jordan's rights and legitimate and vital interests in the economic, agricultural, demographic and ecological fields,

Noting with regret the non-compliance by Israel with General Assembly resolution 36/150,

1. *Deplores* Israel's non-compliance with General Assembly resolution 37/122 and its refusal to receive the team to experts;

2. *Emphasizes* that the canal linking the Mediterranean Sea with the Dead Sea, if constructed, is a violation of the rules and principles of international law, especially those relating to the fundamental rights and duties of States and to belligerent occupation of land;

3. *Demands* that Israel not construct this canal and cease forthwith all actions taken and/or plans made towards the implementation of this project;

4. *Calls upon* all States, specialized agencies and governmental and non-governmental organizations not to assist, directly or indirectly, in the preparation and execution of this project and strongly urges national, international and multinational corporations to do likewise;

5. *Requests* the Secretary-General to monitor and assess, on a continuing basis and through a competent expert organ, all aspects—juridical, political, economic, ecological and demographic—of the adverse effects on Jordan and on the Arab territories occupied since 1967, including Jerusalem, arising from the implementation of the Israeli decision to construct this canal and to forward the findings of that organ on a regular basis to the General Assembly;

6. *Requests* the Secretary-General to report to the General Assembly at its thirty-ninth session on the implementation of the present resolution;

7. *Decides* to include in the provisional agenda of its thirty-ninth session the item entitled "Israel's decision to build a canal linking the Mediterranean Sea to the Dead Sea".

---

[222]On Israel's proposed canal between the Mediterranean and the Dead Seas. [ed. note]
[223]United Nations, *Treaty Series*, vol. 75, no. 973, p. 287.
[224]A/38/502 and Add.1 and 2.

Adopted at the 98th plenary meeting:

In favour: 141

Afghanistan, Albania, Algeria, Angola, Argentina, Australia, Austria, Bahamas, Bahrain, Bangladesh, Barbados, Belgium, Belize, Benin, Bhutan, Bolivia, Botswana, Brazil, Bulgaria, Burma, Burundi, Byelorussia, Canada, Cape Verde, Central African Republic, Chad, Chile, China, Colombia, Congo, Costa Rica, Cuba, Cyprus, Czechoslovakia, Democratic Kampuchea, Democratic Yemen, Denmark, Djibouti, Dominican Republic, Ecuador, Egypt, El Salvador, Equatorial Guinea, Ethiopia, Fiji, Finland, France, Gabon, Gambia, German Democratic Republic, Federal Republic of Germany, Ghana, Greece, Grenada, Guinea, Guinea-Bissau, Guyana, Hungary, Iceland, India, Indonesia, Iran, Iraq, Ireland, Italy, Jamaica, Japan, Jordan, Kenya, Kuwait, Lao People's Democratic Republic, Lebanon, Lesotho, Liberia, Libya, Luxembourg, Madagascar, Malawi, Malaysia, Maldives, Mali, Malta, Mauritania, Mauritius, Mexico, Mongolia, Morocco, Mozambique, Nepal, Netherlands, New Zealand, Nicaragua, Niger, Nigeria, Norway, Oman, Pakistan, Panama, Papua New Guinea, Paraguay, Peru, Philippines, Poland, Portugal, Qatar, Romania, Rwanda, Sao Tome and Principe, Saudi Arabia, Senegal, Seychelles, Sierra Leone, Singapore, Somalia, Spain, Sri Lanka, Sudan, Suriname, Swaziland, Sweden, Syria, Thailand, Togo, Trinidad and Tobago, Tunisia, Turkey, Uganda, Ukraine, USSR, United Arab Emirates, United Kingdom, United Republic of Cameroon, United Republic of Tanzania, Upper Volta, Uruguay, Venezuela, Viet Nam, Yemen, Yugoslavia, Zambia, Zimbabwe.

Against: 2

Israel, United States.

Abstentions: 0

Absent: 14

Antigua and Barbuda, Comoros, Dominica, Guatemala, Haiti, Honduras, Ivory Coast, Saint Lucia, Saint Vincent, Samoa, Solomon Islands, St. Christopher and Nevis, Vanuatu,* Zaire.

---

* Later advised the Secretariat it had intended to vote in favour.

Resolution No. 38/130 of 19 December 1983

URGING ALL STATES TO CONTRIBUTE TO THE ELIMINATION OF THE CAUSES UNDERLYING INTERNATIONAL TERRORISM

The General Assembly,

Recalling its resolutions 3034 (XXVII) of 18 December 1972, 31/102 of 15 December 1976, 32/147 of 16 December 1977, 34/145 of 17 December 1979 and 36/109 of 10 December 1981,[225]

Recalling also the Declaration of Principles of International Law concerning Friendly Relations and Co-operation among States in accordance with the Charter of the

United Nations,[226] the Declaration on the Strengthening of International Security,[227] the Definition of Aggression,[228] and the Protocols Additional to the Geneva Conventions of 1949,[229]

Deeply concerned about continuing acts of international terrorism which take a toll of innocent human lives,

Convinced of the importance of international co-operation for dealing with acts of international terrorism,

Reaffirming the principle of self-determination of peoples enshrined in the Charter of the United Nations,

Reaffirming the inalienable right to self-determination and independence of all peoples under colonial and racist régimes and other forms of alien domination, and upholding the legitimacy of their struggle, in particular the struggle of national liberation movements, in accordance with the purposes and principles of the Charter and of the Declaration on Principles of International Law concerning Friendly Relations and Co-operation among States in accordance with the Charter of the United Nations,

Taking note of the report of the Secretary-General,[230]

1. *Deeply deplores* the loss of innocent human lives and the pernicious impact of acts of international terrorism on friendly relations among States as well as on international co-operation, including co-operation for development;

2. *Urges* all States, unilaterally and in co-operation with other States, as well as relevant United Nations organs to contribute to the progressive elimination of the causes underlying international terrorism;

3. *Invites* all States to take all appropriate measures at the national level with a view to the speedy and final elimination of the problem of international terrorism, such as the harmonization of domestic legislation with international conventions, the implementation of assumed international obligations and the prevention of the preparation and organization in their territory of acts directed against other States;

4. *Calls upon* all States to fulfil their obligations under international law to refrain from organizing, instigating, assisting or participating in acts of civil strife or terrorist acts in another State, or acquiescing in organized activities within their territory directed towards the commission of such acts;

5. *Appeals* to all States that have not yet done so to consider becoming parties to the existing international conventions relating to various aspects of the problem of international terrorism;

6. *Urges* all States to co-operate with one another more closely, especially through the exchange of relevant information concerning the prevention and combating of international terrorism, the apprehension and prosecution of the perpetrators of such acts, the conclusion of special

---

[225]On the problem of international terrorism. [ed. note]

[226]Resolution 2625 (XXV), annex.

[227]Resoluiton 2734 (XXV).

[228]Resolution 3314 (XXIX), annex.

[229]A/32/144, annexes I and II.

[230]A/38/355 and Add.1-3.

treaties and/or the incorporation into appropriate bilateral treaties of special clauses, in particular regarding the extradition or prosecution of international terrorists;

7. *Re-endorses* the recommendations submitted by the *Ad Hoc* Committee on International Terrorism in its report to the General Assembly at its thirty-fourth session relating to practical measures of co-operation for the speedy elimination of the problem of international terrorism;[231]

8. *Calls upon* all States to observe and implement the recommendations submitted by the *Ad Hoc* Committee;

9. *Requests* the Secretary-General to follow up, as appropriate, the implementation of the present resolution and, in particular, of the recommendations submitted by the *Ad Hoc* Committee and to submit a report to the General Assembly at its fortieth session;

10. *Decides* to include the item in the provisional agenda of its fortieth session.

Adopted at the 101st plenary meeting without a vote.

Resolution No. 38/144 of 19 December 1983

REAFFIRMING THE ILLEGALITY OF MEASURES TAKEN BY ISRAEL TO EXPLOIT THE HUMAN AND NATURAL RESOURCES OF THE OCCUPIED ARAB AND PALESTINIAN TERRITORIES, AND CALLING UPON IT TO DESIST FROM SUCH MEASURES

The General Assembly,

Recalling its resolutions 37/135 of 17 December 1982,

Recalling also its previous resolutions on permanent sovereignty over natural resources,

Bearing in mind the relevant principles of international law and the provisions of the international conventions and regulations, in particular Convention IV of The Hague of 1907,[232] and the Geneva Convention Relative to the Protection of Civilian Persons in Time of War, of 12 August 1949,[233] concerning the obligations and responsibilities of the occupying Power,

Bearing in mind also the pertinent provisions of its resolutions 3201 (S-VI) and 3202 (S-VI) of 1 May 1974, containing the Declaration and the Programme of Action on the Establishment of a New International Economic Order, and 3281 (XXIX) of 12 December 1974, containing the Charter of Economic Rights and Duties of States,

1. *Takes note* of the report of the Secretary-General on permanent sovereignty over national resources in the occupied Palestinian and other Arab territories;[234]

2. *Commends* the report of the Secretary-General on the implications, under international law, of the United Nations resolutions on permanent sovereignty over natural resources, on the occupied Palestinian and other Arab territories and on the obligations of Israel concerning its conduct in these territories;[235]

3. *Condemns* Israel for its exploitation of the national resources of the occupied Palestinian and other Arab territories;

4. *Reaffirms* that Convention IV of The Hague of 1907 and the Geneva Convention Relative to the Protection of Civilian Persons in Time of War, of 12 August 1949, are applicable to the occupied Palestinian and other Arab territories;

5. *Emphasizes* the right of the Palestinian and other Arab peoples whose territories are under Israeli occupation to full and effective permanent sovereignty and control over their natural and all other resources, wealth and economic activities;

6. *Also reaffirms* that all measures undertaken by Israel to exploit the human, natural and all other resources, wealth and economic activities in the occupied Palestinian and other Arab territories are illegal, and calls upon Israel to desist immediately from such measures;

7. *Further reaffirms* the right of the Palestinian and other Arab people subjected to Israeli aggression and occupation to the restitution of, and full compensation for the exploitation, depletion and loss of and damage to, their natural, human and all other resources, wealth and economic activities, and calls upon Israel to meet their just claims;

8. *Calls upon* all States to support the Palestinian and other Arab peoples in the exercise of their above-mentioned rights;

9. *Calls upon* all States, international organizations, specialized agencies, business corporations and all other institutions not to recognize, or co-operate with or assist in any manner in, any measures undertaken by Israel to exploit the national resources of the occupied Palestinian and other Arab territories or to effect any changes in the demographic composition, the character and form of use of their natural resources or the institutional structure of those territories;

10. *Requests* the Secretary-General to elaborate on his report[236] in order to cover also, in detail, the resources exploited by the Israeli settlements and the Israeli-imposed regulations and policies hampering the economic development of the occupied Palestinian and other Arab territories, including a comparison between the practices of Israel and its obligations under international law;

11. *Also requests* the Secretary-General to submit the detailed report to the General Assembly at its thirty-ninth session, through the Economic and Social Council.

Adopted at the 102nd plenary meeting:
In favour: 120
Afghanistan, Albania, Algeria, Angola, Argentian, Austria, Bahamas, Bahrain, Bangladesh, Barbados, Belize, Benin, Bhutan, Bolivia, Botswana, Brazil, Bulgaria,

---

[231]*Official Records of the General Assembly, Thirty-fourth Session, Supplement No. 37* (A/34/37), para. 118.

[232]Carnegie Endowment for International Peace, *The Hague Conventions and Declarations of 1899 and 1907* (New York, Oxford University Press, 1915), p. 100.

[233]United Nations, *Treaty Series*, vol. 75, no. 973, p. 287.

[234]A/38/282-E/1983/84.

[235]A/38/265-E/1983/85.

[236]A/38/265-E/1983/85.

Burundi, Byelorussia, Cape Verde, Chile, China, Colombia, Congo, Cuba, Cyprus, Czechoslovakia, Democratic Kampuchea, Democratic Yemen, Djibouti, Dominican Republic, Ecuador, Egypt, El Salvador, Ethiopia, Fiji, Gabon, Gambia, German Democratic Republic, Ghana, Greece, Guinea, Guinea-Bissau, Guyana, Honduras, Hungary, India, Indonesia, Iran, Iraq, Jamaica, Japan, Jordan, Kenya, Kuwait, Lao People's Democratic Republic, Lebanon, Lesotho, Liberia, Libya, Madagascar, Malaysia, Maldives, Mali, Malta, Mauritania, Mauritius, Mexico, Mongolia, Morocco, Mozambique, Nepal, Nicaragua, Niger, Nigeria, Oman, Pakistan, Panama, Papua New Guinea, Paraguay, Peru, Philippines, Poland, Portugal, Qatar, Romania, Rwanda, Saint Vincent, Sao Tome and Principe, Saudi Arabia, Senegal, Sierra Leone, Singapore, Somalia, Spain, Sri Lanka, Sudan, Suriname, Swaziland, Syria, Thailand, Togo, Trinidad and Tobago, Tunisia, Turkey, Uganda, Ukraine, USSR, United Arab Emirates, United Republic of Cameroon, United Republic of Tanzania, Upper Volta, Uruguay, Vanuatu, Venezuela, Viet Nam, Yemen, Yugoslavia, Zaire, Zambia.

Against: 2

Israel, United States.

Abstentions: 18

Australia, Belgium, Burma, Canada, Denmark, Finland, France, Federal Republic of Germany, Iceland, Ireland, Italy, Ivory Coast, Luxembourg, Netherlands, New Zealand, Norway, Sweden, United Kingdom.

Absent: 17

Antigua and Barbuda, Central African Republic, Chad, Comoros, Costa Rica, Dominica, Equatorial Guinea, Grenada, Guatemala, Haiti, Malawi,* Saint Lucia, Samoa, Seychelles, Solomon Islands, St. Christopher and Nevis, Zimbabwe.

---

* Later advised the Secretariat it had intended to vote in favour.

Resolution No. 38/145 of 19 December 1983

CALLING FOR THE PROVISION OF ECONOMIC AND SOCIAL ASSISTANCE TO THE PALESTINIAN PEOPLE, AND REQUESTING THAT UNITED NATIONS ASSISTANCE SHOULD BE RENDERED IN COOPERATION WITH THE PALESTINE LIBERATION ORGANIZATION

The General Assembly,

Recalling its resolution 37/134 of 17 December 1982,

Recalling also Economic and Social Council resolution 1983/43 of 25 July 1983,

Recalling further the Programme of Action for the Achievement of Palestinian Rights, adopted by the International Conference on the Question of Palestine,[237]

Noting the need to provide economic and social assistance to the Palestinian people,

---

[237]*Report of the International Conference on the Question of Palestine, Geneva, 29 August-7 September 1983* (United Nations publication, Sales No. E.83.I.21), chap. I, sect. B.

1. *Endorses* Economic and Social Council resolution 1983/43;

2. *Endorses also* decision 83/11 of 24 June 1983 of the Governing Council of the United Nations Development Programme,[238] in which the Council called upon Governments and intergovernmental organizations to provide additional special contributions to the Programme amounting to at least 8 million dollars during the third programming cycle, so as to ensure the implementation of the United Nations Development Programme assistance programme for the Palestinian people;

3. *Requests* the Secretary-General:

(*a*) To convene in 1984 a meeting of the relevant programmes, organizations, agencies and organs of the United Nations system to develop a co-ordinated programme of economic and social assistance to the Palestinian people and to ensure its implementation;

(*b*) To provide for the participation in the meeting of the Palestine Liberation Organization, the Arab host countries and relevant intergovernmental and non-governmental organizations;

(*c*) To utilize existing inter-agency mechanisms to prepare proposals for assistance projects to be considered at the meeting;

4. *Requests* that the meeting should look into the most effective inter-agency machinery to co-ordinate and intensify United Nations assistance to the Palestinian people;

5. *Requests* the relevant programmes, organizations, agencies and organs of the United Nations system to intensify their efforts, in co-operation with the Palestine Liberation Organization, to provide economic and social assistance to the Palestinian people;

6. *Also requests* that United Nations assistance to the Palestinians in the Arab host countries should be rendered in co-operation with the Palestine Liberation Organization and with the consent of the Arab host Government concerned;

7. *Requests* the Secretary-General to report to the General Assembly at its thirty-ninth session, through the Economic and Social Council, on the progress made in the implementation of the present resolution.

Adopted at the 102nd plenary meeting:

In favour: 140

Afghanistan, Albania, Algeria, Angola, Argentina, Australia, Austria, Bahamas, Bahrain, Bangladesh, Barbados, Belgium, Belize, Benin, Bhutan, Bolivia, Botswana, Brazil, Bulgaria, Burma, Burundi, Byelorussia, Canada, Cape Verde, Central African Republic, Chad, Chile, China, Colombia, Congo, Cuba, Cyprus, Czechoslovakia, Democratic Kampuchea, Democratic Yemen, Denmark, Djibouti, Dominican Republic, Ecuador, Egypt, El Salvador, Ethiopia, Fiji, Finland, France, Gabon, Gambia, German Democratic Republic, Federal Republic of Germany, Ghana, Greece, Guinea, Guinea-Bissau, Guyana, Honduras,

---

[238]See *Official Records of the Economic and Social Council, 1983, Supplement No. 9* (E/1983/20), annex I.

Hungary, Iceland, India, Indonesia, Iran, Iraq, Italy, Ivory Coast, Jamaica, Japan, Jordan, Kenya, Kuwait, Lao People's Democratic Republic, Lebanon, Lesotho, Liberia, Libya, Luxembourg, Madagascar, Malaysia, Maldives, Mali, Malta, Mauritania, Mauritius, Mexico, Mongolia, Morocco, Mozambique, Nepal, Netherlands, New Zealand, Nicaragua, Niger, Nigeria, Norway, Oman, Pakistan, Panama, Papua New Guinea, Paraguay, Peru, Philippines, Poland, Portugal, Qatar, Romania, Rwanda, Saint Lucia, Saint Vincent, Sao Tome and Principe, Saudi Arabia, Senegal, Sierra Leone, Singapore, Somalia, Spain, Sri Lanka, Sudan, Suriname, Swaziland, Sweden, Syria, Thailand, Togo, Trinidad and Tobago, Tunisia, Turkey, Uganda, Ukraine, USSR, United Arab Emirates, United Kingdom, United Republic of Cameroon, United Republic of Tanzania, Upper Volta, Uruguay, Vanuatu, Venezuela, Viet Nam, Yemen, Yugoslavia, Zaire, Zambia.

Against: 2

Israel, United States.

Abstentions: 1

Ireland.*

Absent: 14

Antigua and Barbuda, Comoros, Costa Rica, Dominica, Equatorial Guinea, Grenada, Guatemala, Haiti, Malawi,* Samoa, Seychelles, Solomon Islands, St. Christopher and Nevis, Zimbabwe.

---

* Later advised the Secretariat it had intended to vote in favour.

Resolution No. 38/166 of 19 December 1983

EXPRESSING ALARM AT THE DETERIORATION IN LIVING CONDITIONS IN THE ARAB TERRITORIES UNDER ISRAELI OCCUPATION AND AFFIRMING THAT OCCUPATION IS CONTRADICTORY TO THE BASIC REQUIREMENTS OF THEIR SOCIAL AND ECONOMIC DEVELOPMENT

The General Assembly,

Recalling the Vancouver Declaration on Human Settlements, 1976,[239] and the relevant recommendations for national action[240] adopted by Habitat: United Nations Conference on Human Settlements,

Recalling also resolution 3, entitled "Living conditions of the Palestinians in occupied territories", contained in the recommendations for international co-operation adopted by Habitat: United Nations Conference on Human Settlements,[241]

Recalling further its resolution 37/222 of 20 December 1982,

Taking note of resolution 6/2 adopted by the Commission on Human Settlements on 4 May 1983,[242]

Gravely alarmed by the continuation of the Israeli settlement policies, which have been declared null and void and a major obstacle to peace,

1. *Takes note* of the report of the Secretary-General on the living conditions of the Palestinian people in the occupied Palestinian territories;[243]

2. *Takes note also* of the statement made on 1 November 1983 by the observer of the Palestine Liberation Organization;[244]

3. *Rejects* the Israeli plans and actions intended to change the demographic composition of the occupied Palestinian territories, particularly the increase and expansion of the Israeli settlements, and other plans and actions creating conditions leading to the displacement and exodus of Palestinians from the occupied Palestinian territories;

4. *Expresses its alarm* at the deterioration in the living conditions of the Palestinian people in the Palestinian territories occupied since 1967 as a result of the Israeli occupation;

5. *Affirms* that the Israeli occupation is contradictory to the basic requirements for the social and economic development of the Palestinian people in the occupied West Bank and the Gaza Strip;

6. *Calls upon* the Israeli occupation authorities to give United Nations experts access to the occupied Palestinian territories;

7. *Recognizes* the need for a comprehensive report on the impact of the Israeli settlements on the living conditions of the Palestinian people in the occupied Palestinian territories;

8. *Requests* the Secretary-General to prepare and submit to the General Assembly at its thirty-ninth session, through the Economic and Social Council, a comprehensive report on the current and future impact of the Israeli settlements on the living conditions of the Palestinian people in the occupied Palestinian territories, including a comparison between the living conditions of the latter and those of the residents of the Israeli settlements.

Adopted at the 102nd plenary meeting:

In favour: 142

Afghanistan, Albania, Algeria, Angola, Argentina, Australia, Austria, Bahamas, Bahrain, Bangladesh, Barbados, Belgium, Belize, Benin, Bhutan, Bolivia, Botswana, Brazil, Bulgaria, Burma, Burundi, Byelorussia, Canada, Cape Verde, Central African Republic, Chad, Chile, China, Colombia, Congo, Cuba, Cyprus, Czechoslovakia, Democratic Kampuchea, Democratic Yemen, Denmark, Djibouti, Dominican Republic, Ecuador, Egypt, El Salvador, Ethiopia, Fiji, Finland, France, Gabon, Gambia, German Democratic Republic, Federal Republic of Germany, Ghana, Greece, Guinea, Guinea-Bissau, Guyana, Haiti, Honduras, Hungary, Iceland, India, Indonesia, Iran, Iraq, Ireland, Italy, Ivory Coast, Jamaica, Japan, Jordan, Kenya,

---

[239] *Report of Habitat: United Nations Conference on Human Settlements, Vancouver, 31 May-11 June 1976* (United Nations publication, Sales No. E.76.IV.7 and corrigendum), chap. I.

[240] *Ibid.,* chap. II.

[241] *Ibid.,* chap. III.

[242] See *Official Records of the General Assembly, Thirty-eighth Session, Supplement No. 8* (A/38/8), annex I.

[243] A/38/278-E/1983/77.

[244] *Official Records of the General Assembly, Thirty-eighth Session, Second Committee,* 24th meeting, paras. 1-5.

Kuwait, Lao People's Democratic Republic, Lebanon, Lesotho, Liberia, Libya, Luxembourg, Madagascar, Malawi, Malaysia, Maldives, Mali, Malta, Mauritania, Mauritius, Mexico, Mongolia, Morocco, Mozambique, Nepal, Netherlands, New Zealand, Nicaragua, Niger, Nigeria, Norway, Oman, Pakistan, Panama, Papua New Guinea, Paraguay, Peru, Philippines, Poland, Portugal, Qatar, Romania, Rwanda, Saint Lucia, Saint Vincent, Sao Tome and Principe, Saudi Arabia, Senegal, Sierra Leone, Singapore, Somalia, Spain, Sri Lanka, Sudan, Suriname, Swaziland, Sweden, Syria, Thailand, Togo, Trinidad and Tobago, Tunisia, Turkey, Uganda, Ukraine, USSR, United Arab Emirates, United Kingdom, United Republic of Cameroon, United Republic of Tanzania, Upper Volta, Uruguay, Venezuela, Viet Nam, Yemen, Yugoslavia, Zaire, Zambia.

Against: 2

Israel, United States.

Abstentions: 0

Absent: 13

Antigua and Barbuda, Comoros, Costa Rica, Dominica, Equatorial Guinea, Grenada, Guatemala, Samoa, Seychelles, Solomon Islands, St. Christopher and Nevis, Vanuatu, Zimbabwe.

Resolution No. 38/180 A, B, C, D, E of 19 December 1983

ON THE SITUATION IN THE MIDDLE EAST: CONDEMNING ISRAEL'S POLICIES IN THE OCCUPIED TERRITORIES AND CALLING FOR ITS COMPLETE WITHDRAWAL FROM THEM, CONDEMNING ISRAELI ARMY ACTIONS IN BEIRUT IN 1982, DECLARING THE NEED FOR RECOGNITION OF THE RIGHT OF THE PALESTINIAN PEOPLE, UNDER THE LEADERSHIP OF THE PALESTINE LIBERATION ORGANIZATION, TO SELF-DETERMINATION AND AN INDEPENDENT STATE, CALLING ON ALL STATES TO PUT AN END TO THE FLOW OF AID TO ISRAEL, AND CONDEMNING ISRAELI-SOUTH AFRICAN COLLABORATION

A

The General Assembly,

Having discussed the item entitled "The situation in the Middle East",

Taking note of the report of the Secretary-General of 30 September 1983,[245]

Recalling Security Council resolution 497 (1981) of 17 December 1981,

Reaffirming its resolutions 36/226 B of 17 December 1981, ES-9/1 of 5 February 1982 and 37/123 A of 16 December 1982,

Recalling its resolution 3314 (XXIX) of 14 December 1974, in which it defined an act of aggression, *inter alia*, as "the invasion or attack by the armed fores of a State of the territory of another State, or any military occupation, however temporary, resulting from such invasion or attack, or any annexation by the use of force of the territory

of another State or part thereof" and provided that "no consideration of whatever nature, whether political, economic, military or otherwise, may serve as a justification for aggression",

Reaffirming the fundamental principle of the inadmissibility of the acquisition of territory by force,

Reaffirming once more the applicability of the Geneva Convention relative to the Protection of Civilian Persons in Time of War, of 12 August 1949,[246] to the occupied Palestinian and other Arab territories, including Jerusalem,

Noting that Israel's record, policies and actions establish conclusively that it is not a peace-loving Member State and that it has not carried out its obligations under the Charter of the United Nations,

Noting further that Israel has refused, in violation of Article 25 of the Charter, to accept and carry out the numerous relevant decisions of the Security Council, in particular resolution 497 (1981), thus failing to carry out its obligations under the Charter,

1. *Strongly condemns* Israel for its failure to comply with Security Council resolution 497 (1981) and General Assembly resolutions 36/226 B, ES-9/1 and 37/123 A;

2. *Declares once more* that Israel's continued occupation of the Golan Heights and its decision of 14 December 1981 to impose its laws, jurisdiction and administration on the occupied Syrian Golan Heights constitute an act of aggression under the provisions of Article 39 of the Charter of the United Nations and General Assembly resolution 3314 (XXIX);

3. *Declares once more* that Israel's decision to impose its laws, jurisdiction and administration on the occupied Syrian Golan Heights is illegal and therefore null and void and has no validity whatsoever;

4. *Declares* all Israeli policies and practices of, or aimed at, annexation of the occupied Palestinian and other Arab territories, including Jerusalem, to be illegal and in violation of international law and of the relevant United Nations resolutions;

5. *Determines once more* that all actions taken by Israel to give effect to its decision relating to the occupied Syrian Golan Heights are illegal and invalid and shall not be recognized;

6. *Reaffirms its determination* that all relevant provisions of the Regulations annexed to the Hague Convention IV of 1907,[247] and the Geneva Convention relative to the Protection of Civilian Persons in Time of War, of 12 August 1949, continue to apply to the Syrian territory occupied by Israel since 1967, and calls upon the parties thereto to respect and ensure respect of their obligations under these instruments in all circumstances;

7. *Determines once more* that the continued occupation of the Syrian Golan Heights since 1967 and their annexation

---

[245]A/38/458-S/16015. For the printed text, see *Official Records of the Security Council, Thirty-eighth Year, Supplement for July, August and September 1983,* document S/16015.

[246]United Nations, *Treaty Series,* vol. 75, no. 973, p. 287.

[247]Carnegie Endowment for International Peace, *The Hague Conventions and Declarations of 1899 and 1907* (New York, Oxford University Press, 1915), p. 100.

by Israel on 14 December 1981, following Israel's decision to impose its laws, jurisdiction and administration on that territory, constitute a continuing threat to international peace and security;

8. *Strongly deplores* the negative vote by a permanent member of the Security Council which prevented the Council from adopting against Israel, under Chapter VII of the Charter, the "appropriate measures" referred to in resolution 497 (1981) unanimously adopted by the Council;

9. *Further deplores* any political, economic, financial, military and technological support to Israel that encourages Israel to commit acts of aggression and to consolidate and perpetuate its occupation and annexation of occupied Arab territories;

10. *Firmly emphasizes once more* its demand that Israel, the occupying Power, rescind forthwith its illegal decision of 14 December 1981 to impose its laws, jurisdiction and administration on the Syrian Golan Heights, which resulted in the effective annexation of that territory;

11. *Reaffirms once more* the overriding necessity of the total and unconditional withdrawal by Israel from all the Palestinian and other Arab territories occupied since 1967, including Jerusalem, which is an essential prerequisite for the establishment of a comprehensive and just peace in the Middle East;

12. *Determines once more* that Israel's record, policies and actions confirm that it is not a peace-loving Member State, that it has persistently violated the principles contained in the Charter and that it has carried out neither its obligations under the Charter nor its commitment under General Assembly resolution 273 (III) of 11 May 1949;

13. *Calls once more upon* all Member States to apply the following measures:

(a) To refrain from supplying Israel with any weapons and related equipment and to suspend any military assistance that Israel receives from them;

(b) To refrain from acquiring any weapons or military equipment from Israel;

(c) To suspend economic, financial and technological assistance to and co-operation with Israel;

(d) To sever diplomatic, trade and cultural relations with Israel;

14. *Reiterates its call* to all Member States to cease forthwith, individually and collectively, all dealings with Israel in order totally to isolate it in all fields;

15. *Urges* non-member States to act in accordance with the provisions of the present resolution;

16. *Calls upon* the specialized agencies and other international institutions to conform their relations with Israel to the terms of the present resolution;

17. *Requests* the Secretary-General to report to the General Assembly at its thirty-ninth session on the implementation of the present resolution.

Adopted at the 102nd plenary meeting:
In favour: 85
Afghanistan, Albania, Algeria, Angola, Bahrain, Bangladesh, Benin, Bhutan, Botswana, Bulgaria, Burundi, Byelorussia, Cape Verde, Central African Republic, China, Congo, Cuba, Cyprus, Czechoslovakia, Democratic Yemen, Djibouti, Ethiopia, Gambia, German Democratic Republic, Ghana, Greece, Guinea, Guinea-Bissau, Guyana, Hungary, India, Indonesia, Iran, Iraq, Japan,* Jordan, Kenya, Kuwait, Lao People's Democratic Republic, Lebanon, Libya, Madagascar, Malaysia, Maldives, Mali, Malta, Mauritania, Mexico, Mongolia, Morocco, Mozambique, Nepal, Nicaragua, Niger, Nigeria, Oman, Pakistan, Poland, Qatar, Rwanda, Sao Tome and Principe, Saudi Arabia, Senegal, Seychelles, Sierra Leone, Somalia, Sri Lanka, Sudan, Suriname, Syria, Togo, Tunisia, Turkey, Uganda, Ukraine, USSR, United Arab Emirates, United Republic of Cameroon, United Republic of Tanzania, Upper Volta, Viet Nam, Yemen, Yugoslavia, Zambia, Zimbabwe.

Against: 23
Australia, Belgium, Canada, Chile, Costa Rica, Denmark, Finland, France, Federal Republic of Germany, Haiti, Iceland, Ireland, Israel, Italy, Luxembourg, Netherlands, New Zealand, Norway, Portugal, Saint Lucia, Sweden, United Kingdom, United States.

Abstentions: 31
Argentina, Austria, Bahamas, Barbados, Belize, Bolivia, Brazil, Burma, Chad, Colombia, Dominican Republic, Ecuador, Egypt, El Salvador, Fiji, Guatemala, Honduras, Ivory Coast, Jamaica, Malawi, Papua New Guinea, Paraguay, Peru, Philippines, Saint Vincent, Singapore, Spain, Thailand, Trinidad and Tobago, Uruguay, Venezuela.

Absent: 18
Antigua and Barbuda, Comoros, Democratic Kampuchea, Dominica, Equatorial Guinea, Gabon, Grenada, Lesotho, Liberia, Mauritius, Panama, Romania, Samoa, Solomon Islands, St. Christopher and Nevis, Swaziland, Vanuatu, Zaire.

---

* Later advised the Secretariat that due to an error by the voting machine, its vote against was recorded as in favour.

B

The General Assembly,
Recalling the relevant provisions of the Universal Declaration of Human Rights,[248]

Recalling also the Constitution of the United Nations Educational, Scientific and Cultural Organization,[249] and all other relevant international instruments concerning the right to cultural identity in all its forms,

Having learned that the Israeli army, during its occupation of Beirut, seized and took away archives and documents of every kind concerning Palestinian history and culture, including cultural articles belonging to Palestinian institutions—in particular the Palestine Research Centre—archives, documents, manuscripts and materials such as film documents, literary works by major authors,

---

[248]Resolution 217 A (III).
[249]See *Manual of the General Conference,* 1981 edition (Paris, UNESCO, 1981).

paintings, *objets d'art* and works of folklore, research works and so forth, serving as a foundation for the history, culture, national awareness, unity and solidarity of the Palestinian people,

1. *Condemns* those acts of plundering of the Palestinian cultural heritage;

2. *Calls upon* the Government of Israel to make full restitution, through the United Nations Educational, Scientific and Cultural Organization, of all cultural property belonging to Palestinian institutions, including the archives and documents removed from the Palestine Research Centre and arbitrarily seized by the Israeli forces;

3. *Requests* the Secretary-General to report to the General Assembly at its thirty-ninth session on the implementation of the present resolution.

Adopted at the 102nd plenary meeting:

In favour: 121

Afghanistan, Albania, Algeria, Angola, Argentina, Austria, Bahamas, Bahrain, Bangladesh, Barbados, Belize, Benin, Bhutan, Bolivia, Botswana, Brazil, Bulgaria, Burma, Burundi, Byelorussia, Cape Verde, Central African Republic, Chad, Chile, China, Colombia, Congo, Costa Rica, Cuba, Cyprus, Czechoslovakia, Democratic Kampuchea, Democratic Yemen, Djibouti, Ecuador, Egypt, El Salvador, Ethiopia, Fiji, Gabon, Gambia, German Democratic Republic, Ghana, Greece, Guinea, Guinea-Bissau, Guyana, Haiti, Honduras, Hungary, India, Indonesia, Iran, Iraq, Ivory Coast, Jamaica, Japan, Jordan, Kenya, Kuwait, Lao People's Democratic Republic, Lebanon, Libya, Madagascar, Malawi, Malaysia, Maldives, Mali, Malta, Mauritania, Mauritius, Mexico, Mongolia, Morocco, Mozambique, Nepal, Nicaragua, Niger, Nigeria, Oman, Pakistan, Papua New Guinea, Paraguay, Peru, Philippines, Poland, Portugal, Qatar, Romania, Rwanda, Sao Tome and Principe, Saudi Arabia, Senegal, Seychelles, Sierra Leone, Singapore, Somalia, Spain, Sri Lanka, Sudan, Suriname, Syria, Thailand, Togo, Trinidad and Tobago, Tunisia, Turkey, Uganda, Ukraine, USSR, United Arab Emirates, United Republic of Cameroon, United Republic of Tanzania, Upper Volta, Uruguay, Venezuela, Viet Nam, Yemen, Yugoslavia, Zambia, Zimbabwe.

Against: 1

Israel.

Abstentions: 20

Australia, Belgium, Canada, Denmark, Dominican Republic, Finland, France, Federal Republic of Germany, Iceland, Ireland, Italy, Luxembourg, Netherlands, New Zealand, Norway, Saint Lucia, Saint Vincent, Sweden, United Kingdom, United States.

Absent: 15

Antigua and Barbuda, Comoros, Dominica, Equatorial Guinea, Grenada, Guatemala, Lesotho, Liberia, Panama, Samoa, Solomon Islands, St. Christopher and Nevis, Swaziland, Vanuatu, Zaire.

C

The General Assembly,

Recalling its resolutions 36/120 E of 10 December 1981 and 37/123 C of 16 December 1982, in which it deter-

mined that all legislative and administrative measures and actions taken by Israel, the occupying Power, which had altered or purported to alter the character and status of the Holy City of Jerusalem, in particular the so-called "Basic Law" on Jerusalem and the proclamation of Jerusalem as the capital of Israel, were null and void and must be rescinded forthwith,

Recalling Security Council resolution 478 (1980) of 20 August 1980, in which the Council, *inter alia*, decided not to recognize the "Basic Law" and called upon those States that had established diplomatic missions at Jerusalem to withdraw such missions from the Holy City,

1. *Declares once more* that Israel's decision to impose its laws, jurisdiction and administration on the Holy City of Jerusalem is illegal and therefore null and void and has no validity whatsoever;

2. *Deplores* the transfer by some States of their diplomatic missions to Jerusalem in violation of Security Council resolution 478 (1980);

3. *Calls once again upon* those States to abide by the provisions of the relevant United Nations resolutions, in conformity with the Charter of the United Nations;

4. *Requests* the Secretary-General to report to the General Assembly at its thirty-ninth session on the implementation of the present resolution.

Adopted at the 102nd plenary meeting:

In favour: 137

Afghanistan, Albania, Algeria, Angola, Argentina, Australia, Austria, Bahamas, Bahrain, Bangladesh, Barbados, Belgium, Belize, Benin, Bhutan, Bolivia, Botswana, Brazil, Bulgaria, Burma, Burundi, Byelorussia, Canada, Cape Verde, Central African Republic, Chad, Chile, China, Colombia, Congo, Cuba, Cyprus, Czechoslovakia, Democratic Kampuchea, Democratic Yemen, Denmark, Djibouti, Ecuador, Egypt, El Salvador, Ethiopia, Fiji, Finland, France, Gabon, Gambia, German Democratic Republic, Federal Republic of Germany, Ghana, Greece, Guinea, Guinea-Bissau, Guyana, Honduras, Hungary, Iceland, India, Indonesia, Iran, Iraq, Ireland, Italy, Ivory Coast, Jamaica, Japan, Jordan, Kenya, Kuwait, Lao People's Democratic Republic, Lebanon, Libya, Luxembourg, Madagascar, Malawi, Malaysia, Maldives, Mali, Malta, Mauritania, Mauritius, Mexico, Mongolia, Morocco, Mozambique, Nepal, Netherlands, New Zealand, Nicaragua, Niger, Nigeria, Norway, Oman, Pakistan, Papua New Guinea, Paraguay, Peru, Philippines, Poland, Portugal, Qatar, Romania, Rwanda, Saint Lucia, Saint Vincent, Sao Tome and Principe, Saudi Arabia, Senegal, Seychelles, Sierra Leone, Singapore, Somalia, Spain, Sri Lanka, Sudan, Suriname, Sweden, Syria, Thailand, Togo, Trinidad and Tobago, Tunisia, Turkey, Uganda, Ukraine, USSR, United Arab Emirates, United Kingdom, United Republic of Cameroon, United Republic of Tanzania, Upper Volta, Uruguay, Venezuela, Viet Nam, Yemen, Yugoslavia, Zambia, Zimbabwe.

Against: 1

Israel.

Abstentions: 3

Dominican Republic, Guatemala, United States.
Absent: 16
Antigua and Barbuda, Comoros, Costa Rica, Dominica, Equatorial Guinea, Grenada, Haiti, Lesotho, Liberia, Panama, Samoa, Solomon Islands, St. Christopher and Nevis, Swaziland, Vanuatu, Zaire.

D

The General Assembly,

Having discussed the item entitled "The situation in the Middle East",

Reaffirming its resolutions 36/226 A and B of 17 December 1981, ES-9/1 of 5 February 1982 and 37/123 F of 16 December 1982,

Recalling Security Council resolutions 425 (1978) of 19 March 1978, 497 (1981) of 17 December 1981, 508 (1982) of 5 June 1982, 509 (1982) of 6 June 1982, 511 (1982) of 18 June 1982, 512 (1982) of 19 June 1982, 513 (1982) of 4 July 1982, 515 (1982) of 29 July 1982, 516 (1982) of 1 August 1982, 517 (1982) of 4 August 1982, 518 (1982) of 12 August 1982, 519 (1982) of 17 August 1982, 520 (1982) of 17 September 1982 and 521 (1982) of 19 September 1982,

Taking note of the report of the Secretary-General of 12 October 1982,[250]

Welcoming the world-wide support extended to the just cause of the Palestinian people and the other Arab countries in their struggle against Israeli aggression and occupation in order to achieve a comprehensive, just and lasting peace in the Middle East and the full exercise by the Palestinian people of its inalienable national rights, as affirmed by previous resolutions of the General Assembly relating to the question of Palestine and to the situation in the Middle East,

Gravely concerned that the Arab and Palestinian territories occupied since 1967, including Jerusalem, still remain under Israeli occupation, that the relevant resolutions of the United Nations have not been implemented and that the Palestinian people is still denied the restoration of its land and the exercise of its inalienable national rights in conformity with international law, as reaffirmed by resolutions of the United Nations,

Reaffirming the applicability of the Geneva Convention relative to the Protection of Civilian Persons in Time of War, of 12 August 1949,[251] to all the occupied Palestinian and other Arab territories, including Jerusalem,

Reiterating all relevant United Nations resolutions which emphasize that the acquisition of territory by force is inadmissible under the Charter of the United Nations and the principles of international law and that Israel must withdraw unconditionally from all the Palestinian and other Arab territories occupied by Israel since 1967, including Jerusalem,

Reaffirming further the imperative necessity of establishing a comprehensive, just and lasting peace in the region, based on full respect for the Charter and the principles of international law,

Gravely concerned also at recent Israeli actions involving the escalation and expansion of the conflict in the region which further violate the principles of international law and endanger international peace and security,

Recognizing the great importance of the time factor in the endeavors to achieve a comprehensive, just and lasting peace in the Middle East,

1. *Reaffirms its conviction* that the question of Palestine is the core of the conflict in the Middle East and that no comprehensive, just and lasting peace in the region will be achieved without the full exercise by the Palestinian people of its inalienable national rights and the immediate, unconditional and total withdrawal of Israel from all the Palestinian and other occupied Arab territories;

2. *Reaffirms further* that a just and comprehensive settlement of the situation in the Middle East cannot be achieved without the participation on an equal footing of all the parties to the conflict, including the Palestine Liberation Organization, the representative of the Palestinian people;

3. *Declares once more* that peace in the Middle East is indivisible and must be based on a comprehensive, just and lasting solution of the Middle East problem, under the auspices of the United Nations and on the basis of relevant resolutions of the United Nations, which ensures the complete and unconditional withdrawal of Israel from the Palestinian and other Arab territories occupied since 1967, including Jerusalem, and which enables the Palestinian people, under the leadership of the Palestine Liberation Organization, to exercise its inalienable rights, including the right to return and the right to self-determination, national independence and the establishment of its independent sovereign State in Palestine, in accordance with the resolutions of the United Nations relevant to the question of Palestine, in particular General Assembly resolutions ES-7/2 of 29 July 1980, 36/120 A to F of 10 December 1981, 37/86 A to D of 10 December 1982 and 37/86 E of 20 December 1982;

4. *Welcomes* the Arab Peace Plan adopted unanimously at the Twelfth Arab Summit Conference, held at Fez, Morocco, on 25 November 1981 and from 6 to 9 September 1982;[252]

5. *Condemns* Israel's continued occupation of the Palestinian and other Arab territories including Jerusalem, in violation of the Charter of the United Nations, the principles of international law and the relevant resolutions of the United Nations, and demands the immediate, unconditional and total withdrawal of Israel from all the territories occupied since June 1967;

6. *Rejects* all agreements and arrangements which violate the recognized rights of the Palestinian people and

---

[250]A/37/525-S/15451. For the printed text, see *Official Records of the Security Council, Thirty-seventh Year, Supplement for October, November and December 1982,* document S/15451.

[251]United Nations, *Treaty Series,* vol. 75, no. 973, p. 287.

[252]See A/37/696-S/15510, annex.

contradict the principles of just and comprehensive solutions to the Middle East problem to ensure the establishment of a just peace in the area;

7. *Deplores* Israel's failure to comply with Security Council resolutions 476 (1980) of 30 June 1980 and 478 (1980) of 20 August 1980 and General Assembly resolutions 35/207 of 16 December 1980 and 36/226 A and B of 17 December 1981, determines that Israel's decision to annex Jerusalem and to declare it its "capital" as well as the measures to alter its physical character, demographic composition, institutional structure and status are null and void and demands that they be rescinded immediately, and calls upon all Member States, the specialized agencies and all other international organizations to abide by the present resolution and all other relevant resolutions including Assembly resolutions 37/86 A to E;

8. *Condemns* Israel's aggression, policies and practices against the Palestinian people in the occupied Palestinian territories and outside these territories, particularly Palestinians in Lebanon, including the expropriation and annexation of territory, the establishment of settlements, assassination attempts and other terrorist, aggressive and repressive measures, which are in violation of the Charter and the principles of international law and the relevant international conventions;

9. *Strongly condemns* the imposition by Israel of its laws, jurisdiction and administration on the occupied Syrian Golan Heights, its annexationist policies and practices, the establishment of settlements, the confiscation of lands, the diversion of water resources and the imposition of Israeli citizenship on Syrian nationals and declares that all these measures are null and void and constitute a violation of the rules and principles of international law relating to belligerent occupation, in particular the Geneva Convention relative to the Protection of Civilian Persons in Time of War, of 12 August 1949;

10. *Considers* that the agreements on strategic cooperation between the United States of America and Israel signed on 30 November 1981, together with the recent accords concluded in this context, would encourage Israel to pursue its aggressive and expansionist policies and practices in the Palestinian and other Arab territories occupied since 1967, including Jerusalem, would have adverse effects on efforts for the establishment of a comprehensive, just and lasting peace in the Middle East and would threaten the security of the region;

11. *Calls upon* all States to put an end to the flow to Israel of any military, economic and financial aid, as well as of human resources, aimed at encouraging it to pursue its aggressive policies against the Arab countries and the Palestinian people;

12. *Strongly condemns* the continuing and increasing collaboration between Israel and the racist régime of South Africa, especially in the economic, military and nuclear fields, which constitutes a hostile act against the African and Arab States and enables Israel to enhance its nuclear capabilities, thus subjecting the States of the region to nuclear blackmail;

13. *Reaffirms* the call for the convening of an international peace conference on the Middle East—as specified in paragraph 5 of the Geneva Declaration on Palestine,[253] adopted on 7 September 1983 by the International Conference on the Question of Palestine—under the auspices of the United Nations and on the basis of relevant resolutions of the United Nations;

14. *Requests* the Secretary-General to report to the Security Council periodically on the development of the situation and to submit to the General Assembly at its thirty-ninth session a comprehensive report covering the developments in the Middle East in all their aspects.

Adopted at the 102nd plenary meeting:

In favour: 101

Afghanistan, Albania, Algeria, Angola, Argentina, Bahamas, Bahrain, Bangladesh, Benin, Bhutan, Bolivia, Botswana, Brazil, Bulgaria, Burundi, Byelorussia, Cape Verde, Central African Republic, China, Colombia, Congo, Cuba, Cyprus, Czechoslovakia, Democratic Kampuchea, Democratic Yemen, Djibouti, Ecuador, Egypt, El Salvador, Ethiopia, Gambia, German Democratic Republic, Ghana, Greece, Guinea, Guinea-Bissau, Guyana, Hungary, India, Indonesia, Iran, Iraq, Jordan, Kenya, Kuwait, Lao People's Democratic Republic, Lebanon, Libya, Madagascar, Malaysia, Maldives, Mali, Malta, Mauritania, Mauritius, Mexico, Mongolia, Morocco, Mozambique, Nicaragua, Niger, Nigeria, Oman, Pakistan, Papua New Guinea, Peru, Philippines, Poland, Qatar, Romania, Rwanda, Sao Tome and Principe, Saudi Arabia, Senegal, Seychelles, Sierra Leone, Singapore, Somalia, Sri Lanka, Sudan, Suriname, Syria, Thailand, Togo, Trinidad and Tobago, Tunisia, Turkey, Uganda, Ukraine, USSR, United Arab Emirates, United Republic of Cameroon, United Republic of Tanzania, Upper Volta, Venezuela, Viet Nam, Yemen, Yugoslavia, Zambia, Zimbabwe.

Against: 18

Australia, Belgium, Canada, Denmark, France, Federal Republic of Germany, Haiti, Iceland, Ireland, Israel, Italy, Luxembourg, Netherlands, New Zealand, Norway, Portugal, United Kingdom, United States.

Abstentions: 20

Austria, Barbados, Belize, Burma, Chad, Chile, Dominican Republic, Fiji, Finland, Guatemala, Honduras, Ivory Coast, Jamaica, Japan, Malawi, Saint Lucia, Saint Vincent, Spain, Sweden, Uruguay.

Absent: 18

Antigua and Barbuda, Comoros, Costa Rica, Dominica, Equatorial Guinea, Gabon, Grenada, Lesotho, Liberia, Nepal, Panama, Paraguay, Samoa, Solomon Islands, St. Christopher and Nevis, Swaziland, Vanuatu, Zaire.

E

The General Assembly,

---

[253] *Report of the International Conference on the Question of Palestine, Geneva, 29 August-7 September 1983* (United Nations publication, Sales No. E.83.I.21), chap. I, sect. A.

Having considered the item entitled "The situation in the Middle East",

Recalling its resolutions 36/226 A of 17 December 1981 and 37/123 F of 20 December 1982, in which it stated, *inter alia,* its concern over certain factors which exacerbate the situation in the Middle East,

Deeply concerned at recent developments in the Middle East and the critical situation confronting the region resulting from the continued escalation of Israel's policy of aggression, expansion and annexation in the region,

Expressing grave concern over the continued supply of modern arms and war materials to Israel, augmented by substantial economic aid, without which Israel's policy of aggression and of flouting United Nations resolutions could not be maintained,

Deeply aware that the recent reported agreements following the memorandum of understanding between the United States of America and Israel will increase Israel's intransigence and its war potential and escalate its expansionist and annexationist policies in the Palestinian and other Arab territories occupied since 1967, including Jerusalem, at a time when it is defying United Nations resolutions,

1. *Declares,* accordingly, the international responsibility of any party or parties that supply Israel with arms or economic aid that augment its war potential;

2. *Expresses deep concern* at and condemns all steps which may result in augmenting the capability of Israel and contributing to its policy of aggression against countries in the region;

3. *Demands* that all States, particularly the United States of America, in the light of the said agreements, refrain from taking any step that would support Israel's war capabilities and consequently its aggressive acts, whether in the Palestinian and other Arab territories occupied since 1967 or against countries in the region;

4. *Calls upon* all States to review, in the light of the present resolution, any agreement, whether military, economic or otherwise, concluded with Israel.

Adopted at the 102nd plenary meeting:
In favour: 81
Afghanistan, Albania, Algeria, Angola, Bahrain, Bangladesh, Benin, Bhutan, Botswana, Bulgaria, Burundi, Byelorussia, Cape Verde, China, Congo, Cuba, Cyprus, Czechoslovakia, Democratic Kampuchea, Democratic Yemen, Djibouti, Egypt, Ethiopia, Gambia, German Democratic Republic, Ghana, Greece, Guinea, Guinea-Bissau, Guyana, Hungary, India, Indonesia, Iran, Iraq, Jordan, Kenya, Kuwait, Lao People's Democratic Republic, Libya, Madagascar, Malaysia, Maldives, Mali, Malta, Mauritania, Mongolia, Morocco, Mozambique, Nicaragua, Niger, Nigeria, Oman, Pakistan, Poland, Qatar, Romania, Sao Tome and Principe, Saudi Arabia, Senegal, Seychelles, Sierra Leone, Somalia, Sri Lanka, Sudan, Suriname, Syria, Tunisia, Turkey, Uganda, Ukraine, USSR, United Arab Emirates, United Republic of Cameroon, United Republic of Tanzania, Upper Volta, Viet Nam, Yemen, Yugoslavia, Zambia, Zimbabwe.

Against: 27
Australia, Belgium, Canada, Chile, Costa Rica, Denmark, Dominican Republic, Finland, France, Federal Republic of Germany, Guatemala, Haiti, Honduras, Iceland, Ireland, Israel, Italy, Japan, Luxembourg, Netherlands, New Zealand, Norway, Paraguay, Portugal, Sweden, United Kingdom, United States.

Abstentions: 29
Argentina, Austria, Bahamas, Barbados, Belize, Bolivia, Brazil, Burma, Chad, Colombia, Ecuador, El Salvador, Fiji, Ivory Coast, Jamaica, Malawi, Mexico, Nepal, Papua New Guinea, Peru, Philippines, Saint Lucia, Saint Vincent, Singapore, Spain, Thailand, Trinidad and Tobago, Uruguay, Venezuela.

Absent: 20
Antigua and Barbuda, Central African Republic, Comoros, Dominica, Equatorial Guinea, Gabon, Grenada, Lebanon, Lesotho, Liberia, Mauritius, Panama, Rwanda, Samoa, Solomon Islands, St. Christopher and Nevis, Swaziland, Togo, Vanuatu, Zaire.

Resolution No. 38/220 of 20 December 1983

CALLING FOR ASSISTANCE FOR THE RECONSTRUCTION AND DEVELOPMENT OF LEBANON

The General Assembly,

Recalling its resolutions 33/146 of 20 December 1978, 34/135 of 14 December 1979, 35/85 of 5 December 1980, 36/205 of 17 December 1981 and 37/163 of 17 December 1982 on assistance for the reconstruction and development of Lebanon,

Recalling also Economic and Social Council resolution 1980/15 of 29 April 1980 and decision 1983/112 of 17 May 1983,

Noting with deep concern the continuing heavy loss of life and the additional destruction of property, which have caused further extensive damage to the economic and social structures of Lebanon,

Welcoming the determined efforts of the Government of Lebanon in undertaking its reconstruction and rehabilitation programme,

Reaffirming the urgent need for further international action to assist the Government of Lebanon in its continuing efforts for reconstruction and development,

Taking note of the report of the Secretary-General[254] and of the statement made by the United Nations Coordinator of Assistance for the Reconstruction and Development of Lebanon on 10 November 1983,[255]

1. *Expresses its appreciation* to the Secretary-General for his report and for the steps he has taken to mobilize assistance to Lebanon;

2. *Commends* the United Nations Co-ordinator of Assistance for the Reconstruction and Development of Lebanon and his staff for their valuable and unstinting efforts

---

[254] A/38/217 and Add.1.
[255] A/C.2/38/SR. 35, paras. 1-17.

in the discharge of their duties;

3. *Expresses its appreciation* for the relentless efforts undertaken by the Government of Lebanon in the implementation of the initial phase of the reconstruction of Lebanon, despite adverse circumstances;

4. *Requests* the Secretary-General to continue and intensify his efforts to mobilize all possible assistance within the United Nations system to help the Government of Lebanon in its reconstruction and development efforts;

5. *Requests* the organs, organizations and bodies of the United Nations system to intensify their programmes of assistance and to expand them in response to the needs of Lebanon;

6. *Also requests* the Secretary-General to report to the Economic and Social Council at its second regular session of 1984 and to the General Assembly at its thirty-ninth session on the progress achieved in the implementation of the present resolution.

Adopted at the 104th plenary meeting without a vote.

Resolution No. 39/14 of 16 November 1984

DEMANDING AN UNDERTAKING FROM ISRAEL NOT TO ATTACK NUCLEAR FACILITIES DEVOTED TO PEACEFUL PURPOSES IN IRAQ OR OTHER COUNTRIES

The General Assembly,

Having considered the item entitled "Armed Israeli aggression against the Iraqi nuclear installations and its grave consequences for the established international system concerning the peaceful uses of nuclear energy, the non-proliferation of nuclear weapons and international peace and security",

Recalling the relevant resolutions of the Security Council and the General Assembly,

Taking note of the relevant resolutions of the International Atomic Energy Agency,

Viewing with deep concern Israel's refusal to comply with those resolutions, particularly Security Council resolution 487 (1981) of 19 June 1981,

Noting that Israel's statements contained in its communication of 12 July 1984[256] continue to ignore the safeguards system of the International Atomic Energy Agency and do not specify the Iraqi nuclear installations which were the subject of the Israeli attack and subsequent threats,

Convinced that the Israeli threats to attack nuclear facilities in Iraq and in other countries will continue to endanger peace and security in the region,

1. *Reiterates its condemnation* of Israel's continuing refusal to implement Security Council resolution 487 (1981), unanimously adopted by the Council on 19 June 1981;

2. *Considers* that Israel's statements contained in its communication of 12 July 1984 do not fulfil or, in the view of some, do not completely fulfil the provisions of General Assembly resolution 38/9 of 10 November 1983 which

specifically demanded that Israel withdraw forthwith its threat to attack and destroy nuclear facilities in Iraq and in other countries;

3. *Further considers* that any threat to attack and destroy nuclear facilities in Iraq and in other countries constitutes a violation of the Charter of the United Nations;

4. *Demands* that Israel undertake forthwith not to carry out, in disregard of the safeguards system of the International Atomic Energy Agency, any attack on nuclear facilities in Iraq, or on similar facilities in other countries, devoted to peaceful purposes;

5. *Requests* the Security Council to consider the necessary measures to ensure Israel's compliance with Security Council resolution 487 (1981) and to deter Israel from repeating its attack on nuclear facilities;

6. *Reaffirms its call* for the continuation of the consideration, at the international level, of legal measures to prohibit armed attacks against nuclear facilities, as a contribution to promoting and ensuring the safe development of nuclear energy for peaceful purposes;

7. *Requests* the Secretary-General to report to the General Assembly at its fortieth session on the question of the implementation of Security Council resolution 487 (1981) and on the consequences of Israel's non-compliance with that resolution;

8. *Decides* to include in the provisional agenda of its fortieth session the item entitled "Armed Israeli aggression against the Iraqi nuclear installations and its grave consequences for the established international system concerning the peaceful uses of nuclear energy, the non-proliferation of nuclear weapons and international peace and security".

Adopted at the 65th plenary meeting:
In favour: 106
Afghanistan, Albania, Algeria, Angola, Argentina, Austria, Bahrain, Bangladesh, Benin, Bhutan, Bolivia, Botswana, Brazil, Brunei Darussalam, Bulgaria, Burkina Faso, Burundi, Byelorussia, Cameroon, Cape Verde, Central African Republic, Chad, China, Comoros, Congo, Cuba, Cyprus, Czechoslovakia, Democratic Kampuchea, Democratic Yemen, Djibouti, Egypt, Ethiopia, Gabon, German Democratic Republic, Ghana, Greece, Guinea, Guinea-Bissau, Guyana, Hungary, India, Indonesia, Iran, Iraq, Ireland, Japan, Jordan, Kenya, Kuwait, Lao People's Democratic Republic, Lebanon, Lesotho, Libya, Madagascar, Malaysia, Maldives, Mali, Malta, Mauritania, Mauritius, Mexico, Mongolia, Morocco, Mozambique, Nepal, New Zealand, Nicaragua, Niger, Nigeria, Oman, Pakistan, Peru, Philippines, Poland, Portugal, Qatar, Romania, Rwanda, Sao Tome and Principe, Saudi Arabia, Senegal, Seychelles, Sierra Leone, Singapore, Somalia, Spain, Sri Lanka, Sudan, Syria, Thailand, Togo, Trinidad and Tobago, Tunisia, Turkey, Uganda, Ukraine, USSR, United Arab Emirates, United Republic of Tanzania, Uruguay, Viet Nam, Yemen, Yugoslavia, Zambia, Zimbabwe.
Against: 2
Israel, United States.
Abstentions: 33

---

[256]A/39/349.

Australia, Barbados, Belgium, Canada, Chile, Colombia, Costa Rica, Denmark, Dominican Republic, Ecuador, Equatorial Guinea, Fiji, Finland, France, Federal Republic of Germany, Guatemala, Haiti, Iceland, Italy, Ivory Coast, Jamaica, Liberia, Luxembourg, Malawi, Netherlands, Norway, Panama, Papua New Guinea, Paraguay, Sweden, United Kingdom, Venezuela, Zaire.
Absent: 17
Antigua and Barbuda, Bahamas, Belize, Burma, Dominica, El Salvador, Gambia, Grenada, Honduras, Saint Lucia, Saint Vincent, Samoa, Solomon Islands, St. Christopher and Nevis, Suriname, Swaziland, Vanuatu.

Resolution No. 39/17 of 23 November 1984

REAFFIRMING THE RIGHT OF THE PALESTINIAN PEOPLE TO SELF-DETERMINATION AND INDEPENDENCE [EXCERPT FROM A RESOLUTION ON THE RIGHT OF PEOPLES TO SELF-DETERMINATION]

The General Assembly,

Recalling further its relevant resolutions on the question of Palestine, in particular resolutions 3236 (XXIX) and 3237 (XXIX) of 22 November 1974, 36/120 of 10 December 1981, ES-7/6 of 19 August 1982, 37/86 of 10 December 1982 and 38/58 of 13 December 1983,

Recalling the Geneva Declaration on Palestine and the Programme of Action for the Achievement of Palestinian Rights, adopted by the International Conference on the Question of Palestine,[257]

Considering that the denial of the inalienable rights of the Palestinian people to self-determination, sovereignty, independence and return to Palestine and the repeated acts of aggression by Israel against the people of the region constitute a serious threat to international peace and security,

Deeply shocked and alarmed at the deplorable consequences of the Israeli invasion of Lebanon and recalling all the relevant resolutions of the Security Council, in particular resolutions 508 (1982) of 5 June 1982, 509 (1982) of 6 June 1982, 520 (1982) of 17 September 1982 and 521 (1982) of 19 September 1982,

1. *Calls upon* all States to implement fully and faithfully all the resolutions of the United Nations regarding the exercise of the right to self-determination and independence by peoples under colonial and foreign domination;

2. *Reaffirms* the legitimacy of the struggle of peoples for their independence, territorial integrity, national unity and liberation from colonial domination, *apartheid* and foreign occupation by all available means, including armed struggle;

3. *Reaffirms* the inalienable right of the Namibian people, the Palestinian people and all peoples under foreign and colonial domination to self-determination, national independence, territorial integrity, national unity and sovereignty without foreign interference;

4. *Strongly condemns* those Governments that do not recognize the right to self-determination and independence of all peoples still under colonial domination and alien subjugation, notably the peoples of Africa and the Palestinian people;

5. *Calls* for the full and immediate implementation of the declarations and programmes of action on Namibia and on Palestine adopted by the international conferences on those questions;

17. *Denounces* the collusion between Israel and South Africa and expresses support for the Declaration of the International Conference on the Alliance between South Africa and Israel;[258]

18. *Strongly condemns* the policy of those Western States, Israel and other States whose political, economic, military, nuclear, strategic, cultural and sports relations with the racist minority régime in South Africa encourage that régime to persist in its suppression of the aspirations of peoples to self-determination and independence;

27. *Strongly condemns* the constant and deliberate violations of the fundamental rights of the Palestinian people, as well as the expansionist activities of Israel in the Middle East, which constitute an obstacle to the achievement of the self-determination and independence by the Palestinian people and a threat to peace and stability in the region;

28. *Further strongly condemns* the massacre of Palestinians and other civilians at Beirut and the Israeli aggression against Lebanon, which endangers stability, peace and security in the region;

29. *Demands* the immediate and unconditional release of all persons detained or imprisoned as a result of their struggle for self-determination and independence, full respect for their fundamental individual rights and compliance with article 5 of the Universal Declaration of Human Rights,[259] under which no one shall be subjected to torture or to cruel, inhuman or degrading treatment;

30. *Urges* all States, specialized agencies, competent organizations of the United Nations system and other international organizations to extend their support to the Palestinian people through its sole and legitimate representative, the Palestine Liberation Organization, in its struggle to regain its right to self-determination and independence in accordance with the Charter;

Adopted at the 71st plenary meeting:
In favour: 121

---

[257]*Report of the International Conference on the Question of Palestine, Geneva, 29 August-7 September 1983* (United Nations publication, Sales No. E.83.I.21), chap. I.

[258]See A/38/311-S/15883, annex.
[259]Resolution 217 A (III).

out in Assembly resolution 3101 (XXVIII) and the provisions of section II, paragraphs 2 (*b*) and 2 (*c*), and section V, paragraph 1, of resolution 3374 C (XXX), section V, paragraph 1, of resolution 31/5 D, section V, paragraph 1, of resolution 32/4 C, section V, paragraph 1, of resolution 33/13 D, section V, paragraph 1, of resolution 34/7 C, section V, paragraph 1, of resolution 35/45 A, section V, paragraph 1, of resolution 36/66 A and section V, paragraph 1, of resolution 37/38 A, in the proportions determined by the scale of assessments for the years 1983, 1984 and 1985;

3. *Decides* that there shall be set off against the apportionment among Member States, as provided in paragraph 2 above, their respective share in the estimated income of $10,000 other than staff assessment income aproved for the period from 1 December 1984 to 31 May 1985, inclusive;

4. *Decides* that, in accordance with the provisions of its resolution 973 (X) of 15 December 1955, there shall be set off against the apportionment among Member States, as provided for in paragraph 2 above, their respective share in the Tax Equalization Fund of the estimated staff assessment income of $250,500 approved for the period from 1 December 1984 to 31 May 1985, inclusive;

III

Authorizes the Secretary-General to enter into commitments for the United Nations Disengagement Observer Force at a rate not to exceed $2,975,416 gross ($2,932,000 net) per month for the period from 1 June to 30 November 1985, inclusive, should the Security Council, decide to continue the Force beyond the period of six months authorized under its resolution 557 (1984), the said amount to be apportioned among Member States in accordance with the scheme set out in the present resolution;

IV

1. *Stresses* the need for voluntary contributions to the United Nations Disengagement Observer Force, both in cash and in the form of services and supplies acceptable to the Secretary-General;

2. *Requests* the Secretary-General to take all necessary action to ensure that the United Nations Disengagement Observer Force is conducted with a maximum of efficiency and economy;

V

1. *Decides* that Brunei Darussalam shall be included in the group of Member States mentioned in paragraph 2 (*c*) of General Assembly resolution 3101 (XXVIII) and that its contribution to the United Nations Disengagement Observer Force shall be calculated in accordance with the provisions of the resolution adopted by the Assembly at the current session regarding the scale of assessments;[263]

2. *Decides* that Saint Christopher and Nevis shall be included in the group of Member States mentioned in

paragraph 2 (*d*) of General Assembly resolution 3101 (XXVIII) and that its contribution to the United Nations Disengagement Observer Force shall be calculated in accordance with the provisions of the resolution adopted by the Assembly at the current session regarding the scale of assessments;[264]

3. *Decides further* that, in accordance with regulation 5.2 (*c*) of the Financial Regulations of the United Nations, the contributions to the United Nations Disengagement Observer Force until 30 November 1984 of the Member States referred to in paragraphs 1 and 2 of the present section shall be treated as miscellaneous income to be set off against the appropriations apportioned in section II above.

Adopted at the 81st plenary meeting:
In favour: 98
Against: 2
Abstentions: 12
Absent: 46

[*No voting lists were recorded.*]

B

The General Assembly,
Having regard to the financial position of the Special Account for the United Nations Emergency Force and the United Nations Disengagement Observer Force, as set forth in the report of the Secretary-General,[265] and referring to paragraph 5 of the report of the Advisory Committee on Administrative and Budgetary Questions,[266]

Mindful of the fact that it is essential to provide the United Nations Disengagement Observer Force with the necessary financial resources to enable it to fulfil its responsibilities under the relevant resolutions of the Security Council,

Concerned that the Secretary-General is continuing to face growing difficulties in meeting the obligations of the Forces on a current basis, particularly those due to the Governments of troop-contributing States,

Recalling its resolutions 33/13 E of 14 December 1978, 34/7 D of 17 December 1979, 35/45 B of 1 December 1980, 36/66 B of 30 November 1981, 37/38 B of 30 November 1982 and 38/35 B of 1 December 1983,

Recognizing that, in consequence of the withholding of contributions by certain Member States, the surplus balances in the Special Account for the United Nations Emergency Force and the United Nations Disengagement Observer Force have, in effect, been drawn upon to the full extent to supplement the income received from contributions for meeting expenses of the Forces,

Concerned that the application of the provisions of regulations 5.2 (*b*), 5.2 (*d*), 4.3 and 4.4 of the Financial Regulations of the United Nations would aggravate the already difficult financial situation of the Forces,

---

[263]Resolution 39/247 A, paras. 1 and 4.

[264]*Ibid.*
[265]A/39/468.
[266]A/39/653.

Decides that the provisions of regulations 5.2 (*b*), 5.2 (*d*), 4.3 and 4.4 of the Financial Regulations of the United Nations shall be suspended in respect of the amount of $4,824,613, which otherwise would have to be surrendered pursuant to those provisions, this amount to be entered in the account referred to in the operative part of General Assembly resolution 33/13 E and held in suspense until a further decision is taken by the Assembly.

Adopted at the 81st plenary meeting:

In favour: 98

Against: 11

Abstentions: 5

Absent: 44

[*No voting lists were recorded.*]

Resolution No. 39/49 A, B, C, D of 11 December 1984

ON THE QUESTION OF PALESTINE: ENDORSING THE RECOMMENDATIONS OF THE COMMITTEE ON THE EXERCISE OF THE INALIENABLE RIGHTS OF THE PALESTINIAN PEOPLE, REQUESTING WIDER DISSEMINATION OF INFORMATION ON THE QUESTION OF PALESTINE AND UNITED NATIONS ACTIVITIES RELATING TO IT, AND ENDORSING THE CONVENING OF AN INTERNATIONAL PEACE CONFERENCE ON THE MIDDLE EAST

A

The General Assembly,

Recalling its resolutions 3376 (XXX) of 10 November 1975, 31/20 of 24 November 1976, 32/40 of 2 December 1977, 33/28 of 7 December 1978, 34/65 A and B of 29 November 1979 and 34/65 C and D of 12 December 1979, ES-7/2 of 29 July 1980, 35/169 of 15 December 1980, 36/120 of 10 December 1981, ES-7/4 of 28 April 1982, ES-7/5 of 26 June 1982, ES-7/9 of 24 September 1982, 37/86 A of 10 December 1982 and 38/58 A of 13 December 1983,[267]

Having considered the report of the Committee on the Exercise of the Inalienable Rights of the Palestinian People,[268]

1. *Expresses its appreciation* to the Committee on the Exercise of the Inalienable Rights of the Palestinian People for its efforts in performing the tasks assigned to it by the General Assembly;

2. *Endorses* the recommendations of the Committee contained in paragraphs 155 to 160 of its report and draws the attention of the Security Council to the fact that action on the Committee's recommendations, as repeatedly endorsed by the General Assembly at its thirty-first session and subsequently, is still awaited;

3. *Requests* the Committee to continue to keep under review the situation relating to the question of Palestine as well as the implementation of the Programme of Action for the Achievement of Palestinian Rights[269] adopted by the International Conference on the Question of Palestine and to report and make suggestions to the General Assembly or the Security Council as appropriate;

4. *Authorizes* the Committee to continue to exert all efforts to promote the implementation of its recommendations, to send delegations or representatives to international conferences where such representation would be considered by it to be appropriate, and to report thereon to the General Assembly at its fortieth session and thereafter;

5. *Requests* the Committee to continue to extend its cooperation to non-governmental organizations in their contribution towards heightening international awareness of the facts relating to the question of Palestine;

6. *Requests* the United Nations Conciliation Commission for Palestine, established under General Assembly resolution 194 (III) of 11 December 1948, as well as other United Nations bodies associated with the question of Palestine, to co-operate fully with the Committee and to make available to it, at its request, the relevant information and documentation which they have at their disposal;

7. *Decides* to circulate the report of the Committee to all the competent bodies of the United Nations and urges them to take the necessary action, as appropriate, in accordance with the Committee's programme of implementation;

8. *Requests* the Secretary-General to continue to provide the Committee with all the necessary facilities for the performance of its tasks.

Adopted at the 95th plenary meeting:

In favour: 127

Afghanistan, Albania, Algeria, Angola, Argentina, Bahamas, Bahrain, Bangladesh, Barbados, Belize, Benin, Bhutan, Bolivia, Botswana, Brazil, Brunei Darussalam, Bulgaria, Burkina Faso, Burma, Burundi, Byelorussia, Cameroon, Cape Verde, Central African Republic, Chad, Chile, China, Colombia, Comoros, Congo, Cuba, Cyprus, Czechoslovakia, Democratic Kampuchea, Democratic Yemen, Djibouti, Dominican Republic, Ecuador, Egypt, Equatorial Guinea, Ethiopia, Fiji, Gabon, Gambia, German Democratic Republic, Greece, Guinea, Guinea-Bissau, Guyana, Haiti, Honduras, Hungary, India, Indonesia, Iran, Iraq, Ivory Coast, Jamaica, Jordan, Kenya, Kuwait, Lao People's Democratic Republic, Lebanon, Lesotho, Liberia, Libya, Madagascar, Malawi, Malaysia, Maldives, Mali, Malta, Mauritania, Mauritius, Mexico, Mongolia, Morocco, Mozambique, Nepal, Nicaragua, Niger, Nigeria, Oman, Pakistan, Panama, Papua New Guinea, Paraguay, Peru, Philippines, Poland, Portugal, Qatar, Romania, Rwanda, Saint Lucia, Saint Vincent, Samoa, Sao Tome and Principe, Saudi Arabia, Senegal, Seychelles, Sierra Leone, Singapore, Somalia, Spain, Sri Lanka, Sudan, Suriname, Syria, Thailand, Togo, Trinidad and Tobago, Tunisia, Turkey,

---

[267]The resolutions cited are previous resolutions on the Question of Palestine. [ed. note]

[268]*Official Records of the General Assembly, Thirty-ninth Session, Supplement No. 35* (A/39/35).

[269]*Report of the International Conference on the Question of Palestine, Geneva, 29 August-7 September 1983* (United Nations publication, Sales No. E.83.I.21), chap. I, sect. B.

Uganda, Ukraine, USSR, United Arab Emirates, United Republic of Tanzania, Uruguay, Vanuatu, Venezuela, Viet Nam, Yemen, Yugoslavia, Zambia, Zimbabwe.

Against: 2

Israel, United States.

Abstentions: 21

Australia, Austria, Belgium, Canada, Costa Rica, Denmark, Dominica, Finland, France, Federal Republic of Germany, Guatemala, Iceland, Ireland, Italy, Japan, Luxembourg, Netherlands, New Zealand, Norway, Sweden, United Kingdom.

Absent: 8

Antigua and Barbuda, El Salvador, Ghana,* Grenada, Solomon Islands, St. Christopher and Nevis, Swaziland, Zaire.

---

*Later advised the Secretariat it had intended to vote in favour.

B

The General Assembly,

Having considered the report of the Committee on the Exercise of the Inalienable Rights of the Palestinian People,[270]

Noting the particularly relevant information contained in paragraphs 125 to 132 of that report,

Recalling its resolutions 32/40 B of 2 December 1977, 33/28 C of 7 December 1978, 34/65 D of 12 December 1979, 35/169 D of 15 December 1980, 36/120 B of 10 December 1981, 37/86 B of 10 December 1982 and 38/58 B of 13 December 1983,

1. *Notes with appreciation* the action taken by the Secretary-General in compliance with General Assembly resolution 38/58 B;

2. *Requests* the Secretary-General to ensure that the Division for Palestinian Rights of the Secretariat continues to discharge the tasks detailed in paragraph 1 of General Assembly resolution 32/40 B, paragraph 2(*b*) of resolution 34/65 D, paragraph 3 of resolution 36/120 B and paragraphs 2 and 3 of resolution 38/58 B, in consultation with the Committee on the Exercise of the Inalienable Rights of the Palestinian People and under its guidance;

3. *Also requests* the Secretary-General to ensure the continued co-operation of the Department of Public Information and other units of the Secretariat in enabling the Division for Palestinian Rights to perform its tasks and in covering adequately the various aspects of the question of Palestine;

4. *Invites* all Governments and organizations to lend their co-operation to the Committee on the Exercise of the Inalienable Rights of the Palestinian People and the Division for Palestinian Rights in the performance of their tasks;

5. *Notes with appreciation* the action taken by Member States to observe annually on 29 November the International Day of Solidarity with the Palestinian People and the issuance by them of special postage stamps for the occasion.

Adopted at the 95th plenary meeting:

In favour: 130

Afghanistan, Albania, Algeria, Angola, Argentina, Bahamas, Bahrain, Bangladesh, Barbados, Belize, Benin, Bhutan, Bolivia, Botswana, Brazil, Brunei Darussalam, Bulgaria, Burkina Faso, Burma, Burundi, Byelorussia, Cameroon, Cape Verde, Central African Republic, Chad, Chile, China, Colombia, Comoros, Congo, Costa Rica, Cuba, Cyprus, Czechoslovakia, Democratic Kampuchea, Democratic Yemen, Djibouti, Dominica, Dominican Republic, Ecuador, Egypt, Equatorial Guinea, Ethiopia, Fiji, Gabon, Gambia, German Democratic Republic, Greece, Guatemala, Guinea, Guinea-Bissau, Guyana, Haiti, Honduras, Hungary, India, Indonesia, Iran, Iraq, Ivory Coast, Jamaica, Jordan, Kenya, Kuwait, Lao People's Democratic Republic, Lebanon, Lesotho, Liberia, Libya, Madagascar, Malawi, Malaysia, Maldives, Mali, Malta, Mauritania, Mauritius, Mexico, Mongolia, Morocco, Mozambique, Nepal, Nicaragua, Niger, Nigeria, Oman, Pakistan, Panama, Papua New Guinea, Paraguay, Peru, Philippines, Poland, Portugal, Qatar, Romania, Rwanda, Saint Lucia, Saint Vincent, Samoa, Sao Tome and Principe, Saudi Arabia, Senegal, Seychelles, Sierra Leone, Singapore, Somalia, Spain, Sri Lanka, Sudan, Suriname, Syria, Thailand, Togo, Trinidad and Tobago, Tunisia, Turkey, Uganda, Ukraine, USSR, United Arab Emirates, United Republic of Tanzania, Uruguay, Vanuatu, Venezuela, Viet Nam, Yemen, Yugoslavia, Zambia, Zimbabwe.

Against: 3

Canada, Israel, United States.

Abstentions: 17

Australia, Austria, Belgium, Denmark, Finland, France, Federal Republic of Germany, Iceland, Ireland, Italy, Japan, Luxembourg, Netherlands, New Zealand, Norway, Sweden, United Kingdom.

Absent: 8

Antigua and Barbuda, El Salvador, Ghana,* Grenada, Solomon Islands, St. Christopher and Nevis, Swaziland, Zaire.

---

*Later advised the Secretariat it had intended to vote in favour.

C

The General Assembly,

Having considered the report of the Committee on the Exercise of the Inalienable Rights of the Palestinian People,[271]

Noting, in particular, the information contained in paragraphs 133 to 142 of that report,

---

[270]*Official Records of the General Assembly, Thirty-ninth Session, Supplement No. 35* (A/39/35).

[271]*Official Records of the General Assembly, Thirty-ninth Session, Supplement No. 35* (A/39/35).

Recalling its resolution 38/58 E of 13 December 1983,

Convinced that the world-wide dissemination of accurate and comprehensive information and the role of non-governmental organizations and institutions remain of vital importance in heightening awareness of and support for the inalienable rights of the Palestinian people to self-determination and to the establishment of an independent sovereign Palestinian State,

1. *Notes with appreciation* the action taken by the Department of Public Information of the Secretariat in compliance with General Assembly resolution 38/58 E;

2. *Requests* that the Department of Public Information, in full co-operation and co-ordination with the Committee on the Exercise of the Inalienable Rights of the Palestinian People, should:

(*a*) Continue the implementation of all parts of General Assembly resolution 38/58 E;

(*b*) Disseminate all information on the activities of the United Nations system relating to Palestine;

(*c*) Expand and update publications and audio-visual material on the facts and developments pertaining to the question of Palestine;

(*d*) Publish newsletters and articles in its relevant publications on Israeli violations of the human rights of the Arab inhabitants of the occupied territories;

(*e*) Organize fact-finding missions to the area for journalists;

(*f*) Organize regional and national encounters for journalists.

Adopted at the 95th plenary meeting:
In favour: 131

Afghanistan, Albania, Algeria, Angola, Argentina, Austria, Bahamas, Bahrain, Bangladesh, Barbados, Belize, Benin, Bhutan, Bolivia, Botswana, Brazil, Brunei Darussalam, Bulgaria, Burkina Faso, Burma, Burundi, Byelorussia, Cameroon, Cape Verde, Central African Republic, Chad, China, Colombia, Comoros, Congo, Cuba, Cyprus, Czechoslovakia, Democratic Kampuchea, Democratic Yemen, Djibouti, Dominica, Dominican Republic, Ecuador, Egypt, Equatorial Guinea, Ethiopia, Fiji, Finland, Gabon, Gambia, German Democratic Republic, Greece, Guatemala, Guinea, Guinea-Bissau, Guyana, Haiti, Honduras, Hungary, India, Indonesia, Iran, Iraq, Ivory Coast, Jamaica, Jordan, Kenya, Kuwait, Lao People's Democratic Republic, Lebanon, Lesotho, Liberia, Libya, Madagascar, Malawi, Malaysia, Maldives, Mali, Malta, Mauritania, Mauritius, Mexico, Mongolia, Morocco, Mozambique, Nepal, Nicaragua, Niger, Nigeria, Oman, Pakistan, Panama, Papua New Guinea, Paraguay, Peru, Philippines, Poland, Portugal, Qatar, Romania, Rwanda, Saint Lucia, Saint Vincent, Samoa, Sao Tome and Principe, Saudi Arabia, Senegal, Seychelles, Sierra Leone, Singapore, Somalia, Spain, Sri Lanka, Sudan, Suriname, Sweden, Syria, Thailand, Togo, Trinidad and Tobago, Tunisia, Turkey, Uganda, Ukraine, USSR, United Arab Emirates, United Republic of Tanzania, Uruguay, Vanuatu, Venezuela, Viet Nam, Yemen, Yugoslavia, Zambia, Zimbabwe.

Against: 3
Canada, Israel, United States.

Abstentions: 15
Australia, Belgium, Costa Rica, Denmark, France, Federal Republic of Germany, Iceland, Ireland, Italy, Japan, Luxembourg, Netherlands, New Zealand, Norway, United Kingdom.

Absent: 9
Antigua and Barbuda, Chile, El Salvador, Ghana,* Grenada, Solomon Islands, St. Christopher and Nevis, Swaziland, Zaire.

---

*Later advised the Secretariat it had intended to vote in favour.

D

General Assembly,

Recalling its resolution 38/58 C of 13 December 1984, in which it, *inter alia,* endorsed the convening of an International Peace Conference on the Middle East,

Reaffirming paragraph 5 of its resolution 38/58 C, in which it requested the Secretary-General to undertake preparatory measures to convene the Conference,

Having considered the reports of the Secretary-General of 13 March 1984[272] and 13 September 1984,[273] in which he stated that, *inter alia,* "it is clear from the replies of the Governments of Israel and the United States of America that they are not prepared to participate in the proposed Conference",[274]

Reiterating its conviction that the convening of the Conference would constitute a major contribution by the United Nations towards the achievement of a comprehensive, just and lasting solution to the Arab-Israeli conflict,

1. *Takes note* of the reports of the Secretary-General;

2. *Reaffirms* its endorsement of the call for convening the International Peace Conference on the Middle East in conformity with the provisions of General Assembly resolution 38/58 C;

3. *Expresses its regret* at the negative response of the two Governments and calls upon them to reconsider their position towards the Conference;

4. *Urges* all Governments to make additional constructive efforts and to strengthen their political will in order to convene the Conference without delay and for the achievement of its peaceful objectives;

5. *Requests* the Secretary-General, in consultation with the Security Council, to continue his efforts with a view to convening the Conference and to report thereon to the General Assembly not later than 15 March 1985;[275]

---

[272]A/39/130-S/16409. For the printed text, see *Official Records of the Security Council, Thirty-ninth Year, Supplement for January, February and March 1984,* document S/16409.

[273]A/39/130/Add.1-S/16409/Add.1. For the printed text, see *Official Records of the Security Council, Thirty-ninth Year, Supplement for July, August and September 1984,* document S/16409/Add.1.

[274]*Ibid.,* para. 4.

[275]The report was issued under the symbol A/40/168-S/17014. For the printed text, see *Official Records of the Security Council, Fortieth Year, Supplement for January, February and March 1985,* document S/17014.

6. *Decides* to consider at its fortieth session the report of the Secretary-General on the implementation of the present resolution.

Adopted at the 95th plenary meeting:
In favour: 121
Afghanistan, Algeria, Angola, Argentina, Austria, Bahamas, Bahrain, Bangladesh, Barbados, Belize, Benin, Bhutan, Bolivia, Botswana, Brazil, Brunei Darussalam, Bulgaria, Burkina Faso, Burma, Burundi, Byelorussia, Cameroon, Cape Verde, Central African Republic, Chad, China, Colombia, Comoros, Congo, Cuba, Cyprus, Czechoslovakia, Democratic Kampuchea, Democratic Yemen, Djibouti, Dominican Republic, Ecuador, Egypt, Equatorial Guinea, Ethiopia, Fiji, Finland, Gabon, Gambia, German Democratic Republic, Greece, Guatemala, Guinea, Guinea-Bissau, Guyana, Hungary, India, Indonesia, Iran, Iraq, Jamaica, Jordan, Kenya, Kuwait, Lao People's Democratic Republic, Lebanon, Lesotho, Libya, Madagascar, Malaysia, Maldives, Mali, Malta, Mauritania, Mauritius, Mexico, Mongolia, Morocco, Mozambique, Nepal, Nicaragua, Niger, Nigeria, Oman, Pakistan, Papua New Guinea, Paraguay, Peru, Philippines, Poland, Portugal, Qatar, Romania, Rwanda, Samoa, Sao Tome and Principe, Saudi Arabia, Senegal, Seychelles, Sierra Leone, Singapore, Somalia, Spain, Sri Lanka, Sudan, Suriname, Sweden, Syria, Thailand, Togo, Trinidad and Tobago, Tunisia, Turkey, Uganda, Ukraine, USSR, United Arab Emirates, United Republic of Tanzania, Uruguay, Vanuatu, Venezuela, Viet Nam, Yemen, Yugoslavia, Zambia, Zimbabwe.
Against: 3
Canada, Israel, United States.
Abstentions: 23
Australia, Belgium, Costa Rica, Denmark, Dominica, France, Federal Republic of Germany, Haiti, Iceland, Ireland, Italy, Ivory Coast, Japan, Liberia, Luxembourg, Malawi, Netherlands, New Zealand, Norway, Panama, Saint Lucia, Saint Vincent, United Kingdom.
Absent: 10
Antigua and Barbuda, Chile, El Salvador, Ghana,* Grenada, Honduras, Solomon Islands, St. Christopher and Nevis, Swaziland, Zaire.

Albania announced that it was not participating in the vote.

---

*Later advised the Secretariat it had intended to vote in favour.

Resolution No. 39/50 A, D of 12 December 1984

CONDEMNING THE COLLUSION BETWEEN SOUTH AFRICA AND ISRAEL IN THE NUCLEAR FIELD [EXCERPTS FROM A RESOLUTION ON NAMIBIA]

A

SITUATION IN NAMIBIA RESULTING FROM THE ILLEGAL OCCUPATION OF THE TERRITORY BY SOUTH AFRICA

The General Assembly,

Deeply deploring the continued collaboration with South Africa of certain Western States, in particular the United States of America, as well as that of Israel, in the political, military, economic and nuclear fields, in disregard of the relevant resolutions of the General Assembly and the Security Council,

37. *Condemns* the increased assistance rendered by the major Western countries and Israel to South Africa in the political, economic, financial and particularly the military and nuclear fields, expresses its conviction that this assistance constitutes a hostile action against the people of Namibia and the front-line states since it is bound to strengthen further the aggressive military machine of the racist régime, and therefore demands that such assistance by immediately terminated;

44. *Condemns* the continuing military and nuclear collaboration on the part of certain Western States and Israel with the racist régime of South Africa, in violation of the arms embargo imposed against South Africa under Security Council resolution 418 (1977) of 4 November 1977;

49. *Strongly condemns* the collusion between South Africa, Israel, and certain Western States, particularly the United States of America, in the nuclear field and calls upon France and all other States to refrain from supplying the racist minority régime of South Africa, directly or indirectly, with installations that might enable it to produce uranium, plutonium or other nuclear materials, reactors or military equipment;

Adopted at the 97th plenary meeting:
In favour: 128
Afghanistan, Albania, Algeria, Angola, Antigua and Barbuda, Argentina, Bahamas, Bahrain, Bangladesh, Barbados, Belize, Benin, Bhutan, Bolivia, Botswana, Brazil, Brunei Darussalam, Bulgaria, Burkina Faso, Burma, Burundi, Byelorussia, Cameroon, Cape Verde, Central African Republic, Chad, China, Colombia, Comoros, Congo, Costa Rica, Cuba, Cyprus, Czechoslovakia, Democratic Kampuchea, Democratic Yemen, Djibouti, Dominica, Dominican Republic, Ecuador, Egypt, El Salvador, Equatorial Guinea, Ethiopia, Fiji, Gabon, Gambia, German Democratic Republic, Ghana, Greece, Guatemala, Guinea, Guinea-Bissau, Guyana, Haiti, Honduras, Hungary, India, Indonesia, Iran, Iraq, Jamaica, Jordan, Kenya, Kuwait, Lao People's Democratic Republic, Lebanon, Lesotho, Liberia, Libya, Madagascar, Malaysia, Maldives, Mali, Malta, Mauritania, Mexico, Mongolia, Morocco, Mozambique, Nepal, Nicaragua, Niger, Nigeria, Oman, Pakistan, Panama, Papua New Guinea, Peru, Philippines, Poland, Qatar, Romania, Rwanda, Saint Lucia, Saint Vincent, Samoa, Sao Tome and Principe, Saudi Arabia, Senegal, Seychelles, Sierra Leone, Singapore, Somalia, Sri Lanka, Sudan, Suriname, Swaziland, Syria, Thai-

land, Togo, Trinidad and Tobago, Tunisia, Turkey, Uganda, Ukraine, USSR, United Arab Emirates, United Republic of Tanzania, Uruguay, Vanuatu, Venezuela, Viet Nam, Yemen, Yugoslavia, Zaire, Zambia, Zimbabwe.

Against: 0

Abstentions: 25

Australia, Austria, Belgium, Canada, Denmark, Finland, France, Federal Republic of Germany, Grenada, Iceland, Ireland, Italy, Ivory Coast, Japan, Luxembourg, Malawi, Netherlands, New Zealand, Norway, Paraguay, Portugal, Spain, Sweden, United Kingdom, United States.

Absent: 5

Chile, Israel, Mauritius, Solomon Islands, St. Christopher and Nevis.

D

DISSEMINATION OF INFORMATION AND MOBILIZATION OF INTERNATIONAL PUBLIC OPINION IN SUPPORT OF NAMIBIA

The General Assembly,

Deploring the continued assistance rendered by Israel and certain Western States, especially the United States of America, to South Africa in the political, economic, military and cultural fields and expressing its conviction that this assistance should be exposed by the United Nations Council for Namibia by all means available to it,

5. *Decides* to intensify its international campaign in support of the cause of Namibia and to expose and denounce the collusion of the United States of America, certain other Western countries and Israel with the South African racists and, to this end, requests the United Nations Council for Namibia to include in its programme of dissemination of information for 1985 the following activities:

(*a*) Preparation and dissemination of publications on the political, economic, military and social consequences of the illegal occupation of Namibia by South Africa, as well as on legal matters, on the question of the territorial integrity of Namibia and on contacts between Member States and South Africa;

(*b*) Production and dissemination of radio programmes in English, French, German and Spanish languages designed to draw the attention of world public opinion to the current situation in and around Namibia;

(*c*) Production of material for publicity through radio and television broadcasts;

(*d*) Placement of advertisements in newspapers and magazines;

(*e*) Production of films, film-strips and slide sets on Namibia;

(*f*) Production and dissemination of posters;

(*g*) Full utilization of the resources related to press releases, press conferences and press briefings in order to maintain a constant flow of information to the public on all aspects of the question of Namibia;

(*h*) Production and dissemination of a comprehensive economic map of Namibia;

(*i*) Production and dissemination of booklets on the activities of the Council;

(*j*) Preparation and wide dissemination of a booklet containing resolutions of the General Assembly and the Security Council relating to Namibia, together with relevant portions of Assembly resolutions on the activities of foreign economic interests in Namibia and on military activities in Namibia;

(*k*) Publicity for and distribution of an indexed reference book on transnational corporations which plunder the natural and human resources of Namibia, and on the profits extracted from the Territory;

(*l*) Preparation and dissemination of a booklet based on a study on the implementation of Decree No. 1 for the Protection of the Natural Resources of Namibia,[276] enacted by the Council on 27 September 1974;

(*m*) Acquisition of books, pamphlets, and other materials relating to Namibia for further dissemination;

Adopted at the 97th plenary meeting:

In favour: 130

Afghanistan, Albania, Algeria, Angola, Antigua and Barbuda, Argentina, Bahamas, Bahrain, Bangladesh, Barbados, Belize, Benin, Bhutan, Bolivia, Botswana, Brazil, Brunei Darussalam, Bulgaria, Burkina Faso, Burma, Burundi, Byelorussia, Cameroon, Cape Verde, Central African Republic, Chad, Chile, China, Colombia, Comoros, Congo, Costa Rica, Cuba, Cyprus, Czechoslovakia, Democratic Kampuchea, Democratic Yemen, Djibouti, Dominica, Dominican Republic, Ecuador, Egypt, El Salvador, Equatorial Guinea, Ethiopia, Fiji, Gabon, Gambia, German Democratic Republic, Ghana, Greece, Guatemala, Guinea-Bissau, Guyana, Haiti, Honduras, Hungary, India, Indonesia, Iran, Iraq, Jamaica, Jordan, Kenya, Kuwait, Lao People's Democratic Republic, Lebanon, Lesotho, Liberia, Libya, Madagascar, Malawi, Malaysia, Maldives, Mali, Malta, Mauritania, Mexico, Mongolia, Morocco, Mozambique, Nepal, Nicaragua, Niger, Nigeria, Oman, Pakistan, Panama, Papua New Guinea, Peru, Philippines, Poland, Qatar, Romania, Rwanda, Saint Lucia, Saint Vincent, Samoa, Sao Tome and Principe, Saudi Arabia, Senegal, Seychelles, Sierra Leone, Singapore, Somalia, Sri Lanka, Sudan, Suriname, Swaziland, Syria, Thailand, Togo, Trinidad and Tobago, Tunisia, Turkey, Uganda, Ukraine, USSR, United Arab Emirates, United Republic of Tanzania, Uruguay, Vanuatu, Venezuela, Viet Nam, Yemen, Yugoslavia, Zaire, Zambia, Zimbabwe.

Against: 0

Abstentions: 24

Australia, Austria, Belgium, Canada, Denmark, Finland, France, Federal Republic of Germany, Grenada, Iceland, Ireland, Italy, Ivory Coast, Japan, Luxembourg, Nether-

---

[276]*Official Records of the General Assembly, Thirty-fifth Session, Supplement No. 24* (A/35/24), vol. I, annex II.

lands, New Zealand, Norway, Paraguay, Portugal, Spain, Sweden, United Kingdom, United States.
Absent: 4
Israel, Mauritius, Solomon Islands, St. Christopher and Nevis.

Resolution No. 39/54 of 12 December 1984

CALLING UPON COUNTRIES OF THE MIDDLE EAST TO PLACE THEIR NUCLEAR ACTIVITIES UNDER INTERNATIONAL ATOMIC ENERGY AGENCY SAFEGUARDS

The General Assembly,

Recalling its resolutions 3263 (XXIX) of 9 December 1974, 3474 (XXX) of 11 December 1975, 31/71 of 10 December 1976, 32/82 of 12 December 1977, 33/64 of 14 December 1978, 34/77 of 11 December 1979, 35/147 of 12 December 1980, 36/87 of 9 December 1981, 37/75 of 9 December 1982 and 38/64 of 15 December 1983 on the establishment of a nuclear-weapon-free zone in the region of the Middle East,

Recalling also the recommendations for the establishment of such a zone in the Middle East consistent with paragraphs 60 to 63, in particular paragraph 63 (*d*), of the Final Document of the Tenth Special Session of the General Assembly,[277]

Emphasizing the basic provisions of the above-mentioned resolutions, which call upon all parties directly concerned to consider taking the practical and urgent steps required for the implementation of the proposal to establish a nuclear-weapon-free zone in the region of the Middle East and, pending and during the establishment of such a zone, to declare solemnly that they will refrain, on a reciprocal basis, from producing, acquiring or in any other way possessing nuclear weapons and nuclear explosive devices and from permitting the stationing of nuclear weapons on their territory by any third party, to agree to place all their nuclear facilities under International Atomic Energy Agency safeguards and to declare their support for the establishment of the zone and deposit such declarations with the Security Council for consideration, as appropriate,

Reaffirming the inalienable right of all States to acquire and develop nuclear energy for peaceful purposes,

Emphasizing further the need for appropriate measures on the question of the prohibition of military attacks on nuclear facilities,

Bearing in mind the consensus reached by the General Assembly at its thirty-fifth session that the establishment of a nuclear-weapon-free zone in the region of the Middle East would greatly enhance international peace and security,

Desirous to build on that consensus so that substantial progress can be made towards establishing a nuclear-weapon-free zone in the region of the Middle East,

Emphasizing the essential role of the United Nations in the establishment of a nuclear-weapon-free zone in the region of the Middle East,

Taking note of the report of the Secretary-General,[278]

1. *Urges* all parties directly concerned to consider seriously taking the practical and urgent steps required for the implementation of the proposal to establish a nuclear-weapon-free zone in the region of the Middle East in accordance with the relevant resolutions of the General Assembly and, as a means of promoting this objective, invites the countries concerned to adhere to the Treaty on the Non-Proliferation of Nuclear Weapons;[279]

2. *Calls upon* all countries of the region that have not done so, pending the establishment of the zone, to agree to place all their nuclear activities under International Atomic Energy Agency safeguards;

3. *Invites* those countries, pending the establishment of a nuclear-weapon-free zone in the region of the Middle East, to declare their support for establishing such a zone, consistent with the relevant paragraph of the Final Document of the Tenth Special Session of the General Assembly, and to deposit those declarations with the Security Council;

4. *Further invites* those countries, pending the establishment of the zone, not to develop, produce, test or otherwise acquire nuclear weapons or permit the stationing on their territories, or territories under their control, of nuclear weapons or nuclear explosive devices;

5. *Invites* the nuclear-weapon States and all other States to render their assistance in the establishment of the zone and at the same time to refrain from any action that runs counter to both the letter and spirit of the present resolution;

6. *Requests* the Secretary-General to seek the views of all concerned parties regarding the establishment of a nuclear-weapon-free zone in the region of the Middle East;

7. *Requests* the Secretary-General to submit a report to the General Assembly at its fortieth session on the implementation of the present resolution;

8. *Decides* to include in the provisional agenda of its fortieth session the item entitled "Establishment of a nuclear-weapon-free zone in the region of the Middle East".

Adopted at the 97th plenary meeting without a vote.

Resolution No. 39/71 A, B of 13 December 1984

ON THE FINANCING OF UNIFIL

A

The General Assembly,
Having considered the report of the Secretary-General on the financing of the United Nations Interim Force in

---

[277]Resolution S-10/2.

[278]A/39/472.
[279]Resolution 2373 (XXII), annex.

Lebanon[280] and the related report of the Advisory Committee on Administrative and Budgetary Questions,[281]

Bearing in mind Security Council resolutions 425 (1978) and 426 (1978) of 19 March 1978, 427 (1978) of 3 May 1978, 434 (1978) of 18 September 1978, 444 (1979) of 19 January 1979, 450 (1979) of 14 June 1979, 459 (1979) of 19 December 1979, 474 (1980) of 17 June 1980, 483 (1980) of 17 December 1980, 488 (1981) of 19 June 1981, 498 (1981) of 18 December 1981, 501 (1982) of 25 February 1982, 511 (1982) of 18 June 1982, 519 (1982) of 17 August 1982, 523 (1982) of 18 October 1982, 529 (1983) of 18 January 1983, 536 (1983) of 18 July 1983, 538 (1983) of 18 October 1983, 549 (1984) of 19 April 1984 and 555 (1984) of 12 October 1984,[282]

Recalling its resolutions S-8/2 of 21 April 1978, 33/14 of 3 November 1978, 34/9 B of 17 December 1979, 35/44 of 1 December 1980, 35/115 A of 10 December 1980, 36/138 A of 16 December 1981, 36/138 C of 19 March 1982, 37/127 A of 17 December 1982 and 38/38 A of 5 December 1983,

Reaffirming its previous decisions regarding the fact that, in order to meet the expenditures caused by such operations, a different procedure from the one applied to meet expenditures of the regular budget of the United Nations is required,

Taking into account the fact that the economically more developed countries are in a position to make relatively larger contributions and that the economically less developed countries have a relatively limited capacity to contribute towards peace-keeping operations involving heavy expenditures,

Bearing in mind the special responsibilities of the States permanent members of the Security Council in the financing of the peace-keeping operations decided upon in accordance with the Charter of the United Nations,

I

Decides to appropriate to the Special Account referred to in section I, paragraph 1, of General Assembly resolution S-8/2 an amount of $70,446,000 gross ($69,486,000 net), being the amount authorized with the prior concurrence of the Advisory Committee on Administrative and Budgetary Questions and apportioned under the provisions of section VI of Assembly resolution 38/38 A for the operation of the United Nations Interim Force in Lebanon from 19 April to 18 October 1984, inclusive;

II

Decides to appropriate to the Special Account an amount of $23,482,000 gross ($23,148,667 net), being the amount authorized with the prior concurrence of the Advisory Committee on Administrative and Budgetary Questions and apportioned under the provisions of section VI of

General Assembly resolution 38/38 A for the operation of the United Nations Interim Force in Lebanon from 19 October to 18 December 1984, inclusive;

III

1. *Decides* to appropriate to the Special Account an amount of $46,964,000 for the operation of the United Nations Interim Force in Lebanon for the period from 19 December 1984 to 18 April 1985, inclusive;

2. *Decides further,* as an *ad hoc* arrangement, without prejudice to the positions of principle that may be taken by Member States in any consideration by the General Assembly of arrangements for the financing of peace-keeping operations, to apportion the amount of $46,964,000 among Member States in accordance with the scheme set out in Assembly resolution 33/14 and the provisions of section V, paragraph 1, of resolution 34/9 B, section VI, paragraph 1, of resolution 35/115 A, section VI, paragraph 1, of resolution 36/138 A and section IX, paragraph 1, of resolution 37/127 A, in the proportions determined by the scale of assessments for the years 1983, 1984 and 1985;

3. *Decides* that there shall be set off against the apportionment among Member States, as provided for in paragraph 2 above, their respective share in the estimated income of $13,333 other than staff assessment income approved for the period from 19 December 1984 to 18 April 1985, inclusive;

4. *Decides* that, in accordance with the provisions of its resolution 973 (X) of 15 December 1955, there shall be set off against the apportionment among Member States, as provided for in paragraph 2 above, their respective share in the Tax Equalization Fund of the estimated staff assessment income of $653,334 approved for the period from 19 December 1984 to 18 April 1985, inclusive;

IV

Authorizes the Secretary-General to enter into commitments for the operation of the United Nations Interim Force in Lebanon at a rate not to exceed $11,741,000 gross ($11,574,333 net) per month for the period from 19 April to 18 December 1985, inclusive, should the Security Council decide to continue the Force beyond the period of six months authorized under its resolution 555 (1984), subject to obtaining the prior concurrence of the Advisory Committee on Administrative and Budgetary questions for the actual level of commitments to be entered into for each mandate period that may be approved subsequent to 19 April 1985, the said amount to be apportioned among Member States in accordance with the scheme set out in the present resolution;

V

1. *Renews its invitation* to Member States to make voluntary contributions to the United Nations Interim Force in Lebanon both in cash and in the form of services and supplies acceptable to the Secretary-General;

2. *Invites* Member States to make voluntary contributions in cash to the Suspense Account established in accordance with its resolution 34/9 D of 17 December 1979;

---

[280]A/39/650.

[281]A/39/685.

[282]The resolutions in this and the next paragraph provide for the financing and renewal of mandate of Unifil. [ed. note]

VI

Requests the Secretary-General to take all necessary action to ensure that the United Nations Interim Force in Lebanon shall be administered with a maximum of efficiency and economy;

VII

1. *Decides* that Brunei Darussalam shall be included in the group of Member States mentioned in section I, paragraph 2 (*c*), of General Assembly resolution S-8/2 and that its contribution to the United Nations Interim Force in Lebanon shall be calculated in accordance with the provisions of the resolution adopted by the Assembly at the current session regarding the scale of assessments;[283]

2. *Decides* that Saint Christopher and Nevis shall be included in the group of Member States mentioned in section I, paragraph 2 (*d*), of General Assembly resolution S-8/2 and that its contribution to the United Nations Interim Force in Lebanon shall be calculated in accordance with the provisions of the resolution adopted by the Assembly at the current session regarding the scale of assessments;[284]

3. *Decides further* that, in accordance with regulation 5.2 (*c*) of the Financial Regulations of the United Nations, the contributions to the United Nations Interim Force in Lebanon until 18 December 1984 of the Member States referred to in paragraphs 1 and 2 of the present section shall be treated as miscellaneous income to be set off against the apportionments authorized in section III above.

B

The General Assembly,

Having regard to the financial position of the Special Account for the United Nations Interim Force in Lebanon, as set forth in the report of the Secretary-General,[285] and referring to paragraph 7 of the report of the Advisory Committee on Administrative and Budgetary questions,[286]

Mindful of the fact that it is essential to provide the United Nations Interim Force in Lebanon with the necessary financial resources to enable it to fulfil its responsibilities under the relevant resolutions of the Security Council,

Concerned that the Secretary-General is continuing to face growing difficulties in meeting the obligations of the United Nations Interim Force in Lebanon on a current basis, particularly those due to the Governments of troop-contributing States,

Recalling its resolutions 34/9 E of 17 December 1979, 35/115 B of 10 December 1980, 36/138 B of 16 December 1981, 37/127 B of 17 December 1982 and 38/38 B of 5 December 1983,

Recognizing that, in consequence of the withholding of contributions by certain Member States, the surplus balances in the Special Account for the United Nations Interim Force in Lebanon have, in effect, been drawn upon to the full extent to supplement income received from contributions for meeting expenses of the Force,

Concerned that the application of the provisions of regulations 5.2 (*b*), 5.2 (*d*), 4.3 and 4.4 of the Financial Regulations of the United Nations would aggravate the already difficult financial situation of the United Nations Interim Force in Lebanon,

Decides that the provisions of regulations 5.2 (*b*), 5.2 (*d*), 4.3 and 4.4 of the Financial Regulations of the United Nations shall be suspended in respect of the amount of $6,035,305, which otherwise would have to be surrendered pursuant to those provisions, this amount to be entered in the account referred to in the operative part of General Assembly resolution 34/9 E and held in suspense until a further decision is taken by the Assembly.

Both resolutions were adopted together at the 98th plenary meeting:
In favour: 121
Argentina, Australia, Austria, Bahamas, Bahrain, Bangladesh, Barbados, Belgium, Belize, Bhutan, Bolivia, Botswana, Brazil, Brunei Darussalam, Burkina Faso, Burma, Burundi, Cameroon, Canada, Cape Verde, Central African Republic, Chad, Chile, China, Congo, Costa Rica, Cyprus, Democratic Kampuchea, Denmark, Djibouti, Dominican Republic, Ecuador, Egypt, El Salvador, Equatorial Guinea, Ethiopia, Fiji, Finland, France, Gabon, Gambia, Federal Republic of Germany, Ghana, Greece, Guatemala, Guinea, Guinea-Bissau, Guyana, Haiti, Honduras, Iceland, India, Indonesia, Ireland, Israel, Italy, Ivory Coast, Jamaica, Japan, Jordan, Kenya, Kuwait, Lebanon, Liberia, Luxembourg, Madagascar, Malawi, Malaysia, Mali, Malta, Mauritania, Mauritius, Mexico, Morocco, Nepal, Netherlands, New Zealand, Nicaragua, Niger, Nigeria, Norway, Oman, Pakistan, Panama, Papua New Guinea, Paraguay, Peru, Philippines, Portugal, Qatar, Romania, Rwanda, Saint Lucia, Saint Vincent, Samoa, Saudi Arabia, Senegal, Sierra Leone, Singapore, Somalia, Spain, Sri Lanka, Sudan, Suriname, Sweden, Thailand, Togo, Trinidad and Tobago, Tunisia, Turkey, Uganda, United Arab Emirates, United Kingdom, United Republic of Tanzania, United States, Uruguay, Venezuela, Yugoslavia, Zaire, Zambia, Zimbabwe.
Against: 15
Afghanistan, Albania, Bulgaria, Byelorussia, Cuba, Czechoslovakia, German Democratic Republic, Hungary, Lao People's Democratic Republic, Mongolia, Poland, Syria, Ukraine, USSR, Viet Nam.
Abstentions: 3
Iraq, Maldives, Yemen.
Absent: 19
Algeria, Angola, Antigua and Barbuda, Benin, Colombia,* Comoros, Democratic Yemen, Dominica, Grenada, Iran, Lesotho, Libya, Mozambique, Sao Tome and Principe, Seychelles, Solomon Islands, St. Christopher

---

[283]Resolution 39/247 A, paras. 1 and 4.
[284]*Ibid.*
[285]A/39/650.
[286]A/39/685.

and Nevis, Swaziland, Vanuatu.

---

* Later advised the Secretariat it had intended to vote in favour.

Resolution No. 39/72 A, C of 13 December 1984

CONDEMNING COLLABORATION BETWEEN ISRAEL AND SOUTH AFRICA [EXCERPTS FROM A RESOLUTION ON THE *APARTHEID* POLICIES OF THE SOUTH AFRICAN GOVERNMENT]

A

COMPREHENSIVE SANCTIONS AGAINST THE *APARTHEID* REGIME AND SUPPORT TO THE LIBERATION STRUGGLE IN SOUTH AFRICA

The General Assembly,

....

Recognizing that the policies and actions of certain Western Powers and Israel are the main obstacles which have frustrated international efforts for the elimination of *apartheid,*

Deploring, in particular, the actions of those States, in particular the Western States and Israel, which have continued and increased their political, economic and other collaboration with the Pretoria régime,

Gravely concerned that the racist régime of South Africa has continued, despite the mandatory arms embargo instituted by the Security Council in resolution 418 (1977) of 4 November 1977, to obtain military equipment and ammunition, as well as technology and know-how, to develop its armaments industry and to acquire nuclear-weapon capability,

Expressing alarm at the growing violation of the arms embargo as well as the continued nuclear collaboration by some Western States and Israel with the *apartheid* régime,

....

14. *Condemns* the policies of certain Western States and Israel and of their transnational corporations and financial institutions that have increased political, economic, military and nuclear collaboration with the racist minority régime of South Africa despite repeated appeals by the General Assembly;

....

Adopted at the 99th plenary meeting:
In favour: 123
Afghanistan, Albania, Algeria, Angola, Argentina, Bahrain, Bangladesh, Barbados, Belize, Benin, Bhutan, Bolivia, Brazil, Brunei Darussalam, Bulgaria, Burkina Faso, Burma, Burundi, Byelorussia, Cameroon, Cape Verde, Central African Republic, Chad, China, Colombia, Comoros, Congo, Costa Rica, Cuba, Cyprus, Czechoslovakia, Democratic Kampuchea, Democratic Yemen, Djibouti, Dominica, Dominican Republic, Ecuador, Egypt, El Salvador, Equatorial Guinea, Ethiopia, Gabon, Gambia, German Democratic Republic, Ghana, Grenada, Guatemala, Guinea, Guinea-Bissau, Guyana, Haiti, Honduras, Hungary, India, Indonesia, Iran, Iraq, Jamaica,

Jordan, Kenya, Kuwait, Lao People's Democratic Republic, Lebanon, Liberia, Libya, Madagascar, Malaysia, Maldives, Mali, Malta, Mauritania, Mauritius, Mexico, Mongolia, Morocco, Mozambique, Nepal, Nicaragua, Niger, Nigeria, Oman, Pakistan, Panama, Papua New Guinea, Peru, Philippines, Poland, Qatar, Romania, Rwanda, Saint Lucia, Sao Tome and Principe, Saudi Arabia, Senegal, Seychelles, Sierra Leone, Singapore, Solomon Islands, Somalia, Sri Lanka, St. Christopher and Nevis, Sudan, Suriname, Syria, Thailand, Togo, Trinidad and Tobago, Tunisia, Turkey, Uganda, Ukraine, USSR, United Arab Emirates, United Republic of Tanzania, Uruguay, Vanuatu, Venezuela, Viet Nam, Yemen, Yugoslavia, Zaire, Zambia, Zimbabwe.
Against: 15
Belgium, Canada, Denmark, France, Federal Republic of Germany, Iceland, Ireland, Italy, Japan, Luxembourg, Netherlands, Norway, Portugal, United Kingdom, United States.
Abstentions: 15
Australia, Austria, Bahamas, Botswana, Fiji, Finland, Greece, Ivory Coast, Lesotho, Malawi, New Zealand, Saint Vincent, Samoa, Spain, Sweden.
Absent: 5
Antigua and Barbuda, Chile, Israel, Paraguay, Swaziland.

C

RELATIONS BETWEEN ISRAEL AND SOUTH AFRICA

The General Assembly,

Reaffirming its resolutions on relations between Israel and South Africa,

Having considered the special report of the Special Committee against *Apartheid* on recent developments concerning relations between Israel and South Africa,[287]

Taking note of the declaration and resolutions of the Conference of Arab Solidarity with the Struggle for Liberation in Southern Africa, held at Tunis from 7 to 9 August 1984,[288]

Reiterating that the increasing collaboration by Israel with the racist régime of South Africa, especially in the military and nuclear fields, in defiance of resolutions of the General Assembly and the Security Council is a serious hindrance to international action for the eradication of *apartheid,* an encouragement to the racist régime of South Africa to persist in its criminal policy of *apartheid* and a hostile act against the oppressed people of South Africa and the entire African continent and constitutes a threat to international peace and security,

1. *Commends* the Special Committee against *Apartheid* for publicizing the growing relations between Israel and South Africa and promoting public awareness of the grave

---

[287]*Official Records of the General Assembly, Thirty-ninth Session, Supplement No. 22A* (A/39/22/Add.1).
[288]See A/39/450-S/16726, annex.

dangers of the alliance between Israel and South Africa;

2. *Again strongly condemns* the continuing and increasing collaboration of Israel with the racist régime of South Africa, especially in the military and nuclear fields;

3. *Demands* that Israel desist from and terminate all forms of collaboration with South Africa forthwith, particularly in the military and nuclear fields, and abide scrupulously by the relevant resolutions of the General Assembly and the Security Council;

4. *Calls upon* all Governments and organizations to exert their influence to persuade Israel to desist from such collaboration and abide by the resolutions of the General Assembly;

5. *Requests* the Special Committee to continue to publicize, as widely as possible, information on the relations between Israel and South Africa;

6. *Requests* the Secretary-General to render, through the Department of Public Information and the Centre against *Apartheid* of the Secretariat, all possible assistance to the Special Committee in disseminating information relating to the collaboration between Israel and South Africa;

7. *Further requests* the Special Committee to keep the matter under constant review and to report to the General Assembly and the Security Council as appropriate.

Adopted at the 99th plenary meeting:

In favour: 108

Afghanistan, Albania, Algeria, Angola, Argentina, Bahamas, Bahrain, Bangladesh, Benin, Bhutan, Bolivia, Botswana, Brazil, Brunei Darussalam, Bulgaria, Burkina Faso, Burma, Burundi, Byelorussia, Cameroon, Cape Verde, Central African Republic, Chad, China, Comoros, Congo, Cuba, Cyprus, Czechoslovakia, Democratic Kampuchea, Democratic Yemen, Djibouti, Ecuador, Egypt, Equatorial Guinea, Ethiopia, Gabon, Gambia, German Democratic Republic, Ghana, Greece, Guinea, Guinea-Bissau, Guyana, Hungary, India, Indonesia, Iran, Iraq, Jordan, Kenya, Kuwait, Lao People's Democratic Republic, Lebanon, Lesotho, Libya, Madagascar, Malaysia, Maldives, Mali, Malta, Mauritania, Mauritius, Mexico, Mongolia, Morocco, Mozambique, Nepal, Nicaragua, Niger, Nigeria, Oman, Pakistan, Papua New Guinea, Peru, Philippines, Poland, Qatar, Romania, Rwanda, Sao Tome and Principe, Saudi Arabia, Senegal, Seychelles, Sierra Leone, Singapore, Solomon Islands, Somalia, Sri Lanka, Sudan, Suriname, Syria, Thailand, Togo, Tunisia, Turkey, Uganda, Ukraine, USSR, United Arab Emirates, United Republic of Tanzania, Vanuatu, Venezuela, Viet Nam, Yemen, Yugoslavia, Zambia, Zimbabwe.

Against: 19

Australia, Austria, Belgium, Canada, Denmark, Finland, France, Federal Republic of Germany, Iceland, Ireland, Israel, Italy, Luxembourg, Netherlands, New Zealand, Norway, Sweden, United Kingdom, United States.

Abstentions: 25

Barbados, Belize, Colombia, Costa Rica, Dominica, Dominican Republic, El Salvador, Fiji, Grenada, Guatemala, Haiti, Honduras, Ivory Coast, Jamaica, Japan, Liberia, Malawi, Panama, Portugal, Saint Lucia, Saint Vincent,

Samoa, Spain, St. Christopher and Nevis, Uruguay.

Absent: 6

Antigua and Barbuda, Chile, Paraguay, Swaziland, Trinidad and Tobago, Zaire.

Resolution No. 39/76 of 13 December 1984

CALLING UPON ALL STATES TO ACCORD THE NECESSARY FACILITIES, PRIVILEGES AND IMMUNITIES TO DELEGATIONS OF NATIONAL LIBERATION MOVEMENTS RECOGNIZED BY THE ORGANIZATION OF AFRICAN UNITY AND/OR THE LEAGUE OF ARAB STATES AND ACCORDED OBSERVER STATUS BY INTERNATIONAL ORGANIZATIONS

The General Assembly,

Recalling its resolutions 35/167 of 15 December 1980 and 37/104 of 16 December 1982,

Recalling also its resolutions 3237 (XXIX) of 22 November 1974, 3280 (XXIX) of 10 December 1974 and 31/152 of 20 December 1976,

Taking note of the report of the Secretary-General,[289]

Bearing in mind the resolution of the United Nations Conference on the Representation of States in Their Relations with International Organizations relating to the observer status of national liberation movements recognized by the Organization of African Unity and/or by the League of Arab States,[290]

Noting that the Vienna Convention on the Representation of States in Their Relations with International Organizations of a Universal Character, of 14 March 1975,[291] regulates only the representation of States in their relations with international organizations,

Taking into account the continued and uninterrupted current practice of inviting the above-mentioned national liberation movements to participate as observers in the sessions of the General Assembly, specialized agencies and other organizations of the United Nations system and in the work of the conferences held under the auspices of such international organizations,

Convinced that the participation of the national liberation movements referred to above in the work of international organizations helps to strengthen international peace and co-operation,

Desirous of ensuring the effective participation of the above-mentioned national liberation movements as observers in the work of international organizations and of regulating, to that end, their status and the facilities, privileges and immunities necessary for the performance of their functions,

1. *Urges* all States that have not done so, in particular those which are hosts to international organizations or to conferences convened by, or held under the auspices of,

---

[289]A/39/437.

[290]See *Official Records of the United Nations Conference on the Representation of States in Their Relations with International Organizations, Vienna, 4 February-14 March 1975*, vol. II (United Nations publication, Sales No. E.75.V.12), document A/CONF.67/15, annex.

[291]*Ibid.*, vol. II, p. 207.

international organizations of a universal character, to consider as soon as possible the question of ratifying, or acceding to, the Vienna Convention on the Representation of States in Their Relations with International Organizations of a Universal Character;

2. *Calls once more upon* the States concerned to accord to the delegations of the national liberation movements recognized by the Organization of African Unity and/or by the League of Arab States, and accorded observer status by international organizations, the facilities, privileges and immunities necessary for the performance of their functions in accordance with the provisions of the Vienna Convention on the Representation of States in Their Relations with International Organizations of a Universal Character;

3. *Requests* the Secretary-General to report to the General Assembly at its forty-first session on the implementation of the present resolution.

Adopted at the 99th plenary meeting:

In favour: 106

Afghanistan, Albania, Algeria, Angola, Argentina, Bahamas, Bahrain, Bangladesh, Barbados, Benin, Bhutan, Bolivia, Botswana, Brazil, Brunei Darussalam, Bulgaria, Burkina Faso, Burundi, Byelorussia, Cameroon, Cape Verde, Chad, Chile, China, Congo, Cuba, Cyprus, Czechoslovakia, Democratic Kampuchea, Democratic Yemen, Djibouti, Dominican Republic, Ecuador, Egypt, El Salvador, Ethiopia, Gabon, German Democratic Republic, Ghana, Greece, Guinea, Guyana, Hungary, India, Indonesia, Iran, Iraq, Ivory Coast, Jamaica, Jordan, Kenya, Kuwait, Lao People's Democratic Republic, Lebanon, Lesotho, Liberia, Libya, Madagascar, Malawi, Malaysia, Maldives, Mali, Mauritania, Mauritius, Mexico, Mongolia, Morocco, Mozambique, Nepal, Nicaragua, Niger, Nigeria, Oman, Pakistan, Panama, Papua New Guinea, Peru, Philippines, Poland, Qatar, Romania, Rwanda, Sao Tome and Principe, Saudi Arabia, Senegal, Sierra Leone, Singapore, Somalia, Sri Lanka, Sudan, Syria, Thailand, Togo, Trinidad and Tobago, Tunisia, Turkey, Uganda, Ukraine, USSR, United Arab Emirates, Venezuela, Viet Nam, Yemen, Yugoslavia, Zaire, Zambia.

Against: 10

Belgium, Canada, France, Federal Republic of Germany, Israel, Italy, Luxembourg, Netherlands, United Kingdom, United States.

Abstentions: 21

Australia, Austria, Burma, Colombia, Costa Rica, Denmark, Fiji, Finland, Guatemala, Haiti, Honduras, Iceland, Ireland, Japan, New Zealand, Norway, Paraguay, Portugal, Spain, Sweden, Uruguay.

Absent: 21

Antigua and Barbuda, Belize, Central African Republic, Comoros, Dominica, Equatorial Guinea, Gambia, Grenada, Guinea-Bissau, Malta, Saint Lucia, Saint Vincent, Samoa, Seychelles, Solomon Islands, St. Christopher and Nevis, Suriname, Swaziland, United Republic of Tanzania, Vanuatu, Zimbabwe.

Resolution No. 39/95 A,B,C,D,E,F,G,H of 14 December 1984

ON ISRAELI PRACTICES AFFECTING HUMAN RIGHTS IN THE OCCUPIED TERRITORIES: CONDEMNING ISRAEL FOR FAILING TO HONOR A PRISONER RELEASE AGREEMENT NEGOTIATED THROUGH THE RED CROSS, FOR ITS POLICIES OF SETTLEMENT AND ANNEXATION IN THE OCCUPIED TERRITORIES, AS WELL AS MEASURES AGAINST CIVIL AND EDUCATIONAL FREEDOM THERE, AND FOR ITS EXPULSION OF PALESTINIAN LEADERS

A

The General Assembly,

Recalling its resolution 38/79 A of 15 December 1983,

Taking note of the report of the International Committee of the Red Cross of 13 December 1983,[292]

Taking note of the report of the Secretary-General of 14 November 1984,[293]

1. *Deplores* the fact that the Israeli authorities, at the last minute, took one prisoner, Ziyad Abu Eain, who had been registered before embarkation by delegates of the International Committee of the Red Cross at Tel Aviv airport;

2. *Condemns* Israel for its failure to comply with General Assembly resolution 38/79 A;

3. *Demands again* the immediate release of all prisoners, including Ziyad Abu Eain, who were duly registered to be freed from Insar Camp and other military command posts in southern Lebanon and Israel but have not, in fact, been released, and the securing of their transfer to Algiers in conformity with the agreement reached through the good offices of the International Committee of the Red Cross;

4. *Requests* the Secretary-General to report to the General Assembly as soon as possible and not later than the beginning of its fortieth session on the implementation of the present resolution.

Adopted at the 100th plenary meeting:

In favour: 120

Afghanistan, Albania, Algeria, Angola, Argentina, Austria, Bahrain, Bangladesh, Belgium, Benin, Bhutan, Bolivia, Botswana, Brazil, Brunei Darussalam, Bulgaria, Burkina Faso, Burundi, Byelorussia, Cameroon, Canada, Cape Verde, Chad, China, Colombia, Congo, Costa Rica, Cuba, Cyprus, Czechoslovakia, Democratic Kampuchea, Democratic Yemen, Denmark, Djibouti, Ecuador, Egypt, El Salvador, Equatorial Guinea, Ethiopia, Fiji, Finland, France, Gabon, Gambia, German Democratic Republic, Federal Republic of Germany, Ghana, Greece, Guinea, Guinea-Bissau, Guyana, Haiti, Hungary, India, Indonesia, Iraq, Ireland, Italy, Japan, Jordan, Kenya, Kuwait, Lao People's Democratic Republic, Lebanon, Lesotho, Libya, Luxembourg, Madagascar, Malaysia, Maldives, Mali, Malta, Mauritania, Mauritius, Mexico, Mongolia, Morocco, Mozambique, Netherlands, New Zealand, Nicaragua, Niger, Nigeria, Norway, Oman, Pakistan, Papua New Guinea, Peru, Poland, Portugal, Qatar, Romania, Rwanda, Samoa,

---

[292]See A/38/735.

[293]A/39/665.

Sao Tome and Principe, Saudi Arabia, Senegal, Seychelles, Sierra Leone, Somalia, Spain, Sudan, Suriname, Sweden, Syria, Togo, Tunisia, Turkey, Uganda, Ukraine, USSR, United Arab Emirates, United Kingdom, United Republic of Tanzania, Venezuela, Viet Nam, Yemen, Yugoslavia, Zambia, Zimbabwe.

Against: 2

Israel, United States.

Abstentions: 15

Australia, Bahamas, Barbados, Belize, Guatemala, Ivory Coast, Jamaica, Liberia, Malawi, Nepal, Panama, Paraguay, Sri Lanka, Trinidad and Tobago, Zaire.

Absent: 21

Antigua and Barbuda, Burma, Central African Republic, Chile, Comoros, Dominica, Dominican Republic, Grenada, Honduras, Iceland, Iran,* Philippines, Saint Lucia, Saint Vincent, Singapore, Solomon Islands, St. Christopher and Nevis, Swaziland, Thailand, Uruguay, Vanuatu.

---

*Later advised the Secretariat it had intended to vote in favour.

B

The General Assembly,

Recalling its resolutions 3092 A (XXVIII) of 7 December 1973, 3240 B (XXIX) of 29 November 1974, 3525 B (XXX) of 15 December 1975, 31/106 B of 16 December 1976, 32/91 A of 13 December 1977, 33/113 A of 18 December 1978, 34/90 B of 12 December 1979, 35/122 A of 11 December 1980, 36/147 A of 16 December 1981, 37/88 A of 10 December 1982 and 38/79 B of 15 December 1983,[294]

Recalling also Security Council resolution 465 (1980) of 1 March 1980 in which, *inter alia,* the Council affirmed that the Geneva Convention relative to the Protection of Civilian Persons in Time of War, of 12 August 1949,[295] is applicable to the Arab territories occupied by Israel since 1967, including Jerusalem,

Considering that the promotion of respect for the obligations arising from the Charter of the United Nations and other instruments and rules of international law is among the basic purposes and principles of the United Nations,

Bearing in mind the provisions of the Geneva Convention,

Noting that Israel and those Arab States whose territories have been occupied by Israel since June 1967 are parties to that Convention,

Taking into account that States parties to the Convention undertake, in accordance with article 1 thereof, not only to respect but also to ensure respect for the Convention in all circumstances,

1. *Reaffirms* that the Geneva Convention relative to the Protection of Civilian Persons in Time of War, of 12 August 1949, is applicable to the Palestinian and other Arab territories occupied by Israel since 1967, including Jerusalem;

2. *Condemns once again* the failure of Israel, the occupying Power, to acknowledge the applicability of that Convention to the territories it has occupied since 1967, including Jerusalem;

3. *Strongly demands* that Israel acknowledge and comply with the provisions of that Convention in the Palestinian and other Arab territories it has occupied since 1967, including Jerusalem;

4. *Urgently calls upon* all States parties to that Convention to exert all efforts in order to ensure respect for and compliance with its provisions in the Palestinian and other Arab territories occupied by Israel since 1967, including Jerusalem.

Adopted at the 100th plenary meeting:

In favour: 140

Afghanistan, Albania, Algeria, Angola, Argentina, Australia, Austria, Bahamas, Bahrain, Bangladesh, Barbados, Belgium, Belize, Benin, Bhutan, Bolivia, Botswana, Brazil, Brunei Darussalam, Bulgaria, Burkina Faso, Burma, Burundi, Byelorussia, Cameroon, Canada, Cape Verde, Chad, Chile, China, Colombia, Congo, Costa Rica, Cuba, Cyprus, Czechoslovakia, Democratic Kampuchea, Democratic Yemen, Denmark, Djibouti, Dominican Republic, Ecuador, Egypt, El Salvador, Equatorial Guinea, Ethiopia, Fiji, Finland, France, Gabon, Gambia, German Democratic Republic, Federal Republic of Germany, Ghana, Greece, Guatemala, Guinea, Guinea-Bissau, Guyana, Haiti, Hungary, Iceland, India, Indonesia, Iraq, Ireland, Italy, Ivory Coast, Jamaica, Japan, Jordan, Kenya, Kuwait, Lao People's Democratic Republic, Lebanon, Lesotho, Libya, Luxembourg, Madagascar, Malawi, Malaysia, Maldives, Mali, Malta, Mauritius, Mexico, Mongolia, Morocco, Mozambique, Nepal, Netherlands, New Zealand, Nicaragua, Niger, Nigeria, Norway, Oman, Pakistan, Panama, Papua New Guinea, Paraguay, Peru, Philippines, Poland, Portugal, Qatar, Romania, Rwanda, Samoa, Sao Tome and Principe, Saudi Arabia, Senegal, Seychelles, Sierra Leone, Singapore, Somalia, Spain, Sri Lanka, Sudan, Suriname, Sweden, Syria, Thailand, Togo, Trinidad and Tobago, Tunisia, Turkey, Uganda, Ukraine, USSR, United Arab Emirates, United Kingdom, United Republic of Tanzania, Uruguay, Venezuela, Viet Nam, Yemen, Yugoslavia, Zambia, Zimbabwe.

Against: 1

Israel.

Abstentions: 3

Liberia, United States, Zaire.

Absent: 14

Antigua and Barbuda, Central African Republic, Comoros, Dominica, Grenada, Honduras, Iran,* Mauritania, Saint Lucia, Saint Vincent, Solomon Islands, St. Christopher and Nevis, Swaziland, Vanuatu.

---

*Later advised the Secretariat it had intended to vote in favour.

---

[294]The resolutions cited are previous resolutions on Israeli practices in the occupied territories. [ed. note]

[295]United Nations, *Treaty Series,* vol. 75, no. 973, p. 287.

C

The General Assembly,

Recalling its resolutions 32/5 of 28 October 1977, 33/113 B of 18 December 1978, 34/90 C of 12 December 1979, 35/122 B of 11 December 1980, 36/147 B of 16 December 1981, 37/88 B of 10 December 1982 and 38/79 C of 15 December 1983,[296]

Recalling also Security Council resolution 465 (1980) of 1 March 1980,

Expressing grave anxiety and concern at the present serious situation in the occupied Palestinian and other Arab territories, including Jerusalem, as a result of the continued Israeli occupation and the measures and actions taken by Israel, the occupying Power, designed to change the legal status, geographical nature and demographic composition of those territories,

Confirming that the Geneva Convention relative to the Protection of Civilian Persons in Time of War, of 12 August 1949,[297] is applicable to all Arab territories occupied since June 1967, including Jerusalem,

1. *Determines* that all such measures and actions taken by Israel in the Palestinian and other Arab territories occupied since 1967, including Jerusalem, are in violation of the relevant provisions of the Geneva Convention relative to the Protection of Civilian Persons in Time of War, of 12 August 1949, and constitute a serious obstruction to the efforts to achieve a just and lasting peace in the Middle East and therefore have no legal validity;

2. *Strongly deplores* the persistence of Israel in carrying out such measures, in particular the establishment of settlements in the Palestinian and other occupied Arab territories, including Jerusalem;

3. *Demands* that Israel comply strictly with its international obligations in accordance with the principles of international law and the provisions of the Geneva Convention;

4. *Demands once more* that Israel, the occupying Power, desist forthwith from taking any action which would result in changing the legal status, geographical nature or demographic composition of the Palestinian and other Arab territories occupied since 1967, including Jerusalem;

5. *Urgently calls upon* all States parties to the Geneva Convention to respect and to exert all efforts in order to ensure respect for and compliance with its provisions in all Arab territories occupied by Israel since 1967, including Jerusalem.

Adopted at the 100th plenary meeting:

In favour: 143

Afghanistan, Albania, Algeria, Angola, Argentina, Australia, Austria, Bahamas, Bahrain, Bangladesh, Barbados, Belgium, Belize, Benin, Bhutan, Bolivia, Botswana, Brazil, Brunei Darussalam, Bulgaria, Burkina Faso, Burma, Burundi, Byelorussia, Cameroon, Canada, Central African Republic, Chad, Chile, China, Colombia, Congo, Costa Rica, Cuba, Cyprus, Czechoslovakia, Democratic Kampuchea, Democratic Yemen, Denmark, Djibouti, Dominican Republic, Ecuador, Egypt, El Salvador, Equatorial Guinea, Ethiopia, Fiji, Finland, France, Gabon, Gambia, German Democratic Republic, Federal Republic of Germany, Ghana, Greece, Guatemala, Guinea, Guinea-Bissau, Guyana, Haiti, Hungary, Iceland, India, Indonesia, Iraq, Ireland, Italy, Ivory Coast, Jamaica, Japan, Jordan, Kenya, Kuwait, Lao People's Democratic Republic, Lebanon, Lesotho, Liberia, Libya, Luxembourg, Madagascar, Malawi, Malaysia, Maldives, Mali, Malta, Mauritania, Mauritius, Mexico, Mongolia, Morocco, Mozambique, Nepal, Netherlands, New Zealand, Nicaragua, Niger, Nigeria, Norway, Oman, Pakistan, Panama, Papua New Guinea, Paraguay, Peru, Philippines, Poland, Portugal, Qatar, Romania, Rwanda, Samoa, Sao Tome and Principe, Saudi Arabia, Senegal, Seychelles, Sierra Leone, Singapore, Somalia, Spain, Sri Lanka, Sudan, Suriname, Sweden, Syria, Thailand, Togo, Trinidad and Tobago, Tunisia, Turkey, Uganda, Ukraine, USSR, United Arab Emirates, United Kingdom, United Republic of Tanzania, Uruguay, Venezuela, Viet Nam, Yemen, Yugoslavia, Zaire, Zambia, Zimbabwe.

Against: 1

Israel.

Abstentions: 1

United States.

Absent: 13

Antigua and Barbuda, Cape Verde,* Comoros, Dominica, Grenada, Honduras, Iran,* Saint Lucia, Saint Vincent, Solomon Islands, St. Christopher and Nevis, Swaziland, Vanuatu.

---

*Later advised the Secretariat it had intended to vote in favour.

D

The General Assembly,

Guided by the purposes and principles of the Charter of the United Nations and by the principles and provisions of the Universal Declaration of Human Rights,[298]

Bearing in mind the provisions of the Geneva Convention relative to the Protection of Civilian Persons in Time of War, of 12 August 1949,[299] as well as of other relevant conventions and regulations,

Recalling all its resolutions on the subject, in particular resolutions 32/91 B and C of 13 December 1977, 33/113 C of 18 December 1978, 34/90 A of 12 December 1979, 35/122 C of 11 December 1980, 36/147 C of 16 December 1981, 37/88 C of 10 December 1982 and 38/79 D of 15 December 1983, and also those adopted by the Security Council, the Commission on Human Rights, in particular

---

[296] The resolutions cited are previous resolutions on Israeli practices in the occupied territories. [ed. note]

[297] United Nations, *Treaty Series,* vol. 75, no. 973, p. 287.

[298] Resolution 217 A (III).

[299] United Nations, *Treaty Series,* vol. 75, no. 973, p. 287.

its resolutions 1983/1 of 15 February 1983[300] and 1984/1 of 20 February 1984,[301] and other United Nations organs concerned and by the specialized agencies,

Having considered the report of the Special Committee to Investigate Israeli Practices Affecting the Human Rights of the Population of the Occupied Territories,[302] which contains, *inter alia*, self-incriminating public statements made by officials of Israel, the occupying Power,

Taking note of the report of the Secretary-General of 6 November 1984,[303]

1. *Commends* the Special Committee to Investigate Israeli Practices Affecting the Human Rights of the Population of the Occupied Territories for its efforts in performing the tasks assigned to it by the General Assembly and for its thoroughness and impartiality;

2. *Deplores* the continued refusal by Israel to allow the Special Committee access to the occupied territories;

3. *Demands* that Israel allow the Special Committee access to the occupied territories;

4. *Reaffirms* the fact that occupation itself constitutes a grave violation of the human rights of the civilian population of the occupied Arab territories;

5. *Condemns* the continued and persistent violation by Israel of the Geneva Convention relative to the Protection of Civilian Persons in Time of War, of 12 August 1949, and other applicable international instruments, and condemns in particular those violations which the Convention designates as "grave breaches" thereof;

6. *Declares once more* that Israel's grave breaches of that Convention are war crimes and an affront to humanity;

7. *Strongly condemns* the following Israeli policies and practices:

(a) Annexation of parts of the occupied territories, including Jerusalem;

(b) Imposition of Israeli laws, jurisdiction and administration on the Syrian Golan Heights, which has resulted in the effective annexation of the Syrian Golan Heights;

(c) Illegal imposition and levy of heavy and disproportionate taxes and dues;

(d) Establishment of new Israeli settlements and expansion of the existing settlements on private and public Arab lands, and transfer of an alien population thereto;

(e) Eviction, deportation, expulsion, displacement and transfer of Arab inhabitants of the occupied territories and denial of their right to return;

(f) Confiscation and expropriation of private and public Arab property in the occupied territories and all other transactions for the acquisition of land involving the Israeli authorities, institutions or nationals on the one hand and the inhabitants or institutions of the occupied territories on the other;

(g) Excavations and transformations of the landscape and the historical, cultural and religious sites, especially at Jerusalem;

(h) Pillaging of archaeological and cultural property;

(i) Destruction and demolition of Arab houses, the most recent of which have been in the Jordan Valley;

(j) Collective punishment, mass arrests, administrative detention and ill-treatment of the Arab population;

(k) Ill-treatment and torture of persons under detention;

(l) Interference with religious freedoms and practices as well as family rights and customs;

(m) Interference with the system of education and with the social and economic development of the population in the occupied Palestinian and other Arab territories;

(n) Interference with the freedom of movement of individuals within the occupied Palestinian and other Arab territories;

(o) Illegal exploitation of the natural wealth, resources and population of the occupied territories;

8. *Strongly condemns* the arming of Israeli settlers in the occupied territories to commit acts of violence against Arab civilians and the perpetration of acts of violence by these armed settlers against individuals, causing injury and death and wide-scale damage to Arab property;

9. *Reaffirms* that all measures taken by Israel to change the physical character, demographic composition, institutional structure or legal status of the occupied territories, or any part thereof, including Jerusalem, are null and void, and that Israel's policy of settling parts of its population and new immigrants in the occupied territories constitutes a flagrant violation of the Geneva Convention and of the relevant resolutions of the United Nations;

10. *Demands* that Israel desist forthwith from the policies and practices referred to in paragraphs 7,8, and 9 above;

11. *Calls upon* Israel, the occupying Power, to take immediate steps for the return of all displaced Arab and Palestinian inhabitants to their homes or former places of residence in the territories occupied by Israel since 1967;

12. *Urges* the international organizations and the specialized agencies, in particular the International Labour Organisation, to examine the conditions of Arab workers in the occupied Palestinian and other Arab territories, including Jerusalem;

13. *Reiterates its call* upon all States, in particular those States parties to the Geneva Convention, in accordance with article 1 of that Convention, and upon international organizations and the specialized agencies not to recognize any changes carried out by Israel in the occupied territories and to avoid actions, including those in the field of aid, which might be used by Israel in its pursuit of the policies of annexation and colonization or any of the other policies and practices referred to in the present resolution;

14. *Requests* the Special Committee, pending early termination of Israeli occupation, to continue to investigate Israeli policies and practices in the Arab territories occupied by Israel since 1967, to consult, as appropriate, with

---

[300]See *Official Records of the Economic and Social Council, 1983, Supplement No. 3* (E/1983/13 and Corr.1), chap. XXVII, sect. A.

[301]*Ibid., 1984, Supplement No. 4* (E/1984/14 and Corr.1), chap. II, sect. A.

[302]See A/39/591.

[303]A/39/620.

the International Committee of the Red Cross in order to ensure the safeguarding of the welfare and human rights of the population of the occupied territories and to report to the Secretary-General as soon as possible and whenever the need arises thereafter;

15. *Requests* the Special Committee to continue to investigate the treatment of civilians in detention in the Arab territories occupied by Israel since 1967;

16. *Condemns* Israel's refusal to permit persons from the occupied territories to appear as witnesses before the Special Committee and to participate in conferences and meetings held outside the occupied territories;

17. *Requests* the Secretary-General:

(*a*) To provide all necessary facilities to the Special Committee, including those required for its visits to the occupied territories, with a view to investigating the Israeli policies and practices referred to in the present resolution;

(*b*) To continue to make available additional staff as may be necessary to assist the Special Committee in the performance of its tasks;

(*c*) To ensure the widest circulation of the reports of the Special Committee and of information regarding its activities and findings by all means available through the Department of Public Information of the Secretariat and, where necessary, to reprint those reports of the Special Committee which are no longer available;

(*d*) To report to the General Assembly at its fortieth session on the tasks entrusted to him in the present paragraph;

18. *Requests* the Security Council to ensure Israel's respect for and compliance with all the provisions of the Geneva Convention relative to the Protection of Civilian Persons in Time of War, of 12 August 1949, in the Palestinian and other Arab territories occupied since 1967, including Jerusalem, and to initiate measures to halt Israeli policies and practices in those territories;

19. *Decides* to include in the provisional agenda of its fortieth session the item entitled "Report of the Special Committee to Investigate Israeli Practices Affecting the Human Rights of the Population of the Occupied Territories".

Adopted at the 100th plenary meeting:

In favour: 115

Afghanistan, Albania, Algeria, Angola, Argentina, Bahrain, Bangladesh, Benin, Bhutan, Bolivia, Botswana, Brazil, Brunei Darussalam, Bulgaria, Burkina Faso, Burma, Burundi, Byelorussia, Cameroon, Cape Verde, Central African Republic, Chad, China, Colombia, Congo, Costa Rica,** Cuba, Cyprus, Czechoslovakia, Democratic Kampuchea, Democratic Yemen, Djibouti, Ecuador, Egypt, El Salvador, Equatorial Guinea, Ethiopia, Fiji, Gabon, Gambia, German Democratic Republic, Ghana, Greece, Guatemala, Guinea, Guinea-Bissau, Guyana, Hungary, India, Indonesia, Iraq, Jamaica, Jordan, Kenya, Kuwait, Lao People's Democratic Republic, Lebanon, Lesotho, Libya, Madagascar, Malaysia, Maldives, Mali, Malta, Mauritania, Mauritius, Mexico, Mongolia, Morocco, Mozambique, Nepal, Nicaragua, Niger, Nigeria, Oman, Pakistan, Panama, Papua New Guinea, Peru, Philippines, Poland, Portugal, Qatar, Romania, Rwanda, Samoa, Sao Tome and Principe, Saudi Arabia, Senegal, Seychelles, Sierra Leone, Singapore, Somalia, Spain, Sri Lanka, Sudan, Suriname, Syria, Thailand, Togo, Trinidad and Tobago, Tunisia, Turkey, Uganda, Ukraine, USSR, United Arab Emirates, United Republic of Tanzania, Uruguay, Venezuela, Viet Nam, Yemen, Yugoslavia, Zambia, Zimbabwe.

Against: 2

Israel, United States.

Abstentions: 28

Australia, Austria, Bahamas, Barbados, Belgium, Belize, Canada, Denmark, Dominican Republic, Finland, France, Federal Republic of Germany, Haiti, Iceland, Ireland, Italy, Ivory Coast, Japan, Liberia, Luxembourg, Malawi, Netherlands, New Zealand, Norway, Paraguay, Sweden, United Kingdom, Zaire.

Absent: 13

Antigua and Barbuda, Chile, Comoros, Dominica, Grenada, Honduras, Iran,* Saint Lucia, Saint Vincent, Solomon Islands, St. Christopher and Nevis, Swaziland, Vanuatu.

---

*Later advised the Secretariat it had intended to vote in favour.
**Later advised the Secretariat it had intended not to participate in the vote.

E

The General Assembly,

Recalling Security Council resolutions 468 (1980) of 8 May 1980, 469 (1980) of 20 May 1980 and 484 (1980) of 19 December 1980 and General Assembly resolutions 36/147 D of 16 December 1981, 37/88 D of 10 December 1982 and 38/79 E of 15 December 1983,[304]

Taking note of the report of the Secretary-General of 27 September 1984,[305]

Deeply concerned at the expulsion by the Israeli military occupation authorities of the Mayors of Hebron and Halhul and of the Sharia Judge of Hebron,

Recalling the Geneva Convention relative to the Protection of Civilian Persons in Time of War, of 12 August 1949,[306] in particular article 1 and the first paragraph of article 49, which read as follows:

"Article 1

"The High Contracting Parties undertake to respect and to ensure respect for the present Convention in all circumstances."

Article 49

"Individual or mass forcible transfers, as well as deportations of protected persons from occupied territory to the territory of the occupying Power or to that of any other country, occupied or not, are prohibited, regardless of their motive . . . ",

---

[304]These resolutions refer to Israeli measures against Palestinian leaders. [ed. note]
[305]A/39/527.
[306]United Nations, *Treaty Series*, vol. 75, no. 973, p. 287.

Reaffirming the applicability of the Geneva Convention to the Palestinian and other Arab territories occupied by Israel since 1967, including Jerusalem,

1. *Demands once more* that the Government of Israel, the occupying Power, rescind the illegal measures taken by the Israeli military occupation authorities in expelling and imprisoning the Mayors of Hebron and Halhul and in expelling the Sharia Judge of Hebron and that it facilitate the immediate return of the expelled Palestinian leaders so that they can resume the functions for which they were elected and appointed;

2. *Requests* the Secretary-General to report to the General Assembly as soon as possible and not later than the beginning of its fortieth session on the implementation of the present resolution.

Adopted at the 100th plenary meeting:
In favour: 143
Afghanistan, Albania, Algeria, Angola, Argentina, Australia, Austria, Bahamas, Bahrain, Bangladesh, Barbados, Belgium, Belize, Benin, Bhutan, Bolivia, Botswana, Brazil, Brunei Darussalam, Bulgaria, Burkina Faso, Burma, Burundi, Byelorussia, Cameroon, Canada, Cape Verde, Central African Republic, Chad, Chile, China, Congo, Costa Rica, Cuba, Cyprus, Czechoslovakia, Democratic Kampuchea, Democratic Yemen, Denmark, Djibouti, Dominican Republic, Ecuador, Egypt, El Salvador, Equatorial Guinea, Ethiopia, Fiji, Finland, France, Gabon, Gambia, German Democratic Republic, Federal Republic of Germany, Ghana, Greece, Guatemala, Guinea, Guinea-Bissau, Guyana, Haiti, Hungary, Iceland, India, Indonesia, Iraq, Ireland, Italy, Ivory Coast, Jamaica, Japan, Jordan, Kenya, Kuwait, Lao People's Democratic Republic, Lebanon, Lesotho, Liberia, Libya, Luxembourg, Madagascar, Malawi, Malaysia, Maldives, Mali, Malta, Mauritania, Mauritius, Mexico, Mongolia, Morocco, Mozambique, Nepal, Netherlands, New Zealand, Nicaragua, Niger, Nigeria, Norway, Oman, Pakistan, Panama, Papua New Guinea, Paraguay, Peru, Philippines, Poland, Portugal, Qatar, Romania, Rwanda, Samoa, Sao Tome and Principe, Saudi Arabia, Senegal, Seychelles, Sierra Leone, Singapore, Somalia, Spain, Sri Lanka, Sudan, Suriname, Sweden, Syria, Thailand, Togo, Trinidad and Tobago, Tunisia, Turkey, Uganda, Ukraine, USSR, United Arab Emirates, United Kingdom, United Republic of Tanzania, Uruguay, Venezuela, Viet Nam, Yemen, Yugoslavia, Zaire, Zambia, Zimbabwe.
Against: 1
Israel.
Abstentions: 1
United States.
Absent: 13
Antigua and Barbuda, Colombia,* Comoros, Dominica, Grenada, Honduras, Iran,* Saint Lucia, Saint Vincent, Solomon Islands, St. Christopher and Nevis, Swaziland, Vanuatu.

F

The General Assembly,
Deeply concerned that the Arab territories occupied since 1967 have been under continued Israeli military occupation,

Recalling Security Council resolution 497 (1981) of 17 December 1981 and General Assembly resolutions 36/226 B of 17 December 1981, ES-9/1 of 5 February 1982, 37/88 E of 10 December 1982 and 38/79 F of 15 December 1983,

Having considered the report of the Secretary-General of 1 October 1984,[307]

Recalling its previous resolutions, in particular resolutions 3414 (XXX) of 5 December 1975, 31/61 of 9 December 1976, 32/20 of 25 November 1977, 33/28 and 33/29 of 7 December 1978, 34/70 of 6 December 1979 and 35/122 E of 11 December 1980, in which it, *inter alia,* called upon Israel to put an end to its occupation of the Arab territories and to withdraw from all those territories,

Reaffirming once more the illegality of Israel's decision of 14 December 1981 to impose its laws, jurisdiction and administration on the Syrian Golan Heights, which has resulted in the effective annexation of that territory,

Reaffirming that the acquisition of territory by force is inadmissible under the Charter of the United Nations and that all territories thus occupied by Israel must be returned,

Recalling the Geneva Convention relative to the Protection of Civilian Persons in Time of War, of 12 August 1949,[308]

1. *Strongly condemns* Israel, the occupying Power, for its refusal to comply with the relevant resolutions of the General Assembly and the Security Council, particularly Council resolution 497 (1981), in which the Council, *inter alia,* decided that the Israeli decision to impose its laws, jurisdiction and administration on the occupied Syrian Golan Heights was null and void and without international legal effect and demanded that Israel, the occupying Power, should rescind forthwith its decision;

2. *Condemns* the persistence of Israel in changing the physical character, demographic composition, institutional structure and legal status of the occupied Syrian Arab Golan Heights;

3. *Determines* that all legislative and administrative measures and actions taken or to be taken by Israel, the occupying Power, that purport to alter the character and legal status of the Syrian Golan Heights are null and void and constitute a flagrant violation of international law and of the Geneva Convention relative to the Protection of Civilian Persons in Time of War, of 12 August 1949, and have no legal effect;

4. *Strongly condemns* Israel for its attempts and measures to impose forcibly Israeli citizenship and Israeli identity cards on the Syrian citizens in the occupied Syrian Arab

---

*Later advised the Secretariat it had intended to vote in favour.

[307]A/39/532 and Corr.1.
[308]United Nations, *Treaty Series,* vol. 75, no. 973, p. 287.

Golan Heights and calls upon it to desist from its repressive measures against the population of the Syrian Arab Golan Heights;

5. *Calls once again upon* Member States not to recognize any of the legislative or administrative measures and actions referred to above;

6. *Requests* the Secretary-General to submit to the General Assembly at its fortieth session a report on the implementation of the present resolution.

Adopted at the 100th plenary meeting:
In favour: 141
Afghanistan, Albania, Algeria, Angola, Argentina, Australia, Austria, Bahamas, Bahrain, Bangladesh, Barbados, Belgium, Belize, Benin, Bhutan, Bolivia, Botswana, Brazil, Brunei Darussalam, Bulgaria, Burkina Faso, Burma, Burundi, Byelorussia, Cameroon, Canada, Cape Verde, Central African Republic, Chad, Chile, China, Colombia, Congo, Costa Rica, Cuba, Cyprus, Czechoslovakia, Democratic Kampuchea, Democratic Yemen, Denmark, Djibouti, Dominican Republic, Ecuador, Egypt, El Salvador, Equatorial Guinea, Ethiopia, Fiji, Finland, France, Gabon, Gambia, German Democratic Republic, Federal Republic of Germany, Ghana, Greece, Guatemala, Guinea, Guinea-Bissau, Guyana, Haiti, Hungary, Iceland, India, Indonesia, Iraq, Ireland, Italy, Ivory Coast, Jamaica, Japan, Jordan, Kenya, Kuwait, Lao People's Democratic Republic, Lebanon, Lesotho, Libya, Luxembourg, Madagascar, Malawi, Malaysia, Maldives, Mali, Malta, Mauritania, Mauritius, Mexico, Mongolia, Morocco, Mozambique, Nepal, Netherlands, New Zealand, Nicaragua, Niger, Nigeria, Norway, Oman, Pakistan, Panama, Papua New Guinea, Peru, Philippines, Poland, Portugal, Qatar, Romania, Rwanda, Samoa, Sao Tome and Principe, Saudi Arabia, Senegal, Seychelles, Sierra Leone, Singapore, Somalia, Spain, Sri Lanka, Sudan, Suriname, Sweden, Syria, Thailand, Togo, Trinidad and Tobago, Tunisia, Turkey, Uganda, Ukraine, USSR, United Arab Emirates, United Kingdom, United Republic of Tanzania, Uruguay, Venezuela, Viet Nam, Yemen, Yugoslavia, Zambia, Zimbabwe.
Against: 1
Israel.
Abstentions: 3
Liberia, United States, Zaire.
Absent: 13
Antigua and Barbuda, Comoros, Dominica, Grenada, Honduras, Iran,* Paraguay, Saint Lucia, Saint Vincent, Solomon Islands, St. Christopher and Nevis, Swaziland, Vanuatu.

---

*Later advised the Secretariat it had intended to vote in favour.

G

The General Assembly,
Bearing in mind the Geneva Convention relative to the Protection of Civilian Persons in Time of War, of 12 August 1949,[309]

Deeply concerned at the continued harassment by Israel, the occupying Power, against educational institutions in the occupied Palestinian territories,

Recalling its resolution 38/79 G of 15 December 1983,

Taking note of the report of the Secretary-General of 18 September 1984,[310]

1. *Reaffirms* the applicability of the Geneva Convention relative to the Protection of Civilian Persons in Time of War, of 12 August 1949, to the Palestinian and other Arab territories occupied by Israel since 1967, including Jerusalem;

2. *Condemns* Israeli policies and practices against Palestinian students and faculties in schools, universities and other educational institutions in the occupied Palestinian territories, especially the policy of opening fire on defenceless students, causing many casualties;

3. *Condemns* the systematic Israeli campaign of repression against and closing of universities and other educational and vocational institutions in the occupied Palestinian territories, restricting and impeding the academic activities of Palestinian universities by subjecting the selection of courses, textbooks and educational programmes, the admission of students and the appointment of faculty members to the control and supervision of the military occupation authorities, in clear contravention of the Geneva Convention;

4. *Demands* that Israel, the occupying Power, comply with the provisions of that Convention, rescind all actions and measures against all educational institutions, ensure the freedom of those institutions and refrain forthwith from hindering the effective operation of the universities and other educational institutions;

5. *Requests* the Secretary-General to report to the General Assembly as soon as possible and not later than the beginning of its fortieth session on the implementation of the present resolution.

Adopted at the 100th plenary meeting:
In favour: 117
Afghanistan, Albania, Algeria, Angola, Argentina, Austria, Bahamas, Bahrain, Bangladesh, Belize, Benin, Bhutan, Bolivia, Botswana, Brazil, Brunei Darussalam, Bulgaria, Burkina Faso, Burundi, Byelorussia, Cameroon, Cape Verde, Central African Republic, Chad, China, Colombia, Congo, Costa Rica, Cuba, Cyprus, Czechoslovakia, Democratic Kampuchea, Democratic Yemen, Djibouti, Dominican Republic, Ecuador, Egypt, El Salvador, Equatorial Guinea, Ethiopia, Fiji, Gabon, Gambia, German Democratic Republic, Ghana, Greece, Guinea, Guinea-Bissau, Guyana, Haiti, Hungary, India, Indonesia, Iraq, Jamaica, Jordan, Kenya, Kuwait, Lao People's Democratic Republic, Lebanon, Lesotho, Libya, Madagascar, Malawi, Malaysia, Maldives, Mali, Malta, Mauritania, Mauritius, Mexico, Mongolia, Morocco, Mozambique, Nepal, Nicaragua, Ni-

---

[309]United Nations, *Treaty Series*, vol. 75, no. 973, p. 287.
[310]A/39/501.

ger, Nigeria, Oman, Pakistan, Papua New Guinea, Peru, Philippines, Poland, Portugal, Qatar, Romania, Samoa, Sao Tome and Principe, Saudi Arabia, Senegal, Seychelles, Sierra Leone, Singapore, Somalia, Spain, Sri Lanka, Sudan, Suriname, Sweden, Syria, Thailand, Togo, Trinidad and Tobago, Tunisia, Turkey, Uganda, Ukraine, USSR, United Arab Emirates, United Republic of Tanzania, Venezuela, Viet Nam, Yemen, Yugoslavia, Zambia, Zimbabwe.

Against: 2

Israel, United States.

Abstentions: 26

Australia, Barbados, Belgium, Burma, Canada, Chile, Denmark, Finland, France, Federal Republic of Germany, Guatemala, Iceland, Ireland, Italy, Ivory Coast, Japan, Liberia, Luxembourg, Netherlands, New Zealand, Norway, Panama, Paraguay, United Kingdom, Uruguay, Zaire.

Absent: 13

Antigua and Barbuda, Comoros, Dominica, Grenada, Honduras, Iran,* Rwanda, Saint Lucia, Saint Vincent, Solomon Islands, St. Christopher and Nevis, Swaziland, Vanuatu.

---

*Later advised the Secretariat it had intended to vote in favour.

H

The General Assembly,

Recalling Security Council resolution 471 (1980) of 5 June 1980, in which the Council condemned the assassination attempts against the Mayors of Nablus, Ramallah and Al Bireh and called for the immediate apprehension and prosecution of the perpetrators of those crimes,

Recalling also General Assembly resolutions 36/147 G of 16 December 1981, 37/88 G of 10 December 1982 and 38/79 H of 15 December 1983,

Taking note of the report of the Secretary-General of 9 July 1984,[311]

Recalling once again the Geneva Convention relative to the Protection of Civilian Persons in Time of War, of 12 August 1949,[312] in particular article 27, which states, *inter alia:*

> "Protected persons are entitled, in all circumstances, to respect for their persons . . . They shall at all times be humanely treated, and shall be protected especially against all acts of violence or threats thereof . . . ",

Reaffirming the applicability of that Convention to the Arab territories occupied by Israel since 1967, including Jerusalem,

1. *Demands* that Israel, the occupying Power, inform the Secretary-General of the results of the investigations and prosecution relative to the assassination attempts;

2. *Requests* the Secretary-General to submit to the General Assembly at its fortieth session a report on the implementation of the present resolution.

---

[311]A/39/339.

[312]United Nations, *Treaty Series,* vol. 75, no. 973, p. 287.

Adopted at the 100th plenary meeting:

In favour: 143

Afghanistan, Albania, Algeria, Angola, Argentina, Australia, Austria, Bahamas, Bahrain, Bangladesh, Barbados, Belgium, Belize, Benin, Bhutan, Bolivia, Botswana, Brazil, Brunei Darussalam, Bulgaria, Burkina Faso, Burma, Burundi, Byelorussia, Cameroon, Canada, Cape Verde, Central African Republic, Chad, Chile, China, Colombia, Congo, Costa Rica, Cuba, Cyprus, Czechoslovakia, Democratic Kampuchea, Democratic Yemen, Denmark, Djibouti, Dominican Republic, Ecuador, Egypt, El Salvador, Equatorial Guinea, Ethiopia, Fiji, Finland, France, Gabon, Gambia, German Democratic Republic, Federal Republic of Germany, Ghana, Greece, Guatemala, Guinea, Guinea-Bissau, Guyana, Haiti, Hungary, Iceland, India, Indonesia, Iraq, Ireland, Italy, Ivory Coast, Jamaica, Japan, Jordan, Kenya, Kuwait, Lao People's Democratic Republic, Lebanon, Lesotho, Liberia, Libya, Luxembourg, Madagascar, Malawi, Malaysia, Maldives, Mali, Malta, Mauritania, Mauritius, Mexico, Mongolia, Morocco, Mozambique, Nepal, Netherlands, New Zealand, Nicaragua, Niger, Nigeria, Norway, Oman, Pakistan, Panama, Papua New Guinea, Peru, Philippines, Poland, Portugal, Qatar, Romania, Rwanda, Samoa, Sao Tome and Principe, Saudi Arabia, Senegal, Seychelles, Sierra Leone, Singapore, Somalia, Spain, Sri Lanka, Sudan, Suriname, Sweden, Syria, Thailand, Togo, Trinidad and Tobago, Tunisia, Turkey, Uganda, Ukraine, USSR, United Arab Emirates, United Kingdom, United Republic of Tanzania, Uruguay, Venezuela, Viet Nam, Yemen, Yugoslavia, Zaire, Zambia, Zimbabwe.

Against: 2

Israel, United States.

Abstentions: 0

Absent: 13

Antigua and Barbuda, Comoros, Dominica, Grenada, Honduras, Iran,* Paraguay, Saint Lucia, Saint Vincent, Solomon Islands, St. Christopher and Nevis, Swaziland, Vanuatu.

---

*Later advised the Secretariat it had intended to vote in favour.

Resolution No. 39/99 A,B,C,D,E,F,G,H,I,J,K of 14 December 1984

ON UNRWA: CALLING FOR CONTRIBUTIONS BY GOVERNMENTS TO UNRWA AND ENDORSING ASSISTANCE TO PALESTINIAN REFUGEES, CALLING ON ISRAEL TO PERMIT THE RETURN OF DISPLACED PALESTINIANS AND DEMANDING THAT IT DESIST FROM THE DESTRUCTION OF PALESTINIAN REFUGEE SHELTERS IN THE GAZA STRIP AND REFUGEE CAMPS IN THE WEST BANK, REQUESTING THE SECRETARY-GENERAL TO TAKE APPROPRIATE STEPS FOR THE PROTECTION OF ARAB PROPERTY, ASSETS AND PROPERTY RIGHTS, AND CALLING ON ISRAEL TO REMOVE HINDRANCES TO THE ESTABLISHMENT OF A UNIVERSITY OF JERUSALEM FOR PALESTINIAN REFUGEES

A

ASSISTANCE TO PALESTINE REFUGEES

The General Assembly,

Recalling its resolution 38/83 A of 15 December 1983 and all previous resolutions on the question, including resolution 194 (III) of 11 December 1948,

Taking note of the report of the Commissioner-General of the United Nations Relief and Works Agency for Palestine Refugees in the Near East covering the period from 1 July 1983 to 30 June 1984,[313]

1. *Notes with deep regret* that repatriation or compensation of the refugees as provided for in paragraph 11 of General Assembly resolution 194 (III) has not been effected, that no substantial progress has been made in the programme endorsed by the Assembly in paragraph 2 of its resolution 513 (VI) of 26 January 1952 for the reintegration of refugees either by repatriation or resettlement and that, therefore, the situation of the refugees continues to be a matter of serious concern;

2. *Expresses its thanks* to the Commissioner-General and to all the staff of the United Nations Relief and Works Agency for Palestine Refugees in the Near East, recognizing that the Agency is doing all it can within the limits of available resources, and also expresses its thanks to the specialized agencies and private organizations for their valuable work in assisting the refugees;

3. *Reiterates its request* that the headquarters of the United Nations Relief and Works Agency for Palestine Refugees in the Near East should be relocated to its former site within its area of operations as soon as practicable;

4. *Notes with regret* that the United Nations Conciliation Commission for Palestine has been unable to find a means of achieving progress in the implementation of paragraph 11 of General Assembly resolution 194 (III),[314] and requests the Commission to exert continued efforts towards the implementation of that paragraph and to report to the Assembly as appropriate, but no later than 1 September 1985;

5. *Directs attention* to the continuing seriousness of the financial position of the United Nations Relief and Works Agency for Palestine Refugees in the Near East, as outlined in the report of the Commissioner-General;

6. *Notes with profound concern* that, despite the commendable and successful efforts of the Commissioner-General to collect additional contributions, this increased level of income to the United Nations Relief and Works Agency for Palestine Refugees in the Near East is still insufficient to cover essential budget requirements in the present year and that, at currently foreseen levels of giving, deficits will recur each year;

7. *Calls upon* all Governments as a matter of urgency to make the most generous efforts possible to meet the anticipated needs of the United Nations Relief and Works Agency for Palestine Refugees in the Near East, particularly in the light of the budgetary deficit projected in the report of the Commissioner-General, and therefore urges non-contributing Governments to contribute regularly and contributing Governments to consider increasing their regular contributions.

Adopted at the 100th plenary meeting:

In favour: 145

Afghanistan, Algeria, Angola, Argentina, Australia, Austria, Bahamas, Bahrain, Bangladesh, Barbados, Belgium, Belize, Benin, Bhutan, Bolivia, Botswana, Brazil, Brunei Darussalam, Bulgaria, Burkina Faso, Burma, Burundi, Byelorussia, Cameroon, Canada, Cape Verde, Central African Republic, Chad, Chile, China, Colombia, Congo, Costa Rica, Cuba, Cyprus, Czechoslovakia, Democratic Kampuchea, Democratic Yemen, Denmark, Djibouti, Dominican Republic, Ecuador, Egypt, El Salvador, Equatorial Guinea, Ethiopia, Fiji, Finland, France, Gabon, Gambia, German Democratic Republic, Federal Republic of Germany, Ghana, Greece, Guatemala, Guinea, Guinea-Bissau, Guyana, Haiti, Honduras, Hungary, Iceland, India, Indonesia, Iraq, Ireland, Italy, Ivory Coast, Jamaica, Japan, Jordan, Kenya, Kuwait, Lao People's Democratic Republic, Lebanon, Lesotho, Liberia, Libya, Luxembourg, Madagascar, Malawi, Malaysia, Maldives, Mali, Malta, Mauritania, Mauritius, Mexico, Mongolia, Morocco, Mozambique, Nepal, Netherlands, New Zealand, Nicaragua, Niger, Nigeria, Norway, Oman, Pakistan, Panama, Papua New Guinea, Paraguay, Peru, Philippines, Poland, Portugal, Qatar, Romania, Rwanda, Samoa, Sao Tome and Principe, Saudi Arabia, Senegal, Seychelles, Sierra Leone, Singapore, Somalia, Spain, Sri Lanka, Sudan, Suriname, Sweden, Syria, Thailand, Togo, Trinidad and Tobago, Tunisia, Turkey, Uganda, Ukraine, USSR, United Arab Emirates, United Kingdom, United Republic of Tanzania, United States, Uruguay, Venezuela, Viet Nam, Yemen, Yugoslavia, Zaire, Zambia, Zimbabwe.

Against: 0

Abstentions: 1

Israel.

Absent: 12

Albania, Antigua and Barbuda, Comoros, Dominica, Grenada, Iran,* Saint Lucia, Saint Vincent, Solomon Islands, St. Christopher and Nevis, Swaziland, Vanuatu.

---

*Later advised the Secretariat it had intended to vote in favour.

B

WORKING GROUP ON THE FINANCING OF THE UNITED NATIONS RELIEF AND WORKS AGENCY FOR PALESTINE REFUGEES IN THE NEAR EAST

The General Assembly,

Recalling its resolutions 2656 (XXV) of 7 December 1970, 2728 (XXV) of 15 December 1970, 2791 (XXVI) of 6 December 1971, 2964 (XXVII) of 13 December 1972, 3090 (XXVIII) of 7 December 1973, 3330 (XXIX) of 17

---

[313]*Official Records of the General Assembly, Thirty-ninth Session, Supplement No. 13* (A/39/13).

[314]See A/39/455, annex.

December 1974, 3419 D (XXX) of 8 December 1975, 31/15 C of 23 November 1976, 32/90 D of 13 December 1977, 33/112 D of 18 December 1978, 34/52 D of 23 November 1979, 35/13 D of 3 November 1980, 36/146 E of 16 December 1981, 37/120 A of 16 December 1982 and 38/83 B of 15 December 1983,[315]

Recalling also its decision 36/462 of 16 March 1982, whereby it took note of the special report of the Working Group on the Financing of the United Nations Relief and Works Agency for Palestine Refugees in the Near East,[316] and adopted the recommendations contained therein,

Having considered the report of the Working Group on the Financing of the United Nations Relief and Works Agency for Palestine Refugees in the Near East,[317]

Taking into account the report of the Commissioner-General of the United Nations Relief and Works Agency for Palestine Refugees in the Near East covering the period from 1 July 1983 to 30 June 1984,[318]

Gravely concerned at the critical financial situation of the United Nations Relief and Works Agency for Palestine Refugees in the Near East, which has already reduced the essential minimum services being provided to the Palestine refugees and which threatens even greater reductions in the future,

Emphasizing the urgent need for extraordinary efforts in order to maintain, at least at their present minimum level, the activities of the United Nations Relief and Works Agency for Palestine Refugees in the Near East,

1. *Commends* the Working Group on the Financing of the United Nations Relief and Works Agency for Palestine Refugees in the Near East for its efforts to assist in ensuring the Agency's financial security;

2. *Takes note with approval* of the report of the Working Group;

3. *Requests* the Working Group to continue its efforts, in co-operation with the Secretary-General and the Commissioner-General of the United Nations Relief and Works Agency for Palestine Refugees in the Near East, for the financing of the Agency for a further period of one year;

4. *Requests* the Secretary-General to provide the necessary services and assistance to the Working Group for the conduct of its work.

Adopted at the 100th plenary meeting without a vote.

C

ASSISTANCE TO PERSONS DISPLACED AS A RESULT OF THE JUNE 1967 AND SUBSEQUENT HOSTILITIES

The General Assembly,

Recalling its resolution 38/83 C of 15 December 1983

and all previous resolutions on the question,

Taking note of the report of the Commissioner-General of the United Nations Relief and Works Agency for Palestine Refugees in the Near East, covering the period from 1 July 1983 to 30 June 1984,[319]

Concerned about the continued human suffering resulting from the hostilities in the Middle East,

1. *Reaffirms* its resolution 38/83 C and all previous resolutions on the question;

2. *Endorses,* bearing in mind the objectives of those resolutions, the efforts of the Commissioner-General of the United Nations Relief and Works Agency for Palestine Refugees in the Near East to continue to provide humanitarian assistance as far as practicable, on an emergency basis and as a temporary measure, to other persons in the area who are at present displaced and in a serious need of continued assistance as a result of the June 1967 and subsequent hostilities;

3. *Strongly appeals* to all Governments and to organizations and individuals to contribute generously for the above purposes to the United Nations Relief and Works Agency for Palestine Refugees in the Near East and to the other intergovernmental and non-governmental organizations concerned.

Adopted at the 100th plenary meeting without a vote.

D

OFFERS BY MEMBER STATES OF GRANTS AND SCHOLARSHIPS FOR HIGHER EDUCATION, INCLUDING VOCATIONAL TRAINING, FOR PALESTINE REFUGEES

The General Assembly,

Recalling its resolution 212 (III) of 19 November 1948 on assistance to Palestine refugees,

Recalling also its resolutions 35/13 B of 3 November 1980, 36/146 H of 16 December 1981, 37/120 D of 16 December 1982 and 38/83 D of 15 December 1983,

Cognizant of the fact that the Palestine refugees have, for the last three decades, lost their lands and means of livelihood,

Having examined the report of the Secretary-General[320] on offers of grants and scholarships for higher education for Palestine refugees and on the scope of the implementation of resolution 38/83 D,

Having also examined the report of the Commissioner-General of the United Nations Relief and Works Agency for Palestine Refugees in the Near East, covering the period from 1 July 1983 to 30 June 1984,[321] dealing with this subject,

1. *Urges* all States to respond to the appeal contained in General Assembly resolution 32/90 F of 13 December 1977 in a manner commensurate with the needs of Palestine refugees for higher education and vocational training;

---

[315]These resolutions focus on the financing of the United Nations Relief and Works Agency for Palestine Refugees in the Near East. [ed. note]
[316]A/36/866; see also A/37/591.
[317]A/39/575.
[318]*Official Records of the General Assembly, Thirty-ninth Session, Supplement No. 13* (A/39/13).

[319]*Official Records of the General Assembly, Thirty-ninth Session, Supplement No. 13* (A/39/13).
[320]A/39/375.
[321]*Official Records of the General Assembly, Thirty-ninth Session, Supplement No. 13* (A/39/13).

2. *Strongly appeals* to all States, specialized agencies and non-governmental organizations to augment the special allocations for grants and scholarships to Palestine refugees in addition to their contributions to the regular budget of the United Nations Relief and Works Agency for Palestine Refugees in the Near East;

3. *Expresses its appreciation* to all Governments, specialized agencies and non-governmental organizations that responded favourably to General Assembly resolution 38/83 D;

4. *Invites* the relevant specialized agencies and other organizations of the United Nations system to continue, within their respective spheres of competence, to extend assistance for higher education to Palestine refugee students;

5. *Appeals* to all States, specialized agencies and the United Nations University to contribute generously to the Palestinian universities in the territories occupied by Israel since 1967, including, in due course, the proposed University of Jerusalem "Al-Quds" for Palestine refugees;

6. *Also appeals* to all States, specialized agencies and other international bodies to contribute towards the establishment of vocational training centres for Palestine refugees;

7. *Requests* the United Nations Relief and Works Agency for Palestine Refugees in the Near East to act as the recipient and trustee for such special allocations and scholarships and to award them to qualified Palestine refugee candidates;

8. *Requests* the Secretary-General to report to the General Assembly at its fortieth session on the implementation of the present resolution.

Adopted at the 100th plenary meeting:
In favour: 145
Afghanistan, Algeria, Angola, Argentina, Australia, Austria, Bahamas, Bahrain, Bangladesh, Barbados, Belgium, Belize, Benin, Bhutan, Bolivia, Botswana, Brazil, Brunei Darussalam, Bulgaria, Burkina Faso, Burma, Burundi, Byelorussia, Cameroon, Canada, Cape Verde, Central African Republic, Chad, Chile, China, Colombia, Congo, Costa Rica, Cuba, Cyprus, Czechoslovakia, Democratic Kampuchea, Democratic Yemen, Denmark, Djibouti, Dominican Republic, Ecuador, Egypt, El Salvador, Equatorial Guinea, Ethiopia, Fiji, Finland, France, Gabon, Gambia, German Democratic Republic, Federal Republic of Germany, Ghana, Greece, Guatemala, Guinea, Guinea-Bissau, Guyana, Haiti, Honduras, Hungary, Iceland, India, Indonesia, Iraq, Ireland, Italy, Ivory Coast, Jamaica, Japan, Jordan, Kenya, Kuwait, Lao People's Democratic Republic, Lebanon, Lesotho, Liberia, Libya, Luxembourg, Madagascar, Malawi, Malaysia, Maldives, Mali, Malta, Mauritania, Mauritius, Mexico, Mongolia, Morocco, Mozambique, Nepal, Netherlands, New Zealand, Nicaragua, Niger, Nigeria, Norway, Oman, Pakistan, Panama, Papua New Guinea, Paraguay, Peru, Philippines, Poland, Portugal, Qatar, Romania, Rwanda, Samoa, Sao Tome and Principe, Saudi Arabia, Senegal, Seychelles, Sierra Leone, Singapore, Somalia, Spain, Sri Lanka, Sudan, Suriname, Sweden, Syria, Thailand, Togo, Trinidad and Tobago, Tunisia, Turkey, Uganda, Ukraine, USSR, United Arab Emirates, United Kingdom, United Republic of Tanzania, United States, Uruguay, Venezuela, Viet Nam, Yemen, Yugoslavia, Zaire, Zambia, Zimbabwe.
Against: 0
Abstention: 1
Israel.
Absent: 12
Albania, Antigua and Barbuda, Comoros, Dominica, Grenada, Iran,* Saint Lucia, Saint Vincent, Solomon Islands, St. Christopher and Nevis, Swaziland, Vanuatu.

---

*Later advised the Secretariat it had intended to vote in favour.

E

PALESTINE REFUGEES IN THE GAZA STRIP

The General Assembly,

Recalling Security Council resolution 237 (1967) of 14 June 1967,

Recalling also General Assembly resolutions 2792 C (XXVI) of 6 December 1971, 2963 C (XXVII) of 13 December 1972, 3089 C (XXVIII) of 7 December 1973, 3331 D (XXIX) of 17 December 1974, 3419 C (XXX) of 8 December 1975, 31/15 E of 23 November 1976, 32/90 C of 13 December 1977, 33/112 E of 18 December 1978, 34/52 F of 23 November 1979, 35/13 F of 3 November 1980, 36/146 A of 16 December 1981, 37/120 E of 16 December 1982 and 38/83 E of 15 December 1983,[322]

Having considered the report of the Commissioner-General of the United Nations Relief and Works Agency for Palestine Refugees in the Near East covering the period from 1 July 1983 to 30 June 1984,[323] and the report of the Secretary-General of 4 September 1984,[324]

Recalling the provisions of paragraph 11 of its resolution 194 (III) of 11 December 1948 and considering that measures to resettle Palestine refugees in the Gaza Strip away from the homes and property from which they were displaced constitute a violation of their inalienable right of return,

Alarmed by the reports received from the Commissioner-General that the Israeli occupying authorities, in contravention of Israel's obligation under international law, persist in their policy of demolishing shelters occupied by refugee families,

1. *Reiterates its demand* that Israel desist from the removal and resettlement of Palestine refugees in the Gaza Strip and from the destruction of their shelters;

2. *Requests* the Secretary-General, after consulting with the Commissioner-General of the United Nations Relief and Works Agency for Palestine Refugees in the Near

---

[322]On Israeli actions harmful to Palestinian refugees in the Gaza Strip. [ed. note]
[323]*Official Records of the General Assembly, Thirty-ninth Session, Supplement No. 13* (A/39/13).
[324]A/39/457; reissued for technical reasons on 13 September 1984.

East, to report to the General Assembly, before the opening of its fortieth session, on Israel's compliance with paragraph 1 above.

Adopted at the 100th plenary meeting:
In favour: 145
Afghanistan, Albania, Algeria, Angola, Argentina, Australia, Austria, Bahamas, Bahrain, Bangladesh, Barbados, Belgium, Belize, Benin, Bhutan, Bolivia, Botswana, Brazil, Brunei Darussalam, Bulgaria, Burkina Faso, Burma, Burundi, Byelorussia, Cameroon, Canada, Cape Verde, Central African Republic, Chad, Chile, China, Colombia, Congo, Costa Rica, Cuba, Cyprus, Czechoslovakia, Democratic Kampuchea, Democratic Yemen, Denmark, Djibouti, Dominican Republic, Ecuador, Egypt, El Salvador, Equatorial Guinea, Ethiopia, Fiji, Finland, France, Gabon, Gambia, German Democratic Republic, Federal Republic of Germany, Ghana, Greece, Guatemala, Guinea, Guinea-Bissau, Guyana, Haiti, Honduras, Hungary, Iceland, India, Indonesia, Iraq, Ireland, Italy, Ivory Coast, Jamaica, Japan, Jordan, Kenya, Kuwait, Lao People's Democratic Republic, Lebanon, Lesotho, Liberia, Libya, Luxembourg, Madagascar, Malawi, Malaysia, Maldives, Mali, Malta, Mauritania, Mauritius, Mexico, Mongolia, Morocco, Mozambique, Nepal, Netherlands, New Zealand, Nicaragua, Niger, Nigeria, Norway, Oman, Pakistan, Panama, Papua New Guinea, Paraguay, Peru, Philippines, Poland, Portugal, Qatar, Romania, Rwanda, Samoa, Sao Tome and Principe, Saudi Arabia, Senegal, Seychelles, Sierra Leone, Singapore, Somalia, Spain, Sri Lanka, Sudan, Suriname, Sweden, Syria, Thailand, Togo, Trinidad and Tobago, Tunisia, Turkey, Uganda, Ukraine, USSR, United Arab Emirates, United Kingdom, United Republic of Tanzania, Uruguay, Venezuela, Viet Nam, Yemen, Yugoslavia, Zaire, Zambia, Zimbabwe.
Against: 2
Israel, United States.
Abstentions: 0
Absent: 11
Antigua and Barbuda, Comoros, Dominica, Grenada, Iran,* Saint Lucia, Saint Vincent, Solomon Islands, St. Christopher and Nevis, Swaziland, Vanuatu.

---

*Later advised the Secretariat it had intended to vote in favour.

F
RESUMPTION OF THE RATION DISTRIBUTION TO PALESTINE REFUGEES

The General Assembly,
Recalling its resolutions 36/146 F of 16 December 1981, 37/120 F of 16 December 1982, 38/83 F of 15 December 1983 and all previous resolutions on the question, including resolution 302 (IV) of 8 December 1949,
Having considered the report of the Commissioner-General of the United Nations Relief and Works Agency for Palestine Refugees in the Near East, covering the period from 1 July 1983 to 30 June 1984,[325]

Deeply concerned at the interruption by the United Nations Relief and Works Agency for Palestine Refugees in the Near East, owing to financial difficulties, of the general ration distribution to Palestine refugees in all fields,

1. *Regrets* that resolutions 37/120 F and 38/83 F have not been implemented;

2. *Calls once again upon* all Governments, as a matter of urgency, to make the most generous efforts possible and to offer the necessary resources to meet the needs of the United Nations Relief and Works Agency for Palestine Refugees in the Near East, particularly in the light of the interruption by the Agency of the general ration distribution to Palestine refugees in all fields, and therefore urges non-contributing Governments to contribute regularly and contributing Governments to consider increasing their regular contributions;

3. *Requests* the Commissioner-General of the United Nations Relief and Works Agency for Palestine Refugees in the Near East to resume on a continuing basis the interrupted general ration distribution to Palestine refugees in all fields;

4. *Requests* the Secretary-General, in consultation with the Commissioner-General, to report to the General Assembly at its fortieth session on the implementation of the present resolution.

Adopted at the 100th plenary meeting:
In favour: 122
Afghanistan, Algeria, Angola, Argentina, Bahamas, Bahrain, Bangladesh, Barbados, Belize, Benin, Bhutan, Bolivia, Botswana, Brazil, Brunei Darussalam, Bulgaria, Burkina Faso, Burma, Burundi, Byelorussia, Cameroon, Cape Verde, Central African Republic, Chad, Chile, China, Colombia, Congo, Cuba, Cyprus, Czechoslovakia, Democratic Kampuchea, Democratic Yemen, Djibouti, Dominican Republic, Ecuador, Egypt, El Salvador, Equatorial Guinea, Ethiopia, Fiji, Gabon, Gambia, German Democratic Republic, Ghana, Greece, Guatemala, Guinea, Guinea-Bissau, Guyana, Haiti, Honduras, Hungary, India, Indonesia, Iraq, Ivory Coast, Jamaica, Jordan, Kenya, Kuwait, Lao People's Democratic Republic, Lebanon, Lesotho, Liberia, Libya, Madagascar, Malawi, Malaysia, Maldives, Mali, Malta, Mauritania, Mauritius, Mexico, Mongolia, Morocco, Mozambique, Nepal, Nicaragua, Niger, Nigeria, Oman, Pakistan, Panama, Papua New Guinea, Paraguay, Peru, Philippines, Poland, Qatar, Romania, Rwanda, Samoa, Sao Tome and Principe, Saudi Arabia, Senegal, Seychelles, Sierra Leone, Singapore, Somalia, Sri Lanka, Sudan, Suriname, Syria, Thailand, Togo, Trinidad and Tobago, Tunisia, Turkey, Uganda, Ukraine, USSR, United Arab Emirates, United Republic of Tanzania, Uruguay, Venezuela, Viet Nam, Yemen, Yugoslavia, Zambia, Zimbabwe.
Against: 19

---

[325]*Official Records of the General Assembly, Thirty-ninth Session, Supplement No. 13* (A/39/13).

Australia, Belgium, Canada, Denmark, Finland, France, Federal Republic of Germany, Iceland, Ireland, Israel, Italy, Japan, Luxembourg, Netherlands, New Zealand, Norway, Sweden, United Kingdom, United States.
Abstentions: 4
Austria, Portugal, Spain, Zaire.
Absent: 13
Albania, Antigua and Barbuda, Comoros, Costa Rica, Dominica, Grenada, Iran,* Saint Lucia, Saint Vincent, Solomon Islands, St. Christopher and Nevis, Swaziland, Vanuatu.

———
*Later advised the Secretariat it had intended to vote in favour.

G

POPULATION AND REFUGEES DISPLACED SINCE 1967

The General Assembly,
Recalling Security Council resolution 237 (1967) of 14 June 1967,

Recalling also General Assembly resolutions 2252 (ES-V) of 4 July 1967, 2452 A (XXIII) of 19 December 1968, 2535 B (XXIV) of 10 December 1969, 2672 D (XXV) of 8 December 1970, 2792 E (XXVI) of 6 December 1971, 2963 C and D (XXVII) of 13 December 1972, 3089 C (XXVIII) of 7 December 1973, 3331 D (XXIX) of 17 December 1974, 3419 C (XXX) of 8 December 1975, 31/15 D of 23 November 1976, 32/90 E of 13 December 1977, 33/112 F of 18 December 1978, 34/52 E of 23 November 1979, ES-7/2 of 29 July 1980, 35/13 E of 3 November 1980, 36/146 B of 16 December 1981, 37/120 G of 16 December 1982 and 38/83 G of 15 December 1983,[326]

Having considered the report of the Commissioner-General of the United Nations Relief and Works Agency for Palestine Refugees in the Near East, covering the period from 1 July 1983 to 30 June 1984,[327] and the report of the Secretary-General of 21 August 1984,[328]

1. *Reaffirms* the inalienable right of all displaced inhabitants to return to their homes or former places of residence in the territories occupied by Israel since 1967 and declares once more that any attempt to restrict, or to attach conditions to, the free exercise of the right of return by any displaced person is inconsistent with that inalienable right and inadmissible;

2. *Considers* any and all agreements embodying any restriction on or condition for the return of the displaced inhabitants as null and void;

3. *Strongly deplores* the continued refusal of the Israeli authorities to take steps for the return of the displaced inhabitants;

4. *Calls once more upon* Israel:

(a) To take immediate steps for the return of all displaced inhabitants;

(b) To desist from all measures that obstruct the return of the displaced inhabitants, including measures affecting the physical and demographic structure of the occupied territories;

5. *Requests* the Secretary-General, after consulting with the Commissioner-General of the United Nations Relief and Works Agency for Palestine Refugees in the Near East, to report to the General Assembly before the opening of its fortieth session on Israel's compliance with paragraph 4 above.

Adopted at the 100th plenary meeting:
In favour: 127
Afghanistan, Albania, Algeria, Angola, Argentina, Bahamas, Bahrain, Bangladesh, Barbados, Belize, Benin, Bhutan, Bolivia, Botswana, Brazil, Brunei Darussalam, Bulgaria, Burkina Faso, Burma, Burundi, Byelorussia, Cameroon, Cape Verde, Central African Republic, Chad, Chile, China, Colombia, Congo, Costa Rica, Cuba, Cyprus, Czechoslovakia, Democratic Kampuchea, Democratic Yemen, Djibouti, Dominican Republic, Ecuador, Egypt, El Salvador, Equatorial Guinea, Ethiopia, Fiji, Gabon, Gambia, German Democratic Republic, Ghana, Greece, Guatemala, Guinea, Guinea-Bissau, Guyana, Haiti, Honduras, Hungary, India, Indonesia, Iraq, Ivory Coast, Jamaica, Japan, Jordan, Kenya, Kuwait, Lao People's Democratic Republic, Lebanon, Lesotho, Liberia, Libya, Madagascar, Malawi, Malaysia, Maldives, Mali, Malta, Mauritania, Mauritius, Mexico, Mongolia, Morocco, Mozambique, Nepal, Nicaragua, Niger, Oman, Pakistan, Panama, Papua New Guinea, Paraguay, Peru, Philippines, Poland, Portugal, Qatar, Romania, Rwanda, Samoa, Sao Tome and Principe, Saudi Arabia, Senegal, Seychelles, Sierra Leone, Singapore, Somalia, Spain, Sri Lanka, Sudan, Suriname, Syria, Thailand, Togo, Trinidad and Tobago, Tunisia, Turkey, Uganda, Ukraine, USSR, United Arab Emirates, United Republic of Tanzania, Uruguay, Venezuela, Viet Nam, Yemen, Yugoslavia, Zambia, Zaire, Zimbabwe.
Against: 2
Israel, United States.
Abstentions: 17
Australia, Austria, Belgium, Canada, Denmark, Finland, France, Federal Republic of Germany, Iceland, Ireland, Italy, Luxembourg, Netherlands, New Zealand, Norway, Sweden, United Kingdom.
Absent: 12
Antigua and Barbuda, Comoros, Dominica, Grenada, Iran,* Nigeria, Saint Lucia, Saint Vincent, Solomon Islands, St. Christopher and Nevis, Swaziland, Vanuatu.

———
*Later advised the Secretariat it had intended to vote in favour.

H

REVENUES DERIVED FROM PALESTINE REFUGEE PROPERTIES

The General Assembly,
Recalling its resolutions 35/13 A to F of 3 November

[326]Concerning persons displaced since 1967. [ed. note]
[327]*Official Records of the General Assembly, Thirty-ninth Session, Supplement No. 13* (A/39/13).
[328]A/39/411.

1980, 36/146 C of 16 December 1981, 37/120 H of 16 December 1982, 38/83 H of 15 December 1983 and all its previous resolutions on the question, including resolution 194 (III) of 11 December 1948,

Taking note of the reports of the Secretary-General of 6 September and 12 October 1984,[329]

Taking note also of the report of the United Nations Conciliation Commission for Palestine, covering the period from 1 October 1983 to 30 September 1984,[330]

Recalling that the Universal Declaration of Human Rights[331] and the principles of international law uphold the principle that no one shall be arbitrarily deprived of his or her private property,

Considering that the Palestine Arab refugees are entitled to their property and to the income derived from their property, in conformity with the principles of justice and equity,

Recalling, in particular, its resolution 394 (V) of 14 December 1950, in which it directed the United Nations Conciliation Commission for Palestine, in consultation with the parties concerned, to prescribe measures for the protection of the rights, property and interests of the Palestinian Arab refugees,

Taking note of the completion of the programme of identification and evaluation of Arab property, as announced by the United Nations Conciliation Commission for Palestine in its twenty-second progress report,[332] of 11 May 1964, and of the fact that the Land Office had a schedule of Arab owners and file of documents defining the location, area and other particulars of Arab property,

1. *Requests* the Secretary-General to take all appropriate steps, in consultation with the United Nations Conciliation Commission for Palestine, for the protection and administration of Arab property, assets and property rights in Israel, and to establish a fund for the receipt of income derived therefrom, on behalf of the rightful owners;

2. *Calls upon* Israel to render all facilities and assistance to the Secretary-General in the implementation of the present resolution;

3. *Calls upon* all other Governments of Member States concerned to provide the Secretary-General with any pertinent information in their possession concerning Arab property, assets and property rights in Israel, which would assist the Secretary-General in the implementation of the present resolution;

4. *Deplores* Israel's refusal to co-operate with the Secretary-General in the implementation of the resolutions on the question;

5. *Requests* the Secretary-General to report to the General Assembly at its fortieth session on the implementation of the present resolution.

Adopted at the 100th plenary meeting:

---

[329]A/39/464 and Add.1.
[330]A/39/455, annex.
[331]Resolution 217 A (III).
[332]*Official Records of the General Assembly, Nineteenth Session, Annex No. 11,* document A/5700.

In favour: 123

Afghanistan, Albania, Algeria, Angola, Argentina, Bahamas, Bahrain, Bangladesh, Barbados, Belize, Benin, Bhutan, Bolivia, Botswana, Brazil, Brunei Darussalam, Bulgaria, Burkina Faso, Burma, Burundi, Byelorussia, Cameroon, Cape Verde, Central African Republic, Chad, Chile, China, Colombia, Congo, Costa Rica, Cuba, Cyprus, Czechoslovakia, Democratic Kampuchea, Democratic Yemen, Djibouti, Dominican Republic, Ecuador, Egypt, El Salvador, Equatorial Guinea, Ethiopia, Fiji, Gabon, Gambia, German Democratic Republic, Ghana, Greece, Guatemala, Guinea, Guinea-Bissau, Guyana, Haiti, Honduras, Hungary, India, Indonesia, Iraq, Jamaica, Jordan, Kenya, Kuwait, Lao People's Democratic Republic, Lebanon, Lesotho, Libya, Madagascar, Malawi, Malaysia, Maldives, Malta, Mauritania, Mauritius, Mexico, Mongolia, Morocco, Mozambique, Nepal, Nicaragua, Niger, Nigeria, Oman, Pakistan, Panama, Papua New Guinea, Paraguay, Peru, Philippines, Poland, Portugal, Qatar, Romania, Rwanda, Samoa, Sao Tome and Principe, Saudi Arabia, Senegal, Seychelles, Sierra Leone, Singapore, Somalia, Spain, Sri Lanka, Sudan, Suriname, Syria, Thailand, Togo, Trinidad and Tobago, Tunisia, Turkey, Uganda, Ukraine, USSR, United Arab Emirates, United Republic of Tanzania, Uruguay, Venezuela, Viet Nam, Yemen, Yugoslavia, Zambia, Zimbabwe.

Against: 2

Israel, United States.

Abstentions: 21

Australia, Austria, Belgium, Canada, Denmark, Finland, France, Federal Republic of Germany, Iceland, Ireland, Italy, Ivory Coast, Japan, Liberia, Luxembourg, Netherlands, New Zealand, Norway, Sweden, United Kingdom, Zaire.

Absent: 12

Antigua and Barbuda, Comoros, Dominica, Grenada, Iran,* Mali, Saint Lucia, Saint Vincent, Solomon Islands, St. Christopher and Nevis, Swaziland, Vanuatu.

---

*Later advised the Secretariat it had intended to vote in favour.

I

PROTECTION OF PALESTINE REFUGEES

The General Assembly,

Recalling Security Council resolutions 508 (1982) of 5 June 1982, 509 (1982) of 6 June 1982, 511 (1982) of 18 June 1982, 512 (1982) of 19 June 1982, 513 (1982) of 4 July 1982, 515 (1982) of 29 July 1982, 517 (1982) of 4 August 1982, 518 (1982) of 12 August 1982, 519 (1982) of 17 August 1982, 520 (1982) of 17 September 1982 and 523 (1982) of 18 October 1982,[333]

Recalling General Assembly resolutions ES-7/5 of 26 June 1982, ES-7/6 and ES-7/8 of 19 August 1982, ES-7/9

---

[333]Concerning the provision of assistance to, and the rights of, Palestinian refugees. [ed. note]

of 24 September 1982, 37/120 J of 16 December 1982 and 38/83 I of 15 December 1983,

Having considered the report of the Secretary-General of 2 October 1984,[334]

Having also considered the report of the Commissioner-General of the United Nations Relief and Works Agency for Palestine Refugees in the Near East, covering the period from 1 July 1983 to 30 June 1984,[335]

Referring to the humanitarian principles of the Geneva Convention relative to the Protection of Civilian Persons in Time of War, of 12 August 1949,[336] and to the obligations arising from the Regulations annexed to the Hague Convention IV of 1907,[337]

Deeply concerned at the lack of security for the Palestine refugees in occupied southern Lebanon resulting in scores of violent deaths, woundings, kidnappings, disappearances, evictions in the face of threats, explosions and arsons,

Deeply distressed at the sufferings of the Palestinians resulting from the Israeli invasion of Lebanon,

Reaffirming its support for Lebanese sovereignty, unity and territorial integrity, within its internationally recognized boundaries,

1. *Urges* the Secretary-General, in consultation with the United Nations Relief and Works Agency for Palestine Refugees in the Near East, to undertake effective measures to guarantee the safety and security and the legal and human rights of the Palestine refugees in all the territories under Israeli occupation in 1967 and thereafter;

2. *Holds* Israel responsible for the security of the Palestine refugees in occupied southern Lebanon, and calls upon it to fulfil its obligations as the occupying Power in this regard, in accordance with the pertinent provisions of the Geneva Convention relative to the Protection of Civilian Persons in Time of War, of 12 August 1949;

3. *Calls once again upon* Israel, the occupying Power, to release forthwith all detained Palestine refugees, including the employees of the United Nations Relief and Works Agency for Palestine Refugees in the Near East;

4. *Also calls upon* Israel to desist forthwith from preventing those Palestinians registered as refugees in Lebanon from returning to their camps in Lebanon;

5. *Further calls upon* Israel to allow the resumption of health, medical, educational and social services rendered by the United Nations Relief and Works Agency for Palestine Refugees in the Near East to the Palestinians in the refugee camps in southern Lebanon;

6. *Requests* the Commissioner-General of the United Nations Relief and Works Agency for Palestine Refugees in the Near East to co-ordinate his activities in rendering these services with the Government of Lebanon, the host country;

7. *Urges* the Commissioner-General to provide housing, in consultation with the Government of Lebanon, to the Palestine refugees whose houses were demolished or razed by the Israeli forces;

8. *Calls once again upon* Israel to compensate the United Nations Relief and Works Agency for Palestine Refugees in the Near East for the damage to its property and facilities resulting from the Israeli invasion of Lebanon, without prejudice to Israel's responsibility for all damages resulting from that invasion;

9. *Requests* the Secretary-General, in consultation with the Commissioner-General, to report to the General Assembly, before the opening of its fortieth session, on the implementation of the present resolution.

Adopted at the 100th plenary meeting:

In favour: 127

Afghanistan, Albania, Algeria, Angola, Argentina, Austria, Bahamas, Bahrain, Bangladesh, Barbados, Benin, Bhutan, Bolivia, Botswana, Brazil, Brunei Darussalam, Bulgaria, Burkina Faso, Burma, Burundi, Byelorussia, Cameroon, Cape Verde, Central African Republic, Chad, Chile, China, Colombia, Congo, Costa Rica, Cuba, Cyprus, Czechoslovakia, Democratic Kampuchea, Democratic Yemen, Djibouti, Dominican Republic, Ecuador, Egypt, El Salvador, Equatorial Guinea, Ethiopia, Fiji, Finland, France, Gabon, Gambia, German Democratic Republic, Ghana, Greece, Guatemala, Guinea, Guinea-Bissau, Guyana, Haiti, Honduras, Hungary, India, Indonesia, Iraq, Jamaica, Japan, Jordan, Kenya, Kuwait, Lao People's Democratic Republic, Lebanon, Lesotho, Libya, Madagascar, Malawi, Malaysia, Maldives, Mali, Malta, Mauritania, Mauritius, Mexico, Mongolia, Morocco, Mozambique, Nepal, New Zealand, Nicaragua, Niger, Nigeria, Oman, Pakistan, Papua New Guinea, Paraguay, Peru, Philippines, Poland, Qatar, Romania, Rwanda, Samoa, Sao Tome and Principe, Saudi Arabia, Senegal, Seychelles, Sierra Leone, Singapore, Somalia, Spain, Sri Lanka, Sudan, Suriname, Sweden, Syria, Thailand, Togo, Trinidad and Tobago, Tunisia, Turkey, Uganda, Ukraine, USSR, United Arab Emirates, United Republic of Tanzania, Uruguay, Venezuela, Viet Nam, Yemen, Yugoslavia, Zambia, Zimbabwe.

Against: 2

Israel, United States.

Abstentions: 18

Australia, Belgium, Belize, Canada, Denmark, Federal Republic of Germany, Iceland, Ireland, Italy, Ivory Coast, Liberia, Luxembourg, Netherlands, New Zealand, Norway, Panama, Portugal, United Kingdom, Zaire.

Absent: 11

Antigua and Barbuda, Comoros, Dominica, Grenada, Iran,* Saint Lucia, Saint Vincent, Solomon Islands, St. Christopher and Nevis, Swaziland, Vanuatu.

---

[334]A/39/538.

[335]*Official Records of the General Assembly, Thirty-ninth Session, Supplement No. 13* (A/39/13).

[336]United Nations, *Treaty Series,* vol. 75, no. 973, p. 287.

[337]Carnegie Endowment for International Peace, *The Hague Conventions and Declarations of 1899 and 1907* (New York, Oxford University Press, 1915), p. 100.

---

*Later advised the Secretariat it had intended to vote in favour.

J

PALESTINE REFUGEES IN THE WEST BANK

The General Assembly,

Recalling Security Council resolution 237 (1967) of 14 June 1967,

Recalling also General Assembly resolution 38/83 J of 15 December 1983,

Having considered the report of the Secretary-General of 8 August 1984,[338]

Having also considered the report of the Commissioner-General of the United Nations Relief and Works Agency for Palestine Refugees in the Near East, covering the period from 1 July 1983 to 30 June 1984,[339]

Alarmed by Israel's plans to remove and resettle the Palestine refugees of the West Bank and to destroy their camps,

Recalling the provisions of paragraph 11 of its resolution 194 (III) of 11 December 1948 and considering that measures to resettle Palestine refugees in the West Bank away from the homes and property from which they were displaced constitute a violation of their inalienable right of return,

1. *Calls upon* Israel to abandon its plans and to refrain from the removal, and from any action that may lead to the removal and resettlement, of Palestine refugees in the West Bank and from the destruction of their camps;

2. *Requests* the Secretary-General in co-operation with the Commissioner-General of the United Nations Relief and Works Agency for Palestine Refugees in the Near East, to keep the matter under close supervision and to report to the General Assembly, before the opening of its fortieth session, on any developments regarding this matter.

Adopted at the 100th plenary meeting:

In favour: 145

Afghanistan, Albania, Algeria, Angola, Argentina, Australia, Austria, Bahamas, Bahrain, Bangladesh, Barbados, Belgium, Belize, Benin, Bhutan, Bolivia, Botswana, Brazil, Brunei Darussalam, Bulgaria, Burkina Faso, Burma, Burundi, Byelorussia, Cameroon, Canada, Cape Verde, Central African Republic, Chad, Chile, China, Colombia, Congo, Costa Rica, Cuba, Cyprus, Czechoslovakia, Democratic Kampuchea, Democratic Yemen, Denmark, Djibouti, Dominican Republic, Ecuador, Egypt, El Salvador, Equatorial Guinea, Ethiopia, Fiji, Finland, France, Gabon, Gambia, German Democratic Republic, Federal Republic of Germany, Ghana, Greece, Guatemala, Guinea, Guinea-Bissau, Guyana, Haiti, Honduras, Hungary, Iceland, India, Indonesia, Iraq, Ireland, Italy, Ivory Coast, Jamaica, Japan, Jordan, Kenya, Kuwait, Lao People's Democratic Republic, Lebanon, Lesotho, Liberia, Libya, Luxembourg, Madagascar, Malawi, Malaysia, Maldives, Mali, Malta, Mauritania, Mauritius, Mexico, Mongolia, Morocco, Mozambique, Nepal, Netherlands, New Zealand, Nicaragua, Niger, Nigeria, Norway, Oman, Pakistan, Panama, Papua New Guinea, Paraguay, Peru, Philippines, Poland, Portugal, Qatar, Romania, Rwanda, Samoa, Sao Tome and Principe, Saudi Arabia, Senegal, Seychelles, Sierra Leone, Singapore, Somalia, Spain, Sri Lanka, Sudan, Suriname, Sweden, Syria, Thailand, Togo, Trinidad and Tobago, Tunisia, Turkey, Uganda, Ukraine, USSR, United Arab Emirates, United Kingdom, United Republic of Tanzania, Uruguay, Venezuela, Viet Nam, Yemen, Yugoslavia, Zaire, Zambia, Zimbabwe.

Against: 2

Israel, United States.

Abstentions: 0

Absent: 11

Antigua and Barbuda, Comoros, Dominica, Grenada, Iran,* Saint Lucia, Saint Vincent, Solomon Islands, St. Christopher and Nevis, Swaziland, Vanuatu.

---

*Later advised the Secretariat it had intended to vote in favour.

K

UNIVERSITY OF JERUSALEM "AL-QUDS" FOR PALESTINE REFUGEES

The General Assembly,

Recalling its resolutions 36/146 G of 16 December 1981, 37/120 C of 16 December 1982 and 38/83 K of 15 December 1983,

Having examined the report of the Secretary-General on the question of the establishment of a university at Jerusalem,[340]

Having also examined the report of the Commissioner-General of the United Nations Relief and Works Agency for Palestine Refugees in the Near East, covering the period from 1 July 1983 to 30 June 1984,[341]

1. *Commends* the constructive efforts made by the Secretary-General, the Commissioner-General of the United Nations Relief and Works Agency for Palestine Refugees in the Near East, the Council of the United Nations University and the United Nations Educational, Scientific and Cultural Organization, which worked diligently towards the implementation of General Assembly resolution 38/83 D and other relevant resolutions;

2. *Further commends* the close co-operation of the competent educational authorities concerned;

3. *Emphasizes* the need for strengthening the educational system in the Arab territories occupied since 5 June 1967, including Jerusalem, and specifically the need for the establishment of the proposed university;

4. *Requests* the Secretary-General to continue to take all necessary measures for establishing the University of Je-

---

[338] A/39/372.

[339] *Official Records of the General Assembly, Thirty-ninth Session, Supplement No. 13* (A/39/13).

[340] A/39/528.

[341] *Official Records of the General Assembly, Thirty-ninth Session, Supplement No. 13* (A/39/13).

rusalem, "Al-Quds", in accordance with General Assembly resolution 35/13 B of 3 November 1980, giving due consideration to the recommendations consistent with the provisions of that resolution;

5. *Calls upon* Israel, the occupying Power, to co-operate in the implementation of the present resolution and to remove the hindrances which it has put in the way of establishing the University of Jerusalem;

6. *Requests* the Secretary-General to report to the General Assembly at its fortieth session on the progress made in the implementation of the present resolution.

Adopted at the 100th plenary meeting:
In favour: 144

Afghanistan, Albania, Algeria, Angola, Argentina, Australia, Austria, Bahamas, Bahrain, Bangladesh, Barbados, Belgium, Belize, Benin, Bhutan, Bolivia, Botswana, Brazil, Brunei Darussalam, Bulgaria, Burkina Faso, Burma, Burundi, Byelorussia, Cameroon, Canada, Cape Verde, Central African Republic, Chad, Chile, China, Colombia, Congo, Costa Rica, Cuba, Cyprus, Czechoslovakia, Democratic Kampuchea, Democratic Yemen, Denmark, Djibouti, Dominican Republic, Ecuador, Egypt, El Salvador, Equatorial Guinea, Ethiopia, Fiji, Finland, France, Gabon, Gambia, German Democratic Republic, Federal Republic of Germany, Ghana, Greece, Guatemala, Guinea, Guinea-Bissau, Guyana, Haiti, Honduras, Hungary, Iceland, India, Indonesia, Iraq, Ireland, Italy, Ivory Coast, Jamaica, Japan, Jordan, Kenya, Kuwait, Lao People's Democratic Republic, Lebanon, Lesotho, Liberia, Libya, Luxembourg, Madagascar, Malawi, Malaysia, Maldives, Malta, Mauritania, Mauritius, Mexico, Mongolia, Morocco, Mozambique, Nepal, Netherlands, New Zealand, Nicaragua, Niger, Nigeria, Norway, Oman, Pakistan, Panama, Papua New Guinea, Paraguay, Peru, Philippines, Poland, Portugal, Qatar, Romania, Rwanda, Samoa, Sao Tome and Principe, Saudi Arabia, Senegal, Seychelles, Sierra Leone, Singapore, Somalia, Spain, Sri Lanka, Sudan, Suriname, Sweden, Syria, Thailand, Togo, Trinidad and Tobago, Tunisia, Turkey, Uganda, Ukraine, USSR, United Arab Emirates, United Kingdom, United Republic of Tanzania, Uruguay, Venezuela, Viet Nam, Yemen, Yugoslavia, Zaire, Zambia, Zimbabwe.

Against: 2

Israel, United States.

Abstentions: 0

Absent: 12

Antigua and Barbuda, Comoros, Dominica, Grenada, Iran,* Mali,* Saint Lucia, Saint Vincent, Solomon Islands, St. Christopher and Nevis, Swaziland, Vanuatu.

---

*Later advised the Secretariat it had intended to vote in favour.

Resolution No. 39/101 of 14 December 1984

DEMANDING THAT ISRAEL CEASE ALL PLANS TO BUILD A CANAL LINKING THE MEDITERRANEAN SEA TO THE DEAD SEA

The General Assembly,

Recalling its resolutions 36/150 of 16 December 1981, 37/122 of 16 December 1982 and 38/85 of 15 December 1983,[342]

Recalling the rules and principles of international law relative to the fundamental rights and duties of States,

Bearing in mind the principles of international law relative to belligerent occupation of land, including the Geneva Convention relative to the Protection of Civilian Persons in Time of War, of 12 August 1949,[343] and reaffirming their applicability to all Arab territories occupied since 1967, including Jerusalem,

Having considered the report of the Secretary-General,[344]

Recognizing that the proposed canal, to be constructed partly through the Gaza Strip, a Palestinian territory occupied in 1967, would violate the principles of international law and affect the interests of the Palestinian people,

Confident that the canal linking the Mediterranean Sea with the Dead Sea, if constructed by Israel, will cause direct, serious and irreparable damage to Jordan's rights and legitimate and vital interests in the economic, agricultural, demographic and ecological fields,

Deeply concerned at the digging activities in the Dead Sea area at the envisaged site of that end of the canal,

Noting with regret the non-compliance by Israel with General Assembly resolution 36/150,

1. *Deplores* Israel's non-compliance with General Assembly resolutions 37/122 and 38/85 and its refusal to receive the team of experts;

2. *Emphasizes* that the canal linking the Mediterranean Sea with the Dead Sea, if constructed, is a violation of the rules and principles of international law, especially those relating to the fundmental rights and duties of States and to belligerent occupation of land;

3. *Demands once again* that Israel not contruct this canal and cease forthwith all actions taken and/or digging plans made towards the execution of this project;

4. *Calls upon* all States, specialized agencies and governmental and non-governmental organizations not to assist, directly or indirectly, in the preparation and execution of this project, and strongly urges national, international and multinational corporations to do likewise;

5. *Requests* the Secretary-General to monitor and assess, on a continuing basis and through a competent expert organ, all aspects—juridical, political, economic, ecological, and demographic—of the adverse effects on Jordan and on the Arab territories occupied since 1967, including Jerusalem, arising from the implementation of the Israeli decision to construct this canal and to forward the findings of that organ on a regular basis to the General Assembly;

6. *Requests* the Secretary-General to report to the General Assembly at its fortieth session on the implementation of the present resolution;

---

[342]On Israel's proposed canal between the Mediterranean and the Dead Seas. [ed. note]
[343]United Nations, *Treaty Series,* vol. 75, no. 973, p. 287.
[344]A/39/142.

7. *Decides* to include in the provisional agenda of its fortieth session the item entitled "Israel's decision to build a canal linking the Mediterranean Sea to the Dead Sea".

Adopted at the 100th plenary meeting:
In favour: 143
Afghanistan, Albania, Algeria, Angola, Argentina, Australia, Austria, Bahamas, Bahrain, Bangladesh, Barbados, Belgium, Belize, Benin, Bhutan, Bolivia, Botswana, Brazil, Brunei Darussalam, Bulgaria, Burkina Faso, Burma, Burundi, Byelorussia, Cameroon, Canada, Cape Verde, Central African Republic, Chad, Chile, China, Colombia, Congo, Costa Rica, Cuba, Cyprus, Czechoslovakia, Democratic Kampuchea, Democratic Yemen, Denmark, Djibouti, Dominican Republic, Ecuador, Egypt, El Salvador, Equatorial Guinea, Ethiopia, Fiji, Finland, France, Gabon, Gambia, German Democratic Republic, Federal Republic of Germany, Ghana, Greece, Guatemala, Guinea, Guinea-Bissau, Guyana, Haiti, Honduras, Hungary, Iceland, India, Indonesia, Iraq, Ireland, Italy, Ivory Coast, Jamaica, Japan, Jordan, Kenya, Kuwait, Lao People's Democratic Republic, Lesotho, Liberia, Libya, Luxembourg, Madagascar, Malawi, Malaysia, Maldives, Mali, Malta, Mauritania, Mauritius, Mexico, Mongolia, Morocco, Mozambique, Nepal, Netherlands, New Zealand, Nicaragua, Niger, Nigeria, Norway, Oman, Pakistan, Panama, Papua New Guinea, Paraguay, Peru, Philippines, Poland, Portugal, Qatar, Romania, Rwanda, Samoa, Sao Tome and Principe, Saudi Arabia, Senegal, Seychelles, Sierra Leone, Singapore, Somalia, Spain, Sri Lanka, Sudan, Suriname, Sweden, Syria, Thailand, Togo, Trinidad and Tobago, Tunisia, Turkey, Uganda, Ukraine, USSR, United Arab Emirates, United Kingdom, United Republic of Tanzania, Uruguay, Venezuela, Viet Nam, Yemen, Yugoslavia, Zambia, Zimbabwe.
Against: 2
Israel, United States.
Abstention: 1
Zaire.
Absent: 12
Antigua and Barbuda, Comoros, Dominica, Grenada, Iran,* Lebanon, Saint Lucia, Saint Vincent, Solomon Islands, St. Christopher and Nevis, Swaziland, Vanuatu.

---

*Later advised the Secretariat it had intended to vote in favour.

Resolution No. 39/146 A, B, C of 14 December 1984

ON THE SITUATION IN THE MIDDLE EAST: CONDEMNING ISRAEL'S POLICIES IN THE OCCUPIED TERRITORIES AND CALLING FOR ITS COMPLETE WITHDRAWAL FROM THEM, DECLARING THE NEED FOR RECOGNITION OF THE RIGHT OF THE PALESTINIAN PEOPLE, UNDER THE LEADERSHIP OF THE PALESTINE LIBERATION ORGANIZATION, TO SELF-DETERMINATION AND AN INDEPENDENT STATE, AND CALLING ON ALL STATES TO PUT AN END TO THE FLOW OF AID TO ISRAEL

A

The General Assembly,

Having discussed the item entitled "The situation in the Middle East",

Reaffirming its resolutions 36/226 A and B of 17 December 1981, ES-9/1 of 5 February 1982, 37/123 F of 20 December 1982 and 38/180 A to D of 19 December 1983,[345]

Recalling Security Council resolutions 425 (1978) of 19 March 1978, 497 (1981) of 17 December 1981, 508 (1982) of 5 June 1982, 509 (1982) of 6 June 1982, 511 (1982) of 18 June 1982, 512 (1982) of 19 June 1982, 513 (1982) of 4 July 1982, 515 (1982) of 29 July 1982, 516 (1982) of 1 August 1982, 517 (1982) of 4 August 1982, 518 (1982) of 12 August 1982, 519 (1982) of 17 August 1982, 520 (1982) of 17 September 1982, 521 (1982) of 19 September 1982, and 555 (1984) of 12 October 1984,

Taking note of the reports of the Secretary-General of 13 March 1984,[346] 13 September 1984,[347] 2 October 1984[348] and 26 October 1984,[349]

Welcoming the world-wide support extended to the just cause of the Palestinian people and the other Arab countries in their struggle against Israeli aggression and occupation in order to achieve a comprehensive, just and lasting peace in the Middle East and the full exercise by the Palestinian people of its inalienable national rights, as affirmed by previous resolutions of the General Assembly relating to the question of Palestine and to the situation in the Middle East,

Gravely concerned that the Palestinian and other Arab territories occupied since 1967, including Jerusalem, still remain under Israeli occupation, that the relevant resolutions of the United Nations have not been implemented and that the Palestinian people is still denied the restoration of its land and the exercise of its inalienable national rights in conformity with international law, as reaffirmed by resolutions of the United Nations,

Reaffirming the applicability of the Geneva Convention relative to the Protection of Civilian Persons in Time of War, of 12 August 1949,[350] to all the occupied Palestinian and other Arab territories, including Jerusalem,

Reiterating all relevant United Nations resolutions which emphasize that the acquisition of territory by force is inadmissible under the Charter of the United Nations and the principles of international law and that Israel must withdraw unconditionally from all the Palestinian and other Arab territories occupied by Israel since 1967,

---

[345]The resolutions in this and the next paragraph deal primarily with Israeli policy in Lebanon and the Palestinian dimension of the Middle East conflict. [ed. note]

[346]A/39/130-S/16409. For the printed text, see *Official Records of the Security Council, Thirty-ninth Year, Supplement for January, February and March 1984*, document S/16409.

[347]A/39/130/Add.1-S/16409/Add.1. For the printed text, see *Official Records of the Security Council, Thirty-ninth Year, Supplement for July, August and September 1984*, document S/16409/Add.1.

[348]A/39/533.

[349]A/39/600-S/16792. For the printed text, see *Official Records of the Security Council, Thirty-ninth Year, Supplement for October, November and December 1984*, document S/16792.

[350]United Nations, *Treaty Series*, vol. 75, no. 973, p. 287.

including Jerusalem,

Reaffirming further the imperative necessity of establishing a comprehensive, just and lasting peace in the region, based on full respect for the Charter and the principles of international law,

Gravely concerned also at the continuing Israeli actions involving the escalation and expansion of the conflict in the region, which further violate the principles of international law and endanger international peace and security,

Stressing the great importance of the time factor in the endeavours to achieve a comprehensive, just and lasting peace in the Middle East,

1. *Reaffirms its conviction* that the question of Palestine is the core of the conflict in the Middle East and that no comprehensive, just and lasting peace in the region will be achieved without the full exercise by the Palestinian people of its inalienable national rights and the immediate, unconditional and total withdrawal of Israel from all the Palestinian and other occupied Arab territories;

2. *Reaffirms further* that a just and comprehensive settlement of the situation in the Middle East cannot be achieved without the participation on an equal footing of all the parties to the conflict, including the Palestine Liberation Organization, the representative of the Palestinian people;

3. *Declares once more* that peace in the Middle East is indivisible and must be based on a comprehensive, just and lasting solution of the Middle East problem, under the auspices of the United Nations and on the basis of relevant resolutions of the United Nations, which ensures the complete and unconditional withdrawal of Israel from the Palestinian and other Arab territories occupied since 1967, including Jerusalem, and which enables the Palestinian people, under the leadership of the Palestine Liberation Organization, to exercise its inalienable rights, including the right to return and the right to self-determination, national independence and the establishment of its independent sovereign State in Palestine, in accordance with the resolutions of the United Nations relevant to the question of Palestine, in particular General Assembly resolutions ES-7/2 of 29 July 1980, 36/120 A to F of 10 December 1981, 37/86 A to D of 10 December 1982, 37/86 E of 20 December 1982 and 38/58 A to E of 13 December 1983;

4. *Considers* the Arab Peace Plan adopted unanimously at the Twelfth Arab Summit Conference, held at Fez, Morocco, on 25 November 1981 and from 6 to 9 September 1982,[351] as an important contribution towards the achievement of a comprehensive, just and lasting peace in the Middle East;

5. *Condemns* Israel's continued occupation of the Palestinian and other Arab territories, including Jerusalem, in violation of the Charter of the United Nations, the principles of international law and the relevant resolutions of the United Nations, and demands the immediate, unconditional and total withdrawal of Israel from all the territories occupied since June 1967;

6. *Rejects* all agreements and arrangements which violate the inalienable rights of the Palestinian people and contradict the principles of a just and comprehensive solution to the Middle East problem to ensure the establishment of a just peace in the area;

7. *Deplores* Israel's failure to comply with Security Council resolutions 476 (1980) of 30 June 1980 and 478 (1980) of 20 August 1980 and General Assembly resolutions 35/207 of 16 December 1980 and 36/226 A and B of 17 December 1981, determines that Israel's decision to annex Jerusalem and to declare it as its "capital" as well as the measures to alter its physical character, demographic composition, institutional structure and status are null and void and demands that they be rescinded immediately, and calls upon all Member States, the specialized agencies and all other international organizations to abide by the present resolution and all other relevant resolutions and decisions;

8. *Condemns* Israel's aggression, policies and practices against the Palestinian people in the occupied Palestinian territories and outside these territories, particularly Palestinians in Lebanon, including the expropriation and annexation of territory, the establishment of settlements, assassination attempts and other terrorist, aggressive and repressive measures, which are in violation of the Charter and the principles of international law and the relevant international conventions;

9. *Stongly condemns* the imposition by Israel of its laws, jurisdiction and administration on the occupied Syrian Golan Heights, its annexationist policies and practices, the establishment of settlements, the confiscation of lands, the diversion of water resources and the imposition of Israeli citizenship on Syrian nationals, and declares that all these measures are null and void and constitute a violation of the rules and principles of international law relative to belligerent occupation, in particular the Geneva Convention relative to the Protection of Civilian Persons in Time of War, of 12 August 1949;

10. *Considers* that the agreements on strategic co-operation between the United States of America and Israel signed on 30 November 1981, together with the recent accords concluded in this context, would encourage Israel to pursue its aggressive and expansionist policies and practices in the Palestinian and other Arab territories occupied since 1967, including Jerusalem, would have adverse effects on efforts for the establishment of a comprehensive, just and lasting peace in the Middle East and would threaten the security of the region;

11. *Calls upon* all States to put an end to the flow to Israel of any military, economic and financial aid, as well as of human resources, aimed at encouraging it to pursue its aggressive policies against the Arab countries and the Palestinian people;

12. *Strongly condemns* the continuing and increasing collaboration between Israel and the racist régime of South Africa, especially in the economic, military and nuclear

---

[351] See A/37/696-S/15510, annex.

131

fields, which constitutes a hostile act against the African and Arab States and enables Israel to enhance its nuclear capabilities, thus subjecting the States of the region to nuclear blackmail;

13. *Reaffirms* its call for the convening of an International Peace Conference on the Middle East—as specified in paragraph 5 of the Geneva Declaration on Palestine,[352] adopted on 7 September 1983 by the International Conference on the Question of Palestine—under the auspices of the United Nations and on the basis of relevant resolutions of the United Nations;

14. *Requests* the Secretary-General to report to the Security Council periodically on the development of the situation and to submit to the General Assembly at its fortieth session a comprehensive report covering the developments in the Middle East in all their aspects.

Adopted at the 101st plenary meeting:
In favour: 100
Afghanistan, Albania, Algeria, Angola, Argentina, Bahrain, Bangladesh, Benin, Bhutan, Bolivia, Botswana, Brazil, Brunei Darussalam, Bulgaria, Burkina Faso, Burundi, Byelorussia, Cameroon, Cape Verde, Central African Republic, Chad, China, Colombia, Comoros, Congo, Cuba, Cyprus, Czechoslovakia, Democratic Kampuchea, Democratic Yemen, Djibouti, Ecuador, Egypt, Equatorial Guinea, Ethiopia, Gabon, Gambia, German Democratic Republic, Ghana, Greece, Guinea, Guinea-Bissau, Guyana, Hungary, India, Indonesia, Iran, Iraq, Jordan, Kenya, Kuwait, Lao People's Democratic Republic, Lebanon, Lesotho, Libya, Madagascar, Malaysia, Maldives, Mali, Malta, Mauritania, Mexico, Mongolia, Morocco, Mozambique, Nepal, Nicaragua, Niger, Nigeria, Oman, Pakistan, Peru, Philippines, Poland, Qatar, Romania, Rwanda, Sao Tome and Principe, Saudi Arabia, Senegal, Singapore, Somalia, Sri Lanka, Sudan, Syria, Thailand, Togo, Trinidad and Tobago, Tunisia, Turkey, Uganda, Ukraine, USSR, United Arab Emirates, United Republic of Tanzania, Viet Nam, Yemen, Yugoslavia, Zambia, Zimbabwe.
Against: 16
Australia, Belgium, Canada, Denmark, France, Federal Republic of Germany, Iceland, Ireland, Israel, Italy, Luxembourg, Netherlands, New Zealand, Norway, United Kingdom, United States.
Abstentions: 28
Austria, Bahamas, Barbados, Belize, Burma, Chile, Dominica, Dominican Republic, Fiji, Finland, Guatemala, Haiti, Honduras, Ivory Coast, Jamaica, Japan, Liberia, Malawi, Panama, Papua New Guinea, Paraguay, Portugal, Saint Vincent, Samoa, Spain, Sweden, Uruguay, Venezuela.
Absent: 14
Antigua and Barbuda, Costa Rica, El Salvador, Grenada, Mauritius, Saint Christopher and Nevis, Saint Lucia, Seychelles, Sierra Leone, Solomon Islands, Suriname, Swaziland, Vanuatu, Zaire.

---

[352]*Report of the International Conference on the Question of Palestine, Geneva, 29 August-7 September 1983* (United Nations publication, Sales No. E.83.I.21), chap. I, sect. A.

B

The General Assembly,
Having discussed the item entitled "The situation in the Middle East",
Having considered the report of the Secretary-General of 2 October 1984,[353]
Recalling Security Council resolution 497 (1981) of 17 December 1981,
Reaffirming its resolutions 36/226 B of 17 December 1981, ES-9/1 of 5 February 1982, 37/123 A of 16 December 1982 and 38/180 A of 19 December 1983,
Recalling its resolution 3314 (XXIX) of 14 December 1974, in which it defined an act of aggression, *inter alia,* as "the invasion or attack by the armed forces of a State of the territory of another State, or any military occupation, however temporary, resulting from such invasion or attack, or any annexation by the use of force of the territory of another State or part thereof" and provided that "no consideration of whatever nature, whether political, economic, military or otherwise, may serve as a justification for aggression",
Reaffirming the fundamental principle of the inadmissibility of the acquisition of territory by force,
Reaffirming once more the applicability of the Geneva Convention relative to the Protection of Civilian Persons in Time of War, of 12 August 1949,[354] to the occupied Palestinian and other Arab territories, including Jerusalem,
Noting that Israel's record, policies and actions establish conclusively that it is not a peace-loving Member State and that it has not carried out its obligations under the Charter of the United Nations,
Noting further that Israel has refused, in violation of Article 25 of the Charter, to accept and carry out the numerous relevant decisions of the Security Council, in particular resolution 497 (1981), thus failing to carry out its obligations under the Charter,

1. *Strongly condemns* Israel for its failure to comply with Security Council resolution 497 (1981) and General Assembly resolutions 36/226 B, ES-9/1, 37/123 A and 38/180 A;

2. *Declares once more* that Israel's continued occupation of the Golan Heights and its decision of 14 December 1981 to impose its laws, jurisdiction and administration on the occupied Syrian Golan Heights constitute an act of aggression under the provisions of Article 39 of the Charter of the United Nations and General Assembly resolution 3314 (XXIX);

3. *Declares once more* that Israel's decision to impose its laws, jurisdiction and administration on the occupied Syrian Golan Heights is illegal and therefore null and void and has no validity whatsoever;

4. *Declares* all Israeli policies and practices of, or aimed at, annexation of the occupied Palestinian and other Arab territories, including Jerusalem, to be illegal and in viola-

---

[353]A/39/533.
[354]United Nations, *Treaty Series,* vol. 75, no. 973, p. 287.

Afghanistan, Albania, Algeria, Angola, Antigua and Barbuda, Argentina, Bahamas, Bahrain, Bangladesh, Barbados, Benin, Bhutan, Bolivia, Botswana, Brazil, Brunei Darussalam, Bulgaria, Burkina Faso, Burma, Burundi, Byelorussia, Cameroon, Cape Verde, Central African Republic, Chad, Chile, China, Colombia, Comoros, Congo, Cuba, Cyprus, Czechoslovakia, Democratic Kampuchea, Democratic Yemen, Djibouti, Dominican Republic, Ecuador, Egypt, Equatorial Guinea, Ethiopia, Fiji, Gabon, Gambia, German Democratic Republic, Ghana, Grenada, Guinea, Guinea-Bissau, Guyana, Haiti, Honduras, Hungary, India, Indonesia, Iran, Iraq, Ivory Coast, Jamaica, Jordan, Kenya, Kuwait, Lao People's Democratic Republic, Lebanon, Lesotho, Liberia, Libya, Madagascar, Malaysia, Maldives, Mali, Malta, Mauritania, Mexico, Mongolia, Morocco, Mozambique, Nepal, Nicaragua, Niger, Nigeria, Oman, Pakistan, Panama, Papua New Guinea, Peru, Philippines, Poland, Qatar, Romania, Rwanda, Saint Lucia, Samoa, Sao Tome and Principe, Saudi Arabia, Senegal, Sierra Leone, Singapore, Somalia, Sri Lanka, Sudan, Suriname, Swaziland, Syria, Thailand, Togo, Trinidad and Tobago, Tunisia, Turkey, Uganda, Ukraine, USSR, United Arab Emirates, United Republic of Tanzania, Uruguay, Venezuela, Viet Nam, Yemen, Yugoslavia, Zambia, Zimbabwe.

Against: 17

Australia, Belgium, Canada, Denmark, Finland, France, Federal Republic of Germany, Iceland, Israel, Italy, Luxembourg, Netherlands, New Zealand, Norway, Sweden, United Kingdom, United States.

Abstentions: 7

Austria, Greece, Ireland, Japan, Malawi, Portugal, Spain.

Absent: 13

Belize, Costa Rica, Dominica, El Salvador,* Guatemala, Mauritius, Paraguay, Saint Vincent, Seychelles, Solomon Islands, St. Christopher and Nevis, Vanuatu, Zaire.

---

*Later advised the Secretariat it had intended to vote in favour.

Resolution No. 39/28 A, B of 30 November 1984

ON THE FINANCING OF THE UNITED NATIONS DISENGAGEMENT OBSERVER FORCE

A

The General Assembly,

Having considered the report of the Secretary-General on the financing of the United Nations Disengagement Observer Force,[260] as well as the related report of the Advisory Committee on Administrative and Budgetary Questions,[261]

Bearing in mind Security Council resolutions 350 (1974) of 31 May 1974, 363 (1974) of 29 November 1974, 369 (1975) of 28 May 1975, 381 (1975) of 30 November 1975, 390 (1976) of 28 May 1976, 398 (1976) of 30 November

1976, 408 (1977) of 26 May 1977, 420 (1977) of 30 November 1977, 429 (1978) of 31 May 1978, 441 (1978) of 30 November 1978, 449 (1979) of 30 May 1979, 456 (1979) of 30 November 1979, 470 (1980) of 30 May 1980, 481 (1980) of 26 November 1980, 485 (1981) of 22 May 1981, 493 (1981) of 23 November 1981, 506 (1982) of 26 May 1982, 524 (1982) of 29 November 1982, 531 (1983) of 26 May 1983, 543 (1983) of 29 November 1983, 551 (1984) of 30 May 1984 and 557 (1984) of 28 November 1984,[262]

Recalling its resolutions 3101 (XXVIII) of 11 December 1973, 3211 B (XXIX) of 29 November 1974, 3374 C (XXX) of 2 December 1975, 31/5 D of 22 December 1976, 32/4 C of 2 December 1977, 33/13 D of 8 December 1978, 34/7 C of 3 December 1979, 35/44 of 1 December 1980, 35/45 A of 1 December 1980, 36/66 A of 30 November 1981, 37/38 A of 30 November 1982 and 38/35 A of 1 December 1983,

Reaffirming its previous decisions regarding the fact that, in order to meet the expenditures caused by such operations, a different procedure is required from that applied to meet expenditures of the regular budget of the United Nations,

Taking into account the fact that the economically more developed countries are in a position to make relatively larger contributions and that the economically less developed countries have a relatively limited capacity to contribute towards peace-keeping operations involving heavy expenditures,

Bearing in mind the special responsibilities of the States permanent members of the Security Council in the financing of such operations, as indicated in General Assembly resolution 1874 (S-IV) of 27 June 1963 and other resolutions of the Assembly,

I

Decides to appropriate to the Special Account referred to in section II, paragraph 1, of General Assembly resolution 3211 B (XXIX) the amount of $17,489,496 gross ($17,280,000 net) authorized and apportioned by section III of Assembly resolution 38/35 A for the operation of the United Nations Disengagement Observer Force for the period from 1 June to 30 November 1984, inclusive;

II

1. *Decides* to appropriate to the Special Account an amount of $17,852,500 for the operation of the United Nations Disengagement Observer Force for the period from 1 December 1984 to 31 May 1985, inclusive;

2. *Decides further,* as an *ad hoc* arrangement, without prejudice to the positions of principle that may be taken by Member States in any consideration by the General Assembly of arrangements for the financing of peace-keeping operations, to apportion the amount of $17,852,500 among Member States in accordance with the scheme set

---

[260] A/39/468.

[261] A/39/653.

[262] The resolutions in this and the next paragraph provide for the financing and extension of mandate of UNDOF. [ed. note]

tion of international law and of the relevant United Nations resolutions;

5. *Determines once more* that all actions taken by Israel to give effect to its decision relating to the occupied Syrian Golan Heights are illegal and invalid and shall not be recognized;

6. *Reaffirms its determination* that all relevant provisions of the Regulations annexed to the Hague Convention IV of 1907,[355] and the Geneva Convention relative to the Protection of Civilian Persons in Time of War, of 12 August 1949, continue to apply to the Syrian territory occupied by Israel since 1967, and calls upon the parties thereto to respect and ensure respect of their obligations under these instruments in all circumstances;

7. *Determines once more* that the continued occupation of the Syrian Golan Heights since 1967 and their annexation by Israel on 14 December 1981, following Israel's decision to impose its laws, jurisdiction and administration on that territory, constitute a continuing threat to international peace and security;

8. *Strongly deplores* the negative vote by a permanent member of the Security Council which prevented the Council from adopting against Israel, under Chapter VII of the Charter, the "appropriate measures" referred to in resolution 497 (1981) unanimously adopted by the Council;

9. *Further deplores* any political, economic, financial, military and technological support to Israel that enourages Israel to commit acts of aggression and to consolidate and perpetuate its occupation and annexation of occupied Arab territories;

10. *Firmly emphasizes once more* its demand that Israel, the occupying Power, rescind forthwith its illegal decision of 14 December 1981 to impose its laws, jurisdiction and administration on the Syrian Golan Heights, which resulted in the effective annexation of that territory;

11. *Reaffirms once more* the overriding necessity of the total and unconditional withdrawal by Israel from all the Palestinian and other Arab territories occupied since 1967, including Jerusalem, which is an essential prerequisite for the establishment of a comprehensive and just peace in the Middle East;

12. *Determines once more* that Israel's record, policies and actions confirms that it is not a peace-loving Member State, that it has persistently violated the principles contained in the Charter and that it has carried out neither its obligations under the Charter nor its commitment under General Assembly resolution 273 (III) of 11 May 1949;

13. *Calls once more upon* all Member States to apply the following measures:

(*a*) To refrain from supplying Israel with any weapons and related equipment and to suspend any military assistance that Israel receives from them;

(*b*) To refrain from acquiring any weapons or military equipment from Israel;

(*c*) To suspend economic, financial and technological assistance to and co-operation with Israel;

(*d*) To sever diplomatic, trade and cultural relations with Israel;

14. *Reiterates its call* to all Member States to cease forthwith, individually and collectively, all dealings with Israel in order totally to isolate it in all fields;

15. *Urges* non-Member States to act in accordance with the provisions of the present resolution;

16. *Calls upon* the specialized agencies and other international organizations to conform their relations with Israel to the terms of the present resolution;

17. *Requests* the Secretary-General to report to the General Assembly at its fortieth session on the implementation of the present resolution.

Adopted at the 101st plenary meeting:
In favour: 88
Afghanistan, Albania, Algeria, Angola, Bahrain, Bangladesh, Benin, Bhutan, Botswana, Brunei Darussalam, Bulgaria, Burkina Faso, Burundi, Byelorussia, Cameroon, Cape Verde, Central African Republic, Chad, China, Comoros, Congo, Cuba, Cyprus, Czechoslovakia, Democratic Yemen, Djibouti, Equatorial Guinea, Ethiopia, Gabon, Gambia, German Democratic Republic, Ghana, Greece, Guinea, Guinea-Bissau, Guyana, Hungary, India, Indonesia, Iran, Iraq, Jordan, Kenya, Kuwait, Lao People's Democratic Republic, Lebanon, Lesotho, Libya, Madagascar, Malaysia, Maldives, Mali, Malta, Mauritania, Mexico, Mongolia, Morocco, Mozambique, Nepal, Nicaragua, Niger, Nigeria, Oman, Pakistan, Poland, Qatar, Rwanda, Sao Tome and Principe, Saudi Arabia, Senegal, Seychelles, Somalia, Sri Lanka, Sudan, Syria, Togo, Tunisia, Turkey, Uganda, Ukraine, USSR, United Arab Emirates, United Republic of Tanzania, Viet Nam, Yemen, Yugoslavia, Zambia, Zimbabwe.
Against: 22
Australia, Belgium, Canada, Denmark, Finland, France, Federal Republic of Germany, Haiti, Iceland, Ireland, Israel, Italy, Japan, Liberia, Luxembourg, Netherlands, New Zealand, Norway, Portugal, Sweden, United Kingdom, United States.
Abstentions: 32
Argentina, Austria, Bahamas, Barbados, Belize, Bolivia, Brazil, Burma, Colombia, Dominica, Dominican Republic, Ecuador, Egypt, Fiji, Guatemala, Honduras, Ivory Coast, Jamaica, Malawi, Panama, Papua New Guinea, Paraguay, Peru, Philippines, Saint Vincent, Samoa, Singapore, Spain, Thailand, Trinidad and Tobago, Uruguay, Venezuela.
Absent: 16
Antigua and Barbuda, Chile, Costa Rica, Democratic Kampuchea, El Salvador, Grenada, Mauritius, Romania, Saint Christopher and Nevis, Saint Lucia, Sierra Leone, Solomon Islands, Suriname, Swaziland, Vanuatu, Zaire.

---

[355]Carnegie Endowment for International Peace, *The Hague Conventions and Declarations of 1899 and 1907* (New York, Oxford University Press, 1915), p. 100.

C

The General Assembly,

Recalling its resolutions 36/120 E of 10 December 1981, 37/123 C of 16 December 1982 and 38/180 C of 19 December 1983, in which it determined that all legislative and administrative measures and actions taken by Israel, the occupying Power, which had altered or purported to alter the character and status of the Holy City of Jerusalem, in particular the so-called "Basic Law" on Jerusalem and the proclamation of Jerusalem as the capital of Israel, were null and void and must be rescinded forthwith,

Recalling Security Council resolution 478 (1980) of 20 August 1980, in which the Council, *inter alia,* decided not to recognize the "Basic Law" and called upon those States that had established diplomatic missions at Jerusalem to withdraw such missions from the Holy City,

Having considered the report of the Secretary-General of 2 October 1984,[356]

1. *Declares once more* that Israel's decision to impose its laws, jurisdiction and administration on the Holy City of Jerusalem is illegal and therefore null and void and has no validity whatsoever;

2. *Deplores* the transfer by some States of their diplomatic missions to Jerusalem in violation of Security Council resolution 478 (1980) and their refusal to comply with the provisions of that resolution;

3. *Calls once again upon* those States to abide by the provisions of the relevant United Nations resolutions, in conformity with the Charter of the United Nations;

4. *Requests* the Secretary-General to report to the General Assembly at its fortieth session on the implementation of the present resolution.

Adopted at the 101st plenary meeting:

In favour: 138

Afghanistan, Albania, Algeria, Angola, Argentina, Australia, Austria, Bahamas, Bahrain, Bangladesh, Barbados, Belgium, Belize, Benin, Bhutan, Bolivia, Botswana, Brazil, Brunei Darussalam, Bulgaria, Burkina Faso, Burma, Burundi, Byelorussia, Cameroon, Canada, Cape Verde, Central African Republic, Chad, Chile, China, Colombia, Comoros, Congo, Cuba, Cyprus, Czechoslovakia, Democratic Kampuchea, Democratic Yemen, Denmark, Djibouti, Dominica, Dominican Republic, Ecuador, Egypt, Equatorial Guinea, Ethiopia, Fiji, Finland, France, Gabon, Gambia, German Democratic Republic, Federal Republic of Germany, Ghana, Greece, Guinea, Guinea-Bissau, Guyana, Honduras, Hungary, Iceland, India, Indonesia, Iran, Iraq, Ireland, Italy, Jamaica, Japan, Jordan, Kenya, Kuwait, Lao People's Democratic Republic, Lebanon, Lesotho, Libya, Luxembourg, Madagascar, Malawi, Malaysia, Maldives, Mali, Malta, Mauritania, Mauritius, Mexico, Mongolia, Morocco, Mozambique, Nepal, Netherlands, New Zealand, Nicaragua, Niger, Nigeria, Norway, Oman, Pakistan, Panama, Papua New Guinea, Peru, Philippines, Poland, Portugal, Qatar, Romania, Rwanda, Samoa, Sao Tome and Principe, Saudi Arabia, Senegal, Seychelles, Singapore, Somalia, Spain, Sri Lanka, Sudan, Suriname, Sweden, Syria, Thailand, Togo, Trinidad and Tobago, Tunisia, Turkey, Uganda, Ukraine, USSR, United Arab Emirates, United Kingdom, United Republic of Tanzania, Uruguay, Viet Nam, Yemen, Yugoslavia, Zambia, Zimbabwe.

Against: 1

Israel.

Abstentions: 7

Guatemala, Ivory Coast, Liberia, Paraguay, Saint Vincent, United States, Venezuela.

Absent: 12

Antigua and Barbuda, Costa Rica, El Salvador, Grenada, Haiti, Saint Christopher and Nevis, Saint Lucia, Sierra Leone, Solomon Islands, Swaziland, Vanuatu, Zaire.

Resolution No. 39/147 of 17 December 1984

CONDEMNING ISRAEL'S REFUSAL TO RENOUNCE ANY POSSESSION OF NUCLEAR WEAPONS, AND ITS THREAT TO REPEAT ITS ATTACK ON NUCLEAR FACILITIES IN IRAQ

The General Assembly,

Recalling its previous resolutions on Israeli nuclear armament,

Recalling resolution 38/64 of 15 December 1983, in which, *inter alia,* it called upon all countries of the Middle East, pending the establishment of a nuclear-weapon-free zone in the Middle East, to agree to place all their nuclear activities under International Atomic Energy Agency safeguards, and invited those countries also, pending the establishment of a nuclear-weapon-free zone in the region to declare their support for establishing such a zone and to deposit those declarations with the Security Council,

Considering that the Israeli statements contained in a letter dated 12 July 1984[357] continue to disregard the safeguards system of the International Atomic Energy Agency,

Recalling further Security Council resolution 487 (1981) of 19 June 1981 in which, *inter alia,* the Council called upon Israel urgently to place its nuclear facilities under International Atomic Energy Agency safeguards,

Noting with concern Israel's persistent refusal to commit itself not to manufacture or acquire nuclear weapons, despite repeated calls by the General Assembly, the Security Council and the International Atomic Energy Agency, and to place its nuclear facilities under Agency safeguards,

Conscious of the grave consequences which endanger international peace and security as a result of Israel's development and acquisition of nuclear weapons and Israel's collaboration with South Africa to develop nuclear weapons and their delivery systems,

Recalling its repeated condemnation of nuclear collaboration between Israel and South Africa,

Taking note of the report of the Secretary-General on

---

[356]A/39/533.

[357]A/39/349.

Israeli nuclear armament,[358]

1. *Condemns* Israel's continued refusal to implement Security Council resolution 487 (1981), unanimously adopted by the Council on 19 June 1981, and its refusal to renounce any possession of nuclear weapons;

2. *Requests* the Security Council to take urgent and effective measures to ensure that Israel complies with the resolution and places all its nuclear facilities under International Atomic Energy Agency safeguards;

3. *Requests again* the Security Council to investigate Israel's nuclear activities and the collaboration of other States, parties and institutions in these activities;

4. *Reiterates its request* to the International Atomic Energy Agency to suspend any scientific co-operation with Israel which could contribute to Israel's nuclear capabilities;

5. *Reiterates further* its condemnation of the Israeli threat, in violation of the Charter of the United Nations, to repeat its armed attack on peaceful facilities in Iraq and in other countries;

6. *Reaffirms* its condemnation of the continuing nuclear collaboration between Israel and South Africa;

7. *Requests* the United Nations Institute for Disarmament Research, in co-operation with the Department for Disarmament Affairs of the Secretariat and in consultation with the League of Arab States and the Organization of African Unity, to prepare a report providing data and other relevant information relating to Israeli nuclear armament and further nuclear developments taking into account, *inter alia*, the report of the Secretary-General on Israeli nuclear armament,[359] and to submit it to the General Assembly at its fortieth session;

8. *Requests* the Secretary-General to provide the necessary support to the United Nations Institute for Disarmament Research to enable it to carry out the task entrusted to it under the present resolution and for the Institute to submit a report to the General Assembly at its fortieth session;

9. *Decides* to include in the provisional agenda of its fortieth session the item entitled "Israeli nuclear armament".

Adopted at the 102nd plenary meeting:
In favour: 94

Afghanistan, Albania, Algeria, Angola, Argentina, Bahrain, Bangladesh, Barbados, Benin, Bhutan, Botswana, Brazil, Brunei Darussalam, Bulgaria, Burkina Faso, Burundi, Byelorussia, Cameroon, Cape Verde, Chad, China, Congo, Cuba, Cyprus, Czechoslovakia, Democratic Kampuchea, Democratic Yemen, Djibouti, Egypt, Equatorial Guinea, Ethiopia, Gabon, Gambia, German Democratic Republic, Ghana, Greece, Guinea, Guyana, Hungary, India, Indonesia, Iran, Iraq, Jordan, Kenya, Kuwait, Lao People's Democratic Republic, Lebanon, Lesotho, Libya, Madagascar, Malaysia, Maldives, Mali, Malta, Mauritania,

Mauritius, Mexico, Mongolia, Morocco, Mozambique, Nicaragua, Niger, Nigeria, Oman, Pakistan, Peru, Philippines, Poland, Qatar, Romania, Sao Tome and Principe, Senegal, Seychelles, Sierra Leone, Sri Lanka, Sudan, Suriname, Syria, Thailand, Togo, Trinidad and Tobago, Tunisia, Turkey, Uganda, Ukraine, USSR, United Arab Emirates, United Republic of Tanzania, Venezuela, Viet Nam, Yemen, Yugoslavia, Zambia.

Against: 2

Israel, United States.

Abstentions: 44

Antigua and Barbuda, Australia, Austria, Bahamas, Belgium, Bolivia, Burma, Canada, Chile, Colombia, Costa Rica, Denmark, Dominican Republic, Ecuador, El Salvador, Fiji, Finland, France, Federal Republic of Germany, Haiti, Honduras, Iceland, Ireland, Italy, Ivory Coast, Jamaica, Japan, Liberia, Luxembourg, Malawi, Nepal, Netherlands, New Zealand, Norway, Panama, Paraguay, Portugal, Saint Lucia, Saint Vincent, Spain, Sweden, United Kingdom, Uruguay, Zaire.

Absent: 18

Belize, Central African Republic, Comoros, Dominica, Grenada, Guatemala, Guinea-Bissau,* Papua New Guinea, Rwanda, Samoa, Saudi Arabia,* Singapore, Solomon Islands, Somalia,* St. Christopher and Nevis, Swaziland, Vanuatu, Zimbabwe.

---

*Later advised the Secretariat it had intended to vote in favour.

Resolution No. 39/169 of 17 December 1984

EXPRESSING ALARM AT THE DETERIORATION OF LIVING CONDITIONS IN THE TERRITORIES UNDER ISRAELI OCCUPATION AND AFFIRMING THAT THE OCCUPATION IS CONTRADICTORY TO THE BASIC REQUIREMENTS OF THEIR SOCIAL AND ECONOMIC DEVELOPMENT

The General Assembly,

Recalling the Vancouver Declaration on Human Settlements, 1976,[360] and the relevant recommendations for national action[361] adopted by Habitat: United Nations Conference on Human Settlements,

Recalling also its resolution 38/166 of 19 December 1983,

Gravely alarmed by the continuation of the Israeli settlement policies, which have been declared null and void and a major obstacle to peace,

Recognizing the need to investigate ways and means of arresting the deterioration in the economy of the occupied Palestinian territories,

1. *Takes note with concern* of the report of the Secretary-General on the living conditions of the Palestinian people in the occupied Palestinian territories;[362]

2. *Takes note also* of the statement made on 29 October

---

[358]A/39/435.
[359]A/37/434.
[360]*Report of Habitat: United Nations Conference on Human Settlements, Vancouver, 31 May-11 June 1976* (United Nations publication, Sales No. E.76.IV.7 and corrigendum), chap. I.
[361]*Ibid.*, chap. II.
[362]A/39/233-E/1984/79.

1984 by the Observer of the Palestine Liberation Organization;[363]

3. *Rejects* the Israeli plans and actions intended to change the demographic composition of the occupied Palestinian territories, particularly the increase and expansion of the Israeli settlements, and other plans and actions creating conditions leading to the displacement and exodus of Palestinians from the occupied Palestinian territories;

4. *Expresses its alarm* at the deterrioration, as a result of the Israeli occupation, in the living conditions of the Palestinian people in the Palestinian territories occupied since 1967;

5. *Affirms* that the Israeli occupation is contradictory to the basic requirements for the social and economic development of the Palestinian people in the occupied Palestinian territories;

6. *Requests* the Secretary-General:

(*a*) To organize, in 1985, a seminar on remedies for the deterioration of the economic and social conditions of the Palestinian people in the occupied Palestinian territories;

(*b*) To make the necessary preparations for the seminar providing for the participation of the Palestine Liberation Organization;

(*c*) To invite experts to present papers to the seminar;

(*d*) To invite also relevant intergovernmental and nongovernmental organizations;

(*e*) To report to the General Assembly at its fortieth session, through the Economic and Social Council, on the seminar.

Adopted at the 103rd plenary meeting:
In favour: 143
Afghanistan, Albania, Algeria, Angola, Argentina, Australia, Austria, Bahamas, Bahrain, Bangladesh, Barbados, Belgium, Benin, Bhutan, Bolivia, Botswana, Brazil, Brunei Darussalam, Bulgaria, Burkina Faso, Burma, Burundi, Byelorussia, Cameroon, Canada, Cape Verde, Central African Republic, Chad, Chile, China, Colombia, Congo, Cuba, Cyprus, Czechoslovakia, Democratic Kampuchea, Democratic Yemen, Denmark, Djibouti, Dominican Republic, Ecuador, Egypt, El Salvador, Equatorial Guinea, Ethiopia, Fiji, Finland, France, Gambia, German Democratic Republic, Federal Republic of Germany, Ghana, Greece, Guatemala, Guinea, Guinea-Bissau, Guyana, Haiti, Honduras, Hungary, Iceland, India, Indonesia, Iran, Iraq, Ireland, Italy, Jamaica, Japan, Jordan, Kenya, Kuwait, Lao People's Democratic Republic, Lebanon, Lesotho, Liberia, Libya, Luxembourg, Madagascar, Malawi, Malaysia, Maldives, Mali, Malta, Mauritania, Mauritius, Mexico, Mongolia, Morocco, Mozambique, Nepal, Netherlands, New Zealand, Nicaragua, Niger, Nigeria, Norway, Oman, Pakistan, Panama, Papua New Guinea, Paraguay, Peru, Philippines, Poland, Portugal, Qatar, Romania, Rwanda, Samoa, Sao Tome and Principe, Saudi Arabia, Senegal, Sierra Leone, Singapore, Somalia, Spain, Sri Lanka, Su-

dan, Suriname, Swaziland, Sweden, Syria, Thailand, Togo, Trinidad and Tobago, Tunisia, Turkey, Uganda, Ukraine, USSR, United Arab Emirates, United Kingdom, United Republic of Tanzania, Uruguay, Vanuatu, Venezuela, Viet Nam, Yemen, Yugoslavia, Zaire, Zambia, Zimbabwe.
Against: 2
Israel, United States.
Abstentions: 2
Gabon, Ivory Coast.
Absent: 11
Antigua and Barbuda, Belize, Comoros, Costa Rica, Dominica, Grenada, Saint Lucia, Saint Vincent, Seychelles, Solomon Islands, St. Christopher and Nevis.

Resolution No. 39/197 of 17 December 1984

CALLING FOR ASSISTANCE FOR THE RECONSTRUCTION AND DEVELOPMENT OF LEBANON

The General Assembly,

Recalling its resolutions 33/146 of 20 December 1978, 34/135 of 14 December 1979, 35/85 of 5 December 1980, 36/205 of 17 December 1981, 37/163 of 17 December 1982, 38/220 of 20 December 1983 on assistance for the reconstruction and development of Lebanon,

Recalling also Economic and Social Council resolution 1980/15 of 29 April 1980 and decisions 1983/112 of 17 May 1983 and 1984/174 of 26 July 1984,

Noting with deep concern the continuing heavy loss of life and the additional destruction of property, which have caused further extensive damage to the economic and social structures of Lebanon,

Also noting with concern the serious economic situation in Lebanon,

Welcoming the determined efforts of the Government of Lebanon in undertaking its reconstruction and rehabilitation programme,

Reaffirming the urgent need for further international action to assist the Government of Lebanon in its continuing efforts for reconstruction and development,

Taking note of the report of the Secretary-General[364] and of the statement made on 6 November 1984 by the United Nations Co-ordinator of Assistance for the Reconstruction and Development of Lebanon,[365]

1. *Expresses its appreciation* to the Secretary-General for his report and for the steps he has taken to mobilize assistance to Lebanon;

2. *Commends* the United Nations Co-ordinator of Assistance for the Reconstruction and Development of Lebanon and his staff for their valuable and unstinting efforts in the discharge of their duties;

3. *Expresses its appreciation* for the relentless efforts undertaken by the Government of Lebanon in the implementation of the initial phase of reconstruction of the

[363]*Official Records of the General Assembly, Thirty-ninth Session, Second Committee,* 26th meeting, paras. 51-55.

[364]A/39/390.
[365]See *Official Records of the General Assembly, Thirty-ninth Session, Second Committee,* 37th meeting, paras. 15-24.

country, despite adverse circumstances, and for the steps it has taken to remedy the economic situation;

4. *Requests* the Secretary-General to continue and intensify his efforts to mobilize all possible assistance within the United Nations system to help the Government of Lebanon in its reconstruction and development efforts;

5. *Requests* the organs, organizations and bodies of the United Nations system to intensify their programmes of assistance and to expand them in response to the needs of Lebanon;

6. *Also requests* the Secretary-General to report to the Economic and Social Council at its second regular session of 1985 and to the General Assembly at its fortieth session on the progress achieved in the implementation of the present resolution.

Adopted at the 103rd plenary meeting without a vote.

Resolution No. 39/223 of 18 December 1984

CALLING FOR THE LIFTING OF ISRAELI RESTRICTIONS ON THE ECONOMY OF THE OCCUPIED PALESTINIAN TERRITORIES, AND CALLING FOR THE ESTABLISHMENT OF A SEAPORT IN THE OCCUPIED GAZA STRIP

The General Assembly,

Aware of the Israeli restrictions imposed on the foreign trade of the occupied Palestinian territories,

Aware also of the imposed domination of the Palestinian market by Israel,

Taking into account the need to give Palestinian firms and products direct access to external markets without Israeli interference,

1. *Calls* for the urgent lifting of the Israeli restrictions imposed on the economy of the occupied Palestinian territories;

2. *Recognizes* the Palestinian interest in establishing a seaport in the occupied Gaza Strip to give Palestinian firms and products direct access to external markets;

3. *Calls upon* all concerned to facilitate the establishment of a seaport in the occupied Gaza Strip;

4. *Also calls upon* all concerned to facilitate the establishment of a cement plant in the occupied West Bank and a citrus plant in the occupied Gaza Strip;

5. *Requests* the Secretary-General to report to the General Assembly at its fortieth session, through the Economic and Social Council, on the progress made in the implementation of the present resolution.

Adopted at the 104th plenary meeting:
In favour: 138
Afghanistan, Albania, Algeria, Angola, Argentina, Austria, Bahamas, Bahrain, Bangladesh, Barbados, Belgium, Benin, Bhutan, Bolivia, Botswana, Brazil, Brunei Darussalam, Bulgaria, Burkina Faso, Burma, Burundi, Byelorussia, Cape Verde, Chad, Chile, China, Colombia, Congo, Costa Rica, Cuba, Cyprus, Czechoslovakia, Democratic Kampuchea, Democratic Yemen, Denmark, Djibouti, Dominican Republic, Ecuador, Egypt, El Salvador, Equatorial Guinea, Ethiopia, Fiji, France, Gabon, Gambia, German Democratic Republic, Federal Republic of Germany,

Ghana, Greece, Guatemala, Guinea, Guinea-Bissau, Guyana, Haiti, Honduras, Hungary, India, Indonesia, Iran, Iraq, Ireland, Italy, Ivory Coast, Jamaica, Japan, Jordan, Kenya, Kuwait, Lao People's Democratic Republic, Lebanon, Lesotho, Liberia, Libya, Luxembourg, Madagascar, Malawi, Malaysia, Maldives, Mali, Malta, Mauritania, Mauritius, Mexico, Mongolia, Morocco, Mozambique, Nepal, Netherlands, New Zealand, Nicaragua, Niger, Nigeria, Oman, Pakistan, Panama, Papua New Guinea, Peru, Philippines, Poland, Portugal, Qatar, Romania, Rwanda, Saint Vincent, Samoa, Sao Tome and Principe, Saudi Arabia, Senegal, Sierra Leone, Singapore, Somalia, Spain, Sri Lanka, Sudan, Suriname, Swaziland, Syria, Thailand, Togo, Trinidad and Tobago, Tunisia, Turkey, Uganda, Ukraine, USSR, United Arab Emirates, United Kingdom, United Republic of Tanzania, Uruguay, Vanuatu, Venezuela, Viet Nam, Yemen, Yugoslavia, Zaire, Zambia, Zimbabwe.

Against: 2
Israel, United States.

Abstentions: 7
Australia, Canada, Finland, Iceland, Norway, Paraguay, Sweden.

Absent: 11
Antigua and Barbuda, Belize, Cameroon, Central African Republic, Comoros, Dominica, Grenada, Saint Lucia, Seychelles, Solomon Islands, St. Christopher and Nevis.

Resolution No. 39/224 of 18 December 1984

CALLING FOR THE PROVISION OF ECONOMIC AND SOCIAL ASSISTANCE TO THE PALESTINIAN PEOPLE, AND REQUESTING THAT UNITED NATIONS ASSISTANCE SHOULD BE RENDERED IN COOPERATION WITH THE PALESTINE LIBERATION ORGANIZATION

The General Assembly,

Recalling its resolution 38/145 of 19 December 1983,

Recalling also Economic and Social Council resolution 1984/56 of 25 July 1984,

Recalling further the Programme of Action for the Achievement of Palestinian Rights, adopted by the International Conference on the Question of Palestine,[366]

Noting the need to provide economic and social assistance to the Palestinian people,

1. *Takes note* of the report of the Secretary-General on assistance to the Palestinian people;[367]

2. *Takes note also* of the report of the Secretary-General[368] concerning the meeting on assistance to the Palestinian people which was held at Geneva on 5 and 6 July 1984 in response to General Assembly resolution 38/145;

3. *Expresses its thanks* to the Secretary-General for convening the meeting on assistance to the Palestinian people;

---

[366] *Report of the International Conference on the Question of Palestine, Geneva, 29 August-7 September 1983* (United Nations publication, Sales No. E.83.I.21), chap. I, sect. B.
[367] A/39/265-E/1984/77 and Add. 1.
[368] A/39/474 and Corr.1.

4. *Regards* such a meeting as a valuable opportunity to assess progress in economic and social assistance to the Palestinian people and to explore ways and means of enhancing such assistance;

5. *Draws the attention* of the international community, the United Nations system and intergovernmental and non-governmental organizations to the need to disburse their aid to the occupied Palestinian territories only for the benefit of the Palestinian people and to ensure that it is not used in any manner to serve the interests of the Israeli occupation authorities;

6. *Requests* the Secretary-General:

(*a*) To expedite the finalizing, through existing inter-agency mechanisms, of the co-ordinated programme of economic and social assistance to the Palestinian people requested in General Assembly resolution 38/145;

(*b*) To convene in 1985 a meeting of the relevant programmes, organizations, agencies, funds and organs of the United Nations system to consider the co-ordinated programme of economic and social assistance to the Palestinian people;

(*c*) To provide for the participation in the meeting of the Palestine Liberation Organization, the Arab host countries and relevant intergovernmental and non-governmental organizations;

7. *Requests* the relevant programmes, organizations, agencies, funds and organs of the United Nations system to intensify their efforts, in co-operation with the Palestine Liberation Organization, to provide economic and social assistance to the Palestinian people;

8. *Also requests* that United Nations assistance to the Palestinians in the Arab host countries should be rendered in co-operation with the Palestine Liberation Organization and with the consent of the Arab host Government concerned;

9. *Requests* the Secretary-General to report to the General Assembly at its fortieth session, through the Economic and Social Council, on the progress made in the implementation of the present resolution.

Adopted at the 104th plenary meeting:
In favour: 146
Afghanistan, Albania, Algeria, Angola, Argentina, Australia, Austria, Bahamas, Bahrain, Bangladesh, Barbados, Belgium, Benin, Bhutan, Bolivia, Botswana, Brazil, Brunei Darussalam, Bulgaria, Burkina Faso, Burma, Burundi, Byelorussia, Canada, Cape Verde, Central African Republic, Chad, Chile, China, Colombia, Congo, Costa Rica, Cuba, Cyprus, Czechoslovakia, Democratic Kampuchea, Democratic Yemen, Denmark, Djibouti, Dominican Republic, Ecuador, Egypt, El Salvador, Equatorial Guinea, Ethiopia, Fiji, Finland, France, Gabon, Gambia, German Democratic Republic, Federal Republic of Germany, Ghana, Greece, Guinea, Guinea-Bissau, Guyana, Haiti, Honduras, Hungary, Iceland, India, Indonesia, Iran, Iraq, Ireland, Italy, Ivory Coast, Jamaica, Japan, Jordan, Kenya, Kuwait, Lao People's Democratic Republic, Lebanon, Lesotho, Liberia, Libya, Luxembourg, Madagascar, Malawi, Malaysia, Maldives, Mali, Malta, Mauritania,

Mauritius, Mexico, Mongolia, Morocco, Mozambique, Nepal, Netherlands, New Zealand, Nicaragua, Niger, Nigeria, Norway, Oman, Pakistan, Panama, Papua New Guinea, Peru, Philippines, Poland, Portugal, Qatar, Romania, Rwanda, Saint Lucia, Saint Vincent, Samoa, Sao Tome and Principe, Saudi Arabia, Senegal, Sierra Leone, Singapore, Somalia, Spain, Sri Lanka, St. Christopher and Nevis, Sudan, Suriname, Swaziland, Sweden, Syria, Thailand, Togo, Trinidad and Tobago, Tunisia, Turkey, Uganda, Ukraine, USSR, United Arab Emirates, United Kingdom, United Republic of Tanzania, Uruguay, Vanuatu, Venezuela, Viet Nam, Yemen, Yugoslavia, Zaire, Zambia, Zimbabwe.
Against: 2
Israel, United States.
Abstentions: 0
Absent: 10
Antigua and Barbuda, Belize, Cameroon, Comoros, Dominica, Grenada, Guatemala, Paraguay, Seychelles, Solomon Islands.

Decision No. 39/442 of 18 December 1984

ON ISRAELI ECONOMIC PRACTICES IN THE OCCUPIED TERRITORIES

At its 104th plenary meeting, on 18 December 1984, the General Assembly, on the recommendation of the Second Committee,[369] requested the Secretary-General to submit to the Assembly at its fortieth session, through the Economic and Social Council, the comparative study on the Israeli practices in the occupied Palestinian and other Arab territories and its obligations under international law, requested in Assembly resolution 38/144 of 19 December 1983 as adopted.

Adopted at the 104th plenary meeting:
In favour: 145
Afghanistan, Albania, Algeria, Angola, Argentina, Australia, Austria, Bahamas, Bahrain, Bangladesh, Barbados, Belgium, Benin, Bhutan, Bolivia, Botswana, Brazil, Brunei Darussalam, Bulgaria, Burkina Faso, Burma, Burundi, Byelorussia, Canada, Cape Verde, Central African Republic, Chad, Chile, China, Colombia, Congo, Costa Rica, Cuba, Cyprus, Czechoslovakia, Democratic Kampuchea, Democratic Yemen, Denmark, Djibouti, Dominican Republic, Ecuador, Egypt, El Salvador, Equatorial Guinea, Ethiopia, Fiji, Finland, France, Gabon, Gambia, German Democratic Republic, Federal Republic of Germany, Ghana, Greece, Guatemala, Guinea, Guinea-Bissau, Guyana, Haiti, Honduras, Hungary, Iceland, India, Indonesia, Iran, Iraq, Ireland, Italy, Ivory Coast, Jamaica, Japan, Jordan, Kenya, Kuwait, Lao People's Democratic Republic, Lebanon, Lesotho, Liberia, Libya, Luxembourg, Madagascar, Malawi, Malaysia, Maldives, Mali, Malta, Mauritania, Mexico, Mongolia, Morocco, Mozambique, Nepal,

[369]*Official Records of the General Assembly, Thirty-ninth Session, Annexes,* agenda item 12, document A/39/789, para. 49.

Netherlands, New Zealand, Nicaragua, Niger, Nigeria, Norway, Oman, Pakistan, Panama, Papua New Guinea, Paraguay, Peru, Philippines, Poland, Portugal, Qatar, Romania, Rwanda, Saint Vincent, Samoa, Sao Tome and Principe, Saudi Arabia, Senegal, Sierra Leone, Singapore, Somalia, Spain, Sri Lanka, Sudan, Suriname, Swaziland, Sweden, Syria, Thailand, Togo, Trinidad and Tobago, Tunisia, Turkey, Uganda, Ukraine, USSR, United Arab Emirates, United Kingdom, United Republic of Tanzania, Uruguay, Vanuatu, Venezuela, Viet Nam, Yemen, Yugoslavia, Zaire, Zambia, Zimbabwe.

Against: 2

Israel, United States.

Abstentions: 0

Absent: 11

Antigua and Barbuda, Belize, Cameroon, Comoros, Dominica, Grenada, Mauritius, Saint Lucia, Seychelles, Solomon Islands, St. Christopher and Nevis.

Resolution No. 40/6 of 11 November 1985

CALLING UPON ISRAEL TO PLACE ITS NUCLEAR FACILITIES UNDER INTERNATIONAL ATOMIC ENERGY AGENCY SAFEGUARDS

The General Assembly,

Having considered the item entitled "Armed Israeli aggression against the Iraqi nuclear installations and its grave consequences for the established international system concerning the peaceful uses of nuclear energy, the non-proliferation of nuclear weapons and international peace and security",

Recalling the relevant resolutions of the Security Council and the General Assembly,

Taking note of the relevant resolutions of the International Atomic Energy Agency,

Viewing with deep concern Israel's refusal to comply with Security Council resolution 487 (1981) of 19 June 1981,

Noting with deep concern the threatening statement made by an Israeli cabinet member on 26 March 1985,[370] in which he stated, *inter alia,* "We are prepared to strike against any nuclear reactor built by Iraq in the future",

Deeply alarmed by Israel's failure to state without ambiguity its acceptance of the internationally recognized criteria for the definition of a peaceful nuclear facility and to acknowledge the effectiveness of the safeguards system of the International Atomic Energy Agency as a reliable means of verifying the peaceful operation of nuclear facilities,

Concerned that armed attacks against nuclear facilities raise fears about the safety of present and future nuclear installations,

Aware that all States developing nuclear energy for peaceful purposes need assurances against armed attacks on nuclear facilities,

1. *Strongly condemns* all military attacks on all nuclear installations dedicated to peaceful purposes, including the military attacks by Israel on the nuclear facilities of Iraq;

2. *Considers* that Israel has not yet committed itself not to attack or threaten to attack nuclear facilities in Iraq or elsewhere, including facilities under International Atomic Energy Agency safeguards;

3. *Requests* the Security Council to take urgent and effective measures to ensure that Israel complies without further delay with the provisions of resolution 487 (1981);

4. *Requests* the International Atomic Energy Agency to consider additional measures effectively to ensure that Israel undertakes not to attack or threaten to attack peaceful nuclear facilities in Iraq or elsewhere, in violation of the Charter of the United Nations and in disregard of the safeguards system of the International Atomic Energy Agency;

5. *Calls upon* Israel urgently to place all its nuclear facilities under International Atomic Energy Agency safeguards in accordance with resolution 487 (1981) adopted unanimously by the Security Council;

6. *Reaffirms* that Iraq is entitled to compensation for the damage it has suffered as a result of the Israeli armed attack on 7 June 1981;

7. *Urges* all Member States to provide necessary technical assistance to Iraq to restore its peaceful nuclear programme and to overcome the damage caused by the Israeli attack;

8. *Calls upon* all States and organizations that have not yet done so to discontinue co-operating with and giving assistance to Israel in the nuclear field;

9. *Requests* the Conference on Disarmament to continue negotiations with a view to an immediate conclusion of the agreement on the prohibition of military attacks on nuclear facilities as a contribution to promoting and ensuring the safe development of nuclear energy for peaceful purposes;

10. *Decides* to include in the provisional agenda of its forty-first session the item entitled "Armed Israeli aggression against the Iraqi nuclear installations and its grave consequences for the established international system concerning the peaceful uses of nuclear energy, the non-proliferation of nuclear weapons and international peace and security".

Adopted at the 59th plenary meeting:

In favour: 88

Afghanistan, Albania, Algeria, Angola, Bahrain, Bangladesh, Benin, Bhutan, Brazil, Brunei Darussalam, Bulgaria, Burkina Faso, Burundi, Byelorussia, Cape Verde, Central African Republic, Chad, China, Comoros, Congo, Cuba, Cyprus, Czechoslovakia, Democratic Kampuchea, Democratic Yemen, Djibouti, Egypt, Gabon, German Democratic Republic, Ghana, Guinea, Guinea-Bissau, Guyana, Hungary, India, Indonesia, Iran, Iraq, Jordan, Kenya, Kuwait, Lao People's Democratic Republic, Lebanon, Lesotho, Libya, Madagascar, Malaysia, Maldives, Mali, Malta, Mauritania, Mauritius, Mongolia, Morocco, Mozambique, Nepal, Nicaragua, Niger, Nigeria, Oman, Paki-

---

[370]See A/40/283, annex.

stan, Peru, Philippines, Poland, Qatar, Romania, Rwanda, Saudi Arabia, Senegal, Seychelles, Somalia, Sri Lanka, Sudan, Syria, Togo, Trinidad and Tobago, Tunisia, Turkey, Uganda, Ukraine, USSR, United Arab Emirates, United Republic of Tanzania, Viet Nam, Yemen, Yugoslavia, Zambia, Zimbabwe.

Against: 13

Belgium, Canada, Denmark, Finland, Federal Republic of Germany, Iceland, Israel, Luxembourg, Netherlands, Norway, Sweden, United Kingdom, United States.

Abstentions: 39

Antigua and Barbuda, Argentina, Australia, Austria, Barbados, Bolivia, Cameroon, Chile, Colombia, Costa Rica, Dominican Republic, Ecuador, Equatorial Guinea, Fiji, France, Greece, Grenada, Guatemala, Haiti, Ireland, Italy, Ivory Coast, Jamaica, Japan, Liberia, Malawi, Mexico, New Zealand, Panama, Papua New Guinea, Paraguay, Portugal, Saint Vincent, Samoa, Solomon Islands, Spain, Uruguay, Venezuela, Zaire.

Absent: 18

Bahamas, Belize, Botswana, Burma, Dominica, El Salvador, Ethiopia, Gambia,* Honduras, Saint Lucia, Sao Tome and Principe, Sierra Leone, Singapore, St. Christopher and Nevis, Suriname, Swaziland, Thailand, Vanuatu.

---

*Later advised the Secretariat it had intended to vote in favour.

Resolution No. 40/25 of 29 November 1985

REAFFIRMING THE RIGHT OF THE PALESTINIAN PEOPLE TO SELF-DETERMINATION AND INDEPENDENCE [EXCERPTS FROM A RESOLUTION ON THE RIGHT OF PEOPLES TO SELF-DETERMINATION]

The General Assembly,

Recalling further its relevant resolutions on the question of Palestine, in particular resolutions 3236 (XXIX) and 3237 (XXIX) of 22 November 1974, 36/120 of 10 December 1981, ES-7/6 of 19 August 1982, 37/86 of 10 December 1982, 38/58 of 13 December 1983 and 39/49 D of 11 December 1984,

Recalling the Geneva Declaration on Palestine and the Programme of Action for the Achievement of Palestinian Rights, adopted by the International Conference on the Question of Palestine,[371]

Considering that the denial of the inalienable rights of the Palestinian people to self-determination, sovereignty, independence and return to Palestine and the repeated acts of aggression by Israel against the people of the region constitute a serious threat to international peace and security,

Deeply shocked and alarmed at the deplorable consequences of the Israeli invasion of Lebanon and recalling all the relevant resolutions of the Security Council, in particular resolutions 508 (1982) of 5 June 1982, 509 (1982) of 6 June 1982, 520 (1982) of 17 September 1982 and 521 (1982) of 19 September 1982,

1. *Calls upon* all States to implement fully and faithfully all the resolutions of the United Nations regarding the exercise of the right to self-determination and independence by peoples under colonial and foreign domination;

2. *Reaffirms* the legitimacy of the struggle of peoples for their independence, territorial integrity, national unity and liberation from colonial domination, *apartheid* and foreign occupation by all available means, including armed struggle;

3. *Reaffirms* the inalienable right of the Namibian people, the Palestinian people and all peoples under foreign and colonial domination to self-determination, national independence, territorial integrity, national unity and sovereignty without foreign interference;

4. *Strongly condemns* those Governments that do not recognize the right to self-determination and independence of all peoples still under colonial domination and alien subjugation, notably the peoples of Africa and the Palestinian people;

5. *Calls* for the full and immediate implementation of the declarations and programmes of action on Namibia and on Palestine adopted by the international conferences on those questions;

21. *Denounces* the collusion between Israel and South Africa and expresses support for the Declaration of the International Conference on the Alliance between South Africa and Israel;[372]

22. *Strongly condemns* the policy of those Western States, Israel and other States whose political, economic, military, nuclear, strategic, cultural and sports relations with the racist minority régime of South Africa encourage that régime to persist in its suppression of the aspirations of peoples to self-determination and independence;

31. *Strongly condemns* the constant and deliberate violations of the fundamental rights of the Palestinian people, as well as the expansionist activities of Israel in the Middle East, which constitute an obstacle to the achievement of self-determination and independence by the Palestinian people and a threat to peace and stability in the region;

32. *Demands* the immediate and unconditional release of all persons detained or imprisoned as a result of their struggle for self-determination and independence, full respect for their fundamental individual rights and compliance with article 5 of the Universal Declaration of Human Rights,[373] under which no one shall be subjected to torture or to cruel, inhuman or degrading treatment;

33. *Urges* all States, the specialized agencies, competent

---

[371]*Report of the International Conference on the Question of Palestine, Geneva, 29 August-7 September 1983* (United Nations publication, Sales No. E.83.I.21), chap. I.

[372]See A/38/311-S/15883, annex.
[373]Resolution 217 A (III).

organizations of the United Nations system and other international organizations to extend their support to the Palestinian people through its sole and legitimate representative, the Palestine Liberation Organization, in its struggle to regain its right to self-determination and independence in accordance with the Charter;

....

Adopted at the 96th plenary meeting:
In favour: 118

Afghanistan, Albania, Algeria, Angola, Argentina, Bahamas, Bahrain, Bangladesh, Barbados, Benin, Bhutan, Bolivia, Botswana, Brazil, Brunei Darussalam, Bulgaria, Burkina Faso, Burma, Burundi, Byelorussia, Cameroon, Cape Verde, Central African Republic, Chad, China, Comoros, Congo, Cuba, Cyprus, Czechoslovakia, Democratic Kampuchea, Democratic Yemen, Djibouti, Dominican Republic, Ecuador, Egypt, Equatorial Guinea, Ethiopia, Fiji, Gabon, German Democratic Republic, Ghana, Grenada, Guinea, Guinea-Bissau, Guyana, Hungary, India, Indonesia, Iran, Iraq, Ivory Coast, Jamaica, Jordan, Kenya, Kuwait, Lao People's Democratic Republic, Lebanon, Lesotho, Liberia, Libya, Madagascar, Malawi, Malaysia, Maldives, Mali, Malta, Mauritania, Mauritius, Mexico, Mongolia, Morocco, Mozambique, Nicaragua, Niger, Nigeria, Oman, Pakistan, Panama, Papua New Guinea, Peru, Philippines, Poland, Qatar, Romania, Rwanda, Saint Lucia, Samoa, Sao Tome and Principe, Saudi Arabia, Senegal, Seychelles, Sierra Leone, Singapore, Somalia, Sri Lanka, Sudan, Suriname, Swaziland, Syria, Thailand, Togo, Trinidad and Tobago, Tunisia, Turkey, Uganda, Ukraine, USSR, United Arab Emirates, United Republic of Tanzania, Uruguay, Venezuela, Viet Nam, Yemen, Yugoslavia, Zaire, Zambia, Zimbabwe.

Against: 17

Australia, Belgium, Canada, Denmark, Finland, France, Federal Republic of Germany, Iceland, Israel, Italy, Luxembourg, Netherlands, New Zealand, Norway, Sweden, United Kingdom, United States.

Abstentions: 9

Austria, El Salvador, Greece, Guatemala, Honduras, Ireland, Japan, Portugal, Spain.

Absent: 14

Antigua and Barbuda,* Belize, Chile, Colombia,* Costa Rica, Dominica, Gambia, Haiti, Nepal, Paraguay, Saint Vincent, Solomon Islands, St. Christopher and Nevis, Vanuatu.

_____

* Later advised the Secretariat that it had not intended to vote in favour.

Resolution No. 40/59 A, B of 2 December 1985

ON THE FINANCING OF THE UNITED NATIONS DISENGAGEMENT OBSERVER FORCE

A

The General Assembly,
Having considered the report of the Secretary-General on the financing of the United Nations Disengagement Observer Force,[374] as well as the related report of the Advisory Committee on Administrative and Budgetary Questions,[375]

Bearing in mind Security Council resolutions 350 (1974) of 31 May 1974, 363 (1974) of 29 November 1974, 369 (1975) of 28 May 1975, 381 (1975) of 30 November 1975, 390 (1976) of 28 May 1976, 398 (1976) of 30 November 1976, 408 (1977) of 26 May 1977, 420 (1977) of 30 November 1977, 429 (1978) of 31 May 1978, 441 (1978) of 30 November 1978, 449 (1979) of 30 May 1979, 456 (1979) of 30 November 1979, 470 (1980) of 30 May 1980, 481 (1980) of 26 November 1980, 485 (1981) of 22 May 1981, 493 (1981) of 23 November 1981, 506 (1982) of 26 May 1982, 524 (1982) of 29 November 1982, 531 (1983) of 26 May 1983, 543 (1983) of 29 November 1983, 551 (1984) of 30 May 1984, 557 (1984) of 28 November 1984, 563 (1985) of 21 May 1985 and 576 (1985) of 21 November 1985,[376]

Recalling its resolutions 3101 (XXVIII) of 11 December 1973, 3211 B (XXIX) of 29 November 1974, 3374 C (XXX) of 2 December 1975, 31/5 D of 22 December 1976, 32/4 C of 2 December 1977, 33/13 D of 8 December 1978, 34/7 C of 3 December 1979, 35/44 of 1 December 1980, 35/45 A of 1 December 1980, 36/66 A of 30 November 1981, 37/38 A of 30 November 1982, 38/35 A of 1 December 1983 and 39/28 A of 30 November 1984,

Reaffirming its previous decisions regarding the fact that, in order to meet the expenditures caused by such operations, a different procedure is required from that applied to meet expenditures of the regular budget of the United Nations,

Taking into account the fact that the economically more developed countries are in a position to make relatively larger contributions and that the economically less developed countries have a relatively limited capacity to contribute towards peace-keeping operations involving heavy expenditures,

Bearing in mind the special responsibilities of the States permanent members of the Security Council in the financing of such operations, as indicated in General Assembly resolution 1874 (S-IV) of 27 June 1983 and other resolutions of the Assembly,

I

Decides to appropriate to the Special Account referred to in section II, paragraph 1, of General Assembly resolution 3211 B (XXIX) the amount of $17,852,496 gross ($17,592,000 net) authorized and apportioned by section III of Assembly resolution 39/28 A for the operation of the United Nations Disengagement Observer Force for the period from 1 June to 30 November 1985, inclusive;

II

1. *Decides* to appropriate to the Special Account an

_____

[374]A/40/754.
[375]A/40/948.
[376]The resolutions cited in this paragraph and the next provide for the renewed mandate and financing of the United Nations Disengagement Observer Force. [ed. note]

amount of $18,282,000 for the operation of the United Nations Disengagement Observer Force for the period from 1 December 1985 to 31 May 1986, inclusive;

2. *Decides further,* as an *ad hoc* arrangement, without prejudice to the positions of principle that may be taken by Member States in any consideration by the General Assembly of arrangements for the financing of peace-keeping operations, to apportion the amount of $18,282,000 among Member States in accordance with the scheme set out in Assembly resolution 3101 (XXVIII) and the provisions of section II, paragraphs 2(*b*) and 2(*c*), and section V, paragraph 1, of resolution 3374 C (XXX), section V, paragraph 1, of resolution 31/5 D, section V, paragraph 1, of resolution 32/4 C, section V, paragraph 1, of resolution 33/13 D, section V, paragraph 1, of resolution 34/7 C, section V, paragraph 1, of resolution 35/45 A, section V, paragraph 1, of resolution 36/66 A, section V, paragraph 1, of resolution 37/38 A and section V, paragraphs 1 and 2, of resolution 39/28 A; the scale of assessments for the years 1983, 1984 and 1985 shall be applied against a portion thereof, that is $3,047,000 being the amount pertaining on a *pro rata* basis to the month of December 1985, and the scale of assessments for the years 1986, 1987 and 1988 shall be applied against the balance, that is $15,235,000, for the period thereafter;

3. *Decides* that there shall be set off against the apportionment among Member States, as provided in paragraph 2 above, their respective share in the estimated income of $10,000 other than staff assessment income approved for the period from 1 December 1985 to 31 May 1986, inclusive;

4. *Decides* that, in accordance with the provisions of its resolution 973 (X) of 15 December 1955, there shall be set off against the apportionment among Member States, as provided for in paragraph 2 above, their respective share in the Tax Equalization Fund of the estimated staff assessment income of $337,500 approved for the period from 1 December 1985 to 31 May 1986, inclusive;

III

Authorizes the Secretary-General to enter into commitments for the United Nations Disengagement Observer Force at a rate not to exceed $3,047,000 gross ($2,989,083 net) per month for the period from 1 June to 30 November 1986, inclusive, should the Security Council decide to continue the Force beyond the period of six months authorized under its resolution 576 (1985), the said amount to be apportioned among Member States in accordance with the scheme set out in the present resolution;

IV

1. *Stresses* the need for voluntary contributions to the United Nations Disengagement Observer Force, both in cash and in the form of services and supplies acceptable to the Secretary-General;

2. *Requests* the Secretary-General to take all necessary action to ensure that the United Nations Disengagement Observer Force is conducted with a maximum of efficiency and economy.

Adopted at the 99th plenary meeting:
In favour: 96
Argentina, Australia, Austria, Bahrain, Bangladesh, Barbados, Belgium, Bhutan, Bolivia, Botswana, Brazil, Burkina Faso, Burma, Burundi, Cameroon, Canada, Central African Republic, Chad, Chile, China, Colombia, Congo, Cyprus, Denmark, Dominican Republic, Ecuador, Egypt, El Salvador, Ethiopia, Fiji, Finland, France, Federal Republic of Germany, Greece, Guyana, Honduras, Iceland, India, Indonesia, Ireland, Italy, Ivory Coast, Japan, Jordan, Kenya, Kuwait, Madagascar, Malaysia, Mauritania, Mauritius, Mexico, Nepal, Netherlands, New Zealand, Niger, Nigeria, Norway, Oman, Pakistan, Panama, Papua New Guinea, Peru, Philippines, Poland, Portugal, Qatar, Romania, Rwanda, Saint Lucia, Samoa, Saudi Arabia, Senegal, Sierra Leone, Singapore, Somalia, Spain, Sri Lanka, Sudan, Suriname, Swaziland, Sweden, Thailand, Togo, Trinidad and Tobago, Tunisia, Turkey, Uganda, United Arab Emirates, United Kingdom, United States, Uruguay, Venezuela, Viet Nam,* Zaire, Zambia, Zimbabwe.
Against: 2
Albania, Syria.
Abstentions: 13
Afghanistan, Algeria, Benin, Bulgaria, Byelorussia, Cuba, Czechoslovakia, German Democratic Republic, Hungary, Iraq, Morocco, USSR, Yemen.
Absent: 47
Angola, Antigua and Barbuda, Bahamas, Belize, Brunei Darussalam, Cape Verde, Comoros, Costa Rica, Democratic Kampuchea, Democratic Yemen, Djibouti, Dominica, Equatorial Guinea, Gabon, Gambia, Ghana, Grenada, Guatemala, Guinea, Guinea-Bissau, Haiti, Iran, Israel, Jamaica, Lao People's Democratic Republic, Lebanon, Lesotho, Liberia, Libya, Luxembourg, Malawi, Maldives, Mali, Malta, Mongolia, Mozambique, Nicaragua, Paraguay, Saint Vincent, Sao Tome and Principe, Seychelles, Solomon Islands, St. Christopher and Nevis, Ukraine, United Republic of Tanzania, Vanuatu, Yugoslavia.

---

* Later advised the Secretariat it had intended to abstain

B

The General Assembly,
Having regard to the financial position of the Special Account for the United Nations Emergency Force and the United Nations Disengagement Observer Force, as set forth in the report of the Secretary-General,[377] and referring to paragraph 5 of the report of the Advisory Committee on Administrative and Budgetary Questions,[378]

Mindful of the fact that it is essential to provide the United Nations Disengagement Observer Force with the necessary financial resources to enable it to fulfil its responsibilities under the relevant resolutions of the Secu-

---

[377] A/40/754.
[378] A/40/948.

rity Council,

Concerned that the Secretary-General is continuing to face growing difficulties in meeting the obligations of the Forces on a current basis, particularly those due to the Governments of troop-contributing States,

Recalling its resolutions 33/13 E of 14 December 1978, 34/7 D of 17 December 1979, 35/45 B of 1 December 1980, 36/66 B of 30 November 1981, 37/38 B of 30 November 1982, 38/35 B of 1 December 1983 and 39/28 B of 30 November 1984,

Recognizing that, in consequence of the withholding of contributions by certain Member States, the surplus balances in the Special Account for the United Nations Emergency Force and the United Nations Disengagement Observer Force have, in effect, been drawn upon to the full extent to supplement the income received from contributions for meeting expenses of the Forces,

Concerned that the application of the provisions of regulations 5.2(*b*), 5.2(*d*), 4.3 and 4.4 of the Financial Regulations of the United Nations would aggravate the already difficult financial situation of the Forces,

Decides that the provisions of regulations 5.2(*b*), 5.2(*d*), 4.3 and 4.4 of the Financial Regulations of the United Nations shall be suspended in respect of the amount of $3,250,131, which otherwise would have to be surrendered pursuant to those provisions, this amount to be entered into the account referred to in the operative part of General Assembly resolution 33/13 E and held in suspense until a further decision is taken by the Assembly.

Adopted at the 99th plenary meeting:

In favour: 93

Argentina, Australia, Austria, Bahrain, Bangladesh, Barbados, Belgium, Bhutan, Bolivia, Botswana, Brazil, Burkina Faso, Burma, Burundi, Cameroon, Canada, Central African Republic, Chad, Chile, China, Colombia, Congo, Cyprus, Denmark, Dominican Republic, Ecuador, Egypt, El Salvador, Ethiopia, Fiji, Finland, France, Federal Republic of Germany, Greece, Guyana, Honduras, Iceland, India, Indonesia, Ireland, Italy, Ivory Coast, Japan, Jordan, Kenya, Kuwait, Madagascar, Malaysia, Mauritania, Mauritius, Mexico, Nepal, Netherlands, New Zealand, Niger, Nigeria, Norway, Oman, Pakistan, Panama, Papua New Guinea, Peru, Philippines, Poland, Portugal, Qatar, Rwanda, Saint Lucia, Samoa, Saudi Arabia, Senegal, Sierra Leone, Somalia, Spain, Sri Lanka, Sudan, Suriname, Swaziland, Sweden, Thailand, Togo, Trinidad and Tobago, Tunisia, Turkey, Uganda, United Arab Emirates, United Kingdom, United States, Uruguay, Venezuela, Zaire, Zambia, Zimbabwe.

Against: 10

Afghanistan, Albania, Bulgaria, Byelorussia, Cuba, Czechoslovakia, German Democratic Republic, Hungary, Syria, USSR.

Abstentions: 6

Algeria, Benin, Iraq, Morocco, Romania, Yemen.

Absent: 49

Angola, Antigua and Barbuda, Bahamas, Belize, Brunei Darussalam, Cape Verde, Comoros, Costa Rica, Demo-

cratic Kampuchea, Democratic Yemen, Djibouti, Dominica, Equatorial Guinea, Gabon, Gambia, Ghana, Grenada, Guatemala, Guinea, Guinea-Bissau, Haiti, Iran, Israel, Jamaica, Lao People's Democratic Republic, Lebanon, Lesotho, Liberia, Libya, Luxembourg, Malawi, Maldives, Mali, Malta, Mongolia, Mozambique, Nicaragua, Paraguay, Saint Vincent, Sao Tome and Principe, Seychelles, Singapore, Solomon Islands, St. Christopher and Nevis, Ukraine, United Republic of Tanzania, Vanuatu, Viet Nam, Yugoslavia.

Resolution No. 40/61 of 9 December 1985

INVITING STATES TO TAKE MEASURES WITH A VIEW TO THE ELIMINATION OF INTERNATIONAL TERRORISM, AND URGING THEM TO CONTRIBUTE TO THE ELIMINATION OF THE CAUSES UNDERLYING TERRORISM

The General Assembly,

Recalling its resolutions 3034 (XXVII) of 18 December 1972, 31/102 of 15 December 1976, 32/147 of 16 December 1977, 34/145 of 17 December 1979, 36/109 of 10 December 1981 and 38/130 of 19 December 1983,

Recalling also the Declaration on Principles of International Law concerning Friendly Relations and Co-operation among States in accordance with the Charter of the United Nations,[379] the Declaration on the Strengthening of International Security,[380] the Definition of Aggression[381] and relevant instruments on international humanitarian law applicable in armed conflict,

Further recalling the existing international conventions relating to various aspects of the problem of international terrorism, *inter alia,* the Convention on Offences and Certain Other Acts Committed on Board Aircraft, signed at Tokyo on 14 September 1963,[382] the Convention for the Suppression of Unlawful Seizure of Aircraft, signed at The Hague on 16 December 1970,[383] the Convention for the Suppression of Unlawful Acts against the Safety of Civil Aviation, signed at Montreal on 23 September 1971,[384] the Convention on the Prevention and Punishment of Crimes against Internationally Protected Persons, including Diplomatic Agents, signed at New York on 14 December 1973,[385] and the International Convention against the Taking of Hostages, adopted at New York on 17 December 1979,[386]

Deeply concerned about the world-wide escalation of acts of terrorism in all its forms, which endanger or take innocent human lives, jeopardize fundamental freedoms and seriously impair the dignity of human beings,

Taking note of the deep concern and condemnation of

[379]Resolution 2625 (XXV), annex.
[830]Resolution 2734 (XXV).
[381]Resolution 3314 (XXIX), annex.
[382]United Nations, *Treaty Series,* vol. 704, No. 10106, p.219.
[383]*Ibid.,* vol. 860, No. 12325, p. 106.
[384]*United States Treaties and Other International Agreements,* vol. 24, part one (1973), p. 268.
[385]United Nations, *Treaty Series,* vol. 1035, no. 15410, p. 167.
[386]Resolution 34/146, annex.

all acts of international terrorism expressed by the Security Council and the Secretary-General,

Convinced of the importance of expanding and improving international co-operation among States, on a bilateral and multilateral basis, which will contribute to the elimination of acts of international terrorism and their underlying causes and to the prevention and elimination of this criminal scourge,

Reaffirming the principle of self-determination of peoples enshrined in the Charter of the United Nations,

Reaffirming also the inalienable right to self-determination and independence of all peoples under colonial and racist régimes and other forms of alien domination, and upholding the legitimacy of their struggle, in particular the struggle of national liberation movements, in accordance with the purposes and principles of the Charter and of the Declaration on Principles of International Law concerning Friendly Relations and Co-operation among States in accordance with the Charter of the United Nations,

Mindful of the necessity of maintaining and safeguarding the basic rights of the individual in accordance with the relevant international human rights instruments and generally accepted international standards,

Convinced of the importance of the observance by States of their obligations under the relevant international conventions to ensure that appropriate law enforcement measures are taken in connection with the offences addressed in those Conventions,

Expressing its concern that in recent years terrorism has taken on forms that have an increasingly deleterious effect on international relations, which may jeopardize the very territorial integrity and security of States,

Taking note of the report of the Secretary-General,[387]

1. *Unequivocally condemns,* as criminal, all acts, methods and practices of terrorism wherever and by whomever committed, including those which jeopardize friendly relations among States and their security;

2. *Deeply deplores* the loss of innocent human lives which results from such acts of terrorism;

3. *Also deplores* the pernicious impact of acts of international terrorism on relations of co-operation among States, including co-operation for development;

4. *Appeals* to all States that have not yet done so to consider becoming party to the existing international conventions relating to various aspects of international terrorism;

5. *Invites* all States to take all appropriate measures at the national level with a view to the speedy and final elimination of the problem of international terrorism, such as the harmonization of domestic legislation with existing international conventions, the fulfilment of assumed international obligations, and the prevention of the preparation and organization in their respective territories of acts directed against other States;

6. *Calls upon* all States to fulfil their obligations under international law to refrain from organizing, instigating, assisting or participating in terrorist acts in other States, or acquiescing in activities within their territory directed towards the commission of such acts;

7. *Urges* all States not to allow any circumstances to obstruct the application of appropriate law enforcement measures provided for in the relevant conventions to which they are party to persons who commit acts of international terrorism covered by those conventions;

8. *Also urges* all States to co-operate with one another more closely, especially through the exchange of relevant information concerning the prevention and combating of terrorism, the apprehension and prosecution or extradition of the perpetrators of such acts, the conclusion of special treaties and/or the incorporation into appropriate bilateral treaties of special clauses, in particular regarding the extradition or prosecution of terrorists;

9. *Further urges* all States, unilaterally and in co-operation with other States, as well as relevant United Nations organs, to contribute to the progressive elimination of the causes underlying international terrorism and to pay special attention to all situations, including colonialism, racism and situations involving mass and flagrant violations of human rights and fundamental freedoms and those involving alien occupation, that may give rise to international terrorism and may endanger international peace and security;

10. *Calls upon* all States to observe and implement the recommendations of the *Ad Hoc* Committee on International Terrorism contained in its report to the General Assembly at its thirty-fourth session;[388]

11. *Also calls upon* all States to take all appropriate measures, as recommended by the International Civil Aviation Organization and as set forth in relevant international conventions, to prevent terrorist attacks against civil aviation transport and other forms of public transport;

12. *Encourages* the International Civil Aviation Organization to continue its efforts aimed at promoting universal acceptance of and strict compliance with the international air security conventions;

13. *Requests* the International Maritime Organization to study the problem of terrorism aboard or against ships with a view to making recommendations on appropriate measures;

14. *Requests* the Security-General to follow up, as appropriate, the implementation of the present resolution and to submit a report to the General Assembly at its forty-second session;

15. *Decides* to include the item in the provisional agenda of its forty-second session.

Adopted at the 108th plenary meeting without a vote.

---

[387] A/40/445 and Add.1 and 2.

[388] *Official Records of the General Assembly, Thirty-fourth Session, Supplement No. 37* (A/34/37).

Resolution No. 40/64 A, E of 10 December 1985

CONDEMNING COLLABORATION BETWEEN ISRAEL AND SOUTH AFRICA (EXCERPTS FROM A RESOLUTION CONDEMNING THE POLICIES OF APARTHEID OF THE GOVERNMENT OF SOUTH AFRICA)

A

COMPREHENSIVE SANCTIONS AGAINST THE RACIST REGIME OF SOUTH AFRICA

The General Assembly,

....

Expressing its grave concern at the continued violation of the arms embargo as well as nuclear collaboration by certain Western States and Israel with the racist régime of South Africa,

....

19. *Requests and authorizes* the Special Committee against *Apartheid* to redouble its efforts and intensify its activities for the total isolation of the *apartheid* régime, for promoting comprehensive and mandatory sanctions against South Africa and for mobilizing public opinion and encouraging public action against collaboration with South Africa;

20. *Further requests* the Special Committee to keep the matter of collaboration between South Africa and Israel and between South Africa and any other State under constant review and to report to the General Assembly and the Security Council as appropriate.

Adopted at the 111th plenary meeting:

In favour: 122

Afghanistan, Albania, Algeria, Angola, Antigua and Barbuda, Argentina, Bahamas, Bahrain, Bangladesh, Barbados, Belize, Benin, Bhutan, Bolivia, Brazil, Brunei Darussalam, Bulgaria, Burkina Faso, Burma, Burundi, Byelorussia, Cameroon, Cape Verde, Central African Republic, Chad, China, Colombia, Comoros, Congo, Costa Rica, Cuba, Cyprus, Czechoslovakia, Democratic Kampuchea, Democratic Yemen, Djibouti, Dominican Republic, Ecuador, Egypt, El Salvador, Equatorial Guinea, Ethiopia, Gabon, Gambia, German Democratic Republic, Ghana, Guatemala, Guinea, Guinea-Bissau, Guyana, Haiti, Honduras, Hungary, India, Indonesia, Iran, Iraq, Jamaica, Jordan, Kenya, Kuwait, Lao People's Democratic Republic, Lebanon, Liberia, Libya, Madagascar, Malaysia, Maldives, Mali, Malta, Mauritania, Mauritius, Mexico, Mongolia, Morocco, Mozambique, Nepal, Nicaragua, Niger, Nigeria, Oman, Pakistan, Panama, Papua New Guinea, Peru, Philippines, Poland, Qatar, Romania, Rwanda, Saint Lucia, Saint Vincent, Sao Tome and Principe, Saudi Arabia, Senegal, Seychelles, Sierra Leone, Singapore, Somalia, Sri Lanka, Sudan, Suriname, Syria, Thailand, Togo, Trinidad and Tobago, Tunisia, Turkey, Uganda, Ukraine, USSR, United Arab Emirates, United Republic of Tanzania, Uruguay, Vanuatu, Venezuela, Viet Nam, Yemen, Yugoslavia, Zaire, Zambia, Zimbabwe.

Against: 18

Belgium, Canada, Denmark, France, Federal Republic of Germany, Grenada, Iceland, Ireland, Israel, Italy, Japan, Luxembourg, Netherlands, Norway, Portugal, Spain, United Kingdom, United States.

Abstentions: 14

Australia, Austria, Botswana, Fiji, Finland, Greece, Ivory Coast, Lesotho, Malawi, New Zealand, Samoa, Solomon Islands, Swazilnd, Sweden.

Absent: 4

Chile, Dominica, Paraguay, St. Christopher and Nevis.

E

RELATIONS BETWEEN ISRAEL AND SOUTH AFRICA

The General Assembly,

Reaffirming its resolutions on relations between Israel and South Africa,

Having considered the special report of the Special Committee against *Apartheid* on recent developments concerning relations between Israel and South Africa,[389]

Noting with appreciation the efforts of the Special Committee to expose the increasing and continuing collaboration between Israel and South Africa,

Reiterating that the increasing collaboration by Israel with the racist régime of South Africa, especially in the military and nuclear fields, in defiance of resolutions of the General Assembly and the Security Council is a serious hindrance to international action for the eradication of *apartheid*, an encouragement to the racist régime of South Africa to persist in its criminal policy of *apartheid* and a hostile act against the oppressed people of South Africa and the entire African continent and constitutes a threat to international peace and security,

1. *Commends* the Special Committee against *Apartheid* for publicizing the growing relations between Israel and South Africa and promoting public awareness of the grave dangers of the alliance between Israel and South Africa;

2. *Again strongly condemns* the continuing and increasing collaboration of Israel with the racist régime of South Africa, especially in the military and nuclear fields;

3. *Demands* that Israel desist from and terminate all forms of collaboration with South Africa forthwith, particularly in the military and nuclear fields, and abide scrupulously by the relevant resolutions of the General Assembly and the Security Council;

4. *Calls upon* all Governments and organizations in a position to do so to exert their influence to persuade Israel to desist from such collaboration;

5. *Requests* the Special Committee to continue to publicize, as widely as possible, information on the relations between Israel and South Africa;

6. *Again requests* the Secretary-General to render, through the Department of Public Information and the Centre against *Apartheid* of the Secretariat, all possible assistance to the Special Committee in disseminating information relating to the collaboration between Israel and South Africa;

7. *Further requests* the Special Committee to keep the

---

[389]*Ibid.*, document A/40/22/Add.2.

matter under constant review and to report to the General Assembly and the Security Council as appropriate.

Adopted at the 111th plenary meeting:
In favour: 102
Afghanistan, Albania, Algeria, Angola, Argentina, Bahrain, Bangladesh, Benin, Bhutan, Bolivia, Botswana, Brazil, Brunei Darussalam, Bulgaria, Burkina Faso, Burundi, Byelorussia, Cape Verde, Central African Republic, Chad, China, Comoros, Congo, Cuba, Cyprus, Czechoslovakia, Democratic Kampuchea, Democratic Yemen, Djibouti, Ecuador, Egypt, Ethiopia, Gabon, Gambia, German Democratic Republic, Ghana, Guinea, Guinea-Bissau, Guyana, Haiti, Hungary, India, Indonesia, Iran, Iraq, Jordan, Kenya, Kuwait, Lao People's Democratic Republic, Lebanon, Lesotho, Libya, Madagascar, Malaysia, Maldives, Mali, Malta, Mauritania, Mauritius, Mexico, Mongolia, Morocco, Mozambique, Nicaragua, Niger, Nigeria, Oman, Pakistan, Papua New Guinea, Peru, Philippines, Poland, Qatar, Romania, Rwanda, Sao Tome and Principe, Saudi Arabia, Senegal, Seychelles, Sierra Leone, Singapore, Somalia, Sri Lanka, Sudan, Suriname, Syria, Thailand, Togo, Tunisia, Turkey, Uganda, Ukraine, USSR, United Arab Emirates, United Republic of Tanzania, Vanuatu, Venezuela, Viet Nam, Yemen, Yugoslavia, Zambia, Zimbabwe.
Against: 20
Australia, Austria, Belgium, Canada, Denmark, Finland, France, Federal Republic of Germany, Grenada, Iceland, Ireland, Israel, Italy, Luxembourg, Netherlands, New Zealand, Norway, Sweden, United Kingdom, United States.
Abstentions: 30
Bahamas, Barbados, Belize, Burma, Cameroon, Chile, Colombia, Costa Rica, Dominican Republic, Equatorial Guinea, Fiji, Greece, Guatemala, Honduras, Ivory Coast, Jamaica, Japan, Liberia, Malawi, Nepal, Panama, Portugal, Saint Lucia, Saint Vincent, Samoa, Solomon Islands, Spain, Swaziland, Uruguay, Zaire.
Absent: 6
Antigua and Barbuda, Dominica, El Salvador, Paraguay, St. Christopher and Nevis, Trinidad and Tobago.

Resolution No. 40/82 of 12 December 1985

CALLING UPON ALL COUNTRIES OF THE MIDDLE EAST TO PLACE THEIR NUCLEAR ACTIVITIES UNDER INTERNATIONAL ATOMIC ENERGY AGENCY SAFEGUARDS

The General Assembly,

Recalling its resolutions 3263 (XXIX) of 9 December 1974, 3474 (XXX) of 11 December 1975, 31/71 of 10 December 1976, 32/82 of 12 December 1977, 33/64 of 14 December 1978, 34/77 of 11 December 1979, 35/147 of 12 December 1980, 36/87 of 9 December 1981, 37/75 of 9 December 1982, 38/64 of 15 December 1983 and 39/54 of 12 December 1984 on the establishment of a nuclear-weapon-free zone in the region of the Middle East,

Recalling also the recommendations for the establishment of such a zone in the Middle East consistent with paragraphs 60 to 63, and in particular paragraph 63 (*d*),

of the Final Document of the Tenth Special Session of the General Assembly,[390]

Emphasizing the basic provisions of the above-mentioned resolutions, which call upon all parties directly concerned to consider taking the practical and urgent steps required for the implementation of the proposal to establish a nuclear-weapon-free zone in the region of the Middle East and, pending and during the establishment of such a zone, to declare solemnly that they will refrain, on a reciprocal basis, from producing, acquiring or in any other way possessing nuclear weapons and nuclear explosive devices and from permitting the stationing of nuclear weapons on their territory by any third party, to agree to place all their nuclear facilities under International Atomic Energy Agency safeguards and to declare their support for the establishment of the zone and deposit such declarations with the Security Council for consideration, as appropriate,

Reaffirming the inalienable right of all States to acquire and develop nuclear energy for peaceful purposes,

Emphasizing further the need for appropriate measures on the question of the prohibition of military attacks on nuclear facilities,

Bearing in mind the consensus reached by the General Assembly at its thirty-fifth session that the establishment of a nuclear-weapon-free zone in the region of the Middle East would greatly enhance international peace and security,

Desirous to build on that consensus so that substantial progress can be made towards establishing a nuclear-weapon-free zone in the region of the Middle East,

Emphasizing the essential role of the United Nations in the establishment of a nuclear-weapon-free zone in the region of the Middle East,

Having examined the report of the Secretary-General,[391]

1. *Urges* all parties directly concerned to consider seriously taking the practical and urgent steps required for the implementation of the proposal to establish a nuclear-weapon-free zone in the region of the Middle East in accordance with the relevant resolutions of the General Assembly and, as a means of promoting this objective, invites the countries concerned to adhere to the Treaty on the Non-Proliferation of Nuclear Weapons;[392]

2. *Calls upon* all countries of the region that have not done so, pending the establishment of the zone, to agree to place all their nuclear activities under International Atomic Energy Agency safeguards;

3. *Invites* those countries, pending the establishment of a nuclear-weapon-free zone in the region of the Middle East, to declare their support for establishing such a zone, consistent with the relevant paragraph of the Final Document of the Tenth Special Session of the General Assembly, and to deposit those declarations with the Security Council;

---

[390]Resolution S-10/2.
[391]A/40/442 and Add.1.
[392]Resolution 2373 (XXII), annex.

4. *Further invites* those countries, pending the establishment of the zone, not to develop, produce, test or otherwise acquire nuclear weapons or permit the stationing on their territories, or territories under their control, of nuclear weapons or nuclear explosive devices;

5. *Invites* the nuclear-weapon States and all other States to render their assistance in the establishment of the zone and at the same time to refrain from any action that runs counter to both the letter and spirit of the present resolution;

6. *Extends its thanks* to the Secretary-General for his report containing the views of parties concerned regarding the establishment of a nuclear-weapon-free zone in the region of the Middle East;[393]

7. *Takes note* of the above-mentioned report;

8. *Requests* those parties that have not yet communicated their views to the Secretary-General to do so;

9. *Welcomes* any further comments from those parties that have already communicated their views to the Secretary-General;

10. *Requests* the Secretary-General to submit a report to the General Assembly at its forty-first session on the implementation of the present resolution;

11. *Decides* to include in the provisional agenda of its forty-first session the item entitled "Establishment of a nuclear-weapon-free zone in the region of the Middle East".

Adopted at the 113th plenary meeting without a vote.

Resolution No. 40/93 of 12 December 1985

CONDEMNING ISRAEL'S REFUSAL TO RENOUNCE ANY POSSESSION OF NUCLEAR WEAPONS

The General Assembly,

Bearing in mind its previous resolutions on Israeli nuclear armament, the latest of which is 39/147 of 17 December 1984,

Recalling resolution 39/54 of 12 December 1984, in which, *inter alia*, it called upon all countries of the Middle East, pending the establishment of a nuclear-weapon-free zone in the Middle East, to agree to place all their nuclear activities under International Atomic Energy Agency safeguards,

Recalling further Security Council resolution 487 (1981) of 19 June 1981 in which, *inter alia*, the Council called upon Israel urgently to place its nuclear facilities under International Atomic Energy Agency safeguards,

Noting with grave concern Israel's persistent refusal to commit itself not to manufacture or acquire nuclear weapons, despite repeated calls by the General Assembly, the Security Council and the International Atomic Energy Agency, and to place its nuclear facilities under Agency safeguards,

Aware of the grave consequences that endanger international peace and security as a result of Israel's development and acquisition of nuclear weapons and Israel's collaboration with South Africa to develop nuclear weapons and their delivery systems,

1. *Takes note* of the report of the United Nations Institute for Disarmament Research on this question;[394]

2. *Reiterates its condemnation* of Israel's refusal to renounce any possession of nuclear weapons;

3. *Requests once more* the Security Council to take urgent and effective measures to ensure that Israel complies with Security Council resolution 487 (1981) and places all its nuclear facilities under International Atomic Energy Agency safeguards;

4. *Reiterates its request* to the Security Council to investigate Israel's nuclear activities and the collaboration of other States, parties and institutions in these activities;

5. *Calls upon* all States and organizations that have not yet done so to discontinue co-operating with and giving assistance to Israel in the nuclear field;

6. *Reaffirms its condemnation* of the continuing nuclear collaboration between Israel and South Africa;

7. *Requests* the Secretary-General to follow closely Israeli nuclear activities and to report thereon as appropriate to the General Assembly.

Adopted at the 113th plenary meeting:
In favour: 101
Afghanistan, Albania, Algeria, Angola, Argentina, Bahrain, Bangladesh, Barbados, Benin, Bhutan, Botswana, Brazil, Brunei Darussalam, Bulgaria, Burkina Faso, Burundi, Byelorussia, Cameroon, Cape Verde, Central African Republic, Chad, China, Comoros, Congo, Cuba, Cyprus, Czechoslovakia, Democratic Kampuchea, Democratic Yemen, Djibouti, Egypt, Equatorial Guinea, Ethiopia, Gabon, German Democratic Republic, Ghana, Greece, Guinea, Guinea-Bissau, Guyana, Hungary, India, Indonesia, Iran, Iraq, Jordan, Kenya, Kuwait, Lao People's Democratic Republic, Lebanon, Lesotho, Liberia, Libya, Madagascar, Malaysia, Maldives, Mali, Malta, Mauritania, Mauritius, Mexico, Mongolia, Morocco, Mozambique, Nicaragua, Niger, Nigeria, Oman, Pakistan, Peru, Philippines, Poland, Qatar, Romania, Rwanda, Sao Tome and Principe, Saudi Arabia, Senegal, Seychelles, Sierra Leone, Somalia, Sri Lanka, Sudan, Swaziland, Syria, Thailand, Trinidad and Tobago, Tunisia, Turkey, Uganda, Ukraine, USSR, United Arab Emirates, United Republic of Tanzania, Vanuatu, Venezuela, Viet Nam, Yemen, Yugoslavia, Zambia, Zimbabwe.
Against: 2
Israel, United States.
Abstentions: 47
Antigua and Barbuda, Australia, Austria, Bahamas, Belguim, Bolivia, Burma, Canada, Chile, Colombia, Denmark, Dominican Republic, Ecuador, El Salvador, Fiji, Finland, France, Federal Republic of Germany, Grenada, Guatemala, Haiti, Honduras, Iceland, Ireland, Italy, Ivory Coast, Jamaica, Japan, Luxembourg, Malawi, Nepal, Neth-

---

[393] A/40/442 and Add.1.

[394] A/40/520, annex.

erlands, New Zealand, Norway, Panama, Papua New Guinea, Paraguay, Portugal, Saint Lucia, Saint Vincent, Solomon Islands, Spain, St. Christopher and Nevis, Sweden, United Kingdom, Uruguay, Zaire.

Absent: 8

Belize, Costa Rica, Dominica, Gambia, Samoa, Singapore, Suriname, Togo.

Resolution No. 40/96 A, B, C, D of 12 December 1985

ON THE QUESTION OF PALESTINE: ENDORSING THE REC-OMMENDATIONS OF THE COMMITTEE ON THE EXERCISE OF THE INALIENABLE RIGHTS OF THE PALESTINIAN PEOPLE, URGING WIDER DISSEMINATION OF INFORMATION ON THE QUESTION OF PALESTINE AND UNITED NATIONS ACTIVITIES RELATING TO IT, AND ENDORSING THE CONVENING OF AN INTERNATIONAL PEACE CONFERENCE ON THE MIDDLE EAST

A

The General Assembly,

Recalling its resolutions 3376 (XXX) of 10 November 1975, 31/20 of 24 November 1976, 32/40 of 2 December 1977, 33/28 of 7 December 1978, 34/65 A and B of 29 November 1979 and 34/65 C and D of 12 December 1979, ES-7/2 of 29 July 1980, 35/169 of 15 December 1980, 36/120 of 10 December 1981, ES-7/4 of 28 April 1982, ES-7/5 of 26 June 1982, ES-7/9 of 24 September 1982, 37/86 A of 10 December 1982, 38/58 A of 13 December 1983 and 39/49 A of 11 December 1984,

Having considered the report of the Committee on the Exercise of the Inalienable Rights of the Palestinian People,[395]

1. *Expresses its appreciation* to the Committee on the Exercise of the Inalienable Rights of the Palestinian People for its efforts in performing the tasks assigned to it by the General Assembly;

2. *Endorses* the recommendations contained in paragraphs 163 to 172 of the report of the Committee [396] and draws the attention of the Security Council to the fact that action on the Committee's recommendations, as repeatedly endorsed by the General Assembly at its thirty-first session and subsequently, is still awaited;

3. *Requests* the Committee to continue to keep under review the situation relating to the question of Palestine as well as the implementation of the Programme of Action for the Achievement of Palestinian Rights[397] and to report and make suggestions to the General Assembly or the Security Council, as appropriate;

4. *Authorizes* the Committee to continue to exert all efforts to promote the implementation of its recommendations, including representation at conferences and meet-

ings and the sending of delegations where such activities would be considered by it to be appropriate, and to report thereon to the General Assembly at its forty-first session and thereafter;

5. *Requests* the Committee to continue to extend its co-operation to non-governmental organizations in their contribution towards heightening international awareness of the facts relating to the question of Palestine and in creating a more favourable atmosphere for the full implementation of the Committee's recommendations, and to take the necessary steps to expand its contacts with those organizations;

6. *Requests* the United Nations Conciliation Commission for Palestine, established under General Assembly resolution 194 (III) of 11 December 1948, as well as other United Nations bodies associated with the question of Palestine, to co-operate fully with the Committee and to make available to it, at its request, the relevant information and documentation which they have at their disposal;

7. *Decides* to circulate the report of the Committee to all the competent bodies of the United Nations and urges them to take the necessary action, as appropriate, in accordance with the Committee's programme of implementation;

8. *Requests* the Secretary-General to continue to provide the Committee with all the necessary facilities for the performance of its tasks.

Adopted at the 114th plenary meeting:

In favour: 128

Afghanistan, Albania, Algeria, Angola, Antigua and Barbuda, Argentina, Bahamas, Bahrain, Bangladesh, Barbados, Benin, Bhutan, Bolivia, Botswana, Brazil, Brunei Darussalam, Bulgaria, Burma, Burundi, Byelorussia, Cameroon, Cape Verde, Central African Republic, Chad, Chile, China, Colombia, Comoros, Congo, Cuba, Cyprus, Czechoslovakia, Democratic Kampuchea, Democratic Yemen, Djibouti, Dominican Republic, Ecuador, Egypt, El Salvador, Equatorial Guinea, Ethiopia, Fiji, Gabon, Gambia, German Democratic Republic, Ghana, Greece, Guatemala, Guinea, Guinea-Bissau, Guyana, Haiti, Honduras, Hungary, India, Indonesia, Iraq, Ivory Coast, Jamaica, Jordan, Kenya, Kuwait, Lao People's Democratic Republic, Lebanon, Lesotho, Liberia, Libya, Madagascar, Malaysia, Maldives, Mali, Malta, Mauritania, Mauritius, Mexico, Mongolia, Morocco, Mozambique, Nepal, Nicaragua, Niger, Nigeria, Oman, Pakistan, Panama, Papua New Guinea, Paraguay, Peru, Philippines, Poland, Qatar, Romania, Rwanda, Saint Lucia, Saint Vincent, Samoa, Sao Tome and Principe, Saudi Arabia, Senegal, Seychelles, Sierra Leone, Singapore, Somalia, Spain, Sri Lanka, Sudan, Suriname, Swaziland, Syria, Thailand, Togo, Trinidad and Tobago, Tunisia, Turkey, Uganda, Ukraine, USSR, United Arab Emirates, United Republic of Tanzania, Uruguay, Vanuatu, Venezuela, Viet Nam, Yemen, Yugoslavia, Zaire, Zambia, Zimbabwe.

Against: 2

Israel, United States.

Abstentions: 22

---

[395] *Official Records of the General Assembly, Fortieth Session, Supplement No. 35* (A/40/35).

[396] *Ibid., Supplement No. 35* (A/40/35).

[397] *Report of the International Conference on the Question of Palestine, Geneva, 29 August-7 September 1983* (United Nations publication, Sales No. E.83.1.21), chap. I, sect. B.

Australia, Austria, Belgium, Canada, Denmark, Finland, France, Federal Republic of Germany, Grenada, Iceland, Ireland, Italy, Japan, Luxembourg, Malawi, Netherlands, New Zealand, Norway, Portugal, Solomon Islands, Sweden, United Kingdom.

Absent: 6

Belize, Burkina Faso,* Costa Rica, Dominica, Iran,* St. Christopher and Nevis.

_____

*Later advised the Secretariat it had intended to vote in favour.

B

The General Assembly,

Having considered the report of the Committee on the Exercise of the Inalienable Rights of the Palestinian People,[398]

Noting the particularly relevant information contained in paragraphs 135 to 150 of that report,

Recalling its resolutions 32/40 B of 2 December 1977, 33/28 C of 7 December 1978, 34/65 D of 12 December 1979, 35/169 D of 15 December 1980, 36/120 B of 10 December 1981, 37/86 B of 10 December 1982, 38/58 B of 13 December 1983 and 39/49 B of 11 December 1984,

1. *Takes note with appreciation* of the action taken by the Secretary-General in compliance with General Assembly resolution 39/49 B;

2. *Requests* the Secretary-General to ensure that the Division for Palestinian Rights of the Secretariat continues to discharge the tasks detailed in paragraph 1 of General Assembly resolution 32/40 B, paragraph 2(*b*) of resolution 34/65 D, paragraph 3 of resolution 36/120 B and paragraphs 2 and 3 of resolution 38/58 B, in consultation with the Committee on the Exercise of the Inalienable Rights of the Palestinian People and under its guidance;

3. *Also requests* the Secretary-General to provide the Division for Palestinian Rights with the necessary resources to accomplish its tasks and to expand its work programme, particularly through additional meetings for non-governmental organizations, in order to heighten awareness of the facts relating to the question of Palestine and to create a more favourable atmosphere for the full implementation of the recommendations of the Committee on the Exercise of the Inalienable Rights of the Palestinian People;

4. *Further requests* the Secretary-General to ensure the continued co-operation of the Department of Public Information and other units of the Secretariat in enabling the Division for Palestinian Rights to perform its tasks and in covering adequately the various aspects of the question of Palestine;

5. *Invites* all Governments and organizations to lend their co-operation to the Committee on the Exercise of the Inalienable Rights of the Palestinian People and the Division for Palestinian Rights in the performance of their tasks;

6. *Takes note with appreciation* of the action taken by Member States to observe annually on 29 November the International Day of Solidarity with the Palestinian People and the issuance by them of special postage stamps for the occasion.

Adopted at the 114th plenary meeting:

In favour: 129

Afghanistan, Albania, Algeria, Angola, Antigua and Barbuda, Argentina, Bahamas, Bahrain, Bangladesh, Barbados, Benin, Bhutan, Bolivia, Botswana, Brazil, Brunei Darussalam, Bulgaria, Burma, Burundi, Byelorussia, Cameroon, Cape Verde, Central African Republic, Chad, Chile, China, Colombia, Comoros, Congo, Cuba, Cyprus, Czechoslovakia, Democratic Kampuchea, Democratic Yemen, Djibouti, Dominican Republic, Ecuador, Egypt, El Salvador, Equatorial Guinea, Ethiopia, Fiji, Gabon, Gambia, German Democratic Republic, Ghana, Greece, Guatemala, Guinea, Guinea-Bissau, Guyana, Haiti, Honduras, Hungary, India, Indonesia, Iraq, Ivory Coast, Jamaica, Jordan, Kenya, Kuwait, Lao People's Democratic Republic, Lebanon, Lesotho, Liberia, Libya, Madagascar, Malawi, Malaysia, Maldives, Mali, Malta, Mauritania, Mauritius, Mexico, Mongolia, Morocco, Mozambique, Nepal, Nicaragua, Niger, Nigeria, Oman, Pakistan, Panama, Papua New Guinea, Paraguay, Peru, Philippines, Poland, Qatar, Romania, Rwanda, Saint Lucia, Saint Vincent, Samoa, Sao Tome and Principe, Saudi Arabia, Senegal, Seychelles, Sierra Leone, Singapore, Somalia, Spain, Sri Lanka, Sudan, Suriname, Swaziland, Syria, Thailand, Togo, Trinidad and Tobago, Tunisia, Turkey, Uganda, Ukraine, USSR, United Arab Emirates, United Republic of Tanzania, Uruguay, Vanuatu, Venezuela, Viet Nam, Yemen, Yugoslavia, Zaire, Zambia, Zimbabwe.

Against: 3

Canada, Israel, United States.

Abstentions: 20

Australia, Austria, Belgium, Denmark, Finland, France, Federal Republic of Germany, Grenada, Iceland, Ireland, Italy, Japan, Luxembourg, Netherlands, New Zealand, Norway, Portugal, Solomon Islands, Sweden, United Kingdom.

Absent: 6

Belize, Burkina Faso,* Costa Rica, Dominica, Iran,* St. Christopher and Nevis.

_____

*Later advised the Secretariat it had intended to vote in favour.

C

The General Assembly,

Having considered the report of the Committee on the Exercise of the Inalienable Rights of the Palestinian People,[399]

Noting, in particular, the information contained in para-

_____

[398]*Official Records of the General Assembly Fortieth Session, Supplement No. 35* (A/40/35).

[399]*Ibid., Supplement No. 35* (A/40/35).

graphs 151 to 162 of that report,

Recalling its resolutions 38/58 E of 13 December 1983 and 39/49 C of 11 December 1984,

Convinced that the world-wide dissemination of accurate and comprehensive information and the role of non-governmental organizations and institutions remain of vital importance in heightening awareness of and support for the inalienable rights of the Palestinian people to self-determination and to the establishment of an independent sovereign Palestinian State,

1. *Takes note with appreciation* of the action taken by the Department of Public Information of the Secretariat in compliance with General Assembly resolutions 38/58 E and 39/49 C;

2. *Requests* the Department of Public Information, in full co-operation and co-ordination with the Committee on the Exercise of the Inalienable Rights of the Palestinian People, to continue its special information programme on the question of Palestine for the biennium 1986-1987 and, in particular:

(*a*) To disseminate information on all the activities of the United Nations system relating to the question of Palestine;

(*b*) To continue to update publications on the facts and developments pertaining to the question of Palestine;

(*c*) To publish brochures and booklets on the various aspects of the question of Palestine, including Israeli violations of the human rights of the Arab inhabitants of the occupied territories;

(*d*) To expand its audio-visual material on the question of Palestine, including the production of a new film, special series of radio programmes and television broadcasts;

(*e*) To organize fact-finding news missions to the area for journalists;

(*f*) To organize regional and national encounters for journalists.

Adopted at the 114th plenary meeting:

In favour: 131

Afghanistan, Albania, Algeria, Angola, Antigua and Barbuda, Argentina, Austria, Bahamas, Bahrain, Bangladesh, Barbados, Benin, Bhutan, Bolivia, Botswana, Brazil, Brunei Darussalam, Bulgaria, Burma, Burundi, Byelorussia, Cameroon, Cape Verde, Central African Republic, Chad, Chile, China, Colombia, Comoros, Congo, Cuba, Cyprus, Czechoslovakia, Democratic Kampuchea, Democratic Yemen, Djibouti, Dominican Republic, Ecuador, Egypt, El Salvador, Equatorial Guinea, Ethiopia, Fiji, Finland, Gabon, Gambia, German Democratic Republic, Ghana, Greece, Guatemala, Guinea, Guinea-Bissau, Guyana, Haiti, Honduras, Hungary, India, Indonesia, Iraq, Ivory Coast, Jamaica, Jordan, Kenya, Kuwait, Lao People's Democratic Republic, Lebanon, Lesotho, Liberia, Libya, Madagascar, Malawi, Malaysia, Maldives, Mali, Malta, Mauritania, Mauritius, Mexico, Mongolia, Morocco, Mozambique, Nepal, Nicaragua, Niger, Nigeria, Oman, Pakistan, Panama, Papua New Guinea, Paraguay, Peru, Philippines, Poland, Qatar, Romania, Rwanda, Saint Lucia, Saint Vin-

cent, Samoa, Sao Tome and Principe, Saudi Arabia, Senegal, Seychelles, Sierra Leone, Singapore, Somalia, Spain, Sri Lanka, Sudan, Suriname, Swaziland, Sweden, Syria, Thailand, Togo, Trinidad and Tobago, Tunisia, Turkey, Uganda, Ukraine, USSR, United Arab Emirates, United Republic of Tanzania, Uruguay, Vanuatu, Venezuela, Viet Nam, Yemen, Yugoslavia, Zambia, Zimbabwe.

Against: 3

Canada, Israel, United States.

Abstentions: 18

Australia, Belgium, Denmark, France, Federal Republic of Germany, Grenada, Iceland, Ireland, Italy, Japan, Luxembourg, Netherlands, New Zealand, Norway, Portugal, Solomon Islands, United Kingdom, Zaire.

Absent: 6

Belize, Burkina Faso,* Costa Rica, Dominica, Iran,* St. Christopher and Nevis.

------

*Later advised the Secretariat it had intended to vote in favour.

D

The General Assembly,

Recalling its resolutions 38/58 C of 13 December 1983 and 39/49 D of 11 December 1984, in which it, *inter alia,* endorsed the convening of an International Peace Conference on the Middle East,

Reaffirming its resolution 39/49 D, in which it, *inter alia,* requested the Secretary-General, in consultation with the Security Council, to continue his efforts with a view to convening the Conference,

Having considered the reply of the President of the Security Council to the Secretary-General, dated 26 February 1985, in which he, *inter alia,* stated on the subject of the Conference: "In this context, members of the Council invite the Secretary-General to continue consultations on the subject in any manner he deems appropriate in the light of General Assembly resolution 39/49 D.",[400]

Having considered again the reports of the Secretary-General of 13 March 1984 [401] and 13 September 1984,[402] in which he stated, *inter alia,* that it was clear from the replies of the Governments of Israel and the United States of America that they were not prepared to participate in the proposed Conference, and regretting the continued negative response of these two Governments and the lack of willingness to reconsider their position towards the Conference,

Having considered the reports of the Secretary-General

------

[400]See A/40/168-S/17014, para. 3. For the printed text, see *Official Records of the Security Council, Fortieth Year, Supplement for January, February and March 1985,* document S/17014, para.3.

[401]A/39/130-S/16409. For the printed text, see *Official Records of the Security Council, Thirty-ninth Year, Supplement for January, February and March 1984,* document S/16409.

[402]A/39/130/Add.1-S/16409/Add.1. For the printed text, see *Official Records of the Security Council, Thirty-ninth Year, Supplement for July, August and September 1984,* document S/16409/Add.1.

of 11 March 1985[403] and 22 October 1985,[404] in which he, *inter alia,* referred to the difficulties experienced in his efforts made the previous year with a view to convening the Conference,

Having heard the constructive statements made by numerous representatives, including that of the Palestine Liberation Organization,

Taking note of the positive positions of the concerned parties, including the Palestine Liberation Organization, and of other States on the convening of the Conference,[405]

Taking note also of the position of the Palestine Liberation Organization which condemns all acts of terrorism, whether committed by States or individuals, including acts of terrorism committed by Israel against the Palestinian people and the Arab nation,

Reiterating once again its conviction that the convening of the Conference would constitute a major contribution by the United Nations towards the achievement of a comprehensive, just and lasting solution to the Arab-Israeli conflict,

1. *Takes note with appreciation* of the reports of the Secretary-General;

2. *Reaffirms again* its endorsement of the call for convening the International Peace Conference on the Middle East in conformity with the provisions of its resolution 38/58 C;

3. *Stresses* the urgent need for additional constructive efforts by all Governments in order to convene the Conference without further delay and for the achievement of its peaceful objectives;

4. *Determines* that the question of Palestine is the root-cause of the Arab-Israeli conflict in the Middle East;

5. *Calls upon* the Governments of Israel and the United States of America to reconsider their positions towards the attainment of peace in the Middle East through the convening of the Conference;

6. *Requests* the Secretary-General, in consultation with the Security Council, to continue his efforts with a view to convening the Conference and to report thereon to the General Assembly not later than 15 March 1986;

7. *Decides* to consider at its forty-first session the report of the Secretary-General on the implementation of the present resolution.

Adopted at the 114th plenary meeting:
In favour: 107
Afghanistan, Algeria, Angola, Argentina, Bahamas, Bahrain, Bangladesh, Barbados, Benin, Bhutan, Bolivia, Botswana, Brazil, Brunei Darussalam, Bulgaria, Burma, Burundi, Byelorussia, Cameroon, Cape Verde, Central African Republic, Chad, China, Comoros, Congo, Cuba, Cyprus, Czechoslovakia, Democratic Kampuchea, Democratic Yemen, Djibouti, Egypt, Equatorial Guinea, Ethiopia, Fiji, Gabon, Gambia, German Democratic Republic, Ghana, Guinea, Guinea-Bissau, Guyana, Hungary, India, Indonesia, Iraq, Jamaica, Jordan, Kenya, Kuwait, Lao People's Democratic Republic, Lebanon, Lesotho, Libya, Madagascar, Malaysia, Maldives, Mali, Malta, Mauritania, Mauritius, Mexico, Mongolia, Morocco, Mozambique, Nepal, Nicaragua, Niger, Nigeria, Oman, Pakistan, Peru, Philippines, Poland, Qatar, Romania, Rwanda, Samoa, Sao Tome and Principe, Saudi Arabia, Senegal, Seychelles, Sierra Leone, Singapore, Somalia, Sri Lanka, Sudan, Suriname, Syria, Thailand, Togo, Trinidad and Tobago, Tunisia, Turkey, Uganda, Ukraine, USSR, United Arab Emirates, United Republic of Tanzania, Uruguay, Vanuatu, Venezuela, Viet Nam, Yemen, Yugoslavia, Zambia, Zimbabwe.
Against: 3
Canada, Israel, United States.
Abstentions: 41
Antigua and Barbuda, Australia, Austria, Belgium, Chile, Columbia, Denmark, Dominican Republic, Ecuador, El Salvador, Finland, France, Federal Republic of Germany, Greece, Grenada, Guatemala, Haiti, Honduras, Iceland, Ireland, Italy, Ivory Coast, Japan, Liberia, Luxembourg, Malawi, Netherlands, New Zealand, Norway, Panama, Papua New Guinea, Paraguay, Portugal, Saint Lucia, Saint Vincent, Solomon Islands, Spain, Swaziland, Sweden, United Kingdom, Zaire.
Absent: 6
Belize, Burkina Faso,* Costa Rica, Dominica, Iran,* St. Christopher and Nevis.

Albania announced that it was not participating in the vote.

*Later advised the Secretariat it had intended to vote in favour.

Resolution No. 40/161 A, B, C, D, E, F, G of 16 December 1985

ON ISRAELI PRACTICES AFFECTING HUMAN RIGHTS IN THE OCCUPIED TERRITORIES: CALLING FOR THE LIBERATION OF ARABS DETAINED BY ISRAEL, CONDEMNING ISRAELI POLICIES OF ANNEXATION AND SETTLEMENT IN THE OCCUPIED TERRITORIES AS WELL AS MEASURES AGAINST CIVIL RIGHTS AND EDUCATIONAL FREEDOMS THERE, AND FOR ITS EXPULSION OF PALESTINIAN LEADERS

A

The General Assembly,
Recalling its resolutions 38/79 A of 15 December 1983 and 39/95 A of 14 December 1984,
Taking note of the report of the International Commit-

[403]A/40/168-S/17014. For the printed text, see *Official Records of the Security Council, Fortieth Year, Supplement for January, February and March 1985,* document S/17014.
[404]A/40/779-S/17581 and Corr.1. For the printed text, see *Official Records of the Security Council, Fortieth Year, Supplement for October, November and December 1985,* document S/17581.

[405]A/39/130/Add. I-S/16409/Add.1. For the printed text, see *Official Records of the Security Council, Thirty-ninth year, Supplement for July, August and September 1984,* document S/16409/Add.1.

tee of the Red Cross of 13 December 1983,[406]

Taking note also of the report of the Secretary-General of 30 September 1985,[407]

Taking note further of the report of the Special Committee to Investigate Israeli Practices Affecting the Human Rights of the Population of the Occupied Territories,[408]

1. *Calls upon* Israel to release all Arabs arbitrarily detained and/or imprisoned as a result of their struggle for self-determination and for the liberation of their territories;

2. *Notes* the initial release of Ziyad Abu Eain, among others, from prison on 20 May 1985;

3. *Deplores* the Israeli subsequent arbitrary detention of Ziyad Abu Eain and others;

4. *Demands* that the Government of Israel, the occupying Power, rescind its action against Ziyad Abu Eain and others and release them immediately;

5. *Requests* the Secretary-General to report to the General Assembly as soon as possible and not later than the beginning of its forty-first session on the implementation of the present resolution.

Adopted at the 118th plenary meeting:

In favour: 95

Afghanistan, Albania, Algeria, Argentina, Bahrain, Bangladesh, Benin, Bhutan, Bolivia, Botswana, Brazil, Brunei Darussalam, Bulgaria, Burkina Faso, Burundi, Byelorussia, Cape Verde, Central African Republic, Chad, China, Congo, Cuba, Cyprus, Czechoslovakia, Democratic Kampuchea, Democratic Yemen, Djibouti, Dominican Republic, Ecuador, Egypt, El Salvador, Ethiopia, Gabon, Gambia, German Democratic Republic, Guinea, Guinea-Bissau, Guyana, Hungary, India, Indonesia, Iraq, Jordan, Kenya, Kuwait, Lao People's Democratic Republic, Lebanon, Lesotho, Libya, Madagascar, Malaysia, Maldives, Mali, Malta, Mauritania, Mauritius, Mexico, Mongolia, Morocco, Mozambique, Nicaragua, Niger, Nigeria, Oman, Pakistan, Panama, Peru, Poland, Qatar, Romania, Rwanda, Sao Tome and Principe, Saudi Arabia, Senegal, Seychelles, Sierra Leone, Sri Lanka, Sudan, Suriname, Syria, Togo, Tunisia, Turkey, Uganda, Ukraine, USSR, United Arab Emirates, United Republic of Tanzania, Vanuatu, Venezuela, Viet Nam, Yemen, Yugoslavia, Zambia, Zimbabwe.

Against: 2

Israel, United States.

Abstentions: 37

Antigua and Barbuda, Australia, Austria, Bahamas, Belgium, Cameroon, Canada, Costa Rica, Denmark, Dominica, Fiji, Finland, France, Federal Republic of Germany, Greece, Grenada, Iceland, Ireland, Italy, Ivory Coast, Jamaica, Japan, Liberia, Luxembourg, Malawi, Nepal, Netherlands, New Zealand, Norway, Portugal, Saint Lucia, Samoa, Spain, Swaziland, Sweden, United Kingdom, Zaire.

Absent: 24

Angola, Barbados, Belize, Burma, Chile, Colombia, Comoros, Equatorial Guinea, Ghana, Guatemala, Haiti, Honduras, Iran,* Papua New Guinea, Paraguay, Philippines, Saint Vincent, Singapore, Solomon Islands, Somalia,* St. Christopher and Nevis, Thailand, Trinidad and Tobago, Uruguay.

---

*Later advised the Secretariat it had intended to vote in favour.

B

The General Assembly,

Recalling Security Council resolution 465 (1980) of 1 March 1980, in which, *inter alia*, the Council affirmed that the Geneva Convention relative to the Protection of Civilian Persons in Time of War, of 12 August 1949,[409] is applicable to the Arab territories occupied by Israel since 1967, including Jerusalem,

Recalling also its resolutions 3092 A (XXVIII) of 7 December 1973, 3240 B (XXIX) of 29 November 1974, 3525 B (XXX) of 15 December 1975, 31/106 B of 16 December 1976, 32/91 A of 13 December 1977, 33/113 A of 18 December 1978, 34/90 B of 12 December 1979, 35/122 A of 11 December 1980, 36/147 A of 16 December 1981, 37/88 A of 10 December 1982, 38/79 B of 15 December 1983 and 39/95 B of 14 December 1984,[410]

Considering that the promotion of respect for the obligations arising from the Charter of the United Nations and other instruments and rules of international law is among the basic purposes and principles of the United Nations,

Bearing in mind the provisions of the Geneva Convention,

Noting that Israel and the Arab States whose territories have been occupied by Israel since June 1967 are parties to that Convention,

Taking into account that States parties to the Convention undertake, in accordance with article 1 thereof, not only to respect but also to ensure respect for the Convention in all circumstances,

1. *Reaffirms* that the Geneva Convention relative to the Protection of Civilian Persons in Time of War, of 12 August 1949, is applicable to the Palestinian and other Arab territories occupied by Israel since 1967, including Jerusalem;

2. *Condemns once again* the failure of Israel, the occupying Power, to acknowledge the applicability of that Convention to the territories it has occupied since 1967, including Jerusalem;

3. *Strongly demands* that Israel acknowledge and comply with the provisions of that Convention in the Palestinian and other Arab territories it has occupied since 1967, including Jerusalem;

4. *Urgently calls upon* all States parties to that Convention to exert all efforts in order to ensure respect for and compliance with its provisions in the Palestinian and other Arab territories occupied by Israel since 1967, including Jerusalem;

---

[406] See A/38/735.
[407] A/40/686.
[408] See A/40/702.

[409] United Nations, *Treaty Series,* vol. 75, no. 973, p. 287.
[410] The resolutions cited are previous resolutions on Israeli practices in the occupied territories. [ed. note]

5. *Requests* the Secretary-General to report to the General Assembly at its forty-first session on the implementation of the present resolution.

Adopted at the 118th plenary meeting:
In favour: 137
Afghanistan, Albania, Algeria, Antigua and Barbuda, Argentina, Australia, Austria, Bahamas, Bahrain, Bangladesh, Belgium, Benin, Bhutan, Bolivia, Botswana, Brazil, Brunei Darussalam, Bulgaria, Burkina Faso, Burma, Burundi, Byelorussia, Canada, Cape Verde, Central African Republic, Chad, Chile, China, Colombia, Congo, Costa Rica, Cuba, Cyprus, Czechoslovakia, Democratic Kampuchea, Democratic Yemen, Denmark, Djibouti, Dominica, Dominican Republic, Ecuador, Egypt, El Salvador, Equatorial Guinea, Ethiopia, Fiji, Finland, France, Gabon, Gambia, German Democratic Republic, Federal Republic of Germany, Greece, Grenada, Guatemala, Guinea, Guinea-Bissau, Guyana, Hungary, Iceland, India, Indonesia, Iraq, Ireland, Italy, Jamaica, Japan, Jordan, Kenya, Kuwait, Lao People's Democratic Republic, Lebanon, Lesotho, Libya, Luxembourg, Madagascar, Malaysia, Maldives, Mali, Malta, Mauritania, Mauritius, Mexico, Mongolia, Morocco, Mozambique, Nepal, Netherlands, New Zealand, Nicaragua, Niger, Nigeria, Norway, Oman, Pakistan, Panama, Peru, Philippines, Poland, Portugal, Qatar, Romania, Rwanda, Saint Vincent, Samoa, Sao Tome and Principe, Saudi Arabia, Senegal, Seychelles, Sierra Leone, Singapore, Spain, Sri Lanka, Sudan, Suriname, Swaziland, Sweden, Syria, Thailand, Togo, Trinidad and Tobago, Tunisia, Turkey, Uganda, Ukraine, USSR, United Arab Emirates, United Kingdom, United Republic of Tanzania, Uruguay, Vanuatu, Venezuela, Viet Nam, Yemen, Yugoslavia, Zambia, Zimbabwe.
Against: 1
Israel.
Abstentions: 6
Cameroon, Ivory Coast, Liberia, Malawi, United States, Zaire.
Absent: 14
Angola, Barbados, Belize, Comoros, Ghana, Haiti, Honduras, Iran,* Papua New Guinea, Paraguay, Saint Lucia, Solomon Islands, Somalia,* St. Christopher and Nevis.

---

*Later advised the Secretariat it had intended to vote in favour.

C

The General Assembly,
Recalling Security Council resolution 465 (1980) of 1 March 1980,
Recalling also its resolutions 32/5 of 28 October 1977, 33/113 B of 18 December 1978, 34/90 C of 12 December 1979, 35/122 B of 11 December 1980, 36/147 B of 16 December 1981, 37/88 B of 10 December 1982, 38/79 C of 15 December 1983 and 39/95 C of 14 December 1984,[411]

Expressing grave anxiety and concern at the present serious situation in the occupied Palestinian and other Arab territories, including Jerusalem, as a result of the continued Israeli occupation and the measures and actions taken by Israel, the occupying Power, designed to change the legal status, geographical nature and demographic composition of those territories,
Confirming that the Geneva Convention relative to the Protection of Civilian Persons in Time of War, of 12 August 1949,[412] is applicable to all Arab territories occupied since June 1967, including Jerusalem,
1. *Determines* that all such measures and actions taken by Israel in the Palestinian and other Arab territories occupied since 1967, including Jerusalem, are in violation of the relevant provisions of the Geneva Convention relative to the Protection of Civilian Persons in Time of War, of 12 August 1949, and constitute a serious obstacle to the efforts to achieve a comprehensive, just and lasting peace in the Middle East and therefore have no legal validity;
2. *Strongly deplores* the persistence of Israel in carrying out such measures, in particular the establishment of settlements in the Palestinian and other occupied Arab territories, including Jerusalem;
3. *Demands* that Israel comply strictly with its international obligations in accordance with the principles of international law and the provisions of the Geneva Convention;
4. *Demands once more* that Israel, the occupying Power, desist forthwith from taking any action which would result in changing the legal status, geographical nature or demographic composition of the Palestinian and other Arab territories occupied since 1967, including Jerusalem;
5. *Urgently calls upon* all States parties to the Geneva Convention to respect and to exert all efforts in order to ensure respect for and compliance with its provisions in all Arab territories occupied by Israel since 1967, including Jerusalem;
6. *Requests* the Secretary-General to report to the General Assembly at its forty-first session on the implementation of the present resolution.

Adopted at the 118th plenary session:
In favour: 138
Afghanistan, Albania, Algeria, Antigua and Barbuda, Argentina, Australia, Austria, Bahamas, Bahrain, Bangladesh, Belgium, Benin, Bhutan, Bolivia, Botswana, Brazil, Brunei Darussalam, Bulgaria, Burkina Faso, Burma, Burundi, Byelorussia, Cameroon, Canada, Cape Verde, Central African Republic, Chad, Chile, China, Colombia, Congo, Cuba, Cyprus, Czechoslovakia, Democratic Kampuchea, Democratic Yemen, Denmark, Djibouti, Dominica, Dominican Republic, Ecuador, Egypt, El Salvador, Equatorial Guinea, Ethiopia, Fiji, Finland, France, Gabon, Gambia, German Democratic Republic, Federal Republic of Germany, Greece, Guatemala, Guinea, Guinea-Bissau, Guyana, Hungary, Iceland, India, Indonesia, Iraq, Ireland, Italy,

---

[411]The resolutions cited are previous resolutions on Israeli practices in the occupied territories. [ed. note]

[412]United Nations, *Treaty Series*, vol. 75, no. 973, p. 287.

Jamaica, Japan, Jordan, Kenya, Kuwait, Lao People's Democratic Republic, Lebanon, Lesotho, Liberia, Libya, Luxembourg, Madagascar, Malaysia, Maldives, Mali, Malta, Mauritania, Mauritius, Mexico, Mongolia, Morocco, Mozambique, Nepal, Netherlands, New Zealand, Nicaragua, Niger, Nigeria, Norway, Oman, Pakistan, Panama, Peru, Philippines, Poland, Portugal, Qatar, Romania, Rwanda, Saint Vincent, Samoa, Sao Tome and Principe, Saudi Arabia, Senegal, Seychelles, Sierra Leone, Singapore, Spain, Sri Lanka, Sudan, Suriname, Swaziland, Sweden, Syria, Thailand, Togo, Trinidad and Tobago, Tunisia, Turkey, Uganda, Ukraine, USSR, United Arab Emirates, United Kingdom, United Republic of Tanzania, Uruguay, Vanuatu, Venezuela, Viet Nam, Yemen, Yugoslavia, Zaire, Zambia, Zimbabwe.

Against: 1

Israel.

Abstentions: 6

Costa Rica, Grenada, Ivory Coast, Malawi, Saint Lucia, United States.

Absent: 13

Angola, Barbados, Belize, Comoros, Ghana, Haiti, Honduras, Iran, Papua New Guinea, Paraguay, Solomon Islands, Somalia,* St. Christopher and Nevis.

---

*Later advised the Secretariat it had intended to vote in favour.

D

The General Assembly,

Guided by the purposes and principles of the Charter of the United Nations and by the principles and provisions of the Universal Declaration of Human Rights,[413]

Bearing in mind the provisions of the Geneva Convention relative to the Protection of Civilian Persons in Time of War, of 12 August 1949,[414] as well as of other relevant conventions and regulations,

Recalling all its resolutions on the subject, in particular, resolutions 32/91 B and C of 13 December 1977, 33/113 C of 18 December 1978, 34/90 A of 12 December 1979, 35/122 C of 11 December 1980, 36/147 C of 16 December 1981, 37/88 C of 10 December 1982, 38/79 D of 15 December 1983 and 39/95 D of 14 December 1984,

Recalling also the relevant resolutions adopted by the Security Council, by the Commission on Human Rights, in particular its resolutions 1983/1 of 15 February 1983,[415] 1984/1 of 20 February 1984,[416] 1985/1 A and B of 19 February 1985,[417] and 1985/2 of 19 February 1985,[418] and by other United Nations organs concerned and by the specialized agencies,

Having considered the report of the Special Committee to Investigate Israeli Practices Affecting the Human Rights of the Population of the Occupied Territories,[419] which contains, *inter alia*, self-incriminating public statements made by officials of Israel, the occupying Power,

Taking note of the letter dated 29 July 1985 from the Permanent Representative of Jordan addressed to the Secretary-General,[420] concerning the closing down of the Roman Catholic Medical Facility Hospice at Jerusalem,

1. *Commends* the Special Committee to Investigate Israeli Practices Affecting the Human Rights of the Population of the Occupied Territories for its efforts in performing the tasks assigned to it by the General Assembly and for its thoroughness and impartiality;

2. *Deplores* the continued refusal by Israel to allow the Special Committee access to the occupied territories;

3. *Demands* that Israel allow the Special Committee access to the occupied territories;

4. *Reaffirms* the fact that occupation itself constitutes a grave violation of the human rights of the civilian population of the occupied Arab territories;

5. *Condemns* the continued and persistent violation by Israel of the Geneva Convention relative to the Protection of Civilian Persons in Time of War, of 12 August 1949, and other applicable international instruments, and condemns in particular those violations which the Convention designates as "grave breaches" thereof;

6. *Declares once more* that Israel's grave breaches of that Convention are war crimes and an affront to humanity;

7. *Reaffirms,* in accordance with the Convention, that the Israeli military occupation of the Palestinian and other Arab territories is of a temporary nature, thus giving no right whatsoever to the occupying Power over the territorial integrity of the occupied territories;

8. *Strongly condemns* the following Israeli policies and practices:

(*a*) Annexation of parts of the occupied territories, including Jerusalem;

(*b*) Imposition of Israeli laws, jurisdiction and administration on the Syrian Golan Heights, which has resulted in the effective annexation of the Syrian Golan Heights;

(*c*) Illegal imposition and levy of heavy and disproportionate taxes and dues;

(*d*) Establishment of new Israeli settlements and expansion of the existing settlements on private and public Arab lands, and transfer of an alien population thereto;

(*e*) Eviction, deportation, expulsion, displacement and transfer of Arab inhabitants of the occupied territories and denial of their right to return;

(*f*) Confiscation and expropriation of private and public Arab property in the occupied territories and all other transactions for the acquisition of land involving the Israeli authorities, institutions or nationals on the one hand

---

[413]Resolution 217 A (III).

[414]United Nations, *Treaty Series,* vol. 75, no. 973, p. 287.

[415]See *Official Records of the Economic and Social Council, 1983, Supplement No. 3* (E/1983/13 and Corr.1), chap. XXVII, sect. A.

[416]*Ibid., 1984, Supplement No. 4* (E/1984/14 and Corr.1), chap. II, sect. A.

[417]*Ibid. 1985, Supplement No. 22* (E/1985/22), chap. II, sect. A.

[418]*Ibid.*

[419]See A/40/702.

[420]A/40/517-S/17371. For the printed text, see *Official Records of the Security Council, Fortieth Year, Supplement for July, August and September 1985,* document S/17371.

and the inhabitants or institutions of the occupied territories on the other;

(*g*) Excavation and transformation of the landscape and the historical, cultural and religious sites, especially at Jerusalem;

(*h*) Pillaging of archaeological and cultural property;

(*i*) Destruction and demolition of Arab houses;

(*j*) Collective punishment, mass arrests, administrative detention and ill-treatment of the Arab population;

(*k*) Ill-treatment and torture of persons under detention;

(*l*) Interference with religious freedoms and practices as well as family rights and customs;

(*m*) Interference with the system of education and with the social and economic and health development of the population in the occupied Palestinian and other Arab territories;

(*n*) Interference with the freedom of movement of individuals within the occupied Palestinian and other Arab territories;

(*o*) Illegal exploitation of the natural wealth, resources and population of the occupied territories;

9. *Condemns also* the Israeli repression against and closing of the educational institutions in the occupied Syrian Golan Heights, particularly the prohibition of Syrian textbooks, Syrian educational system, the deprivation of Syrian students from pursuing their higher education in Syrian universities, the denial of the right to return to Syrian students receiving their higher education in the Syrian Arab Republic, the forcing of Hebrew on Syrian students, the imposition of courses that promote hatred, prejudice and religious intolerance and the dismissal of teachers, all in clear violation of the Geneva Convention;

10. *Strongly condemns* the arming of Israeli settlers in the occupied territories to commit acts of violence against Arab civilians and the perpetration of acts of violence by these armed settlers against individuals, causing injury and death and wide-scale damage to Arab property;

11. *Reaffirms* that all measures taken by Israel to change the physical character, demographic composition, institutional structure or legal status of the occupied territories, or any part thereof, including Jerusalem, are null and void, and that Israel's policy of settling parts of its population and new immigrants in the occupied territories constitutes a flagrant violation of the Geneva Convention and of the relevant resolutions of the United Nations;

12. *Demands* that Israel desist forthwith from the policies and practices referred to in paragraphs 8, 9, and 10 above;

13. *Calls upon* Israel, the occupying Power, to take immediate steps for the return of all displaced Arab and Palestinian inhabitants to their homes or former places of residence in the territories occupied by Israel since 1967, in implementation of Security Council resolution 237 (1967) of 14 June 1967;

14. *Urges* international organizations, including the specialized agencies, in particular the International Labour Organisation, to examine the conditions of Arab workers in the occupied Palestinian and other Arab territories, including Jerusalem;

15. *Reiterates its call* upon all States, in particular those States parties to the Geneva Convention, in accordance with article 1 of that Convention, and upon international organizations, including the specialized agencies, not to recognize any changes carried out by Israel in the occupied territories and to avoid actions, including those in the field of aid, which might be used by Israel in its pursuit of the policies of annexation and colonization or any of the other policies and practices referred to in the present resolution;

16. *Requests* the Special Committee, pending early termination of Israeli occupation, to continue to investigate Israeli policies and practices in the Arab territories occupied by Israel since 1967, to consult, as appropriate, with the International Committee of the Red Cross in order to ensure the safeguarding of the welfare and human rights of the population of the occupied territories and to report to the Secretary-General as soon as possible and whenever the need arises thereafter;

17. *Requests* the Special Committee to continue to investigate the treatment of civilians in detention in the Arab territories occupied by Israel since 1967;

18. *Condemns* Israel's refusal to permit persons from the occupied territories to appear as witnesses before the Special Committee and to participate in conferences and meetings held outside the occupied territories;

19. *Requests* the Secretary-General:

(*a*) To provide all necessary facilities to the Special Committee, including those required for its visits to the occupied territories, with a view to investigating the Israeli policies and practices referred to in the present resolution;

(*b*) To continue to make available additional staff as may be necessary to assist the Special Committee in the performance of its tasks;

(*c*) To ensure the widest circulation of the reports of the Special Committee and of information regarding its activities and findings, by all means available through the Department of Public Information of the Secretariat and, where necessary, to reprint those reports of the Special Committee that are no longer available;

(*d*) To report to the General Assembly at its forty-first session on the tasks entrusted to him in the present paragraph;

20. *Requests* the Security Council to ensure Israel's respect for and compliance with all the provisions of the Geneva Convention relative to the Protection of Civilian Persons in Time of War, of 12 August 1949, in the Palestinian and other Arab territories occupied since 1967, including Jerusalem, and to initiate measures to halt Israeli policies and practices in those territories;

21. *Calls upon* Israel, the occupying Power, to allow the reopening of the Roman Catholic Medical Facility Hospice at Jerusalem in order to continue to provide needed health and medical services to the Arab population in the city;

22. *Decides* to include in the provisional agenda of its

forty-first session the item entitled "Report of the Special Committee to Investigate Israeli Practices Affecting the Human Rights of the Population of the Occupied Territories".

Adopted at the 118th plenary meeting:
In favour: 109
Afghanistan, Albania, Algeria, Antigua and Barbuda, Argentina, Bahrain, Bangladesh, Benin, Bhutan, Bolivia, Botswana, Brazil, Brunei Darussalam, Bulgaria, Burkina Faso, Burma, Burundi, Byelorussia, Cape Verde, Central African Republic, Chad, China, Colombia, Congo, Cuba, Cyprus, Czechoslovakia, Democratic Kampuchea, Democratic Yemen, Djibouti, Ecuador, Egypt, Equatorial Guinea, Ethiopia, Gabon, Gambia, German Democratic Republic, Greece, Guatemala, Guinea, Guinea-Bissau, Guyana, Hungary, India, Indonesia, Iran, Iraq, Jamaica, Jordan, Kenya, Kuwait, Lao People's Democratic Republic, Lebanon, Lesotho, Libya, Madagascar, Malaysia, Maldives, Mali, Malta, Mauritania, Mauritius, Mexico, Mongolia, Morocco, Mozambique, Nepal, Nicaragua, Niger, Nigeria, Oman, Pakistan, Panama, Peru, Philippines, Poland, Qatar, Romania, Rwanda, Samoa, Sao Tome and Principe, Saudi Arabia, Senegal, Seychelles, Sierra Leone, Singapore, Spain, Sri Lanka, Sudan, Suriname, Syria, Thailand, Togo, Trinidad and Tobago, Tunisia, Turkey, Uganda, Ukraine, USSR, United Arab Emirates, United Republic of Tanzania, Uruguay, Vanuatu, Venezuela, Viet Nam, Yemen, Yugoslavia, Zambia, Zimbabwe.
Against: 2
Israel, United States.
Abstentions: 34
Australia, Austria, Bahamas, Belgium, Cameroon, Canada, Costa Rica, Denmark, Dominica, Dominican Republic, El Salvador, Fiji, Finland, France, Federal Republic of Germany, Grenada, Iceland, Ireland, Italy, Ivory Coast, Japan, Liberia, Luxembourg, Malawi, Netherlands, New Zealand, Norway, Portugal, Saint Lucia, Saint Vincent, Swaziland, Sweden, United Kingdom, Zaire.
Absent: 13
Angola, Barbados, Belize, Chile, Comoros, Ghana, Haiti, Honduras, Papua New Guinea, Paraguay, Solomon Islands, Somalia,* St. Christopher and Nevis.

---

*Later advised the Secretariat it had intended to vote in favour.

E

The General Assembly,
Recalling Security Council resolutions 468 (1980) of 8 May 1980, 469 (1980) of 20 May 1980 and 484 (1980) of 19 December 1980,
Recalling also its resolutions 36/147 D of 16 December 1981, 37/88 D of 10 December 1982, 38/79 E of 15 December 1983 and 39/95 E of 14 December 1984,[421]
Taking note of the report of the Secretary-General of 14

August 1985,[422]
Deeply concerned at the expulsion by the Israeli military occupation authorities of the Mayor of Halhul, the Mayor of Hebron who has since died, the Sharia Judge of Hebron and, in 1985, other Palestinians,
Alarmed by the decision of the Israeli military occupation authorities on 26 October 1985 to expel four Palestinian leaders,
Recalling the Geneva Convention relative to the Protection of Civilian Persons in Time of War, of 12 August 1949,[423] in particular article 1 and the first paragraph of article 49, which read as follows:

"Article 1

"The High Contracting Parties undertake to respect and to ensure respect for the present Convention in all circumstances."

"Article 49

"Individual or mass forcible transfers, as well as deportations of protected persons from occupied territory to the territory of the occupying Power or to that of any other country, occupied or not, are prohibited, regardless of their motive...",
Reaffirming the applicability of the Geneva Convention to the Palestinian and other Arab territories occupied by Israel since 1967, including Jerusalem,
1. *Strongly condemns* Israel, the occupying Power, for its persistent refusal to comply with the relevant resolutions of the Security Council and the General Assembly;
2. *Demands* that the Government of Israel, the occupying Power, rescind the illegal measures taken by the Israeli military occupation authorities in expelling the Mayor of Halhul, the Sharia Judge of Hebron and, in 1985, other Palestinians and that it facilitate the immediate return of the expelled Palestinians so that they can, *inter alia*, resume the functions for which they were elected and appointed;
3. *Calls upon* Israel, the occupying Power, to rescind its illegal decision taken on 26 October 1985 and refrain from deporting the four Palestinian leaders;
4. *Further calls upon* Israel, the occupying Power, to cease forthwith the expulsion of Palestinians and to abide scrupulously by the provisions of the Geneva Convention relative to the Protection of Civilian Persons in Time of War, of 12 August 1949;
5. *Requests* the Secretary-General to report to the General Assembly as soon as possible and not later than the beginning of its forty-first session on the implementation of the present resolution.

Adopted at the 118th plenary meeting:
In favour: 126
Afghanistan, Albania, Algeria, Antigua and Barbuda, Argentina, Australia, Austria, Bahamas, Bahrain, Bangladesh, Benin, Bhutan, Bolivia, Botswana, Brazil, Brunei Darus-

---

[421]These resolutions refer to Israeli measures against Palestinian leaders. [ed. note]

[422]A/40/541.
[423]United Nations, *Treaty Series*, vol. 75, no. 973, p. 287.

salam, Bulgaria, Burkina Faso, Burma, Burundi, Byelorussia, Cape Verde, Central African Republic, Chad, Chile, China, Colombia, Congo, Cuba, Cyprus, Czechoslovakia, Democratic Kampuchea, Democratic Yemen, Djibouti, Dominica, Dominican Republic, Ecuador, Egypt, El Salvador, Equatorial Guinea, Ethiopia, Fiji, Finland, France, Gabon, Gambia, German Democratic Republic, Greece, Guatemala, Guinea, Guinea-Bissau, Guyana, Hungary, India, Indonesia, Iran, Iraq, Ireland, Italy, Jamaica, Japan, Jordan, Kenya, Kuwait, Lao People's Democratic Republic, Lebanon, Lesotho, Libya, Madagascar, Malaysia, Maldives, Mali, Malta, Mauritania, Mauritius, Mexico, Mongolia, Morocco, Mozambique, Nepal, New Zealand, Nicaragua, Niger, Nigeria, Oman, Pakistan, Panama, Peru, Philippines, Poland, Portugal, Qatar, Romania, Rwanda, Saint Vincent, Samoa, Sao Tome and Principe, Saudi Arabia, Senegal, Seychelles, Sierra Leone, Singapore, Spain, Sri Lanka, Sudan, Suriname, Sweden, Syria, Thailand, Togo, Trinidad and Tobago, Tunisia, Turkey, Uganda, Ukraine, USSR, United Arab Emirates, United Republic of Tanzania, Uruguay, Vanuatu, Venezuela, Viet Nam, Yemen, Yugoslavia, Zambia, Zimbabwe.

Against: 1

Israel.

Abstentions: 19

Belgium, Cameroon, Canada, Costa Rica, Denmark, Federal Republic of Germany, Grenada, Iceland, Ivory Coast, Liberia, Luxembourg, Malawi, Netherlands, Norway, Saint Lucia, Swaziland, United Kingdom, United States, Zaire.

Absent: 12

Angola, Barbados, Belize, Comoros, Ghana, Haiti, Honduras, Papua New Guinea, Paraguay, Solomon Islands, Somalia,* St. Christopher and Nevis.

---

*Later advised the Secretariat it had intended to vote in favour.

F

The General Assembly,

Deeply concerned that the Arab territories occupied since 1967 have been under continued Israeli military occupation,

Recalling Security Council resolution 497 (1981) of 17 December 1981,

Recalling also its resolutions 36/226 B of 17 December 1981, ES-9/1 of 5 February 1982, 37/88 E of 10 December 1982, 38/79 F of 15 December 1983 and 39/95 F of 14 December 1984,[424]

Having considered the report of the Secretary-General of 18 September 1985,[425]

Recalling its previous resolutions, in particular resolutions 3414 (XXX) of 5 December 1975, 31/61 of 9 December 1976, 32/20 of 25 November 1977, 33/28 and 33/29 of 7 December 1978, 34/70 of 6 December 1979 and 35/122

E of 11 December 1980, in which it, *inter alia,* called upon Israel to put an end to its occupation of the Arab territories and to withdraw from all those territories,

Reaffirming once more the illegality of Israel's decision of 14 December 1981 to impose laws, jurisdiction and administration on the Syrian Golan Heights, which has resulted in the effective annexation of that territory,

Reaffirming that the acquisition of territory by force is inadmissible under the Charter of the United Nations and that all territories thus occupied by Israel must be returned,

Recalling the Geneva Convention relative to the Protection of Civilian Persons in Time of War, of 12 August 1949,[426]

1. *Strongly condemns* Israel, the occupying Power, for its refusal to comply with the relevant resolutions of the General Assembly and the Security Council, particularly Council resolution 497 (1981), in which the Council, *inter alia,* decided that the Israeli decision to impose its laws, jurisdiction and administration on the occupied Syrian Golan Heights was null and void and without international legal effect and demanded that Israel, the occupying Power, should rescind forthwith its decision;

2. *Condemns* the persistence of Israel in changing the physical character, demographic composition, institutional structure and legal status of the occupied Syrian Arab Golan Heights;

3. *Determines* that all legislative and administrative measures and actions taken or to be taken by Israel, the occupying Power, that purport to alter the character and legal status of the Syrian Golan Heights are null and void and constitute a flagrant violation of international law and of the Geneva Convention relative to the Protection of Civilian Persons in Time of War, of 12 August 1949, and have no legal effect;

4. *Strongly condemns* Israel for its attempts and measures to impose forcibly Israeli citizenship and Israeli identity cards on the Syrian citizens in the occupied Syrian Arab Golan Heights and calls upon it to desist from its repressive measures against the population of the Syrian Arab Golan Heights;

5. *Calls once again upon* Member States not to recognize any of the legislative or administrative measures and actions referred to above;

6. *Requests* the Secretary-General to submit to the General Assembly at its forty-first session a report on the implementation of the present resolution.

Adopted at the 118th plenary meeting:

In favour: 136

Afghanistan, Albania, Algeria, Antigua and Barbuda, Argentina, Australia, Austria, Bahamas, Bahrain, Bangladesh, Belgium, Benin, Bhutan, Bolivia, Botswana, Brazil, Brunei Darussalam, Bulgaria, Burkina Faso, Burma, Burundi, Byelorussia, Canada, Cape Verde, Central African Republic, Chad, Chile, China, Colombia, Congo, Cuba, Cy-

---

[424]The resolutions cited are previous resolutions on Israeli practices in the occupied territories. [ed. note]
[425]A/40/649 and Add.1.

[426]United Nations, *Treaty Series,* vol. 75, no. 973, p. 287.

prus, Czechoslovakia, Democratic Kampuchea, Democratic Yemen, Denmark, Djibouti, Dominica, Dominican Republic, Ecuador, Egypt, El Salvador, Equatorial Guinea, Ethiopia, Fiji, Finland, France, Gabon, Gambia, German Democratic Republic, Federal Republic of Germany, Greece, Guatemala, Guinea, Guinea-Bissau, Guyana, Hungary, Iceland, India, Indonesia, Iran, Iraq, Ireland, Italy, Jamaica, Japan, Jordan, Kenya, Kuwait, Lao People's Democratic Republic, Lebanon, Lesotho, Libya, Luxembourg, Madagascar, Malaysia, Maldives, Mali, Malta, Mauritania, Mauritius, Mexico, Mongolia, Morocco, Mozambique, Nepal, Netherlands, New Zealand, Nicaragua, Niger, Nigeria, Norway, Oman, Pakistan, Panama, Peru, Philippines, Poland, Portugal, Qatar, Romania, Rwanda, Saint Vincent, Samoa, Sao Tome and Principe, Saudi Arabia, Senegal, Seychelles, Sierra Leone, Singapore, Somalia, Spain, Sri Lanka, Sudan, Suriname, Sweden, Syria, Thailand, Togo, Trinidad and Tobago, Tunisia, Turkey, Uganda, Ukraine, USSR, United Arab Emirates, United Kingdom, United Republic of Tanzania, Uruguay, Vanuatu, Venezuela, Viet Nam, Yemen, Yugoslavia, Zambia, Zimbabwe.

Against: 1

Israel.

Abstentions: 10

Cameroon, Costa Rica, Grenada, Ivory Coast, Liberia, Malawi, Saint Lucia, Swaziland, United States, Zaire.

Absent: 11

Angola, Barbados, Belize, Comoros, Ghana, Haiti, Honduras, Papua New Guinea, Paraguay, Solomon Islands, St. Christopher and Nevis.

G

The General Assembly,

Bearing in mind the Geneva Convention relative to the Protection of Civilian Persons in Time of War, of 12 August 1949,[427]

Deeply concerned at the continued harassment by Israel, the occupying Power, against educational institutions in the occupied Palestinian territories,

Recalling its resolutions 38/79 G of 15 December 1983 and 39/95 G of 14 December 1984,

Taking note of the report of the Secretary-General of 14 August 1985,[428]

Taking note of the relevant decisions adopted by the Executive Board of the United Nations Educational, Scientific and Cultural Organization concerning the educational and cultural situation in the occupied territories,

1. *Reaffirms* the applicability of the Geneva Convention relative to the Protection of Civilian Persons in Time of War, of 12 August 1949, to the Palestinian and other Arab territories occupied by Israel since 1967, including Jerusalem;

2. *Condemns* Israeli policies and practices against Palestinian students and faculties in schools, universities and other educational institutions in the occupied Palestinian territories, especially the policy of opening fire on defenceless students, causing many casualties;

3. *Condemns* the systematic Israeli campaign of repression against and closing of universities and other educational and vocational institutions in the occupied Palestinian territories, restricting and impeding the academic activities of Palestinian universities by subjecting the selection of courses, textbooks and educational programmes, the admission of students and the appointment of faculty members to the control and supervision of the military occupation authorities, in clear contravention of the Geneva Convention;

4. *Demands* that Israel, the occupying Power, comply with the provisions of that Convention, rescind all actions and measures against all educational institutions, ensure the freedom of those institutions and refrain forthwith from hindering the effective operation of the universities and other educational institutions;

5. *Requests* the Secretary-General to report to the General Assembly as soon as possible and not later than the beginning of its forty-first session on the implementation of the present resolution.

Adopted at the 118th plenary meeting:

In favour: 112

Afghanistan, Albania, Algeria, Antigua and Barbuda, Argentina, Austria, Bahamas, Bahrain, Bangladesh, Benin, Bhutan, Bolivia, Botswana, Brazil, Brunei Darussalam, Bulgaria, Burkina Faso, Burundi, Byelorussia, Cape Verde, Central African Republic, Chad, China, Colombia, Congo, Cuba, Cyprus, Czechoslovakia, Democratic Kampuchea, Democratic Yemen, Djibouti, Dominican Republic, Ecuador, Egypt, Equatorial Guinea, Ethiopia, Fiji, Gabon, Gambia, German Democratic Republic, Greece, Guinea, Guinea-Bissau, Guyana, Hungary, India, Indonesia, Iran, Iraq, Jamaica, Jordan, Kenya, Kuwait, Lao People's Democratic Republic, Lebanon, Lesotho, Libya, Madagascar, Malaysia, Maldives, Mali, Malta, Mauritania, Mauritius, Mexico, Mongolia, Morocco, Mozambique, Nepal, Nicaragua, Niger, Nigeria, Oman, Pakistan, Peru, Philippines, Poland, Qatar, Romania, Rwanda, Samoa, Sao Tome and Principe, Saudi Arabia, Senegal, Seychelles, Sierra Leone, Singapore, Somalia, Spain, Sri Lanka, Sudan, Suriname, Sweden, Syria, Thailand, Togo, Trinidad and Tobago, Tunisia, Turkey, Uganda, Ukraine, USSR, United Arab Emirates, United Republic of Tanzania, Uruguay, Vanuatu, Venezuela, Viet Nam, Yemen, Yugoslavia, Zambia, Zimbabwe.

Against: 2

Israel, United States.

Abstentions: 32

Australia, Belgium, Cameroon, Canada, Chile, Costa Rica, Denmark, Dominica, El Salvador, Finland, France, Federal Republic of Germany, Grenada, Guatemala, Iceland, Ireland, Italy, Ivory Coast, Japan, Liberia, Luxembourg, Malawi, Netherlands, New Zealand, Norway, Panama, Portugal, Saint Lucia, Saint Vincent, Swaziland, United Kingdom, Zaire.

Absent: 12

---

[427]*Ibid.*

[428]A/40/542.

Angola, Barbados, Belize, Burma, Comoros, Ghana, Haiti, Honduras, Papua New Guinea, Paraguay, Solomon Islands, St. Christopher and Nevis.

Resolution No. 40/165 A, B, C, D, E, F, G, H, I, J, K of 16 December 1985

ON THE UNITED NATIONS RELIEF AND WORKS AGENCY FOR PALESTINIAN REFUGEES IN THE NEAR EAST: CALLING FOR CONTRIBUTIONS BY GOVERNMENTS TO THE AGENCY AND ENDORSING ASSISTANCE TO PALESTINIAN REFUGEES, CALLING ON ISRAEL TO PERMIT THE RETURN OF DISPLACED PALESTINIANS AND TO REMOVE OBSTACLES TO THE ESTABLISHMENT OF A UNIVERSITY OF JERUSALEM FOR PALESTINIAN REFUGEES, AND REQUESTING THE SECRETARY-GENERAL TO TAKE APPROPRIATE STEPS FOR THE PROTECTION AND ADMINISTRATION OF ARAB REFUGEE PROPERTY, ASSETS AND PROPERTY RIGHTS

A

ASSISTANCE TO PALESTINE REFUGEES

The General Assembly,

Recalling its resolution 39/99 A of 14 December 1984 and all its previous resolutions on the question, including resolution 194 (III) of 11 December 1948,

Taking note of the report of the Commissioner-General of the United Nations Relief and Works Agency for Palestine Refugees in the Near East, covering the period from 1 July 1984 to 30 June 1985,[429]

1. *Notes with deep regret* that repatriation or compensation of the refugees as provided for in paragraph 11 of General Assembly resolution 194 (III) has not been effected, that no substantial progress has been made in the programme endorsed by the Assembly in paragraph 2 of its resolution 513 (VI) of 26 January 1952 for the reintegration of refugees either by repatriation or resettlement and that, therefore, the situation of the refugees continues to be a matter of serious concern;

2. *Expresses its thanks* to the Commissioner-General and to all the staff of the United Nations Relief and Works Agency for Palestine Refugees in the Near East, recognizing that the Agency is doing all it can within the limits of available resources, and also expresses its thanks to the specialized agencies and private organizations for their valuable work in assisting the refugees;

3. *Expresses its deep appreciation* to the former Commissioner-General, Mr. Olof Rydbeck, for his many years of effective service to the Agency and his dedication to the welfare of the refugees;

4. *Reiterates its request* that the headquarters of the Agency should be relocated to its former site within its area of operations as soon as practicable;

5. *Notes with regret* that the United Nations Conciliation Commission for Palestine has been unable to find a means of achieving progress in the implementation of paragraph 11 of General Assembly resolution 194 (III),[430] and re-

quests the Commission to exert continued efforts towards the implementation of that paragraph and to report to the Assembly as appropriate, but no later than 1 September 1986;

6. *Directs attention* to the continuing seriousness of the financial position of the Agency, as outlined in the report of the Commissioner-General;

7. *Notes with profound concern* that, despite the commendable and successful efforts of the Commissioner-General to collect additional contributions, this increased level of income to the Agency is still insufficient to cover essential budget requirements in the present year and that, at currently foreseen levels of giving, deficits will recur each year;

8. *Calls upon* all Governments, as a matter of urgency, to make the most generous efforts possible to meet the anticipated needs of the Agency, particularly in the light of the budgetary deficit projected in the report of the Commissioner-General, and therefore urges non-contributing Governments to contribute regularly and contributing Governments to consider increasing their regular contributions.

Adopted at the 118th plenary meeting:

In favour: 149

Afghanistan, Algeria, Antigua and Barbuda, Argentina, Australia, Austria, Bahamas, Bahrain, Bangladesh, Barbados, Belgium, Benin, Bhutan, Bolivia, Botswana, Brazil, Brunei Darussalam, Bulgaria, Burkina Faso, Burma, Burundi, Byelorussia, Cameroon, Canada, Cape Verde, Central African Republic, Chad, Chile, China, Colombia, Congo, Costa Rica, Cuba, Cyprus, Czechoslovakia, Democratic Kampuchea, Democratic Yemen, Denmark, Djibouti, Dominica, Dominican Republic, Ecuador, Egypt, El Salvador, Equatorial Guinea, Ethiopia, Fiji, Finland, France, Gabon, Gambia, German Democratic Republic, Federal Republic of Germany, Ghana, Greece, Grenada, Guatemala, Guinea, Guinea-Bissau, Guyana, Haiti, Honduras, Hungary, Iceland, India, Indonesia, Iran, Iraq, Ireland, Italy, Ivory Coast, Jamaica, Japan, Jordan, Kenya, Kuwait, Lao People's Democratic Republic, Lebanon, Lesotho, Liberia, Libya, Luxembourg, Madagascar, Malawi, Malaysia, Maldives, Mali, Malta, Mauritania, Mauritius, Mexico, Mongolia, Morocco, Mozambique, Nepal, Netherlands, New Zealand, Nicaragua, Niger, Nigeria, Norway, Oman, Pakistan, Panama, Peru, Philippines, Poland, Portugal, Qatar, Romania, Rwanda, Saint Lucia, Saint Vincent, Samoa, Sao Tome and Principe, Saudi Arabia, Senegal, Seychelles, Sierra Leone, Singapore, Somalia, Spain, Sri Lanka, Sudan, Suriname, Swaziland, Sweden, Syria, Thailand, Togo, Trinidad and Tobago, Tunisia, Turkey, Uganda, Ukraine, USSR, United Arab Emirates, United Kingdom, United Republic of Tanzania, United States, Uruguay, Vanuatu, Venezuela, Viet Nam, Yemen, Yugoslavia, Zaire, Zambia, Zimbabwe.

Against: 0

Abstention: 1

Israel.

Absent: 8

---

[429]*Official Records of the General Assembly, Fortieth Session, Supplement No. 13* (A/40/13 and Corr. 1 and Add.1 and Add.1/Corr.1).
[430]See A/40/580, annex.

Albania, Angola, Belize, Comoros, Papua New Guinea, Paraguay, Solomon Islands, St. Christopher and Nevis.

B

WORKING GROUP ON THE FINANCING OF THE UNITED NATIONS RELIEF AND WORKS AGENCY FOR PALESTINE REFUGEES IN THE NEAR EAST

The General Assembly,

Recalling its resolutions 2656 (XXV) of 7 December 1970, 2728 (XXV) of 15 December 1970, 2791 (XXVI) of 6 December 1971, 2964 (XXVII) of 13 December 1972, 3090 (XXVIII) of 7 December 1973, 3330 (XXIX) of 17 December 1974, 3419 D (XXX) of 8 December 1975, 31/15 C of 23 November 1976, 32/90 D of 13 December 1977, 33/112 D of 18 December 1978, 34/52 D of 23 November 1979, 35/13 D of 3 November 1980, 36/146 E of 16 December 1981, 37/120 A of 16 December 1982, 38/83 B of 15 December 1983 and 39/99 B of 14 December 1984,[431]

Recalling also its decision 36/462 of 16 March 1982, whereby it took note of the special report of the Working Group on the Financing of the United Nations Relief and Works Agency for Palestine Refugees in the Near East,[432] and adopted the recommendations contained therein,

Having considered the report of the Working Group on the Financing of the United Nations Relief and Works Agency for Palestine Refugees in the Near East,[433]

Taking into account the report of the Commissioner-General of the United Nations Relief and Works Agency for Palestine Refugees in the Near East, covering the period from 1 July 1984 to 30 June 1985,[434]

Gravely concerned at the critical financial situation of the Agency, which has already reduced the essential minimum services being provided to the Palestine refugees and which threatens even greater reductions in the future,

Emphasizing the urgent need for extraordinary efforts in order to maintain, at least at their present minimum level, the activities of the Agency,

1. *Commends* the Working Group on the Financing of the United Nations Relief and Works Agency for Palestine Refugees in the Near East for its efforts to assist in ensuring the Agency's financial security;

2. *Takes note with approval* of the report of the Working Group;

3. *Requests* the Working Group to continue its efforts, in co-operation with the Secretary-General and the Commissioner-General, for the financing of the Agency for a further period of one year;

4. *Requests* the Secretary-General to provide the necessary services and assistance to the Working Group for the

conduct of its work.

Adopted at the 118th plenary meeting without a vote.

C

ASSISTANCE TO PERSONS DISPLACED AS A RESULT OF THE JUNE 1967 AND SUBSEQUENT HOSTILITIES

The General Assembly,

Recalling its resolution 39/99 C of 14 December 1984 and all its previous resolutions on the question,

Taking note of the report of the Commissioner-General of the United Nations Relief and Works Agency for Palestine Refugees in the Near East, covering the period from 1 July 1984 to 30 June 1985,[435]

Concerned about the continued human suffering resulting from the hostilities in the Middle East,

1. *Reaffirms* its resolution 39/99 C and all its previous resolutions on the question;

2. *Endorses*, bearing in mind the objectives of those resolutions, the efforts of the Commissioner-General of the United Nations Relief and Works Agency for Palestine Refugees in the Near East to continue to provide humanitarian assistance as far as practicable, on an emergency basis and as a temporary measure, to other persons in the area who are at present displaced and in serious need of continued assistance as a result of the June 1967 and subsequent hostilities;

3. *Strongly appeals* to all Governments and to organizations and individuals to contribute generously for the above purposes to the United Nations Relief and Works Agency for Palestine Refugees in the Near East and to the other intergovernmental and non-governmental organizations concerned.

Adopted at the 118th plenary meeting without a vote.

D

OFFERS BY MEMBER STATES OF GRANTS AND SCHOLARSHIPS FOR HIGHER EDUCATION, INCLUDING VOCATIONAL TRAINING, FOR PALESTINE REFUGEES

The General Assembly,

Recalling its resolution 212 (III) of 19 November 1948 on assistance to Palestine refugees,

Recalling also its resolutions 35/13 B of 3 November 1980, 36/146 H of 16 December 1981, 37/120 D of 16 December 1982, 38/83 D of 15 December 1983 and 39/99 D of 14 December 1984,

Cognizant of the fact that the Palestine refugees have, for the last three decades, lost their lands and means of livelihood,

Having examined the report of the Secretary-General,[436]

Having also examined the report of the Commissioner-General of the United Nations Relief and Works Agency

---

[431]These resolutions focus on the financing of the United Nations Relief and Works Agency for Palestine Refugees in the Near East. [ed. note]
[432]A/36/866; see also A/37/591.
[433]A/40/736; see also the special report adopted on 26 March 1985 (A/40/207).
[434]*Official Records of the General Assembly, Fortieth Session, Supplement No. 13* (A/40/13 and Corr. 1 and Add.1 and Add. 1./Corr.1).

[435]*Official Records of the General Assembly, Fortieth Session, Supplement No. 13* (A/40/13 and Corr. 1 and Add.1 and Add.1./Corr.1).
[436]A/40/612.

for Palestine Refugees in the Near East, covering the period from 1 July 1984 to 30 June 1985,[437]

1. *Urges* all States to respond to the appeal contained in General Assembly resolution 32/90 F of 13 December 1977 in a manner commensurate with the needs of Palestine refugees for higher education and vocational training;

2. *Strongly appeals* to all States, specialized agencies and non-governmental organizations to augment the special allocations for grants and scholarships to Palestine refugees in addition to their contributions to the regular budget of the United Nations Relief and Works Agency for Palestine Refugees in the Near East;

3. *Expresses its appreciation* to all Governments, specialized agencies and non-governmental organizations that responded favourably to General Assembly resolution 39/99 D;

4. *Invites* the relevant specialized agencies and other organizations of the United Nations system to continue, within their respective spheres of competence, to extend assistance for higher education to Palestine refugee students;

5. *Appeals* to all States, specialized agencies and the United Nations University to contribute generously to the Palestinian universities in the territories occupied by Israel since 1967, including, in due course, the proposed University of Jerusalem "Al-Quds" for Palestine refugees;

6. *Also appeals* to all States, specialized agencies and other international bodies to contribute towards the establishment of vocational training centres for Palestine refugees;

7. *Requests* the United Nations Relief and Works Agency for Palestine Refugees in the Near East to act as the recipient and trustee for such special allocations and scholarships and to award them to qualified Palestine refugee candidates;

8. *Requests* the Secretary-General to report to the General Assembly at its forty-first session on the implementation of the present resolution.

Adopted at the 118th plenary meeting:
In favour: 147
Afghanistan, Algeria, Antigua and Barbuda, Argentina, Australia, Austria, Bahamas, Bahrain, Bangladesh, Barbados, Belgium, Benin, Bhutan, Bolivia, Botswana, Brazil, Brunei Darussalam, Bulgaria, Burkina Faso, Burma, Burundi, Byelorussia, Cameroon, Canada, Central African Republic, Chad, Chile, China, Colombia, Congo, Costa Rica, Cuba, Cyprus, Czechoslovakia, Democratic Kampuchea, Democratic Yemen, Denmark, Djibouti, Dominica, Ecuador, Egypt, El Salvador, Equatorial Guinea, Ethiopia, Fiji, Finland, France, Gabon, Gambia, German Democratic Republic, Federal Republic of Germany, Ghana, Greece, Grenada, Guatemala, Guinea, Guinea-Bissau, Guyana, Haiti, Honduras, Hungary, Iceland, India, Indonesia, Iran, Iraq, Ireland, Italy, Ivory Coast, Jamaica, Japan,

Jordan, Kenya, Kuwait, Lao People's Democratic Republic, Lebanon, Lesotho, Liberia, Libya, Luxembourg, Madagascar, Malawi, Malaysia, Maldives, Mali, Malta, Mauritania, Mauritius, Mexico, Mongolia, Morocco, Mozambique, Nepal, Netherlands, New Zealand, Nicaragua, Niger, Nigeria, Norway, Oman, Pakistan, Panama, Peru, Philippines, Poland, Portugal, Qatar, Romania, Rwanda, Saint Lucia, Saint Vincent, Samoa, Sao Tome and Principe, Saudi Arabia, Senegal, Seychelles, Sierra Leone, Singapore, Somalia, Spain, Sri Lanka, Sudan, Suriname, Swaziland, Sweden, Syria, Thailand, Togo, Trinidad and Tobago, Tunisia, Turkey, Uganda, Ukraine, USSR, United Arab Emirates, United Kingdom, United Republic of Tanzania, United States, Uruguay, Vanuatu, Venezuela, Viet Nam, Yemen, Yugoslavia, Zaire, Zambia, Zimbabwe.
Against: 0
Abstention: 1
Israel.
Absent: 10
Albania, Angola, Belize, Cape Verde, Comoros, Dominican Republic,* Papua New Guinea, Paraguay, Solomon Islands, St. Christopher and Nevis.

---

* Later advised the Secretariat it had intended to vote in favour.

E

PALESTINE REFUGEES IN THE GAZA STRIP

The General Assembly,

Recalling Security Council resolution 237 (1967) of 14 June 1967,

Recalling also General Assembly resolutions 2792 C (XXVI) of 6 December 1971, 2963 C (XXVII) of 13 December 1972, 3089 C (XXVIII) of 7 December 1973, 3331 D (XXIX) of 17 December 1974, 3419 C (XXX) of 8 December 1975, 31/15 E of 23 November 1976, 32/90 C of 13 December 1977, 33/112 E of 18 December 1978, 34/52 F of 23 November 1979, 35/13 F of 3 November 1980, 36/146 A of 16 December 1981, 37/120 E of 16 December 1982, 38/83 E of 15 December 1983 and 39/99 E of 14 December 1984,[438]

Having considered the report of the Commissioner-General of the United Nations Relief and Works Agency for Palestine Refugees in the Near East, covering the period from 1 July 1984 to 30 June 1985,[439] and the report of the Secretary-General,[440]

Recalling the provisions of paragraph 11 of its resolution 194 (III) of 11 December 1948 and considering that measures to resettle Palestine refugees in the Gaza Strip away from the homes and property from which they were displaced constitute a violation of their inalienable right of return,

---

[437]*Official Records of the General Assembly, Fortieth Session, Supplement No. 13,* (A/40/13 and Corr. 1 and Add.1 and Add.1/Corr.1).

[438]On Israeli actions harmful to Palestinian refugees in the Gaza Strip. [ed. note]
[439]*Official Records of the General Assembly, Fortieth Session,* Supplement No. 13(A/40/13 and Corr. 1 and Add.1 and Add.1/Corr.1).
[440]A/40/613.

Alarmed by the reports received from the Commissioner-General that the Israeli occupying authorities, in contravention of Israel's obligation under international law, persist in their policy of demolishing shelters occupied by refugee families,

1. *Reiterates strongly its demand* that Israel desist from the removal and resettlement of Palestine refugees in the Gaza Strip and from the destruction of their shelters;

2. *Requests* the Secretary-General, after consulting with the Commissioner-General of the United Nations Relief and Works Agency for Palestine refugees in the Near East, to report to the General Assembly, before the opening of its forty-first session, on Israel's compliance with paragraph 1 above.

Adopted at the 118th plenary meeting:
In favour: 146

Afghanistan, Albania, Algeria, Antigua and Barbuda, Argentina, Australia, Austria, Bahamas, Bahrain, Bangladesh, Barbados, Belgium, Benin, Bhutan, Bolivia, Botswana, Brazil, Brunei Darussalam, Bulgaria, Burkina Faso, Burma, Burundi, Byelorussia, Cameroon, Canada, Cape Verde, Central African Republic, Chad, Chile, China, Colombia, Congo, Costa Rica, Cuba, Cyprus, Czechoslovakia, Democratic Kampuchea, Democratic Yemen, Denmark, Djibouti, Dominica, Dominican Republic, Ecuador, Egypt, El Salvador, Equatorial Guinea, Ethiopia, Fiji, Finland, France, Gabon, Gambia, German Democratic Republic, Federal Republic of Germany, Ghana, Guatemala, Guinea, Guinea-Bissau, Guyana, Haiti, Honduras, Hungary, Iceland, India, Indonesia, Iran, Iraq, Ireland, Italy, Ivory Coast, Jamaica, Japan, Jordan, Kenya, Kuwait, Lao People's Democratic Republic, Lebanon, Lesotho, Liberia, Libya, Luxembourg, Madagascar, Malawi, Malaysia, Maldives, Mali, Malta, Mauritania, Mauritius, Mexico, Mongolia, Morocco, Mozambique, Nepal, Netherlands, New Zealand, Nicaragua, Niger, Nigeria, Norway, Oman, Pakistan, Panama, Paraguay, Peru, Philippines, Poland, Portugal, Qatar, Romania, Rwanda, Saint Lucia, Saint Vincent, Samoa, Sao Tome and Principe, Saudi Arabia, Senegal, Seychelles, Sierra Leone, Singapore, Spain, Sri Lanka, Sudan, Suriname, Swaziland, Sweden, Syria, Thailand, Togo, Trinidad and Tobago, Tunisia, Turkey, Uganda, Ukraine, USSR, United Arab Emirates, United Kingdom, United Republic of Tanzania, Uruguay, Vanuatu, Venezuela, Viet Nam, Yemen, Yugoslavia, Zambia, Zimbabwe.

Against: 2
Israel, United States.

Abstentions: 2
Grenada, Zaire.

Absent: 8
Angola, Belize, Comoros, Greece,* Papua New Guinea, Solomon Islands, Somalia, St. Christopher and Nevis.

---

* Later advised the Secretariat it had intended to vote in favour.

F

RESUMPTION OF THE RATION DISTRIBUTION TO
PALESTINE REFUGEES

The General Assembly,

Recalling its resolutions 36/146 F of 16 December 1981, 37/120 F of 16 December 1982, 38/83 F of 15 December 1983, 39/99 F of 14 December 1984 and all its previous resolutions on the question, including resolution 302 (IV) of 8 December 1949,

Having considered the report of the Commissioner-General of the United Nations Relief and Works Agency for Palestine Refugees in the Near East, covering the period from 1 July 1984 to 30 June 1985,[441] and the report of the Secretary-General,[442]

Deeply concerned at the interruption by the Agency, owing to financial difficulties, of the general ration distribution to Palestine refugees in all fields,

1. *Regrets* that its resolutions 37/120 F, 38/83 F and 39/99 F have not been implemented;

2. *Calls once again upon* all Governments, as a matter of urgency, to make the most generous efforts possible and to offer the necessary resources to meet the needs of the United Nations Relief and Works Agency for Palestine Refugees in the Near East, particularly in the light of the interruption by the Agency of the general ration distribution to Palestine refugees in all fields, and therefore urges non-contributing Governments to contribute regularly and contributing Governments to consider increasing their regular contributions;

3. *Requests* the Commissioner-General to resume on a continuing basis the interrupted general ration distribution to Palestine refugees in all fields;

4. *Requests* the Secretary-General, in consultation with the Commissioner-General, to report to the General Assembly at its forty-first session on the implementation of the present resolution.

Adopted at the 118th plenary meeting:
In favour: 127

Afghanistan, Algeria, Antigua and Barbuda, Argentina, Bahamas, Bahrain, Bangladesh, Barbados, Benin, Bhutan, Bolivia, Botswana, Brazil, Brunei Darussalam, Bulgaria, Burkina Faso, Burma, Burundi, Byelorussia, Cameroon, Cape Verde, Central African Republic, Chad, Chile, China, Colombia, Congo, Cuba, Cyprus, Czechoslovakia, Democratic Kampuchea, Democratic Yemen, Djibouti, Dominica, Dominican Republic, Ecuador, Egypt, El Salvador, Equatorial Guinea, Ethiopia, Fiji, Gabon, Gambia, German Democratic Republic, Ghana, Greece, Guatemala, Guinea, Guinea-Bissau, Guyana, Haiti, Honduras, Hungary, India, Indonesia, Iran, Iraq, Ivory Coast, Jamaica, Jordan, Kenya, Kuwait, Lao People's Democratic Republic, Lebanon, Lesotho, Liberia, Libya, Madagascar, Malawi, Malaysia, Maldives, Mali, Malta, Mauritania, Mauritius, Mexico, Mongolia, Morocco, Mozambique, Nepal, Nicaragua, Niger, Nigeria, Oman, Pakistan, Panama, Paraguay, Peru, Philippines, Poland, Qatar, Romania, Rwanda, Saint

---

[441]*Official Records of the General Assembly, Fortieth Session*, Supplement No. 13 (A/40/13 and Corr. 1 and Add.1/Corr.1).
[442]A/40/766.

Lucia, Saint Vincent, Samoa, Sao Tome and Principe, Saudi Arabia, Senegal, Seychelles, Sierra Leone, Singapore, Somalia, Sri Lanka, Sudan, Suriname, Swaziland, Syria, Thailand, Togo, Trinidad and Tobago, Tunisia, Turkey, Uganda, Ukraine, USSR, United Arab Emirates, United Republic of Tanzania, Uruguay, Vanuatu, Venezuela, Viet Nam, Yemen, Yugoslavia, Zaire, Zambia, Zimbabwe.

Against: 20

Australia, Belgium, Canada, Denmark, Finland, France, Federal Republic of Germany, Iceland, Ireland, Israel, Italy, Japan, Luxembourg, Netherlands, New Zealand, Norway, Portugal, Sweden, United Kingdom, United States.

Abstentions: 4

Austria, Costa Rica, Grenada, Spain.

Absent: 7

Albania, Angola, Belize, Comoros, Papua New Guinea, Solomon Islands, St. Christopher and Nevis.

G

POPULATION AND REFUGEES DISPLACED SINCE 1967

The General Assembly,

Recalling Security Council resolution 237 (1967) of 14 June 1967,

Recalling also General Assembly resolutions 2252 (ES-V) of 4 July 1967, 2452 A (XXIII) of 19 December 1968, 2535 B (XXIV) of 10 December 1969, 2672 D (XXV) of 8 December 1970, 2792 E (XXVI) of 6 December 1971, 2963 C and D (XXVII) of 13 December 1972, 3089 C (XXVIII) of 7 December 1973, 3331 D (XXIX) of 17 December 1974, 3419 C (XXX) of 8 December 1975, 31/15 D of 23 November 1976, 32/90 E of 13 December 1977, 33/112 F of 18 December 1978, 34/52 E of 23 November 1979, ES-7/2 of 29 July 1980, 35/13 E of 3 November 1980, 36/146 B of 16 December 1981, 37/120 G of 16 December 1982, 38/83 G of 15 December 1983 and 39/99 G of 14 December 1984,[443]

Having considered the report of the Commissioner-General of the United Nations Relief and Works Agency for Palestine Refugees in the Near East, covering the period from 1 July 1984 to 30 June 1985,[444] and the report of the Secretary-General,[445]

1. *Reaffirms* the inalienable right of all displaced inhabitants to return to their homes or former places of residence in the territories occupied by Israel since 1967, and declares once more that any attempt to restrict, or to attach conditions to, the free exercise of the right to return by any displaced person is inconsistent with that inalienable right and inadmissible;

2. *Considers* any and all agreements embodying any restriction on, or condition for, the return of the displaced inhabitants as null and void;

3. *Strongly deplores* the continued refusal of the Israeli authorities to take steps for the return of the displaced inhabitants;

4. *Calls once more upon* Israel:

(*a*) To take immediate steps for the return of all displaced inhabitants;

(*b*) To desist from all measures that obstruct the return of the displaced inhabitants, including measures affecting the physical and demographic structure of the occupied territories;

5. *Requests* the Secretary-General, after consulting with the Commissioner-General of the United Nations Relief and Works Agency for Palestine Refugees in the Near East, to report to the General Assembly before the opening of its forty-first session on Israel's compliance with paragraph 4 above.

Adopted at the 118th plenary meeting:

In Favour: 127

Afghanistan, Albania, Algeria, Antigua and Barbuda, Argentina, Bahamas, Bahrain, Bangladesh, Barbados, Benin, Bhutan, Bolivia, Botswana, Brazil, Brunei Darussalam, Bulgaria, Burkina Faso, Burma, Burundi, Byelorussia, Cameroon, Cape Verde, Central African Republic, Chad, Chile, China, Colombia, Congo, Cuba, Cyprus, Czechoslovakia, Democratic Kampuchea, Democratic Yemen, Djibouti, Dominica, Dominican Republic, Ecuador, Egypt, El Salvador, Equatorial Guinea, Ethiopia, Fiji, Gabon, Gambia, German Democratic Republic, Ghana, Greece, Guatemala, Guinea, Guinea-Bissau, Guyana, Haiti, Honduras, Hungary, India, Indonesia, Iran, Iraq, Ivory Coast, Jamaica, Japan, Jordan, Kenya, Kuwait, Lao People's Democratic Republic, Lebanon, Lesotho, Liberia, Libya, Madagascar, Malaysia, Maldives, Mali, Malta, Mauritania, Mauritius, Mexico, Mongolia, Morocco, Mozambique, Nepal, Nicaragua, Niger, Nigeria, Oman, Pakistan, Panama, Peru, Philippines, Poland, Portugal, Qatar, Romania, Rwanda, Saint Lucia, Saint Vincent, Samoa, Sao Tome and Principe, Saudi Arabia, Senegal, Seychelles, Sierra Leone, Singapore, Somalia, Spain, Sri Lanka, Sudan, Suriname, Syria, Thailand, Togo, Trinidad and Tobago, Tunisia, Turkey, Uganda, Ukraine, USSR, United Arab Emirates, United Republic of Tanzania, Uruguay, Vanuatu, Venezuela, Viet Nam, Yemen, Yugoslavia, Zambia, Zimbabwe.

Against: 2

Israel, United States.

Abstentions: 23

Australia, Austria, Belgium, Canada, Costa Rica, Denmark, Finland, France, Federal Republic of Germany, Grenada, Iceland, Ireland, Italy, Luxembourg, Malawi, Netherlands, New Zealand, Norway, Paraguay, Swaziland, Sweden, United Kingdom, Zaire.

Absent: 6

Angola, Belize, Comoros, Papua New Guinea, Solomon Islands, St. Christopher and Nevis.

---

[443]Concerning persons displaced since 1967. [ed. note]
[444]*Official Records of the General Assembly, Fortieth Session,* Supplement No. 13 (A/40/13 and Corr. 1 and Add. 1 and Add.1/Corr.1).
[445]A/40/614.

H

REVENUES DERIVED FROM PALESTINE REFUGEE PROPERTIES

The General Assembly,

Recalling its resolutions 35/13 A to F of 3 November 1980, 36/146 C of 16 December 1981, 37/120 H of 16 December 1982, 38/83 H of 15 December 1983, 39/99 H of 14 December 1984 and all its previous resolutions on the question, including resolution 194 (III) of 11 December 1948,

Taking note of the report of the Secretary-General,[446]

Taking note also of the report of the United Nations Conciliation Commission for Palestine, covering the period from 1 September 1984 to 31 August 1985,[447]

Recalling that the Universal Declaration of Human Rights and the principles of international law uphold the principle that no one shall be arbitrarily deprived of his or her private property,

Considering that the Palestine Arab refugees are entitled to their property and to the income derived from their property, in conformity with the principles of justice and equity,

Recalling, in particular, its resolution 394 (V) of 14 December 1950, in which it directed the United Nations Conciliation Commission for Palestine, in consultation with the parties concerned, to prescribe measures for the protection of the rights, property and interests of the Palestine Arab refugees,

Taking note of the completion of the programme of identification and evaluation of Arab property, as announced by the United Nations Conciliation Commission for Palestine in its twenty-second progress report,[448] and of the fact that the Land Office had a schedule of Arab owners and file of documents defining the location, area and other particulars of Arab property,

1. *Requests* the Secretary-General to take all appropriate steps, in consultation with the United Nations Conciliation Commission for Palestine, for the protection and administration of Arab property, assets and property rights in Israel, and to establish a fund for the receipt of income derived therefrom, on behalf of the rightful owners;

2. *Calls once again upon* Israel to render all facilities and assistance to the Secretary-General in the implementation of the present resolution;

3. *Calls upon* all other Governments of Member States concerned to provide the Secretary-General with any pertinent information in their possession concerning Arab property, assets and property rights in Israel, which would assist the Secretary-General in the implementation of the present resolution;

4. *Deplores* Israel's refusal to co-operate with the Secretary-General in the implementation of the resolutions on the question;

5. *Requests* the Secretary-General to report to the General Assembly at its forty-first session on the implementation of the present resolution.

Adopted at the 118th plenary meeting:

In favour: 122

Afghanistan, Albania, Algeria, Antigua and Barbuda, Argentina, Bahamas, Bahrain, Bangladesh, Barbados, Benin, Bhutan, Bolivia, Botswana, Brazil, Brunei Darussalam, Bulgaria, Burkina Faso, Burma, Burundi, Byelorussia, Cameroon, Cape Verde, Central African Republic, Chad, Chile, China, Colombia, Congo, Cuba, Cyprus, Czechoslovakia, Democratic Kampuchea, Democratic Yemen, Djibouti, Dominica, Dominican Republic, Ecuador, Egypt, El Salvador, Equatorial Guinea, Ethiopia, Fiji, Gabon, Gambia, German Democratic Republic, Ghana, Greece, Guatemala, Guinea, Guinea-Bissau, Guyana, Honduras, Hungary, India, Indonesia, Iran, Iraq, Jamaica, Jordan, Kenya, Kuwait, Lao People's Democratic Republic, Lebanon, Lesotho, Libya, Madagascar, Malaysia, Maldives, Mali, Malta, Mauritania, Mauritius, Mexico, Mongolia, Morocco, Mozambique, Nepal, Nicaragua, Niger, Nigeria, Oman, Pakistan, Panama, Peru, Philippines, Poland, Portugal, Qatar, Romania, Rwanda, Saint Lucia, Saint Vincent, Samoa, Sao Tome and Principe, Saudi Arabia, Senegal, Seychelles, Sierra Leone, Singapore, Spain, Sri Lanka, Sudan, Suriname, Syria, Thailand, Togo, Trinidad and Tobago, Tunisia, Turkey, Uganda, Ukraine, USSR, United Arab Emirates, United Republic of Tanzania, Uruguay, Vanuatu, Venezuela, Viet Nam, Yemen, Yugoslavia, Zambia, Zimbabwe.

Against: 2

Israel, United States.

Abstentions: 26

Australia, Austria, Belgium, Canada, Costa Rica, Denmark, Finland, France, Federal Republic of Germany, Grenada, Iceland, Ireland, Italy, Ivory Coast, Japan, Liberia, Luxembourg, Malawi, Netherlands, New Zealand, Norway, Paraguay, Swaziland, Sweden, United Kingdom, Zaire.

Absent: 8

Angola, Belize, Comoros, Haiti, Papua New Guinea, Solomon Islands, Somalia, St. Christopher and Nevis.

I

PROTECTION OF PALESTINE REFUGEES

The General Assembly,

Recalling Security Council resolutions 508 (1982) of 5 June 1982, 509 (1982) of 6 June 1982, 511 (1982) of 18 June 1982, 512 (1982) of 19 June 1982, 513 (1982) of 4 July 1982, 515 (1982) of 29 July 1982, 517 (1982) of 4 August 1982, 518 (1982) of 12 August 1982, 519 (1982) of 17 August 1982, 520 (1982) of 17 September 1982 and

---

[446]A/40/616.

[447]A/40/580, annex.

[448]*Official Records of the General Assembly, Nineteenth Session, Annex No. 11,* document A/5700.

523 (1982) of 18 October 1982,[449]

Recalling General Assembly resolutions ES-7/5 of 26 June 1982, ES-7/6 and ES-7/8 of 19 August 1982, ES-7/9 of 24 September 1982, 37/120 J of 16 December 1982, 38/83 I of 15 December 1983 and 39/99 I of 14 December 1984,

Having considered the report of the Secretary-General,[450]

Having also considered the report of the Commissioner-General of the United Nations Relief and Works Agency for Palestine Refugees in the Near East, covering the period from 1 July 1984 to 30 June 1985,[451]

Referring to the humanitarian principles of the Geneva Convention relative to the Protection of Civilian Persons in Time of War, of 12 August 1949,[452] and to the obligations arising from the Regulations annexed to the Hague Convention IV of 1907,[453]

Taking into consideration the marked deterioration in the security situation experienced by the refugees living in the Gaza Strip as reported by the Commissioner-General in his statement of 4 November 1985,[454]

Deeply concerned at the lack of security for the Palestine refugees in the Palestinian and other Arab territories occupied since 1967, including Jerusalem, resulting in scores of violent deaths, woundings, kidnappings, disappearances, evictions in the face of threats, explosions and arsons,

Deeply distressed at the sufferings of the Palestinians resulting from the Israeli invasion of Lebanon,

Reaffirming its support for the sovereignty, unity and territorial integrity of Lebanon, within its internationally recognized boundaries,

1. *Urges* the Secretary-General, in consultation with the United Nations Relief and Works Agency for Palestine Refugees in the Near East, to undertake effective measures to guarantee the safety and security and the legal and human rights of the Palestine refugees in all the territories under Israeli occupation in 1967 and thereafter;

2. *Holds* Israel responsible for the security of the Palestine refugees in the Palestinian and other Arab territories occupied since 1967, including Jerusalem, and calls upon it to fulfil its obligations as the occupying Power in this regard, in accordance with the pertinent provisions of the Geneva Convention relative to the Protection of Civilian Persons in Time of War, of 12 August 1949;

3. *Calls once again upon* Israel, the occupying Power, to release forthwith all detained Palestine refugees, includ-ing the employees of the United Nations Relief and Works Agency for Palestine Refugees in the Near East;

4. *Urges* the Commissioner-General to provide housing, in consultation with the Government of Lebanon, to the Palestine refugees whose houses were demolished or razed by the Israeli forces;

5. *Calls once again upon* Israel to compensate the Agency for the damage to its property and facilities resulting from the Israeli invasion of Lebanon, without prejudice to Israel's responsibility for all damages resulting from that invasion;

6. *Requests* the Secretary-General, in consultation with the Commissioner-General, to report to the General Assembly, before the opening of its forty-first session, on the implementation of the present resolution.

Adopted at the 118th plenary meeting:

In favour: 116

Afghanistan, Albania, Algeria, Antigua and Barbuda, Argentina, Bahamas, Bahrain, Bangladesh, Barbados, Benin, Bhutan, Bolivia, Botswana, Brazil, Brunei Darussalam, Bulgaria, Burkina Faso, Burma, Burundi, Byelorussia, Cameroon, Cape Verde, Central African Republic, Chad, Chile, China, Colombia, Congo, Cuba, Cyprus, Czechoslovakia, Democratic Kampuchea, Democratic Yemen, Djibouti, Dominica, Dominican Republic, Ecuador, Egypt, Equatorial Guinea, Ethiopia, Fiji, Gabon, Gambia, German Democratic Republic, Ghana, Guinea, Guinea-Bissau, Guyana, Honduras, Hungary, India, Indonesia, Iran, Iraq, Jamaica, Jordan, Kenya, Kuwait, Lao People's Democratic Republic, Lebanon, Lesotho, Libya, Madagascar, Malaysia, Maldives, Mali, Malta, Mauritania, Mauritius, Mexico, Mongolia, Morocco, Mozambique, Nepal, Nicaragua, Niger, Nigeria, Oman, Pakistan, Peru, Philippines, Poland, Qatar, Romania, Rwanda, Saint Lucia, Saint Vincent, Samoa, Sao Tome and Principe, Saudi Arabia, Senegal, Seychelles, Sierra Leone, Singapore, Somalia, Sri Lanka, Sudan, Syria, Thailand, Togo, Trinidad and Tobago, Tunisia, Turkey, Uganda, Ukraine, USSR, United Arab Emirates, United Republic of Tanzania, Uruguay, Vanuatu, Venezuela, Viet Nam, Yemen, Yugoslavia, Zambia, Zimbabwe.

Against: 2

Israel, United States.

Abstentions: 33

Australia, Austria, Belgium, Canada, Costa Rica, Denmark, El Salvador, Finland, France, Federal Republic of Germany, Greece, Grenada, Guatemala, Haiti, Iceland, Ireland, Italy, Ivory Coast, Japan, Liberia, Luxembourg, Malawi, Netherlands, New Zealand, Norway, Panama, Paraguay, Portugal, Spain, Swaziland, Sweden, United Kingdom, Zaire.

Absent: 7

Angola, Belize, Comoros, Papua New Guinea, Solomon Islands, St. Christopher and Nevis, Suriname.

J

PALESTINE REFUGEES IN THE WEST BANK

The General Assembly,

Recalling Security Council resolution 237 (1967) of 14

---

[449]The resolutions cited in this paragraph and the next focus principally upon the Israeli invasion of Lebanon and the condition of Palestinian refugees there. [ed. note]

[450]A/40/756.

[451]*Official Records of the General Assembly, Fortieth Session,* Supplement No. 13 (A/40/13 and Corr.1 and Add.1 and Add.1/Corr.1).

[452]United Nations, *Treaty Series,* vol. 75, no. 973, p. 287.

[453]Carnegie Endowment for International Peace, The Hague Conventions and Declarations of 1899 and 1907 (New York, Oxford University Press, 1915), p. 100.

[454]See *Official Records of the General Assembly, Fortieth Session, Special Political Committee,* 22nd meeting, paras. 27-38.

June 1967,

Recalling also General Assembly resolutions 38/83 J of 15 December 1983 and 39/99 J of 14 December 1984,

Having considered the report of the Security-General,[455]

Having also considered the report of the Commissioner-General of the United Nations Relief and Works Agency for Palestine Refugees in the Near East, covering the period from 1 July 1984 to 30 June 1985,[456]

Alarmed by Israel's plans to remove and resettle the Palestine refugees of the West Bank and to destroy their camps,

Recalling the provisions of paragraph 11 of its resolution 194 (III) of 11 December 1948 and considering that measures to resettle Palestine refugees in the West Bank away from the homes and property from which they were displaced constitute a violation of their inalienable right of return,

1. *Calls once again upon* Israel to abandon its plans and to refrain from the removal, and from any action that may lead to the removal and resettlement, of Palestine refugees in the West Bank and from the destruction of their camps,

2. *Requests* the Secretary-General, in co-operation with the Commissioner-General of the United Nations Relief and Works Agency for Palestine Refugees in the Near East, to keep the matter under close supervision and to report to the General Assembly, before the opening of its forty-first session, on any developments regarding this matter.

Adopted at the 118th plenary meeting:

In favour: 146

Afghanistan, Albania, Algeria, Antigua and Barbuda, Argentina, Australia, Austria, Bahamas, Bahrain, Bangladesh, Barbados, Belgium, Benin, Bhutan, Bolivia, Botswana, Brazil, Brunei Darussalam, Bulgaria, Burkina Faso, Burma, Burundi, Byelorussia, Cameroon, Canada, Cape Verde, Central African Republic, Chad, Chile, China, Colombia, Congo, Costa Rica, Cuba, Cyprus, Czechoslovakia, Democratic Kampuchea, Democratic Yemen, Denmark, Djibouti, Dominica, Dominican Republic, Ecuador, Egypt, El Salvador, Equatorial Guinea, Ethiopia, Fiji, Finland, France, Gabon, Gambia, German Democratic Republic, Federal Republic of Germany, Ghana, Greece, Guatemala, Guinea, Guinea-Bissau, Guyana, Haiti, Honduras, Hungary, Iceland, India, Indonesia, Iran, Iraq, Ireland, Italy, Ivory Coast, Jamaica, Japan, Jordan, Kenya, Kuwait, Lao People's Democratic Republic, Lebanon, Lesotho, Liberia, Libya, Luxembourg, Madagascar, Malaysia, Maldives, Mali, Malta, Mauritania, Mauritius, Mexico, Mongolia, Morocco, Mozambique, Nepal, Netherlands, New Zealand, Nicaragua, Niger, Nigeria, Norway, Oman, Pakistan, Panama, Paraguay, Peru, Philippines, Poland, Portugal, Qatar, Romania, Saint Lucia, Saint Vincent, Samoa, Sao Tome and Principe, Saudi Arabia, Senegal, Seychelles, Sierra Leone, Singapore, Spain, Sri Lanka, Sudan, Suriname, Swaziland, Sweden, Syria, Thailand, Togo, Trinidad and Tobago, Tunisia, Turkey, Uganda, Ukraine, USSR, United Arab Emirates, United Kingdom, United Republic of Tanzania, Uruguay, Vanuatu, Venezuela, Viet Nam, Yemen, Yugoslavia, Zaire, Zambia, Zimbabwe.

Against: 2

Israel, United States.

Abstentions: 2

Grenada, Malawi.

Absent: 8

Angola, Belize, Comoros, Papua New Guinea, Rwanda, Solomon Islands, Somalia,* St. Christopher and Nevis.

---

* Later advised the Secretariat it had intended to vote in favour.

K

UNIVERSITY OF JERUSALEM "AL-QUDS" FOR PALESTINE REFUGEES

The General Assembly,

Recalling its resolutions 36/146 G of 16 December 1981, 37/120 C of 16 December 1982, 38/83 K of 15 December 1983 and 39/99 K of 14 December 1984,

Having examined the report of the Secretary-General on the question of the establishment of a university of Jerusalem,[457]

Having also examined the report of the Commissioner-General of the United Nations Relief and Works Agency for Palestine Refugees in the Near East, covering the period from 1 July 1984 to 30 June 1985,[458]

1. *Commends* the constructive efforts made by the Secretary-General, the Commissioner-General of the United Nations Relief and Works Agency for Palestine Refugees in the Near East, the Council of the United Nations University and the United Nations Educational, Scientific and Cultural Organization, which worked diligently towards the implementation of General Assembly resolution 38/83 D of 15 December 1983 and other relevant resolutions;

2. *Further commends* the close co-operation of the competent educational authorities concerned;

3. *Emphasizes* the need for strengthening the educational system in the Arab territories occupied since 5 June 1967, including Jerusalem, and specifically the need for the establishment of the proposed university;

4. *Requests* the Secretary-General to continue to take all necessary measures for establishing the University of Jerusalem, "Al-Quds," in accordance with General Assembly resolution 35/13 B of 3 November 1980, giving due consideration to the recommendations consistent with the provisions of that resolution;

5. *Calls upon* Israel, the occupying Power, to co-operate

---

[455]A/40/615.

[456]*Official Records of the General Assembly, Fortieth Session,* Supplement No. 13 (A/40/13 and Corr.1 and Add.1 and Add.1/Corr.1).

[457]A/40/543.

[458]*Official Records of the General Assembly, Fortieth Session,* Supplement No. 13 (A/40/13 and Corr.1 and Add.1 and Add.1/Corr.1).

in the implementation of the present resolution and to remove the hindrances which it has put in the way of establishing the University of Jerusalem;

6. *Requests* the Secretary-General to report to the General Assembly at its forty-first session on the progress made in the implementation of the present resolution.

Adopted at the 118th plenary meeting:
In favour: 149

Afghanistan, Albania, Algeria, Antigua and Barbuda, Argentina, Australia, Austria, Bahamas, Bahrain, Bangladesh, Barbados, Belgium, Benin, Bhutan, Bolivia, Botswana, Brazil, Brunei Darussalam, Bulgaria, Burkina Faso, Burma, Burundi, Byelorussia, Cameroon, Canada, Cape Verde, Central African Republic, Chad, Chile, China, Colombia, Congo, Costa Rica, Cuba, Cyprus, Czechoslovakia, Democratic Kampuchea, Democratic Yemen, Denmark, Djibouti, Dominica, Dominican Republic, Ecuador, Egypt, El Salvador, Equatorial Guinea, Ethiopia, Fiji, Finland, France, Gabon, Gambia, German Democratic Republic, Federal Republic of Germany, Ghana, Greece, Guatemala, Guinea, Guinea-Bissau, Guyana, Haiti, Honduras, Hungary, Iceland, India, Indonesia, Iran, Iraq, Ireland, Italy, Ivory Coast, Jamaica, Japan, Jordan, Kenya, Kuwait, Lao People's Democratic Republic, Lebanon, Lesotho, Liberia, Libya, Luxembourg, Madagascar, Malawi, Malaysia, Maldives, Mali, Malta, Mauritania, Mauritius, Mexico, Mongolia, Morocco, Mozambique, Nepal, Netherlands, New Zealand, Nicaragua, Niger, Nigeria, Norway, Oman, Pakistan, Panama, Paraguay, Peru, Philippines, Poland, Portugal, Qatar, Romania, Rwanda, Saint Lucia, Saint Vincent, Samoa, Sao Tome and Principe, Saudi Arabia, Senegal, Seychelles, Sierra Leone, Singapore, Somalia, Spain, Sri Lanka, Sudan, Suriname, Swaziland, Sweden, Syria, Thailand, Togo, Trinidad and Tobago, Tunisia, Turkey, Uganda, Ukraine, USSR, United Arab Emirates, United Kingdom, United Republic of Tanzania, Uruguay, Vanuatu, Venezuela, Viet Nam, Yemen, Yugoslavia, Zaire, Zambia, Zimbabwe.

Against: 2
Israel, United States.
Abstention: 1
Grenada.
Absent: 6

Angola, Belize, Comoros, Papua New Guinea, Solomon Islands, St. Christopher and Nevis.

Resolution No. 40/167 of 16 December 1985

REQUESTING THE SECRETARY-GENERAL TO MONITOR ANY NEW DEVELOPMENT RELATING TO THE ISRAELI PROPOSAL TO BUILD A CANAL LINKING THE MEDITERRANEAN SEA TO THE DEAD SEA

The General Assembly,
Recalling its resolutions 36/150 of 16 December 1981, 37/122 of 16 December 1982, 38/85 of 15 December 1983

and 39/101 of 14 December 1984,[459]

Taking note of the report of the Secretary-General,[460]

1. *Requests* the Secretary-General to monitor on a continuing basis any new development relating to the proposed canal linking the Mediterranean Sea to the Dead Sea and to report all findings in this regard to the General Assembly;

2. *Decides* to resume consideration of this item in case activities by Israel relating to the said canal are resumed.

Adopted at the 118th plenary meeting:
In favour: 150

Afghanistan, Albania, Algeria, Argentina, Australia, Austria, Bahamas, Bahrain, Bangladesh, Barbados, Belgium, Benin, Bhutan, Bolivia, Botswana, Brazil, Brunei Darussalam, Bulgaria, Burkina Faso, Burma, Burundi, Byelorussia, Cameroon, Canada, Cape Verde, Central African Republic, Chad, Chile, China, Colombia, Comoros, Congo, Costa Rica, Cuba, Cyprus, Czechoslovakia, Democratic Kampuchea, Democratic Yemen, Denmark, Djibouti, Dominica, Dominican Republic, Ecuador, Egypt, El Salvador, Equatorial Guinea, Ethiopia, Fiji, Finland, France, Gabon, Gambia, German Democratic Republic, Federal Republic of Germany, Ghana, Greece, Grenada, Guatemala, Guinea, Guinea-Bissau, Guyana, Haiti, Honduras, Hungary, Iceland, India, Indonesia, Iran, Iraq, Ireland, Italy, Ivory Coast, Jamaica, Japan, Jordan, Kenya, Kuwait, Lao People's Democratic Republic, Lebanon, Lesotho, Liberia, Libya, Luxembourg, Madagascar, Malawi, Malaysia, Maldives, Mali, Malta, Mauritania, Mauritius, Mexico, Mongolia, Morocco, Mozambique, Nepal, Netherlands, New Zealand, Nicaragua, Niger, Nigeria, Norway, Oman, Pakistan, Panama, Paraguay, Peru, Philippines, Poland, Portugal, Qatar, Romania, Rwanda, Saint Lucia, Saint Vincent, Samoa, Sao Tome and Principe, Saudi Arabia, Senegal, Seychelles, Sierra Leone, Singapore, Somalia, Spain, Sri Lanka, Sudan, Suriname, Swaziland, Sweden, Syria, Thailand, Togo, Trinidad and Tobago, Tunisia, Turkey, Uganda, Ukraine, USSR, United Arab Emirates, United Kingdom, United Republic of Tanzania, United States, Uruguay, Vanuatu, Venezuela, Viet Nam, Yemen, Yugoslavia, Zaire, Zambia, Zimbabwe.

Against: 1
Israel.
Abstentions: 0
Absent: 7

Angola, Antigua and Barbuda, Belize, Comoros, Papua New Guinea, Solomon Islands, St. Christopher and Nevis.

---

[459]On Israel's proposed canal between the Mediterranean and the Dead Sea. [ed. note]
[460]A/40/803.

Resolution No. 40/168 A, B, C of 16 December 1985

ON THE SITUATION IN THE MIDDLE EAST: CONDEMNING ISRAEL'S POLICIES IN THE OCCUPIED TERRITORIES AND CALLING FOR ITS COMPLETE WITHDRAWAL FROM THEM, DECLARING THE NEED FOR RECOGNITION OF THE RIGHT OF THE

PALESTINIAN PEOPLE, UNDER THE LEADERSHIP OF THE PALESTINE LIBERATION ORGANIZATION, TO SELF-DETERMINATION AND AN INDEPENDENT STATE, AND CALLING ON ALL STATES TO PUT AN END TO THE FLOW OF AID TO ISRAEL

The General Assembly,

Having discussed the item entitled "The situation in the Middle East",

Reaffirming its resolutions 36/226 A and B of 17 December 1981, ES-9/1 of 5 February 1982, 37/123 F of 20 December 1982, 38/58 A to E of 13 December 1983, 38/180 A to D of 19 December 1983 and 39/146 A to C of 14 December 1984,

Recalling Security Council resolutions 425 (1978) of 19 March 1978, 497 (1981) of 17 December 1981, 508 (1982) of 5 June 1982, 509 (1982) of 6 June 1982, 511 (1982) of 18 June 1982, 512 (1982) of 19 June 1982, 513 (1982) of 4 July 1982, 515 (1982) of 29 July 1982, 516 (1982) of 1 August 1982, 517 (1982) of 4 August 1982, 518 (1982) of 12 August 1982, 519 (1982) of 17 August 1982, 520 (1982) of 17 September 1982, 521 (1982) of 19 September 1982 and 555 (1984) of 12 October 1984,[461]

Taking note of the reports of the Secretary-General of 11 March 1985,[462] 24 September 1985,[463] and 22 October 1985,[464]

Reaffirming the need for continued collective support for the resolutions adopted by the Twelfth Arab Summit Conference, held at Fez, Morocco, on 25 November 1981 and from 6 to 9 September 1982,[465] reiterating its previous resolutions regarding the Palestinian question and its support for the Palestine Liberation Organization as the sole, legitimate representative of the Palestinian people, and considering that the convening of an International Peace Conference on the Middle East, under the auspices of the United Nations, in accordance with General Assembly resolution 38/58 C and other relevant resolutions related to the question of Palestine, would contribute to the promotion of peace in the region,

Welcoming all efforts contributing towards the realization of the inalienable rights of the Palestinian people through the achievement of a comprehensive, just and lasting peace in the Middle East, in accordance with the United Nations resolutions relating to the question of Palestine and to the situation in the Middle East,

Welcoming the world-wide support extended to the just cause of the Palestinian people and the other Arab countries in their struggle against Israeli aggression and occupation in order to achieve a comprehensive, just and lasting peace in the Middle East and the full exercise by the Palestinian people of its inalienable national rights, as affirmed by previous resolutions of the General Assembly relating to the question of Palestine and to the situation in the Middle East,

Gravely concerned that the Palestinian and other Arab territories occupied since 1967, including Jerusalem, still remain under Israeli occupation, that the relevant resolutions of the United Nations have not been implemented and that the Palestinian people is still denied the restoration of its land and the exercise of its inalienable national rights in conformity with international law, as reaffirmed by resolutions of the United Nations,

Reaffirming the applicability of the Geneva Convention relative to the Protection of Civilian Persons in Time of War, of 12 August 1949,[466] to all the occupied Palestinian and other Arab territories, including Jerusalem,

Reaffirming also all relevant United Nations resolutions which stipulate that the acquisition of territory by force is inadmissible under the Charter of the United Nations and the principles of international law and that Israel must withdraw unconditionally from all the Palestinian and other Arab territories occupied by Israel since 1967, including Jerusalem,

Reaffirming further the imperative necessity of establishing a comprehensive, just and lasting peace in the region, based on full respect for the Charter and the principles of international law,

Gravely concerned also at the continuing Israeli policies involving the escalation and expansion of the conflict in the region, which further violate the principles of international law and endanger international peace and security,

Stressing once again the great importance of the time factor in the endeavours to achieve an early comprehensive, just and lasting peace in the Middle East,

1. *Reaffirms its conviction* that the question of Palestine is the core of the conflict in the Middle East and that no comprehensive, just and lasting peace in the region will be achieved without the full exercise by the Palestinian people of its inalienable national rights and the immediate, unconditional and total withdrawal of Israel from all the Palestinian and other occupied Arab territories;

2. *Reaffirms further* that a just and comprehensive settlement of the situation in the Middle East cannot be achieved without the participation on an equal footing of all the parties to the conflict, including the Palestine Liberation Organization, the representative of the Palestinian people;

3. *Declares once more* that peace in the Middle East is indivisible and must be based on a comprehensive, just and lasting solution of the Middle East problem, under the auspices and on the basis of the relevant resolutions of the United Nations, which ensures the complete and unconditional withdrawal of Israel from the Palestinian and other Arab territories occupied since 1967, including Jerusalem, and which enables the Palestinian people, under the leadership of the Palestine Liberation Organization, to exercise its inalienable rights, including the right to return and the right to self-determination, national independence and the establishment of its independent sovereign State in Palestine, in accordance with the resolutions

---

[461]Most of these resolutions focus on the situation arising from Israel's invasions of Lebanon in 1978 and 1982. [ed. note]

[462]A/40/168-S/17014.

[463]A/40/668 and Add.1.

[464]A/40/779-S/17581 and Corr.1.

[465]See A/37/696-S/15510, annex.

[466]United Nations, *Treaty Series*, vol. 75, no. 973, p. 287.

of the United Nations relevant to the question of Palestine, in particular General Assembly resolutions ES-7/2 of 29 July 1980, 36/120 A to F of 10 December 1981, 37/86 A to D of 10 December 1982, 37/86 E of 20 December 1982, 38/58 A to E of 13 December 1983 and 39/49 A to D of 11 December 1984;

4. *Considers* the Arab Peace Plan adopted unanimously at the Twelfth Arab Summit Conference, held at Fez, Morocco, on 25 November 1981 and from 6 to 9 September 1982,[467] and reiterated by the Extraordinary Summit Conference of the Arab States held at Casablanca, Morocco, from 7 to 9 August 1985,[468] as well as relevant efforts and action to implement the Fez Plan, as an important contribution towards the realization of the inalienable rights of the Palestinian people through the achievement of a comprehensive, just and lasting peace in the Middle East;

5. *Condemns* Israel's continued occupation of the Palestinian and other Arab territories, including Jerusalem, in violation of the Charter of the United Nations, the principles of international law and the relevant resolutions of the United Nations, and demands the immediate, unconditional and total withdrawal of Israel from all the territories occupied since 1967;

6. *Rejects* all agreements and arrangements which violate the inalienable rights of the Palestinian people and contradict the principles of a just and comprehensive solution to the Middle East problem to ensure the establishment of a just peace in the area;

7. *Deplores* Israel's failure to comply with Security Council resolutions 476 (1980) of 30 June 1980 and 478 (1980) of 20 August 1980 and General Assembly resolutions 35/207 of 16 December 1980 and 36/226 A and B of 17 December 1981; determines that Israel's decision to annex Jerusalem and to declare it as its "capital" as well as the measures to alter its physical character, demographic composition, institutional structure and status are null and void and demands that they be rescinded immediately; and calls upon all Member States, the specialized agencies and all other international organizations to abide by the present resolution and all other relevant resolutions and decisions;

8. *Condemns* Israel's aggression, policies and practices against the Palestinian people in the occupied Palestinian territories and outside these territories, including expropriation, the establishment of settlements, annexation and other terrorist, aggressive and repressive measures, which are in violation of the Charter and the principles of international law and the relevant international conventions;

9. *Strongly condemns* the imposition by Israel of its laws, jurisdiction and administration on the occupied Syrian Golan Heights, its annexationist policies and practices, the establishment of settlements, the confiscation of lands, the diversion of water resources and the imposition of Israeli citizenship on Syrian nationals, and declares that all these measures are null and void and constitute a violation of the rules and principles of international law relative to belligerent occupation, in particular the Geneva Convention relative to the Protection of Civilian Persons in Time of War, of 12 August 1949;

10. *Considers* that the agreements on strategic co-operation between the United States of America and Israel, signed on 30 November 1981, and the continued supply of modern arms and *matériel* to Israel, augmented by substantial economic aid, including the recently concluded Agreement on the Establishment of a Free Trade Area between the two Governments, have encouraged Israel to pursue its aggressive and expansionist policies and practices in the Palestinian and other Arab territories occupied since 1967, including Jerusalem, have had adverse effects on efforts for the establishment of a comprehensive, just and lasting peace in the Middle East and threaten the security of the region;

11. *Calls once more upon* all States to put an end to the flow to Israel of any military, economic, financial and technological aid, as well as of human resources, aimed at encouraging it to pursue its aggressive policies against the Arab countries and the Palestinian people;

12. *Strongly condemns* the continuing and increasing collaboration between Israel and the racist régime of South Africa, especially in the economic, military and nuclear fields, which constitutes a hostile act against the African and Arab States and enables Israel to enhance its nuclear capabilities, thus subjecting the States of the region to nuclear blackmail;

13. *Reaffirms its call* for the convening of an International Peace Conference on the Middle East under the auspices of the United Nations and on the basis of its relevant resolutions—as specified in paragraph 5 of the Geneva Declaration on Palestine[469] and endorsed by General Assembly resolution 38/58 C of 13 December 1983;

14. *Requests* the Secretary-General to report to the Security Council periodically on the development of the situation and to submit to the General Assembly at its forty-first session a comprehensive report covering the developments in the Middle East in all their aspects.

Adopted at the 118th plenary meeting:
In favour: 98

Afghanistan, Albania, Algeria, Argentina, Bahrain, Bangladesh, Benin, Bhutan, Bolivia, Botswana, Brazil, Brunei Darussalam, Bulgaria, Burkina Faso, Burundi, Byelorussia, Cape Verde, Central African Republic, Chad, China, Congo, Cuba, Cyprus, Czechoslovakia, Democratic Kampuchea, Democratic Yemen, Djibouti, Ecuador, Egypt, Equatorial Guinea, Ethiopia, Gabon, Gambia, German Democratic Republic, Ghana, Greece, Guinea, Guinea-Bissau, Guyana, Hungary, India, Indonesia, Iran, Iraq, Jordan, Kenya, Kuwait, Lao People's Democratic Repub-

---

[467]See A/37/696-S/15510, annex.
[468]See A/40/564 and Corr.1, annex.

[469]*Report of the International Conference on the Question of Palestine, Geneva, 29 August - 7 September 1983* (United Nations publication, Sales No. E.83.1.21), chap. I, sect. A.

lic, Lebanon, Lesotho, Libya, Madagascar, Malaysia, Maldives, Mali, Malta, Mauritania, Mexico, Mongolia, Morocco, Mozambique, Nepal, Nicaragua, Niger, Nigeria, Oman, Pakistan, Peru, Philippines, Poland, Qatar, Romania, Rwanda, Sao Tome and Principe, Saudi Arabia, Senegal, Singapore, Somalia, Sri Lanka, Sudan, Syria, Thailand, Togo, Trinidad and Tobago, Tunisia, Turkey, Uganda, Ukraine, USSR, United Arab Emirates, United Republic of Tanzania, Vanuatu, Venezuela, Viet Nam, Yemen, Yugoslavia, Zambia, Zimbabwe.

Against: 19

Australia, Belgium, Canada, Costa Rica, Denmark, El Salvador, France, Federal Republic of Germany, Iceland, Ireland, Israel, Italy, Luxembourg, Netherlands, New Zealand, Norway, Portugal, United Kingdom, United States.

Abstentions: 31

Antigua and Barbuda, Austria, Bahamas, Barbados, Burma, Cameroon, Chile, Colombia, Dominica, Dominican Republic, Fiji, Finland, Grenada, Guatemala, Haiti, Honduras, Ivory Coast, Jamaica, Japan, Liberia, Malawi, Panama, Paraguay, Saint Lucia, Saint Vincent, Samoa, Spain, Swaziland, Sweden, Uruguay, Zaire.

Absent: 10

Angola, Belize, Comoros,* Mauritius, Papua New Guinea, Seychelles, Sierra Leone, Solomon Islands, St. Christopher and Nevis, Suriname.

---

*Later advised the Secretariat it had intended to vote in favour.

B

The General Assembly,

Having discussed the item entitled "The situation in the Middle East",

Taking note of the report of the Secretary-General of 22 October 1985,[470]

Recalling Security Council resolution 497 (1981) of 17 December 1981,

Reaffirming its resolutions 36/226 B of 17 December 1981, ES-9/1 of 5 February 1982, 37/123 A of 16 December 1982, 38/180 A of 19 December 1983 and 39/146 B of 14 December 1984,

Recalling its resolution 3314 (XXIX) of 14 December 1974, in which it defined an act of aggression, *inter alia,* as "the invasion or attack by the armed forces of a State of the territory of another State, or any military occupation, however temporary, resulting from such invasion or attack, or any annexation by the use of force of the territory of another State or part thereof" and provided that "no consideration of whatever nature, whether political, economic, military or otherwise, may serve as a justification for aggression",

Reaffirming the fundamental principle of the inadmissibility of the acquisition of territory by force,

Reaffirming once more the applicability of the Geneva Convention relative to the Protection of Civilian Persons

in Time of War, of 12 August 1949,[471] to the occupied Palestinian and other Arab territories, including Jerusalem,

Noting that Israel's record, policies and actions establish conclusively that it is not a peace-loving Member State and that it has not carried out its obligations under the Charter of the United Nations,

Noting further that Israel has refused, in violation of Article 25 of the Charter, to accept and carry out the numerous relevant decisions of the Security Council, in particular resolution 497 (1981), thus failing to carry out its obligations under the Charter,

1. *Strongly condemns* Israel for its failure to comply with Security Council resolution 497 (1981) and General Assembly resolutions 36/226 B, ES-9/1, 37/123 A, 38/180 A and 39/146 B;

2. *Declares once more* that Israel's continued occupation of the Golan Heights and its decision of 14 December 1981 to impose its laws, jurisdiction and administration on the occupied Syrian Golan Heights constitute an act of aggression under the provisions of Article 39 of the Charter of the United Nations and General Assembly resolution 3314 (XXIX);

3. *Declares once more* that Israel's decision to impose its laws, jurisdiction and administration on the occupied Syrian Golan Heights is illegal and therefore null and void and has no validity whatsoever;

4. *Declares* all Israeli policies and practices of, or aimed at, annexation of the occupied Palestinian and other Arab territories, including Jerusalem, to be illegal and in violation of international law and of the relevant United Nations resolutions;

5. *Determines once more* that all actions taken by Israel to give effect to its decision relating to the occupied Syrian Golan Heights are illegal and invalid and shall not be recognized;

6. *Reaffirms its determination* that all relevant provisions of the Regulations annexed to the Hague Convention IV of 1907,[472] and the Geneva Convention relative to the Protection of Civilian Persons in Time of War, of 12 August 1949, continue to apply to the Syrian territory occupied by Israel since 1967, and calls upon the parties thereto to respect and ensure respect for their obligations under these instruments in all circumstances;

7. *Determines once more* that the continued occupation of the Syrian Golan Heights since 1967 and their annexation by Israel on 14 December 1981, following Israel's decision to impose its laws, jurisdiction and administration on that territory, constitute a continuing threat to international peace and security;

8. *Strongly deplores* the negative vote by a permanent member of the Security Council which prevented the Council from adopting against Israel, under Chapter VII of the Charter, the "appropriate measures" referred to in

---

[470]A/40/779-S/17581 and Corr.1.

[471]United Nations, *Treaty Series,* vol. 75, no. 973, p. 287.

[472]Carnegie Endowment for International Peace, *The Hague Conventions and Declarations of 1899 and 1907* (New York, Oxford University Press, 1915), p. 100.

resolution 497 (1981) unanimously adopted by the Council;

9. *Further deplores* any political, economic, financial, military and technological support to Israel that encourages Israel to commit acts of aggression and to consolidate and perpetuate its occupation and annexation of occupied Arab territories;

10. *Firmly emphasizes once more* its demand that Israel, the occupying Power, rescind forthwith its illegal decision of 14 December 1981 to impose its laws, jurisdiction and administration on the Syrian Golan Heights, which resulted in the effective annexation of that territory;

11. *Reaffirms once more* the overriding necessity of the total and unconditional withdrawal by Israel from all the Palestinian and other Arab territories occupied since 1967, including Jerusalem, which is an essential prerequisite for the establishment of a comprehensive and just peace in the Middle East;

12. *Determines once more* that Israel's record, policies and actions confirm that it is not a peace-loving Member State, that it has persistently violated the principles contained in the Charter and that it has carried out neither its obligations under the Charter nor its commitment under General Assembly resolution 273 (III) of 11 May 1949;

13. *Calls once more upon* all Member States to apply the following measures:

(*a*) To refrain from supplying Israel with any weapons and related equipment and to suspend any military assistance that Israel receives from them;

(*b*) To refrain from acquiring any weapons or military equipment from Israel;

(*c*) To suspend economic, financial and technological assistance to and co-operation with Israel;

(*d*) To sever diplomatic, trade and cultural relations with Israel;

14. *Reiterates its call* to all Member States to cease forthwith, individually and collectively, all dealings with Israel in order totally to isolate it in all fields;

15. *Urges* non-member States to act in accordance with the provisions of the present resolution;

16. *Calls upon* the specialized agencies and other international organizations to conform their relations with Israel to the terms of the present resolution;

17. *Requests* the Secretary-General to report to the General Assembly at its forty-first session on the implementation of the present resolution.

Adopted at the 118th plenary meeting:
In favour: 86
Afghanistan, Albania, Algeria, Argentina, Bahrain, Bangladesh, Barbados,* Benin, Bhutan, Botswana, Brunei Darussalam, Bulgaria, Burkina Faso, Burundi, Byelorussia, Cape Verde, Chad, China, Comoros, Congo, Cuba, Cyprus, Czechoslovakia, Democratic Kampuchea, Democratic Yemen, Djibouti, Ethiopia, Gabon, Gambia, German Democratic Republic, Ghana, Greece, Guinea, Guinea-Bissau, Guyana, Hungary, India, Indonesia, Iran, Iraq, Jordan, Kenya, Kuwait, Lao People's Democratic Republic, Lebanon, Lesotho, Libya, Madagascar, Malaysia, Maldives, Mali, Malta, Mauritania, Mexico, Mongolia, Morocco, Mozam-

bique, Nicaragua, Niger, Nigeria, Oman, Pakistan, Poland, Qatar, Rwanda, Sao Tome and Principe, Saudi Arabia, Senegal, Somalia, Sri Lanka, Sudan, Syria, Togo, Trinidad and Tobago, Tunisia, Turkey, Uganda, Ukraine, USSR, United Arab Emirates, United Republic of Tanzania, Viet Nam, Yemen, Yugoslavia, Zambia, Zimbabwe.
Against: 23
Australia, Belgium, Canada, Costa Rica, Denmark, El Salvador, Finland, France, Federal Republic of Germany, Haiti, Iceland, Ireland, Israel, Italy, Japan, Luxembourg, Netherlands, New Zealand, Norway, Portugal, Sweden, United Kingdom, United States.
Abstentions: 37
Antigua and Barbuda, Austria, Bahamas, Bolivia, Brazil, Burma, Cameroon, Colombia, Dominica, Dominican Republic, Ecuador, Egypt, Equatorial Guinea, Fiji, Grenada, Guatemala, Honduras, Ivory Coast, Jamaica, Liberia, Malawi, Nepal, Panama, Paraguay, Peru, Philippines, Saint Lucia, Saint Vincent, Samoa, Sierra Leone, Singapore, Spain, Swaziland, Thailand, Uruguay, Venezuela, Zaire.
Absent: 12
Angola, Belize, Central African Republic, Chile, Mauritius Papua New Guinea, Romania, Seychelles, Solomon Islands, St. Christopher and Nevis, Suriname, Vanuatu.

---

*Later advised the Secretariat that it had intended to abstain.

C

The General Assembly,
Recalling its resolutions 36/120 E of 10 December 1981, 37/123 C of December 1982, 38/180 C of 19 December 1983 and 39/146 C of 14 December 1984, in which it determined that all legislative and administrative measures and actions taken by Israel, the occupying Power, which had altered or purported to alter the character and status of the Holy City of Jerusalem, in particular the so-called "Basic Law" on Jerusalem and the proclamation of Jerusalem as the capital of Israel, were null and void and must be rescinded forthwith,

Recalling Security Council resolution 478 (1980) of 20 August 1980, in which the Council, *inter alia*, decided not to recognize the "Basic Law" and called upon those States that had established diplomatic missions at Jerusalem to withdraw such missions from the Holy City,

Having considered the report of the Secretary-General of 22 October 1985,[473]

1. *Determines* that Israel's decision to impose its laws, jurisdiction and administration on the Holy City of Jerusalem is illegal and therefore null and void and has no validity whatsoever;

2. *Deplores* the transfer by some States of their diplomatic missions to Jerusalem in violation of Security Council resolution 478 (1980) and their refusal to comply with the provisions of that resolution;

3. *Calls once again upon* those States to abide by the provisions of the relevant United Nations resolutions, in

---

[473]A/40/779-S/17581 and Corr.1.

171

conformity with the Charter of the United Nations;

4. *Requests* the Secretary-General to report to the General Assembly at its forty-first session on the implementation of the present resolution.

Adopted at the 118th plenary meeting:
In favour: 137

Afghanistan, Albania, Algeria, Argentina, Australia, Austria, Bahamas, Bahrain, Bangladesh, Barbados, Belgium, Benin, Bhutan, Bolivia, Botswana, Brazil, Brunei Darussalam, Bulgaria, Burkina Faso, Burma, Burundi, Byelorussia, Cameroon, Canada, Cape Verde, Central African Republic, Chad, Chile, China, Colombia, Comoros, Congo, Cuba, Cyprus, Czechoslovakia, Democratic Kampuchea, Democratic Yemen, Denmark, Djibouti, Dominican Republic, Ecuador, Egypt, Equatorial Guinea, Ethiopia, Fiji, Finland, France, Gabon, Gambia, German Democratic Republic, Federal Republic of Germany, Ghana, Greece, Guinea, Guinea-Bissau, Guyana, Honduras, Hungary, Iceland, India, Indonesia, Iran, Iraq, Ireland, Italy, Ivory Coast, Jamaica, Japan, Jordan, Kenya, Kuwait, Lao People's Democratic Republic, Lebanon, Lesotho, Libya, Luxembourg, Madagascar, Malaysia, Maldives, Mali, Malta, Mauritania, Mauritius, Mexico, Mongolia, Morocco, Mozambique, Nepal, Netherlands, New Zealand, Nicaragua, Niger, Nigeria, Norway, Oman, Pakistan, Panama, Peru, Philippines, Poland, Portugal, Qatar, Romania, Rwanda, Saint Lucia, Saint Vincent, Samoa, Sao Tome and Principe, Saudi Arabia, Senegal, Singapore, Somalia, Spain, Sri Lanka, Sudan, Suriname, Sweden, Syria, Thailand, Togo, Trinidad and Tobago, Tunisia, Turkey, Uganda, Ukraine, USSR, United Arab Emirates, United Kingdom, United Republic of Tanzania, Uruguay, Vanuatu, Venezuela, Viet Nam, Yemen, Yugoslavia, Zambia, Zimbabwe.

Against: 2

Costa Rica, Israel.

Abstentions: 10

Antigua and Barbuda, Dominica, Grenada, Guatemala, Liberia, Malawi, Paraguay, Swaziland, United States, Zaire.

Absent: 9

Angola, Belize, El Salvador, Haiti, Papua New Guinea, Seychelles, Sierra Leone, Solomon Islands, St. Christopher and Nevis.

Resolution No. 40/169 of 17 December 1985

CALLING FOR THE LIFTING OF ISRAELI RESTRICTIONS ON THE ECONOMY OF THE OCCUPIED TERRITORIES AND FOR THE ESTABLISHMENT OF A SEAPORT IN THE OCCUPIED GAZA STRIP

The General Assembly,

Aware of the Israeli restrictions imposed on the foreign trade of the occupied Palestinian territories,

Aware also of the imposed domination of the Palestinian market by Israel,

Taking into account the need to give Palestinian firms and products direct access to external markets without Israeli interference,

Noting with regret the lack of progress in the implemen-

tation of General Assembly resolution 39/223 of 18 December 1984, as reflected in the report of the Secretary-General on economic development projects in the occupied Palestinian territories,[474]

1. *Calls* for the urgent lifting of the Israeli restrictions imposed on the economy of the occupied Palestinian territories;

2. *Recognizes* the Palestinian interest in establishing a seaport in the occupied Gaza Strip to give Palestinian firms and products direct access to external markets;

3. *Calls upon* all concerned to facilitate the establishment of a seaport in the occupied Gaza Strip;

4. *Also calls upon* all concerned to facilitate the establishment of a cement plant in the occupied West Bank and a citrus plant in the occupied Gaza Strip;

5. *Requests* the Secretary-General to continue his efforts to facilitate the establishment of the above-mentioned projects and to report to the General Assembly at its forty-first session, through the Economic and Social Council, on the progress made in the implementation of the present resolution.

Adopted at the 119th plenary meeting:
In favour: 138

Afghanistan, Albania, Algeria, Angola, Antigua and Barbuda, Argentina, Austria, Bahamas, Bahrain, Bangladesh, Barbados, Belgium, Benin, Bhutan, Bolivia, Botswana, Brazil, Brunei Darussalam, Bulgaria, Burkina Faso, Burma, Burundi, Byelorussia, Cameroon, Cape Verde, Central African Republic, Chad, Chile, China, Colombia, Comoros, Congo, Cuba, Cyprus, Czechoslovakia, Democratic Kampuchea, Democratic Yemen, Denmark, Djibouti, Dominica, Dominican Republic, Ecuador, Egypt, El Salvador, Equatorial Guinea, Ethiopia, Fiji, France, Gabon, German Democratic Republic, Federal Republic of Germany, Ghana, Greece, Guatemala, Guinea, Guinea-Bissau, Haiti, Honduras, Hungary, India, Indonesia, Iran, Iraq, Ireland, Italy, Ivory Coast, Jamaica, Japan, Jordan, Kuwait, Lao People's Democratic Republic, Lebanon, Lesotho, Liberia, Libya, Luxembourg, Madagascar, Malawi, Malaysia, Maldives, Mali, Malta, Mauritania, Mauritius, Mexico, Mongolia, Morocco, Mozambique, Nepal, Netherlands, New Zealand, Nicaragua, Niger, Nigeria, Oman, Pakistan, Panama, Papua New Guinea, Paraguay, Peru, Philippines, Poland, Portugal, Qatar, Romania, Rwanda, Saint Vincent, Samoa, Sao Tome and Principe, Saudi Arabia, Senegal, Sierra Leone, Singapore, Somalia, Spain, Sri Lanka, Sudan, Suriname, Swaziland, Syria, Thailand, Togo, Trinidad and Tobago, Tunisia, Turkey, Uganda, Ukraine, USSR, United Arab Emirates, United Kingdom, United Republic of Tanzania, Uruguay, Venezuela, Viet Nam, Yemen, Yugoslavia, Zaire, Zambia.

Against: 2

Israel, United States.

Abstentions: 7

Australia, Canada, Finland, Grenada, Iceland, Norway, Sweden.

---

[474]A/40/367-E/1985/116.

Absent: 11

Belize, Costa Rica, Gambia, Guyana,* Kenya, Saint Lucia, Seychelles, Solomon Islands, St. Christopher and Nevis, Vanuatu, Zimbabwe.*

---

*Later advised the Secretariat it had intended to vote in favour.

Resolution No. 40/170 of 17 December 1985

CALLING FOR THE PROVISION OF ECONOMIC AND SOCIAL ASSISTANCE TO THE PALESTINIAN PEOPLE AND REQUESTING THAT UNITED NATIONS ASSISTANCE SHOULD BE RENDERED IN CO-OPERATION WITH THE PALESTINE LIBERATION ORGANIZATION

The General Assembly,

Recalling its resolution 39/224 of 18 December 1984,

Recalling also Economic and Social Council resolution 1985/57 of 25 July 1985,

Recalling further the Programme of Action for the Achievement of Palestinian Rights, adopted by the International Conference on the Question of Palestine,[475]

Noting the need to provide economic and social assistance to the Palestinian people,

1. *Takes note* of the report of the Secretary-General on assistance to the Palestinian people;[476]

2. *Notes* the meeting on assistance to the Palestinian people that was held at Geneva on 5 and 8 July 1985 in response to Geneva Assembly resolution 39/224;

3. *Expresses its thanks* to the Secretary-General for convening the meeting on assistance to the Palestinian people;

4. *Regards* such a meeting as a valuable opportunity to assess progress in economic and social assistance to the Palestinian people and to explore ways and means of enhancing such assistance;

5. *Draws the attention* of the international community, the United Nations system and intergovernmental and non-governmental organizations to the need to disburse their aid to the occupied Palestinian territories only for the benefit of the Palestinian people;

6. *Requests* the Secretary-General:

(a) To review the progress made in the implementation of the proposed activities and projects described in his report on assistance to the Palestinian people;

(b) To take all necessary steps to finalize the programme of economic and social assistance to the Palestinian people requested in General Assembly resolution 38/145 of 19 December 1983;

(c) To convene in 1986 a meeting of the relevant programmes, organizations, agencies, funds and organs of the United Nations system to consider economic and social assistance to the Palestinian people;

(d) To provide for the participation in the meeting of the Palestine Liberation Organization, the Arab host countries and relevant intergovernmental and non-governmental organizations;

7. *Requests* the relevant programmes, organizations, agencies, funds and organs of the United Nations system to intensify their efforts, in co-operation with the Palestine Liberation Organization, to provide economic and social assistance to the Palestinian people;

8. *Also requests* that United Nations assistance to the Palestinians in the Arab host countries should be rendered in co-operation with the Palestine Liberation Organization and with the consent of the Arab host Government concerned;

9. *Requests* the Secretary-General to report to the General Assembly at its forty-first session, through the Economic and Social Council, on the progress made in the implementation of the present resolution.

Adopted at the 119th plenary meeting:

In favour: 145

Afghanistan, Albania, Algeria, Angola, Antigua and Barbuda, Argentina, Australia, Austria, Bahamas, Bahrain, Bangladesh, Barbados, Belgium, Benin, Bhutan, Bolivia, Botswana, Brazil, Brunei Darussalam, Bulgaria, Burkina Faso, Burma, Burundi, Byelorussia, Cameroon, Canada, Cape Verde, Central African Republic, Chad, Chile, China, Colombia, Comoros, Congo, Cuba, Cyprus, Czechoslovakia, Democratic Kampuchea, Democratic Yemen, Denmark, Djibouti, Dominica, Dominican Republic, Ecuador, Egypt, Equatorial Guinea, Ethiopia, Fiji, Finland, France, Gabon, German Democratic Republic, Federal Republic of Germany, Ghana, Greece, Guatemala, Guinea, Guinea-Bissau, Guyana, Haiti, Honduras, Hungary, Iceland, India, Indonesia, Iran, Iraq, Ireland, Italy, Ivory Coast, Jamaica, Japan, Jordan, Kuwait, Lao People's Democratic Republic, Lebanon, Lesotho, Liberia, Libya, Luxembourg, Madagascar, Malawi, Malaysia, Maldives, Mali, Malta, Mauritania, Mauritius, Mexico, Mongolia, Morocco, Mozambique, Nepal, Netherlands, New Zealand, Nicaragua, Niger, Nigeria, Norway, Oman, Pakistan, Panama, Papua New Guinea, Paraguay, Peru, Philippines, Poland, Portugal, Qatar, Romania, Rwanda, Saint Vincent, Samoa, Sao Tome and Principe, Saudi Arabia, Senegal, Sierra Leone, Singapore, Somalia, Spain, Sri Lanka, St. Christopher and Nevis, Sudan, Suriname, Swaziland, Sweden, Syria, Thailand, Togo, Trinidad and Tobago, Tunisia, Turkey, Uganda, Ukraine, USSR, United Arab Emirates, United Kingdom, United Republic of Tanzania, Uruguay, Venezuela, Viet Nam, Yemen, Yugoslavia, Zaire, Zambia.

Against: 2

Israel, United States.

Abstention: 1

Grenada.

Absent: 10

Belize, Costa Rica, El Salvador,* Gambia,* Kenya, Saint Lucia, Seychelles, Solomon Islands, Vanuatu, Zimbabwe.*

---

[475] *Report of the International Conference on the Question of Palestine, Geneva, 29 August-7 September 1983* (United Nations publication, Sales No. E.83.1.21), chap. I, sect. B.

[476] A/40/353-E/1985/115 and Corr.1 and Add.1 and Add.1/Corr.1.

---

*Later advised the Secretariat it had intended to vote in favour.

Resolution No. 40/201 of 17 December 1985

EXPRESSING ALARM AT THE DETERIORATION OF LIVING CONDITIONS IN THE TERRITORIES UNDER ISRAELI OCCUPATION, AND AFFIRMING THAT THE OCCUPATION IS CONTRADICTORY TO THE BASIC REQUIREMENTS OF THEIR SOCIAL AND ECONOMIC DEVELOPMENT

The General Assembly,

Recalling the Vancouver Declaration on Human Settlements, 1976,[477] and the relevant recommendations for national action[478] adopted by Habitat: United Nations Conference on Human Settlements,

Recalling also its resolution 39/169 of 17 December 1984,

Taking note of Commission on Human Settlements resolution 8/3 of 10 May 1985,[479]

Gravely alarmed by the continuation of the Israeli settlement policies, which have been declared null and void and a major obstacle to peace,

Recognizing the need to identify priority development projects needed for improving the living conditions of the Palestinian people in the occupied Palestinian territories,

1. *Takes note with concern* of the report of the Secretary-General on the living conditions of the Palestinian people in the occupied Palestinian territories;[480]

2. *Takes note also* of the statement made on 25 October 1985 by the observer of the Palestine Liberation Organization;[481]

3. *Rejects* the Israeli plans and actions intended to change the demographic composition of the occupied Palestinian territories, particularly the increase and expansion of the Israeli settlements, and other plans and actions creating conditions leading to the displacement and exodus of Palestinians from the occupied Palestinian territories;

4. *Expresses its alarm* at the deterioration, as a result of the Israeli occupation, in the living conditions of the Palestinian people in the Palestinian territories occupied since 1967;

5. *Affirms* that the Israeli occupation is contradictory to the basic requirements for the social and economic development of the Palestinian people in the occupied Palestinian territories;

6. *Requests* the Secretary-General;

(*a*) To organize, by April 1987, a seminar on priority development projects needed for improving the living conditions of the Palestinian people in the occupied Palestinian territories, including a comprehensive general housing programme, as recommended in resolution 8/3 of the Commission on Human Settlements;

(*b*) To make the necessary preparations for the seminar,

providing for the participation of the Palestine Liberation Organization;

(*c*) To invite experts to present papers to the seminar;

(*d*) To invite also relevant intergovernmental and non-governmental organizations;

(*e*) To report to the General Assembly at its forty-first session, through the Economic and Social Council, on the preparations for the seminar;

(*f*) To report to the General Assembly at its forty-second session, through the Economic and Social Council, on the seminar.

Adopted at the 119th plenary meeting:

In favour: 153

Afghanistan, Albania, Algeria, Angola, Antigua and Barbuda, Argentina, Australia, Austria, Bahamas, Bahrain, Bangladesh, Barbados, Belgium, Belize, Benin, Bhutan, Bolivia, Botswana, Brazil, Brunei Darussalam, Bulgaria, Burkina Faso, Burma, Burundi, Byelorussia, Cameroon, Canada, Cape Verde, Central African Republic, Chad, Chile, China, Colombia, Comoros, Congo, Costa Rica, Cuba, Cyprus, Czechoslovakia, Democratic Kampuchea, Democratic Yemen, Denmark, Djibouti, Dominica, Dominican Republic, Ecuador, Egypt, El Salvador, Equatorial Guinea, Ethiopia, Fiji, Finland, France, Gabon, Gambia, German Democratic Republic, Federal Republic of Germany, Ghana, Greece, Guatemala, Guinea, Guinea-Bissau, Guyana, Haiti, Honduras, Hungary, Iceland, India, Indonesia, Iran, Iraq, Ireland, Italy, Ivory Coast, Jamaica, Japan, Jordan, Kenya, Kuwait, Lao People's Democratic Republic, Lebanon, Lesotho, Liberia, Libya, Luxembourg, Madagascar, Malawi, Malaysia, Maldives, Mali, Malta, Mauritania, Mauritius, Mexico, Mongolia, Morocco, Mozambique, Nepal, Netherlands, New Zealand, Nicaragua, Niger, Nigeria, Norway, Oman, Pakistan, Panama, Papua New Guinea, Paraguay, Peru, Philippines, Poland, Portugal, Qatar, Romania, Rwanda, Saint Lucia, Saint Vincent, Samoa, Sao Tome and Principe, Saudi Arabia, Senegal, Sierra Leone, Singapore, Somalia, Spain, Sri Lanka, St. Christopher and Nevis, Sudan, Suriname, Swaziland, Sweden, Syria, Thailand, Togo, Trinidad and Tobago, Tunisia, Turkey, Uganda, Ukraine, USSR, United Arab Emirates, United Kingdom, United Republic of Tanzania, Uruguay, Vanuatu, Venezuela, Viet Nam, Yemen, Yugoslavia, Zaire, Zambia, Zimbabwe.

Against: 2

Israel, United States.

Abstention: 1

Grenada.

Absent: 2

Seychelles, Solomon Islands.

---

[477]*Report of Habitat: United Nations Conference on Human Settlements, Vancouver, 31 May-11 June 1976* (United Nations publication, Sales No. E.76.IV.7 and corrigendum), chap.I.

[478]*Ibid.,* chap.II.

[479]See *Official Records of the General Assembly, Fortieth Session, Second Committee,* 17th meeting, paras. 93-99.

[480]A/40/373-E/1985/99.

[481]*Official Records of the General Assembly, Fortieth Session, Second Committee,* 17th meeting, paras. 93-99.

Resolution No. 40/229 of 17 December 1985

REQUESTING ASSISTANCE FOR THE RECONSTRUCTION AND DEVELOPMENT OF LEBANON

The General Assembly,

Recalling its resolutions 33/146 of 20 December 1978, 34/135 of 14 December 1979, 35/85 of 5 December 1980,

36/205 of 17 December 1981, 37/163 of 17 December 1982, 38/220 of 20 December 1983 and 39/197 of 17 December 1984 on assistance for the reconstruction and development of Lebanon,

Recalling also Economic and Social Council resolutions 1980/15 of 29 April 1980 and 1985/56 of 25 July 1985 and decisions 1983/112 of 17 May 1983 and 1984/174 of 26 July 1984,

Noting with deep concern the continuing heavy loss of life and the additional destruction of property, which have caused further extensive damage to the economic and social structures of Lebanon,

Also noting with concern the serious economic situation in Lebanon,

Welcoming the determined efforts of the Government of Lebanon in undertaking its reconstruction and rehabilitation programme,

Reaffirming the urgent need for further international action to assist the Government of Lebanon in its continuing efforts for reconstruction and development,

Considering that filling the vacant post of United Nations Co-ordinator of Assistance for the Reconstruction and Development of Lebanon would facilitate the normal operations of international assistance to Lebanon,

Taking note of the report of the Secretary-General[482] and of the statement made on 12 November 1985 by the Under-Secretary-General for Political and General Assembly Affairs,[483]

1. *Expresses* its appreciation to the Secretary-General for his report and for the steps he has taken to mobilize assistance to Lebanon;

2. *Commends* the Under-Secretary-General for Political and General Assembly Affairs for his co-ordination of system-wide assistance for Lebanon, as well as the staff of the Office of the United Nations Co-ordinator of Assistance for the Reconstruction and Development of Lebanon for their invaluable efforts in the discharge of their duties;

3. *Expresses its appreciation* for the relentless efforts undertaken by the Government of Lebanon in the implementation of the initial phase of reconstruction of the country, despite adverse circumstances, and for the steps it has taken to remedy the economic situation;

4. *Requests* the Secretary-General to continue and intensify his efforts to mobilize all possible assistance within the United Nations system to help the Government of Lebanon in its reconstruction and development efforts;

5. *Invites* the Secretary-General to consider arranging, under the terms of resolution 33/146, for the United Nations Co-ordinator of Assistance for the Reconstruction and Development of Lebanon to resume his functions in Lebanon;

6. *Requests* the organs, organizations and bodies of the United Nations system to intensify their programmes of assistance and to expand them in response to the needs of Lebanon, and to take the necessary steps to ensure that their offices in Beirut are adequately staffed at the senior level;

7. *Also requests* the Secretary-General to report to the General Assembly at its forty-first session on the progress achieved in the implementation of the present resolution.

Adopted at the 120th plenary meeting without a vote.

Resolution No. 40/246 A, B of 18 December 1985

ON THE FINANCING OF THE UNITED NATIONS INTERIM FORCE IN LEBANON

A

The General Assembly,

Having considered the report of the Secretary-General on the financing of the United Nations Interim Force in Lebanon[484] and the related report of the Advisory Committee on Administrative and Budgetary Questions,[485]

Bearing in mind Security Council resolutions 425 (1978) and 426 (1978) of 19 March 1978, 427 (1978) of 3 May 1978, 434 (1978) of 18 September 1978, 444 (1979) of 19 January 1979, 450 (1979) of 14 June 1979, 459 (1979) of 19 December 1979, 474 (1980) of 17 June 1980, 483 (1980) of 17 December 1980, 488 (1981) of 19 June 1981, 498 (1981) of 18 December 1981, 501 (1982) of 25 February 1982, 511 (1982) of 18 June 1982, 519 (1982) of 17 August 1982, 523 (1982) of 18 October 1982, 529 (1983) of 18 January 1983, 536 (1983) of 18 July 1983, 538 (1983) of 18 October 1983, 549 (1984) of 19 April 1984, 555 (1984) of 12 October 1984, 561 (1985) of 17 April 1985 and 575 (1985) of 17 October 1985,[486]

Recalling its resolutions S-8/2 of 21 April 1978, 33/14 of 3 November 1978, 34/9 B of 17 December 1979, 35/44 of 1 December 1980, 35/115 A of 10 December 1980, 36/138 A of 16 December 1981, 36/138 C of 19 March 1982, 37/127 A of 17 December 1982, 38/38 A of 5 December 1983 and 39/71 A of 13 December 1984,

Reaffirming its previous decisions regarding the fact that, in order to meet the expenditures caused by such operations, a different procedure from the one applied to meet expenditures of the regular budget of the United Nations is required,

Taking into account the fact that the economically more developed countries are in a position to make relatively larger contributions and that the economically less developed countries have a relatively limited capacity to contribute towards peace-keeping operations involving heavy expenditures,

Bearing in mind the special responsibilities of the States permanent members of the Security Council in the fi-

---

[482]A/40/434 and Add.1.
[483]*Official Records of the General Assembly, Fortieth Session, Second Committee,* 31st meeting, paras. 34-41.

[484]A/40/844.
[485]A/40/954.
[486]The resolutions cited in this and the next paragraph refer to the renewal of the mandate and the financing of the United Nations Interim Force in Lebanon. [ed. note]

nancing of peace-keeping operations decided upon in accordance with the Charter of the United Nations,

I

Decides to appropriate to the Special Account referred to in section I, paragraph 1, of General Assembly resolution S-8/2 an amount of $70,446,000 gross ($69,446,000 net), being the amount authorized with the prior concurrence of the Advisory Committee on Administrative and Budgetary Questions and apportioned under the provisions of section IV of Assembly resolution 39/71 A for the operation of the United Nations Interim Force in Lebanon from 19 April to 18 October 1985, inclusive;

II

Decides to appropriate to the Special Account an amount of $23,482,000 gross ($23,148,666 net), being the amount authorized with the prior concurrence of the Advisory Committee on Administrative and Budgetary Questions and apportioned under the provisions of section IV of Assembly resolution 39/71 A for the operation of the United Nations Interim Force in Lebanon from 19 October to 18 December 1985, inclusive;

III

1. *Decides* to appropriate to the Special Account an amount of $48,263,000 for the operation of the United Nations Interim Force in Lebanon for the period from 19 December 1985 to 18 April 1986, inclusive;

2. *Decides further,* as an *ad hoc* arrangement, without prejudice to the positions of principle that may be taken by Member States in any consideration by the General Assembly of arrangements for the financing of peace-keeping operations, to apportion the amount of $48,263,000 among Member States in accordance with the scheme set out in Assembly resolution 33/14 and the provisions of section V, paragraph 1, of resolution 34/9 B, section VI, paragraph 1, of resolution 35/115 A, section VI, paragraph 1, of resolution 36/138 A, section IX, paragraph 1, of resolution 37/127 A and section VII, paragraphs 1 and 2, of resolution 39/71 A; the scale of assessments for the years 1983, 1984 and 1985 shall be applied against a portion thereof, that is $5,185,281, being the amount pertaining on a *pro rata* basis to the period from 19 to 31 December 1985, inclusive, and the scale of assessments for the years 1986, 1987 and 1988 shall be applied against the balance, that is $43,077,719, for the period thereafter;

3. *Decides* that there shall be set off against the apportionment among Member States, as provided for in paragraph 2 above, their respective share in the estimated income of $13,333 other than staff assessment income approved for the period from 19 December 1985 to 18 April 1986, inclusive;

4. *Decides* that, in accordance with the provisions of its resolution 973 (X) of 15 December 1955, there shall be set off against the apportionment among Member States, as provided for in paragraph 2 above, their respective share in the Tax Equalization Fund of the estimated staff assessment income of $823,333 approved for the period from

19 December 1985 to 18 April 1986, inclusive;

IV

Authorizes the Secretary-General to enter into commitments for the operation of the United Nations Interim Force in Lebanon at a rate not to exceed $11,957,500 gross ($11,762,500 net) per month for the period from 19 April to 18 December 1986, inclusive, should the Security Council decide to continue the Force beyond the period of six months authorized under its resolution 575 (1985), subject to obtaining the prior concurrence of the Advisory Committee on Administrative and Budgetary Questions for the actual level of commitments to be entered into for each mandate period that may be approved subsequent to 19 April 1986, the said amount to be apportioned among Member States in accordance with the scale of assessments for the years 1986, 1987 and 1988;

V

1. *Renews its invitation* to Member States to make voluntary contributions to the United Nations Interim Force in Lebanon both in cash and in the form of services and supplies acceptable to the Secretary-General;

2. *Invites* Member States to make voluntary contributions in cash to the Suspense Account established in accordance with its resolution 34/9 D of 17 December 1979;

VI

Requests the Secretary-General to take all necessary action to ensure that the United Nations Interim Force in Lebanon shall be administered with a maximum of efficiency and economy.

Adopted at the 121st plenary meeting:
In favour: 124
Antigua and Barbuda, Argentina, Australia, Austria, Bahamas, Bahrain, Bangladesh, Barbados, Belgium, Belize, Benin, Bhutan, Bolivia, Botswana, Brazil, Brunei Darussalam, Burkina Faso, Burma, Burundi, Cameroon, Canada, Cape Verde, Central African Republic, Chad, Chile, China, Colombia, Congo, Costa Rica, Cyprus, Democratic Kampuchea, Denmark, Djibouti, Dominican Republic, Ecuador, Egypt, El Salvador, Equatorial Guinea, Ethiopia, Fiji, Finland, France, Gabon, Gambia, Federal Republic of Germany, Ghana, Greece, Grenada, Guatemala, Guyana, Honduras, Iceland, India, Indonesia, Ireland, Israel, Italy, Ivory Coast, Jamaica, Japan, Jordan, Kenya, Kuwait, Lebanon, Lesotho, Liberia, Luxembourg, Madagascar, Malawi, Malaysia, Malta, Mauritania, Mauritius, Mexico, Morocco, Nepal, Netherlands, New Zealand, Nicaragua, Niger, Nigeria, Norway, Oman, Pakistan, Panama, Papua New Guinea, Peru, Philippines, Portugal, Qatar, Romania, Rwanda, Saint Lucia, Saint Vincent, Samoa, Sao Tome and Principe, Saudi Arabia, Senegal, Sierra Leone, Singapore, Solomon Islands, Somalia, Spain, Sri Lanka, Sudan, Suriname, Swaziland, Sweden, Thailand, Togo, Trinidad and Tobago, Tunisia, Turkey, Uganda, United Arab Emirates, United Kingdom, United Republic of Tanzania, United States, Uruguay, Venezuela, Yugoslavia, Zaire, Zambia, Zimbabwe.

Against: 15

Afghanistan, Albania, Bulgaria, Byelorussia, Cuba, Czechoslovakia, German Democratic Republic, Hungary, Lao People's Democratic Republic, Mongolia, Poland, Syria, Ukraine, USSR, Viet Nam.

Abstentions: 4

Democratic Yemen, Iraq, Maldives, Yemen.

Absent: 15

Algeria, Angola, Comoros, Dominica, Guinea, Guinea-Bissau, Haiti, Iran, Libya, Mali, Mozambique, Paraguay, Seychelles, St. Christopher and Nevis, Vanuatu.

B

The General Assembly,

Having regard to the financial position of the Special Account for the United Nations Interim Force in Lebanon, as set forth in the report of the Secretary-General,[487] and referring to paragraph 7 of the report of the Advisory Committee on Administrative and Budgetary Questions,[488]

Mindful of the fact that it is essential to provide the United Nations Interim Force in Lebanon with the necessary financial resources to enable it to fulfil its responsibilities under the relevant resolutions of the Security Council,

Concerned that the Secretary-General is continuing to face growing difficulties in meeting the obligations of the United Nations Interim Force in Lebanon on a current basis, particularly those due to the Governments of troop-contributing States,

Recalling its resolutions 34/9 E of 17 December 1979, 35/115 B of 10 December 1980, 36/138 B of 16 December 1981, 37/127 B of 17 December 1982, 38/38 B of 5 December 1983 and 39/71 B of 13 December 1984,

Recognizing that, in consequence of the withholding of contributions by certain Member States, the surplus balances in the Special Account for the United Nations Interim Force in Lebanon have, in effect, been drawn upon to the full extent to supplement the income received from contributions for meeting expenses of the Force,

Concerned that the application of the provisions of regulations 5.2(*b*), 5.2 (*d*), 4.3 and 4.4 of the Financial Regulations of the United Nations would aggravate the already difficult financial situation of the United Nations Interim Force in Lebanon,

Decides that the provisions of regulations 5.2(*b*), 5.2(*d*), 4.3 and 4.4 of the Financial Regulations of the United Nations shall be suspended in respect of the amount of $8,868,174, which otherwise would have to be surrendered pursuant to those provisions, this amount to be entered in the account referred to in the operative part of General Assembly resolution 34/9 E and held in suspense until a further decision is taken by the Assembly.

Adopted at the 121st plenary meeting:

In favour: 122

Antigua and Barbuda, Argentina, Australia, Austria, Bahamas, Bahrain, Bangladesh, Barbados, Belgium, Belize, Bhutan, Bolivia, Botswana, Brazil, Brunei Darussalam, Burkina Faso, Burma, Burundi, Cameroon, Canada, Cape Verde, Central African Republic, Chad, Chile, China, Colombia, Congo, Costa Rica, Cyprus, Democratic Kampuchea, Denmark, Djibouti, Dominican Republic, Ecuador, Egypt, El Salvador, Equatorial Guinea, Ethiopia, Fiji, Finland, France, Gabon, Gambia, Federal Republic of Germany, Ghana, Greece, Grenada, Guatemala, Guyana, Honduras, Iceland, India, Indonesia, Ireland, Israel, Italy, Ivory Coast, Jamaica, Japan, Jordan, Kenya, Kuwait, Lebanon, Lesotho, Liberia, Luxembourg, Madagascar, Malawi, Malaysia, Malta, Mauritania, Mauritius, Mexico, Morocco, Nepal, Netherlands, New Zealand, Nicaragua, Niger, Nigeria, Norway, Oman, Pakistan, Panama, Papua New Guinea, Peru, Philippines, Poland,* Portugal, Qatar, Rwanda, Saint Lucia, Saint Vincent, Samoa, Saudi Arabia, Senegal, Sierra Leone, Singapore, Solomon Islands, Somalia, Spain, Sri Lanka, Sudan, Suriname, Swaziland, Sweden, Thailand, Togo, Trinidad and Tobago, Tunisia, Turkey, Uganda, United Arab Emirates, United Kingdom, United Republic of Tanzania, United States, Uruguay, Venezuela, Yugoslavia, Zaire, Zambia, Zimbabwe.

Against: 14

Afghanistan, Albania, Bulgaria, Byelorussia, Cuba, Czechoslovakia, German Democratic Republic, Hungary, Lao People's Democratic Republic, Mongolia, Syria, Ukraine, USSR, Viet Nam.

Abstentions: 5

Democratic Yemen, Iraq, Maldives, Romania, Yemen.

Absent: 17

Algeria, Angola, Benin, Comoros, Dominica, Guinea, Guinea-Bissau, Haiti, Iran, Libya, Mali, Mozambique, Paraguay, Sao Tome and Principe, Seychelles, St. Christopher and Nevis, Vanuatu.

*Later advised the Secretariat it had intended to vote against.

Decision No. 40/432 of 17 December 1985

ON ISRAELI ECONOMIC PRACTICES IN THE OCCUPIED TERRITORIES

At its 119th plenary meeting, on 17 December 1985, the General Assembly, on the recommendation of the Second Committee:[489]

(*a*) Took note, with concern, of the report of the Secretary-General prepared in pursuance of Assembly decision 39/442;[490]

(*b*) Requested the Secretary-General to prepare a report on the financial and trade practices of the Israeli occupation authorities in the occupied Palestinian and other Arab territories;

(*c*) Invited the Secretary-General to utilize the services

---

[487]A/40/844.
[488]A/40/954.

[489]*Ibid.,* document A/40/1009/Add.1, para. 38.
[490]A/40/381-E/1985/105.

of competent United Nations bodies in preparing the report;

(d) Requested the Secretary-General to submit the report to the General Assembly at its forty-first session, through the Economic and Social Council.

Adopted at the 119th plenary meeting:
In favour: 147

Afghanistan, Albania, Algeria, Angola, Antigua and Barbuda, Argentina, Australia, Austria, Bahamas, Bahrain, Bangladesh, Barbados, Belgium, Benin, Bhutan, Bolivia, Botswana, Brazil, Brunei Darussalam, Bulgaria, Burkina Faso, Burma, Burundi, Byelorussia, Cameroon, Canada, Cape Verde, Central African Republic, Chad, Chile, China, Colombia, Comoros, Congo, Costa Rica, Cuba, Cyprus, Czechoslovakia, Democratic Kampuchea, Democratic Yemen, Denmark, Djibouti, Dominica, Dominican Republic, Ecuador, Egypt, El Salvador, Equatorial Guinea, Ethiopia, Fiji, Finland, France, Gabon, German Democratic Republic, Federal Republic of Germany, Ghana, Greece, Guatemala, Guinea, Guinea-Bissau, Guyana, Haiti, Honduras, Hungary, Iceland, India, Indonesia, Iran, Iraq, Ireland, Italy, Ivory Coast, Jamaica, Japan, Jordan, Kuwait, Lao People's Democratic Republic, Lebanon, Lesotho, Liberia, Libya, Luxembourg, Madagascar, Malawi, Malaysia, Maldives, Mali, Malta, Mauritania, Mauritius, Mexico, Mongolia, Morocco, Mozambique, Nepal, Netherlands, New Zealand, Nicaragua, Niger, Nigeria, Norway, Oman, Pakistan, Panama, Papua New Guinea, Paraguay, Peru, Philippines, Poland, Portugal, Qatar, Romania, Rwanda, Saint Lucia, Saint Vincent, Samoa, Sao Tome and Principe, Saudi Arabia, Senegal, Sierra Leone, Singapore, Somalia, Spain, Sri Lanka, Sudan, Suriname, Swaziland, Sweden, Syria, Thailand, Togo, Trinidad and Tobago, Tunisia, Turkey, Uganda, Ukraine, USSR, United Arab Emirates, United Kingdom, United Republic of Tanzania, Uruguay, Venezuela, Viet Nam, Yemen, Yugoslavia, Zaire, Zambia.

Against: 2

Israel, United States.

Abstentions: 2

Grenada, St. Christopher and Nevis.

Absent: 7

Belize, Gambia,* Kenya, Seychelles, Solomon Islands, Vanuatu, Zimbabwe.*

---

*Later advised the Secretariat it had intended to vote in favour.

Resolution No. 41/12 of 29 October 1986

CALLING ON ISRAEL TO PLACE ITS NUCLEAR FACILITIES UNDER INTERNATIONAL ATOMIC ENERGY AGENCY SAFEGUARDS

The General Assembly,

Having considered the item entitled "Armed Israeli aggression against the Iraqi nuclear installations and its grave consequences for the established international system concerning the peaceful uses of nuclear energy, the non-proliferation of nuclear weapons and international

peace and security",

Recalling the relevant resolutions of the Security Council and the General Assembly,

Taking note of the relevant resolutions of the International Atomic Energy Agency,

Viewing with deep concern Israel's refusal to comply with Security Council resolution 487 (1981) of 19 June 1981,

Concerned that armed attacks on nuclear facilities raise fears about the safety of present and future nuclear installations,

Aware that all States developing nuclear energy for peaceful purposes need assurances against armed attacks on nuclear facilities,

1. *Calls upon* Israel urgently to place all its nuclear facilities under International Atomic Energy Agency safeguards in accordance with resolution 487 (1981) adopted unanimously by the Security Council;

2. *Considers* that Israel has not yet committed itself not to attack or threaten to attack nuclear facilities in Iraq or elsewhere, including facilities under International Atomic Energy Agency safeguards;

3. *Reaffirms* that Iraq is entitled to compensation for the damage it has suffered as a result of the Israeli armed attack on 7 June 1981;

4. *Requests* the Conference on Disarmament to continue negotiations with a view to reaching an immediate conclusion of the agreement on the prohibition of military attacks on nuclear facilities as a contribution to promoting and ensuring the safe development of nuclear energy for peaceful purposes;

5. *Decides* to include in the provisional agenda of its forty-second session the item entitled "Armed Israeli aggression against the Iraqi nuclear installations and its grave consequences for the established international system concerning the peaceful uses of nuclear energy, the non-proliferation of nuclear weapons and international peace and security".

Adopted at the fifty-first plenary meeting:
In favour: 86

Afghanistan, Albania, Algeria, Angola, Bahrain, Bangladesh, Bhutan, Botswana, Brazil, Brunei Darussalam, Bulgaria, Burkina Faso, Burundi, Byelorussia, Central African Republic, Chad, China, Comoros, Congo, Cuba, Cyprus, Czechoslovakia, Democratic Kampuchea, Democratic Yemen, Djibouti, Egypt, Gabon, Gambia, German Democratic Republic, Ghana, Guinea, Guyana, Hungary, India, Indonesia, Iran, Iraq, Jordan, Kenya, Kuwait, Lao People's Democratic Republic, Lebanon, Lesotho, Libya, Madagascar, Malaysia, Maldives, Mali, Malta, Mauritania, Mongolia, Morocco, Nepal, Nicaragua, Niger, Nigeria, Oman, Pakistan, Papua New Guinea, Philippines, Poland, Qatar, Romania, Rwanda, Saudi Arabia, Senegal, Seychelles, Somalia, Sri Lanka, Sudan, Syria, Thailand, Togo, Trinidad and Tobago, Tunisia, Turkey, Uganda, Ukraine, USSR, United Arab Emirates, United Republic of Tanzania, Viet Nam, Yemen, Yugoslavia, Zambia, Zimbabwe.

Against: 5

El Salvador, Honduras, Israel, St. Christopher and Nevis,

United States.

Abstentions: 55

Antigua and Barbuda, Argentina, Australia, Austria, Bahamas, Barbados, Belgium, Bolivia, Cameroon, Canada, Chile, Colombia, Costa Rica, Denmark, Dominican Republic, Ecuador, Equatorial Guinea, Fiji, Finland, France, Federal Republic of Germany, Greece, Grenada, Guatemala, Haiti, Iceland, Ireland, Italy, Ivory Coast, Jamaica, Japan, Liberia, Luxembourg, Malawi, Mauritius, Mexico, Netherlands, New Zealand, Norway, Panama, Paraguay, Peru, Portugal, Saint Lucia, Saint Vincent, Samoa, Sierra Leone, Solomon Islands, Spain, Swaziland, Sweden, United Kingdom, Uruguay, Venezuela, Zaire.

Absent: 12

Belize, Benin, Burma, Cape Verde, Dominica, Ethiopia, Guinea-Bissau, Mozambique, Sao Tome and Principe, Singapore, Suriname, Vanuatu.

Resolution No. 41/35 C of 10 November 1986

CONDEMNING COLLABORATION BETWEEN ISRAEL AND SOUTH AFRICA [EXCERPT FROM A RESOLUTION ON SOUTH AFRICAN POLICIES OF *APARTHEID*]

C

RELATIONS BETWEEN ISRAEL AND SOUTH AFRICA

The General Assembly,

Reaffirming its resolutions on relations between Israel and South Africa,

Having considered the special report of the Special Committee against *Apartheid* on recent developments concerning relations between Israel and South Africa,[491]

Taking note of the relevant provision of the Political Declaration of the Eighth Conference of Heads of State or Government of Non-Aligned Countries, held at Harare from 1 to 6 September 1986,[492]

Noting with appreciation the efforts of the Special Committee to disclose the increasing collaboration between Israel and South Africa,

Reiterating that the increasing collaboration by Israel with the racist régime of South Africa, especially in the economic, military and nuclear fields, in defiance of resolutions of the General Assembly and the Security Council, is a serious hindrance to international action for the eradication of *apartheid*, an encouragement to the racist régime of South Africa to persist in its criminal policy of *apartheid* and a hostile act against the oppressed people of South Africa and the entire African continent and constitutes a threat to international peace and security,

1. *Again strongly condemns* the continuing and increasing collaboration of Israel with the racist régime of South Africa, especially in the economic, military and nuclear fields;

2. *Demands* that Israel desist from and terminate forth-

with all forms of collaboration with South Africa, particularly in the economic, military and nuclear fields, and abide scrupulously by the relevant resolutions of the General Assembly and the Security Council;

3. *Calls upon* all Governments and organizations in a position to do so to exert their influence to persuade Israel to desist from such collaboration;

4. *Commends* the Special Committee against *Apartheid* for publicizing information on the growing relations between Israel and South Africa and promoting public awareness of the grave dangers of the alliance between Israel and South Africa;

5. *Requests* the Special Committee to continue to publicise, as widely as possible, information on the relations between Israel and South Africa;

6. *Requests* the Secretary-General to render, through the Department of Public Information and the Centre Against *Apartheid* of the Secretariat, all possible assistance to the Special Committee in disseminating information relating to the collaboration between Israel and South Africa;

7. *Further requests* the Special Committee to keep the matter under constant review and to report to the General Assembly and the Security Council as appropriate.

Adopted at the sixty-fourth plenary meeting:

In favour: 102

Afghanistan, Albania, Algeria, Angola, Antigua and Barbuda, Argentina, Bahrain, Bangladesh, Benin, Bhutan, Bolivia, Botswana, Brazil, Brunei Darussalam, Bulgaria, Burkina Faso, Burundi, Byelorussia, Cape Verde, Chad, China, Comoros, Congo, Cuba, Cyprus, Czechoslovakia, Democratic Kampuchea, Democratic Yemen, Djibouti, Ecuador, Egypt, Ethiopia, Gabon, Gambia, German Democratic Republic, Ghana, Guinea, Guinea-Bissau, Guyana, Haiti, Hungary, India, Indonesia, Iran, Iraq, Jordan, Kenya, Kuwait, Lao People's Democratic Republic, Lebanon, Libya, Madagascar, Malaysia, Maldives, Mali, Malta, Mauritania, Mauritius, Mexico, Mongolia, Morocco, Mozambique, Nicaragua, Niger, Nigeria, Oman, Pakistan, Peru, Philippines, Poland, Qatar, Romania, Rwanda, Sao Tome and Principe, Saudi Arabia, Senegal, Seychelles, Sierra Leone, Singapore, Solomon Islands, Somalia, Sri Lanka, Sudan, Suriname, Syria, Thailand, Togo, Trinidad and Tobago, Tunisia, Turkey, Uganda, Ukraine, USSR, United Arab Emirates, United Republic of Tanzania, Vanuatu, Venezuela, Viet Nam, Yemen, Yugoslavia, Zambia, Zimbabwe.

Against: 29

Australia, Austria, Belgium, Canada, Costa Rica, Denmark, Dominican Republic, El Salvador, Finland, France, Federal Republic of Germany, Honduras, Iceland, Ireland, Israel, Italy, Luxembourg, Malawi, Netherlands, New Zealand, Norway, Portugal, Saint Lucia, Spain, St. Christopher and Nevis, Sweden, United Kingdom, United States, Zaire.

Abstentions: 26

Bahamas, Barbados, Belize, Burma, Cameroon, Central African Republic, Chile, Colombia, Dominica, Equatorial Guinea, Fiji, Greece, Grenada, Guatemala, Ivory Coast,

---

[491]A/41/22/Add.1 and Corr.1.

[492]A/41/697-S/18392, annex.

Jamaica, Japan, Lesotho, Liberia, Nepal, Panama, Papua New Guinea, Saint Vincent, Samoa, Swaziland, Uruguay.
Absent: 1
Paraguay.

Resolution No. 41/43 A,B,C,D of 2 December 1986

ON THE QUESTION OF PALESTINE: ENDORSING THE RECOMMENDATIONS OF THE COMMITTEE ON THE EXERCISE OF THE INALIENABLE RIGHTS OF THE PALESTINIAN PEOPLE, REQUESTING THE DISSEMINATION OF INFORMATION ON THE QUESTION OF PALESTINE AND UNITED NATIONS ACTIVITIES RELATING TO IT, AND ENDORSING THE CONVENING OF AN INTERNATIONAL PEACE CONFERENCE ON THE MIDDLE EAST

A

The General Assembly,

Recalling its resolutions 181 (II) of 29 November 1947, 194 (III) of 11 December 1948, 3236 (XXIX) of 22 November 1974, 3375 (XXX) and 3376 (XXX) of 10 November 1975, 31/20 of 24 November 1976, 32/40 of 2 December 1977, 33/28 of 7 December 1978, 34/65 A and B of 29 November 1979 and 34/65 C and D of 12 December 1979, ES-7/2 of 29 July 1980, 35/169 of 15 December 1980, 36/120 of 10 December 1981, ES-7/4 of 28 April 1982, ES-7/5 of 26 June 1982, ES-7/9 of 24 September 1982, 37/86 A of 10 December 1982, 38/58 A of 13 December 1983, 39/49 A of 11 December 1984 and 40/96 A of 12 December 1985,

Having considered the report of the Committee on the Exercise of the Inalienable Rights of the Palestinian People,[493]

1. *Expresses its appreciation* to the Committee on the Exercise of the Inalienable Rights of the Palestinian People for its efforts in performing the tasks assigned to it by the General Assembly;

2. *Endorses* the recommendations of the Committee contained in paragraphs 112 to 120 of its report[494] and draws the attention of the Security Council to the fact that action on the Committee's recommendations, as repeatedly endorsed by the General Assembly at its thirty-first session and subsequently, is still awaited;

3. *Requests* the Committee to continue to keep under review the situation relating to the question of Palestine as well as the implementation of the Programme of Action for the Achievement of Palestinian Rights[495] and to report and make suggestions to the General Assembly or the Security Council, as appropriate;

4. *Authorizes* the Committee to continue to exert all efforts to promote the implementation of its recommenda-

tions, including representation at conferences and meetings and the sending of delegations where such activities would be considered by it to be appropriate, and to report thereon to the General Assembly at its forty-second session and thereafter;

5. *Requests* the Committee to continue to extend its cooperation to non-governmental organizations in their contribution towards heightening international awareness of the facts relating to the question of Palestine and in creating a more favourable atmosphere for the full implementation of the Committee's recommendations, and to take the necessary steps to expand its contacts with those organizations;

6. *Requests* the United Nations Conciliation Commission for Palestine, established under General Assembly resolution 194 (III), as well as other United Nations bodies associated with the question of Palestine, to co-operate fully with the Committee and to make available to it, at its request, the relevant information and documentation which they have at their disposal;

7. *Decides* to circulate the report of the Committee to all the competent bodies of the United Nations and urges them to take the necessary action, as appropriate, in accordance with the Committee's programme of implementation;

8. *Requests* the Secretary-General to continue to provide the Committee with all the necessary facilities for the performance of its tasks.

Adopted at the 93rd plenary meeting:
In favour: 121
Afghanistan, Albania, Algeria, Angola, Antigua and Barbuda, Argentina, Bahamas, Bahrain, Bangladesh, Barbados, Belize, Benin, Bhutan, Bolivia, Botswana, Brazil, Brunei Darussalam, Bulgaria, Burkina Faso, Burma, Burundi, Byelorussia, Cameroon, Cape Verde, Central African Republic, Chad, Chile, China, Colombia, Congo, Cuba, Cyprus, Czechoslovakia, Democratic Yemen, Djibouti, Dominican Republic, Ecuador, Egypt, Ethiopia, Gabon, German Democratic Republic, Ghana, Greece, Grenada, Guatemala, Guinea, Guinea-Bissau, Guyana, Haiti, Hungary, India, Indonesia, Iran, Iraq, Ivory Coast, Jamaica, Jordan, Kuwait, Lao People's Democratic Republic, Lebanon, Lesotho, Liberia, Libya, Madagascar, Malaysia, Maldives, Mali, Malta, Mauritania, Mauritius, Mexico, Mongolia, Morocco, Mozambique, Nepal, Nicaragua, Niger, Nigeria, Oman, Pakistan, Papua New Guinea, Peru, Philippines, Poland, Qatar, Romania, Rwanda, Saint Lucia, Samoa, Sao Tome and Principe, Saudi Arabia, Senegal, Seychelles, Sierra Leone, Singapore, Solomon Islands, Somalia, Spain, Sri Lanka, Sudan, Suriname, Swaziland, Syria, Thailand, Togo, Trinidad and Tobago, Tunisia, Turkey, Uganda, Ukraine, USSR, United Arab Emirates, United Republic of Tanzania, Uruguay, Venezuela, Viet Nam, Yemen, Yugoslavia, Zaire, Zambia, Zimbabwe.
Against: 2
Israel, United States.
Abstentions: 21
Australia, Austria, Belgium, Canada, Costa Rica, Den-

---

[493]*Official Records of the General Assembly, Forty-first Session, Supplement No. 35* (A/41/35).
[494]*Ibid.*
[495]*Report of the International Conference on the Question of Palestine, Geneva, 29 August-7 September 1983* (United Nations publication, Sales No. E.83.I.21), chap. I, sect. B.

mark, El Salvador, Finland, France, Federal Republic of Germany, Iceland, Ireland, Italy, Japan, Luxembourg, Netherlands, New Zealand, Norway, Portugal, Sweden, United Kingdom.

Absent: 14

Comoros,* Democratic Kampuchea,* Dominica, Equatorial Guinea, Fiji, Gambia,* Honduras, Kenya,* Malawi, Panama,* Paraguay, Saint Vincent,* St. Christopher and Nevis, Vanuatu.*

---

* Later advised the Secretariat it had intended to vote in favour.

B

The General Assembly,

Having considered the report of the Committee on the Exercise of the Inalienable Rights of the Palestinian People,[496]

Taking note, in particular, of relevant information contained in paragraphs 73 to 101 of that report,

Recalling its resolutions 32/40 B of 2 December 1977, 33/28 C of 7 December 1978, 34/65 D of 12 December 1979, 35/169 D of 15 December 1980, 36/120 B of 10 December 1981, 37/86 B of 10 December 1982, 38/58 B of 13 December 1983, 39/49 B of 11 December 1984 and 40/96 B of 12 December 1985

1. *Takes note with appreciation* of the action taken by the Secretary-General in compliance with General Assembly resolution 40/96 B;

2. *Requests* the Secretary-General to provide the Division for Palestinian Rights of the Secretariat with the necessary resources and to ensure that it continues to discharge the tasks detailed in paragraphs 2 and 3 of General Assembly resolution 40/96 B in consultation with the Committee on the Exercise of the Inalienable Rights of the Palestinian People and under its guidance;

3. *Also requests* the Secretary-General to ensure the continued co-operation of the Department of Public Information and other units of the Secretariat in enabling the Division for Palestinian Rights to perform its tasks and in covering adequately the various aspects of the question of Palestine;

4. *Invites* all Governments and organizations to lend their co-operation to the Committee on the Exercise of the Inalienable Rights of the Palestinian People and the Division for Palestinian Rights in the performance of their tasks;

5. *Takes note with appreciation* of the action taken by Member States to observe annually on 29 November the International Day of Solidarity with the Palestinian People and the issuance by them of special postage stamps for the occasion.

Adopted at the 93rd plenary meeting:

In favour: 125

Afghanistan, Albania, Algeria, Angola, Antigua and Barbuda, Argentina, Bahamas, Bahrain, Bangladesh, Barba-

dos, Belize, Benin, Bhutan, Bolivia, Botswana, Brazil, Brunei Darussalam, Bulgaria, Burkina Faso, Burma, Burundi, Byelorussia, Cameroon, Cape Verde, Central African Republic, Chad, Chile, China, Colombia, Congo, Costa Rica, Cuba, Cyprus, Czechoslovakia, Democratic Yemen, Djibouti, Dominican Republic, Ecuador, Egypt, El Salvador, Ethiopia, Gabon, German Democratic Republic, Ghana, Greece, Grenada, Guatemala, Guinea, Guinea-Bissau, Guyana, Haiti, Hungary, India, Indonesia, Iran, Iraq, Ivory Coast, Jamaica, Jordan, Kenya, Kuwait, Lao People's Democratic Republic, Lebanon, Lesotho, Liberia, Libya, Madagascar, Malaysia, Maldives, Mali, Malta, Mauritania, Mauritius, Mexico, Mongolia, Morocco, Mozambique, Nepal, Nicaragua, Niger, Nigeria, Oman, Pakistan, Papua New Guinea, Peru, Philippines, Poland, Qatar, Romania, Rwanda, Saint Lucia, Samoa, Sao Tome and Principe, Saudi Arabia, Senegal, Seychelles, Sierra Leone, Singapore, Solomon Islands, Somalia, Spain, Sri Lanka, Sudan, Suriname, Swaziland, Syria, Thailand, Togo, Trinidad and Tobago, Tunisia, Turkey, Uganda, Ukraine, USSR, United Arab Emirates, United Republic of Tanzania, Uruguay, Vanuatu, Venezuela, Viet Nam, Yemen, Yugoslavia, Zaire, Zambia, Zimbabwe.

Against: 3

Canada, Israel, United States.

Abstentions: 18

Australia, Austria, Belgium, Denmark, Finland, France, Federal Republic of Germany, Iceland, Ireland, Italy, Japan, Luxembourg, Netherlands, New Zealand, Norway, Portugal, Sweden, United Kingdom.

Absent: 12

Comoros,* Democratic Kampuchea,* Dominica, Equatorial Guinea, Fiji, Gambia,* Honduras, Malawi, Panama,* Paraguay, Saint Vincent,* St. Christopher and Nevis.

---

* Later advised the Secretariat it had intended to vote in favour.

C

The General Assembly,

Having considered the report of the Committee on the Exercise of the Inalienable Rights of the Palestinian People,[497]

Taking note, in particular, of the information contained in paragraphs 102 to 111 of that report,

Recalling its resolution 40/96 C of 12 December 1985,

Convinced that the world-wide dissemination of accurate and comprehensive information and the role of non-governmental organizations and institutions remain of vital importance in heightening awareness of and support for the inalienable rights of the Palestinian people to self-determination and to the establishment of an independent sovereign Palestinian State,

1. *Takes note with appreciation* of the action taken by the Department of Public Information of the Secretariat in compliance with General Assembly resolution 40/96 C,

---

[496]*Official Records of the General Assembly, Forty-first Session, Supplement No. 35* (A/41/35).

[497]*Official Records of the General Assembly, Forty-first Session, Supplement No. 35* (A/41/35).

2. *Requests* the Department of Public Information, in full co-operation and co-ordination with the Committee on the Exercise of the Inalienable Rights of the Palestinian People, to continue its special information programme on the question of Palestine for the biennium 1986-1987 and, in particular:

(*a*) To disseminate information on all the activities of the United Nations system relating to the question of Palestine;

(*b*) To continue to update publications on the facts and developments pertaining to the question of Palestine;

(*c*) To publish brochures and booklets on various aspects of the question of Palestine, including Israeli violations of the human rights of the Arab inhabitants of the occupied territories;

(*d*) To expand its audio-visual material on the question of Palestine, including the production of a new film in 1987 and special series of radio programmes and television broadcasts;

(*e*) To organize fact-finding news missions to the area for journalists;

(*f*) To organize regional and national encounters for journalists.

Adopted at the 93rd plenary meeting:
In favour: 124
Afghanistan, Albania, Algeria, Angola, Antigua and Barbuda, Argentina, Austria, Bahamas, Bahrain, Bangladesh, Barbados, Belize, Benin, Bhutan, Bolivia, Botswana, Brazil, Brunei Darussalam, Bulgaria, Burkina Faso, Burma, Burundi, Byelorussia, Cape Verde, Central African Republic, Chad, Chile, China, Colombia, Congo, Cuba, Cyprus, Czechoslovakia, Democratic Yemen, Djibouti, Dominican Republic, Ecuador, Egypt, Ethiopia, Finland, Gabon, German Democratic Republic, Ghana, Greece, Grenada, Guatemala, Guinea, Guinea-Bissau, Guyana, Haiti, Hungary, India, Indonesia, Iran, Iraq, Ivory Coast, Jamaica, Jordan, Kenya, Kuwait, Lao People's Democratic Republic, Lebanon, Lesotho, Liberia, Libya, Madagascar, Malaysia, Maldives, Mali, Malta, Mauritania, Mauritius, Mexico, Mongolia, Morocco, Mozambique, Nepal, Nicaragua, Niger, Nigeria, Oman, Pakistan, Papua New Guinea, Peru, Philippines, Poland, Qatar, Romania, Rwanda, Samoa, Sao Tome and Principe, Saudi Arabia, Senegal, Seychelles, Sierra Leone, Singapore, Solomon Islands, Somalia, Spain, Sri Lanka, Sudan, Suriname, Swaziland, Sweden, Syria, Thailand, Togo, Trinidad and Tobago, Tunisia, Turkey, Uganda, Ukraine, USSR, United Arab Emirates, United Republic of Tanzania, Uruguay, Vanuatu, Venezuela, Viet Nam, Yemen, Yugoslavia, Zaire, Zambia, Zimbabwe.
Against: 3
Canada, Israel, United States.
Abstentions: 19
Australia, Belgium, Cameroon, Costa Rica, Denmark, El Salvador, France, Federal Republic of Germany, Iceland, Ireland, Italy, Japan, Luxembourg, Netherlands, New Zealand, Norway, Portugal, Saint Lucia, United Kingdom.
Absent: 12

Comoros,* Democratic Kampuchea,* Dominica, Equatorial Guinea, Fiji, Gambia,* Honduras, Malawi, Panama,* Paraguay, Saint Vincent,** St. Christopher and Nevis.

---

*Later advised the Secretariat it had intended to vote in favour.
**Later advised the Secretariat it had intended to abstain.

D

The General Assembly,

Recalling its resolutions 38/58 C of 13 December 1983, 39/49 D of 11 December 1984 and 40/96 D of 12 December 1985, in which it, *inter alia,* endorsed the call for convening the International Peace Conference on the Middle East,

Recalling also the relevant resolutions of the Security Council,

Reaffirming its resolutions 39/49 D and 40/96 D, in which it, *inter alia,* requested the Secretary-General, in consultation with the Security Council, to continue his efforts with a view to convening the Conference,

Having considered the report of the Secretary-General of 14 March 1986, in which he, *inter alia,* stated that "the obstacles which have so far prevented the convening of the International Peace Conference on the Middle East as called for by the General Assembly still exist",[498] and his report of 29 October 1986,[499]

Expressing its regret that, owing to the negative attitude of some Member States, the difficulties regarding the convening of the Conference "have remained essentially the same",[500] and expressing its hope that those Member States will reconsider their attitude,

Having heard the constructive statements made by numerous representatives, including that of the Palestine Liberation Organization,

Emphasizing the need to bring about a just and comprehensive settlement to the Arab-Israeli conflict which has persisted for nearly four decades,

Recognizing that the persistence of the Arab-Israeli conflict in the Middle East constitutes a threat to security and stability in the region and to world peace, and, therefore, directly involves the responsibility of the United Nations,

Stressing its conviction that the convening of the Conference will constitute a major contribution by the United Nations towards the realization of a just solution to the question of Palestine conducive to the achievement of a comprehensive, just and lasting solution to the Arab-Israeli conflict,

Appreciating the concern about the exacerbating situation in the Middle East as voiced in a great many statements during the general debate at the current session and at previous sessions,

1. *Takes note with appreciation* of the reports of the Secretary-General;[501]

---

[498]See A/41/215-S/17916, para. 2.
[499]A/41/768-S/18427.
[500]*Ibid.*, para. 31.
[501]See A/41/215-S/17916, para. 2 and A/41/768-S/18427.

2. *Determines* that the question of Palestine is the core of the Arab-Israeli conflict in the Middle East;

3. *Reaffirms once again* its endorsement of the call for convening the International Peace Conference on the Middle East in conformity with the provisions of the resolution 38/58 C;

4. *Stresses* the urgent need for additional concrete and constructive efforts by all Governments in order to convene the Conference without further delay;

5. *Endorses the call* for setting up a preparatory committee, within the framework of the Security Council, with the participation of the permanent members of the Council, to take the necessary action to convene the Conference;

6. *Requests* the Secretary-General, in consultation with the Security Council, to continue his efforts with a view to convening the Conference and to report thereon to the General Assembly not later than 15 May 1987;

7. *Decides* to consider at its forty-second session the report of the Secretary-General on the implementation of the present resolution.

Adopted at the 93rd plenary meeting:

In favour: 123

Afghanistan, Algeria, Angola, Argentina, Austria, Bahamas, Bahrain, Bangladesh, Barbados, Belize, Benin, Bhutan, Bolivia, Botswana, Brazil, Brunei Darussalam, Bulgaria, Burkina Faso, Burma, Burundi, Byelorussia, Cameroon, Cape Verde, Central African Republic, Chad, Chile, China, Colombia, Congo, Cuba, Cyprus, Czechoslovakia, Democratic Yemen, Djibouti, Dominican Republic, Ecuador, Egypt, Ethiopia, Finland, Gabon, German Democratic Republic, Ghana, Greece, Guatemala, Guinea, Guinea-Bissau, Guyana, Haiti, Hungary, India, Indonesia, Iran, Iraq, Ivory Coast, Jamaica, Japan, Jordan, Kenya, Kuwait, Lao People's Democratic Republic, Lebanon, Lesotho, Liberia, Libya, Madagascar, Malaysia, Maldives, Mali, Malta, Mauritania, Mauritius, Mexico, Mongolia, Morocco, Mozambique, Nepal, Nicaragua, Niger, Nigeria, Oman, Pakistan, Papua New Guinea, Peru, Philippines, Poland, Qatar, Romania, Rwanda, Samoa, Sao Tome and Principe, Saudi Arabia, Senegal, Seychelles, Sierra Leone, Singapore, Solomon Islands, Somalia, Spain, Sri Lanka, Sudan, Suriname, Swaziland, Sweden, Syria, Thailand, Togo, Trinidad and Tobago, Tunisia, Turkey, Uganda, Ukraine, USSR, United Arab Emirates, United Republic of Tanzania, Uruguay, Vanuatu, Venezuela, Viet Nam, Yemen, Yugoslavia, Zaire, Zambia, Zimbabwe.

Against: 3

Antigua and Barbuda, Israel, United States.

Abstentions: 19

Australia, Belgium, Canada, Costa Rica, Denmark, El Salvador, France, Federal Republic of Germany, Grenada, Iceland, Ireland, Italy, Luxembourg, Netherlands, New Zealand, Norway, Portugal, Saint Lucia, United Kingdom.

Absent: 13

Albania, Comoros,* Democratic Kampuchea,* Dominica, Equatorial Guinea, Fiji, Gambia,* Honduras, Malawi, Panama,* Paraguay, Saint Vincent,** St. Christopher and Nevis.

---

*Later advised the Secretariat it had intended to vote in favour.

**Later advised the Secretariat it had intended to abstain.

Resolution No. 41/44 A, B of 3 December 1986

ON THE FINANCING OF THE UNITED NATIONS DISENGAGEMENT OBSERVER FORCE

A

The General Assembly,

Having considered the report of the Secretary-General on the financing of the United Nations Disengagement Observer Force,[502] as well as the related report of the Advisory Committee on Administrative and Budgetary Questions,[503]

Bearing in mind Security Council resolutions 350 (1974) of 31 May 1974, 363 (1974) of 29 November 1974, 369 (1975) of 28 May 1975, 381 (1975) of 30 November 1975, 390 (1976) of 28 May 1976, 398 (1976) of 30 November 1976, 408 (1977) of 26 May 1977, 420 (1977) of 30 November 1977, 429 (1978) of 31 May 1978, 441 (1978) of 30 November 1978, 449 (1979) of 30 May 1979, 456 (1979) of 30 November 1979, 470 (1980) of 30 May 1980, 481 (1980) of 26 November 1980, 485 (1981) of 22 May 1981, 493 (1981) of 23 November 1981, 506 (1982) of 26 May 1982, 524 (1982) of 29 November 1982, 531 (1983) of 26 May 1983, 543 (1983) of 29 November 1983, 551 (1984) of 30 May 1984, 557 (1984) of 28 November 1984, 563 (1985) of 21 May 1985, 576 (1985) of 21 November 1985, 584 (1986) of 29 May 1986 and 590 (1986) of 26 November 1986,[504]

Recalling its resolutions 3101 (XXVIII) of 11 December 1973, 3211 B (XXIX) of 29 November 1974, 3374 C (XXX) of 2 December 1975, 31/5 D of 22 December 1976, 32/4 C of 2 December 1977, 33/13 D of 8 December 1978, 34/7 C of 3 December 1979, 35/44 of 1 December 1980, 35/45 A of 1 December 1980, 36/66 A of 30 November 1981, 37/38 A of 30 November 1982, 38/35 A of 1 December 1983, 39/28 A of 30 November 1984 and 40/59 A of 2 December 1985,

Reaffirming its previous decisions regarding the fact that, in order to meet the expenditures caused by such operations, a different procedure is required from that applied to meet expenditures of the regular budget of the United Nations,

Taking into account the fact that the economically more developed countries are in a position to make relatively larger contributions and that the economically less developed countries have a relatively limited capacity to contribute towards peace-keeping operations involving heavy expenditures,

Bearing in mind the special responsibilities of the States

---

[502]A/41/705.

[503]A/41/820.

[504]The resolutions cited in this paragraph and the next provide for the renewed mandate and financing of the United Nations Disengagement Observer Force. [ed. note]

permanent members of the Security Council in the financing of such operations, as indicated in General Assembly resolution 1874 (S-IV) of 27 June 1963 and other resolutions of the Assembly,

I

Decides to appropriate to the Special Account referred to in section II, paragraph 1, of General Assembly resolution 3211 B (XXIX) the amount of $18,282,000 gross ($17,934,498 net) authorized and apportioned by section III of Assembly resolution 40/59 A for the operation of the United Nations Disengagement Observer Force for the period from 1 June to 30 November 1986, inclusive;

II

1. *Decides* to appropriate to the Special Account an amount of $17,400,000 for the operation of the United Nations Disengagement Observer Force for the period from 1 December 1986 to 31 May 1987, inclusive;

2. *Decides further,* as an *ad hoc* arrangement, without prejudice to the positions of principle that may be taken by Member States in any consideration by the General Assembly of arrangements for the financing of peace-keeping operations, to apportion the amount of $17,400,000 among Member States in accordance with the scheme set out in Assembly resolution 3101 (XXVIII) and the provisions of section II, paragraphs 2(*b*) and 2(*c*), and section V, paragraph 1, of resolution 3374 C (XXX), section V, paragraph 1, of resolution 31/5 D, section V, paragraph 1, of resolution 32/4 C, section V, paragraph 1, of resolution 33/13 D, section V, paragraph 1, of resolution 34/7 C, section V, paragraph 1, of resolution 35/45 A, section V, paragraph 1, of resolution 36/66 A, section V, paragraph 1, of resolution 37/38 A and section V, paragraphs 1 and 2, of resolution 39/28 A, in the proportions determined by the scale of assessments of the years 1986, 1987 and 1988;

3. *Decides* that there shall be set off against the apportionment among Member States, as provided in paragraph 2 above, their respective share in the estimated income of $10,000 other than staff assessment income approved for the period from 1 December 1986 to 31 May 1987, inclusive;

4. *Decides* that, in accordance with the provisions of its resolution 973 (X) of 15 December 1955, there shall be set off against the apportionment among Member States, as provided for in paragraph 2 above, their respective share in the Tax Equalization Fund of the estimated staff assessment income of $290,000 approved for the period from 1 December 1986 to 31 May 1987, inclusive;

III

Authorizes the Secretary-General to enter into commitments for the United Nations Disengagement Observer Force at a rate not to exceed $2,900,000 gross ($2,850,000 net) per month for the period from 1 June to 30 November 1987, inclusive, should the Security Council decide to continue the Force beyond the period of six months authorized under its resolution 590 (1986), the said amount to be apportioned among Member States in accordance with the scheme set out in the present resolution;

IV

1. *Stresses* the need for voluntary contributions to the United Nations Disengagement Observer Force, both in cash and in the form of services and supplies acceptable to the Secretary-General;

2. *Requests* the Secretary-General to take all necessary action to ensure that the United Nations Disengagement Observer Force is conducted with a maximum of efficiency and economy.

Adopted at the 94th plenary meeting:
In favour: 110
Antigua and Barbuda, Argentina, Australia, Austria, Bahamas, Bangladesh, Barbados, Belgium, Bhutan, Bolivia, Botswana, Brazil, Brunei Darussalam, Burkina Faso, Burma, Burundi, Cameroon, Canada, Cape Verde, Central African Republic, Chad, Chile, China, Colombia, Costa Rica, Cyprus, Democratic Kampuchea, Denmark, Dominican Republic, Ecuador, Egypt, Equatorial Guinea, Ethiopia, Fiji, Finland, France, Gabon, Federal Republic of Germany, Ghana, Greece, Grenada, Guinea-Bissau, Guyana, Iceland, India, Indonesia, Ireland, Israel, Italy, Ivory Coast, Jamaica, Japan, Jordan, Kenya, Kuwait, Lebanon, Liberia, Luxembourg, Madagascar, Malawi, Malaysia, Malta, Mauritania, Mauritius, Mexico, Morocco, Nepal, Netherlands, New Zealand, Nicaragua, Niger, Norway, Oman, Pakistan, Panama, Peru, Philippines, Poland, Portugal, Qatar, Romania, Saint Lucia, Saint Vincent, Samoa, Sao Tome and Principe, Saudi Arabia, Senegal, Sierra Leone, Singapore, Spain, Sri Lanka, Sudan, Suriname, Swaziland, Sweden, Thailand, Togo, Trinidad and Tobago, Tunisia, Turkey, Uganda, United Arab Emirates, United Kingdom, United Republic of Tanzania, United States, Uruguay, Venezuela, Yugoslavia, Zaire, Zambia.
Against: 3
Albania, Comoros,* Syria.
Abstentions: 21
Algeria, Angola, Benin, Bulgaria, Byelorussia, Cuba, Czechoslovakia, Democratic Yemen, German Democratic Republic, Hungary, Iraq, Lao People's Democratic Republic, Libya, Maldives, Mali, Mongolia, Seychelles, Ukraine, USSR, Viet Nam, Yemen.
Absent: 24
Afghanistan,* Bahrain,** Belize, Congo, Djibouti, Dominica, El Salvador, Gambia, Guatemala, Guinea, Haiti, Honduras, Iran, Lesotho, Mozambique, Nigeria, Papua New Guinea,** Paraguay, Rwanda, Solomon Islands, Somalia, St. Christopher and Nevis, Vanuatu, Zimbabwe.

---

*Later advised the Secretariat it had intended to abstain.
**Later advised the Secretariat it had intended to vote in favour.

B

The General Assembly,
Having regard to the financial position of the Special

Account for the United Nations Emergency Force and the United Nations Disengagement Observer Force, as set forth in the report of the Secretary-General,[505] and referring to paragraph 6 of the report of the Advisory Committee on Administrative and Budgetary Questions,[506]

Mindful of the fact that it is essential to provide the United Nations Disengagement Observer Force with the necessary financial resources to enable it to fulfil its responsibilities under the relevant resolutions of the Security Council,

Concerned that the Secretary-General is continuing to face growing difficulties in meeting the obligations of the Forces on a current basis, particularly those due to the Governments of troop-contributing States,

Recalling its resolutions 33/13 E of 14 December 1978, 34/7 D of 17 December 1979, 35/45 B of 1 December 1980, 36/66 B of 30 November 1981, 37/38 B of 30 November 1982, 38/35 B of 1 December 1983, 39/28 B of 30 November 1984 and 40/59 B of 2 December 1985,

Recognizing that, in consequence of the withholding of contributions by certain Member States, the surplus balances in the Special Account for the United Nations Emergency Force and the United Nations Disengagement Observer Force have, in effect, been drawn upon to the full extent to supplement the income received from contributions for meeting expenses of the Forces,

Concerned that the application of the provisions of regulations 5.2(*b*), 5.2(*d*), 4.3 and 4.4 of the Financial Regulations of the United Nations would aggravate the already difficult financial situation of the Forces,

Decides that the provisions of regulations 5.2(*b*), 5.2(*d*), 4.3 and 4.4 of the Financial Regulations of the United Nations shall be suspended in respect of the amount of $1,496,703, which otherwise would have to be surrendered pursuant to those provisions, this amount to be entered into the account referred to in the operative part of General Assembly resolution 33/13 E and held in suspense until a further decision is taken by the Assembly.

Adopted at the 94th plenary meeting:

In favour: 115

Argentina, Australia, Austria, Bahamas, Bahrain, Bangladesh, Barbados, Belgium, Bhutan, Bolivia, Botswana, Brazil, Brunei Darussalam, Burkina Faso, Burma, Burundi, Cameroon, Canada, Cape Verde, Central African Republic, Chad, Chile, China, Colombia, Comoros, Congo, Costa Rica, Cyprus, Democratic Kampuchea, Denmark, Dominican Republic, Ecuador, Egypt, Equatorial Guinea, Ethiopia, Fiji, Finland, France, Gabon, Federal Republic of Germany, Ghana, Greece, Grenada, Guatemala, Guinea-Bissau, Guyana, Iceland, India, Indonesia, Ireland, Israel, Italy, Ivory Coast, Jamaica, Japan, Jordan, Kenya, Kuwait, Lebanon, Lesotho, Liberia, Luxembourg, Madagascar, Malawi, Malaysia, Malta, Mauritania, Mauritius, Mexico, Morocco, Nepal, Netherlands, New Zealand, Nicaragua, Niger, Norway, Oman, Pakistan, Panama, Papua New Guinea, Peru, Philippines, Portugal, Qatar, Romania, Saint Lucia, Saint Vincent, Samoa, Sao Tome and Principe, Saudi Arabia, Senegal, Sierra Leone, Singapore, Spain, Sri Lanka, Sudan, Suriname, Sweden, Syria,* Thailand, Togo, Trinidad and Tobago, Tunisia, Turkey, Uganda, United Arab Emirates, United Kingdom, United Republic of Tanzania, United States, Uruguay, Venezuela, Yugoslavia, Zaire, Zambia.

Against: 1

Albania.

Abstentions: 22

Algeria, Angola, Benin, Bulgaria, Byelorussia, Cuba, Czechoslovakia, Democratic Yemen, German Democratic Republic, Hungary, Iraq, Lao People's Democratic Republic, Libya, Maldives, Mali, Mongolia, Poland, Seychelles, Ukraine, USSR, Viet Nam, Yemen.

Absent: 20

Afghanistan,** Antigua and Barbuda, Belize, Djibouti, Dominica, El Salvador, Gambia, Guinea, Haiti, Honduras, Iran, Mozambique, Nigeria, Paraguay, Rwanda, Solomon Islands, Somalia, St. Christopher and Nevis, Vanuatu, Zimbabwe.

---

*Later advised the Secretariat it had intended to vote against.
**Later advised the Secretariat it had intended to abstain.

Resolution No. 41/48 of 3 December 1986

CALLING UPON ALL COUNTRIES OF THE MIDDLE EAST TO PLACE THEIR NUCLEAR ACTIVITIES UNDER INTERNATIONAL ATOMIC ENERGY AGENCY SAFEGUARDS

The General Assembly,

Recalling its resolutions 3263 (XXIX) of 9 December 1974, 3474 (XXX) of 11 December 1975, 31/71 of 10 December 1976, 32/82 of 12 December 1977, 33/64 of 14 December 1978, 34/77 of 11 December 1979, 35/147 of 12 December 1980, 36/87 of 9 December 1981, 37/75 of 9 December 1982, 38/64 of 15 December 1983, 39/54 of 12 December 1984 and 40/82 of 12 December 1985 on the establishment of a nuclear-weapon-free zone in the region of the Middle East,

Recalling also the recommendations for the establishment of such a zone in the Middle East consistent with paragraphs 60 to 63, and in particular paragraph 63 (*d*) of the Final Document of the Tenth Special Session of the General Assembly,[507]

Emphasizing the basic provisions of the above-mentioned resolutions, which call upon all parties directly concerned to consider taking the practical and urgent steps required for the implementation of the proposal to establish a nuclear-weapon-free zone in the region of the Middle

---

[505]A/41/705.
[506]A/41/820.

[507]General Assembly resolution S-10/2.

East and, pending and during the establishment of such a zone, to declare solemnly that they will refrain, on a reciprocal basis, from producing, acquiring or in any other way possessing nuclear weapons and nuclear explosive devices and from permitting the stationing of nuclear weapons in their territory by any third party, to agree to place all their nuclear facilities under International Atomic Energy Agency safeguards and to declare their support for the establishment of the zone and deposit such declarations with the Security Council for consideration, as appropriate,

Reaffirming the inalienable right of all States to acquire and develop nuclear energy for peaceful purposes,

Emphasizing further the need for appropriate measures on the question of the prohibition of military attacks on nuclear facilities,

Bearing in mind the consensus reached by the General Assembly at its thirty-fifth session that the establishment of a nuclear-weapon-free zone in the region of the Middle East would greatly enhance international peace and security,[508]

Desirous to build on that consensus so that substantial progress can be made towards establishing a nuclear-weapon-free zone in the region of the Middle East,

Emphasizing the essential role of the United Nations in the establishment of a nuclear-weapon-free zone in the region of the Middle East,

Having examined the report of the Secretary-General,[509]

1. *Urges* all parties directly concerned to consider seriously taking the practical and urgent steps required for the implementation of the proposal to establish a nuclear-weapon-free zone in the region of the Middle East in accordance with the relevant resolutions of the General Assembly and, as a means of promoting this objective, invites the countries concerned to adhere to the Treaty on the Non-Proliferation of Nuclear Weapons;[510]

2. *Calls upon* all countries of the region that have not done so, pending the establishment of the zone, to agree to place all their nuclear activities under International Atomic Energy safeguards;

3. *Invites* those countries, pending the establishment of a nuclear-weapon-free zone in the region of the Middle East, to declare their support for establishing such a zone, consistent with the relevant paragraph of the Final Document of the Tenth Special Session of the General Assembly,[511] the first special session devoted to disarmament, and to deposit those declarations with the Security Council;

4. *Further invites* those countries, pending the establishment of the zone, not to develop, produce, test or otherwise acquire nuclear weapons or permit the stationing on their territories, or territories under their control, of nuclear weapons or nuclear explosive devices;

5. *Invites* the nuclear-weapon States and all other States

to render their assistance in the establishment of the zone and at the same time to refrain from any action that runs counter to both the letter and spirit of the present resolution;

6. *Extends its thanks* to the Secretary-General for his report containing the views of parties concerned regarding the establishment of a nuclear-weapon-free zone in the region of the Middle East;[512]

7. *Takes note* of the above-mentioned report;

8. *Requests* those parties that have not yet communicated their views to the Secretary-General to do so;

9. *Welcomes* any further comments from those parties that have already communicated their views to the Secretary-General;

10. *Requests* the Secretary-General to submit a report to the General Assembly at its forty-second session on the implementation of the present resolution;

11. *Decides* to include in the provisional agenda of its forty-second session the item entitled "Establishment of a nuclear-weapon-free zone in the region of the Middle East".

Adopted at the 94th plenary meeting without a vote.

Resolution No. 41/63 A, B, C, D, E, F, G of 3 December 1986

ON ISRAELI PRACTICES AFFECTING HUMAN RIGHTS IN THE OCCUPIED TERRITORIES: CALLING ON ISRAEL TO RELEASE ARAB PRISONERS, CONDEMNING IT FOR ITS POLICIES OF SETTLEMENT AND ANNEXATION IN THE OCCUPIED TERRITORIES, AS WELL AS MEASURES AGAINST CIVIL AND EDUCATIONAL FREEDOM THERE, AND FOR ITS EXPULSION OF PALESTINIAN LEADERS

A

The General Assembly,

Recalling its resolutions 38/79 A of 15 December 1983, 39/95 A of 14 December 1984 and 40/161 A of 16 December 1985,

Taking note of the report of the Special Committee to Investigate Israeli Practices Affecting the Human Rights of the Population of the Occupied Territories,[513]

Taking note also of the reports of the Secretary-General of 21 and 29 July 1986,[514]

1. *Calls upon* Israel to release all Arabs arbitrarily detained and imprisoned as a result of their struggle for self-determination and for the liberation of their territories;

2. *Notes* the initial release of Palestinian prisoners from prison on 20 May 1985;

3. *Deplores* the Israeli subsequent arbitrary detention and imprisonment of hundreds of Palestinians;

4. *Demands* that the Government of Israel, the occupying Power, rescind its action against the detainees and imprisoned Palestinians and release them immediately;

---

[508]See General Assembly resolution 35/147.
[509]A/41/465 and Add.1.
[510]General Assembly resolution 2373 (XXII), annex.
[511]General Assembly resolution S-10/2.

[512]A/41/465 and Add.1.
[513]A/41/680.
[514]A/41/469 and Add.1.

5. *Requests* the Secretary-General to report to the General Assembly as soon as possible and not later than the beginning of its forty-second session on the implementation of the present resolution.

Adopted at the 95th plenary meeting:
In favour: 108
Afghanistan, Albania, Algeria, Angola, Antigua and Barbuda, Argentina, Bahamas, Bahrain, Bangladesh, Barbados, Benin, Bhutan, Bolivia, Botswana, Brazil, Brunei Darussalam, Bulgaria, Burkina Faso, Burma, Burundi, Byelorussia, Cape Verde, Central African Republic, Chad, China, Congo, Cuba, Cyprus, Czechoslovakia, Democratic Kampuchea, Democratic Yemen, Djibouti, Dominican Republic, Ecuador, Egypt, El Salvador, Ethiopia, Gabon, German Democratic Republic, Ghana, Guatemala, Guinea, Guinea-Bissau, Guyana, Honduras, Hungary, India, Indonesia, Iran, Iraq, Jordan, Kenya, Kuwait, Lao People's Democratic Republic, Lebanon, Lesotho, Libya, Madagascar, Malaysia, Maldives, Mali, Malta, Mauritania, Mauritius, Mexico, Mongolia, Morocco, Mozambique, Nicaragua, Niger, Oman, Pakistan, Panama, Papua New Guinea, Paraguay, Peru, Philippines, Poland, Qatar, Romania, Rwanda, Sao Tome and Principe, Saudi Arabia, Senegal, Sierra Leone, Solomon Islands, Somalia, Sri Lanka, Sudan, Suriname, Swaziland, Syria, Togo, Trinidad and Tobago, Tunisia, Turkey, Uganda, Ukraine, USSR, United Arab Emirates, United Republic of Tanzania, Vanuatu, Venezuela, Viet Nam, Yemen, Yugoslavia, Zambia, Zimbabwe.
Against: 2
Israel, United States.
Abstentions: 34
Australia, Austria, Belgium, Cameroon, Canada, Costa Rica, Denmark, Equatorial Guinea, Fiji, Finland, France, Federal Republic of Germany, Greece, Grenada, Iceland, Ireland, Italy, Ivory Coast, Jamaica, Japan, Liberia, Luxembourg, Malawi, Nepal, Netherlands, New Zealand, Norway, Portugal, Saint Lucia, Saint Vincent, Samoa, Spain, Sweden, United Kingdom.
Absent: 14
Belize, Chile, Colombia, Comoros, Dominica, Gambia,* Haiti, Nigeria, Seychelles, Singapore, St. Christopher and Nevis, Thailand, Uruguay, Zaire.**

---

*Later advised the Secretariat it had intended to vote in favour.
**Later advised the Secretariat it had intended to abstain.

B

The General Assembly,
Recalling Security Council resolution 465 (1980) of 1 March 1980, in which, *inter alia*, the Council affirmed that the Geneva Convention relative to the Protection of Civilian Persons in Time of War, of 12 August 1949,[515] is applicable to the Arab territories occupied by Israel since 1967, including Jerusalem,
Recalling also its resolutions 3092 A (XXVIII) of 7 De-

cember 1973, 3240 B (XXIX) of 29 November 1974, 3525 B (XXX) of 15 December 1975, 31/106 B of 16 December 1976, 32/91 A of 13 December 1977, 33/133 A of 18 December 1978, 34/90 B of 12 December 1979, 35/122 A of 11 December 1980, 36/147 A of 16 December 1981, 37/88 A of 10 December 1982, 38/79 B of 15 December 1983, 39/95 B of 14 December 1984 and 40/161 B of 16 December 1985,[516]
Taking note of the report of the Secretary-General of 7 October 1986,[517]
Considering that the promotion of respect for the obligations arising from the Charter of the United Nations and other instruments and rules of international law is among the basic purposes and principles of the United Nations,
Bearing in mind the provisions of the Geneva Convention,
Noting that Israel and the Arab States whose territories have been occupied by Israel since June 1967 are parties to that Convention,
Taking into account that States parties to the Convention undertake, in accordance with article 1 thereof, not only to respect but also to ensure respect for the Convention in all circumstances,
1. *Reaffirms* that the Geneva Convention relative to the Protection of Civilian Persons in Time of War, of 12 August 1949,[518] is applicable to the Palestinian and other Arab territories occupied by Israel since 1967, including Jerusalem;
2. *Condemns once again* the failure of Israel, the occupying Power, to acknowledge the applicability of that Convention to the territories it has occupied since 1967, including Jerusalem;
3. *Strongly demands* that Israel acknowledge and comply with the provisions of that Convention in the Palestinian and other Arab territories it has occupied since 1967, including Jerusalem;
4. *Urgently calls upon* all States parties to that Convention to exert all efforts in order to ensure respect for and compliance with its provisions in the Palestinian and other Arab territories occupied by Israel since 1967, including Jerusalem;
5. *Requests* the Secretary-General to report to the General Assembly at its forty-second session on the implementation of the present resolution.

Adopted at the 95th plenary meeting:
In favour: 145
Afghanistan, Albania, Algeria, Angola, Antigua and Barbuda, Argentina, Australia, Austria, Bahamas, Bahrain, Bangladesh, Barbados, Belgium, Benin, Bhutan, Bolivia, Botswana, Brazil, Brunei Darussalam, Bulgaria, Burkina Faso, Burma, Burundi, Byelorussia, Cameroon, Canada, Cape Verde, Central African Republic, Chad, Chile, China, Colombia, Congo, Cuba, Cyprus, Czechoslovakia, Democratic Kampuchea, Democratic Yemen, Denmark, Djibouti,

---

[515]United Nations, *Treaty Series*, vol. 75, no. 973, p. 287.

[516]The resolutions cited are previous resolutions on Israeli practices in the occupied territories. [ed. note]
[517]A/41/681.
[518]United Nations, *Treaty Series*, vol. 75, no. 973, p. 287.

Dominican Republic, Ecuador, Egypt, Ethiopia, Fiji, Finland, France, Gabon, German Democratic Republic, Federal Republic of Germany, Ghana, Greece, Grenada, Guatemala, Guinea, Guinea-Bissau, Guyana, Haiti, Honduras, Hungary, Iceland, India, Indonesia, Iran, Iraq, Ireland, Italy, Jamaica, Japan, Jordan, Kenya, Kuwait, Lao People's Democratic Republic, Lebanon, Lesotho, Libya, Luxembourg, Madagascar, Malawi, Malaysia, Maldives, Mali, Malta, Mauritania, Mauritius, Mexico, Mongolia, Morocco, Mozambique, Nepal, Netherlands, New Zealand, Nicaragua, Niger, Norway, Oman, Pakistan, Panama, Papua New Guinea, Paraguay, Peru, Philippines, Poland, Portugal, Qatar, Romania, Rwanda, Saint Lucia, Saint Vincent, Samoa, Sao Tome and Principe, Saudi Arabia, Senegal, Sierra Leone, Singapore, Solomon Islands, Somalia, Spain, Sri Lanka, St. Christopher and Nevis, Sudan, Suriname, Swaziland, Sweden, Syria, Thailand, Togo, Trinidad and Tobago, Tunisia, Turkey, Uganda, Ukraine, USSR, United Arab Emirates, United Kingdom, United Republic of Tanzania, Uruguay, Vanuatu, Venezuela, Viet Nam, Yemen, Yugoslavia, Zaire,** Zambia, Zimbabwe.

Against: 1

Israel.

Abstentions: 6

Costa Rica, El Salvador, Equatorial Guinea, Ivory Coast, Liberia, United States.

Absent: 6

Belize, Comoros, Dominica, Gambia,* Nigeria, Seychelles.

---

*Later advised the Secretariat it had intended to vote in favour.
**Later advised the Secretariat it had intended to abstain.

C

The General Assembly,

Recalling Security Council resolution 465 (1980) of 1 March 1980,

Recalling also its resolutions 32/5 of 28 October 1977, 33/113 B of 18 December 1978, 34/90 C of 12 December 1979, 35/122 B of 11 December 1980, 36/147 B of 16 December 1981, 37/88 B of 10 December 1982, 38/79 C of 15 December 1983, 39/95 C of 14 December 1984 and 40/161 C of 16 December 1985,

Expressing grave anxiety and concern at the present serious situation in the occupied Palestinian and other Arab territories, including Jerusalem, as a result of the continued Israeli occupation and the measures and actions taken by Israel, the occupying Power, designed to change the legal status, geographical nature and demographic composition of those territories,

Taking note of the report of the Secretary-General of 7 October 1986,[519]

Confirming that the Geneva Convention relative to the Protection of Civilian Persons in Time of War, of 12 August 1949,[520] is applicable to all Arab territories occupied since June 1967, including Jerusalem,

1. *Determines* that all such measures and actions taken by Israel in the Palestinian and other Arab territories occupied since 1967, including Jerusalem, are in violation of the relevant provisions of the Geneva Convention relative to the Protection of Civilian Persons in Time of War, of 12 August 1949,[521] and constitute a serious obstacle to the efforts to achieve a comprehensive, just and lasting peace in the Middle East and therefore have no legal validity;

2. *Strongly deplores* the persistence of Israel in carrying out such measures, in particular the establishment of settlements in the Palestinian and other occupied Arab territories, including Jerusalem;

3. *Demands* that Israel comply strictly with its international obligations in accordance with the principles of international law and the provisions of the Geneva Convention;

4. *Demands once more* that Israel, the occupying Power, desist forthwith from taking any action which would result in changing the legal status, geographical nature or demographic composition of the Palestinian and other Arab territories occupied since 1967, including Jerusalem;

5. *Urgently calls upon* all States parties to the Geneva Convention to respect and to exert all efforts in order to ensure respect for and compliance with its provisions in all Arab territories occupied by Israel since 1967, including Jerusalem;

6. *Requests* the Secretary-General to report to the General Assembly at its forty-second session on the implementation of the present resolution.

Adopted at the 95th plenary meeting:

In favour: 145

Afghanistan, Albania, Algeria, Angola, Antigua and Barbuda, Argentina, Australia, Austria, Bahamas, Bahrain, Bangladesh, Barbados, Belgium, Benin, Bhutan, Bolivia, Botswana, Brazil, Brunei Darussalam, Bulgaria, Burkina Faso, Burma, Burundi, Byelorussia, Cameroon, Canada, Cape Verde, Central African Republic, Chad, Chile, China, Colombia, Congo, Cuba, Cyprus, Czechoslovakia, Democratic Kampuchea, Democratic Yemen, Denmark Djibouti, Dominican Republic, Ecuador, Egypt, El Salvador, Ethiopia, Fiji, Finland, France, Gabon, German Democratic Republic, Federal Republic of Germany, Ghana, Greece, Grenada, Guatemala, Guinea, Guinea-Bissau, Guyana, Haiti, Honduras, Hungary, Iceland, India, Indonesia, Iran, Iraq, Ireland, Italy, Jamaica, Japan, Jordan, Kenya, Kuwait, Lao People's Democratic Republic, Lebanon, Lesotho, Liberia, Libya, Luxembourg, Madagascar, Malawi, Malaysia, Maldives, Mali, Malta, Mauritania, Mauritius, Mexico, Mongolia, Morocco, Mozambique, Nepal, Netherlands, New Zealand, Nicaragua, Niger, Norway, Oman, Pakistan, Panama, Papua New Guinea, Paraguay, Peru, Philippines, Poland, Portugal, Qatar, Romania, Rwanda, Saint Vincent, Samoa, Sao Tome and Principe, Saudi Arabia, Senegal, Sierra Leone, Singapore, Solomon Islands, Somalia, Spain, Sri Lanka, Sudan, Suriname, Swaziland, Sweden,

---

[519]A/41/682.
[520]United Nations, *Treaty Series,* vol. 75, no. 973, p. 287.
[521]*Ibid.*

Syria, Thailand, Togo, Trinidad and Tobago, Tunisia, Turkey, Uganda, Ukraine, USSR, United Arab Emirates, United Kingdom, United Republic of Tanzania, Uruguay, Vanuatu, Venezuela, Viet Nam, Yemen, Yugoslavia, Zaire, Zambia, Zimbabwe.

Against: 1

Israel.

Abstentions: 5

Costa Rica, Equatorial Guinea, Ivory Coast, Saint Lucia, United States.

Absent: 7

Belize, Comoros, Dominica, Gambia,* Nigeria, Seychelles, St. Christopher and Nevis.

---

* Later advised the Secretariat that it had intended to vote in favour.

D

The General Assembly,

Guided by the purposes and principles of the Charter of the United Nations and by the principles and provisions of the Universal Declaration of Human Rights,[522]

Bearing in mind the provisions of the Geneva Convention relative to the Protection of Civilian Persons in Time of War, of 12 August 1949,[523] as well as of other relevant conventions and regulations,

Recalling all its resolutions on the subject, in particular resolutions 32/91 B and C of 13 December 1977, 33/113 C of 18 December 1978, 34/90 A of 12 December 1979, 35/122 C of 11 December 1980, 36/147 C of 16 December 1981, 37/88 C of 10 December 1982, 38/79 D of 15 December 1983, 39/95 D of 14 December 1984 and 40/161 D of 16 December 1985,

Recalling also the relevant resolutions adopted by the Security Council, by the Commission on Human Rights, in particular its resolutions 1983/1 of 15 February 1983,[524] 1984/1 of 20 February 1984,[525] 1985/1 A and B and 1985/2 of 19 February 1985,[526] 1986/1 A and B and 1986/2 of 20 February 1986,[527] and by other United Nations organs concerned and by the specialized agencies,

Having considered the report of the Special Committee to Investigate Israeli Practices Affecting the Human Rights of the Population of the Occupied Territories, dated 20 October 1986,[528] which contains, *inter alia,* self-incriminating public statements made by officials of Israel, the occupying Power,

1. *Commends* the Special Committee to Investigate Israeli Practices Affecting the Human Rights of the Population of the Occupied Territories for its efforts in perform-

ing the tasks assigned to it by the General Assembly and for its thoroughness and impartiality;

2. *Deplores* the continued refusal by Israel to allow the Special Committee access to the occupied territories;

3. *Demands* that Israel allow the Special Committee access to the occupied territories;

4. *Reaffirms* the fact that occupation itself constitutes a grave violation of the human rights of the civilian population of the occupied Arab territories;

5. *Condemns* the continued and persistent violation by Israel of the Geneva Convention relative to the Protection of Civilian Persons in Time of War, of 12 August 1949,[529] and other applicable international instruments, and condemns, in particular, those violations which the Convention designates as "grave breaches" thereof;

6. *Declares once more* that Israel's grave breaches of that Convention are war crimes and an affront to humanity;

7. *Reaffirms,* in accordance with the Convention, that the Israeli military occupation of the Palestinian and other Arab territories is of a temporary nature, thus giving no right whatsoever to the occupying Power over the territorial integrity of the occupied territories;

8. *Strongly condemns* the following Israeli policies and practices:

(*a*) Annexation of parts of the occupied territories, including Jerusalem;

(*b*) Imposition of Israeli laws, jurisdiction and administration on the Syrian Golan Heights, which has resulted in the effective annexation of the Syrian Golan Heights;

(*c*) Illegal imposition and levy of heavy and disproportionate taxes and dues;

(*d*) Establishment of new Israeli settlements and expansion of the existing settlements on private and public Arab lands, and transfer of an alien population thereto;

(*e*) Eviction, deportation, expulsion, displacement and transfer of Arab inhabitants of the occupied territories and denial of their right to return;

(*f*) Confiscation and expropriation of private and public Arab property in the occupied territories and all other transactions for the acquisition of land involving the Israeli authorities, institutions or nations on the one hand and the inhabitants or institutions of the occupied territories on the other;

(*g*) Excavation and transformation of the landscape and the historical, cultural and religious sites, especially at Jerusalem;

(*h*) Pillaging of archaeological and cultural property;

(*i*) Destruction and demolition of Arab houses;

(*j*) Collective punishment, mass arrests, administrative detention and ill-treatment of the Arab population;

(*k*) Ill-treatment and torture of persons under detention;

(*l*) Interference with religious freedoms and practices as well as family rights and customs;

(*m*) Interference with the system of education and with the social and economic and health development of the

---

[522]General Assembly resolution 217 A (III).

[523]United Nations, *Treaty Series,* vol. 75, no. 973, p. 287.

[524]See *Official Records of the Economic and Social Council, 1983, Supplement No. 3* (E/1983/13 and Corr. 1), chap. XXVII, sect. A.

[525]*Ibid., 1984, Supplement No. 4* (E/1984/14 and Corr.1), chap. II, sect. A.

[526]*Ibid., 1985, Supplement No. 2* (E/1985/22), chap. II, sect. A.

[527]*Ibid., 1986, Supplement No. 2* (E/1986/22), chap. II, sect. A.

[528]A/41/680.

[529]United Nations, *Treaty Series,* vol. 75, no. 973, p. 287.

population in the occupied Palestinian and other Arab territories;

(*n*) Interference with the freedom of movement of individuals within the occupied Palestinian and other Arab territories;

(*o*) Illegal exploitation of the natural wealth, resources and population of the occupied territories;

9. *Strongly condemns also* the following particular Israeli policies and practices:

(*a*) Implementation of an "iron-fist policy" against the inhabitants of the occupied territories since 4 August 1985;

(*b*) Ill-treatment and torture of children and minors under detention and/or imprisonment;

(*c*) Closure of headquarters and/or offices of trade unions and harassment of trade union leaders;

(*d*) Interference with the freedom of the press including censorship, closure and suspension of newspapers and magazines;

10. *Condemns also* the Israeli repression against and closing of the educational institutions in the occupied Syrian Golan Heights, particularly the prohibition of Syrian textbooks, Syrian educational system, the deprivation of Syrian students from pursuing their higher education in Syrian universities, the denial of the right to return to Syrian students receiving their higher education in the Syrian Arab Republic, the forcing of Hebrew on Syrian students, the imposition of courses that promote hatred, prejudice and religious intolerance and the dismissal of teachers, all in clear violation of the Geneva Convention;

11. *Strongly condemns* the arming of Israeli settlers in the occupied territories to commit acts of violence against Arab civilians and the perpetration of acts of violence by these armed settlers against individuals, causing injury and death and wide-scale damage to Arab property;

12. *Reaffirms* that all measures taken by Israel to change the physical character, demographic composition, institutional structure or legal status of the occupied territories, or any part thereof, including Jerusalem, are null and void, and that Israel's policy of settling parts of its population and new immigrants in the occupied territories constitutes a flagrant violation of the Geneva Convention and of the relevant resolutions of the United Nations;

13. *Demands* that Israel desist forthwith from the policies and practices referred to in paragraphs 8, 9, 10 and 11 above;

14. *Calls upon* Israel, the occupying Power, to take immediate steps for the return of all displaced Arab and Palestinian inhabitants to their homes or former places of residence in the territories occupied by Israel since 1967, in implementation of Security Council resolution 237 (1967) of 14 June 1967;

15. *Urges* international organizations, including the specialized agencies, in particular the International Labour Organisation, to continue to examine the conditions of Arab workers in the occupied Palestinian and other Arab territories, including Jerusalem;

16. *Reiterates its call* upon all States, in particular those States parties to the Geneva Convention, in accordance with article 1 of that Convention, and upon international organizations, including the specialized agencies, not to recognize any changes carried out by Israel in the occupied territories and to avoid actions, including those in the field of aid, which might be used by Israel in its pursuit of the policies of annexation and colonization or any of the other policies and practices referred to in the present resolution;

17. *Requests* the Special Committee, pending early termination of Israeli occupation, to continue to investigate Israeli policies and practices in the Arab territories occupied by Israel since 1967, to consult, as appropriate, with the International Committee of the Red Cross in order to ensure the safeguarding of the welfare and human rights of the population of the occupied territories and to report to the Secretary-General as soon as possible and whenever the need arises thereafter;

18. *Requests* the Special Committee to continue to investigate the treatment of civilians in detention in the Arab territories occupied by Israel since 1967;

19. *Condemns* Israel's refusal to permit persons from the occupied territories to appear as witnesses before the Special Committee and to participate in conferences and meetings held outside the occupied territories;

20. *Requests* the Secretary-General:

(*a*) To provide all necessary facilities to the Special Committee, including those required for its visits to the occupied territories, with a view to investigating the Israeli policies and practices referred to in the present resolution;

(*b*) To continue to make available additional staff as may be necessary to assist the Special Committee in the performance of its tasks;

(*c*) To ensure the widest circulation of the reports of the Special Committee and of information regarding its activities and findings by all means available through the Department of Public Information of the Secretariat and, where necessary, to reprint those reports of the Special Committee that are no longer available;

(*d*) To report to the General Assembly at its forty-second session on the tasks entrusted to him in the present paragraph;

21. *Requests* the Security Council to ensure Israel's respect for and compliance with all the provisions of the Geneva Convention relative to the Protection of Civilian Persons in Time of War, of 12 August 1949, in the Palestinian and other Arab territories occupied since 1967, including Jerusalem, and to initiate measures to halt Israeli policies and practices in those territories;

22. *Calls upon* Israel, the occupying Power, to allow the reopening of the Roman Catholic Medical Facility Hospice at Jerusalem in order to continue to provide needed health and medical services to the Arab population in the city;

23. *Decides* to include in the provisional agenda of its forty-second session the item entitled "Report of the Special Committee to Investigate Israeli Practices Affecting the Human Rights of the Population of the Occupied Territories".

Adopted at the 95th plenary meeting:

In favour: 114

Afghanistan, Albania, Algeria, Angola, Argentina, Bahamas, Bahrain, Bangladesh, Benin, Bhutan, Bolivia, Botswana, Brazil, Brunei Darussalam, Bulgaria, Burkina Faso, Burma, Burundi, Byelorussia, Cape Verde, Central African Republic, Chad, China, Colombia, Congo, Cuba, Cyprus, Czechoslovakia, Democratic Kampuchea, Democratic Yemen, Djibouti, Ecuador, Egypt, Ethiopia, Gabon, German Democratic Republic, Ghana, Greece, Guatemala, Guinea, Guinea-Bissau, Guyana, Haiti, Honduras, Hungary, India, Indonesia, Iran, Iraq, Jamaica, Jordan, Kenya, Kuwait, Lao People's Democratic Republic, Lebanon, Lesotho, Libya, Madagascar, Malaysia, Maldives, Mali, Malta, Mauritania, Mauritius, Mexico, Mongolia, Morocco, Mozambique, Nepal, Nicaragua, Niger, Nigeria, Oman, Pakistan, Panama, Papua New Guinea, Paraguay, Peru, Philippines, Poland, Qatar, Romania, Rwanda, Samoa, Sao Tome and Principe, Saudi Arabia, Senegal, Sierra Leone, Singapore, Solomon Islands, Somalia, Spain, Sri Lanka, Sudan, Suriname, Syria, Thailand, Togo, Trinidad and Tobago, Tunisia, Turkey, Uganda, Ukraine, USSR, United Arab Emirates, United Republic of Tanzania, Uruguay, Vanuatu, Venezuela, Viet Nam, Yemen, Yugoslavia, Zambia, Zimbabwe.

Against: 2

Israel, United States.

Abstentions: 36

Antigua and Barbuda, Australia, Austria, Barbados, Belgium, Cameroon, Canada, Costa Rica, Denmark, Dominican Republic, El Salvador, Equatorial Guinea, Fiji, Finland, France, Federal Republic of Germany, Grenada, Iceland, Ireland, Italy, Ivory Coast, Japan, Liberia, Luxembourg, Malawi, Netherlands, New Zealand, Norway, Portugal, Saint Lucia, Saint Vincent, St. Christopher and Nevis, Swaziland, Sweden, United Kingdom, Zaire.

Absent: 6

Belize, Chile, Comoros, Dominica, Gambia,* Seychelles.

----

*Later advised the Secretariat it had intended to vote in favour.

E

The General Assembly,

Recalling Security Council resolutions 468 (1980) of 8 May 1980, 469 (1980) of 20 May 1980 and 484 (1980) of 19 December 1980,

Recalling also its resolutions 36/147 D of 16 December 1981, 37/88 D of 10 December 1982, 38/79 E of 15 December 1983, 39/95 E of 14 December 1984 and 40/161 E of 16 December 1985,

Taking note of the report of the Secretary-General of 16 July 1986,[530]

Deeply concerned at the expulsion by the Israeli military occupation authorities of the Mayor of Halhul, the Mayor of Hebron who has since died, the Sharia Judge of Hebron and, in 1985 and 1986, other Palestinians,

Alarmed by the expulsion of many Palestinian leaders

from the occupied Palestinian territories by the Israeli military occupation authorities in 1985 and 1986,

Recalling the Geneva Convention relative to the Protection of Civilian Persons in Time of War, of 12 August 1949,[531] in particular article 1 and the first paragraph of article 49, which read as follows:

"Article 1

"The High Contracting Parties undertake to respect and to ensure respect for the present Convention in all circumstances."

"Article 49

"Individual or mass forcible transfers, as well as deportations of protected persons from occupied territory to the territory of the occupying Power or to that of any other country, occupied or not, are prohibited, regardless of their motive ... ",

Reaffirming the applicability of the Geneva Convention to the Palestinian and other Arab territories occupied by Israel since 1967, including Jerusalem,

1. *Strongly condemns* Israel, the occupying Power, for its persistent refusal to comply with the relevant resolutions of the Security Council and the General Assembly;

2. *Demands* that the Government of Israel, the occupying Power, rescind the illegal measures taken by the Israeli military occupation authorities in expelling the Mayor of Halhul, the Sharia Judge of Hebron and, in 1985 and 1986, other Palestinian leaders and that it facilitate the immediate return of the expelled Palestinians so that they can, *inter alia*, resume the functions for which they were elected and appointed;

3. *Calls upon* Israel, the occupying Power, to cease forthwith the expulsion of Palestinians and to abide scrupulously by the provisions of the Geneva Convention relative to the Protection of Civilian Persons in Time of War, of 12 August 1949;[532]

4. *Requests* the Secretary-General to report to the General Assembly as soon as possible and not later than the beginning of its forty-second session on the implementation of the present resolution.

Adopted at the 95th plenary meeting:

In favour: 131

Afghanistan, Albania, Algeria, Angola, Argentina, Australia, Austria, Bahamas, Bahrain, Bangladesh, Benin, Bhutan, Bolivia, Botswana, Brazil, Brunei Darussalam, Bulgaria, Burkina Faso, Burma, Burundi, Byelorussia, Cape Verde, Central African Republic, Chad, Chile, China, Colombia, Comoros, Congo, Cuba, Cyprus, Czechoslovakia, Democratic Kampuchea, Democratic Yemen, Djibouti, Dominican Republic, Ecuador, Egypt, El Salvador, Equatorial Guinea, Ethiopia, Fiji, Finland, France, Gabon, German Democratic Republic, Ghana, Greece, Guatemala, Guinea, Guinea-Bissau, Guyana, Honduras, Hungary, In-

----

[530]A/41/454.

[531]United Nations, *Treaty Series*, vol. 75, no. 973, p. 287.

[532]*Ibid.*

dia, Indonesia, Iran, Iraq, Ireland, Italy, Jamaica, Japan, Jordan, Kenya, Kuwait, Lao People's Democratic Republic, Lebanon, Lesotho, Libya, Madagascar, Malaysia, Maldives, Mali, Malta, Mauritania, Mauritius, Mexico, Mongolia, Morocco, Mozambique, Nepal, New Zealand, Nicaragua, Niger, Nigeria, Norway, Oman, Pakistan, Panama, Papua New Guinea, Paraguay, Peru, Philippines, Poland, Portugal, Qatar, Romania, Rwanda, Samoa, Sao Tome and Principe, Saudi Arabia, Senegal, Sierra Leone, Singapore, Solomon Islands, Somalia, Spain, Sri Lanka, Sudan, Suriname, Sweden, Syria, Thailand, Togo, Trinidad and Tobago, Tunisia, Turkey, Uganda, Ukraine, USSR, United Arab Emirates, United Republic of Tanzania, Uruguay, Vanuatu, Venezuela, Viet Nam, Yemen, Yugoslavia, Zaire,* Zambia, Zimbabwe.

Against: 1

Israel.

Abstentions: 21

Antigua and Barbuda, Barbados, Belgium, Cameroon, Canada, Costa Rica, Denmark, Federal Republic of Germany, Grenada, Iceland, Ivory Coast, Liberia, Luxembourg, Malawi, Netherlands, Saint Lucia, Saint Vincent, St. Christopher and Nevis, Swaziland, United Kingdom, United States.

Absent: 5

Belize, Dominica, Gambia,** Haiti, Seychelles.

---

*Later advised the Secretariat it had intended to abstain.
**Later advised the Secretariat it had intended to vote in favour.

F

The General Assembly,

Deeply concerned that the Arab territories occupied since 1967 have been under continued Israeli military occupation,

Recalling Security Council resolution 497 (1981) of 17 December 1981,

Recalling also its resolutions 36/226 B of 17 December 1981, ES-9/1 of 5 February 1982, 37/88 E of 10 December 1982, 38/79 F of 15 December 1983, 39/95 F of 14 December 1984 and 40/161 F of 16 December 1985,

Having considered the report of the Secretary-General of 16 July and 19 September 1986,[533]

Recalling its previous resolutions, in particular resolutions 3414 (XXX) of 5 December 1975, 31/61 of 9 December 1976, 32/20 of 25 November 1977, 33/28 and 33/29 of 7 December 1978, 34/70 of 6 December 1979 and 35/122 E of 11 December 1980, in which it, *inter alia,* called upon Israel to put an end to its occupation of the Arab territories and to withdraw from all those territories,

Reaffirming once more the illegality of Israel's decision of 14 December 1981 to impose its laws, jurisdiction and administration on the Syrian Golan Heights, which has resulted in the effective annexation of that territory,

Reaffirming that the acquisition of territory by force is inadmissible under the Charter of the United Nations and that all territories thus occupied by Israel must be returned,

Recalling the Geneva Convention relative to the Protection of Civilian Persons in Time of War of 12 August 1949,[534]

1. *Strongly condemns* Israel, the occupying Power, for its refusal to comply with the relevant resolutions of the General Assembly and the Security Council, particularly Council resolution 497 (1981), in which the Council, *inter alia,* decided that the Israeli decision to impose its laws, jurisdiction and administration on the occupied Syrian Golan Heights was null and void and without international legal effect and demanded that Israel, the occupying Power, should rescind forthwith its decision;

2. *Condemns* the persistence of Israel in changing the physical character, demographic composition, institutional structure and legal status of the occupied Syrian Golan Heights;

3. *Determines* that all legislative and administrative measures and actions taken or to be taken by Israel, the occupying Power, that purport to alter the character and legal status of the Syrian Golan Heights are null and void and constitute a flagrant violation of international law and of the Geneva Convention relative to the Protection of Civilian Persons in Time of War, of 12 August 1949,[535] and have no legal effect;

4. *Strongly condemns* Israel for its attempts and measures to impose forcibly Israeli citizenship and Israeli identity cards on the Syrian citizens in the occupied Syrian Arab Golan Heights and calls upon it to desist from its repressive measures against the population of the Syrian Arab Golan Heights;

5. *Calls once again upon* Member States not to recognize any of the legislative or administrative measures and actions referred to above;

6. *Requests* the Secretary-General to submit to the General Assembly at its forty-second session a report on the implementation of the present resolution.

Adopted at the 95th plenary meeting:

In favour: 142

Afghanistan, Albania, Algeria, Angola, Antigua and Barbuda, Argentina, Australia, Austria, Bahamas, Bahrain, Bangladesh, Barbados, Belgium, Benin, Bhutan, Bolivia, Botswana, Brazil, Brunei Darussalam, Bulgaria, Burkina Faso, Burma, Burundi, Byelorussia, Canada, Cape Verde, Central African Republic, Chad, Chile, China, Colombia, Comoros, Congo, Cuba, Cyprus, Czechoslovakia, Democratic Kampuchea, Democratic Yemen, Denmark, Djibouti, Dominican Republic, Ecuador, Egypt, Equatorial Guinea, Ethiopia, Fiji, Finland, France, Gabon, German Democratic Republic, Federal Republic of Germany, Ghana, Greece, Guatemala, Guinea, Guinea-Bissau, Guyana, Haiti, Honduras, Hungary, Iceland, India, Indonesia, Iran, Iraq,

---

[533]A/41/455 and Add.1.

[534]United Nations, *Treaty Series,* vol. 75, no. 973, p. 287.
[535]*Ibid.*

Ireland, Italy, Jamaica, Japan, Jordan, Kenya, Kuwait, Lao People's Democratic Republic, Lebanon, Lesotho, Libya, Luxembourg, Madagascar, Malaysia, Maldives, Mali, Malta, Mauritania, Mauritius, Mexico, Mongolia, Morocco, Mozambique, Nepal, Netherlands, New Zealand, Nicaragua, Niger, Nigeria, Norway, Oman, Pakistan, Panama, Papua New Guinea, Paraguay, Peru, Philippines, Poland, Portugal, Qatar, Romania, Rwanda, Samoa, Sao Tome and Principe, Saudi Arabia, Senegal, Sierra Leone, Singapore, Solomon Islands, Somalia, Spain, Sri Lanka, Sudan, Suriname, Swaziland, Sweden, Syria, Thailand, Togo, Trinidad and Tobago, Tunisia, Turkey, Uganda, Ukraine, USSR, United Arab Emirates, United Kingdom, United Republic of Tanzania, Uruguay, Vanuatu, Venezuela, Viet Nam, Yemen, Yugoslavia, Zaire,* Zambia, Zimbabwe.

Against: 1

Israel.

Abstentions: 11

Cameroon, Costa Rica, El Salvador, Grenada, Ivory Coast, Liberia, Malawi, Saint Lucia, Saint Vincent, St. Christopher and Nevis, United States.

Absent: 4

Belize, Dominica, Gambia,** Seychelles.

---

*Later advised the Secretariat it had intended to abstain.
**Later advised the Secretariat it had intended to vote in favour.

G

The General Assembly,

Bearing in mind the Geneva Convention relative to the Protection of Civilian Persons in Time of War, of 12 August 1949,[536]

Deeply concerned at the continued harassment by Israel, the occupying Power, against educational institutions in the occupied Palestinian territories,

Recalling its resolutions 38/79 G of 15 December 1983, 39/95 G of 14 December 1984 and 40/161 G of 16 December 1985,

Taking note of the report of the Secretary-General of 18 July 1986,[537]

Taking note of the relevant decisions adopted by the Executive Board of the United Nations Educational, Scientific and Cultural Organization concerning the educational and cultural situation in the occupied territories,

1. *Reaffirms* the applicability of the Geneva Convention relative to the Protection of Civilian Persons in Time of War, of 12 August 1949,[538] to the Palestinian and other Arab territories occupied by Israel since 1967, including Jerusalem;

2. *Condemns* Israeli policies and practices against Palestinian students and faculties in schools, universities and other educational institutions in the occupied Palestinian territories, especially the policy of opening fire on defenceless students, causing many casualties;

3. *Condemns* the systematic Israeli campaign of repression against and closing of universities and other educational and vocational institutions in the occupied Palestinian territories, restricting and impeding the academic activities of Palestinian universities by subjecting the selection of courses, textbooks and educational programmes, the admission of students and the appointment of faculty members to the control and supervision of the military occupation authorities, in clear contravention of the Geneva Convention;

4. *Demands* that Israel, the occupying Power, comply with the provisions of that Convention, rescind all actions and measures against all educational institutions, ensure the freedom of those institutions and refrain forthwith from hindering the effective operation of the universities and other educational institutions;

5. *Requests* the Secretary-General to report to the General Assembly as soon as possible and not later than the beginning of its forty-second session on the implementation of the present resolution.

Adopted at the 95th plenary meeting:

In favour: 119

Afghanistan, Albania, Algeria, Angola, Argentina, Austria, Bahamas, Bahrain, Bangladesh, Barbados, Benin, Bhutan, Bolivia, Botswana, Brazil, Brunei Darussalam, Bulgaria, Burkina Faso, Burundi, Byelorussia, Cape Verde, Central African Republic, Chad, China, Colombia, Comoros, Congo, Cuba, Cyprus, Czechoslovakia, Democratic Kampuchea, Democratic Yemen, Djibouti, Ecuador, Egypt, Ethiopia, Fiji, France, Gabon, German Democratic Republic, Ghana, Greece, Guinea, Guinea-Bissau, Guyana, Haiti, Hungary, India, Indonesia, Iran, Iraq, Italy, Jamaica, Jordan, Kenya, Kuwait, Lao People's Democratic Republic, Lebanon, Lesotho, Libya, Madagascar, Malaysia, Maldives, Mali, Malta, Mauritania, Mauritius, Mexico, Mongolia, Morocco, Mozambique, Nepal, Nicaragua, Niger, Nigeria, Oman, Pakistan, Papua New Guinea, Paraguay, Peru, Philippines, Poland, Qatar, Romania, Rwanda, Samoa, Sao Tome and Principe, Saudi Arabia, Senegal, Sierra Leone, Singapore, Solomon Islands, Somalia, Spain, Sri Lanka, Sudan, Suriname, Swaziland, Sweden, Syria, Thailand, Togo, Trinidad and Tobago, Tunisia, Turkey, Uganda, Ukraine, USSR, United Arab Emirates, United Republic of Tanzania, Uruguay, Vanuatu, Venezuela, Viet Nam, Yemen, Yugoslavia, Zaire,* Zambia, Zimbabwe.

Against: 2

Israel, United States.

Abstentions: 32

Antigua and Barbuda, Australia, Belgium, Cameroon, Canada, Chile, Costa Rica, Denmark, Dominican Republic, El Salvador, Equatorial Guinea, Finland, Federal Republic of Germany, Grenada, Guatemala, Honduras, Iceland, Ireland, Ivory Coast, Japan, Liberia, Luxembourg, Malawi, Netherlands, New Zealand, Norway, Panama, Portugal, Saint Lucia, Saint Vincent, St. Christopher and Nevis, United Kingdom.

Absent: 5

---

[536]*Ibid.*
[537]A/41/456.
[538]United Nations, *Treaty Series,* vol. 75, no. 973, p. 287.

Belize, Buma, Dominica, Gambia,** Seychelles.

---

*Later advised the Secretariat it had intended to abstain.
**Later advised the Secretariat it had intended to vote in favour.

Resolution No. 41/69 A, B, C, D, E, F, G, H, I, J, K of 3 December 1986

ON THE UNITED NATIONS RELIEF AND WORKS AGENCY FOR PALESTINE REFUGEES IN THE NEAR EAST: CALLING FOR CONTRIBUTIONS BY GOVERNMENTS TO THE AGENCY AND ENDORSING ASSISTANCE TO PALESTINIAN REFUGEES, CALLING UPON ISRAEL TO PERMIT THE RETURN OF DISPLACED PALESTINIANS AND TO REMOVE OBSTACLES TO THE ESTABLISHMENT OF A UNIVERSITY OF JERUSALEM FOR PALESTINIAN REFUGEES, AND REQUESTING THE SECRETARY-GENERAL TO TAKE APPROPRIATE STEPS FOR THE PROTECTION AND ADMINISTRATION OF ARAB REFUGEE PROPERTY, ASSETS AND PROPERTY RIGHTS

A

ASSISTANCE TO PALESTINE REFUGEES

The General Assembly,

Recalling its resolution 40/165 A of 16 December 1985 and all its previous resolutions on the question, including resolution 194 (III) of 11 December 1948,

Taking note of the report of the Commissioner-General of the United Nations Relief and Works Agency for Palestine Refugees in the Near East, covering the period from 1 July 1985 to 30 June 1986,[539]

1. *Notes with deep regret* that repatriation or compensation of the refugees as provided for in paragraph 11 of General Assembly resolution 194 (III) has not been effected, that no substantial progress has been made in the programme endorsed by the Assembly in paragraph 2 of its resolution 513 (VI) of 26 January 1952 for the reintegration of refugees either by repatriation or resettlement and that, therefore, the situation of the refugees continues to be a matter of serious concern;

2. *Expresses its thanks* to the Commissioner-General and to all the staff of the United Nations Relief and Works Agency for Palestine Refugees in the Near East, recognizing that the Agency is doing all it can within the limits of available resources, and also expresses its thanks to the specialized agencies and private organizations for their valuable work in assisting the refugees;

3. *Reiterates its request* that the headquarters of the Agency should be relocated to its former site within its area of operations as soon as practicable;

4. *Notes with regret* that the United Nations Conciliation Commission for Palestine has been unable to find a means of achieving progress in the implementation of paragraph 11 of General Assembly resolution 194 (III),[540] and requests the Commission to exert continued efforts towards the implementation of that paragraph and to report to the Assembly as appropriate, but no later than 1 September ber 1987;

5. *Directs attention* to the continuing seriousness of the financial position of the Agency, as outlined in the report of the Commissioner-General;[541]

6. *Notes with profound concern* that, despite the commendable and successful efforts of the Commissioner-General to collect additional contributions, this increased level of income to the Agency is still insufficient to cover essential budget requirements in the present year and that, at currently foreseen levels of giving, deficits will recur each year;

7. *Calls upon* all Governments, as a matter of urgency, to make the most generous efforts possible to meet the anticipated needs of the Agency, particularly in the light of the budgetary deficit projected in the report of the Commissioner-General, and therefore urges non-contributing Governments to contribute regularly and contributing Governments to consider increasing their regular contributions;

8. *Decides* to extend until 30 June 1990, without prejudice to the provisions of paragraph 11 of General Assembly resolution 194 (III), the mandate of the United Nations Relief and Works Agency for Palestine Refugees in the Near East.

Adopted at the 95th plenary meeting:

In favour: 150

Afghanistan, Algeria, Angola, Antigua and Barbuda, Argentina, Australia, Austria, Bahamas, Bahrain, Bangladesh, Barbados, Belgium, Benin, Bhutan, Bolivia, Botswana, Brazil, Brunei Darussalam, Bulgaria, Burkina Faso, Burma, Burundi, Byelorussia, Cameroon, Canada, Cape Verde, Central African Republic, Chad, Chile, China, Colombia, Comoros, Congo, Costa Rica, Cuba, Cyprus, Czechoslovakia, Democratic Kampuchea, Democratic Yemen, Denmark, Djibouti, Dominican Republic, Ecuador, Egypt, El Salvador, Equatorial Guinea, Ethiopia, Fiji, Finland, France, Gabon, German Democratic Republic, Federal Republic of Germany, Ghana, Greece, Grenada, Guatemala, Guinea, Guyana, Haiti, Honduras, Hungary, Iceland, India, Indonesia, Iran, Iraq, Ireland, Italy, Ivory Coast, Jamaica, Japan, Jordan, Kenya, Kuwait, Lao People's Democratic Republic, Lebanon, Lesotho, Liberia, Libya, Luxembourg, Madagascar, Malawi, Malaysia, Maldives, Mali, Malta, Mauritania, Mauritius, Mexico, Mongolia, Morocco, Mozambique, Nepal, Netherlands, New Zealand, Nicaragua, Niger, Nigeria, Norway, Oman, Pakistan, Panama, Papua New Guinea, Paraguay, Peru, Philippines, Poland, Portugal, Qatar, Romania, Rwanda, Saint Lucia, Saint Vincent, Samoa, Sao Tome and Principe, Saudi Arabia, Senegal, Sierra Leone, Singapore, Solomon Islands, Somalia, Spain, Sri Lanka, St. Christopher and Nevis, Sudan, Suriname, Swaziland, Sweden, Syria, Thailand, Togo, Trinidad and Tobago, Tunisia, Turkey, Uganda, Ukraine, United Arab Emirates, United Kingdom, United

---

[539]*Official Records of the General Assembly, Forty-first Session, Supplement No. 13* (A/41/13 and Add.1).
[540]A/41/555, annex.

---

[541]*Official Records of the General Assembly, Forty-first Session, Supplement No. 13* (A/41/13 and Add.1).

Republic of Tanzania, United States, Uruguay, Vanuatu, Venezuela, Viet Nam, Yemen, Yugoslavia, Zaire, Zambia, Zimbabwe.
Against: 0
Abstention: 1
Israel.
Absent: 7
Albania, Belize, Dominica, Gambia, Guinea-Bissau,* Seychelles, USSR.*

---

* Later advised the Secretariat it had intended to vote in favour.

B

WORKING GROUP ON THE FINANCING OF THE UNITED NATIONS RELIEF AND WORKS AGENCY FOR PALESTINE REFUGEES IN THE NEAR EAST

The General Assembly,

Recalling its resolutions 2656 (XXV) of 7 December 1970, 2728 (XXV) of 15 December 1970, 2791 (XXVI) of 6 December 1971, 2964 (XXVII) of 13 December 1972, 3090 (XXVIII) of 7 December 1973, 3330 (XXIX) of 17 December 1974, 3419 D (XXX) of 8 December 1975, 31/15 C of 23 November 1976, 32/90 D of 13 December 1977, 33/112 D of 18 December 1978, 34/52 D of 23 November 1979, 35/13 D of 3 November 1980, 36/146 E of 16 December 1981, 37/120 A of 16 December 1982, 38/83 B of 15 December 1983, 39/99 B of 14 December 1984 and 40/165 B of 16 December 1985,[542]

Recalling also its decision 36/462 of 16 March 1982, whereby it took note of the special report of the Working Group on the Financing of the United Nations Relief and Works Agency for Palestine Refugees in the Near East[543] and adopted the recommendations contained therein,

Having considered the report of the Working Group on the Financing of the United Nations Relief and Works Agency for Palestine Refugees in the Near East,[544]

Taking into account the report of the Commissioner-General of the United Nations Relief and Works Agency for Palestine Refugees in the Near East, covering the period from 1 July 1985 to 30 June 1986,[545]

Gravely concerned at the critical financial situation of the Agency, which has already reduced the essential minimum services being provided to the Palestine refugees and which threatens even greater reductions in the future;

Emphasizing the urgent need for extraordinary efforts in order to maintain, at least at their present minimum level, the activities of the Agency,

1. *Commends* the Working Group on the Financing of the United Nations Relief and Works Agency for Palestine Refugees in the Near East for its efforts to assist in ensuring the Agency's financial security;

2. *Takes note with approval* of the report of the Working Group;[546]

3. *Requests* the Working Group to continue its efforts, in co-operation with the Secretary-General and the Commissioner-General, for the financing of the Agency for a further period of one year;

4. *Requests* the Secretary-General to provide the necessary services and assistance to the Working Group for the conduct of its work.

Adopted at the 95th plenary meeting without a vote.

C

ASSISTANCE TO PERSONS DISPLACED AS A RESULT OF THE JUNE 1967 AND SUBSEQUENT HOSTILITIES

The General Assembly,

Recalling its resolution 40/165 C of 16 December 1985 and all its previous resolutions on the question,

Taking note of the report of the Commissioner-General of the United Nations Relief and Works Agency for Palestine Refugees in the Near East, covering the period from 1 July 1985 to 30 June 1986,[547]

Concerned about the continued human suffering resulting from the hostilities in the Middle East,

1. *Reaffirms* its resolution 40/165 C and all its previous resolutions on the question;

2. *Endorses,* bearing in mind the objectives of those resolutions, the efforts of the Commissioner-General of the United Nations Relief and Works Agency for Palestine Refugees in the Near East to continue to provide humanitarian assistance as far as practicable, on an emergency basis and as a temporary measure, to other persons in the area who are at present displaced and in serious need of continued assistance as a result of the June 1967 and subsequent hostilities;

3. *Strongly appeals* to all Governments and to organizations and individuals to contribute generously for the above purposes to the United Nations Relief and Works Agency for Palestine Refugees in the Near East and to the other intergovernmental and non-governmental organizations concerned.

Adopted at the 95th plenary meeting without a vote.

D

OFFERS BY MEMBER STATES OF GRANTS AND SCHOLARSHIPS FOR HIGHER EDUCATION, INCLUDING VOCATIONAL TRAINING FOR PALESTINE REFUGEES

The General Assembly,

Recalling its resolution 212 (III) of 19 November 1948 on assistance to Palestine refugees,

Recalling also its resolutions 35/13 B of 3 November 1980, 36/146 H of 16 December 1981, 37/120 D of 16 December 1982, 38/83 D of 15 December 1983, 39/99 D of 14 December 1984 and 40/165 D of 16 December 1985,

---

[542]These resolutions focus on the financing of the United Nations Relief and Works Agency for Palestine Refugees in the Near East. [ed. note]
[543]A/36/866; see also A/37/591.
[544]A/41/702.
[545]*Official Records of the General Assembly, Forty-first Session, Supplement No. 13* (A/41/13 and Add.1).

[546]A/41/702.
[547]*Official Records of the General Assembly, Forty-first Session, Supplement No. 13* (A/41/13 and Add.1).

Cognizant of the fact that the Palestine refugees have, for the last three decades, lost their lands and means of livelihood,

Having examined the report of the Secretary-General,[548]

Having also examined the report of the Commissioner-General of the United Nations Relief and Works Agency for Palestine Refugees in the Near East, covering the period from 1 July 1985 to 30 June 1986,[549]

1. *Urges* all States to respond to the appeal contained in General Assembly resolution 32/90 F of 13 December 1977 in a manner commensurate with the needs of Palestine refugees for higher education, including vocational training;

2. *Strongly appeals* to all States, specialized agencies and non-governmental organizations to augment the special allocations for grants and scholarships to Palestine refugees in addition to their contributions to the regular budget of the United Nations Relief and Works Agency for Palestine Refugees in the Near East;

3. *Expresses its appreciation* to all Governments, specialized agencies and non-governmental organizations that responded favourably to General Assembly resolution 40/165 D;

4. *Invites* the relevant specialized agencies and other organizations of thé United Nations system to continue, within their respective spheres of competence, to extend assistance for higher education to Palestine refugee students;

5. *Appeals* to all States, specialized agencies and the United Nations University to contribute generously to the Palestinian universities in the territories occupied by Israel since 1967, including, in due course, the proposed University of Jerusalem "Al-Quds" for Palestine refugees;

6. *Also appeals* to all States, specialized agencies and other international bodies to contribute towards the establishment of vocational training centres for Palestine refugees;

7. *Requests* the United Nations Relief and Works Agency for Palestine Refugees in the Near East to act as the recipient and trustee of such special allocations and scholarships and to award them to qualified Palestine refugee candidates;

8. *Requests* the Secretary-General to report to the General Assembly at its forty-second session on the implementation of the present resolution.

Adopted at the 95th plenary meeting:

In favour: 153

Afghanistan, Albania, Algeria, Angola, Antigua and Barbuda, Argentina, Australia, Austria, Bahamas, Bahrain, Bangladesh, Barbados, Belgium, Benin, Bhutan, Bolivia, Botswana, Brazil, Brunei Darussalam, Bulgaria, Burkina Faso, Burma, Burundi, Byelorussia, Cameroon, Canada, Cape Verde, Central African Republic, Chad, Chile, China, Colombia, Comoros, Congo, Costa Rica, Cuba, Cyprus, Czechoslovakia, Democratic Kampuchea, Democratic Yemen, Denmark, Djibouti, Dominican Republic, Ecuador, Egypt, El Salvador, Equatorial Guinea, Ethiopia, Fiji, Finland, France, Gabon, German Democratic Republic, Federal Republic of Germany, Ghana, Greece, Grenada, Guatemala, Guinea, Guinea-Bissau, Guyana, Haiti, Honduras, Hungary, Iceland, India, Indonesia, Iran, Iraq, Ireland, Italy, Ivory Coast, Jamaica, Japan, Jordan, Kenya, Kuwait, Lao People's Democratic Republic, Lebanon, Lesotho, Liberia, Libya, Luxembourg, Madagascar, Malawi, Malaysia, Maldives, Mali, Malta, Mauritania, Mauritius, Mexico, Mongolia, Morocco, Mozambique, Nepal, Netherlands, New Zealand, Nicaragua, Niger, Nigeria, Norway, Oman, Pakistan, Panama, Papua New Guinea, Paraguay, Peru, Philippines, Poland, Portugal, Qatar, Romania, Rwanda, Saint Lucia, Saint Vincent, Samoa, Sao Tome and Principe, Saudi Arabia, Senegal, Sierra Leone, Singapore, Solomon Islands, Somalia, Spain, Sri Lanka, St. Christopher and Nevis, Sudan, Suriname, Swaziland, Sweden, Syria, Thailand, Togo, Trinidad and Tobago, Tunisia, Turkey, Uganda, Ukraine, USSR, United Arab Emirates, United Kingdom, United Republic of Tanzania, United States, Uruguay, Vanuatu, Venezuela, Viet Nam, Yemen, Yugoslavia, Zaire, Zambia, Zimbabwe.

Against: 0

Abstention: 1

Israel.

Absent: 4

Belize, Dominica, Gambia, Seychelles.

E

PALESTINE REFUGEES IN THE GAZA STRIP

The General Assembly,

Recalling Security Council resolution 237 (1967) of 14 June 1967,

Recalling also General Assembly resolutions 2792 C (XXVI) of 6 December 1971, 2963 C (XXVII) of 13 December 1972, 3089 C (XXVIII) of 7 December 1973, 3331 D (XXIX) of 17 December 1974, 3419 C (XXX) of 8 December 1975, 31/15 E of 23 November 1976, 32/90 C of 13 December 1977, 33/112 E of 18 December 1978, 34/52 F of 23 November 1979, 35/13 F of 3 November 1980, 36/146 A of 16 December 1981, 37/120 E of 16 December 1982, 38/83 E of 15 December 1983, 39/99 E of 14 December 1984 and 40/165 E of 16 December 1985,[550]

Having considered the report of the Commissioner-General of the United Nations Relief and Works Agency for Palestine Refugees in the Near East, covering the period from 1 July 1985 to 30 June 1986,[551] and the report of the Secretary-General,[552]

Recalling the provisions of paragraph 11 of its resolu-

---

[548]A/41/563.

[549]*Official Records of the General Assembly, Forty-first Session, Supplement No. 13* (A/41/13 and Add.1).

[550]On Israeli actions harmful to Palestinian refugees in the Gaza Strip. [ed. note]

[551]*Official Records of the General Assembly, Forty-first Session, Supplement No. 13* (A/41/13 and Add.1).

[552]A/41/564.

tion 194 (III) of 11 December 1948 and considering that measures to resettle Palestine refugees in the Gaza Strip away from the homes and property from which they were displaced constitute a violation of their inalienable right of return,

Alarmed by the reports received from the Commissioner-General that the Israeli occupying authorities, in contravention of Israel's obligation under international law, persist in their policy of demolishing shelters occupied by refugee families,

Emphasizing the statement contained in paragraph 16 of the report of the Commissioner-General of the United Nations Relief and Works Agency for Palestine Refugees in the Near East, which reads as follows:

"I believe I have a duty to draw the attention of Member States to the deteriorating conditions in the Gaza Strip and urge that the international community give serious consideration to what can be done to ease conditions there. This problem warrants immediate attention",

1. *Reiterates strongly its demand* that Israel desist from the removal and resettlement of Palestine refugees in the Gaza Strip and from the destruction of their shelters;

2. *Requests the Commissioner-General* to extend all services of the United Nations Relief and Works Agency for Palestine Refugees in the Near East to Palestine refugees in the Gaza Strip;

3. *Requests* the Secretary-General, after consulting with the Commissioner-General of the United Nations Relief and Works Agency for Palestine Refugees in the Near East, to report to the General Assembly, before the opening of its forty-second session, on Israel's compliance with paragraph 1 above.

Adopted at the 95th plenary meeting:

In favour: 146

Afghanistan, Albania, Algeria, Angola, Antigua and Barbuda, Argentina, Australia, Austria, Bahamas, Bahrain, Bangladesh, Barbados, Belgium, Benin, Bhutan, Bolivia, Botswana, Brazil, Brunei Darussalam, Bulgaria, Burkina Faso, Burma, Burundi, Byelorussia, Canada, Cape Verde, Central African Republic, Chad, Chile, China, Colombia, Comoros, Congo, Cuba, Cyprus, Czechoslovakia, Democratic Kampuchea, Democratic Yemen, Denmark, Djibouti, Dominican Republic, Ecuador, Egypt, El Salvador, Equatorial Guinea, Ethiopia, Fiji, Finland, France, Gabon, German Democratic Republic, Federal Republic of Germany, Ghana, Greece, Grenada, Guatemala, Guinea, Guinea-Bissau, Guyana, Haiti, Honduras, Hungary, Iceland, India, Indonesia, Iran, Iraq, Ireland, Italy, Ivory Coast, Jamaica, Japan, Jordan, Kenya, Kuwait, Lao People's Democratic Republic, Lebanon, Lesotho, Libya, Luxembourg, Madagascar, Malaysia, Maldives, Mali, Malta, Mauritania, Mauritius, Mexico, Mongolia, Morocco, Mozambique, Nepal, Netherlands, New Zealand, Nicaragua, Niger, Nigeria, Norway, Oman, Pakistan, Panama, Papua New Guinea, Paraguay, Peru, Philippines, Poland, Portugal, Qatar, Romania, Rwanda, Saint Lucia, Saint Vincent, Samoa, Sao Tome and Principe, Saudi Arabia, Senegal, Sierra Leone, Singapore, Solomon Islands, Somalia, Spain, Sri Lanka, Sudan, Suriname, Swaziland, Sweden, Syria, Thailand, Togo, Trinidad and Tobago, Tunisia, Turkey, Uganda, Ukraine, USSR, United Arab Emirates, United Kingdom, United Republic of Tanzania, Uruguay, Vanuatu, Venezuela, Viet Nam, Yemen, Yugoslavia, Zambia, Zimbabwe.

Against: 2

Israel, United States.

Abstentions: 5

Cameroon, Costa Rica, Liberia, Malawi, Zaire.

Absent: 5

Belize, Dominica, Gambia, Seychelles, St. Christopher and Nevis.

F

RESUMPTION OF THE RATION DISTRIBUTION TO PALESTINE REFUGEES

The General Assembly,

Recalling its resolutions 36/146 F of 16 December 1981, 37/120 F of 16 December 1982, 38/83 F of 15 December 1983, 39/99 F of 14 December 1984 and 40/165 F of 16 December 1985 and all its previous resolutions on the question, including resolution 302 (IV) of 8 December 1949,

Having considered the report of the Commissioner-General of the United Nations Relief and Works Agency for Palestine Refugees in the Near East, covering the period from 1 July 1985 to 30 June 1986,[553] and the report of the Secretary-General,[554]

Deeply concerned at the interruption by the Agency, owing to financial difficulties, of the general ration distribution to Palestine refugees in all fields,

1. *Regrets* that its resolutions 37/120 F, 38/83 F, 39/99 F and 40/165 F have not been implemented;

2. *Calls once again upon* all Governments, as a matter of urgency, to make the most generous efforts possible and to offer the necessary resources to meet the needs of the United Nations Relief and Works Agency for Palestine Refugees in the Near East, particularly in the light of the interruption by the Agency of the general ration distribution to Palestine refugees in all fields, and therefore urges non-contributing Governments to contribute regularly and contributing Governments to consider increasing their regular contributions;

3. *Requests* the Comissioner-General to resume on a continuing basis the interrupted general ration distribution to Palestine refugees in all fields;

4. *Requests* the Secretary-General, in consultation with the Commissioner-General, to report to the General Assembly at its forty-second session on the implementation of the present resolution.

Adopted at the 95th plenary meeting:

In favour: 130

Afghanistan, Albania, Algeria, Angola, Antigua and Bar-

---

[553] *Official Records of the General Assembly, Forty-first Session, Supplement No. 13* (A/41/13 and Add.1).
[554] A/41/565.

buda, Argentina, Bahamas, Bahrain, Bangladesh, Barba-
dos, Benin, Bhutan, Bolivia, Botswana, Brazil, Brunei
Darussalam, Bulgaria, Burkina Faso, Burma, Burundi,
Byelorussia, Cape Verde, Central African Republic, Chad,
Chile, China, Colombia, Comoros, Congo, Cuba, Cyprus,
Czechoslovakia, Democratic Kampuchea, Democratic Ye-
men, Djibouti, Dominican Republic, Ecuador, Egypt, El
Salvador, Equatorial Guinea, Ethiopia, Fiji, Gabon, Ger-
man Democratic Republic, Ghana, Greece, Grenada, Guate-
mala, Guinea, Guinea-Bissau, Guyana, Haiti, Honduras,
Hungary, India, Indonesia, Iran, Iraq, Ivory Coast, Ja-
maica, Jordan, Kenya, Kuwait, Lao People's Democratic
Republic, Lebanon, Lesotho, Liberia, Libya, Madagascar,
Malawi, Malaysia, Maldives, Mali, Malta, Mauritania,
Mauritius, Mexico, Mongolia, Morocco, Mozambique,
Nepal, Nicaragua, Niger, Nigeria, Oman, Pakistan, Pan-
ama, Papua New Guinea, Paraguay, Peru, Philippines,
Poland, Qatar, Romania, Rwanda, Saint Lucia, Saint Vin-
cent, Samoa, Sao Tome and Principe, Saudi Arabia, Sene-
gal, Sierra Leone, Singapore, Solomon Islands, Somalia,
Sri Lanka, St. Christopher and Nevis, Sudan, Suriname,
Swaziland, Syria, Thailand, Togo, Trinidad and Tobago,
Tunisia, Turkey, Uganda, Ukraine, USSR, United Arab
Emirates, United Republic of Tanzania, Uruguay, Vanuatu,
Venezuela, Viet Nam, Yemen, Yugoslavia, Zaire, Zambia,
Zimbabwe.

Against: 20

Australia, Belgium, Canada, Denmark, Finland, France,
Federal Republic of Germany, Iceland, Ireland, Israel,
Italy, Japan, Luxembourg, Netherlands, New Zealand,
Norway, Portugal, Sweden, United Kingdom, United States.

Abstentions: 4

Austria, Cameroon, Costa Rica, Spain.

Absent: 4

Belize, Dominica, Gambia, Seychelles.

G

POPULATION AND REFUGEES DISPLACED SINCE 1967

The General Assembly,

Recalling Security Council resolution 237 (1967) of 14
June 1967,

Recalling also General Assembly resolutions 2252 (ES-
V) of 4 July 1967, 2452 A (XXIII) of 19 December 1968,
2535 B (XXIV) of 10 December 1969, 2672 D (XXV) of 8
December 1970, 2792 E (XXVI) of 6 December 1971,
2963 C and D (XXVII) of 13 December 1972, 3089 C
(XXVIII) of 7 December 1973, 3331 D (XXIX) of 17
December 1974, 3419 C (XXX) of 8 December 1975,
31/15 D of 23 November 1976, 32/90 E of 13 December
1977, 33/112 F of 18 December 1978, 34/52 E of 23
November 1979, ES-7/2 of 29 July 1980, 35/13 E of 3
November 1980, 36/146 B of 16 December 1981, 37/120
G of 16 December 1982, 38/83 G of 15 December 1983,
39/99 G of 14 December 1984 and 40/165 G of 16 December 1985,[555]

Having considered the report of the Commissioner-General

of the United Nations Relief and Works Agency for Palestine Refugees in the Near East, covering the period from
1 July 1985 to 30 June 1986,[556] and the report of the
Secretary-General,[557]

1. *Reaffirms* the inalienable right of all displaced inhabitants to return to their homes or former places of residence in the territories occupied by Israel since 1967, and
declares once more that any attempt to restrict, or to attach
conditions to, the free exercise of the right to return by
any displaced person is inconsistent with that inalienable
right and inadmissible;

2. *Considers* any and all agreements embodying any restriction on, or condition for, the return of the displaced
inhabitants as null and void;

3. *Strongly deplores* the continued refusal of the Israeli
authorities to take steps for the return of the displaced
inhabitants;

4. *Calls once more upon* Israel:

(a) To take immediate steps for the return of all displaced inhabitants;

(b) To desist from all measures that obstruct the return
of the displaced inhabitants, including measures affecting
the physical and demographic structure of the occupied
territories;

5. *Requests* the Secretary-General, after consulting with
the Commissioner-General of the United Nations Relief
and Works Agency for Palestine Refugees in the Near
East, to report to the General Assembly before the opening of its forty-second session on Israel's compliance with
paragraph 4 above.

Adopted at the 95th plenary meeting:
In favour: 126

Afghanistan, Albania, Algeria, Angola, Antigua and Bar-
buda, Argentina, Bahamas, Bahrain, Bangladesh, Barba-
dos, Benin, Bhutan, Bolivia, Botswana, Brazil, Brunei
Darussalam, Bulgaria, Burkina Faso, Burma, Burundi,
Byelorussia, Cape Verde, Central African Republic, Chad,
Chile, China, Colombia, Comoros, Congo, Cuba, Cyprus,
Czechoslovakia, Democratic Kampuchea, Democratic Ye-
men, Djibouti, Dominican Republic, Ecuador, Egypt, El
Salvador, Equatorial Guinea, Ethiopia, Fiji, Gabon, Ger-
man Democratic Republic, Ghana, Greece, Guatemala,
Guinea, Guinea-Bissau, Guyana, Haiti, Honduras, Hun-
gary, India, Indonesia, Iran, Iraq, Ivory Coast,* Jamaica,
Japan, Jordan, Kenya, Kuwait, Lao People's Democratic
Republic, Lebanon, Lesotho, Libya, Madagascar, Malay-
sia, Maldives, Mali, Malta, Mauritania, Mauritius, Mexico,
Mongolia, Morocco, Mozambique, Nepal, Nicaragua, Ni-
ger, Nigeria, Oman, Pakistan, Panama, Papua New Guinea,
Paraguay, Peru, Philippines, Poland, Portugal, Qatar, Ro-
mania, Rwanda, Saint Vincent, Samoa, Sao Tome and
Principe, Saudi Arabia, Senegal, Sierra Leone, Singapore,
Solomon Islands, Somalia, Spain, Sri Lanka, Sudan,
Suriname, Syria, Thailand, Togo, Trinidad and Tobago,

---

[555]Concerning persons displaced since 1967. [ed. note]

---

[556]*Official Records of the General Assembly, Forty-first Session, Supplement No.
13* (A/41/13 and Add.1).
[557]A/41/566.

Tunisia, Turkey, Uganda, Ukraine, USSR, United Arab Emirates, United Republic of Tanzania, Uruguay, Vanuatu, Venezuela, Viet Nam, Yemen, Yugoslavia, Zambia, Zimbabwe.

Against: 2
Israel, United States.

Abstentions: 25
Australia, Austria, Belgium, Cameroon, Canada, Costa Rica, Denmark, Finland, France, Federal Republic of Germany, Grenada, Iceland, Ireland, Italy, Liberia, Luxembourg, Malawi, Netherlands, New Zealand, Norway, Saint Lucia, Swaziland, Sweden, United Kingdom, Zaire.

Absent: 5
Belize, Dominica, Gambia, Seychelles, St. Christopher and Nevis.

---

*Later advised the Secretariat it had intended to abstain.

H

REVENUES DERIVED FROM PALESTINE REFUGEE PROPERTIES

The General Assembly,

Recalling its resolutions 35/13 A to F of 3 November 1980, 36/146 C of 16 December 1981, 37/120 H of 16 December 1982, 38/83 H of 15 December 1983, 39/99 H of 14 December 1984, 40/165 H of 16 December 1985 and all its previous resolutions on the question, including resolution 194 (III) of 11 December 1948,

Taking note of the report of the Secretary-General,[558]

Taking note also of the report of the United Nations Conciliation Commission for Palestine, covering the period from 1 September 1985 to 31 August 1986,[559]

Recalling that the Universal Declaration of Human Rights[560] and the principles of international law uphold the principle that no one shall be arbitrarily deprived of his or her private property,

Considering that the Palestine Arab refugees are entitled to their property and to the income derived from their property, in conformity with the principles of justice and equity,

Recalling, in particular, its resolution 394 (V) of 14 December 1950, in which it directed the United Nations Conciliation Commission for Palestine, in consultation with the parties concerned, to prescribe measures for the protection of the rights, property and interests of the Palestine Arab refugees,

Taking note of the completion of the programme of identification and evaluation of Arab property, as announced by the United Nations Conciliation Commission for Palestine in its twenty-second progress report,[561] and of the fact that the Land Office had a schedule of Arab owners and file of documents defining the location, area

and other particulars of Arab property,

1. *Requests* the Secretary-General to take all appropriate steps, in consultation with the United Nations Conciliation Commission for Palestine, for the protection and administration of Arab property, assets and property rights in Israel, and to establish a fund for the receipt of income derived therefrom, on behalf of the rightful owners;

2. *Calls once more upon* Israel to render all facilities and assistance to the Secretary-General in the implementation of the present resolution;

3. *Calls upon* all other Governments of Member States concerned to provide the Secretary-General with any pertinent information in their possession concerning Arab property, assets and property rights in Israel, which would assist the Secretary-General in the implementation of the present resolution;

4. *Deplores* Israel's refusal to co-operate with the Secretary-General in the implementation of the resolutions on the question;

5. *Requests* the Secretary-General to report to the General Assembly at its forty-second session on the implementation of the present resolution.

Adopted at the 95th plenary meeting:

In favour: 124
Afghanistan, Albania, Algeria, Angola, Antigua and Barbuda, Argentina, Bahamas, Bahrain, Bangladesh, Barbados, Benin, Bhutan, Bolivia, Botswana, Brazil, Brunei Darussalam, Bulgaria, Burkina Faso, Burma, Burundi, Byelorussia, Cape Verde, Central African Republic, Chile, China, Colombia, Comoros, Congo, Cuba, Cyprus, Czechoslovakia, Democratic Kampuchea, Democratic Yemen, Djibouti, Dominican Republic, Ecuador, Egypt, El Salvador, Equatorial Guinea, Ethiopia, Gabon, German Democratic Republic, Ghana, Greece, Grenada, Guatemala, Guinea, Guinea-Bissau, Guyana, Haiti, Honduras, Hungary, India, Indonesia, Iran, Iraq, Jamaica, Jordan, Kenya, Kuwait, Lao People's Democratic Republic, Lebanon, Lesotho, Libya, Madagascar, Malaysia, Maldives, Mali, Malta, Mauritania, Mauritius, Mexico, Mongolia, Morocco, Mozambique, Nepal, Nicaragua, Niger, Nigeria, Oman, Pakistan, Panama, Paraguay, Peru, Philippines, Poland, Portugal, Qatar, Romania, Rwanda, Saint Lucia, Saint Vincent, Samoa, Sao Tome and Principe, Saudi Arabia, Senegal, Sierra Leone, Singapore, Solomon Islands, Somalia, Spain, Sri Lanka, Sudan, Suriname, Swaziland, Syria, Thailand, Togo, Trinidad and Tobago, Tunisia, Turkey, Uganda, Ukraine, USSR, United Arab Emirates, United Republic of Tanzania, Uruguay, Vanuatu, Venezuela, Viet Nam, Yemen, Yugoslavia, Zambia, Zimbabwe.

Against: 2
Israel, United States.

Abstentions: 28
Australia, Austria, Belgium, Cameroon, Canada, Chad, Costa Rica, Denmark, Fiji, Finland, France, Federal Republic of Germany, Iceland, Ireland, Italy, Ivory Coast, Japan, Liberia, Luxembourg, Malawi, Netherlands, New Zealand, Norway, Papua New Guinea, St. Christopher and Nevis, Sweden, United Kingdom, Zaire.

---

[558]A/41/543.

[559]A/41/555.

[560]General Assembly resolution 217 A (III).

[561]*Official Records of the General Assembly, Nineteenth Session, Annex No. 11,* document A/5700.

Absent: 4
Belize, Dominica, Gambia, Seychelles.

I

PROTECTION OF PALESTINE REFUGEES

The General Assembly,

Recalling Security Council resolutions 508 (1982) of 5 June 1982, 509 (1982) of 6 June 1982, 511 (1982) of 18 June 1982, 512 (1982) of 19 June 1982, 513 (1982) of 4 July 1982, 515 (1982) of 29 July 1982, 517 (1982) of 4 August 1982, 518 (1982) of 12 August 1982, 519 (1982) of 17 August 1982, 520 (1982) of 17 September 1982 and 523 (1982) of 18 October 1982,[562]

Recalling General Assembly resolutions ES-7/5 of 26 June 1982, ES-7/6 and ES-7/8 of 19 August 1982, ES-7/9 of 24 September 1982, 37/120 J of 16 December 1982, 38/83 I of 15 December 1983, 39/99 I of 14 December 1984 and 40/165 I of 16 December 1985,

Having considered the report of the Secretary-General,[563]

Having also considered the report of the Commissioner-General of the United Nations Relief and Works Agency for Palestine Refugees in the Near East, covering the period from 1 July 1985 to 30 June 1986,[564]

Referring to the humanitarian principles of the Geneva Convention relative to the Protection of Civilian Persons in Time of War, of 12 August 1949,[565] and to the obligations arising from the Regulations annexed to the Hague Convention IV of 1907,[566]

Deeply concerned at the marked deterioration in the security situation experienced by the Palestine refugees as stated by the Commissioner-General of the United Nations Relief and Works Agency for Palestine Refugees in the Near East, in his report,

Deeply distressed at the continuous suffering of the Palestinians resulting from the Israeli invasion of Lebanon, and its consequences,

Reaffirming its support for the sovereignty, unity and territorial integrity of Lebanon, within its internationally recognized boundaries,

1. *Urges* the Secretary-General, in consultation with the Commissioner-General of the United Nations Relief and Works Agency for Palestine Refugees in the Near East, to undertake effective measures to guarantee the safety and security and the legal and human rights of the Palestine refugees in all the territories under Israeli occupation in 1967 and thereafter;

2. *Holds* Israel responsible for the security of the Palestine refugees in the Palestinan and other Arab territories occupied since 1967, including Jerusalem, and calls upon it to fulfil its obligations as the occupying Power in this regard, in accordance with the pertinent provisions of the Geneva Convention relative to the Protection of Civilian Persons in Time of War, of 12 August 1949;[567]

3. *Calls once again upon* Israel, the occupying Power, to release forthwith all detained Palestine refugees, including the employees of the United Nations Relief and Works Agency for Palestine Refugees in the Near East;

4. *Urges* the Commissioner-General, in consultation with the Government of Lebanon, to provide housing to the Palestine refugees whose houses were demolished or razed by the Israeli forces;

5. *Calls once again upon* Israel to compensate the Agency for the damage to its property and facilities resulting from the Israeli invasion of Lebanon, without prejudice to Israel's responsiblility for all damages resulting from that invasion;

6. *Requests* the Secretary-General, in consultation with the Commissioner-General, to report to the General Assembly, before the opening of its forty-second session, on the implementation of the present resolution.

Adopted at the 95th plenary meeting:

In favour: 121

Afghanistan, Albania, Algeria, Angola, Antigua and Barbuda, Argentina, Austria, Bahamas, Bahrain, Bangladesh, Barbados, Benin, Bhutan, Bolivia, Botswana, Brazil, Brunei Darussalam, Bulgaria, Burkina Faso, Burma, Burundi, Byelorussia, Cape Verde, Central African Republic, Chad, Chile, China, Colombia, Comoros, Congo, Cuba, Cyprus, Czechoslovakia, Democratic Kampuchea, Djibouti, Dominican Republic, Ecuador, Egypt, Equatorial Guinea, Ethiopia, Fiji, Finland, Gabon, German Democratic Republic, Ghana, Grenada, Guinea, Guinea-Bissau, Guyana, Honduras, Hungary, India, Indonesia, Iran, Iraq, Ivory Coast, Jamaica, Jordan, Kenya, Kuwait, Lao People's Democratic Republic, Lebanon, Lesotho, Liberia, Libya, Madagascar, Malaysia, Maldives, Mali, Malta, Mauritania, Mauritius, Mexico, Mongolia, Morocco, Mozambique, Nepal, Nicaragua, Niger, Nigeria, Oman, Pakistan, Papua New Guinea, Paraguay, Peru, Philippines, Poland, Qatar, Romania, Rwanda, Samoa, Sao Tome and Principe, Saudi Arabia, Senegal, Sierra Leone, Singapore, Solomon Islands, Somalia, Sri Lanka, Sudan, Suriname, Swaziland, Sweden, Syria, Thailand, Togo, Trinidad and Tobago, Tunisia, Turkey, Uganda, Ukraine, USSR, United Arab Emirates, United Republic of Tanzania, Vanuatu, Venezuela, Viet Nam, Yemen, Yugoslavia, Zambia, Zimbabwe.

Against: 2

Israel, United States.

Abstentions: 29

Australia, Belgium, Cameroon, Canada, Costa Rica, Denmark, El Salvador, France, Federal Republic of Germany, Greece, Guatemala, Iceland, Ireland, Italy, Japan, Lux-

---

[562]The resolutions in this and the next paragraph refer principally to Israel's invasion of Lebanon in 1982 and the situation of Palestinian refugees there.

[563]A/41/567.

[564]*Official Records of the General Assembly, Forty-first Session, Supplement No. 13* (A/41/13 and Add.1).

[565]United Nations, *Treaty Series,* vol. 75, no. 973, p. 287.

[566]Carnegie Endowment for International Peace, *The Hague Conventions and Declarations of 1899 and 1907* (New York, Oxford University Press, 1915), p. 100.

[567]United Nations, *Treaty Series,* vol. 75, no. 973, p. 287.

embourg, Malawi, Netherlands, New Zealand, Norway, Panama, Portugal, Saint Lucia, Saint Vincent, Spain, St. Christopher and Nevis, United Kingdom, Uruguay, Zaire.

Absent: 6

Belize, Democratic Yemen, Dominica, Gambia, Haiti, Seychelles.

J

PALESTINE REFUGEES IN THE WEST BANK

The General Assembly,

Recalling Security Council resolution 237 (1967) of 14 June 1967,

Recalling also General Assembly resolutions 38/83 J of 15 December 1983, 39/99 J of 14 December 1984 and 40/165 J of 16 December 1985,

Having considered the report of the Secretary-General,[568]

Having also considered the report of the Commissioner-General of the United Nations Relief and Works Agency for Palestine Refugees in the Near East, covering the period from 1 July 1985 to 30 June 1986,[569]

Alarmed by Israel's demolition of Palestine refugees' camps in the West Bank,

Alarmed also by Israel's plans to remove and resettle the Palestine refugees of the West Bank and to destroy their camps,

Recalling the provisions of paragraph 11 of its resolution 194 (III) of 11 December 1948 and considering that measures to resettle Palestine refugees in the West Bank away from the homes and property from which they were displaced constitute a violation of their inalienable right of return,

1. *Calls once again upon* Israel to abandon those plans and to refrain from any action that leads to the removal and resettlement of Palestine refugees in the West Bank and from the destruction of their camps;

2. *Requests* the Secretary-General, in co-operation with the Commissioner-General of the United Nations Relief and Works Agency for Palestine Refugees in the Near East, to keep the matter under close supervision and to report to the General Assembly, before the opening of its forty-second session, on any developments regarding this matter.

Adopted at the 95th plenary meeting:

In favour: 145

Afghanistan, Albania, Algeria, Angola, Antigua and Barbuda, Argentina, Australia, Austria, Bahamas, Bahrain, Bangladesh, Barbados, Belgium, Benin, Bhutan, Bolivia, Botswana, Brazil, Brunei Darussalam, Bulgaria, Burkina Faso, Burma, Burundi, Byelorussia, Cameroon, Canada, Cape Verde, Central African Republic, Chad, Chile, China, Colombia, Comoros, Congo, Cuba, Cyprus, Czechoslovakia, Democratic Kampuchea, Democratic Yemen, Den-

mark, Djibouti, Dominican Republic, Ecuador, Egypt, Equatorial Guinea, Ethiopia, Fiji, Finland, France, Gabon, German Democratic Republic, Federal Republic of Germany, Ghana, Greece, Grenada, Guatemala, Guinea, Guinea-Bissau, Guyana, Haiti, Honduras, Hungary, Iceland, India, Indonesia, Iran, Iraq, Ireland, Italy, Jamaica, Japan, Jordan, Kenya, Kuwait, Lao People's Democratic Republic, Lebanon, Lesotho, Libya, Luxembourg, Madagascar, Malaysia, Maldives, Mali, Malta, Mauritania, Mauritius, Mexico, Mongolia, Morocco, Mozambique, Nepal, Netherlands, New Zealand, Nicaragua, Niger, Nigeria, Norway, Oman, Pakistan, Panama, Papua New Guinea, Paraguay, Peru, Philippines, Poland, Portugal, Qatar, Romania, Rwanda, Saint Lucia, Saint Vincent, Samoa, Sao Tome and Principe, Saudi Arabia, Senegal, Sierra Leone, Singapore, Solomon Islands, Somalia, Spain, Sri Lanka, Sudan, Suriname, Swaziland, Sweden, Syria, Thailand, Togo, Trinidad and Tobago, Tunisia, Turkey, Uganda, Ukraine, USSR, United Arab Emirates, United Kingdom, United Republic of Tanzania, Uruguay, Vanuatu, Venezuela, Viet Nam, Yemen, Yugoslavia, Zambia, Zimbabwe.

Against: 2

Israel, United States.

Abstentions: 6

Costa Rica, El Salvador, Ivory Coast, Liberia, Malawi, Zaire.

Absent: 5

Belize, Dominica, Gambia, Seychelles, St. Christopher and Nevis.

K

UNIVERSITY OF JERUSALEM "AL-QUDS" FOR PALESTINE REFUGEES

The General Assembly,

Recalling its resolutions 36/146 G of 16 December 1981, 37/120 C of 16 December 1982, 38/83 K of 15 December 1983, 39/99 K of 14 December 1984 and 40/165 D and K of 16 December 1985

Having examined the report of the Secretary-General,[570]

Having also examined the report of the Commissioner-General of the United Nations Relief and Works Agency for Palestine Refugees in the Near East, covering the period from 1 July 1985 to 30 June 1986,[571]

1. *Emphasizes* the need for strengthening the educational system in the Arab territories occupied since 5 June 1967, including Jerusalem, and specifically the need for the establishment of the proposed university;

2. *Requests* the Secretary-General to continue to take all necessary measures for establishing the University of Jerusalem, "Al-Quds", in accordance with General Assembly resolution 35/13 B of 3 November 1980, giving due consideration to the recommendations consistent with the

---

[568]A/41/568.

[569]*Official Records of the General Assembly, Forty-first Session, Supplement No. 13* (A/41/13 and Add.1).

[570]A/41/457.

[571]*Official Records of the General Assembly, Forty-first Session, Supplement No. 13* (A/41/13 and Add.1).

provisions of that resolution;

3. *Calls once more upon* Israel, the occupying Power, to co-operate in the implementation of the present resolution and to remove the hindrances that it has put in the way of establishing the University of Jerusalem "Al-Quds";

4. *Requests* the Secretary-General to report to the General Assembly at its forty-second session on the progress made in the implementation of the present resolution.

Adopted at the 95th plenary meeting:

In favour: 152

Afghanistan, Albania, Algeria, Angola, Antigua and Barbuda, Argentina, Australia, Austria, Bahamas, Bahrain, Bangladesh, Barbados, Belgium, Benin, Bhutan, Bolivia, Botswana, Brazil, Brunei Darussalam, Bulgaria, Burkina Faso, Burma, Burundi, Byelorussia, Cameroon, Canada, Cape Verde, Central African Republic, Chad, Chile, China, Colombia, Comoros, Congo, Costa Rica, Cuba, Cyprus, Czechoslovakia, Democratic Kampuchea, Democratic Yemen, Denmark, Djibouti, Dominican Republic, Ecuador, Egypt, El Salvador, Equatorial Guinea, Ethiopia, Fiji, Finland, France, Gabon, German Democratic Republic, Federal Republic of Germany, Ghana, Greece, Grenada, Guatemala, Guinea, Guinea-Bissau, Guyana, Haiti, Honduras, Hungary, Iceland, India, Indonesia, Iran, Iraq, Ireland, Italy, Ivory Coast, Jamaica, Japan, Jordan, Kenya, Kuwait, Lao People's Democratic Republic, Lebanon, Lesotho, Liberia, Libya, Luxembourg, Madagascar, Malawi, Malaysia, Maldives, Mali, Malta, Mauritania, Mauritius, Mexico, Mongolia, Morocco, Mozambique, Nepal, Netherlands, New Zealand, Nicaragua, Niger, Nigeria, Norway, Oman, Pakistan, Panama, Papua New Guinea, Paraguay, Peru, Philippines, Poland, Portugal, Qatar, Romania, Rwanda, Saint Lucia, Saint Vincent, Samoa, Sao Tome and Principe, Saudi Arabia, Senegal, Sierra Leone, Singapore, Solomon Islands, Somalia, Spain, Sri Lanka, St. Christopher and Nevis, Sudan, Suriname, Swaziland, Sweden, Syria, Thailand, Togo, Trinidad and Tobago, Tunisia, Turkey, Uganda, Ukraine, USSR, United Arab Emirates, United Kingdom, United Republic of Tanzania, Uruguay, Vanuatu, Venezuela, Viet Nam, Yemen, Yugoslavia, Zaire, Zambia, Zimbabwe.

Against: 2

Israel, United States.

Abstentions: 0

Absent: 4

Belize, Dominica, Gambia, Seychelles.

Resolution No. 41/71 of 3 December 1986

CALLING UPON ALL STATES TO ACCORD THE NECESSARY FACILITIES, PRIVILEGES AND IMMUNITIES TO DELEGATIONS OF NATIONAL LIBERATION MOVEMENTS RECOGNIZED BY THE ORGANIZATION OF AFRICAN UNITY AND/OR THE LEAGUE OF ARAB STATES AND ACCORDED OBSERVER STATUS BY INTERNATIONAL ORGANIZATIONS

The General Assembly,

Recalling its resolutions 35/167 of 15 December 1980, 37/104 of 16 December 1982 and 39/76 of 13 December

1984,

Recalling also its resolutions 3237 (XXIX) of 22 November 1974, 3280 (XXIX) of 10 December 1974 and 31/152 of 20 December 1976,

Taking note of the report of the Secretary-General,[572]

Bearing in mind the resolution of the United Nations Conference on the Representation of States in Their Relations with International Organizations relating to the observer status of national liberation movements recognized by the Organization of African Unity and/or by the League of Arab States,[573]

Noting that the Vienna Convention on Representation of States in Their Relations with International Organizations of a Universal Character, of 14 March 1975,[574] regulates only the representation of States in their relations with international organizations,

Taking into account the current practice of inviting the above-mentioned national liberation movements to participate as observers in the sessions of the General Assembly, specialized agencies and other organizations of the United Nations system and in the work of the conference held under the auspices of such international organizations,

Convinced that the participation of the national liberation movements referred to above in the work of international organizations helps to strengthen international peace and co-operation,

Desirous of ensuring the effective participation of the above-mentioned national liberation movements as observers in the work of international organizations and of regulating, to that end, their status and the facilities, privileges and immunities necessary for the performance of their functions,

Noting also that many States have recognized those national liberation movements and have granted them in their countries facilities, privileges and immunities,

1. *Urges* all States that have not done so, in particular those which are hosts to international organizations or to conferences convened by, or held under the auspices of, international organizations of a universal character, to consider as soon as possible the question of ratifying, or acceding to, the Vienna Convention on the Representation of States in Their Relations with International Organizations of a Universal Character;[575]

2. *Calls once more upon* the States concerned to accord to the delegations of the national liberation movements recognized by the Organization of African Unity and/or by the League of Arab States and accorded observer status by international organizations, the facilities, privileges and

---

[572]A/41/534.

[573]See *Official Records of the United Nations Conference on the Representation of States in Their Relations with International Organizations, Vienna, 4 February-14 March 1975,* vol. II (United Nations publication, Sales No. E.75.V.12), document A/CONF.67/15, annex.

[574]*Ibid.,* vol. II, p. 207.

[575]See *Official Records of the United Nations Conference on the Representation of States in Their Relations with International Organizations, Vienna, 4 February-14 March 1975,* vol. II (United Nations publication, Sales No. E.75.V.12), document A/CONF.67/15, p. 207.

immunities necessary for the performance of their functions in accordance with the provisions of the Vienna Convention on the Representation of States in Their Relations with International Organizations of a Universal Character;

3. *Requests* the Secretary-General to report to the General Assembly at its forty-third session on the implementation of the present resolution.

Adopted at the 95th plenary meeting:
In favour: 125

Afghanistan, Albania, Algeria, Angola, Antigua and Barbuda, Argentina, Bahamas, Bahrain, Bangladesh, Barbados, Benin, Bhutan, Bolivia, Botswana, Brazil, Brunei Darussalam, Bulgaria, Burkina Faso, Burundi, Byelorussia, Cameroon, Cape Verde, Central African Republic, Chad, Chile, China, Colombia, Comoros, Congo, Cuba, Cyprus, Czechoslovakia, Democratic Kampuchea, Democratic Yemen, Djibouti, Dominican Republic, Ecuador, Egypt, Equatorial Guinea, Ethiopia, Gabon, Gambia, German Democratic Republic, Ghana, Greece, Grenada, Guinea, Guinea-Bissau, Guyana, Haiti, Hungary, India, Indonesia, Iran, Iraq, Ivory Coast, Jamaica, Jordan, Kenya, Kuwait, Lao People's Democratic Republic, Lebanon, Lesotho, Liberia, Libya, Madagascar, Malawi, Malaysia, Maldives, Mali, Malta, Mauritania, Mauritius, Mexico, Mongolia, Morocco, Mozambique, Nepal, Nicaragua, Niger, Nigeria, Oman, Pakistan, Panama, Papua New Guinea, Peru, Philippines, Poland, Qatar, Romania, Rwanda, Saint Lucia, Saint Vincent, Samoa, Sao Tome and Principe, Saudi Arabia, Senegal, Sierra Leone, Singapore, Solomon Islands, Somalia, Sri Lanka, St. Christopher and Nevis, Sudan, Suriname, Swaziland, Syria, Thailand, Togo, Trinidad and Tobago, Tunisia, Turkey, Uganda, Ukraine, USSR, United Arab Emirates, United Republic of Tanzania, Vanuatu, Venezuela, Viet Nam, Yemen, Yugoslavia, Zaire, Zambia, Zimbabwe.

Against: 10

Belgium, Canada, France, Federal Republic of Germany, Israel, Italy, Luxembourg, Netherlands, United Kingdom, United States.

Abstentions: 17

Australia, Austria, Burma, Denmark, Fiji, Finland, Guatemala, Honduras, Iceland, Ireland, Japan, New Zealand, Norway, Paraguay, Portugal, Spain, Sweden.

Absent: 6

Belize, Costa Rica, Dominica, El Salvador, Seychelles, Uruguay.

Resolution No. 41/93 of 4 December 1986

CONDEMNING ISRAEL'S REFUSAL TO RENOUNCE ANY POSSESSION OF NUCLEAR WEAPONS

The General Assembly,

Bearing in mind its previous resolutions on Israeli nuclear armament, the latest of which is 40/93 of 12 December 1985,

Recalling resolution 40/82 of 12 December 1985, in

which, *inter alia,* it called upon all countries of the region that had not done so, pending the establishment of a nuclear-weapon-free zone in the Middle East, to agree to place all their nuclear activities under Internationl Atomic Energy Agency safeguards,

Recalling further Security Council resolution 487 (1981) of 19 June 1981 in which, *inter alia,* the Council called upon Israel urgently to place all its nuclear facilities under International Atomic Energy Agency safeguards,

Noting with grave concern Israel's persistent refusal to commit itself not to manufacture or acquire nuclear weapons, despite repeated calls by the General Assembly, the Security Council and the International Atomic Energy Agency, and to place its nuclear facilities under Agency safeguards,

Aware of the grave consequences that endanger international peace and security as a result of Israel's development and acquisition of nuclear weapons and Israel's collaboration with South Africa to develop nuclear weapons and their delivery systems,

Deeply concerned over the continuing development and acquisition of nuclear weapons by Israel,

1. *Reiterates its condemnation* of Israel's refusal to renounce any possession of nuclear weapons;

2. *Requests once more* the Security Council to take urgent and effective measures to ensure that Israel complies with Security Council resolution 487 (1981) and place all its nuclear facilities under International Atomic Energy Agency safeguards;

3. *Reiterates its request* to the Security Council to investigate Israel's nuclear activities and the collaboration of other States, parties and institutions in the nuclear field;

4. *Reiterates its request* to the International Atomic Energy Agency to suspend any scientific co-operation with Israel which could contribute to its nuclear capabilities;

5. *Calls upon* all States and organizations that have not yet done so to discontinue co-operating with and giving assistance to Israel in the nuclear field;

6. *Reaffirms its condemnation* of the continuing nuclear collaboration between Israel and South Africa;

7. *Requests* the Secretary-General to closely follow up Israeli nuclear activities in the light of the latest available information, to update the study on Israeli nuclear armament[576] and to submit it to the General Assembly at its forty-second session;

8. *Decides* to include in the provisional agenda of its forty-second session the item entitled "Israeli nuclear armament".

Adopted at the 96th plenary meeting:
In favour: 95

Afghanistan, Albania, Algeria, Angola, Argentina, Bahrain, Bangladesh, Benin, Bhutan, Botswana, Brazil, Brunei Darussalam, Bulgaria, Burkina Faso, Burundi, Byelorussia, Cape Verde, Central African Republic, China, Comoros,

---

[576]A/36/431.

Congo, Cuba, Cyprus, Czechoslovakia, Democratic Kampuchea, Democratic Yemen, Djibouti, Egypt, Ethiopia, Gabon, German Democratic Republic, Ghana, Greece, Guinea, Guinea-Bissau, Guyana, Hungary, India, Indonesia, Iran, Iraq, Jordan, Kenya, Kuwait, Lao People's Democratic Republic, Lebanon, Libya, Madagascar, Malaysia, Maldives, Mali, Malta, Mauritania, Mauritius, Mexico, Mongolia, Morocco, Mozambique, Nicaragua, Niger, Nigeria, Oman, Pakistan, Peru, Philippines, Poland, Qatar, Romania, Rwanda, Sao Tome and Principe, Saudi Arabia, Senegal, Seychelles, Sierra Leone, Somalia, Sri Lanka, Sudan, Suriname, Syria, Thailand, Togo, Trinidad and Tobago, Tunisia, Turkey, Uganda, Ukraine, USSR, United Arab Emirates, United Republic of Tanzania, Venezuela, Viet Nam, Yemen, Yugoslavia, Zambia, Zimbabwe.

Against: 2

Israel, United States.

Abstentions: 56

Antigua and Barbuda, Australia, Austria, Bahamas, Barbados, Belgium, Belize, Bolivia, Burma, Cameroon, Canada, Chad, Chile, Colombia, Costa Rica, Denmark, Dominican Republic, Ecuador, Equatorial Guinea, Fiji, Finland, France, Federal Republic of Germany, Grenada, Guatemala, Haiti, Honduras, Iceland, Ireland, Italy, Ivory Coast, Jamaica, Japan, Lesotho,* Liberia, Luxembourg, Malawi, Nepal, Netherlands, New Zealand, Norway, Panama, Papua New Guinea, Paraguay, Portugal, Saint Lucia, Saint Vincent, Samoa, Solomon Islands, Spain, St. Christopher and Nevis, Swaziland, Sweden, United Kingdom, Uruguay, Zaire.

Absent: 5

Dominica, El Salvador, Gambia, Singapore, Vanuatu.

---

*Later advised the Secretariat it had intended to vote in favour.

Resolution No. 41/95 of 4 December 1986

CONDEMNING COLLABORATION BETWEEN ISRAEL AND SOUTH AFRICA [EXCERPTS FROM A RESOLUTION ON THE PROVISION OF ASSISTANCE TO THE SOUTH AFRICAN REGIME]

The General Assembly,

....

Alarmed at the continued collaboration of certain Western States and Israel with the racist régime of South Africa in the nuclear field,

....

3. *Vigorously condemns* the collaboration of certain Western States, Israel and other States, as well as the transnational corporations and other organizations which maintain or continue to increase their collaboration with the racist régime of South Africa, especially on the political, economic, military and nuclear fields, thus encouraging that régime to persist in its inhuman and criminal policy of brutal oppression of the peoples of southern Africa and denial of their human rights;

....

Adopted at the 97th plenary meeting:

In favour: 126

Afghanistan, Albania, Algeria, Angola, Antigua and Barbuda, Argentina, Bahamas, Bahrain, Bangladesh, Barbados, Belize, Benin, Bolivia, Botswana, Brazil, Brunei Darussalam, Bulgaria, Burkina Faso, Burma, Burundi, Byelorussia, Cape Verde, Central African Republic, Chad, China, Colombia, Comoros, Congo, Cuba, Cyprus, Czechoslovakia, Democratic Kampuchea, Democratic Yemen, Djibouti, Dominican Republic, Ecuador, Egypt, Equatorial Guinea, Ethiopia, Fiji, Gabon, Gambia, German Democratic Republic, Ghana, Grenada, Guatemala, Guinea, Guinea-Bissau, Guyana, Haiti, Honduras, Hungary, India, Indonesia, Iran, Iraq, Ivory Coast, Jamaica, Jordan, Kenya, Kuwait, Lao People's Democratic Republic, Lebanon, Lesotho, Liberia, Libya, Madagascar, Malaysia, Maldives, Mali, Malta, Mauritania, Mauritius, Mexico, Mongolia, Morocco, Mozambique, Nepal, Nicaragua, Niger, Nigeria, Oman, Pakistan, Panama, Papua New Guinea, Peru, Philippines, Poland, Qatar, Romania, Rwanda, Saint Lucia, Saint Vincent, Samoa, Sao Tome and Principe, Saudi Arabia, Senegal, Seychelles, Sierra Leone, Singapore, Solomon Islands, Somalia, Sri Lanka, St. Christopher and Nevis, Sudan, Suriname, Swaziland, Syria, Thailand, Togo, Trinidad and Tobago, Tunisia, Turkey, Uganda, Ukraine, USSR, United Arab Emirates, United Republic of Tanzania, Uruguay, Venezuela, Viet Nam, Yemen, Yugoslavia, Zaire, Zambia, Zimbabwe.

Against: 10

Belgium, Cameroon, France, Federal Republic of Germany, Israel, Italy, Luxembourg, Netherlands, United Kingdom, United States.

Abstentions: 17

Australia, Austria, Bhutan,* Canada, Costa Rica, Denmark, Finland, Greece, Iceland, Ireland, Japan, Malawi, New Zealand, Norway, Portugal, Spain, Sweden.

Absent: 5

Chile, Dominica, El Salvador, Paraguay, Vanuatu.*

---

*Later advised the Secretariat it had intended to vote in favour.

Resolution No. 41/101 of 4 December 1986

REAFFIRMING THE RIGHT OF THE PALESTINIAN PEOPLE TO SELF-DETERMINATION AND INDEPENDENCE (EXCERPTS FROM A RESOLUTION ON THE RIGHT TO SELF-DETERMINATION OF COLONIAL COUNTRIES AND PEOPLES)

The General Assembly,

....

Recalling the Political Declaration adopted by the First Conference of Heads of State and Government of the Organization of African Unity and the League of Arab States, held at Cairo from 7 to 9 March 1977,[577]

Recalling further its relevant resolutions on the question of Palestine, in particular resolution 40/96 of 12 Decem-

---

[577]A/32/61, annex I.

ber 1985,

Recalling the Geneva Declaration on Palestine and the Programme of Action for the Achievement of Palestinian Rights, adopted by the International Conference on the Question of Palestine,[578]

Considering that the denial of the inalienable rights of the Palestinian people to self-determination, sovereignty, independence and return to Palestine and the repeated acts of aggression by Israel against the people of the region constitute a serious threat to international peace and security,

Deeply shocked and alarmed at the deplorable consequences of the Israeli invasion of Lebanon and recalling all the relevant resolutions of the Security Council, in particular resolutions 508 (1982) of 5 June 1982, 509 (1982) of 6 June 1982, 520 (1982) of 17 September 1982 and 521 (1982) of 19 September 1982,

1. *Calls upon* all States to implement fully and faithfully all the resolutions of the United Nations regarding the exercise of the right to self-determination and independence by peoples under colonial and foreign domination;

2. *Reaffirms* the legitimacy of the struggle of peoples for their independence, territorial integrity, national unity and liberation from colonial domination, *apartheid* and foreign occupation by all available means, including armed struggle;

3. *Reaffirms* the inalienable right of the Namibian people, the Palestinian people and all peoples under foreign and colonial domination to self-determination, national independence, territorial integrity, national unity and sovereignty without foreign interference;

4. *Strongly condemns* those Governments that do not recognize the right to self-determination and independence of all people still under colonial domination and alien subjugation, notably the peoples of Africa and the Palestinian people;

5. *Calls* for the full and immediate implementation of the declarations and programmes of action on Namibia and on Palestine adopted by the international conferences on those questions;

....

18. *Strongly condemns* the continued violation of the human rights of the peoples still under colonial domination and alien subjugation, the continuation of the illegal occupation by the racist minority régime in southern Africa and the denial to the Palestinian people of their inalienable national rights;

....

21. *Denounces* the collusion between Israel and South Africa and expresses support for the Declaration of the International Conference on the Alliance between South Africa and Israel;[579]

22. *Strongly condemns* the policy of those Western States,

Israel and other States whose political, economic, military, nuclear, strategic, cultural and sports relations with the racist minority régime of South Africa encourage that régime to persist in its suppression of the aspirations of peoples to self-determination and independence;

....

31. *Strongly condemns* the constant and deliberate violations of the fundamental rights of the Palestinian people, as well as the expansionist activities of Israel in the Middle East, which constitute an obstacle to the achievement of self-determination and independence by the Palestinian people and a threat to peace and stability in the region;

32. *Demands* the immediate and unconditional release of all persons detained or imprisoned as a result of their struggle for self-determination and independence, full respect for their fundamental individual rights and compliance with article 5 of the Universal Declaration of Human Rights[580] under which no one shall be subjected to torture or to cruel, inhuman or degrading treatment;

33. *Urges* all States, the specialized agencies, organizations of the United Nations system and other international organizations to extend their support to the Palestinian people through its sole and legitimate representative, the Palestine Liberation Organization, in its struggle to regain its right to self-determination and independence in accordance with the Charter;

....

Adopted at the 97th plenary meeting:

In favour: 126

Afghanistan, Albania, Algeria, Angola, Antigua and Barbuda, Argentina, Bahamas, Bahrain, Bangladesh, Barbados, Belize, Benin, Bhutan, Bolivia, Botswana, Brazil, Brunei Darussalam, Bulgaria, Burkina Faso, Burma, Burundi, Byelorussia, Cameroon, Cape Verde, Central African Republic, Chad, China, Colombia, Comoros, Congo, Cuba, Cyprus, Czechoslovakia, Democratic Kampuchea, Democratic Yemen, Djibouti, Dominican Republic, Ecuador, Egypt, Ethiopia, Gabon, Gambia, German Democratic Republic, Ghana, Grenada, Guatemala, Guinea, Guinea-Bissau, Guyana, Haiti, Hungary, India, Indonesia, Iran, Iraq, Ivory Coast, Jamaica, Jordan, Kenya, Kuwait, Lao People's Democratic Republic, Lebanon, Lesotho, Liberia, Libya, Madagascar, Malawi, Malaysia, Maldives, Mali, Malta, Mauritania, Mauritius, Mexico, Mongolia, Morocco, Mozambique, Nepal, Nicaragua, Niger, Nigeria, Oman, Pakistan, Panama, Papua New Guinea, Peru, Philippines, Poland, Qatar, Romania, Rwanda, Saint Lucia, Saint Vincent, Sao Tome and Principe, Saudi Arabia, Senegal, Seychelles, Sierra Leone, Singapore, Solomon Islands, Somalia, Sri Lanka, St. Christopher and Nevis, Sudan, Suriname, Swaziland, Syria, Thailand, Togo, Trinidad and Tobago, Tunisia, Turkey, Uganda, Ukraine, USSR, United Arab Emirates, United Republic of Tanzania, Uruguay, Vanuatu, Venezuela, Viet Nam, Yemen, Yugoslavia, Zaire, Zambia, Zimbabwe.

---

[578]*Report of the International Conference on the Question of Palestine, Geneva, 29 August-7 September 1983* (United Nations publication, Sales No. E.83.I.21), chap. I

[579]See A/38/311-S/15883, annex.

[580]General Assembly resolution 217 A (III).

Against: 18

Australia, Belgium, Canada, Denmark, El Salvador, Finland, France, Federal Republic of Germany, Iceland, Israel, Italy, Luxembourg, Netherlands, New Zealand, Norway, Sweden, United Kingdom, United States.

Abstentions: 12

Austria, Costa Rica, Equatorial Guinea, Fiji, Greece, Honduras, Ireland, Japan, Paraguay, Portugal, Samoa, Spain.

Absent: 2

Chile, Dominica.

Resolution No. 41/162 A, B, C of 4 December 1986

ON THE SITUATION IN THE MIDDLE EAST: CONDEMNING ISRAEL'S POLICIES IN THE OCCUPIED TERRITORIES AND CALLING FOR ITS COMPLETE WITHDRAWAL FROM THEM, DECLARING THE NEED FOR RECOGNITION OF THE RIGHT OF THE PALESTINIAN PEOPLE, UNDER THE LEADERSHIP OF THE PALESTINE LIBERATION ORGANIZATION, TO SELF-DETERMINATION AND INDEPENDENCE, AND CALLING ON ALL STATES TO END AID TO ISRAEL

A

The General Assembly,

Having discussed the item entitled "The situation in the Middle East",

Reaffirming its resolutions 36/226 A and B of 17 December 1981, ES-9/1 of 5 February 1982, 37/123 F of 20 December 1982, 38/58 A to E of 13 December 1983, 38/180 A to D of 19 December 1983, 39/146A to C of 14 December 1984 and 40/168A to C of 16 December 1985,[581]

Recalling Security Council resolutions 425 (1978) of 19 March 1978, 497 (1981) of 17 December 1981, 508 (1982) of 5 June 1982, 509 (1982) of 6 June 1982, 511 (1982) of 18 June 1982, 512 (1982) of 19 June 1982, 513 (1982) of 4 July 1982, 515 (1982) of 29 July 1982, 516 (1982) of 1 August 1982, 517 (1982) of 4 August 1982, 518 (1982) of 12 August 1982, 519 (1982) of 17 August 1982, 520 (1982) of 17 September 1982, 521 (1982) of 19 September 1982 and 555 (1984) of 12 October 1984,

Taking note of the reports of the Secretary-General of 14 March 1986,[582] 19 September 1986[583] and 18 November 1986,[584]

Reaffirming the need for continued collective support for the resolutions adopted by the Twelfth Arab Summit Conference, held at Fez, Morocco, on 25 November 1981 and from 6 to 9 September 1982,[585] reiterating its previous resolutions regarding the Palestinian question and its support for the Palestine Liberation Organization as the sole, legitimate representative of the Palestinian people, and considering that the convening of the International Peace Conference on the Middle East, under the auspices of the United Nations in accordance with General Assembly resolution 38/58 C and other relevant resolutions related to the question of Palestine, would contribute to the promotion of peace in the region,

Welcoming all efforts contributing towards the realization of the inalienable rights of the Palestinian people through the achievement of a comprehensive, just and lasting peace in the Middle East, in accordance with the United Nations resolutions relating to the question of Palestine and to the situation in the Middle East,

Welcoming the world-wide support extended to the just cause of the Palestinian people and the other Arab countries in their struggle against Israeli aggression and occupation in order to achieve a comprehensive, just and lasting peace in the Middle East and the full exercise by the Palestinian people of its inalienable national rights, as affirmed by previous resolutions of the General Assembly relating to the question of Palestine and to the situation in the Middle East,

Gravely concerned that the Palestinian and other Arab territories occupied since 1967, including Jerusalem, still remain under Israeli occupation, that the relevant resolutions of the United Nations have not been implemented and that the Palestinian people is still denied the restoration of its land and the exercise of its inalienable national rights in conformity with international law, as reaffirmed by resolutions of the United Nations,

Reaffirming the applicability of the Geneva Convention relative to the Protection of Civilian Persons in Time of War, of 12 August 1949,[586] to all the occupied Palestinian and other Arab territories, including Jerusalem,

Reaffirming also all relevant United Nations resolutions which stipulate that the acquisition of territory by force is inadmissible under the Charter of the United Nations and the principles of international law and that Israel must withdraw unconditionally from all the Palestinian and other Arab territories occupied by Israel since 1967, including Jerusalem,

Reaffirming further the imperative necessity of establishing a comprehensive, just and lasting peace in the region, based on full respect for the Charter and the principles of international law,

Gravely concerned also at the continuing Israeli policies involving the escalation and expansion of the conflict in the region, which further violate the principles of international law and endanger international peace and security,

Stressing once again the great importance of the time factor in the endeavours to achieve an early comprehensive, just and lasting peace in the Middle East,

1. *Reaffirms its conviction* that the question of Palestine is the core of the conflict in the Middle East and that no comprehensive, just and lasting peace in the region will be achieved without the full exercise by the Palestinian people of its inalienable national rights and the immediate, unconditional and total withdrawal of Israel from all the Palestinian and other occupied Arab territories;

---

[581]Most resolutions cited in this and the next paragraph are previous resolutions on "The situation in the Middle East," and on the situation created by Israel's invasions of Lebanon in 1978 and 1982. [ed. note]

[582]A/41/215-S/17916.

[583]A/41/453 and Add.1.

[584]A/41/768-S/18427.

[585]See A/37/696-S/15510, annex.

[586]United Nations, *Treaty Series,* vol. 75, no. 973, p. 287.

2. *Reaffirms further* that a just and comprehensive settlement of the situation in the Middle East cannot be achieved without the participation on an equal footing of all the parties to the conflict, including the Palestine Liberation Organization, the representative of the Palestinian people;

3. *Declares once more* that peace in the Middle East is indivisible and must be based on a comprehensive, just and lasting solution of the Middle East problem, under the auspices of the United Nations and on the basis of its relevant resolutions, which ensures the complete and unconditional withdrawal of Israel from the Palestinian and other Arab territories occupied since 1967, including Jerusalem, and which enables the Palestinian people, under the leadership of the Palestine Liberation Organization, to exercise its inalienable rights, including the right to return and the right to self-determination, national independence and the establishment of its independent sovereign State in Palestine, in accordance with the resolutions of the United Nations relevant to the question of Palestine, in particular General Assembly resolutions ES-7/2 of 29 July 1980, 36/120 A to F of 10 December 1981, 37/86 A to D of 10 December 1982, 37/86 E of 20 December 1982, 38/58 A to E of 13 December 1983, 39/146 A to C of 14 December 1984 and 40/168 A to C of 16 December 1985;

4. *Considers* the Arab Peace Plan adopted unanimously at the Twelfth Summit Conference, held at Fez, Morocco, on 25 November 1981 and from 6 to 9 September 1982,[587] reiterated by the Extraordinary Summit Conference of the Arab States held at Casablanca, Morocco, from 7 to 9 August 1985,[588] as well as relevant efforts and action to implement the Fez Plan, as an important contribution towards the realization of the inalienable rights of the Palestinian people through the achievement of a comprehensive, just and lasting peace in the Middle East;

5. *Condemns* Israel's continued occupation of the Palestinian and other Arab territories, including Jerusalem, in violation of the Charter of the United Nations, the principles of international law and the relevant resolutions of the United Nations, and demands the immediate, unconditional and total withdrawal of Israel from all the territories occupied since 1967;

6. *Rejects* all agreements and arrangements which violate the inalienable rights of the Palestinian people and contradict the principles of a just and comprehensive solution to the Middle East problem to ensure the establishment of a just peace in the area;

7. *Deplores* Israel's failure to comply with Security Council resolutions 476 (1980) of 30 June 1980 and 478 (1980) of 20 August 1980 and General Assembly resolutions 35/207 of 16 December 1980 and 36/226 A and B of 17 December 1981; determines that Israel's decision to annex Jerusalem and to declare it as its "capital" as well as the measures to alter its physical character, demographic composition, institutional structure and status are null

and void and demands that they be rescinded immediately; and calls upon all Member States, the specialized agencies and all other international organizations to abide by the present resolution and all other relevant resolutions and decisions;

8. *Condemns* Israel's aggression, policies and practices against the Palestinian people in the occupied Palestinian territories and outside these territories, including expropriation, establishment of settlements, annexation and other terrorist, aggressive and repressive measures, which are in violation of the Charter and principles of international law and the relevant international conventions;

9. *Strongly condemns* the imposition by Israel of its laws, jurisdiction and administration on the occupied Syrian Golan Heights, its annexationist policies and practices, the establishment of settlements, the confiscation of lands, the diversion of water resources and imposition of Israeli citizenship on Syrian nationals, and declares that all these measures are null and void and constitute a violation of the rules and principles of international law relative to belligerent occupation, in particular the Geneva Convention relative to the Protection of Civilian Persons in Time of War, of 12 August 1949;[589]

10. *Considers* that the agreements on strategic co-operation between the United States of America and Israel, signed on 30 November 1981, and the continued supply of modern arms and *matériel* to Israel, augmented by substantial economic aid, including the recently concluded Agreement on the Establishment of a Free Trade Area between the two Governments, have encouraged Israel to pursue its aggressive and expansionist policies and practices in the Palestinian and other Arab territories occupied since 1967, including Jerusalem, and have had adverse effects on efforts for the establishment of a comprehensive, just and lasting peace in the Middle East and threaten the security of the region;

11. *Calls once more upon* all States to put an end to the flow to Israel of any military, economic, financial and technological aid, as well as of human resources, aimed at encouraging it to pursue its aggressive policies against the Arab countries and the Palestinian people;

12. *Strongly condemns* the continuing and increasing collaboration between Israel and the racist régime of South Africa, especially in the economic, military and nuclear fields, which constitutes a hostile act against the African and Arab States and enables Israel to enhance its nuclear capabilities, thus subjecting the States of the region to nuclear blackmail;

13. *Reaffirms its call* for the convening of the International Peace Conference on the Middle East under the auspices of the United Nations as specified in paragraph 5 of the Geneva Declaration on Palestine[590] and endorsed by General Assembly resolution 38/58 C of 13 December

---

[587]See A/37/696-S/15510, annex.
[588]See A/40/564 and Corr.1, annex.

[589]United Nations, *Treaty Series*, vol. 75, no. 973, p. 287.
[590]*Report of the International Conference on the Question of Palestine, Geneva, 29 August-7 September 1983* (United Nations publication, Sales No. E.83.I.21), chap. I, sect. A.

1983 and on the basis of its relevant resolutions;

14. *Endorses the call* for setting up a preparatory committee, within the framework of the Security Council, with the participation of the permanent members of the Council, to take the necessary action to convene the Conference;

15. *Requests* the Secretary-General to report to the Security Council periodically on the development of the situation and to submit to the General Assembly at its forty-second session a comprehensive report covering the developments in the Middle East in all their aspects.

Adopted at the 97th plenary meeting:

In favour: 104

Afghanistan, Albania, Algeria, Angola, Argentina, Bahrain, Bangladesh, Benin, Bhutan, Bolivia, Botswana, Brazil, Brunei Darussalam, Bulgaria, Burkina Faso, Burundi, Byelorussia, Cape Verde, Central African Republic, Chad, China, Comoros, Congo, Cuba, Cyprus, Czechoslovakia, Democratic Kampuchea, Democratic Yemen, Djibouti, Ecuador, Egypt, Ethiopia, Gabon, Gambia, German Democratic Republic, Ghana, Greece, Guinea, Guinea-Bissau, Guyana, Hungary, India, Indonesia, Iran, Iraq, Jordan, Kenya, Kuwait, Lao People's Democratic Republic, Lebanon, Lesotho, Libya, Madagascar, Malaysia, Maldives, Mali, Malta, Mauritania, Mauritius, Mexico, Mongolia, Morocco, Mozambique, Nepal, Nicaragua, Niger, Nigeria, Oman, Pakistan, Papua New Guinea, Peru, Philippines, Poland, Qatar, Romania, Rwanda, Sao Tome and Principe, Saudi Arabia, Senegal, Sierra Leone, Singapore, Solomon Islands, Somalia, Sri Lanka, Sudan, Suriname, Syria, Thailand, Togo, Trinidad and Tobago, Tunisia, Turkey, Uganda, Ukraine, USSR, United Arab Emirates, United Republic of Tanzania, Vanuatu, Venezuela, Viet Nam, Yemen, Yugoslavia, Zambia, Zimbabwe.

Against: 19

Australia, Belgium, Canada, Costa Rica, Denmark, El Salvador, France, Federal Republic of Germany, Iceland, Ireland, Israel, Italy, Luxembourg, Netherlands, New Zealand, Norway, Portugal, United Kingdom, United States.

Abstentions: 32

Antigua and Barbuda, Austria, Bahamas, Barbados, Belize, Burma, Cameroon, Chile, Colombia, Dominican Republic, Equatorial Guinea, Finland, Grenada, Guatemala, Haiti, Honduras, Ivory Coast, Jamaica, Japan, Liberia, Malawi, Panama, Paraguay, Saint Lucia, Saint Vincent, Samoa, Spain, St. Christopher and Nevis, Swaziland, Sweden, Uruguay, Zaire.

Absent: 3

Dominica, Fiji, Seychelles.

B

The General Assembly,

Having discussed the item entitled "The situation in the Middle East",

Taking note of the report of the Secretary-General of 18 November 1986,[591]

Recalling Security Council resolution 497 (1981) of 17 December 1981,

Reaffirming its resolutions 36/226 B of 17 December 1981, ES-9/1 of 5 February 1982, 37/123 A of 16 December 1982, 38/180 A of 19 December 1983, 39/146 B of 14 December 1984 and 40/168 B of 16 December 1985,

Recalling its resolution 3314 (XXIX) of 14 December 1974, in which it defined an act of aggression, *inter alia*, as "the invasion or attack by the armed forces of a State of the territory of another State, or any military occupation, however temporary, resulting from such invasion or attack, or any annexation by the use of force of the territory of another State or part thereof" and provided that "no consideration of whatever nature, whether political, economic, military or otherwise, may serve as a justification for aggression",

Reaffirming the fundamental principle of the inadmissibility of the acquisition of territory by force,

Reaffirming once more the applicability of the Geneva Convention relative to the Protection of Civilian Persons in Time of War, of 12 August 1949,[592] to the occupied Palestinian and other Arab territories, including Jerusalem,

Noting that Israel's record, policies and actions establish conclusively that it is not a peace-loving State and that it has not carried out its obligations under the Charter of the United Nations,

Noting further that Israel has refused, in violation of Article 25 of the Charter, to accept and carry out the numerous relevant decisions of the Security Council, in particular resolution 497 (1981), thus failing to carry out its obligations under the Charter,

1. *Strongly condemns* Israel for its failure to comply with Security Council resolution 497 (1981) and General Assembly resolutions 36/226 B, ES-9/1, 37/123 A, 38/180 A, 39/146 B and 40/168 B;

2. *Declares once more* that Israel's continued occupation of the Golan Heights and its decision of 14 December 1981 to impose its laws, jurisdiction and administration on the occupied Syrian Golan Heights constitute an act of aggression under the provisions of Article 39 of the Charter of the United Nations and General Assembly resolution 3314 (XXIX);

3. *Declares once more* that Israel's decision to impose its laws, jurisdiction and administration on the occupied Syrian Golan Heights is illegal and therefore null and void and has no validity whatsoever;

4. *Declares* all Israeli policies and practices of, or aimed at, annexation of the occupied Palestinian and other Arab territories, including Jerusalem, to be illegal and in violation of international law and of the relevant United Nations resolutions;

5. *Determines once more* that all actions taken by Israel to give effect to its decision relating to the occupied Syrian Golan Heights are illegal and invalid and shall not be recognized;

---

[591]A/41/768-S/18427.

[592]United Nations, *Treaty Series*, vol. 75, no. 973, p. 287.

6. *Reaffirms its determination* that all relevant provisions of the Regulations annexed to the Hague Convention IV of 1907,[593] and the Geneva Convention relative to the Protection of Civilian Persons in Time of War, of 12 August 1949,[594] continue to apply to the Syrian territory occupied by Israel since 1967, and calls upon the parties thereto to respect and ensure respect for their obligations under these instruments in all circumstances;

7. *Determines once more* that the continued occupation of the Syrian Golan Heights since 1967 and their annexation by Israel on 14 December 1981, following Israel's decision to impose its laws, jurisdiction and administration on that territory, constitute a continuing threat to international peace and security;

8. *Strongly deplores* the negative vote by a permanent member of the Security Council which prevented the Council from adopting against Israel, under Chapter VII of the Charter, the "appropriate measures" referred to in resolution 497 (1981) unanimously adopted by the Council;

9. *Further deplores* any political, economic, financial, military and technological support to Israel that encourages Israel to commit acts of aggression and to consolidate and perpetuate its occupation and annexation of occupied Arab territories;

10. *Firmly emphasizes once more* its demand that Israel, the occupying Power, rescind forthwith its illegal decision of 14 December 1981 to impose its laws, jurisdiction and administration on the Syrian Golan Heights, which resulted in the effective annexation of that territory;

11. *Reaffirms once more* the overriding necessity of the total and unconditional withdrawal by Israel from all the Palestinian and other Arab territories occupied since 1967, including Jerusalem, which is an essential prerequisite for the establishment of a comprehensive and just peace in the Middle East;

12. *Determines once more* that Israel's record, policies and actions confirm that it is not a peace-loving Member State, that it has persistently violated the principles contained in the Charter and that it has carried out neither its obligations under the Charter nor its commitment under General Assembly resolution 273 (III) of 11 May 1949;

13. *Calls once more upon* all Member States to apply the following measures:

(*a*) To refrain from supplying Israel with any weapons and related equipment and to suspend any military assistance that Israel receives from them;

(*b*) To refrain from acquiring any weapons or military equipment from Israel;

(*c*) To suspend economic, financial and technological assistance to, and co-operation with, Israel;

(*d*) To sever diplomatic, trade and cultural relations with Israel;

14. *Reiterates its call* to all Member States to cease forthwith, individually and collectively, all dealings with Israel in order totally to isolate it in all its fields;

15. *Urges* non-member States to act in accordance with the provisions of the present resolution;

16. *Calls upon* the specialized agencies and other international organizations to conform their relations with Israel to the terms of the present resolution;

17. *Requests* the Secretary-General to report to the General Assembly at its forty-second session on the implementation of the present resolution.

Adopted at the 97th plenary meeting:

In favour: 90
Afghanistan, Albania, Algeria, Angola, Bahrain, Bangladesh, Benin, Bhutan, Botswana, Brunei Darussalam, Bulgaria, Burkina Faso, Burundi, Byelorussia, Cape Verde, Central African Republic, Chad, China, Comoros, Congo, Cuba, Cyprus, Czechoslovakia, Democratic Kampuchea, Democratic Yemen, Djibouti, Ethiopia, Gabon, Gambia, German Democratic Republic, Ghana, Greece, Guinea, Guinea-Bissau, Guyana, Hungary, India, Indonesia, Iran, Iraq, Jordan, Kenya, Kuwait, Lao People's Democratic Republic, Lebanon, Libya, Madagascar, Malaysia, Maldives, Mali, Malta, Mauritania, Mauritius, Mexico, Mongolia, Morocco, Mozambique, Nicaragua, Niger, Nigeria, Oman, Pakistan, Peru,* Poland, Qatar, Rwanda, Sao Tome and Principe, Saudi Arabia, Senegal, Sierra Leone, Solomon Islands, Somalia, Sri Lanka, Sudan, Suriname, Syria, Togo, Tunisia, Turkey, Uganda, Ukraine, USSR, United Arab Emirates, United Republic of Tanzania, Vanuatu, Viet Nam, Yemen, Yugoslavia, Zambia, Zimbabwe.

Against: 29
Antigua and Barbuda, Australia, Belgium, Canada, Costa Rica, Denmark, El Salvador, Finland, France, Federal Republic of Germany, Grenada, Haiti, Honduras, Iceland, Ireland, Israel, Italy, Japan, Luxembourg, Netherlands, New Zealand, Norway, Portugal, Saint Lucia, Saint Vincent, St. Christopher and Nevis, Sweden, United Kingdom, United States.

Abstentions: 34
Argentina, Austria, Bahamas, Barbados, Belize, Bolivia, Brazil, Burma, Cameroon, Colombia, Dominican Republic, Ecuador, Egypt, Equatorial Guinea, Guatemala, Ivory Coast, Jamaica, Lesotho, Liberia, Malawi, Nepal, Panama, Papua New Guinea, Paraguay, Philippines, Samoa, Singapore, Spain, Swaziland, Thailand, Trinidad and Tobago, Uruguay, Venezuela, Zaire.

Absent: 5
Chile, Dominica, Fiji, Romania, Seychelles.

---

*Later advised the Secretariat it had intended to abstain.

---

[593]Carnegie Endowment for International Peace, *The Hague Conventions and Declarations of 1899 and 1907* (New York, Oxford University Press, 1915), p. 100.
[594]United Nations, *Treaty Series*, vol. 75, no. 973, p. 287.

C

The General Assembly,

Recalling its resolutions 36/120 E of 10 December 1981, 37/123 C of 16 December 1982, 38/180 C of 19 December 1983, 39/146 C of 14 December 1985 and 40/168 C of 16 December 1985, in which it determined that all legislative and administrative measures and actions taken by Israel, the occupying Power, which had altered or purported to alter the character and status of the Holy City of Jerusalem, in particular the so-called "Basic Law" on Jerusalem and the proclamation of Jerusalem as the capital of Israel, were null and void and must be rescinded forthwith,

Recalling Security Council resolution 478 (1980) of 20 August 1980, in which the Council, *inter alia,* decided not to recognize the "Basic Law" and called upon those States that had established diplomatic missions at Jerusalem to withdraw such missions from the Holy City,

Having considered the report of the Secretary-General of 18 November 1986,[595]

1. *Determines* that Israel's decision to impose its laws, jurisdiction and administration on the Holy City of Jerusalem is illegal and therefore null and void and has no validity whatsoever;

2. *Deplores* the transfer by some States of their diplomatic missions to Jerusalem in violation of Security Council resolution 478 (1980) and their refusal to comply with the provisions of that resolution;

3. *Calls once again upon* those States to abide by the provisions of the relevant United Nations resolutions, in conformity with the Charter of the United Nations;

4. *Requests* the Secretary-General to report to the General Assembly at its forty-second session on the implementation of the present resolution.

Adopted at the 97th plenary meeting:

In favour: 141

Afghanistan, Albania, Algeria, Angola, Argentina, Australia, Austria, Bahamas, Bahrain, Bangladesh, Barbados, Belgium, Belize, Benin, Bhutan, Bolivia, Botswana, Brazil, Brunei Darussalam, Bulgaria, Burkina Faso, Burma, Burundi, Byelorussia, Canada, Cape Verde, Central African Republic, Chad, Chile, China, Colombia, Comoros, Congo, Cuba, Cyprus, Czechoslovakia, Democratic Kampuchea, Democratic Yemen, Denmark, Djibouti, Dominican Republic, Ecuador, Egypt, Equatorial Guinea, Ethiopia, Finland, France, Gabon, Gambia, German Democratic Republic, Federal Republic of Germany, Ghana, Greece, Guinea, Guinea-Bissau, Guyana, Haiti, Hungary, Iceland, India, Indonesia, Iran, Iraq, Ireland, Italy, Ivory Coast, Jamaica, Japan, Jordan, Kenya, Kuwait, Lao People's Democratic Republic, Lebanon, Lesotho, Libya, Luxembourg, Madagascar, Malaysia, Maldives, Mali, Malta, Mauritania, Mauritius, Mexico, Mongolia, Morocco, Mozambique, Nepal, Netherlands, New Zealand, Nicaragua, Niger, Nigeria, Norway, Oman, Pakistan, Panama, Papua New Guinea, Paraguay, Peru, Philippines, Poland, Portu-

gal, Qatar, Romania, Rwanda, Samoa, Sao Tome and Principe, Saudi Arabia, Senegal, Sierra Leone, Singapore, Solomon Islands, Somalia, Spain, Sri Lanka, Sudan, Suriname, Swaziland, Sweden, Syria, Thailand, Togo, Trinidad and Tobago, Tunisia, Turkey, Uganda, Ukraine, USSR, United Arab Emirates, United Kingdom, United Republic of Tanzania, Uruguay, Vanuatu, Venezuela, Viet Nam, Yemen, Yugoslavia, Zaire, Zambia, Zimbabwe.

Against: 3

Costa Rica, El Salvador, Israel.

Abstentions: 11

Antigua and Barbuda, Cameroon, Grenada, Guatemala, Honduras, Liberia, Malawi, Saint Lucia, Saint Vincent, St. Christopher and Nevis, United States.

Absent: 3

Dominica, Fiji, Seychelles.

Resolution No. 41/179 A,B of 5 December 1986

ON THE FINANCING OF THE UNITED NATIONS INTERIM FORCE IN LEBANON

A

The General Assembly,

Having considered the report of the Secretary-General on the financing of the United Nations Interim Force in Lebanon[596] and the related report of the Advisory Committee on Administrative and Budgetary Questions,[597]

Bearing in mind Security Council resolutions 425 (1978) and 426 (1978) of 19 March 1978, 427 (1978) of 3 May 1978, 434 (1978) of 18 September 1978, 444 (1979) of 19 January 1979, 450 (1979) of 14 June 1979, 459 (1979) of 19 December 1979, 474 (1980) of 17 June 1980, 483 (1980) of 17 December 1980, 488 (1981) of 19 June 1981, 498 (1981) of 18 December 1981, 501 (1982) of 25 February 1982, 511 (1982) of 18 June 1982, 519 (1982) of 17 August 1982, 523 (1982) of 18 October 1982, 529 (1983) of 18 January 1983, 536 (1983) of 18 July 1983, 538 (1983) of 18 October 1983, 549 (1984) of 19 April 1984, 555 (1984) of 12 October 1984, 561 (1985) of 17 April 1985, 575 (1985) of 17 October 1984, 561 (1985) of 17 April 1985, 575 (1985) of 17 October 1985, 583 (1986) of 18 April 1986 and 586 (1986) of 18 July 1986,[598]

Recalling its resolutions S-8/2 of 21 April 1978, 33/14 of 3 November 1978, 34/9 B of 17 December 1979, 35/44 of 1 December 1980, 35/115 A of 10 December 1980, 36/138 A of 16 December 1981, 36/138 C of 19 March 1982, 37/127 A of 17 December 1982, 38/38 A of 5 December 1983, 39/71 A of 13 December 1984 and 40/246 A of 18 December 1985,

Reaffirming its previous decisions regarding the fact

---

[595]A/41/768-S/18427.

[596]A/41/783 and Corr.1.

[597]A/41/820.

[598]The resolutions cited in this paragraph and the next provide for the renewed mandate and financing of the United Nations Interim Force in Lebanon and (in 1978) for the withdrawal of Israeli forces from Lebanese territory. [ed. note]

that, in order to meet the expenditures caused by such operations, a different procedure from the one applied to meet expenditures of the regular budget of the United Nations is required,

Taking into account the fact that the economically more developed countries are in a position to make relatively larger contributions and that the economically less developed countries have a relatively limited capacity to contribute towards peace-keeping operations involving heavy expenditures,

Bearing in mind the special responsibilities of the States permanent members of the Security Council in the financing of peace-keeping operations decided upon in accordance with the Charter of the United Nations,

I

Decides to appropriate to the Special Account referred to in section I, paragraph 1, of General Assembly resolution S-8/2 an amount of $35,872,000 gross ($35,287,000 net), being the amount authorized with the prior concurrence of the Advisory Committee on Administrative and Budgetary Questions and apportioned under the provisions of section IV of Assembly resolution 40/246 A for the operation of the United Nations Interim Force in Lebanon from 19 April to 18 July 1986, inclusive;

II

Decides to appropriate to the Special Account an amount of $59,787,500 gross ($58,812,500 net), being the amount authorized with the prior concurrence of the Advisory Committee on Administrative and Budgetary Questions and apportioned under the provisions of section IV of Assembly resolution 40/246 A for the operation of the United Nations Interim Force in Lebanon from 19 July to 18 December 1986, inclusive;

III

1. *Decides* to appropriate to the Special Account an amount of $16,579,000 for the operation of the United Nations Interim Force in Lebanon for the period from 19 December 1986 to 18 January 1987, inclusive;

2. *Decides further*, as an *ad hoc* arrangement, without prejudice to the positions of principle that may be taken by Member States in any consideration by the General Assembly of arrangements for the financing of peace-keeping operations, to apportion the amount of $16,579,000 among Member States in accordance with the scheme set out in Assembly resolution 33/14 and the provisions of section V, paragraph 1, of resolution 34/9 B, section VI, paragraph 1, of resolution 35/115 A, section VI, paragraph 1, of resolution 36/138 A, section IX, paragraph 1, of resolution 37/127 A and section VII, paragraphs 1 and 2, of resolution 39/71 A, in the proportions determined by the scale of assessments for the years 1986, 1987 and 1988;

3. *Decides* that there shall be set off against the apportionment among Member States, as provided in paragraph 2 above, their respective share in the estimated income of $3,000 other than staff assessment income approved for the period from 19 December 1986 to 18 January 1987, inclusive;

4. *Decides* that, in accordance with the provisions of its resolution 973 (X) of 15 December 1955, there shall be set off against the apportionment among Member States, as provided for in paragraph 2 above, their respective share in the Tax Equalization Fund of the estimated staff assessment income of $192,000 approved for the period from 19 December 1986 to 18 January 1987, inclusive;

IV

Authorizes the Secretary-General to enter into commitments for the operation of the United Nations Interim Force in Lebanon at a rate not to exceed $12,125,000 gross ($11,922,000 net) per month for the 12-month period beginning 19 January 1987, should the Security Council decide to continue the Force beyond the period of six months authorized under its resolution 586 (1986), the said amount to be apportioned among Member States in accordance with the scheme set out in the present resolution;

V

1. *Renews its invitation* to Member States to make voluntary contributions to the United Nations Interim Force in Lebanon both in cash and in the form of services and supplies acceptable to the Secretary-General;

2. *Invites* Member States to make voluntary contributions in cash to the Suspense Account established in accordance with its resolution 34/9 D of 17 December 1979;

VI

Requests the Secretary-General to take all necessary action to ensure that the United Nations Interim Force in Lebanon shall be administered with a maximum of efficiency and economy.

Adopted at the 99th plenary meeting:
In favour: 125
Afghanistan, Antigua and Barbuda, Argentina, Australia, Austria, Bahrain, Bangladesh, Barbados, Belgium, Bhutan, Bolivia, Botswana, Brazil, Brunei Darussalam, Bulgaria, Burkina Faso, Burma, Burundi, Byelorussia, Cameroon, Canada, Cape Verde, Central African Republic, Chad, Chile, China, Colombia, Comoros, Congo, Costa Rica, Cyprus, Czechoslovakia, Democratic Kampuchea, Denmark, Djibouti, Dominican Republic, Ecuador, Egypt, Equatorial Guinea, Ethiopia, Fiji, Finland, France, Gabon, German Democratic Republic, Federal Republic of Germany, Ghana, Greece, Grenada, Guatemala, Guinea-Bissau, Guyana, Haiti, Honduras, Hungary, Iceland, India, Indonesia, Ireland, Israel, Italy, Ivory Coast, Jamaica, Japan, Jordan, Kenya, Kuwait, Lebanon, Lesotho, Liberia, Luxembourg, Malawi, Malaysia, Malta, Mauritania, Mauritius, Mexico, Mongolia, Morocco, Nepal, Netherlands, Niger, Nigeria, Norway, Oman, Pakistan, Panama, Paraguay, Peru, Philippines, Portugal, Romania, Rwanda, Saint Lucia, Saint Vincent, Samoa, Sao Tome and Principe, Saudi Arabia, Senegal, Sierra Leone, Singapore, Somalia, Spain, Sri Lanka, St. Christopher and Nevis,

Sudan, Suriname, Swaziland, Sweden, Thailand, Togo, Tunisia, Turkey, Uganda, Ukraine, USSR, United Arab Emirates, United Kingdom, United Republic of Tanzania, United States, Venezuela, Yugoslavia, Zaire, Zambia, Zimbabwe.

Against: 2

Albania, Syria.

Abstentions: 9

Angola, Cuba, Iraq, Lao People's Democratic Republic, Libya, Maldives, Poland, Viet Nam, Yemen.

Absent: 22

Algeria, Bahamas, Belize, Benin, Democratic Yemen, Dominica, El Salvador, Gambia, Guinea, Iran, Madagascar, Mali, Mozambique, New Zealand, Nicaragua, Papua New Guinea, Qatar,* Seychelles, Solomon Islands, Trinidad and Tobago, Uruguay, Vanuatu.

---

*Later advised the Secretariat it had intended to vote in favour.

B

The General Assembly,

Having regard to the financial position of the Special Account for the United Nations Interim Force in Lebanon, as set forth in the report of the Secretary-General,[599] and referring to paragraph 18 of the report of the Advisory Committee on Administrative and Budgetary Questions,[600]

Mindful of the fact that it is essential to provide the United Nations Interim Force in Lebanon with the necessary financial resources to enable it to fulfil its responsibilities under the relevant resolutions of the Security Council,

Concerned that the Secretary-General is continuing to face growing difficulties in meeting the obligations of the United Nations Interim Force in Lebanon on a current basis, particularly those due to the Governments of troop-contributing States,

Recognizing that, in consequence of the shortfall of financial contributions, troop-contributing States are not being reimbursed to the full extent of the established rates, thus bearing considerably larger portions of the costs for their troops serving in the United Nations peacekeeping forces than those indicated by the Secretary-General in his report to the fortieth session,[601]

Recalling its resolutions 34/9 E of 17 December 1979, 35/115 B of 10 December 1980, 36/138 B of 16 December 1981, 37/127 B of 17 December 1982, 38/38 B of 5 December 1983, 39/71 B of 13 December 1984 and 40/246 B of 18 December 1985,

Recognizing that, in consequence of the withholding of contributions by certain Member States, the surplus balances in the Special Account for the United Nations Interim Force in Lebanon have, in effect, been drawn upon

to the full extent to supplement the income received from contributions for meeting expenses of the Force,

Concerned that the application of the provisions of regulations 5.2 (*b*), 5.2 (*d*), 4.3 and 4.4 of the Financial Regulations of the United Nations would aggravate the already difficult financial situation of the United Nations Interim Force in Lebanon,

Decides that the provisions of regulations 5.2 (*b*), 5.2 (*d*), 4.3 and 4.4 of the Financial Regulations of the United Nations shall be suspended in respect of the amount of $4,763,620, which otherwise would have to be surrendered pursuant to those provisions, this amount to be entered in the account referred to in the operative part of General Assembly resolution 34/9 E and held in suspense until a further decision is taken by the Assembly.

Adopted at the 99th plenary meeting:

In favour: 116

Antigua and Barbuda, Argentina, Australia, Austria, Bahrain, Bangladesh, Barbados, Belgium, Bhutan, Bolivia, Botswana, Brazil, Brunei Darussalam, Burkina Faso, Burma, Burundi, Cameroon, Canada, Cape Verde, Central African Republic, Chad, Chile, China, Colombia, Comoros, Congo, Costa Rica, Côte d'Ivoire, Cyprus, Democratic Kampuchea, Denmark, Djibouti, Dominican Republic, Ecuador, Egypt, Equatorial Guinea, Ethiopia, Fiji, Finland, France, Gabon, Federal Republic of Germany, Ghana, Greece, Grenada, Guatemala, Guinea-Bissau, Guyana, Haiti, Honduras, Iceland, India, Indonesia, Ireland, Israel, Italy, Jamaica, Japan, Kenya, Kuwait, Lebanon, Lesotho, Liberia, Luxembourg, Malawi, Malaysia, Malta, Mauritania, Mauritius, Mexico, Morocco, Nepal, Netherlands, New Zealand, Niger, Nigeria, Norway, Oman, Pakistan, Panama, Paraguay, Peru, Philippines, Portugal, Rwanda, Saint Lucia, Saint Vincent, Samoa, Sao Tome and Principe, Saudi Arabia, Senegal, Sierra Leone, Singapore, Somalia, Spain, Sri Lanka, St. Christopher and Nevis, Sudan, Suriname, Swaziland, Sweden, Thailand, Togo, Tunisia, Turkey, Uganda, United Arab Emirates, United Kingdom, United Republic of Tanzania, United States, Uruguay, Venezuela, Yugoslavia, Zaire, Zambia, Zimbabwe.

Against: 2

Albania, Syria.

Abstentions: 19

Afghanistan, Angola, Bulgaria, Byelorussia, Cuba, Czechoslovakia, German Democratic Republic, Hungary, Iraq, Lao People's Democratic Republic, Libya, Maldives, Mongolia, Poland, Romania, Ukraine, USSR, Viet Nam, Yemen.

Absent: 21

Algeria, Bahamas, Belize, Benin, Democratic Yemen, Dominica, El Salvador, Gambia, Guinea, Iran, Jordan,* Madagascar, Mali, Mozambique, Nicaragua, Papua New Guinea, Qatar,* Seychelles, Solomon Islands, Trinidad and Tobago,* Vanuatu.

---

*Later advised the Secretariat it had intended to vote in favour.

---

[599]A/41/783 and Corr.1.

[600]A/41/820.

[601]A/40/845.

Resolution No. 41/181 of 8 December 1986

REQUESTING THE INTERNATIONAL COMMUNITY TO PROVIDE ASSISTANCE TO THE PALESTINIAN PEOPLE IN CO-OPERATION WITH THE PALESTINE LIBERATION ORGANIZATION

The General Assembly,

Recalling its resolution 40/170 of 17 December 1985,

Recalling also Economic and Social Council resolution 1986/49 of 22 July 1986,

Recalling further the Programme of Action for the Achievement of Palestinian Rights, adopted by the International Conference on the Question of Palestine,[602]

Noting that the programme of economic and social assistance to the Palestinian people requested in General Assembly resolution 38/145 of 19 December 1983 has not been prepared,

Noting the increasing need to provide economic and social assistance to the Palestinian people,

1. *Takes note* of the report of the Secretary-General on assistance to the Palestinian people;[603]

2. *Welcomes* the decision of the Secretary-General to send a mission to prepare the programme of economic and social assistance to the Palestinian people requested in General Assembly resolution 38/145;

3. *Notes* the meeting on assistance to the Palestinian people held at Geneva on 2 July 1986 in response to General Assembly resolution 40/170;[604]

4. *Expresses its thanks* to the Secretary-General for convening the meeting on assistance to the Palestinian people;

5. *Regards* such a meeting as a valuable opportunity to assess progress in economic and social assistance to the Palestinian people and to explore ways and means of enhancing such assistance;

6. *Urges* the international community, the United Nations system and intergovernmental and non-governmental organizations to disburse their aid or any other form of assistance to the occupied Palestinian territories only for the benefit of the Palestinian people and in a manner that will not serve to prolong the Israeli occupation;

7. *Requests* the Secretary-General;

(*a*) To convene in 1987 a meeting of the relevant programmes, organizations, agencies, funds and organs of the United Nations system to consider economic and social assistance to the Palestinian people;

(*b*) To invite the Palestine Liberation Organization, the Arab host countries and relevant intergovernmental and non-governmental organizations to participate in the meeting;

8. *Requests* the international community, the United Nations system and intergovernmental and non-governmental organizations to sustain and increase their assistance to the Palestinian people in co-operation with the Palestine Liberation Organization;

9. *Also requests* that United Nations assistance to the Palestinians in the Arab host countries should be rendered in co-operation with the Palestine Liberation Organization with the consent of the Arab host Government concerned;

10. *Requests* the Secretary-General to report to the General Assembly at its forty-second session, through the Economic and Social Council, on the progress made in the implementation of the present resolution.

Adopted at the 100th plenary meeting:

In favour: 142

Afghanistan, Albania, Algeria, Angola, Antigua and Barbuda, Argentina, Australia, Austria, Bahamas, Bahrain, Bangladesh, Barbados, Belgium, Bhutan, Bolivia, Botswana, Brazil, Brunei Darussalam, Bulgaria, Burkina Faso, Burma, Burundi, Byelorussia, Cameroon, Canada, Cape Verde, Central African Republic, Chad, Chile, China, Colombia, Côte d'Ivoire, Cuba, Czechoslovakia, Democratic Kampuchea, Democratic Yemen, Denmark, Djibouti, Dominican Republic, Ecuador, Egypt, El Salvador, Equatorial Guinea, Ethiopia, Fiji, Finland, France, Gabon, German Democratic Republic, Federal Republic of Germany, Ghana, Greece, Grenada, Guatemala, Guinea, Guinea-Bissau, Guyana, Haiti, Honduras, Hungary, Iceland, India, Indonesia, Iran, Iraq, Ireland, Italy, Jamaica, Japan, Jordan, Kenya, Kuwait, Lao People's Democratic Republic, Lebanon, Lesotho, Liberia, Libya, Luxemboug, Madagascar, Malawi, Malaysia, Maldives, Mali, Malta, Mauritania, Mauritius, Mexico, Morocco, Mozambique, Nepal, Netherlands, New Zealand, Nicaragua, Niger, Nigeria, Norway, Oman, Pakistan, Panama, Paraguay, Peru, Philippines, Poland, Portugal, Qatar, Romania, Rwanda, Saint Lucia, Saint Vincent, Samoa, Sao Tome and Principe, Saudi Arabia, Senegal, Sierra Leone, Singapore, Solomon Islands, Somalia, Spain, Sri Lanka, Sudan, Suriname, Swaziland, Sweden, Syria, Thailand, Togo, Trinidad and Tobago, Tunisia, Turkey, Uganda, Ukraine, USSR, United Arab Emirates, United Kingdom, United Republic of Tanzania, Uruguay, Vanuatu, Venezuela, Viet Nam, Yemen, Yugoslavia, Zambia.

Against: 2

Israel, United States.

Abstention: 1

Costa Rica.

Absent: 13

Belize, Benin, Comoros, Congo, Cyprus, Dominica, Gambia, Mongolia, Papua New Guinea, Seychelles, St. Christopher and Nevis, Zaire, Zimbabwe.

Resolution No. 41/196 of 8 December 1986

REQUESTING ASSISTANCE FOR THE RECONSTRUCTION AND DEVELOPMENT OF LEBANON

The General Assembly,

Recalling its resolutions 33/146 of 20 December 1978, 34/135 of 14 December 1979, 35/85 of 5 December 1980, 36/205 of 17 December 1981, 37/163 of 17 December 1982, 38/220 of 20 December 1983, 39/197 of 17 Decem-

---

[602]*Report of the International Conference on the Question of Palestine, Geneva, 29 August-7 September 1983* (United Nations publication, Sales No. E.83.I.21), chap. I, sect. B.

[603]A/41/319-E/1986/72 and Corr.1 and Add.1-2.

[604]See A/41/319/Add.1-E/1986/72/Add.1.

ber 1984 and 40/229 of 17 December 1985,

Recalling also Economic and Social Council resolutions 1980/15 of 29 April 1980, 1985/56 of 25 July 1985 and 1986/46 of 22 July 1986, and decisions 1983/112 of 17 May 1983 and 1984/174 of 26 July 1984,

Noting with deep concern the continuing heavy loss of life and the additional destruction of property, which have caused further extensive damage to the economic and social structures of Lebanon,

Noting with concern the serious economic situation in Lebanon,

Welcoming the determined efforts of the Government of Lebanon in undertaking its reconstruction and rehabilitation programme,

Reaffirming the urgent need for further international action to assist the Government of Lebanon in its continuing efforts for reconstruction and development,

Considering that filling the vacant post of United Nations Co-ordinator of Assistance for the Reconstruction and Development of Lebanon would facilitate the normal operations of international assistance to Lebanon,

Taking note of the report of the Secretary-General[605] and of the statement made on 22 October 1986 by the Under-Secretary-General for Political and General Assembly Affairs,[606]

1. *Expresses its appreciation* to the Secretary-General for his report[607] and for the steps he has taken to mobilize assistance to Lebanon;

2. *Commends* the Under-Secretary-General for Political and General Assembly Affairs for his co-ordination of system-wide assistance for Lebanon;

3. *Commends further* the efforts undertaken by the Government of Lebanon in the implementation of the initial phase of reconstruction of the country, despite adverse circumstances, and of the steps it has taken to remedy the economic situation;

4. *Requests* the Secretary-General, in accordance with the provisions of General Assembly resolution 41/192, to continue and intensify his efforts to mobilize all possible assistance within the United Nations system to help the Government of Lebanon in its reconstruction and development efforts;

5. *Invites* the Secretary-General to consider the urgent need to nominate a United Nations Co-ordinator of Assistance for the Reconstruction and Development of Lebanon and the implementation of his functions therein;

6. *Requests* the organs, organizations and bodies of the United Nations system to intensify their programmes of assistance and to expand them in response to the needs of Lebanon, and to take the necessary steps to ensure that their offices at Beirut are adequately staffed at the senior level;

7. *Requests* the Secretary-General to report to the General Assembly at its forty-second session on the progress made in the implementation of the present resolution.

Adopted at the 100th plenary meeting without a vote.

---

[605]A/41/679.
[606]A/C.2/41/SR.19.
[607]A/41/679.

II. RESOLUTIONS OF THE SECURITY COUNCIL

Resolution No. 500 (1982) of 28 January 1982

DECIDING TO CALL AN EMERGENCY SPECIAL SESSION OF THE GENERAL ASSEMBLY TO EXAMINE THE SITUATION IN THE OCCUPIED ARAB TERRITORIES

The Security Council,

Having considered the item on the agenda of its 2329th meeting, as contained in document S/Agenda/2329/Rev.1,[1]

Taking into account that the lack of unanimity of its permanent members at the 2329th meeting has prevented it from exercising its primary responsibility for the maintenance of international peace and security,

Decides to call an emergency special session of the General Assembly to examine the question contained in document S/Agenda/2329/Rev.1.

Adopted at the 2330th meeting:
In favour: 13
China, France, Guyana, Ireland, Japan, Jordan, Panama, Poland, Spain, Togo, Uganda, USSR, Zaire.
Against: 0
Abstentions: 2
United Kingdom, United States.

Resolution No. 501 (1982) of 25 February 1982

CALLING UPON ISRAEL TO CEASE MILITARY ACTION IN LEBANON IMMEDIATELY AND WITHDRAW ITS FORCES FROM LEBANESE TERRITORY AND DECIDING TO APPROVE AN IMMEDIATE INCREASE IN THE STRENGTH OF UNIFIL

The Security Council,

Recalling its resolutions 425 (1978), 426 (1978), 427 (1978), 434 (1978), 444 (1979), 450 (1979), 459 (1979), 467 (1980), 474 (1980), 483 (1980), 488 (1981), 490 (1981) and 498 (1981),[2]

Acting in accordance with its resolution 498 (1981), and in particular with paragraph 10 of that resolution in which it decided to review the situation as a whole,

Having studied the special report of the Secretary-General on the United Nations Interim Force in Lebanon,[3]

Taking note of the letter of the Permanent Representative of Lebanon to the President of the Security Council,[4]

Having reviewed the situation as a whole in the light of the report of the Secretary-General and of the letter of the Permanent Representative of Lebanon,

Noting from the report of the Secretary-General that it is the strong recommendation of the Commander of the United Nations Interim Force in Lebanon, and also the wish of the Government of Lebanon, that the ceiling for troops of the Force should be increased, and that the Secretary-General fully supports the recommendation for an increase by one thousand of the troop strength of the Force,

1. *Reaffirms* its resolution 425 (1978) which reads:
"*The Security Council,*
"*Taking note* of the letters from the Permanent Representative of Lebanon[5] and from the Permanent Representative of Israel,[6]
"*Having heard* the statements of the Permanent Representatives of Lebanon and Israel,[7]
"*Gravely concerned* at the deterioration of the situation in the Middle East and its consequences to the maintenance of international peace,
"*Convinced* that the present situation impedes the achievement of a just peace in the Middle East,
"1. *Calls* for the strict respect for the territorial integrity, sovereignty and political independence of Lebanon within its internationally recognized boundaries;
"2. *Calls upon* Israel immediately to cease its military action against Lebanese territorial integrity and withdraw forthwith its forces from all Lebanese territory;
"3. *Decides,* in the light of the request of the Government of Lebanon, to establish immediately under its authority a United Nations interim force for southern Lebanon for the purpose of confirming the withdrawal of Israeli forces, restoring international peace and security and assisting the Government of Lebanon in ensuring the return of its effective authority in the area, the force to be composed of personnel drawn from Member States;
"4. *Requests* the Secretary-General to report to the Council within twenty-four hours on the implementation of the present resolution."

2. *Decides* to approve the immediate increase in the strength of the United Nations Interim Force in Lebanon recommended by the Secretary-General in paragraph 6 of his report,[8] from six thousand to approximately seven thousand troops, to reinforce present operations as well as to make further deployment possible on the lines of resolution 425 (1978);

3. *Re-emphasizes* the terms of reference and general guidelines of the Force as stated in the report of the Secretary-General of 19 March 1978[9] confirmed by resolution 426 (1978), and particularly:

(a) That the Force "must be able to function as an integrated and efficient military unit";

---

[1]Concerning the situation in the occupied Arab territories. [ed. note]
[2]These resolutions focus upon different aspects of the situation in Lebanon. Resolution 425 calls for Israel to cease military actions in Lebanon and to withdraw its forces from Lebanese territory. It also provides for the establishment of the United Nations Interim Force in Lebanon (UNIFIL). Resolution 427 calls for the withdrawal of Israeli forces from Lebanon, and Resolutions 450 and 467 call for an end to Israeli assistance to armed groups in the country. Resolution 490 calls for a cease-fire. Resolutions 434, 444, 450, 459, 474, 483, 488 and 498 provide for the financing and extension of the mandate of UNIFIL. [ed. note]
[3]*Official Records of the Security Council, Thirty-seventh Year, Supplement for January, February and March 1982,* document S/14869.
[4]*Ibid.,* document S/14875.

[5]*Ibid., Thirty-third Year, Supplement for January, February and March 1978,* documents S/12600 and S/12606.
[6]*Ibid.,* document S/12607.
[7]*Ibid., Thirty-third Year,* 2071st meeting.
[8]*Official Records of the Security Council, Thirty-seventh Year, Supplement for January, February and March 1982,* document S/14869.
[9]*Ibid., Thirty-third Year, Supplement for January, February and March 1978,* document S/12611.

(b) That the Force "must enjoy the freedom of movement and communication and other facilities that are necessary to the performance of its tasks";

(c) That the Force "will not use force except in self-defence";

(d) That "self-defence would include resistance to attempts by forceful means to prevent it from discharging its duties under the mandate of the Security Council";

4. *Calls upon* the Secretary-General to renew his efforts to reactivate the General Armistice Agreement between Lebanon and Israel of 23 March 1949[10] and, in particular, to convene an early meeting of the Mixed Armistice Commission;

5. *Requests* the Secretary-General to continue his discussions with the Government of Lebanon and the parties concerned with a view to submitting a report by 10 June 1982 on the necessary requirements for achieving further progress in a phased programme of activities with the Government of Lebanon;

6. *Decides* to remain seized of the question and invites the Secretary-General to report to the Security Council on the situation as a whole within two months.

Adopted at the 2332nd meeting:

In favour: 13

China, France, Guyana, Ireland, Japan, Jordan, Panama, Spain, Togo, Uganda, United Kingdom, United States, Zaire.

Against: 0

Abstentions: 2

Poland, USSR.

Resolution No. 506 (1982) of 26 May 1982

RENEWING THE MANDATE OF THE UNITED NATIONS DISENGAGEMENT OBSERVER FORCE UNTIL 30 NOVEMBER 1982[11]

The Security Council,

Having considered the report of the Secretary-General on the United Nations Disengagement Observer Force,[12]

Decides:

(a) To call upon the parties concerned to implement immediately Security Council resolution 338 (1973);[13]

(b) To renew the mandate of the United Nations Disengagement Observer Force for another period of six months, that is, until 30 November 1982;

(c) To request the Secretary-General to submit, at the end of this period, a report on the developments in the

situation and the measures taken to implement resolution 338 (1973).

Adopted unanimously at the 2369th meeting.

Resolution No. 508 (1982) of 5 June 1982

CALLING FOR AN IMMEDIATE CEASE-FIRE IN LEBANON AND ACROSS THE LEBANESE-ISRAELI BORDER

The Security Council,

Recalling its resolutions 425 (1978), 426 (1978) and its ensuing resolutions and, more particularly, resolution 501 (1982),[14]

Taking note of the letters of the Permanent Representative of Lebanon dated 4 June 1982,[15]

Deeply concerned at the deterioration of the present situation in Lebanon and in the Lebanese-Israeli border area, and its consequences for peace and security in the region,

Gravely concerned at the violation of the territorial integrity, independence and sovereignty of Lebanon,

Reaffirming and supporting the statement made by the President and the members of the Security Council on 4 June 1982,[16] as well as the urgent appeal issued by the Secretary-General on 4 June 1982,

Taking note of the report of the Secretary-General,[17]

1. *Calls upon* all the parties to the conflict to cease immediately and simultaneously all military activities within Lebanon and across the Lebanese-Israeli border and not later than 0600 hours, local time, on Sunday, 6 June 1982;

2. *Requests* all Member States which are in a position to do so to bring their influence to bear upon those concerned so that the cessation of hostilities declared by Security Council resolution 490 (1981) can be respected;

3. *Requests* the Secretary-General to undertake all possible efforts to ensure the implementation of and compliance with the present resolution and to report to the Security Council as early as possible and not later than forty-eight hours after the adoption of the present resolution.

Adopted unanimously at the 2374th meeting.

Resolution No. 509 (1982) of 6 June 1982

DEMANDING THAT ISRAEL WITHDRAW ITS MILITARY FORCES FROM LEBANON FORTHWITH AND UNCONDITIONALLY

The Security Council,

Recalling its resolutions 425 (1978) and 508 (1982),

Gravely concerned at the situation as described by the Secretary-General in his report to the Council,[18]

---

[10]*Ibid., Fourth Year, Special Supplement No. 4.*

[11]The United Nations Disengagement Observer Force (UNDOF) between Israeli and Syrian forces in the Golan Heights was established by virtue of Security Council Resolution No. 350 (1974) for an initial period of six months, subject to renewal by further resolution of the Security Council. [ed. note]

[12]*Official Records of the Security Council, Thirty-seventh Year, Supplement for April, May and June 1982,* document S/15079.

[13]This resolution was passed on 22 October 1973, and called for a cease-fire in the Middle East and the implementation of Security Council Resolution 242 of 1967. [ed. note]

---

[14]Calling for the withdrawal of Israeli forces from Lebanon. [ed. note]

[15]*Official Records of the Security Council, Thirty-seventh Year, Supplement for April, May and June 1982,* documents S/15161 and S/15162.

[16]S/15163.

[17]*Ibid., Thirty-seventh Year,* 2374th meeting.

[18]*Ibid.,* 2375th meeting.

Reaffirming the need for strict respect for the territorial integrity, sovereignty and political independence of Lebanon within its internationally recognized boundaries,

1. *Demands* that Israel withdraw all its military forces forthwith and unconditionally to the internationally recognized boundaries of Lebanon;

2. *Demands* that all parties observe strictly the terms of paragraph 1 of resolution 508 (1982) which called on them to cease immediately and simultaneously all military activities within Lebanon and across the Lebanese-Israeli border;

3. *Calls* on all parties to communicate to the Secretary-General their acceptance of the present resolution within twenty-four hours;

4. *Decides* to remain seized of the question.

Adopted unanimously at the 2375th meeting.

Resolution No. 511 of 18 June 1982

EXTENDING THE MANDATE OF THE UNITED NATIONS INTERIM FORCE IN LEBANON UNTIL 19 AUGUST 1982

The Security Council,

Recalling its resolutions 425 (1978), 426 (1978), 427 (1978), 434 (1978), 444 (1979), 450 (1979), 459 (1979), 467 (1980), 483 (1980), 488 (1981), 490 (1981), 498 (1981) and 501 (1982),[19]

Reaffirming its resolutions 508 (1982) and 509 (1982),

Having studied the report of the Secretary-General on the United Nations Interim Force in Lebanon[20] and taking note of the conclusions and recommendations expressed therein,

Bearing in mind the need to avoid any developments which could further aggravate the situation and the need, pending an examination of the situation by the Security Council in all its aspects, to preserve in place the capacity of the United Nations to assist in the restoration of the peace,

1. *Decides,* as an interim measure, to extend the present mandate of the United Nations Interim Force in Lebanon for a period of two months, that is, until 19 August 1982;

2. *Authorizes* the Force during that period to carry out, in addition, the interim tasks referred to in paragraph 17 of the report of the Secretary-General on the Force;[21]

3. *Calls on* all concerned to extend full co-operation to the Force in the discharge of its tasks;

4. *Requests* the Secretary-General to keep the Security Council regularly informed of the implementation of resolutions 508 (1982) and 509 (1982) and the present resolution.

Adopted at the 2379th meeting:
In favour: 13
China, France, Guyana, Ireland, Japan, Jordan, Panama, Spain, Togo, Uganda, United Kingdom, United States, Zaire.
Against: 0
Abstentions: 2
Poland, USSR.

Resolution No. 512 (1982) of 19 June 1982

CALLING UPON PARTIES TO THE CONFLICT IN LEBANON TO RESPECT THE RIGHTS AND ALLEVIATE THE SUFFERING OF THE CIVILIAN POPULATION IN LEBANON

The Security Council,

Deeply concerned at the sufferings of the Lebanese and Palestinian civilian populations,

Referring to the humanitarian principles of the Geneva Conventions of 1949[22] and to the obligations arising from the regulations annexed to The Hague Convention of 1907,[23]

Reaffirming its resolutions 508 (1982) and 509 (1982),

1. *Calls upon* all the parties to the conflict to respect the rights of the civilian populations, to refrain from all acts of violence against those populations and to take all appropriate measures to alleviate the suffering caused by the conflict, in particular, by facilitating the dispatch and distribution of aid provided by United Nations agencies and by non-governmental organizations, in particular, the International Committee of the Red Cross;

2. *Appeals* to Member States to continue to provide the most extensive humanitarian aid possible;

3. *Stresses* the particular humanitarian responsibilities of the United Nations and its agencies, including the United Nations Relief and Works Agency for Palestine Refugees in the Near East, towards civilian populations and calls upon all the parties to the conflict not to hamper the exercise of those responsibilities and to assist in humanitarian efforts;

4. *Takes note* of the measures taken by the Secretary-General to co-ordinate the activities of the international agencies in this field and requests him to make every effort to ensure the implementation of and compliance with the present resolution and to report on these efforts to the Security Council as soon as possible.

Adopted unanimously at the 2380th meeting.

Resolution No. 513 (1982) of 4 July 1982

CALLING FOR RESPECT FOR THE RIGHTS OF THE CIVILIAN POPULATION IN LEBANON

---

[19]Most of these resolutions provide for the financing and renewal of mandate of UNIFIL. The remainder deal with different episodes of conflict in the country: Resolution 425 calls for Israel to cease military actions in Lebanon and to withdraw its forces from Lebanese territory; Resolution 427 calls for the withdrawal of Israeli forces from Lebanon; and Resolutions 450 and 467 call for an end to Israeli assistance to armed groups in the country. [ed. note]

[20]*Official Records of the Security Council, Thirty-seventh Year, Supplement for April, May and June 1982,* documents S/15194 and Add. 1 and 2.

[21]*Ibid.,* document S/15194/Add.2.

[22]United Nations, *Treaty Series,* vol. 75, nos. 970-973.

[23]Carnegie Endowment for International Peace, *The Hague Conventions and Declarations of 1899 and 1907* (New York, Oxford University Press, 1915).

The Security Council,

Alarmed by the continued sufferings of the Lebanese and Palestinian civilian populations in southern Lebanon and in west Beirut,

Referring to the humanitarian principles of the Geneva Conventions of 1949[24] and to the obligations arising from the regulations annexed to The Hague Convention of 1907,[25]

Reaffirming its resolutions 508 (1982), 509 (1982) and 512 (1982),

1. *Calls* for respect for the rights of the civilian populations without any discrimination and repudiates all acts of violence against those populations;

2. *Calls further* for the restoration of the normal supply of vital facilities such as water, electricity, food and medical provisions, particularly in Beirut;

3. *Commends* the efforts of the Secretary-General and the action of international agencies to alleviate the sufferings of the civilian population and requests them to continue their efforts to ensure their success.

Adopted unanimously at the 2382nd meeting.

Resolution No. 515 (1982) of 29 July 1982

DEMANDING THAT ISRAEL LIFT ITS BLOCKADE OF BEIRUT IMMEDIATELY

The Security Council,

Deeply concerned at the situation of the civilian population of Beirut,

Referring to the humanitarian principles of the Geneva Conventions of 1949[26] and to the obligations arising from the regulations annexed to The Hague Convention of 1907,[27]

Recalling its resolutions 512 (1982) and 513 (1982),

1. *Demands* that the Government of Israel lift immediately the blockade of the city of Beirut in order to permit the dispatch of supplies to meet the urgent needs of the civilian population and allow the distribution of aid provided by United Nations agencies and by non-governmental organizations, particularly the International Committee of the Red Cross;

2. *Requests* the Secretary-General to transmit the text of the present resolution to the Government of Israel and to keep the Security Council informed of its implementation.

Adopted at the 2385th meeting:
In favour: 14
China, France, Guyana, Ireland, Japan, Jordan, Panama, Poland, Spain, Togo, Uganda, USSR, United Kingdom,

Zaire.
Against: 0
Not participating in the vote: 1
United States.

Resolution No. 516 (1982) of 1 August 1982

DEMANDING AN IMMEDIATE CEASE-FIRE IN LEBANON AND ACROSS THE LEBANESE-ISRAELI BORDER

The Security Council,

Reaffirming its resolutions 508 (1982), 509 (1982), 511 (1982), 512 (1982) and 513 (1982),

Recalling its resolution 515 (1982),

Alarmed by the continuation and intensification of military activities in and around Beirut,

Taking note of the latest massive violations of the cease-fire in and around Beirut,

1. *Confirms* its previous resolutions and demands an immediate cease-fire, and a cessation of all military activities within Lebanon and across the Lebanese-Israeli border;

2. *Authorizes* the Secretary-General to deploy immediately, on the request of the Government of Lebanon, United Nations observers to monitor the situation in and around Beirut;

3. *Requests* the Secretary-General to report back to the Security Council on compliance with the present resolution as soon as possible and not later than four hours from now.

Adopted unanimously at the 2386th meeting.

Resolution No. 517 (1982) of 4 August 1982

CONFIRMING A PREVIOUS DEMAND FOR AN IMMEDIATE CEASE-FIRE AND ISRAELI WITHDRAWAL FROM LEBANON

The Security Council,

Deeply shocked and alarmed by the deplorable consequences of the Israeli invasion of Beirut on 3 August 1982,

1. *Reconfirms* its resolutions 508 (1982), 509 (1982), 512 (1982), 513 (1982), 515 (1982) and 516 (1982);

2. *Confirms once again* its demand for an immediate cease-fire and withdrawal of Israeli forces from Lebanon;

3. *Censures* Israel for its failure to comply with the above resolutions;

4. *Calls* for the prompt return of Israeli troops which have moved forward subsequent to 1325 hours, eastern daylight time, on 1 August 1982;

5. *Takes note* of the decision of the Palestine Liberation Organization to move the Palestinian armed forces from Beirut;

6. *Expresses its appreciation* for the efforts and steps taken by the Secretary-General to implement the provisions of resolution 516 (1982) and authorizes him, as an immediate step, to increase the number of United Nations observers in and around Beirut;

7. *Requests* the Secretary-General to report to the Security Council on the implementation of the present resolu-

---

[24]United Nations, *Treaty Series,* vol. 75, nos. 970-973.

[25]Carnegie Endowment for International Peace, *The Hague Conventions and Declarations of 1899 and 1907* (New York, Oxford University Press, 1915).

[26]United Nations, *Treaty Series,* vol. 75, nos. 970-973.

[27]Carnegie Endowment for International Peace, *The Hague Conventions and Declarations of 1899 and 1907* (New York, Oxford University Press, 1915).

tion as soon as possible and not later than 1000 hours, eastern daylight time, on 5 August 1982;

8. *Decides* to meet at that time, if necessary, in order to consider the report of the Secretary-General and, in case of failure to comply by any of the parties to the conflict, to consider adopting effective ways and means in accordance with the provisions of the Charter of the United Nations.

Adopted at the 2389th meeting:
In favour: 14
China, France, Guyana, Ireland, Japan, Jordan, Panama, Poland, Spain, Togo, Uganda, USSR, United Kingdom, Zaire.
Against: 0
Abstention: 1
United States.

Resolution No. 518 (1982) of 12 August 1982

DEMANDING THAT ISRAEL AND ALL PARTIES TO THE CONFLICT CEASE MILITARY ACTIVITIES AND THAT RESTRICTIONS ON SUPPLIES TO BEIRUT BE LIFTED IMMEDIATELY

The Security Council,
Recalling its resolutions 508 (1982), 509 (1982), 511 (1982), 512 (1982), 513 (1982), 515 (1982), 516 (1982) and 517 (1982),

Expressing its most serious concern about continued military activities in Lebanon and, particularly, in and around Beirut,

1. *Demands* that Israel and all parties to the conflict observe strictly the terms of Security Council resolutions relevant to the immediate cessation of all military activities within Lebanon and, particularly, in and around Beirut;

2. *Demands* the immediate lifting of all restrictions on the city of Beirut in order to permit the free entry of supplies to meet the urgent needs of the civilian population in Beirut;

3. *Requests* the United Nations observers in, and in the vicinity of, Beirut to report on the situation;

4. *Demands* that Israel co-operate fully in the effort to secure the effective deployment of the United Nations observers, as requested by the Government of Lebanon, and in such a manner as to ensure their safety;

5. *Requests* the Secretary-General to report as soon as possible to the Security Council on the implementation of the present resolution;

6. *Decides* to meet, if necessary, in order to consider the situation upon receipt of the report of the Secretary-General.

Adopted unanimously at the 2392nd meeting.

Resolution No. 519 (1982) of 17 August 1982

EXTENDING THE MANDATE OF THE UNITED NATIONS INTERIM FORCE IN LEBANON UNTIL 19 OCTOBER 1982

The Security Council,

Recalling its resolutions 425 (1978), 426 (1978), 427 (1978), 434 (1978), 444 (1979), 450 (1979), 459 (1979), 467 (1980), 483 (1980), 488 (1981), 490 (1981), 498 (1981), 501 (1982) and 511 (1982),[28]

Reaffirming its resolutions 508 (1982) and 509 (1982), as well as subsequent resolutions on the situation in Lebanon,

Having studied with grave concern the report of the Secretary-General on the United Nations Interim Force in Lebanon[29] and noting its conclusions and recommendations and the wishes of the Government of Lebanon as set out therein,

Bearing in mind the need, pending an examination by the Security Council of the situation in all its aspects, to preserve in place the capacity of the United Nations to assist in the restoration of the peace and of the authority of the Government of Lebanon throughout Lebanon,

1. *Decides* to extend the present mandate of the United Nations Interim Force in Lebanon for a further interim period of two months, that is, until 19 October 1982;

2. *Authorizes* the Force during that period to continue to carry out, in addition, the interim tasks in the humanitarian and administrative fields assigned to it in paragraph 2 of resolution 511 (1982);

3. *Calls on* all concerned, taking into account paragraphs 5, 8, and 9 of the report of the Secretary-General on the Force, to extend full co-operation to it in the discharge of its tasks;

4. *Supports* the efforts of the Secretary-General, with a view to optimum use of observers of the United Nations Truce Supervision Organization, as envisaged by relevant resolutions of the Security Council;

5. *Decides* to consider the situation fully and in all its aspects before 19 October 1982.

Adopted at the 2393rd meeting:
In favour: 13
China, France, Guyana, Ireland, Japan, Jordan, Panama, Spain, Togo, Uganda, United Kingdom, United States, Zaire.
Against: 0
Abstentions: 2
Poland, USSR.

Resolution No. 520 (1982) of 17 September 1982

CONDEMNING ISRAELI INCURSIONS INTO BEIRUT IN VIOLATION OF THE CEASE-FIRE AGREEMENTS AND DEMANDING ISRAEL'S RETURN TO ITS PREVIOUS POSITIONS

The Security Council,
Having considered the report of the Secretary-General of 15 September 1982,[30]

Condemning the murder of Bashir Gemayel, the constitutionally elected President-elect of Lebanon, and every

---

[28]See note 19 above.
[29]*Official Records of the Security Council Thirty-seventh Year, Supplement for July, August and September 1982*, document S/15357.
[30]*Ibid.*, document S/15382/Add.1.

effort to disrupt by violence the restoration of a strong, stable government in Lebanon,

Having listened to the statement by the Permanent Representative of Lebanon,[31]

Taking note of the determination of Lebanon to ensure the withdrawal of all non-Lebanese forces from Lebanon,

1. *Reaffirms* its resolutions 508 (1982), 509 (1982) and 516 (1982) in all their components;

2. *Condemns* the recent Israeli incursions into Beirut in violation of the cease-fire agreements and of Security Council resolutions;

3. *Demands* an immediate return to the positions occupied by Israel before 15 September 1982, as a first step towards the full implementation of Security Council resolutions;

4. *Calls again* for the strict respect of the sovereignty, territorial integrity, unity and political independence of Lebanon under the sole and exclusive authority of the Government of Lebanon through the Lebanese Army throughout Lebanon;

5. *Reaffirms* its resolutions 512 (1982) and 513 (1982), which call for respect for the rights of the civilian populations without any discrimination, and repudiates all acts of violence against those populations;

6. *Supports* the efforts of the Secretary-General to implement resolution 516 (1982), concerning the deployment of United Nations observers to monitor the situation in and around Beirut, and requests all the parties concerned to co-operate fully in the application of that resolution;

7. *Decides* to remain seized of the question and asks the Secretary-General to keep the Security Council informed of developments as soon as possible and not later than within twenty-four hours.

Adopted unanimously at the 2395th meeting.

Resolution No. 521 (1982) of 19 September 1982

CONDEMNING THE MASSACRE OF PALESTINIAN CIVILIANS IN BEIRUT

The Security Council,

Appalled at the massacre of Palestinian civilians in Beirut,

Having heard the report of the Secretary-General[32] at its 2396th meeting,

Noting that the Government of Lebanon has agreed to the dispatch of United Nations observers to the sites of greatest human suffering and losses in and around that city,

1. *Condemns* the criminal massacre of Palestinian civilians in Beirut;

2. *Reaffirms* once again its resolutions 512 (1982) and 513 (1982), which call for respect for the rights of the

civilian populations without any discrimination, and repudiates all acts of violence against those populations;

3. *Authorizes* the Secretary-General, as an immediate step, to increase the number of United Nations observers in and around Beirut from ten to fifty, and insists that there shall be no interference with the deployment of the observers and that they shall have full freedom of movement;

4. *Requests* the Secretary-General, in consultation with the Government of Lebanon, to ensure the rapid deployment of those observers in order that they may contribute in every way possible within their mandate to the effort to ensure full protection for the civilian populations;

5. *Requests* the Secretary-General, as a matter of urgency, to initiate appropriate consultations and, in particular, consultations with the Government of Lebanon on additional steps which the Security Council might take, including the possible deployment of United Nations forces, to assist that Government in ensuring full protection for the civilian populations in and around Beirut and requests him to report to the Council within forty-eight hours;

6. *Insists* that all concerned must permit United Nations observers and forces established by the Security Council in Lebanon to be deployed and to discharge their mandates and, in this connection, solemnly calls attention to the obligation of all Member States, under Article 25 of the Charter of the United Nations, to accept and carry out the decisions of the Council in accordance with the Charter;

7. *Requests* the Secretary-General to keep the Security Council informed on an urgent and continuing basis.

Adopted unanimously at the resumed 2396th meeting.

Resolution No. 523 (1982) of 18 October 1982

EXTENDING THE MANDATE OF THE UNITED NATIONS INTERIM FORCE IN LEBANON UNTIL 19 JANUARY 1983

The Security Council,

Having heard the statement of the President of the Republic of Lebanon,[33]

Recalling its resolutions 425 (1978), 426 (1978) and 519 (1982),

Reaffirming its resolutions 508 (1982) and 509 (1982), as well as all subsequent resolutions on the situation in Lebanon,

Having studied the report of the Secretary-General[34] and taking note of its conclusions and recommendations,

Responding to the request of the Government of Lebanon,

1. *Decides* to extend the present mandate of the United Nations Interim Force in Lebanon for a further interim period of three months, that is, until 19 January 1983;

2. *Insists* that there shall be no interference under any

---

[31] *Ibid., Thirty-seventh Year,* 2394th meeting.

[32] *Ibid., Thirty-seventh Year, Supplement for July, August and September 1982,* document S/15400.

[33] *Ibid., Thirty-seventh Year,* 2400th meeting.

[34] *Ibid., Thirty-seventh Year, Supplement for October, November and December 1982,* document S/15455 and Corr.1.

pretext with the operations of the Force and that it shall have full freedom of movement in the discharge of its mandate;

3. *Authorizes* the Force during that period to carry out with the consent of the Government of Lebanon, interim tasks in the humanitarian and administrative fields, as indicated in resolutions 511 (1982) and 519 (1982), and to assist the Government of Lebanon in ensuring the security of all the inhabitants of the area without any discrimination;

4. *Requests* the Secretary-General, within the three-month period, to consult with the Government of Lebanon and to report to the Security Council on ways and means of ensuring the full implementation of the mandate of the Force as defined in resolutions 425 (1978) and 426 (1978), and the relevant decisions of the Council;

5. *Requests* the Secretary-General to report to the Security Council on the progress of his consultations.

Adopted at the 2400th meeting:
In favour: 13
China, France, Guyana, Ireland, Japan, Jordan, Panama, Spain, Togo, Uganda, United Kingdom, United States, Zaire.
Against: 0
Abstentions: 2
Poland, USSR.

Resolution No. 524 (1982) of 29 November 1982

RENEWING THE MANDATE OF THE UNITED NATIONS DISENGAGEMENT OBSERVER FORCE UNTIL 31 MAY 1983

The Security Council,
Having considered the report of the Secretary-General on the United Nations Disengagement Observer Force,[35]
Decides:

(a) To call upon the parties concerned to implement immediately Security Council resolution 338 (1973);

(b) To renew the mandate of the United Nations Disengagement Observer Force for another period of six months, that is, until 31 May 1983;

(c) To request the Secretary-General to submit, at the end of this period, a report on the developments in the situation and the measures taken to implement resolution 338 (1973).

Adopted unanimously at the 2403rd meeting.

Resolution No. 529 (1983) of 18 January 1983

EXTENDING THE MANDATE OF THE UNITED NATIONS INTERIM FORCE IN LEBANON UNTIL 19 JULY 1983

The Security Council,
Recalling its resolutions 425 (1978) and 426 (1978), and all subsequent resolutions on the United Nations Interim Force in Lebanon,

Recalling further its resolutions 508 (1982) and 509 (1982),

Having taken note of the letter of the Permanent Representative of Lebanon to the President of the Security Council and to the Secretary-General of 13 January 1983,[36] and of the statement he made at the 2411th meeting of the Council,

Having studied the report of the Secretary-General[37] and taking note of his observations,

Responding to the request of the Government of Lebanon,

1. *Decides* to extend the present mandate of the United Nations Interim Force in Lebanon for a further interim period of six months, that is, until 19 July 1983;

2. *Calls upon* all parties concerned to co-operate with the Force for the full implementation of the present resolution;

3. *Requests* the Secretary-General to report to the Security Council on the progress made in this respect.

Adopted at the 2411th meeting:
In favour: 13
China, France, Guyana, Jordan, Malta, Netherlands, Nicaragua, Pakistan, Togo, United Kingdom, United States, Zaire, Zimbabwe.
Against: 0
Abstentions: 2
Poland, USSR.

Resolution No. 531 (1983) of 26 May 1983

RENEWING THE MANDATE OF THE UNITED NATIONS DISENGAGEMENT OBSERVER FORCE UNTIL 30 NOVEMBER 1983

The Security Council,
Having considered the report of the Secretary-General on the United Nations Disengagement Observer Force,[38]
Decides:

(a) To call upon the parties concerned to implement immediately Security Council resolution 338 (1973);

(b) To renew the mandate of the United Nations Disengagement Observer Force for another period of six months, that is, until 30 November 1983;

(c) To request the Secretary-General to submit, at the end of this period, a report on the developments in the situation and the measures taken to implement resolution 338 (1973).

Adopted unanimously at the 2445th meeting.

[35] *Official Records of the Security Council Thirty-seventh Year, Supplement for October, November and December 1982*, document S/15493.

[36] *Official Records of the Security Council, Thirty-eighth Year, Supplement for January, February and March 1983*, document S/15557, annex I.
[37] *Ibid.*, document S/15557.
[38] *Official Records of the Security Council, Thirty-eighth Year, Supplement for April, May and June 1983*, document S/15777.

Resolution No. 536 (1983) of 18 July 1983

EXTENDING THE MANDATE OF THE UNITED NATIONS IN-
TERIM FORCE IN LEBANON UNTIL 19 OCTOBER 1983

The Security Council,

Having heard the statement of the Minister for Foreign
Affairs of the Republic of Lebanon,[39]

Recalling its resolutions 425 (1978) and 426 (1978), and
all subsequent resolutions on the United Nations Interim
Force in Lebanon,

Recalling further its resolutions 508 (1982), 509 (1982)
and 520 (1982), as well as all its other resolutions on the
situation in Lebanon,

Reiterating its strong support for the territorial integrity,
sovereignty and political independence of Lebanon within
its internationally recognized boundaries,

Having taken note of the letter of the Permanent Representative of Lebanon to the President of the Security
Council of 5 July 1983,[40]

Having studied the report of the Secretary-General[41]
and taking note of his observations and recommendation
expressed therein,

Responding to the request of the Government of
Lebanon,

1. *Decides* to extend the present mandate of the United
Nations Interim Force in Lebanon for a further interim
period of three months, that is, until 19 October 1983;

2. *Calls upon* all parties concerned to co-operate with
the Force for the full implementation of its mandate as
defined in resolutions 425 (1978) and 426 (1978) and the
relevant decisions of the Security Council;

3. *Requests* the Secretary-General to report to the Council on the progress made in this respect.

Adopted at the 2456th meeting:
In favour: 13
China, France, Guyana, Jordan, Malta, Netherlands, Nic-
aragua, Pakistan, Togo, United Kingdom, United States,
Zaire, Zimbabwe.
Against: 0
Abstentions: 2
Poland, USSR.

Resolution No. 538 (1983) of 18 October 1983

EXTENDING THE MANDATE OF THE UNITED NATIONS IN-
TERIM FORCE IN LEBANON UNTIL 19 APRIL 1984

The Security Council,

Having heard the statements of the representative of
Lebanon,[42]

Recalling its resolutions 425 (1978) and 426 (1978) and
all subsequent resolutions on the United Nations Interim

Force in Lebanon,

Recalling further its resolutions 508 (1982), 509 (1982)
and 520 (1982), as well as all its other resolutions on the
situation in Lebanon,

Reiterating its strong support for the territorial integrity,
sovereignty and political independence of Lebanon within
its internationally recognized boundaries,

Having studied the report of the Secretary-General on
the United Nations Interim Force in Lebanon[43] and taking note of the conclusions and recommendations expressed therein,

Taking note of the letter of the Permanent Representative of Lebanon to the Secretary-General,[44]

Responding to the request of the Government of
Lebanon,

1. *Decides* to extend the present mandate of the United
Nations Interim Force in Lebanon for a further interim
period of six months, that is, until 19 April 1984;

2. *Calls upon* all parties concerned to co-operate fully
with the Force for the full implementation of its mandate,
as defined in resolutions 425 (1978) and 426 (1978) and
the relevant decisions of the Security Council;

3. *Requests* the Secretary-General to report to the Council on the progress made in this respect.

Adopted at the 2480th meeting:
In favour: 13
China, France, Guyana, Jordan, Malta, Netherlands,
Nicaragua, Pakistan, Togo, United Kingdom, United
States, Zaire, Zimbabwe.
Against: 0
Abstentions: 2
Poland, USSR.

Resolution No. 542 (1983) of 23 November 1983

CALLING FOR AN IMMEDIATE CEASE-FIRE IN NORTHERN
LEBANON

The Security Council,

Having considered the situation prevailing in northern
Lebanon,

Recalling the statement made on this question by the
President of the Security Council on 11 November 1983,[45]

Deeply concerned by the intensification of the fighting,
which continues to cause great suffering and loss of human
life,

1. *Deplores* the loss of human life caused by the events
taking place in northern Lebanon;

2. *Reiterates its call* for the strict respect for the sovereignty, political independence and territorial integrity of
Lebanon within its internationally recognized boundaries;

3. *Requests* the parties concerned immediately to accept
a cease-fire and scrupulously to observe the cessation of
hostilities;

---

[39]*Official Records of the Security Council, Thirty-eighth Year, Supplement for
July, August and September 1983,* 2456th meeting.
[40]*Ibid.,* document S/15868.
[41]*Ibid.,* document S/15863.
[42]*Ibid., Thirty-eighth Year, Supplement for October, November and December
1983,* 2480th meeting.

[43]*Ibid.,* document S/16036.
[44]*Ibid.,* para. 20.
[45]Document S/16142, incorporated in the record of the 2496th meeting.

4. *Invites* the parties concerned to settle their differences exclusively by peaceful means and to refrain from the threat or use of force;

5. *Pays tribute* to the work done by the United Nations Relief and Works Agency for Palestine Refugees in the Near East and by the International Committee of the Red Cross in providing emergency humanitarian assistance to the Palestinian and Lebanese civilians in Tripoli and its surroundings;

6. *Calls upon* the parties concerned to comply with the provisions of the present resolution;

7. *Requests* the Secretary-General to follow the situation in northern Lebanon, to consult with the Government of Lebanon, and to report to the Security Council, which remains seized of the question.

Adopted unanimously at the 2501st meeting.

Resolution No. 543 (1983) of 29 November 1983

RENEWING THE MANDATE OF THE UNITED NATIONS DISENGAGEMENT OBSERVER FORCE UNTIL 31 MAY 1984

The Security Council,
Having considered the report of the Secretary-General on the United Nations Disengagement Observer Force,[46]
Decides:

(a) To call upon the parties concerned to implement immediately Security Council resolution 338 (1973);

(b) To renew the mandate of the United Nations Disengagement Observer Force for another period of six months, that is, until 31 May 1984;

(c) To request the Secretary-General to submit, at the end of this period, a report on the developments in the situation and the measures taken to implement resolution 338 (1973).

Adopted unanimously at the 2502nd meeting.

Resolution No. 549 (1984) of 19 April 1984

EXTENDING THE MANDATE OF THE UNITED NATIONS INTERIM FORCE IN LEBANON UNTIL 19 OCTOBER 1984

The Security Council,
Recalling its resolutions 425 (1978), 426 (1978), 501 (1982), 508 (1982), 509 (1982) and 520 (1982),[47] as well as all its resolutions on the situation in Lebanon,
Having studied the report of the Secretary-General on the United Nations Interim Force in Lebanon of 9 April 1984[48] and taking note of the observations expressed therein,
Taking note of the letter of the Permanent Representa-

tive of Lebanon to the Secretary-General of 9 April 1984,[49]
Responding to the request of the Government of Lebanon,

1. *Decides* to extend the present mandate of the United Nations Interim Force in Lebanon for a further interim period of six months, that is, until 19 October 1984;

2. *Reiterates* its strong support for the territorial integrity, sovereignty and independence of Lebanon within its internationally recognized boundaries;

3. *Re-emphasizes* the terms of reference and general guidelines of the Force as stated in the report of the Secretary-General of 19 March 1978,[50] approved by resolution 426 (1978), and calls upon all parties concerned to co-operate fully with the Force for the full implementation of its mandate;

4. *Reiterates* that the Force should fully implement its mandate as defined in resolutions 425 (1978), 426 (1978) and all other relevant resolutions;

5. *Requests* the Secretary-General to continue consultations with the Government of Lebanon and other parties directly concerned on the implementation of the present resolution and to report to the Council thereon.

Adopted at the 2530th meeting:
In favour: 13
Burkina Faso, China, Egypt, France, India, Malta, Netherlands, Nicaragua, Pakistan, Peru, United Kingdom, United States, Zimbabwe.
Against: 0
Abstentions: 2
Ukrainian SSR, USSR.

Resolution No. 551 (1984) of 30 May 1984

RENEWING THE MANDATE OF THE UNITED NATIONS DISENGAGEMENT OBSERVER FORCE UNTIL 30 NOVEMBER 1984

The Security Council,
Having considered the report of the Secretary-General on the United Nations Disengagement Observer Force,[51]
Decides:

(a) To call upon the parties concerned to implement immediately Security Council resolution 338 (1973);

(b) To renew the mandat of the United Nations Disengagement Observer Force for another period of six months, that is, until 30 November 1984;

(c) To request the Secretary-General to submit, at the end of this period, a report on the developments in the situation and the measures taken to implement resolution 338 (1973).

Adopted unanimously at the 2544th meeting.

---

[46]*Official Records of the Security Council, Thirty-eighth Year, Supplement for October, November and December 1983,* document S/16169.

[47]Most of these resolutions call for a cease-fire in Lebanon and/or for Israeli withdrawal from Lebanese territory. [ed. note]

[48]*Official Records of the Security Council, Thirty-ninth Year, Supplement for April, May and June 1984,* document S/16472.

[49]*Ibid.,* document S/16471.

[50]*Ibid., Thirty-third Year, Supplement for January, February and March 1978,* document S/12611.

[51]*Official Records of the Security Council, Thirty-ninth Year, Supplement for April, May and June 1984,* document S/16573.

Resolution No. 555 (1984) of 12 October 1984

EXTENDING THE MANDATE OF THE UNITED NATIONS IN-
TERIM FORCE IN LEBANON UNTIL 19 APRIL 1985

The Security Council,

Recalling its resolutions 425 (1978), 426 (1978), 501 (1982), 508 (1982), 509 (1982) and 520 (1982),[52] as well as all its resolutions on the situation in Lebanon,

Having studied the report of the Secretary-General on the United Nations Interim Force in Lebanon of 9 October 1984,[53] and taking note of the observations expressed therein,

Taking note of the letter of the Permanent Representative of Lebanon addressed to the Secretary-General of 8 October 1984,[54]

Responding to the request of the Government of Lebanon,

1. *Decides* to extend the present mandate of the United Nations Interim Force in Lebanon for a further interim period of six months, that is, until 19 April 1985;

2. *Reiterates* its strong support for the territorial integrity, sovereignty and independence of Lebanon within its internationally recognized boundaries;

3. *Re-emphasizes* the terms of reference and general guidelines of the Force as stated in the report of the Secretary-General of 19 March 1978,[55] approved by resolution 426 (1978), and calls upon all parties concerned to co-operate fully with the Force for the full implementation of its mandate;

4. *Reiterates* that the Force should fully implement its mandate as defined in resolutions 425 (1978), 426 (1978) and all other relevant resolutions;

5. *Requests* the Secretary-General to continue consultations with the Government of Lebanon and other parties directly concerned on the implementation of the present resolution and to report to the Council thereon.

Adopted at the 2559th meeting:

In favour: 13
Burkina Faso, China, Egypt, France, India, Malta, Netherlands, Nicaragua, Pakistan, Peru, United Kingdom, United States, Zimbabwe.

Against: 0

Abstentions: 2
Ukrainian SSR, USSR.

Resolution No. 557 (1984) of 28 November 1984

RENEWING THE MANDATE OF THE UNITED NATIONS DISEN-
GAGEMENT OBSERVER FORCE UNTIL 31 MAY 1985

The Security Council,

Having considered the report of the Secretary-General on the United Nations Disengagement Observer Force,[56]

Decides:

(a) To call upon the parties concerned to implement immediately Security Council resolution 338 (1973);

(b) To renew the mandate of the United Nations Disengagement Observer Force for another period of six months, that is, until 31 May 1985;

(c) To request the Secretary-General to submit, at the end of this period, a report on the developments in the situation and the measures taken to implement resolution 338 (1973).

Adopted unanimously at the 2563rd meeting.

Resolution No. 561 (1985) of 17 April 1985

EXTENDING THE MANDATE OF THE UNITED NATIONS IN-
TERIM FORCE IN LEBANON UNTIL 19 OCTOBER 1985

The Security Council,

Recalling its resolutions 425 (1978), 426 (1978), 501 (1982), 508 (1982), 509 (1982) and 520 (1982), as well as all its resolutions on the situation in Lebanon,

Having studied the report of the Secretary-General on the United Nations Interim Force in Lebanon of 11 April 1985,[57] and taking note of the observations expressed therein,

Taking note of the letter of the Permanent Representative of Lebanon addressed to the Secretary-General of 27 March 1985,[58]

Responding to the request of the Government of Lebanon,

1. *Decides* to extend the present mandate of the United Nations Interim Force in Lebanon for a further interim period of six months, that is, until 19 October 1985;

2. *Reiterates* its strong support for the territorial integrity, sovereignty and independence of Lebanon within its internationally recognized boundaries;

3. *Re-emphasizes* the terms of reference and general guidelines of the Force as stated in the report of the Secretary-General of 19 March 1978,[59] approved by resolution 426 (1978), and calls upon all parties concerned to co-operate fully with the Force for the full implementation of its mandate;

4. *Reiterates* that the Force should fully implement its mandate as defined in resolutions 425 (1978), 426 (1978) and all other relevant resolutions;

5. *Requests* the Secretary-General to continue consultations with the Government of Lebanon and other parties directly concerned on the implementation of the present

---

[52]Most of these resolutions call for a cease-fire in Lebanon and/or for Israeli withdrawal from Lebanese territory. [ed. note]

[53]*Official Records of the Security Council, Thirty-ninth Year, Supplement for October, November and December 1984,* document S/16776.

[54]*Ibid.,* document S/16772.

[55]*Ibid., Thirty-third Year, Supplement for January, February and March 1978,* document S/12611.

[56]*Official Records of the Security Council, Thirty-ninth Year, Supplement for October, November and December 1984,* document S/16829.

[57]*Official Records of the Security Council, Fortieth Year, Supplement for April, May and June 1985,* document S/17093.

[58]*Ibid., Fortieth Year, Supplement for January, February and March 1985,* document S/17062.

[59]*Ibid., Thirty-third Year, Supplement for January, February and March 1978,* document S/12611.

resolution and to report to the Council thereon.

Adopted at the 2575th meeting:
In favour: 13
Australia, Burkina Faso, China, Denmark, Egypt, France, India, Madagascar, Peru, Thailand, Trinidad and Tobago, United Kingdom, United States.
Against: 0
Abstentions: 2
Ukrainian SSR, USSR.

Resolution No. 563 (1985) of 21 May 1985

RENEWING THE MANDATE OF THE UNITED NATIONS DISENGAGEMENT OBSERVER FORCE UNTIL 30 NOVEMBER 1985

The Security Council,
Having considered the report of the Secretary-General on the United Nations Disengagement Observer Force,[60]
Decides:

(*a*) To call upon the parties concerned to implement immediately Security Council resolution 338 (1973);

(*b*) To renew the mandate of the United Nations Disengagement Observer Force for another period of six months, that is, until 30 November 1985;

(*c*) To request the Secretary-General to submit, at the end of this period, a report on the developments in the situation and the measures taken to implement resolution 338 (1973).

Adopted unanimously at the 2581st meeting.

Resolution No. 564 (1985) of 31 May 1985

CALLING UPON ALL CONCERNED TO END ACTS OF VIOLENCE AGAINST THE CIVILIAN POPULATION IN LEBANON AND PARTICULARLY IN AND AROUND PALESTINIAN REFUGEE CAMPS

The Security Council,
Recalling the statement made by the President on 24 May 1985[61] on behalf of the members of the Council on the heightened violence in certain parts of Lebanon,
Alarmed at the continued escalation of violence involving the civilian population, including Palestinians in refugee camps, resulting in grievous casualties and material destruction on all sides,

1. *Expresses anew* its deepest concern at the heavy costs in human lives and material destruction affecting the civilian population in Lebanon, and calls on all concerned to end acts of violence against the civilian population in Lebanon and, in particular, in and around Palestinian refugee camps;

2. *Reiterates* its calls for respect for the sovereignty, independence and territorial integrity of Lebanon;

3. *Calls upon* all parties to take necessary measures to alleviate the suffering resulting from acts of violence, in

particular by facilitating the work of United Nations agencies, especially the United Nations Relief and Works Agency for Palestine Refugees in the Near East, and non-governmental organizations, including the International Committee of the Red Cross, in providing humanitarian assistance to all those affected and emphasizes the need to ensure the safety of all the personnel of these organizations;

4. *Appeals* to all interested parties to co-operate with the Lebanese Government and the Secretary-General with a view to ensuring the implementation of this resolution, and requests the Secretary-General to report to the Security Council thereon;

5. *Reaffirms* its intention to continue to follow the situation closely.

Adopted unanimously at the 2582nd meeting.

Resolution No. 573 (1985) of 4 October 1985

CONDEMNING ISRAEL'S ATTACK ON TUNISIA, AND URGING MEMBERS OF THE UNITED NATIONS TO TAKE MEASURES DISSUADING ISRAEL FROM SUCH ACTS OF AGGRESSION

The Security Council,
Having considered the letter dated 1 October 1985,[62] in which Tunisia made a complaint against Israel following the act of aggression which the latter committed against the sovereignty and territorial integrity of Tunisia,
Having heard the statement by the Minister for Foreign Affairs of Tunisia,[63]
Having noted with concern that the Israeli attack has caused heavy loss of human life and extensive material damage,
Considering that, in accordance with Article 2, paragraph 4, of the Charter of the United Nations, all States Members shall refrain in their international relations from the threat or use of force against the territorial integrity or political independence of any State, or acting in any other manner inconsistent with the purposes of the United Nations,
Gravely concerned at the threat to peace and security in the Mediterranean region posed by the air raid perpetrated on 1 October by Israel in the area of Hammam Plage, situated in the southern suburb of Tunis,
Drawing attention to the serious effect which the aggression carried out by Israel and all acts contrary to the Charter cannot but have on any initiative designed to establish an overall, just and lasting peace in the Middle East,
Considering that the Israeli Government claimed responsibility for the attack as soon as it had been carried out,

1. *Condemns vigorously* the act of armed aggression perpetrated by Israel against Tunisian territory in flagrant violation of the Charter of the United Nations, interna-

---

[60]*Official Records of the Security Council, Fortieth Year, Supplement for April, May and June 1985,* document S/17177.
[61]S/17215.

[62]*Official Records of the Security Council, Fortieth Year, Supplement for October, November and December 1985,* document S/17509.
[63]*Ibid., Fortieth Year,* 2610th meeting.

tional law and norms of conduct;

2. *Demands* that Israel refrain from perpetrating such acts of aggression or from threatening to do so;

3. *Urges* Member States to take measures to dissuade Israel from resorting to such acts against the sovereignty and territorial integrity of all States;

4. *Considers* that Tunisia has the right to appropriate reparations as a result of the loss of human life and material damage which it has suffered and for which Israel has claimed responsibility;

5. *Requests* the Secretary-General to report to the Security Council on the implementation of the present resolution by 30 November 1985 at the latest;

6. *Decides* to remain seized of the matter.

Adopted at the 2615th meeting:
In favour: 14
Australia, Burkina Faso, China, Denmark, Egypt, France, India, Madagascar, Peru, Thailand, Trinidad and Tobago, Ukrainian SSR, USSR, United Kingdom.
Against: 0
Abstention: 1
United States.

Resolution No. 575 (1985) of 17 October 1985

EXTENDING THE MANDATE OF THE UNITED NATIONS INTERIM FORCE IN LEBANON UNTIL 19 APRIL 1986

The Security Council,
Recalling its resolutions 425 (1978), 426 (1978), 501 (1982), 508 (1982), 509 (1982) and 520 (1982),[64] as well as all its resolutions on the situation in Lebanon,

Having studied the report of the Secretary-General on the United Nations Interim Force in Lebanon of 10 October 1985[65] and taking note of the observations expressed therein,

Taking note of the letter of the Permanent Representative of Lebanon addressed to the Secretary-General of 3 October 1985,[66]

Responding to the request of the Government of Lebanon,

1. *Decides* to extend the present mandate of the United Nations Interim Force in Lebanon for a further interim period of six months, that is, until 19 April 1986;

2. *Reiterates* its strong support for the territorial integrity, sovereignty and independence of Lebanon within its internationally recognized boundaries;

3. *Re-emphasizes* the terms of reference and general guidelines of the Force as stated in the report of the Secretary-General of 19 March 1978,[67] approved by resolution 426 (1978), and calls upon all parties concerned to

co-operate fully with the Force for the full implementation of its mandate;

4. *Reiterates* that the Force should fully implement its mandate as defined in resolutions 425 (1978), 426 (1978) and all other relevant resolutions;

5. *Requests* the Secretary-General to continue consultations with the Government of Lebanon and other parties directly concerned on the implementation of the present resolution and to report to the Council thereon.

Adopted at the 2623rd meeting:
In favour: 13
Australia, Burkina Faso, China, Denmark, Egypt, France, India, Madagascar, Peru, Thailand, Trinidad and Tobago, United Kingdom, United States.
Against: 0
Abstentions: 2
Ukrainian SSR, USSR.

Resolution No. 576 (1985) of 21 November 1985

RENEWING THE MANDATE OF THE UNITED NATIONS DISENGAGEMENT OBSERVER FORCE UNTIL 31 MAY 1986

The Security Council,
Having considered the report of the Secretary-General on the United Nations Disengagement Observer Force,[68]
Decides:

(*a*) To call upon the parties concerned to implement immediately Security Council resolution 338 (1973);

(*b*) To renew the mandate of the United Nations Disengagement Observer Force for another period of six months, that is, until 31 May 1986;

(*c*) To request the Secretary-General to submit, at the end of this period, a report on the developments in the situation and the measures taken to implement resolution 338 (1973).

Adopted unanimously at the 2630th meeting.

Resolution No. 579 (1985) of 18 December 1985

CONDEMNING THE TAKING OF HOSTAGES AND URGING INTERNATIONAL COOPERATION TO PREVENT, PROSECUTE AND PUNISH ACTS OF HOSTAGE-TAKING

The Security Council,
Deeply disturbed at the prevalence of incidents of hostage-taking and abduction, several of which are of protracted duration and have included loss of life,

Considering that the taking of hostages and abductions are offences of grave concern to the international community, having severe adverse consequences for the rights of the victims and for the promotion of friendly relations and co-operation among States,

Recalling the statement of 9 October 1985 by the President of the Security Council, resolutely condemning all acts of terrorism, including hostage-taking,

---

[64]Most of these resolutions call for a cease-fire in Lebanon and/or for Israeli withdrawal from Lebanese territory. [ed. note]
[65]*Official Records of the Security Council, Fortieth Year, Supplement for October, November and December 1985*, document S/17557.
[66]*Ibid.*, document S/17526.
[67]*Ibid., Thirty-third Year, Supplement for January, February and March 1978*, document S/12611.

[68]*Ibid.*, document S/17628.

Recalling also resolution 40/61 of 9 December 1985 of the General Assembly,

Bearing in mind the International Convention against the Taking of Hostages, adopted on 17 December 1979,[69] the Convention on the Prevention and Punishment of Crimes against Internationally Protected Persons, including Diplomatic Agents, adopted on 14 December 1973,[70] the Convention for the Suppression of Unlawful Acts against the Safety of Civil Aviation, signed on 23 September 1971,[71] the Convention for the Suppression of Unlawful Seizure of Aircraft, signed on 16 December 1970,[72] and other relevant conventions,

1. *Condemns unequivocally* all acts of hostage-taking and abduction;

2. *Calls for* the immediate safe release of all hostages and abducted persons wherever and by whomever they are being held;

3. *Affirms* the obligation of all States in whose territory hostages or abducted persons are held urgently to take all appropriate measures to secure their safe release and to prevent the commission of acts of hostage-taking and abduction in the future;

4. *Appeals* to all States that have not yet done so to consider the possibility of becoming parties to the International Convention against the Taking of Hostages, the Convention on the Prevention and Punishment of Crimes against Internationally Protected Persons, including Diplomatic Agents, the Convention for the Suppression of Unlawful Acts against the Safety of Civil Aviation, the Convention for the Suppression of Unlawful Seizure of Aircraft and other relevant conventions;

5. *Urges* the further development of international co-operation among States in devising and adopting effective measures which are in accordance with the rules of international law to facilitate the prevention, prosecution and punishment of all acts of hostage-taking and abduction as manifestations of international terrorism.

Adopted unanimously at the 2637th meeting.

Resolution No. 583 (1986) of 18 April 1986

EXTENDING THE MANDATE OF THE UNITED NATIONS INTERIM FORCE IN LEBANON UNTIL 19 JULY 1986

The Security Council,

Recalling its resolutions 425 (1978), 426 (1978), 501 (1982), 508 (1982), 509 (1982), and 520 (1982),[73] as well as all its resolutions on the situation in Lebanon,

Having studied the report of the Secretary-General on the United Nations Interim Force in Lebanon of 9 April 1986 (S/17965) and taking note of the observations expressed therein,

Taking note of the letter of the Permanent Representative of Lebanon addressed to the Secretary-General of 1 April 1986 (S/17968),

Responding to the request of the Government of Lebanon,

1. *Decides* to extend the present mandate of the United Nations Interim Force in Lebanon for a further interim period of three months, that is, until 19 July 1986;

2. *Reiterates* its strong support for the territorial integrity, sovereignty and independence of Lebanon within its internationally recognized boundaries;

3. *Re-emphasizes* the terms of reference and general guidelines of the Force as stated in the report of the Secretary-General of 19 March 1978, approved by resolution 426 (1978), and calls upon all parties concerned to co-operate fully with the Force for the full implementation of its mandate;

4. *Reiterates* that the United Nations Interim Force in Lebanon should fully implement its mandate as defined in resolutions 425 (1978), 426 (1978) and all other relevant resolutions;

5. *Requests* the Secretary-General to continue consultations with the Government of Lebanon and other parties directly concerned on the implementation of the present resolution and to report to the Council by 19 June 1986.

Adopted unanimously at the 2681st meeting.

Resolution No. 584 (1986) of 29 May 1986

RENEWING THE MANDATE OF THE UNITED NATIONS DISENGAGEMENT OBSERVER FORCE UNTIL 30 NOVEMBER 1986

The Security Council,

Having considered the report of the Secretary-General on the United Nations Disengagement Observer Force (S/18061),

Decides:

(*a*) To call upon the parties concerned to implement immediately Security Council resolution 338 (1973) of 22 October 1973;

(*b*) To renew the mandate of the United Nations Disengagement Observer Force for another period of six months, that is, until 30 November 1986;

(*c*) To request the Secretary-General to submit, at the end of this period, a report on the developments in the situation and the measures taken to implement Security Council resolution 338 (1973).

Adopted unanimously at the 2697th meeting.

Resolution No. 586 (1986) of 18 July 1986

EXTENDING THE MANDATE OF THE UNITED NATIONS INTERIM FORCE IN LEBANON UNTIL 19 JANUARY 1987

The Security Council,

Recalling its resolutions 425 (1978), 426 (1978), 501 (1982), 508 (1982), 509 (1982) and 520 (1982), as well as all its resolutions on the situation in Lebanon,

---

[69]General Assembly resolution 34/146, annex.
[70]General Assembly resolution 3166 (XXVIII), annex.
[71]United Nations, *Treaty Series,* vol. 974, no. 14118, p. 178.
[72]United Nations, *Treaty Series,* vol. 860, no. 12325, p. 105.
[73]Most of these resolutions call for a cease-fire in Lebanon and/or for Israeli withdrawal from Lebanese territory. [ed note]

Having studied the report of the Secretary-General on the United Nations Interim Force in Lebanon of 17 June and 10 July 1986 (S/18164 and Add.1 and Add. 1/Corr.1) and taking note of the observations expressed therein,

Taking note of the letter of the Permanent Representative of Lebanon to the United Nations addressed to the Secretary-General of 7 July 1986 (S/18202),

Responding to the request of the Government of Lebanon,

1. *Decides* to extend the present mandate of the United Nations Interim Force in Lebanon for a further interim period of six months, that is, until 19 January 1987;

2. *Reiterates* its strong support for the territorial integrity, sovereignty and independence of Lebanon within its internationally recognized boundaries;

3. *Re-emphasizes* the terms of reference and general guidelines of the Force as stated in the report of the Secretary-General of 19 March 1978, approved by resolution 426 (1978), and calls upon all parties concerned to co-operate fully with the Force for the full implementation of its mandate;

4. *Reiterates* that the Force should fully implement its mandate as defined in resolutions 425 (1978), 426 (1978) and all other relevant resolutions;

5. *Requests* the Secretary-General to continue consultations with the Government of Lebanon and other parties directly concerned on the implementation of the present resolution and to report to the Security Council thereon.

Adopted unanimously at the 2699th meeting.

Resolution No. 587 (1986) of 23 September 1986

CONDEMNING ATTACKS AGAINST THE UNITED NATIONS INTERIM FORCE IN LEBANON AND CALLING AGAIN FOR AN END TO ANY MILITARY PRESENCE IN SOUTHERN LEBANON NOT ACCEPTED BY THE LEBANESE AUTHORITIES

The Security Council,

Recalling its resolutions 425 (1978) and 426 (1978), as well as resolutions 511 (1982), 519 (1982) and 523 (1982) and all the resolutions relating to the United Nations Interim Force in Lebanon,

Recalling the mandate entrusted to the United Nations Interim Force in Lebanon by resolution 425 (1978) and the guidelines of the Force set forth in the report of the Secretary-General dated 19 March 1978 (S/12611) and approved in resolution 426 (1978),

Further recalling its resolutions 508 (1982), 509 (1982) and 520 (1982), as well as all its other resolutions relating to the situation in Lebanon,

Solemnly reaffirming that it firmly supports the unity, territorial integrity, sovereignty and independence of Lebanon within its internationally recognized boundaries,

Deeply grieved over the tragic loss of human life and indignant at the harassment and attacks to which the soldiers of the Force are being subjected,

Recalling in this connection the statement made on 5 September by the President of the Council on its behalf (S/18320),

Expressing its concern at the new obstacles to the freedom of movement of the Force and at the threats to its security,

Noting with regret that the Force, whose mandate has been renewed for the twenty-first time, has so far been prevented from fulfilling the task entrusted to it,

Recalling its resolutions 444 (1979), 450 (1979), 459 (1979), 474 (1980), 483 (1980) and 488 (1981), in which it expressed its determination, in the event of continuing obstruction of the mandate of the Force, to examine practical ways and means to secure full and unconditional implementation of resolution 425 (1978),

Emphasizing its conviction that this deterioration of the situation constitutes a challenge to its authority and its resolutions,

1. *Condemns in the strongest terms* the attacks committed against the United Nations Interim Force in Lebanon;

2. *Expresses indignation* at the support which such criminal actions may receive;

3. *Pays homage* to the courage, spirit of discipline and composure of the soldiers of the Force;

4. *Takes note* of the report of the Secretary-General prepared after the recent mission by his Representative in the region (S/18348), particularly the paragraphs relating to the security of the Force and the withdrawal of Israeli military forces from southern Lebanon;

5. *Takes note* of the preliminary security measures decided on by the Secretary-General and requests him to take any further measures needed to enhance the security of the men of the Force in their peace mission;

6. *Urges* all the parties concerned to co-operate unreservedly with the Force in the fulfilment of its mandate;

7. *Again calls* for an end in southern Lebanon to any military presence which is not accepted by the Lebanese authorities;

8. *Requests* the Secretary-General to make the necessary arrangements for a deployment of the Force to the southern border of Lebanon, and solemnly calls on all the parties concerned to co-operate in the achievement of that objective;

9. *Requests* the Secretary-General to report to it within twenty-one days on the application of this resolution.

Adopted at the 2708th meeting:

In favour: 14

Australia, Bulgaria, China, Congo, Denmark, France, Ghana, Madagascar, Thailand, Trinidad and Tobago, USSR, United Arab Emirates, United Kingdom, Venezuela.

Against: 0

Abstention: 1

United States.

Resolution No. 590 (1986) of 26 November 1986

RENEWING THE MANDATE OF THE UNITED NATIONS DISENGAGEMENT OBSERVER FORCE UNTIL 31 MAY 1987

The Security Council,

Having considered the report of the Secretary-General

on the United Nations Disengagement Observer Force (S/18453),

Decides:

(*a*) To call upon the parties concerned to implement immediately Security Council resolution 338 (1973) of 22 October 1973;

(*b*) To renew the mandate of the United Nations Disengagement Observer Force for another period of six months, that is, until 31 May 1987;

(*c*) To request the Secretary-General to submit, at the end of this period, a report on the developments in the situation and the measures taken to implement Security Council resolution 338 (1973).

Adopted unanimously at the 2722nd meeting.

Resolution No. 592 (1986) of 8 December 1986

DEPLORING THE OPENING OF FIRE BY THE ISRAELI ARMY RESULTING IN THE DEATH AND WOUNDING OF STUDENTS AT BIR ZEIT UNIVERSITY

The Security Council,

Having considered the letter dated 4 December 1986 from the Permanent Representative of Zimbabwe to the United Nations, in his capacity as the Chairman of the Movement of Non-Aligned Countries, contained in document S/18501,

Recalling the Geneva Convention relative to the Protection of Civilian Persons in Time of War, of 12 August 1949,

Seriously concerned about the situation in the Palestinian and other Arab territories occupied by Israel since 1967, including Jerusalem,

Bearing in mind the specific status of Jerusalem,

1. *Reaffirms* that the Geneva Convention relative to the Protection of Civilian Persons in Time of War, of 12 August 1949, is applicable to the Palestinian and other Arab territories occupied by Israel since 1967, including Jerusalem;

2. *Strongly deplores* the opening of fire by the Israeli army resulting in the death and the wounding of defenceless students;

3. *Calls upon* Israel to abide immediately and scrupulously by the Geneva Convention relative to the Protection of Civilian Persons in Time of War, of 12 August 1949;

4. *Further calls upon* Israel to release any person or persons detained as a result of the recent events at Bir Zeit University in violation of the above-mentioned Geneva Convention;

5. *Also calls on* all concerned parties to exercise maximum restraint, to avoid violent acts, and to contribute towards the establishment of peace;

6. *Requests* the Secretary-General to report to the Council on the implementation of the present resolution not later than 20 December 1986.

Adopted at the 2727th meeting:
In favour: 14

Australia, Bulgaria, China, Congo, Denmark, France, Ghana, Madagascar, Thailand, Trinidad and Tobago, USSR, United Arab Emirates, United Kingdom, Venezuela.
Against: 0
Abstention: 1
United States.

III. RESOLUTIONS OF THE ECONOMIC AND SOCIAL COUNCIL
A. ECONOMIC AND SOCIAL COUNCIL
B. COMMISSION ON HUMAN RIGHTS
C. ECONOMIC COMMISSION FOR WESTERN ASIA
D. GOVERNING COUNCIL OF THE UNITED NATIONS DEVELOPMENT
PROGRAMME

A. ECONOMIC AND SOCIAL COUNCIL

Resolution No. 1982/18 of 4 May 1982

APPEALING FOR ASSISTANCE TO PALESTINIAN WOMEN IN THEIR STRUGGLE FOR THEIR RIGHTS

The Economic and Social Council,

Deeply concerned about the prevailing conditions of the Palestinian people, particularly the women and children,

Noting the great sacrifices of the Palestinian women and children in pursuit of their inalienable right to have their own homeland,

Considering that international co-operation and peace are threatened by colonialism, neo-colonialism, fascism, zionism, *apartheid* and foreign occupation, alien domination and racial discrimination in all its forms,

Affirming its full solidarity with the Palestinian women in their struggle for independence under the leadership of the Palestine Liberation Organization,

Expressing its grave concern that the Palestinian women and people continue to be denied their inalienable rights, in particular their right to return to their homes and property from which they have been displaced and uprooted, the right to self-determination and the right to national independence and sovereignty,

Recognizing that the mass uprooting from their homeland obstructs the participation and integration of women in efforts to achieve progress,

1. *Appeals* to all women of the world to proclaim their solidarity with and support for the Palestinian women and people in their drive to put an end to the flagrant violation by Israel of fundamental human rights in the occupied territories;

2. *Also appeals* to all States and international organizations to extend all moral and material assistance to the Palestinian and Arab women and people in their struggle for the restoration of their inalienable right to return to their homes and property from which they have been displaced and uprooted;

3. *Further appeals* to all women of the world to take the necessary measures to secure the release of thousands of persons, including women and children, fighters for the cause of self-determination, liberation and independence, held arbitrarily in the prisons of the occupying forces;

4. *Requests* the United Nations and its organs and specialized agencies, as well as all national, regional and international women's organizations, to extend their help, both moral and material, to the Palestinian women and their organizations and institutes.

Adopted at the 22nd plenary meeting:

In favour: 28

Argentina, Bangladesh, Benin, Brazil, Bulgaria, Burundi, Byelorussian SSR, China, Ethiopia, India, Iraq, Jordan, Kenya, Libyan Arab Jamahiriya, Mali, Nepal, Nicaragua, Nigeria, Pakistan, Poland, Qatar, Romania, Sudan, Tunisia, USSR, United Republic of Cameroon, Yugoslavia, Zaire.

Against: 9

Australia, Belgium, Canada, Denmark, Federal Republic of Germany, Italy, Norway, United Kingdom, United States.

Abstentions: 15

Austria, Bahamas, Chile, Colombia, Fiji, France, Greece, Japan, Liberia, Malawi, Mexico, Portugal, Saint Lucia, Thailand, Venezuela.

Resolution No. 1982/48 of 27 July 1982

CALLING FOR EMERGENCY ASSISTANCE TO THE PALESTINIAN POPULATION IN LEBANON

The Economic and Social Council,

Recalling General Assembly resolution ES-7/5 of 26 June 1982,

Recalling further Security Council resolution 512 (1982) of 19 June 1982,

Expressing its deep alarm at the Israeli invasion of Lebanon, which claimed the lives of a very large number of civilian Palestinians,

Gravely concerned at the Israeli destruction in Lebanon of Palestinian camps and other areas heavily inhabited by civilian Palestinians, together with their social and economic structures,

Noting with deep concern the dire need of the Palestinians in Lebanon for urgent humanitarian assistance as a result of the Israeli invasion,

Referring to the humanitarian principles of the Geneva Convention relative to the Protection of Civilian Persons in Time of War, of 12 August 1949,[1] and to the obligations arising from the regulations annexed to the Hague Conventions of 1907,[2]

1. *Endorses* General Assembly resolution ES-7/5, in which the Assembly condemned Israel for its non-compliance with Security Council resolutions 508 (1982) of 5 June 1982 and 509 (1982) of 6 June 1982 and stressed its support for victims of the Israeli invasion of Lebanon, which inflicted severe damage on the civilian population, including the heavy loss of human lives and social and economic structures;

2. *Calls upon* all Governments to provide, as a matter of urgency, emergency assistance to the Palestinians in Lebanon;

3. *Urges* the relevant programmes, organizations, agencies and organs of the United Nations system to initiate and provide, in co-operation with the Palestine Liberation Organization, urgent humanitarian assistance to the Palestinians in Lebanon;

---

[1]United Nations, *Treaty Series,* vol. 75, no. 973, p. 287.
[2]See Carnegie Endowment for International Peace, *The Hague Conventions and Declarations of 1899 and 1907* (New York, Oxford University Press, 1915).

4. *Calls upon* Israel to release civilians detained by the Israeli occupation army in Lebanon and to apply fully to the civilians the Geneva Convention relative to the Protection of Civilian Persons in Time of War;

5. *Also calls upon* Israel to apply fully the Geneva Conventions to imprisoned combatants;

6. *Requests* the Secretary-General to report to the General Assembly at its thirty-seventh session and to the Economic and Social Council at its second regular session of 1983 on the progress made in the implementation of the present resolution.

Adopted at the 48th plenary meeting:

In favour: 48

Against: 1

Abstentions: 0

Resolution No. 1983/43 of 25 July 1983

REQUESTING UNITED NATIONS BODIES TO PROVIDE ECONOMIC AND SOCIAL ASSISTANCE FOR THE PALESTINIAN PEOPLE IN CO-OPERATION WITH THE PALESTINE LIBERATION ORGANIZATION

The Economic and Social Council,

Recalling General Assembly resolution 37/134 of 17 December 1982,

Recalling also Council resolution 1982/48 of 27 July 1982,

Noting with deep concern that the continued detention of Palestinian civilians in Al Ansar camp by the Israeli invasion army has deprived many of their dependants of their sole source of income, in addition to having other adverse economic and social consequences,

Noting also the need to provide economic and social assistance to the Palestinian people,

1. *Takes note* of the report of the Secretary-General on assistance to the Palestinian people;[3]

2. *Expresses its gratitude* to the Governments and United Nations bodies which provided humanitarian assistance to the Palestinian victims of the Israeli invasion of Lebanon;

3. *Takes note with appreciation* of the assistance provided by United Nations bodies to the Palestinian people;

4. *Deplores* the non-compliance of Israel with Economic and Social Council resolution 1982/48;

5. *Calls upon* the Israeli occupation authorities to facilitate the efforts of all United Nations bodies intending to implement assistance projects for the Palestinian people in the occupied Palestinian territories;

6. *Requests* the competent programmes, organizations, agencies and organs of the United Nations system to sustain and intensify their efforts, in co-operation with the Palestine Liberation Organization, in providing economic and social assistance to the Palestinian people;

7. *Also requests* that United Nations assistance to the Palestinians in the Arab host countries should be rendered in co-operation with the Palestine Liberation Organization and with the consent of the Arab host Governments concerned;

8. *Requests* the Secretary-General to report to the General Assembly at its thirty-ninth session, through the Economic and Social Council, on the progress made in the implementation of the present resolution.

Adopted at the 39th plenary meeting:

In favour: 48
Algeria, Argentina, Austria, Bangladesh, Benin, Botswana, Brazil, Bulgaria, Burundi, Byelorussian SSR, Canada, China, Colombia, Congo, Denmark, Djibouti, Ecuador, France, German Democratic Republic, Federal Republic of Germany, Greece, India, Japan, Kenya, Lebanon, Luxembourg, Malaysia, Mali, Mexico, Netherlands, New Zealand, Norway, Pakistan, Peru, Poland, Portugal, Qatar, Romania, Saint Lucia, Saudi Arabia, Sudan, Suriname, Swaziland, Thailand, Tunisia, USSR, United Kingdom, Venezuela.

Against: 1
United States.

Abstentions: 1
Liberia.

Resolution No. 1984/18 of 24 May 1984

REQUESTING A COMPREHENSIVE REPORT BY THE SECRETARY-GENERAL ON THE SITUATION OF PALESTINIAN WOMEN LIVING IN AND OUTSIDE THE OCCUPIED ARAB TERRITORIES

The Economic and Social Council,

Deeply concerned about the prevailing living conditions of Palestinian women within and outside the occupied Arab territories,

Recognizing that the mass uprooting of Palestinian women from their homeland seriously affects their participation and integration in the development process,

Noting that no comprehensive study relating to the status of Palestinian women within and outside the occupied Arab territories has been conducted in the United Nations system since the World Conference of the United Nations Decade for Women: Equality, Development and Peace, held at Copenhagen from 14 to 30 July 1980,

Recalling the relevant resolutions of the General Assembly, the Economic and Social Council and other appropriate United Nations organizations,

Taking note of chapter II of the report of the Secretary-General on the situation of Palestinian women and children in the occupied Arab territories,[4] submitted to the Commission on the Status of Women at its thirtieth session,

1. *Requests* the Secretary-General to submit an updated version of that report to the Commission on the Status of Women at its thirty-first session;

---

[3]E/1983/72 and Add.1.

[4]E/CN.6/1984/10.

2. *Also requests* the Secretary-General to prepare a comprehensive report on the situation of Palestinian women living within and outside the occupied Arab territories and to submit it to the Commission on the Status of Women at its thirty-second session;

3. *Further requests* the Secretary-General to submit an interim report on the preparation of that study to the Commission on the Status of Women at its thirty-first session;

4. *Invites* all Governments, intergovernmental and non-governmental organizations and United Nations bodies to extend all necessary assistance to the Secretary-General in this regard.

Adopted at the 19th plenary meeting.

Resolution No. 1984/56 of 25 July 1984

REQUESTING UNITED NATIONS BODIES TO PROVIDE ECONOMIC AND SOCIAL ASSISTANCE FOR THE PALESTINIAN PEOPLE IN CO-OPERATION WITH THE PALESTINE LIBERATION ORGANIZATION

The Economic and Social Council,

Recalling General Assembly resolution 38/145 of 19 December 1983,

Recalling also Council resolution 1983/43 of 25 July 1983,

Noting the need to provide economic and social assistance to the Palestinian people,

Noting also the oral report made by the representative of the Secretary-General before the Third (Programme and Co-ordination) Committee of the Council on 9 July 1984, concerning the meeting on assistance to the Palestinian people held at Geneva on 5 and 6 July 1984 in response to General Assembly resolution 38/145,

1. *Takes note* of the report of the Secretary-General on assistance to the Palestinian people;[5]

2. *Expresses its thanks* to the Secretary-General for convening the meeting on assistance to the Palestinian people, pursuant to General Assembly resolution 38/145;

3. *Regards* such a meeting as a valuable opportunity to assess progress in economic and social assistance to the Palestinian people and to explore ways and means of enhancing such assistance;

4. *Draws the attention* of the international community, the United Nations system and intergovernmental and non-governmental organizations to the need to ensure that their aid to the occupied Palestinian territories is disbursed only for the benefit of the Palestinian people and is not used in any manner to serve the interests of the Israeli occupation authorities;

5. *Requests* the competent programmes, organizations, agencies and organs of the United Nations system to intensify their efforts, in co-operation with the Palestine Liberation Organization, to provide economic and social assistance to the Palestinian people;

6. *Also requests* that United Nations assistance to the Palestinians in the Arab host countries should be rendered in co-operation with the Palestine Liberation Organization and with the consent of the Arab host Government concerned;

7. *Requests* the Secretary-General to report to the General Assembly at its fortieth session, through the Economic and Social Council, on the progress made in the provision of assistance to the Palestinian people.

Adopted at the 48th plenary meeting:

In favour: 48

Algeria, Argentina, Austria, Benin, Brazil, Bulgaria, Canada, China, Colombia, Congo, Costa Rica, Djibouti, Finland, France, German Democratic Republic, Federal Republic of Germany, Greece, Guyana, Indonesia, Japan, Lebanon, Luxembourg, Malaysia, Mexico, Netherlands, New Zealand, Pakistan, Papua New Guinea, Poland, Portugal, Qatar, Romania, Rwanda, Saint Lucia, Saudi Arabia, Sierra Leone, Somalia, Sri Lanka, Suriname, Sweden, Thailand, Tunisia, Uganda, USSR, United Kingdom, Venezuela, Yugoslavia, Zaire.

Against: 1

United States.

Abstentions: 0

Resolution No. 1985/57 of 25 July 1985

REQUESTING UNITED NATIONS BODIES TO PROVIDE ECONOMIC AND SOCIAL ASSISTANCE FOR THE PALESTINIAN PEOPLE IN CO-OPERATION WITH THE PALESTINE LIBERATION ORGANIZATION

The Economic and Social Council,

Recalling General Assembly resolution 39/224 of 18 December 1984,

Recalling also Council resolution 1984/56 of 25 July 1984,

Recalling further the Programme of Action for the Achievement of Palestinian Rights, adopted by the International Conference on the Question of Palestine,[6]

Noting the need to provide economic and social assistance to the Palestinian people,

1. *Takes note* of the report of the Secretary-General on assistance to the Palestinian people;[7]

2. *Notes* the meeting on assistance to the Palestinian people which was held at Geneva on 5 and 8 July 1985 in response to General Assembly resolution 39/224;

3. *Expresses its thanks* to the Secretary-General for convening the meeting on assistance to the Palestinian people;

4. *Regards* such a meeting as a valuable opportunity to assess progress in economic and social assistance to the Palestinian people and to explore ways and means of

---

[5]A/39/265-E/1984/77.

[6]*Report of the International Conference on the Question of Palestine, Geneva, 29 August-7 September 1983* (United Nations publication, Sales No. E.83.1.21), chap. I, sect. B.

[7]A/40/353-E/1985/115 and Corr.1 and Add.1 and Add.1/Corr.1.

enhancing such assistance;

5. *Draws the attention* of the international community, the United Nations system and intergovernmental and non-governmental organizations to the need to disburse their aid to the occupied Palestinian territories only for the benefit of the Palestinian people;

6. *Requests* the Secretary-General:

(*a*) To review the progress made in the implementation of the proposed activities and projects described in the report of the Secretary-General on assistance to the Palestinian people;

(*b*) To take all necessary steps to finalize the programme of economic and social assistance to the Palestinian people requested in General Assembly resolution 38/145 of 19 December 1983;

(*c*) To convene in 1986 a meeting of the relevant programmes, organizations, agencies, funds and organs of the United Nations system to consider economic and social assistance to the Palestinian people;

(*d*) To provide for the participation in the meeting of the Palestine Liberation Organization, the Arab host countries and relevant intergovernmental and non-governmental organizations;

7. *Requests* the relevant programmes, organizations, agencies, funds and organs of the United Nations system to intensify their efforts, in co-operation with the Palestine Liberation Organization, to provide economic and social assistance to the Palestinian people;

8. *Also requests* that United Nations assistance to the Palestinians in the Arab host countries should be rendered in co-operation with the Palestine Liberation Organization and with the consent of the Arab host Government concerned;

9. *Requests* the Secretary-General to report to the General Assembly at its forty-first session, through the Economic and Social Council, on the progress made in the implementation of the present resolution.

Adopted at the 52nd plenary meeting:

In favour: 44*

Algeria, Argentina, Bangladesh, Botswana, Brazil, Bulgaria, Canada, China, Congo, Ecuador, Finland, France, German Democratic Republic, Federal Repulic of Germany, Iceland, India, Indonesia, Japan, Luxembourg, Malaysia, Mexico, Morocco, Netherlands, New Zealand, Nigeria, Poland, Romania, Rwanda, Saudi Arabia, Senegal, Sierra Leone, Somalia, Spain, Suriname, Sweden, Thailand, Turkey, Uganda, USSR, United Kingdom, Venezuela, Yugoslavia, Zaire, Zimbabwe.

Against: 1
United States.

Abstentions: 0

---

*The delegation of Sri Lanka subsequently indicated that, had it been present during the voting, it would have voted in favour.

Resolution No. 1985/58 of 25 July 1985

CALLING FOR THE LIFTING OF RESTRICTIONS ON THE ECONOMY OF THE OCCUPIED PALESTINIAN TERRITORIES AND FOR THE ESTABLISHMENT OF A SEAPORT IN THE GAZA STRIP

The Economic and Social Council,

Aware of the Israeli restrictions imposed on the foreign trade of the occupied Palestinian territories,

Aware also of the imposed domination of the Palestinian market by Israel,

Taking into account the need to give Palestinian firms and products direct access to external markets without Israeli interference,

Noting the lack of progress in the implementation of General Assembly resolution 39/223 of 18 December 1984, as reflected in the report of the Secretary-General on economic development projects in the occupied Palestinian territories,

1. *Calls* for the urgent lifting of the Israeli restrictions imposed on the economy of the occupied Palestinian territories;

2. *Recognizes* the Palestinian interest in establishing a seaport in the occupied Gaza Strip to give Palestinian firms and products direct access to external markets;

3. *Calls upon* all concerned to facilitate the establishment of a seaport in the occupied Gaza Strip;

4. *Also calls upon* all concerned to facilitate the establishment of a cement plant in the occupied West Bank and a citrus plant in the occupied Gaza Strip;

5. *Requests* the Secretary-General to continue his efforts to facilitate the establishment of the above-mentioned projects and to report to the General Assembly at its forty-first session, through the Economic and Social Council, on the progress made in the implementation of the present resolution.

Adopted at the 52nd plenary meeting:

In favour: 41*

Algeria, Argentina, Bangladesh, Botswana, Brazil, Bulgaria, China, Congo, France, German Democratic Republic, Federal Republic of Germany, Haiti, India, Indonesia, Japan, Luxembourg, Malaysia, Mexico, Morocco, Netherlands, New Zealand, Nigeria, Poland, Romania, Rwanda, Saudi Arabia, Senegal, Sierra Leone, Somalia, Spain, Suriname, Thailand, Turkey, Uganda, USSR, United Kingdom, Venezuela, Yugoslavia, Zaire, Zimbabwe.

Against: 1
United States.

Abstentions: 4
Canada, Finland, Iceland, Sweden.

---

*The delegation of Sri Lanka subsequently indicated that, had it been present during the voting, it would have voted in favour.

Resolution No. 1986/49 of 22 July 1986

REQUESTING UNITED NATIONS BODIES TO PROVIDE ECONOMIC AND SOCIAL ASSISTANCE FOR THE PALESTINIAN PEOPLE IN COOPERATION WITH THE PALESTINE LIBERATION ORGANIZATION

The Economic and Social Council,

Recalling General Assembly resolution 40/170 of 17 December 1985,

Recalling also Economic and Social Council resolution 1985/57 of 27 July 1985,

Recalling further the Programme of Action for the Achievement of Palestinian Rights, adopted by the International Conference on the Question of Palestine,[8]

Noting that the programme of economic and social assistance to the Palestinian people requested in General Assembly resolution 38/145 of 19 December 1983 has not been prepared,

Noting the increasing need to provide economic and social assistance to the Palestinian people;

1. *Takes note* of the report of the Secretary-General on assistance to the Palestinian people;[9]

2. *Notes* the meeting on assistance to the Palestinian people held at Geneva on 2 July 1986 in response to General Assembly resolution 40/170;

3. *Expresses its thanks* to the Secretary-General for convening the meeting on assistance to the Palestinian people;

4. *Regards* such a meeting as a valuable opportunity to assess progress in economic and social assistance to the Palestinian people and to explore ways and means of enhancing such assistance;

5. *Urges* the international community, the United Nations system and intergovernmental and non-governmental organizations to disburse their aid or any other form of assistance to the occupied Palestinian territories only for the benefit of the Palestinian people and in a manner which will not serve to prolong the Israeli occupation;

6. *Requests* the Secretary-General:

(*a*) To prepare without further delay the programme of economic and social assistance to the Palestinian people requested in General Assembly resolution 38/145;

(*b*) To convene in 1987 a meeting of the relevant programmes, organizations, agencies, funds and organs of the United Nations system to consider economic and social assistance to the Palestinian people;

(*c*) To invite the Palestine Liberation Organization, the Arab host countries and relevant intergovernmental and non-governmental organizations to participate in the meeting;

7. *Requests* the international community, the United Nations system and intergovernmental and non-governmental organizations to sustain and increase their assistance to the Palestinian people in co-operation with the Palestine Liberation Organization;

8. *Also requests* that United Nations assistance to the Palestinians in the Arab host countries should be rendered in co-operation with the Palestine Liberation Organization and with the consent of the Arab host Government concerned;

9. *Requests* the Secretary-General to report to the General Assembly at its forty-second session, through the Economic and Social Council, on the progress made in the implementation of the present resolution.

Adopted at the 38th plenary meeting.

Resolution No. 1986/67 of 23 July 1986

CONCERNING ISRAEL'S APPLICATION FOR MEMBERSHIP IN THE ECONOMIC COMMISSION FOR EUROPE

The Economic and Social Council,

Noting the letter dated 2 May 1986 from the Permanent Representative of Israel to the United Nations addressed to the President of the Economic and Social Council,[10] containing an application for admission to membership in the Economic Commission for Europe,

Noting the draft decision entitled "Membership of Israel in the Economic Commission for Europe",[11] sponsored by the United States of America,

Conscious of the right of all States Members of the United Nations to be admitted to a regional commission as full members,

Recognizing that the members of a regional commission should be consulted before the admission of any new member,

Recognizing that the question of admitting Israel to a regional commission as a full member should be resolved at the earliest possible time,

1. *Decides* to transmit the draft decision regarding Israel's membership in the Economic Commission for Europe[12] to the Economic and Social Council at its second regular session of 1987;

2. *Requests* the Executive Secretary of the Economic Commission for Europe to consult with States members of the Commission on the question of admitting Israel to the Commission and to report thereon to the Economic and Social Council at its second regular session of 1987, with a view to taking action on the question of Israel's full participation in the regional economic activities of the United Nations.

Adopted at the 38th plenary meeting.

---

[8] *Report of the International Conference on the Question of Palestine, Geneva, 29 August-7 September 1983* (United Nations publication, Sales No. E.83.I.21), chap. I, sect. B.

[9] A/41/319-E/1986/72 and Corr.1.

[10] E/1986/82.

[11] E/1986/C.1/L.7; see *Official Records of the General Assembly, Forty-first Session, Supplement No. 3* (A/41/3), chap. IV.

[12] *Ibid.*

B. COMMISSION ON HUMAN RIGHTS

Resolution No. 1982/1 A, B of 11 February 1982

CONDEMNING ISRAELI POLICIES AND PRACTICES AFFECTING THE HUMAN RIGHTS OF THE INHABITANTS OF THE OCCUPIED TERRITORIES

A

The Commission on Human Rights,

Guided by the purposes and principles of the Charter of the United Nations as well as the principles and provisions of the Universal Declaration of Human Rights,

Bearing in mind the provisions of the Geneva Convention relative to the Protection of Civilian Persons in Time of War of 12 August 1949[13] and of other relevant conventions and regulations,

Taking into consideration that the General Assembly has adopted resolution 3314 (XXIX) of 14 December 1974, which defined as an act of aggression the invasion or attack by the armed forces of a State of the territory of another State, or any military occupation, however temporary, resulting from such invasion or attack, or any annexation by the use of force of the territory of another State or part thereof,

Recalling General Assembly resolutions ES-7/2 of 29 July 1980, 36/15 of 28 October 1981, 36/120 of 10 December 1981, 36/147 of 16 December 1981 and 36/226 of 17 December 1981, and all General Assembly resolutions on Israeli violations of the human rights of the population of occupied Arab territories,

Recalling, in particular, Security Council resolutions 237 (1967) of 14 June 1967, 465 (1980) of 1 March 1980, 468 (1980) of 8 May 1980, 469 (1980) of 20 May 1980, 471 (1980) of 5 June 1980, 476 (1980) of 30 June 1980, 478 (1980) of 20 August 1980 and 484 (1980) of 19 December 1980,

Taking note of the reports and resolutions of the International Labour Organisation, the World Health Organization and the United Nations Educational, Scientific and Cultural Organization concerning the conditions of the population in the Palestinian and other occupied Arab territories since 1967, including Jerusalem,

Taking note of the report "Review of the economic conditions of the Palestinian people in the occupied Arab territories"[14] prepared by the secretariat of the United Nations Conference on Trade and Development,

Recalling its resolution 1 (XXXVII) of 11 February 1981 on the "Question of the violation of human rights in the occupied Arab territories, including Palestine", and previous resolutions of the Commission on Human Rights on this subject,

1. *Reaffirms* the fact that occupation itself constitutes a fundamental violation of the human rights of the civilian population of the Palestinian and other Arab occupied territories;

2. *Reiterates* the alarm deeply expressed by the Special Committee to Investigate Israeli Practices Affecting the Human Rights of the Population of the Occupied Territories in its reports submitted to the General Assembly at its thirty-fourth,[15] thirty-fifth[16] and thirty-sixth[17] sessions, that Israel's policy in the occupied territories is based on the so-called "Homeland" doctrine which envisages a mono-religious (Jewish) State that includes also territories occupied by Israel since June 1967, and the affirmation by the Special Committee that this policy not only denies the rights to self-determination of the population of the occupied territories but also constitutes the source of the continuing and systematic violation of human rights;

3. *Declares* that Israel's grave breaches of the Geneva Convention relative to the Protection of Civilian Persons in Time of War of 12 August 1949 and of the Additional Protocols to the Geneva Conventions[18] are war crimes and an affront to humanity;

4. *Firmly rejects and reiterates its condemnation* of Israel's decision to annex Jerusalem and alter its physical character, demographic composition, institutional structure and status, and considers all these measures and their consequences null and void;

5. *Strongly condemns* Israeli policies and practices, administrative and legislative measures to promote and expand the establishment of settler colonies in the occupied territories as well as the following practices:

(*a*) The annexation of parts of the occupied territories, including Jerusalem;

(*b*) The establishment of new Israeli settlements and expansion of the existing settlements on private and public Arab lands, and the transfer of an alien population thereto;

(*c*) The arming of settlers in the occupied territories to commit acts of violence against Arab civilians, the perpetration of acts of violence by these armed settlers against individuals, causing injury and death and wide-scale damage to Arab property;

(*d*) The evacuation, deportation, expulsion, displacement and transfer of Arab inhabitants of the occupied territories, and the denial of their right to return;

(*e*) The confiscation and expropriation of Arab property in the occupied territories and all other transactions for the acquisition of land involving Israeli authorities, institutions or nationals on the one hand, and inhabitants or institutions of the occupied territories on the other;

(*f*) The destruction and demolition of Arab houses;

(*g*) Mass arrests, collective punishments, administrative detention and ill-treatment of the Arab population and the torture of persons under detention, and the inhuman

---

[13]United Nations, *Treaty Series,* vol. 75, p. 287.
[14]TD/B/870.

[15]A/34/631.
[16]A/35/425.
[17]A/36/632/Add.1 and Add.1/Corr.1.
[18]A/32/144, annexes I and II.

conditions in prisons;

(h) The pillaging of archaeological and cultural property;

(i) The interference with religious freedoms and practices as well as with family rights and customs;

(j) The systematic Israeli repression against universities in the occupied Palestinian territories, restricting and impeding academic activities of Palestinian universities by subjecting selections of courses, textbooks and educational programmes, admission of students and appointment of faculty members to the control and supervision of the military occupation authorities;

(k) The illegal exploitation of the natural wealth, resources and population of the occupied territories;

6. *Calls upon* Israel to take immediate steps for the return of the displaced Arab inhabitants to their homes and property in Palestine and the other Arab territories occupied since June 1967;

7. *Calls upon* the Israeli authorities to implement forthwith Security Council resolution 484 (1980) of 19 December 1980 and previous resolutions calling for the immediate return of the expelled Mayors of Hebron and Halhoul so that they can assume the functions for which they were elected and appointed;

8. *Demands* that Israel desist forthwith from the policies and practices referred to in paragraphs 4 and 5 above;

9. *Calls upon* Israel to release all Arabs detained or imprisoned as a result of their struggle for self-determination and for the liberation of their territories, and to accord them, pending their release, the protection envisaged in the relevant provisions of the international instruments concerning the treatment of prisoners of war, and demands that Israel cease forthwith all acts of torture and ill-treatment of Arab detainees and prisoners;

10. *Reiterates* its call to all States, in particular the States parties to the Geneva Convention relative to the Protection of Civilian Persons in Time of War, in accordance with article 1 of that Convention, and to international organizations and specialized agencies, not to recognize any changes carried out by Israel in the occupied territories, including Jerusalem, and to avoid taking any action or extending any aid which might be used by Israel in its pursuit of the policies of annexation and colonization or any other policies and practices referred to in the present resolution;

11. *Calls upon* Israel to report, through the Secretary-General, to the Commission at its thirty-ninth session on the implementation of paragraphs 4, 5 and 9 above;

12. *Renews its request* to the Secretary-General to collect all relevant information concerning detainees, such as their number, identity, place and duration of detention, and to make this information available to the Commission at its thirty-ninth session;

13. *Requests* the Secretary-General to bring the present resolution to the attention of all Governments, the competent United Nations organs, the specialized agencies, the regional intergovernmental organizations and the international humanitarian organizations and to give it the widest possible publicity, and to report to the Commission on Human Rights at its thirty-ninth session;

14. *Further requests* the Secretary-General to bring to the attention of the Commission all United Nations reports appearing between sessions of the Commission that deal with the situation of the population of those occupied territories;

15. *Decides* that a seminar on "Violations of human rights in the Palestinian and other Arab territories occupied by Israel" be held at the United Nations Office at Geneva and requests the Secretary-General to make the appropriate arrangements for the organization of this seminar and to report to the Commission on Human Rights at its thirty-ninth session;

16. *Decides* to place on the provisional agenda of the thirty-ninth session as a matter of high priority the item entitled "Question of the violation of human rights in the Arab occupied territories, including Palestine".

Adopted at the 17th meeting:
In favour: 32*
Algeria, Argentina, Brazil, Bulgaria, Byelorussian SSR, China, Costa Rica, Cuba, Cyprus, Ethiopia, Fiji, Gambia, Ghana, Greece, India, Jordan, Mexico, Pakistan, Panama, Peru, Philippines, Poland, Senegal, Syrian Arab Republic, Togo, Uganda, USSR, Uruguay, Yugoslavia, Zaire, Zambia, Zimbabwe.
Against: 3

---

* The representative of Rwanda subsequently noted that he would have voted in favour had he been present.

B

The Commission on Human Rights,

Recalling its resolution 1 B (XXXVII) of 11 February 1981 and General Assembly resolutions 3092 A (XXVIII) of 7 December 1973, 32/91 A of 13 December 1977, 33/113 A of 18 December 1978, 34/90 B of 12 December 1979, 35/122 A of 11 December 1980 and 36/147 of 16 December 1981,

Recalling Security Council resolutions 465 (1980) of 1 March 1980, 468 (1980) of 8 May 1980, 469 (1980) of 20 May 1980, 471 (1980) of 5 June 1980, 476 (1980) of 30 June 1980, 478 (1980) of 20 August 1980 and 484 (1980) of 19 December 1980,

Recalling resolution III on the application of the Fourth Geneva Convention of 12 August 1949 adopted by the XXIVth International Conference of the Red Cross held at Manila in November 1981,

Bearing in mind that the provisions of the Geneva Conventions of 12 August 1949 must be fully applied in all circumstances to all persons who are protected by those instruments, without any adverse distinction based on the nature or origin of the armed conflict or on the causes espoused by or attributed to the conflict,

Recognizing that the persistent failure of Israel to apply the Geneva Convention relative to the Protection of Civilian Persons in Time of War of 12 August 1949[19] creates a situation fraught with danger,

Taking into account that States parties to the Fourth Geneva Convention of 12 August 1949 undertake, in accordance with article 1 thereof, not only to respect but also to ensure respect for the Convention in all circumstances,

1. *Expresses its deep concern* at the consequences of Israel's systematic refusal to apply the Geneva Convention relative to the Protection of Civilian Persons in Time of War of 12 August 1949 in all its provisions to Palestinian and other Arab territories occupied since 1967, including Jerusalem;

2. *Reaffirms* that the Geneva Convention relative to the Protection of Civilian Persons in Time of War is applicable to all the Arab territories occupied by Israel since 1967, including Jerusalem;

3. *Condemns* the failure of Israel to acknowledge the applicability of that Convention to the territories it has occupied since 1967, including Jerusalem;

4. *Calls upon* Israel to abide by and respect the obligations arising from the Charter of the United Nations and other instruments and rules of international law, in particular the provisions of the Geneva Convention relative to the Protection of Civilian Persons in Time of War, in Palestinian and other Arab territories occupied since 1967, including Jerusalem;

5. *Urges once more* all States parties to that Convention to exert all efforts in order to ensure respect for and compliance with the provisions thereof in all the Arab territories occupied by Israel since 1967, including Jerusalem;

6. *Requests* the Secretary-General to bring the present resolution to the attention of all Governments, the competent United Nations organs, the specialized agencies, the regional intergovernmental organizations, the international humanitarian organizations and non-governmental organizations.

Adopted at the 17th meeting:
In favour: 41*
Algeria, Argentina, Australia, Brazil, Bulgaria, Byelorussian SSR, Canada, China, Costa Rica, Cuba, Cyprus, Denmark, Ethiopia, Fiji, France, Gambia, Federal Republic of Germany, Ghana, Greece, India, Italy, Japan, Jordan, Mexico, Netherlands, Pakistan, Panama, Peru, Philippines, Poland, Senegal, Syrian Arab Republic, Togo, Uganda, USSR, United Kingdom, Uruguay, Yugoslavia, Zaire, Zambia, Zimbabwe.
Against: 1
United States.

---

* The representative of Rwanda subsequently stated that he would have voted in favour of the resolution had he been present.

---

[19]United Nations, *Treaty Series*, vol. 75, no. 973, p. 287.

Resolution No. 1982/2 of 11 February 1982

CONDEMNING ISRAEL'S DECISION OF 1981 ANNEXING THE GOLAN HEIGHTS AND DECLARING IT TO BE NULL AND VOID

The Commission on Human Rights,

Guided by the purposes and principles of the Charter of the United Nations as well as by the principles of international law,

Gravely alarmed by Israel's behaviour in ignoring all the relevant resolutions of the Security Council, the General Assembly, the Commission on Human Rights and other international organs of the United Nations concerning the Arab territories occupied by Israel and its persistent violations of human rights in those territories,

Reaffirming that the acquisition of territories by force is inadmissible, according to the Charter of the United Nations, the principles of international law, and relevant Security Council resolutions,

Recalling General Assembly resolution 3314 (XXIX) of 14 December 1974, which defined as an act of aggression the invasion or attack by the armed forces of a State of the territory of another State, or any military occupation resulting from such invasion or attack or any annexation by the use of force of the territory of another State or part thereof,

Recalling Security Council resolution 497/1981 of 17 December 1981, in which the Security Council decided that the Israeli decision to impose its laws, jurisdiction and administration in the occupied Syrian Golan Heights is null and void and without international legal effect,

Recalling its resolution 1 (XXXVII) of 11 February 1981 by which the Commission on Human Rights condemned the Israeli policies and practices of annexing parts of the occupied Arab territories,

Recalling General Assembly resolution 36/226 B of 17 December 1981 by which the General Assembly reaffirmed once more the applicability of the Geneva Convention relative to the Protection of Civilian Persons in Time of War of 12 August 1949[20] to the occupied Syrian territory,

Recalling General Assembly resolution ES-9/1 of 5 February 1982 in which the Assembly strongly deplored the negative vote by a permanent member of the Security Council which prevented the Council from adopting against Israel, under Chapter VII of the Charter, the "appropriate measures" referred to in resolution 497 (1981) unanimously adopted by the Council,

1. *Resolutely condemns* the Israeli decision, dated 14 December 1981, annexing the Golan Syrian territory occupied since 1967, through the imposition of its laws, jurisdiction and administration on the occupied territory;

2. *Declares* that the Israeli decision is null and void and without any international legal effect and demands that Israel, the occupying Power, rescind its illegal and pernicious act;

3. *Determines* that the persistent defiance by Israel of the

---

[20]*Ibid.*

resolutions and authority of the United Nations and the systematic violations of human rights in the occupied Arab territories, including Palestine, constitute a continuing threat to international peace and security;

4. *Calls upon* all Member States to apply against Israel the measures referred to in paragraphs 11, 12, 13 and 15 of General Assembly resolution ES-9/1 of 5 February 1982.

Adopted at the 17th meeting:
In favour: 22*
Algeria, Bulgaria, Byelorussian SSR, China, Cuba, Cyprus, Ethiopia, Gambia, Ghana, Greece, India, Jordan, Pakistan, Poland, Senegal, Syrian Arab Republic, Togo, Uganda, USSR, Yugoslavia, Zambia, Zimbabwe.
Against: 11
Australia, Canada, Denmark, Fiji, France, Federal Republic of Germany, Italy, Japan, Netherlands, United Kingdom, United States.
Abstentions: 7
Argentina, Brazil, Costa Rica, Mexico, Panama, Uruguay, Zaire.

---

* The representative of Rwanda subsequently stated that he would have voted in favour of the resolution had he been present.

Resolution No. 1982/3 of 11 February 1982

REAFFIRMING THE INALIENABLE RIGHT OF THE PALESTINIAN PEOPLE TO SELF-DETERMINATION AND AN INDEPENDENT STATE AND RETURN TO THEIR HOMES AND PROPERTY

The Commission on Human Rights,

Recalling General Assembly resolutions 1514 (XV) of 14 December 1960, 3236 (XXIX) of 22 November 1974, 3375 (XXX) and 3376 (XXX) of 10 November 1975, 32/14 of 7 November 1977, 32/20 of 25 November 1977, 32/40 of 2 December 1977, 32/42 of 7 December 1977, 33/28 of 7 December 1978, 34/65 of 29 November 1979, ES.7/2 of 29 July 1980, 35/169 of 15 December 1980, 36/120 of 10 December 1981 and 36/226 of 17 December 1981,

Recalling further Economic and Social Council resolutions 1865 (LVI) and 1866 (LVI) of 17 May 1974,

Reaffirming its resolutions 2 (XXXVII) of 11 February 1981 and 14 (XXXVII) of 6 March 1981,

Bearing in mind the report of the Committee on the Exercise of the Inalienable Rights of the Palestinian People,[21] and especially paragraphs 49 to 72 of that report,

Reaffirming that the Palestinian people are entitled to self-determination in accordance with the Charter of the United Nations and other relevant United Nations resolutions, and expressing its grave concern that the Palestinian people have been prevented by force from enjoying their inalienable rights, in particular their right to self-determination,

---

[21] *Official Records of the General Assembly, Thirty-sixth Session, Supplement No. 35* (A/36/35).

Expressing its grave concern that no just solution to the problem of Palestine has been achieved and that this problem therefore continues to aggravate the Middle East conflict, of which it is the core, and to endanger international peace and security,

1. *Reaffirms* the inalienable right of the Palestinian people to self-determination without external interference and the establishment of a fully independent and sovereign State of Palestine;

2. *Reaffirms* the inalienable right of the Palestinians to return to their homes and property, from which they have been displaced and uprooted by Israel, and calls for their return in the exercise of their right to self-determination;

3. *Recognizes* the right of the Palestinian people to regain their rights by all means in accordance with the purposes and principles of the Charter of the United Nations;

4. *Reaffirms* the basic principle that the future of the Palestinian people can only be decided with its full participation in all efforts, through its representative, the Palestine Liberation Organization;

5. *Expresses its strong opposition* to all partial agreements and separate treaties which constitute a flagrant violation of the rights of the Palestinian people, the principles of the Charter and the resolutions adopted in the various international forums on the Palestinian issue, as well as the principles of international law, and declares that all agreements and separate treaties have no validity in so far as they purport to determine the future of the Palestinian people and of the Palestinian territories occupied by Israel since 1967, including Jerusalem;

6. *Strongly rejects* the continuation of the negotiations on the question of "autonomy", within the framework of the "Camp David accords" and declares that these accords have no validity in so far as they purport to determine the future of the Palestinian people and of the Palestinian territories occupied by Israel since 1967;

7. *Urges* all States, United Nations organs, specialized agencies and other international organizations to extend their support to the Palestinian people through its representative, the Palestine Liberation Organization, in its struggle to restore its rights in accordance with the Charter and the relevant resolutions of the United Nations;

8. *Requests* the Secretary-General to make available to the Commission on Human Rights and to the Sub-Commission on Prevention of Discrimination and Protection of Minorities the reports, studies and publications prepared by the Special Unit on Palestinian Rights, which was established by General Assembly resolution 32/40 B of 2 December 1977.

Adopted at the 17th meeting:
In favour: 26
Algeria, Argentina, Bulgaria, Byelorussian SSR, China, Cuba, Cyprus, Ethiopia, Gambia, Ghana, Greece, India, Jordan, Pakistan, Peru, Poland, Senegal, Syrian Arab Republic, Togo, Uganda, USSR, Uruguay, Yugoslavia, Zimbabwe.

Against: 7

Australia, Canada, Denmark, Federal Republic of Germany, Italy, Netherlands, United Kingdom, United States.
Abstentions: 10

Brazil, Costa Rica, Fiji, France, Japan, Mexico, Panama, Philippines, Zaire, Zambia.

Resolution No. 1983/1 A, B of 15 February 1983

CONDEMNING ISRAELI POLICY AND PRACTICES AFFECTING THE HUMAN RIGHTS OF THE INHABITANTS OF THE OCCUPIED TERRITORIES

A

The Commission on Human Rights,

Guided by the purposes and principles of the Charter of the United Nations as well as the principles and provisions of the Universal Declaration of Human Rights,

Also guided by the provisions of the International Covenant on Economic, Social and Cultural Rights and the International Covenant on Civil and Political Rights,

Bearing in mind the provisions of the Geneva Convention relative to the Protection of Civilian Persons in Time of War of 12 August 1949 and of other relevant conventions and regulations,

Taking into consideration that the General Assembly has adopted resolution 3314 (XXIX) of 14 December 1974, which defined as an act of aggression "the invasion or attack by the armed forces of a State of the territory of another State, or any military occupation, however temporary, resulting from such invasion or attack, or any annexation by the use of force of the territory of another State or part thereof",

Recalling General Assembly resolutions ES-7/2 of 29 July 1980, 37/88 of 10 December 1982, 37/123 of 16/20 December 1982 and all relevant General Assembly resolutions on Israeli violations of the human rights of the population of occupied Arab territories,

Recalling, in particular, Security Council resolutions 237 (1967) of 14 June 1967, 465 (1980) of 1 March 1980, 468 (1980) of 8 May 1980, 469 (1980) of 20 May 1980, 471 (1980) of 5 June 1980, 476 (1980) of 30 June 1980, 478 (1980) of 20 August 1980 and 484 (1980) of 19 December 1980,

Taking note of the reports and resolutions of the International Labour Organisation, the World Health Organization and the United Nations Educational, Scientific and Cultural Organization concerning the conditions of the population in the Palestinian and other occupied Arab territories since 1967, including Jerusalem,

Recalling its resolution 1982/1 of 11 February 1982 on the "Question of the violation of human rights in the occupied Arab territories, including Palestine", and previous resolutions of the Commission on Human Rights on this subject,

Taking note of the report of the seminar on violations of human rights in the Palestinian and other Arab territories occupied by Israel, held at Geneva from 29 November to

3 December 1982,[22]

1. *Reaffirms* the fact that occupation itself constitutes a fundamental violation of the human rights of the civilian population of the Palestinian and other occupied Arab territories;

2. *Reiterates* the alarm deeply expressed by the Special Committee to Investigate Israeli Practices Affecting the Human Rights of the Population of the Occupied Territories in its reports submitted to the General Assembly at its thirty-fourth,[23] thirty-fifth,[24] thirty-sixth,[25] and thirty-seventh[26] sessions, that Israel's policy in the occupied territories is based on the so-called "Homeland" doctrine which envisages a mono-religious (Jewish) State that includes also territories occupied by Israel since June 1967, and the affirmation by the Special Committee that this policy not only denies the right to self-determination of the population of the occupied territories but also constitutes the source of the continuing and systematic violation of human rights;

3. *Declares* that Israel's continuous grave breaches of the Geneva Convention relative to the Protection of Civilian Persons in Time of War of 12 August 1949[27] and of the Additional Protocols[28] to the Geneva Conventions are war crimes and an affront to humanity;

4. *Firmly rejects and reiterates its condemnation of* Israel's decision to annex Jerusalem and to change the physical character, demographic composition, institutional structure or status of the occupied territories, including the Holy City, and considers all these measures and their consequences null and void;

5. *Strongly condemns* Israeli policies and practices, administrative and legislative measures to promote and expand the establishment of settler colonies in the occupied territories as well as the following practices:

(*a*) The annexation of parts of the occupied territories, including Jerusalem;

(*b*) The continuing establishment of new Israeli settlements and expansion of the existing settlements on private and public Arab lands, and the transfer of an alien population thereto;

(*c*) The arming of settlers in the occupied territories to commit acts of violence against Arab civilians, and the perpetration of acts of violence by these armed settlers against individuals, causing injury and death and wide-scale damage to Arab property;

(*d*) The evacuation, deportation, expulsion, displacement and transfer of Arab inhabitants of the occupied territories, and the denial of their right to return;

(*e*) The confiscation and expropriation of Arab property in the occupied territories and all other transactions for the acquisition of land involving Israeli authorities,

---

[22]ST/HR/SER.A/14.
[23]A/34/631.
[24]A/35/425.
[25]A/36/632 and Add.1 and Add.1/Corr.1.
[26]A/37/485.
[27]United Nations, *Treaty Series,* vol. 75, p. 287.
[28]A/32/144, annexes I and II.

institutions or nationals on the one hand, and inhabitants or institutions of the occupied territories on the other;

(*f*) The destruction and demolition of Arab houses;

(*g*) Mass arrests, collective punishments, administrative detention and ill-treatment of the Arab population and the torture of persons under detention, and the inhuman conditions in prisons;

(*h*) The pillaging of archaeological and cultural property;

(*i*) The interference with religious freedoms and practices as well as with family rights and customs;

(*j*) The systematic Israeli repression against cultural and educational institutions, especially universities, in the occupied Palestinian territories, closing them or restricting and impeding their academic activities by subjecting selection of courses, textbooks and educational programmes, admission of students and appointment of faculty members to the control and supervision of the military occupation authorities and by the expulsion of numerous faculty members of several universities for refusing to sign statements containing political positions, in flagrant defiance and disregard of their right to academic freedom;

(*k*) The illegal exploitation of the natural wealth, water and other resources and the population of the occupied territories;

(*l*) The dismantlement of the municipal services by dismissing the elected mayors as well as the municipal councils and forbidding Arab aid funds;

6. *Calls upon* Israel to take immediate steps for the return of the displaced Arab inhabitants to their homes and property in Palestine and the other Arab territories occupied since June 1967;

7. *Calls upon* the Israeli authorities to implement forthwith Security Council resolution 484 (1980) of 19 December 1980 and previous resolutions calling for the immediate return of the expelled Mayors of Hebron and Halhoul so that they can resume the functions for which they were elected and appointed;

8. *Calls upon* Israel to release all Arabs detained or imprisoned as a result of their struggle for self-determination and for the liberation of their territories, and to accord them, pending their release, the protection envisaged in the relevant provisions of the international instruments concerning the treatment of prisoners of war, and demands that Israel cease forthwith all acts of torture and ill-treatment of Arab detainees and prisoners;

9. *Reiterates* its call to all States, in particular the States parties to the Geneva Convention relative to the Protection of Civilian Persons in Time of War, in accordance with article 1 of that Convention, and to international organizations and specialized agencies, not to recognize any changes carried out by Israel in the occupied territories, including Jerusalem, and to avoid taking any action or extending any aid which might be used by Israel in its pursuit of the policies of annexation and colonization or any other policies and practices referred to in the present resolution;

10. *Urges* Israel to refrain from the policies and practices violating human rights in the occupied territories,

and to report, through the Secretary-General, to the Commission at its fortieth session on the implementation of this resolution;

11. *Requests* the General Assembly, through the Economic and Social Council, to recommend to the Security Council the adoption against Israel of the measures referred to in Chapter VII of the Charter of the United Nations for its persistence in violating the human rights of the population of the Palestinian and other occupied Arab territories;

12. *Requests* the Secretary-General to submit the report of the seminar on violations of human rights in the Palestinian and other Arab territories occupied by Israel to the General Assembly at its thirty-eighth session and to draw its attention particularly to the conclusions, recommendations and appeal adopted by the seminar;

13. *Renews its request* to the Secretary-General to collect all relevant information concerning detainees, such as their number, identity, place and duration of detention, and to make this information available to the Commission at its fortieth session;

14. *Requests* the Secretary-General to bring the present resolution to the attention of all Governments, the competent United Nations organs, the specialized agencies, the regional intergovernmental organizations and the international humanitarian organizations and to give it the widest possible publicity, and to report to the Commission on Human Rights at its fortieth session;

15. *Further requests* the Secretary-General to bring to the attention of the Commission all United Nations reports appearing between sessions of the Commission that deal with the situation of the population of those occupied territories;

16. *Decides* to place on the provisional agenda of the fortieth session as a matter of high priority the item entitled "Question of the violation of human rights in the occupied Arab territories, including Palestine".

Adopted at the 22nd meeting:
In favour: 29
Argentina, Bangladesh, Brazil, Bulgaria, China, Colombia, Cuba, Cyprus, Fiji, Gambia, Ghana, India, Jordan, Libyan Arab Jamahiriya, Mexico, Mozambique, Nicaragua, Pakistan, Philippines, Poland, Senegal, Togo, Uganda, Ukrainian SSR, USSR, United Republic of Tanzania, Uruguay, Yugoslavia, Zimbabwe.
Against: 1
United States.
Abstentions: 13
Australia, Canada, Costa Rica, Finland, France, Federal Republic of Germany, Ireland, Italy, Japan, Netherlands, Rwanda, United Kingdom, Zaire.

B

The Commission on Human Rights,
Recalling its resolution 1982/1 B of 11 February 1982 and General Assembly resolutions 3092 A (XXVIII) of 7 December 1973, 32/91 A of 13 December 1977, 33/113 A of 18 December 1978, 34/90 B of 12 December 1979,

35/122 A of 11 December 1980, 36/147 of 16 December 1981, and 37/88 A of 10 December 1982,

Recalling Security Council resolutions 465 (1980) of 1 March 1980, 468 (1980) of 8 May 1980, 469 (1980) of 20 May 1980, 471 (1980) of 5 June 1980, 476 (1980) of 30 June 1980, 478 (1980) of 20 August 1980 and 484 (1980) of 19 December 1980,

Recalling resolution III on the application of the Geneva Convention relative to the Protection of Civilian Persons in Time of War of 12 August 1949 adopted by the Twenty-fourth International Conference of the Red Cross held at Manila in November 1981,

Bearing in mind that the provisions of the Geneva Conventions of 12 August 1949 must be fully applied in all circumstances to all persons who are protected by those instruments, without any adverse distinction based on the nature or origin of the armed conflict or on the causes espoused by or attributed to the conflict,

Recognizing that the persistent failure of Israel to apply the Geneva Convention relative to the Protection of Civilian Persons in Time of War creates a situation fraught with danger,

Taking into account that States parties to the fourth Geneva Convention of 12 August 1949 undertake, in accordance with article 1 thereof, not only to respect but also to ensure respect for the Convention in all circumstances,

1. *Expresses its deep concern* at the consequence of Israel's systematic refusal to apply the Geneva Convention relative to the Protection of Civilian Persons in Time of War of 12 August 1949 in all its provisions to Palestinian and other Arab territories occupied since 1967, including Jerusalem;

2. *Reaffirms* that the Geneva Convention relative to the Protection of Civilian Persons in Time of War is applicable to all Arab territories occupied by Israel since 1967, including Jerusalem;

3. *Condemns* the failure of Israel to acknowledge the applicability of that Convention to the territories it has occupied since 1967, including Jerusalem;

4. *Calls upon* Israel to abide by and respect the obligations arising from the Charter of the United Nations and other instruments and rules of international law, in particular the provisions of the Geneva Convention relative to the Protection of Civilian Persons in Time of War, in Palestinian and other Arab territories occupied since 1967, including Jerusalem;

5. *Urges once more* all States parties to that Convention to exert all efforts in order to ensure respect for and compliance with the provisions thereof in all the Arab territories occupied by Israel since 1967, including Jerusalem;

6. *Requests* the Secretary-General to bring the present resolution to the attention of all Governments, the competent United Nations organs, the specialized agencies, the regional intergovernmental organizations, the international humanitarian organizations and non-governmental organizations.

Adopted at the 22nd meeting:
In favour: 39

Argentina, Australia, Bangladesh, Brazil, Bulgaria, Canada, China, Colombia, Cuba, Cyprus, Finland, France, Gambia, Federal Republic of Germany, Ghana, India, Ireland, Italy, Japan, Jordan, Libyan Arab Jamahiriya, Mexico, Mozambique, Netherlands, Nicaragua, Pakistan, Philippines, Poland, Rwanda, Senegal, Togo, Uganda, Ukrainian SSR, USSR, United Kingdom, United Republic of Tanzania, Uruguay, Yugoslavia, Zimbabwe.
Against: 1
United States.
Abstentions: 3
Costa Rica, Fiji,* Zaire.

---

* The representative of Fiji subsequently informed the Secretariat that his delegation had intended to vote in favour.

Resolution No. 1983/2 of 15 February 1983

DECLARING ISRAEL'S DECISION OF 1981 TO IMPOSE ITS LAWS, JURISDICTION AND ADMINISTRATION ON THE GOLAN HEIGHTS TO BE NULL AND VOID, AND CALLING ON ISRAEL TO RESCIND IT

The Commission on Human Rights,

Having examined the situation in the occupied Arab territories, including Palestine and the occupied Syrian Golan Heights,

Recalling its resolution 1982/2 of 11 February 1982,

Taking note of the report of the Special Committee to Investigate Israeli Practices Affecting the Human Rights of the Population of the Occupied Territories,[29]

Gravely alarmed by Israel's behaviour in systematically ignoring all relevant resolutions of the Security Council, the General Assembly, the Commission on Human Rights and other organs of the United Nations concerning the Arab territories occupied by Israel and its persistent violations of human rights in those territories,

Reaffirming that the acquisition of territories by force is inadmissible under the Charter of the United Nations, the principles of international law and relevant United Nations resolutions,

Recalling General Assembly resolution 3314 (XXIX) of 14 December 1974, in which the Assembly defined an act of aggression, *inter alia*, as "the invasion or attack by the armed forces of a State of the territory of another State, or any military occupation, however temporary, resulting from such invasion or attack, or any annexation by the use of force of the territory of another State or part thereof" and provided that "no consideration of whatever nature, whether political, economic, military or otherwise, may serve as a justification for aggression",

Recalling Security Council resolution 497 (1981) of 17 December 1981 and General Assembly resolutions 36/226 B of 17 December 1981, ES-9/1 of 5 February 1982 and 37/123 A of 16 December 1982,

Reaffirming once more the applicability of the Geneva Convention relative to the Protection of Civilian Persons

---

[29] A/37/485.

in Time of War of 12 August 1949 to the occupied Palestinian and other Arab territories, including the occupied Syrian Golan Heights,

Gravely alarmed by the inhuman treatment imposed by the occupying Israeli authorities on the Syrian population of the Golan Heights and noting that "The continued protests [by the Syrian population] led to a wave of arrests, dismissals and a rupture in communications and, on 25 February 1982, a blockade was imposed on the villages ... the population was even prevented from obtaining medical aid outside the area",[30]

1. *Resolutely condemns* Israel for its failure to comply with Security Council resolution 497 (1981) and General Assembly resolutions 36/226 B, ES-9/1 and 37/123 A;

2. *Declares once more* that Israel's decision of 14 December 1981 to impose its laws, jurisdiction and administration on the occupied Syrian Golan Heights constitutes an act of aggression under the provisions of Article 39 of the Charter of the United Nations and General Assembly resolution 3314 (XXIX);

3. *Declares once more* that Israel's decision to impose its laws, jurisdiction and administration on the occupied Syrian Golan Heights is null and void and has no legal validity and/or effect;

4. *Reaffirms its determination* that all provisions of the Hague Convention of 1907 and the Geneva Convention relative to the Protection of Civilian Persons in Time of War of 12 August 1949[31] continue to apply to the Syrian territory occupied by Israel since 1967, and calls upon parties thereto to respect their obligations under these instruments in all circumstances;

5. *Determines once more* that continued occupation of the Syrian Golan Heights since 1967 and its effective annexation by Israel on 14 December 1981, as well as the inhuman treatment of the Syrian population, constitute a grave violation of the Universal Declaration of Human Rights, the Geneva Convention and the relevant United Nations resolutions;

6. *Strongly deplores* the negative vote of a permanent member of the Security Council which prevented the Council from adopting against Israel, under chapter VII of the Charter of the United Nations, the "appropriate measures" referred to in resolution 497 (1981), adopted unanimously by the Security Council;

7. *Calls upon* Israel, the occupying Power, to rescind forthwith its decision of 14 December 1981 to impose its laws, jurisdiction and administration on the Syrian Golan Heights, and firmly emphasizes the overriding necessity of the total and unconditional withdrawal by Israel from all Palestinian and Syrian territories occupied since 1967, including Jerusalem, which is an essential prerequisite for the establishment of a comprehensive and just peace in the Middle East;

8. *Decides* to place on the provisional agenda of its fortieth session as a matter of high priority the item entitled "Question of the violation of human rights in the occupied Arab territories, including Palestine".

Adopted at the 22nd meeting:
In favour: 27
Argentina, Bangladesh, Brazil, Bulgaria, China, Colombia, Cuba, Cyprus, Gambia, Ghana, India, Jordan, Libyan Arab Jamahiriya, Mexico, Mozambique, Nicaragua, Pakistan, Poland, Rwanda, Senegal, Togo, Uganda, Ukrainian SSR, USSR, United Republic of Tanzania, Yugoslavia, Zimbabwe.
Against: 2
Australia, United States.
Abstentions: 13
Canada, Costa Rica, Fiji, Finland, France, Federal Republic of Germany, Ireland, Italy, Japan, Netherlands, United Kingdom, Uruguay, Zaire.

The representative of the Philippines announced that his delegation had not participated in the vote.

Resolution No. 1983/3 of 15 February 1983

REAFFIRMING THE INALIENABLE RIGHT OF THE PALESTINIAN PEOPLE TO SELF-DETERMINATION AND AN INDEPENDENT STATE AND TO RETURN TO THEIR HOMES AND PROPERTY

The Commission on Human Rights,

Recalling General Assembly resolutions 181 (II) of 29 November 1947, 194 (III) of 11 December 1948, 1514 (XV) of 14 December 1960, 3236 (XXIX) of 22 November 1974, 3375 (XXX) and 3376 (XXX) of 10 November 1975, 32/14 of 7 November 1977, 32/20 of 25 November 1977, 32/40 of 2 December 1977, 32/42 of 7 December 1977, 33/28 of 7 December 1978, 34/65 of 29 November 1979, ES-7/2 of 29 July 1980, 35/169 of 15 December 1980, 36/120 of 10 December 1981, 36/226 of 17 December 1981, ES-7/9 of 24 September 1982 and 37/86 of 10/20 December 1982,

Recalling further Economic and Social Council resolutions 1865 (LVI) and 1866 (LVI) of 17 May 1974,

Reaffirming its resolution 1982/3 of 11 February 1982,

Bearing in mind the report of the Committee on the Exercise of the Inalienable Rights of the Palestinian People,[32] and especially paragraphs 49 to 72 of that report,

Emphasizing once more that the Palestinian people are entitled to self-determination in accordance with the Charter of the United Nations and other relevant United Nations resolutions, and expressing its grave concern that Israel has prevented the Palestinian people by force from enjoying their inalienable rights, in particular their right to self-determination, in defiance of the principles of international law,

Expressing its grave concern that no just solution to the problem of Palestine has been achieved and that this problem therefore continues to aggravate the Middle East

[30]*Ibid.*, para. 43.
[31]United Nations, *Treaty Series,* vol. 75, p. 287.

[32]*Official Records of the General Assembly, Thirty-sixth Session, Supplement No. 35* (A/36/35).

conflict, of which it is the core, and to endanger international peace and security, as has been tragically illustrated by the Israeli invasion of Lebanon,

Welcoming the Arab peace plan adopted at the Twelfth Arab Summit Conference, held at Fez, Morocco, on 25 November 1981 and 9 September 1982,

1. *Condemns* Israel's continued occupation of the Palestinian and other Arab territories, including Jerusalem, in violation of the Charter of the United Nations, the principles of international law and the relevant resolutions of the United Nations, and demands the immediate, unconditional and total withdrawal of Israel from all these occupied territories;

2. *Condemns* Israel's aggression and practices against the Palestinian people in the occupied Palestinian territories and outside these territories, particularly Palestinians in Lebanon, as a result of the Israeli invasion of Lebanon which claimed the lives of thousands of Lebanese and Palestinian civilians;

3. *Condemns in the strongest terms* the large-scale massacre of Palestinian civilians in the Sabra and Shatila refugee camps for which the responsibility of the Israeli Government has been established;

4. *Decides* that the massacre was an act of genocide;

5. *Requests* the General Assembly to declare 17 September a day to commemorate the memory of the victims of Sabra and Shatila;

6. *Expresses its grave concern* that, until a just and equitable solution to the problem of Palestine has been implemented, the Palestinian people will be exposed to grave dangers such as the appalling massacre perpetrated in the Sabra and Shatila refugee camps;

7. *Reaffirms* the inalienable right of the Palestinian people to self-determination without external interference and the establishment of a fully independent and sovereign State of Palestine;

8. *Reaffirms* the inalienable right of the Palestinians to return to their homes and property, from which they have been displaced and uprooted by Israel, and calls for their return in the exercise of their right to self-determination;

9. *Recognizes* the right of the Palestinian people to regain their rights by all means in accordance with the purposes and principles of the Charter of the United Nations;

10. *Reaffirms* the basic principle that the future of the Palestinian people can only be decided with its full participation in all efforts, through its representative, the Palestine Liberation Organization;

11. *Rejects* all partial agreements and separate treaties in so far as they violate the inalienable rights of the Palestinian people and contradict the principles of just and comprehensive solutions to the Middle East problem to ensure the establishment of a just peace in the area, in accordance with the principles of the Charter of the United Nations and with relevant United Nations resolutions;

12. *Strongly rejects* the plan of "autonomy" within the framework of the "Camp David accords" and declares that these accords have no validity in so far as they purport to determine the future of the Palestinian people and of the Palestinian territories occupied by Israel since 1967;

13. *Urges* all States, United Nations organs, specialized agencies and other international organizations to extend their support to the Palestinian people through its representative, the Palestine Liberation Organization, in its struggle to restore its rights in accordance with the Charter and the relevant resolutions of the United Nations;

14. *Requests* the Secretary-General to make available to the Commission on Human Rights and to the Sub-Commission on Prevention of Discrimination and Protection of Minorities the reports, studies and publications prepared by the Division for Palestinian Rights.

Adopted at the 22nd meeting:
In favour: 26
Argentina, Bangladesh, Brazil, Bulgaria, China, Colombia, Cuba, Cyprus, Gambia, Ghana, India, Jordan, Libyan Arab Jamahiriya, Mozambique, Nicaragua, Pakistan, Poland, Rwanda, Senegal, Togo, Uganda, Ukrainian SSR, USSR, United Republic of Tanzania, Yugoslavia, Zimbabwe.
Against: 7
Australia, Canada, Federal Republic of Germany, Italy, Netherlands, United Kingdom, United States.
Abstentions: 10
Costa Rica, Fiji, Finland, France, Ireland, Japan, Mexico, Philippines, Uruguay, Zaire.

Resolution No. 1984/1 A, B of 20 February 1984

CONDEMNING ISRAELI POLICIES AND PRACTICES AFFECTING THE HUMAN RIGHTS OF THE INHABITANTS OF THE OCCUPIED TERRITORIES

A

The Commission on Human Rights,

Guided by the purposes and principles of the Charter of the United Nations as well as the principles and provisions of the Universal Declaration of Human Rights,

Also guided by the provisions of the International Covenant on Economic, Social and Cultural Rights and the International Covenant on Civil and Political Rights,

Bearing in mind the provisions of the Geneva Convention relative to the Protection of Civilian Persons in Time of War, of 12 August 1949,[33] and of other relevant conventions and regulations,

Taking into consideration that the General Assembly has adopted resolution 3314 (XXIX) of 14 December 1974, which defined as an act of aggression "the invasion or attack by the armed forces of a State of the territory of another State, or any military occupation, however temporary, resulting from such invasion or attack, or any annexation by the use of force of the territory of another State or part thereof",

---
[33]United Nations, *Treaty Series,* vol. 75, no. 973, p. 287.

Recalling General Assembly resolutions ES-7/2 of 29 July 1980, 37/88 A to G of 10 December 1982, 37/123 A to F of 16 and 20 December 1982, 38/58 A to E of 13 December 1983 and 38/79 A to H of 15 December 1983, and all other relevant General Assembly resolutions on Israeli violations of the human rights of the population of occupied Arab territories,

Recalling, in particular, Security Council resolutions 237 (1967) of 14 June 1967, 465 (1980) of 1 March 1980, 468 (1980) of 8 May 1980, 469 (1980) of 20 May 1980, 471 (1980) of 5 June 1980, 476 (1980) of 30 June 1980, 478 (1980) of 20 August 1980 and 484 (1980) of 19 December 1980,

Taking note of the reports and resolutions of the International Labour Organisation, the World Health Organization and the United Nations Educational, Scientific and Cultural Organization as well as the report of the seminar on violations of human rights in the Palestinian and other Arab territories occupied by Israel, held at Geneva from 29 November to 3 December 1982,[34] the Geneva Declaration adopted by the International Conference on the Question of Palestine held at Geneva from 29 August to 7 September 1983,[35] and the reports of the Special Committee to Investigate Israeli Practices Affecting the Human Rights of the Population of the Occupied Territories,

Recalling the International Committee of the Red Cross press release No. 1478 of 13 December 1983 on Israeli violations of the agreement for the exchange of prisoners between the Palestine Liberation Organization and Israel which involved the retaining of prisoners and detainees whose release was provided for in the agreement,

Recalling its resolutions 1982/1 A and B of 11 February 1982 and 1983/1 A and B and 1983/2 of 15 February 1983 on the "Question of the violation of human rights in the occupied Arab territories, including Palestine", and previous resolutions of the Commission on Human Rights on this subject,

1. *Reaffirms* the fact that occupation itself constitutes a fundamental violation of the human rights of the civilian population of the Palestinian and other occupied Arab territories;

2. *Denounces* the continued refusal of Israel to allow the Special Committee to Investigate Israeli Practices Affecting the Human Rights of the Population of the Occupied Territories access to the occupied territories;

3. *Reiterates* the deep alarm expressed by the Special Committee in its reports submitted to the General Assembly at its thirty-fourth,[36] thirty-fifth,[37] thirty-sixth,[38] thirty-seventh,[39] and thirty-eighth[40] sessions that Israel's policy

in the occupied territories is based on the so-called "Homeland" doctrine which envisages a monoreligious (Jewish) State that includes territories occupied by Israel since June 1967, and the affirmation by the Special Committee that this policy not only denies the right to self-determination of the population of the occupied territories but also constitutes the source of the continuing and systematic violation of human rights;

4. *Confirms its declaration* that Israel's continuous grave breaches of the Geneva Convention relative to the Protection of Civilian Persons in Time of War of 12 August 1949 and of the Additional Protocols[41] to the Geneva Conventions are war crimes and an affront to humanity;

5. *Firmly rejects and reiterates its condemnation of* Israel's decision to annex Jerusalem and to change the physical character, demographic composition, institutional structure or status of the occupied territories, including the Holy City, and considers all these measures and their consequences null and void;

6. *Strongly condemns* Israel's attempts to subject the West Bank and the Gaza Strip to Israeli laws;

7. *Strongly condemns* Israeli policies and practices, administrative and legislative measures to promote and expand the establishment of settler colonies in the occupied territories as well as the following practices:

(*a*) The annexation of parts of the occupied territories, including Jerusalem;

(*b*) The continuing establishment of new Israeli settlements and expansion of the existing settlements on private and public Arab lands, and the transfer of an alien population thereto;

(*c*) The arming of settlers in the occupied territories to commit acts of violence against Arab civilians, and the perpetration of acts of violence by these armed settlers against individuals, causing injury and death and wide-scale damage to Arab property;

(*d*) The arming of settlers in the occupied territories to strike at Muslim and Christian religious and holy places;

(*e*) The evacuation, deportation, expulsion, displacement and transfer of Arab inhabitants of the occupied territories, and the denial of their right to return;

(*f*) The confiscation and expropriation of Arab property in the occupied territories and all other transactions for the acquisition of land involving Israeli authorities, institutions or nationals on the one hand, and inhabitants or institutions of the occupied territories on the other;

(*g*) The destruction and demolition of Arab houses;

(*h*) Mass arrests, collective punishments, administrative detention and ill-treatment of the Arab population, the torture of persons under detention and the inhuman conditions in prisons;

(*i*) The pillaging of archaeological and cultural property;

(*j*) The interference with religious freedoms and practices as well as with family rights and customs;

(*k*) The systematic Israeli repression against cultural

[34] ST/HR/SER.A/14.

[35] *Report of the International Conference on the Question of Palestine, Geneva, 29 August-7 September 1983* (United Nations publication, Sales No. E.83.I.21), part one, chap. I, sect. A.

[36] A/34/631.

[37] A/35/425.

[38] A/36/632 and Add.1 and Add.1/Corr.1.

[39] A/37/485.

[40] A/38/409.

[41] International Committee of the Red Cross, *Protocols additional to the Geneva Conventions of 12 August 1949* (Geneva, 1977).

and educational institutions, especially universities, in the occupied Palestinian territories, closing them or restricting and impeding their academic activities by subjecting selection of courses, textbooks and educational programmes, admission of students and appointment of faculty members to the control and supervision of the military occupation authorities and by the expulsion of numerous faculty members of several universities for refusing to sign statements containing political positions, in flagrant defiance and disregard of their right to academic freedom;

(*l*) The illegal exploitation of the natural wealth, water and other resources and the population of the occupied territories;

(*m*) The dismantling of municipal services, the dismissing of the elected mayors as well as the municipal councils and forbidding Arab aid funds;

8. *Calls upon* Israel to take immediate steps for the return of the displaced Arab inhabitants to their homes and property in Palestine and the other Arab territories occupied since June 1967;

9. *Calls upon* the Israeli authorities to implement forthwith Security Council resolution 484 (1980) of 19 December 1980 and previous resolutions calling for the immediate return of the municipal chiefs to their municipalities so that they can resume the functions for which they were elected;

10. *Calls upon* Israel to release all Arabs detained or imprisoned as a result of their struggle for self-determination and for the liberation of their territories, and, pending their release, to accord them the protection envisaged in the relevant provisions of the international instruments concerning the treatment of prisoners of war, and demands that Israel cease forthwith all acts of torture and ill-treatment of Arab detainees and prisoners;

11. *Condemns* Israel for its continued detention of Ziad Abu Ain, and calls on Israel to implement fully the agreement on the exchange of prisoners with the Palestine Liberation Organization concluded with the International Committee of the Red Cross in November 1983; and further calls on Israel to release Ziad Abu Ain and others whom it continues to detain and who were in Ansar Camp, which must be closed under the provisions of the above-mentioned agreement;

12. *Reiterates* its call to all States, in particular the States parties to the Geneva Convention relative to the Protection of Civilian Persons in Time of War, in accordance with article 1 of that Convention, and to international organizations and specialized agencies, not to recognize any changes carried out by Israel in the occupied territories, including Jerusalem, and to avoid taking any action or extending any aid which might be used by Israel in its pursuit of the policies of annexation and colonization or any other policies and practices referred to in the present resolution;

13. *Urges* Israel to refrain from the policies and practices violating human rights in the occupied territories, and to report, through the Secretary-General, to the

Commission at its forty-first session on the implementation of this resolution;

14. *Requests* the General Assembly, through the Economic and Social Council, to recommend to the Security Council the adoption against Israel of the measures referred to in Chapter VII of the Charter of the United Nations for its persistent violation of the human rights of the population of the Palestinian and other occupied Arab territories;

15. *Requests* the Secretary-General to bring the present resolution to the attention of all Governments, the competent United Nations organs, the specialized agencies, the regional intergovernmental organizations and the international humanitarian organizations and to give it the widest possible publicity, and to report to the Commission on Human Rights at its forty-first session;

16. *Further requests* the Secretary-General to bring to the attention of the Commission all United Nations reports appearing between sessions of the Commission that deal with the situation of the population of those occupied territories;

17. *Decides* to place on the provisional agenda of the forty-first session as a matter of high priority the item entitled "Question of the violation of human rights in the occupied Arab territories, including Palestine".

Adopted at the 19th meeting:
In favour: 29
Against: 1
Abstentions: 11

B

The Commission on Human Rights,

Recalling its resolutions 1982/1 B of 11 February 1982 and 1982/1 B of 15 February 1983 and General Assembly resolutions 3092 A (XXVIII) of 7 December 1973, 32/91 A of 13 December 1977, 33/113 A of 18 December 1978, 34/90 B of 12 December 1979, 35/122 A of 11 December 1980, 36/147 A of 16 December 1981, 37/88 of 10 December 1982 and 38/79 B of 15 December 1983,

Recalling Security Council resolutions 465 (1980) of 1 March 1980, 468 (1980) of 8 May 1980, 469 (1980) of 20 May 1980, 471 (1980) of 5 June 1980, 476 (1980) of 30 June 1980, 478 (1980) of 20 August 1980 and 484 (1980) of 19 December 1980,

Recalling resolution III on the application of the Geneva Convention relative to the Protection of Civilian Persons in Time of War of 12 August 1949 adopted by the Twenty-fourth International Conference of the Red Cross held at Manila in November 1981,

Bearing in mind that the provisions of the Geneva Conventions of 12 August 1949 must be fully applied in all circumstances to all persons who are protected by those instruments, without any adverse distinction based on the nature or origin of the armed conflict or on the causes espoused by or attributed to the conflict,

Recognizing that the persistent failure of Israel to apply the Geneva Convention relative to the Protection of Civilian Persons in Time of War creates a situation fraught with danger, and considering that it persists in violating human rights,

Taking into account that States parties to the Geneva Convention relative to the Protection of Civilian Persons in Time of War undertake, in accordance with article 1 thereof, not only to respect but also to ensure respect for the Convention in all circumstances,

1. *Reaffirms* that the Geneva Convention relative to the Protection of Civilian Persons in Time of War is applicable to all the Arab territories occupied by Israel since 1967, including Jerusalem;

2. *Expresses* its deep concern at the consequence of Israel's systematic refusal to apply that Convention in all its provisions to Palestinian and other Arab territories occupied since 1967, including Jerusalem;

3. *Condemns* the failure of Israel to acknowledge the applicability of that Convention to the territories it has occupied since 1967, including Jerusalem;

4. *Calls upon* Israel to abide by and respect the obligations arising from the Charter of the United Nations and other instruments and rules of international law, in particular the provisions of the Geneva Convention relative to the Protection of Civilian Persons in Time of War, in Palestinian and other Arab territories occupied since 1967, including Jerusalem; requests Israel to release all Arabs detained or imprisoned as a result of their struggle for self-determination and the liberation of their territories and to accord them, pending their release, the protection envisaged in the relevant provisions of the international instruments concerning the treatment of prisoners of war; and demands that Israel cease forthwith all acts of torture and ill-treatment of Arab detainees and prisoners;

5. *Urges once more* all States parties to that Convention to make every effort to ensure respect for and compliance with the provisions thereof in all the Arab territories occupied by Israel since 1967, including Jerusalem;

6. *Requests* the Secretary-General to bring the present resolution to the attention of all Governments, the competent United Nations organs, the specialized agencies, the regional intergovernmental organizations, the international humanitarian organizations and non-governmental organizations, and to submit a report on progress in its implementation to the Commission on Human Rights at its forty-first session.

Adopted at the 19th meeting:
In favour: 32
Against: 1
Abstentions: 8

Resolution No. 1984/2 of 20 February 1984

REPEATING THAT ISRAEL'S DECISION OF 1981 TO IMPOSE ITS LAWS, JURISDICTION AND ADMINISTRATION ON THE GOLAN HEIGHTS IS NULL AND VOID, AND CALLING UPON ISRAEL TO RESCIND IT

The Commission on Human Rights,
Having examined the ever deteriorating situation in the

occupied Arab territories, including Palestine and the occupied Syrian Golan Heights,

Recalling its resolution 1983/2 of 15 February 1983,

Taking note of the report of the Special Committee of Experts appointed to study the health conditions of the inhabitants of the occupied territories[42] and the relevant resolution of the World Health Assembly,[43]

Having considered the report of the Special Committee to Investigate Israeli Practices Affecting the Human Rights of the Population of the Occupied Territories,[44]

Gravely alarmed by Israel's increasingly arrogant behaviour in systematically ignoring and openly defying all relevant resolutions of the Security Council, the General Assembly, the Commission on Human Rights, the World Health Organization, and other organs and agencies of the United Nations concerning the Arab territories occupied by Israel and its persistent violations of human rights in those territories,

Reaffirming that the acquisition of territories by force is inadmissible under the Charter of the United Nations, the principles of international law and relevant United Nations resolutions,

Recalling General Assembly resolution 3314 (XXIX) of 14 December 1974, in which the Assembly defined an act of aggression, *inter alia*, as "the invasion or attack by the armed forces of a State of the territory of another State, or any military occupation, however temporary, resulting from such invasion or attack, or any annexation by the use of force of the territory of another State or part thereof" and provided that "no consideration of whatever nature, whether political, economic, military or otherwise, may serve as a justification for aggression",

Recalling Security Council resolution 497 (1981) of 17 December 1981 and General Assembly resolutions 36/226 B of 17 December 1981, ES-9/1 of 5 February 1982 and 37/123 A of 16 December 1982 in connection with the Israeli occupation of the Syrian Golan Heights, and the imposition of its laws, jurisdiction and administration on the Syrian occupied territory,

Reiterating its grave alarm at the inhuman treatment which the occupying Israeli authorities continue to impose on the Syrian population of the occupied Golan Heights, and the measures and actions designed to change the legal status, geographic nature and demographic composition of these occupied territories,

Recalling General Assembly resolutions 38/79 D and F of 15 December 1983 and 38/180 A and D of 19 December 1983 on the situation in the Middle East and the report of the Special Committee to Investigate Israeli Practices Affecting the Human Rights of the Population of the Occupied Territories,

1. *Resolutely condemns* Israel for its failure to comply with Security Council resolution 497 (1981) and General Assembly resolutions 36/226 B, ES-9/1 and 37/123 A;

---

[42]World Health Organization, document A36/14, 28 April 1983.
[43]World Health Organization, document WHA36.27, 16 May 1983.
[44]A/38/409.

2. *Declares once more* that Israel's decision of 14 December 1981 to impose its laws, jurisdiction and administration on the occupied Syrian Golan Heights, whose outcome has been the effective annexation of this territory, is null and void and has no legal validity and no effect, and that Israeli practices and inhuman treatment of the Syrian Arab population constitute a grave violation of the Universal Declaration of Human Rights, the Geneva Convention relative to the Protection of Civilian Persons in Time of War of 12 August 1949[45] and the relevant United Nations resolutions as well as a continuing threat to international peace and security;

3. *Strongly condemns* Israel for its attempts and measures to impose Israeli citizenship and identity cards on the Syrian citizens in the occupied Golan Heights by force;

4. *Strongly deplores* the negative vote and pro-Israeli position of a permanent member of the Security Council which prevented the Council from adopting against Israel, under Chapter VII of the Charter of the United Nations, the "appropriate measures" referred to in resolution 497 (1981), adopted unanimously by the Security Council;

5. *Reaffirms* its determination that all provisions of The Hague Convention of 1907[46] and the Geneva Convention relative to the Protection of Civilian Persons in Time of War continue to apply to the Syrian territory occupied by Israel since 1967, strongly demands that Israel recognize the provisions of these Conventions and apply them in the occupied Arab territories, and calls upon parties to these Conventions to respect their obligations thereunder in all circumstances;

6. *Calls upon* Israel, the occupying Power, to rescind forthwith its decision of 14 December 1981 to impose its laws, jurisdiction and administration on the Syrian Golan Heights, emphasizes that Israel must allow the evacuees from among the Golan population to return to their homes and to recover their former property and residences occupied by Israel since 1967, and firmly emphasizes the overriding necessity of the total and unconditional withdrawal by Israel from all Palestinian and Syrian territories occupied since 1967, including Jerusalem, which is an essential prerequisite for the establishment of a comprehensive and just peace in the Middle East;

7. *Decides* to place on the provisional agenda of its forty-first session as a matter of high priority the item entitled "Question of the violation of human rights in the occupied Arab territories, including Palestine".

Adopted at the 19th meeting:
In favour: 30
Argentina, Bangladesh, Brazil, Bulgaria, Cameroon, China, Colombia, Cuba, Cyprus, Gambia, German Democratic Republic, India, Jordan, Kenya, Libyan Arab Jamahiriya, Mauritania, Mexico, Mozambique, Nicaragua, Pakistan,

Philippines, Rwanda, Senegal, Spain, Syrian Arab Republic, Ukrainian SSR, USSR, United Republic of Tanzania, Yugoslavia, Zimbabwe.
Against: 1
United States.
Abstentions: 11
Canada, Costa Rica, Finland, France, Federal Republic of Germany, Ireland, Italy, Japan, Netherlands, United Kingdom, Uruguay.

The representative of Togo subsequently stated that he would have voted in favour of the resolution had he been present.

Resolution No. 1984/3 of 20 February 1984

CONDEMNING ISRAEL'S POLICIES OF OCCUPATION AND SETTLEMENT IN THE OCCUPIED TERRITORIES, AND CALLING FOR ITS COMPLETE WITHDRAWAL FROM THEM

The Commission on Human Rights,

1. *Condemns* Israel for its continued occupation of the Palestinian territories, including Jerusalem, and of other Arab territories in violation of relevant United Nations resolutions and of the provisions of international law;

2. *Condemns* Israel for its persistence in developing the colonization of these territories which aims at changing the demographic composition, institutional structure and status of the occupied territories, including Jerusalem;

3. *Reaffirms* that measures such as those described in the above paragraph constitute grave violations of the Geneva Convention relative to the Protection of Civilian Persons in Time of War of 12 August 1949,[47] and The Hague Convention of 1907,[48] and that they are null and void with regard to international law;

4. *Calls upon* Israel to withdraw immediately from the occupied Palestinian territories, including Jerusalem, in order to restore to the Palestinian people their inalienable national rights, and from all the other occupied Arab territories.

Adopted at the 19th meeting:
In favour: 30
Against: 1
Abstentions: 11

Resoltuion No. 1985/1 A, B of 19 February 1985

CONDEMNING ISRAELI POLICIES AND PRACTICES AFFECTING THE HUMAN RIGHTS OF THE INHABITANTS OF THE OCCUPIED TERRITORIES

The Commission on Human Rights,

Guided by the purposes and principles of the Charter of the United Nations as well as the principles and provis-

---

[45]United Nations, *Treaty Series*, vol. 75, No. 973, p. 287.
[46]Carnegie Endowment for International Peace, *The Hague Conventions and Declarations of 1899 and 1907* (New York, Oxford University Press, 1915), p. 100.

[47]United Nations, *Treaty Series*, vol. 75, no. 973, p. 287.
[48]Carnegie Endowment for International Peace, *The Hague Conventions and Declarations of 1899 and 1907* (New York, Oxford University Press, 1915), p. 100.

ions of the Universal Declaration of Human Rights,

Guided also by the provisions of the International Covenant on Economic, Social and Cultural Rights and the International Covenant on Civil and Political Rights,

Bearing in mind the provisions of the Geneva Convention relative to the Protection of Civilian Persons in Time of War, of 12 August 1949,[49] and of other relevant conventions and regulations,

Taking into consideration General Assembly resolution 3314 (XXIX) of 14 December 1974, which defined as an act of aggression "the invasion or attack by the armed forces of a State of the territory of another State, or any military occupation, however temporary, resulting from such invasion or attack, or any annexation by the use of force of the territory of another State or part thereof",

Recalling General Assembly resolutions ES-7/2 of 29 July 1980, 37/88 A to G of 10 December 1982, 37/123 A to F of 16 and 20 December 1982, 38/58 A to E of 13 December 1983, 38/79 A to H of 15 December 1983, 39/49 A to D of 11 December 1984 and 39/95 A to H of 14 December 1984 and all other relevant General Assembly resolutions on Israeli violations of the human rights of the population of occupied Arab territories,

Recalling, in particular, Security Council resolutions 237 (1967) of 14 June 1967, 465 (1980) of 1 March 1980, 468 (1980) of 8 May 1980, 469 (1980) of 20 May 1980, 471 (1980) of 5 June 1980, 476 (1980) of 30 June 1980, 478 (1980) of 20 August 1980 and 484 (1980) of 19 December 1980,

Taking note of the reports and resolutions of the International Labour Organisation, the World Health Organization and the United Nations Educational, Scientific and Cultural Organization as well as the report of the seminar on violations of human rights in the Palestinian and other Arab territories occupied by Israel, held at Geneva from 29 November to 3 December 1982,[50] the Geneva Declaration adopted by the International Conference on the Question of Palestine held at Geneva from 29 August to 7 September 1983,[51] and the reports of the Special Committee to Investigate Israeli Practices Affecting the Human Rights of the Population of the Occupied Territories,

Recalling the International Committee of the Red Cross press release No. 1478 of 13 December 1983 on Israeli violations of the agreement for the exchange of prisoners between the Palestine Liberation Organization and Israel which involved the retaining of prisoners and detainees whose release was provided for in the agreement,

Recalling its resolutions 1982/1 A and B of 11 February 1982, 1983/1 A and B and 1983/2 of 15 February 1983 and 1984/1 A and B and 1984/2 of 20 February 1984 on the "Question of the violation of human rights in the occupied Arab territories, including Palestine", and previous resolutions of the Commission on Human Rights on this subject,

1. *Reaffirms* the fact that occupation itself constitutes a fundamental violation of the human rights of the civilian population of the Palestinian and other occupied Arab territories;

2. *Denounces* the continued refusal of Israel to allow the Special Committee to Investigate Israeli Practices Affecting the Human Rights of the Population of the Occupied Territories access to the occupied territories;

3. *Reiterates* the deep alarm expressed by the Special Committee in its reports submitted to the General Assembly at its thirty-fourth,[52] thirty-fifth,[53] thirty-sixth,[54] thirty-seventh,[55] thirty-eighth[56] and thirty-ninth[57] sessions that Israel's policy in the occupied territories is based on the so-called "Homeland" doctrine which envisages a mono-religious (Jewish) State that includes territories occupied by Israel since June 1967, and the affirmation by the Special Committee that this policy not only denies the right to self-determination of the population of the occupied territories but also constitues the source of the continuing and systematic violation of human rights;

4. *Confirms its declaration* that Israel's continuous grave breaches of the Geneva Convention relative to the Protection of Civilian Persons in Time of War, of 12 August 1949, and of the Additional Protocols[58] to the Geneva Conventions are war crimes and an affront to humanity;

5. *Firmly rejects and reiterates its condemnation* of Israel's decision to annex Jerusalem and to change the physical character, demographic composition, institutional structure or status of the occupied territories, including the Holy City, and considers all these measures and their consequences null and void;

6. *Strongly condemns* Israel's attempts to subject the West Bank and the Gaza Strip to Israeli laws;

7. *Strongly condemns* all the terrorist actions perpetrated against the Palestinian inhabitants of the occupied territories by Jewish gangs, led by Rabbi Meir Kahane, member of the Knesset, and the racist Rabbi Moshe Levinger, the leader of the Gush Emunim gang, and other racist Zionists;

8. *Strongly condemns* Israeli policies and practices, administrative and legislative measures to promote and expand the establishment of settler colonies in the occupied territories as well as the following practices:

(*a*) The annexation of parts of the occupied territories, including Jerusalem;

(*b*) The continuing establishment of new Israeli settlements and expansion of the existing settlements on private and public Arab lands, and the transfer of an alien population thereto;

---

[49]United Nations, *Treaty Series*, vol. 75, no. 973, p. 287.

[50]ST/HR/SER.A/14.

[51]*Report of the International Conference on the Question of Palestine, Geneva, 29 August-7 September 1983* (United Nations publication, Sales No. E.83.I.21), part one, chap. I, sect. A.

[52]A/34/631.

[53]A/35/425.

[54]A/36/632 and Add.1 and Add.1/Corr.1.

[55]A/37/485.

[56]A/38/409.

[57]A/39/591.

[58]International Committee of the Red Cross, *Protocols additional to the Geneva Conventions of 12 August 1949* (Geneva, 1977).

(c) The arming of settlers in the occupied territories to commit acts of violence against Arab civilians, and the perpetration of acts of violence by these armed settlers against individuals, causing injury and death and wide-scale damage to Arab property;

(d) The arming of settlers in the occupied territories to strike at Muslim and Christian religious and holy places;

(e) The evacuation, deportation, expulsion, displacement and transfer of Arab inhabitants of the occupied territories, the denial of their right to return to their homeland and the transfer and settlement of alien populations brought from other parts of the world in the place of the original Palestinian owners of land;

(f) The confiscation and expropriation of Arab property in the occupied territories and all other transactions for the acquisition of land involving Israeli authorities, institutions or nationals on the one hand, and inhabitants or institutions of the occupied territories on the other;

(g) The destruction and demolition of Arab houses;

(h) Mass arrests, collective punishments, administrative detention and ill-treatment of the Arab population, the torture of persons under detention and the inhuman conditions in prisons;

(i) The pillaging of archaelogical and cultural property;

(j) The interference with religious freedoms and practices as well as with family rights and customs;

(k) The systematic Israeli repression of cultural and educational institutions, especially universities, schools and institutes, in the occupied Palestinian territories, closing them or restricting and impeding their academic activities by subjecting selection of courses, textbooks and educational programmes, admission of students and appointment of faculty members to the control and supervision of the military occupation authorities and by expelling numerous faculty members of several universities for refusing to sign statements containing political positions, in flagrant defiance and disregard of their right to academic freedom;

(l) The illegal expropriation and exploitation of the natural wealth, water and other resources which belong to the inhabitants of the occupied territories;

(m) The dismantling of municipal services, dismissing the elected mayors as well as the municipal councils and preventing the flow of Arab aid funds to the population of the occupied territories;

9. *Calls upon* Israel to take immediate steps for the return of the displaced Arab inhabitants to their homes and property in Palestine and the other Arab territories occupied since June 1967;

10. *Calls upon* the Israeli authorities to implement forthwith Security Council resolution 484 (1980) of 19 December 1980 and previous resolutions calling for the immediate return of the municipal chiefs to their municipalities so that they can resume the functions for which they were elected;

11. *Calls upon* Israel to release all Arabs detained or imprisoned as a result of their struggle for self-determination and for the liberation of their territories, and, pending their release, to accord them the protection en-

visaged in the relevant provisions of the international instruments concerning the treatment of prisoners of war, and demands that Israel cease forthwith all acts of torture and ill-treatment of Arab detainees and prisoners;

12. *Condemns* Israel for its continued detention of Ziad Abu Ain, and calls on Israel to implement fully the agreement concluded with the International Committee of the Red Cross in November 1983 for the exchange of prisoners between the Palestine Liberation Organization and Israel; and further calls on Israel to release Ziad Abu Ain and others whom it continues to detain and who were in Ansar Camp, which must be closed under the provisions of the above-mentioned agreement;

13. *Reiterates* its call to all States, in particular the States parties to the Geneva Convention relative to the protection of Civilian Persons in Time of War, in accordance with article 1 of that Convention, and to international organizations and specialized agencies, not to recognize any changes carried out by Israel in the occupied territories, including Jerusalem, and to avoid taking any action or extending any aid which might be used by Israel in its pursuit of the policies of annexation and colonization or any other policies and practices referred to in the present resolution;

14. *Urges* Israel to refrain from the policies and practices violating human rights in the occupied territories, and to report, through the Secretary-General, to the Commission at its forty-second session on the implementation of this resolution;

15. *Requests* the General Assembly, through the Economic and Social Council, to recommend to the Security Council the adoption against Israel of the measures referred to in Chapter VII of the Charter of the United Nations for its persistent violation of the human rights of the population of the Palestinian and other occupied Arab territories;

16. *Requests* the Secretary-General to bring the present resolution to the attention of all Governments, the competent United Nations organs, the specialized agencies, the regional intergovernmental organizations and the international humanitarian organizations and to give it the widest possible publicity, and to report to the Commission on Human Rights at its forty-second session;

17. *Further requests* the Secretary-General to bring to the attention of the Commission all United Nations reports appearing between sessions of the Commission that deal with the situation of the population of those occupied territories;

18. *Decides* to place on the provisional agenda of the forty-second session as a matter of high priority the item entitled "Question of the violation of human rights in the occupied Arab territories, including Palestine".

Adopted at the 21st meeting:
In favour: 28
Argentina, Bangladesh, Brazil, Bulgaria, Cameroon, China, Colombia, Congo, Cyprus, Gambia, German Democratic Republic, India, Jordan, Kenya, Liberia, Libyan Arab Jamahiriya, Mozambique, Nicaragua, Peru, Philippines,

Senegal, Sri Lanka, Syrian Arab Republic, Ukrainian SSR, USSR, United Republic of Tanzania, Venezuela, Yugoslavia.
Against: 5
France, Federal Republic of Germany, Netherlands, United Kingdom, United States.
Abstentions: 8
Australia, Austria, Costa Rica, Finland, Ireland, Japan, Mexico, Spain.

B

The Commission on Human Rights,

Recalling its resolutions 1982/1 B of 11 February 1982, 1983/1 B of 15 February 1983 and 1984/1 B of 20 February 1984 and General Assembly resolutions 3092 A (XXVIII) of 7 December 1973, 32/91 A of 13 December 1977, 33/113 A of 18 December 1978, 34/90 B of 12 December 1979, 35/122 A of 11 December 1980, 36/147 A of 16 December 1981, 37/88 of 10 December 1982, 38/79 B of 15 December 1983 and 39/95 D of 14 December 1984,

Recalling Security Council resolutions 465 (1980) of 1 March 1980, 468 (1980) of 8 May 1980, 469 (1980) of 20 May 1980, 471 (1980) of 5 June 1980, 476 (1980) of 30 June 1980, 478 (1980) of 20 August 1980 and 484 (1980) of 19 December 1980,

Recalling resolution III on the application of the Geneva Convention relative to the Protection of Civilian Persons in Time of War, of 12 August 1949, adopted by the Twenty-fourth International Conference of the Red Cross held at Manila in November 1981,

Bearing in mind that the provisions of the Geneva Conventions of 12 August 1949[59] must be fully applied in all circumstances to all persons protected by those instruments, without any adverse distinction based on the nature or origin of the armed conflict or on the causes espoused by or attributed to the conflict,

Recognizing that the persistent failure of Israel to apply the Geneva Convention relative to the Protection of Civilian Persons in Time of War creates a situation fraught with danger, and considering that it persists in violating human rights,

Taking into account that States parties to the Geneva Convention relative to the Protection of Civilian Persons in Time of War undertake, in accordance with article 1 thereof, not only to respect but also to ensure respect for the Convention in all circumstances,

1. *Reaffirms* that the Geneva Convention relative to the Protection of Civilian Persons in Time of War is applicable to all the Arab territories occupied by Israel since 1967, including Jerusalem;

2. *Expresses its deep concern* at the consequences of Israel's systematic refusal to apply that Convention in all its provisions to Palestinian and other Arab territories occupied since 1967, including Jerusalem;

3. *Condemns* the failure of Israel to acknowledge the applicability of that Convention to the territories it has occupied since 1967, including Jerusalem;

4. *Calls upon* Israel to abide by and respect the obligations arising from the Charter of the United Nations and other instruments and rules of international law, in particular the provisions of the Geneva Convention relative to the Protection of Civilian Persons in Time of War, in Palestinian and other Arab territories occupied since 1967, including Jerusalem; requests Israel to release all Arabs detained or imprisoned as a result of their struggle for self-determination and the liberation of their territories and to accord them, pending their release, the protection envisaged in the relevant provisions of the international instruments concerning the treatment of prisoners of war; and demands that Israel cease forthwith all acts of torture and ill-treatment of Arab detainees and prisoners;

5. *Urges once more* all States parties to that Convention to make every effort to ensure respect for and compliance with the provisions thereof in all the Arab territories occupied by Israel since 1967, including Jerusalem;

6. *Requests* the Secretary-General to bring the present resolution to the attention of all Governments, the competent United Nations organs, the specialized agencies, the regional intergovernmental organizations, the international humanitarian oganizations and non-governmental organizations, and to submit a report on progress in its implementation to the Commission on Human Rights at its forty-second session.

Adopted at the 21st meeting:
In favour: 33
Argentina, Austria, Bangladesh, Brazil, Bulgaria, Cameroon, China, Colombia, Congo, Cyprus, Finland, Gambia, German Democratic Republic, India, Japan, Jordan, Kenya, Liberia, Libyan Arab Jamahiriya, Mexico, Mozambique, Nicaragua, Peru, Philippines, Senegal, Spain, Sri Lanka, Syrian Arab Republic, Ukrainian SSR, USSR, United Republic of Tanzania, Venezuela, Yugoslavia.
Against: 1
United States.
Abstentions: 7
Australia, Costa Rica, France, Federal Republic of Germany, Ireland, Netherlands, United Kingdom.

Resolution No. 1985/2 of 19 February 1985

REPEATING THAT ISRAEL'S DECISION OF 1981 TO IMPOSE ITS LAWS, JURISDICTION AND ADMINISTRATION ON THE GOLAN HEIGHTS IS NULL AND VOID, AND CALLING UPON ISRAEL TO RESCIND IT

The Commission on Human Rights,

Gravely concerned at the fact that Israel is continuing its occupation of the Arab territories, including Palestine and the Syrian Golan Heights, in spite of all the condemnations of Israel that have been expressed due to that occupation,

Recalling its resolution 1984/2 of 20 February 1984,

Noting with severe disapproval, having considered the re-

---

[59]United Nations, *Treaty Series,* vol. 75, nos. 970-73.

port of the Special Committee to Investigate Israeli Practices Affecting the Human Rights of the Population of the Occupied Territories,[60] the deteriorating situation in the occupied Arab territories,

Recalling the resolution adopted by the 71st Inter-Parliamentary Conference, held at Geneva from 2 to 7 April 1984, which condemned all Israeli policies and practices relating to the annexation of occupied Arab territories in Jerusalem and the Syrian Golan Heights,

Recalling World Health Assembly resolution WHA37.26 of 17 May 1984,[61] which condemned Israel for its continuing occupation of the Arab territories, including Palestine, and its continuing arbitrary practices against the Arab population,

Reaffirming that the acquisition of territory by force is inadmissible under the Charter of the United Nations, the principles of international law and the relevant resolutions of the United Nations,

Recalling General Assembly resolution 3314 (XXIX) of 14 December 1974, in which the Assembly defined an act of aggression, *inter alia*, as "the invasion or attack by the armed forces of a State of the territory of another State, or any military occupation, however temporary, resulting from such invasion or attack, or any annexation by the use of force of the territory of another State or part thereof" and provided that "no consideration of whatever nature, whether political, economic, military or otherwise, may serve as a justification for aggression",

Recalling Security Council resolution 497 (1981) of 17 December 1981 and General Assembly resolutions 36/226 B of 17 December 1981, ES-9/1 of 5 February 1982, 37/88 E of 10 December 1982, 37/123 A of 16 December 1982, 38/79 D of 15 December 1983 and 39/146 B of 14 December 1984, relating to the Israeli occupation of the Syrian Golan Heights and the imposition of its laws, jurisdiction and administration on the occupied Syrian territory,

Reaffirming once more that the Geneva Convention relative to the Protection of Civilian Persons in Time of War, of 12 August 1949,[62] continues to apply to the Syrian territory that has been occupied since 1967,

1. *Resolutely condemns* Israel for its persistent failure to comply with, and its defiance of, Security Council resolution 497 (1981) and all other resolutions relating to the Syrian Golan Heights adopted by the General Assembly and other United Nations bodies, and strongly deprecates Israel's annexation of the occupied Syrian territory;

2. *Declares once more* that Israel's decision of 14 December 1981 to impose its laws, jurisdiction and administration on the occupied Syrian Golan Heights, which has resulted in the effective annexation of this territory, is null and void, has no international legal validity or effect, constitutes a grave violation of international law and the

Charter of the United Nations and is an affront to the international community;

3. *Strongly deplores* the negative vote and pro-Israeli position of a permanent member of the Security Council which prevented the Council from adopting against Israel, under Chapter VII of the Charter of the United Nations, the "appropriate measures" referred to in resolution 497 (1981), adopted unanimously by the Security Council;

4. *Deplores* the inhuman treatment, terror and practices contrary to human rights which the Israeli occupation authorities continue to apply against Syrian citizens in the occupied Syrian Golan Heights by reason of their refusal of Israeli nationality and in order to force them to carry Israeli identity cards, which practices constitute a flagrant violation of the Universal Declaration of Human Rights, the Geneva Convention relative to the Protection of Civilian Persons in Time of War, of 12 August 1949, and the relevant resolutions adopted by the Security Council, the General Assembly and other international bodies and also constitute a threat to peace and international security;

5. *Reaffirms* its request to all States Members of the United Nations not to recognize any jurisdiction, laws or measures established by Israel in respect of occupied Syrian and other Arab territories;

6. *Calls upon* Israel, the occupying Power, to rescind without delay its decision of 14 December 1981 and to cease its acts of terrorism directed against Syrian citizens in the occupied Syrian Golan Heights in order to impose Israeli citizenship upon them and force them to carry Israeli identity cards, emphasizes that Israel must allow the evacuees from among the Golan population to return to their homes and to recover their property and residences occupied by Israel since 1967, and firmly emphasizes the overriding necessity of the total and unconditional withdrawal by Israel from all Palestinian and Syrian territories occupied since 1967, including Jerusalem, which is an essential prerequisite for the establishment of a just and comprehensive peace in the Middle East;

7. *Decides* to place on the provisional agenda of its forty-second session as a matter of high priority the item entitled "Question of the violation of human rights in the occupied Arab territories, including Palestine".

Adopted at the 21st meeting:

In favour: 30
Argentina, Bangladesh, Brazil, Bulgaria, Cameroon, China, Colombia, Congo, Cyprus, Gambia, German Democratic Republic, India, Jordan, Kenya, Liberia, Libyan Arab Jamahiriya, Mexico, Mozambique, Nicaragua, Peru, Philippines, Senegal, Spain, Sri Lanka, Syrian Arab Republic, Ukrainian SSR, USSR, United Republic of Tanzania, Venezuela, Yugoslavia.

Against: 1
United States.

Abstentions: 10
Australia, Austria, Costa Rica, Finland, France, Federal Republic of Germany, Ireland, Japan, Netherlands, United Kingdom.

---

[60]A/39/591.
[61]World Health Organization, *Thirty-seventh World Health Assembly, Geneva, 7-17 May 1984, Resolutions and Decisions* (WHA37/1984/REC/1), Geneva, 1984.
[62]United Nations, *Treaty Series*, vol. 75, No. 973, p. 287.

Resolution No. 1985/4 of 26 February 1985

REAFFIRMING THE INALIENABLE RIGHTS OF THE PALESTIN-
IAN PEOPLE TO SELF-DETERMINATION AND AN INDEPEN-
DENT STATE AND TO RETURN TO THEIR HOMES AND PROP-
ERTY

The Commission on Human Rights,

Recalling General Assembly resolutions 181 A and B
(II) of 29 November 1947, 194 (III) of 11 December
1948, 1514 (XV) of 14 December 1960, 3236 (XXIX) of
22 November 1974, 3375 (XXX) and 3376 (XXX) of 10
November 1975, 32/14 of 7 November 1977, 32/20 of 25
November 1977, 32/40 A and B of 2 December 1977,
32/42 of 7 December 1977, 33/28 A to C of 7 December
1978, 34/65 A to D of 29 November and 12 December
1979, ES-7/2 of 29 July 1980, 35/169 A to E of 15 December 1980, 36/120 A to F of 10 December 1981, 36/226 A
and B of 17 December 1981, ES-7/9 of 24 September
1982, 37/86 A to E of 10 and 20 December 1982, 38/58 A
to E of 13 December 1983 and 39/49 A to D of 11
December 1984,

Recalling further Economic and Social Council resolutions 1865 (LVI) and 1866 (LVI) of 17 May 1974,

Reaffirming its resolutions 1982/3 of 11 February 1982,
1983/3 of 15 February 1983 and 1984/11 of 29 February
1984,

Bearing in mind the reports and recommendations of
the Committee on the Exercise of the Inalienable Rights
of the Palestinian People,

Emphasizing once more that the Palestinian people are
entitled to self-determination in accordance with the Charter of the United Nations and the relevant United Nations resolutions, and expressing its grave concern that
Israel has prevented the Palestinian people by force from
enjoying their inalienable rights, in particular their right
to self-determination, in defiance of the principles of
international law and in disregard of the will of the international community,

Expressing its grave concern that no just solution to the
problem of Palestine has been achieved and that this
problem therefore continues to aggravate the Middle East
conflict, of which it is the core, and to endanger international peace and security, as has been tragically illustrated
by Israel's invasion and continued occupation of Lebanon,

Welcoming the Arab peace plan adopted by the Twelfth
Arab Summit Conference, held at Fez, Morocco, on 9
September 1982,

Noting with satisfaction the outcome of the proceedings
of the International Conference on the Question of Palestine held at Geneva from 29 August to 7 September 1983,

Gravely concerned at the agreements on strategic co-
operation between the United States of America and Israel signed on 30 November 1981, as well as the agreements recently concluded in that respect, which would
encourage and support Israeli policies of aggression and
expansion,

1. *Condemns* Israel's continued occupation of the Palestinian and other Arab territories, including Jerusalem,
in violation of the Charter of the United Nations, the
principles of international law and the relevant resolutions of the United Nations, and demands the immediate,
unconditional and total withdrawal of Israel from all those
occupied territories;

2. *Condemns* Israel's aggression and practices against the
Palestinian people in the occupied Palestinian territories
and outside those territories, particularly against Palestinians in Lebanon, as a result of the Israeli invasion of
Lebanon which claimed the lives of thousands of Lebanese and Palestinian civilians;

3. *Strongly condemns anew* Israel's responsibility for the
large-scale massacre in the Sabra and Shatila refugee camps,
which constituted an act of genocide, and expresses its
grave concern that, until a just and equitable solution to
the problem of Palestine has been implemented, the Palestinian people will be exposed to grave dangers such as
the appalling massacre perpetrated in the Sabra and Shatila
refugee camps;

4. *Reaffirms* the inalienable right of the Palestinian people to self-determination without external interference
and the establishment of a fully independent and sovereign State of Palestine;

5. *Reaffirms* the inalienable right of the Palestinians to
return to their homes and property, from which they
have been uprooted by force, and calls for their return
and the exercise of their right to self-determination;

6. *Recognizes* the right of the Palestinian people to regain their rights by all means in accordance with the
purposes and principles of the Charter of the United
Nations;

7. *Reaffirms* the basic principle that the future of the
Palestinian people can only be decided with its full participation in all efforts, through its legitimate and sole representative, the Palestine Liberation Organization;

8. *Reaffirms* its rejection of all partial agreements and
separate treaties in so far as they violate the inalienable
rights of the Palestinian people and contradict the principles of just and comprehensive solutions to the Middle
East problem that ensure the establishment of a just peace
in the area, in accordance with the principles of the Charter of the United Nations and with relevant United Nations resolutions;

9. *Strongly rejects* the plan for "autonomy" within the
framework of the "Camp David accords" and declares
that these accords have no validity in determining the
future of the Palestinian people and of the Palestinian
territories occupied by Israel since 1967;

10. *Reaffirms its support* for the Geneva Declaration on
Palestine adopted by the International Conference on the
Question of Palestine,[63] and welcomes the call to convene
an international peace conference on the Middle East
under the auspices of the United Nations, in which all
parties to the Arab-Israeli conflict, including the Palestine
Liberation Organization, the Union of Soviet Socialist

---

[63]*Report of the International Conference on the Question of Palestine, Geneva,
29 August-7 September 1983* (United Nations publication, Sales No.
E.83.I.21), part 1, chap. I, sect. A.

Republics and the United States of America, as well as other concerned States, participate on an equal footing and with equal rights;

11. *Expresses its deep regret* at the negative reaction of the United States of America and Israel towards the above-mentioned international conference and calls upon the United States and Israel to reconsider their attitude, so as to facilitate the convening of the conference under the auspices of the United Nations and with the participation of the Palestine Liberation Organization on an equal footing with all parties concerned in the Arab-Israeli conflict;

12. *Urges* all States, United Nations organs, specialized agencies and other international organizations to extend their support to the Palestinian people through its representative, the Palestine Liberation Organization, in its struggle to restore its rights in accordance with the Charter and the relevant resolutions of the United Nations;

13. *Requests* the Secretary-General to make available to the Commission on Human Rights all information pertaining to the implementation of this resolution;

14. *Decides* to place on the provisional agenda of its forty-second session as a matter of priority the item entitled "The right of peoples to self-determination and its application to peoples under colonial or alien domination or foreign occupation".

Adopted at the 21st meeting:
In favour: 29
Argentina, Bangladesh, Brazil, Bulgaria, Cameroon, China, Colombia, Congo, Cyprus, Gambia, German Democratic Republic, India, Jordan, Kenya, Lesotho, Libyan Arab Jamahiriya, Mauritania, Mozambique, Nicaragua, Peru, Philippines, Senegal, Sri Lanka, Syrian Arab Republic, Ukrainian SSR, USSR, United Republic of Tanzania, Venezuela, Yugoslavia.
Against: 7
Australia, Costa Rica, Federal Republic of Germany, Ireland, Netherlands, United Kingdom, United States.
Abstentions: 7
Austria, Finland, France, Japan, Liberia, Mexico, Spain.

Resolution No. 1985/41 of 13 March 1985

CONDEMNING ISRAEL FOR VIOLATIONS OF HUMAN RIGHTS IN SOUTHERN LEBANON

The Commission on Human Rights,

Gravely concerned by Israeli action in southern Lebanon which constitutes a flagrant violation of the Geneva Convention relative to the Protection of Civilian Persons in Time of War, of 12 August 1949,[64] the Universal Declaration of Human Rights, the principles of international law and the objectives of the Charter of the United Nations,

1. *Strongly condemns* Israel for its human rights violations: assassinations, mass arrests among the civilian population, abductions, demolition of houses, desecration of

places of worship and other inhuman acts;

2. *Calls on* Israel to put an immediate end to such repressive practices and to release persons detained and abducted, and demands the immediate and total withdrawal of Israel from southern Lebanon, in accordance with Security Council resolution 509 (1982) of 6 June 1982;

3. *Calls on* those Governments which continue to give Israel economic, political and military aid to put an end to support to Israel which encouraged it to persevere with its policy of aggression, expansion and colonial settlements;

4. *Requests* the Secretary-General to monitor the implementation of the present resolution and to submit to the General Assembly a report on the results of his efforts in that regard.

Adopted at the 21st meeting:
In favour: 24
Bangladesh, Brazil, Bulgaria, Cameroon, China, Congo, Cyprus, Gambia, German Democratic Republic, India, Jordan, Kenya, Lesotho, Libyan Arab Jamahiriya, Mozambique, Nicaragua, Philippines, Senegal, Sri Lanka, Syrian Arab Republic, Ukrainian SSR, USSR, United Republic of Tanzania, Yugoslavia.
Against: 1
United States.
Abstentions: 16
Argentina, Australia, Austria, Colombia, Finland, France, Federal Republic of Germany, Ireland, Japan, Liberia, Mexico, Netherlands, Peru, Spain, United Kingdom, Venezuela.

Resolution No. 1986/1 A, B of 20 February 1986

CONDEMNING ISRAELI POLICIES AND PRACTICES AFFECTING THE HUMAN RIGHTS OF THE INHABITANTS OF THE OCCUPIED TERRITORIES

A

The Commission on Human Rights,

Guided by the purposes and principles of the Charter of the United Nations as well as the principles and provisions of the Universal Declaration of Human Rights,

Guided also by the provisions of the International Covenant on Economic, Social and Cultural Rights and the International Covenant on Civil and Political Rights,

Bearing in mind the provisions of the Geneva Convention relative to the Protection of Civilian Persons in Time of War, of 12 August 1949,[65] of The Hague Convention of 1907,[66] and of other relevant conventions and regulations,

Taking into consideration General Assembly resolution

---

[64]United Nations, *Treaty Series,* vol. 75, no. 973, p. 287.

[65]United Nations, *Treaty Series,* vol. 75, no. 973, p. 287.
[66]Carnegie Endowment for International Peace, *The Hague Conventions and Declarations of 1899 and 1907* (New York, Oxford University Press, 1915, p. 100.

3314 (XXIX) of 14 December 1974, which defined as an act of aggression "the invasion or attack by the armed forces of a State of the territory of another State, or any military occupation, however temporary, resulting from such invasion or attack, or any annexation by the use of force of the territory of another State or part thereof",

Recalling General Assembly resolutions ES-7/2 of 29 July 1980, 37/88 A to G of 10 December 1982, 37/123 A to F of 16 and 20 December 1982, 38/58 A to E of 13 December 1983, 38/79 A to H of 15 December 1983, 39/49 A to D of 11 December 1984, 39/95 A to H of 14 December 1984 and 40/161 A to G of 16 December 1985 and all other relevant General Assembly resolutions on Israeli violations of the human rights of the population of occupied Arab territories,

Recalling, in particular, Security Council resolutions 237 (1967) of 14 June 1967, 465 (1980) of 1 March 1980, 468 (1980) of 8 May 1980, 469 (1980) of 20 May 1980, 471 (1980) of 5 June 1980, 476 (1980) of 30 June 1980, 478 (1980) of 20 August 1980 and 484 (1980) of 19 December 1980,

Taking note of the reports and resolutions of the International Labour Organization, the United Nations Educational, Scientific and Cultural Organization and the World Health Organization as well as the report of the seminar on violations of human rights in the Palestinian and other Arab territories occupied by Israel, held at Geneva from 29 November to 3 December 1982,[67] the Geneva Declaration adopted by the International Conference on the Question of Palestine, held at Geneva from 29 August to 7 September 1983,[68] and the reports of the Special Committee to Investigate Israeli Practices Affecting the Human Rights of the Population of the Occupied Territories, particularly its report to the General Assembly at its fortieth session,[69]

Recalling its previous resolutions in this connection, particularly resolutions 1982/1 A and B of 11 February 1982, 1983/1 A and B and 1983/2 of 15 February 1983, 1984/1 A and B and 1984/2 of 20 February 1984 and 1985/1 A and B of 19 February 1985 on the "Question of the violation of human rights in the occupied Arab territories, including Palestine",

1. *Reaffirms* the fact that occupation itself constitutes a fundamental violation of the human rights of the civilian population of the occupied Arab territories, including Palestine;

2. *Denounces* the continued refusal of Israel to allow the Special Committee to Investigate Israeli Practices Affecting the Human Rights of the Population of the Occupied Territories access to the occupied territories;

3. *Reiterates* the deep concern expressed by the Special Committee in its reports submitted to the General Assem-

bly that Israel's policy in the occupied territories is based on the so-called "Homeland" doctrine which envisages a monoreligious (Jewish) State that includes territories occupied by Israel since June 1967, and the affirmation by the Special Committee that this policy not only denies the right to self-determination of the population of the occupied territories but also constitutes the source of the continuing and systematic violation of human rights;

4. *Reaffirms* the fact that Israel's continuous grave breaches of the Geneva Convention relative to the Protection of Civilian Persons in Time of War, of 12 August 1949, and of the Additional Protocols[70] to the Geneva Conventions of 1949 are war crimes and an affront to humanity;

5. *Firmly rejects* and reiterates its condemnation of Israel's decision to annex Jerusalem and to change the physical character, demographic composition, institutional structure or status of the occupied territories, including Jerusalem, and considers all these measures and their consequences null and void;

6. *Strongly condemns* Israel's attempts to subject the West Bank and the Gaza Strip to Israeli laws;

7. *Strongly condemns* all the terrorist actions perpetrated against the Palestinian inhabitants of the occupied territories by Jewish gangs, led by Rabbi Meir Kahane, member of the Knesset, and the racist Rabbi Moshe Levinger, the leader of the Gush Emunim gang, and other racist Zionists;

8. *Strongly condemns* Israeli policies and practices, administrative and legislative measures to promote and expand the establishment of settler colonies in the occupied territories, as well as the following practices:

(a) The annexation of parts of the occupied territories, including Jerusalem;

(b) The continuing establishment of new Israeli settlements and expansion of the existing settlements on private and public Arab lands, and the transfer of an alien population thereto;

(c) The arming of settlers in the occupied territories to commit acts of violence against Arab civilians, and the perpetration of acts of violence by these armed settlers against individuals from Palestinian camps and institutions, causing injury and death and wide-scale damage to Arab property;

(d) Striking at Muslim and Christian religious and holy places and repeated attacks on Al-Aqsa Mosque aimed at seizing and destroying it;

(e) The evacuation, deportation, expulsion, displacement and transfer of Arab inhabitants of the occupied territories, the denial of their right to return to their homeland and the transfer and settlement of alien populations brought from other parts of the world in the place of the original Palestinian owners of land;

(f) The confiscation and expropriation of Arab property in the occupied territories and all other transactions

---

[67]ST/HR/SER.A/14.

[68]*Report of the International Conference on the Question of Palestine, Geneva, 29 August-7 September 1983* (United Nations publication, Sales No. E.83.I.21), part one, chap. I, sect. A.

[69]A/40/702.

[70]International Committee of the Red Cross, *Protocols additional to the Geneva Conventions of 12 August 1949* (Geneva, 1977).

for the acquisition of land involving Israeli authorities, institutions or nationals on the one hand, and inhabitants or institutions of the occupied territories on the other;

(g) The destruction and demolition of Arab houses;

(h) Mass arrests, collective punishments, administrative detention and ill-treatment of the Arab population, the torture of persons under detention and the inhuman conditions in prisons;

(i) The pillaging of archaeological and cultural property;

(j) The interference with religious freedoms and practices as well as with family rights and customs;

(k) The systematic Israeli repression of cultural and educational institutions, especially universities, schools and institutes, in the occupied Palestinian territories, closing them or restricting and impeding their academic activities by subjecting selection of courses, textbooks and educational programmes, admission of students and appointment of faculty members to the control and supervision of the military occupation authorities and by expelling numerous faculty members of several universities for refusing to sign statements containing political positions, in flagrant defiance and disregard of their right to academic freedom;

(l) Expropriation and exploitation of the natural wealth, water and other resources which belong to the inhabitants of the occupied territories;

(m) The dismantling of municipal services by dismissal of the elected mayors as well as the municipal councils and prevention of the flow of Arab aid funds to the population of the occupied territories;

9. *Calls upon* Israel to take immediate steps for the return of the displaced Arab inhabitants to their homes and property in Palestine and other Arab territories occupied since June 1967;

10. *Calls upon* the Israeli authorities to implement forthwith Security Council resolution 484 (1980) of 19 December 1980 and previous resolutions calling for the immediate return of the municipal chiefs to their municipalities so that they can resume the functions for which they were elected;

11. *Calls upon* Israel to release all Arabs detained or imprisoned as a result of their struggle for self-determination and for the liberation of their territories, and, pending their release, to accord them the protection envisaged in the relevant provisions of the international instruments concerning the treatment of prisoners of war, and demands that Israel cease forthwith all acts of torture and ill-treatment of Arab detainees and prisoners;

12. *Reiterates* its call to all States, in particular the States parties to the Geneva Convention relative to the Protection of Civilian Persons in Time of War, in accordance with article 1 of that Convention, and to international organizations and specialized agencies, not to recognize any changes carried out by Israel in the occupied territories, including Jerusalem, and to avoid taking any action or extending any aid which might be used by Israel in its pursuit of the policies of annexation and colonization or any other policies and practices referred to in the present resolution;

13. *Urges* Israel to refrain from the policies and practices violating human rights in the occupied territories, and to report, through the Secretary-General, to the Commission at its forty-third session on the implementation of the present resolution;

14. *Requests* the General Assembly, through the Economic and Social Council, to recommend to the Security Council the adoption against Israel of the measures referred to in Chapter VII of the Charter of the United Nations for its persistent violation of the human rights of the population of the Palestinian and other occupied Arab territories;

15. *Requests* the Secretary-General to bring the present resolution to the attention of all Governments, the competent United Nations organs, the specialized agencies, the regional intergovernmental organizations and the international humanitarian organizations and to give it the widest possible publicity, and to report to the Commission on Human Rights at its forty-third session;

16. *Further requests* the Secretary-General to provide the Commission with all United Nations reports appearing between sessions of the Commission and dealing with the situation of the population of those occupied territories;

17. *Decides* to place on the provisional agenda of the forty-third session, as a matter of high priority, the item entitled "Question of the violation of human rights in the occupied Arab territories, including Palestine".

Adopted at the 25th meeting:
In favour: 29
Algeria, Argentina, Bangladesh, Brazil, Bulgaria, Byelorussian SSR, Cameroon, China, Colombia, Congo, Cyprus, Ethiopia, German Democratic Republic, India, Jordan, Kenya, Lesotho, Liberia, Mauritania, Mozambique, Nicaragua, Peru, Philippines, Senegal, Sri Lanka, Syrian Arab Republic, USSR, Venezuela, Yugoslavia.
Against: 7
Australia, Belgium, France, Federal Republic of Germany, Norway, United Kingdom, United States.
Abstentions: 6
Austria, Costa Rica, Ireland, Japan, Mexico, Spain.

B

The Commission on Human Rights,

Recalling its resolutions 1982/1 B of 11 February 1982, 1983/1 B of 15 February 1983, 1984/1 B of 20 February 1984 and 1985/1 B of 19 February 1985 and General Assembly resolutions 2674 (XXV) and 2675 (XXV) of 9 December 1970, 3092 A (XXVIII) of 7 December 1973, 32/91 A of 13 December 1977, 33/113 A of 18 December 1978, 34/90 B of 12 December 1979, 35/122 A of 11 December 1980, 36/147 A of 16 December 1981, 37/88 of 10 December 1982, 38/79 B of 15 December 1983, 39/95 D of 14 December 1984 and 40/161 A to G of 16 December 1985,

Recalling Security Council resolutions 465 (1980) of 1 March 1980, 468 (1980) of 8 May 1980, 469 (1980) of 20 May 1980, 471 (1980) of 5 June 1980, 476 (1980) of 30 June 1980, 478 (1980) of 20 August 1980 and 484 (1980)

of 19 December 1980,

Recalling resolution III on the application of the Geneva Convention relative to the Protection of Civilian Persons in Time of War, of 12 August 1949, adopted by the Twenty-fourth International Conference of the Red Cross held at Manila in November 1981,

Bearing in mind that the provisions of the Geneva Conventions of 12 August 1949[71] must be fully applied in all circumstances to all persons protected by those instruments, without any adverse distinction based on the nature or origin of the armed conflict or on the causes espoused by or attributed to the conflict,

Deeply alarmed at the situation of Palestinians detained by Israel in Israeli prisons,

Recognizing that the persistent refusal of Israel to apply the Geneva Convention relative to the Protection of Civilian Persons in Time of War creates a situation fraught with danger, and considering that it persists in violating human rights,

Taking into account that States parties to the Geneva Convention relative to the Protection of Civilian Persons in Time of War undertake, in accordance with article 1 thereof, not only to respect but also to ensure respect for the Convention in all circumstances,

1. *Reaffirms* the fact that the fundamental human rights as established by international law and set forth in international instruments remain fully applicable in cases of armed conflict;

2. *Reaffirms* that the Geneva Convention relative to the Protection of Civilian Persons in Time of War, of 12 August 1949, is applicable to all Palestinian and other Arab territories occupied by Israel since 1967, including Jerusalem;

3. *Expresses its deep concern* at the consequences of Israel's systematic refusal to apply that Convention in all its provisions to Palestinian and other Arab territories occupied since 1967, including Jerusalem;

4. *Condemns* the failure of Israel to acknowledge the applicability of that Convention to the territories it has occupied since 1967, including Jerusalem;

5. *Strongly condemns* Israel for its policies of ill-treatment and torture of Palestinian detainees and prisoners in Israeli prisons;

6. *Urges* Israel to grant prisoner-of-war status, in accordance with the Geneva Convention relative to the Treatment of Prisoners of War, of 12 August 1949,[72] to all Palestinian fighters captured by Israel, and to treat them accordingly;

7. *Calls upon* Israel to abide by and respect the obligations arising from the Charter of the United Nations and other instruments and rules of international law, in particular the provisions of the Geneva Convention relative to the Protection of Civilian Persons in Time of War, in Palestinian and other Arab territories occupied since 1967, including Jerusalem; requests Israel to release all Arabs detained or imprisoned as a result of their struggle for self-determination and the liberation of their territories and to accord them, pending their release, the protection envisaged in the relevant provisions of the international instruments concerning the treatment of prisoners of war, in particular the Geneva Convention relative to the Protection of Civilian Persons in Time of War and The Hague Convention of 1907; and demands that Israel cease forthwith all acts of torture and ill-treatment of Arab detainees and prisoners;

8. *Urges once more* all States parties to the Geneva Convention relative to the Protection of Civilian Persons in Time of War to make every effort to ensure respect for and compliance with the provisions of that Convention in all the Arab territories occupied by Israel since 1967, including Jerusalem;

9. *Strongly condemns* Israel for its deportation of the liberated Palestinian prisoners in contravention of the agreement for the exchange of prisoners, and in violation of the principles of international law and United Nations resolutions, and calls upon Israel, the occupying Power, to refrain forthwith from the deportation of Palestinians, to rescind the deportation decision in order to enable those who were deported to return to their homeland and property, and to comply strictly with the provisions of the Geneva Convention relative to the Protection of Civilian Persons in Time of War;

10. *Urges* Israel to co-operate with the International Committee of the Red Cross and to allow it to visit all Palestinian detainees in Israeli prisons;

11. *Requests* the Secretary-General to bring the present resolution to the attention of all Governments, the competent United Nations organs, the specialized agencies, the regional intergovernmental organizations, the international humanitarian organizations and non-governmental organizations, and to submit a report on progress in its implementation to the Commission on Human Rights at its forty-third session;

12. *Decides* to consider this subject at its forty-third session as a matter of high priority.

Adopted at the 25th meeting:
In favour: 32
Algeria, Argentina, Austria, Bangladesh, Brazil, Bulgaria, Byelorussian SSR, Cameroon, China, Colombia, Congo, Cyprus, Ethiopia, German Democratic Republic, India, Jordan, Kenya, Lesotho, Liberia, Mauritania, Mexico, Mozambique, Nicaragua, Peru, Philippines, Senegal, Spain, Sri Lanka, Syrian Arab Republic, USSR, Venezuela, Yugoslavia.
Against: 1
United States.
Abstentions: 9
Australia, Belgium, Costa Rica, France, Federal Republic of Germany, Ireland, Japan, Norway, United Kingdom.

---

[71]United Nations, *Treaty Series,* vol. 75, nos. 970-73.
[72]*Ibid.,* no. 972, p. 135.

Resolution No. 1986/2 of 20 February 1986

REPEATING THAT ISRAEL'S DECISION OF 1981 TO IMPOSE ITS LAWS, JURISDICTION AND ADMINISTRATION ON THE GOLAN HEIGHTS IS NULL AND VOID, AND CALLING UPON ISRAEL TO RESCIND IT

The Commission on Human Rights,

Gravely concerned at the fact that Syrian Arab territories occupied by Israel in 1967 are still suffering from the Israeli military occupation, which is becoming increasingly severe and vicious,

Recalling once again the provisions of the Charter of the United Nations and the Universal Declaration of Human Rights and guided by the provisions of the International Covenant on Economic, Social and Cultural Rights and the International Covenant on Civil and Political Rights,

Recalling the resolution adopted by the 71st Inter-Parliamentary Conference, held at Geneva from 2 to 7 April 1984, which condemned all Israeli policies and practices relating to the annexation of occupied Arab territories in Jerusalem and the Syrian Golan Heights,

Taking note with deep concern of the report of the Special Committee to Investigate Israeli Practices Affecting the Human Rights of the Population of the Occupied Territories,[73]

Noting with severe disapproval, after having considered the above report, that Israel continues its flagrant violations of human rights in Syrian and other Arab territories occupied by Israel since 1967, despite the resolutions on occupied Arab territories adopted by the Commission, the Security Council, the General Assembly and other United Nations organs and specialized agencies,

Affirming its resolution 1985/2 of 19 February 1985,

Recalling World Health Assembly resolution WHA38.15 of 16 May 1985,[74] which condemns Israel for its policy aiming at making the population of the occupied Arab territories, including Palestine and the Syrian Golan Heights, dependent on the Israeli health system, by hindering the normal development of the Arab health institutions, as part of Israel's overall plan of annexation of those territories,

Reaffirming the resolutions of the Security Council, the General Assembly and other bodies which state that the acquisition of territory by force is inadmissible under the principles of international law and relevant United Nations resolutions,

Recalling General Assembly resolution 3314 (XXIX) of 14 December 1974, in which the Assembly defined an act of aggression, *inter alia,* as "the invasion or attack by the armed forces of a State of the territory of another State or any military occupation, however temporary, resulting from such invasion or attack, or any annexation by the use of force of the territory of another State or part thereof" and provided that "no consideration of whatever nature, whether political, economic, military or otherwise, may serve as a justification for aggression",

Recalling Security Council resolution 497 (1981) of 17 December 1981,

Recalling General Assembly resolutions 36/226 B of 17 December 1981, ES-9/1 of 5 February 1982, 37/88 E of 10 December 1982, 37/123 A of 16 December 1982, 38/79 D of 15 December 1983, 39/146 B of 14 December 1984 and 40/161 D to F of 16 December 1985, relating to the population of the Syrian territory that has been occupied since 1967,

Reaffirming that the Geneva Convention relative to the Protection of Civilian Persons in Time of War, of 12 August 1949,[75] applies to the Syrian territory that has been occupied since 1967,

1. *Strongly condemns* Israel for its persistent disregard for, and defiance of, the provisions of Security Council resolution 497 (1981) and all other resolutions relating to occupied Syrian territory adopted by the General Assembly and other United Nations bodies and specialized agencies, and strongly deprecates Israel's failure to implement the provisions of these resolutions by ending its occupation and ceasing its repressive measures and violations of human rights;

2. *Declares once more* that Israel's decision of 14 December 1981 to impose its laws, jurisdiction and administration on the occupied Syrian Golan Heights, which has resulted in the effective annexation of this territory, is null and void, has no international legal validity or effect, constitutes a grave violation of international law and the Charter of the United Nations and is in defiance of the international community;

3. *Strongly deplores* the negative vote and pro-Israeli position of a permanent member of the Security Council which prevented the Council from adopting against Israel, under Chapter VII of the Charter of the United Nations, the "appropriate measures" referred to in resolution 497 (1981), adopted unanimously by the Security Council;

4. *Deplores* the inhuman treatment, terror and practices contrary to human rights which the Israeli occupation authorities continue to apply against Syrian citizens in the occupied Syrian Golan Heights by reason of their refusal of Israeli nationality and in order to force them to carry Israeli identity cards, which practices constitute a flagrant violation of the Universal Declaration of Human Rights, the Geneva Convention relative to the Protection of Civilian Persons in Time of War, of 12 August 1949, and the relevant resolutions adopted by the Security Council, General Assembly and other international bodies and also constitute a threat to peace and international security;

5. *Reaffirms* its request to all States Members of the United Nations not to recognize any jurisdiction, laws or measures established by Israel in respect of occupied Syrian and other Arab territories;

---

[73]A/40/702.
[74]World Health Organization, *Thirty-eighth World Health Assembly, Geneva, 6-20 May 1985, Resolutions and Decisions* (WHA38/1985/REC/1), Geneva, 1985.

[75]United Nations, *Treaty Series,* vol. 75, no. 973, p. 287.

6. *Calls upon* Israel, the occupying Power, to rescind forthwith its decision of 14 December 1981 and to cease its acts of terrorism directed against Syrian citizens in the occupied Syrian Golan Heights in order to impose Israeli citizenship upon them and force them to carry Israeli identity cards, emphasizes that Israel must allow the evacuees from among the Golan population to return to their homes and to recover their property and residences occupied by Israel since 1967, and firmly emphasizes the overriding necessity of the total and unconditional withdrawal by Israel from all Palestinian and Syrian territories occupied since 1967, including Jerusalem, which is an essential prerequisite for the establishment of a just and comprehensive peace in the Middle East;

7. *Requests* the Secretary-General to bring the present resolution to the attention of all Governments, the competent United Nations organs, the specialized agencies, the regional intergovernmental organizations and the international humanitarian organizations and to give it the widest possible publicity, and to report to the Commission on Human Rights at its forty-third session;

8. *Decides* to place on the provisional agenda of its forty-third session, as a matter of high priority, the item entitled "Question of the violation of human rights in the occupied Arab territories, including Palestine".

Adopted at the 25th meeting:
In favour: 31
Algeria, Argentina, Bangladesh, Brazil, Bulgaria, Byelorussian SSR, Cameroon, China, Colombia, Congo, Cyprus, Ethiopia, German Democratic Republic, India, Jordan, Kenya, Lesotho, Liberia, Mauritania, Mexico, Mozambique, Nicaragua, Peru, Philippines, Senegal, Spain, Sri Lanka, Syrian Arab Republic, USSR, Venezuela, Yugoslavia.
Against: 1
United States.
Abstentions: 10
Australia, Austria, Belgium, Costa Rica, France, Federal Republic of Germany, Ireland, Japan, Norway, United Kingdom.

Resolution No. 1986/22 of 10 March 1986

REAFFIRMING THE INALIENABLE RIGHT OF THE PALESTINIAN PEOPLE TO SELF-DETERMINATION AND AN INDEPENDENT STATE AND TO RETURN TO THEIR HOMES AND PROPERTY

The Commission on Human Rights,

Recalling General Assembly resolutions 181 A and B (II) of 29 November 1947, which called for the establishment of a Palestinian State in Palestine, 194 (III) of 11 December 1948, 1514 (XV) of 14 December 1960, 3236 (XXIX) of 22 November 1974, 3375 (XXX) and 3376 (XXX) of 10 November 1975, 32/14 of 7 November 1977, 32/20 of 25 November 1977, 32/40 A and B of 2 December 1977, 32/42 of 7 December 1977, 33/28 A to C of 7 December 1978, 34/65 A to D of 29 November and 12 December 1979, ES-7/2 of 29 July 1980, 35/169 A to E of

15 December 1980, 36/120 A to F of 10 December 1981, 36/226 A and B of 17 December 1981, ES-7/9 of 24 September 1982, 37/86 A to E of 10 and 20 December 1982, 38/58 A to E of 13 December 1983, 39/49 A to D of 11 December 1984 and 40/96 A to D of 12 December 1985,

Recalling further Economic and Social Council resolutions 1865 (LVI) and 1866 (LVI) of 17 May 1974,

Reaffirming its resolutions 1982/3 of 11 February 1982, 1983/3 of 15 February 1983, 1984/11 of 29 February 1984 and 1985/4 of 26 February 1985,

Recalling Security Council resolution 573 (1985) of 4 October 1985,

Bearing in mind the reports and recommendations of the Committee on the Exercise of the Inalienable Rights of the Palestinian People,

Emphasizing once more the right of the Palestinian people to self-determination in accordance with the Charter of the United Nations and the relevant United Nations resolutions, and expressing its grave concern that Israel continues to prevent the Palestinian people by force from enjoying their inalienable rights, in particular their right to self-determination, in defiance of the principles of international law and in disregard of the will of the international community and of United Nations resolutions,

Expresses its grave concern that no just solution to the problem of Palestine has been achieved and that this problem therefore continues to aggravate the Middle East conflict, of which it is the core, and to endanger international peace and security, as has been tragically illustrated by Israel's invasion and continued occupation of part of Lebanon, in addition to its continued occupation of Palestinian and other Arab territories,

Welcoming once again the Arab peace plan adopted by the Twelfth Arab Summit Conference, held at Fez, Morocco, on 9 September 1982,

Reiterating its grave concern at the agreements on strategic co-operation between the United States of America and Israel signed on 30 November 1981, as well as the agreements recently concluded in that respect, which would encourage and support Israeli policies of aggression, expansion and continued occupation of Palestinian and other Arab territories,

Reaffirming its support for the outcome of the proceedings of the International Conference on the Question of Palestine held at Geneva in 1983,

1. *Strongly condemns* Israel, the occupying Power, for its non-compliance with the relevant resolutions of the Security Council, the General Assembly and the Commission on Human Rights;

2. *Condemns* Israel's continued occupation of the Palestinian and other Arab territories, including Jerusalem, in violation of the Charter of the United Nations, the principles of international law and the relevant resolutions of the United Nations, and demands the immediate, unconditional and total withdrawal of Israel from all those occupied territories, because the Israeli occupation of the Palestinian territories constitutes the major obstacle hindering

the exercise of the right to self-determination by the Palestinian people;

3. *Condemns* Israel's aggression and practices against the Palestinian people in the occupied Palestinian territories and outside those territories, particularly against Palestinians in Lebanon, as a result of the Israeli invasion of Lebanon which claimed the lives of thousands of Lebanese and Palestinian civilians;

4. *Strongly condemns* the Israeli armed aggression on Tunisia and on offices of the Palestine Liberation Organization in Tunisia on 1 October 1985;

5. *Strongly condemns anew* Israel's responsibility for the large-scale massacre in the Sabra and Shatila refugee camps, which constituted an act of genocide, and expresses its grave concern that, until a just and equitable solution to the problem of Palestine has been implemented, the Palestinian people will be exposed to grave dangers, such as the appalling massacre perpetrated in the Sabra and Shatila refugee camps in September 1982;

6. *Reaffirms* the inalienable right of the Palestinian people to self-determination without external interference and the establishment of their independent and sovereign State on their national soil in accordance with General Assembly resolutions;

7. *Reaffirms* the inalienable right of the Palestinians to return to their homes and property, from which they have been uprooted by force, and calls for their return and the exercise of their right to self-determination in accordance with the principles of international law and General Assembly resolutions;

8. *Affirms* the right of the Palestinian people to regain their rights by all means in accordance with the purposes and principles of the Charter of the United Nations and with relevant United Nations resolutions;

9. *Reaffirms* the basic principle that the future of the Palestinian people can only be decided with its full participation, through its legitimate and sole representative, the Palestine Liberation Organization, in all efforts and international conferences concerning the question of Palestine and the future of the Palestinian people;

10. *Reaffirms* its rejection of all partial agreements and separate treaties in so far as they violate the inalienable rights of the Palestinian people and contradict the principles of just and comprehensive solutions to the Middle East problem that ensure the establishment of a just peace in the area, in accordance with the principles of the Charter of the United Nations and with relevant United Nations resolutions;

11. *Reiterates* its strong rejection of any plan for "autonomy" which would constitute flagrant disregard of the inalienable right of the Palestinian people to self-determination without external interference, in accordance with the provisions of the Charter of the United Nations and with relevant United Nations resolutions;

12. *Reaffirms its support* for the Geneva Declaration on Palestine adopted by the International Conference on the Question of Palestine,[76] and affirms its support for the call to convene an international peace conference on the Middle East, in accordance with the provisions of General Assembly resolution 38/58 C, and appeals to all States to make further constructive efforts towards the convening of such a conference without delay, with a view to achieving a just peace in the region;

13. *Expresses its deep regret* at the negative reaction of the United States of America and Israel towards the above-mentioned international conference and calls upon the United States and Israel to reconsider their attitude towards the question of peace in the area, so as to facilitate the convening of the conference under the auspices of the United Nations and with the participation of the Palestine Liberation Organization on an equal footing with all parties concerned in the Arab-Israeli conflict, as well as of the Union of Soviet Socialist Republics and the United States of America;

14. *Urges* all States, United Nations organs, specialized agencies and other international organizations to extend their support to the Palestinian people through its representative, the Palestine Liberation Organization, in its struggle to restore its rights in accordance with the Charter of the United Nations and with relevant United Nations resolutions;

15. *Requests* the Secretary-General to make available to the Commission on Human Rights all information pertaining to the implementation of the present resolution;

16. *Decides* to place on the provisional agenda of its forty-third session as a matter of priority the item entitled "The right of peoples to self-determination and its application to peoples under colonial or alien domination or foreign occupation".

Adopted at the 50th meeting:
In favour: 28
Algeria, Argentina, Bangladesh, Brazil, Bulgaria, Byelorussian SSR, Cameroon, China, Colombia, Congo, Cyprus, Ethiopia, Gambia, German Democratic Republic, India, Jordan, Kenya, Mauritania, Mozambique, Nicaragua, Peru, Philippines, Senegal, Sri Lanka, Syrian Arab Republic, USSR, Venezuela, Yugoslavia.
Against: 8
Australia, Belgium, Costa Rica, Federal Republic of Germany, Ireland, Norway, United Kingdom, United States.
Abstentions: 7
Austria, France, Japan, Lesotho, Liberia, Mexico, Spain.

Resolution No. 1986/33 of 11 March 1986

CONDEMNING ISRAEL'S POLICIES OF OCCUPATION AND SETTLEMENT IN ARAB TERRITORIES AND CALLING FOR ITS COMPLETE WITHDRAWAL FROM THEM

---

[76]*Report of the International Conference on the Question of Palestine, Geneva, 29 August-7 September 1983* (United Nations publication, Sales No. E.83.I.21), part 1, chap. I, sect. A.

The Commission on Human Rights,

1. *Condemns* Israel for its continued occupation of the Palestinian territories, including Jerusalem, and of other Arab territories in violation of relevant United Nations resolutions and of the provisions of international law;

2. *Strongly condemns* Israeli policies and practices of terrorist action perpetrated against the Palestinian inhabitants of the occupied territories, such as killing, detention and torture, deportation, and confiscation and annexation of land, which constitute grave violations of the Charter of the United Nations, the Universal Declaration of Human Rights and all relevant United Nations resolutions;

3. *Condemns* Israel for its persistence in developing the colonization of these territories which aims at changing the demographic composition, the institutional structure and the status of the occupied territories, including Jerusalem;

4. *Reaffirms* that such measures as are described in the foregoing paragraphs constitute grave violations of the Geneva Convention relative to the Protection of Civilian Persons in Time of War, of 12 August 1949,[77] and of The Hague Convention IV of 1907,[78] and that they are null and void with regard to international law;

5. *Calls upon* Israel to withdraw immediately from the occupied Palestinian territories, including Jerusalem, in order to restore to the Palestinian people their inalienable national rights, and from all the other occupied Arab territories.

Adopted at the 52nd meeting:
In favour: 28

Algeria, Argentina, Bangladesh, Brazil, Bulgaria, Byelorussian SSR, China, Colombia, Congo, Ethiopia, Gambia, German Democratic Republic, India, Jordan, Kenya, Lesotho, Mauritania, Mexico, Mozambique, Nicaragua, Peru, Philippines, Senegal, Sri Lanka, Syrian Arab Republic, USSR, Venezuela, Yugoslavia.
Against: 6

Belgium, France, Federal Republic of Germany, Norway, United Kingdom, United States.
Abstentions: 5

Australia, Austria, Ireland, Japan, Spain.

Resolution No. 1986/43 of 12 March 1986

CONDEMNING ISRAEL FOR VIOLATIONS OF HUMAN RIGHTS IN SOUTHERN LEBANON

The Commission on Human Rights,
Gravely concerned by the continuous acts of aggression and the arbitrary practices of the Israeli occupation forces in southern Lebanon which constitute a flagrant violation of the Geneva Convention relative to the Protection of Civilian Persons in Time of War, of 12 August 1949,[79] the provisions of The Hague Convention of 1907,[80] the Universal Declaration of Human Rights, the principles of international law and the objectives of the Charter of the United Nations,

Reaffirming its resolution 1985/41 of 13 March 1985,
Reiterating what has been previously confirmed by the resolutions of the Security Council, the General Assembly and other United Nations organs, that the continued occupation and repeated acts of aggression constitute a violation of both the will of the international community and the conventions in force in this field,

1. *Strongly condemns* Israel for its human rights violations such as acts of aggression and the arbitrary practices against civilian populations, assassinations, detentions, abductions, demolition of houses, desecration of places of worship and other inhuman acts;

2. *Calls on* Israel to put an immediate end to such repressive practices and demands the immediate, total and unconditional withdrawal of Israel from Lebanese territory to the internationally recognized boundaries and respect for the sovereignty, independence and territorial integrity of Lebanon, in accordance with Security Council resolutions 425 (1978) of 19 March 1978 and 509 (1982) of 6 June 1982;

3. *Calls on* those Governments which are continuing to give Israel economic, political and military aid to refrain from providing Israel with support which is encouraging it to persevere with its policy of aggression and expansion;

4. *Requests* the Secretary-General to monitor the implementation of the present resolution and to submit to the General Assembly a report on the results of his efforts in that regard.

Adopted at the 54th meeting:
In favour: 25

Algeria, Bangladesh, Brazil, Bulgaria, Byelorussian SSR, China, Colombia, Congo, Cyprus, Ethiopia, Gambia, German Democratic Republic, India, Jordan, Kenya, Lesotho, Mauritania, Mozambique, Nicaragua, Philippines, Senegal, Sri Lanka, Syrian Arab Republic, USSR, Yugoslavia.
Against: 1

United States.
Abstentions: 17

Argentina, Australia, Austria, Belgium, Cameroon, Costa Rica, France, Federal Republic of Germany, Ireland, Japan, Liberia, Mexico, Norway, Peru, Spain, United Kingdom, Venezuela.

---

[77]United Nations, *Treaty Series*, vol. 75, no. 973, p. 287.
[78]Carnegie Endowment for International Peace, *The Hague Conventions and Declarations of 1899 and 1907* (New York, Oxford University Press, 1915), p. 100.

[79]United Nations, *Treaty Series*, vol. 75, no. 973, p. 287.
[80]Carnegie Endowment for International Peace, *The Hague Conventions and Declarations of 1899 and 1907* (New York, Oxford University Press, 1915), p. 100.

C. ECONOMIC AND SOCIAL COMMISSION FOR WESTERN ASIA[81]

Resolution No. 108 (IX) of 11 May 1982

ON ASSISTANCE TO THE PALESTINE LIBERATION ORGANIZATION

The Economic Commission for Western Asia,

Having considered the note by the Executive Secretary (E/ECWA/144), concerning the least developed countries of the ECWA region, and document E/ECWA/CMTP/WP.2/Rev.1 concerning the work programme and priorities for the period 1984-1989,

Considering the present economic and social conditions of the Palestinian Arab people,

Requests the Executive Secretary, in receiving requests for assistance from the Palestine Liberation Organization, to be guided by the scale on which the Commission provides assistance to the least developed countries of the region.

Adopted at the 7th meeting.

Resolution No. 109 (IX) of 11 May 1982

URGING STATES HOSTING THE PALESTINIAN PEOPLE TO COLLABORATE WITH THE PALESTINE LIBERATION ORGANIZATION FOR THE PURPOSE OF A CENSUS OF THE PALESTINIAN PEOPLE

The Economic Commission for Western Asia,

Recalling the note by the Executive Secretary (E/ECWA/141) on follow-up action on the implementation of resolution 28 (III) on the Census of the Palestinian Arab People,

Taking note of the agreement reached between the Palestine Liberation Organization and the Secretariat of the Commission as referred to in paragraph 4(c) and paragraph 6 of document E/ECWA/141,

1. *Urges* States which are hosting the Palestinian Arab People to provide the Palestine Liberation Organization with all the information needed to implement the project for a Census of the Palestinian Arab People, and to allow the Organization to make the arrangements and take the measures necessary to carry out the census operation in a manner compatible with the regulations and laws in force in the States concerned;

2. *Requests* the United Nations Fund for Population Activities to continue its financing of the project for a Census of the Palestinian Arab People;

3. *Requests* the Executive Secretary of the Commission to transmit this resolution to the Director of the United Nations Fund for Population Activities.

Adopted at the 7th meeting.

Resolution No. 116 (X) of 11 May 1983

REQUESTING THAT THE PALESTINE LIBERATION ORGANIZATION BE ASSIGNED A QUOTA OF POSTS IN THE SECRETARIAT OF THE ECONOMIC COMMISSION FOR WESTERN ASIA IN ITS CAPACITY AS A FULL MEMBER OF THE COMMISSION

The Economic Commission for Western Asia,

Considering the note by the Executive Secretary on the retrospect and perspective of the Commission's work contained in document E/ECWA/161,

Agreeing with the content of that note concerning the administrative constraints encountered by the secretariat in dealing with issues which limit or impede the discharge of its functions,

Reaffirming the need to strengthen the role of ECWA as an instrument for co-operation and regional integration in a manner consistent with General Assembly resolution 32/197 on restructuring of the economic and social sectors of the United Nations system,

Emphasizing that the discharge by the secretariat of its functions of preparing and servicing meetings of the Commission and its subsidiary bodies, carrying out research in connection with economic problems in the ECWA region, preparing studies and reports requested by the Commission and maintaining contacts with the Governments of member countries requires a full staffing level appropriate to the needs and circumstances of the region in which the Commission is functioning,

Noting with appreciation the efforts of the Executive Secretary to ensure that competent staff members from all members of the Commission are appointed to the ECWA secretariat,

1. *Recommends* that vacant posts be filled by qualified and experienced staff thoroughly acquainted with the situation and circumstances of the region in which the Commission is functioning;

2. *Recommends* further that at least 75 per cent of the vacant posts be filled by nationals of its member States, as applied in other regional economic commissions;

3. *Urges* member States which are unrepresented or under-represented to endeavor to second for fixed-term periods to the Commission's secretariat competent candidates and in the event of the non-availability of such candidates, to examine the possibility of temporarily relinquishing their quota for the next two bienniums in favour of other member countries;

4. *Requests* the Economic and Social Council to propose to the General Assembly that the Palestine Liberation Organization be assigned a quota of posts in the secretariat of the Economic Commission for Western Asia in its capacity as a full member of the Commission.

Adopted at the 7th meeting.

---

[81]The Economic Commission for Western Asia became the Economic and Social Commission for Western Asia in 1985.

Resolution No. 123 (X) of 11 May 1983

ON THE STUDY OF THE ECONOMIC AND SOCIAL SITUATION AND POTENTIAL OF THE PALESTINIAN ARAB PEOPLE

The Economic Commission for Western Asia,

Recalling its resolution 27 (III) of 1976 which provided for the preparation of a study of the economic and social situation and potential of the Palestinian Arab people,

Also recalling General Assembly resolution 36/120C of 10 December 1981 on convening an International Conference on the Question of Palestine which will be held at Paris from 16 to 27 August 1983,

Noting the submission by the Executive Secretary concerning the study under consideration,

Decides:

(*a*) *To refer* the report contained in document E/ECWA/166/Add.1 of 5 May 1983 entitled "Final report on the economic and social situation and potential of the Palestinian Arab people in the region of Western Asia" to member States for study with a view to the submission of their observations or amendments to the ECWA secretariat not later than 15 June 1983;

(*b*) *To establish,* in accordance with the desire of member States for the submission of adequate information on the situation of the Palestinian people to the International Conference due to be held at Paris from 16 to 27 August 1983 at Unesco headquarters, a sub-committee composed of the following members: Egypt, Iraq, Jordan, Kuwait, Lebanon, Palestine Liberation Organization, Saudi Arabia and any other member States wishing to participate therein, which will meet from 28 June to 1 July 1983 at the headquarters of the ECWA secretariat at Baghdad in order to redraft the report mentioned in document E/ECWA/166/Add.1, in the light of the observations received from member States and the deliberations of the sub-committee and with the omission of the list of documents contained on pages 131 and 132 of the said document, and to put the report into final form as a document issued by the Economic Commission for Western Asia for submission to the above-mentioned International Conference on the Question of Palestine;

(*c*) *To request* the Executive Secretary to send the study prepared by TEAM, the Arab engineering and management consultancy firm, on "The economic and social situation and potential of the Palestinian Arab people in the region of Western Asia", together with the documents annexed thereto, to the member States for study prior to its discussion at the eleventh session of the Economic Commission for Western Asia;

(*d*) *To request* the Executive Secretary to follow-up the implementation of this resolution.

Adopted at the 7th meeting.

Resolution No. 124 (XI) of 26 April 1984

ON THE STUDY OF THE ECONOMIC AND SOCIAL SITUATION AND POTENTIAL OF THE PALESTINIAN ARAB PEOPLE

The Economic Commission for Western Asia,

Recalling its resolution 27(III) of 1976 which provided for the preparation of a comprehensive study of the economic and social situation and potential of the Palestinian Arab people,

Further recalling its resolution 123(X) of 1983,

Taking cognizance of the note submitted by the Executive Secretary concerning the study under consideration,

1. *Decides* to refer to member States the complete study together with its summary, and the report of the sub-committee established pursuant to its resolution 123(X), so that they may make observations thereon within a period not exceeding four months;

2. *Requests* the sub-committee to meet after that period has lapsed, in order to consider the observations of member States and revise the complete and summarized versions of the study on the basis of those observations with a view to the production of a new study and summary thereof, within a period not exceeding eight months;

3. *Invites* member States to finance the emoluments of the members of the sub-committee and the costs of translating the complete study into Arabic if required after its revision, on the basis of the financial estimate presented by the Executive Secretary of the Commission;

4. *Decides* to distribute to non-members neither the study nor its summary until these have been revised and approved at the twelfth session of the Economic Commission for Western Asia.

Adopted at the 6th meeting.

Resolution No. 132 (XI) of 16 April 1984

ON THE ECONOMIC AND SOCIAL CONDITIONS OF THE PALESTINIAN PEOPLE UNDER OCCUPATION

The Economic Commission for Western Asia,

Recalling its resolution 30 (III) of 14 May 1976 urging the Economic and Social Council to work towards the speedy adoption of practical measures to ensure the improvement of the economic and social conditions of the Palestinian Arab people in their homeland, and its resolution 108 (IX) of 11 May 1982 on assistance to the Palestine Liberation Organization,

Recalling also the substance of paragraphs 14 and 15 of section (b) of the Geneva Declaration on Palestine and the work programme on the exercise of Palestinian rights which, respectively, contained recommendations to "undertake measures to alleviate the economic and social burdens borne by the Palestinian people as a result of the continued Israeli occupation of their territories since 1967" and to "consider contributing or increasing special contributions to the proposed budgets, programmes and projects of the relevant organs, funds and agencies of the United Nations system that have been requested to provide humanitarian, economic and social assistance to the Palestinian people",

1. *Expresses gratitude* to the Executive Secretary for the secretariat's efforts to conduct social and economic studies on the Palestinian people;

2. *Calls upon* the Executive Secretary to continue to devote special attention to social and economic studies on the Palestinian people in the occupied territories.

Adopted at the 6th meeting.

Resolution No. 139 (XII) of 24 April 1985

ON THE ECONOMIC AND SOCIAL CONDITIONS OF THE PALESTINIAN PEOPLE UNDER OCCUPATION

The Economic Commission for Western Asia,

Recalling its resolution 30 (III) of 14 May 1976 in which it appealed to the Economic and Social Council for prompt action to take practical measures to ensure the improvement of the economic and social conditions of the Palestinian Arab people in their homeland, its resolution 108 (IX) of 11 May 1982 on assistance to the Palestine Liberation Organization, and its resolution 132 (XI) of 26 April 1984 calling for special attention to be devoted to social and economic studies on the Palestinian people in the occupied territories,

Recalling the provisions of the Geneva Declaration on Palestine and Programme of Action for the Achievement of Palestinian Rights,[82] concerning the adoption of measures to alleviate the economic and social burdens borne by the Palestinian people as a result of the continued Israeli occupation of their territories and with regard to contributing or increasing special contributions to the proposed budgets, programmes and projects of the relevant organs, funds and agencies of the United Nations system that have been requested to provide humanitarian and social assistance to the Palestinian people,

1. *Expresses gratitude* to the Executive Secretary for the secretariat's efforts to conduct social and economic studies on the Palestinian Arab people;

2. *Calls upon* the Executive Secretary to ensure that all available data and information relating to the occupied Palestinian territories are included in all studies and statistical abstracts issued by the Commission at the regional level;

3. *Calls upon* the Executive Secretary to include in the programme of work and priorities for the period 1986-1987 studies, in co-operation with the concerned Arab and international organizations, on economic and social conditions in the occupied Palestinian territories, such as may serve to strengthen the resistance of the Palestinian people in those areas, and to prepare studies on the population situation, the Israeli settlement policy aimed at changing the demographic structure and destroying the Palestinian character of the occupied Palestinian territories, and studies relating to support for the industrial sector, particularly existing industries and the solution of the problems from which they suffer, such as those of marketing, finance, manpower and raw materials;

4. *Appeals* to the international and Arab organizations

concerned with the problems of social and economic development to assist the Executive Secretary in the preparation and execution of such specialized studies.

Adopted at the 3rd plenary meeting.

Resolution No. 141 (XII) of 24 April 1985

ON THE STUDY OF THE ECONOMIC AND SOCIAL SITUATION AND POTENTIAL OF THE PALESTINIAN PEOPLE

The Economic Commission for Western Asia,

Recalling its resolution 27 (III) of 14 May 1976 deciding on the preparation of a comprehensive study of the economic and social situation of the Palestinian Arab people,

Recalling also its resolutions 123(X) of 11 May 1983 and 124(XI) of 26 April 1984,

Noting that the sub-committee referred to in the two above-mentioned resolutions has not met,

1. *Decides* to refer the study to the secretariat for revision with the participation of the Palestine Liberation Organization and the Hashemite Kingdom of Jordan and any other members that wish to participate, it being understood that the observations made or those that might be communicated up to the end of June 1985 will be taken into account;

2. *Also decides* that the sub-committee shall begin its work within not more than one month after 25 April 1985 and that it is to complete the task entrusted to it by the end of August 1985 at the latest;

3. *Requests* the Executive Secretary to invite members to an intergovernmental meeting of the Economic Commission for Western Asia at a time no later than the end of October 1985 to approve the study.

Adopted at the 3rd plenary meeting.

Resolution No. 145 (XIII) of 24 April 1986

ON THE ECONOMIC AND SOCIAL CONDITIONS OF THE PALESTINIAN PEOPLE UNDER OCCUPATION

The Economic and Social Commission for Western Asia,

Recalling its resolution 30(III) of 14 May 1976 in which it appealed to the Economic and Social Council for prompt action to take practical measures to ensure the improvement of the economic and social conditions of the Palestinian Arab people in their homeland, its resolution 108(IX) of 11 May 1982 on assistance to the Palestine Liberation Organization, and its resolution 132(XI) of 26 April 1984 calling for special attention to be devoted to social and economic studies on the Palestinian people in the occupied territories,

Further recalling its resolution 139(XII) of 24 April 1985 in which it called upon the Executive Secretary to ensure that all available data and information relating to the occupied Palestinian territories are included in all studies and statistical abstracts issued by the Commission at the regional level and to include in the programme of work

---

[82]See the report of the International Conference on the Question of Palestine, held at Geneva from 29 August to 7 September 1983.

and priorities for the period 1986-1987 studies, in co-operation with the concerned Arab and international organizations, on economic and social conditions in the occupied Palestinian territories,

1. *Stresses* its deep appreciation of the efforts of the secretariat in this connection;

2. *Requests* the secretariat to continue such efforts.

Adopted at the 3rd plenary meeting.

Resolution No. 146 (XIII) of 24 April 1986

ON THE STUDY OF THE ECONOMIC AND SOCIAL SITUATION AND POTENTIAL OF THE PALESTINIAN PEOPLE

The Economic and Social Commission for Western Asia,

Recalling its resolution 27(III) of 14 May 1976 deciding on the preparation of a general study of the economic and social situation and potential of the Palestinian Arab people,

Recalling also its resolutions 123(X) of 11 May 1983 and 124(XI) of 26 April 1984,

Noting with satisfaction the follow-up on its resolution 141(XII) of 24 April 1985,

1. *Decides* to adopt the "Economic and social situation and potential of the Palestinian Arab people in the region of Western Asia: Summary"[83] and those individual parts of the general study revised and approved by the Intergovernmental Meeting on the General Study of the Economic and Social Situation and Potential of the Palestinian Arab People in the region of Western Asia, held at Baghdad from 28 to 31 October 1985, together with the recommendations contained in the report of the Intergovernmental Meeting;[84]

2. *Further decides* to publish the summary and those individual parts of the general study revised and approved by the Intergovernmental Meeting in stages, in accordance with the capacities of the Commission, provided that publication shall be completed no later than the end of 1987;

3. *Requests* the Executive Secretary to submit to the Commission at its fourteenth session a report on the implementation of the present resolution.

Adopted at the 3rd plenary meeting.

Resolution No. 151 (XIII) of 24 April 1986

AFFIRMING THE RIGHT OF THE PALESTINIAN PEOPLE TO SELF-DETERMINATION UNDER THE LEADERSHIP OF THE PALESTINE LIBERATION ORGANIZATION

The Economic and Social Commission for Western Asia,

Recalling General Assembly resolutions 37/16 of 16 November 1982 and 40/3 of 24 October 1985,

Recognizing that the promotion and achievement of the ideals of peace by all possible means constitutes a funda-

mental purpose of the Charter of the United Nations,

Inspired by the proclamation by the United Nations of the International Year of Peace, which states that international peace and security constitute a universal ideal and that their promotion requires continuing and positive action by States and peoples aimed at the prevention of war, removal of various threats to peace—including the nuclear threat—respect for the principle of non-use of force, the resolution of conflicts and peaceful settlement of disputes,

Proceeding from the principles of the Islamic religion and of those revealed religions which call for peace and good-neighbourliness,

Recalling its terms of reference, whose objective it is to raise the level of economic activity, to maintain and strengthen economic relations and to deal with the social aspects of economic development and the interrelationship of economic and social factors,

Expressing the belief that aggression in all its forms, the woes of war suffered by the region of Western Asia and the cumulative devastating effects of continuing hostilities cause aggravated material, human, economic and social damage where, instead, the full potential of the countries concerned should be made available for effective participation in development efforts and the promotion of the interests of their peoples,

Proclaims:

(a) *Its determination* to work for peace in accordance with the purposes and principles of the Charter of the United Nations;

(b) *Its affirmation* of the need to find a just solution to the Palestine question, by means of the full application of United Nations resolutions, in order that the Palestinian people may be enabled to exercise its legitimate right to self-determination under the leadership of its sole legitimate representative, the Palestine Liberation Organization;

(c) *Its affirmation* that the prolongation of the armed conflict between Iran and Iraq constitutes a violation of the purposes and principles of the Charter of the United Nations with respect to peace and depletes the human and material capacities of the two parties and of the countries of the region, thus threatening the interests of the peoples of the region in regard to economic and social development, particularly in view of the fact that Iraq has adopted a positive attitude towards United Nations resolutions calling for an end to the war and for the establishment of peace;

(d) *Its affirmation* that the continuation of the current situation in Lebanon has posed a threat to that country's sovereignty, security and territorial integrity and caused a deterioration in its economic and social situation;

(e) *Calls upon* the Secretary-General, the General Assembly and the international community to provide further support for efforts to solve these issues in accordance with the Charter of the United Nations and in keeping with the spirit of the International Year of Peace.

Adopted at the 3rd plenary meeting.

---

[83]E/ESCWA/85/IG.1/WP.1/Rev.1.

[84]E/ESCWA/85/IG.1/4.

D. GOVERNING COUNCIL OF THE
UNITED NATIONS DEVELOPMENT PROGRAMME

Decision No. 82/13 of 18 June 1982

AUTHORIZING ASSISTANCE TO HELP TO MEET THE ECONOMIC AND SOCIAL NEEDS OF THE PALESTINIAN PEOPLE

The Governing Council,

Taking note of the progress achieved in the implementation of its decisions 79/18 of 26 June 1979 and 81/13 of 23 June 1981,

Recalling its decisions 80/30 of 26 June 1980 and 81/16 of 27 June 1981 regarding the use of Special Programme Resources during the third programming cycle, 1982–1986,

1. *Endorses* the approach that has been followed by the Administrator in the implementation of decision 79/13, which is described in his report on the programme of assistance to the Palestinian people (DP/1982/18);

2. *Authorizes* the Administrator to draw up to $4 million from the Special Programme Resources during the remainder of the third programming cycle for the implementation of projects designed to help meet the economic and social needs of the Palestinian people;

3. *Appeals* to Governments and intergovernmental organizations to provide at least an additional $8 million during the third programming cycle to supplement the resources available from the Special Programme Resources for the purpose of helping to meet the economic and social needs of the Palestinian people.

Adopted at the 37th meeting.

Decision No. 83/11 of 24 June 1983

REITERATING ITS APPEAL FOR ASSISTANCE TO HELP TO MEET THE ECONOMIC AND SOCIAL NEEDS OF THE PALESTINIAN PEOPLE

The Governing Council,

Recalling its decisions 79/18 of 26 June 1979, 81/13 of 23 June 1981 and 82/13 of 18 June 1982 and the relevant provisions of General Assembly resolutions,

Recognizing that the economic and social situation of the Palestinian people continues to require the special and urgent attention of the international community,

Recalling also its decisions 80/30 of 26 June 1980, 81/16 of 27 June 1981 and 82/13 of 18 June 1982, concerning the use of Special Programme Resources during the third programming cycle, 1982-1986, in particular, paragraph 3 of decision 82/13, in which the Governing Council appealed to Governments and intergovernmental organizations to provide at least an additional $8 million during the third programming cycle to supplement the resources available from the Special Programme Resources for the purpose of helping to meet the economic and social needs of the Palestinian people,

Noting the obstacles encountered in efforts by the international community to bring meaningful and comprehensive development assistance to the Palestinian people

in the occupied territories,

Taking note of the report of the Administrator on assistance to the Palestinian people (DP/1983/14),

1. *Expresses its appreciation* to the Administrator for his continuous efforts in the implementation of the programme of assistance to the Palestinian people;

2. *Recommends* that further and vigorous efforts should be made urgently, in collaboration and direct consultation with all parties concerned, as requested by the General Assembly in various relevant resolutions, to achieve the goals with regard to meeting the economic and social needs of the Palestinian people;

3. *Strongly reiterates* its appeal to Governments and intergovernmental organizations to provide additional special contributions amounting to at least $8 million during the third programming cycle for the purpose of helping to meet the economic and social needs of the Palestinian people;

4. *Requests* the Administrator to report to the Governing Council at its thirty-first session on the concrete measures taken for the full implementation of the present decision and on the results achieved in that respect.

Adopted at the 39th meeting.

Decision No. 84/13 of 29 June 1984

REQUESTING THE ADMINISTRATOR TO MAKE PROPOSALS CONCERNING SUPPORT FOR PROGRAMMES OF ASSISTANCE TO THE PALESTINIAN PEOPLE

The Governing Council,

Recalling its decisions 79/18 of 26 June 1979, 81/13 of 23 June 1981, 82/13 of 18 June 1982 and 83/11 of 24 June 1983 and the relevant provisions of General Assembly resolutions,

Reaffirming the commitment of the United Nations Development Programme to assist the Palestinian people in advancing their economic and social development,

Taking note of the report of the Administrator concerning the programme of assistance to the Palestinian people (DP/1984/16),

1. *Expresses its satisfaction* with the efforts of the Administrator in assisting the Palestinian people in the West Bank and the Gaza Strip;

2. *Notes with regret* that previous appeals by the Governing Council and the General Assembly for additional special contributions amounting to at least $8 million in the third programming cycle have drawn only a very modest response so far;

3. *Reconfirms* the need for such special contributions, now made even more urgent by the full commitment of all funds made available from Special Programme Resources;

4. *Notes further* that, unless additional contributions are received, it will not be possible to undertake in timely and

fully effective fashion the ready pipeline of basic development projects in the West Bank and the Gaza Strip;

5. *Requests* the Administrator, when the total amount available for allocations to Special Programme Resources for the fourth cycle has been determined, to make proposals, for consideration by the Governing Council, concerning the amount which could appropriately be utilized from those resources, having regard to the other claims thereon, to support programmes of assistance to the Palestinian people.

Adopted at the 33rd meeting.

Decision No. 85/15 of 29 June 1985

RECOMMENDING EFFORTS TO ACHIEVE GOALS ON MEETING THE ECONOMIC AND SOCIAL NEEDS OF THE PALESTINIAN PEOPLE

The Governing Council,

Recalling its decisions 79/18 of 26 June 1979, 81/13 of 23 June 1981, 82/13 of 18 June 1982, 83/11 of 24 June 1983 and 84/13 of 29 June 1984 and the relevant provisions of General Assembly resolutions,

Recognizing that the economic and social situation of the Palestinian people continues to require the special and urgent attention of the international community,

Reaffirming the commitment of the United Nations Development Programme to assist the Palestinian people in advancing their economic and social development,

Noting the difficulties encountered in efforts by the international community to bring meaningful and comprehensive development assistance to the Palestinian people in the occupied territories,

Taking note of the report of the Administrator of the United Nations Development Programme concerning the programme of assistance to the Palestinian people (DP/1985/18),

1. *Expresses its appreciation* to the Administrator of the United Nations Development Program for his continuous efforts in the implementation of the programme of assistance to the Palestinian people;

2. *Recommends* that further and vigorous efforts be made urgently in collaboration and direct consultation with all parties concerned, as requested in various relevant resolutions of the General Assembly, to achieve the goals regarding meeting the economic and social needs of the Palestinian people;

3. *Expresses its gratitude* to those Governments and funds which have responded generously to appeals by the Governing Council and the General Assembly for additional special contributions to the third programming cycle;

4. *Reconfirms* the need for additional special contributions, now made even more urgent by the full commitment of all funds made available from Special Programme Resources, and other sources;

5. *Notes* that, unless additional contributions are received, it will not be possible to undertake in a timely and fully effective fashion the ready pipeline of basic development projects in the West Bank and the Gaza Strip;

6. *Authorizes* the allocation of an additional $2 million from the third cycle Special Programme Resources in order to maintain the Programme's momentum and ensure a smooth transition into the fourth cycle;

7. *Requests* the Administrator to report to the Governing Council at its thirty-third session (1986) on the concrete measures taken for the full implementation of the present decision and the result achieved in that respect.

Adopted at the 38th meeting.

Decision No. 86/55 of 19 June 1986

TAKING NOTE OF THE REPORT OF THE ADMINISTRATOR ON ASSISTANCE TO THE PALESTINIAN PEOPLE

The Governing Council,
Takes note of the following:

....

(*e*) Report of the Administrator on assistance to the Palestinian people (DP/1986/22).

....

Adopted at the 27th meeting.

RESOLUTIONS OF UNESCO
A. GENERAL CONFERENCE
B. EXECUTIVE BOARD

A. GENERAL CONFERENCE

Resolution No. 4XC/2.13 of 3 December 1982

INVITING THE DIRECTOR-GENERAL TO PLAN TO REINFORCE COOPERATION IN UNESCO'S FIELDS OF COMPETENCE WITH THE PALESTINE LIBERATION ORGANIZATION [EXCERPT FROM A RESOLUTION ON MAJOR PROGRAMME XIII, ('PEACE, INTERNATIONAL UNDERSTANDING, HUMAN RIGHTS AND THE RIGHTS OF PEOPLES')]

The General Conference,

Recalling that, under the terms of its Constitution, the purpose of Unesco is 'to contribute to peace and security by promoting collaboration among the nations through education, science and culture in order to further universal respect for justice, for the rule of law and for the human rights and fundamental freedoms which are affirmed for the peoples of the world, without distinction of race, sex, language or religion, by the Charter of the United Nations',

....

2. *Approves* the lines of emphasis of Major Programme XIII, 'Peace, international understanding, human rights and the rights of peoples', and *invites* the Director-General to base the biennial programming for the period 1984-1989 on the constituent programmes:

....

2.2 *Programme XIII.2 'Respect for human rights'*
  (a) which aims, within the framework of increased co-operation and co-ordination with scientific institutions and international governmental and non-governmental organizations:
    (i) to contribute to a more searching analysis of the causes of violations of human rights, fundamental freedoms and peoples' rights, *inter alia* in situations of occupation or colonial domination, adopting an interdisciplinary approach;
    (ii) to promote the effective exercise of cultural rights, the right to education, freedom of opinion and expression and the right to communicate, *inter alia* in situations of occupation or colonial domination;
    (iii) to strengthen the protection of human rights in Unesco's fields of competence;
    (iv) to reinforce co-operation in Unesco's fields of competence with the national liberation movements recognized by the Organization of African Unity and the Palestine Liberation Organization, recognized by the League of Arab States,
  (b) and which comprises the following subprogrammes:
    (i) Reflection about human rights;
    (ii) The effective exercise of human rights in specific social and economic situations;
    (iii) Promotion and protection of human rights;

....

Adopted at the 17th plenary meeting [of the fourth extraordinary General Conference]

Resolution No. 22C/2.1 of 21 November 1983

INVITING THE DIRECTOR-GENERAL TO CONTINUE COOPERATION WITH UN INSTITUTIONS PROVIDING EDUCATIONAL ASSISTANCE TO THE PALESTINE LIBERATION ORGANIZATION. [EXCERPT FROM A RESOLUTION ON MAJOR PROGRAMME II, 'EDUCATION FOR ALL']

The General Conference,

Recalling resolution 2/02 adopted at its fourth extraordinary session relating to Major Programme II, 'Education for all', of the second Medium-Term Plan,

Recognizing that the right to education is one of the basic human rights and that education is one of the prerequisites for the exercise of the other human rights,

....

1. *Authorizes* the Director-General to implement the programmes and subprogrammes for which provision is made in Major Programme II, 'Education for all';

2. In particular, *invites* the Director General:

....

  (f) under Programme II.6, 'Promotion of the right to education of particular groups':
    (i) to develop education and training activities for handicapped persons, especially activities that can help to foster the integration of the handicapped into regular educational systems;
    (ii) to continue co-operation with the United Nations Relief and Works Agency for Palestine Refugees in the Near East (UNRWA), and also with the Office of the United Nations High Commissioner for Refugees (UNHCR), the United Nations Development Programme (UNDP) and the other institutions providing educational assistance to refugees and national liberation movements recognized by the Organization of African Unity (OAU) and to the Palestine Liberation Organization (PLO), recognized by the League of Arab States, and to strengthen activities aimed at training the professional personnel of these movements;

....

Adopted at the 27th plenary meeting.

Resolution No. 22C/11.8 of 25 November 1983

CONDEMNING ISRAELI POLICIES IN THE CITY OF JERUSALEM

The General Conference,

Recalling the Constitution of Unesco and its objectives relating to the preservation and protection of the world heritage of monuments of historical and scientific value,

Considering the exceptional importance of the cultural property in the City of Jerusalem, not only to the countries directly concerned but to all humanity,

Recalling all the relevant resolutions and decisions adopted by the General Conference and the Executive Board of Unesco, in particular 21C/Resolution 4/14,

Recalling that the General Conference, by that resolution, invited the Executive Board to review developments in the situation regarding Jerusalem and to take any measures that it might consider appropriate, and invited the Director-General to keep a constant watch on the execution of the resolutions and decisions concerning Jerusalem,

Having noted the report contained in document 22C/90, and in particular the report (116EX/18) submitted by the Director-General to the Executive Board at its 116th session,

Considering with consternation and concern that the Israeli occupying authorities are persisting in their refusal to apply the above-mentioned resolutions and decisions,

Noting specifically:

(a) that those authorities are continuing to carry out excavations and are undertaking civil engineering and building operations detrimental to the historical and cultural character of the Holy City,

(b) that the archaeological excavations and constructions begun and continued since 1967 are causing irreparable damage and harm to the Holy City of Jerusalem,

(c) that the Al-Aqsa Mosque is more and more seriously and gravely endangered as a result of excavations and of the acts of armed aggression that have been perpetrated against it by fanatical groups,

(d) that the objective of the establishment of Jewish colonies around the City of Jerusalem and of small Jewish religious communities inside the city is the judaization of the City of Jerusalem,

Considering further that, in persisting in their policy of annexation of Jerusalem, the Israeli authorities are deliberately refusing to abide by the decisions of the United Nations and Unesco in the matter,

Considering that the above-mentioned policy and practices, which have repeatedly been denounced and condemned by the international community, constitute a constant violation of the Charter of the United Nations, the Constitution of Unesco and the international conventions and recommendations relating to the protection of cultural property in the occupied territories,

1. *Reaffirms* the previous resolutions and decisions of the General Conference and the Executive Board concerning cultural property in Jerusalem;

2. *Endorses* decision 5.4.1 adopted by the Executive Board at its 116th session;

3. *Strongly condemns* Israel's persistent refusal to abide by those resolutions and decisions, and its policy of judaization and annexation of the City of Jerusalem;

4. *Invites* the Member States of Unesco to undertake all necessary action, by such means as they may deem appropriate, to put an end to this situation;

5. *Thanks* the World Heritage Committee for its decision to include the Old City of Jerusalem and its walls on the List of World Heritage in Danger and *invites* it to continue its activities for the protection and safeguarding of cultural property in the city;

6. *Thanks* the Director-General for the continued efforts he has made to ensure implementation of the relevant resolutions and decisions, while maintaining Unesco's presence in the city;

7. *Requests* the Director-General to keep the Executive Board informed of the developments in the situation;

8. *Decides* to include this question in the agenda of its twenty-third session.

Adopted at the 32nd plenary meeting.

Resolution No. 22C/11.16 of 25 November 1983

ON THE PRESERVATION OF THE CULTURAL HERITAGE AND IDENTITY OF THE PALESTINIAN PEOPLE

The General Conference,

Recalling the significance attached by Unesco's Constitution to the respect, conservation and preservation of all cultures,

Recalling in this connection Article I of the Declaration of the Principles of International Cultural Co-operation, adopted by the General Conference of Unesco at its fourteenth session, which reads: 'Each culture has a dignity and value . . . Every people has the right and the duty to develop its culture . . . all cultures form part of the common heritage belonging to all mankind',

Recalling Resolution No. 3 of the Intergovernmental Conference on Institutional, Administrative and Financial Aspects of Cultural Policies (Venice, 1970), recommending that 'any state occupying the territory of another people should fully respect, protect and preserve the cultural property and heritage of that people, and that such occupation should end as soon as possible',

Considering that cultural identity is the very essence of a people's destiny and the living core of its culture,

Referring to Recommendation No. 11 on the cultural identity and heritage of the Palestinian people, adopted by the World Conference on Cultural Policies (Mexico City, 1982),

Noting that the monumental, artistic and traditional heritage of the Palestinian people has been and still is being plundered and that the cultural property of this people is in danger,

Taking note with satisfaction of the efforts made by Unesco for the safeguarding of the Palestinian heritage, in particular by way of the application of the following conventions:

Convention for the Protection of Cultural Property in the Event of Armed Conflict (1954)

Convention on the Means of Prohibiting and Preventing the Illicit Import, Export and Transfer of Ownership of Cultural Property (1970)

Convention for the Protection of the World Cultural and Natural Heritage (1972),

Invites the Director-General to take action within the limits of the budget in document 22C/5 to ensure that Unesco:

(*a*) strengthens its efforts to preserve the cultural identity of the Palestinian people and safeguard its heritage;

(*b*) strengthens its efforts to preserve the Palestinian cultural heritage in the occupied territories;

(*c*) takes action to protect and promote Palestinian cultural institutions;

(*d*) lends its intellectual and technical co-operation for

the preparation by ALECSO of a book on the cultural history of the Palestinian people.

Adopted at the 32nd plenary meeting.

Resolution No. 22C/23 of 25 November 1983

ON THE IMPLEMENTATION OF A PREVIOUS RESOLUTION ON EDUCATIONAL AND CULTURAL INSTITUTIONS IN THE OCCUPIED ARAB TERRITORIES

The General Conference,

Affirming that the forcible occupation of the territories of others constitutes a grave violation of the Charter of the United Nations, the Constitution of Unesco and the Universal Declaration of Human Rights, in particular the right of access to national education and culture, and also constitutes a permanent danger to peace, development and stability,

Recalling all resolutions of the General Conference and decisions of the Executive Board relating to educational and cultural institutions in the occupied Arab territories,

Recalling further the resolutions adopted by the United Nations relating to the Palestinian question and the occupied Arab territories,

Noting with keen anxiety, after taking cognizance of the report of the Director-General set forth in document 22C/18 and addenda and in the light of the available facts and information, that Israel continues:

(*a*) to refuse to implement the General Conference resolutions and Executive Board decisions, and to refuse to authorize the Director-General to keep a permanent watch on the functioning of educational and cultural institutions in the occupied Arab territories through an effective Unesco presence in those territories;

(*b*) to close, by arbitrary military orders, educational and cultural institutions in the occupied Arab territories or to restrict their academic freedoms; to restrict the freedom of thought, opinion and expression of the inhabitants of those territories; to persecute students and teachers; and systematically to apply a policy designed to efface Arab culture in all the occupied territories, including Jerusalem and the Golan;

(*c*) to refuse to rescind Military Order No. 854; to compel teachers to sign written undertakings in order to obtain work permits, linking those undertakings to unjust military orders; to open fire on students and teachers during demonstrations; to resort to collective punishments and other means of repression which jeopardize human lives and fundamental human rights; and to paralyse educational and cultural institutions,

1. *Reaffirms* the previous resolutions and decisions adopted by the General Conference and the Executive Board on this subject;

2. *Strongly condemns* the measures taken by Israel to efface the cultural identity of the Palestinian people, and the actions of the Israeli authorities in closing universities and other educational institutions, violating academic freedoms and opening fire on Arab students and teachers;

3. *Expresses once again its thanks and profound gratitude* to the Director-General for his tireless efforts with a view to the implementation of the Unesco resolutions relating to educational and cultural institutions in the occupied Arab territories;

4. *Invites* Member States to take the necessary measures to induce Israel to comply with the resolutions of Unesco;

5. *Urges* Israel to rescind Military Order No. 854 immediately, to cancel the undertakings required in order to obtain work permits, and to rescind the two orders under which such undertakings are required (Orders Nos. 65 and 938) and all other military orders limiting the academic freedom of educational institutions and restricting the right to education;

6. *Invites* the Director-General:

(*a*) to make all necessary efforts with a view to the reopening of the University of Bethlehem and the other educational institutions closed by military orders, and to enabling all teachers who have been dismissed to resume their work in universities and educational institutions;

(*b*) to strengthen the technical and material support provided by Unesco to educational and cultural institutions in the occupied Arab territories in order to give effect to the recommendations of the mission sent by Unesco to the occupied territories;

(*c*) to continue efforts to enable Unesco to keep a permanent watch on the functioning of educational and cultural institutions in the occupied Arab territories and to submit a report on this matter to the Executive Board at its 120th session;

(*d*) to see to it that a scholarship fund, to be financed by donations, is set up for the higher education of students of the occupied territories in order to improve and develop the skills of the staff of the educational and cultural institutions of the occupied Arab territories;

7. *Decides* to place this matter on the agenda of the twenty-third session of the General Conference.

Adopted at the 32nd plenary meeting.

Resolution No. 23C/18.8 of 1 November 1985

ON AN INTERNATIONAL DAY OF SOLIDARITY WITH THE PALESTINIAN PEOPLE

The General Conference,

Invites the Director-General to associate Unesco, as from 1986, with the celebration, on 29 November, of the International Day of Solidarity with the Palestinian People by means of a cultural event intended to make known the cultural identity and cultural heritage of the Palestinian people.

Adopted at the 35th plenary meeting.

Resolution No. 23C/2.1 of 5 November 1985

INVITING THE DIRECTOR TO CONTINUE TO SUPPORT EDUCATIONAL ACTIVITIES BY THE UNITED NATIONS SYSTEM FOR PALESTINIAN REFUGEES AND THE TRAINING OF TEACH-

ERS FOR NATIONAL LIBERATION MOVEMENTS [EXCERPT FROM A RESOLUTION ON MAJOR PROGRAMME II, 'EDUCATION FOR ALL']

The General Conference,

Recalling resolution 2/02, adopted at its fourth extraordinary session, on Major Programme II, 'Education for all',

Reaffirming that the right to education is one of the fundamental human rights, and that education is one of the prerequisites for exercising the other human rights,

....

1. *Authorizes* the Director-General to continue on this basis the implementation of Major Programme II, "Education for all";

2. *Invites* the Director-General in particular:

....

(*f*) under Programme II.6, 'Promotion of the right to education of particular groups',

(i) to continue, and to develop, activities to foster the education of the disabled and activities aimed at improving the vocational qualifications of persons engaged in the education of the disabled, with a view to facilitating the integration of disabled children, adolescents and adults into normal educational and training structures and helping them to take their place in the working life of the societies to which they belong;

(ii) to continue to support, within the framework of co-operation with the United Nations Relief and Works Agency for Palestine Refugees in the Near East (UNRWA), the Office of the United Nations High Commissioner for Refugees (UNHCR) and the United Nations Development Programme (UNDP) and with the other institutions providing educational assistance to refugees and national liberation movements recognized by the Organization of African Unity (OAU) and to the Palestine Liberation Organization (PLO), recognized by the League of Arab States, the educational activities being conducted in this context and the activities aimed at training the teachers and key personnel of these movements;

(iii) to continue the efforts made to enable Unesco to monitor on a permanent basis the functioning of the educational and cultural institutions in the occupied Arab territories, and to strengthen Unesco's technical and material support for the educational and cultural institutions in those territories;

(iv) to encourage the creation of a scholarship fund, to be financed by donations, with a view to assisting students of the occupied Arab territories to continue their higher education and to improving and developing the skills of the personnel of the educational and cultural institutions in those territories;

(v) to promote educational activities on behalf of migrant workers and their families, particularly activities concerned with the teaching of their mother tongue, the preservation of their cultural identity, literacy training for women and girls and pre-vocational education, with a view to facilitating their integration into the host country and their subsequent reintegration into their country of origin; and to undertake an evaluation of the impact of the Organization's activities in the education of migrant workers and their families.

Adopted at the 35th plenary meeting.

Resolution No. 23C/2.9 of 5 November 1985

ON THE CREATION OF A PALESTINIAN OPEN UNIVERSITY

The General Conference,

Recalling resolution 1/06 on the Palestinian Open University, adopted at its twenty-first session,

Noting the technical and financial assistance provided by Unesco for the purpose of carrying out the feasibility study on the creation of a Palestinian Open University,

Aware that this study contributes directly to the development and improvement of the educational systems of developing countries,

Considering that this innovatory system of education will benefit the largest possible number of people who are at present deprived of formal and non-formal education,

Convinced that the implementation of this project will offer the Palestinian people the opportunity to benefit from adequate educational facilities while at the same time helping to preserve its cultural identity,

1. *Thanks* Unesco and the Arab Fund for Economic and Social Development for their contribution to the preparation of the feasibility study;

2. *Invites* the Director-General to provide technical and financial assistance with the limits of the available resources.

Adopted at the 35th plenary meeting.

Resolution No. 23C/11.3 of 8 November 1985

DEPLORING ASSAULTS ON THE HOLY PLACES OF ISLAM IN JERUSALEM

The General Conference,

Recalling the provisions of the Constitution of Unesco relating to the conservation and protection of and respect for the natural heritage and cultural property, especially property of outstanding universal value,

Recalling The Hague Convention and Protocol of 1954 concerning the protection of cultural property in the event of armed conflict,

Recalling that the conventions, recommendations and resolutions that have been adopted by the international community on behalf of the natural heritage and cultural property demonstrate the importance for humanity of safeguarding such property,

Considering that it is of importance to the entire international community that the natural and cultural heritage should be protected,

Considering the unique role of the city of Jerusalem in the history of humanity as a holy city for the three monotheistic religions that share the same philosophical, ethical and religious values, which are fundamental for more than 2,000 million people in all the continents of the world,

Considering that the entire city and its heritage of monuments bear living witness to this exceptional role,

Considering that it is the eternal vocation of Jerusalem to promote peace and understanding among men, in accordance with the message that was delivered there,

1. *Recalls* that it is for that reason that the city of Jerusalem has been recognized as of universal importance by being included in the World Heritage List;

2. *Recalls* that the Israeli military occupation and the present status of the city entail dangers for the safeguarding of its essential vocation;

3. *Recalls and reaffirms* the previous resolutions adopted by the General Conference, which seek to ensure the safeguarding of all the spiritual, cultural, historical and other values of the holy city;

4. *Deplores* the fact that assaults and attempted assaults have been perpetrated on the holy places of Islam, which constitutes a grave derogation from the ecumenical vocation of the city;

5. *Deplores* the fact that works carried out in the old holy city have imperilled important historical monuments, which embody the cultural identity of the indigenous population;

6. *Recommends* that all Member States combine their efforts to ensure the total and effective safeguarding of the occupied holy city and the preservation and restoration of the historical monuments of the city and its universal heritage belonging to all religions;

7. *Draws the attention* of the international community more particularly to the state of degradation of a large part of the Islamic cultural and religious heritage and *urges* Member States to support the efforts of the Waqf, owner of this heritage, by making voluntary contribution to the financing of safeguarding operations;

8. *Thanks* the Director-General for everything he has done in this context and *requests* him to assist by appropriate means in implementing this resolution, in accordance with the conclusions of Professor Lemaire's report set out in document 23C/15;

9. *Decides* to include this question in the agenda of the twenty-fourth session of the General Conference, with a view to taking such decisions as may be required by the situation obtaining at that time.

Adopted at the 36th plenary meeting.

Resolution No. 23C/11.6 of 8 November 1985

ON THE PRESERVATION OF THE CULTURAL HERITAGE AND IDENTITY OF THE PALESTINIAN PEOPLE

The General Conference,

Recalling the importance that the Constitution of Unesco attaches to respect for and the preservation and protection of all cultures,

Recalling in this connection Article I of the Declaration of the Principles of International Cultural Co-operation,

adopted at its fortieth session, stating that 'Each culture has a dignity and value which must be respected and preserved . . . Every people has the right and duty to develop its culture . . . all cultures form part of the common heritage belonging to all mankind',

Recalling Resolution No. 3 of the Intergovernmental Conference on Institutional, Administrative and Financial Aspects of Cultural Policies (Venice, 1970), recommending 'that any State occupying the territory of another people should fully respect, protect and preserve the cultural property and heritage of that people, and that such occupation should end as soon as possible',

Considering that cultural identity is the very essence of a people's destiny and the living core of its culture,

Noting with satisfaction the efforts made by Unesco to safeguard the Palestinian heritage, in pursuance *inter alia* of the following instruments:

Convention for the Protection of Cultural Property in the Event of Armed Conflict (1954),

Convention on the Means of Prohibiting and Preventing the Illicit Import, Export and Transfer of Ownership of Cultural Property (1970),

Convention concerning the Protection of the World Cultural and Natural Heritage (1972),

Invites the Director-General to see to it that Unesco:

(*a*) continues its action for the preservation of the cultural identity of the Palestinian people and the safeguarding of its heritage;

(*b*) continues its action for the preservation of the Palestinian cultural heritage in the occupied territories;

(*c*) ensures the protection and promotion of the Palestinian cultural institutions;

(*d*) undertakes a study on the identity of the Palestinian people in its various aspects (origin, historical development, present state), it being understood that this study will be financed by means of extra-budgetary funds.

Adopted at the 36th plenary meeting.

Resolution No. 23C/27 of 8 November 1985

ON THE IMPLEMENTATION OF A PREVIOUS RESOLUTION ON EDUCATIONAL AND CULTURAL INSTITUTIONS IN THE OCCUPIED ARAB TERRITORIES

The General Conference,

Recalling the Geneva Convention (1949) relative to the protection of civilian persons in time of war and the Convention for the Protection of Cultural Property in the Event of Armed Conflict (The Hague Convention, 1954),

Affirming that everyone has the right to education (Universal Declaration of Human Rights, Article 26, paragraph 1) and that this right is not limited to primary and secondary education but also applies to higher education (International Covenant on Economic, Social and Cultural Rights, Article 13, paragraph 2),

Considering that higher educational institutions should be free communities of intellectuals and students enjoying universally recognized university freedoms,

Considering that the existence and free functioning of these institutions are fundamental and essential elements in the affirmation and consolidation of the cultural identity of the Palestinian people,

Expressing its keen desire to see the inhabitants of the occupied territories enjoy the fundamental right to receive an education adapted to their needs and their cultural identity like all other peoples,

Noting with grave concern, after consideration of the report of the Director-General contained in documents 23C/22 and Add. 1 and 2, that the Israeli occupation authorities are continuing to obstruct the normal functioning of educational institutions, UNRWA/Unesco training centres, universities, institutes for advanced studies and cultural institutions,

1. *Reaffirms* all the resolutions and decisions adopted by the General Conference and by the Executive Board concerning the educational and cultural institutions in the occupied Arab territories;

2. *Deplores* the obstruction and repression practiced by the occupation authorities against educational and cultural institutions in the Palestinian territories and other occupied Arab territories, which could threaten the very existence of those institutions;

3. *Asks* the occupation authorities to respect the Geneva and Hague Conventions, by cancelling all the measures taken, all the acts committed and all the military orders issued against educational and cultural institutions, and to preserve the academic freedoms of the universities and other educational and cultural institutions so that they may conduct their activities without let or hindrance;

4. *Warmly thanks* the Director-General for his continuing efforts to enable Unesco to keep a watch on the functioning of educational and cultural institutions in the occupied Arab territories and on the implementation of the resolutions and decisions of Unesco relating to these institutions;

5. *Invites* the Director-General to appoint a leading academic personality with responsibility for conducting a comprehensive study of the conditions in which academic freedoms are guaranteed and exercised in the occupied Arab territories, the said mission to gather the necessary information in the occupied territories, hear testimony at the Headquarters of the Organization and prepare a report to be submitted, when completed, to the Executive Board for consideration at a future session;

6. *Decides* to place this question on the agenda of its twenty-fourth session, with a view to ascertaining the development of the situation in those territories.

Adopted at the 36th plenary meeting.

B. EXECUTIVE BOARD[1]

Decision No. 114 EX/5.1.2 of 1982[2]

ON THE IMPLEMENTATION OF A UNESCO GENERAL CONFERENCE RESOLUTION ON EDUCATIONAL AND CULTURAL INSTITUTIONS IN THE OCCUPIED ARAB TERRITORIES

The Executive Board,

1. *Recalling* all the relevant resolutions and decisions adopted by the General Conference and the Executive Board of Unesco, and in particular resolution 14.1 adopted by the General Conference at its twenty-first session concerning educational and cultural institutions in the occupied Arab territories, which requests Israel 'to cancel . . . Military Order [No. 854] immediately' and 'to observe and implement previous Unesco resolutions and decisions concerning this matter',

2. *Recalling further* the resolutions adopted by the United Nations, in particular:

(*a*) resolution ES-9/1, adopted on 5 February 1982 by the United Nations General Assembly at its ninth emergency special session, which calls upon all Member States to apply a set of measures including the severance of cultural relations with Israel and calls upon the Specialized Agencies and international organizations to conform to the terms of the said resolution, and which, in its third operative paragraph, '*declares once more* that Israel's decision to impose its laws, jurisdiction and administration on the occupied Syrian Golan Heights is null and void and has no legal validity and/or effect whatsoever';

(*b*) resolution ES-7/4 adopted by the United Nations General Assembly on 28 April 1982 at its resumed seventh emergency special session, which 'declares once again that Israel's record and actions confirm that it is not a peace-loving Member State and that it has carried out neither its obligations under the Charter nor its commitment under General Assembly resolution 273 (III) of 11 May 1949';

3. *Considering* that Israel's annexation of Jerusalem and the Golan undoubtedly has grave consequences upon the population of those territories, in its cultural identity and its right to education, already seriously affected by the Israeli occupation,

4. *Reaffirming* that Israel's occupation of the Arab territories by force constitutes a flagrant violation of the fundamental principles of the Charter of the United Nations, the Constitution of Unesco and the Universal Declaration of Human Rights, and in particular of the right of access

---

[1]Not included in this section are excerpts from a number of Unesco Executive Board decisions on invitations to a variety of Unesco-sponsored conferences, in which invitations to the Palestine Liberation Organization to participate as an observer were among those agreed upon.

Decisions relating to Lebanon are only included if they are relevant to the Palestine problem and Arab-Israeli conflict. [ed. note]

[2]Adopted at the 114th session of the Executive Board, held in Paris between 5 and 21 May 1982. [ed. note]

to a national education and culture,

5. *Noting,* after studying the report submitted by the Director-General (114 EX/13 and Add. 1 and 2) and in the light of the available facts and information, that Israel:

(*a*) refuses and persists in its refusal to cancel its Military Order No. 854 and to abide by the decisions and resolutions adopted by Unesco;

(*b*) practises a policy of Judaization and annexation in all the occupied Arab territories, including Jerusalem and the Golan, and imposes by force upon their populations an educational and cultural policy entirely alien to their history and culture;

(*c*) to that end resorts to all means and forms of repression which jeopardize human lives and fundamental human rights and paralyse the functioning of educational and cultural institutions;

(*d*) is persevering in its policy of destroying Arab culture and education in all the occupied Arab territories;

6. *Noting with profound regret* that the Israeli authorities have refused the mission designated by the Director-General of Unesco access to Jerusalem and the Golan to carry out the mandate entrusted to it,

7. *Reaffirms* all the relevant previous resolutions and decisions of the General Conference and Executive Board of Unesco;

8. *Takes into consideration:*

(*a*) resolution ES-9/1 adopted on 5 February 1982 by the United Nations General Assembly at its ninth emergency special session;

(*b*) resolution ES-7/4 on the question of Palestine adopted on 28 April 1982 by the United Nations General Assembly at its resumed seventh emergency special session;

9. *Strongly condemns* Israel's policy and measures of repression, Judaization and annexation of the territories;

10. *Reaffirms* the importance of Unesco's role, which is to preserve the spirit and culture of the peoples and, hence, the right of the Arab people in the occupied Arab territories, including Jerusalem and the Golan, to its own education and culture;

11. *Strongly deplores* the refusal by the Israeli authorities to allow the mission designated by the Director-General to carry out its mandate in Jerusalem and the Golan;

12. *Thanks* the Director-General for his continued efforts to ensure the implementation of Unesco's resolutions and decisions concerning the occupied Arab territories;

13. *Invites* the Director-General to continue his action on behalf of the educational and cultural institutions in the occupied Arab territories, in particular by providing technical and financial assistance to the universities and scientific and technological institutes, in accordance with such procedures as he may judge necessary;

14. *Invites* the Director-General to undertake any action necessary to the proper functioning of the educational and cultural institutions in the occupied Arab territories, including Jerusalem and the Golan, to continue his efforts to enable the mission designated by him to fulfil its mandate without any restriction, and to communicate to the Executive Board any information and suggestions which would enable it to take, at its 116th session, such measures as it deems necessary.

Adopted at the 114th session.

Decision No. 114 EX/5.4.2 of 1982[3]

CONDEMNING ISRAEL'S REPEATED REFUSAL TO IMPLEMENT THE RESOLUTIONS AND DECISIONS OF UNESCO ON THE CITY OF JERUSALEM

The Executive Board,

1. *Recalling* all the resolutions and decisions adopted by the General Conference of Unesco and its Executive Board concerning the preservation of cultural property in Jerusalem,

2. *Recalling:*

(*a*) that the General Conference, in its 21 C/Resolution 4/14, invited Member States to 'withhold all recognition of the modifications made by Israel to the character and status of Jerusalem and to abstain from any act that might imply any recognition whatsoever of those modifications', and that it also invited the Executive Board 'to review developments in the situation regarding Jerusalem and to take any measures that it might consider appropriate, in conformity with the prerogatives conferred upon it by the Constitution',

(*b*) that the Executive Board, in its decision 113 EX/5.5.1, invited the Director-General 'to undertake a study of the situation of all the cultural property located in Jerusalem and of the dangers to which it is exposed so that the Executive Board can identify the facts making it possible to take the decision that the situation warrants',

3. *Having taken note* of the tragic machine-gunning incident at the Al Aqsa Mosque, which caused several casualties among the faithful and defaced the Holy Sanctuary of the Mosque,

4. *Noting with extreme concern* that Israel:

(*a*) persists in its refusal to abide by the resolutions and decisions adopted by Unesco concerning the City of Jerusalem,

(*b*) perseveres in its policy of annexing and Judaizing the City of Jerusalem,

(*c*) persists in carrying out excavations and destruction and in threatening the cultural character of Jerusalem,

(*d*) does not respect the sacred character of the Holy Places, which are continually subjected to assaults and profanation with the full knowledge of the Israeli authorities,

5. *Noting with profound disquiet* the refusal of the occupation authorities to allow the Director-General's mission, comprising five specialists, to go to the occupied City of Jerusalem,

6. *Having noted,* after consideration of the report of the Director-General contained in document 114 EX/17 and Add. 1, 2 and 3, the request submitted by Jordan that the

---

[3]*Ibid.*

Old City of Jerusalem and its walls, which are already included in the World Heritage List, be included in the List of World Heritage in Danger,

7. *Reaffirms* the previous resolutions and decisions of the General Conference and the Executive Board concerning cultural property in Jerusalem;

8. *Strongly condemns* Israel's repeated refusal to implement those resolutions and decisions;

9. *Recommends* to the General Conference that at its twenty-second session it consider the situation brought about by Israel's refusal to implement the resolutions and decisions adopted by the General Conference and the Executive Board, and that it take such action as it may deem appropriate in the matter;

10. *Strongly denounces* the act of aggression committed by Israeli soldiers against the Al-Aqsa Mosque, which led to the death of several of the faithful;

11. *Recommends* to the World Heritage Committee that it speed up the procedure for including the Old City of Jerusalem and its walls in the List of World Heritage in Danger;

12. *Invites* the Director-General to continue his efforts to enable a mission to be sent to study the situation in occupied Jerusalem on the spot, in order that a report on this subject may be submitted to the Executive Board at its 116th session.

Adopted at the 114th session.

Decision No. 115 EX/5.1.1 II, III and IV of 1982[4]

ASKING THE DIRECTOR-GENERAL TO TAKE MEASURES TO MAKE POSSIBLE ASSISTANCE TO LEBANON, STRONGLY CONDEMNING THE ISRAELI ACTIONS OF DESTRUCTION AND PLUNDER AGAINST PALESTINIAN AND LEBANESE EDUCATIONAL AND CULTURAL INSTITUTIONS, AND CONDEMNING UNRESERVEDLY THOSE WHO CARRIED OUT AND MADE POSSIBLE THE MASSACRES OF SABRA AND CHATILA

....

II

Assistance to Lebanon

The Executive Board,

1. *Considering* resolution 36/205 of the United Nations General Assembly, which requests the Secretary-General to continue and intensify his efforts to provide all possible assistance within the United Nations system for the reconstruction and development of Lebanon,

2. *Recalling* 112 EX/Decision 5.6, which invites the Director-General to continue to extend all possible assistance to Lebanon in Unesco's fields of competence,

3. *Congratulating* the Director-General on the action that he has taken to aid Lebanese institutions which have been severely affected by the events that have taken place in that country and to preserve the archaeological site of

Tyre, which is part of the common heritage of mankind,

4. *Aware* of the extent of the fresh destruction of all kinds suffered by Lebanon, particularly in its administrative, university and cultural structures,

5. *Asks* the Director-General to examine as a matter of urgency any request from the Lebanese authorities and to take the fullest possible range of measures to make possible assistance activities meeting Lebanon's most pressing reconstruction needs within Unesco's fields of competence, and to that end, to dispatch to Lebanon, at the earliest opportunity, an intersectoral mission to examine the needs of the Lebanese authorities;

6. *Requests* the Director-General to report to the Executive Board on this matter at its 116th session.

III

Damage caused to Palestinian and Lebanese educational and cultural institutions

The Executive Board,

1. *Having taken note* of the oral report by the Director-General and other available information concerning the tragic impact on school and university activities and cultural life of the acts of violence perpetrated, in the course of the Israeli invasion, against educational and cultural institutions, especially Palestinian institutions, in Lebanon,

2. *Having noted with profound indignation* the reports indicating that the Israeli army has made arbitrary arrests of intellectuals, teachers, students and pupils, many of whom belong to the system established by UNRWA,

3. *Having learned with deep concern* that the international community is without news, since the time of their arrest, of the persons held in custody,

4. *Having learned* that the Israeli army has seized and taken away with it archives and documents of every kind concerning Palestinian history and culture, including cultural articles belonging to those institutions—in particular the Palestinian Research Centre—archives, documents and materials such as film documents, literary works by major authors, paintings, objets d'art and works of folklore, research works, etc., serving as a foundation for the history, culture, national awareness, unity and solidarity of the Palestinian people,

5. *Strongly condemns* all these acts of destruction and plunder, which constitute serious violations of the human rights defined by the Universal Declaration of Human Rights, Unesco's Constitution and all other relevant international instruments concerning in particular the right to education and the right to cultural identity in all its forms;

6. *Requests* the international community to take every suitable measure to put an immediate halt to these deplorable acts of violence not only against the rights of individuals but also against the educational and cultural values of the Palestinian people;

7. *Requests* the Israeli Government to release immediately the intellectuals, teachers and students who have been arbitrarily arrested and to make full restitution of all the archives and documents removed from the Palestinian Research Centre as a result of the Israeli ag-

[4]Adopted at the 115th session of the Executive Board, held in Paris between 8 September and 7 October 1982. [ed. note]

gression, together with the other cultural property belonging to Palestinian institutions and arbitrarily seized by the Israeli forces;

8. *Requests* the Director-General, by agreement with the Lebanese Government and in collaboration with the other competent organizations of the United Nations system, especially UNRWA, to dispatch, at the earliest possible opportunity, an on-the-spot mission to assess the extent of the destruction of Palestinian educational and cultural institutions in Lebanon and to determine their priority needs within Unesco's spheres of competence;

9. *Emphasizes* the need for the international community to make the necessary effort to provide forthwith the 39 million dollars which, as estimated in the Director-General's oral report, are required to enable UNRWA to meet its immediate needs and ensure the resumption of the activities of the educational and cultural institutions destroyed by the Israeli aggression;

10. *Requests* the Director-General to report to the Executive Board at its 116th session,

IV

Massacre of Sabra and Chatila

The Executive Board,

1. *Shocked* by the horror of the dreadful massacre perpetrated on the civilian Palestinian population in Beirut,

2. *Recalling* the terms of Article I of the Constitution of Unesco which defines the Organization's responsibilities in contributing to peace and security, respect for human rights and fundamental freedoms for all,

3. *Condemns unreservedly* those who carried out and all those who made it possible to carry out the dastardly and criminal act committed against the civilian population of Beirut, notably unarmed civilian Palestinian refugees, who were aged persons, women and children living in the camps of Sabra and Chatila, an act which is in contradiction to the pursuit of peace and is repugnant to the human conscience;

4. *Appeals* to the conscience of the world community to exert the maximum effort to remove, once and for all, the immediate and fundamental causes that have brought about this wanton extermination of innocent and defenceless human beings and to mobilize all efforts to ensure a speedy return to normal life by the population, and particularly the children in the affected area, and send urgent relief to alleviate the sufferings of the Palestinian refugees and Lebanese civilian victims.

Adopted at the 115th session.

Decision No. 116 EX/5.1.5 of 1983[5]

CONDEMNING ISRAELI POLICIES AFFECTING EDUCATIONAL AND CULTURAL FREEDOM IN THE OCCUPIED ARAB TERRITORIES

The Executive Board,

1. *Recalling* all resolutions and decisions adopted by the General Conference of Unesco and the Executive Board concerning educational and cultural institutions in the occupied Arab territories,

2. *Having taken cognizance* of document 116 EX/16 and Addenda,

3. *Noting* that the occupying Israeli forces are continuing to:

(*a*) refuse to implement the General Conference resolutions and Executive Board decisions inviting the Director-General to exercise full supervision of the operation of educational and cultural institutions in the occupied Arab territories through an effective Unesco presence in those territories,

(*b*) arbitrarily close educational institutions in the occupied Arab territories, to restrict academic freedom and freedom of thought, conscience, opinion and expression, to persecute students and teachers and systematically to apply a policy of cultural assimilation in all the occupied territories, including Jerusalem and the Golan,

4. *Taking note* of the encroachments on academic freedom mentioned in the Director-General's report (116 EX/16), in paragraphs 13 and 18 in particular, inasmuch as teachers are being obliged to sign written undertakings; of the violations committed against UNRWA/Unesco educational institutions in the occupied Arab territories, as described in paragraphs 16, 27, 28 and 29 and including the arrest of teachers and pupils, opening fire on demonstrators, the closing of educational institutions and the violation of their campuses; and of the deteriorating situation of educational and cultural institutions resulting from the occupation as referred to in paragraphs 33 and 34 of the report of the mission sent to the occupied territories by the Director-General,

5. *Reaffirming* all previous General Conference resolutions and Executive Board decisions on this subject,

6. *Strongly condemns* the arbitrary arrests of teachers and pupils by the occupying power, the closing of educational institutions and the placing of obstacles in the way of the advancement and full development of cultural institutions, together with the violation of academic freedom and attempts to eliminate Palestinian Arab cultural identity;

7. *Reiterates its profound gratitude* to the Director-General for the efforts he has constantly made to apply Unesco resolutions concerning educational and cultural institutions in the occupied territories;

8. *Invites* the Director-General to pursue his efforts with a view to implementing these resolutions and enabling Unesco—through its permanent presence—to exercise full supervision of the educational and cultural institutions in all the occupied territories, including Jerusalem and the Golan;

9. *Invites* the Director-General to urge the Israeli occupying authorities immediately to cancel Military Order 854, as well as the undertaking governing the issue of work permits and the Military Orders—Nos. 65 and

---

[5]Adopted at the 116th session of the Executive Board, held in Paris between 25 May and 29 June 1983. [ed. note]

938—which regulate this;

10. *Requests* the Director-General to urge the Israeli authorities to reopen forthwith the universities and educational establishments which have been closed on military orders, and to allow all teachers who have been expelled to take up their duties once more;

11. *Invites* the Director-General to continue his efforts to implement the recommendations of the mission sent by Unesco to the occupied territories;

12. *Further invites* the Director-General to continue his action to help to improve the financial situation of UNRWA and of its educational programmes;

13. *Decides* to include this matter on the agenda of the twenty-second session of the General Conference with a view to adopting the necessary measures.

Adopted at the 116th session.

Decision No. 116 EX/5.4.1 of 1983[6]

CONDEMNING ISRAEL'S ANNEXATIONIST POLICIES AFFECTING THE CULTURAL AND RELIGIOUS CHARACTER OF JERUSALEM

The Executive Board,

1. *Recalling* all the resolutions and decisions adopted by the Unesco General Conference and Executive Board on the preservation of cultural property in Jerusalem, in particular 21 C/Resolution 4/14,

2. *Recalling* that in 21 C/Resolution 4/14, the General Conference invited the Executive Board to review developments in the situation regarding Jerusalem and to take any measures that it might consider appropriate, and invited the Director-General to keep a constant watch on the execution of the resolutions and decisions concerning Jerusalem,

3. *Observing* with deep disquiet that in addition to the tragic machine-gun attack in the Al-Aqsa Mosque on 13 April 1982, in which there were several victims among the faithful and damage to the Holy Sanctuary of the Mosque, the Mosque has again, in 1983, been the object of an attempted attack on the part of a group of Jewish religious extremists, and that there has been a substantial theft of rare historical objects from the Jerusalem Museum,

4. *Considering* with dismay that the responsibility for all these acts lies with the occupying authority which, where there has not been actual complicity, has omitted to take the necessary preventive and protective measures,

5. *Having noted* the Director-General's report contained in document 116 EX/18, especially paragraphs 4.1, 4.2, 6.2, 6.3, 6.4, 7, 8, 9, 10.2 and 10.4,

6. *Observing* with deep disquiet that the picture painted by the report is largely as follows:

(a) Israel persists in its refusal to conform to the Unesco resolutions and decisions stipulating that there should be a halt to the excavations and to all work in progress which affects or modifies the historical and cultural

character of the monuments and sites of the city of Jerusalem,

(b) the consequence of this negative attitude is to allow destruction, alteration and other serious threats to the unique historical character of the city of Jerusalem,

(c) the large-scale building work in progress is in grave danger of marring the whole landscape of the city for a long time to come,

(d) not only have the archaeological excavations in progress since 1967 not been suspended but are being pursued on an ever-increasing scale, thereby causing irreparable damage to the city of Jerusalem,

(e) in particular, the Haram al-Sharif, which has already been damaged as a result of the holes and tunnels that have been dug beneath it, remains exposed to more serious dangers, a situation that justifies the anxiety of all communities, especially Muslim circles,

7. *Considering* with emotion that new forms of Judaization of the Arab city of Jerusalem can be seen, with the settlement of small Jewish religious communities in houses in the vicinity of the Haram al-Sharif, which is seen as a first step towards eventually occupying the Haram al-Sharif itself,

8. *Considering* that this new situation is likely to exacerbate the tensions that already exist,

9. *Reaffirms* the previous resolutions and decisions of the General Conference and the Executive Board concerning cultural property in Jerusalem;

10. *Strongly condemns* Israel's persistent refusal to implement those resolutions and decisions, its deliberate policy of Judaization and annexation of the city of Jerusalem and the acts of aggression committed against the Al-Aqsa Mosque;

11. *Notes with satisfaction* the decision of the World Heritage Committee to include the Old City of Jerusalem and its walls on the List of World Heritage in Danger;

12. *Invites* that Committee to continue taking action to safeguard Jerusalem, in accordance with the provisions of the Convention for the Protection of the World Cultural and Natural Heritage;

13. *Thanks* the Director-General for his efforts to secure implementation of Unesco's resolutions and decisions on the question of Jerusalem;

14. *Invites* him to extend Unesco's necessary assistance for the safeguarding of the historical and religious heritage of Jerusalem, including the archives kept in the Al-Aqsa Library.

Adopted at the 116th session.

Decision No. 116 EX/7.3 of 1983[7]

URGING MEMBER STATES TO ASSIST PALESTINIAN EDUCATIONAL AND CULTURAL INSTITUTIONS IN LEBANON TO RESUME THEIR ACTIVITIES

---

[6] *Ibid.*

[7] *Ibid.*

The Executive Board,

1. *Recalling* decision 5.1.1 which it adopted at its 115th session, in which among other things it:

requested the Director-General, by agreement with the Lebanese Government and in collaboration with UNRWA, to dispatch a mission to Lebanon to assess the extent of the destruction of Palestinian educational and cultural institutions in Lebanon and to determine their priority needs within Unesco's spheres of competence,

invited the international community to provide UNRWA with aid worth $39 million to enable it to ensure the resumption of the activities of the educational and cultural institutions destroyed by the Israeli aggression,

requested the Israeli Government to make full restitution of all the archives and documents removed from the Palestinian Research Centre,

2. *Reaffirming* the right of the Palestinian people to education and culture,

3. *Having taken note* of the report of the Director-General contained in document 116 EX/35,

4. *Reaffirms* its decision 5.1.1 referred to above;

5. *Thanks* the Member States, organizations and institutions that have answered the Director-General's appeal for contributions to the resources of the UNRWA/Unesco educational programme in Lebanon;

6. *Urges* the other Member States to make their contribution to the effort needed to enable the Palestinian educational and cultural institutions in Lebanon to resume their activities;

7. *Takes note of and thanks* the Director-General for the efforts he has made to ensure implementation of that decision, in particular the assistance he has decided to provide for the implementation of four projects relating to Palestinian educational and cultural institutions in Lebanon;

8. *Invites* the Director-General to continue to make the necessary representations with a view to achieving, with the agreement of the Lebanese Government, implementation of decision 5.1.1 in its entirety;

9. *Requests* the Director-General to report to it at its 119th session on the application of the present decision.

Adopted at the 116th session.

Decision No. 119 EX/5.6 of 1984[8]

ON DAMAGE CAUSED TO PALESTINIAN AND LEBANESE CULTURAL AND EDUCATIONAL INSTITUTIONS

Having considered the report of the Programme and External Relations Commission (119 EX/37), the Executive Board *endorsed* the statement by the Chairman of the Commission in paragraph 129 of that report, which is

worded as follows:

'Closing the discussions, the Chairman of the Commission expressed his confidence that the Secretariat would explore all possible ways and means of carrying out the study requested by the Executive Board'.

Decision No. 120 EX/5.3.1 of 1984[9]

CONCERNING ISRAELI ANNEXATIONIST POLICIES AFFECTING THE CULTURAL AND RELIGIOUS CHARACTER OF JERUSALEM

The Executive Board,

1. *Recalling* all the resolutions and decisions adopted by the General Conference and the Executive Board of Unesco regarding the protection and safeguarding of the cultural property in the city of Jerusalem, in particular 22 C/Resolution 11.8,

2. *Having noted* the report of the Director-General contained in document 120 EX/14,

3. *Considering* it necessary, after examination of the above-mentioned report and in the light of the relevant discussions, to provide additional detailed information, in particular on the following:

the effects of the digging of a tunnel along the western wall of Haram al-Sharif; the experts' study on the fabric of the Al-Madrasa Al-Manjakiyya,

4. *Considering also* that the Israeli occupation authorities have not yet replied to the letter of the Director-General dated 27 July 1984,

5. *Invites* the Director-General to take whatever steps he deems necessary to obtain the additional detailed information required, and to report to the 121st session of the Executive Board;

6. *Decides* to include this topic on the agenda of its 121st session so as to take an appropriate decision on the matter in the light of the Director-General's report.

Adopted at the 120th session.

Decision No. 121 EX/5.1.3 of 1985[10]

DEPLORING ISRAELI PRACTICES AFFECTING EDUCATIONAL AND CULTURAL INSTITUTIONS IN THE OCCUPIED ARAB TERRITORIES

The Executive Board,

1. *Recalling* the Convention Relative to the Protection of Civilian Persons in Time of War (Geneva, 1949) and the Convention for the Protection of Cultural Property in the Event of Armed Conflict (The Hague, 1954),

2. *Affirming* that everyone has the right to education (Universal Declaration of Human Rights, Article 26, paragraph 1) and that that right is not restricted to primary

---

[8]*Ibid.*

[9]Adopted at the 120th session of the Executive Board, held in Paris between 26 September and 22 October 1984. [ed. note]

[10]Adopted at the 121st session of the Executive Board, held in Paris between 9 May and 21 June 1985. [ed. note]

and secondary education but also extends to higher education (International Covenant on Economic, Social and Cultural Rights, Article 13, paragraph 2),

3. *Considering* that institutions of higher education should constitute free communities of scholars and students that should enjoy the universally recognized academic freedoms,

4. *Deeming* the existence and free functioning of those institutions as constituting fundamental and essential elements in the affirmation and strengthening of the cultural identity of the Palestinian people,

5. *Expressing* its strong desire to see the inhabitants of the occupied territories enjoy the same essential rights as are enjoyed by all people with respect to an education suited to their needs and cultural identity,

6. *Noting* with grave apprehension, after examining the report of the Director-General contained in documents 120 EX/10 and Add.1 and 121 EX/40, that the Israeli occupying authority continues to obstruct the natural functioning of educational institutions, UNRWA/Unesco training centres, universities, institutes of advanced studies and cultural institutions,

7. *Reaffirms* all the resolutions adopted by the General Conference and the decisions of the Executve Board concerning educational and cultural institutions in the occupied Arab territories;

8. *Deplores* the acts of obstruction and harassment practised by the occupying authorities against educational and cultural institutions in the Palestinian territories and other occupied Arab territories, which could imperil the very existence of those institutions;

9. *Calls upon* the occupying authority to comply with the Geneva and The Hague Conventions by rescinding all the measures taken, acts committed and military orders issued against educational and cultural institutions, and to safeguard the academic freedoms of universities and other educational and cultural institutions so that they can engage in their activities without let or hindrance;

10. *Warmly thanks* the Director-General for his assiduous efforts to have Unesco monitor the functioning of educational and cultural institutions in the occupied Arab territories and the implementation of the resolutions and decisions of Unesco concerning those institutions;

11. *Invites* the Director-General to appoint a mission of academics with responsibility for conducting a comprehensive study of the conditions in which academic freedoms are guaranteed and exercised in the occupied Arab territories, the said mission to gather the necessary information in the occupied territories, bear testimony at the Headquarters of the Organization and prepare a report to be submitted when completed, to the Executive Board for consideration at a future session;

12. *Decides* to include this question on the agenda of the 125th session of the Executive Board with a view to the taking of such decisions as may be appropriate.

Adopted at the 121st session.

Decision No. 121 EX/5.4.1 of 1985[11]

REQUESTING THAT ISRAEL TAKE ACTION TO GIVE EFFECT TO RECOMMENDATIONS OF THE UNESCO EXECUTIVE BOARD ON JERUSALEM

The Executive Board,

1. *Recalling* the provisions of the Constitution of Unesco relating to the conservation and protection of and respect for the natural heritage and cultural property, especially property of outstanding universal value,

2. *Recalling* The Hague Convention of 1954 and the Recommendation on International Principles Applicable to Archaeological Excavations adopted on 5 December 1956 by the General Conference at its ninth session, in particular paragraph 32, which states: 'In the event of armed conflict, any Member State occupying the territory of another State should refrain from carrying out archaeological excavations in the occupied territory',

3. *Recalling* that existing international conventions, recommendations and resolutions on behalf of the natural heritage and cultural property demonstrate the importance for humanity of safeguarding such property, to whatever people it may belong,

4. *Considering* that it is of importance to the entire international community that the natural and cultural heritage should be protected,

5. *Considering* that the historic site of Jerusalem constitutes a homogeneous, balanced and unique cultural property of outstanding universal value, and that accordingly the international community has deemed it to be one of the invaluable and irreplaceable properties of humanity as a whole, worthy of being included on the World Heritage List,

6. *Recalling* the decision of the World Heritage Committee to include the 'Old City of Jerusalem and its walls' on the List of World Heritage in Danger, with a view to preserving it from the serious and specific dangers threatening it, in particular the increasingly rapid deterioration of monuments, the appalling disfigurement of the environment, the destruction resulting from changes in the use of monuments or the ownership of land and the distortion of the cultural authenticity of properties,

7. *Having examined* the Director-General's report contained in documents 120 EX/14 and 121 EX/11 and *noted* the results achieved by the mission of Professor Lemaire, personal representative of the Director-General,

8. *Nevertheless deplores* the fact that those results do not entirely measure up to the expectations of the international community, which has constantly opposed all violations of The Hague Convention of 1954;

9. *Reaffirms* the previous resolutions of the General Conference and decisions of the Executive Board pertaining to the protection of the cultural properties of Jerusalem;

10. *Urges* Member States of Unesco to continue to seek, by such means as they may deem appropriate, to safeguard the cultural and natural heritage of Jerusalem and

---

[11]*Ibid.*

to preserve its homogeneity, its unique nature and its authenticity;

11. *Requests* the World Heritage Committee to continue its activities in connection with the inclusion of the Holy City on the List of World Heritage in Danger, with a view to taking appropriate follow-up action;

12. *Appeals* to the international community to help by means of voluntary contributions to safeguard the cultural heritage of Jerusalem;

13. *Requests*, inter alia, that action be taken without delay by the Israeli occupying authorities to give effect to the recommendation of the Executive Board at its 120th session calling for detailed information, prepared by an expert approved by both parties, regarding:

the effects of the digging of a tunnel along the western wall of Haram-al-Sharif;

the study concerning the stability of Al-Madrasa Al-Manjakiyya;

and *regrets* that this has not so far been done;

14. *Warmly thanks* the Director-General for his continuing efforts to maintain a Unesco presence in the occupied Holy City and to ensure the monitoring of the condition of endangered cultural properties;

15. *Invites* the Director-General to keep the Executive Board informed of the evolution of the situation in the occupied Holy City and to publicize all information about specific threats;

16. *Decides* to include this question on the agenda of the 125th session of the Executive Board with a view to taking such decisions as the new situation may require.

Adopted at the 121st session.

Decision No. 125 EX/5.2.2 of 1986[12]

ON A MISSION TO OBTAIN INFORMATION ON EDUCATIONAL AND CULTURAL INSTITUTIONS IN THE OCCUPIED ARAB TERRITORIES

The Executive Board,

1. *Recalling* 23 C/Resolution 27 in which the General Conference, *inter alia*, invited the Director-General 'to appoint a leading academic personality with responsibility for conducting a comprehensive study of the conditions in which academic freedoms are guaranteed and exercised in the occupied Arab Territories, the said mission to gather the necessary information in the occupied territories, hear testimony at the Headquarters of the Organization and prepare a report to be submitted, when completed, to the Executive Board for consideration at a future session',

2. *Having examined* the report of the Director-General contained in document 125 EX/11 and Add.,

3. *Noting* that as a consequence, the Director-General proposed to the occupation authorities that that mission

take place in October 1986,

4. *Takes note* of document 125 EX/11 and Add.;

5. *Invites* the Director-General to take all measures necessary for the accomplishment of the mission of the academic personality whom he has designated, on the understanding that that mission shall also investigate the new developments mentioned in the aforesaid report;

6. *Decides* to consider this question at its 126th session on the basis of the report to be submitted by the Director-General.

Adpted at the 125th session.

Decision No. 125 EX/5.4.1 of 1986[13]

DEPLORING ASSAULTS PERPETRATED ON THE HOLY PLACES OF ISLAM IN JERUSALEM

The Executive Board,

1. *Recalling* the provisions of the Constitution of Unesco relating to the conservation and protection of and respect for the natural heritage and cultural property, especially property of outstanding universal value,

2. *Recalling* The Hague Convention and Protocol of 1954 concerning the protection of cultural property in the event of armed conflict,

3. *Recalling* that the conventions, recommendations and resolutions that have been adopted by the international community on behalf of the natural heritage and cultural property demonstrate the importance for humanity of safeguarding such property,

4. *Considering* that it is of importance to the entire international community that the natural and cultural heritage should be protected,

5. *Considering* the unique role of the city of Jerusalem in the history of humanity as a holy city for the three monotheistic religions that share the same philosophical, ethical and religious values, which are fundamental for more than 2,000 million people in all the continents of the world,

6. *Considering* that the historic city of Jerusalem constitutes a homogeneous, balanced and unique cultural property of outstanding universal value, and that accordingly the international community has deemed it to be one of the invaluable and irreplaceable properties of humanity as a whole, worthy of being included on the World Heritage List,

7. *Considering* that it is the eternal vocation of Jerusalem to promote peace and understanding among men, in accordance with the message that was delivered there,

8. *Having examined* the Director-General's report on this matter (125 EX/15 and Add.1),

9. *Takes note* of the report by Professor Lemaire (125 EX/15 Add.1), and in particular of the cessation of archaeological excavations in the holy city of Jerusalem;

10. *Requests* consequently that, in accordance with the provisions of the 1954 Hague Convention and the resolu-

---

[12]Adopted at the 125th session of the Executive Board, held in Paris between 10 September and 8 October 1986. [ed. note]

[13]*Ibid.*

tion of the General Conference adopted at its ninth session (New Delhi, 1956), no excavation should be resumed;

11. *Recalls* that the Israeli occupation of the city entails risks for the safeguarding of its essential vocation;

12. *Recalls and reaffirms* the previous decisions adopted by the Executive Board, which seek to ensure the safeguarding of all the spiritual, cultural, historical and other values of the holy city;

13. *Deplores* the fact that assaults and attempted assaults have been perpetrated on the holy places of Islam, which constitutes a grave derogation from the ecumenical vocation of the city, and *requests,* consequently, that the occupation authorities should reinforce security measures so as to prevent any further attempted assault;

14. *Urges* the Israeli occupation authorities to follow up immediately the recommendation of the Executive Board at its 120th session regarding the effects of the digging of a tunnel along the western wall of Haram Al-Sharif (Professor Lemaire's reports of 19 March 1985 and 28 July 1986);

15. *Thanks* the Director-General for all that he has done to ensure the application of Unesco resolutions and decisions regarding the occupied city of Jerusalem;

16. *Invites* the Director-General to submit a synoptic report to it at its 127th session on the application of Unesco resolutions and decisions regarding the cultural heritage of Jerusalem;

17. *Requests* the Director-General to launch a solemn appeal to the international community to contribute to the financing of the works for safeguarding the Islamic cultural and religious heritage in order to support the efforts of the Waqf, the owner of this heritage;

18. *Decides* to include this question on the agenda of its 127th session with a view to taking such decisions as may be required by the situation obtaining at that time.

Adopted at the 125th session.

V. RESOLUTIONS OF THE
WORLD HEALTH ORGANIZATION

Resolution No. WHA 35.15 of 14 May 1982

CONDEMNING ISRAELI PRACTICES IN THE OCCUPIED TERRITORIES AND URGING THE ESTABLISHMENT OF NEW PALESTINIAN MEDICAL INSTITUTIONS

The Thirty-fifth World Health Assembly,

Mindful of the basic principle laid down in the WHO Constitution which provides that the health of all peoples is fundamental to the attainment of peace and security;

Aware of its responsibility for ensuring proper health conditions for all peoples who suffer from exceptional situations, including foreign occupation and especially settler colonialism;

Bearing in mind that the WHO Constitution provides that "health is a state of complete physical, mental and social wellbeing and not merely the absence of disease or infirmity";

Affirming the principle that the acquisition of territories by force is inadmissible and that any occupation of territories by force gravely affects the health, social, psychological, mental and physical conditions of the population under occupation, and that this can be rectified only by the complete and immediate termination of the occupation;

Considering that the States parties to the Geneva Convention of 12 August 1949 pledged, under Article One thereof, not only to respect the Convention but also to ensure its respect in all circumstances;

Recalling the United Nations resolutions concerning the inalienable right of the Palestinian people to self-determination;

Affirming the right of Arab refugees and displaced persons to return to their homes and properties from which they were forced to emigrate;

Recalling all the previous WHO resolutions on this matter, especially resolution WHA26.56, dated 23 May 1973, and subsequent resolutions;

Recalling resolution 1-2 (XXXVIII), 1982, adopted by the Commission on Human Rights, which condemns Israel's violations of human rights in occupied Arab territories, including Palestine and the Golan, and United Nations General Assembly resolutions ES-9/1, dated 5 February 1982, and ES-7/L.3, dated 28 April 1982;

Taking note of the report[1] of the Special Committee of Experts, especially paragraph 3.7 stressing that international co-operation to promote health should be more dynamic in the occupied territories and that involvement of international institutions and organizations, including WHO, is necessary;

Observing with great concern the increasing violence and oppression practised against the civilians in the occupied Arab territories, including Palestine and the Golan, which have resulted in the isolation of cities and villages under strike and in depriving them of basic necessities of life such as water and medicaments, and which have caused:

(1) the paralysis of all institutions, including municipalities and medical, social and educational establishments;

(2) killing and injuring of a great number of civilians by the military authorities and the armed settlers;

(3) precluding the population in the occupied territories from practising their religious rites, as occurred in the attack on the Aqsa Mosque and the Church of the Holy Sepulchre and the arrest of religious personalities;

I

1. *Calls* upon the occupying authorities to desist from all continued acts of violence and oppression and to reinstate the dismissed mayors in their offices so that they may perform their duties in the public health and social spheres;

2. *Condemns* Israel for its annexation of Jerusalem and the Golan and considers this procedure null and void and with no legal validity; condemns, too, all the procedures aimed at the annexation of other occupied Arab territories;

3. *Expresses* its deep concern at the poor health and psychological conditions endured by the inhabitants of the occupied Arab territories, including Palestine and the Golan, and condemns Israel's attempts to incorporate Arab health institutions into the occupation authorities' institutions;

4. *Condemns* all acts undertaken by Israel to change the physical aspects, the geography, the institutional and legal status or context of the occupied Arab territories, including Palestine and the Golan, and considers Israel's policy in settling part of its population and new settlers in the occupied territories a flagrant violation of the Geneva Convention Relative to the Protection of Civilian Persons in Time of War and the relevant United Nations resolutions;

5. *Condemns* Israel for the continued establishment of Israeli settlements in the occupied Arab territories, including Palestine and the Golan, and the illicit exploitation of the natural wealth and resources of the Arab inhabitants in those territories, especially the confiscation of Arab water sources and their diversion for the purpose of occupation and settlement;

6. *Condemns* the inhuman practices to which Arab prisoners and detainees are subject in Israeli prisons, resulting in the deterioration of their health, psychological and mental conditions, and causing death and permanent physical disability;

7. *Condemns* Israel for its refusal to apply the Fourth Geneva Convention Relative to the Protection of Civilian Persons in Time of War, of 12 August 1949;

8. *Condemns* Israel for its refusal to implement resolutions of the Health Assembly and other international organizations calling upon it to allow refugees and displaced persons to return to their homes;

9. *Condemns* Israel for continuing its aggressive policy, its arbitrary practices and its continuous shelling of

---

[1]Document A35/16.

residential areas in Lebanon, which have caused death, injury and mutilation to hundreds of civilians;

10. *Endorses* the opinion of the Special Committee of Experts, expressed in paragraphs 4 and 8 of its report A34/17, that the "socioeconomic situation of a population and its state of health are closely related" and that the sociopolitical situation existing in the occupied Arab territories, including Palestine, is favourable neither to the improvement of the state of health of the population concerned nor to the full development of services adapted to the promotion of human welfare;

11. *Condemns* Israel for not allowing the Special Committee to carry out its tasks fully according to World Health Assembly resolution WHA33.18;

12. *Thanks* the Special Committee of Experts, and requests it to continue its task with respect to all the implications of occupation and the policies of the occupying Israeli authorities and their various practices which adversely affect the health conditions of the Arab inhabitants in the occupied Arab territories, including Palestine, and to report to the Thirty-sixth World Health Assembly, bearing in mind all the provisions of this resolution, in coordination with the Arab States concerned and the Palestine Liberation Organization;

II

Having examined the annual report of the United Nations Relief and Works Agency for Palestine Refugees in the Near East;

Deeply concerned at the deterioration of the Agency's situation with regard to its budget and the services provided owing to the repeated Israeli aggression;

1. *Requests* States to increase their contributions so that the Agency can continue carrying out the tasks assigned to it;

2. *Requests* the Director-General to continue his collaboration with the United Nations Relief and Works Agency for Palestine Refugees in the Near East, by all possible means and to the extent necessary to ease the difficulties it is facing and increase the services it provides to the Palestinian people;

III

Requests the Director-General:

(1) to increase collaboration and coordination with the Palestine Liberation Organization concerning the provision of the necessary assistance to the Palestinian people;

(2) to establish three health centres in the occupied Arab territories, including Palestine, provided that the centres shall be under the direct supervision of WHO.

Adopted at the 13th plenary meeting:
In favour: 59
Against: 25
Abstentions: 17

Resolution No. WHA 36.27 of 16 May 1983

CONDEMNING ISRAELI PRACTICES IN THE OCCUPIED TERRITORIES AND URGING THE ESTABLISHMENT OF NEW PALES-

TINIAN MEDICAL INSTITUTIONS THERE

The Thirty-sixth World Health Assembly,

Mindful of the basic principles established in the WHO Constitution, which provides that the health of all peoples is fundamental to the attainment of peace and security;

Aware of its responsibility for ensuring proper health conditions for all peoples who suffer from exceptional situations, including foreign occupation and especially settler colonialism;

Affirming the principle that the acquisition of territories by force is inadmissible and that any occupation of territories by force gravely affects the health, social, psychological, mental and physical conditions of the people under occupation, and that this can be rectified only by the complete and immediate termination of the occupation;

Considering that the States parties to the Geneva Convention of 12 August 1949 pledged, under Article One thereof, not only to respect the Convention but also to ensure that it be respected in all circumstances;

Recalling the United Nations resolutions concerning the inalienable right of the Palestinian people to self-determination;

Affirming the right of Arab refugees and displaced persons to return to their homes and properties from which they were forced to emigrate;

Recalling resolutions 1983/1, 1983/2 and 1983/3, of 15 February 1983, adopted by the Commission on Human Rights, which condemn Israel's violations of human rights in occupied Arab territories, including Palestine and the Golan, and United Nations General Assembly resolutions ES-7/5 of 26 June 1982, ES-7/6 of 19 August 1982 and ES-7/9 of 24 September 1982;

Stressing that international cooperation to promote health should be more dynamic in the occupied territories and that involvement of international institutions and organizations, including WHO, is necessary;

Taking note of the report of the Special Committee of Experts;[2]

Considering the right of the peoples to organize for themselves the provision of their own health and social services;

Observing with great concern the clinical syndrome which spread amongst the female students in the West Bank and gave rise to the effects mentioned in the report of the Special Committee of Experts of 28 April 1983;[3]

1. *Endorses* resolution WHA35.15 and previous relevant resolutions of the Health Assembly;

2. *Condemns* Israel for its continuous aggressive policy, its arbitrary practices and its continuous shelling of Arab residential areas, including refugee camps, especially during the last ferocious war launched by Israel against Lebanon, which has resulted in the destruction of cities and camps, killing and injuring tens of thousands of civilians, children, women and elderly people, as well as the bar-

---

[2]Document A36/14.
[3]Document A36/14, paragraph 4.1.3.3.

baric collective massacre of Sabra and Shatila, for which the responsibility of the Government of Israel has been established;

3. *Demands* the immediate end to occupation, violence and oppression, to enable the Palestinian people to exercise its inalienable national rights;

4. *Thanks* the Special Committee of Experts, and requests it to continue its task with respect to all the implications of occupation and the policies of the occupying Israeli authorities and their various practices which adversely affect the health conditions of the Arab inhabitants in the occupied Arab territories, including Palestine, and to report to the Thirty-seventh World Health Assembly, bearing in mind all the provisions of this resolution, in coordination with the Arab States concerned and the Palestine Liberation Organization;

5. *Takes note* of the successive reports of the Special Committee of Experts submitted to the Health Assembly at its previous sessions, and the statement in its report of 28 April 1983 that "there is a public health problem which should not be minimized";[4]

6. *Recommends* that every possible measure be taken to continue monitoring any developments in the health conditions of the population and requests the World Health Organization directly to supervise the health conditions of the Arab population in the occupied Arab territories, including Palestine, to ensure a proper health environment for the population;

7. *Condemns* Israel for the continued establishment of Israeli settlements in the occupied Arab territories, including Palestine and the Golan, and the illegal exploitation of the natural wealth and resources of the Arab inhabitants in those territories, especially the appropriation of water sources and their diversion for the purpose of occupation and settlement, and requests that the establishment of new settlements be stopped immediately and that those already established be dismantled;

8. *Affirms* the right of the Palestinian people to have its own social institutions which provide medical and social services, and requests the Director-General:

(1) to further collaboration and coordination with the Palestine Liberation Organization concerning the provision of the necessary assistance to the Palestinian people;

(2) to establish three medical centres in the occupied Arab territories, including Palestine, with funds allotted for this purpose, provided that the centres shall be under the direct supervision of WHO, and to submit a report to the Thirty-seventh World Health Assembly;

(3) to follow up the health conditions of the population in the occupied Arab territories, including that of the sufferers from the above-mentioned clinical syndrome, or

other similar cases, and to report regularly to the Health Assembly.

Adotped at the 13th plenary meeting:
In favour: 81
Against: 16
Abstentions: 28

Resolution No. WHA 37.26 of 17 May 1984

CONDEMNING ISRAELI PRACTICES AND HEALTH POLICY IN THE OCCUPIED TERRITORIES AND REAFFIRMING THE RIGHT OF THE PALESTINIAN POPULATION TO HAVE ITS OWN MEDICAL INSTITUTIONS

The Thirty-seventh World Health Assembly,

Mindful of the basic principle established in the WHO Constitution, which affirms that the health of all peoples is fundamental to the attainment of peace and security;

Aware of its responsibility for ensuring proper health conditions for all peoples who suffer from exceptional situations, including foreign occupation and especially settler colonialism;

Affirming the principle that the acquisition of territories by force is inadmissible and that any occupation of territories by force gravely affects the health, social, psychological, mental and physical conditions of the people under occupation, and that this can be rectified only by the complete and immediate termination of the occupation;

Considering that the States parties to the Geneva Convention of 12 August 1949 pledged themselves, under Article One thereof, not only to respect the Convention but also to ensure that it was respected in all circumstances;

Recalling United Nations General Assembly resolutions 38/58 of 13 December 1983 and 38/79 of 15 December 1983 and all other United Nations resolutions relative to the questions of Palestine and the Middle East;

Mindful of the struggle that the Palestinian people, led by the Palestine Liberation Organization, their sole legitimate representative, have waged for their rights to self-determination, to return to their homeland and to establish their independent State in Palestine;

Reiterating the support to this struggle expressed in many resolutions of the United Nations and other international institutions and organizations that call for the immediate and unconditional withdrawal of Israel from the occupied Arab territories, including Palestine;

Taking note of the report of the Special Committee of Experts;[5]

Considering the right of the peoples to organize for

---

[4]Document A36/14, paragraph 4.1.3.3.

[5]Document A37/13.

themselves the provision of their own health and social services;

1. *Endorses* resolution WHA36.27 and previous relevant resolutions of the Health Assembly;

2. *Condemns* Israel for its continuing occupation of the Arab territories, including Palestine, and its continuing arbitrary practices against the Arab population;

3. *Condemns* Israel for the continued establishment of Israeli settlements in the occupied Arab territories, including Palestine and the Golan, and the illegal exploitation of the natural wealth and resources of the Arab inhabitants in those territories, especially the appropriation of water resources and their diversion for the purpose of occupation and settlement, and demands that the establishment of new settlements be stopped immediately and that those already established be dismantled;

4. *Demands* an immediate end to occupation, violence and oppression to enable the Palestinian people to exercise its inalienable national rights, which is a prerequisite to the establishment of a health and social system that would include all necessary institutions to meet its needs;

5. *Condemns* Israel for its policy aiming, as part of its overall plan of annexation of the occupied territories, at making the Arab population dependent on the Israeli health system by paralyzing the services in the Arab health and social institutions;

6. *Condemns* Israel for continuously raising obstacles to the implementation of resolution WHA36.27, sub-paragraph 8(2), which requests the establishment of three health centres in the occupied Arab territories, including Palestine, under the direct supervision of WHO;

7. *Thanks* the Director-General for his efforts to implement sub-paragraph 8(2) of resolution WHA36.27 and requests that he pursue these efforts until the full implementation of this resolution and submit a report to the Thirty-eighth World Health Assembly;

8. *Reaffirms* the right of the Palestinian people to have its own institutions which provide medical and social services, and requests the Director-General:

(1) to collaborate and coordinate further with the Arab States concerned and with the Palestine Liberation Organization regarding the provision of the necessary assistance to the Palestinian people;

(2) to take suitable steps to ensure WHO participation in the implementation of the programme of action adopted by the International Conference on the Question of Palestine convened in Geneva on 29 August 1983;

(3) to monitor the health conditions of the Arab population in the occupied Arab territories, including Palestine, and report regularly to the Health Assembly;

9. *Thanks* the Special Committee of Experts for its report and requests it to continue its task with respect to all the implications of occupation and the policies of the occupying Israeli authorities and their various practices which

adversely affect the health conditions of the Arab inhabitants in the occupied Arab territories, including Palestine, both physically and psychologically, and to report to the Thirty-eighth World Health Assembly, in coordination with the Arab States concerned and the Palestine Liberation Organization.

Adopted at the 14th plenary meeting:

In favour: 75
Against: 23
Abstentions: 28

Resolution No. WHA 38.15 of 16 May 1985

CONDEMNING ISRAELI PRACTICES AND HEALTH POLICY IN THE OCCUPIED TERRITORIES AND REAFFIRMING THE RIGHT OF THE PALESTINIAN POPULATION TO HAVE ITS OWN MEDICAL INSTITUTIONS

The Thirty-eighth World Health Assembly,

Mindful of the basic principle established in the WHO Constitution, which affirms that the health of all peoples is fundamental to the attainment of peace and security;

Aware of its responsibility for ensuring proper health conditions for all peoples who suffer from exceptional situations, including foreign occupation and especially settler colonialism;

Affirming the principle that the acquisition of territories by force is inadmissible and that any occupation of territories by force gravely affects the health, social, psychological, mental and physical conditions of the people under occupation, and that this can be rectified only by the complete and immediate termination of the occupation;

Considering that the States parties to the Geneva Convention of 12 August 1949 pledged themselves, under Article One thereof, not only to respect the Convention but also to ensure that it was respected in all circumstances;

Recalling United Nations General Assembly resolutions 39/49, 39/95 and 39/169 as well as all other United Nations resolutions relative to the questions of Palestine and the Middle East:

Mindful of the struggle that the Palestinian people, led by the Palestine Liberation Organization, their sole legitimate representative, have waged for their rights to self-determination, to return to their homeland and to establish their independent State in Palestine;

Reiterating the support to this struggle expressed in many resolutions of the United Nations and other international institutions and organizations that call for the immediate and unconditional withdrawal of Israel from the occupied Arab territories, including Palestine;

Taking note of the report of the Special Committee of Experts;[6]

Considering the right of the peoples to organize for themselves the provision of their own health and social services;

1. *Reaffirms* resolutions WHA37.26, WHA36.27 and previous relevant resolutions of the World Health Assembly;

2. *Condemns* Israel for its continuing occupation, its arbitrary practices against the Arab population, and its continuing establishment of Israeli settlements in the Arab Occupied Territories, including Palestine and the Golan; and for its illegal exploitation of the natural wealth and resources of the Arab inhabitants in those territories, especially the appropriation of water resources and their diversion for the purpose of occupation and settlement, all of which have devastating and long-term effects on the mental and physical health conditions of the population under occupation;

3. *Condemns* Israel for its policy aiming at making the population of the occupied Arab territories, including Palestine and the Golan, dependent on the Israeli health system, by hindering the normal course and development of the Arab health institutions, as part of Israel's overall plan of annexation of those territories;

4. *Condemns* Israel for continuously raising obstacles to the implementation of resolution WHA36.27, sub-paragraph 8(2), which requests the establishment of three health centres in the occupied Arab territories, including Palestine, under the direct supervision of WHO;

5. *Demands* an immediate end to occupation, violence and repression, and to the establishment of new settlements; also demands that those settlements already established be dismantled, in order to enable the Palestinian people to exercise its inalienable national rights, as a prerequisite to the establishment of a social and health system that would be able to ensure health for all by the year 2000;

6. *Thanks* the Director-General for his efforts to implement sub-paragraph 8(2) of resolution WHA36.27 and requests that he pursue these efforts until the full implementation of this resolution and submit a report to the Thirty-ninth World Health Assembly;

7. *Reaffirms* the right of the Palestinian people to have its own institutions which provide medical and social services, and requests the Director-General:

(1) to collaborate and coordinate further with the Arab States concerned and with the Palestine Liberation Or-

ganization regarding the provision of the necessary assistance to the Palestinian people;

(2) to help the Palestinian people and their health institutions to promote primary health care inside and outside the occupied Palestinian territories, by developing sufficient health and social services, and the training of the health personnel, in order to reach health for all by the year 2000;

(3) to monitor the health conditions of the Arab population in the occupied Arab territories, including Palestine, and report regularly to the Health Assembly;

8. *Thanks* the Special Committee of Experts for its report and requests it to continue its task with respect to all the implications of occupation and the policies of the occupying Israeli authorities and their various practices which adversely affect the health conditions of the Arab inhabitants in the occupied Arab territories, including Palestine, both physically and psychologically, and to report to the Thirty-ninth World Health Assembly, in coordination with the Arab States concerned and the Palestine Liberation Organization.

Adopted at the 14th plenary meeting:

In favour: 76

Afghanistan, Algeria, Angola, Bahrain, Bangladesh, Benin, Bhutan, Botswana, Brunei Darussalam, Bulgaria, Burkina Faso, Burundi, Cape Verde, Central African Republic, China, Comoros, Congo, Cuba, Cyprus, Czechoslovakia, Democratic Kampuchea, Democratic People's Republic of Korea, Democratic Yemen, Djibouti, Egypt, Ethiopia, German Democratic Republic, Greece, Guinea, Guinea-Bissau, Hungary, India, Indonesia, Islamic Republic of Iran, Iraq, Jordan, Kuwait, Lebanon, Libyan Arab Jamahiriya, Madagascar, Malaysia, Maldives, Mali, Malta, Mauritania, Mongolia, Morocco, Mozambique, Nicaragua, Niger, Nigeria, Oman, Pakistan, Philippines, Poland, Qatar, Saudi Arabia, Senegal, Sierra Leone, Sri Lanka, Sudan, Suriname, Syrian Arab Republic, Thailand, Tunisia, Turkey, Uganda, USSR, United Arab Emirates, United Republic of Tanzania, Vanuatu, Viet Nam, Yemen, Yugoslavia, Zambia, Zimbabwe.

Against: 28

Australia, Belgium, Canada, Cook Islands, Costa Rica, Denmark, El Salvador, France, Federal Republic of Germany, Grenada, Haiti, Iceland, Ireland, Israel, Italy, Liberia, Luxembourg, Monaco, Netherlands, New Zealand, Norway, Papua New Guinea, Paraguay, Switzerland, Tonga, Trinidad and Tobago, United Kingdom, United States.

Abstentions: 22

Argentina, Austria, Bolivia, Brazil, Chile, Colombia, Dominican Republic, Finland, Guatemala, Ivory Coast, Jamaica, Japan, Kiribati, Malawi, Mexico, Panama, Peru, Portugal, Samoa, San Marino, Sweden, Venezuela.

Absent: 33

Albania, Antigua and Barbuda, Bahamas, Barbados, Burma, Cameroon, Chad, Ecuador, Equatorial Guinea, Fiji, Gabon, Gambia, Ghana, Guyana, Honduras, Kenya, Lao People's Democratic Republic, Lesotho, Mauritius,

---

[6]Document A38/10.

Nepal, Republic of Korea, Romania, Rwanda, Sao Tome and Principe, Seychelles, Singapore, Solomon Islands, Somalia, Spain, Swaziland, Togo, Uruguay, Zaire.

Resolution No. WHA 39.10 of 15 May 1986

CONDEMNING ISRAELI PRACTICES AND HEALTH POLICY IN THE OCCUPIED TERRITORIES AND REAFFIRMING THE RIGHT OF THE PALESTINIAN POPULATION TO HAVE ITS OWN MEDICAL INSTITUTIONS

The Thirty-ninth World Health Assembly,

Mindful of the basic principle established in the WHO Constitution, which affirms that the health of all peoples is fundamental to the attainment of peace and security;

Aware of its responsibility for ensuring proper health conditions for all peoples who suffer from exceptional situations, including foreign occupation and especially settler colonialism;

Affirming the principle that acquisition of territories by force is inadmissible and that any occupation of territories by force has serious repercussions on the health and psychosocial conditions of the people under occupation, including mental and physical health, and that this can be rectified only by the complete and immediate termination of the occupation;

Mindful of the struggle that the Palestinian people, led by the Palestine Liberation Organization, their sole legitimate representative, have waged and are waging for their rights to self-determination, to return to their homeland and to establish their independent state in Palestine, and calling upon Israel to end its occupation of the occupied Arab territories, including Palestine;

Recalling and reaffirming previous resolutions of the Health Assembly regarding the health conditions of the Arab population in the occupied Arab territories, including Palestine, especially resolutions WHA36.27, WHA37.26 and WHA38.15;

Considering the right of the peoples to organize for themselves, and through their institutions, the provision of their own humanitarian health and social services;

1. *Condemns* Israel for its continuing occupation of Arab territories, its arbitrary practices against the Arab populations, and its continuing establishment of Israeli settlements in the occupied Arab territories, including Palestine and the Golan; and for its illegal exploitation of the natural wealth and resources of the Arab inhabitants in those territories, especially the appropriation of water resources and their diversion for the purpose of occupation and settlement, all of which have devastating and long-term effects on the mental and physical health conditions of the population under occupation;

2. *Condemns* Israel for its policy aiming at the annexation of the occupied Arab territories, its attempt at linking the Arab population in Palestine and the Golan to the Israeli health system, its hindering the normal development of the Arab health institutions and its closure of some of these institutions such as the hospice-hospital in the city of Jerusalem;

3. *Condemns* Israel for its refusal to allow the Special Committee of Experts to visit the occupied Arab territories, including Palestine and the Golan, and its refusal to implement resolution WHA38.15;

4. *Affirms* the need for continuously informing the Health Assembly of the health conditions of the Arab population under occupation, through regular reporting by the Special Committee of Experts, and the need for the Committee to continue its mission and to submit its report to the Fortieth World Health Assembly concerning the effects of occupation, the policies of the Israeli occupying forces and their various practices which have adverse effects on the health conditions of the Arab population under occupation;

5. *Thanks* the Director-General for his efforts to implement the resolutions of the Health Assembly and requests that he pursue the implementation of resolution WHA38.15 especially regarding the visit of the Special Committee of Experts to the occupied Arab territories;

6. *Reaffirms* the right of the Palestinian people to have their own institutions which provide health and social services, and requests the Director-General:

(1) to collaborate and coordinate further with the Arab States concerned and with the Palestine Liberation Organization regarding the provision of the necessary assistance to the Palestinian people;

(2) to help the Palestinian people and their health institutions to promote primary health care inside and outside the occupied Palestinian territories, by developing adequate health and social services, and by the training of additional health personnel, in order to achieve health for all by the year 2000;

(3) to monitor the health conditions of the Arab population in the occupied Arab territories, including Palestine, and report to the Fortieth World Health Assembly;

(4) to strengthen the health centres in the occupied Arab territories that are under the direct supervision of WHO, and further to increase the services they provide;

(5) to provide financial and moral support to all local and international institutions, societies and organizations that seek to establish hospitals and health units in the occupied Arab territories.

Adopted at the 14th plenary meeting:
In favour: 64
Afghanistan, Algeria, Angola, Bahrain, Bangladesh, Botswana, Brazil, Bulgaria, Burkina Faso, Burundi, China, Congo, Cuba, Cyprus, Czechoslovakia, Democratic People's Republic of Korea, Egypt, Ethiopia, Gambia, German Democratic Republic, Greece, Guinea, Guyana, Hungary, India, Indonesia, Islamic Republic of Iran, Iraq, Jordan, Kuwait, Lebanon, Madagascar, Malaysia, Maldives, Mali, Malta, Mauritania, Mauritius, Mongolia, Morocco, Mozambique, Nepal, Nicaragua, Niger, Oman, Pakistan, Poland, Qatar, Romania, Rwanda, Saudi Arabia, Senegal, Sri Lanka, Sudan, Syrian Arab Republic, Thailand, Tunisia, Turkey, USSR, United Arab Emirates, United

Republic of Tanzania, Viet Nam, Yugoslavia, Zambia.

Against: 21

Australia, Belgium, Canada, Costa Rica, Denmark, El Salvador, France, Federal Republic of Germany, Iceland, Ireland, Israel, Italy, Luxembourg, Monaco, Netherlands, New Zealand, Norway, Portugal, Switzerland, United Kingdom, United States.

Abstentions: 27

Antigua and Barbuda, Argentina, Austria, Central African Republic, Chile, Colombia, Cook Islands, Ecuador, Finland, Guatemala, Haiti, Honduras, Jamaica, Japan, Kenya, Liberia, Malawi, Mexico, Panama, Peru, Samoa, San Marino, Spain, Suriname, Sweden, Trinidad and Tobago, Venezuela.

Absent: 46

Albania, Bahamas, Benin, Bhutan, Bolivia, Brunei Darussalam, Burma, Cameroon, Cape Verde, Chad, Comoros, Democratic Kampuchea, Democratic Yemen, Djibouti, Dominican Republic, Equatorial Guinea, Fiji, Gabon, Ghana, Grenada, Guinea-Bissau, Ivory Coast, Kiribati, Lao People's Democratic Republic, Lesotho, Libyan Arab Jamahiriya, Nigeria, Papua New Guinea, Paraguay, Philippines, Republic of Korea, Sao Tome and Principe, Seychelles, Sierra Leone, Singapore, Solomon Islands, Somalia, Swaziland, Togo, Tonga, Uganda, Uruguay, Vanuatu, Yemen, Zaire, Zimbabwe.

VI. RESOLUTIONS OF THE INTERNATIONAL
ATOMIC ENERGY AGENCY

Resolution No. GC (XXVII)/RES/409 of 14 October 1983

CALLING ON ISRAEL TO WITHDRAW ITS THREAT TO REPEAT ITS ATTACK ON IRAQI NUCLEAR FACILITIES

The General Conference,

(a) *Having* considered agenda item 8,

(b) *Recalling* resolution GC(XXV)/RES/381 adopted by the General Conference on 26 September 1981, which, inter alia, expressed grave concern that Israel's military aggression against a safeguarded nuclear research facility has caused considerable damage to the safeguards regime and could seriously jeopardize the development of nuclear energy for peaceful purposes,

(c) *Taking note* of resolution A/RES/37/19 adopted by the General Assembly of the United Nations on 22 November 1982 which "considers that Israel's threat to repeat its armed attack against such facilities, as well as any other attack against such facilities, constitutes, inter alia, a serious threat to the role and activities of the International Atomic Energy Agency in the development and further promotion of nuclear energy for peaceful purposes",

(d) *Aware* that the promotion of application of nuclear energy for peaceful purposes and the ensurance that these activities are not used to further any military purposes are the main objectives of the Agency as envisaged in the Statute,

(e) *Noting* that serious radiological effects would follow from an armed attack with conventional weapons on a nuclear installation,

(f) *Noting further* that radiological warfare could also in this manner be initiated through the use of conventional weapons,

1. *Notes* that statements made so far by Israel have not removed apprehension that its threat to repeat its armed attack against nuclear facilities, as well as any similar action against such facilities will continue to endanger the role and activities of the Agency, and other international instruments, in the development of nuclear energy for peaceful purposes, and in safeguarding against further proliferation of nuclear weapons;

2. *Urgently calls on* Israel to withdraw forthwith its threat to attack and destroy nuclear facilities in Iraq and in other countries;

3. *Decides* to withhold Agency research contracts to Israel, to discontinue the purchase of equipment and materials from Israel and to refrain from holding seminars, scientific and technical meetings in Israel if, by the next General Conference, Israel has not complied with paragraph 2 of the present resolution;

4. *Requests* the Director-General to re-examine and report to the Board of Governors with respect to Israel on the Agency's research contracts, purchase of equipment and materials, and the holding of meetings outside Agency Headquarters;

5. *Calls* for the early consideration of the conclusion of an international agreement to prohibit military attacks on nuclear installations;

6. *Urges* Member States to initiate or support actions in the proper international fora with the aim to prohibit military attacks against "civilian" nuclear installations since such attacks could result in the release of dangerous forces and could be tantamount to an attack by nuclear weapons;

7. *Reaffirms* the right of Iraq and all other developing countries in exercising their right to acquire and develop nuclear technology for peaceful purposes and for their development programmes;

8. *Considers* that Iraq is entitled to appropriate redress for the destruction it has suffered, responsibility for which has been acknowledged by Israel, and urges the Security Council to take the appropriate measures in accordance with its resolution 487 of 19 June 1981;

9. *Requests* the Director-General to prepare a report on the consequences of an armed attack on peaceful nuclear installations and the threats thereof on the Agency safeguards system and the peaceful applications of atomic energy; and to submit this report to the twenty-eighth regular session of the General Conference; and

10. *Further requests* the Director-General to report to the twenty-eighth regular session of the General Conference on the implementation of the present resolution.

Adopted at the 27th regular session.

Resolution No. GC (XXVIII)/RES/425 of 28 September 1984

DEMANDING THAT ISRAEL UNDERTAKE NOT TO CARRY OUT FURTHER ATTACKS ON NUCLEAR FACILITIES IN IRAQ AND CALLING ON ISRAEL TO PLACE ITS NUCLEAR FACILITIES UNDER IAEA SAFEGUARDS

The General Conference,

(a) *Having* considered agenda item 10,

(b) *Recalling* resolution GC (XXVII)/RES/409(1983) and other relevant General Conference resolutions,

(c) *Taking note* of Security Council resolution 487 adopted unanimously on 19 June 1981, which, inter alia, called upon Israel to refrain in the future from any such acts or threats thereof, and urgently to place its nuclear facilities under IAEA safeguards,

(d) *Taking note* further of the relevant resolutions of the General Assembly of the United Nations,

(e) *Taking note* of the report of the Director-General contained in document GC(XXVIII)/719 on the consequences of the Israeli military attack on the Iraqi Nuclear Research Reactor and the standing threat to repeat this attack for: (i) the development of nuclear energy for peaceful purposes and (ii) the role and activities of the International Atomic Energy Agency,

(f) *Considering* that the Israeli statements contained in

document GC(XXVIII)/720 continue to ignore the Agency's safeguards system under the Statute and do not specify the Iraqi nuclear installations which were subjected to Israeli attack and subsequent threats,

(g) *Convinced* that the stated Israeli threats to attack nuclear facilities in Iraq and in other countries will continue to endanger the role and activities of the Agency, and other international instruments in the development of nuclear energy for peaceful purposes, and in safeguarding against further proliferation of nuclear weapons,

(h) *Mindful* of the fact that all Iraqi nuclear installations are under Agency safeguards, and

(i) *Reaffirming* its confidence in the effectiveness of the Agency's safeguards system as a reliable means of verifying the peaceful use of a nuclear facility,

1. *Considers* that Israeli statements contained in document GC(XXVIII)/720 do not fulfil or, in the view of some do not completely fulfil, the provisions of resolution GC(XXVII)/RES/409, which urgently called on Israel to withdraw forthwith its threat to attack and destroy nuclear facilities in Iraq and in other countries;

2. *Further considers* that any threat to attack and destroy nuclear facilities in Iraq and in other countries constitutes a violation of the Charter of the United Nations and of the Statute of the Agency;

3. *Demands* that Israel undertake forthwith not to carry out any further attacks on nuclear facilities in Iraq or on similar facilities in other countries, devoted to peaceful purposes, in disregard of the Agency's safeguards system;

4. *Requests* the Director-General to seek personally from the Government of Israel the undertakings required by paragraph 3 above, to keep the Board of Governors informed of his progress, and to report to the twenty-ninth session of the General Conference, which shall then consider the implementation of paragraph 3 of General Conference resolution GC(XXVII)/RES/409;

5. *Calls upon* all Member States to assist and support the Director-General's efforts in this regard;

6. *Calls upon* Israel urgently to place all its nuclear facilities under Agency safeguards; and

7. *Reaffirms* the right of all nations in exercising their right to acquire and develop nuclear technology for peaceful purposes and for their development programme.

Adopted at the 28th regular session.

Resolution No. GC (XXIX)/RES/443 of 27 September 1985

CONSIDERING THAT ISRAEL HAS COMMITTED ITSELF NOT TO ATTACK PEACEFUL NUCLEAR FACILITIES IN IRAQ, AND CALLING ON ISRAEL TO PLACE ITS NUCLEAR FACILITIES UNDER IAEA SAFEGUARDS

The General Conference,

(a) *Having considered* agenda item 10,

(b) *Taking note* of Security resolution 487 unanimously adopted on 19 June 1981, which, inter alia, called upon Israel to refrain in the future from any such acts or threats thereof, and urgently to place its nuclear facilities under IAEA safeguards,

(c) *Recalling* relevant General Conference resolutions, particularly GC(XXVII)/RES/407 (1983) and GC(XXVIII)/RES/425 (1984), which, inter alia, demanded that Israel undertake forthwith not to carry out any further attacks on nuclear facilities in Iraq or on similar facilities in other countries, devoted to peaceful purposes, in disregard of the Agency's safeguards system,

(d) *Taking note* of the United Nations General Assembly resolution 39/14 and earlier relevant resolutions of the United Nations General Assembly on the same subject,

(e) *Recalling* that, as stated in resolution GC(XXVII)/RES/407, it is an objective of the International Atomic Energy Agency to "seek to accelerate and enlarge the contribution of atomic energy to peace, health and prosperity throughout the world" and that in carrying out its functions the Agency shall "conduct its activities in accordance with the purposes and principles of the United Nations to promote peace and international co-operation, and in conformity with policies of the United Nations furthering the establishment of safeguarded worldwide disarmament and in conformity with any international agreements entered into pursuant to such policies",

(f) *Reaffirming* the right of all nations to acquire and develop nuclear technology for peaceful purposes for their development programmes under effective international safeguards,

(g) *Considering* that any attacks or threats of attack against peaceful nuclear facilities jeopardize the development and further promotion of the peaceful uses of nuclear energy, and, therefore, the achievement of one of the main objectives of the International Atomic Energy Agency,

(h) *Concerned* that such attacks raise fears about the safety of present and future nuclear facilities,

(i) *Aware* that all States developing nuclear energy for peaceful purposes need assurances against armed attacks on peaceful nuclear facilities,

(j) *Reaffirming* its confidence in the effectiveness of the Agency's safeguards system as a reliable means of verifying the peaceful use of a nuclear facility,

(k) *Taking into account* that the question of the protection of nuclear facilities against armed attack is under consideration in other international organizations, including the Conference on Disarmament,

(l) *Bearing in mind* the report of the Director-General of the IAEA contained in document GC(XXVIII)/719,

(m) *Having heard* the Director-General's report, in his statement of 23 September 1985, on his discussions in compliance with GC(XXVIII)/RES/425,

(n) *Having studied* the letter of 23 September 1985 addressed to the Director-General by the Resident Representative of Israel, and circulated to the members of the Conference, and

(o) *Taking note* of the statement made on 26 September 1985 in the General Conference by the Representative of Israel, as directed by the Minister for Foreign Affairs of Israel and on behalf of his Government, according to which:

(1) Israel holds that all States must refrain from attacking or threatening to attack nuclear facilities devoted to peaceful purposes, and that the safeguards system operated by the IAEA brings evidence of the peaceful operation of a facility;

(2) Israel reconfirms that under its stated policy it will not attack or threaten to attack any nuclear facilities devoted to peaceful purposes either in the Middle East or anywhere else and emphasizes specifically that Iraq is included;

(3) Israel will support any subsequent action in competent fora convened to work out binding agreements protecting nuclear installations devoted to peaceful purposes from attack and threat of attack.

1. *Thanks* the Director-General for the skill and perseverance with which he carried out the task entrusted to him by resolution GC(XXVIII)/RES/425;

2. *Declares* that all States must refrain from attacking or threatening to attack peaceful nuclear facilities in other countries;

3. *Considers* that the letter of 23 September 1985 from the Resident Representative of Israel and the statement by the Representative of Israel on 26 September 1985 contain undertakings on behalf of their Government in response to resolution GC(XXVIII)/RES/425 and notes in particular the statement that Israel will not attack or threaten to attack any nuclear facilities devoted to peaceful purposes either in the Middle East, including Iraq, or anywhere else;

4. *Notes* that Israel has thereby committed itself not to attack peaceful nuclear facilities in Iraq, elsewhere in the Middle East, or anywhere else;

5. *Calls upon* Israel urgently to place all its nuclear facilities under IAEA safeguards;

6. *Considers* that the safeguards system of the IAEA brings evidence of and an opportunity to review the peaceful nature of nuclear facilities subject to such safeguards;

7. *Reaffirms* that any attack on a peaceful nuclear facility subject to IAEA safeguards would constitute a serious threat to the safeguards system of the IAEA;

8. *Appeals* to competent international organs to take steps, in accordance with their mandates, to ensure the inviolability of peaceful nuclear facilities and to contribute thereby to the safe development of nuclear energy;

9. *Affirms* the readiness of the International Atomic Energy Agency to assist the competent international organs, if they so request, in any technical and safeguards aspects of this matter; and

10. *Declares* that, if such attacks or threats of attack were to occur again, the matter will be examined by the International Atomic Energy Agency in accordance with its Statute and the relevant resolutions.

Adopted at the 29th regular session.

SOURCES OF TEXTS OF RESOLUTIONS

General Assembly

1982 Resolution No.ES-9/1: *Resolutions and Decisions Adopted by the General Assembly at its Ninth Emergency Special Session, 29 January to 5 February 1982*, UN Document GA/6560, pp. 1-3.

Decision No. 36/462: *Resolutions and Decisions Adopted by the General Assembly at its Resumed Thirty-sixth Regular Session, 16 to 19 March and 29 March 1982*, UN Document GA/6546/Add. 1, p. 5.

Resolution No. 36/138 C: *Ibid.*, pp. 1-2.

Resolution No. ES-7/4: *Resolutions and Decisions Adopted by the General Assembly at its Resumed Seventh Emergency Special Session, 20-28 April 1982*, UN Document GA/6245/Add. 1, pp. 1-4.

Resolution No. ES-7/5: *Resolutions and Decisions Adopted by the General Assembly at its Resumed Seventh Emergency Special Session, 25-26 June 1982*, UN Document GA/6245/Add. 2, pp. 1-3.

Resolution No. ES-7/6: *Resolutions and Decisions Adopted by the General Assembly at its Resumed Seventh Emergency Special Session, 16-19 August 1982*, UN Document GA/6245/Add. 3, pp. 1-4.

Resolution No. ES-7/7: *Ibid.*, pp. 5-6.

Resolution No. ES-7/8: *Ibid.*, p. 7.

Resolution No. ES-7/9: *Resolutions and Decisions Adopted by the General Assembly at its Seventh Emergency Special Session on the Question of Palestine, 24 September 1982*, UN Document GA/6245/Add. 4, pp. 1-3.

Resolution No. 37/18: *Resolutions and Decisions Adopted by the General Assembly during its Thirty-seventh Session, 21 September-21 December 1982 and 10-13 May 1983*. General Assembly Official Records, Thirty-seventh Session, Supplement No. 51, p. 22.

Resolution No. 37/19 : *Ibid.*, pp. 22-23.

Resolution No. 37/38 A, B: *Ibid.*, pp. 239-40.

Resolution No. 37/39: *Ibid.*, pp. 172-74.

Resolution No. 37/40: *Ibid.*, pp. 174-75.

Resolution No. 37/43: *Ibid.*, pp. 177-79.

Resolution No. 37/46: *Ibid.*, pp. 180-81.

Resolution No. 37/69 A, C, D, F: *Ibid.*, pp. 28-34.

Resolution No. 37/75: *Ibid.*, pp. 56-57.

Resolution No. 37/82: *Ibid.*, pp. 67-68.

Resolution No. 37/86 A, B, C, D, E: *Ibid.*, pp. 34-36.

Resolution No. 37/88 A, B, C, D, E, F, G: *Ibid.*, pp. 92-95.

Resolution No. 37/104: *Ibid.*, pp. 265-66.

Resolution No. 37/120 A, B, C, D, E, F, G, H, I, J, K: *Ibid.*, pp. 103-107.

Resolution No. 37/122: *Ibid.*, pp. 107-108.

Resolution No. 37/123 A, B, C, D, E, F: *Ibid.*, pp. 36-39.

Resolution No. 37/127 A, B: *Ibid.*, pp. 244-46.

Resolution No. 37/134: *Ibid.*, p. 111.

Resolution No. 37/135: *Ibid.*, pp. 111-12.

Resolution No. 37/163: *Ibid.*, p. 133.

Resolution No. 37/222: *Ibid.*, p. 149.

1983 Resolution No. 38/9: *Resolutions and Decisions Adopted by the General Assembly during its Thirty-eighth Session, 20 September-20 December 1983 and 26 June 1984*, General Assembly Official Records, Thirty-eighth Session, Supplement No. 47, pp. 14-15.

Resolution No. 38/17: *Ibid.*, pp. 185-87.

Resolution No. 38/35 A, B: *Ibid.*, pp. 241-42.

Resolution No. 38/36 A, D: *Ibid.*, pp. 25-36.

Resolution No. 38/38 A, B: *Ibid.*, pp. 242-43.

Resolution No. 38/39 A, F, G: *Ibid.*, pp. 36-42.

Resolution No. 38/58 A, B, C, D, E: *Ibid.*, pp. 46-48.

Resolution No. 38/64: *Ibid.*, p. 57.

Resolution No. 38/69: *Ibid.*, pp. 60-61.

Resolution No. 38/79 A, B, C, D, E, F, G, H: *Ibid.*, pp. 94-98.

Resolution No. 38/83 A, B, C, D, E, F, G, H, I, J, K: *Ibid.*, pp. 107-12.

Resolution No. 38/85: *Ibid.*, pp. 112-13.

Resolution No. 38/130: *Ibid.*, pp. 266-67.

Resolution No. 38/144: *Ibid.*, pp. 117-18.

Resolution No. 38/145: *Ibid.*, p. 118.

Resolution No. 38/166: *Ibid.*, pp. 134-35.

Resolution No. 38/180 A, B, C, D, E: *Ibid.*, pp. 49-52.

Resolution No. 38/220: *Ibid.*, p. 171.

1984 Resolution No. 39/14: *Resolutions and Decisions Adopted by the General Assembly during its Thirty-ninth Session 18 September-18 December 1984 and 9-12 April 1985*, General Assembly Official Records, Thirty-ninth Session, Supplement No. 51, pp. 23-24.

Resolution No. 39/17: *Ibid.*, pp. 187-89.

Resolution No. 39/28 A, B: *Ibid.*, pp. 256-58.

Resolution No. 39/49 A, B, C, D: *Ibid.*, pp. 27-28.

Resolution No. 39/50 A, D: *Ibid.*, pp. 28-39.

Resolution No. 39/54: *Ibid.*, pp. 59-60.

Resolution No. 39/71 A, B: *Ibid.*, pp. 264-65.

Resolution No. 39/72 A, C: *Ibid.*, pp. 40-45.

Resolution No. 39/76: *Ibid.*, p. 284.

Resolution No. 39/95 A, B, C, D, E, F, G, H: *Ibid.*, pp. 102-106.

Resolution No. 39/99 A, B, C, D, E, F, G, H, I, J, K: *Ibid.*, pp. 115-20.

Resolution No. 39/101: *Ibid.*, pp. 120-21.

Resolution No. 39/146 A, B, C: *Ibid.*, pp. 50-53.

Resolution No. 39/147: *Ibid.*, pp. 75-76.

Resolution No. 39/169: *Ibid.*, pp. 130-31.

Resolution No. 39/197: *Ibid.*, p. 150.

Resolution No. 39/223: *Ibid.*, p. 170.

Resolution No. 39/224: *Ibid.*, pp. 170-71.

Decision No. 39/442: *Ibid.*, pp. 313-14.

1985 Resolution No. 40/6: *Resolutions and Decisions Adopted by the General Assembly during its Fortieth Session, 17 September-18 December 1985, 28 April-9 May and 20 June 1986*, General Assembly Official Records, Fortieth Session, Supplement No. 53, pp. 17-18.

Resolution No. 40/25: *Ibid.*, p. 196.

Resolution No. 40/59 A, B: *Ibid.*, pp. 278-79.

Resolution No. 40/61: *Ibid.*, pp. 301-302.

Resolution No. 40/64 A, E: *Ibid.*, pp. 32-41.

Resolution No. 40/82: *Ibid.*, pp. 68-69.

Resolution No. 40/93: *Ibid.*, p. 79.

Resolution No. 40/96 A, B, C, D: *Ibid.*, pp. 42-44.

Resolution No. 40/161 A, B, C, D, E, F, G,: *Ibid.*, pp. 112-16.

Resolution No. 40/165 A, B, C, D, E, F, G, H, I, J, K: *Ibid.*, pp. 127-31.

Resolution No. 40/167: *Ibid.*, p. 132.

Resolution No. 40/168 A, B, C: *Ibid.*, pp. 57-60.

Resolution No. 40/169: *Ibid.*, p. 135.

Resolution No. 40/170: *Ibid.*, p. 135.

Resolution No. 40/201: *Ibid.*, p. 155.

Resolution No. 40/229: *Ibid.*, p. 184.

Resolution No. 40/246 A, B: *Ibid.*, pp. 288-89.

Decision No. 40/432: *Ibid.*, p. 334.

1986 Resolution No. 41/12: *Resolutions and Decisions Adopted by the General Assembly during the First Part of its Forty-first Session from 16 September to 19 December 1986*, United Nations Department of Public Information Press Release GA/7463, pp.17-18.

Resolution No. 41/35 C: *Ibid.*, pp. 28-39.

Resolution No. 41/43 A, B, C, D: *Ibid.*, pp. 87-92.

Resolution No. 41/44 A, B: *Ibid.*, pp. 457-59.

Resolution No. 41/48: *Ibid.*, pp. 107-109.

Resolution No. 41/63 A, B, C, D, E, F, G: *Ibid.*, pp. 207-14.

Resolution No. 41/69 A, B, C, D, E, F, G, H, I, J, K: *Ibid.*, pp. 239-48.

Resolution No. 41/71: *Ibid.*, pp. 499-500.

Resolution No. 41/93: *Ibid.*, pp. 202-203.

Resolution No. 41/95: *Ibid.*, pp. 310-12.

Resolution No. 41/101: *Ibid.*, pp. 320-24.

Resolution No. 41/162 A, B, C: *Ibid.*, pp. 87-92.

Resolution No. 41/179 A, B: *Ibid.*, pp. 466-68.

Resolution No. 41/181: *Ibid.*, pp. 275-76.

Resolution No. 41/196: *Ibid.*, pp. 294-95.

Security Council

1982 Resolution No. 500 (1982): *Resolutions and Decisions of the Security Council, 1982*, Security Council Official Records, Thirty-seventh Year, p. 2.

Resolution No. 501 (1982): *Ibid.*, pp. 2-3.

Resolution No. 506 (1982): *Ibid.*, p. 5.

Resolution No. 508 (1982): *Ibid.*, pp. 5-6.

Resolution No. 509 (1982): *Ibid.*, p. 6.

Resolution No. 511 (1982): *Ibid.*, pp. 6-7.

Resolution No. 512 (1982): *Ibid.*, p. 7.

Resolution No. 513 (1982): *Ibid.*, p. 7.

Resolution No. 515 (1982): *Ibid.*, pp. 7-8.

Resolution No. 516 (1982): *Ibid.*, p. 8.

Resolution No. 517 (1982): *Ibid.*, pp. 8-9.

Resolution No. 518 (1982): *Ibid.*, p. 9.

Resolution No. 519 (1982): *Ibid.*, p. 9.

Resolution No. 520 (1982): *Ibid.*, p. 10.

Resolution No. 521 (1982): *Ibid.*, p. 10.

Resolution No. 523 (1982): *Ibid.*, p. 11.

Resolution No. 524 (1982): *Ibid.*, p. 12.

1983   Resolution No. 529 (1983): *Resolutions and Decisions of the Security Council, 1983*, Security Council Official Records, Thirty-eighth Year, p. 1.

Resolution No. 531 (1983): *Ibid.*, p. 2.

Resolution No. 536 (1983): *Ibid.*, p. 3.

Resolution No. 538 (1983): *Ibid.*, p. 4.

Resolution No. 542 (1983): *Ibid.*, pp. 4-5.

Resolution No. 543 (1983): *Ibid.*, p. 5.

1984   Resolution No. 549 (1984): *Resolutions and Decisions of the Security Council, 1984*, Security Council Official Records, Thirty-ninth Year, p. 6.

Resolution No. 551 (1984): *Ibid.*, p. 7.

Resolution No. 555 (1984): *Ibid.*, p. 8.

Resolution No. 557 (1984): *Ibid.*, p. 9.

1985   Resolution No. 561 (1985): *Resolutions and Decisions of the Security Council, 1985*, Security Council Official Records, Fortieth Year, p. 2.

Resolution No. 563 (1985): *Ibid.*, pp. 2-3.

Resolution No. 564 (1985): *Ibid.*, pp. 3-4.

Resolution No. 573 (1985): *Ibid.*, p. 23.

Resolution No. 575 (1985): *Ibid.*, p. 5.

Resolution No. 576 (1985): *Ibid.*

Resolution No. 579 (1985): *Ibid.*, pp. 24-25.

1986   Resolution No. 583 (1986): *Resolutions and Decisions of the Security Council, 1986*, Security Council Official Records, Forty-first Year, pp. 1-2.

Resolution No. 584 (1986): *Ibid.*, p. 2.

Resolution No. 586 (1986): *Ibid.*, p. 3.

Resolution No. 587 (1986): *Ibid.*, p. 4.

Resolution No. 590 (1986): *Ibid.*, p. 5.

Resolution No. 592 (1986): *Ibid.*, p. 7.

Economic and Social Council

1982   Resolution No. 1982/18: *Resolutions and Decisions of the Economic and Social Council, First Regular Session of 1982*, Economic and Social Council Official Records, 1982, Supplement No. 1, pp. 14-15.

Resolution No. 1982/48: *Resolutions and Decisions of the Economic and Social Council, Second Regular Session of 1982*, Economic and Social Council Official Records, 1982, Supplement No. 1A, pp. 10-11.

1983   Resolution No. 1983/43: *Resolutions and Decisions of the Economic and Social Council, Second Regular Session of 1983*, Economic and Social Council Official Records, 1983, Supplement No. 1A, p. 7.

1984   Resolution No. 1984/18: *Resolutions and Decisions of the Economic and Social Council, First Regular Session of 1984*, Economic and Social Council Official Records, 1984, Supplement No. 1, p. 17.

Resolution No. 1984/56: *Resolutions and Decisions of the Economic and Social Council, Second Regular Session of 1984*, Economic and Social Council Official Records, 1984, Supplement No. 1A, p. 9.

1985   Resolution No. 1985/57: *Resolutions and Decisions of the Economic and Social Council, Second Regular Session of 1985*, Economic and Social Council Official Records, 1985, Supplement No. 1A, p. 12.

Resolution No. 1985/58: *Resolutions and Decisions of the Economic and Social Council, Second Regular Session of 1985*, Economic and Social Council Official Records, 1985, Supplement No. 1A, pp. 12-13.

1986 Resolution No. 1986/49: *Resolutions and Decisions of the Economic and Social Council, Second Regular Session of 1986*, Economic and Social Council Official Records, 1986, Supplement No. 1A, p. 9.

Resolution No. 1986/67: *Resolutions and Decisions of the Economic and Social Council, Second Regular Session of 1986*, Economic and Social Council Official Records, Supplement No. 1A, pp. 20-21.

Commission on Human Rights

1982 Resolution No. 1982/1 A, B: Commission on Human Rights, *Report on the Thirty-eighth Session*, Economic and Social Council Official Records, 1982, Supplement No. 2, pp. 102-106.

Resolution No. 1982/2: Commission on Human Rights, *Report on the Thirty-eighth Session*, Economic and Social Council Official Records, 1982, Supplement No. 2, pp. 107-108.

Resolution No. 1982/3: Commission on Human Rights, *Report on the Thirty-eighth Session*, Economic and Social Council Official Records, 1982, Supplement No. 2, pp. 108-109.

1983 Resolution No. 1983/1 A, B: Commission on Human Rights, *Report on the Thirty-ninth Session*, Economic and Social Council Official Records, 1983, Supplement No. 3, pp. 112-16.

Resolution No. 1983/2: Commission on Human Rights, *Report on the Thirty-ninth Session*, Economic and Social Council Official Records, 1983, Supplement No. 3, pp. 116-18.

Resolution No. 1983/3: Commission on Human Rights, *Report on the Thirty-ninth Session*, Economic and Social Council Official Records, 1983, Supplement No. 3, pp. 118-20.

1984 Resolution No. 1984/1 A, B: Commission on Human Rights, *Report on the Fortieth Session*, Economic and Social Council Official Records, 1984, Supplement No. 4, pp. 18-22.

Resolution No. 1984/2: Commission on Human Rights, *Report on the Fortieth Session*, Economic and Social Council Official Records, 1984, Supplement No. 4, pp. 23-25.

Resolution No. 1984/3: Commission on Human Rights, *Report on the Fortieth Session*, Economic and Social Council Official Records, 1984, Supplement No. 4, p. 25.

1985 Resolution No. 1985/1 A, B: Commission on Human Rights, *Report on the Forty-first Session*, Economic and Social Council Official Records, 1985, Supplement No. 2, pp. 12-17.

Resolution No. 1985/2: Commission on Human Rights, *Report on the Forty-first Session*, Economic and Social Council Official Records, 1985, Supplement No. 2, pp. 18-19.

Resolution No. 1985/4: Commission on Human Rights, *Report on the Forty-first Session*, Economic and Social Council Official Records, 1985, Supplement No. 2, pp. 22-24.

Resolution No. 1985/41: Commission on Human Rights, *Report on the Forty-first Session*, Economic and Social Council Official Records, 1985, Supplement No. 2, p. 85.

1986 Resolution No. 1986/1 A, B: Commission on Human Rights, *Report on the Forty-second Session*, Economic and Social Council Official Records, 1986, Supplement No. 2, pp. 14-20.

Resolution No. 1986/2: Commission on Human Rights, *Report on the Forty-second Session*, Economic and Social Council Official Records, 1986, Supplement No. 2, pp. 21-24.

Resolution No. 1986/22: Commission on Human Rights, *Report on the Forty-second Session*, Economic and Social Council Official Records, 1986, Supplement No. 2, pp. 69-72.

Resolution No. 1986/33: Commission on Human Rights, *Report on the Forty-second Session*, Economic and Social Council Official Records, 1986, Supplement No. 2, p. 94.

Resolution No. 1986/43: Commission on Human Rights, *Report on the Forty-second Session*, Economic and Social Council Official Records, 1986, Supplement No. 2, pp. 110-11.

Economic Commission for Western Asia/ Economic and Social Commission for Western Asia

1982 Resolution No. 108 (IX): Economic Commission for Western Asia, *Report on the Ninth Session*, Economic and Social Council Official Records, 1982, Supplement No. 12, p. 41.

Resolution No. 109 (IX): Economic Commission for Western Asia, *Report on the Ninth Session*, Economic and Social Council Official Records, 1982, Supplement No. 12, p. 47.

1983   Resolution No. 116 (X): Economic Commission for Western Asia, *Report on the Tenth Session*, Economic and Social Council Official Records, 1983, Supplement No. 14, p. 3.

Resolution No. 123 (X): Economic Commission for Western Asia, *Report on the Tenth Session*, Economic and Social Council Official Records, 1983, Supplement No. 14, p. 38.

1984   Resolution No. 124 (XI): Economic Commission for Western Asia, *Report on the Eleventh Session*, Economic and Social Council Official Records, 1984, Supplement No. 25, p. 40.

Resolution No. 132 (XI): Economic Commission for Western Asia, *Report on the Eleventh Session*, Economic and Social Council Official Records, 1984, Supplement No. 25, p. 49.

1985   Resolution No. 139 (XII): Economic Commission for Western Asia, *Report on the Twelfth Session*, Economic and Social Council Official Records, 1985, Supplement No. 14, pp. 26-27.

Resolution No. 141 (XII): Economic Commission for Western Asia, *Report on the Twelfth Session*, Economic and Social Council Official Records, 1985, Supplement No. 14, p. 29.

1986   Resolution No. 145 (XIII): Economic Commission for Western Asia, *Report on the Thirteenth Session*, Economic and Social Council Official Records, 1986, Supplement No. 14, p. 21.

Resolution No. 146 (XIII): Economic Commission for Western Asia, *Report on the Thirteenth Session*, Economic and Social Council Official Records, 1986, Supplement No. 14, p. 22.

Resolution No. 151 (XIII): Economic Commission for Western Asia, *Report on the Thirteenth Session*, Economic and Social Council Official Records, 1986, Supplement No. 14, pp. 28-29.

Governing Council of the United Nations Development Programme

1982   Decision No. 82/13: Governing Council of the United Nations Development Programme, *Report on the Organizational Meeting for 1982, the Special Meeting for the Consideration of Country and Inter-Country Programmes and Projects and the Twenty-ninth Session*, Economic and Social Council Official Records, 1982, Supplement No. 6, p. 55.

1983   Decision No. 83/11: Governing Council of the United Nations Development Programme, *Report on the Organizational Meeting for 1983, the Special Meeting for the Consideration of Country and Inter-Country Programmes and Projects and the Thirtieth Session*, Economic and Social Council Official Records, 1983, Supplement No. 9, pp. 57-58.

1984   Decision No. 84/13: Governing Council of the United Nations Development Programme, *Report on the Organizational Meeting for 1984 and the Thirty-first Session*, Economic and Social Council Official Records, 1984, Supplement No. 10, p. 48.

1985   Decision No. 85/15: Governing Council of the United Nations Development Programme, *Report on the Organizational Meeting for 1985, the Special Meeting on Preparations for the Fourth Programming Cycle and the Thirty-second Session*, Economic and Social Council Official Records, 1985, Supplement No. 11, p. 54.

1986   Decision No. 86/55: Governing Council of the United Nations Development Programme, *Report on the Organizational Meeting for 1986, the Special Session on Preparations for the Fourth Programming Cycle and the Thirty-third Session*, Economic and Social Council Official Records, 1986, Supplement No. 9, pp. 100Å101.

UNESCO (General Conference)

1982   Resolution No. 4XC/2.13: UNESCO, *Records of the General Conference, Fourth Extraordinary Session, 23 November-3 December 1982, Vol. I, Resolutions*, pp. 46-50.

1983   Resolution No. 22C/2.1: UNESCO, *Records of the General Conference, Twenty-second Session, 25 October to 26 November 1983, Vol. I, Resolutions*, pp. 20-22.

Resolution No. 22C/11.8: *Ibid.*, pp. 58-59.

Resolution No. 22C/11.16: *Ibid.*, pp. 62-63.

Resolution No. 22C/23: *Ibid.*, pp. 102-103.

1985   Resolution No. 23C/18.8: UNESCO, *Records of the General Conference, Twenty-third Session, 8 October to 9 November 1985, Vol. I, Resolutions*, p. 87.

Resolution No. 23C/2.1: *Ibid.*, pp. 21-24.

Resolution No. 23C/2.9: *Ibid.*, pp. 28-29.

Resolution No. 23C/11.3: *Ibid.*, pp. 63-64.

Resolution No. 23C/11.6: *Ibid.*, p. 65.

Resolution No. 23C/27: *Ibid.*, p. 107.

UNESCO (Executive Board)

1982 Decision No. 114 EX/5.1.2 II, III, IV: UNESCO, Executive Board, *Decisions Adopted by the Executive Board at its 114th Session* (Paris, 5-21 May 1982), pp. 17-19.

Decision No. 114 EX/5.4.2: *Ibid.*, pp. 22-23.

Decision No. 115 EX/5.1.1: UNESCO, Executive Board, *Decisions Adopted by the Executive Board at its 115th Session* (Paris, 8 September-7 October 1982), pp. 72-74.

1983 Decision No. 116 EX/5.1.5: UNESCO, Executive Board, *Decisions Adopted by the Executive Board at its 116th Session* (Paris, 25 May-29 June 1983), pp. 23-24.

Decision No. 116 EX/5.4.1: *Ibid.*, pp. 28-29.

Decision No. 116 EX/7.3: *Ibid.*, p. 46.

1984 Decision No. 119 EX/5.6: UNESCO, Executive Board, *Decisions Adopted by the Executive Board at its 119th Session* (Paris, 9-24 May 1984), pp. 25-26.

Decision No. 120 EX/5.3.1: UNESCO, Executive Board, *Decisions Adopted by the Executive Board at its 120th Session* (Paris, 26 September-22 October 1984), pp. 19-20.

1985 Decision No. 121 EX/5.1.3: UNESCO, Executive Board, *Decisions Adopted by the Executive Board at its 121st Session* (Paris, 9 May-21 June 1985), pp. 30-31.

Decision No. 121 EX/5.4.1: *Ibid.*, pp. 34-35.

1986 Decision No. 125 EX/5.2.2: UNESCO, Executive Board, *Decisions Adopted by the Executive Board at its 125th Session* (Paris, 10 September-8 October 1986), pp. 27-28.

Decision No. 125 EX/5.4.1: *Ibid.*, pp. 32-33.

World Health Organization

1982 Resolution No. WHA 35.15: World Health Organization, *Thirty-fifth World Health Assembly, Geneva, 3-14 May 1982: Resolutions and Decisions, Annexes*, pp. 373-74.

1983 Resolution No. WHA 36.27: World Health Organization, *Thirty-sixth World Health Assembly, Geneva, 5-16 May 1983: Resolutions and Decisions, Annexes*, pp. 23-24.

1984 Resolution No. WHA 37.26: World Health Organization, *ThirtyÅseventh World Health Assembly, Geneva, 7-17 May 1984: Resolutions and Decisions, Annexes*, pp. 15-16.

1985 Resolution No. WHA 38.15: World Health Organization Document A38/VR/14, obtained from internally distributed microfilm records of the World Health Organization.

1986 Resolution No. WHA 39.10: World Health Organization, *Thirty-ninth World Health Assembly, Geneva, 5-16 May 1986: Resolutions and Decisions, Annexes*, pp. 11-12.

International Atomic Energy Agency

1983 Resolution No. GC (XXVII)/RES/409: International Atomic Energy Agency, *Resolutions and Other Decisions of the General Conference, Twenty-seventh Regular Session, 10-14 October 1983*, pp. 4-5.

1984 Resolution No. GC (XXVIII)/RES/425: International Atomic Energy Agency, *Resolutions and Other Decisions of the General Conference, Twenty-eighth Regular Session, 24-28 September 1984*, pp. 3-5.

1985 Resolution No. GC (XXIX)/RES/443: International Atomic Energy Agency, *Resolutions and Other Decisions of the General Conference, Twenty-ninth Regular Session, 23-27 September 1985*, pp. 5-7.

SOURCES OF VOTING INFORMATION

General Assembly

1982 Resolution No. ES-9/1: *Resolutions and Decisions Adopted by the General Assembly at its Ninth Emergency Special Session, 29 January to 5 February 1982*, UN Document GA/6560, p. 4.

Decision No. 36/462: *Resolutions and Decisions Adopted by the General Assembly at its Resumed Thirty-sixth Regular Session, 16 to 19 March and 29 March 1982*, UN Document GA/6546/Add. 1, p. 5.

Resolution No. 36/138 C: *Ibid.*, pp. 2-3.

Resolution No. ES-7/4: *Resolutions and Decisions Adopted by the General Assembly at its Resumed Seventh Emergency Special Session, 20-28 April 1982*, UN Document GA/6245/Add. 1, p. 5.

Resolution No. ES-7/5: *Resolutions and Decisions Adopted by the General Assembly at its Resumed Seventh Emergency Special Session, 25-26 June 1982*, UN Document GA/6245/Add. 2, p. 4.

Resolution No. ES-7/6: *Resolutions and Decisions Adopted by the General Assembly at its Resumed Seventh Emergency Special Session, 16-19 August 1982*, UN Document GA/6245/Add. 3, p. 4.

Resolution No. ES-7/7: *Ibid.*, p. 6.

Resolution No. ES-7/8: *Ibid.*, pp. 7-8.

Resolution No. ES-7/9: *Resolutions and Decisions Adopted by the General Assembly at its Seventh Emergency Special Session on the Question of Palestine, 24 September 1982*, UN Document GA/6245/Add. 4, p. 3.

Resolution No. 37/18: *Resolutions and Decisions Adopted by the General Assembly during the First Part of its Thirty-seventh Session from 21 September to 21 December 1982*, United Nations Department of Public Information Press Release GA/6787, p. 20.

Resolution No. 37/19 : *Ibid.*, p. 22.

Resolution No. 37/38 A, B: *Ibid.*, pp. 465-66.

Resolution No. 37/39: *Ibid.*, p. 337.

Resolution No. 37/40: *Ibid.*, p. 340.

Resolution No. 37/43: *Ibid.*, p. 348.

Resolution No. 37/46: *Ibid.*, p. 351.

Resolution No. 37/69 A, C, D, F: *Ibid.*, pp. 45-49.

Resolution No. 37/75: *Ibid.*, p. 94.

Resolution No. 37/82: *Ibid.*, pp. 121-22.

Resolution No. 37/86 A, B, C, D, E: *Ibid.*, pp. 53-55.

Resolution No. 37/88 A, B, C, D, E, F, G: *Ibid.*, pp. 182-85.

Resolution No. 37/104: *Ibid.*, pp. 523-24.

Resolution No. 37/120 A, B, C, D, E, F, G, H, I, J, K: *Ibid.*, pp. 209-13.

Resolution No. 37/122: *Ibid.*, pp. 214-15.

Resolution No. 37/123 A, B, C, D, E, F: *Ibid.*, pp. 62-64.

Resolution No. 37/127 A, B: *Ibid.*, pp. 477-78.

Resolution No. 37/134: *Ibid.*, p. 218.

Resolution No. 37/135: *Ibid.*, p. 220.

Resolution No. 37/163: *Ibid.*, p. 260.

Resolution No. 37/222: *Ibid.*, p. 293.

1983 Resolution No. 38/9: *Resolutions and Decisions Adopted by the General Assembly during the First Part of its Thirty-eighth Session from 20 September to 20 December 1983*, United Nations Department of Public Information Press Release GA/6935, pp. 14-15.

Resolution No. 38/17: *Ibid.*, p. 364.

Resolution No. 38/35 A, B: *Ibid.*, pp. 468-69.

Resolution No. 38/36 A, D: *Ibid.*, pp. 43-45.

Resolution No. 38/38 A, B: *Ibid.*, pp. 471-72.

Resolution No. 38/39 A, F, G: *Ibid.*, pp. 59-63.

Resolution No. 38/58 A, B, C, D, E: *Ibid.*, pp. 74-76.

Resolution No. 38/64: *Ibid.*, p. 94.

Resolution No. 38/69: *Ibid.*, p. 104.

Resolution No. 38/79 A, B, C, D, E, F, G, H: *Ibid.*, pp. 191-94.

Resolution No. 38/83 A, B, C, D, E, F, G, H, I, J, K: *Ibid.*, pp. 224-28.

Resolution No. 38/85: *Ibid.*, p. 230.

Resolution No. 38/130: *Ibid.*, p. 516.

Resolution No. 38/144: *Ibid.*, p. 233.

Resolution No. 38/145: *Ibid.*, p. 234.

Resolution No. 38/166: *Ibid.*, p. 267.

Resolution No. 38/180 A, B, C, D, E: *Ibid.*, pp. 86-88.

Resolution No. 38/220: *Ibid.*, p. 335.

1984 Resolution No. 39/14: *Resolutions and Decisions Adopted by the General Assembly during the First Part of its Thirty-Ninth Session from 18 September to 18 December 1984,* United Nations Department of Public Information Press Release GA/7095, p. 22.

Resolution No. 39/17: *Ibid.*, p. 367.

Resolution No. 39/28 A, B: *Ibid.*, p. 499.

Resolution No. 39/49 A, B, C, D: *Ibid.*, pp. 31-33.

Resolution No. 39/50 A and D: *Ibid.*, pp. 53-55.

Resolution No. 39/54: *Ibid.*, p. 94.

Resolution No. 39/71 A, B: *Ibid.*, p. 515.

Resolution No. 39/72 A and C: *Ibid.*, pp. 66-68.

Resolution No. 39/76: *Ibid.*, p. 549.

Resolution No. 39/95 A, B, C, D, E, F, G, H: *Ibid.*, pp. 203-207.

Resolution No. 39/99 A, B, C, D, E, F, G, H, I, J, K: *Ibid.*, pp. 236-40.

Resolution No. 39/101: *Ibid.*, pp. 243.

Resolution No. 39/146 A, B, C: *Ibid.*, pp. 85-86.

Resolution No. 39/147: *Ibid.*, p. 135.

Resolution No. 39/169: *Ibid.*, p. 258.

Resolution No. 39/197: *Ibid.*, p. 294.

Resolution No. 39/223: *Ibid.*, p. 336.

Resolution No. 39/224: *Ibid.*, pp. 337-38.

Decision No. 39/442: *Ibid.*, p. 597.

1985 Resolution No. 40/6: *Resolutions and Decisions Adopted by the General Assembly during the First Part of its Fortieth Session from 17 September to 18 December 1985*, United Nations Department of Public Information Press Release GA/7272, pp. 8-9.

Resolution No. 40/25: *Ibid.*, p. 397.

Resolution No. 40/59 A, B: *Ibid.*, pp. 559-60.

Resolution No. 40/61: *Ibid.*, p. 607.

Resolution No. 40/64 A, E: *Ibid.*, pp. 59-63.

Resolution No. 40/82: *Ibid.*, p. 114.

Resolution No. 40/93: *Ibid.*, p. 139.

Resolution No. 40/96 A, B, C, D: *Ibid.*, pp. 67-69.

Resolution No. 40/161 A, B, C, D, E, F, G,: *Ibid.*, pp. 224-27.

Resolution No. 40/165 A, B, C, D, E, F, G, H, I, J, K: *Ibid.*, pp. 258-62.

Resolution No. 40/167: *Ibid.*, p. 264.

Resolution No. 40/168 A, B, C: *Ibid.*, pp. 100-101.

Resolution No. 40/169: *Ibid.*, p. 266.

Resolution No. 40/170: *Ibid.*, p. 267.

Resolution No. 40/201: *Ibid.*, p. 311.

Resolution No. 40/229: *Ibid.*, p. 370.

Resolution No. 40/246: *Ibid.*, pp. 581-82.

Decision No. 40/432: *Ibid.*, p. 664.

1986 Resolution No. 41/12: *Resolutions and Decisions Adopted by the General Assembly during the First Part of its Forty-first Session from 16 September to 19 December 1986*, United Nations Department of Public Information Press Release GA/7463, pp. 17-18.

Resolution No. 41/35 C: *Ibid.*, pp. 40-43.

Resolution No. 41/43 A, B, C, D: *Ibid.*, pp. 92-93.

Resolution No. 41/44 A, B: *Ibid.*, pp. 459-60.

Resolution No. 41/48: *Ibid.*, p. 107.

Resolution No. 41/63 A, B, C, D, E, F, G: *Ibid.*, pp. 215-18.

Resolution No. 41/69 A, B, C, D, E, F, G, H, I, J, K: *Ibid.*, pp. 248-52.

Resolution No. 41/71: *Ibid.*, p. 500.

Resolution No. 41/93: *Ibid.*, p. 203.

Resolution No. 41/95: *Ibid.*, p. 313.

Resolution No. 41/101: *Ibid.*, pp. 320, 324.

Resolution No. 41/162 A, B, C: *Ibid.*, pp. 92-93.

Resolution No. 41/179 A, B: *Ibid.*, pp. 468-69.

Resolution No. 41/181: *Ibid.*, p. 277.

Resolution No. 41/196: *Ibid.*, p. 294.

Security Council

[When one or more countries abstain or absent themselves from a Security Council vote, the sources provide the name of this country or these countries, but only the number (not the names) of countries voting in favour. The names of the latter have been derived from the list of Security Council members provided at the beginning of each annual volume of the Security Council records listed here.]

1982 Resolution No. 500 (1982): *Resolutions and Decisions of the Security Council, 1982*, Security Council Official Records, Thirty-seventh Year, p. 2.

Resolution No. 501 (1982): *Ibid.*, p. 3.

Resolution No. 506 (1982): *Ibid.*, p. 5.

Resolution No. 508 (1982): *Ibid.*, p. 6.

Resolution No. 509 (1982): *Ibid.*, p. 6.

Resolution No. 511 (1982): *Ibid.*, p. 7.

Resolution No. 512 (1982): *Ibid.*, p. 7.

Resolution No. 513 (1982): *Ibid.*, p. 7.

Resolution No. 515 (1982): *Ibid.*, p. 8.

Resolution No. 516 (1982): *Ibid.*, p. 8.

Resolution No. 517 (1982): *Ibid.*, p. 9.

Resolution No. 518 (1982): *Ibid.*, p. 9.

Resolution No. 519 (1982): *Ibid.*, p. 9.

Resolution No. 520 (1982): *Ibid.*, p. 10.

Resolution No. 521 (1982): *Ibid.*, p. 10.

Resolution No. 523 (1982): *Ibid.*, p. 11.

Resolution No. 524 (1982): *Ibid.*, p. 12.

1983   Resolution No. 529 (1983): *Resolutions and Decisions of the Security Council, 1983*, Security Council Official Records, Thirty-eighth Year, p. 1.

Resolution No. 531 (1983): *Ibid.*, p. 2.

Resolution No. 536 (1983): *Ibid.*, p. 3.

Resolution No. 538 (1983): *Ibid.*, p. 4.

Resolution No. 542 (1983): *Ibid.*, p. 5.

Resolution No. 543 (1983): *Ibid.*, p. 5.

1984   Resolution No. 549 (1984): *Resolutions and Decisions of the Security Council, 1984*, Security Council Official Records, Thirty-ninth Year, p. 6.

Resolution No. 551 (1984): *Ibid.*, p. 7.

Resolution No. 555 (1984): *Ibid.*, p. 8.

Resolution No. 557 (1984): *Ibid.*, p. 9.

1985   Resolution No. 561 (1985): *Resolutions and Decisions of the Security Council, 1985*, Security Council Official Records, Fortieth Year, p. 2.

Resolution No. 563 (1985): *Ibid.*, p. 3.

Resolution No. 564 (1985): *Ibid.*, p. 4.

Resolution No. 573 (1985): *Ibid.*, p. 23.

Resolution No. 575 (1985): *Ibid.*, p. 5.

Resolution No. 576 (1985): *Ibid.*

Resolution No. 579 (1985): *Ibid.*, p. 25.

1986   Resolution No. 583 (1986): *Resolutions and Decisions of the Security Council, 1986*, Security Council Official Records, Forty-first Year, p. 2.

Resolution No. 584 (1986): *Ibid.*, p. 2.

Resolution No. 586 (1986): *Ibid.*, p. 3.

Resolution No. 587 (1986): *Ibid.*, p. 4.

Resolution No. 590 (1986): *Ibid.*, p. 5.

Resolution No. 592 (1986): *Ibid.*, p. 7.

Economic and Social Council

Resolution No. 1982/18: *Report of the Economic and Social Council for the Year 1982*, General Assembly Official Records, Thirty-seventh Session, Supplement No. 3, p. 54.

Resolution No. 1982/48: *Report of the Economic and Social Council for the Year 1982*, General Assembly Official Records, Thirty-Seventh Session, Supplement No. 3, p. 68.

Resolution No. 1983/43: *Report of the Economic and Social Council for the Year 1983*, General Assembly Official Records, Thirty-Eighth Session, Supplement No. 3, pp. 59-60.

Resolution No. 1984/18: Voting information unobtainable.

Resolution No. 1984/56: *Report of the Economic and Social Council for the Year 1984*, General Assembly Official Records, Thirty-ninth Session, Supplement No. 3, p. 65.

Resolution No. 1985/57: *Report of the Economic and Social Council for the Year 1985*, General Assembly Official Records, Fortieth Session, Supplement No. 3, p. 168.

Resolution No. 1985/58: *Report of the Economic and Social Council for the Year 1985*, General Assembly Official Records, Fortieth Session, Supplement No. 3, p. 168.

Resolution No. 1986/49: Voting information unobtainable.

Resolution No. 1986/67: Voting information unobtainable.

Commission on Human Rights

Resolution No. 1982/1 A, B: Commission on Human Rights, *Report on the Thirty-eighth Session*, Economic and Social Council Official Records, 1982, Supplement No. 2, p. 15.

Resolution No. 1982/2: Commission on Human Rights, *Report on the Thirty-eighth Session*, Economic and Social Council Official Records, 1982, Supplement No. 2, p. 16.

Resolution No. 1982/3: Commission on Human Rights, *Report on the Thirty-eighth Session*, Economic and Social Council Official Records, 1982, Supplement No. 2, p. 41.

Resolution No. 1983/1 A, B: Commission on Human Rights, *Report on the Thirty-ninth Session*, Economic and Social Council Official Records, 1983, Supplement No. 3, pp. 18-19.

Resolution No. 1983/2: Commission on Human Rights, *Report on the Thirty-ninth Session*, Economic and Social Council Official Records, 1983, Supplement No. 3, p. 20.

Resolution No. 1983/3: Commission on Human Rights, *Report on the Thirty-ninth Session*, Economic and Social Council Official Records, 1983, Supplement No. 3, p. 45.

Resolution No. 1984/1 A, B: Commission on Human Rights, *Report on the Fortieth Session*, Economic and Social Council Official Records, 1984, Supplement No. 4, p. 115.

Resolution No. 1984/2: Commission on Human Rights, *Report on the Fortieth Session*, Economic and Social Council Official Records, 1984, Supplement No. 4, p. 115.

Resolution No. 1984/3: Commission on Human Rights, *Report on the Fortieth Session*, Economic and Social Council Official Records, 1984, Supplement No. 4, p. 116.

Resolution No. 1985/1 A, B: Commission on Human Rights, *Report on the Forty-first Session*, Economic and Social Council Official Records, 1985, Supplement No. 2, pp. 116-17.

Resolution No. 1985/2: Commission on Human Rights, *Report on the Forty-first Session*, Economic and Social Council Official Records, 1985, Supplement No. 2, p. 118.

Resolution No. 1985/4: Commission on Human Rights, *Report on the Forty-first Session*, Economic and Social Council Official Records, 1985, Supplement No. 2, pp. 145-46.

Resolution No. 1985/41: Commission on Human Rights, *Report on the Forty-first Session*, Economic and Social Council Official Records, 1985, Supplement No. 2, pp. 170-71.

Resolution No. 1986/1 A, B: Commission on Human Rights, *Report on the Forty-second Session*, Economic and Social Council Official Records, 1986, Supplement No. 2, pp. 156-58.

Resolution No. 1986/2: Commission on Human Rights, *Report on the Forty-second Session*, Economic and Social Council Official Records, 1986, Supplement No. 2, pp. 159-60.

Resolution No. 1986/22: Commission on Human Rights, *Report on the Forty-second Session*, Economic and Social Council Official Records, 1986, Supplement No. 2, p. 194.

Resolution No. 1986/33: Commission on Human Rights, *Report on the Forty-second Session*, Economic and Social Council Official Records, 1986, Supplement No. 2, p. 252.

Resolution No. 1986/43: Commission on Human Rights, *Report on the Forty-second Session*, Economic and Social Council Official Records, 1986, Supplement No. 2, p. 221.

Economic Commission for Western Asia/ Economic and Social Commission for Western Asia, Governing Council of the United Nations Development Programme, UNESCO (General Conference and Executive Board)

Voting information unobtainable

World Health Organization

1982 Resolution No. WHA 35.15: World Health Organization, *Thirty-fifth World Health Assembly, Geneva, 3-14 May 1982: Verbatim Records of Plenary Meetings, Reports of Committees*, p. 234.

1983 Resolution No. WHA 36.27: World Health Organization, *Thirty-sixth World Health Assembly, Geneva, 2-16 May 1983: Verbatim Records of Plenary Meetings, Reports of Committees*, p. 267.

1984 Resolution No. WHA 37.26: World Health Organization, *Thirty-seventh World Health Assembly, Geneva, 7-17 May 1984*, Document No. A37/B/SR/7, p. 9. The list of countries voting represents the votes cast at the seventh meeting of Committee B on May 15, 1984. No detailed breakdown of votes at the 14th plenary meeting is given in the records, which supply only the vote totals (75-23Å28) in World Health Organization, *Thirty-seventh World Health Assembly, Geneva, 7-17 May 1984, Verbatim Records of Plenary Meetings, Reports of Committees*, p. 256.

1985 Resolution No. WHA 38.15: World Health Organization, *Thirty-eighth World Health Assembly, Geneva, 6-20 May 1985: Verbatim Records of Plenary Meetings, Reports of Committees*, p. 243.

1986 Resolution No. WHA 39.10: World Health Organization, *Thirty-ninth World Health Assembly, Geneva, 5-16 May 1986: Verbatim Records of Plenary Meetings, Reports of Committees*, pp. 273-74.

International Atomic Energy Agency

Voting information unobtainable.

I. ATTEMPTS TO CONTROL ARMED CONFLICT

A. Outbreaks of hostilities and military attacks

i) Lebanon

SC Resolution No. 501 (1982) of 25 February 1982: Calling upon Israel to cease military action in Lebanon immediately and withdraw its forces from Lebanese territory and deciding to approve an immediate increase in the strength of UNIFIL, *pp. 217-18.*

SC Resolution No. 508 (1982) of 5 June 1982: Calling for an immediate cease-fire in Lebanon and across the Lebanese-Israeli border, *p. 218.*

SC Resolution No. 509 (1982) of 6 June 1982: Demanding that Israel withdraw its military forces from Lebanon forthwith and unconditionally, *pp. 218-19.*

SC Resolution No. 512 (1982) of 19 June 1982: Calling upon parties to the conflict in Lebanon to respect the rights and alleviate the suffering of the civilian population in Lebanon, *p. 219.*

GA Resolution No. ES-7/5 of 26 June 1982: On the question of Palestine: Demanding a cease-fire in Lebanon, and the withdrawal of Israeli forces from Lebanese territory, *pp. 7-8.*

SC Resolution No. 513 (1982) of 4 July 1982: Calling for respect for the rights of the civilian population in Lebanon, *pp. 219-20.*

ECOSOC Resolution No. 1982/48 of 27 July 1982: Calling for emergency assistance to the Palestinian population in Lebanon, *pp. 235-36.*

SC Resolution No. 515 (1982) of 29 July 1982: Demanding that Israel lift its blockade of Beirut immediately, *p. 220.*

SC Resolution No. 516 (1982) of 1 August 1982: Demanding an immediate cease-fire in Lebanon and across the Lebanese-Israeli border, *p. 220.*

SC Resolution No. 517 (1982) of 4 August 1982: Confirming a previous demand for an immediate cease-fire and Israeli withdrawal from Lebanon, *pp. 220-21.*

SC Resolution No. 518 (1982) of 12 August 1982: Demanding that Israel and all parties to the conflict cease military activities and that restrictions on supplies to Beirut be lifted immediately, *p. 221*.

GA Resolution No. ES-7/6 of 19 August 1982: On the question of Palestine: Calling for the free exercise of the rights of the Palestinian people to self-determination and independence, demanding that Israel carry out previous resolutions of the General Assembly relating to the occupied territories, and urging the Secretary-General to take measures to guarantee the safety of the Palestinian and Lebanese civilian population, *pp. 9-10*.

GA Resolution No. ES-7/8 of 19 August 1982: Deciding to commemorate innocent children who are victims of aggression, *p. 11*.

SC Resolution No. 520 (1982) of 17 September 1982: Condemning Israeli incursions into Beirut in violation of the cease-fire agreements, and demanding Israel's return to its previous positions, *pp. 221-22*.

SC Resolution No. 521 (1982) of 19 September 1982: Condemning the massacre of Palestinian civilians in Beirut, *p. 222*.

GA Resolution No. ES-7/9 of 24 September 1982: On the question of Palestine: Urging an investigation of the massacre of innocent civilians in Beirut, demanding a cease-fire in Lebanon and a withdrawal of Israeli forces from Lebanese territory, and resolving that the Palestinian refugees should be enabled to return to their homes, *pp. 11-13*.

GA Resolution No. 37/43 of 3 December 1982: Reaffirming the right of the Palestinian people to self-determination, condemning Israeli attacks on civilians in Lebanon, and calling for support for the Palestine Liberation Organization [Excerpts from a resolution on the right of peoples under colonial and foreign domination to self-determination and independence], *pp. 18-19*.

GA Resolution No. 37/123 A, B, C, D, E, F of 16 December 1982: Condemning Israel's policies in the occupied Arab territories and calling for its complete withdrawal from them, condemning the massacres of Sabra and Shatila in Lebanon and calling for the restoration of the authority of the Lebanese state in Lebanese territory, condemning Israeli practices in Lebanon, calling for recognition of the right of the Palestinian people, under the leadership of the PLO, to self-determination and an independent state, and calling upon all states to put an end to the flow of aid to Israel, *pp. 45-50*.

GA Resolution No. 37/134 of 17 December 1982: Calling for the provision of humanitarian assistance to the Palestinian people, and requesting that United Nations assistance should be rendered in cooperation with the Palestine Liberation Organization, *pp. 53-54*.

UNESCO Decision No. 115 EX/5.1.1 of 1982: Asking the Director-General to take measures to make possible assistance to Lebanon, strongly condemning Israeli actions of destruction and plunder against Palestinian and Lebanese educational and cultural institutions, and condemning unreservedly those who carried out and made possible the massacres of Sabra and Chatila, *pp. 282-83*.

CHR Resolution No. 1983/3 of 15 February 1983: Reaffirming the inalienable right of the Palestinian people to self-determination and an independent state and to return to their homes and property, *pp. 247-48*.

WHO Resolution No. WHA 36.27 of 16 May 1983: Condemning Israeli practices in the occupied territories and urging the establishment of new Palestinian medical institutions there, *pp. 292-93*.

ECOSOC Resolution No. 1983/43 of 25 July 1983: Requesting United Nations bodies to provide economic and social assistance for the Palestinian people in cooperation with the Palestine Liberation Organization, *p. 236*.

GA Resolution No. 38/17 of 22 November 1983: Condemning Israel's expansionist policies as an obstacle to the achievement of self-determination and independence by the Palestinian people, and condemning the massacre of Palestinians and other civilians in Beirut, as well as Israel's policies in Lebanon [Excerpts from a resolution on the right to self-determination of colonial countries and peoples], *pp. 57-58*.

SC Resolution No. 542 (1983) of 23 November 1983: Calling for an immediate cease-fire in northern Lebanon, *pp. 224-25*.

GA Resolution No. 38/180 A, B, C, D, E of 19 December 1983: On the situation in the Middle East: Condemning Israel's policies in the occupied territories and calling for its complete withdrawal from them; condemning Israeli army actions in Beirut in 1982; declaring the need for recognition of the right of the Palestinian people, under the leadership of the Palestine Liberation Organization, to self-determination and an independent state; calling on all states to put an end to the flow of aid to Israel and condemning Israeli-South African collaboration, *pp. 93-98*.

UNESCO Decision No. 116 EX/7.3 of 1983: Urging member states to assist Palestinian educational and cultural institutions in Lebanon to resume their activities, *pp. 284-85*.

UNESCO Decision No. 119 EX/5.6 of 1984: On damage caused to Palestinian and Lebanese cultural and educational institutions, *p. 285*.

CHR Resolution No. 1985/4 of 26 February 1985: Reaffirming the inalienable right of the Palestinian people to self-determination and an independent state and to return to their homes and property, *p. 257-58.*

CHR Resolution No. 1985/41 of 13 March 1985: Condemning Israel for violations of human rights in southern Lebanon, *pp. 258.*

SC Resolution No. 564 (1985) of 31 May 1985: Calling upon all concerned to end acts of violence against the civilian population in Lebanon and particularly in and around Palestinian refugee camps, *p. 227.*

CHR Resolution No. 1986/22 of 10 March 1986: Reaffirming the inalienable right of the Palestinian people to self-determination and an independent state and to return to their homes and property, *pp. 263-64.*

CHR Resolution No. 1986/43 of 12 March 1986: Condemning Israel for violations of human rights in southern Lebanon, *p. 265.*

SC Resolution No. 587 (1986) of 23 September 1986: Condemning attacks against the United Nations Interim Force in Lebanon and calling again for an end to any military presence in southern Lebanon not accepted by the Lebanese authority, *p. 230.*

ii) Iraq

GA Resolution No. 37/18 of 16 November 1982: Condemning Israel's threat to repeat its attack against Iraqi nuclear installations and demanding that it be withdrawn, *pp. 13-14.*

GA Resolution No. 37/19 of 19 November 1982: Considering that Israel's threat to repeat its attack against Iraqi nuclear installations is a serious threat to the role and activities of the International Atomic Energy Agency, *pp. 14-15.*

IAEA Resolution No. GC (XXVII)/RES/409 of 14 October 1983: Calling on Israel to withdraw its threat to repeat its attack on Iraqi nuclear facilities, *p. 301.*

GA Resolution No. 38/9 of 10 November 1983: Reiterating its demand that Israel withdraw its threat to attack and destroy nuclear facilities in Iraq and other countries, *pp. 56-57.*

IAEA Resolution No. GC (XXVIII)/RES/425 of 28 September 1984: Demanding that Israel undertake not to carry out further attacks on nuclear facilities in Iraq and calling on Israel to place its nuclear facilities under IAEA safeguards, *pp. 301-2.*

GA Resolution No. 39/14 of 16 November 1984: Demanding an undertaking from Israel not to attack nuclear facilities devoted to peaceful purposes in Iraq or other countries, *pp. 99-100.*

GA Resolution No. 39/147 of 17 December 1984: Condemning Israel's refusal to renounce any possession of nuclear weapons, and its threat to repeat its attack on nuclear facilities in Iraq, *pp. 134-35.*

IAEA Resolution No. GC (XXIX)/RES/443 of 27 September 1985: Considering that Israel has committed itself not to attack peaceful nuclear facilities in Iraq, and calling on Israel to place its nuclear facilities under IAEA safeguards, *pp. 302-3.*

GA Resolution No. 40/6 of 11 November 1985: Calling upon Israel to place its nuclear facilities under International Atomic Energy Agency safeguards, *pp. 139-40.*

GA Resolution No. 41/12 of 29 October 1986: Calling on Israel to place its nuclear facilities under International Atomic Energy Agency safeguards, *pp. 178-79.*

iii) Tunisia

SC Resolution No. 573 (1985) of 4 October 1985: Condemning Israel's attack on Tunisia, and urging members of the United Nations to take measures dissuading Israel from such acts of aggression, *pp. 227-28.*

B. Peace-keeping forces: mandates, budgets and discharge of duties

SC Resolution No. 501 (1982) of 25 February 1982: Calling upon Israel to cease military action in Lebanon immediately and withdraw its forces from Lebanese territory and deciding to approve an immediate increase in the strength of UNIFIL, *pp. 217-18.*

GA Resolution No. 36/138 C of 19 March 1982: On the financing of the United Nations Interim Force in Lebanon, *p. 5.*

SC Resolution No. 506 (1982) of 26 May 1982: Renewing the mandate of the United Nations Disengagement Observer Force until 30 November 1982, *p. 218.*

SC Resolution No. 511 (1982) of 18 June 1982: Extending the mandate of the United Nations Interim Force in Lebanon until 19 August 1982, *p. 219.*

SC Resolution No. 519 (1982) of 17 August 1982: Extending the mandate of the United Nations Interim Force in Lebanon until 19 October 1982, *p. 221.*

SC Resolution No. 523 (1982) of 18 October 1982: Extending the mandate of the United Nations Interim Force in Lebanon until 19 January 1983, *pp. 222-23.*

SC Resolution No. 524 (1982) of 29 November 1982: Renewing the mandate of the United Nations Disengagement Observer Force until 31 May 1983, *p. 223.*

GA Resolution No. 37/38 A, B of 30 November 1982: On the financing of the United Nations Disengagement Observer Force, *pp. 115-17.*

GA Resolution No. 37/127 A, B of 17 December 1982: On the financing of the United Nations Interim Force in Lebanon, *pp. 50-53.*

SC Resolution No. 529 (1983) of 18 January 1983: Extending the mandate of the United Nations Interim Force in Lebanon until 19 July 1983, *p. 223.*

SC Resolution No. 531 (1983) of 26 May 1983: Renewing the mandate of the United Nations Disengagement Observer Force until 30 November 1983, *p. 223.*

SC Resolution No. 536 (1983) of 18 July 1983: Extending the mandate of the United Nations Interim Force in Lebanon until 19 October 1983, *p. 224.*

SC Resolution No. 538 (1983) of 18 October 1983: Extending the mandate of the United Nations Interim Force in Lebanon until 19 April 1984, *p. 224.*

SC Resolution No. 543 (1983) of 29 November 1983: Renewing the mandate of the United Nations Disengagement Observer Force until 31 May 1984, *p. 225.*

GA Resolution No. 38/35 A, B of 1 December 1983: On the financing of the United Nations Disengagement Observer Force, *pp. 59-61.*

GA Resolution No. 38/38 A, B of 5 December 1983: On the financing of the United Nations Interim Force in Lebanon, *pp. 62-64.*

SC Resolution No. 549 (1984) of 19 April 1984: Extending the mandate of the United Nations Interim Force in Lebanon until 19 October 1984, *p. 225.*

SC Resolution No. 551 (1984) of 30 May 1984: Renewing the mandate of the United Nations Disengagement Observer Force until 30 November 1984, *p. 225.*

SC Resolution No. 555 (1984) of 12 October 1984: Extending the mandate of the United Nations Interim Force in Lebanon until 19 April 1985, *p. 226.*

SC Resolution No. 557 (1984) of 28 November 1984: Renewing the mandate of the United Nations Disengagement Observer Force until 31 May 1985, *p. 226.*

GA Resolution No. 39/28 A, B of 30 November 1984: On the financing of the United Nations Disengagement Observer Force, *pp. 101-3.*

GA Resolution No. 39/71 A, B of 13 December 1984: On the financing of UNIFIL, *pp. 108-11.*

SC Resolution No. 561 (1985) of 17 April 1985: Extending the mandate of the United Nations Interim Force in Lebanon until 19 October 1985, *pp. 226-27.*

SC Resolution No. 563 (1985) of 21 May 1985: Renewing the mandate of the United Nations Disengagement Observer Force until 30 November 1985, *p. 227.*

SC Resolution No. 575 (1985) of 17 October 1985: Extending the mandate of the United Nations Interim Force in Lebanon until 19 April 1986, *p. 228.*

SC Resolution No. 576 (1985) of 21 November 1985: Renewing the mandate of the United Nations Disengagement Observer Force until 31 May 1986, *p. 228*

GA Resolution No. 40/59 A, B of 2 December 1985: On the financing of the United Nations Disengagement Observer Force, *pp. 141-43.*

GA Resolution No. 40/246 A, B of 18 December 1985: On the financing of the United Nations Interim Force in Lebanon, *pp. 175-77.*

SC Resolution No. 583 (1986) of 18 April 1986: Extending the mandate of the United Nations Interim Force in Lebanon until 19 July 1986, *p. 229.*

SC Resolution No. 584 (1986) of 29 May 1986: Renewing the mandate of the United Nations Disengagement Observer Force until 30 November 1986, *p. 229.*

SC Resolution No. 586 (1986) of 18 July 1986: Extending the mandate of the United Nations Interim Force in Lebanon until 19 January 1987, *pp. 229-30.*

SC Resolution No. 590 (1986) of 26 November 1986: Renewing the mandate of the United Nations Disengagement Observer Force until 31 May 1987, *pp. 230-31.*

GA Resolution No. 41/44 A, B of 3 December 1986: On the financing of the United Nations Disengagement Observer Force, *pp. 183-85.*

GA Resolution No. 41/179 A, B of 5 December 1986: On the financing of the United Nations Interim Force in Lebanon, *pp. 210-12.*

C. Peace conferences

GA Resolution 38/58 A, B, C, D, E of 13 December 1983: On the question of Palestine: Endorsing the right of the Palestinian people to self-determination, including the right to establish an independent state, the right of the Palestine Liberation Organization to participate in peace negotiations on an equal footing, the need for a complete withdrawal of Israeli forces from the occupied territories, and the right of all states in the region to existence within secure and internationally recognized boundaries, *pp. 67-71.*

GA Resolution No. 39/49 A, B, C, D of 11 December 1984: On the question of Palestine: Endorsing the recommendations of the Committee on the Exercise of the Inalienable Rights of the Palestinian People, requesting wider dissemination of information on the question of Palestine and United Nations activities relating to it, and endorsing the convening of an international peace conference on the Middle East, *pp. 103-6.*

GA Resolution No. 40/96 A, B, C, D of 12 December 1985: On the question of Palestine: Endorsing the recommendations of the Committee on the Exercise of the Inalienable Rights of the Palestinian People, urging wider dissemination of information on the question of Palestine and United Nations activities relating to it, and endorsing the convening of an international peace conference on the Middle East, *pp. 148-51.*

GA Resolution No. 41/43 A, B, C, D of 2 December 1986: On the question of Palestine: Endorsing the recommendations of the Committee on the Exercise of the Inalienable Rights of the Palestinian People, requesting the dissemination of information on the question of Palestine and United Nations activities relating to it, and endorsing the convening of an international peace conference on the Middle East, *pp. 180-83.*

D. Terrorism and national liberation movements[1]

UNESCO Resolution No. 4XC/2.13 of 3 December 1982: Inviting the Director-General to plan to reinforce cooperation in UNESCO's fields of competence with the Palestine Liberation Organization [Excerpt from a resolution on Major Programme XIII, 'Peace, international understanding, human rights and the rights of peoples'], *p. 275.*

GA Resolution No. 37/104 of 16 December 1982: Calling on all states to accord the necessary facilities, privileges and immunities to delegations of national liberation movements recognized by the Organization of African Unity and/or the League of Arab States and accorded observer status by international organizations, *pp. 35-36.*

UNESCO Resolution No. 22C/2.1 of 21 November 1983: Inviting the Director-General to continue cooperation with UN institutions providing educational assistance to the Palestine Liberation Organization [Excerpt from a resolution on Major Programme II, 'Education for all'], *p. 275.*

GA Resolution No. 38/130 of 19 December 1983: Urging all states to contribute to the elimination of the causes underlying international terrorism, *pp. 89-90.*

GA Resolution No. 39/76 of 13 December 1984: Calling upon all states to accord the necessary facilities, privileges and immunities to delegations of national liberation movements recognized by the Organization of African Unity and/or the League of Arab States and accorded observer status by international organizations, *pp. 112-13.*

CHR Resolution No. 1985/1 A, B of 19 February 1985: Condemning Israeli policies and practices affecting the human rights of the inhabitants of the occupied territories, *pp. 252-55.*

SC Resolution No. 573 (1985) of 4 October 1985: Condemning Israel's attack on Tunisia, and urging members of the United Nations to take measures dissuading Israel from such acts of aggression, *pp. 227-28.*

UNESCO Resolution No. 23C/2.1 of 5 November 1985: Inviting the Director to continue to support educational activities by the United Nations system for Palestinian refugees and the training of teachers for national liberation movements [Excerpt from a resolution on Major Programme II, 'Education for all'], *pp. 277-78.*

---

[1] *This new heading has been created in this volume to categorize resolutions reflecting the growing international concern with terrorism and attempts to differentiate legitimate national liberation movements from terrorist organizations. Resolutions condemning unsanctioned acts of coercion through fear or tolerated state terrorism, and state-sponsored groups practicing terrorism in occupied territories reflect a concern of the United Nations and its agencies that was not given clear expression in previous volumes.*

GA Resolution No. 40/61 of 9 December 1985: Inviting states to take measures with a view to the elimination of international terrorism, and urging them to contribute to the elimination of the causes underlying terrorism, *pp. 143-44*.

SC Resolution No. 579 (1985) of 18 December 1985: Condemning the taking of hostages and urging international cooperation to prevent, prosecute and punish acts of hostage-taking, *pp. 228-29*.

CHR Resolution No. 1986/1 A, B of 20 February 1986: Condemning Israeli policies and practices affecting the human rights of the inhabitants of the occupied territories, *pp. 258-61*.

CHR Resolution No. 1986/22 of 10 March 1986: Reaffirming the inalienable right of the Palestinian people to self-determination and an independent state and to return to their homes and property, *pp. 263-64*.

CHR Resolution No. 1986/33 of 11 March 1986: Condemning Israel's policies of occupation and settlement in Arab territories and calling for its complete withdrawal from them, *pp. 264-65*.

GA Resolution No. 41/71 of 3 December 1986: Calling upon all states to accord the necessary facilities, privileges and immunities to delegations of national liberation movements recognized by the Organization of African Unity and/or the League of Arab States and accorded observer status by international organizations, *pp. 202-3*.

II. PALESTINIAN RIGHTS AND THE OCCUPIED ARAB TERRITORIES

A. Israeli settlements

SC Resolution No. 500 (1982) of 28 January 1982: Deciding to call an emergency special session of the General Assembly to examine the situation in the occupied Arab territories, *p. 217*.

GA Resolution No. 37/88 A, B, C, D, E, F, G of 10 December 1982: On Israeli practices affecting human rights in the occupied territories: Condemning Israel's policies of annexation and settlement in the occupied Arab territories, as well as the measures of the occupation authorities against civil, political and educational freedom and their failure to apprehend and prosecute persons guilty of assassination attempts against Arab mayors, *pp. 29-35*.

GA Resolution No. 38/79 A, B, C, D, E, F, G, H of 15 December 1983: On Israeli practices affecting human rights in the occupied territories: Condemning Israel for failing to honor a prisoner release agreement negotiated through the Red Cross, for its policies of annexation and settlement in the occupied territories, as well as measures against civil, political and educational freedom there, and for its expulsion of Palestinian leaders and its failure to apprehend and prosecute persons guilty of assassination attempts against Arab mayors, *pp. 73-80*.

GA Resolution No. 39/95 A, B, C, D, E, F, G, H of 14 December 1984: On Israeli practices affecting human rights in the occupied territories: Condemning Israel for failing to honor a prisoner release agreement negotiated through the Red Cross, for its policies of settlement and annexation in the occupied territories, as well as measures against civil and educational freedom there, and for its expulsion of Palestinian leaders, *pp. 113-20*.

GA Resolution No. 40/161 A, B, C, D, E, F, G of 16 December 1985: On Israeli practices affecting human rights in the occupied territories: Calling for the liberation of Arabs detained by Israel, condemning Israeli policies of annexation and settlement in the occupied territories as well as measures against civil rights and educational freedom there, and for its expulsion of Palestinian leaders, *pp. 151-59*.

B. Annexation of territory/changes of status

SC Resolution No. 500 (1982) of 28 January 1982: Deciding to call an emergency special session of the General Assembly to examine the situation in the occupied Arab territories, *p. 217*.

GA Resolution No. ES-9/1 of 5 February 1982: Declaring Israel's decision to impose its laws, jurisdiction and administration on the Golan Heights to be null and void, *pp. 3-4*.

CHR Resolution No. 1982/2 of 11 February 1982: Condemning Israel's decision of 1981 annexing the Golan Heights and declaring it to be null and void, *pp. 242-43*.

GA Resolution No. ES-7/4 of 28 April 1982: On the question of Palestine: Condemning Israel for its policies in the occupied territories, urging states not to provide Israel with assistance, and urging the Security Council to recognize the inalienable rights of the Palestinian people, *pp. 6-7*.

GA Resolution No. 37/88 A, B, C, D, E, F, G of 10 December 1982: On Israeli practices affecting human rights in the occupied territories: Condemning Israel's policies of annexation and settlement in the occupied Arab territories, as well as the measures of the occupation authorities against civil, political and educational freedom and their failure to apprehend and prosecute persons guilty of assassination attempts against Arab mayors, *pp. 29-35*.

GA Resolution No. 37/123 A, B, C, D, E, F of 16 December 1982: Condemning Israel's policies in the occupied Arab territories and calling for its complete withdrawal from them, condemning the massacres of Sabra and Shatila in Lebanon and calling for the restoration of the authority of the Lebanese state in Lebanese territory, condemning Israeli practices in Lebanon, calling for recognition of the right of the Palestinian people, under the leadership of the PLO, to self-determination and an independent state, and calling upon all states to put an end to the flow of aid to Israel, *pp. 45-50.*

UNESCO Decision No. 114 EX/5.4.2 of 1982: Concerning Israel's annexationist policies affecting the cultural and religious character of Jerusalem, *pp. 281-82.*

CHR Resolution No. 1983/2 of 15 February 1983: Declaring Israel's decision of 1981 to impose its laws, jurisdiction and administration on the Golan Heights to be null and void, and calling on Israel to rescind it, *pp. 246-47.*

UNESCO Resolution No. 22C/11.8 of 25 November 1983: Condemning Israeli policies in the City of Jerusalem, *pp. 275-76.*

GA Resolution No. 38/79 A, B, C, D, E, F, G, H of 15 December 1983: On Israeli practices affecting human rights in the occupied territories: Condemning Israel for failing to honor a prisoner release agreement negotiated through the Red Cross, for its policies of annexation and settlement in the occupied territories, as well as measures against civil, political and educational freedom there, and for its expulsion of Palestinian leaders and its failure to apprehend and prosecute persons guilty of assassination attempts against Arab mayors, *pp. 73-80.*

GA Resolution No. 38/180 A, B, C, D, E of 19 December 1983: On the situation in the Middle East: Condemning Israel's policies in the occupied territories and calling for its complete withdrawal from them; condemning Israeli army actions in Beirut in 1982; declaring the need for recognition of the right of the Palestinian people, under the leadership of the Palestine Liberation Organization, to self-determination and an independent state; calling on all states to put an end to the flow of aid to Israel; and condemning Israeli-South African collaboration *pp. 93-98.*

UNESCO Decision No. 116 EX/5.4.1 of 1983: Condemning Israel's annexationist policies affecting the cultural and religious character of Jerusalem, *p. 284.*

CHR Resolution No. 1984/2 of 20 February 1984: Repeating that Israel's decision of 1981 to impose its laws, jurisdiction and administration on the Golan Heights is null and void, and calling upon Israel to rescind it, *pp. 251-52.*

CHR Resolution No. 1984/3 of 20 February 1984: Condemning Israel's policies of occupation and settlement in the occupied territories, and calling for its complete withdrawal from them, *p. 252.*

GA Resolution No. 39/95 A, B, C, D, E, F, G, H of 14 December 1984: On Israeli practices affecting human rights in the occupied territories: Condemning Israel for failing to honor a prisoner release agreement negotiated through the Red Cross, for its policies of settlement and annexation in the occupied territories, as well as measures against civil and educational freedom there, and for its expulsion of Palestinian leaders, *pp. 113-20.*

GA Resolution 39/146 A, B, C of 14 December 1984: On the situation in the Middle East: Condemning Israel's policies in the occupied territories and calling for its complete withdrawal from them; declaring the need for recognition of the right of the Palestinian people, under the leadership of the Palestine Liberation Organization, to self-determination and an independent state; and calling on all states to put an end to the flow of aid to Israel, *pp. 130-34.*

UNESCO Decision No. 120 EX/5.3.1 of 1984: Concerning Israeli annexationist policies affecting the cultural and religious character of Jerusalem, *p. 285.*

CHR Resolution No. 1985/2 of 19 February 1985: Repeating that Israel's decision of 1981 to impose its laws, jurisdiction and administration on the Golan Heights is null and void, and calling upon Israel to rescind it, *pp. 255-56.*

UNESCO Resolution No. 23C/11.3 of 8 November 1985: Deploring assaults on the holy places of Islam in Jerusalem, *pp. 278-79.*

GA Resolution No. 40/161 A, B, C, D, E, F, G of 16 December 1985: On Israeli practices affecting human rights in the occupied territories: Calling for the liberation of Arabs detained by Israel, condemning Israeli policies of annexation and settlement in the occupied territories as well as measures against civil rights and educational freedoms there, and for its expulsion of Palestinian leaders, *pp. 151-59.*

GA Resolution No. 40/168 A, B, C of 16 December 1985: On the situation in the Middle East: Condemning Israel's policies in the occupied territories and calling for its complete withdrawal from them; declaring the need for recognition of the right of the Palestinian people, under the leadership of the Palestine Liberation Organization, to self-determination and an independent state; and calling on all states to put an end to the flow of aid to Israel, *pp. 167-72.*

UNESCO Decision No. 121 EX/5.4.1 of 1985: Requesting that Israel take action to give effect to recommendations of the Unesco Executive Board on Jerusalem, *pp. 286-87.*

CHR Resolution No. 1986/2 of 20 February 1986: Repeating that Israel's decision of 1981 to impose its laws, jurisdiction and administration on the Golan Heights is null and void, and calling upon Israel to rescind it, *pp. 262-63.*

CHR Resolution No. 1986/33 of 11 March 1986: Condemning Israel's policies of occupation and settlement in Arab territories and calling for its complete withdrawal from them, *pp. 264-65.*

GA Resolution No. 41/63 A, B, C, D, E, F, G of 3 December 1986: On Israeli practices affecting human rights in the occupied territories: Calling on Israel to release Arab prisoners, condemning it for its policies of settlement and annexation in the occupied territories, as well as measures against civil and educational freedom there, and for its expulsion of Palestinian leaders, *pp. 186-94.*

GA Resolution No. 41/162 A, B, C of 4 December 1986: On the situation in the Middle East: Condemning Israel's policies in the occupied territories and calling for its complete withdrawal from them; declaring the need for recognition of the right of the Palestinian people, under the leadership of the Palestine Liberation Organization, to self-determination and independence; and calling on all states to end aid to Israel, *pp. 206-10.*

UNESCO Decision No. 125 EX/5.4.1 of 1986: Deploring assaults perpetrated on the holy places of Islam in Jerusalem, *pp. 287-88.*

C. The "inalienable rights" of the Palestinian people and human rights in the occupied territories

SC Resolution No. 500 (1982) of 28 January 1982: Deciding to call an emergency special session of the General Assembly to examine the situation in the occupied Arab territories, *p. 217.*

CHR Resolution No. 1982/1 A, B of 11 February 1982: Condemning Israeli policies and practices affecting the human rights of the inhabitants of the occupied territories, *pp. 240-42.*

CHR Resolution No. 1982/3 of 11 February 1982: Reaffirming the inalienable right of the Palestinian people to self-determination and an independent state and to return to their homes and property, *pp. 243-44.*

GA Resolution No. ES-7/4 of 28 April 1982: On the question of Palestine: Condemning Israel for its policies in the occupied territories, urging states not to provide Israel with assistance, and urging the Security Council to recognize the inalienable rights of the Palestinian people, *pp. 6-7.*

ECOSOC Resolution No. 1982/18 of 4 May 1982: Appealing for assistance to Palestinian women in their struggle for their rights, *p. 235.*

WHO Resolution No. WHA 35.15 of 14 May 1982: Condemning Israeli practices in the occupied territories and urging the establishment of new Palestinian medical institutions there, *pp. 291-92.*

GA Resolution No. ES-7/5 of 26 June 1982: On the question of Palestine: Demanding a cease-fire in Lebanon, and the withdrawal of Israeli forces from Lebanese territory, *pp. 7-8.*

GA Resolution No. ES-7/6 of 19 August 1982: On the question of Palestine: Calling for the free exercise of the rights of the Palestinian people to self-determination and independence, demanding that Israel carry out previous resolutions of the General Assembly relating to the occupied territories, and urging the Secretary-General to take measures to guarantee the safety of the Palestinian and Lebanese civilian population, *pp. 9-10.*

GA Resolution No. ES-7/7 of 19 August 1982: Deciding to convene an International Conference on the Question of Palestine, *pp. 10-11.*

GA Resolution No. ES-7/9 of 24 September 1982: On the question of Palestine: Urging an investigation of the massacre of innocent civilians in Beirut, demanding a cease-fire in Lebanon and a withdrawal of Israeli forces from Lebanese territory, and resolving that the Palestinian refugees should be enabled to return to their homes, *pp. 11-13.*

GA Resolution No. 37/43 of 3 December 1982: Reaffirming the right of the Palestinian people to self-determination, condemning Israeli attacks on civilians in Lebanon and calling for support for the Palestine Liberation Organization [Excerpts from a resolution on the right of peoples under colonial and foreign domination to self-determination and independence], *pp. 18-19.*

UNESCO Resolution No. 4XC/2.13 of 3 December 1982: Inviting the Director-General to plan to reinforce cooperation in Unesco's fields of competence with the Palestine Liberation Organization [Excerpt from a resolution on Major Programme XIII ('Peace, international understanding, human rights and the rights of peoples')], *p. 275.*

GA Resolution No. 37/86 A, B, C, D, E of 10 December 1982: On the question of Palestine: Calling for the complete withdrawal of Israel from the Arab territories occupied since 1967, for the exercise of self-determination by the Palestinian people, including the right to establish an independent state, and for the United Nations to supervise the occupied territories for a short transitional period, *pp. 25-29.*

GA Resolution No. 37/88 A, B, C, D, E, F, G of 10 December 1982: On Israeli practices affecting human rights in the occupied territories: Condemning Israel's policies of annexation and settlement in the occupied Arab territories, as well as the measures of the occupation authorities against civil, political and educational freedom and their failure to apprehend and prosecute persons guilty of assassination attempts against Arab mayors, *pp. 29-35*.

GA Resolution No. 37/120 A, B, C, D, E, F, G, H, I, J, K of 16 December 1982: On the United Nations Relief and Works Agency for Palestine Refugees in the Near East: Endorsing assistance to Palestinian refugees, calling upon Israel to remove obstacles to the establishment of a University of Jerusalem for Palestinian refugees and to permit the return of displaced Palestinians, and requesting the Secretary-General to take all appropriate steps for the protection and administration of Arab property, assets and property rights in Israel, and to issue identification cards to all Palestinian refugees and their descendants, *pp. 36-44*.

GA Resolution No. 37/123 A, B, C, D, E, F of 16 December 1982: Condemning Israel's policies in the occupied Arab territories and calling for its complete withdrawal from them, condemning the massacres of Sabra and Shatila in Lebanon and calling for the restoration of the authority of the Lebanese state in Lebanese territory, condemning Israeli practices in Lebanon, calling for recognition of the right of the Palestinian people, under the leadership of the PLO, to self-determination and an independent state, and calling upon all states to put an end to the flow of aid to Israel, *pp. 45-50*.

GA Resolution No. 37/222 of 20 December 1982: Affirming that Israeli occupation is contradictory to the social and economic development of the Palestinian people in the occupied territories and that the exercise of their right to self-determination is a prerequisite to their social and economic development, *pp. 55-56*.

UNESCO Decision No. 114 EX/5.1.2 II, III and IV of 1982: On the implementation of a Unesco General Conference resolution on educational and cultural institutions in the occupied Arab territories, *pp. 280-81*.

UNESCO Decision No. 115 EX/5.1.1 of 1982: Asking the Director-General to take measures to make possible assistance to Lebanon, strongly condemning Israeli actions of destruction and plunder against Palestinian and Lebanese educational and cultural institutions, and condemning unreservedly those who carried out and made possible the massacres of Sabra and Chatila, *pp. 282-83*.

CHR Resolution No. 1983/1 A, B of 15 February 1983: Condemning Israeli policy and practices affecting the human rights of the inhabitants of the occupied territories, *pp. 244-46*.

CHR Resolution No. 1983/3 of 15 February 1983: Reaffirming the inalienable right of the Palestinian people to self-determination and an independent state and to return to their homes and property, *pp. 247-48*.

WHO Resolution No. WHA 36.27 of 16 May 1983: Condemning Israeli practices in the occupied territories and urging the establishment of new Palestinian medical institutions there, *pp. 292-93*.

UNESCO Resolution No. 22C/2.1 of 21 November 1983: Inviting the Director-General to continue cooperation with UN institutions providing educational assistance to the Palestine Liberation Organization [Excerpt from a resolution on Major Programme II, 'Education for all'], *p. 275*.

GA Resolution No. 38/17 of 22 November 1983: Condemning Israel's expansionist policies as an obstacle to the achievement of self-determination and independence by the Palestinian people, and condemning the massacre of Palestinians and other civilians in Beirut, as well as Israel's policies in Lebanon [Excerpts from a resolution on the right to self-determination of colonial countries and peoples], *pp. 57-58*.

UNESCO Resolution No. 22C/11.16 of 25 November 1983: On the preservation of the cultural heritage and identity of the Palestinian people, *pp. 276-77*.

UNESCO Resolution No. 22C/23 of 25 November 1983: On the implementation of a previous resolution on educational and cultural institutions in the occupied Arab territories, *p. 277*.

GA Resolution No. 38/58 A, B, C, D, E of 13 December 1983: On the question of Palestine: Endorsing the right of the Palestinian people to self-determination, including the right to establish an independent state, the right of the Palestine Liberation Organization to participate in peace negotiations on an equal footing, the need for a complete withdrawal of Israeli forces from the occupied territories, and the right of all states in the region to existence within secure and internationally recognized boundaries, *pp. 67-71*.

GA Resolution No. 38/79 A, B, C, D, E, F, G, H of 15 December 1983: On Israeli practices affecting human rights in the occupied territories: Condemning Israel for failing to honor a prisoner release agreement negotiated through the Red Cross, for its policies of annexation and settlement in the occupied territories, as well as measures against civil, political and educational freedom there, and for its expulsion of Palestinian leaders and its failure to apprehend and prosecute persons guilty of assassination attempts against Arab mayors, *pp. 73-80*.

GA Resolution No. 38/83 A, B, C, D, E, F, G, H, I, J, K of 15 December 1983: On the United Nations Relief and Works Agency for Palestine Refugees in the Near East: Calling for contributions by governments to the Agency and endorsing assistance to Palestinian refugees, calling on Israel to permit the return of displaced Palestinians and to remove obstacles to the establishment of a University of Jerusalem for Palestinian refugees, and requesting the Secretary-General to take appropriate steps for the protection and administration of Arab refugee property, assets and property rights, *pp. 80-88.*

GA Resolution No. 38/180 A, B, C, D, E of 19 December 1983: On the situation in the Middle East: Condemning Israel's policies in the occupied territories and calling for its complete withdrawal from them; condemning Israeli army actions in Beirut in 1982; declaring the need for recognition of the right of the Palestinian people, under the leadership of the Palestine Liberation Organization, to self-determination and an independent state; calling on all states to put an end to the flow of aid to Israel, *pp. 93-98.*

UNESCO Decision No. 116 EX/5.1.5 of 1983: Condemning Israeli policies affecting educational and cultural freedom in the occupied Arab territories, *pp. 283-84.*

CHR Resolution No. 1984/1 A, B of 20 February 1984: Condemning Israeli policies and practices affecting the human rights of the inhabitants of the occupied territories, *pp. 248-51.*

WHO Resolution No. WHA 37.26 of 17 May 1984: Condemning Israeli practices and health policy in the occupied territories and reaffirming the right of the Palestinian population to have its own medical institutions, *pp. 293-94.*

ECOSOC Resolution No. 1984/18 of 24 May 1984: Requesting a comprehensive report by the Secretary-General on the situation of Palestinian women living in and outside the occupied Arab territories, *pp. 236-37.*

GA Resolution No. 39/17 of 23 November 1984: Reaffirming the right of the Palestinian people to self-determination and independence [Excerpts from a resolution on the right of peoples to self-determination], *pp. 100-1.*

GA Resolution No. 39/49 A, B, C, D of 11 December 1984: On the question of Palestine: Endorsing the recommendations of the Committee on the Exercise of the Inalienable Rights of the Palestinian People, requesting wider dissemination of information on the question of Palestine and United Nations activities relating to it, and endorsing the convening of an international peace conference on the Middle East, *pp. 103-6.*

GA Resolution No. 39/95 A, B, C, D, E, F, G, H of 14 December 1984: On Israeli practices affecting human rights in the occupied territories: Condemning Israel for failing to honor a prisoner release agreement negotiated through the Red Cross, for its policies of settlement and annexation in the occupied territories, as well as measures against civil and educational freedom there, and for its expulsion of Palestinian leaders, *pp. 113-20.*

GA Resolution No. 39/99 A, B, C, D, E, F, G, H, I, J, K of 14 December 1984: On UNRWA: Calling for contributions by governments to UNRWA and endorsing assistance to Palestinian refugees; calling on Israel to permit the return of displaced Palestinians, and demanding that it desist from the destruction of Palestinian refugee shelters in the Gaza Strip and refugee camps in the West Bank; requesting the Secretary-General to take appropriate steps for the protection of Arab property, assets and property rights; and calling on Israel to remove hindrances to the establishment of a University of Jerusalem for Palestinian refugees, *pp. 120-29.*

GA Resolution No. 39/146 A, B, C of 14 December 1984: On the situation in the Middle East: Condemning Israel's policies in the occupied territories and calling for its complete withdrawal from them; declaring the need for recognition of the right of the Palestinian people, under the leadership of the Palestine Liberation Organization, to self-determination and an independent state; and calling on all states to put an end to the flow of aid to Israel, *pp. 130-34.*

CHR Resolution No. 1985/1 A, B of 19 February 1985: Condemning Israeli policies and practices affecting the human rights of the inhabitants of the occupied territories, *pp. 252-55.*

CHR Resolution No. 1985/4 of 26 February 1985: Reaffirming the inalienable right of the Palestinian people to self-determination and an independent state and to return to their homes and property, *pp. 257-58.*

WHO Resolution No. WHA 38.15 of 16 May 1985: Condemning Israeli practices and health policy in the occupied territories and reaffirming the right of the Palestinian population to have its own medical institutions, *pp. 294-96.*

UNESCO Resolution No. 23C/18.8 of 1 November 1985: On an international day of solidarity with the Palestinian people, *p. 277.*

UNESCO Resolution No. 23C/2.1 of 5 November 1985: Inviting the Director to continue to support educational activities by the United Nations system for Palestinian refugees and the training of teachers for national liberation movements [Excerpt from a resolution on Major Programme II, 'Education for all'], *pp. 277-78.*

UNESCO Resolution No. 23C/2.9 of 5 November 1985: On the creation of a Palestinian Open University, *p. 278.*

UNESCO Resolution No. 23C/11.6 of 8 November 1985: On the preservation of the cultural heritage and identity of the Palestinian people, *p. 279.*

UNESCO Resolution No. 23C/27 of 8 November 1985: On the implementation of a previous resolution on educational and cultural institutions in the occupied Arab territories, *pp. 279-80.*

GA Resolution No. 40/25 of 29 November 1985: Reaffirming the right of the Palestinian people to self-determination and independence [Excerpt from a resolution on the right of peoples to self-determination], *pp. 140-41.*

GA Resolution No. 40/96 A, B, C, D of 12 December 1985: On the question of Palestine: Endorsing the recommendations of the Committee on the Exercise of the Inalienable Rights of the Palestinian People, urging wider dissemination of information on the question of Palestine and United Nations activities relating to it, and endorsing the convening of an international peace conference on the Middle East, *pp. 148-51.*

GA Resolution No. 40/161 A, B, C, D, E, F, G of 16 December 1985: On Israeli practices affecting human rights in the occupied territories: Calling for the liberation of Arabs detained by Israel, condemning Israeli policies of annexation and settlement in the occupied territories as well as measures against civil rights and educational freedoms there, and for its expulsion of Palestinian leaders, *pp. 151-59.*

GA Resolution No. 40/165 A, B, C, D, E, F, G, H, I, J, K of 16 December 1985: On the United Nations Relief and Works Agency for Palestine Refugees in the Near East: Calling for contributions by governments to the Agency and endorsing assistance to Palestinian refugees, calling on Israel to permit the return of displaced Palestinans and to remove obstacles to the establishment of a University of Jerusalem for Palestinian refugees, and requesting the Secretary-General to take appropriate steps for the protection and administration of Arab refugee property, assets and property rights, *pp. 159-67.*

GA Resolution No. 40/168 A, B, C of 16 December 1985: On the situation in the Middle East: Condemning Israel's policies in the occupied territories and calling for its complete withdrawal from them; declaring the need for recognition of the right of the Palestinian people, under the leadership of the Palestine Liberation Organization, to self-determination and an independent state; and calling on all states to put an end to the flow of aid to Israel, *pp. 167-72.*

UNESCO Decision No. 121 EX/5.1.3 of 1985: Deploring Israeli policies affecting educational and cultural institutions in the occupied Arab territories, *pp. 285-86.*

CHR Resolution No. 1986/1 A, B of 20 February 1986: Condemning Israeli policies and practices affecting the human rights of the inhabitants of the occupied territories, *pp. 258-61.*

CHR Resolution No. 1986/22 of 10 March 1986: Reaffirming the inalienable right of the Palestinian people to self-determination and an independent state and to return to their homes and property, *pp. 263-64.*

CHR Resolution No. 1986/33 of 11 March 1986: Condemning Israel's policies of occupation and settlement in Arab territories and calling for its complete withdrawal from them, *pp. 264-65.*

ECWA Resolution No. 151 (XIII) of 24 April 1986: Affirming the right of the Palestinian people to self-determination under the leadership of the Palestine Liberation Organization, *p. 269.*

WHO Resolution No. WHA 39.10 of 15 May 1986: Condemning Israeli practices and health policy in the occupied territories and reaffirming the right of the Palestinian population to have its own medical institutions, *pp. 296-97.*

GA Resolution No. 41/43 A, B, C, D of 2 December 1986: On the question of Palestine: Endorsing the recommendations of the Committee on the Exercise of the Inalienable Rights of the Palestinian People, requesting the dissemination of information on the question of Palestine and United Nations activities relating to it, and endorsing the convening of an international peace conference on the Middle East, *pp. 180-83.*

GA Resolution No. 41/63 A, B, C, D, E, F, G of 3 December 1986: On Israeli practices affecting human rights in the occupied territories: Calling on Israel to release Arab prisoners, condemning it for its policies of settlement and annexation in the occupied territories, as well as measures against civil and educational freedom there, and for its expulsion of Palestinian leaders, *pp. 186-94.*

GA Resolution No. 41/69 A, B, C, D, E, F, G, H, I, J, K of 3 December 1986: On the United Nations Relief and Works Agency for Palestine Refugees in the Near East: Calling for contributions by governments to the Agency and endorsing assistance to Palestinian refugees, calling upon Israel to permit the return of displaced Palestinians and to remove obstacles to the establishment of a University of Jerusalem for Palestinian refugees, and requesting the Secretary-General to take appropriate steps for the protection and administration of Arab refugee property, assets and property rights, *pp. 194-202.*

GA Resolution No. 41/101 of 4 December 1986: Reaffirming the right of the Palestinian people to self-determination and independence [Excerpts from a resolution on the right to self-determination and independence of colonial countries and peoples], *pp. 204-6.*

GA Resolution No. 41/162 A, B, C of 4 December 1986: On the situation in the Middle East: Condemning Israel's policies in the occupied territories and calling for its complete withdrawal from them; declaring the need for recognition of the right of the Palestinian people, under the leadership of the Palestine Liberation Organization, to self-determination and independence; and calling on all states to end aid to Israel, *pp. 206-10.*

SC Resolution No. 592 (1986) of 8 December 1986: Deploring the opening of fire by the Israeli army resulting in the death and wounding of students at Bir Zeit University, *p. 231.*

UNESCO Decision No. 125 EX/5.2.2 of 1986: On a mission to obtain information on educational and cultural institutions in the occupied Arab territories, *p. 287.*

D. Economic and social situation of the Palestinian people

ECWA Resolution No. 108 (IX) of 11 May 1982: On assistance to the Palestine Liberation Organization, *p. 266.*

ECWA Resolution No. 109 (IX) of 11 May 1982: Urging states hosting the Palestinian people to collaborate with the Palestine Liberation Organization for the purpose of a census of the Palestinian people, *p. 266.*

WHO Resolution No. WHA 35.15 of 14 May 1982: Condemning Israeli practices in the occupied territories and urging the establishment of new Palestinian medical institutions there, *pp. 291-92.*

UNDP Decision No. 82/13 of 18 June 1982: Authorizing assistance to help to meet the economic and social needs of the Palestinian people, *p. 270.*

GA Resolution No. 37/120 A, B, C, D, E, F, G, H, I, J, K of 16 December 1982: On the United Nations Relief and Works Agency for Palestine Refugees in the Near East: Endorsing assistance to Palestinian refugees, calling upon Israel to remove obstacles to the establishment of a University of Jerusalem for Palestinian refugees and to permit the return of displaced Palestinians, and requesting the Secretary-General to take all appropriate steps for the protection and administration of Arab property, assets and property rights in Israel, and to issue identification cards to all Palestinian refugees and their descendants, *pp. 36-44.*

GA Resolution No. 37/122 of 16 December 1982: Demanding that Israel cease all actions and/or plans to build a canal linking the Mediterranean Sea to the Dead Sea, *pp. 44-45.*

GA Resolution No. 37/135 of 17 December 1982: Reaffirming the illegality of measures taken by Israel to exploit the human and natural resources of the occupied Arab and Palestinian territories, and calling upon it to desist from such measures, *pp. 54-55.*

GA Resolution No. 37/222 of 20 December 1982: Affirming that Israeli occupation is contradictory to the social and economic development of the Palestinian people in the occupied territories and that the exercise of their right to self-determination is a prerequisite to their social and economic development, *pp. 55-56.*

UNESCO Decision No. 114 EX/5.1.2 II, III, and IV of 1982: On the implementation of a Unesco General Conference resolution on educational and cultural institutions in the occupied Arab territories, *pp. 280-81.*

ECWA Resolution No. 123 (X) of 11 May 1983: On the study of the economic and social potential of the Palestinian Arab people, *p. 267.*

WHO Resolution No. WHA 36.27 of 16 May 1983: Condemning Israeli practices in the occupied territories and urging the establishment of new Palestinian medical institutions there, *pp. 292-93.*

UNDP Decision No. 83/11 of 24 June 1983: Reiterating its appeal for assistance to help to meet the economic and social needs of the Palestinian people, *p. 270.*

ECOSOC Resolution No. 1983/43 of 25 July 1983: Requesting United Nations bodies to provide economic and social assistance for the Palestinian people in cooperation with the Palestine Liberation Organization, *p. 236.*

GA Resolution No. 38/83 A, B, C, D, E, F, G, H, I, J, K of 15 December 1983: On the United Nations Relief and Works Agency for Palestine Refugees in the Near East: Calling for contributions by governments to the Agency and endorsing assistance to Palestinian refugees, calling on Israel to permit the return of displaced Palestinians and to remove obstacles to the establishment of a University of Jerusalem for Palestinian refugees, and requesting the Secretary-General to take appropriate steps for the protection and administration of Arab refugee property, assets and property rights, *pp. 80-88.*

GA Resolution No. 38/85 of 15 December 1983: Demanding that Israel cease all actions and/or plans to build a canal linking the Mediterranean Sea to the Dead Sea, *pp. 88-89.*

GA Resolution No. 38/144 of 19 December 1983: Reaffirming the illegality of measures taken by Israel to exploit the human and natural resources of the occupied Arab and Palestinian territories, and calling upon it to desist from such measures, *pp. 90-91.*

GA Resolution No. 38/145 of 19 December 1983: Calling for the provision of economic and social assistance to the Palestinian people, and requesting that United Nations assistance should be rendered in cooperation with the Palestine Liberation Organization, *pp. 91-92.*

GA Resolution No. 38/166 of 19 December 1983: Expressing alarm at the deterioration in living conditions in the Arab territories under Israeli occupation and affirming that occupation is contradictory to the basic requirements of their social and economic development, *pp. 92-93.*

ECWA Resolution No. 124 (XI) of 26 April 1984: On the study of the economic and social situation and potential of the Palestinian Arab people, *p. 267.*

ECWA Resolution No. 132 (XI) of 26 April 1984: On the economic and social conditions of the Palestinian people under occupation, *pp. 267-68.*

WHO Resolution No. WHA 37.26 of 17 May 1984: Condemning Israeli practices and health policy in the occupied territories and reaffirming the right of the Palestinian population to have its own medical institutions, *pp. 293-94.*

UNDP Decision No. 84/13 of 29 June 1984: Requesting the Administrator to make proposals concerning support for programmes of assistance to the Palestinian people, *pp. 270-71.*

ECOSOC Resolution No. 1984/56 of 25 July 1984: Requesting United Nations bodies to provide economic and social assistance for the Palestinian people in cooperation with the Palestine Liberation Organization, *p. 237.*

GA Resolution No. 39/99 A, B, C, D, E, F, G, H, I, J, K of 14 December 1984: On UNRWA: Calling for contributions by governments to UNRWA and endorsing assistance to Palestinian refugees; calling on Israel to permit the return of displaced Palestinians, and demanding that it desist from the destruction of Palestinian refugee shelters in the Gaza Strip and refugee camps in the West Bank; requesting the Secretary-General to take appropriate steps for the protection of Arab property, assets and property rights; and calling on Israel to remove hindrances to the establishment of a University of Jerusalem for Palestinian refugees, *pp. 120-29.*

GA Resolution No. 39/101 of 14 December 1984: Demanding that Israel cease all plans to build a canal linking the Mediterranean Sea to the Dead Sea, *pp. 129-30.*

GA Resolution No. 39/169 of 17 December 1984: Expressing alarm at the deterioration of living conditions in the territories under Israeli occupation and affirming that the occupation is contradictory to the basic requirements of their social and economic development, *pp. 135-36.*

GA Resolution No. 39/223 of 18 December 1984: Calling for the lifting of Israeli restrictions on the economy of the occupied Palestinian territories, and calling for the establishment of a seaport in the occupied Gaza Strip, *p. 137.*

GA Resolution No. 39/224 of 18 December 1984: Calling for the provision of economic and social assistance to the Palestinian people, and requesting that United Nations assistance should be rendered in cooperation with the Palestine Liberation Organization, *pp. 137-38.*

GA Decision No. 39/442 of 18 December 1984: On Israeli economic practices in the occupied territories, *pp. 138-39.*

ECWA Resolution No. 139 (XII) of 24 April 1985: On the economic and social conditions of the Palestinian people, *p. 268.*

ECWA Resolution No. 141 (XII) of 24 April 1985: On the study of the economic and social situation and potential of the Palestinian people, *p. 268.*

WHO Resolution No. WHA 38.15 of 16 May 1985: Condemning Israeli practices and health policy in the occupied territories and reaffirming the right of the Palestinian population to have its own medical institutions, *pp. 294-96.*

UNDP Decision No. 85/15 of 29 June 1985: Recommending efforts to achieve goals on meeting the economic and social needs of the Palestinian people, *p. 271.*

ECOSOC Resolution No. 1985/57 of 25 July 1985: Requesting United Nations bodies to provide economic and social assistance for the Palestinian people in cooperation with the Palestine Liberation Organization, *pp. 237-38.*

ECOSOC Resolution No. 1985/58 of 25 July 1985: Calling for the lifting of restrictions on the economy of the occupied Palestinian territories and for the establishment of a seaport in the Gaza Strip, *pp. 238-39.*

GA Resolution No. 40/165 A, B, C, D, E, F, G, H, I, J, K of 16 December 1985: On the United Nations Relief and Works Agency for Palestine Refugees in the Near East: Calling for contributions by governments to the Agency and endorsing assistance to Palestinian refugees, calling on Israel to permit the return of displaced Palestinians and to remove obstacles to the establishment of a University of Jerusalem for Palestinian refugees, and requesting the Secretary-General to take appropriate steps for the protection and administration of Arab refugee property, assets and property rights, *pp. 159-67.*

GA Resolution No. 40/167 of 16 December 1985: Requesting the Secretary-General to monitor any new development relating to the Israeli proposal to build a canal linking the Mediterranean Sea to the Dead Sea, *p. 167*.

GA Resolution No. 40/169 of 17 December 1985: Calling for the lifting of Israeli restrictions on the economy of the occupied territories and for the establishment of a seaport in the occupied Gaza Strip, *pp. 172-73*.

GA Resolution No. 40/170 of 17 December 1985: Calling for the provision of economic and social assistance to the Palestinian people and requesting that United Nations assistance should be rendered in cooperation with the Palestine Liberation Organization, *p. 173*.

GA Resolution No. 40/201 of 17 December 1985: Expressing alarm at the deterioration of living conditions in the territories under Israeli occupation, and affirming that the occupation is contradictory to the basic requirements of their social and economic development, *p. 174*.

GA Decision No. 40/432 of 17 December 1985: On Israeli economic practices in the occupied territories, *pp. 177-78*.

ECWA Resolution No. 145 (XIII) of 24 April 1986: On the economic and social conditions of the Palestinian people under occupation, *pp. 268-69*.

ECWA Resolution No. 146 (XIII) of 24 April 1986: On the study of the economic and social situation and potential of the Palestinian people, *p. 269*.

WHO Resolution No. WHA 39.10 of 15 May 1986: Condemning Israeli practices and health policy in the occupied territories and reaffirming the right of the Palestinian population to have its own medical institutions, *pp. 296-97*.

UNDP Decision No. 86/55 of 19 June 1986: Taking note of the Report of the Administrator on assistance to the Palestinian people, *pp. 271*.

ECOSOC Resolution No. 1986/49 of 22 July 1986: Requesting economic and social assistance for the Palestinian people, *p. 239*.

GA Resolution No. 41/69 A, B, C, D, E, F, G, H, I, J, K of 3 December 1986: On the United Nations Relief and Works Agency for Palestine Refugees in the Near East: Calling for contributions by governments to the Agency and endorsing assistance to Palestinian refugees, calling upon Israel to permit the return of displaced Palestinians and to remove obstacles to the establishment of a University of Jerusalem for Palestinian refugees, and requesting the Secretary-General to take appropriate steps for the protection and administration of Arab refugee property, assets and property rights, *pp. 194-202*.

GA Resolution No. 41/181 of 8 December 1986: Requesting the international community to provide assistance to the Palestinian people in cooperation with the Palestine Liberation Organization, *p. 213*.

III. PLO ACCREDITATION AND PARTICIPATION

ECWA Resolution No. 108 (IX) of 11 May 1982: On assistance to the Palestine Liberation Organization, *p. 266*.

ECWA Resolution No. 109 (IX) of 11 May 1982: Urging states hosting the Palestinian people to collaborate with the Palestine Liberation Organization for the purpose of a census of the Palestinian people, *p. 266*.

WHO Resolution No. WHA 35.15 of 14 May 1982: Condemning Israeli practices in the occupied territories and urging the establishment of new Palestinian medical institutions there, *pp. 291-92*.

GA Resolution No. 37/43 of 3 December 1982: Reaffirming the right of the Palestinian people to self-determination, condemning Israeli attacks on civilians in Lebanon and calling for support for the Palestine Liberation Organization [Excerpts from a resolution on the right of peoples under colonial and foreign domination to self-determination and independence], *pp. 18-19*.

UNESCO Resolution No. 4XC/2.13 of 3 December 1982: Inviting the Director-General to plan to reinforce cooperation in Unesco's fields of competence with the Palestine Liberation Organization [Excerpt from a resolution on Major Programme XIII ('Peace, international understanding, human rights and the rights of peoples')], *p. 275*.

GA Resolution No. 37/104 of 16 December 1982: Calling on all states to accord the necessary facilities and privileges and immunities to delegations of national liberation movements recognized by the Organization of African Unity and/or the League of Arab States and accorded observer status by international organizations, *pp. 35-36*.

GA Resolution No. 37/123 A, B, C, D, E, F of 16 December 1982: Condemning Israel's policies in the occupied Arab territories and calling for its complete withdrawal from them, condemning the massacres of Sabra and Shatila in Lebanon and calling for the restoration of the authority of the Lebanese state in Lebanese territory, condemning Israeli practices in Lebanon, calling for recognition of the right of the Palestinian people, under the leadership of the PLO, to self-determination and an independent state, and calling upon all states to put an end to the flow of aid to Israel, *pp. 45-50*.

GA Resolution No. 37/134 of 17 December 1982: Calling for the provision of humanitarian assistance to the Palestinian people, and requesting that United Nations assistance should be rendered in cooperation with the Palestine Liberation Organization, *pp. 53-54.*

ECWA Resolution No. 116 (X) of 11 May 1983: Requesting that the Palestine Liberation Organization be assigned a quota of posts in the secretariat of the Economic Commission for Western Asia [Excerpt from a resolution on staff and administrative questions], *p. 266.*

WHO Resolution No. WHA 36.27 of 16 May 1983: Condemning Israeli practices in the occupied territories and urging the establishment of new Palestinian medical institutions there, *pp. 292-93.*

ECOSOC Resolution No. 1983/43 of 25 July 1983: Requesting United Nations bodies to provide economic and social assistance for the Palestinian people in cooperation with the Palestine Liberation Organization, *p. 236.*

UNESCO Resolution No. 22C/2.1 of 21 November 1983: Inviting the Director-General to continue cooperation with UN institutions providing educational assistance to the Palestine Liberation Organization [Excerpt from a resolution on Major Programme II, 'Education for all'], *p. 275.*

GA Resolution 38/58 A, B, C, D, E of 13 December 1983: On the question of Palestine: Endorsing the right of the Palestinian people to self-determination, including the right to establish an independent state, the right of the Palestine Liberation Organization to participate in peace negotiations on an equal footing, the need for a complete withdrawal of Israeli forces from the occupied territories, and the right of all states in the region to existence within secure and internationally recognized boundaries, *pp. 67-71.*

GA Resolution No. 38/145 of 19 December 1983: Calling for the provision of economic and social assistance to the Palestinian people, and requesting that United Nations assistance should be rendered in cooperation with the Palestine Liberation Organization, *pp. 91-92.*

GA Resolution No. 38/180 A, B, C, D, E of 19 December 1983: On the situation in the Middle East: Condemning Israel's policies in the occupied territories and calling for its complete withdrawal from them; condemning Israeli army actions in Beirut in 1982; declaring the need for recognition of the right of the Palestinian people, under the leadership of the Palestine Liberation Organization, to self-determination and an independent state; calling on all states to put an end to the flow of aid to Israel; and condemning Israeli-South African collaboration *pp. 93-98.*

WHO Resolution No. WHA 37.26 of 17 May 1984: Condemning Israeli practices and health policy in the occupied territories and reaffirming the right of the Palestinian population to have its own medical institutions, *pp. 293-94.*

ECOSOC Resolution No. 1984/56 of 25 July 1984: Requesting United Nations bodies to provide economic and social assistance for the Palestinian people in cooperation with the Palestine Liberation Organization, *p. 237.*

GA Resolution No. 39/49 A, B, C, D of 11 December 1984: On the question of Palestine: Endorsing the recommendations of the Committee on the Exercise of the Inalienable Rights of the Palestinian People, requesting wider dissemination of information on the question of Palestine and United Nations activities relating to it, and endorsing the convening of an international peace conference on the Middle East, *pp. 103-6.*

GA Resolution No. 39/76 of 13 December 1984: Calling upon all states to accord the necessary facilities, privileges and immunities to delegations of national liberation movements recognized by the Organization of African Unity and/or the League of Arab States and accorded observer status by international organizations, *pp. 112-13.*

GA Resolution No. 39/146 A, B, C of 14 December 1984: On the situation in the Middle East: Condemning Israel's policies in the occupied territories and calling for its complete withdrawal from them; declaring the need for recognition of the right of the Palestinian people, under the leadership of the Palestine Liberation Organization, to self-determination and an independent state; and calling on all states to put an end to the flow of aid to Israel, *pp. 130-34.*

GA Resolution No. 39/224 of 18 December 1984: Calling for the provision of economic and social assistance to the Palestinian people, and requesting that United Nations assistance should be rendered in cooperation with the Palestine Liberation Organization, *pp. 137-38.*

WHO Resolution No. WHA 38.15 of 16 May 1985: Condemning Israeli practices and health policy in the occupied territories and reaffirming the right of the Palestinian population to have its own medical institutions, *pp. 294-96.*

ECOSOC Resolution No. 1985/57 of 25 July 1985: Requesting the United Nations bodies to provide economic and social assistance for the Palestinian people in cooperation with the Palestine Liberation Organization, *pp. 237-38.*

UNESCO Resolution No. 23C/2.1 of 5 November 1985: Inviting the Director to continue to support educational activities by the United Nations system for Palestinian refugees and the training of teachers for national liberation movements [Excerpt from a resolution on Major Programme II, 'Education for all'], *pp. 277-78.*

GA Resolution No. 40/96 A, B, C, D of 12 December 1985: On the question of Palestine: Endorsing the recommendations of the Committee on the Exercise of the Inalienable Rights of the Palestinian People, urging wider dissemination of information on the question of Palestine and United Nations activities relating to it, and endorsing the convening of an international peace conference on the Middle East, *pp. 148-51.*

GA Resolution No. 40/168 A, B, C of 16 December 1985: On the situation in the Middle East: Condemning Israel's policies in the occupied territories and calling for its complete withdrawal from them; declaring the need for recognition of the right of the Palestinian people, under the leadership of the Palestine Liberation Organization, to self-determination and an independent state; and calling on all states to put an end to the flow of aid to Israel, *pp. 167-72.*

GA Resolution No. 40/170 of 17 December 1985: Calling for the provision of economic and social assistance to the Palestinian people and requesting that United Nations assistance should be rendered in cooperation with the Palestine Liberation Organization, *p. 173.*

WHO Resolution No. WHA 39.10 of 15 May 1986: Condemning Israeli practices and health policy in the occupied territories and reaffirming the right of the Palestinian population to have its own medical institutions, *pp. 296-97.*

ECOSOC Resolution No. 1986/49 of 22 July 1986: Requesting economic and social assistance for the Palestinian people, *p. 239.*

GA Resolution No. 41/43 A, B, C, D of 2 December 1986: On the question of Palestine: Endorsing the recommendations of the Committee on the Exercise of the Inalienable Rights of the Palestinian People, requesting the dissemination of information on the question of Palestine and United Nations activities relating to it, and endorsing the convening of an international peace conference on the Middle East, *pp. 180-83.*

GA Resolution No. 41/71 of 3 December 1986: Calling upon all states to accord the necessary facilities, privileges and immunities to delegations of national liberation movements recognized by the Organization of African Unity and/ or the League of Arab States and accorded observer status by international organizations, *pp. 202-3.*

GA Resolution No. 41/162 A, B, C of 4 December 1986: On the situation in the Middle East: Condemning Israel's policies in the occupied territories and calling for its complete withdrawal from them; declaring the need for recognition of the right of the Palestinian people, under the leadership of the Palestine Liberation Organization, to self-determination and independence; and calling on all states to end aid to Israel, *pp. 206-10.*

GA Resolution No. 41/181 of 8 December 1986: Requesting the international community to provide assistance to the Palestinian people in cooperation with the Palestine Liberation Organization, *p. 213.*

IV. CONDEMNATION OF RACISM, COLONIALISM AND/OR LINKS WITH SOUTH AFRICA

GA Resolution No. 37/39 of 3 December 1982: Condemning Israel and certain Western states for collaboration with South Africa in the economic, military and nuclear fields [Excerpts from a resolution on assistance to South Africa], *pp. 17-18.*

GA Resolution No. 37/40 of 3 December 1982: Condemning racism in South Africa and the occupied Arab territories [Excerpts from a resolution on the implementation of the Programme for the Decade for Action to Combat Racism and Racial Discrimination], *p. 18.*

GA Resolution No. 37/43 of 3 December 1982: Reaffirming the right of the Palestinian people to self-determination, condemning Israeli attacks on civilians in Lebanon and calling for support for the Palestine Liberation Organization [Excerpts from a resolution on the right of peoples under colonial and foreign domination to self-determination and independence], *pp. 18-19.*

GA Resolution No. 37/46 of 3 December 1982: Expressing concern at Israel's defiance of the International Convention on the Elimination of all Forms of Racial Discrimination [Excerpts from a resolution on racial discrimination], *p. 20.*

GA Resolution No. 37/69 A, C, D, F of 9 December 1982: Condemning collaboration between Israel and certain Western states and South Africa, especially in the military and nuclear fields [Excerpts from a resolution on South African policies of *apartheid*], *pp. 20-23.*

GA Resolution No. 37/104 of 16 December 1982: Calling on all states to accord the necessary facilities, privileges and immunities to delegations of national liberation movements recognized by the Organization of African Unity and/or the League of Arab States and accorded observer status by international organizations, *pp. 35-36.*

GA Resolution No. 38/17 of 22 November 1983: Condemning Israel's expansionist policies as an obstacle to the achievement of self-determination and independence by the Palestinian people, and condemning the massacre of Palestinians and other civilians in Beirut, as well as Israel's policies in Lebanon [Excerpts from a resolution on the right to self-determination of colonial countries and peoples], *pp. 57-58.*

GA Resolution No. 38/36 A, D of 1 December 1983: Condemning military and nuclear collaboration on the part of Israel and certain Western states and South Africa [Excerpts from a resolution on Namibia], *pp. 61-62*.

GA Resolution No. 38/39 A, F, G of 5 December 1983: Condemning collaboration between Israel and South Africa, especially in the military and nuclear fields. [Excerpts from a resolution on the *apartheid* policies of the South African government], *pp. 64-67*.

GA Resolution No. 39/17 of 23 November 1984: Reaffirming the right of the Palestinian people to self-determination and independence [Excerpts from a resolution on the right of peoples to self-determination], *pp. 100-1*.

GA Resolution No. 39/50 A, D of 12 December 1984: Condemning the collusion between South Africa and Israel in the nuclear field [Excerpts from a resolution on Namibia], *pp. 106-8*.

GA Resolution No. 39/72 A, C of 13 December 1984: Condemning collaboration between Israel and South Africa [Excerpts from a resolution on the *apartheid* policies of the South African government], *pp. 111-12*.

GA Resolution No. 39/76 of 13 December 1984: Calling upon all states to accord the necessary facilities, privileges and immunities to delegations of national liberation movements recognized by the Organization of African Unity and/or the League of Arab States and accorded observer status by international organizations, *pp. 112-13*.

GA Resolution No. 40/25 of 29 November 1985: Reaffirming the right of the Palestinian people to self-determination and independence [Excerpt from a resolution on the right of peoples to self-determination], *pp. 140-41*.

GA Resolution No. 40/64 A, E of 10 December 1985: Condemning collaboration between Israel and South Africa [Excerpts from a resolution condemning the policies of *apartheid* of the government of South Africa], *pp. 145-46*.

GA Resolution No. 41/35 C of 10 November 1986: Condemning collaboration between Israel and South Africa [Excerpt from a resolution on South African policies of *apartheid*], *pp. 179-80*.

GA Resolution No. 41/71 of 3 December 1986: Calling upon all states to accord the necessary facilities, privileges and immunities to delegations of national liberation movements recognized by the Organization of African Unity and/or the League of Arab States and accorded observer status by international organizations, *pp. 202-3*.

GA Resolution No. 41/95 of 4 December 1986: Condemning collaboration between Israel and South Africa [Excerpt from a resolution on the provision of assistance to the South African régime], *p. 204*.

GA Resolution No. 41/101 of 4 December 1986: Reaffirming the right of the Palestinian people to self-determination and independence [Excerpts from a resolution on the right to self-determination of colonial countries and peoples], *pp. 204-6*.

V. JERUSALEM

GA Resolution No. ES-7/4 of 28 April 1982: On the question of Palestine: Condemning Israel for its policies in the occupied territories, urging states not to provide Israel with assistance, and urging the Security Council to recognize the inalienable rights of the Palestinian people, *pp. 6-7*.

GA Resolution No. 37/120 A, B, C, D, E, F, G, H, I, J, K of 16 December 1982: On the United Nations Relief and Works Agency for Palestine Refugees in the Near East: Endorsing assistance to Palestinian refugees, calling upon Israel to remove obstacles to the establishment of a University of Jerusalem for Palestinian refugees and to permit the return of displaced Palestinians, and requesting the Secretary-General to take all appropriate steps for the protection and administration of Arab property, assets and property rights in Israel, and to issue identification cards to all Palestinian refugees their descendants, *pp. 36-44*.

GA Resolution No. 37/123 A, B, C, D, E, F of 16 December 1982: Condemning Israel's policies in the occupied Arab territories and calling for its complete withdrawal from them, condemning the massacres of Sabra and Shatila in Lebanon and calling for the restoration of the authority of the Lebanese state in Lebanese territory, condemning Israeli practices in Lebanon, calling for recognition of the right of the Palestinian people, under the leadership of the PLO, to self-determination and an independent state, and calling upon all states to put an end to the flow of aid to Israel, *pp. 45-50*.

UNESCO Decision No. 114 EX/5.4.2 of 1982: Concerning Israel's annexationist policies affecting the cultural and religious character of Jerusalem, *pp. 281-82*.

UNESCO Resolution No. 22C/11.8 of 25 November 1983: Condemning Israeli policies in the City of Jerusalem, *pp. 275-76*.

GA Resolution No. 38/83 A, B, C, D, E, F, G, H, I, J, K of 15 December 1983: On the United Nations Relief and Works Agency for Palestine Refugees in the Near East: Calling for contributions by governments to the Agency and endorsing assistance to Palestinian refugees, calling on Israel to permit the return of displaced Palestinians and to remove obstacles to the establishment of a University of Jerusalem for Palestinian refugees, and requesting the Secretary-General to take appropriate steps for the protection and administration of Arab refugee property, assets and property rights, *pp. 80-88*.

GA Resolution No. 38/180 A, B, C, D, E of 19 December 1983: On the situation in the Middle East: Condemning Israel's policies in the occupied territories and calling for its complete withdrawal from them; condemning Israeli army actions in Beirut in 1982; declaring the need for recognition of the right of the Palestinian people, under the leadership of the Palestine Liberation Organization, to self-determination and an independent state; calling on all states to put an end to the flow of aid to Israel; and condemning Israeli-South African collaboration, *pp. 93-98*.

UNESCO Decision No. 116 EX/5.4.1 of 1983: Condemning Israel's annexationist policies affecting the cultural and religious character of Jerusalem, *p. 284*.

GA Resolution No. 39/99 A, B, C, D, E, F, G, H, I, J, K of 14 December 1984: On UNRWA: Calling for contributions by governments to UNRWA and endorsing assistance to Palestinian refugees; calling on Israel to permit the return of displaced Palestinians, and demanding that it desist from the destruction of Palestinian refugee shelters in the Gaza Strip and refugee camps in the West Bank; requesting the Secretary-General to take appropriate steps for the protection of Arab property, assets and property rights; and calling on Israel to remove hindrances to the establishment of a University of Jerusalem for Palestinian refugees, *pp. 120-29*.

GA Resolution No. 39/146 A, B, C of 14 December 1984: On the situation in the Middle East: Condemning Israel's policies in the occupied territories and calling for its complete withdrawal from them; declaring the need for recognition of the right of the Palestinian people, under the leadership of the Palestine Liberation Organization, to self-determination and an independent state; and calling on all states to put an end to the flow of aid to Israel, *pp. 130-34*.

UNESCO Decision No. 120 EX/5.3.1 of 1984: Concerning Israeli annexationist policies affecting the cultural and religious character of Jerusalem, *p. 285*.

UNESCO Resolution No. 23C/11.3 of 8 November 1985: Deploring assaults on the holy places of Islam in Jerusalem, *pp. 278-79*.

GA Resolution No. 40/165 A, B, C, D, E, F, G, H, I, J, K of 16 December 1985: On the United Nations Relief and Works Agency for Palestine Refugees in the Near East: Calling for contributions by governments to the Agency and endorsing assistance to Palestinian refugees, calling on Israel to permit the return of displaced Palestinian refugees, and requesting the Secretary-General to take appropriate steps for the protection and administration of Arab refugee property, assets and property rights, *pp. 159-67*.

GA Resolution No. 40/168 A, B, C of 16 December 1985: On the situation in the Middle East: Condemning Israel's policies in the occupied territories and calling for its complete withdrawal from them; declaring the need for recognition of the right of the Palestinian people, under the leadership of the Palestine Liberation Organization, to self-determination and an independent state; and calling on all states to put an end to the flow of aid to Israel, *pp. 167-72*.

UNESCO Decision No. 121 EX/5.4.1 of 1985: Requesting that Israel take action to give effect to recommendations of the UNESCO Executive Board on Jerusalem, *pp. 286-87*.

GA Resolution No. 41/69 A, B, C, D, E, F, G, H, I, J, K of 3 December 1986: On the United Nations Relief and Works Agency for Palestine Refugees in the Near East: Calling for contributions by governments to the Agency and endorsing assistance to Palestinian refugees, calling upon Israel to permit the return of displaced Palestinians and to remove obstacles to the establishment of a University of Jerusalem for Palestinian refugees, and requesting the Secretary-General to take appropriate steps for the protection and administration of Arab refugee property, assets and property rights, *pp. 194-202*.

GA Resolution No. 41/162 A, B, C of 4 December 1986: On the situation in the Middle East: Condemning Israel's policies in the occupied territories and calling for its complete withdrawal from them; declaring the need for recognition of the right of the Palestinian people, under the leadership of the Palestine Liberation Organization, to self-determination and independence; and calling on all states to end aid to Israel, *pp. 206-210*.

UNESCO Decision No. 125 EX/5.4.1 of 1986: Deploring assaults perpetrated on the holy places of Islam in Jerusalem, *pp. 287-88*.

VI. ASSISTANCE TO PALESTINE REFUGEES AND OTHER VICTIMS OF CONFLICT

A. Services to Palestinians of UNRWA and other UN agencies

WHO Resolution No. WHA 35.15 of 14 May 1982: Condemning Israeli practices in the occupied territories and urging the establishment of new Palestinian medical institutions there, *p. 291-92*.

GA Resolution No. 37/120 A, B, C, D, E, F, G, H, I, J, K of 16 December 1982: On the United Nations Relief and Works Agency for Palestine Refugees in the Near East: Endorsing assistance to Palestinian refugees, calling upon Israel to remove obstacles to the establishment of a University of Jerusalem for Palestinian refugees and to permit the return of displaced Palestinians, and requesting the Secretary-General to take all appropriate steps for the protection and administration of Arab property, assets and property rights in Israel, and to issue identification cards to all Palestinian refugees and their descendants, *pp. 36-44.*

GA Resolution No. 37/134 of 17 December 1982: Calling for the provision of humanitarian assistance to the Palestinian people, and requesting that United Nations assistance should be rendered in cooperation with the Palestine Liberation Organization, *pp. 53-54.*

UNESCO Resolution No. 22C/2.1 of 21 November 1983: Inviting the Director-General to continue cooperation with UN institutions providing educational assistance to the Palestine Liberation Organization [Excerpt from a resolution on Major Programme II, 'Education for all'], *p. 275.*

GA Resolution No. 38/83 A, B, C, D, E, F, G, H, I, J, K of 15 December 1983: On the United Nations Relief and Works Agency for Palestine Refugees in the Near East: Calling for contributions by governments to the Agency and endorsing assistance to Palestinian refugees, calling on Israel to permit the return of displaced Palestinians and to remove obstacles to the establishment of a University of Jerusalem for Palestinian refugees, and requesting the Secretary-General to take appropriate steps for the protection and administration of Arab refugee property, assets and property rights, *pp. 80-88.*

UNESCO Decision No. 116 EX/7.3 of 1983: Urging member states to assist Palestinian educational and cultural institutions in Lebanon to resume their activities, *pp. 284-85.*

GA Resolution No. 39/99 A, B, C, D, E, F, G, H, I, J, K of 14 December 1984: On UNRWA: Calling for contributions by governments to UNRWA and endorsing assistance to Palestinian refugees; calling on Israel to permit the return of displaced Palestinians, and demanding that it desist from the destruction of Palestinian refugee shelters in the Gaza Strip and refugee camps in the West Bank; requesting the Secretary-General to take appropriate steps for the protection of Arab property, assets and property rights; and calling on Israel to remove hindrances to the establishment of a University of Jerusalem for Palestinian refugees, *pp. 120-29.*

UNESCO Resolution No. 23C/2.1 of 5 November 1985: Inviting the Director to continue to support educational activities by the United Nations system for Palestinian refugees and the training of teachers for national liberation movements [Excerpt from a resolution on Major Programme II, 'Education for all'], *pp. 277-78.*

GA Resolution No. 40/165 A, B, C, D, E, F, G, H, I, J, K of 16 December 1985: On the United Nations Relief and Works Agency for Palestine Refugees in the Near East: Calling for contributions by governments to the Agency and endorsing assistance to Palestinian refugees, calling on Israel to permit the return of displaced Palestinians and to remove obstacles to the establishment of a University of Jerusalem for Palestinian refugees, and requesting the Secretary-General to take appropriate steps for the protection and administration of Arab refugee property, assets and property rights, *pp. 159-67.*

GA Resolution No. 41/69 A, B, C, D, E, F, G, H, I, J, K of 3 December 1986: On the United Nations Relief and Works Agency for Palestine Refugees in the Near East: Calling for contributions by governments to the Agency and endorsing assistance to Palestinian refugees, calling upon Israel to permit the return of displaced Palestinians and to remove obstacles to the establishment of a University of Jerusalem for Palestinian refugees, and requesting the Secretary-General to take appropriate steps for the protection and administration of Arab refugee property, assets and property rights, *pp. 194-202.*

B. Accounts and financing of U.N. agencies

GA Decision No. 36/462 of 16 March 1982: On the financing of the United Nations Relief and Works Agency for Palestine refugees in the Near East, *p. 4.*

UNDP Decision No. 82/13 of 18 June 1982: Authorizing assistance to help to meet the economic and social needs of the Palestinian people, *p. 270.*

GA Resolution No. 37/120 A, B, C, D, E, F, G, H, I, J, K of 16 December 1982: On the United Nations Relief and Works Agency for Palestine Refugees in the Near East: Endorsing assistance to Palestinian refugees, calling upon Israel to remove obstacles to the establishment of a University of Jerusalem for Palestinian refugees and to permit the return of displaced Palestinians, and requesting the Secretary-General to take all appropriate steps for the protection and administration of Arab property, assets and property rights in Israel, and to issue identification cards to all Palestinian refugees and their descendants, *pp. 36-44.*

UNDP Decision No. 83/11 of 24 June 1983: Reiterating its appeal for assistance to help to meet the economic and social needs of the Palestinian people, *p. 270.*

UNESCO Decision No. 116 EX/7.3 of 1983: Urging member states to assist Palestinian educational and cultural institutions in Lebanon to resume their activities, *pp. 284-85.*

GA Resolution No. 38/83 A, B, C, D, E, F, G, H, I, J, K of 15 December 1983: On the United Nations Relief and Works Agency for Palestine Refugees in the Near East: Calling for contributions by governments to the Agency and endorsing assistance to Palestinian refugees, calling on Israel to permit the return of displaced Palestinians and to remove obstacles to the establishment of a University of Jerusalem for Palestinian refugees, and requesting the Secretary-General to take appropriate steps for the protection and administration of Arab refugee property, assets and property rights, *pp. 80-88*.

UNDP Decision No. 84/13 of 29 June 1984: Requesting the Administrator to make proposals concerning support for programmes of assistance to the Palestinian people, *pp. 270-71*.

GA Resolution No. 39/99 A, B, C, D, E, F, G, H, I, J, K of 14 December 1984: On UNRWA: Calling for contributions by governments to UNRWA and endorsing assistance to Palestinian refugees; calling on Israel to permit the return of displaced Palestinians, and demanding that it desist from the destruction of Palestinian refugee shelters in the Gaza Strip and refugee camps in the West Bank; requesting the Secretary-General to take appropriate steps for the protection of Arab property, assets and property rights; and calling on Israel to remove hindrances to the establishment of a University of Jerusalem for Palestinian refugees, *pp. 120-29*.

UNDP Decision No. 85/15 of 29 June 1985: Recommending efforts to achieve goals on meeting the economic and social needs of the Palestinian people, *p. 271*.

GA Resolution No. 40/165 A, B, C, D, E, F, G, H, I, J, K of 16 December 1985: On the United Nations Relief and Works Agency for Palestine Refugees in the Near East: Calling for contributions by governments to the Agency and endorsing assistance to Palestinian refugees, calling on Israel to permit the return of displaced Palestinians and to remove obstacles to the establishment of a University of Jerusalem for Palestinian refugees, and requesting the Secretary-General to take appropriate steps for the protection and administration of Arab refugee property, assets and property rights, *pp. 159-67*.

UNDP Decision No. 86/55 of 19 June 1986: Taking note of the Report of the Administrator on assistance to the Palestinian people, *p. 271*.

GA Resolution No. 41/69 A, B, C, D, E, F, G, H, I, J, K of 3 December 1986: On the United Nations Relief and Works Agency for Palestine Refugees in the Near East: Calling for contributions by governments to the Agency and endorsing assistance to Palestinian refugees, calling upon Israel to permit the return of displaced Palestinians and to remove obstacles to the establishment of a University of Jerusalem for Palestinian refugees, and requesting the Secretary-General to take appropriate steps for the protection and administration of Arab refugee property, assets and property rights, *pp. 194-202*.

C. Aid to Lebanon

GA Resolution No. 37/163 of 17 December 1982: Calling for assistance for the reconstruction and development of Lebanon, *p. 55*.

UNESCO Decision No. 115 EX/5.1.1 of 1982: Asking the Director-General to take measures to make possible assistance to Lebanon, strongly condemning Israeli actions of destruction and plunder against Palestinian and Lebanese educational and cultural institutions, and condemning unreservedly those who carried out and made possible the massacres of Sabra and Chatila, *pp. 282-83*.

GA Resolution No. 38/220 of 20 December 1983: Calling for assistance for the reconstruction and development of Lebanon, *pp. 98-99*.

GA Resolution No. 39/197 of 17 December 1984: Calling for assistance for the reconstruction and development of Lebanon, *pp. 136-37*.

GA Resolution No. 40/229 of 17 December 1985: Requesting assistance for the reconstruction and development of Lebanon, *pp. 174-75*.

GA Resolution No. 41/196 of 8 December 1986: Requesting assistance for the reconstruction and development of Lebanon, *pp. 213-14*.

VII. A NUCLEAR-FREE ZONE IN THE MIDDLE EAST AND THE NON-PROLIFERATION TREATY

GA Resolution No. 37/18 of 16 November 1982: Condemning Israel's threat to repeat its attack against Iraqi nuclear installations and demanding that it be withdrawn, *pp. 13-14*.

GA Resolution No. 37/19 of 19 November 1982: Considering that Israel's threat to repeat its attack against Iraqi nuclear installations is a serious threat to the role and activities of the International Atomic Energy Agency, *pp. 14-15*.

GA Resolution No. 37/39 of 3 December 1982: Condemning Israel and certain Western states for collaboration with South Africa in the economic, military and nuclear fields [Excerpts from a resolution on assistance to South Africa], *pp. 17-18*.

GA Resolution No. 37/69 A, C, D, F of 9 December 1982: Condemning collaboration between Israel and certain Western states and South Africa, especially in the military and nuclear fields [Excerpts from a resolution on South African policies of *apartheid*], *pp. 20-23*.

GA Resolution No. 37/75 of 9 December 1982: Urging the creation of a nuclear-weapon-free zone in the Middle East, and calling on all countries of the region to place their nuclear activities under International Atomic Energy Agency safeguards, *pp. 23-24*.

GA Resolution No. 37/82 of 9 December 1982: Demanding that Israel renounce the possession of nuclear weapons and place its nuclear activities under international safeguards, *pp. 24-25*.

IAEA Resolution No. GC (XXVII)/RES/409 of 14 October 1983: Calling on Israel to withdraw its threat to repeat its attack on Iraqi nuclear facilities, *p. 301*.

GA Resolution No. 38/36 A, D of 1 December 1983: Condemning military and nuclear collaboration on the part of Israel and certain Western states and South Africa [Excerpts from a resolution on Namibia], *pp. 61-62*.

GA Resolution No. 38/39 A, F, G of 5 December 1983: Condemning collaboration between Israel and South Africa, especially in the military and nuclear fields [Excerpts from a resolution on the *apartheid* policies of the South African government], *pp. 64-67*.

GA Resolution No. 38/64 of 15 December 1983: Calling upon countries of the Middle East to place their nuclear activities under International Atomic Energy Agency safeguards, *pp. 71-72*.

GA Resolution No. 38/69 of 15 December 1983: Condemning Israel's refusal to renounce any possession of nuclear weapons and to place its nuclear activities under international safeguards, *pp. 72-73*.

IAEA Resolution No. GC (XXVIII)/RES/425 of 28 September 1984: Demanding that Israel undertake not to carry out further attacks on nuclear facilities in Iraq and calling on Israel to place its nuclear facilities under IAEA safeguards, *pp. 301-2*.

GA Resolution No. 39/14 of 16 November 1984: Demanding an undertaking from Israel not to attack nuclear facilities devoted to peaceful purposes in Iraq or other countries, *pp. 99-100*.

GA Resolution No. 39/50 A, D of 12 December 1984: Condemning the collusion between South Africa and Israel in the nuclear field [Excerpts from a resolution on Namibia], *pp. 106-8*.

GA Resolution No. 39/54 of 12 December 1984: Calling upon countries of the Middle East to place their nuclear activities under International Atomic Energy Agency safeguards, *p. 108*.

GA Resolution No. 39/147 of 17 December 1984: Condemning Israel's refusal to renounce any possession of nuclear weapons, and its threat to repeat its attack on nuclear facilities in Iraq, *p. 134-35*.

IAEA Resolution No. GC (XXIX)/RES/443 of 27 September 1985: Considering that Israel has committed itself not to attack peaceful nuclear facilities in Iraq, and calling on Israel to place its nuclear facilities under IAEA safeguards, *pp. 302-3*.

GA Resolution No. 40/6 of 11 November 1985: Calling upon Israel to place its nuclear facilities under International Atomic Energy Agency safeguards, *pp. 139-40*.

GA Resolution No. 40/82 of 12 December 1985: Calling upon all countries of the Middle East to place their nuclear activities under International Atomic Energy Agency safeguards, *p. 146-47*.

GA Resolution No. 40/93 of 12 December 1985: Condemning Israel's refusal to renounce any possession of nuclear weapons, *pp. 147-48*.

GA Resolution No. 41/12 of 29 October 1986: Calling on Israel to place its nuclear facilities under International Atomic Energy Agency safeguards, *pp. 178-79*.

GA Resolution No. 41/48 of 3 December 1986: Calling upon all countries of the Middle East to place their nuclear activities under International Atomic Energy Agency safeguards, *185-6*.

GA Resolution No. 41/93 of 4 December 1986: Condemning Israel's refusal to renounce any possession of nuclear weapons, *p. 203-4*.

APPENDICES

THE GENEVA DECLARATION ON PALESTINE AND PROGRAMME OF ACTION FOR THE ACHIEVEMENT OF PALESTINIAN RIGHTS ISSUED BY THE INTERNATIONAL CONFERENCE ON THE QUESTION OF PALESTINE, GENEVA, 1983[1]

A. Geneva Declaration on Palestine

1. The Conference, having thoroughly considered the question of Palestine in all its aspects, expresses the grave concern of all nations and peoples regarding the international tension that has persisted for several decades in the Middle East, the principal cause of which is the denial by Israel, and those supporting its expansionist policies, of the inalienable legitimate rights of the Palestinian people. The Conference reaffirms and stresses that a just solution of the question of Palestine, the core of the problem, is the crucial element in a comprehensive, just and lasting political settlement in the Middle East.

2. The Conference recognizes that, as one of the most acute and complex problems of our time, the question of Palestine—inherited by the United Nations at the time of its establishment—requires a comprehensive, just and lasting political settlement. This settlement must be based on the implementation of the relevant United Nations resolutions concerning the question of Palestine and the attainment of the legitimate, inalienable rights of the Palestinian people, including the right to self-determination and the right to the establishment of its own independent state in Palestine and should also be based on the provision by the Security Council of guarantees for peace and security among all States in the region, including the independent Palestinian State, within secure and internationally recognized boundaries. The Conference is convinced that the attainment by the Palestinian people of their inalienable rights, as defined by General Assembly Resolution 3236 (XXIX) of 22 November 1974, will contribute substantially to the achievement of peace and stability in the Middle East.

3. The Conference considers the role of the United Nations in the achievement of a comprehensive, just and lasting peace in the Middle East to be essential and paramount. It emphasizes the need for respect for, and application of, the provisions of the Charter of the United Nations, the resolutions of the United Nations relevant to the question of Palestine and the observance of the principles of international law.

4. The Conference considers that the various propos-

als, consistent with the principles of international law, which have been presented on this question, such as the Arab peace plan adopted unanimously at the Twelfth Arab Summit Conference held at Fez, Morocco, in September 1982, should serve as guidelines for concerted international effort to resolve the question of Palestine. These guidelines include the following:

(a) The attainment by the Palestinian people of its legitimate inalienable rights, including the right to return, the right to self-determination and the right to establish its own independent state in Palestine;

(b) The right of the Palestine Liberation Organization, the representative of the Palestinian people, to participate on an equal footing with other parties in all efforts, deliberations and conferences on the Middle East;

(c) The need to put an end to Israel's occupation of the Arab territories, in accordance with the principle of the inadmissibility of the acquisition of territory by force, and, consequently, the need to secure Israeli withdrawal from the territories occupied since 1967, including Jerusalem;

(d) The need to oppose and reject such Israeli policies and practices in the occupied territories, including Jerusalem, and any *de facto* situation created by Israel as are contrary to international law and relevant United Nations resolutions, particularly the establishment of settlements, as these policies and practices constitute major obstacles to the achievement of peace in the Middle East;

(e) The need to reaffirm as null and void all legislative and administrative measures and actions taken by Israel, the occupying Power, which have altered or purported to alter the character and status of the Holy City of Jerusalem, including the expropriation of land and property situated thereon, and in particular the so-called "Basic Law" on Jerusalem and the proclamation of Jerusalem as the capital of Israel;

(f) The right of all States in the region to existence within secure and internationally recognized boundaries, with justice and security for all the people, the *sine qua non* of which is the recognition and attainment of the legitimate, inalienable rights of the Palestinian people as stated in paragraph (a) above.

5. In order to give effect to these guidelines, the Conference considers it essential that an international peace conference on the Middle East be convened on the basis of the principles of the Charter of the United Nations and the relevant resolutions of the United Nations, with the aim of achieving a comprehensive, just and lasting solution to the Arab-Israeli conflict, an essential element of which would be the establishment of an independent Palestinian State in Palestine. This peace conference should be convened under the auspices of the United Nations, with the participation of all parties to the Arab-Israeli conflict, including the Palestine Liberation Organization, as well as the United States of America, the Union of Soviet Socialist Republics, and other concerned States, on an equal footing. In this context the Security Council has

---

[1]The International Conference on the Question of Palestine was convened at the United Nations office in Geneva from 29 August to 7 September 1983 in pursuance of General Assembly resolutions 36/120 C of 10 December 1981, ES-7/7 of 19 August 1982, and 37/86 C of 1 December 1982. Its objective was to seek effective ways and means for the Palestinian people to attain and exercise their inalienable rights. The conference was opened by the Secretary-General of the United Nations, Javier Pérez de Cuéllar, and presided over by the Minister of Foreign Affairs of Senegal, Moustapha Niassé. These documents are reprinted from the *UN Chronicle* (November 1983), pp. 48-56. [ed. note]

a primary responsibility to create appropriate institutional arrangements on the basis of relevant United Nations resolutions in order to guarantee and to carry out the accords of the International Peace Conference.

6. The International Conference on the Question of Palestine emphasizes the importance of the time factor in achieving a just solution to the problem of Palestine. The Conference is convinced that partial solutions are inadequate and delays in seeking a comprehensive solution do not eliminate tensions in the region.

B. Programme of Action for the Achievement of Palestinian Rights

I

The International Conference on the Question of Palestine recommends that all States, individually or collectively, consistent with their respective constitutions and their obligations under the Charter of the United Nations and in conformity with the principles of international law:

1. Recognize the great importance of the time factor in solving the question of Palestine;

2. Intensify efforts for the establishment of an independent Palestinian State within the framework of a comprehensive, just and lasting settlement to the Arab-Israeli conflict in accordance with the Charter of the United Nations, the relevant United Nations resolutions and the guidelines of the Geneva Declaration on Palestine;

3. Consider the continued presence of Israel in the occupied Palestinian and other Arab territories, including Jerusalem, as exacerbating instability in the region and endangering international peace and security;

4. Oppose and reject, as a serious and continuing obstacle to peace, the expansionist policies pursued by Israel in the Palestinian and other Arab territories occupied since 1967, including Jerusalem, and in particular the alteration of the geographic nature and demographic composition, and the Israeli attempt to alter through domestic legislation the legal status of those territories and all the measures taken in violation of the Geneva Convention relative to the Treatment of Prisoners of War[2] and the Geneva Convention relative to the Protection of Civilian Persons in Time of War,[3] both of 12 August 1949, and of the Hague Regulations of 1907,[4] such as the establishment and expansion of settlements, the transfer of Israeli civilians into those territories and the individual and mass transfers therefrom of the Arab Palestinian population;

5. Refrain from providing Israel with assistance of such a nature as to encourage it militarily, economically and financially to continue its aggression, occupation and disregard of its obligations under the Charter and the relevant resolutions of the United Nations;

6. Not encourage migration to the occupied Arab territories until Israel has put a definitive end to the implementation of its illegal policy of establishing settlements in the Palestinian and other Arab territories occupied since 1967;

7. Fully comply with the relevant resolutions of the United Nations and its specialized agencies on the Holy City of Jerusalem, including those which reject Israel's annexation of Jerusalem and its declaration of that city as its capital;

8. Undertake universal efforts to protect the Holy Places and urge Israel to take measures to prevent their desecration;

9. Consider ways and means of meeting the threat that Israel poses to the regional security in Africa in view of Israel's disregard of United Nations resolutions, and its close collaboration with the *apartheid* régime in the economic, military and nuclear fields, thereby contributing to the continued illegal occupation of Namibia and enhancing the régime's repressive and aggressive capacity;

10. Encourage, through bilateral and multilateral contacts, all States, including Western European and North American States which have not done so, to welcome all peace initiatives based on the recognition of the inalienable rights of the Palestinian people, which were also welcomed by Chairman Yasser Arafat in his address to the International Conference on the Question of Palestine;

11. Seek and develop ways and means to enable the Palestinian people to exercise sovereignty over their national resources;

12. Express concern that Israel debars Palestinians from economic activity and access to national resources on Palestinian territory, in consistent violation of General Assembly resolutions on the right of the Palestinians to permanent sovereignty over their national resources;

13. Declare null and void, and counter such measures and practices applied by Israel in the occupied Palestinian and other Arab territories, including Jerusalem, as the annexation and the expropriation of land, water resources, and property and the alteration of the demographic, geographic, historical and cultural features thereof;

14. Undertake measures to alleviate the economic and social burdens borne by the Palestinian people as a result of the continued Israeli occupation of their territories since 1967;

15. Consider contributing or increasing special contributions to the proposed budgets, programmes and projects of the relevant organs, funds and agencies of the United Nations system that have been requested to provide humanitarian, economic and social assistance to the Palestinian people, with particular reference to:

(a) General Assembly resolution 33/147 of 20 December 1978, and the appeal of the Governing Council of the United Nations Development Programme at its thirtieth session, for additional special contributions amounting to at least $8 million during the third programming cycle

---

[2]United Nations, *Treaty Series,* vol. 75 no. 972, p. 135.
[3]*Ibid.,* No. 973, p. 187.
[4]Carnegie Endowment for International Peace, *The Hague Conventions and Declarations of 1899 and 1907* (New York, Oxford University Press), 1915, p. 100.

(1982-1986) aimed at helping to meet the economic and social needs of the Palestinian people;[5]

(b) The proposed programme budget of the United Nations Conference on Trade and Development (UNCTAD) for the biennium 1984/1985 regarding the establishment within UNCTAD of a special economic unit, as requested by UNCTAD at its sixth session at Belgrade;

(c) Establishing a special legal aid fund to assist Palestinians in securing their rights under conditions of occupation, in accordance with the Geneva Convention relative to the Protection of Civilian Persons in Time of War;

16. Ensure that the United Nations Relief and Works Agency for Palestine Refugees in the Near East can meet the essential needs of the Palestinians without interruption or any diminution in the effectiveness of its services;

17. Review the situation of Palestinian women in Israeli occupied territories and, in view of their special hardships, urge the Preparatory Committee of the World Conference to Review and Appraise the Achievements of the United Nations Decade for Women, to be held at Nairobi in 1985, to include this item on the agenda of the Conference;

18. Review, if they have not yet done so, in conformity with their national legislation, their economic, cultural, technical and other relations with Israel, and the agreements governing them with the aim of ensuring that these regulations and agreements will not be interpreted or construed as implying in any way recognition of any modification of the legal status of Jerusalem and of the Palestinian and other Arab territories occupied by Israel since 1967, or an acceptance of Israel's illegal presence in those territories;

19. Recognize that the process of enabling the Palestinian people to exercise its inalienable rights in Palestine is a significant contribution to the restoration of the rule of law in international relations;

20. Assure the observance of the stipulations provided in General Assembly resolution 181 (II) guaranteeing to all persons equal and non-discriminatory rights in civil, political, economic and religious matters and the enjoyment of human rights and fundamental freedoms, including freedom of religion, speech, publication, education, assembly and association;

21. Express concern that the laws applicable in the occupied Arab territories have been totally eclipsed by a plethora of military orders that have been designed to establish a new "legal régime" in violation of the Hague Regulations of 1907, and the Geneva Convention relative to the Protection of Civilian Persons in Time of War;

22. Act in accordance with their obligations under existing international law, in particular with regard to the Geneva Conventions of 1949 which require States Parties to respect and to ensure respect for those conventions in all circumstances, and in particular ensure the respect by Israel for the Geneva Conventions of 1949 in the occupied Palestinian and other Arab territories;

23. Express concern that the Palestinians and other Arabs in the occupied territories are deprived of juridical and other kinds of protection, that they are victims of repressive legislation, involving mass arrests, acts of torture, destruction of houses, and the expulsion of people from their homes, acts which constitute flagrant violations of human rights;

24. Recognize the necessity that Palestinian and Lebanese prisoners detained by Israel be accorded the status of prisoners of war in accordance with the Geneva Convention relative to the Treatment of Prisoners of War of 1949,[6] if combatants, or in accordance with the Geneva Convention relative to the Protection of Civilian Persons in Time of War of 1949,[7] if civilians;

25. Strive for the adoption of international measures so that Israel will implement in the West Bank and Gaza the provisions of the Hague Regulations of 1907 and the Geneva Convention relative to the Protection of Civilian Persons, in the light of Security Council Resolution 465 (1980);

26. Recognize, if they have not yet done so, the Palestine Liberation Organization as the representative of the Palestinian people and establish with it appropriate relations;

27. Encourage, in conformity with their national legislations, the formation of national committees in support of the Palestinian people;

28. Encourage the observance of 29 November as the International Day of Solidarity with the Palestinian People, in a most effective and meaningful way;

29. Request the General Assembly at its thirty-eighth session to designate a Year of Palestine, to be observed at the earliest possible time, taking into consideration the factors necessary to ensure its effective preparation for the purpose of galvanizing world-wide public opinion and support for further implementation of the Geneva Declaration on Palestine and the Programme of Action.

II

The International Conference on the Question of Palestine stresses the obligation of all Member States, under the Charter of the United Nations, to enable the United Nations through an expanded and more effective role to fulfil its responsibility for achieving a solution to the question of Palestine. To this end:

A

States participating in the Conference invite the Security Council, as the organ with primary responsibility for the maintenance of international peace and security:

1. To suppress continuing and growing acts of aggression and other breaches of peace in the Middle East which endanger peace and security in the region and the world

---

[5]See *Official Records of the Economic and Social Council, 1983, Supplement No. 9* (E/1983/20).

[6]United Nations, *Treaty Series*, vol. 75, no. 972, p. 135.
[7]*Ibid.*, no. 973, p. 187.

as a whole;

2. To take prompt, firm and effective steps and actions to establish an independent sovereign Palestinian State in Palestine through the implementation of the relevant United Nations resolutions, by facilitating the organization of the international peace conference on the Middle East, as called for in paragraph 5 of the Geneva Declaration on Palestine, and by creating in this context the appropriate institutional arrangements on the basis of relevant United Nations resolutions in order to guarantee and carry out the accords of the international peace conference, including the following:

(a) Taking measures consistent with the principle of the inadmissibility of the acquisition of territory by force to ensure Israel's withdrawal from the Palestinian and other Arab territories occupied since 1967, including Jerusalem, within a specific time-table;

(b) Undertaking effective measures to guarantee the safety and security and legal and human rights of the Palestinians in the occupied territories pending the withdrawal of the Israeli forces from the Palestinian and other Arab territories occupied by Israel since 1967, including Jerusalem;

(c) Subjecting those territories, following the withdrawal of Israel, to a short transitional period, under the supervision of the United Nations, during which period the Palestinian people would exercise its right to self-determination;

(d) Facilitating the implementation of the right to return of the Palestinians to their homes and property;

(e) Supervising elections to the constituent assembly of the independent Palestinian State in which all Palestinians shall participate, in the exercise of their right to self-determination;

(f) Providing, if necessary, temporary peace-keeping forces in order to facilitate the implementation of subparagraphs (a)-(e) above.

B

Meanwhile the Security Council is also invited:

1. To take urgent action to bring about an immediate and complete cessation of such Israeli policies in the occupied territories, and in particular, the establishment of settlements as have been determined by the Security Council to have no legal validity and as a serious obstruction to achieving a comprehensive, just and lasting peace in the Middle East;

2. To consider urgently the reports of the Commission established under its resolution 446 (1979) of 22 March 1979, which examined the situation concerning settlements in the Arab territories occupied since 1967, including Jerusalem, and to reactivate the above-mentioned Commission;

3. To initiate action to terminate Israel's exploitative policies which go against the indigenous economic development of the occupied territories, and to compel Israel to lift its restrictions on water use and well-drilling by Palestinian farmers as well as its diversion of West Bank water resources into the Israeli water grid systems;

4. To keep under its constant attention the actions committed by Israel against the Palestinian people in violation of the stipulations provided for in relevant General Assembly resolutions, in particular the stipulations of resolution 181 (II) of 29 November 1947 guaranteeing to all persons equal and non-discriminatory rights and freedoms;

5. To consider, in the event of Israel's persistent non-compliance with the relevant United Nations resolutions which embody the will of the international community, appropriate measures in accordance with the Charter of the United Nations, to ensure Israel's compliance with these resolutions.

C

1. Taking into account the recommendations of the five regional preparatory meetings of the International Conference on the Question of Palestine[8] and United Nations resolutions concerning economic and social assistance to the Palestinian people, the Secretary-General of the United Nations is requested to convene a meeting of the specialized agencies and other organizations associated with the United Nations, as well as representatives of the Palestine Liberation Organization and of those countries which are hosts to Palestinian refugees, and other potential sources of assistance, to develop a co-ordinated programme of economic and social assistance to the Palestinian people and to ensure its implementation.

2. The meeting should also look into the most effective inter-agency machinery to co-ordinate and sustain and intensify United Nations assistance to the Palestinian people.

D

The dissemination of accurate and comprehensive information world-wide, and the role of non-governmental organizations and institutions, remains of vital importance in heightening awareness of and support for the inalienable rights of the Palestinian people to self-determination and to the establishment of an independent sovereign Palestinian State. To these ends:

1. The Department for Public Information of the United Nations, in full co-operation and constant consultations with the Committee on the Exercise of the Inalienable Rights of the Palestinian People should:

(a) Co-ordinate all information activities of the United Nations system on Palestine through the Joint United Nations Information Committee (JUNIC);

(b) Expand publications and audio and visual coverage of the facts and of developments pertaining to the question of Palestine;

(c) Publish newsletters and articles in its respective publications on Israeli violations of human rights of the Arab inhabitants in the occupied territories and organize fact-finding missions for journalists to the area;

---

[8]African region, A/CONF.114/1; Latin American region, A/CONF.114/2; Western Asian region, A/CONF.114/3; Asian region, A/CONF.114/4; European region, A/CONF.114/5.

(d) Organize regional encounters for journalists;

(e) Disseminate appropriate information on the results of the International Conference on the Question of Palestine;

2. Relevant organizations of the United Nations systems should organize meetings, symposia and seminars on topics within their terms of reference and relating to specific problems of the Palestinian people by establishing closer liaison with non-governmental organizations, the media and other groups interested in the question of Palestine.

III

The International Conference on the Question of Palestine, convinced of the important role of world-wide public opinion in resolving the Question of Palestine, and in the implementation of the Declaration and Programme of Action, urges and encourages:

1. Intergovernmental and non-governmental organizations to increase awareness by the international community of the economic and social burdens borne by the Palestinian people as a result of the continued Israeli occupation and its negative effects on the economic development of the West Asian region as a whole;

2. Non-governmental organizations and professional and popular associations to intensify their efforts to support the rights of the Palestinian people in every possible way;

3. Organizations such as those of women, teachers, workers, youths and students to undertake exchanges and other programmes of joint action with their Palestinian counterparts;

4. Women's associations, in particular, to investigate the conditions of Palestinian women and children in all occupied territories;

5. The media and other institutions to disseminate relevant information to increase public awareness and understanding of the question of Palestine;

6. Institutions of higher education to promote the study of the question of Palestine in all its aspects;

7. Various jurists' associations to establish special investigative commissions to determine the violations by Israel of the Palestinians' legal rights and to disseminate their findings accordingly;

8. Jurists to initiate with their Palestinian counterparts consultations, research and investigations on the juridical aspects of problems affecting the southern African and Palestinian struggles, in particular the detention of political prisoners and the denial of prisoner-of-war status to detained members of the national liberation movements of southern Africa and Palestine;

9. Parliamentarians, political parties, trade unions, organizations for solidarity and intellectuals particularly in Western Europe and North America, to join their counterparts in other parts of the world in giving their support, where it has not been done, to an initiative which would express the desire of the international community to see the Palestinian people at last living in their own independent homeland in peace, freedom and dignity.

APPENDIX B

TABLES OF VOTING IN THE GENERAL ASSEMBLY 1982-1986

Y = Yes N = No A = Abstention NP = Not Present

Year / Session / Res.	1982 / 37 ES9/1	36/462	36/138 C	ES7/4	ES7/5	ES7/6	ES7/7	ES7/8	ES7/9	37/18	37/19	37/38 A	37/38 B	37/39	37/40	37/43	37/46	37/69 A
Afghanistan	Y	ADOPTED WITHOUT A VOTE	NP	Y	Y	Y	Y	Y	Y	NP	Y	NP	NP	NP*	NP*	NP*	NP*	Y
Albania	Y		N	Y	Y	Y	Y	Y	Y	Y	Y	N	N	Y	Y	Y	Y	Y
Algeria	Y		NP	Y	Y	Y	Y	Y	Y	Y	Y	A	A	Y	Y	Y	Y	Y
Angola	Y		NP	Y	Y	Y	Y	Y	Y	Y	Y	NP	NP	Y	Y	Y	Y	Y
Antigua and Barbuda	NP		NP	NP	NP	NP	NP	NP	NP	NP	NP	NP	NP	Y	Y	Y	Y	Y
Argentina	A		Y	A	Y	Y	Y	Y	Y	Y	Y	Y	Y	Y	Y	Y	Y	Y
Australia	N		Y	N	Y	A	A	A	Y	A	A	Y	Y	A	N	N	A	A
Austria	A		Y	N	Y	Y	Y	A	Y	Y	A	Y	Y	A	N	A	A	A
Bahamas	A		Y	A	Y	Y	Y	Y	Y	A	NP	Y	Y	Y	Y	Y	Y	Y
Bahrain	Y		Y	Y	Y	Y	Y	Y	Y	Y	Y	Y	Y	Y	Y	Y	Y	Y
Bangladesh	Y		Y	Y	Y	Y	Y	Y	Y	Y	Y	Y	Y	Y	Y	Y	Y	Y
Barbados	A		Y	A	Y	Y	Y	Y	Y	Y	Y	Y	Y	Y	Y	Y	Y	Y
Belgium	N		Y	N	Y	A	A	A	Y	Y	A	Y	Y	N	N	N	A	N
Belize	NP		NP	NP	NP	NP	NP	NP	NP	NP	NP	NP	NP	Y	Y	Y	A*	NP
Benin	Y		NP	Y	Y	Y	Y	Y	Y	Y	Y	NP	NP	Y	Y	Y	Y	Y
Bhutan	Y		Y	Y	Y	Y	Y	Y	Y	Y	Y	Y	Y	Y	Y	Y	Y	Y
Bolivia	A		Y	A	Y	Y	Y	A	Y	NP	NP	NP	NP	Y	Y	Y	Y	Y
Botswana	Y		NP	Y	Y	Y	Y	Y	Y	NP	NP	NP	NP	Y	Y	Y	Y	Y
Brazil	A		Y	A	Y	Y	Y	Y	Y	Y	Y	Y	Y	Y	Y	Y	Y	Y
Brunei Darussalam																		
Bulgaria	Y		NP	Y	Y	Y	Y	Y	Y	Y	Y	A	N	Y	Y	Y	Y	Y
Burkina Faso (Upper Volta)	Y		NP	Y	Y	Y	Y	NP	Y	Y	NP	NP	NP	Y	Y	Y	Y	Y
Burma	Y		Y	A	Y	Y	Y	A	Y	NP	NP	Y	Y	Y	Y	NP	Y	Y
Burundi	Y		NP	Y	Y	Y	Y	Y	Y	Y	Y	Y	Y	Y	Y	Y	Y	Y
Byelorussian SSR	Y		N	Y	Y	Y	Y	Y	Y	Y	Y	A	N	Y	Y	Y	Y	Y
Canada	N		Y	N	Y	A	A	A	Y	A	A	Y	Y	N	N	N	A	N
Cape Verde	Y		NP	Y	Y	Y	Y	Y	Y	Y	Y	NP	NP	Y	Y	Y	Y	Y
Central African Republic	NP		NP	NP	NP	NP	NP	NP	★	Y	Y	Y	Y	Y	Y	Y	Y	Y
Chad	NP		A	Y	NP	Y	Y	Y	Y	Y	Y	NP	NP	Y	Y	Y	Y	Y
Chile	A		Y	A	Y	Y	Y	NP	Y	A	Y	Y	Y	Y	Y	Y	Y	NP
China	Y		Y	Y	Y	Y	Y	Y	Y	Y	NP	Y	Y	Y	Y	Y	Y	Y
Colombia	A		Y	A	Y	Y	Y	A	Y	A	Y	Y	Y	Y	Y	Y	Y	Y
Comoros	NP		NP	NP	NP	NP	NP	NP	Y	Y	NP	Y	Y	Y	Y	Y	Y	Y
Congo	Y		NP	Y	Y	Y	Y	Y	Y	Y	Y	Y	Y	NP	NP	Y	Y	Y
Costa Rica	A		Y	A	Y	NP	Y	NP	Y	NP	NP	Y	Y	Y	Y	NP	Y	Y
Cuba	Y		NP	Y	Y	Y	Y	Y	Y	Y	Y	A	A	Y	Y	Y	Y	Y
Cyprus	Y		NP	Y	Y	Y	Y	Y	Y	Y	Y	Y	Y	Y	Y	Y	Y	Y
Czechoslovakia	Y		N	Y	Y	Y	Y	Y	Y	Y	Y	A	N	Y	Y	Y	Y	Y
Democratic Kampuchea	NP•		NP	NP	Y	Y	Y	Y	Y	Y	NP	NP	NP	Y	Y	Y	Y	Y
Democratic Yemen	Y		A	Y	Y	Y	Y	Y	Y	Y	Y	A	A	Y	Y	Y	Y	Y
Denmark	N		Y	N	Y	A	A	A	Y	Y	A	Y	Y	A	N	N	A	N
Djibouti	Y		Y	Y	Y	Y	Y	Y	Y	Y	NP	NP	NP	Y	Y	Y	Y	Y
Dominica	NP		NP	NP	NP	NP	NP	NP	NP	NP	NP	NP	NP	NP	NP	NP	NP	NP
Dominican Republic	A		NP	A	NP	A	Y	A	Y	A	Y	A	A	Y	Y	Y	Y	Y
Ecuador	A		Y	A	Y	Y	Y	Y	Y	Y	Y	Y	Y	Y	Y	Y	Y	Y
Egypt	A		Y	A	Y	Y	Y	Y	Y	Y	Y	Y	Y	Y	Y	Y	Y	Y
El Salvador	A		NP	A	NP*	Y	Y	A	Y	Y	NP	NP	NP	Y	Y	Y	Y	NP
Equatorial Guinea	NP		NP	NP	NP	NP	NP	NP	NP	Y	Y	NP	NP	Y	Y	Y	Y	Y
Ethiopia	Y		Y	Y	NP*	Y	Y	Y	Y	Y	Y	A	A	Y	Y	Y	Y	Y
Fiji	N		Y	A	Y	Y	Y	A	Y	A	Y	Y	Y	Y	Y	Y	Y	Y
Finland	N		Y	N	Y	Y	A	A	Y	Y	A	Y	Y	A	N	N	A	A
France	N		Y	N	Y	A	A	A	Y	Y	A	Y	Y	N	N	N	Y	N
Gabon	A		Y	NP	Y	Y	Y	Y	Y	Y	Y	Y	Y	Y	Y	Y	Y	Y
Gambia	Y		NP	Y	Y	Y	Y	Y	Y	Y	Y	Y	Y	NP*	NP*	NP*	NP*	Y
German Democratic Republic	Y		N	Y	Y	Y	Y	Y	Y	Y	Y	A	N	Y	Y	Y	Y	Y
Germany (Federal Republic of)	N		Y	N	Y	A	A	A	Y	Y	A	Y	Y	N	N	N	A	N
Ghana	Y		Y	Y	Y	Y	Y	Y	Y	Y	Y	Y	Y	Y	Y	Y	Y	Y
Greece	Y		Y	Y	Y	Y	Y	Y	Y	Y	A	Y	Y	A	A	A	Y	A
Grenada	Y		NP	Y	NP	Y	Y	Y	Y	Y	NP	A	A	Y	Y	Y	Y	Y
Guatemala	A		NP	A	NP	NP	NP	NP	Y	A	Y	NP	NP	NP	NP	NP	NP	NP
Guinea	Y		A	Y	NP	Y	Y	Y	Y	Y	Y	NP	NP	Y	Y	Y	Y	Y
Guinea-Bissau	Y		NP	Y	Y	Y	Y	Y	Y	NP	Y	NP	NP	Y	Y	Y	Y	Y
Guyana	Y		NP	Y	Y	Y	Y	Y	Y	Y	Y	Y	Y	Y	Y	Y	Y	Y
Haiti	A		NP	A	NP	A	Y	A	Y	A	NP	NP	NP	Y	Y	Y	Y	Y
Honduras	A		NP	A	NP	Y	Y	A	Y	Y	Y	Y	Y	NP	NP	NP	NP	NP
Hungary	Y		N	Y	Y	Y	Y	Y	Y	Y	Y	A	N	Y	Y	Y	Y	Y
Iceland	N		Y	N	Y	A	A	A	Y	Y	A	Y	Y	A	N	N	Y	N
India	Y		Y	Y	Y	Y	Y	Y	Y	Y	Y	Y	Y	Y	Y	Y	Y	Y
Indonesia	Y		Y	Y	Y	Y	Y	Y	Y	Y	Y	Y	Y	Y	Y	Y	Y	Y
Iran	Y		NP	Y	Y	Y	Y	Y	Y	NP	NP	NP	NP	Y	Y	Y	Y	Y
Iraq	Y		NP	Y	Y	Y	Y	Y	Y	Y	Y	N	N	Y	Y	Y	Y	Y
Ireland	N		Y	N	Y	A	A	A	Y	Y	A	Y	Y	A	N	A	A	A
Israel	N		Y	N	N	N	N	N	N	N	N	Y	Y	N	N	N	N	★
Italy	N		Y	N	Y	A	A	A	Y	Y	A	Y	Y	N	N	N	Y	N
Ivory Coast	Y		Y	A	NP	Y	Y	NP	Y	A	Y	Y	Y	A	Y	Y	Y	A
Jamaica	NP		Y	A	Y	A	Y	Y	Y	A	Y	NP*	NP*	Y	Y	Y	Y	Y
Japan	N		Y	A	Y	Y	A	A	Y	Y	A	Y	Y	A	A	A	Y	A*
Jordan	Y		Y	Y	Y	Y	Y	Y	Y	Y	Y	Y	Y	Y	Y	Y	Y	Y
Kenya	Y		Y	Y	Y	Y	Y	Y	Y	Y	Y	Y	Y	Y	Y	Y	Y	Y
Kuwait	Y		Y	Y	Y	Y	Y	Y	Y	Y	Y	Y	Y	Y	Y	Y	Y	Y

★Did not participate in the vote.
• Later announced it was not participating in the vote or had intended not to participate in the vote.
* Later advised the Secretariat it had intended to vote in favour.

										1982 37												
37/69 C	37/69 D	37/69 F	37/75	37/82	37/86 A	37/86 B	37/86 C	37/86 D	37/86 E	37/88 A	37/88 B	37/88 C	37/88 D	37/88 E	37/88 F	37/88 G	37/104	37/120 A	37/120 B	37/120 C	37/120 D	37/120 E
Y	Y	Y		Y	Y	Y	Y	Y	Y	Y	Y	Y	Y	Y	Y	Y	Y				Y	Y
Y	Y	Y		Y	Y	Y	Y	Y	★	Y	Y	Y	Y	Y	Y	Y	Y			Y	NP	Y
Y	Y	Y		Y	Y	Y	Y	Y	Y	NP	NP	Y	Y	Y	Y	Y	Y			Y	Y	Y
Y	Y	Y		NP	Y	Y	Y	Y	NP	NP	NP	NP	NP	NP	NP	NP	Y			NP	NP	NP
Y	Y	Y		Y	Y	Y	Y	Y	Y	Y	Y	Y	Y	Y	Y	Y	Y			Y	Y	Y
A	A	N		A	A	A	A	A	A	Y	Y	A	Y	Y	A	A	A			Y	Y	Y
A	Y	Y		Y	Y	Y	Y	A	Y	NP	NP	NP	NP	NP	NP	NP	Y			Y	Y	Y
Y	Y	Y		Y	Y	Y	Y	Y	Y	Y	Y	Y	Y	Y	Y	Y	Y			Y	Y	Y
Y	Y	Y		Y	Y	Y	Y	A	Y	Y	Y	A	Y	Y	A	Y	Y			Y	Y	Y
N	N	N		A	A	A	A	A	A	Y	Y	A	Y	Y	A	Y	N			Y	Y	Y
NP	NP	NP		Y	Y	Y	Y	Y	NP	NP	NP	NP	NP	NP	NP	NP	Y			Y	Y	Y
Y	Y	Y		Y	Y	Y	Y	Y	Y	Y	Y	Y	Y	Y	Y	Y	Y			Y	Y	Y
Y	Y	Y		Y	NP*	NP*	NP*	NP*	Y	Y	Y	Y	Y	Y	Y	Y	Y			Y	Y	Y
A	Y	Y		Y	NP	NP	NP	NP	Y	Y	Y	Y	Y	Y	Y	Y	Y			Y	Y	Y
Y	Y	Y		Y	Y	Y	Y	Y	Y	Y	Y	Y	Y	Y	Y	Y	Y			Y	Y	Y
Y	Y	Y		Y	Y	Y	Y	Y	Y	Y	Y	Y	Y	Y	Y	Y	Y			Y	Y	Y
Y	Y	Y		Y	Y	Y	Y	Y	Y	Y	Y	Y	Y	Y	Y	Y	Y			Y	Y	Y
Y	Y	A		A	A	Y	Y	A	Y	Y	Y	Y	Y	A	Y	A	Y			Y	Y	Y
Y	Y	Y		Y	Y	Y	Y	Y	Y	Y	Y	Y	Y	Y	Y	Y	Y			Y	Y	Y
N	N	N		A	A	N	A	N	A	Y	Y	A	Y	Y	A	N	N			Y	Y	Y
Y	Y	Y		Y	Y	Y	Y	Y	Y	NP	NP	NP	NP	NP	NP	NP	NP			NP	NP	Y
Y	Y	Y		Y	Y	Y	Y	Y	Y	Y	Y	Y	Y	Y	Y	Y	Y			Y	Y	Y
Y	Y	Y		Y	Y	Y	Y	Y	Y	Y	Y	Y	NP	Y	Y	Y	Y			Y	Y	Y
NP	Y	A		A	Y	Y	Y	Y	Y	Y	Y	NP	Y	Y	A	Y	Y			Y	Y	Y
Y	Y	Y		A	Y	Y	Y	Y	Y	Y	Y	Y	Y	Y	Y	Y	Y			Y	Y	Y
Y	Y	Y		A	Y	Y	Y	Y	Y	Y	Y	NP*	Y	Y	Y	Y	Y			Y	Y	Y
Y	Y	Y		Y	Y	Y	Y	Y	Y	Y	Y	Y	Y	Y	Y	Y	Y			Y	Y	Y
Y	Y	★		NP	A	A	A	N	NP	Y	Y	A	Y	Y	A	Y	NP			Y	Y	Y
Y	Y	Y		Y	Y	Y	Y	Y	Y	Y	Y	Y	Y	Y	Y	Y	Y			Y	Y	Y
Y	Y	Y		Y	Y	Y	Y	Y	Y	Y	Y	Y	Y	Y	Y	Y	Y			Y	Y	Y
Y	Y	Y		Y	Y	Y	Y	Y	Y	Y	Y	Y	Y	Y	Y	Y	Y			Y	Y	Y
A	A	N		A	A	A	A	A	A	Y	Y	A	Y	Y	A	Y	A			Y	Y	Y
Y	Y	Y		Y	Y	Y	Y	Y	Y	Y	Y	Y	Y	Y	Y	Y	Y			Y	Y	Y
NP	NP	NP		NP	NP	NP	NP	NP	NP	NP	NP	NP	NP	NP	NP	NP	NP			NP	NP	NP
Y	Y	Y		A	A	Y	Y	A	Y	Y	Y	A	Y	Y	Y	Y	NP			Y	Y	Y
Y	Y	Y		Y	Y	Y	Y	Y	Y	Y	Y	Y	Y	Y	Y	Y	NP			Y	Y	Y
Y	Y	Y		Y	Y	Y	Y	Y	Y	Y	Y	Y	Y	Y	Y	Y	Y			Y	Y	Y
NP	NP	NP		Y	Y	Y	Y	Y	Y	NP	NP	NP	NP	NP	NP	NP	NP			Y	Y	NP
Y	Y	Y		NP	Y	Y	Y	Y	Y	NP	NP	NP	NP	NP	NP	NP	Y			NP	NP	NP
Y	Y	A		Y	Y	Y	Y	A	A	Y	Y	Y	Y	Y	Y	Y	NP			NP	NP	NP
NP	NP	NP		Y	Y	Y	Y	A	NP	Y	Y	Y	Y	Y	Y	Y	NP			Y	Y	Y
Y	A	N		A	A	A	A	A	A	Y	Y	A	Y	Y	A	Y	A			Y	Y	Y
Y	Y	Y		Y	Y	Y	Y	Y	Y	Y	Y	Y	Y	Y	Y	Y	Y			Y	Y	Y
Y	Y	N		Y	Y	Y	Y	Y	Y	Y	Y	Y	Y	Y	Y	Y	N			Y	Y	Y
Y	Y	Y		A	Y	Y	Y	A	A	Y	Y	Y	Y	Y	A	Y	NP			NP	NP	NP
NP	NP	NP		Y	Y	Y	Y	Y	A	Y	Y	Y	Y	Y	Y	Y	Y			Y	Y	Y
A	A	N		A	A	A	A	A	A	Y	Y	A	Y	Y	A	A	A			Y	Y	Y
Y	Y	Y		Y	Y	Y	Y	Y	Y	Y	Y	Y	Y	Y	Y	Y	Y			Y	Y	Y
Y	Y	Y		Y	Y	Y	Y	Y	Y	Y	Y	Y	Y	Y	Y	Y	Y			Y	Y	Y
Y	Y	N		A	Y	Y	Y	A	A	Y	Y	Y	Y	Y	A	Y	A			Y	Y	Y
★	★	★		N	N	N	N	N	N	N	N	N	N	N	N	N	N			N	A	N
A	A	A		A	Y	Y	Y	NP	Y	NP	NP	NP	NP	NP	NP	A	NP			Y	Y	Y
A	A	A		A	Y	Y	Y	A	Y	Y	Y	A	Y	Y	Y	A	Y			Y	Y	Y
N	A	A		Y	Y	Y	Y	Y	Y	Y	Y	Y	Y	Y	Y	Y	Y			Y	Y	Y
Y	Y	Y		Y	Y	Y	Y	Y	Y	Y	Y	Y	Y	Y	Y	Y	Y			Y	Y	Y
Y	Y	Y		Y	Y	Y	Y	Y	Y	Y	Y	Y	Y	Y	Y	Y	Y			Y	Y	Y

37/75, 37/120 A and 37/120 B: ADOPTED WITHOUT A VOTE

★ Did not participate in the vote.
* Later advised the Secretariat it had intended to vote in favour.

TABLES OF VOTING IN THE GENERAL ASSEMBLY 1982-1986

Y = Yes   N = No   A = Abstention   NP = Not Present

Year / Session / Res.	37/120 F	37/120 G	37/120 H	37/120 I	37/120 J	37/120 K	37/122	37/123 A	37/123 B	37/123 C	37/123 D	37/123 E	37/123 F	37/127 A	37/127 B	37/134	37/135	37/163
Afghanistan	Y	Y	Y	Y	Y	Y	Y	Y	Y	Y	Y	Y	Y	N	N	Y	Y	
Albania	NP	Y	Y	Y	Y	NP	Y	Y	Y	Y	Y	★	★	N	N	Y	Y	
Algeria	Y	Y	Y	Y	Y	Y	Y	Y	Y	Y	Y	Y	Y	NP	NP	Y	Y	
Angola	Y	Y	Y	Y	Y	Y	Y	Y	Y	Y	Y	Y	Y	Y	Y	Y	Y	
Antigua and Barbuda	NP	NP	NP	NP	NP	NP	NP	NP	NP	NP	NP	NP	A	NP	NP	NP	NP	
Argentina	Y	Y	Y	Y	Y	Y	Y	A	Y	Y	Y	Y	Y	Y	Y	Y	Y	
Australia	A	A	A	N	A	Y	Y	N	Y	Y	A	Y	N	Y	Y	Y	A	
Austria	A	A	A	A	Y	Y	Y	A	Y	Y	Y	Y	A	Y	Y	Y	A	
Bahamas	Y	Y	A	A	Y	Y	Y	Y	Y	Y	Y	Y	Y	Y	Y	Y	Y	
Bahrain	Y	Y	Y	Y	Y	Y	Y	Y	Y	Y	Y	Y	Y	Y	Y	Y	Y	
Bangladesh	Y	Y	Y	Y	Y	Y	Y	Y	Y	Y	Y	Y	Y	Y	Y	Y	Y	
Barbados	Y	Y	Y	A	Y	Y	Y	A	Y	Y	A	Y	A	Y	Y	Y	Y	
Belgium	N	A	A	N	A	Y	Y	N	Y	Y	A	Y	N	Y	Y	Y	A	
Belize	Y	Y	Y	NP	Y	Y	Y	NP	Y	NP	Y	Y	NP	NP	NP	NP	NP	
Benin	Y	Y	Y	Y	Y	Y	Y	Y	Y	Y	Y	Y	Y	NP	NP	Y	Y	
Bhutan	Y	Y	Y	Y	Y	Y	Y	Y	Y	Y	Y	Y	Y	Y	Y	Y	Y	
Bolivia	Y	Y	Y	Y	Y	Y	Y	NP	Y	Y	Y	Y	Y	Y	Y	NP*	Y	
Botswana	Y	Y	Y	Y	Y	Y	Y	Y	Y	Y	Y	Y	Y	Y	Y	Y	Y	
Brazil	Y	Y	Y	Y	Y	Y	Y	A	Y	Y	Y	Y	Y	Y	Y	Y	Y	
Brunei Darussalam																		
Bulgaria	Y	Y	Y	Y	Y	Y	Y	Y	Y	Y	Y	Y	Y	N	N	Y	Y	
Burkina Faso (Upper Volta)	Y	Y	Y	Y	Y	Y	Y	A	Y	Y	Y	Y	Y	Y	Y	Y	Y	
Burma	Y	Y	Y	NP	Y	Y	Y	A	Y	Y	Y	Y	A	Y	Y	Y	A	
Burundi	Y	Y	Y	Y	Y	Y	Y	Y	Y	Y	Y	Y	Y	Y	Y	Y	Y	
Byelorussian SSR	A	Y	Y	Y	Y	Y	Y	Y	Y	Y	Y	Y	Y	N	N	Y	A	
Canada	A	A	A	N	A	Y	Y	N	Y	Y	A	Y	N	Y	Y	Y	A	
Cape Verde	Y	Y	Y	Y	Y	Y	Y	Y	Y	Y	Y	Y	Y	Y	Y	Y	Y	
Central African Republic	Y	Y	Y	Y	Y	Y	Y	A	Y	Y	Y	Y	Y	Y	Y	Y	Y	
Chad	Y	Y	Y	Y	Y	Y	Y	Y	Y	Y	Y	Y	Y	Y	Y	Y	Y	
Chile	Y	Y	Y	A	Y	Y	Y	A	Y	Y	Y	Y	Y	Y	Y	Y	Y	
China	Y	Y	Y	Y	Y	Y	Y	Y	Y	Y	Y	Y	Y	Y	Y	Y	Y	
Colombia	Y	Y	Y	Y	Y	Y	Y	A	Y	Y	Y	Y	Y	Y	Y	Y	Y	
Comoros	Y	Y	Y	Y	Y	Y	Y	Y	Y	Y	Y	Y	Y	Y	Y	Y	Y	
Congo	Y	Y	Y	Y	Y	Y	Y	Y	Y	Y	Y	Y	Y	Y	Y	Y	Y	
Costa Rica	Y	Y	Y	A	A	Y	Y	N	Y	NP	Y	Y	NP	Y	Y	Y	Y	
Cuba	Y	Y	Y	Y	Y	Y	Y	Y	Y	Y	Y	Y	Y	A	A	Y	Y	
Cyprus	Y	Y	Y	Y	Y	Y	Y	Y	Y	Y	Y	Y	Y	Y	Y	Y	Y	
Czechoslovakia	Y	Y	Y	Y	Y	Y	Y	Y	Y	Y	Y	Y	Y	N	N	Y	Y	
Democratic Kampuchea	Y	Y	Y	Y	Y	Y	Y	Y	Y	Y	Y	Y	Y	NP	NP	Y	Y	
Democratic Yemen	Y	Y	Y	Y	Y	Y	Y	Y	Y	Y	Y	Y	Y	NP	NP	Y	Y	
Denmark	N	A	A	N	A	Y	Y	N	Y	Y	A	Y	N	Y	Y	Y	A	
Djibouti	Y	Y	Y	Y	Y	Y	Y	Y	Y	Y	Y	Y	Y	Y	Y	Y	Y	
Dominica	NP	NP	NP	NP	NP	NP	NP	NP	NP	NP	NP	NP	NP	Y	Y	Y	Y	
Dominican Republic	Y	Y	Y	Y	Y	Y	Y	A	A	A	A	Y	A	Y	Y	Y	Y	
Ecuador	Y	Y	Y	Y	Y	Y	Y	A	Y	Y	Y	Y	Y	Y	Y	Y	Y	
Egypt	Y	Y	Y	Y	Y	Y	Y	NP	Y	Y	Y	Y	Y	Y	Y	Y	Y	
El Salvador	Y	Y	Y	Y	Y	Y	Y	A	NP	Y	Y	Y	Y	Y	Y	Y	Y	
Equatorial Guinea	NP	NP	NP	NP	NP	NP	NP	NP	NP	NP	NP	NP	Y	NP	NP	NP	NP	
Ethiopia	Y	Y	Y	Y	Y	Y	Y	Y	Y	Y	Y	Y	Y	NP	NP	Y	Y	
Fiji	Y	Y	A	A	Y	Y	Y	A	Y	NP	Y	Y	A	Y	Y	Y	A	
Finland	A	A	A	A	Y	Y	Y	N	Y	Y	Y	Y	A	Y	Y	Y	A	
France	N	A	A	N	Y	Y	Y	N	Y	Y	A	Y	N	Y	Y	Y	A	
Gabon	Y	Y	Y	Y	Y	Y	Y	NP	A	Y	Y	Y	Y	Y	Y	Y	Y	
Gambia	Y	Y	Y	Y	Y	Y	Y	Y	Y	Y	Y	Y	Y	Y	Y	Y	Y	
German Democratic Republic	Y	Y	Y	Y	Y	Y	Y	Y	Y	Y	Y	Y	Y	N	N	Y	Y	
Germany (Federal Republic of)	N	A	A	N	A	Y	Y	N	Y	Y	A	Y	N	Y	Y	Y	A	
Ghana	Y	Y	Y	Y	Y	Y	Y	Y	Y	Y	Y	Y	Y	Y	Y	Y	Y	
Greece	Y	Y	Y	Y	Y	Y	Y	Y	Y	Y	Y	Y	Y	Y	Y	Y	Y	
Grenada	A	A	A	A	A	Y	Y	Y	Y	Y	Y	Y	Y	A	A	Y	Y	
Guatemala	A	A	A	A	A	Y	NP	N	NP	A	Y	Y	NP	Y	Y	NP	NP	
Guinea	Y	Y	Y	Y	Y	Y	Y	Y	Y	Y	Y	Y	Y	Y	Y	Y	Y	
Guinea-Bissau	Y	Y	Y	Y	Y	Y	Y	Y	Y	Y	Y	Y	Y	Y	Y	Y	Y	
Guyana	Y	Y	Y	Y	Y	Y	Y	Y	Y	Y	Y	Y	Y	Y	Y	Y	Y	
Haiti	NP	NP	NP	NP	NP	NP	NP	NP	NP	NP	NP	NP	A	NP	NP	NP	NP	
Honduras	Y	Y	Y	Y	Y	Y	NP	NP	Y	Y	Y	NP	Y	Y	Y	Y	Y	
Hungary	Y	Y	Y	Y	Y	Y	Y	Y	Y	Y	Y	Y	Y	N	N	Y	Y	
Iceland	N	A	A	N	A	Y	Y	N	Y	Y	A	Y	N	Y	Y	Y	A	
India	Y	Y	Y	Y	Y	Y	Y	Y	Y	Y	Y	Y	Y	Y	Y	Y	Y	
Indonesia	Y	Y	Y	Y	Y	Y	Y	Y	Y	Y	Y	Y	Y	Y	Y	Y	Y	
Iran	Y	Y	Y	Y	Y	Y	Y	Y	Y	Y	Y	Y	Y	NP	N	Y	Y	
Iraq	Y	Y	Y	Y	Y	Y	Y	Y	Y	Y	Y	Y	Y	N	N	Y	Y	
Ireland	N	A	A	A	A	Y	Y	N	Y	Y	A	Y	N	Y	Y	Y	A	
Israel	N	N	N	N	N	A	N	N	N	N	A	Y	N	Y	Y	N	N	
Italy	N	A	A	N	A	Y	Y	N	Y	Y	A	Y	N	Y	Y	Y	A	
Ivory Coast	Y	Y	Y	Y	Y	Y	Y	A	Y	Y	A	Y	A	Y	Y	Y	A	
Jamaica	Y	Y	Y	A	Y	Y	Y	A	Y	Y	Y	Y	Y	Y	Y	Y	Y	
Japan	N	Y	A	N	Y	Y	Y	N	Y	Y	Y	Y	A	Y	Y	Y	Y	
Jordan	Y	Y	Y	Y	Y	Y	Y	Y	Y	Y	Y	Y	Y	Y	Y	Y	Y	
Kenya	Y	Y	Y	Y	Y	Y	Y	Y	Y	Y	Y	Y	Y	Y	Y	Y	Y	
Kuwait	Y	Y	Y	Y	Y	Y	Y	Y	Y	Y	Y	Y	Y	Y	Y	Y	Y	

(Column 37/163 — ADOPTED WITHOUT A VOTE)

★ Did not participate in the vote.
* Later advised the Secretariat it had intended to vote in favour.

1982 37/222	1983 38/9	38/17	38/35 A	38/35 B	38/36 A	38/36 D	38/38 A+	38/38 B+	38/39 A	38/39 F	38/39 G	38/58 A	38/58 B	38/58 C	38/58 D	38/58 E	38/64	38/69	38/79 A	38/79 B	38/79 C	38/79 D
Y	Y	Y	NP	NP	Y	Y	A	A	Y	Y	Y	Y	Y	Y	Y	Y		Y	Y	Y	Y	Y
Y	Y	Y	N	N	Y	Y	N	N	Y	Y	Y	Y	Y	Y	Y	Y		Y	Y	Y	Y	Y
Y	Y	Y	A	A	Y	Y	NP	NP	Y	Y	Y	Y	Y	Y	Y	Y		Y	Y	Y	Y	Y
Y	Y	Y	NP	NP	Y	Y	NP	NP	Y	Y	Y	Y	Y	Y	Y	Y		Y	Y	Y	Y	Y
Y	NP	NP	Y	Y	Y	Y	NP	NP	Y	Y	Y	NP	NP	NP	NP	NP		NP	NP	NP	NP	NP
Y	A	N	Y	Y	A	A	Y	Y	N	N	N	A	A	N	Y	Y		A	A	Y	Y	A
Y	A	A	Y	Y	A	A	Y	Y	A	N	A	Y	Y	N	Y	Y		A	Y	Y	Y	A
Y	A	Y	NP*	NP*	Y	Y	NP	NP	Y	A	Y	Y	Y	Y	Y	Y		Y	A	Y	Y	A
Y	Y	Y	NP*	Y	Y	Y	Y	Y	Y	Y	Y	Y	Y	Y	Y	Y		Y	Y	Y	Y	Y
Y	A	NP	Y	Y	Y	Y	NP	NP	Y	NP	Y	NP	NP	NP	NP	NP		Y	A	Y	Y	A
Y	N	N	Y	Y	Y	Y	Y	Y	N	N	A	A	A	Y	Y	A		A	A	Y	Y	A
NP	NP	NP	Y	Y	Y	Y	NP	NP	Y	NP	Y	Y	Y	A	Y	A		NP	A	Y	Y	Y
Y	Y	NP*	NP	NP	Y	Y	NP	NP	Y	Y	Y	Y	Y	Y	Y	Y		Y	Y	Y	Y	Y
Y	Y	Y	Y	NP	Y	Y	Y	Y	Y	Y	Y	Y	Y	Y	Y	Y		Y	A*	Y	Y	Y
Y	NP	Y	Y	NP	Y	Y	NP	NP	Y	Y	Y	Y	Y	Y	Y	Y		Y	A	Y	Y	Y
Y	Y	Y	Y	Y	Y	Y	Y	Y	Y	Y	Y	Y	Y	Y	Y	Y		Y	A	Y	Y	Y
Y	Y	Y	A	N	Y	Y	N	N	Y	Y	Y	Y	Y	Y	Y	Y		Y	Y	Y	Y	Y
Y	Y	Y	Y	Y	Y	Y	NP	NP	Y	Y	Y	Y	Y	Y	Y	Y		Y	Y	Y	Y	Y
A	NP	Y	Y	Y	Y	Y	NP*	NP*	Y	Y	Y	Y	Y	Y	Y	Y		A	NP	Y	Y	Y
Y	Y	Y	NP	NP	Y	Y	A	A	Y	Y	Y	Y	Y	Y	Y	Y		Y	Y	Y	Y	Y
A	Y	Y	A	N	Y	Y	N	N	Y	Y	Y	Y	Y	Y	Y	Y	A D O P T E D W I T H O U T A V O T E	A	A	Y	Y	A
Y	Y	N	Y	Y	Y	Y	A	A	Y	Y	Y	Y	Y	Y	Y	Y		Y	Y	Y	Y	A
Y	Y	NP	Y	Y	A	NP	NP	NP	Y	Y	Y	Y	Y	Y	Y	Y		Y	Y	Y	Y	Y
Y	Y	NP	Y	Y	Y	Y	Y	Y	Y	Y	Y	Y	Y	Y	Y	Y		Y	Y	Y	Y	Y
Y	A	Y	Y	Y	NP	Y	Y	Y	NP	NP	Y	Y	Y	NP	Y	NP		A	NP	Y	Y	NP
Y	Y	Y	Y	Y	Y	Y	Y	Y	NP	NP	Y	Y	Y	Y	Y	Y		Y	Y	Y	Y	Y
Y	A	NP*	Y	Y	NP	Y	NP	NP	Y	A	Y	Y	Y	Y	Y	Y		A	A	Y	Y	Y
Y	Y	NP	Y	Y	Y	Y	NP	NP	Y	Y	Y	Y	Y	Y	Y	Y		NP	NP	NP	NP	NP
Y	Y	Y	A	A	Y	Y	A	A	Y	Y	Y	Y	Y	Y	Y	Y		Y	Y	Y	Y	Y
Y	NP	Y	Y	Y	Y	Y	Y	Y	Y	A	NP	A	Y	Y	A	NP		★	A	Y	Y	A
Y	Y	Y	Y	A	N	Y	Y	N	Y	Y	Y	Y	Y	Y	Y	Y		Y	Y	Y	Y	Y
Y	Y	Y	Y	Y	Y	Y	Y	Y	Y	Y	Y	Y	Y	Y	Y	Y		Y	Y	Y	Y	Y
Y	Y	Y	N	N	Y	Y	NP	NP	Y	Y	Y	Y	Y	Y	Y	Y		Y	Y	Y	Y	A
Y	Y	Y	NP	NP	Y	Y	NP	NP	Y	Y	Y	Y	Y	Y	Y	Y		Y	Y	Y	Y	Y
NP	NP	NP	NP	NP	NP	NP	NP	NP	NP	NP	NP	NP	NP	NP	NP	NP		NP	NP	Y	Y	NP
Y	NP	Y	NP	NP	Y	Y	NP	NP	NP	A	Y	Y	Y	NP	Y	Y		A	A	Y	Y	A
Y	Y	Y	Y	Y	Y	Y	Y	Y	Y	Y	Y	Y	Y	Y	Y	Y		Y	A	Y	Y	Y
NP	NP	Y	Y	Y	Y	Y	NP	NP	Y	Y	Y	Y	Y	Y	Y	Y		NP	Y	Y	Y	NP
Y	Y	Y	NP	NP	Y	Y	NP	NP	Y	Y	Y	Y	Y	Y	Y	Y		Y	Y	Y	Y	Y
Y	A	Y	Y	Y	A	Y	Y	Y	Y	Y	Y	Y	Y	Y	Y	Y		A	A	Y	Y	A
Y	Y	Y	Y	Y	A	A	N	N	A	N	N	A	A	Y	Y	A		A	Y	Y	Y	A
Y	Y	Y	Y	Y	A	Y	Y	Y	Y	Y	Y	Y	Y	Y	Y	Y		Y	Y	Y	Y	Y
Y	Y	NP	NP	NP	NP*	NP*	NP	NP	Y	Y	Y	Y	Y	Y	Y	Y		Y	Y	Y	Y	Y
Y	Y	N	Y	Y	A	A	N	N	N	N	N	A	A	A	Y	A		Y	Y	Y	Y	A
Y	Y	NP	Y	Y	Y	Y	NP	NP	A	Y	Y	Y	Y	Y	Y	Y		Y	Y	Y	Y	Y
Y	A	NP	NP	NP	NP	NP	NP	NP	NP	NP	NP	NP	NP	NP	NP	NP		A	NP	NP	NP	NP
NP	A	NP	Y	Y	NP	NP	Y	Y	A	A	A	NP	NP	NP	NP	NP		A	NP	NP	NP	NP
Y	NP	NP	Y	Y	NP	NP	Y	Y	Y	Y	Y	Y	Y	Y	Y	Y		Y	NP	NP	NP	NP
Y	Y	Y	NP	NP	Y	Y	NP	NP	Y	Y	Y	Y	Y	Y	Y	Y		NP	Y	Y	Y	Y
Y	Y	Y	NP	NP	Y	Y	NP	NP	Y	Y	Y	Y	Y	Y	Y	Y		Y	Y	Y	Y	Y
Y	A	NP	NP	NP	Y	Y	NP	NP	Y	A	Y	Y	★	Y	Y	Y		A	NP	NP	NP	NP
Y	NP	NP	Y	Y	Y	Y	Y	Y	Y	NP	NP	Y	★	Y	Y	Y		A	NP	NP	NP	NP
Y	Y	N	Y	Y	Y	Y	N	N	Y	Y	Y	A	A	A	Y	A		Y	A	Y	Y	Y
Y	Y	Y	Y	Y	Y	Y	Y	Y	Y	Y	Y	A	A	Y	Y	Y		Y	Y	Y	Y	Y
Y	Y	Y	Y	NP	Y	Y	NP	NP	Y	Y	Y	Y	Y	Y	Y	Y		Y	Y	Y	Y	Y
Y	NP*	Y	NP	Y	Y	Y	NP	NP	Y	Y	Y	Y	Y	Y	Y	Y		Y	Y	Y	Y	Y
Y	Y	Y	A	A	Y	Y	A	A	Y	Y	Y	Y	Y	A	A	A		Y	Y	Y	Y	Y
N	N	N	Y	Y	NP	NP	Y	Y	★	★	★	N	N	N	Y	A		A	N	N	N	A
Y	Y	N	Y	Y	A	A	Y	Y	N	N	N	A	A	Y	Y	A		A	Y	N	Y	A
Y	A	NP	Y	Y	Y	Y	NP	NP	Y	A	Y	A	A	Y	Y	A		A	A	Y	Y	Y
Y	Y	A	NP	NP	A	A	Y	Y	A	A	A	A	A	Y	Y	A		NP	A	Y	Y	A
Y	Y	Y	NP	NP	Y	Y	NP	NP	Y	Y	Y	Y	Y	Y	NP	Y		Y	Y	NP	Y	Y
Y	Y	Y	Y	Y	Y	Y	Y	Y	Y	Y	Y	Y	Y	Y	Y	Y		Y	Y	Y	Y	Y

★ Did not participate in the vote.
* Later advised the Secretariat it had intended to vote in favour.
+ Adopted together

APPENDIX B
TABLES OF VOTING IN THE GENERAL ASSEMBLY 1982-1986

Y = Yes   N = No   A = Abstention   NP = Not Present

Columns 38/83 B, 38/83 C, 38/85 and 38/130 were ADOPTED WITHOUT A VOTE.

	38/79 E	38/79 F	38/79 G	38/79 H	38/83 A	38/83 B	38/83 C	38/83 D	38/83 E	38/83 F	38/83 G	38/83 H	38/83 I	38/83 J	38/83 K	38/85	38/130	38/144
Afghanistan	Y	Y	Y	Y	Y			Y	Y	Y	Y	Y	Y	Y	Y	Y		Y
Albania	Y	Y	Y	Y	NP			NP	Y	NP	Y	Y	Y	Y	Y	Y		Y
Algeria	Y	Y	Y	Y	Y			Y	Y	Y	Y	Y	Y	Y	Y	Y		Y
Angola	Y	Y	Y	Y	Y			Y	Y	Y	Y	Y	Y	Y	Y	Y		Y
Antigua and Barbuda	NP	NP	NP	NP	NP			NP	NP	NP	NP	NP	NP	NP	NP	NP		NP
Argentina	Y	Y	Y	Y	Y			Y	Y	N	Y	Y	Y	Y	Y	Y		Y
Australia	Y	Y	A	Y	Y			Y	Y	A	A	A	Y	Y	Y	Y		A
Austria	Y	Y	Y	Y	Y			Y	Y	A	A	A	Y	Y	Y	Y		Y
Bahamas	Y	Y	Y	Y	Y			Y	Y	Y	Y	Y	Y	Y	Y	Y		Y
Bahrain	Y	Y	Y	Y	Y			Y	Y	Y	Y	Y	Y	Y	Y	Y		Y
Bangladesh	Y	Y	Y	Y	Y			Y	Y	Y	Y	Y	Y	Y	Y	Y		Y
Barbados	Y	Y	A	Y	Y			Y	Y	Y	Y	Y	Y	Y	Y	Y		Y
Belgium	Y	Y	A	Y	Y			Y	Y	N	A	A	A	Y	Y	Y		A
Belize	Y	Y	Y	Y	Y			Y	Y	Y	Y	Y	Y	Y	Y	Y		Y
Benin	Y	Y	Y	Y	Y			Y	Y	Y	Y	Y	Y	Y	Y	Y		Y
Bhutan	Y	Y	Y	Y	Y			Y	Y	Y	Y	Y	Y	Y	Y	Y		Y
Bolivia	Y	Y	Y	Y	Y			Y	Y	Y	Y	Y	Y	Y	Y	Y		Y
Botswana	Y	Y	Y	Y	Y			Y	Y	Y	Y	Y	Y	Y	Y	Y		Y
Brazil	Y	Y	Y	Y	Y			Y	Y	Y	Y	Y	Y	Y	Y	Y		Y
Brunei Darussalam																		
Bulgaria	Y	Y	Y	Y	Y			Y	Y	Y	Y	Y	Y	Y	Y	Y		Y
Burkina Faso (Upper Volta)	Y	Y	Y	Y	Y			Y	Y	Y	Y	Y	Y	Y	Y	Y		Y
Burma	Y	Y	A	Y	Y			Y	Y	Y	Y	Y	Y	Y	Y	Y		A
Burundi	Y	Y	Y	Y	Y			Y	Y	Y	Y	Y	Y	Y	Y	Y		Y
Byelorussian SSR	Y	Y	Y	Y	Y			Y	Y	Y	Y	Y	Y	Y	Y	Y		Y
Canada	Y	Y	A	Y	Y			Y	Y	N	A	A	A	Y	Y	Y		A
Cape Verde	Y	Y	Y	Y	Y			Y	Y	Y	Y	Y	Y	Y	Y	Y		NP
Central African Republic	Y	Y	Y	Y	Y			Y	Y	Y	Y	Y	Y	Y	Y	Y		NP
Chad	Y	Y	Y	Y	Y			Y	Y	Y	Y	Y	Y	Y	Y	Y		Y
Chile	Y	Y	A	Y	Y			Y	Y	Y	Y	Y	Y	Y	Y	Y		Y
China	Y	Y	Y	Y	Y			Y	Y	Y	Y	Y	Y	Y	Y	Y		Y
Colombia	Y	Y	A	Y	Y			Y	Y	Y	Y	Y	Y	Y	Y	Y		Y
Comoros	NP	NP	NP	NP	NP			NP	NP	NP	NP	NP	NP	NP	NP	NP		NP
Congo	Y	Y	Y	Y	Y			Y	Y	Y	Y	Y	Y	Y	Y	Y		NP
Costa Rica	Y	Y	A	Y	Y			Y	Y	Y	Y	Y	A	Y	Y	Y		NP
Cuba	Y	Y	Y	Y	Y			Y	Y	Y	Y	Y	A	Y	Y	Y		Y
Cyprus	Y	Y	Y	Y	Y			Y	Y	Y	Y	Y	Y	Y	Y	Y		Y
Czechoslovakia	Y	Y	Y	Y	Y			Y	Y	Y	Y	Y	Y	Y	Y	Y		Y
Democratic Kampuchea	Y	Y	Y	Y	Y			Y	Y	Y	Y	Y	Y	Y	Y	Y		Y
Democratic Yemen	Y	Y	Y	Y	Y			Y	Y	Y	Y	Y	Y	Y	Y	Y		Y
Denmark	Y	Y	A	Y	Y			Y	Y	N	A	A	A	Y	Y	Y		A
Djibouti	Y	Y	Y	Y	Y			Y	Y	Y	Y	Y	Y	Y	Y	Y		A
Dominica	NP	NP	NP	NP	Y			Y	NP	NP	NP	NP	NP	NP	NP	NP		NP
Dominican Republic	Y	Y	Y	Y	Y			Y	Y	Y	Y	Y	Y	Y	Y	Y		Y
Ecuador	Y	Y	Y	Y	Y			Y	Y	Y	Y	Y	Y	Y	Y	Y		Y
Egypt	Y	Y	Y	Y	Y			Y	Y	Y	Y	Y	Y	Y	Y	Y		Y
El Salvador	Y	Y	NP	Y	Y			Y	Y	Y	Y	Y	Y	Y	Y	Y		NP
Equatorial Guinea	Y	Y	Y	Y	Y			Y	Y	Y	Y	Y	Y	Y	Y	Y		Y
Ethiopia	Y	Y	Y	Y	Y			Y	Y	Y	Y	Y	Y	Y	Y	Y		Y
Fiji	Y	Y	Y	Y	Y			Y	Y	Y	Y	Y	Y	Y	Y	Y		Y
Finland	Y	Y	A	Y	Y			Y	Y	N	A	A	A	Y	Y	Y		A
France	Y	Y	A	Y	Y			Y	Y	Y	Y	Y	Y	Y	Y	Y		A
Gabon	Y	Y	Y	Y	Y			Y	Y	Y	Y	Y	Y	Y	Y	Y		Y
Gambia	Y	Y	Y	Y	Y			Y	Y	Y	Y	Y	Y	Y	Y	Y		Y
German Democratic Republic	Y	Y	Y	Y	Y			Y	Y	Y	Y	Y	Y	Y	Y	Y		Y
Germany (Federal Republic of)	Y	Y	A	Y	Y			Y	Y	N	A	A	A	Y	Y	Y		A
Ghana	Y	Y	Y	Y	Y			Y	Y	Y	Y	Y	Y	Y	Y	Y		Y
Greece	Y	Y	Y	Y	Y			Y	Y	Y	Y	Y	Y	Y	Y	Y		NP
Grenada	Y	Y	Y	Y	Y			Y	Y	Y	Y	Y	Y	Y	Y	Y		NP
Guatemala	NP	NP	NP	NP	NP			NP	NP	NP	NP	NP	NP	NP	NP	NP		NP
Guinea	Y	Y	Y	Y	Y			Y	Y	Y	Y	Y	Y	Y	Y	Y		Y
Guinea-Bissau	Y	Y	Y	Y	Y			Y	Y	Y	Y	Y	Y	Y	Y	Y		Y
Guyana	Y	Y	Y	Y	Y			Y	Y	Y	Y	Y	Y	Y	Y	Y		Y
Haiti	NP	NP	NP	NP	NP			NP	NP	NP	NP	NP	NP	NP	NP	NP		NP
Honduras	NP	NP	NP	NP	Y			Y	Y	Y	Y	Y	Y	Y	Y	Y		Y
Hungary	Y	Y	Y	Y	Y			Y	Y	Y	Y	Y	Y	Y	Y	Y		Y
Iceland	Y	Y	A	Y	Y			Y	Y	N	A	A	A	Y	Y	Y		A
India	Y	Y	Y	Y	Y			Y	Y	Y	Y	Y	Y	Y	Y	Y		Y
Indonesia	Y	Y	Y	Y	Y			Y	Y	Y	Y	Y	Y	Y	Y	Y		Y
Iran	Y	Y	Y	Y	Y			Y	Y	Y	Y	Y	Y	Y	Y	Y		Y
Iraq	Y	Y	Y	Y	Y			Y	Y	N	A	A	A	Y	Y	Y		A
Ireland	N	N	A	N	A			A	N	N	N	N	N	N	N	N		A
Israel	N	N	A	N	A			A	N	N	N	N	N	N	N	N		A
Italy	Y	Y	A	Y	Y			Y	Y	N	A	A	A	Y	Y	Y		A
Ivory Coast	Y	Y	Y	Y	Y			Y	Y	Y	Y	Y	Y	Y	Y	NP		A
Jamaica	Y	Y	A	Y	Y			Y	Y	Y	Y	Y	A*	Y	Y	Y		Y
Japan	Y	Y	Y	Y	Y			Y	Y	N	Y	Y	A	Y	Y	Y		Y
Jordan	Y	Y	Y	Y	Y			Y	Y	Y	Y	Y	Y	Y	Y	Y		Y
Kenya	Y	Y	Y	Y	Y			Y	Y	Y	Y	Y	Y	Y	Y	Y		Y
Kuwait	Y	Y	Y	Y	Y			Y	Y	Y	Y	Y	Y	Y	Y	Y		Y

* Later advised the Secretariat it had intended to vote in favour.

38/145	38/166	38/180 A	38/180 B	38/180 C	38/180 D	38/180 E	38/220	39/14	39/17	39/28 A	39/28 B	39/49 A	39/49 B	39/49 C	39/49 D	39/50 A	39/50 D	39/54	39/71 A,B	39/72 A	38/72 C	39/76
Y	Y	Y	Y	Y	Y	Y		Y	Y			Y	Y	Y	Y	Y	Y		N	Y	Y	Y
Y	Y	Y	Y	Y	Y	Y		Y	Y			Y	Y	Y	Y	Y	Y		N	Y	Y	Y
Y	Y	Y	Y	Y	Y	Y		Y	Y			Y	Y	Y	Y	Y	Y		NP	NP	NP	NP
NP	NP	NP	NP	NP	NP	NP		NP	Y			NP	NP	NP	NP	Y	Y		NP	Y	Y	Y
Y	Y	A	Y	Y	Y	Y		Y	Y			Y	Y	Y	Y	Y	Y		Y	Y	Y	Y
Y	Y	N	A	Y	Y	N		A	N			A	A	Y	A	A	A		Y	A	N	A
Y	Y	A	Y	Y	Y	A		Y	N			A	A	Y	Y	A	A		Y	A	N	A
Y	Y	A	Y	Y	Y	A		NP	Y			Y	Y	Y	Y	Y	Y		Y	Y	Y	Y
Y	Y	Y	Y	Y	Y	Y		Y	Y			Y	Y	Y	Y	Y	Y		Y	A	Y	Y
Y	Y	A	Y	Y	Y	A		A	Y			Y	Y	Y	Y	Y	Y		Y	Y	Y	Y
Y	Y	N	A	Y	N	N		A	N			•A	A	A	Y	A	A		Y	N	A	N
Y	Y	A	Y	Y	Y	A		NP	NP			Y	Y	Y	Y	Y	Y		Y	Y	A	NP
Y	Y	Y	Y	Y	Y	Y		Y	Y			Y	Y	Y	Y	Y	Y		NP	Y	Y	Y
Y	Y	Y	Y	Y	Y	Y		Y	Y			Y	Y	Y	Y	Y	Y		Y	Y	Y	Y
Y	Y	A	Y	Y	Y	A		Y	Y			Y	Y	Y	Y	Y	Y		Y	A	Y	Y
Y	Y	Y	Y	Y	Y	Y		Y	Y			Y	Y	Y	Y	Y	Y		Y	Y	Y	Y
Y	Y	A	Y	Y	Y	A		Y	Y			Y	Y	Y	Y	Y	Y		Y	A	Y	Y
Y	Y	Y	Y	Y	Y	Y		Y	Y			Y	Y	Y	Y	Y	Y		N	Y	Y	Y
Y	Y	A	Y	Y	Y	A		Y	Y			Y	Y	Y	Y	Y	Y		Y	Y	Y	Y
Y	Y	A	Y	Y	Y	A		NP	Y			Y	Y	Y	Y	Y	Y		Y	Y	Y	A
Y	Y	Y	Y	Y	Y	Y		Y	Y			Y	Y	Y	Y	Y	Y		N	Y	Y	Y
Y	Y	N	A	Y	N	N		A	N			A	N	N	N	A	A		Y	N	N	N
Y	Y	A	Y	Y	Y	NP		Y	Y			Y	Y	Y	Y	Y	Y		Y	Y	Y	Y
Y	Y	N	Y	Y	A	A		Y	Y			Y	Y	NP	NP	NP	Y		Y	NP	Y	Y
Y	Y	A	Y	Y	A	Y		A	Y			Y	Y	Y	Y	Y	Y		A	Y	A	A
NP	Y	NP	NP	NP	NP	Y		Y	Y			Y	Y	Y	Y	Y	Y		NP*	Y	A	Y
NP	NP	N	Y	NP	NP	N		A	NP			A	Y	A	A	Y	Y		NP	Y	Y	Y
Y	Y	Y	Y	Y	Y	Y		A	Y			A	Y	A	A	Y	Y		N	Y	A	A
Y	Y	Y	Y	Y	Y	Y		Y	Y			Y	Y	Y	Y	Y	Y		N	Y	Y	Y
Y	Y	NP	Y	Y	Y	Y		Y	Y			Y	Y	Y	Y	Y	Y		NP	Y	Y	Y
Y	Y	N	A	Y	N	N		A	N			A	A	A	A	A	A		Y	N	N	N
Y	Y	Y	Y	Y	Y	Y	ADOPTED WITHOUT A VOTE	Y	Y	NO VOTING LISTS WERE RECORDED Y = 98, N = 2, A = 12, NP = 46	NO VOTING LISTS WERE RECORDED Y = 98, N = 11, A = 5, NP = 44	Y	Y	Y	Y	Y	Y	ADOPTED WITHOUT A VOTE	Y	Y	Y	Y
NP	NP	NP	NP	NP	NP	NP		NP	NP			A	Y	A	A	A	A		NP	Y	A	NP
Y	Y	A	Y	Y	Y	A		A	Y			Y	Y	Y	Y	Y	Y		Y	Y	Y	Y
Y	Y	A	Y	Y	Y	A		A	Y			Y	Y	Y	Y	Y	Y		Y	Y	Y	Y
NP	NP	NP	NP	NP	NP	NP		NP	NP			NP	NP	NP	NP	Y	Y		Y	Y	Y	NP
Y	Y	Y	Y	Y	Y	Y		A	Y			Y	Y	Y	Y	Y	Y		Y	A	Y	Y
Y	Y	N	A	Y	N	N		A	N			A	A	A	A	A	A		Y	A	N	A
Y	Y	NP	Y	Y	NP	Y		NP	Y			Y	Y	Y	Y	Y	Y		Y	Y	Y	NP
Y	Y	Y	Y	Y	Y	Y		Y	N			Y	Y	Y	Y	Y	Y		N	Y	N	N
Y	Y	N	Y	Y	N	Y		A	N			A	A	A	A	A	A		Y	N	N	N
Y	Y	Y	Y	Y	Y	Y		Y	Y			NP*	NP*	NP*	NP*	Y	Y		NP	A	Y	Y
NP	NP	NP	NP	NP	NP	NP		NP	Y			NP	NP	NP	NP	A	A		Y	Y	A	NP
NP	NP	A	NP	A	A	N		A	NP			A	Y	Y	Y	Y	Y		Y	Y	A	A
Y	Y	Y	Y	Y	Y	Y		Y	Y			Y	Y	Y	Y	Y	Y		Y	Y	Y	NP
Y	Y	Y	Y	Y	Y	Y		A	Y			Y	Y	Y	Y	Y	Y		Y	Y	Y	Y
NP	Y	N	Y	Y	NP	N		NP	Y			Y	Y	Y	A	Y	Y		Y	Y	A	A
Y	Y	A	Y	Y	Y	N		NP	Y			Y	Y	Y	NP	Y	Y		N	Y	A	Y
Y	Y	N	Y	Y	N	Y		A	N			A	A	A	A	A	A		Y	N	N	A
Y	Y	Y	Y	Y	Y	Y		Y	Y			Y	Y	Y	Y	Y	Y		Y	Y	Y	Y
A*	Y	N	A	N	N	N		N	A			A	A	A	A	A	A		Y	N	N	N
N	N	N	N	N	N	N		N	N			N	N	N	N	NP	NP		Y	NP	N	N
Y	Y	A	Y	Y	Y	A		A	Y			Y	Y	Y	Y	Y	Y		Y	A	A	Y
Y	Y	Y▲	Y	Y	A	N		A	A			A	A	Y	Y	A	A		Y	N	A	Y
Y	Y	Y	Y	Y	A	Y		Y	Y			Y	Y	Y	Y	Y	Y		Y	Y	Y	Y
Y	Y	Y	Y	Y	Y	Y		Y	Y			Y	Y	Y	Y	Y	Y		Y	Y	Y	Y

▲ Later advised the Secretariat that due to an error by the voting
machine its vote against was recorded in favour.

APPENDIX B

TABLES OF VOTING IN THE GENERAL ASSEMBLY 1982-1986

Y = Yes   N = No   A = Abstention   NP = Not Present

Note: Columns 39/99 **B** and **C** are marked "ADOPTED WITHOUT A VOTE" (no votes recorded).

Year Session Res.	39/95 A	39/95 B	39/95 C	39/95 D	39/95 E	39/95 F	39/95 G	39/95 H	39/99 A	39/99 B	39/99 C	39/99 D	39/99 E	39/99 F	39/99 G	39/99 H	39/99 I	39/99 J
Afghanistan	Y	Y	Y	Y	Y	Y	Y	Y	Y			Y	Y	Y	Y	Y	Y	Y
Albania	Y	Y	Y	Y	Y	Y	Y	Y	NP			NP	Y	NP	Y	Y	Y	Y
Algeria	Y	Y	Y	Y	Y	Y	Y	Y	Y			Y	Y	Y	Y	Y	Y	Y
Angola	NP	NP	NP	NP	NP	NP	NP	NP	NP			NP	NP	NP	NP	Y	Y	Y
Antigua and Barbuda	Y	Y	Y	Y	Y	Y	Y	Y	Y			Y	Y	Y	Y	NP	NP	NP
Argentina	Y	Y	Y	Y	Y	Y	Y	Y	Y			Y	Y	N	A	A	A	Y
Australia	A	Y	Y	A	Y	Y	A	Y	Y			Y	Y	A	A	A	A	Y
Austria	Y	Y	Y	A	Y	Y	Y	Y	Y			Y	Y	A	A	A	A	Y
Bahamas	A	Y	Y	A	Y	Y	Y	Y	Y			Y	Y	Y	Y	Y	Y	Y
Bahrain	Y	Y	Y	Y	Y	Y	Y	Y	Y			Y	Y	Y	Y	Y	Y	Y
Bangladesh	Y	Y	Y	Y	Y	Y	Y	Y	Y			Y	Y	Y	Y	Y	Y	Y
Barbados	A	Y	Y	A	Y	Y	A	Y	Y			Y	Y	Y	Y	Y	Y	Y
Belgium	Y	Y	Y	A	Y	Y	A	Y	Y			Y	Y	N	A	A	A	Y
Belize	A	Y	Y	A	Y	Y	Y	Y	Y			Y	Y	Y	Y	Y	A	Y
Benin	Y	Y	Y	Y	Y	Y	Y	Y	Y			Y	Y	Y	Y	Y	Y	Y
Bhutan	Y	Y	Y	Y	Y	Y	Y	Y	Y			Y	Y	Y	Y	Y	Y	Y
Bolivia	Y	Y	Y	Y	Y	Y	Y	Y	Y			Y	Y	Y	Y	Y	Y	Y
Botswana	Y	Y	Y	Y	Y	Y	Y	Y	Y			Y	Y	Y	Y	Y	Y	Y
Brazil	Y	Y	Y	Y	Y	Y	Y	Y	Y			Y	Y	Y	Y	Y	Y	Y
Brunei Darussalam	Y	Y	Y	Y	Y	Y	Y	Y	Y			Y	Y	Y	Y	Y	Y	Y
Bulgaria	Y	Y	Y	Y	Y	Y	Y	Y	Y			Y	Y	Y	Y	Y	Y	Y
Burkina Faso (Upper Volta)	Y	Y	Y	Y	Y	Y	Y	Y	Y			Y	Y	Y	Y	Y	Y	Y
Burma	NP	Y	Y	Y	Y	Y	A	Y	Y			Y	Y	Y	Y	Y	Y	Y
Burundi	Y	Y	Y	Y	Y	Y	Y	Y	Y			Y	Y	Y	Y	Y	Y	Y
Byelorussian SSR	Y	Y	Y	Y	Y	Y	Y	Y	Y			Y	Y	Y	Y	Y	Y	Y
Canada	Y	Y	Y	A	Y	Y	A	Y	Y			Y	Y	N	A	A	A	Y
Cape Verde	Y	Y	NP*	Y	Y	Y	Y	Y	Y			Y	Y	Y	Y	Y	Y	Y
Central African Republic	NP	NP	Y	Y	Y	Y	Y	Y	Y			Y	Y	Y	Y	Y	Y	Y
Chad	Y	Y	Y	Y	Y	Y	Y	Y	Y			Y	Y	Y	Y	Y	Y	Y
Chile	NP	Y	Y	NP	Y	Y	A	Y	Y			Y	Y	Y	Y	Y	Y	Y
China	Y	Y	Y	Y	Y	Y	Y	Y	Y	ADOPTED WITHOUT A VOTE	ADOPTED WITHOUT A VOTE	Y	Y	Y	Y	Y	Y	Y
Colombia	Y	Y	Y	Y	NP*	Y	Y	Y	Y			Y	Y	NP	Y	Y	Y	Y
Comoros	NP	NP	NP	NP	NP	NP	NP	NP	NP			NP	NP	NP	NP	NP	NP	NP
Congo	Y	Y	Y	Y	Y	Y	Y	Y	Y			Y	Y	Y	Y	Y	Y	Y
Costa Rica	Y	Y	Y•	Y	Y	Y	Y	Y	A			Y	Y	NP	Y	Y	Y	Y
Cuba	Y	Y	Y	Y	Y	Y	Y	Y	Y			Y	Y	Y	Y	Y	Y	Y
Cyprus	Y	Y	Y	Y	Y	Y	Y	Y	Y			Y	Y	Y	Y	Y	Y	Y
Czechoslovakia	Y	Y	Y	Y	Y	Y	Y	Y	Y			Y	Y	Y	Y	Y	Y	Y
Democratic Kampuchea	Y	Y	Y	Y	Y	Y	Y	Y	Y			Y	Y	Y	Y	Y	Y	Y
Democratic Yemen	Y	Y	Y	Y	Y	Y	Y	Y	Y			Y	Y	Y	Y	Y	Y	Y
Denmark	Y	Y	Y	A	Y	Y	A	Y	Y			Y	Y	N	A	A	A	Y
Djibouti	Y	Y	Y	Y	Y	Y	Y	Y	Y			Y	Y	Y	Y	Y	Y	Y
Dominica	NP	NP	NP	NP	NP	NP	NP	NP	NP			NP	NP	NP	NP	NP	NP	NP
Dominican Republic	NP	Y	Y	A	Y	Y	Y	Y	Y			Y	Y	Y	Y	Y	Y	Y
Ecuador	Y	Y	Y	Y	Y	Y	Y	Y	Y			Y	Y	Y	Y	Y	Y	Y
Egypt	Y	Y	Y	Y	Y	Y	Y	Y	Y			Y	Y	Y	Y	Y	Y	Y
El Salvador	Y	Y	Y	Y	Y	Y	Y	Y	Y			Y	Y	Y	Y	Y	Y	Y
Equatorial Guinea	Y	Y	Y	Y	Y	Y	Y	Y	Y			Y	Y	Y	Y	Y	Y	Y
Ethiopia	Y	Y	Y	Y	Y	Y	Y	Y	Y			Y	Y	Y	Y	Y	Y	Y
Fiji	Y	Y	Y	Y	Y	Y	Y	Y	Y			Y	Y	Y	Y	Y	Y	Y
Finland	Y	Y	Y	A	Y	Y	A	Y	Y			Y	Y	N	A	A	Y	Y
France	Y	Y	Y	A	Y	Y	A	Y	Y			Y	Y	N	A	A	Y	Y
Gabon	Y	Y	Y	Y	Y	Y	Y	Y	Y			Y	Y	Y	Y	Y	Y	Y
Gambia	Y	Y	Y	Y	Y	Y	Y	Y	Y			Y	Y	Y	Y	Y	Y	Y
German Democratic Republic	Y	Y	Y	Y	Y	Y	Y	Y	Y			Y	Y	Y	Y	Y	Y	Y
Germany (Federal Republic of)	Y	Y	Y	A	Y	Y	A	Y	Y			Y	Y	N	A	A	A	Y
Ghana	Y	Y	Y	Y	Y	Y	Y	Y	Y			Y	Y	Y	Y	Y	A	Y
Greece	Y	Y	Y	Y	Y	Y	Y	Y	Y			Y	Y	Y	Y	Y	Y	Y
Grenada	NP	NP	NP	NP	NP	NP	NP	NP	NP			NP	NP	NP	NP	NP	NP	NP
Guatemala	A	Y	Y	Y	Y	Y	A	Y	Y			Y	Y	Y	Y	Y	Y	Y
Guinea	Y	Y	Y	Y	Y	Y	Y	Y	Y			Y	Y	Y	Y	Y	Y	Y
Guinea-Bissau	Y	Y	Y	Y	Y	Y	Y	Y	Y			Y	Y	Y	Y	Y	Y	Y
Guyana	Y	Y	Y	Y	Y	Y	Y	Y	Y			Y	Y	Y	Y	Y	Y	Y
Haiti	Y	Y	Y	A	Y	Y	Y	Y	Y			Y	Y	Y	Y	Y	Y	Y
Honduras	NP	NP	NP	NP	NP	NP	NP	NP	Y			Y	Y	Y	Y	Y	Y	Y
Hungary	Y	Y	Y	Y	Y	Y	Y	Y	Y			Y	Y	Y	Y	Y	Y	Y
Iceland	NP	Y	Y	A	Y	Y	A	Y	Y			Y	Y	N	A	A	A	Y
India	Y	Y	Y	Y	Y	Y	Y	Y	Y			Y	Y	Y	Y	Y	Y	Y
Indonesia	Y	Y	Y	Y	Y	Y	Y	Y	Y			Y	Y	Y	Y	Y	Y	Y
Iran	NP*	NP*	NP*	NP*	NP*	NP*	NP*	NP*	NP*			NP*	NP*	NP*	NP*	NP*	NP*	NP*
Iraq	Y	Y	Y	Y	Y	Y	Y	Y	Y			Y	Y	N	A	Y	A	Y
Ireland	Y	Y	Y	A	Y	Y	A	Y	Y			Y	Y	N	A	A	A	Y
Israel	N	N	N	N	N	N	N	N	A			A	A	N	A	N	A	N
Italy	Y	Y	Y	A	Y	Y	A	Y	Y			Y	Y	N	A	A	A	Y
Ivory Coast	A	Y	Y	A	Y	Y	A	Y	Y			Y	Y	Y	Y	Y	A	Y
Jamaica	Y	Y	Y	A	Y	Y	A	Y	Y			Y	Y	N	A	Y	A	Y
Japan	Y	Y	Y	A	Y	Y	A	Y	Y			Y	Y	N	A	A	Y	Y
Jordan	Y	Y	Y	Y	Y	Y	Y	Y	Y			Y	Y	Y	Y	Y	Y	Y
Kenya	Y	Y	Y	Y	Y	Y	Y	Y	Y			Y	Y	Y	Y	Y	Y	Y
Kuwait	Y	Y	Y	Y	Y	Y	Y	Y	Y			Y	Y	Y	Y	Y	Y	Y

• Later advised the Secretariat it was not participating in the vote or had intended not to participate in the vote.

* Later advised the Secretariat it had intended to vote in favour.

	1984 39										1985 40											
39/99 K	39/101	39/146 A	39/146 B	39/146 C	39/147	39/169	39/197	39/223	39/224	39/442	40/6	40/25	40/59 A	40/59 B	40/61	40/64 A	40/64 E	40/82	40/93	40/96 A	40/96 B	40/96 C
Y	Y	Y	Y	Y	Y	Y		Y	Y	Y	Y	Y	A	N		Y	Y		Y	Y	Y	Y
Y	Y	Y	Y	Y	Y	Y		Y	Y	Y	Y	Y	A	N		Y	Y		Y	Y	Y	Y
Y	Y	Y	Y	Y	Y	Y		Y	Y	Y	Y	Y	NP	NP		Y	Y		Y	Y	Y	Y
NP	NP	NP	NP	NP	A	NP		NP	NP	NP	A	NP*	NP	NP		Y	NP		A	Y	Y	Y
Y	Y	Y	A	Y	Y	Y		A	Y	Y	Y	Y	Y	Y		Y	Y		Y	Y	Y	Y
Y	Y	N	A	Y	A	Y		Y	Y	Y	A	A	Y	Y		A	N		A	A	A	A
Y	Y	A	A	Y	A	Y		Y	Y	Y	NP	Y	NP	NP		Y	A		A	Y	Y	Y
Y	Y	A	Y	Y	Y	Y		Y	Y	Y	Y	Y	Y	Y		Y	Y		Y	Y	Y	Y
Y	Y	Y	Y	Y	Y	Y		Y	Y	Y	A	Y	Y	Y		Y	A		Y	Y	Y	Y
Y	Y	N	N	Y	A	Y		Y	Y	Y	N	N	Y	Y		N	A		A	A	A	NP
Y	Y	A	A	Y	NP	NP		NP	NP	NP	NP	NP	A	A		Y	A		Y	Y	Y	Y
Y	Y	Y	Y	Y	Y	Y		Y	Y	Y	A	Y	Y	Y		Y	Y		Y	Y	Y	Y
Y	Y	Y	A	Y	Y	Y		Y	Y	Y	NP	Y	Y	Y		Y	Y		Y	Y	Y	Y
Y	Y	Y	Y	Y	Y	Y		Y	Y	Y	Y	Y	NP	NP		Y	Y		Y	Y	Y	Y
Y	Y	Y	Y	Y	Y	Y		Y	Y	Y	Y	Y	A	N		Y	Y		Y	Y	Y	Y
Y	Y	A	A	Y	A	Y		Y	Y	Y	NP	Y	Y	Y		Y	A		A	Y	Y	Y
Y	Y	Y	Y	Y	A	Y		Y	Y	Y	Y	Y	Y	Y		Y	A		Y	NP*	NP*	NP*
Y	Y	N	N	Y	A	Y		A	Y	Y	N	N	Y	Y		N	N		A	A	N	N
Y	Y	Y	Y	Y	Y	Y		A	Y	Y	Y	Y	NP	NP		Y	Y		Y	Y	Y	Y
Y	Y	Y	NP	Y	NP	Y		NP	Y	Y	Y	Y	Y	Y		Y	Y		Y	Y	Y	Y
Y	Y	A	NP	Y	A	Y		Y	Y	Y	A	NP	Y	Y		NP	A		A	Y	Y	Y
NP	NP	Y	A	Y	A	Y		Y	Y	Y	A	Y	NP	NP		Y	A		A	Y	Y	Y
NP	NP	Y	Y	Y	NP	NP		NP	NP	NP	Y	Y	NP	Y		Y	Y		Y	Y	Y	Y
Y	Y	NP	NP	NP	Y	NP		Y	Y	Y	A	NP	NP	NP		Y	A		NP	NP	NP	NP
Y	Y	Y	Y	Y	Y	Y		Y	Y	Y	Y	Y	A	N		Y	Y		Y	Y	Y	Y
Y	Y	A	A	Y	Y	Y		Y	Y	Y	NP	A	Y	Y		Y	Y		Y	Y	Y	Y
Y	Y	NP	NP	NP	Y	Y		Y	Y	Y	A	A	NP	NP		Y	NP		Y	Y	Y	Y
Y	Y	Y	Y	Y	Y	Y		Y	Y	Y	NP	Y	Y	Y		NP	A		Y	Y	Y	Y
Y	Y	A	A	Y	A	Y		A	Y	Y	A	N	Y	Y		NP	N		A	A	A	A
Y	Y	N	N	Y	Y	Y		Y	Y	Y	NP*	NP	A	N		Y	Y		N	N	A	A
Y	Y	Y	Y	Y	Y	Y		Y	Y	Y	Y	N	A	Y		N	N		Y	Y	Y	Y
NP	NP	NP	NP	NP	NP	NP		NP	NP	NP	A	Y	NP	NP		NP	A		A	A	A	A
Y	Y	A	A	A	NP	Y		Y	NP	Y	A	A	NP	N		Y	A		A	A	Y	Y
Y	Y	A	A	Y	NP*	Y		Y	Y	Y	Y	Y	NP	NP		Y	Y		Y	Y	Y	Y
Y	Y	Y	Y	Y	A	Y		Y	Y	Y	A	NP	Y	Y		Y	A		Y	Y	Y	Y
Y	Y	Y	A	Y	A	Y		Y	Y	Y	NP	A	Y	N		Y	Y		A	Y	Y	Y
Y	Y	Y	Y	Y	Y	Y		A	Y	Y	Y	Y	Y	Y		Y	N		Y	A	A	A
NP*	NP*	Y	Y	Y	Y	Y		Y	Y	Y	Y	Y	NP	NP		Y	Y		Y	NP*	NP*	NP*
Y	Y	Y	Y	Y	Y	Y		Y	Y	Y	Y	Y	A	Y		Y	Y		Y	A	Y	Y
N	N	N	N	N	N	N		N	N	N	A	N	NP	NP		N	N		A	N	N	N
Y	Y	A	A	Y	A	A		Y	Y	Y	Y	Y	Y	Y		Y	A		A	Y	Y	Y
Y	Y	A	A	A	A	Y		Y	Y	Y	A	Y	NP	NP		Y	A		A	A	Y	Y
Y	Y	Y	A	Y	Y	Y		Y	Y	Y	A	A	Y	Y		Y	A		A	A	A	A
Y	Y	Y	Y	Y	Y	Y		Y	Y	Y	Y	Y	Y	Y		Y	Y		Y	Y	Y	Y

Columns 39/197, 40/61 and 40/82: ADOPTED WITHOUT A VOTE

* Later advised the Secretariat it had intended to vote in favour.

APPENDIX B

TABLES OF VOTING IN THE GENERAL ASSEMBLY 1982-1986

Y = Yes   N = No   A = Abstention   NP = Not Present

	40/96	40/161	40/161	40/161	40/161	40/161	40/161	40/161	40/165	40/165	40/165	40/165	40/165	40/165	40/165	40/165	40/165	40/165
1985 / 40 Res.	D	A	B	C	D	E	F	G	A	B	C	D	E	F	G	H	I	J
Afghanistan	Y	Y	Y	Y	Y	Y	Y	Y	Y			Y	Y	Y	Y	Y	Y	Y
Albania	★	Y	Y	Y	Y	Y	Y	Y	NP			NP	Y	NP	Y	Y	Y	Y
Algeria	Y	Y	Y	Y	Y	Y	Y	Y	Y			Y	Y	Y	Y	Y	Y	Y
Angola	Y	NP	NP	NP	NP	NP	NP	NP	NP			NP	NP	NP	NP	NP	NP	NP
Antigua and Barbuda	A	A	Y	Y	Y	Y	Y	Y	Y			Y	Y	Y	Y	Y	Y	Y
Argentina	Y	Y	Y	Y	Y	Y	Y	Y	Y			Y	Y	Y	Y	Y	Y	Y
Australia	A	A	Y	Y	A	Y	Y	A	Y			Y	Y	N	A	A	A	Y
Austria	A	A	Y	Y	A	Y	Y	Y	Y			Y	Y	A	A	A	A	Y
Bahamas	Y	A	Y	Y	A	Y	Y	Y	Y			Y	Y	Y	Y	Y	Y	Y
Bahrain	Y	Y	Y	Y	Y	Y	Y	Y	Y			Y	Y	Y	Y	Y	Y	Y
Bangladesh	Y	Y	Y	Y	Y	Y	Y	Y	Y			Y	Y	Y	Y	Y	Y	Y
Barbados	Y	NP	NP	NP	NP	NP	NP	NP	NP			Y	Y	Y	Y	Y	Y	Y
Belgium	A	A	Y	Y	A	A	Y	A	Y			Y	Y	N	A	A	A	Y
Belize	NP	NP	NP	NP	NP	NP	NP	NP	NP			NP	NP	NP	NP	NP	NP	NP
Benin	Y	Y	Y	Y	Y	Y	Y	Y	Y			Y	Y	Y	Y	Y	Y	Y
Bhutan	Y	Y	Y	Y	Y	Y	Y	Y	Y			Y	Y	Y	Y	Y	Y	Y
Bolivia	Y	Y	Y	Y	Y	Y	Y	Y	Y			Y	Y	Y	Y	Y	Y	Y
Botswana	Y	Y	Y	Y	Y	Y	Y	Y	Y			Y	Y	Y	Y	Y	Y	Y
Brazil	Y	Y	Y	Y	Y	Y	Y	Y	Y			Y	Y	Y	Y	Y	Y	Y
Brunei Darussalam	Y	Y	Y	Y	Y	Y	Y	Y	Y			Y	Y	Y	Y	Y	Y	Y
Bulgaria	Y	Y	Y	Y	Y	Y	Y	Y	Y			Y	Y	Y	Y	Y	Y	Y
Burkina Faso (Upper Volta)	NP*	Y	Y	Y	Y	Y	Y	Y	Y			Y	Y	Y	Y	Y	Y	Y
Burma	Y	NP	Y	Y	Y	Y	Y	Y	NP			Y	Y	Y	Y	Y	Y	Y
Burundi	Y	Y	Y	Y	Y	Y	Y	Y	Y			Y	Y	Y	Y	Y	Y	Y
Byelorussian SSR	Y	Y	Y	Y	Y	Y	Y	Y	Y			Y	Y	Y	Y	Y	Y	Y
Canada	N	A	Y	A	A	A	Y	A	Y			Y	Y	N	A	A	A	Y
Cape Verde	Y	Y	Y	Y	Y	Y	Y	Y	Y			NP	Y	Y	Y	Y	Y	Y
Central African Republic	Y	Y	Y	Y	Y	Y	Y	Y	Y			Y	Y	Y	Y	Y	Y	Y
Chad	Y	Y	Y	Y	Y	Y	Y	Y	Y			Y	Y	Y	Y	Y	Y	Y
Chile	A	NP	Y	Y	NP	Y	Y	A	Y			Y	Y	Y	Y	Y	Y	Y
China	Y	Y	Y	Y	Y	Y	Y	Y	Y			Y	Y	Y	Y	Y	Y	Y
Colombia	A	NP	Y	Y	Y	Y	Y	Y	Y			Y	Y	Y	Y	Y	Y	Y
Comoros	Y	NP	NP	NP	NP	NP	NP	NP	NP			NP	NP	NP	NP	NP	NP	NP
Congo	Y	Y	Y	Y	Y	Y	Y	Y	Y			Y	Y	Y	Y	Y	Y	Y
Costa Rica	NP	A	Y	A	A	A	A	A	Y			Y	Y	A	A	A	A	Y
Cuba	Y	Y	Y	Y	Y	Y	Y	Y	Y			Y	Y	Y	Y	Y	Y	Y
Cyprus	Y	Y	Y	Y	Y	Y	Y	Y	Y			Y	Y	Y	Y	Y	Y	Y
Czechoslovakia	Y	Y	Y	Y	Y	Y	Y	Y	Y			Y	Y	Y	Y	Y	Y	Y
Democratic Kampuchea	Y	Y	Y	Y	Y	Y	Y	Y	Y			Y	Y	Y	Y	Y	Y	Y
Democratic Yemen	Y	Y	Y	Y	Y	Y	Y	Y	Y			Y	Y	Y	Y	Y	Y	Y
Denmark	A	A	Y	Y	A	A	Y	A	Y			Y	Y	N	A	A	A	Y
Djibouti	Y	Y	Y	Y	Y	Y	Y	Y	Y			Y	Y	Y	Y	Y	Y	Y
Dominica	NP	A	Y	A	A	Y	A	Y	Y			Y	Y	Y	Y	Y	Y	Y
Dominican Republic	A	Y	Y	Y	Y	Y	Y	Y	Y			NP*	Y	Y	Y	Y	Y	Y
Ecuador	A	Y	Y	Y	Y	Y	Y	Y	Y			Y	Y	Y	Y	Y	Y	Y
Egypt	Y	Y	Y	Y	Y	Y	Y	Y	Y			Y	Y	Y	Y	Y	Y	Y
El Salvador	A	Y	Y	Y	Y	Y	Y	A	Y			Y	Y	Y	Y	Y	A	Y
Equatorial Guinea	Y	NP	Y	Y	Y	Y	Y	Y	Y			Y	Y	Y	Y	Y	Y	Y
Ethiopia	Y	Y	Y	Y	Y	Y	Y	Y	Y			Y	Y	Y	Y	Y	Y	Y
Fiji	Y	A	Y	Y	A	Y	Y	Y	Y			Y	Y	Y	Y	Y	Y	Y
Finland	A	A	Y	Y	A	Y	Y	A	Y			Y	Y	N	A	A	A	Y
France	A	A	Y	Y	A	Y	Y	A	Y			Y	Y	N	A	A	A	Y
Gabon	Y	Y	Y	Y	Y	Y	Y	Y	Y			Y	Y	Y	Y	Y	Y	Y
Gambia	Y	Y	Y	Y	Y	Y	Y	Y	Y			Y	Y	Y	Y	Y	Y	Y
German Democratic Republic	Y	Y	Y	Y	Y	Y	Y	Y	Y			Y	Y	Y	Y	Y	Y	Y
Germany (Federal Republic of)	A	A	Y	Y	A	A	Y	A	Y			Y	Y	N	A	A	A	Y
Ghana	Y	NP	NP	NP	NP	NP	NP	NP	NP			Y	Y	Y	Y	Y	Y	Y
Greece	A	A	Y	Y	Y	Y	Y	Y	Y			Y	NP*	Y	Y	Y	A	Y
Grenada	A	A	Y	A	A	A	A	A	Y			Y	A	A	A	A	A	Y
Guatemala	A	NP	Y	Y	Y	Y	Y	Y	Y			Y	Y	Y	Y	Y	A	Y
Guinea	Y	Y	Y	Y	Y	Y	Y	Y	Y			Y	Y	Y	Y	Y	Y	Y
Guinea-Bissau	Y	Y	Y	Y	Y	Y	Y	Y	Y			Y	Y	Y	Y	Y	Y	Y
Guyana	Y	Y	Y	Y	Y	Y	Y	Y	Y			Y	Y	Y	Y	Y	Y	Y
Haiti	A	NP	NP	NP	NP	NP	NP	NP	Y			Y	Y	Y	Y	NP	A	Y
Honduras	A	NP	NP	NP	NP	NP	NP	NP	Y			Y	Y	Y	Y	Y	Y	Y
Hungary	Y	Y	Y	Y	Y	Y	Y	Y	Y			Y	Y	Y	Y	Y	Y	Y
Iceland	A	A	Y	Y	A	A	Y	A	Y			Y	Y	N	A	A	A	Y
India	Y	Y	Y	Y	Y	Y	Y	Y	Y			Y	Y	Y	Y	Y	Y	Y
Indonesia	Y	NP	Y	Y	Y	Y	Y	Y	Y			Y	Y	Y	Y	Y	Y	Y
Iran	NP*	NP*	NP*	NP	Y	Y	Y	Y	Y			Y	Y	Y	Y	Y	Y	Y
Iraq	Y	Y	Y	Y	Y	Y	Y	Y	Y			Y	Y	Y	Y	Y	Y	Y
Ireland	A	A	Y	Y	A	Y	Y	A	Y			Y	Y	N	A	A	A	Y
Israel	N	N	N	N	N	N	N	N	A			A	N	N	N	N	N	N
Italy	A	A	Y	Y	A	Y	Y	A	Y			Y	Y	N	A	A	A	Y
Ivory Coast	A	A	Y	A	A	A	Y	A	Y			Y	Y	Y	Y	Y	Y	Y
Jamaica	Y	A	Y	Y	Y	Y	Y	Y	Y			Y	Y	Y	Y	Y	Y	Y
Japan	A	A	Y	Y	A	Y	Y	Y	Y			Y	Y	N	Y	A	A	Y
Jordan	Y	Y	Y	Y	Y	Y	Y	Y	Y			Y	Y	Y	Y	Y	Y	Y
Kenya	Y	Y	Y	Y	Y	Y	Y	Y	Y			Y	Y	Y	Y	Y	Y	Y
Kuwait	Y	Y	Y	Y	Y	Y	Y	Y	Y			Y	Y	Y	Y	Y	Y	Y

Columns 40/165 B and 40/165 C: ADOPTED WITHOUT A VOTE

★Did not participate in the vote.

* Later advised the Secretariat it had intended to vote in favour.

	1985 — 40											1986 — 41										
40/165 K	40/167	40/168 A	40/168 B	40/168 C	40/169	40/170	40/201	40/229	40/246 A	40/246 B	40/432	41/12	41/35 C	41/43 A	41/43 B	41/43 C	41/43 D	41/44 A	41/44 B	41/48	41/63 A	41/63 B
Y	Y	Y	Y	Y	Y	Y	Y		Y	N	Y	Y	Y	Y	Y	Y	NP	NP*	NP‡		Y	Y
Y	Y	Y	NP	Y	Y	Y	Y		N	N	Y	Y	Y	Y	Y	Y	Y	N	N		Y	Y
Y	Y	Y	A	Y	Y	Y	Y		NP	NP	Y	Y	Y	Y	Y	Y	Y	A	A		Y	Y
NP	NP	NP	A	NP	Y	Y	Y		NP	NP	Y	A	Y	Y	Y	Y	N	A	NP		Y	Y
Y	NP	A	Y	A	Y	Y	Y		Y	Y	Y	A	Y	Y	Y	Y	N	Y	A		Y	Y
Y	Y	N	N	Y	A	Y	Y		Y	Y	Y	A	N	A	A	A	A	Y	Y		A	Y
Y	Y	A	A	Y	Y	Y	Y		Y	Y	Y	A	N	A	A	Y	Y	Y	Y		A	Y
Y	Y	Y	Y	Y	Y	Y	Y		Y	Y	Y	Y	Y	Y	Y	Y	Y	Y	Y		Y	Y
Y	Y	A	Y‡	Y	Y	Y	Y		Y	Y	Y	A	Y	Y	Y	Y	Y	NP‡	Y		Y	Y
Y	Y	N	N	Y	Y	Y	Y		Y	Y	Y	A	N	A	A	A	A	Y	Y		Y	Y
NP	NP	NP	NP	NP	NP	NP	Y		Y	Y	NP	NP	A	Y	Y	Y	Y	NP	NP		NP	NP
Y	Y	Y	Y	Y	Y	Y	Y		Y	NP	Y	NP	Y	Y	Y	Y	Y	A	A		Y	Y
Y	Y	Y	A	Y	Y	Y	Y		Y	Y	Y	A	Y	Y	Y	Y	Y	Y	Y		Y	Y
Y	Y	Y	A	Y	Y	Y	Y		Y	Y	Y	Y	Y	Y	Y	Y	Y	Y	Y		Y	Y
Y	Y	Y	Y	Y	Y	Y	Y		Y	Y	Y	Y	Y	Y	Y	Y	Y	Y	Y		Y	Y
Y	Y	A	A	Y	Y	Y	Y		Y	Y	Y	NP	A	Y	Y	Y	Y	Y	Y		Y	Y
Y	Y	Y	A	Y	Y	Y	Y		Y	Y	Y	Y	Y	Y	Y	Y	Y	A	A		Y	Y
Y	Y	N	N	Y	A	Y	Y		Y	Y	Y	A	N	A	N	N	A	Y	Y		A	Y
Y	Y	Y	NP	Y	Y	Y	Y		Y	Y	Y	NP	Y	Y	Y	Y	Y	Y	Y		Y	Y
Y	Y	Y	NP	Y	Y	Y	Y		Y	Y	Y	A	A	Y	Y	Y	Y	Y	Y		Y	Y
Y	Y	A	A	Y	Y	Y	Y		Y	Y	Y	A	A	Y	Y	Y	Y	Y	Y		NP	Y
Y	Y	A	A	Y	Y	Y	Y		A	A	Y	A	A	Y	Y	Y	Y	Y	Y		NP	Y
NP	NP	NP*	A	Y	Y	Y	Y		NP	NP	Y	Y	Y	NP*	NP*	NP*	NP*	N*	N*		NP	NP
Y	Y	N	N	N	NP	NP	Y		Y	Y	Y	A	N	A	Y	A	A	NP	NP		A	Y
Y	Y	Y	Y	Y	Y	Y	Y		Y	Y	Y	Y	Y	Y	Y	Y	Y	A	A		Y	Y
Y	Y	Y	Y	Y	Y	Y	N		Y	Y	Y	Y	Y	NP*	NP*	NP*	NP*	A	A		Y	Y
Y	Y	N	N	Y	Y	Y	Y		A	A	Y	Y	N	A	A	A	A	Y	Y		Y	Y
Y	Y	A	A	A	Y	Y	Y		NP	NP	Y	NP	A	NP	NP	NP	NP	Y	Y		NP	NP
Y	Y	A	A	A	Y	Y	Y		Y	Y	Y	A	N	Y	Y	Y	Y	Y	Y		Y	Y
Y	Y	N	N	NP	Y	NP*	Y		Y	Y	Y	N	N	A	Y	A	A	NP	NP		Y	Y
Y	Y	Y	Y	Y	Y	Y	Y		Y	Y	Y	A	N	NP	NP	NP	NP	Y	Y		A	Y
Y	Y	Y	Y	Y	Y	Y	Y		Y	Y	Y	NP	Y	NP	NP	NP	NP	Y	Y		A	Y
A	Y	A	A	A	Y	A	A		Y	Y	A	A	A	Y	Y	Y	A	Y	Y		A	Y
Y	Y	Y	Y	Y	Y	Y	Y		Y	Y	Y	A	A	Y	Y	Y	Y	Y	Y		A	Y
Y	Y	Y	Y	Y	NP	NP	Y		NP	NP	Y	Y	Y	Y	Y	Y	Y	NP	NP		Y	Y
Y	Y	A	N	NP	Y	Y	Y		NP	NP	Y	A	Y	Y	Y	Y	Y	Y	Y		NP	Y
Y	Y	A	Y	Y	Y	Y	Y		Y	N	Y	A	Y	Y	Y	Y	Y	NP	NP		Y	Y
Y	Y	N	N	Y	Y	A	Y		Y	Y	Y	Y	N	A	A	A	A	Y	Y		A	Y
Y	Y	Y	Y	Y	A	Y	Y		Y	Y	Y	A	A	Y	Y	Y	Y	Y	Y		Y	Y
A	Y	A	A	A	Y	A	A		Y	Y	A	A	A	Y	Y	Y	Y	A	A		A	Y
Y	Y	Y	Y	Y	Y	Y	Y		NP	NP	Y	A	A	Y	Y	Y	Y	NP	NP		Y	Y
Y	Y	Y	Y	Y	Y	Y	Y		NP	NP	Y	A	Y	Y	Y	Y	Y	Y	Y		Y	Y
Y	Y	A	N	NP	Y	Y	Y		NP	NP	Y	A	Y	Y	Y	Y	Y	NP	NP		NP	Y
Y	Y	A	Y	Y	Y	Y	Y		Y	N	Y	N	N	NP	NP	NP	NP	A	A		A	Y
Y	Y	N	N	Y	Y	A	Y		Y	Y	Y	Y	N	Y	Y	Y	Y	Y	Y		Y	Y
Y	Y	A	A	Y	Y	Y	Y		Y	Y	Y	A	A	Y	Y	Y	Y	Y	Y		A	Y
Y	Y	Y	Y	Y	Y	Y	Y		NP	NP	Y	Y	Y	Y	Y	Y	Y	NP	NP		Y	Y
Y	Y	A	A	Y	Y	Y	Y		Y	Y	Y	A	Y	Y	Y	Y	Y	A	A		Y	Y
N	Y	N	N	N	Y	N	Y		Y	Y	N	N	N	A	A	A	A	Y	Y		A	N
Y	Y	Y	Y	Y	Y	Y	Y		Y	Y	Y	A	A	A	Y	Y	Y	Y	Y		A	Y
Y	Y	A	N	Y	Y	Y	Y		Y	Y	Y	A	A	A	A	A	A	Y	Y		A	Y
Y	Y	A	A	Y	Y	Y	Y		Y	Y	Y	Y	Y	A	Y	Y	Y	Y	Y		A	Y
Y	Y	Y	Y	Y	NP	NP	Y		Y	Y	Y	Y	Y	NP*	Y	Y	Y	Y	Y		Y	Y

Note: columns 40/229 and 41/48 — ADOPTED WITHOUT A VOTE.

* Later advised the Secretariat it had intended to vote in favour.
‡ Later advised the Secretariat it had intended to abstain.

APPENDIX B

TABLES OF VOTING IN THE GENERAL ASSEMBLY 1982-1986

Y = Yes N = No A = Abstention NP = Not Present

Year / Session	1986 / 41																	
Res.	41/63 C	41/63 D	41/63 E	41/63 F	41/63 G	41/69 A	41/69 B	41/69 C	41/69 D	41/69 E	41/69 F	41/69 G	41/69 H	41/69 I	41/69 J	41/69 K	41/71	41/93
Afghanistan	Y	Y	Y	Y	Y	Y	ADOPTED WITHOUT A VOTE	ADOPTED WITHOUT A VOTE	Y	Y	Y	Y	Y	Y	Y	Y	Y	Y
Albania	Y	Y	Y	Y	Y	NP			Y	Y	Y	Y	Y	Y	Y	Y	Y	Y
Algeria	Y	Y	Y	Y	Y	Y			Y	Y	Y	Y	Y	Y	Y	Y	Y	Y
Angola	Y	Y	Y	Y	Y	Y			Y	Y	Y	Y	Y	Y	Y	Y	Y	Y
Antigua and Barbuda	Y	A	A	Y	A	Y			Y	Y	Y	Y	Y	Y	Y	Y	Y	A
Argentina	Y	Y	Y	Y	Y	Y			Y	Y	Y	Y	Y	Y	Y	Y	Y	Y
Australia	Y	A	Y	Y	A	Y			Y	Y	N	A	A	A	Y	Y	A	A
Austria	Y	A	Y	Y	Y	Y			Y	Y	A	A	A	Y	Y	Y	A	A
Bahamas	Y	Y	Y	Y	Y	Y			Y	Y	Y	Y	Y	Y	Y	Y	Y	A
Bahrain	Y	Y	Y	Y	Y	Y			Y	Y	Y	Y	Y	Y	Y	Y	Y	Y
Bangladesh	Y	Y	Y	Y	Y	Y			Y	Y	Y	Y	Y	Y	Y	Y	Y	Y
Barbados	Y	A	A	Y	Y	Y			Y	Y	Y	Y	Y	Y	Y	Y	Y	A
Belgium	Y	A	A	Y	A	Y			Y	Y	N	A	A	A	Y	Y	N	A
Belize	NP	NP	NP	NP	NP	NP			NP	NP	NP	NP	NP	NP	NP	NP	NP	A
Benin	Y	Y	Y	Y	Y	Y			Y	Y	Y	Y	Y	Y	Y	Y	Y	Y
Bhutan	Y	Y	Y	Y	Y	Y			Y	Y	Y	Y	Y	Y	Y	Y	Y	Y
Bolivia	Y	Y	Y	Y	Y	Y			Y	Y	Y	Y	Y	Y	Y	Y	Y	A
Botswana	Y	Y	Y	Y	Y	Y			Y	Y	Y	Y	Y	Y	Y	Y	Y	Y
Brazil	Y	Y	Y	Y	Y	Y			Y	Y	Y	Y	Y	Y	Y	Y	Y	Y
Brunei Darussalam	Y	Y	Y	Y	Y	Y			Y	Y	Y	Y	Y	Y	Y	Y	Y	Y
Bulgaria	Y	Y	Y	Y	Y	Y			Y	Y	Y	Y	Y	Y	Y	Y	Y	Y
Burkina Faso (Upper Volta)	Y	Y	Y	Y	Y	Y			Y	Y	Y	Y	Y	Y	Y	Y	Y	Y
Burma	Y	Y	Y	Y	NP	Y			Y	Y	Y	Y	Y	Y	Y	Y	A	A
Burundi	Y	Y	Y	Y	Y	Y			Y	Y	Y	Y	Y	Y	Y	Y	Y	Y
Byelorussian SSR	Y	Y	Y	Y	Y	Y			Y	Y	Y	Y	Y	Y	Y	Y	Y	Y
Canada	Y	A	A	Y	A	Y			Y	Y	N	A	A	A	Y	Y	N	A
Cape Verde	Y	Y	Y	Y	Y	Y			Y	Y	Y	Y	Y	Y	Y	Y	Y	Y
Central African Republic	Y	Y	Y	Y	Y	Y			Y	Y	Y	Y	Y	Y	Y	Y	Y	Y
Chad	Y	Y	Y	Y	Y	Y			Y	Y	Y	Y	A	Y	Y	Y	Y	A
Chile	Y	NP	Y	Y	A	Y			Y	Y	Y	Y	Y	Y	Y	Y	Y	A
China	Y	Y	Y	Y	Y	Y			Y	Y	Y	Y	Y	Y	Y	Y	Y	Y
Colombia	Y	Y	Y	Y	Y	Y			Y	Y	Y	Y	Y	Y	Y	Y	Y	A
Comoros	NP	NP	Y	Y	Y	Y			Y	Y	Y	Y	Y	Y	Y	Y	Y	Y
Congo	Y	Y	Y	Y	Y	Y			Y	Y	Y	Y	Y	Y	Y	Y	Y	Y
Costa Rica	Y	A	A	A	A	Y			Y	A	A	A	A	A	A	Y	NP	A
Cuba	Y	Y	Y	Y	Y	Y			Y	Y	Y	Y	Y	Y	Y	Y	Y	Y
Cyprus	Y	Y	Y	Y	Y	Y			Y	Y	Y	Y	Y	Y	Y	Y	Y	Y
Czechoslovakia	Y	Y	Y	Y	Y	Y			Y	Y	Y	Y	Y	Y	Y	Y	Y	Y
Democratic Kampuchea	Y	Y	Y	Y	Y	Y			Y	Y	Y	Y	Y	Y	Y	Y	Y	Y
Democratic Yemen	Y	Y	Y	Y	Y	Y			Y	Y	Y	Y	Y	NP	Y	Y	Y	Y
Denmark	Y	A	A	Y	A	Y			Y	Y	N	A	A	A	Y	Y	A	A
Djibouti	Y	Y	Y	Y	Y	Y			Y	Y	Y	Y	Y	Y	Y	Y	Y	Y
Dominica	NP	NP	NP	NP	NP	NP			NP	NP	NP	NP	NP	NP	NP	NP	NP	NP
Dominican Republic	Y	A	Y	Y	A	Y			Y	Y	Y	Y	Y	Y	Y	Y	Y	A
Ecuador	Y	Y	Y	Y	Y	Y			Y	Y	Y	Y	Y	Y	Y	Y	Y	A
Egypt	Y	Y	Y	Y	Y	Y			Y	Y	Y	Y	Y	Y	Y	Y	Y	Y
El Salvador	Y	A	Y	A	A	Y			Y	Y	Y	Y	Y	A	A	Y	NP	NP
Equatorial Guinea	A	A	Y	Y	A	Y			Y	Y	Y	Y	Y	Y	Y	Y	Y	A
Ethiopia	Y	Y	Y	Y	Y	Y			Y	Y	Y	Y	Y	Y	Y	Y	Y	Y
Fiji	Y	A	Y	Y	Y	Y			Y	Y	Y	Y	A	Y	Y	Y	A	A
Finland	Y	A	Y	Y	A	Y			Y	Y	N	A	A	Y	Y	Y	A	A
France	Y	A	Y	Y	Y	Y			Y	Y	N	A	A	A	Y	Y	N	A
Gabon	Y	Y	Y	Y	Y	Y			Y	Y	Y	Y	Y	Y	Y	Y	Y	Y
Gambia	NP*	NP*	NP*	NP*	NP*	NP			NP	NP	NP	NP	NP	NP	NP	NP	Y	NP
German Democratic Republic	Y	Y	Y	Y	Y	Y			Y	Y	Y	Y	Y	Y	Y	Y	Y	Y
Germany (Federal Republic of)	Y	A	A	Y	A	Y			Y	Y	N	A	A	A	Y	Y	N	A
Ghana	Y	Y	Y	Y	Y	Y			Y	Y	Y	Y	Y	Y	Y	Y	Y	Y
Greece	Y	Y	Y	Y	Y	Y			Y	Y	Y	Y	Y	A	Y	Y	Y	Y
Grenada	Y	A	A	A	A	Y			Y	Y	Y	Y	Y	Y	Y	Y	Y	A
Guatemala	Y	Y	Y	Y	A	Y			Y	Y	Y	A	Y	A	Y	Y	A	A
Guinea	Y	Y	Y	Y	Y	Y			Y	Y	Y	Y	Y	Y	Y	Y	Y	Y
Guinea-Bissau	Y	Y	Y	Y	Y	NP*			Y	Y	Y	Y	Y	Y	Y	Y	Y	Y
Guyana	Y	Y	Y	Y	Y	Y			Y	Y	Y	Y	Y	Y	Y	Y	Y	Y
Haiti	Y	Y	NP	Y	Y	Y			Y	Y	Y	Y	Y	NP	Y	Y	Y	A
Honduras	Y	Y	Y	Y	A	Y			Y	Y	Y	Y	Y	Y	Y	Y	A	A
Hungary	Y	Y	Y	Y	Y	Y			Y	Y	Y	Y	Y	Y	Y	Y	Y	Y
Iceland	Y	A	A	Y	A	Y			Y	Y	N	A	A	A	Y	Y	A	A
India	Y	Y	Y	Y	Y	Y			Y	Y	Y	Y	Y	Y	Y	Y	Y	Y
Indonesia	Y	Y	Y	Y	Y	Y			Y	Y	Y	Y	Y	Y	Y	Y	Y	Y
Iran	Y	Y	Y	Y	Y	Y			Y	Y	Y	Y	Y	Y	Y	Y	Y	Y
Iraq	Y	Y	Y	Y	Y	Y			Y	Y	Y	Y	Y	Y	Y	Y	Y	Y
Ireland	Y	A	Y	Y	A	Y			Y	Y	N	A	A	A	Y	Y	A	A
Israel	Y	N	N	N	N	A			A	N	N	N	N	N	N	N	N	N
Italy	Y	A	Y	Y	Y	Y			Y	Y	N	A	A	A	Y	Y	N	A
Ivory Coast	A	A	A	A	A	Y			Y	Y	Y	Y‡	A	Y	A	Y	Y	A
Jamaica	Y	Y	Y	Y	Y	Y			Y	Y	Y	Y	Y	Y	Y	Y	Y	A
Japan	Y	A	Y	Y	A	Y			Y	Y	N	Y	A	A	Y	Y	A	A
Jordan	Y	Y	Y	Y	Y	Y			Y	Y	Y	Y	Y	Y	Y	Y	Y	Y
Kenya	Y	Y	Y	Y	Y	Y			Y	Y	Y	Y	Y	Y	Y	Y	Y	Y
Kuwait	Y	Y	Y	Y	Y	Y			Y	Y	Y	Y	Y	Y	Y	Y	Y	Y

* Later advised the Secretariat it had intended to vote in favour.
‡ Later advised the Secretariat it had intended to abstain.

		1986 41						
41/95	41/101	41/162 A	41/162 B	41/162 C	41/179 A	41/179 B	41/181	41/196
Y	Y	Y	Y	Y	Y	A	Y	
Y	Y	Y	Y	Y	N	N	Y	
Y	Y	Y	Y	Y	NP	NP	Y	
Y	Y	A	N	A	A	A	Y	
Y	Y	Y	A	Y	Y	Y	Y	
A	N	N	N	Y	Y	Y	Y	
Y	Y	A	A	Y	Y	Y	Y	
Y	Y	Y	Y	Y	NP	NP	Y	
Y	Y	Y	Y	Y	Y	Y	Y	
N	N	A	N	Y	Y	Y	Y	
Y	Y	A	A	Y	NP	NP	NP	
A*	Y	Y	Y	Y	NP	NP	NP	
Y	Y	Y	Y	Y	Y	Y	Y	
Y	Y	Y	A	Y	Y	Y	Y	
Y	Y	Y	A	Y	Y	Y	Y	
Y	Y	Y	Y	Y	Y	A	Y	
Y	Y	A	Y	Y	Y	Y	Y	
Y	Y	A	A	Y	Y	Y	Y	
Y	Y	Y	Y	Y	Y	A	Y	
A	N	N	N	Y	Y	Y	Y	
Y	Y	Y	Y	Y	Y	Y	Y	
Y	Y	Y	Y	Y	Y	Y	Y	
NP	NP	A	NP	Y	Y	Y	Y	ADOPTED WITHOUT A VOTE
Y	Y	A	Y	Y	Y	Y	Y	
Y	Y	Y	Y	Y	Y	Y	NP	
A	A	N	N	N	Y	Y	NP	
Y	Y	Y	Y	Y	A	A	A	
Y	Y	Y	Y	Y	Y	A	NP	
A	Y	Y	Y	Y	NP	NP	Y	
A	Y	Y	Y	Y	Y	Y	Y	
NP	NP	NP	NP	NP	NP	NP	NP	
Y	Y	A	A	Y	Y	Y	Y	
Y	Y	Y	A	Y	Y	Y	Y	
NP	N	N	A	N	NP	NP	Y	
Y	Y	N	A	Y	Y	Y	Y	
Y	A	Y	A	Y	Y	Y	Y	
Y	A	NP	NP	NP	Y	Y	Y	
A	N	A	N	Y	Y	Y	Y	
N	Y	Y	Y	Y	NP	NP	NP	
Y	Y	Y	Y	Y	Y	A	Y	
N	N	N	N	Y	Y	Y	Y	
Y	A	Y	Y	Y	Y	Y	Y	
A	Y	A	A	Y	NP	NP	Y	
Y	Y	Y	Y	Y	Y	Y	Y	
Y	Y	A	N	Y	Y	Y	Y	
Y	A	A	A	Y	Y	A	Y	
Y	N	N	N	Y	Y	Y	Y	
A	Y	Y	Y	Y	Y	Y	Y	
Y	Y	A	Y	Y	NP	NP	Y	
Y	Y	Y	Y	Y	Y	Y	Y	
Y	Y	Y	Y	Y	NP	NP	Y	
Y	Y	A	Y	Y	Y	Y	Y	
A	N	N	N	N	Y	Y	N	
N	N	N	N	N	Y	Y	Y	
Y	Y	N	A	A	Y	Y	Y	
Y	A	A	A	Y	Y	Y	Y	
Y	Y	Y	Y	Y	Y	NP*	Y	
Y	Y	Y	Y	Y	Y	Y	Y	

* Later advised the Secretariat it had intended to vote in favour.

APPENDIX B
TABLES OF VOTING IN THE GENERAL ASSEMBLY 1982-1986

Y = Yes N = No A = Abstention NP = Not Present

Year Session	1982 37																	
Res.	ES9/1	36/462	36/138 C	ES7/4	ES7/5	ES7/6	ES7/7	ES7/8	ES7/9	37/18	37/19	37/38 A	37/38 B	37/39	37/40	37/43	37/46	37/69 A
Lao People's Democratic Republic	Y	ADOPTED WITHOUT A VOTE	N	Y	Y	Y	Y	Y	Y	Y	Y	A•	A•	Y	Y	Y	Y	Y
Lebanon	Y		Y	Y	Y	Y	Y	Y	Y	NP	Y	NP*	NP*	Y	Y	NP	Y	NP
Lesotho	Y		NP	NP	Y	Y	Y	Y	Y	NP	NP	Y	Y	Y	Y	Y	Y	Y
Liberia	A		NP	A	Y	Y	Y	A	Y	Y	A	NP	NP	Y	Y	Y	Y	Y
Libyan Arab Jamahiriya	Y		NP	Y	Y	Y	Y	Y	Y	Y	Y	NP	NP	Y	Y	Y	Y	Y
Luxembourg	N		Y	N	Y	A	A	A	Y	Y	A	Y	Y	N	N	N	A	N
Madagascar	Y		Y	Y	Y	Y	Y	Y	Y	Y	Y	NP	NP	Y	Y	Y	Y	Y
Malawi	A		Y	A	NP	A	Y	A	NP	A	A	Y	Y	NP‡	NP‡	NP‡	A	A
Malaysia	Y		Y	Y	Y	Y	Y	Y	Y	Y	Y	Y	Y	Y	Y	Y	Y	Y
Maldives	Y		Y	Y	Y	Y	Y	Y	Y	Y	Y	NP	NP	Y	Y	Y	Y	Y
Mali	Y		Y	Y	Y	Y	Y	Y	Y	Y	Y	Y	Y	Y	Y	Y	Y	Y
Malta	Y		Y	Y	Y	Y	Y	Y	Y	Y	Y	Y	Y	Y	Y	Y	Y	Y
Mauritania	Y		Y	Y	Y	Y	Y	Y	Y	Y	Y	Y	Y	Y	Y	Y	Y	Y
Mauritius	NP		NP*	NP	Y	Y	Y	Y	Y	Y	Y	Y	Y	Y	Y	Y	Y	Y
Mexico	NP		Y	A	Y	Y	Y	Y	Y	Y	Y	Y	Y	Y	Y	Y	Y	Y
Mongolia	Y		N	Y	Y	Y	Y	Y	Y	Y	Y	A	N	Y	Y	Y	Y	Y
Morocco	Y		Y	Y	Y	Y	Y	Y	Y	Y	Y	Y	Y	Y	Y	Y	Y	Y
Mozambique	Y		NP	Y	Y	Y	Y	Y	Y	Y	Y	NP	NP	Y	Y	Y	Y	Y
Nepal	Y		Y	Y	Y	Y	Y	Y	Y	Y	Y	Y	Y	Y	Y	Y	Y	Y
Netherlands	N		Y	N	Y	A	A	A	Y	Y	A	Y	Y	N	N	N	Y	N
New Zealand	N		Y	N	Y	A	A	A	Y	Y	A	Y	Y	A	N	N	A	N
Nicaragua	Y		NP	Y	Y	Y	Y	Y	Y	Y	Y	NP	NP	Y	Y	Y	Y	Y
Niger	Y		Y	Y	Y	Y	Y	Y	Y	Y	Y	Y	Y	Y	Y	Y	Y	Y
Nigeria	Y		NP	Y	NP	Y	Y	Y	Y	Y	Y	Y	Y	Y	Y	Y	Y	Y
Norway	N		Y	N	Y	A	A	A	Y	Y	A	Y	Y	A	N	N	A	N
Oman	Y		Y	Y	Y	Y	Y	Y	Y	Y	Y	Y	Y	Y	Y	Y	Y	Y
Pakistan	Y		Y	Y	Y	Y	Y	Y	Y	Y	Y	Y	Y	Y	Y	Y	Y	Y
Panama	A		Y	A	Y	Y	Y	Y	Y	Y	Y	NP	NP	Y	Y	Y	Y	Y
Papua New Guinea	A		NP	A	NP	NP	NP	NP	Y	Y	Y	NP	NP	Y	Y	Y	Y	Y
Paraguay	A		Y	A	Y	Y	Y	A	Y	A	A	Y	Y	NP	A	NP	NP	NP
Peru	Y		Y	A	Y	Y	Y	Y	Y	Y	Y	Y	Y	Y	Y	Y	Y	Y
Philippines	★		Y	A	Y	Y	Y	Y	Y	Y	Y	Y	Y	Y	Y	Y	Y	Y
Poland	Y		N	Y	Y	Y	Y	Y	Y	Y	Y	Y	A	Y	Y	Y	Y	Y
Portugal	N		Y	N	Y	A	A	A	Y	Y	A	Y	Y	A	A	A	Y	N
Qatar	Y		Y	Y	Y	Y	Y	Y	Y	Y	Y	Y	Y	Y	Y	Y	Y	Y
Romania	★		Y	Y	Y	Y	Y	Y	Y	Y	Y	Y	A	Y	Y	Y	Y	Y
Rwanda	Y		Y	Y	NP*	Y	Y	Y	Y	NP	NP	Y	Y	Y	Y	Y	Y	Y
Saint Christopher and Nevis																		
Saint Lucia	A		Y	NP	NP	NP	NP	NP	Y	NP	Y	NP	NP	Y	Y	Y	Y	NP
Saint Vincent	A		NP	NP	NP	NP	NP	NP	NP	NP	NP	NP	NP	NP	NP	NP	NP	NP
Samoa	A		Y	A	NP*	Y	Y	A	Y	NP	Y	Y	Y	Y	Y	Y	Y	NP*
Sao Tome and Principe	Y		NP	Y	Y	Y	Y	Y	Y	Y	Y	NP	NP	Y	Y	Y	Y	Y
Saudi Arabia	Y		Y	Y	Y	Y	Y	Y	Y	Y	Y	NP	NP	Y	Y	Y	Y	Y
Senegal	Y		Y	Y	Y	Y	Y	Y	Y	Y	Y	Y	Y	Y	Y	Y	Y	Y
Seychelles	Y		NP	Y	Y	Y	Y	Y	Y	Y	NP	NP	NP	NP	NP	NP	NP	NP*
Sierra Leone	Y		Y	Y	Y	Y	Y	Y	Y	NP	Y	NP*	Y	Y	Y	Y	Y	Y
Singapore	A		Y	A	Y	Y	Y	Y	Y	Y	Y	Y	Y	Y	Y	Y	Y	A
Solomon Islands	NP		NP	NP	NP	NP	NP	NP	Y	NP	Y	Y	Y	Y	Y	Y	Y	Y
Somalia	Y		NP	Y	Y	Y	Y	Y	Y	Y	Y	Y	Y	Y	Y	Y	Y	Y
Spain	A		Y	A	Y	Y	Y	Y	Y	Y	A	Y	Y	A	A	A	Y	A
Sri Lanka	Y		NP	Y	Y	Y	Y	Y	Y	Y	Y	Y	Y	Y	Y	Y	Y	Y
Sudan	Y		NP	Y	Y	Y	Y	Y	Y	Y	Y	Y	Y	Y	Y	Y	Y	Y
Suriname	Y		NP	Y	Y	NP	NP	NP	Y	Y	Y	NP	NP	Y	Y	Y	Y	Y
Swaziland	A		NP	A	NP	Y	Y	A	Y	Y	NP	NP	Y	Y	Y	Y	Y	Y
Sweden	N		Y	N	Y	A	A	A	Y	Y	A	Y	Y	A	N	N	A	A
Syrian Arab Republic	Y		N	Y	Y	Y	Y	Y	Y	Y	Y	N	N	Y	Y	Y	Y	Y
Thailand	A		Y	A	Y	Y	Y	Y	Y	Y	Y	Y	Y	Y	Y	Y	Y	Y
Togo	Y		Y	Y	Y	Y	Y	NP	Y	Y	Y	Y	Y	Y	Y	Y	Y	Y
Trinidad and Tobago	A		Y	Y	Y	Y	Y	Y	Y	Y	Y	Y	Y	Y	Y	Y	Y	Y
Tunisia	Y		Y	Y	Y	Y	Y	Y	Y	Y	Y	Y	Y	Y	Y	Y	Y	Y
Turkey	A		Y	Y	Y	Y	Y	Y	Y	Y	A	Y	Y	Y	Y	Y	Y	Y
Uganda	Y		NP	Y	Y	Y	Y	Y	Y	Y	Y	NP	NP	Y	Y	Y	Y	Y
Ukrainian SSR	Y		N	Y	Y	Y	Y	Y	Y	Y	Y	A	N	Y	Y	Y	Y	Y
USSR	Y		N	Y	Y	Y	Y	Y	Y	Y	Y	A	N	Y	Y	Y	Y	Y
United Arab Emirates	Y		Y	Y	Y	Y	Y	Y	Y	NP*	Y	Y	Y	Y	Y	Y	Y	Y
United Kingdom	N		Y	N	Y	A	A	A	Y	Y	A	Y	Y	N	N	N	A	N
United Republic of Cameroon	Y		Y	Y	Y	Y	Y	Y	Y	Y	Y	Y	Y	NP	NP	NP	Y	Y
United Republic of Tanzania	Y		Y	Y	Y	Y	Y	Y	Y	Y	Y	Y	Y	Y	Y	Y	Y	Y
United States	N		Y	N	N	N	N	N	N	N	N	Y	Y	N	N	N	N	N
Uruguay	A		Y	A	Y	Y	Y	A	Y	Y	Y	Y	Y	Y	Y	Y	Y	Y
Vanuatu	NP		NP	NP	NP	NP	NP	NP	Y	NP	Y	NP	NP	Y	Y	Y	Y	Y
Venezuela	A		Y	A	Y	Y	Y	Y	Y	Y	Y	Y	Y	Y	Y	Y	Y	Y
Viet Nam	Y		N	Y	Y	Y	Y	Y	Y	Y	Y	A	A	Y	Y	Y	Y	Y
Yemen	Y		NP	Y	Y	Y	Y	Y	Y	Y	Y	A	A	Y	Y	Y	Y	Y
Yugoslavia	Y		Y	Y	Y	Y	Y	Y	Y	Y	Y	Y	Y	Y	Y	Y	Y	Y
Zaire	A		Y	A	Y	Y	Y	A	Y	NP	NP	Y	Y	Y	Y	Y	Y	Y
Zambia	Y		Y	Y	Y	Y	Y	Y	Y	Y	Y	Y	Y	Y	Y	Y	Y	Y
Zimbabwe	Y		NP	Y	NP	Y	Y	Y	Y	NP	NP	NP	NP	Y	Y	Y	Y	Y

★Did not participate in the vote
• Later announced it was not participating in the vote or had intended not to participate in the vote.
* Later advised the Secretariat it had intended to vote in favour.
‡ Later advised the Secretariat it had intended to abstain.

1982
37

37/69 C	37/69 D	37/69 F	37/75	37/82	37/86 A	37/86 B	37/86 C	37/86 D	37/86 E	37/88 A	37/88 B	37/88 C	37/88 D	37/88 E	37/88 F	37/88 G	37/104	37/120 A	37/120 B	37/120 C	37/120 D	37/120 E
Y	Y	Y		Y	Y	Y	Y	Y	★	Y	Y	Y	Y	Y	Y	Y				Y	Y	Y
Y	Y	Y		Y	Y	Y	Y	Y		Y	Y	Y	Y	Y	Y	Y				Y	NP	Y
Y	Y	Y		Y	Y	Y	Y	Y	Y	NP	NP	NP	NP	NP	NP	Y				Y	Y	Y
Y	Y	Y		NP	Y	Y	Y	Y	NP	NP	NP	NP	NP	NP	NP	NP				NP	NP	NP
A	A	N		Y	A	A	A	A	A	Y	Y	A	Y	Y	A	Y				Y	Y	Y
A	A	N		Y	A	A	A	Y	A	Y	Y	A	Y	Y	A	A				Y	Y	Y
Y	Y	Y		Y	Y	Y	Y	A	Y	NP	NP	NP	NP	NP	NP	Y				Y	Y	Y
Y	Y	Y		Y	Y	Y	Y	Y	Y	Y	Y	A	Y	Y	A	Y				Y	Y	Y
N	N	N		A	A	A	A	A	A	Y	Y	A	Y	Y	A	N				Y	Y	Y
NP	NP	NP		Y	Y	Y	Y	Y	NP	NP	NP	NP	NP	NP	NP	NP				Y	Y	Y
Y	Y	Y		Y	Y	Y	Y	Y	Y	Y	Y	Y	Y	Y	Y	Y				Y	Y	Y
Y	Y	Y		Y	NP*	NP*	NP*	NP*	Y	Y	Y	Y	Y	Y	Y	Y				Y	Y	Y
A	Y	Y		Y	NP	NP	NP	NP	Y	Y	Y	Y	Y	Y	Y	NP				Y	Y	Y
Y	Y	Y		Y	Y	Y	Y	Y	Y	Y	Y	Y	Y	Y	Y	Y				Y	Y	Y
Y	Y	Y		Y	Y	Y	Y	Y	Y	Y	Y	Y	Y	Y	Y	Y				Y	Y	Y
Y	Y	Y		Y	Y	Y	Y	Y	Y	Y	Y	Y	Y	Y	Y	Y				Y	Y	Y
Y	Y	A		A	A	Y	Y	Y	A	Y	Y	Y	Y	Y	Y	A				Y	Y	Y
Y	Y	Y		Y	Y	Y	Y	Y	Y	Y	Y	Y	Y	Y	Y	Y				Y	Y	Y
N	N	N		A	A	N	A	A	Y	Y	Y	A	Y	Y	Y	N				NP	NP	Y
Y	Y	Y		Y	Y	Y	Y	Y	Y	NP	NP	NP	NP	NP	NP	NP				Y	Y	Y
Y	Y	Y		Y	Y	Y	Y	Y	Y	Y	Y	Y	Y	Y	Y	Y				Y	Y	Y
NP	Y	A		A	Y	Y	Y	Y	Y	Y	Y	NP	Y	Y	A	Y				Y	Y	Y
Y	Y	Y		Y	Y	Y	Y	Y	Y	Y	Y	Y	Y	Y	Y	Y				Y	Y	Y
Y	Y	Y		A	Y	Y	Y	Y	Y	Y	Y	Y	NP*	Y	Y	Y				Y	Y	Y
Y	Y	Y		Y	Y	Y	Y	Y	Y	Y	Y	Y	Y	Y	Y	Y				Y	Y	Y
Y	Y	Y		Y	Y	Y	Y	Y	Y	Y	Y	Y	Y	Y	Y	Y				Y	Y	Y
Y	Y	Y		NP	A	A	A	N	NP	Y	Y	A	Y	Y	A	NP				Y	Y	Y
Y	Y	Y		Y	Y	Y	Y	Y	Y	Y	Y	Y	Y	Y	Y	Y				Y	Y	Y
Y	Y	Y		Y	Y	Y	Y	Y	Y	Y	Y	Y	Y	Y	Y	Y				Y	Y	Y
A	A	N		A	A	A	A	A	A	Y	Y	A	Y	Y	A	A				Y	Y	Y
Y	A	Y		NP	NP	NP	NP	NP	Y	Y	Y	Y	Y	Y	Y	NP				NP	NP	NP
Y	Y	Y		Y	Y	Y	Y	Y	Y	Y	Y	Y	Y	Y	Y	Y				Y	Y	Y
NP	NP	NP		NP	NP	NP	NP	NP	NP	Y	Y	A	Y	Y	A	NP				NP	NP	NP
Y	Y	Y		Y	Y	Y	Y	A	Y	Y	Y	Y	Y	Y	Y	Y				Y	Y	Y
NP	NP	NP		NP	Y	Y	Y	Y	Y	Y	Y	Y	Y	Y	Y	NP				NP	NP	NP
Y	Y	NP		NP	Y	Y	Y	Y	Y	NP	NP	NP	NP	NP	NP	NP				Y	Y	Y
Y	Y	Y		A	Y	Y	Y	Y	Y	Y	Y	Y	Y	Y	Y	A				Y	Y	Y
A	A	N		A	A	A	A	A	A	Y	Y	A	Y	Y	A	N				Y	Y	Y
Y	Y	Y		NP	Y	Y	Y	Y	Y	Y	Y	Y	Y	Y	Y	Y				Y	Y	Y
Y	Y	Y		Y	Y	Y	Y	Y	NP	Y	Y	Y	Y	Y	Y	N				Y	Y	Y
N	A	Y		A	A	A	A	A	A	Y	Y	A	Y	Y	A	Y				Y	Y	Y
A	A	Y		Y	Y	Y	Y	Y	Y	Y	Y	Y	Y	Y	Y	Y				Y	Y	Y
Y	Y	Y		Y	NP	NP	NP	NP	Y	NP	NP	NP	NP	NP	NP	Y				Y	Y	NP
NP	NP	NP		A	NP	NP	NP	NP	A	NP	NP	NP	NP	NP	NP	A				Y	Y	Y
Y	Y	Y		Y	Y	Y	Y	A	Y	NP	NP	NP	NP	NP	NP	NP				Y	Y	Y
Y	Y	Y		Y	Y	Y	Y	Y	Y	Y	Y	Y	Y	Y	Y	NP				Y	Y	Y
Y	Y	Y		A	Y	Y	Y	Y	Y	Y	Y	Y	Y	Y	Y	NP				NP	NP	NP
NP	NP	NP		NP	Y	Y	Y	Y	NP	Y	Y	Y	Y	Y	Y	NP				Y	Y	Y
Y	A	N		Y	A	A	A	A	A	Y	Y	A	Y	Y	A	A				Y	Y	Y
Y	Y	Y		Y	Y	Y	Y	Y	Y	Y	Y	Y	Y	Y	Y	Y				Y	Y	Y
Y	Y	Y		Y	Y	Y	Y	Y	Y	Y	Y	Y	Y	Y	Y	Y				Y	Y	Y
A	A	N		A	A	A	A	A	A	Y	Y	A	Y	Y	A	A				Y	Y	Y
★	A	★		A	N	N	N	N	N	N	N	N	N	N	N	N				N	A	N
A	A	N		A	A	Y	Y	NP	Y	NP	NP	NP	NP	NP	NP	Y				Y	Y	Y
Y	A	Y		A	A	A	A	A	A	Y	Y	A	Y	Y	A	A				Y	Y	Y
N	Y	Y		Y	Y	Y	Y	Y	Y	Y	Y	Y	Y	Y	Y	Y				Y	Y	Y
Y	Y	Y		Y	Y	Y	Y	Y	Y	Y	Y	Y	Y	Y	Y	Y				Y	Y	Y

(Columns 37/75, 37/104, 37/120 A and 37/120 B: ADOPTED WITHOUT A VOTE)

★Did not participate in the vote.
* Later advised the Secretariat it had intended to vote in favour.

APPENDIX B
TABLES OF VOTING IN THE GENERAL ASSEMBLY 1982-1986

Y = Yes   N = No   A = Abstention   NP = Not Present

Year Session Res.	37/120 F	37/120 G	37/120 H	37/120 I	37/120 J	37/120 K	37/122	37/123 A	37/123 B	37/123 C	37/123 D	37/123 E	37/123 F	37/127 A	37/127 B	37/134	37/135	37/163
Lao People's Democratic Republic	Y	Y	Y	Y	Y	Y	Y	Y	Y	Y	Y	Y	Y	NP	NP	Y	Y	
Lebanon	Y	Y	Y	N	Y	Y	Y	Y	Y	Y	NP	Y	Y	Y	Y	Y	Y	
Lesotho	NP	Y	Y	Y	Y	Y	NP	Y	Y	Y	Y	Y	Y	Y	Y	Y	Y	
Liberia	Y	Y	Y	Y	Y	Y	Y	Y	Y	Y	Y	Y	Y	Y	Y	Y	Y	
Libyan Arab Jamahiriya	Y	Y	Y	Y	Y	Y	Y	Y	Y	Y	Y	Y	Y	NP	NP	Y	Y	
Luxembourg	N	A	A	N	A	Y	Y	N	Y	Y	A	Y	N	Y	Y	Y	A	
Madagascar	Y	Y	Y	Y	Y	Y	Y	Y	Y	Y	Y	Y	Y	Y	Y	Y	Y	
Malawi	Y	A	Y	A	Y	Y	A	A	A	A	Y	Y	A	Y	Y	Y	Y	
Malaysia	Y	Y	Y	Y	Y	Y	Y	Y	Y	Y	Y	Y	Y	Y	Y	Y	Y	
Maldives	Y	Y	Y	Y	Y	Y	Y	Y	Y	Y	Y	Y	Y	A	A	Y	Y	
Mali	Y	Y	Y	Y	Y	Y	Y	Y	Y	Y	Y	Y	Y	Y	Y	Y	Y	
Malta	Y	Y	Y	Y	Y	Y	Y	Y	Y	Y	Y	Y	Y	Y	Y	Y	Y	
Mauritania	Y	Y	Y	Y	Y	Y	Y	Y	Y	Y	Y	Y	Y	Y	Y	Y	Y	
Mauritius	Y	Y	Y	Y	Y	Y	Y	Y	Y	Y	Y	Y	Y	Y	Y	Y	Y	
Mexico	Y	Y	Y	Y	Y	Y	Y	Y	Y	Y	Y	Y	Y	Y	Y	Y	Y	
Mongolia	Y	Y	Y	Y	Y	Y	Y	Y	Y	Y	Y	Y	Y	N	N	Y	Y	
Morocco	Y	Y	Y	Y	Y	Y	Y	Y	Y	Y	Y	Y	Y	Y	Y	Y	Y	
Mozambique	Y	Y	Y	Y	Y	Y	Y	Y	Y	Y	Y	Y	Y	NP	NP	Y	Y	
Nepal	Y	Y	Y	Y	Y	Y	Y	Y	Y	Y	Y	Y	Y	Y	Y	Y	Y	
Netherlands	N	A	A	N	A	Y	Y	N	Y	Y	A	Y	N	Y	Y	Y	A	
New Zealand	A	A	A	A	Y	Y	Y	N	Y	Y	A	Y	N	Y	Y	Y	A	
Nicaragua	Y	Y	Y	Y	Y	Y	Y	Y	Y	Y	Y	Y	Y	Y	Y	Y	Y	
Niger	NP	NP	NP	NP	NP	NP	NP	NP	NP	NP	NP	NP	Y	Y	Y	Y	Y	
Nigeria	Y	Y	Y	Y	Y	Y	Y	Y	Y	Y	Y	Y	Y	NP	NP	Y	Y	
Norway	A	A	A	N	A	Y	Y	N	Y	Y	A	Y	N	Y	Y	Y	A	
Oman	Y	Y	Y	Y	Y	Y	Y	Y	Y	Y	Y	Y	Y	Y	Y	Y	Y	
Pakistan	Y	Y	Y	Y	Y	Y	Y	Y	Y	Y	Y	Y	Y	Y	Y	Y	Y	
Panama	Y	Y	Y	Y	Y	Y	Y	A	Y	Y	Y	Y	Y	Y	Y	Y	Y	
Papua New Guinea	Y	Y	A	A	Y	Y	Y	A	A	NP	A	Y	Y	Y	Y	Y	Y	
Paraguay	Y	Y	Y	A	A	Y	Y	A	Y	Y	Y	Y	Y	Y	Y	Y	Y	
Peru	Y	Y	Y	Y	Y	Y	Y	A	Y	Y	Y	Y	Y	Y	Y	Y	Y	
Philippines	Y	Y	Y	A	Y	Y	Y	A	Y	Y	Y	Y	Y	N	N	Y	Y	
Poland	Y	Y	Y	Y	Y	Y	Y	Y	Y	Y	Y	Y	Y	N	N	Y	Y	
Portugal	A	Y	Y	A	A	Y	Y	N	Y	Y	A	Y	N	Y	Y	Y	Y	
Qatar	Y	Y	Y	Y	Y	Y	Y	Y	Y	Y	Y	Y	Y	Y	Y	Y	Y	
Romania	Y	Y	Y	Y	Y	Y	Y	NP	Y	Y	Y	Y	Y	Y	A	Y	Y	
Rwanda	Y	Y	Y	Y	Y	Y	Y	Y	Y	Y	Y	Y	Y	Y	Y	Y	Y	
Saint Christopher and Nevis																		
Saint Lucia	NP	NP	NP	NP	NP	NP	NP	NP	NP	NP	NP	NP	NP	NP	NP	NP	NP	
Saint Vincent	NP	NP	NP	NP	NP	NP	NP	NP	NP	NP	NP	NP	NP	NP	NP	NP	NP	
Samoa	Y	Y	A*	NP	Y	Y	Y	A	Y	Y	Y	Y	Y	Y	Y	Y	Y	
Sao Tome and Principe	Y	Y	Y	Y	Y	Y	Y	Y	Y	Y	Y	Y	Y	A	A	Y	Y	
Saudi Arabia	Y	Y	Y	Y	Y	Y	Y	Y	Y	Y	Y	Y	Y	A	Y	Y	Y	
Senegal	Y	Y	Y	Y	Y	Y	Y	Y	Y	Y	Y	Y	Y	Y	Y	Y	Y	
Seychelles	Y	Y	Y	Y	Y	Y	Y	Y	Y	Y	Y	Y	Y	NP	NP	NP	NP	
Sierra Leone	Y	Y	Y	Y	Y	Y	Y	Y	Y	Y	Y	Y	Y	Y	Y	Y	Y	
Singapore	NP	Y	Y	NP	NP	Y	Y	A	Y	Y	Y	Y	Y	Y	Y	Y	Y	
Solomon Islands	NP	NP	NP	NP	NP	NP	NP	NP	NP	NP	NP	NP	Y	Y	Y	Y	Y	
Somalia	Y	Y	Y	Y	Y	Y	Y	Y	Y	Y	Y	Y	Y	Y	Y	Y	Y	
Spain	A	Y	Y	A	Y	Y	Y	A	Y	Y	Y	Y	Y	Y	Y	Y	Y	
Sri Lanka	Y	Y	Y	Y	Y	Y	Y	Y	Y	Y	Y	Y	Y	Y	Y	Y	Y	
Sudan	Y	Y	Y	Y	Y	Y	Y	Y	Y	Y	Y	Y	Y	Y	Y	NP*	NP*	
Suriname	Y	Y	Y	Y	Y	Y	Y	Y	Y	Y	Y	Y	Y	Y	Y	Y	Y	
Swaziland	NP	NP	NP	NP	NP	NP	NP	NP	NP	NP	NP	NP	Y	Y	Y	Y	Y	
Sweden	A	A	A	A	Y	Y	Y	N	Y	Y	A	Y	A	Y	Y	Y	A	
Syrian Arab Republic	Y	Y	Y	Y	Y	Y	Y	Y	Y	Y	Y	Y	Y	N	N	NP*	NP*	
Thailand	Y	Y	Y	Y	Y	Y	Y	A	Y	Y	Y	Y	Y	Y	Y	Y	Y	
Togo	Y	Y	Y	Y	Y	Y	Y	Y	Y	Y	Y	Y	Y	Y	Y	Y	Y	
Trinidad and Tobago	Y	Y	Y	Y	Y	Y	Y	A	Y	Y	Y	Y	Y	Y	Y	Y	Y	
Tunisia	Y	Y	Y	Y	Y	Y	Y	Y	Y	Y	Y	Y	Y	Y	Y	Y	Y	
Turkey	Y	Y	Y	Y	Y	Y	Y	Y	Y	Y	Y	Y	Y	Y	Y	Y	Y	
Uganda	Y	Y	Y	Y	Y	Y	Y	Y	Y	Y	Y	Y	Y	Y	Y	Y	Y	
Ukrainian SSR	Y	Y	Y	Y	Y	Y	Y	Y	Y	Y	Y	Y	Y	N	N	Y	Y	
USSR	Y	Y	Y	Y	Y	Y	Y	Y	Y	Y	Y	Y	Y	N	N	Y	Y	
United Arab Emirates	Y	Y	Y	Y	Y	Y	Y	Y	Y	Y	Y	Y	Y	Y	Y	Y	Y	
United Kingdom	N	A	A	N	A	Y	Y	N	Y	Y	A	Y	N	Y	Y	Y	A	
United Republic of Cameroon	Y	Y	Y	Y	Y	Y	Y	Y	Y	Y	Y	Y	Y	Y	Y	Y	Y	
United Republic of Tanzania	Y	Y	Y	Y	Y	Y	Y	Y	Y	Y	Y	Y	Y	Y	Y	Y	Y	
United States	N	N	N	N	N	Y	N	N	A	A	A	Y	N	Y	Y	N	N	
Uruguay	Y	Y	Y	A	Y	Y	Y	A	Y	Y	Y	Y	A	Y	A	Y	Y	
Vanuatu	Y	Y	Y	Y	Y	Y	Y	NP	NP*	Y	Y	Y	Y	NP	NP	NP	Y	
Venezuela	Y	Y	Y	Y	Y	Y	Y	A	Y	Y	Y	Y	Y	Y	Y	Y	Y	
Viet Nam	Y	Y	Y	Y	Y	Y	Y	Y	Y	Y	Y	Y	Y	N	N	Y	Y	
Yemen	Y	Y	Y	Y	Y	Y	Y	Y	Y	Y	Y	Y	Y	A	A	Y	Y	
Yugoslavia	Y	Y	Y	Y	Y	Y	Y	Y	Y	Y	Y	Y	Y	Y	Y	Y	Y	
Zaire	Y	Y	A	A	Y	Y	Y	A	Y	Y	Y	Y	A	Y	Y	Y	Y	
Zambia	Y	Y	Y	Y	Y	Y	Y	Y	Y	Y	Y	Y	Y	Y	Y	Y	Y	
Zimbabwe	Y	Y	Y	NP	NP	NP	NP	NP	NP	NP	NP	NP	Y	Y	Y	Y	Y	

Column 37/163: ADOPTED WITHOUT A VOTE

* Later advised the Secretariat it had intended to vote in favour.

1982 37/222	38/9	38/17	38/35 A	38/35 B	38/36 A	38/36 D	38/38 A+	38/38 B+	38/39 A	38/39 F	38/39 G	38/58 A	38/58 B	38/58 C	38/58 D	38/58 E	38/64	38/69	38/79 A	38/79 B	38/79 C	38/79 D
Y	Y	Y	NP	NP	Y	Y	NP	NP	Y	Y	Y	Y	Y	Y	Y	Y		Y	Y	Y	Y	Y
Y	Y	Y	Y	Y	Y	Y	Y	Y	Y	Y	Y	Y	Y	Y	Y	Y		Y	Y	Y	Y	Y
Y	Y	Y	NP	NP	NP‡	NP*	Y	Y	Y	Y	Y	Y	Y	Y	Y	Y		NP	A	Y	Y	Y
Y	NP	NP	Y	Y	NP	NP	NP	NP	NP	Y	Y	NP	Y	NP	Y	NP		A	A	Y	Y	Y
Y	Y	Y	★	★	Y	Y	★	★	Y	Y	Y	Y	Y	Y	Y	Y		A	Y	Y	Y	Y
Y	Y	N	Y	Y	A	A	NP	NP	N	N	A	A	A	A	Y	A		A	Y	Y	Y	A
Y	A	NP‡	Y	Y	Y	Y	NP*	NP*	A	A	A	Y	Y	Y	Y	Y		A	A	Y	Y	A
Y	Y	Y	NP	NP	Y	Y	A	A	Y	Y	Y	Y	Y	Y	Y	Y		Y	Y	Y	Y	Y
Y	Y	Y	Y	Y	Y	Y	Y	Y	Y	Y	Y	Y	Y	Y	Y	Y		Y	Y	Y	Y	Y
Y	Y	Y	Y	Y	Y	Y	Y	Y	Y	Y	Y	Y	Y	Y	Y	Y		NP	Y	Y	Y	Y
Y	Y	Y	Y	Y	Y	Y	NP	NP	Y	Y	Y	Y	Y	Y	Y	Y		Y	Y	Y	Y	Y
Y	Y	Y	A	N	Y	Y	N	N	Y	Y	Y	Y	Y	Y	Y	Y		Y	Y	Y	Y	Y
Y	Y	Y	NP	NP	Y	Y	NP*	NP*	Y	Y	Y	Y	Y	Y	Y	Y		Y	Y	Y	Y	Y
Y	Y	Y	NP	NP	Y	Y	NP	NP	Y	Y	Y	Y	Y	Y	Y	Y		A	A	Y	Y	Y
Y	Y	N	Y	Y	A	A	Y	Y	N	N	A	A	A	A	Y	A		A	Y	Y	Y	A
Y	Y	Y	NP	Y	Y	Y	Y	Y	Y	Y	Y	Y	Y	Y	Y	Y		Y	Y	Y	Y	Y
Y	Y	NP*	Y	Y	Y	Y	NP	NP	Y	Y	Y	Y	Y	Y	Y	Y		Y	Y	Y	Y	Y
Y	NP	Y	Y	Y	Y	Y	Y	Y	Y	Y	Y	Y	Y	Y	Y	Y		Y	Y	Y	Y	Y
Y	Y	N	Y	Y	A	A	Y	Y	N	N	A	A	A	A	Y	A		A	A	Y	Y	A
Y	Y	Y	Y	Y	Y	Y	Y	Y	Y	Y	Y	Y	Y	Y	Y	Y		A	A	Y	Y	Y
Y	Y	Y	Y	Y	Y	Y	Y	Y	Y	Y	A	Y	Y	Y	Y	Y		A	A	Y	Y	Y
Y	A	Y•	NP	NP	NP	NP	NP	NP	N	A	N	Y	Y	Y	Y	Y		A	A	Y	Y	A
Y	Y	Y	Y	Y	Y	Y	NP	NP	Y	Y	Y	Y	Y	Y	Y	Y		A	A	Y	Y	Y
Y	Y	Y	Y	Y	A	Y	N	N	Y	Y	Y	Y	Y	Y	Y	Y		A	NP	Y	Y	Y
Y	Y	A	Y	Y	A	A	Y	Y	N	A	N	Y	Y	Y	Y	Y		A	Y	Y	Y	Y
Y	Y	Y	Y	A	Y	Y	NP*	NP*	Y	Y	Y	Y	Y	Y	Y	Y		Y	Y	Y	Y	Y
Y	Y	Y	Y	Y	Y	Y	NP	NP	Y	Y	Y	Y	Y	Y	Y	Y		Y	Y	Y	Y	Y
	NP	NP	NP	NP	NP	NP	NP	NP	NP	NP	NP	NP	NP	NP	NP	NP		NP	NP	NP	NP	NP
	NP	Y	Y	Y	A	Y	Y	Y	Y	Y	NP	NP	NP	NP	NP	NP		NP	NP	Y	Y	NP
Y	NP	NP	NP	NP	Y	Y	NP	NP	Y	NP	Y	NP	NP	NP	NP	NP		NP	NP	NP	NP	NP
Y	Y	Y	NP	NP	A	NP	Y	Y	Y	A	Y	Y	Y	Y	Y	Y		Y	Y	Y	Y	Y
Y	Y	Y	Y	Y	Y	Y	Y	Y	Y	Y	Y	Y	Y	Y	Y	Y		Y	Y	Y	Y	Y
NP	NP*	NP	NP	NP	Y	Y	NP	NP	Y	Y	Y	Y	Y	Y	Y	Y		Y	Y	Y	Y	Y
Y	Y	NP	NP	NP	Y	Y	NP	NP	Y	Y	Y	Y	Y	Y	Y	Y		Y	Y	Y	Y	Y
Y	Y	Y	Y	Y	Y	Y	Y	Y	Y	Y	Y	Y	Y	Y	Y	Y		NP	NP	Y	Y	Y
NP	Y	NP	Y	Y	Y	Y	NP*	NP*	Y	A	Y	Y	Y	A	Y	A		NP	Y	Y	Y	NP
Y	Y	Y	Y	Y	NP*	NP*	Y	Y	A	A	A	Y	Y	Y	Y	Y		Y	Y	Y	Y	Y
Y	Y	A	Y	Y	A	A	Y	Y	A	A	A	Y	Y	Y	Y	Y		Y	Y	Y	Y	Y
Y	Y	Y	Y	Y	Y	Y	NP	NP	Y	Y	Y	Y	Y	Y	Y	Y		Y	Y	Y	Y	Y
Y	NP	Y	Y	Y	Y	Y	Y	Y	Y	NP	Y	Y	Y	Y	Y	Y		Y	A	Y	Y	Y
Y	NP	Y	NP	NP	Y	Y	Y	Y	NP	NP	Y	NP	NP	NP	NP	NP		A	A	Y	Y	A
Y	Y	N	N	N	Y	Y	N	N	Y	Y	Y	Y	Y	Y	Y	Y		A	A	Y	Y	Y
Y	Y	Y	Y	Y	Y	Y	NP*	NP*	Y	Y	Y	Y	Y	Y	Y	Y		Y	NP	Y	Y	Y
Y	Y	Y	Y	Y	Y	Y	Y	Y	Y	NP	Y	Y	Y	Y	Y	Y		Y	A	Y	Y	Y
Y	Y	Y	Y	Y	Y	Y	Y	Y	Y	Y	Y	Y	Y	Y	Y	Y		Y	Y	Y	Y	Y
Y	Y	Y	A	N	Y	Y	N	N	Y	Y	Y	Y	Y	Y	Y	Y		Y	Y	Y	Y	Y
Y	Y	Y	A	N	Y	Y	N	N	Y	Y	Y	Y	Y	Y	Y	Y		Y	Y	Y	Y	Y
Y	N	Y	Y	Y	Y	Y	N	N	N	N	N	A	A	A	Y	A		A	Y	Y	Y	Y
Y	Y	Y	Y	Y	Y	Y	Y	Y	Y	Y	Y	Y	Y	Y	Y	Y		Y	Y	Y	Y	Y
N	Y	Y	Y	Y	A	A	N	N	Y‡	Y	N	N	N	N	N	N		N	N	A	A	N
Y	NP	NP	Y	Y	Y	Y	NP	NP	Y	Y	Y	Y	Y	Y	Y	Y		Y	Y	Y	Y	Y
Y	Y	Y	NP	NP	Y	Y	NP†	NP†	Y	Y	Y	Y	Y	Y	Y	Y		Y	Y	Y	Y	Y
Y	Y	Y	A	A	Y	Y	A	A	Y	Y	Y	Y	Y	Y	Y	Y		Y	Y	Y	Y	Y
Y	NP	NP	Y	Y	Y	Y	NP*	NP*	Y	NP	Y	Y	Y	NP	Y	NP		A	A	Y	Y	A
Y	Y	NP	Y	Y	Y	Y	NP	NP	Y	Y	Y	Y	Y	Y	Y	Y		Y	Y	Y	Y	Y

38/64 column: ADOPTED WITHOUT A VOTE

★ Did not participate in the vote.
† Later advised the Secretariat it had intended to vote against.
* Later advised the Secretariat it had intended to vote in favour.
‡ Later advised the Secretariat it had intended to abstain.
+ Adopted together.

363

APPENDIX B
TABLES OF VOTING IN THE GENERAL ASSEMBLY 1982-1986

Y = Yes   N = No   A = Abstention   NP = Not Present

Year: 1983 — Session: 38

Columns 38/83 B, 38/83 C and 38/130 were ADOPTED WITHOUT A VOTE.

Res.	38/79 E	38/79 F	38/79 G	38/79 H	38/83 A	38/83 B	38/83 C	38/83 D	38/83 E	38/83 F	38/83 G	38/83 H	38/83 I	38/83 J	38/83 K	38/85	38/130	38/144
Lao People's Democratic Republic	Y	Y	Y	Y	Y			Y	Y	Y	Y	Y	Y	Y	Y	Y		Y
Lebanon	Y	Y	Y	Y	Y			Y	Y	Y	Y	Y	NP	Y	Y	Y		Y
Lesotho	Y	Y	Y	Y	Y			Y	Y	Y	Y	A	Y	Y	Y	Y		Y
Liberia	Y	Y	A	Y	Y			Y	Y	Y	Y	A	Y	Y	Y	Y		Y
Libyan Arab Jamahiriya	Y	Y	Y	Y	Y			Y	Y	Y	Y	A	Y	Y	Y	Y		A
Luxembourg	Y	Y	Y	Y	Y			Y	Y	N	A	A	A	Y	Y	A		Y
Madagascar	Y	Y	A	Y	Y			Y	Y	Y	Y	Y	Y	Y	Y	Y		NP*
Malawi	Y	Y	Y	Y	Y			Y	Y	Y	Y	Y	Y	Y	Y	Y		Y
Malaysia	Y	Y	Y	Y	Y			Y	Y	Y	Y	Y	Y	Y	Y	Y		Y
Maldives	Y	Y	Y	Y	Y			Y	Y	Y	Y	Y	Y	Y	Y	Y		Y
Mali	Y	Y	Y	Y	Y			Y	Y	Y	Y	Y	Y	Y	Y	Y		Y
Malta	Y	Y	Y	Y	Y			Y	Y	Y	Y	Y	Y	Y	Y	Y		Y
Mauritania	Y	Y	Y	Y	Y			Y	Y	Y	Y	Y	Y	Y	Y	Y		Y
Mauritius	Y	Y	Y	Y	Y			Y	Y	Y	Y	Y	Y	Y	Y	Y		Y
Mexico	Y	Y	Y	Y	Y			Y	Y	Y	Y	Y	Y	Y	Y	Y		Y
Mongolia	Y	Y	Y	Y	Y			Y	Y	Y	Y	Y	Y	Y	Y	Y		Y
Morocco	Y	Y	Y	Y	Y			Y	Y	Y	Y	Y	Y	Y	Y	Y		Y
Mozambique	Y	Y	Y	Y	Y			Y	Y	Y	Y	Y	Y	Y	Y	Y		Y
Nepal	Y	Y	Y	Y	Y			Y	Y	Y	Y	Y	Y	Y	Y	Y		Y
Netherlands	Y	Y	A	Y	Y			Y	Y	N	A	A	A	Y	Y	Y		A
New Zealand	Y	Y	A	Y	Y			Y	Y	N	A	A	Y	Y	Y	Y		A
Nicaragua	Y	Y	Y	Y	Y			Y	Y	Y	Y	Y	Y	Y	Y	Y		Y
Niger	Y	Y	Y	Y	Y			Y	Y	Y	Y	Y	Y	Y	Y	Y		Y
Nigeria	Y	Y	A	Y	Y			Y	Y	N	A	A	A	Y	Y	Y		A
Norway	Y	Y	Y	Y	Y			Y	Y	Y	Y	A	NP	Y	Y	Y		A
Oman	Y	Y	Y	Y	Y			Y	Y	Y	Y	A	Y	NP	Y	Y		Y
Pakistan	Y	Y	Y	Y	Y			Y	Y	Y	Y	Y	Y	Y	Y	Y		Y
Panama	Y	Y	Y	Y	Y			Y	Y	Y	Y	Y	Y	Y	Y	Y		Y
Papua New Guinea	Y	Y	Y	Y	Y			Y	Y	Y	Y	Y	Y	Y	Y	Y		Y
Paraguay	Y	Y	A	Y	Y			Y	Y	Y	Y	Y	Y	Y	Y	Y		Y
Peru	Y	Y	Y	Y	Y			Y	Y	Y	Y	Y	Y	Y	Y	Y		Y
Philippines	Y	Y	Y	Y	Y			Y	Y	Y	Y	Y	Y	Y	Y	Y		Y
Poland	Y	Y	Y	Y	Y			Y	Y	Y	Y	Y	Y	Y	Y	Y		Y
Portugal	Y	Y	Y	Y	Y			Y	Y	A	Y	Y	A	Y	Y	Y		Y
Qatar	Y	Y	Y	Y	Y			Y	Y	Y	Y	Y	Y	Y	Y	Y		Y
Romania	Y	Y	Y	Y	Y			Y	Y	Y	Y	Y	Y	Y	Y	Y		Y
Rwanda	NP	NP	NP	NP	NP			NP	NP	NP	NP	NP	NP	NP	NP	NP		NP
Saint Christopher and Nevis	NP	NP	NP	NP	NP			Y	Y	NP	NP	NP	NP	Y	Y	NP		NP
Saint Lucia	Y	NP	NP	Y	Y			Y	Y	NP	NP	NP	NP	Y	Y	NP		Y
Saint Vincent	NP	NP	NP	NP	NP			NP	NP	NP	NP	NP	NP	NP	NP	NP		NP
Samoa	NP	NP	NP	NP	NP			NP	NP	NP	NP	NP	NP	NP	NP	NP		NP
Sao Tome and Principe	Y	Y	Y	Y	Y			Y	Y	Y	Y	Y	Y	Y	Y	Y		Y
Saudi Arabia	Y	Y	Y	Y	Y			Y	Y	Y	Y	Y	Y	Y	Y	Y		Y
Senegal	Y	Y	Y	Y	Y			Y	Y	Y	Y	Y	Y	Y	Y	Y		NP
Seychelles	Y	Y	Y	Y	Y			Y	Y	Y	Y	Y	Y	Y	Y	Y		Y
Sierra Leone	Y	Y	Y	Y	Y			Y	Y	Y	Y	Y	Y	Y	Y	Y		Y
Singapore	Y	Y	Y	Y	Y			Y	Y	Y	Y	Y	Y	Y	Y	Y		Y
Solomon Islands	Y	Y	A	Y	NP			NP	NP	NP	NP	NP	NP	NP	NP	NP		NP
Somalia	Y	Y	Y	Y	Y			Y	Y	Y	Y	Y	Y	Y	Y	Y		Y
Spain	Y	Y	Y	Y	Y			Y	Y	A	Y	Y	Y	Y	Y	Y		Y
Sri Lanka	Y	Y	Y	Y	Y			Y	Y	Y	Y	Y	Y	Y	Y	Y		Y
Sudan	Y	Y	Y	Y	Y			Y	Y	Y	Y	Y	Y	Y	Y	Y		Y
Suriname	Y	Y	Y	Y	Y			Y	Y	Y	Y	Y	Y	Y	Y	Y		Y
Swaziland	Y	Y	A	Y	Y			Y	Y	Y	Y	Y	Y	Y	Y	Y		Y
Sweden	Y	Y	A	Y	Y			Y	Y	N	A	A	Y	Y	Y	Y		A
Syrian Arab Republic	Y	Y	Y	Y	Y			Y	Y	Y	Y	Y	Y	Y	Y	Y		Y
Thailand	Y	Y	Y	Y	Y			Y	Y	Y	Y	Y	Y	Y	Y	Y		Y
Togo	Y	Y	Y	Y	Y			Y	Y	Y	Y	Y	Y	Y	Y	Y		Y
Trinidad and Tobago	Y	Y	Y	Y	Y			Y	Y	Y	Y	Y	Y	Y	Y	Y		Y
Tunisia	Y	Y	Y	Y	Y			Y	Y	Y	Y	Y	Y	Y	Y	Y		Y
Turkey	Y	Y	Y	Y	Y			Y	Y	Y	Y	Y	Y	Y	Y	Y		Y
Uganda	Y	Y	Y	Y	Y			Y	Y	Y	Y	Y	Y	Y	Y	Y		Y
Ukrainian SSR	Y	Y	Y	Y	Y			Y	Y	Y	Y	Y	Y	Y	Y	Y		Y
USSR	Y	Y	Y	Y	Y			Y	Y	Y	Y	Y	Y	Y	Y	Y		Y
United Arab Emirates	Y	Y	A	Y	Y			Y	Y	N	A	A	A	Y	Y	Y		A
United Republic of Cameroon	Y	Y	Y	Y	Y			Y	Y	Y	Y	Y	Y	Y	Y	Y		Y
United Republic of Tanzania	Y	Y	Y	Y	Y			Y	Y	Y	Y	N	Y	Y	N	N		Y
United States	A	A	N	A	Y			Y	N	N	N	N	Y	N	N	Y		N
Uruguay	Y	Y	A	Y	Y			Y	Y	Y	Y	Y	Y	Y	Y	NP*		Y
Vanuatu	Y	Y	Y	Y	Y			Y	Y	Y	Y	Y	Y	Y	Y	Y		Y
Venezuela	Y	Y	Y	Y	Y			Y	Y	Y	Y	Y	Y	Y	Y	Y		Y
Viet Nam	Y	Y	Y	Y	Y			Y	Y	Y	Y	Y	Y	Y	Y	Y		Y
Yemen	Y	Y	Y	Y	Y			Y	Y	Y	Y	Y	Y	Y	Y	Y		Y
Yugoslavia	Y	Y	Y	Y	Y			Y	Y	Y	Y	Y	Y	Y	Y	Y		Y
Zaire	Y	NP	A	NP	Y			Y	Y	NP	Y	A	Y	Y	Y	NP		Y
Zambia	Y	Y	Y	Y	Y			Y	Y	Y	Y	Y	Y	Y	Y	Y		Y
Zimbabwe	Y	Y	Y	Y	Y			Y	Y	Y	Y	Y	Y	Y	Y	Y		NP

* Later advised the Secretariat it had intended to vote in favour.

| | 1983 38 | | | | | | | 1984 39 | | | | | | | | | | | | | | |
38/145	38/166	38/180 A	38/180 B	38/180 C	38/180 D	38/180 E	38/220	39/14	39/17	39/28 A	39/28 B	39/49 A	39/49 B	39/49 C	39/49 D	39/50 A	39/50 D	39/54	39/71 A,B	39/72 A	38/72 C	39/76
Y	Y	Y	Y	Y	Y	Y		Y	Y			Y	Y	Y	Y	Y	Y		N	Y	Y	Y
Y	Y	NP	NP	NP	NP	NP		Y	Y			Y	Y	Y	Y	Y	Y		N	Y	Y	Y
Y	Y	NP	NP	NP	NP	NP		A	Y			Y	Y	Y	A	Y	Y		NP	A	Y	Y
Y	Y	Y	Y	Y	Y	Y		Y	Y			Y	Y	Y	A	Y	Y		NP	Y	A	Y
Y	Y	N	A	Y	N	N		A	N			A	A	A	A	A	A		Y	N	N	N
Y	Y	Y	Y	Y	Y	Y		Y	Y			Y	Y	Y	A	Y	Y		Y	Y	Y	Y
NP*	Y	A	Y	Y	A	A		A	A			Y	Y	Y	A	A	Y		Y	A	A	Y
Y	Y	Y	Y	Y	Y	Y		Y	Y			Y	Y	Y	Y	Y	Y		A	Y	Y	Y
Y	Y	Y	Y	Y	Y	Y		Y	Y			Y	Y	Y	Y	Y	Y		Y	Y	Y	Y
Y	Y	Y	Y	Y	Y	Y		Y	Y			Y	Y	Y	Y	Y	Y		Y	Y	Y	NP
Y	Y	NP	Y	Y	Y	NP		Y	NP			Y	Y	Y	Y	NP	NP		Y	Y	Y	Y
Y	Y	Y	Y	Y	Y	A		Y	Y			Y	Y	Y	Y	Y	Y		N	Y	Y	Y
Y	Y	Y	Y	Y	Y	Y		Y	Y			Y	Y	Y	Y	Y	Y		NP	Y	Y	Y
Y	Y	Y	Y	Y	NP	A		Y	Y			Y	Y	Y	Y	Y	Y		Y	Y	Y	Y
Y	Y	N	A	Y	N	N		A	N			A	A	A	A	A	A		Y	N	N	N
Y	Y	N	A	Y	N	N		A	N			A	A	A	A	A	A		Y	A	N	Y
Y	Y	Y	Y	Y	Y	Y		Y	Y			Y	Y	Y	Y	Y	Y		Y	Y	Y	Y
Y	Y	N	A	Y	N	N		A	N			A	A	A	A	A	A		Y	N	N	A
Y	Y	Y	Y	Y	Y	Y		Y	Y			Y	Y	Y	Y	Y	Y		Y	Y	Y	Y
Y	Y	NP	NP	NP	NP	NP		A	Y			Y	Y	Y	Y	Y	Y		Y	Y	A	Y
Y	Y	A	Y	Y	Y	A		A	NP			Y	Y	Y	Y	Y	Y		Y	NP	NP	A
Y	Y	A	Y	Y	NP	N		Y	Y			Y	Y	Y	Y	A	A		Y	Y	Y	A
Y	Y	A	Y	Y	Y	A		Y	Y			Y	Y	Y	Y	Y	Y		Y	Y	Y	A
Y	Y	N	Y	Y	Y	N		Y	A			Y	Y	Y	Y	A	A		N	Y	A	A
Y	Y	Y	Y	Y	Y	Y		Y	Y			Y	Y	Y	Y	Y	Y		Y	Y	Y	Y
Y	Y	NP	Y	Y	Y	NP		Y	Y			Y	Y	Y	Y	A	A		Y	Y	Y	Y
NP	NP	NP	NP	NP	NP	NP		NP	NP			NP	NP	NP	NP	NP	NP		NP	NP	A	NP
Y	Y	N	A	Y	A	A		NP	NP			Y	Y	Y	A	Y	NP		Y	Y	Y	NP
Y	Y	A	A	Y	A	A		NP	NP			Y	Y	Y	Y	Y	Y		Y	A	A	NP
NP	NP	NP	NP	NP	NP	NP		NP	Y			Y	Y	Y	Y	Y	Y		Y	A	A	NP
Y	Y	Y	Y	Y	Y	Y		Y	Y			Y	Y	Y	Y	Y	Y		NP	Y	Y	Y
Y	Y	Y	Y	Y	Y	Y		Y	Y			Y	Y	Y	Y	Y	Y		Y	Y	Y	Y
NP	NP	Y	Y	Y	Y	Y	ADOPTED WITHOUT A VOTE	NP	NP	NO VOTING LISTS WERE RECORDED Y = 98, N = 2, A = 12, NP = 46	NO VOTING LISTS WERE RECORDED Y = 98, N = 11, A = 5, NP = 44	Y	Y	Y	Y	Y	Y	ADOPTED WITHOUT A VOTE	NP	Y	Y	NP
Y	Y	A	Y	Y	Y	Y		Y	Y			Y	Y	Y	Y	Y	Y		Y	Y	Y	Y
NP	NP	NP	NP	NP	NP	NP		NP	NP			NP	NP	NP	NP	NP	NP		NP	Y	Y	NP
Y	Y	A	Y	Y	A	A		Y	A			Y	Y	Y	Y	A	A		Y	A	A	A
Y	Y	Y	Y	Y	Y	Y		Y	Y			Y	Y	Y	Y	Y	Y		Y	Y	Y	Y
Y	Y	Y	Y	Y	Y	Y		NP	Y			Y	Y	Y	Y	Y	Y		Y	Y	Y	NP
Y	Y	NP	NP	NP	NP	NP		NP	Y			NP	NP	NP	NP	Y	Y		NP	NP	NP	NP
Y	Y	N	A	Y	A	N		A	N			A	A	Y	Y	A	A		N	Y	Y	Y
Y	Y	Y	Y	Y	Y	Y		Y	Y			Y	Y	Y	Y	Y	Y		Y	Y	Y	Y
Y	Y	Y	Y	Y	Y	NP		Y	Y			Y	Y	Y	Y	Y	Y		Y	Y	NP	Y
Y	Y	Y	Y	Y	Y	Y		Y	Y			Y	Y	Y	Y	Y	Y		Y	Y	Y	Y
Y	Y	Y	Y	Y	Y	Y		Y	Y			Y	Y	Y	Y	Y	Y		N	Y	Y	Y
Y	Y	Y	Y	Y	Y	Y		Y	Y			Y	Y	Y	Y	Y	Y		N	Y	Y	Y
Y	Y	N	A	Y	N	N		Y	N			A	A	A	A	A	A		Y	N	N	Y
Y	Y	Y	Y	Y	Y	Y		Y	Y			Y	Y	Y	Y	Y	Y		Y	Y	Y	Y
N	N	N	A	Y	A	N		Y	N			N	N	N	Y	A	A		Y	N	N	NP
Y	Y	A	Y	A	Y	A		Y	N			Y	Y	Y	Y	A	A		Y	N	A	N
Y	NP	NP	NP	NP	NP	NP		NP	NP			Y	Y	Y	Y	Y	Y		NP	A	Y	NP
Y	Y	A	Y	Y	Y	A		A	Y			Y	Y	Y	Y	Y	Y		N	Y	Y	Y
Y	Y	Y	Y	Y	Y	Y		Y	Y			Y	Y	Y	Y	Y	Y		A	Y	Y	Y.
X	Y	Y	Y	Y	Y	Y		Y	Y			Y	Y	Y	Y	Y	Y		A	Y	Y	Y
Y	Y	NP	NP	NP	NP	NP		A	NP			NP	NP	NP	NP	Y	Y		Y	Y	NP	Y
Y	Y	Y	Y	Y	Y	Y		A	Y			Y	Y	Y	Y	Y	Y		Y	Y	Y	Y
NP	NP	Y	Y	Y	Y	Y		Y	Y			Y	Y	Y	Y	Y	Y		Y	Y	Y	NP

* Later advised the Secretariat it had intended to vote in favour.

APPENDIX B

TABLES OF VOTING IN THE GENERAL ASSEMBLY 1982-1986

Y = Yes N = No A = Abstention NP = Not Present

Year / Session	1984 / 39																	
Res.	39/95 A	39/95 B	39/95 C	39/95 D	39/95 E	39/95 F	39/95 G	39/95 H	39/99 A	39/99 B	39/99 C	39/99 D	39/99 E	39/99 F	39/99 G	39/99 H	39/99 I	39/99 J
Lao People's Democratic Republic	Y	Y	Y	Y	Y	Y	Y	Y	Y	ADOPTED WITHOUT A VOTE	ADOPTED WITHOUT A VOTE	Y	Y	Y	Y	Y	Y	Y
Lebanon	Y	Y	Y	Y	Y	Y	Y	Y	Y			Y	Y	Y	Y	Y	Y	Y
Lesotho	Y	Y	Y	Y	Y	Y	Y	Y	Y			Y	Y	Y	Y	Y	Y	Y
Liberia	A	A	Y	A	Y	A	A	Y	Y			Y	Y	Y	Y	A	A	Y
Libyan Arab Jamahiriya	Y	Y	Y	Y	Y	Y	Y	Y	Y			Y	Y	Y	Y	Y	Y	Y
Luxembourg	Y	Y	Y	A	Y	Y	A	Y	Y			Y	Y	N	A	A	A	Y
Madagascar	Y	Y	Y	Y	Y	Y	Y	Y	Y			Y	Y	Y	Y	Y	Y	Y
Malawi	A	Y	Y	A	Y	Y	Y	Y	Y			Y	Y	Y	Y	Y	Y	Y
Malaysia	Y	Y	Y	Y	Y	Y	Y	Y	Y			Y	Y	Y	Y	Y	Y	Y
Maldives	Y	Y	Y	Y	Y	Y	Y	Y	Y			Y	Y	Y	Y	Y	Y	Y
Mali	Y	Y	Y	Y	Y	Y	Y	Y	Y			Y	Y	Y	Y	NP	Y	Y
Malta	Y	Y	Y	Y	Y	Y	Y	Y	Y			Y	Y	Y	Y	Y	Y	Y
Mauritania	Y	NP	Y	Y	Y	Y	Y	Y	Y			Y	Y	Y	Y	Y	Y	Y
Mauritius	Y	Y	Y	Y	Y	Y	Y	Y	Y			Y	Y	Y	Y	Y	Y	Y
Mexico	Y	Y	Y	Y	Y	Y	Y	Y	Y			Y	Y	Y	Y	Y	Y	Y
Mongolia	Y	Y	Y	Y	Y	Y	Y	Y	Y			Y	Y	Y	Y	Y	Y	Y
Morocco	Y	Y	Y	Y	Y	Y	Y	Y	Y			Y	Y	Y	Y	Y	Y	Y
Mozambique	Y	Y	Y	Y	Y	Y	Y	Y	Y			Y	Y	Y	Y	Y	Y	Y
Nepal	A	Y	Y	Y	Y	Y	Y	Y	Y			Y	Y	Y	Y	Y	Y	Y
Netherlands	Y	Y	Y	A	Y	Y	A	Y	Y			Y	Y	N	A	A	A	Y
New Zealand	Y	Y	Y	A	Y	Y	A	Y	Y			Y	Y	N	A	A	Y	Y
Nicaragua	Y	Y	Y	Y	Y	Y	Y	Y	Y			Y	Y	Y	Y	Y	Y	Y
Niger	Y	Y	Y	Y	Y	Y	Y	Y	Y			Y	Y	Y	Y	Y	Y	Y
Nigeria	Y	Y	Y	Y	Y	Y	Y	Y	Y			Y	Y	Y	NP	Y	Y	Y
Norway	Y	Y	Y	A	Y	Y	A	Y	Y			Y	Y	N	A	A	A	Y
Oman	Y	Y	Y	Y	Y	Y	Y	Y	Y			Y	Y	Y	Y	Y	Y	Y
Pakistan	Y	Y	Y	Y	Y	Y	Y	Y	Y			Y	Y	Y	Y	Y	Y	Y
Panama	A	Y	Y	Y	Y	Y	A	Y	Y			Y	Y	Y	Y	Y	A	Y
Papua New Guinea	Y	Y	Y	Y	Y	Y	Y	Y	Y			Y	Y	Y	Y	Y	Y	Y
Paraguay	A	Y	Y	A	Y	NP	A	NP	Y			Y	Y	Y	Y	Y	Y	Y
Peru	Y	Y	Y	Y	Y	Y	Y	Y	Y			Y	Y	Y	Y	Y	Y	Y
Philippines	NP	Y	Y	Y	Y	Y	Y	Y	Y			Y	Y	Y	Y	Y	Y	Y
Poland	Y	Y	Y	Y	Y	Y	Y	Y	Y			Y	Y	Y	Y	Y	Y	Y
Portugal	Y	Y	Y	Y	Y	Y	Y	Y	Y			Y	Y	A	Y	Y	A	Y
Qatar	Y	Y	Y	Y	Y	Y	Y	Y	Y			Y	Y	Y	Y	Y	Y	Y
Romania	Y	Y	Y	Y	Y	Y	Y	Y	Y			Y	Y	Y	Y	Y	Y	Y
Rwanda	Y	Y	Y	Y	Y	Y	NP	Y	Y			Y	Y	Y	Y	Y	Y	Y
Saint Christopher and Nevis	NP	NP	NP	NP	NP	NP	NP	NP	NP			NP	NP	NP	NP	NP	NP	NP
Saint Lucia	NP	NP	NP	NP	NP	NP	NP	NP	NP			NP	NP	NP	NP	NP	NP	NP
Saint Vincent	NP	NP	NP	NP	NP	NP	NP	NP	NP			NP	NP	NP	NP	NP	NP	NP
Samoa	Y	Y	Y	Y	Y	Y	Y	Y	Y			Y	Y	Y	Y	Y	Y	Y
Sao Tome and Principe	Y	Y	Y	Y	Y	Y	Y	Y	Y			Y	Y	Y	Y	Y	Y	Y
Saudi Arabia	Y	Y	Y	Y	Y	Y	Y	Y	Y			Y	Y	Y	Y	Y	Y	Y
Senegal	Y	Y	Y	Y	Y	Y	Y	Y	Y			Y	Y	Y	Y	Y	Y	Y
Seychelles	Y	Y	Y	Y	Y	Y	Y	Y	Y			Y	Y	Y	Y	Y	Y	Y
Sierra Leone	Y	Y	Y	Y	Y	Y	Y	Y	Y			Y	Y	Y	Y	Y	Y	Y
Singapore	NP	Y	Y	Y	Y	Y	Y	Y	Y			Y	Y	Y	Y	Y	Y	Y
Solomon Islands	NP	NP	NP	NP	NP	NP	NP	NP	NP			NP	NP	NP	NP	NP	NP	NP
Somalia	Y	Y	Y	Y	Y	Y	Y	Y	Y			Y	Y	Y	Y	Y	Y	Y
Spain	Y	Y	Y	Y	Y	Y	Y	Y	Y			Y	Y	A	Y	Y	Y	Y
Sri Lanka	A	Y	Y	Y	Y	Y	Y	Y	Y			Y	Y	Y	Y	Y	Y	Y
Sudan	Y	Y	Y	Y	Y	Y	Y	Y	Y			Y	Y	Y	Y	Y	Y	Y
Suriname	Y	Y	Y	Y	Y	Y	Y	Y	Y			Y	Y	Y	Y	Y	Y	Y
Swaziland	NP	NP	NP	NP	NP	NP	NP	NP	NP			NP	NP	NP	NP	NP	NP	NP
Sweden	Y	Y	Y	A	Y	Y	Y	Y	Y			Y	Y	N	A	A	Y	Y
Syrian Arab Republic	Y	Y	Y	Y	Y	Y	Y	Y	Y			Y	Y	Y	Y	Y	Y	Y
Thailand	NP	Y	Y	Y	Y	Y	Y	Y	Y			Y	Y	Y	Y	Y	Y	Y
Togo	Y	Y	Y	Y	Y	Y	Y	Y	Y			Y	Y	Y	Y	Y	Y	Y
Trinidad and Tobago	A	Y	Y	Y	Y	Y	Y	Y	Y			Y	Y	Y	Y	Y	Y	Y
Tunisia	Y	Y	Y	Y	Y	Y	Y	Y	Y			Y	Y	Y	Y	Y	Y	Y
Turkey	Y	Y	Y	Y	Y	Y	Y	Y	Y			Y	Y	Y	Y	Y	Y	Y
Uganda	Y	Y	Y	Y	Y	Y	Y	Y	Y			Y	Y	Y	Y	Y	Y	Y
Ukrainian SSR	Y	Y	Y	Y	Y	Y	Y	Y	Y			Y	Y	Y	Y	Y	Y	Y
USSR	Y	Y	Y	Y	Y	Y	Y	Y	Y			Y	Y	Y	Y	Y	Y	Y
United Arab Emirates	Y	Y	Y	Y	Y	Y	Y	Y	Y			Y	Y	Y	Y	Y	Y	Y
United Kingdom	Y	Y	Y	A	Y	Y	A	Y	Y			Y	Y	N	A	A	A	Y
United Republic of Cameroon	Y	Y	Y	Y	Y	Y	Y	Y	Y			Y	Y	Y	Y	Y	Y	Y
United Republic of Tanzania	Y	Y	Y	Y	Y	Y	Y	Y	Y			Y	Y	Y	Y	Y	Y	Y
United States	N	A	A	N	A	A	N	N	Y			Y	A	N	N	N	N	N
Uruguay	NP	Y	Y	Y	Y	Y	A	Y	Y			Y	Y	Y	Y	Y	Y	Y
Vanuatu	NP	NP	NP	NP	NP	NP	NP	NP	NP			NP	NP	NP	NP	NP	NP	NP
Venezuela	Y	Y	Y	Y	Y	Y	Y	Y	Y			Y	Y	Y	Y	Y	Y	Y
Viet Nam	Y	Y	Y	Y	Y	Y	Y	Y	Y			Y	Y	Y	Y	Y	Y	Y
Yemen	Y	Y	Y	Y	Y	Y	Y	Y	Y			Y	Y	Y	Y	Y	Y	Y
Yugoslavia	Y	Y	Y	Y	Y	Y	Y	Y	Y			Y	Y	Y	Y	Y	Y	Y
Zaire	A	A	Y	A	Y	A	A	Y	Y			Y	Y	A	Y	A	A	Y
Zambia	Y	Y	Y	Y	Y	Y	Y	Y	Y			Y	Y	Y	Y	Y	Y	Y
Zimbabwe	Y	Y	Y	Y	Y	Y	Y	Y	Y			Y	Y	Y	Y	Y	Y	Y

Resolutions 39/197, 40/61 and 40/82 were **ADOPTED WITHOUT A VOTE** (no recorded votes in those columns).

	1984 — 39										1985 — 40									
	39/99 K	39/101	39/146 A	39/146 B	39/146 C	39/147	39/169	39/223	39/224	39/442	40/6	40/25	40/59 A	40/59 B	40/64 A	40/64 E	40/93	40/96 A	40/96 B	40/96 C
	Y	Y	Y	Y	Y	Y	Y	Y	Y	Y	Y	Y	NP	NP	Y	Y	Y	Y	Y	Y
	Y	NP	Y	Y	Y	Y	Y	Y	Y	Y	Y	Y	NP	NP	NP	Y	Y	Y	Y	Y
	Y	Y	A	N	A	A	Y	Y	Y	Y	A	Y	NP	NP	Y	A	Y	Y	Y	Y
	Y	Y	Y	Y	Y	Y	Y	Y	Y	Y	Y	Y	NP	NP	Y	Y	Y	Y	Y	A
	Y	Y	N	N	Y	A	Y	Y	Y	Y	N	N	NP	NP	N	N	A	A	A	A
	Y	Y	Y	Y	Y	Y	Y	Y	Y	Y	Y	Y	Y	Y	Y	Y	Y	A	A	Y
	Y	Y	A	A	Y	A	Y	Y	Y	Y	A	Y	NP	NP	NP	A	Y	A	A	Y
	Y	Y	Y	Y	Y	Y	Y	Y	Y	Y	Y	Y	Y	Y	Y	Y	Y	Y	Y	Y
	NP*	Y	Y	Y	Y	Y	Y	Y	Y	Y	Y	Y	NP	NP	Y	Y	Y	Y	Y	Y
	Y	Y	Y	Y	Y	Y	Y	Y	Y	Y	Y	Y	NP	NP	Y	Y	Y	Y	Y	Y
	Y	Y	NP	NP	Y	Y	Y	Y	NP	NP	Y	Y	Y	Y	Y	Y	Y	Y	Y	Y
	Y	Y	Y	Y	Y	Y	Y	Y	Y	Y	A	Y	NP	NP	Y	Y	Y	Y	Y	Y
	Y	Y	Y	Y	Y	Y	Y	Y	Y	Y	Y	Y	A	A	Y	Y	Y	Y	Y	Y
	Y	Y	Y	Y	Y	A	Y	Y	Y	Y	Y	NP	Y	Y	A	A	A	A	A	Y
	Y	Y	N	N	Y	A	Y	Y	Y	Y	N	N	Y	Y	N	N	A	A	A	A
	Y	Y	N	N	Y	A	Y	Y	Y	Y	A	N	NP	NP	NP	N	A	A	A	A
	Y	Y	Y	Y	Y	Y	Y	Y	Y	Y	Y	Y	NP	NP	Y	Y	Y	Y	Y	Y
	Y	Y	N	N	Y	A	Y	A	Y	Y	N	N	Y	Y	N	N	Y	A	A	A
	Y	Y	Y	Y	Y	Y	Y	Y	Y	Y	Y	Y	Y	Y	Y	Y	Y	Y	Y	Y
	Y	Y	A	A	Y	A	Y	Y	Y	Y	A	Y	Y	Y	Y	A	Y	A	Y	Y
	Y	Y	A	A	A	NP	Y	Y	Y	Y	A	Y	Y	Y	Y	Y	Y	A	Y	Y
	Y	Y	Y	A	Y	Y	Y	Y	Y	Y	Y	Y	Y	Y	Y	Y	Y	Y	Y	Y
	Y	Y	Y	Y	Y	Y	Y	Y	Y	Y	A	A	Y	Y	N	A	Y	A	Y	Y
	Y	Y	A	N	Y	Y	Y	Y	Y	Y	A	Y	Y	Y	Y	Y	Y	Y	Y	Y
	Y	Y	NP	NP	Y	Y	Y	Y	Y	Y	A	Y	Y	Y	NP	NP	Y	Y	Y	Y
	NP	NP	NP	NP	NP	NP	NP	NP	Y	NP	NP	NP	NP	NP	NP	NP	A	NP	NP	NP
	NP	NP	NP	NP	NP	A	NP	NP	Y	NP	A	NP	NP	NP	Y	A	A	Y	Y	Y
	NP	NP	A	A	A	A	NP	Y	Y	Y	A	NP	NP	NP	Y	A	NP	Y	Y	Y
	Y	Y	A	A	Y	NP	Y	Y	Y	Y	NP	Y	Y	Y	NP	A	Y	Y	Y	Y
	Y	Y	Y	Y	Y	NP*	Y	Y	Y	Y	Y	Y	NP	NP	Y	Y	Y	Y	Y	Y
	Y	Y	NP	Y	Y	Y	NP	NP	NP	NP	Y	Y	NP	NP	Y	Y	Y	Y	Y	Y
	Y	Y	NP	NP	Y	NP	Y	Y	Y	Y	NP	Y	Y	Y	Y	Y	Y	NP	Y	Y
	NP	NP	NP	NP	NP	NP	NP	NP	NP	NP	A	NP	NP	NP	NP	A	A	A	A	A
	Y	Y	Y	Y	Y	NP*	Y	Y	Y	Y	A	A	Y	Y	N	A	A	Y	Y	Y
	Y	Y	A	A	Y	A	Y	Y	Y	Y	A	A	Y	Y	N	A	A	Y	Y	Y
	Y	Y	Y	Y	Y	Y	Y	Y	Y	Y	Y	Y	Y	Y	Y	Y	Y	Y	Y	Y
	Y	Y	NP	NP	Y	NP	Y	Y	Y	Y	NP	Y	Y	Y	Y	Y	NP	Y	Y	Y
	NP	NP	NP	NP	NP	NP	Y	Y	Y	Y	NP	Y	Y	Y	NP	A	Y	Y	Y	Y
	Y	Y	A	N	Y	A	Y	A	Y	Y	N	N	Y	Y	N	N	A	A	A	Y
	Y	Y	Y	A	Y	Y	Y	Y	Y	Y	NP	Y	Y	Y	Y	Y	Y	Y	Y	Y
	Y	Y	Y	Y	Y	Y	Y	Y	Y	Y	Y	Y	Y	Y	NP	NP	Y	Y	Y	Y
	Y	Y	Y	Y	Y	Y	Y	Y	Y	Y	Y	Y	Y	Y	Y	Y	Y	Y	Y	Y
	Y	Y	Y	Y	Y	Y	Y	Y	Y	Y	Y	Y	NP	NP	Y	Y	Y	Y	Y	Y
	Y	Y	Y	Y	Y	Y	Y	Y	Y	Y	Y	Y	A	N	Y	Y	Y	Y	Y	Y
	Y	Y	N	N	Y	A	Y	Y	Y	Y	N	N	Y	Y	N	N	A	A	A	A
	N	N	N	N	A	N	N	N	N	N	N	N	Y	Y	N	N	N	N	N	N
	NP	NP	NP	NP	NP	NP	Y	Y	Y	Y	NP	NP	NP	Y	Y	Y	A	Y	Y	Y
	Y	Y	A	A	Y	Y	Y	Y	Y	Y	A	Y	Y‡	NP	Y	Y	Y	Y	Y	Y
	Y	Y	Y	Y	Y	Y	Y	Y	Y	Y	Y	Y	A	A	Y	Y	Y	Y	Y	Y
	Y	Y	NP	NP	NP	A	Y	Y	Y	Y	A	Y	NP	Y	Y	A	Y	A	A	A
	Y	A	Y	Y	Y	Y	Y	Y	Y	Y	Y	Y	Y	Y	Y	Y	Y	Y	Y	Y
	Y	Y	Y	Y	Y	NP	Y	Y	Y	Y	Y	Y	Y	Y	Y	Y	Y	Y	Y	Y

* Later advised the Secretariat it had intended to vote in favour.
‡ Later advised the Secretariat it had intended to abstain.

APPENDIX B

TABLES OF VOTING IN THE GENERAL ASSEMBLY 1982-1986

Y = Yes   N = No   A = Abstention   NP = Not Present

	Year Session	1985 40																
Res.	40/96 D	40/161 A	40/161 B	40/161 C	40/161 D	40/161 E	40/161 F	40/161 G	40/165 A	40/165 B	40/165 C	40/165 D	40/165 E	40/165 F	40/165 G	40/165 H	40/165 I	40/165 J
Lao People's Democratic Republic	Y	Y	Y	Y	Y	Y	Y	Y	Y			Y	Y	Y	Y	Y	Y	Y
Lebanon	Y	Y	Y	Y	Y	Y	Y	Y	Y			Y	Y	Y	Y	Y	Y	Y
Lesotho	Y	Y	Y	Y	Y	Y	Y	Y	Y			Y	Y	Y	Y	Y	Y	Y
Liberia	A	A	A	Y	A	A	A	A	Y			Y	Y	Y	Y	A	A	Y
Libyan Arab Jamahiriya	Y	Y	Y	Y	Y	Y	Y	Y	Y			Y	Y	Y	Y	Y	Y	Y
Luxembourg	A	A	Y	Y	A	A	Y	Y	Y			Y	Y	N	A	A	A	Y
Madagascar	Y	Y	Y	Y	Y	Y	Y	Y	Y			Y	Y	Y	Y	Y	Y	Y
Malawi	A	A	A	A	A	A	A	A	Y			Y	Y	Y	A	A	A	Y
Malaysia	Y	Y	Y	Y	Y	Y	Y	Y	Y			Y	Y	Y	Y	Y	Y	Y
Maldives	Y	Y	Y	Y	Y	Y	Y	Y	Y			Y	Y	Y	Y	Y	Y	Y
Mali	Y	Y	Y	Y	Y	Y	Y	Y	Y			Y	Y	Y	Y	Y	Y	Y
Malta	Y	Y	Y	Y	Y	Y	Y	Y	Y			Y	Y	Y	Y	Y	Y	Y
Mauritania	Y	Y	Y	Y	Y	Y	Y	Y	Y			Y	Y	Y	Y	Y	Y	Y
Mauritius	Y	Y	Y	Y	Y	Y	Y	Y	Y			Y	Y	Y	Y	Y	Y	Y
Mexico	Y	Y	Y	Y	Y	Y	Y	Y	Y			Y	Y	Y	Y	Y	Y	Y
Mongolia	Y	Y	Y	Y	Y	Y	Y	Y	Y			Y	Y	Y	Y	Y	Y	Y
Morocco	Y	Y	Y	Y	Y	Y	Y	Y	Y			Y	Y	Y	Y	Y	Y	Y
Mozambique	Y	Y	Y	Y	Y	Y	Y	Y	Y			Y	Y	Y	Y	Y	Y	Y
Nepal	Y	A	Y	Y	Y	Y	Y	Y	Y			Y	Y	Y	Y	Y	Y	Y
Netherlands	A	A	Y	Y	A	A	Y	A	Y			Y	Y	N	A	A	A	Y
New Zealand	A	A	Y	Y	A	A	Y	A	Y			Y	Y	N	A	A	A	Y
Nicaragua	Y	Y	Y	Y	Y	Y	Y	Y	Y			Y	Y	Y	Y	Y	Y	Y
Niger	Y	Y	Y	Y	Y	Y	Y	Y	Y			Y	Y	Y	Y	Y	Y	Y
Nigeria	Y	Y	Y	Y	Y	Y	Y	Y	Y			Y	Y	Y	Y	Y	Y	Y
Norway	A	A	Y	Y	A	A	Y	A	Y			Y	Y	N	A	A	A	Y
Oman	Y	Y	Y	Y	Y	Y	Y	Y	Y			Y	Y	Y	Y	Y	Y	Y
Pakistan	Y	Y	Y	Y	Y	Y	Y	Y	Y			Y	Y	Y	Y	Y	Y	Y
Panama	A	Y	Y	Y	Y	Y	Y	A	Y			Y	Y	Y	Y	Y	A	Y
Papua New Guinea	A	NP	NP	NP	NP	NP	NP	NP	NP			NP	NP	NP	NP	NP	NP	NP
Paraguay	A	NP	NP	NP	NP	NP	NP	NP	NP			NP	Y	Y	A	A	A	Y
Peru	Y	Y	Y	Y	Y	Y	Y	Y	Y			Y	Y	Y	Y	Y	Y	Y
Philippines	Y	NP	Y	Y	Y	Y	Y	Y	Y	ADOPTED WITHOUT A VOTE	ADOPTED WITHOUT A VOTE	Y	Y	Y	Y	Y	Y	Y
Poland	Y	Y	Y	Y	Y	Y	Y	Y	Y			Y	Y	Y	Y	Y	Y	Y
Portugal	A	A	Y	Y	A	A	Y	A	Y			Y	Y	N	Y	Y	A	Y
Qatar	Y	Y	Y	Y	Y	Y	Y	Y	Y			Y	Y	Y	Y	Y	Y	Y
Romania	Y	Y	Y	Y	Y	Y	Y	Y	Y			Y	Y	Y	Y	Y	Y	Y
Rwanda	Y	Y	Y	Y	Y	Y	Y	Y	Y			Y	Y	Y	Y	Y	Y	NP
Saint Christopher and Nevis	NP	NP	NP	NP	NP	NP	NP	NP	NP			NP	NP	NP	NP	NP	NP	NP
Saint Lucia	A	A	NP	A	A	A	A	A	Y			Y	Y	Y	Y	Y	Y	Y
Saint Vincent	A	NP	Y	Y	A	Y	Y	A	Y			Y	Y	Y	Y	Y	Y	Y
Samoa	Y	A	Y	Y	Y	Y	Y	Y	Y			Y	Y	Y	Y	Y	Y	Y
Sao Tome and Principe	Y	Y	Y	Y	Y	Y	Y	Y	Y			Y	Y	Y	Y	Y	Y	Y
Saudi Arabia	Y	Y	Y	Y	Y	Y	Y	Y	Y			Y	Y	Y	Y	Y	Y	Y
Senegal	Y	Y	Y	Y	Y	Y	Y	Y	Y			Y	Y	Y	Y	Y	Y	Y
Seychelles	Y	Y	Y	Y	Y	Y	Y	Y	Y			Y	Y	Y	Y	Y	Y	Y
Sierra Leone	Y	Y	Y	Y	Y	Y	Y	Y	Y			Y	Y	Y	Y	Y	Y	Y
Singapore	Y	NP	Y	Y	Y	Y	Y	Y	Y			Y	Y	Y	Y	Y	Y	Y
Solomon Islands	A	NP	NP	NP	NP	NP	NP	NP	NP			NP	NP	NP	NP	NP	NP	NP
Somalia	Y	NP*	NP*	NP*	NP*	NP*	Y	Y	Y			Y	NP	Y	Y	NP	Y	NP*
Spain	A	A	Y	Y	Y	Y	Y	Y	Y			Y	Y	A	Y	Y	A	Y
Sri Lanka	Y	Y	Y	Y	Y	Y	Y	Y	Y			Y	Y	Y	Y	Y	Y	Y
Sudan	Y	Y	Y	Y	Y	Y	Y	Y	Y			Y	Y	Y	Y	Y	Y	Y
Suriname	Y	Y	Y	Y	Y	Y	Y	Y	Y			Y	Y	Y	Y	Y	NP	Y
Swaziland	A	A	Y	Y	A	A	A	A	Y			Y	Y	Y	A	A	A	Y
Sweden	A	A	Y	Y	A	A	Y	A	Y			Y	Y	N	A	A	A	Y
Syrian Arab Republic	Y	Y	Y	Y	Y	Y	Y	Y	Y			Y	Y	Y	Y	Y	Y	Y
Thailand	Y	NP	Y	Y	Y	Y	Y	Y	Y			Y	Y	Y	Y	Y	Y	Y
Togo	Y	Y	Y	Y	Y	Y	Y	Y	Y			Y	Y	Y	Y	Y	Y	Y
Trinidad and Tobago	Y	NP	Y	Y	Y	Y	Y	Y	Y			Y	Y	Y	Y	Y	Y	Y
Tunisia	Y	Y	Y	Y	Y	Y	Y	Y	Y			Y	Y	Y	Y	Y	Y	Y
Turkey	Y	Y	Y	Y	Y	Y	Y	Y	Y			Y	Y	Y	Y	Y	Y	Y
Uganda	Y	Y	Y	Y	Y	Y	Y	Y	Y			Y	Y	Y	Y	Y	Y	Y
Ukrainian SSR	Y	Y	Y	Y	Y	Y	Y	Y	Y			Y	Y	Y	Y	Y	Y	Y
USSR	Y	Y	Y	Y	Y	Y	Y	Y	Y			Y	Y	Y	Y	Y	Y	Y
United Arab Emirates	Y	Y	Y	Y	Y	Y	Y	Y	Y			Y	Y	Y	Y	Y	Y	Y
United Kingdom	A	A	Y	Y	A	A	Y	A	Y			Y	Y	N	A	A	A	Y
United Republic of Cameroon	Y	A	A	Y	A	A	A	A	Y			Y	Y	Y	Y	Y	Y	Y
United Republic of Tanzania	Y	Y	Y	Y	Y	Y	Y	Y	Y			Y	Y	Y	Y	Y	Y	Y
United States	N	N	A	A	N	A	A	N	Y			Y	N	N	N	N	N	N
Uruguay	Y	NP	Y	Y	Y	Y	Y	Y	Y			Y	Y	Y	Y	Y	Y	Y
Vanuatu	Y	Y	Y	Y	Y	Y	Y	Y	Y			Y	Y	Y	Y	Y	Y	Y
Venezuela	Y	Y	Y	Y	Y	Y	Y	Y	Y			Y	Y	Y	Y	Y	Y	Y
Viet Nam	Y	Y	Y	Y	Y	Y	Y	Y	Y			Y	Y	Y	Y	Y	Y	Y
Yemen	Y	Y	Y	Y	Y	Y	Y	Y	Y			Y	Y	Y	Y	Y	Y	Y
Yugoslavia	Y	Y	Y	Y	Y	Y	Y	Y	Y			Y	Y	Y	Y	Y	Y	Y
Zaire	A	A	A	Y	A	A	A	A	Y			Y	A	Y	A	A	A	Y
Zambia	Y	Y	Y	Y	Y	Y	Y	Y	Y			Y	Y	Y	Y	Y	Y	Y
Zimbabwe	Y	Y	Y	Y	Y	Y	Y	Y	Y			Y	Y	Y	Y	Y	Y	Y

Note: Columns 40/165 B and 40/165 C were ADOPTED WITHOUT A VOTE.

* Later advised the Secretariat it had intended to vote in favour.

40/165 K	40/167	40/168 A	40/168 B	40/168 C	40/169	40/170	40/201	40/229	40/246 A	40/246 B	40/432	41/12	41/35 C	41/43 A	41/43 B	41/43 C	41/43 D	41/44 A	41/44 B	41/48	41/63 A	41/63 B
Y	Y	Y	Y	Y	Y	Y	Y		Y	N	Y	Y	Y	Y	Y	Y	Y	A	A		Y	Y
Y	Y	Y	Y	Y	Y	Y	Y		Y	Y	Y	Y	A	Y	Y	Y	Y	NP	Y		Y	Y
Y	Y	Y	A	Y	A	Y	Y		Y	Y	Y	A	A	Y	Y	Y	Y	Y	Y		A	A
Y	Y	A	Y	Y	Y	Y	Y		NP	NP	Y	A	Y	Y	Y	Y	Y	A	A		A	Y
Y	Y	N	N	Y	Y	Y	Y		Y	Y	Y	Y	Y	A	A	A	A	Y	Y		A	Y
Y	Y	Y	A	A	A	Y	Y		Y	Y	Y	A	N	NP	NP	NP	NP	Y	Y		A	Y
Y	Y	Y	Y	Y	Y	Y	Y		A	A	Y	Y	Y	Y	Y	Y	Y	A	A		Y	Y
Y	Y	Y	Y	Y	Y	Y	Y		NP	NP	Y	Y	Y	Y	Y	Y	Y	A	A		Y	Y
Y	Y	Y	Y	Y	Y	Y	Y		Y	Y	Y	Y	Y	Y	Y	Y	Y	Y	Y		Y	Y
Y	Y	NP	NP	Y	Y	Y	Y		Y	Y	Y	A	Y	Y	Y	Y	Y	Y	Y		Y	Y
Y	Y	Y	Y	Y	Y	Y	Y		Y	N	Y	Y	Y	Y	Y	Y	Y	A	A		Y	Y
Y	Y	Y	Y	Y	Y	Y	Y		NP	NP	Y	NP	Y	Y	Y	Y	Y	NP	NP		Y	Y
Y	Y	Y	A	Y	Y	Y	Y		Y	Y	Y	A	A	A	A	A	A	Y	Y		A	Y
Y	Y	N	N	Y	Y	Y	Y		Y	Y	Y	A	N	A	A	A	A	Y	Y		A	Y
Y	Y	N	N	Y	Y	Y	Y		Y	Y	Y	Y	Y	Y	Y	Y	Y	Y	Y		Y	Y
Y	Y	Y	Y	Y	Y	Y	Y		Y	Y	Y	Y	Y	Y	Y	Y	Y	NP	Y		NP	NP
Y	Y	N	N	Y	A	Y	Y		Y	Y	Y	A	N	A	A	A	A	Y	Y		Y	Y
Y	Y	Y	Y	Y	Y	Y	Y		Y	Y	Y	Y	Y	Y	Y	Y	Y	Y	Y		Y	Y
Y	Y	A	A	Y	Y	Y	Y		Y	Y	Y	A	A	NP*	NP*	NP*	NP*	Y	Y		Y	Y
NP	NP	NP	NP	NP	Y	Y	Y		Y	Y	Y	A	A	Y	Y	Y	Y	NP‡	Y		Y	Y
Y	Y	A	A	A	Y	Y	Y		NP	NP	Y	A	NP	NP	NP	NP	NP	NP	NP		Y	Y
Y	Y	A	A	Y	Y	Y	Y		Y	Y	Y	A	Y	Y	Y	Y	Y	Y	Y		Y	Y
Y	Y	N	N	Y	Y	Y	Y		Y	Y†	Y	A	N	A	A	A	A	Y	A		A	A
Y	Y	Y	NP	Y	Y	Y	Y		Y	Y	Y	Y	Y	Y	Y	Y	Y	Y	Y		Y	Y
NP	NP	NP	NP	NP	NP	Y	Y	ADOPTED WITHOUT A VOTE	NP	NP	A	N	N	Y	Y	A	A	Y	Y	ADOPTED WITHOUT A VOTE	NP	A
Y	Y	A	A	Y	NP	NP	Y		Y	Y	Y	A	A	NP*	NP*	Y	Y	Y	Y		A	A
Y	Y	A	A	Y	Y	Y	Y		Y	Y	Y	A	A	Y	Y	Y	Y	Y	Y		Y	Y
Y	Y	Y	Y	Y	Y	Y	Y		Y	NP	Y	NP	Y	Y	Y	Y	Y	Y	Y		Y	Y
Y	Y	Y	Y	Y	Y	Y	Y		Y	Y	Y	Y	Y	Y	Y	Y	Y	Y	Y		Y	Y
NP	NP	NP	NP	NP	NP	NP	NP		NP	NP	NP	Y	Y	Y	Y	Y	Y	A	A		NP	NP
Y	Y	NP	A	NP	Y	Y	Y		Y	Y	Y	A	Y	Y	Y	Y	Y	Y	Y		Y	Y
Y	Y	Y	A	Y	Y	Y	Y		Y	Y	Y	NP	Y	Y	Y	Y	Y	NP	NP		NP	Y
NP	NP	NP	NP	NP	NP	NP	NP		Y	Y	NP	A	Y	Y	Y	Y	Y	NP	NP		Y	Y
Y	Y	Y	Y	Y	Y	Y	Y		Y	Y	Y	Y	N	Y	Y	Y	Y	Y	Y		A	Y
Y	Y	A	A	Y	Y	Y	Y		Y	Y	Y	Y	Y	Y	Y	Y	Y	Y	Y		Y	Y
Y	Y	NP	NP	Y	Y	Y	Y		Y	Y	Y	NP	A	Y	Y	Y	Y	Y	Y		Y	Y
Y	Y	A	A	A	Y	Y	Y		Y	Y	Y	A	N	A	A	Y	Y	Y	Y		A	Y
Y	Y	A	N	Y	Y	A	Y		Y	N	Y	Y	Y	Y	Y	Y	Y	N	Y†		A	Y
Y	Y	Y	A	Y	Y	Y	Y		Y	N	Y	Y	Y	Y	Y	Y	Y	Y	Y		NP	Y
Y	Y	Y	Y	Y	Y	Y	Y		Y	Y	Y	Y	Y	Y	Y	Y	Y	Y	Y		Y	Y
Y	Y	Y	Y	Y	Y	Y	Y		Y	Y	Y	Y	Y	Y	Y	Y	Y	Y	Y		Y	Y
Y	Y	Y	Y	Y	Y	Y	Y		Y	Y	Y	Y	Y	Y	Y	Y	Y	Y	Y		Y	Y
Y	Y	Y	Y	Y	Y	Y	Y		Y	N	Y	Y	Y	Y	Y	Y	Y	A	A		Y	Y
Y	Y	Y	Y	Y	Y	Y	Y		Y	N	Y	Y	Y	Y	Y	Y	Y	A	A		A	Y
Y	Y	Y	Y	Y	Y	Y	Y		Y	Y	Y	A	N	A	Y	A	A	Y	Y		A	Y
Y	Y	N	N	Y	Y	Y	Y		Y	Y	Y	A	A	Y	Y	A	Y	Y	Y		A	A
N	Y	N	N	A	N	Y	N		Y	Y	N	N	N	N	N	N	N	Y	Y		N	A
Y	Y	A	NP	Y	NP	NP	Y		NP	NP	NP	NP	Y	NP*	Y	Y	Y	NP	NP		Y	Y
Y	Y	Y	Y	Y	Y	Y	Y		Y	N	Y	A	Y	Y	Y	Y	Y	A	A		Y	Y
Y	Y	Y	Y	Y	Y	Y	Y		A	A	Y	Y	Y	Y	Y	Y	Y	A	A		Y	Y
Y	Y	A	A	A	A	A	Y		Y	Y	Y	A	N	Y	Y	Y	Y	Y	Y		NP‡	Y‡
Y	Y	Y	Y	Y	NP*	NP*	Y		Y	Y	NP*	Y	Y	Y	Y	Y	Y	NP	NP		Y	Y

* Later advised the Secretariat it had intended to vote in favour.
† Later advised the Secretariat it had intended to vote against.
‡ Later advised the Secretariat it had intended to abstain.

APPENDIX B

TABLES OF VOTING IN THE GENERAL ASSEMBLY 1982-1986

Y = Yes   N = No   A = Abstention   NP = Not Present

Year Session Res.	1986 41																	
	41/63 C	41/63 D	41/63 E	41/63 F	41/63 G	41/69 A	41/69 B	41/69 C	41/69 D	41/69 E	41/69 F	41/69 G	41/69 H	41/69 I	41/69 J	41/69 K	41/71	41/93
Lao People's Democratic Republic	Y	Y	Y	Y	Y	Y			Y	Y	Y	Y	Y	Y	Y	Y	Y	Y
Lebanon	Y	Y	Y	Y	Y	Y			Y	Y	Y	Y	Y	Y	Y	Y	Y	Y
Lesotho	Y	Y	Y	Y	Y	Y			Y	Y	Y	Y	Y	Y	Y	Y	Y	A*
Liberia	Y	A	A	A	A	Y			Y	A	Y	A	A	Y	A	Y	Y	A
Libyan Arab Jamahiriya	Y	Y	Y	Y	Y	Y			Y	Y	Y	Y	Y	Y	Y	Y	Y	Y
Luxembourg	Y	A	A	Y	A	Y			Y	Y	N	A	A	A	Y	Y	N	A
Madagascar	Y	Y	Y	Y	Y	Y			Y	Y	Y	Y	Y	Y	Y	Y	Y	Y
Malawi	Y	A	A	A	A	Y			Y	A	Y	A	A	A	A	Y	Y	A
Malaysia	Y	Y	Y	Y	Y	Y			Y	Y	Y	Y	Y	Y	Y	Y	Y	Y
Maldives	Y	Y	Y	Y	Y	Y			Y	Y	Y	Y	Y	Y	Y	Y	Y	Y
Mali	Y	Y	Y	Y	Y	Y			Y	Y	Y	Y	Y	Y	Y	Y	Y	Y
Malta	Y	Y	Y	Y	Y	Y			Y	Y	Y	Y	Y	Y	Y	Y	Y	Y
Mauritania	Y	Y	Y	Y	Y	Y			Y	Y	Y	Y	Y	Y	Y	Y	Y	Y
Mauritius	Y	Y	Y	Y	Y	Y			Y	Y	Y	Y	Y	Y	Y	Y	Y	Y
Mexico	Y	Y	Y	Y	Y	Y			Y	Y	Y	Y	Y	Y	Y	Y	Y	Y
Mongolia	Y	Y	Y	Y	Y	Y			Y	Y	Y	Y	Y	Y	Y	Y	Y	Y
Morocco	Y	Y	Y	Y	Y	Y			Y	Y	Y	Y	Y	Y	Y	Y	Y	Y
Mozambique	Y	Y	Y	Y	Y	Y			Y	Y	Y	Y	Y	Y	Y	Y	Y	Y
Nepal	Y	Y	Y	Y	Y	Y			Y	Y	Y	Y	Y	Y	Y	Y	Y	A
Netherlands	Y	A	A	Y	A	Y			Y	Y	N	A	A	A	Y	Y	N	A
New Zealand	Y	A	Y	A	A	Y			Y	Y	N	A	A	A	Y	Y	A	A
Nicaragua	Y	Y	Y	Y	Y	Y			Y	Y	Y	Y	Y	Y	Y	Y	Y	Y
Niger	Y	Y	Y	Y	Y	Y			Y	Y	Y	Y	Y	Y	Y	Y	Y	Y
Nigeria	NP	Y	Y	Y	Y	Y			Y	Y	Y	Y	Y	Y	Y	Y	Y	Y
Norway	Y	A	Y	Y	A	Y			Y	Y	N	A	A	A	Y	Y	A	A
Oman	Y	Y	Y	Y	Y	Y			Y	Y	Y	Y	Y	Y	Y	Y	Y	Y
Pakistan	Y	Y	Y	Y	Y	Y			Y	Y	Y	Y	Y	Y	Y	Y	Y	Y
Panama	Y	Y	Y	Y	A	Y			Y	Y	Y	Y	A	Y	Y	Y	Y	A
Papua New Guinea	Y	Y	Y	Y	Y	Y			Y	Y	Y	Y	A	Y	Y	Y	Y	A
Paraguay	Y	Y	Y	Y	Y	Y			Y	Y	Y	Y	Y	Y	Y	Y	A	A
Peru	Y	Y	Y	Y	Y	Y			Y	Y	Y	Y	Y	Y	Y	Y	Y	Y
Philippines	Y	Y	Y	Y	Y	Y			Y	Y	Y	Y	Y	Y	Y	Y	Y	Y
Poland	Y	Y	Y	Y	Y	Y			Y	Y	Y	Y	Y	Y	Y	Y	Y	Y
Portugal	Y	A	A	Y	A	Y			Y	Y	N	Y	A	Y	A	Y	A	A
Qatar	Y	Y	Y	Y	Y	Y			Y	Y	Y	Y	Y	Y	Y	Y	Y	Y
Romania	Y	Y	Y	Y	Y	Y			Y	Y	Y	Y	Y	Y	Y	Y	Y	Y
Rwanda	Y	Y	Y	Y	Y	Y			Y	Y	Y	Y	Y	Y	Y	Y	Y	Y
Saint Christopher and Nevis	NP	A	A	A	A	Y			Y	NP	Y	NP	A	A	NP	Y	Y	A
Saint Lucia	A	A	A	A	A	Y			Y	Y	Y	A	Y	A	Y	Y	Y	A
Saint Vincent	Y	A	A	A	A	Y			Y	Y	Y	Y	Y	A	Y	Y	Y	A
Samoa	Y	Y	Y	Y	Y	Y			Y	Y	Y	Y	Y	Y	Y	Y	Y	A
Sao Tome and Principe	Y	Y	Y	Y	Y	Y			Y	Y	Y	Y	Y	Y	Y	Y	Y	Y
Saudi Arabia	Y	Y	Y	Y	Y	Y			Y	Y	Y	Y	Y	Y	Y	Y	Y	Y
Senegal	Y	Y	Y	Y	Y	Y			Y	Y	Y	Y	Y	Y	Y	Y	Y	Y
Seychelles	NP	NP	NP	NP	NP	NP	ADOPTED WITHOUT A VOTE	ADOPTED WITHOUT A VOTE	NP	NP	NP	NP	NP	NP	NP	NP	NP	Y
Sierra Leone	Y	Y	Y	Y	Y	Y			Y	Y	Y	Y	Y	Y	Y	Y	Y	Y
Singapore	Y	Y	Y	Y	Y	Y			Y	Y	Y	Y	Y	Y	Y	Y	Y	NP
Solomon Islands	Y	Y	Y	Y	Y	Y			Y	Y	Y	Y	Y	Y	Y	Y	Y	A
Somalia	Y	Y	Y	Y	Y	Y			Y	Y	Y	Y	Y	Y	Y	Y	Y	A
Spain	Y	Y	Y	Y	Y	Y			Y	Y	A	Y	Y	A	Y	Y	A	A
Sri Lanka	Y	Y	Y	Y	Y	Y			Y	Y	Y	Y	Y	Y	Y	Y	Y	A
Sudan	Y	Y	Y	Y	Y	Y			Y	Y	Y	Y	Y	Y	Y	Y	Y	Y
Suriname	Y	Y	Y	Y	Y	Y			Y	Y	Y	Y	Y	Y	Y	Y	Y	Y
Swaziland	Y	A	A	Y	Y	Y			Y	Y	N	Y	A	Y	Y	Y	Y	A
Sweden	Y	A	A	Y	Y	Y			Y	Y	N	A	A	Y	Y	Y	A	A
Syrian Arab Republic	Y	Y	Y	Y	Y	Y			Y	Y	Y	Y	Y	Y	Y	Y	Y	Y
Thailand	Y	Y	Y	Y	Y	Y			Y	Y	Y	Y	Y	Y	Y	Y	Y	Y
Togo	Y	Y	Y	Y	Y	Y			Y	Y	Y	Y	Y	Y	Y	Y	Y	Y
Trinidad and Tobago	Y	Y	Y	Y	Y	Y			Y	Y	Y	Y	Y	Y	Y	Y	Y	Y
Tunisia	Y	Y	Y	Y	Y	Y			Y	Y	Y	Y	Y	Y	Y	Y	Y	Y
Turkey	Y	Y	Y	Y	Y	Y			Y	Y	Y	Y	Y	Y	Y	Y	Y	Y
Uganda	Y	Y	Y	Y	Y	Y			Y	Y	Y	Y	Y	Y	Y	Y	Y	Y
Ukrainian SSR	Y	Y	Y	Y	Y	Y			Y	Y	Y	Y	Y	Y	Y	Y	Y	Y
USSR	Y	Y	Y	Y	Y	NP*			Y	Y	Y	Y	Y	Y	Y	Y	Y	Y
United Arab Emirates	Y	Y	Y	Y	Y	Y			Y	Y	Y	Y	Y	Y	Y	Y	Y	Y
United Kingdom	Y	A	A	Y	A	Y			Y	Y	N	A	A	A	Y	Y	N	A
United Republic of Cameroon	Y	A	A	A	A	Y			Y	A	A	A	A	A	Y	Y	N	A
United Republic of Tanzania	Y	Y	Y	Y	Y	Y			Y	Y	Y	Y	Y	Y	Y	Y	Y	N
United States	A	N	A	A	N	Y			Y	N	N	N	N	N	N	N	N	N
Uruguay	Y	Y	Y	Y	Y	Y			Y	Y	Y	Y	Y	A	Y	Y	NP	A
Vanuatu	Y	Y	Y	Y	Y	Y			Y	Y	Y	Y	Y	A	Y	Y	Y	NP
Venezuela	Y	Y	Y	Y	Y	Y			Y	Y	Y	Y	Y	Y	Y	Y	Y	Y
Viet Nam	Y	Y	Y	Y	Y	Y			Y	Y	Y	Y	Y	Y	Y	Y	Y	Y
Yemen	Y	Y	Y	Y	Y	Y			Y	Y	Y	Y	Y	Y	Y	Y	Y	Y
Yugoslavia	Y	Y	Y	Y	Y	Y			Y	Y	Y	Y	Y	Y	Y	Y	Y	Y
Zaire	Y	A	Y‡	Y‡	Y‡	Y			Y	A	Y	A	A	A	A	Y	Y	A
Zambia	Y	Y	Y	Y	Y	Y			Y	Y	Y	Y	Y	Y	Y	Y	Y	Y
Zimbabwe	Y	Y	Y	Y	Y	Y			Y	Y	Y	Y	Y	Y	Y	Y	Y	Y

* Later advised the Secretariat it had intended to vote in favour.
‡ Later advised the Secretariat it had intended to abstain.

		1986 41						
41/95	41/101	41/162 A	41/162 B	41/162 C	41/179 A	41/179 B	41/181	41/196
Y	Y	Y	Y	Y	A	A	Y	
Y	Y	Y	Y	Y	Y	Y	Y	
Y	Y	Y	A	Y	Y	Y	Y	
Y	Y	A	A	Y	Y	Y	Y	
Y	Y	Y	Y	Y	A	A	Y	
N	N	N	N	Y	Y	Y	Y	
Y	Y	Y	Y	Y	NP	NP	Y	
A	Y	A	A	A	Y	Y	Y	
Y	Y	Y	Y	Y	Y	Y	Y	
Y	Y	Y	Y	Y	A	A	Y	
Y	Y	Y	Y	Y	NP	NP	Y	
Y	Y	Y	Y	Y	Y	Y	Y	
Y	Y	Y	Y	Y	Y	Y	Y	
Y	Y	Y	Y	Y	Y	Y	Y	
Y	Y	Y	Y	Y	Y	A	NP	
Y	Y	Y	Y	Y	Y	Y	Y	
Y	Y	Y	Y	Y	NP	NP	Y	
Y	Y	Y	A	Y	Y	Y	Y	
N	N	N	N	Y	Y	Y	Y	
A	N	N	N	Y	NP	NP	Y	
Y	Y	Y	Y	Y	Y	Y	Y	
Y	Y	Y	Y	Y	Y	Y	Y	
A	N	N	N	Y	Y	Y	Y	
Y	Y	Y	Y	Y	Y	Y	Y	
Y	Y	Y	Y	Y	Y	Y	Y	ADOPTED WITHOUT A VOTE
Y	Y	A	A	Y	NP	NP	NP	
NP	A	A	A	Y	Y	Y	Y	
Y	Y	Y	Y	Y‡	Y	Y	Y	
Y	Y	Y	A	Y	Y	Y	Y	
Y	Y	Y	Y	Y	A	A	Y	
A	A	N	N	Y	Y	Y	Y	
Y	Y	Y	Y	Y	NP*	NP*	Y	
Y	Y	Y	NP	Y	Y	A	Y	
Y	Y	Y	Y	Y	Y	Y	Y	
Y	Y	A	N	A	Y	Y	NP	
Y	Y	A	N	A	Y	Y	Y	
Y	A	A	A	Y	Y	Y	Y	
Y	Y	Y	Y	Y	Y	Y	Y	
Y	Y	Y	Y	Y	Y	Y	Y	
Y	Y	NP	NP	NP	NP	NP	NP	
Y	Y	Y	Y	Y	Y	Y	Y	
Y	Y	Y	A	Y	Y	Y	Y	
Y	Y	Y	Y	Y	NP	NP	Y	
A	A	A	A	Y	Y	Y	Y	
Y	Y	Y	Y	Y	Y	Y	Y	
Y	Y	Y	Y	Y	Y	Y	Y	
Y	Y	A	A	Y	Y	Y	Y	
A	N	A	N	Y	Y	Y	Y	
Y	Y	Y	A	Y	N	N	Y	
Y	Y	Y	A	Y	Y	Y	Y	
Y	Y	Y	A	Y	Y	Y	Y	
Y	Y	Y	Y	Y	NP	NP*	Y	
Y	Y	Y	Y	Y	Y	Y	Y	
Y	Y	Y	Y	Y	Y	Y	Y	
Y	Y	Y	Y	Y	Y	A	Y	
Y	Y	Y	Y	Y	Y	A	Y	
N	Y	N	N	Y	Y	Y	Y	
N	Y	A	A	A	Y	Y	Y	
Y	Y	Y	Y	A	Y	Y	Y	
N	N	N	N	A	Y	Y	N	
Y	Y	A	A	Y	NP	Y	Y	
NP*	Y	Y	Y	Y	NP	NP	Y	
Y	Y	Y	A	Y	Y	Y	Y	
Y	Y	Y	Y	Y	A	A	Y	
Y	Y	Y	Y	Y	Y	Y	Y	
Y	Y	A	A	Y	Y	Y	NP	
Y	Y	Y	Y	Y	Y	Y	Y	
Y	Y	Y	Y	Y	Y	Y	NP	

* Later advised the Secretariat it had intended to vote in favour.
‡ Later advised the Secretariat it had intended to abstain.

APPENDIX C

TABLES OF VOTING IN THE
SECURITY COUNCIL, 1982-1986

Y = Yes;   N = No;   A = Abstention;   NP = Not Present

1982

Resolutions	China	France	UK	USA	USSR	Guyana	Ireland	Japan	Jordan	Panama	Poland	Spain	Togo	Uganda	Zaire
	Permanent members					*Non-permanent members*									
500	Y	Y	A	A	Y	Y	Y	Y	Y	Y	Y	Y	Y	Y	Y
501	Y	Y	Y	Y	A	Y	Y	Y	Y	Y	A	Y	Y	Y	Y
506				Adopted unanimously											
508				Adopted unanimously											
509				Adopted unanimously											
511	Y	Y	Y	Y	A	Y	Y	Y	Y	Y	A	Y	Y	Y	Y
512				Adopted unanimously											
513				Adopted unanimously											
515	Y	Y	Y	*	Y	Y	Y	Y	Y	Y	Y	Y	Y	Y	Y
516				Adopted unanimously											
517	Y	Y	Y	A	Y	Y	Y	Y	Y	Y	Y	Y	Y	Y	Y
518				Adopted unanimously											
519	Y	Y	Y	Y	A	Y	Y	Y	Y	Y	A	Y	Y	Y	Y
520				Adopted unanimously											
521				Adopted unanimously											
523	Y	Y	Y	Y	A	Y	Y	Y	Y	Y	A	Y	Y	Y	Y
524				Adopted unanimously											

* Did not participate in the vote

1983

Resolutions	China	France	UK	USA	USSR	Guyana	Jordan	Malta	Netherlands	Nicaragua	Pakistan	Poland	Togo	Zaire	Zimbabwe
529	Y	Y	Y	Y	A	Y	Y	Y	Y	Y	Y	A	Y	Y	Y
531				Adopted unanimously											
536	Y	Y	Y	Y	A	Y	Y	Y	Y	Y	Y	A	Y	Y	Y
538	Y	Y	Y	Y	A	Y	Y	Y	Y	Y	Y	A	Y	Y	Y
542				Adopted unanimously											
543				Adopted unanimously											

1984

Permanent members — **1984** — *Non-permanent members*

Resolutions	China	France	UK	USA	USSR	Burkina Faso	Egypt	India	Malta	Netherlands	Nicaragua	Pakistan	Peru	Ukrainian SSR	Zimbabwe
549	Y	Y	Y	Y	A	Y	Y	Y	Y	Y	Y	Y	Y	A	Y
551	Adopted unanimously														
555	Y	Y	Y	Y	A	Y	Y	Y	Y	Y	Y	Y	Y	A	Y
557	Adopted unanimously														

1985

	China	France	UK	USA	USSR	Australia	Burkina Faso	Denmark	Egypt	India	Madagascar	Peru	Thailand	Trinidad and Tobago	Ukrainian SSR
561	Y	Y	Y	Y	A	Y	Y	Y	Y	Y	Y	Y	Y	Y	A
563	Adopted unanimously														
564	Adopted unanimously														
573	Y	Y	Y	A	Y	Y	Y	Y	Y	Y	Y	Y	Y	Y	Y
575	Y	Y	Y	Y	A	Y	Y	Y	Y	Y	Y	Y	Y	Y	A
576	Adopted unanimously														
579	Adopted unanimously														

1986

	China	France	UK	USA	USSR	Australia	Bulgaria	Congo	Denmark	Ghana	Madagascar	Thailand	Trinidad and Tobago	United Arab Emirates	Venezuela
583	Adopted unanimously														
584	Adopted unanimously														
586	Adopted unanimously														
587	Y	Y	Y	A	Y	Y	Y	Y	Y	Y	Y	Y	Y	Y	Y
590	Adopted unanimously														
592	Y	Y	Y	A	Y	Y	Y	Y	Y	Y	Y	Y	Y	Y	Y

INDEX

Abu 'Ain, Ziyad: **II**, 173, 207; **III**, 73, 113, 152, 250, 254

Advisory Committee on Administrative and Budgetary Questions: *see* under Committees

Afghanistan: **I**, 106; committee/commission memberships, **I**, 60n; **II**, 36n

African National Congress: **II**, 230

Aggression, Definition of: **III**, 89, 143

Aiken, Frank: **I**, 62

Algeria: committee/commission memberships, **I**, 60n

Algiers: **III**, 73, 113

American Friends Service Committee: **I**, 19, 22, 193

Ammundsen, Esther: **I**, 214

Angola: **I**, 184; **II**, 8, 37, 39, 58, 142, 144; right of its people to self-determination, **I**, 83

Ansar Camp (Lebanon): **III**, 73, 113, 250, 254

Antigua and Barbuda: **III**, 16, 52

al-Aqsa Mosque: **I**, 146-47, 196-97; **II**, 146; **III**, 259, 276, 278-79, 281-82, 284-85, 291; *see* also Holy places

Arab Fund for Economic and Social Development: **II**, 244; **III**, 278

Arab Higher Committee: UN hearing granted (1947), **I**, 3; called on to help arrange truce and cease-fire in Palestine, **I**, 125-26

Arab League: *see* League of Arab States

Argentina: committee/commission memberships, **I**, 31n, 39n, 42n, 44n, 46n, 54n, 60n

Armed conflict:

1947-49: call for abstention from use of force in Palestine (1947), **I**, 4; hostilities in Palestine, **I**, 125-30; refusal of Syria to sit on Truce Commission for Palestine, **I**, 126; mission and assassination of Count Bernadotte, **I**, 128-29; Armistice agreements, **I**, 129-32

1950-55: fighting on Israeli-Syrian armistice line (1951), **I**, 133; Israeli aerial action on Syrian front (1951), **I**, 134; Israeli attack on Qibya (1953), **I**, 135-36; Israeli attack on Gaza Strip (1955), **I**, 136; violence on Israeli-Egyptian armistice line (1955), **I**, 137

1956-57: Israeli attack on Syria (1956), **I**, 137

Suez crisis: **I**, 31-40, 139; calls for cease-fire, **I**, 31-32; calls for French and British withdrawal, **I**, 32, 34-35; Israel called on to withdraw to armistice lines, **I**, 31-32, 34-35, 39-40

1958-66: Israel requested to refrain from military action in Tiberias area (1962), **I**, 140-41; Israeli attack on Samu', **I**, 141

1967: situation arising from 1967 war, **I**, 66-69; call for cease-fire, **I**, 141-42; calls for Israeli withdrawal from

territories occupied in 1967, *see* Occupied territories and Peace settlement

1968-72: Israeli attack on Karameh (1968), **I**, 143; Israeli attacks on Salt (1968-69), **I**, 144-46; call for respect for cease-fire (1968), **I**, 144-45; Israeli attacks on Lebanon (1968-72), **I**, 145-50, 154; call for extension of cease-fire (1970), **I**, 76-77; abduction of Syrian and Lebanese military personnel (1972), **I**, 149-50

1973-74: Israeli attacks on Lebanon, **I**, 150-51; situation arising from 1973 war, **I**, 109, 151-52; disengagement of forces (1973-74), **I**, 153-55; **II**, 86n, 119n

1975-81: Israeli attacks on civilian targets, **II**, 65, 73, 117, 145, 176, 189, 200n, 229; call for cease-fire in Lebanon (1978), **II**, 184-85, 187n, 189, 192n, 200-1; call for Israeli withdrawal from Lebanon (1978), **II**, 57-58, 159n, 184-85, 187n, 189n, 192n; Israeli attacks on Lebanon (1979-81), **II**, 140, 145, 176, 189, 192-93, 200-1; Israeli assistance to militias in Lebanon, (1979-80), **II**, 187, 189, 192-93; **III**, 217n, 219n; Israeli lack of cooperation with UNIFIL (1979), **II**, 187; acts of violence in South Lebanon condemned (1980), **II**, 195

Iraq: Israeli attack on Iraq (1981), **II**, 147-49, 151-52, 198-99, 271-72; **III**, 178, 301

1982-86, Israeli attacks on/invasion of Lebanon, **III**, 7-12, 42-43, 53, 58, 86, 168n, 200, 205, 217-22, 248, 257, 264, 282, 292-93; cease-fires called for (1982), **III**, 7-8, 11-12, 218-22, 224-25, 226n, 228n, 229n; Israeli blockade of Beirut (1982), **III**, 220-21; Israeli invasion of Beirut (1982), **III**, 19, 47, 94-95, 220-22; massacre of Sabra and Shatila, **III**, 11-12, 19, 45, 48, 53, 57-58, 100, 222, 248, 257, 264, 282-83, 292-293; civilian victims in Lebanon, **III**, 7-12, 19, 53, 219-20, 248, 257, 264, 291-92; Israeli withdrawal from Lebanon called for, **III**, 7-8, 11-12, 19, 210n, 217-20, 225n, 226n, 228n, 229n, 230, 258, 265

Iraq: Israeli threats against Iraq, **III**, 13-14, 56-57, 72, 99, 134-35, 139, 178, 301-3; Israel called on not to carry out further attacks on Iraq, **III**, 301-3

Tunisia: Israeli attack on Tunisia (1985), **III**, 227-28, 264; Israel called on to refrain from further aggression against Tunisia, **III**, 228

Armistice agreements (1949): **I**, 26n, 31-32, 34-35, 39-40, 131, 137-39; call for armistice, **I**, 130; Israel-Egypt, **I**, 31, 34-35, 39-40, 132-37; Israel-Jordan, **I**, 132, 139-41; Israel-Lebanon, **I**, 146, 150; **II**, 189, 191; **III**, 218; Israel-Syria, **I**, 133-34, 137, 140-41; procedure for settlement of complaints, **I**, 132-33; supervision of, **I**,